Reference and Information Services

Recent Titles in Library and Information Science Text Series

Guide to the Library of Congress Classification, Sixth Edition
Lois Mai Chan, Sheila S. Intner, and Jean Weihs

Research Methods in Library and Information Science, Sixth Edition
Lynn Silipigni Connaway and Marie L. Radford

Information Services to Diverse Populations: Developing Culturally Competent Library Professionals
Nicole A. Cooke

The School Librarian as Curriculum Leader
Jody K. Howard

The School Library Manager: Surviving and Thriving, Sixth Edition
Blanche Woolls and Sharon Coatney

The Organization of Information, Fourth Edition
Daniel N. Joudrey and Arlene G. Taylor, with the assistance of Katherine M. Wisser

Library and Information Center Management, Ninth Edition
Barbara B. Moran and Claudia J. Morner

Collection Management Basics, Seventh Edition
Margaret Zarnosky Saponaro and G. Edward Evans

Young Adult Literature in Action: A Librarian's Guide, Third Edition
Rose Brock

Children's Literature in Action: A Librarian's Guide, Third Edition
Sylvia M. Vardell

Library Information Systems, Second Edition
Joseph R. Matthews and Carson Block

Data Science for Librarians
Yunfei Du and Hammad Rauf Khan

REFERENCE AND INFORMATION SERVICES

An Introduction

Sixth Edition

Melissa A. Wong and Laura Saunders, Editors

Foreword by Linda C. Smith

Library and Information Science Text Series

An Imprint of ABC-CLIO, LLC
Santa Barbara, California • Denver, Colorado

Library of Congress Cataloging-in-Publication Data

Names: Saunders, Laura, 1975– editor. | Wong, Melissa Autumn, editor.
Title: Reference and information services : an introduction / Melissa A. Wong and Laura Saunders, editors.
Description: Sixth edition. | Santa Barbara, California : Libraries Unlimited, [2020] | Series: Library and information science text series | Includes bibliographical references and index.
Identifiers: LCCN 2019057161 (print) | LCCN 2019057162 (ebook) | ISBN 9781440868832 (hardcover ; acid–free paper) | ISBN 9781440875045 (paper ; acid-free paper) | ISBN 9781440868849 (ebook)
Subjects: LCSH: Reference services (Libraries) | Information services.
Classification: LCC Z711 .R443 2020 (print) | LCC Z711 (ebook) | DDC 025.5/2—dc23
LC record available at https://lccn.loc.gov/2019057161
LC ebook record available at https://lccn.loc.gov/2019057162

ISBN: 978-1-4408-6883-2 (hardcover)
978-1-4408-7504-5 (paperback)
978-1-4408-6884-9 (ebook)

24 23 22 21 20 1 2 3 4 5

This book is also available as an eBook.

Libraries Unlimited
An Imprint of ABC-CLIO, LLC

ABC-CLIO, LLC
147 Castilian Drive
Santa Barbara, California 93117
www.abc-clio.com

This book is printed on acid-free paper ∞

Manufactured in the United States of America

Contents

Foreword

As the coeditor of the first five editions of *Reference and Information Services: An Introduction* (published by Libraries Unlimited in 1991, 1995, 2001, 2011, and 2016 in their Library and Information Science Text Series), I welcome the publication of this new sixth edition in 2020. Nearly thirty years have passed since the first edition appeared in 1991. On December 17 of that year, I attended the Third ACM Conference on Hypertext in San Antonio, Texas, and saw Tim Berners-Lee demonstrate the World Wide Web project (https://cds.cern.ch/record/1164398). I certainly did not anticipate how the Web would transform reference and information services. But by the third edition, in 2001, website URLs appeared for some sources discussed in the chapters on information sources and their use. Now, in 2020, each chapter has been updated to encompass a much more extensive list of Web resources, both freely available and licensed.

This new sixth edition reflects both continuity and change from the preceding editions. Coeditors Melissa A. Wong (a chapter author beginning with the fourth edition and coeditor of the fifth edition) and Laura Saunders (a chapter author beginning with the fifth edition) have guided chapter authors to ensure that the content reflects how reference and information services continue to be affected by rapidly developing technologies and increasing volumes of digital content. They have also placed increased attention on issues of diversity, equity, and inclusion and insights from critical theory. The resulting text achieves its goal to provide students and practitioners with an overview of current reference sources, issues, and services.

Continuity is reflected in the basic structure of the text. Chapters are divided into two major parts: Part I—Concepts and Processes and Part II—Information Sources and Their Use. Part III, The Future of Reference Service, was added beginning with the fifth edition. All chapters have elements to enhance student learning and engagement through the use of boxes to generate thought and discussion and a carefully selected annotated list of suggested readings. In Part II, rather than merely describing selected reference tools, chapters emphasize the formulation of strategies for their effective use. Continuity is also reflected in the collaborative nature of the text, involving many different chapter authors who draw on their expertise as practitioners and/or teachers of reference.

Change is evident in the gradual expansion of the scope, from twenty chapters in the first edition to thirty-two chapters in the sixth edition. Comparing the lists of chapter titles for the first and sixth editions in Part I, one finds "Ethics" replacing "A Philosophy of Service"; "Reference Services to Special Groups" split into chapters titled "Reference Services for Children and Young Adults" and "Reference Services for Diverse Populations"; and new chapters titled "Consortia and Cooperation," "Models of Reference Services," and "Marketing and Promotion of Reference Services." Comparing the two lists of chapter titles in Part II, one finds "Government Documents and Statistics Sources" split into chapters titled "Government Information" and "Data and Statistical Sources"; multiple source types grouped in a new chapter titled "Ready Reference Sources"; and new chapters titled "Introduction to Information Creation and Dissemination," "Licensing and Managing Electronic Resources," "Search Strategies for Online Sources," "Readers' Advisory Services and Sources," "News Sources," "Business Sources," "Health and Medicine Sources," "Primary and Archival Sources," and "Legal Sources." Finally, the new Part III has a chapter titled "Creating the Future of Reference Service."

Not surprisingly, given the passage of nearly three decades since the first edition, I am the only author who has contributed one or more chapters to each edition of the text. Authors of the first edition all had some type of affiliation with the University of Illinois at Urbana-Champaign during their careers—as a student, librarian, and/or faculty member. Over time, new chapter authors have been recruited as experts with a much wider range of affiliations, including one from Canada beginning with the fifth edition and now one from Australia in the sixth edition. Beginning with the second edition, an effort has been made to include more reference sources specific to Canada. A search of *WorldCat* reveals translations of some earlier editions into Spanish, Korean, and even Mongolian, expanding the potential readership even further.

My University of Illinois Library colleague Richard E. Bopp (1944–2011), lead editor for the first four editions, needs to be recognized for first proposing the idea of a collaboratively authored reference textbook in the late 1980s. His influence continues to be felt in the commitment to creating a high-quality text to prepare a new generation of reference librarians. I am grateful to Melissa A. Wong and Laura Saunders for all their work to accomplish this through the publication of this sixth edition.

Linda C. Smith

Preface

This new sixth edition of *Reference and Information Services* reflects the dramatic changes shaped by rapidly developing technologies and increasing volumes of digital content over the past four years. In addition, the editors and authors have made an effort to increase attention to issues of diversity, equity, and inclusion and to integrate more critical theory throughout the text. In Part I, "Concepts and Processes," chapters have been revised and updated to reflect new ideas and methods in the provision of reference service in an era of increased accountability and emphasis on critical reflection in professional practice. In Part II, "Information Sources and Their Use," discussion of each source type has been updated to encompass a much more extensive list of Web resources, both freely available and licensed. A new introduction to this section provides an overview of the information life cycle and outlines some of the more pressing issues with regard to locating, selecting, and evaluating information sources. A new chapter on news sources confronts the challenges of misinformation and disinformation and offers a thorough overview of a range of resources for accessing current and historical news. A single final chapter makes up Part III, exploring how professionals can create the future of reference service.

A number of new authors are contributors to this sixth edition, bringing to their chapters their experience as teachers of reference or as practitioners in various types of libraries. Throughout the text, boxes are used to generate thought and discussion. Despite these updates and changes, the sixth edition has the same goal as its predecessors', to provide students and practitioners with an overview of current reference sources, issues, and services.

Melissa A. Wong
Laura Saunders

Acknowledgments

A number of individuals assisted the editors and authors in the creation of this sixth edition of *Reference and Information Services*. We would like here to express our gratitude for their valuable contributions.

First, we would like to thank the editorial and production staff of Libraries Unlimited, an imprint of ABC-CLIO, for their support in publishing this new edition.

The authors of several chapters in the sixth edition built on the work of authors who had contributed to previous editions. We would like to acknowledge our debt to Marcia A. Brandt, Rick Burke, David A. Cobb, Prudence W. Dalrymple, Eric Forte, Jim Hahn, Frances Jacobson Harris, Wendy Holliday, Jenny Marie Johnson, Josephine Z. Kibbee, Kathleen M. Kluegel, Elizabeth Leonard, Mary Mallory, Lori S. Mestre, Carol Bates Penka, Richard E. Rubin, Joseph E. Straw, Rosalind Tedford, Jo Bell Whitlatch, Lynn Wiley, and Beth S. Woodward for helping shape earlier editions of this text.

Thanks go to Corinne M. Henderson for creating the reference interview figure in Chapter 3, Holly Soboroff for creating the Venn diagram figures in Chapter 16, and Matthew Beth for his assistance.

We are deeply indebted to Richard E. Bopp (1944–2011) and Linda C. Smith. Rich first proposed the idea of a collaboratively authored reference textbook in the late 1980s and served as the lead editor for the first four editions published in 1991, 1995, 2001, and 2011. Linda C. Smith served as coeditor from the launch of the textbook in 1991 through the fifth edition in 2016. Through their diligent work and persistent effort, these authors created a seminal textbook that has served as the foundation for countless library careers. We are honored to carry on Rich and Linda's legacy. Finally, we would like to extend a special thank-you to Blanche Woolls, who served as editor for the fourth through sixth editions and who provided invaluable advice and guidance on this sixth edition, as she did for so many authors during her time at Libraries Unilimited.

Melissa would like to thank her family, Bob, Erica, and Craig, for their patience all the times this book went on vacation with us. You make it a wonderful world every day.

Laura would also like to thank her family, David, Lissa, and Will, for their support, humor, and patience.

Part I

Concepts and Processes

Chapter 1

History and Functions of Reference Service

Dave A. Tyckoson

INTRODUCTION

This is the information age, where information is available everywhere all the time. With the devices in their pockets, people are able to find, collect, and utilize the information that they seek—no matter when it is needed or where it is located. People can collect statistics on climate change, quote *Macbeth*, watch the rise and fall of the stock market, read news stories from around the corner and around the world, listen to their favorite music, find out when the bus will reach its stop, figure out which store has the best price on the product they want to purchase, and watch cat videos—all at the same time. Every person with an Internet connection has the power to retrieve the information that they need—so why do we still need libraries? And why do libraries still need reference librarians?

There are obviously many answers to those questions—and this book will provide a variety of opinions, options, and actions that will keep libraries and reference services growing and thriving. To fully understand the roles, responsibilities, and continuing need for reference librarians, it is important to look back at the reasons that reference service was established, the things reference librarians have traditionally done, and how those activities have evolved to the present day.

THE LIBRARY AND THE COMMUNITY

The library is not an independent institution in and of itself, but it exists to serve and support the community for which it was established. Public libraries serve the residents of a defined geographic area, most often a city or county.

Academic libraries serve the faculty, staff, and students at the college or university. School libraries serve the teachers and students attending a specific school. Medical libraries serve the doctors, nurses, staff, and patients of the clinic or hospital. Law libraries serve the attorneys and staff of the firm. Corporate libraries serve the management and employees of a specific company.

When members of the community need information services, the primary objective of the library is to fill that need. Whether that need relates to research, business, or entertainment, members of the community often turn to the library. Most libraries, especially public and academic libraries, also allow people from outside the primary community to use their collections, facilities, and services. However, the primary focus needs to be on the people who make up the parent community. A library that is perceived as vital to its community will receive the support, staff, and funding to maintain its role as an information utility for the community. A library that does not fill the needs of its parent community will slowly wither, will become marginalized, and may even close. To serve the community effectively, librarians must learn who comprises that community, what their information needs are, and how those needs are changing. Know the community, and the librarian will know what the library should contain, which services to offer, and what level of support to expect in return.

WHAT LIBRARIES DO

Libraries perform four basic functions in order to fill the information needs of their communities. Each is extremely detailed and highly complex, yet all of the activities of the library can be included in one of these four functions. The functions of the library have evolved over time as libraries and their parent communities have coevolved.

Collections

Historically, the first function of libraries was to select, collect, and preserve information. From ancient times, librarians have collected and retained documents of interest to their parent communities. From the scrolls in the Great Library of Alexandria to the books chained to the desks of the Bodleian Library to the scientific journals of the National Library of Medicine to the children's books of the local public library to the digital content of a university repository, every library has had as its first role the accumulation of information of interest to its community. This information takes many forms, which today include books, journals, photographs, videos, DVDs, websites, MP3s, computer files, and any other form of information storage that has been used in the past. In response to the needs of the community, librarians will also collect any new information formats that will be developed in the future. The popular image of the library as a warehouse for materials—whether those materials are row after row of books on shelving, cabinets of microfilm or audio CDs, or a web page full of links—comes directly from this collection function. This is the oldest historical function of libraries: to find, select, acquire, and preserve documents of interest to the community. It remains a vital role to this day. Part II of this book (Chapters 13–31) discusses collections.

Organization

The second function of libraries is to organize the information that they collect. The fact that librarians organize information may seem obvious, but it is a much more recent function than collecting. Historically, this was the second function to arise in libraries, evolving as a corollary to the first function. When libraries were very small, a user or librarian could simply browse the entire collection to find what was needed. As the size of libraries grew, other methods of organization were required.

From alphabetical order to RDA and from MARC to metadata, librarians have developed a wide variety of methods for organizing and finding materials in their collections. Most of these tools were initially developed by librarians primarily for self-assistance. As libraries grew larger, it became much more difficult for librarians to know where to find specific documents or pieces of information within the overall collection. As a result, librarians developed concepts such as subject headings, main entries, authority files, call numbers, metadata tags, and controlled vocabularies. Although libraries must have always had some kind of organization, the first modern catalogs were developed as inventory control devices in the latter half of the 15th century. The first published catalog was the book catalog of the Bodleian Library in Oxford, which was printed in book form in 1620. Although no precise date can be given for when librarians began to organize information on a large scale, they have been doing so for at least 500 years (Hanson and Daily 1970).

Librarians have become quite sophisticated in organizing and indexing the materials contained within their collections. Using the technology of the times, from scrolls to books to cards to databases, librarians have been and continue to be leaders in the theory and practice of indexing and cataloging information. *Google* may tell library users what exists out on the Web, but librarian-developed tools such as OCLC's *WorldCat* and Springshare's *LibGuides* make useful material easier to find. For more on the organization function, see Chapter 14.

Service

The third function of libraries is to provide direct assistance to users in their search and retrieval of information, which is what librarians now call reference service. This aspect of librarianship began much more recently than the first two and was first discussed in the mid- to late 1800s. Although everyone today has grown up with this function of the library and tends to take reference service for granted, it was truly a revolutionary concept when first introduced.

Publishing

The fourth and newest function of the library is to serve as a publisher and distributor of information of value to its local community. With the free and open Web, everyone has access to the same publicly available content. It is the unique, local material that is the most valuable to the community. Many libraries have developed repositories for exactly this type of content, including local histories, photographs, government documents, and dissertations and theses. By digitizing these collections, libraries are making them available to the wider world—and promoting the local community at the same time.

HISTORICAL DEVELOPMENT OF REFERENCE SERVICE

Universal Education and Public Libraries

That reference service developed at all is linked to two different, yet related 19th-century ideals: universal education and public libraries. These two movements transformed the fabric of American society and had a lasting impact that remains today. Universal education was the concept that all children in the United States, no matter what class, race, or religion, would be able to receive free public education. Reasons for establishing universal education for all school-aged children varied widely and were often at cross-purposes to each other (Gutek 1970, 51–52). Regardless of the motivations for establishing universal education, state and local governments throughout the nation established free public schools, which did, in fact, result in a more highly educated society. As a direct result of universal education, the literacy rate in the United States rose significantly during the 19th century. And as more and more people learned to read, they became more and more interested in doing so.

At the same time that universal education was becoming the norm, the concept of the free public library was being established. To convince the city fathers that such an institution would be a necessary and valuable component of the community, the trustees of the Boston Public Library made these arguments: "The question is not what will be brought about by a few individuals of indomitable will and an ardent thirst for improvement, but what is most for the advantage of the mass of the community. In this point of view we consider that a large public library is of the utmost importance as the means of completing our system of public education" (Trustees of the Public Library of the City of Boston [1852] 1975, 9). That the public library was viewed as a component of universal education is emphasized again later in that same report (emphases in the original document):

> And yet there can be no doubt that such reading ought to be furnished to all, as a matter of public policy and duty, on the same principle that we furnish free education, and in fact, as a part, and the most important part, of the education of all. For it has been rightly judged that,—under political, social and religious institutions like ours,—it is of paramount importance that the means of general information should so diffused that the largest possible number of persons should be induced to read and understand questions going down to the very foundations of social order, which are constantly presenting themselves, and which we, as a people, are constantly required to decide, and do decide, either ignorantly or wisely. That this *can* be done,—that is, that such libraries *can* be collected, and that they will be used to a much wider extent than libraries have ever been used before, and with much more important results, there can be no doubt; and if it can be done *anywhere*, it can be done *here* in Boston; for no population of one hundred and fifty thousand souls, lying so compactly together as to be able, with tolerable convenience, to resort to one library, was ever before so well fitted to become a reading, self-cultivating population, as the population of our own city is at this moment.
>
> To accomplish this object, however,—which has never yet been attempted,—we must use means which have never before been used; otherwise the library we propose to establish, will not be adjusted to its especial purposes. Above all, while the rightful claim of no class,—however highly educated already,—should be overlooked, the first regard should be shown, as in the case of our Free Schools, to the wants of those, who can, in no other way supply themselves with the interesting and healthy reading necessary for their farther education. (Trustees of the Public Library of the City of Boston [1852] 1975, 15–16)

The Boston Public Library did, in fact, become a reality and opened its doors to the public—all of the public—on March 20, 1854. It was an instant success. In less than six months of operation, more than 35,000 volumes were borrowed (Stone 1977, 158). When given an opportunity to read, the public responded at an overwhelming rate, borrowing an average of one book for every two people living in the city, and this at a time when the concept of borrowing books was new to the majority of the population and not yet a common practice. The concept of the free public library was rapidly adopted by other municipalities, with 188 such libraries having been established in 11 different states by 1876 (Poole 1876).

Reference service came about as a direct result of these two innovations. Universal education taught the public to read, and public libraries offered material to read. As Melvil Dewey put it,

> The school teaches them to read; the library must supply them with reading which will serve to educate, and so it is that we are forced to divide popular education into two parts of almost equal importance and deserving equal attention: the free school and the free library. (Dewey 1876, 6)

The newly literate members of society knew how to read and sought out materials that would allow them to practice that newly learned skill. Unlike today's society, where information is ubiquitous, information was somewhat scarce in that time period. Few families owned reading materials, and books were relatively expensive, so people turned to the newly formed public libraries for their reading material. However, they had no idea how to use a library. Naturally, they asked the librarians for advice. By 1876, the idea of reference service had been born.

Samuel Green and the Founding of Reference Service

The first discussion of any type of direct service by librarians to help library users was in a paper presented by Samuel Swett Green at the first conference of the American Library Association in Philadelphia in 1876. His paper, "Personal Intercourse and Relations between Librarians and Readers in Popular Libraries," outlined the concept of the librarian interacting with and assisting the reader. He did not use the phrase "reference service" because that term had not yet been developed. His paper was published with a shorter title in the first volume of *Library Journal* and is universally recognized as the first professional discussion of what we now call reference service (Green 1876). See Box 1.1 for an explanation of how the term "reference service" developed.

That reference service originated in public libraries is proof positive of the democratic ideals on which those institutions were founded. Instead of being developed within the walls of academe, where students were theoretically seeking to build upon the knowledge of the past, it was in the *people's university*, the *free public library*, that the concept took hold. Samuel Rothstein (1972, 25–27), who studied the development of reference services in academic libraries, accounts for the lack of interest among academics as follows: "Actually, the student of that era was little inclined to make much use of the college librarian in any case. The idea of research had as yet scarcely reached American universities, and the teaching methods in undergraduate courses still emphasized the traditional reliance upon the textbook. The student had little occasion to borrow

Box 1.1 Why Do We Call It "Reference Service"?

When the idea of helping library users was first proposed, the terms "reference service" and "reference librarian" had yet to be coined. However, the term "reference book" was already widely in use. Reference books earned that name because they were the books, such as catalogs, indexes, and bibliographies, that one consulted to find references to other sources. By the 1870s, any library book that did not circulate was being called a reference book.

In the first paper discussing reference service, Samuel Green called it "personal intercourse between librarians and readers." Fortunately, that phrase was quickly shortened to "aid to readers." Later, the term "assistance to readers" came into more widespread use as the service end of reference began to be more widely recognized. Because the librarians who helped readers tended to use the books that were located in the reference collection, they gradually became known as reference librarians. In 1885, Melvil Dewey became the first to hire staff with the title of "reference librarian" when he organized the first multiple-librarian (i.e., two-person) reference department at Columbia College. "Reference work" was what "reference librarians" did. That name caught on, and the rest, as they say, is history.

(Rothstein 1972, 25–27)

books from the library, and his demands for personal assistance must have been even more rare."

However, some positive reaction to the concept of personal assistance was found in academic institutions. In the discussion that followed Green's presentation, Otis Robinson of the University of Rochester heartily endorsed the concept (Robinson 1876, 123–124). At the London Conference the following year, Reuben Guild of Brown University described the availability of librarians to the public (faculty and students) at his university (Guild 1878, 278). Within a decade of Green's paper, Melvil Dewey had embraced the idea of reference service in the Columbia College (now Columbia University) Library. As the teaching methods used in colleges and universities evolved into a more research-based model, the use of the library by students increased to the point where reference service became established in academic libraries. More traditional academic institutions took longer to adopt this idea, but eventually reference service was available in virtually any public or academic library in the United States.

Original Functions of the Reference Librarian

So what exactly does a reference librarian do? Green's original paper on the topic consists primarily of examples of the types of questions asked by a variety of users of his public library. However, embedded within those examples are four distinct functions of the reference librarian.

1. **Teach people how to use the library and its resources.** Although some scholars may have known their way around catalogs, indexes, and the stacks, most of the newly literate members of society were unfamiliar with what libraries contained and how to find it. The first function of the librarian

providing personal assistance to readers was to teach them how to find things in the library. Green (1876, 80) states, "Give them as much assistance as they need, but try at the same time to teach them to rely upon themselves and become independent."

2. **Answer readers' questions.** Green's paper provides myriad examples of the types of questions asked by users of the public library, ranging from simple factual queries to in-depth research projects. The librarian was expected to be able to answer—or, more accurately, to provide sources that would answer—all of these types of questions. As Green (1876, 74) states so succinctly, "Persons who use a popular library for purposes of investigation generally need a great deal of assistance." He then presents three pages of examples of the type of assistance that readers in his library requested.
3. **Aid the reader in the selection of good works.** People wanted to read but did not know what was worth reading. One of the major roles of the librarian was to serve as a readers' advisor, recommending material that fit each reader's interests and ability. Green (1876, 79), in discussing his reference librarian, comments, "I am confident that in some such way as this a great influence can be exerted in the direction of causing good books to be used. . . . Only let her aim at providing every person who applies for aid with the best book he is willing to read."
4. **Promote the library within the community.** Underlying all of Green's examples is the concept that by being personally available to members of the community, the librarian would generate support from the community, which of course would lead to more use of the library and greater financial support. Green (1876, 81) closes his paper by stating, "The more freely a librarian mingles with readers, and the greater the amount of assistance he renders them, the more intense does the conviction of citizens, also, become, that the library is a useful institution, and the more willing do they grow to grant money in larger and larger sums to be used in buying books and employing additional assistants." In other words, if you help them, they will come—and provide funding!

Changes Since 1876

Technology

Of course, society has changed significantly since 1876. The area that is most obviously different is the technology used in libraries. Whereas librarians in Green's time had essentially two formats, books and periodicals, librarians today use a wide range of resources. The reference librarian today almost always starts with a computer rather than a book when responding to a question. A wide range of types of machines are found throughout the library. Technology has transformed the way that libraries operate and the way that readers use the library. Over the decades, the library has gone from a place that relied on paper and pencil to one that uses silicon chips and electrons. Table 1.1 illustrates the parade of technology through libraries by decade.

Although this is a vast array of technologies, each of which has had a profound impact on libraries, all of these technologies can be broken down into three distinct categories: technology that stores information, technology that reproduces

TABLE 1.1 Technology Arranged Chronologically: A List of Technologies Impacting Library Services, Arranged by Decade

1890s	Typewriter	1980s	Personal computer
1920s	Telephone		Printer
	Radio		Floppy disk
1930s	Phonodisc		Audio compact disc
1940s	Television		CD-ROM
	Microfilm		E-mail
1950s	Tape recording		Electronic mailing lists
	Punch card	1990s	World Wide Web
	Slide		Internet chat
	Thermofax copier		E-commerce
1960s	Photocopier		Laptop computer
	Filmstrip		Wireless telecommunication
	Microfiche	2000s	iPod
	Microcard		USB storage device
	Telex		Smartphones
1970s	Mainframe computer		Text messaging
	Modem	2010s	Social media
	Video recording		Tablets
	Cassette tape		
	Telefacsimile		

information, and technology that communicates information. The technologies in Table 1.1 can be divided into these three categories, as listed in Table 1.2.

Some of these technologies are used to perform more than one of the three listed functions (such as the computer, which can do all of them), but each technology enhances the ability of the library to function in one or more ways. While each of these technologies is a tool that enhances library service, it does not fundamentally change the nature of that service. The next several years will undoubtedly bring about even more technological developments, and libraries will adopt those technologies that help them improve service to their communities. The chapters in Part I (Chapters 1–12) address many aspects of reference and discuss how technology continues to influence reference services.

Diversity

The other major change in libraries over the past 130 years has been in the nature of the populations that libraries serve. Since the 19th century, the population of the United States has become much more diverse. Whereas the users of libraries in Green's time were primarily English speakers of European descent, users of libraries in the United States today come from all over the world and speak hundreds of languages. As our communities have changed to incorporate immigrants from Asia, Africa, and Latin America, our libraries also have changed to include more materials about other cultures in more and more languages.

Diversity is not only ethnic in nature. In the 1870s, libraries existed to serve adults. During the ensuing years, libraries have established a number of specialized

TABLE 1.2 Technology Arranged by Function: A List of Technologies Impacting Library Services, Categorized as Technologies That Store, Reproduce, or Communicate Information

Storage	Reproduction	Communication
Phonodisc	Typewriter	Telephone
Microfilm	Thermofax copier	Radio
Punch card	Photocopier	Television
Tape recording	Mainframe computer	Telex
Slide	Telefacsimile	Modem
Filmstrip	Personal computer	Telefacsimile
Microfiche	Printer	E-mail
Microcard	Laptop computer	Electronic mailing lists
Video recording	Tablet	World Wide Web
Cassette tape		Internet chat
Mainframe computer		E-commerce
Personal computer		Wireless telecommunication
Floppy disk		Smartphones
Audio compact disc		Text messaging
CD-ROM		Social media
Laptop computer		
iPod		
USB storage		
Tablet		

services and departments for various segments of the population, including children, teens, senior citizens, veterans, persons with disabilities, students, teachers, the business community, unemployed persons, and virtually any other discrete population with needs that go beyond basic library programs or collections. Diversity has had an impact on reference service by creating the need to respond to these demographic changes. It is important to note that libraries have not always lived up to the ideal of providing equitable service to all people and instead left many communities underserved. Many public libraries in the late 19th and early 20th centuries were segregated, and services to immigrants during this time focused largely on assimilation, with little attention to the languages and cultures of the newly arrived. With a focus on culturally competent services and an emphasis on outreach and community engagement, libraries can continue to make strides in engaging with and providing better services to historically underserved and marginalized groups. For more on diversity, equity, and inclusion issues within reference service, see Chapters 11 and 12.

FUNCTIONS OF THE REFERENCE LIBRARIAN TODAY

So what do reference librarians do today? With all of these changes in technology and the growing diversity of users, what is reference like now? Surprisingly (or perhaps not), the actual functions of the reference librarian have changed very little over the years. A century after Green first discussed reference service, Thomas Galvin (1978) listed the functions of the modern reference librarian as follows:

- Assistance and instruction (formal or informal) in the use of the library
- Assistance in the identification and selection of books, journals, and other materials relevant to a particular information need
- Provision of brief, factual information of the "ready-reference" variety

More recently, in her dictionary of librarianship, Joan Reitz (2004, 602) defined reference services as including but not limited to answering substantive questions, instructing users in the selection of appropriate tools and techniques for finding information, conducting searches on behalf of the patron, directing users to the location of library resources, assisting in the evaluation of information, referring patrons to resources outside the library when appropriate, keeping reference statistics, and participating in the development of the reference collection.

The role of the reference librarian today is also reflected in the definitions of a reference transaction and reference work, adopted by the Reference and User Services Association (RUSA) of the American Library Association (ALA):

> **Reference Transactions** are information consultations in which library staff recommend, interpret, evaluate, and/or use information resources to help others to meet particular information needs. Reference transactions do not include formal instruction or exchanges that provide assistance with locations, schedules, equipment, supplies, or policy statements.
>
> **Reference work** includes reference transactions and other activities that involve the creation, management, and assessment of information or research resources, tools, and services. (Reference and User Services Association 2008a, emphasis in original)

Although these definitions do not mention the public relations role of the librarian, the functions described today are otherwise essentially the same as those mentioned by Green. While technology and information sources today are entirely different than they were in Green's era, the reference process and function are essentially the same.

REFERENCE WORK: VARIETIES AND APPROACHES

Styles of Reference Service

Although what librarians do has remained fairly constant over the years, the relative importance of those functions has varied tremendously. From the time that the first questions were asked by curious readers, the librarian has had to determine whether it is appropriate to *conduct* research for the patron or to *instruct* the patron in how to do that research. Do we give users the specific information they request, or do we teach them how to find it on their own? This debate has raged for at least a century and is one that is still appropriate today.

In one of the early textbooks on reference service, James Wyer (1930, 6–7) described three different philosophies of reference service, which he labeled "conservative," "moderate," and "liberal." In his landmark history of reference service, Samuel Rothstein (1961) calls these same philosophies "minimum," "middling," and "maximum." No matter what one calls them, these philosophies define the range of possible reference services. Simply stated, these alternatives are as follows:

1. **Conservative or minimum.** The primary role of the librarian is to teach patrons how to use the library. The librarian helps users find sources but does not read or interpret those sources for the user. The library is seen as an extension of instruction. Not surprisingly, this approach is most common in academic libraries.
2. **Moderate or middling.** The librarian not only teaches the user how to use sources but also provides answers to many questions. The librarian does not do homework assignments for students but will search exhaustively to find answers for research and factual questions. This model is most common in public libraries.
3. **Liberal or maximum.** The librarian takes the user's question, conducts the research, finds appropriate material, and presents it to the user. In some cases, the librarian even writes a summary or analysis of the information found. This type of reference service is most often found in special libraries, including medical libraries, law libraries, and corporate libraries.

The conservative/minimum philosophy emphasizes instruction over answers, the liberal/maximum philosophy emphasizes answers over instruction, and the moderate/middling philosophy comprises equal parts of each. All reference services fall somewhere within this overall spectrum; exactly where depends on the needs and expectations of the parent community.

Types of Reference Service

Within these philosophies and functions of the reference librarian, several particular types of reference service have been developed. Some common forms of reference service include readers' advisory, ready reference, research consulting, subject specialists, bibliographic verification and citation, interlibrary loan and document delivery, instruction, literacy programs, and outreach and marketing.

Readers' Advisory

Readers' advisory is the process of recommending titles, particularly fiction, for leisure reading to library users. In her dictionary, Joan Reitz (2004, 592) defines this service as follows: "A readers' advisor recommends specific titles and/or authors, based on knowledge of the patron's past reading preferences, and may also compile lists of recommended titles."

Commercial information suppliers have also jumped on the popularity of readers' advisory services by creating their own recommendation services. Shopping sites use aggregated data to recommend additional titles to consumers, music streaming sites recommend similar artists or styles to listeners, and video sites recommend similar themes to viewers. Recommendation has become a ubiquitous component of the always-online information age and is an example of how work originally done primarily by reference librarians has evolved into a standard service in a wide range of environments. For more on readers' advisory, see Chapter 21.

Ready Reference

Ready reference is the provision of short, factual answers to highly specific questions. Answers to these questions are usually verifiable as accurate or inaccurate. The following are examples of ready-reference questions: "What is the population of Chicago?" "How many apples were grown in Washington State in 2017?" "Who played the role of Stella in the film version of *A Streetcar Named Desire*?" "What is the address of the headquarters of Microsoft?" "In which year did Yugoslavia cease to be a single nation?"

Answering ready-reference questions is the most common image of the reference librarian. This image has been popularized by media, as in the portrayals by Katharine Hepburn and her staff in the film *Desk Set* (Lang 1957). However, ready reference has never been the primary function of reference service and is rapidly becoming an even smaller component of the reference librarian's duties. In the past, reference librarians did more ready reference simply because the sources required to answer such questions were in library collections and not in the hands of the users. With the development of the Web and sites such as *Wikipedia* and *Google*, users have access to this type of information on their own. As a result, there is less need to consult a librarian for ready reference. This is another example of how today's information age has changed reference services.

Research Consulting

A more common form of reference service is assisting users with research questions. These questions do not have single, factual answers but have many possible results that vary depending on the researcher's interests and needs. In this case, the librarian may suggest sources, search terms, and pathways that will lead to material relevant to the research project. Following are some examples of research questions: "Why did the various ethnic groups in Chicago settle in the neighborhoods that they now occupy?" "What is the effect of pesticides on apple production?" "What is Stella's psychological background in *A Streetcar Named Desire*?" "How did Microsoft grow into a company that dominates the information industry?" "What political, economic, and social issues led to the breakup of Yugoslavia?"

Each of these examples corresponds to one of the ready-reference examples in the previous section, but in each case the question touches on issues that are much more complex. There are a wide range of possible approaches, search strategies, and potential sources for every question, each leading the user in a different direction. The role of the librarian as a research consultant is to find out what aspects of the problem the user is interested in and to suggest possible search strategies that will lead the user toward the best possible sources. As a research consultant, the librarian may get the user started in the research, but the user will do most of the actual searching, potentially returning to the librarian for additional assistance several times during the process. Research consulting is more common in academic and research libraries than in other types, but it is becoming the dominant form of reference service in all libraries.

Subject Specialists

Many large libraries hire librarians to be specialists in a specific subject field or discipline. These librarians immerse themselves in the subject area, usually selecting materials for the collection as well as assisting users with specialized research. Although subject specialists can be assigned to cover any discipline, they are most common in areas that society sees as requiring more specialized knowledge to succeed, such as law, medicine, the sciences, and business. Subject specialists often have advanced degrees within their field of specialization. They work closely with the researchers who comprise their community and often handle very complex questions. Subject specialists are most often found in academic libraries, large public libraries, and special libraries.

Bibliographic Verification and Citation

Bibliographic verification is the process of reading, identifying, and interpreting citations to information sources. Those sources include books, journals, theses, web pages, manuscripts, or any other form of publication. In the process of verification, the librarian usually finds other reference sources that cite the same publication, corrects errors, and determines where to find the desired publication. As information becomes more complex, verification is a growing activity for reference librarians. Another function that is related to bibliographic verification is helping users to correctly cite the information sources that they have used. Students, researchers, and the general public all need to be able to provide accurate citations to their materials so that others will be able to find those same sources. With the wide range of available citation styles and an ever-growing number of information formats, users find it increasingly difficult to accurately cite the information sources that they use. This is extremely common in academic and school libraries where students are learning how to cite material, but citations are frequent queries in public and special libraries as well. Reference librarians are often the people behind the scenes who are most responsible for maintaining good standards in citations and references.

Interlibrary Loan and Document Delivery

Interlibrary loan is the process of sharing materials among and between libraries. The owning library may loan an item to another library for a specific period of time or may copy the original and deliver it to the requesting library. Interlibrary loan is a common service in most libraries of all types because it extends the range of material available to users beyond their home library's collection. Most libraries belong to consortia that determine which materials may be borrowed or photocopied. Using established codes and copyright guidelines (Reference and User Services Association 2008b), libraries regularly exchange material in all formats. When cooperative union catalogs such as OCLC were adapted for interlibrary loan, the process was made significantly easier, and the volume of traffic among lending libraries rose tremendously.

Interlibrary loan librarians spend a lot of time doing bibliographic verification. Their primary responsibility is to search for material requested by users, verify that the information is accurate, determine that the home library does not own it, and identify potential lending partners who can provide the material. Software such as OCLC's ILLiad and Tipasa make the processing of requests much easier for the librarian, allowing the same staff to handle an increasing volume of requests. For more about interlibrary loan, see Chapter 5.

Instruction

Green's first function of the reference librarian was to instruct readers about the library, and that instructional role continues well into the 21st century. Instruction tends to take two forms: direct and indirect. Direct instruction is characterized by the librarian communicating directly to the user and may be delivered through any of a number of channels. It may come in a one-on-one situation in which the librarian teaches the user as they work together on a query; it may be done in a voluntary group environment, through workshops or classes that teach general or specific skills to those who choose to attend; or it may be a required part of a specific course or assignment in which the instructor wants all students to use library resources. Required instruction is more common in academic and school libraries, whereas voluntary and one-on-one instruction are features of reference service in all libraries.

In indirect instruction, the librarian does not communicate directly with the user but communicates through instructional tools. Indirect instruction is provided in anticipation of user needs rather than in response to a specific request. In order to assist users with common problems, librarians create guides, pathfinders, videos, and tutorials that describe how and where to approach various research problems. Some guides cover specific issues, such as how to use the catalog, a specific database, or a specific reference source. Other guides may be directed at a specific discipline, such as bibliographies or web pages of useful materials in music or education. Guides may be in print or in electronic form and are updated as needed. For more about instruction, see Chapter 4.

Literacy Programs

Libraries have continued to play a role in education itself. Many librarians conduct literacy programs that are designed to teach reading and writing skills to those members of the community who have not acquired those skills through other channels. Frequently, these programs are aimed at adults who have not completed their schooling, for whom English is a second language, or who are new immigrants to the community. Literacy programs are most common in public libraries. These programs continue the historic role of the public library in educating members of the communities that they serve.

Outreach and Marketing

Public relations is as important in today's libraries as it was back in Samuel Green's time. Green realized the value of having the public interact directly with librarians, and this type of personal interaction has been a symbol of reference service ever since. However, librarians today have gone beyond a passive approach of waiting for users to come to the library and now work to generate interest in their communities. Academic and public libraries frequently have staff whose primary responsibility is to work with specific segments of the community to increase library awareness and use within those populations. In the academic environment, the library may target outreach efforts at specific disciplines or departments or specific types of users, such as faculty, graduate students, or first-year students. In public libraries, outreach is often directed at segments of the community, such as teens, senior citizens, veterans, or members of clubs or interest groups. Outreach activities continue to grow in libraries and are often a part of the reference librarian's duties. Some reference librarians spend more time on outreach and marketing than they do in ready reference and research consulting. Marketing and outreach are discussed in Chapter 10.

Models of Reference Service

As described in detail in Chapter 6, reference service takes many different forms, including service at a reference desk, roving reference, tiered reference, reference by appointment, and service to remote users.

Reference Desk

In this traditional model of reference service, the librarian staffs a desk or counter at a fixed location within the library. That location is usually in a prominent position within the building so that users can easily find it, often near the entrance to the library. The materials consulted by the reference librarians—books, indexes, computers, and so on—are usually found adjacent to the librarian for easy access. Users approach the desk when they have a question. The librarian may work with the user at the desk or take the user to the appropriate sources or facilities elsewhere in the building. One distinguishing characteristic of the reference desk model is that the user initiates the transaction, not the librarian.

Roving Reference

In order to provide more proactive reference service, some reference librarians wander through the library looking for users who may have questions. This has the advantage of offering assistance to users where they are already working on their research; of allowing more hesitant users to be helped; and of eliminating any physical barriers that the desk itself poses to users. The roving method is distinguished by the fact that the librarian is the one who initiates the reference transaction by approaching the potential user. Roving is used in many libraries, most often as a supplement to the traditional reference desk.

Tiered Reference Service

Tiered service is a model in which staff members with varying levels of skill answer different levels of queries. The theory behind tiered reference is that each level of staff will answer questions that best fit their training. Paraprofessionals or student assistants staff an information desk and answer directional questions and basic questions regarding library holdings, as well as ready-reference questions, freeing up reference librarians to answer all of the research-level questions. When a user comes to the desk with a complex question, that user is referred to the reference librarian on duty, who is often in a private office or another area of the building, away from the busy atmosphere of the information desk. A benefit of tiered reference is that high-level staff are not wasted on routine directional questions. The problem with this method is that many users simply accept the information provided at the first level of service and do not follow through with the referral. Tiered reference is slowly growing as a service model, especially in academic libraries.

Reference by Appointment

A more extreme version of tiered reference is reference service by appointment. In this method, users make an appointment to meet with the librarian. The benefit of this method is that the individual has the full attention of the librarian for an extended period of time. The disadvantage of appointment-based service is that many users do not want to wait for an appointment and simply accept whatever information they can find on their own. Appointment-based reference service is most often used with subject specialists in research and special libraries.

Service to Remote Users

All of the service models mentioned previously require that the user be physically in the library building in order to receive assistance. In Green's day, that was always the case. Unless a user wrote a letter to the librarian, the only way to make any use of the library was to go in person to the physical library building. In today's environment, individuals can communicate instantly with librarians at a distance using technologies such as the telephone, e-mail, chat, instant messaging, and social networking tools. As a result, many libraries have developed special reference services based on those technologies.

Reference service has been available by telephone for many years. This was such a popular service in urban public libraries that large public libraries often had separate telephone reference departments handling hundreds or thousands of calls each day. More recently, most libraries have established e-mail accounts or web forms that allow users to submit questions. Some have initiated virtual reference services using chat, instant messaging, or other software that allows the librarian to communicate over the Web with users. Because of the technical requirements of some of these virtual reference services, they are often established in cooperative ventures with other libraries or with commercial companies, such as Springshare's *LibAnswers +Social*. These services succeed when the community members served by the library are frequent users of those communication technologies. Virtual reference is now offered by many libraries of all types and has grown to become a standard service in many libraries. Today, a user outside the library building is as likely to use instant messaging or chat to communicate with the librarian as that user is to call on the telephone. Reference service via some form of communications technology is a standard component of almost all reference departments.

THE PERSONAL NATURE OF REFERENCE SERVICE

Whether they are physically present or not, people who ask reference librarians for assistance are often at a psychological disadvantage. In today's information environment, where information is available everywhere all the time, people feel that if they cannot find what they want then they have failed. Having to approach another person for help implies that they have to admit that they are a failure, which some users are not willing to do. Of course, the librarian does not see the user as a failure, but the user does not know that. Because users are not certain how to proceed, they rarely state exactly what they want.

It is very important that people feel comfortable in asking for the reference librarian's help and that each user is treated with dignity and respect. Most of the time, reference librarians are not helping users find specific, factual information but are helping the user to identify sources and suggesting search strategies. In this regard, reference service is more like counseling the user than it is providing the user with specific answers. Reference service is about developing a relationship between the user and the librarian, not about a specific answer to a question. In order to help librarians work with users, RUSA has developed a set of guidelines to assist librarians with the behavioral nature of the reference process (Reference and User Services Association 2013). This is where the reference interview comes into play.

The reference interview is a set of listening and questioning skills that enables the librarian to work with the user to figure out what the query really is. A good interview is a conversation between the librarian and user that identifies and clarifies what the user is looking for. In many cases, the user has not thought through their topic, and the librarian helps the user determine the parameters of the information need. By using good interview skills, the librarian can help the user define the information need and come up with some search possibilities to satisfy that need. For more information on the reference interview, see Chapter 3.

Even the most skilled reference librarians have limits to what they can offer. In some subject areas, especially law and medicine, the librarian needs to be very careful about giving advice to users. Even in his original paper, Green (1876, 78) recognized that librarians cannot provide answers to all questions:

> There are obvious limits to the assistance which a librarian can undertake to render. Common-sense will dictate them. Thus, no librarian would take the responsibility of recommending books to give directions for the treatment of diseases. Nor would he give legal advice nor undertake to instruct applicants in regard to the practical manipulations of the workshop or laboratory.

In light of recent events and the current political climate, formerly theoretical ethical issues for reference librarians have become practical realities. Ethical questions such as the provision of information that has the potential to harm society (e.g., how to build a bomb) are now concrete issues that reference librarians encounter in their daily lives. For more on the ethics of reference service, see Chapter 2.

HOW ARE REFERENCE LIBRARIANS DOING?

Reference service has become a standard component of library services, but is it achieving its goals? Are reference librarians really effective in teaching people to use the library, answering their questions, recommending resources, and promoting the library in the community? The evaluation and assessment of reference service present a number of challenges.

On a superficial level, reference staff can easily measure the quantity of reference transactions. Most reference departments keep statistical tallies that indicate how many users ask questions. This data is used to fill annual reports and is an indication of the busyness of the reference department. Sometimes these statistical tallies are divided by type of question, by subject field, or by type of user. Many different methods of tracking statistics are used, from simple tick marks to data tracking software. No matter what method of statistics collection is being used, a disturbing trend has arisen: fewer and fewer reference transactions are occurring each year.

The decline in reference statistics first emerged as a trend in the 1990s and, in the beginning, was reported anecdotally. More detailed analysis of reference statistics indicates that the decline in questions is a reality. The Public Library Data Service shows a 19 percent decline in reference questions at public libraries from 2012 to 2016, which was the largest decline in any service area measured (Reid 2017, 3). The decline in academic libraries is almost twice as large. During that same time period, the cumulative number of reference questions answered at all academic libraries dropped 35 percent (ACRL 2018). Collectively, reference librarians are answering far fewer questions than a decade ago.

Statistics such as this are measures of quantity, but how can one also measure quality? In the 1970s, the idea of unobtrusive testing of reference service was developed. This assessment method involves asking questions of librarians and comparing the answers received with the previously known correct answer. This method was popularized by Peter Hernon and Charles McClure in the 1980s. The results of these studies were disturbing: reference librarians gave correct answers only slightly more than one half of the time. This gave rise to what Hernon and McClure (1986) called the "55 percent rule": whenever a user asks a question, there is a 55 percent chance of getting the correct answer. This is clearly not very good. The results of unobtrusive testing have pointed out areas in which improvement can be made through staff training, collection enhancement, and other techniques to improve the accuracy of responses to factual questions. For more on reference assessment, see Chapter 8.

Because assessment techniques were producing such discouraging results, reference librarians went through a crisis of conscience during the 1980s and 1990s. This era was bracketed by two classic articles on the state of reference service: William Miller's (1984) "What's Wrong with Reference?" and the follow-up fifteen years later by David Tyckoson's (1999) "What's Right with Reference?" In between these two publications, reference librarians did a lot of collective soul searching. The most critical viewpoint about reference service was expressed by Jerry Campbell (1992), who attempted to shake reference to its conceptual foundation by proposing that libraries essentially eliminate the reference component of library service.

Some of the most prominent efforts to review reference services were the "Rethinking Reference" institutes organized by Anne Lipow (1993). These seminars reexamined each of the roles traditionally played by reference librarians, from the reference desk to instruction to management. Some librarians, including Steve Coffman (1999), looked to the commercial sector for ideas about customer service. Some very innovative new services came out of this period of reflection, most notably the concept of cooperative 24/7 virtual reference. Reference librarians may answer fewer questions now than in the past, but their time is taken with complex questions that require more sophisticated research skills.

THE FUTURE OF REFERENCE

What will happen next for reference service? Will the service side of the library remain a standard feature for years to come, will it fade into history, or will something else take its place? In another century, will reference service be viewed as an aberration of the 20th century, or will it still be a common service offered by libraries to their future communities? Of course, no one can say for sure. Many have made an attempt to predict what reference service will be like in future years, including a panel of experts who were invited to write papers for ALA/RUSA on this topic (Rockman 2003). The best indication of the value of reference service comes from its most important critics: the users. When asked, users consistently rate reference service as one of the most important features of the library. In survey after survey in every type of library, it is clear that users still place a very high value on Samuel Green's "personal intercourse between librarians and readers."

However, the fact that reference is popular now does not necessarily mean it will remain so in the future. Following are three possible scenarios in which the current model of reference service will cease to exist:

1. **Information tools become so easy to use that people no longer need assistance.** Users currently have the ability to find and retrieve more information than at any previous time in human history, but they still need help finding the information that they actually want amid the torrent of results. Although new tools do get better and make information easier to acquire, reference librarians still have a role in teaching people how to use them and in evaluating the results. In addition, the quantity and complexity of information are so vast that people will always need assistance in finding and using that information. Despite the advances in technology and tools, this scenario is extremely unlikely to occur.
2. **Information becomes entirely commercialized, requiring each user to pay for any and all information obtained.** This scenario is slightly more likely than the first but still highly unlikely. Although information has become more of a commodity in the past few decades, libraries serve as information utilities, purchasing information collectively for the use of all members of their communities. In addition, in a democratic society, federal and state governments will have an obligation to make information produced by government agencies widely available. Even when some information is privatized, other sources are available that will provide similar information at no cost. *Wikipedia* is the prime example of this phenomenon. Although it may not be as good an encyclopedia as *Britannica* or *World Book*, it is the single most heavily used reference source in human history. It has achieved that status because it is free, instantly available, and up to date. Those factors outweigh the scholarship—and the cost—of commercial encyclopedias. Information that is free is the information that will be used.
3. **Communities no longer value libraries and the services that they provide.** Sadly, this is the most likely scenario to occur. A few public libraries have actually shut down in recent years, including the Douglas County Public Library system in Oregon and the Norlina Public Library in North Carolina, both of which closed in 2017. School libraries have fared even worse. In the decade ending in 2015, 368 California school librarian positions were eliminated, a reduction of over 30 percent (California Department of Education n.d.), while across the country nearly 20 percent of school library positions have been lost over the past fifteen years (Lance 2018). Many corporations have already closed their libraries in efforts to reduce costs. Some students (and a few professors) have the idea that everything that they need is on the Web. If reference service is to wither away, it will be due to the decline of the library as a useful institution in the community. For this reason, Green's concept of promoting the value of the library to the community is becoming ever more important. Marketing and outreach activities are designed to prevent this scenario from occurring.

Reference librarians continue to provide personal service to the people in their communities. And reference librarians continue to instruct users, answer questions, recommend sources, and promote the library within the community. The amount of each activity is changing, most likely with answering questions going down and marketing and instruction going up, but the reference librarian of the future will continue to provide direct, personal service to members of the community. And the personal nature of that service is what will bring people back to the library, ensuring that it remains a vital institution in the collective mind of the community. Box 1.2 provides an argument for why reference librarians are still relevant.

Box 1.2 Why Do We Still Need Reference Librarians When We Have *Wikipedia* and *Google*?

It is the question that we have all heard before in one variation or another. After all, we live in a world in which every individual has instant access to more information than at any previous time in human history. With any networked device, we can all find information, take classes, make purchases, listen to music, watch videos, get directions, see what our friends are doing, and find out just about anything. In this connected world, why do we need libraries—or reference librarians?

It is a valid, but naive, question. The popular image of the reference librarian is of someone who dispenses answers. The question assumes that what librarians do is dispense facts. Do you need to find a biography of Einstein, the dates of the Norman invasion, the distance to the closest star, or the names of the seven dwarfs? You used to ask a reference librarian. But with the Internet, people no longer need to ask those questions—they can find that information themselves. Therefore, they naively make the assumption that reference librarians are no longer needed.

The problem with the question is that it misses the more subtle—and more important—nature of libraries and reference service. Yes, librarians sometimes give out factual answers. But most of the time, the questions that we get have no single answer. Is global warming real? Does listening to music while asleep improve memory skills when awake? Do diet soft drinks increase a risk of cancer? Are the beaches nicer in the Caribbean or in Hawai'i? We help our users with many more of those kinds of questions than we do for factual ones—and we always have. Finding facts is easy—answering complex questions is difficult. And it is for those complex questions that reference librarians are needed.

Reference librarians know how to search and how to evaluate information. We understand how to judge which sources are credible, and we know search techniques that find resources that simple searching cannot. We know how to determine an author's biases. We know how to identify the underlying political aspects of a document. And we never tell anyone else what we helped you with.

But the biggest impact of the reference librarian—and of the library—is on the community. Every library is designed to serve a specific community. Public libraries serve the people of a specific city or county. Academic libraries serve the faculty, staff, and students of a specific college or university. School libraries serve the students and teachers of a specific school. Medical libraries serve doctors, nurses, and patients at a specific hospital. Law libraries serve the attorneys and staff of a specific law firm. Each library is designed to add value to the specific community that it serves.

Some of that value comes from the library collections, which provide access to specific information resources that support the community. Yes, librarians purchase sources, build guides, and link to sites that meet the needs of members of our specific community. But the real value comes from the librarians who guide users to their information. Reference librarians serve as advisors, recommending the best information sources for each community member. Reference librarians serve as searchers, using specialized skills to retrieve the best information from the overwhelming number of documents available. Reference librarians serve as evaluators, identifying which sources are credible and which are not. And reference librarians serve as instructors, teaching community members skills to make them information independent.

The library—and the reference librarian—exists to serve the community. By interacting with reference librarians, community members become more information literate. And when a community is composed of members with a higher degree of information literacy, it becomes a better community. Libraries and reference librarians help the community learn and grow. Libraries and reference librarians help the community survive. Communities become better places when libraries and reference librarians are part of them. And that is why we still need reference librarians.

Adapted from Tyckoson (2014)
Used with permission from the American Library Association

REFERENCES

ACRL. 2018. "ACRL*Metrics*." https://www.acrlmetrics.com.

California Department of Education. n.d. "Statistics about California School Libraries." https://www.cde.ca.gov/ci/cr/lb/schoollibrstats08.asp.

Campbell, Jerry D. 1992. "Shaking the Conceptual Foundations of Reference: A Perspective." *Reference Services Review* 20 (Winter): 29–35.

Coffman, Steve. 1999. "Reference as Others Do It." *American Libraries* 30 (May): 54–56.

Dewey, Melvil. 1876. "The Profession." *American Library Journal* 1 (September 30): 5–6.

Encyclopaedia Britannica. http://www.britannica.com/.

Galvin, Thomas J. 1978. "Reference Services and Libraries." In *Encyclopedia of Library and Information Science*, vol. 25, edited by Allen Kent and Harold Lancour, 210–26. New York: Marcel Dekker.

Google. http://www.google.com.

Green, Samuel S. 1876. "Personal Relations between Librarians and Readers." *American Library Journal* 1 (November 30): 74–81.

Guild, Reuben A. 1878. "Access to Librarians." *Library Journal* 2 (January–February): 278.

Gutek, Gerald Lee. 1970. *An Historical Introduction to American Education.* New York: Crowell.

Hanson, Eugene R., and Jay E. Daily. 1970. "Catalogs and Cataloging." In *Encyclopedia of Library and Information Science*, vol. 4, edited by Allen Kent and Harold Lancour, 242–305. New York: Marcel Dekker.

Hernon, Peter, and Charles McClure. 1986. "Unobtrusive Reference Testing: The 55 Percent Rule." *Library Journal* 111 (April 15): 37–41.

Lance, Keith Curry. 2018. "School Librarian, Where Art Thou?" *School Library Journal* 64 (3): 36–44.

Lang, Walter, dir. 1957. *Desk Set.* Los Angeles, CA: 20th Century Fox, 2013. DVD.

LibGuides. Miami, FL: Springshare. https://springshare.com/libguides/. Subscription required.

LibAnswers +Social. Miami, FL: Springshare. https://www.springshare.com/libanswers/.

Lipow, Anne G. 1993. *Rethinking Reference in Academic Libraries.* Berkeley, CA: Library Solutions Institute.

Miller, William. 1984. "What's Wrong with Reference?" *American Libraries* 15 (May): 303–6, 321–22.

Poole, William F. 1876. "Some Popular Objections to the Public Libraries." *American Library Journal* 1 (November 30): 45–51.

Reference and User Services Association. 2008a. "Definitions of Reference." American Library Association. Last modified January 14, 2008. http://www.ala.org/rusa/guidelines/definitionsreference.

Reference and User Services Association. 2008b. "Interlibrary Loan Code for the United States." American Library Association. Last modified January 11, 2016. http://www.ala.org/rusa/guidelines/interlibrary.

Reference and User Services Association. 2013. "Guidelines for Behavioral Performance of Reference and Information Service Providers." American Library Association. Last modified May 28, 2013. http://www.ala.org/rusa/resources/guidelines/guidelinesbehavioral.

Reid, Ian. 2017. "The 2017 Public Library Data Service: Characteristics and Trends." *Public Libraries Online* (September/October). http://publiclibrariesonline.org/2017/12/the-2017-public-library-data-service-report-characteristics-and-trends/.

Reitz, Joan M. 2004. *Dictionary for Library and Information Science.* Westport, CT: Libraries Unlimited.

Robinson, O.H. 1876. "Librarians and Readers." *American Library Journal* 1 (November 30): 123–24.

Rockman, Ilene, ed. 2003. "Special Issue: The Future of Reference." *Reference Services Review* 31: 7–104.

Rothstein, Samuel. 1961. "Reference Service: The New Dimension in Librarianship." *College & Research Libraries* 22 (January): 11–18.

Rothstein, Samuel. 1972. *The Development of Reference Services through Academic Traditions, Public Library Practice and Special Librarianship.* ACRL Monographs 14. Boston, MA: Gregg Press.

Stone, Elizabeth W. 1977. *American Library Development, 1600–1899.* New York: H.W. Wilson.

Trustees of the Public Library of the City of Boston. (1852) 1975. *Upon the Objects to Be Attained by the Establishment of a Public Library*, City Document no. 37. Boston: J. H. Eastburn, Printer. Reprint, G. K. Hall. Citations refer to the Hall edition.

Tyckoson, Dave. 2014. "Talking Shop with Dave Tyckoson: The Importance of Being a Reference Librarian." *Booklist Online.* http://www.booklistonline.com/Talking-Shop-with-Dave-Tyckoson-The-Importance-of-Being-a-Reference-Librarian-Tyckoson-Dave/pid=7112623.

Tyckoson, David A. 1999. "What's Right with Reference?" *American Libraries* 30 (May): 57–63.

Wikipedia. http://www.wikipedia.com.

World Book Encyclopedia. 2019. 22 vols. Chicago: World Book.

Worldcat. http://www.worldcat.org.

Wyer, James I. 1930. *Reference Work: A Textbook for Students of Library Work and Librarians.* Chicago: American Library Association.

SUGGESTED READINGS

Cheng, Yungrang Laura, ed. 2008. "Special Section on Virtual Reference Services." *Bulletin of the American Society for Information Science and Technology* 34 (2): 6–28. https://asistdl.onlinelibrary.wiley.com/toc/15508366/2008/34/2.

This series of five papers discusses different aspects of virtual reference services: the history (and possible future) of virtual reference services, participatory librarianship, evaluation of virtual reference services, implementation of professional and ethical standards, and understanding nonusers of virtual reference services.

Green, Samuel S. 1876. "Personal Relations between Librarians and Readers." *American Library Journal* 1 (November 30): 74–81.

In the very first article ever published about reference service, Green discusses the need for providing service, gives examples of the types of service needed, and outlines the role of the librarian in providing service.

Kenney, Brian. 2015. "For Future Reference." *Publisher's Weekly* 262 (September 14): 20–21.

This article questions the role of reference service in today's libraries, highlighting that library users need help doing things, not finding things. Along with its follow-up article in the same journal on August 29, 2016, it presents a good debate about reference services today.

Lipow, Anne G., ed. 1993. *Rethinking Reference in Academic Libraries*. Berkeley, CA: Library Solutions Press.

The institutes on which this volume is based explore the need for changes in reference services to respond to changes in user needs, information delivery, and society, in general. Topics discussed include new staffing patterns, new administrative structures, new physical arrangements, and serving users who are at a distance from the library. Among several useful appendices is an annotated bibliography on the topic of rethinking reference.

Miller, William, and Rita M. Pellen, eds. 2007. "Reforming Reference." *Reference Librarian* 48 (2): 1–60.

This collection includes four papers presented by William Miller, Brian Mathews, James Rettig, and Jerry Campbell at a session at the 2007 national conference of the Association of College and Research Libraries titled "The Reference Question—Where Has Reference Been? Where Is Reference Going?" In addition, Anna Carlin's selective annotated bibliography of literature about reference services from 1984 to the present highlights factors that have contributed to challenge and change in reference services over the past twenty years.

O'Gorman, Jack, and Barry Trott. 2009. "What Will Become of Reference in Academic and Public Libraries?" *Journal of Library Administration* 49 (4): 327–39.

A thoughtful article on what is changing in reference and what the future may look like, it covers collections, services, delivery methods, and user expectations, with a base in the core values of reference service.

Rettig, James. 2006. "Reference Service: From Certainty to Uncertainty." *Advances in Librarianship* 30: 105–43.

Drawing on his own experience in academic libraries as well as the published literature, Rettig traces changes in reference service over a period of thirty years, highlighting trends in the areas of technology, rethinking reference, development of new services, assessment, collaboration, reference collections, and instruction.

Rockman, Ilene, ed. 2003. "Special Issue on 'The Future of Reference.'" *Reference Services Review* 31 (1): 7–104.

Five prominent reference librarians present their personal views of what the future of reference may look like, and other authors respond to these forecasts.

Rothstein, Samuel. 1955. *The Development of Reference Services through Academic Traditions, Public Library Practice and Special Librarianship*. ACRL Monographs Number 14. Chicago: Association of College and Research Libraries. Reprinted by Gregg Press in 1972.

Rothstein's comprehensive history of the first few decades of reference service compares the development of reference work in academic, public, and special libraries.

Schlachter, Gail A., ed. 1982. *The Service Imperative for Libraries: Essays in Honor of Margaret E. Monroe*. Littleton, CO: Libraries Unlimited.

Compiled in honor of a reference instructor, these essays present a thorough review of the four functions of reference service (instruction, answering questions, readers' advisory, and public relations), in addition to providing discussions of education for and assessment of reference services.

Thomsen, Elizabeth. 1999. *Rethinking Reference: The Reference Librarian's Practical Guide for Surviving Constant Change*. New York: Neal-Schuman.

Thomsen provides an overview of reference service in modern times, covering all aspects of reference service, including the history of reference, communication skills, answering questions, instruction, and the Internet.

Zabel, Diane, ed. 2011. *Reference Reborn: Breathing New Life into Public Services Librarianship*. Santa Barbara, CA: Libraries Unlimited.

Another in the long line of reference reform books, this one reviews developments in service models, the role of the reference librarian, technologies, collections, and the education and training of reference staff.

Chapter 2

Ethics

Emily J. M. Knox

MAKING ETHICAL JUDGMENTS

As Jean Preer notes in *Library Ethics*, ethics is about choices (2008, 1). Though many equate the job of reference librarians with simply politely answering patrons' questions all day, reference librarians make professional ethical judgments both large and small every day. Even the prosaic act of answering questions can involve ethical dilemmas that are not always readily apparent. Some of the ethical judgments that reference librarians make concern larger social and community issues such as what types of information to include in the collection and how to manage patrons' records, while others center on the questions that an individual patron might ask regarding, for example, health information. These decisions might seem to have little consequence, but even minor choices can have a huge accumulated impact. This chapter is a very short introduction to ethics and some of the ethical challenges that a reference librarian might encounter on the job. It is hoped that the information presented here will provide some understanding of the principles that guide contemporary librarianship. However, the chapter is not intended to be comprehensive, and readers are strongly encouraged to explore the Suggested Reading listed at the end of the chapter.

In *Our Enduring Values: Librarianship in the 21st Century*, Michael Gorman (2000, 5) defines values as "something that is of deep interest . . . to an individual or a group." For Gorman, librarianship's enduring values are stewardship, service, intellectual freedom, rationalism, literacy and learning, equity of access to recorded knowledge and information, privacy, and democracy. Ethics, or the application of values, is, along with metaphysics, logic, epistemology, and aesthetics, one of the major areas of study in philosophy. Ethics does not provide answers but frameworks for choosing a path forward among competing obligations and responsibilities. Ethics in the workplace is known as applied ethics and has long been the concern of scholars and practitioners of library and information science (LIS). Information ethics and its close and more recent counterpart, computer ethics, have a long history of scholarship. As will be seen later, because LIS is fundamentally concerned with the storage, organization, and circulation of knowledge, the ethics in the field is also closely related to epistemology or the study of knowledge. Debates over what sort of information should be provided in libraries; whether or not librarians should protect the privacy of all patrons, regardless of status; and how librarians should weigh their competing obligations to society, the profession, their institutions, and individuals have been part of the landscape of LIS since its inception.

One of the best historical examples of information ethics discourse in LIS concerns the so-called fiction question. Although librarians are now known for their commitment to provide all of their patrons with access to information, this was not always the case. As a profession, librarianship has often wavered between paternalism and autonomy with regard to patrons. Evelyn Geller (1984, 11) notes that "the freedom to read as it has come to be perceived, had little to do with the aspirations of the founders of the first public libraries, for the knowledge relevant to their goals was linked to quite different preoccupations. In a period that predated widespread secondary and higher education, the diffusion of knowledge meant certified knowledge of value to elites. . . . Libraries were established in opposition not to censorship but to [social] privilege." Libraries were intended to be places of social assimilation and, in order to fulfill this mission, they were expected to include only "good" reading material in their collections. In the late 19th and early 20th centuries, librarians held what might be called a traditional-modernist view of the effects of new knowledge on individuals and society wherein reading good books would lead to good outcomes while reading bad books would lead to the opposite (Knox 2014a, 11–26). As a result, "immoral" books, especially popular, naturalistic fiction, were excluded from libraries.

This attitude slowly started to shift during the early and mid-20th century. Geller (1984) attributes this to new ideas regarding the library as an educational institution; educational freedom required an open shelf. According to Joyce M. Latham (2009), the Chicago Public Library Board passed the first statement on intellectual freedom in the United States in 1936 followed by the Des Moines Public Library policy that is often cited by historians as the basis for the American Library Association's first code. This growing commitment to intellectual freedom and other liberal information ethics principles was eventually codified in the profession when the American Library Association (ALA) adopted its first code of ethics in 1939. In 1950, Leon Carnovsky, a professor of library science at the Graduate Library School at the University of Chicago, wrote that the public library has "no nobler function" than to "put teeth to the principle of free speech" (25). Over the latter part of the 20th century, librarians solidified their commitment to intellectual freedom primarily because they accepted two ideas. First, they accepted the epistemology of reader-response theory, which holds that different readers have different responses to the same text. Second, they accepted an agnostic-postmodernist view of reading effects wherein it is impossible to know how any one person might be affected by reading a particular text (Knox 2014a). Acceptance of these two premises gave librarians the philosophical foundation to invite any and all ideas into their collections.

Other ethical issues would gain importance in librarianship depending on current events. For example, the development of the copier in the 1960s and 1970s spearheaded the discussion regarding the rights of creators and protecting the rights of patrons to access information. After 9/11 and the passage of the USA PATRIOT Act and again with the revelations regarding federal surveillance of electronic information by Edward Snowden in 2013, protecting patron privacy moved to the fore. More recently, shifts in the political landscape, including the rise of nationalist political movements and ubiquity of social media hacking across the globe, have led to increased calls for carefully weighing the rights of individuals and groups against the stability of institutions, including public institutions such as the library. However, as will be shown later, even though these events have been the catalyst for various ethical discussions in the literature, librarians have remained committed to providing the best service possible for their patrons while weighing their various obligations to society, the profession, their institutions, and individuals.

MAJOR ETHICAL CODES FOR REFERENCE LIBRARIANS

Librarians do not work in a vacuum. As part of a profession, they receive both training and guidance to make ethical judgments in their work. Training happens in workshops, in classes, in continuing professional education, and on the job. Institutionalized guidance is provided through the codes of ethics and other statements of values and principles by various professional organizations, including the American Library Association, the Association for Information Science and Technology (ASIS&T), and the Medical Library Association (MLA). These statements are the codification of the values of the profession (Knox 2014b). However, it should be noted that codes of ethics can be quite controversial. Preer (2008, 5) notes that the first ALA Code of Ethics from 1938 was outdated before it appeared in that it embodied a "nineteenth-century view of libraries as repositories of collections and librarians as their keepers." Currently there are debates over the purpose of these statements along with calls to update and/or revise the Code of Ethics and the Library Bill of Rights. Ilana Newman's (2018) article in *Medium* on the 2018 dispute over the Library Bill of Rights Meeting Room Interpretation provides a good overview of some of the tensions currently being explored in the field.

Although all of the LIS codes of ethics described later have a slightly different emphasis, they all have several themes in common. All espouse varying levels of obligation: to the individual, to the profession, to the organization or institution, and to society (Rubin 2011, 40). The individual level refers to the obligations that the librarian has to each individual patron. The professional level refers to the idea that librarians should promote and adhere to the standards and principles of professional conduct that have been established by the professional organizations that have created the codes of conduct. The institutional level refers to the obligations that librarians have to uphold the mission of their institutions, while the societal level refers to the obligations that librarians have to serve the best interests of their society.

It should not come as a surprise that these obligations can sometimes conflict with each other. This is where training and practice becomes of the utmost importance, as it is the only way that librarians can gain the knowledge to balance the competing obligations enumerated in the codes of ethics discussed later. It should be noted that codes of ethics tend to be reactionary documents; an accumulation of outside events, such as changes in society, technology, or the law, will eventually spur a change in one of the levels of obligation, and the organizations will respond to that change by revising their codes.

The Code of Ethics of the American Library Association (2008)

The code of ethics that is most familiar to members of the information profession is the Code of Ethics of the American Library Association (see Appendix at the end of this chapter), most recently amended in 2008. The ALA originally adopted the code in 1939 in response to the spread of propaganda in the run-up to World War II and has amended it three times since then. It is considered by many to be the most general statement of ethics in librarianship.

ASIS&T (1992)

The ASIS&T approved a set of professional guidelines instead of a code of ethics. As noted in the document, because ASIS&T's membership has a less institutionally focused membership than the ALA's, the guidelines address information professionals who might work outside of traditional information institutions. The guidelines have not been amended since their initial adoption in 1992.

Medical Library Association (2010)

The Medical Library Association's (MLA's) Code of Ethics for Health Sciences Librarianship addresses a particular subset of librarians whose work may come in conflict with the expertise of another group of professionals, members of the medical community. It was most recently updated in 2010 and addresses not only librarians in traditional medical settings but also those who work in academic libraries and research organizations. MLA's code specifically addresses the impact that access to knowledge can have on health.

American Association of Law Libraries (2019)

The American Association of Law Libraries (AALL) updated their ethical principles in 2019. Like the MLA code, the AALL document addresses a particular subset of librarians, those who provide legal information services to both the legal profession and the public. Members of the organization work in law firms, academic law libraries, and other legal settings.

Society of American Archivists (2011)

Unlike the statements previously, the Society of American Archivists' (SAA's) code addresses a group of information professionals whose guiding principles are somewhat different from those found in traditional librarianship. It is divided into both a statement of principles available on the SAA website and a code of ethics that are intended to be used in tandem. Although access to information is still a guiding principle for archivists, the framework differs in that emphasis is placed on providing access to specific aspects of humankind's cultural heritage. For example, the code of ethics recognizes the privacy rights of users, donors, and "individuals and groups who have no voice or role in collections' creation, retention or public use."

OTHER ETHICAL GUIDELINES AND STATEMENTS

Along with the codes of ethics statements discussed previously, there are other guidelines and statements of principles that librarians use to guide their ethical practice. These vary according to country but are often mentioned when discussing ethics and librarianship.

The Library Bill of Rights (2019)

The Library Bill of Rights (see Appendix) is also a document from the ALA. It is often used as a guiding principle in many different library settings for developing policy along with the Code of Ethics. It differs from codes of ethics in that it addresses the purpose of the library as an institution rather than the various levels of obligations of the librarian. Many libraries also adhere to the Freedom to Read (2004) and Freedom to View (1990) statements, which enumerate the principles of intellectual freedom. The Library Bill of Rights was first adopted in 1953 and last amended in 2019. As it still refers to "books and other library resources," there are calls for the Library Bill of Rights to be revised in the near future.

The First and Fourth Amendments to the U.S. Constitution

Many libraries in the United States include a reference to the First Amendment of the U.S. Constitution in their policies along with the Code of Ethics and Library Bill of Rights. The familiar words of the First Amendment (see Appendix) cover many freedoms granted to U.S. citizens. Most importantly for libraries and ethics in librarianship, it prohibits the U.S. government from passing any law that curtails the freedom of speech. As noted earlier, many in American society consider the library to be the embodiment of this amendment in their local communities. The Fourth Amendment (see Appendix), while not often explicitly stated in library policy, protects the privacy of U.S. citizens and ensures that library records cannot be searched without a warrant.

The Universal Declaration of Human Rights (1948)

Outside of the United States, many libraries base their policies on the Universal Declaration of Human Rights. This document, which was passed by the General Assembly of the United Nations in 1948, enumerates the rights of all human beings, including, for example, the right to a fair hearing by a court (see Appendix). Articles 18 and 19 of the Declaration are most directly related to ethics in librarianship and discuss the right to freedom of thought and to freedom of expression.

The IFLA Code of Ethics (2012)

In 2012, the Committee on Freedom of Access to Information and Freedom of Expression of the International Federation of Library Associations and Institutions (IFLA) developed an international code of ethics for information professionals. Like the ALA Code of Ethics, it includes several levels of obligation. Librarians outside of the United States often base their policies on this statement of ethics. There are two versions—one long, one short. The long version discusses each of the enumerated principles in depth and is available on the IFLA website. The short version is found in the chapter's Appendix.

All of these guidelines and principles can be used as a framework for ethical conduct for reference librarians. In particular, these statements are used in the development of policy in information settings. The process for moving from a statement of guidelines to policy is discussed next.

WRITING ETHICAL POLICY AND COMPETENCIES

Although policy is often considered to be a dry subject, it is the written embodiment of an institution's values. Without thorough written policies, it is impossible to know, for example, what a particular library's stance is on privacy or how staff are expected to treat patrons. In essence, policies transform values into action (Nelson, Garcia, and Public Library Association 2003). They may be dry, but written policy provides guidance for many different stakeholders to understand the purpose of an institution and how it will enact this purpose in everyday transactions. Policies should be current, truthful, and accessible. That is, they must be updated on a regular basis, they should match what is actually done in an institution and should not discuss ideals, and they should be accessible both on the institution's website and, if feasible, in hard copy.

In their book on developing library policy, Sandra S. Nelson, June Garcia, and the Public Library Association (2003, 4) note that there are four different elements in policy documents: guidelines, statements, regulations, and procedures. Guidelines are the codes of ethics and other statements of principles listed earlier. They are philosophical in nature and provide a framework for the policy. Guidelines like the ALA Code of Ethics and the Library Bill of Rights are often referenced in the preamble to policies in libraries. Statements describe why an institution provides a particular service. For example, reference departments often include a statement of objectives that addresses the information services the department provides to patrons. Regulations define the policy statement and are what is generally understood as "policy" although, as mentioned previously, all four elements constitute policy for institutions. Reference services department policies often detail such regulations as the mode of delivery, how much time staff will spend answering a question, and sometimes which types of questions staff will not answer. Finally, procedures are step-by-step instructions for carrying out tasks, such as steps for answering questions using a chat reference client. Taken as a whole, policies provide guidelines for ethical behavior of librarians within a particular institution.

Along with policies, reference librarians are subject to certain competencies. These are lists of behaviors and best practices that reference librarians should exhibit in their work. Many information organizations have published competencies, including the Special Libraries Association, the MLA, and the SAA.

The Professional Competencies from the Reference and User Services Association (RUSA), a division of the ALA, serve as guidelines for reference librarians in many different settings and institutions. RUSA's guidelines build on eight core competencies:

1. Foundations of the profession
2. Information resources
3. Organization of recorded knowledge and information
4. Technological knowledge and skills
5. Reference and user services
6. Research
7. Continuing education and lifelong learning
8. Administration and management

These competencies specifically refer to behaviors that a librarian must be able to exhibit in order to succeed at their job and are available in full on the RUSA website (Reference and User Services Association 2017). It is important to note that reference librarians are not expected to have these skills on their first day of work; instead, they are expected to apply the knowledge they have learned in their coursework and should be open to "learning on the job" and further continuing education.

MAJOR ETHICAL AREAS AND ISSUES

Right of Access and Protecting Individuals and Society from Harm

Few areas of ethics are more at the forefront of reference librarianship than the protection of the right of individuals to access information and of both individuals and society from harm. Note that many of the codes of ethics as well as the RUSA competencies have some reference to access to information. For example, the ALA Code of Ethics (2008) states that "we are members of a profession explicitly committed to intellectual freedom and the freedom of access to information." Providing this access can take many different forms, and reference librarians are often the key to matching information seekers with materials that meets their information need. Richard Rubin (2011) notes that librarians are often seen as neutral arbiters of information. That is, when someone asks any question, the ALA Code of Ethics, Library Bill of Rights, and the Freedom to Read statements hold that librarians must answer the question to the best of their ability and "resist all efforts to censor library resources" (American Library Association 2008). However, it is important to note that this is not, in fact, a neutral stand. By answering any and all questions, reference librarians take a stand, one that holds that all questions should be answered (Jensen 2008). Instead of being neutral, librarians must define what it means to provide access to information for all and navigate the various tensions between providing information and serving both individual and societal interests.

These tensions manifest themselves in several ways. First, one of the most persistent situations focuses on the harm that the questioner might cause to oneself. The case study in Box 2.1 focuses on a patron who is giving signs of having depression and asks for a book about suicide. Other questions that involve harm to the individual include when patrons ask about information that concerns drug use or for materials that include extreme violence. According to the Code of Ethics and the Library Bill of Rights, no judgments should be made regarding the appropriateness of these materials for any individual. As discussed previously, because it is impossible to know how any one person might react to information, it is best err on the side of providing access.

Box 2.1 Activity: To Be or Not to Be

Melissa, a fifteen-year-old, comes into the Jonestown Public Library from time to time. None of the reference librarians in the library knows her well, but when Melissa passes the desk, she usually says "hi" as she goes by to any staff member who is stationed there. She is not a behavioral problem, although occasionally a staff member may have to tell her to keep her voice down. The reference staff are aware that Melissa has had "some problems," and there is a rumor that last year she tried to hurt herself.

Melissa approaches the reference librarian. She looks like she has been crying; her eyes are a little red and her face is slightly puffy. In a slightly shaky voice, she asks, "I've been looking for a book, but it's not on the shelf. It's called *Final Exit*. Can you tell me where it is?" You know that *Final Exit* is a book on how to commit suicide. You also know that it has just been returned and is on a cart ready for re-shelving.

Questions for Reflection and Discussion:

1. Should the librarian retrieve the book from the cart and give it to Melissa?
2. Should any other actions be taken?
3. Exactly what would you say to Melissa?
4. How would your reaction differ if you were a state-designated mandatory reporter?

Based on a scenario developed by Richard Rubin (2011).

Another tension concerns the issue of how much and what kinds of information should be available to patrons of the library, as illustrated by the case study in Box 2.2, which focuses on a so-called trashy book. Access to many different kinds of information of varying quality has become particularly salient with the rise in the ubiquity of the Internet in everyday life. Almost all libraries provide some sort of patron access to the Internet, and these computers often become a contested space in the library, especially those that provide services to children and young adults. In 2000, the U.S. Congress passed the Children's Internet Protection Act and held that institutions that use the E-rate, or the Universal Service Program for Schools and Libraries administered by the Federal Communications Commission's Universal Service Fund, to provide access to the Internet (usually public libraries and schools) must filter the Internet for information that might cause harm to children. The Supreme Court held that this is legal as long as adults are permitted to ask for the filters to be removed. Internet filters are clearly a violation of the ALA Code of Ethics as they restrict access to information; however, there are often good reasons for libraries to use them (Caldwell-Stone 2013). For example, libraries may be unable to afford the provision of Internet access to their patrons without using

E-rate. In this case, providing even limited, restricted access to resources on the Internet might outweigh the restrictions that filters impose on patrons.

With regard to harming both individuals and society, there is considerable debate over controversial materials in the library's collections, including materials that might be considered harmful to diverse groups, including, to use We Need Diverse Book's definition of diversity, "ethnic and racial minorities, people with disabilities, LGBTQIA, people of color, gender diversity, people with disabilities, and ethnic, cultural, and religious minorities" (We Need Diverse Books 2018). Answers to this debate depend on the mission of the institution. Reference librarians are encouraged to review both professional guidelines and local policies when making selection decisions. Lester Asheim's (1953) classic statement regarding the difference between censorship and selection can be helpful in this situation: "To the selector, the important thing is to find reasons to keep the book. Given such a guiding principle, the selector looks for values, for strengths, for virtues which will over shadow minor objections. For the censor, on the other hand, the important thing is to find reasons to reject the book; his guiding principle leads him to seek out the objectionable features, the weaknesses, the possibilities for misinterpretation."

The question of harm to society is addressed in a classic controversial request for information about explosives and other massively destructive materials. In 1976, Robert Hauptman went to thirteen different reference desks and asked for information on how to build a bomb. All of the librarians gave him the information (Hauptman 1976). Hauptman was quite horrified by this and stated in an interview from 2008 that he was "aghast" that they helped him (Buchanan 2008, 252). The Hauptman case is the embodiment of the tensions that exist between protecting the needs of the individual and protecting the needs of society. Most librarians, strictly following the code of ethics, would choose to answer patrons' questions even if the questions seem suspect. Librarians hold that since it is impossible to know what any one person might do with the information, one must err on the side of protecting individual rights (Knox 2014a).

Box 2.2 Activity: "Trashy" Books in the School Library

Mrs. Smith, a parent of one of the ninth graders at your affluent, suburban public high school, approaches the reference desk holding a copy of Lauren Myracle's *yolo*. Her daughter brought the book home last night, and Mrs. Smith is appalled that the school library would include such "poorly written trash." The book is written in a series of texts and chat messages and employs "text speech." You know that all of the books in Myracle's *Internet Girls* series circulate well.

Questions for Reflection and Discussion:

1. How would you respond to Mrs. Smith?
2. What resources would you use to support your response?
3. What other actions might be taken?

Equality of Access

Another ethical issue that affects both individuals and society concerns equality of access to information. It should also be noted that there is a difference between equality and equity of access. Equality means that all things are equal, that all libraries have the same services, while equity means the level of service is equal. As Betty J. Turock and Gustav W. Friedrich (2009, 24) note, "Equity adds the denotation of fairness, impartiality, freedom from favoritism, and justice."

One of the most important issues regarding equality of access in the 21st century is the digital divide. The digital divide (or, more accurately, digital divides) is a complex issue that can be understood on many different levels. For example, there is a divide among nations (how many citizens have access to the Web) and also among different types of communities within a nation (which communities lack broadband access). There have been many attempts to close the digital divide across the world. For example, UNESCO is highly involved in programs to create inclusive knowledge societies, particularly through the implementation of the goals of the World Summit on the Information Society (WSIS) held in 2005 (Souter 2010). The WSIS holds follow-up forums for implementation and review every year in Geneva. In the United States, the American Recovery and Reinvestment Act of 2009 included provisions for expanding broadband access across the country (National Telecommunications and Information Administration n.d.). The Federal Communications Commission presents an updated broadband deployment report every year. Libraries are an integral part of bridging access divides in the digital age and provide information for patrons in many different forms. In some respects, the presence of a library as an institution within a community can help alleviate this divide and facilitate equality of access. Non-information professionals often focus on books in library collections, but libraries also provide information through many types of media (magazines, newspapers, the Internet) and for many different purposes. Technology in libraries also supports patrons engaged in all aspects of the information cycle, including creation, for example, using a word processor to write a novel, and interaction, for example, providing access to e-mail, job sites, and coursework.

Another aspect of equality of access concerns levels of service that libraries provide. Should libraries provide an equal level of service to all individuals regardless of status? This is often harder to do than it might seem, as the library itself has its own interests. Discussions regarding whether or not public libraries should provide services for fees or the types of services that should be given to children are always a part of the LIS landscape. What is most important for reference librarians is to consider who or what benefits when policies are written that are onerous on the poor or deprive children from accessing particular types of information. For example, charging to use popular new books at public libraries will mean that people without disposable income have less access to those books. Also, children often do not have jobs, so it does not always make sense to charge them fines for overdue books. Navigating these issues is not always straightforward, but it is important to keep them in mind when developing ethical policies and guidelines for information institutions.

Copyright Issues

Copyright issues are ubiquitous in the information profession. Article IV of the ALA (2008) Code of Ethics states that librarians must "respect intellectual property rights and advocate balance between the interests of information users and rights holders." This has proven a thorny area in the digital age. Now that most serials and many books are available electronically, previous methods of balancing between rights of users and creators are proving untenable since the creation, copying, and storage of digital materials can often be done for a fraction of the cost of physical materials. For many years, the fair use guidelines of the 1976 Copyright law found in Title 17 of the U.S. Code and Title 37 of the Code of Federal Regulations have been seen as out of date. Seven different sections of the copyright code apply to libraries. One is the right of first sale, which was recently under scrutiny by the U.S. Supreme Court in the *Kirtsaeng v. John Wiley & Sons, Inc.* case. The Court found for Kirtsaeng and stated that it is not an infringement of copyright to sell copies of books purchased overseas. Another important section of the copyright code in the United States is Section 108, which describes how librarians may copy a work for use in their collections. Fair use, found in Section 107, is an exception to copyright, meaning that although the right to copy remains with the owner, when material is used under "fair use," this is an exception to these laws.

It is imperative that reference librarians understand Section 107 and "fair use." Although the vagaries of copyright law and fair use are too complex to go into detail here, it is important to at least be aware that there are four factors that must be considered whenever one is judging whether or not materials can be used under the fair use guidelines. These factors are purpose, nature, amount, and effect. Purpose refers to how the user or institution that wants the material will use it, including whether it is for noncommercial or educational use. Nature refers to the type of work. How the law considers books, images, videos, and journal articles differs as well as whether a work is creative or factual. Amount refers to how much of a particular work the entity wants to use. Obviously, there are different considerations for longer works such as books or movies as opposed to images or articles. Effect concerns the effect that using the copyrighted work will have on market value of the work. As an example, consider the fair use implication of using one chapter from a nonfiction, edited work versus a single chapter from a novella. Intellectual property law is complex, and reference librarians are not expected to be attorneys; thus, there are guidelines, such as the National Commission on New Technological Uses of Copyrighted Works, that librarians follow to guide the copying and sharing of works. Also note that due to the influence of Disney and other major content makers, copyright law in the United States will probably be reviewed and updated by Congress before 2023.

Confidentiality, Privacy, and Security

Concerns with confidentiality, privacy, and security have long been of interest to librarians. The 1939 ALA Code of Ethics stated that "it is the librarian's obligation to treat as confidential any private information obtained through contact with library patrons." In the United States, privacy is protected in the First and Fourth Amendments to the U.S. Constitution. With the rise of the Internet, the passage of the USA PATRIOT Act in the wake of 9/11, and the revelations of Edward Snowden regarding the National Security Administration's surveillance of private citizens, this area of ethics has become even more salient (Greenwald and MacAskill 2013).

Note that there is a difference between privacy and confidentiality. Privacy refers to the person, while confidentiality refers to data. That is, a librarian keeps facts about a person such as their address and birthdate private, but records of the books that they read are confidential. Before the digital age, librarians were primarily concerned with keeping patrons' records confidential. In *Library Ethics*,

Preer (2008, 183) discusses privacy as the paradox of access. In order to know what someone needs, they must be willing to open up about their need.

Reference librarians protect their patrons' privacy in many different ways. Chat reference (discussed in more detail in Chapter 6) is often conducted anonymously, and any personal information that is shared by the patron should be purged from the records. However, note that these records are often kept on servers that are owned by private businesses and not the library, which may lead to additional privacy issues. Librarians do not discuss individuals' questions with other people, including their fellow librarians, in ways that will identify the patron. For example, when sending an e-mail to colleagues for help on a question, the e-mail writer usually writes, "A patron asked. . . ." This is often done automatically, but this is an important aspect of protecting a patron's privacy.

With the revelations by Snowden and the ubiquity of sharing data online, it often falls to frontline librarians to inform patrons of what it means to agree to the terms of service for social media sites like *Facebook* or *Twitter* or Internet-services and product corporations like *Google*. In addition, the development of data analytics systems, such as Ex Libris's Alma Analytics, has led to new privacy questions with regard to the use of services and collections in libraries and how patron data is protected. For example, although libraries often delete patron circulation records to protect their privacy, this means that they do not have an overall view of the reading interests of a particular patron. Alma Analytics and similar services seek to harness this information to provide more tailored recommendations to each patron.

The issues involved in confidentiality, privacy, and security explore the tensions between information professionals' obligations to individuals and to society. In this area, librarians tend to lean on the side of protecting individuals from harm by society. Daniel Solove (2007) argues that privacy is made up of a plurality of things that mitigate the power relationship between the individual and the modern state. Although in common parlance privacy is about concealment and hiding things, Solove argues that privacy is actually about power, and it is important for reference librarians to both know and inform their patrons of what is happening with their data.

CONCLUSION

The aforementioned discussions have probably raised more questions for the reader than they answered. In some respects, this is always true of ethical discussions. Making ethical choices pervades every aspect of library service and is a continually moving target. New technologies and service models change some aspect of how the various levels of obligations mentioned in the information codes of ethics are weighed against one another. Although learning to make ethical decisions and keeping up with changes in the field can seem daunting, it is important to remember that, as discussed earlier, everyone makes ethical decisions every day. In a profession dedicated to acting in an ethical manner, LIS provides many different resources and tools to aid librarians in making these decisions in their professional lives.

Appendix
Code of Ethics of the American Library Association

As members of the American Library Association, we recognize the importance of codifying and making known to the profession and to the general public the ethical principles that guide the work of librarians, other professionals providing information services, library trustees and library staffs.

Ethical dilemmas occur when values are in conflict. The American Library Association Code of Ethics states the values to which we are committed, and embodies the ethical responsibilities of the profession in this changing information environment.

We significantly influence or control the selection, organization, preservation, and dissemination of information. In a political system grounded in an informed citizenry, we are members of a profession explicitly committed to intellectual freedom and the freedom of access to information. We have a special obligation to ensure the free flow of information and ideas to present and future generations.

The principles of this Code are expressed in broad statements to guide ethical decision making. These statements provide a framework; they cannot and do not dictate conduct to cover particular situations.

Adopted at the 1939 Midwinter Meeting by the ALA Council; amended June 30, 1981; June 28, 1995; and January 22, 2008.

I. We provide the highest level of service to all library users through appropriate and usefully organized resources; equitable service policies; equitable access; and accurate, unbiased, and courteous responses to all requests.

II. We uphold the principles of intellectual freedom and resist all efforts to censor library resources.

III. We protect each library user's right to privacy and confidentiality with respect to information sought or received and resources consulted, borrowed, acquired or transmitted.

IV. We respect intellectual property rights and advocate balance between the interests of information users and rights holders.

V. We treat co-workers and other colleagues with respect, fairness, and good faith, and advocate conditions of employment that safeguard the rights and welfare of all employees of our institutions.

VI. We do not advance private interests at the expense of library users, colleagues, or our employing institutions.

VII. We distinguish between our personal convictions and professional duties and do not allow our personal beliefs to interfere with fair representation of the aims of our institutions or the provision of access to their information resources.

VIII. We strive for excellence in the profession by maintaining and enhancing our own knowledge and skills, by encouraging the professional development of co-workers, and by fostering the aspirations of potential members of the profession.

Library Bill of Rights

The American Library Association affirms that all libraries are forums for information and ideas, and that the following basic policies should guide their services.

I. Books and other library resources should be provided for the interest, information, and enlightenment of all people of the community the library serves. Materials should not be excluded because of the origin, background, or views of those contributing to their creation.

II. Libraries should provide materials and information presenting all points of view on current and historical issues. Materials should not be proscribed or removed because of partisan or doctrinal disapproval.

III. Libraries should challenge censorship in the fulfillment of their responsibility to provide information and enlightenment.

IV. Libraries should cooperate with all persons and groups concerned with resisting abridgment of free expression and free access to ideas.

V. A person's right to use a library should not be denied or abridged because of origin, age, background, or views.

VI. Libraries which make exhibit spaces and meeting rooms available to the public they serve should make such facilities available on an equitable basis, regardless of the beliefs or affiliations of individuals or groups requesting their use.

VII. All people, regardless of origin, age, background, or views, possess a right to privacy and confidentiality in their library use. Libraries should advocate for, educate about, and protect people's privacy, safeguarding all library use data, including personally identifiable information.

Adopted June 19, 1939, by the ALA Council; amended October 14, 1944; June 18, 1948; February 2, 1961; June 27, 1967; January 23, 1980; January 29, 2019. Inclusion of "age" reaffirmed January 23, 1996.

United States Constitution

FIRST AMENDMENT

Congress shall make no law respecting an establishment of religion, or prohibiting the free exercise thereof; or abridging the freedom of speech, or of the press; or the right of the people peaceably to assemble, and to petition the Government for a redress of grievances.

FOURTH AMENDMENT

The right of the people to be secure in their persons, houses, papers, and effects, against unreasonable searches and seizures, shall not be violated, and no Warrants shall issue, but upon probable cause, supported by Oath or affirmation, and particularly describing the place to be searched, and the persons or things to be seized.

Universal Declaration of Human Rights

ARTICLE 18

Everyone has the right to freedom of thought, conscience and religion; this right includes freedom to change his religion or belief, and freedom, either alone or in community with others and in public or private, to manifest his religion or belief in teaching, practice, worship and observance.

ARTICLE 19

Everyone has the right to freedom of opinion and expression; this right includes freedom to hold opinions without interference and to seek, receive and impart information and ideas through any media and regardless of frontiers.

IFLA Code of Ethics for Librarians and Other Information Workers (short version)

PREAMBLE

This Code of Ethics and Professional Conduct is offered as a series of ethical propositions for the guidance of individual librarians as well as other information workers, and for the consideration of Library and Information Associations when creating or revising their own codes.

The function of codes of ethics can be described as

- encouraging reflection on principles on which librarians and other information workers can form policies and handle dilemmas
- improving professional self-awareness
- providing transparency to users and society in general.

This code is not intended to replace existing codes or to remove the obligation on professional associations to develop their own codes through a process of research, consultation and cooperative drafting. Full compliance with this code is not expected.

Endorsed by the IFLA Governing Board, August 2012. Reprinted with permission from the International Federation of Library Associations and Institutions (IFLA).

The clauses of this code of ethics build on the core principles outlined in this preamble to provide a set of suggestions on the conduct of professionals. IFLA recognises that whilst these core principles should remain at the heart of any such code, the specifics of codes will necessarily vary according to the particular society, community of practice or virtual community. Code making is an essential function of a professional association, just as ethical reflection is a necessity for all professionals. IFLA recommends the Code of Ethics for IFLA to all its member associations and institutions and to individual librarians and information workers for these purposes.

IFLA undertakes to revise this code whenever appropriate.

1. ACCESS TO INFORMATION

   The core mission of librarians and other information workers is to ensure access to information for all for personal development, education, cultural enrichment, leisure, economic activity and informed participation in and enhancement of democracy.

   To this end, librarians and other information workers reject censorship in all its forms, support provision of services free of cost to the user, promote collections and services to potential users, and seek the highest standards of accessibility to both physical and virtual services.

2. RESPONSIBILITIES TOWARDS INDIVIDUALS AND SOCIETY

   In order to promote inclusion and eradicate discrimination, librarians and other information workers ensure that the right of accessing information is not denied and that equitable services are provided for everyone whatever their age, citizenship, political belief, physical or mental ability, gender identity, heritage, education, income, immigration and asylum-seeking status, marital status, origin, race, religion or sexual orientation.

   To enhance access for all, librarians and other information workers support people in their information searching, assist them to develop their reading skills and information literacy, and encourage them in the ethical use of information (with particular attention to the welfare of young people).

3. PRIVACY, SECRECY AND TRANSPARENCY

   Librarians and other information workers respect personal privacy, and the protection of personal data, necessarily shared between individuals and institutions. At the same time they support the fullest possible transparency for information relating to public bodies, private sector companies and all other institutions whose activities effect the lives of individuals and society as a whole.

4. OPEN ACCESS AND INTELLECTUAL PROPERTY

   Librarians and other information workers' interest is to provide the best possible access for library users to information and ideas in any media or format, whilst recognising that they are partners of authors, publishers and other creators of copyright protected works. Librarians and other information workers seek to ensure that both users' rights and creators' rights are respected. They promote the principles of open access, open source, and open licenses. They seek appropriate and necessary limitations and exceptions for libraries and, in particular, seek to limit the expansion of copyright terms.

5. NEUTRALITY, PERSONAL INTEGRITY AND PROFESSIONAL SKILLS

   Librarians and other information workers are strictly committed to neutrality and an unbiased stance regarding collection, access and service. They seek to acquire balanced collections, apply fair service policies, avoid allowing personal convictions to hinder the carrying out of their professional duties, combat corruption and seek the highest standards of professional excellence.

6. COLLEAGUE AND EMPLOYER/EMPLOYEE RELATIONSHIP
   Librarians and other information workers treat each other with fairness and respect. To this end they oppose discrimination in any aspect of employment because of age, citizenship, political belief, physical or mental ability, gender, marital status, origin, race, religion or sexual orientation. They support equal payment for equal work between men and women, share their professional experience, and contribute towards the work of their professional associations.

REFERENCES

American Association of Law Libraries. 2019. "Ethical Principles." Last modified August 30, 2019. https://www.aallnet.org/about-us/what-we-do/policies/public-policies/aall-ethical-principles/.

American Library Association. 1990. "Freedom to View Statement." Last modified January 10, 1990. http://www.ala.org/advocacy/intfreedom/freedomviewstatement.

American Library Association. 2004. "Freedom to Read Statement." Last modified June 30, 2004. http://www.ala.org/advocacy/intfreedom/freedomreadstatement.

American Library Association. 2008. "Code of Ethics." Last modified January 22, 2008. http://www.ala.org/tools/ethics.

American Library Association. 2019. "Library Bill of Rights." Last modified January 29, 2019. http://www.ala.org/advocacy/intfreedom/librarybill.

Asheim, L. 1953. "Not Censorship but Selection." *Wilson Library Bulletin* 28: 63–67.

Association for Information Science and Technology (ASIS&T). 1992. "Professional Guidelines." Last modified May 30, 1992. https://www.asist.org/about/asist-professional-guidelines/.

Buchanan, Elizabeth. 2008. "On Theory, Practice, and Responsibilities: A Conversation with Robert Hauptman." *Library & Information Science Research* 30 (4): 250–56.

Caldwell-Stone, Deborah. 2013. "Filtering and the First Amendment." *American Libraries* 44 (3/4): 58–61.

Carnovsky, Leon. 1950. "The Obligations and Responsibilities of the Librarian Concerning Censorship." *The Library Quarterly* 20 (1): 21–32.

Ex Libris. 2018. "Alma." https://www.exlibrisgroup.com/products/alma-library-services-platform/.

Facebook. http://www.facebook.com

Geller, Evelyn. 1984. *Forbidden Books in American Public Libraries, 1876–1939: A Study in Cultural Change*. Westport, CT: Greenwood.

Google. http://www.google.com.

Gorman, Michael. 2000. *Our Enduring Values: Librarianship in the 21st Century*. Chicago, IL: American Library Association.

Greenwald, Glenn, and Ewen MacAskill. 2013. "NSA Prism Program Taps in to User Data of Apple, Google and Others." *The Guardian*, June 7. http://www.theguardian.com/world/2013/jun/06/us-tech-giants-nsa-data.

Hauptman, Robert. 1976. "Professionalism or Culpability? An Experiment in Ethics." *Wilson Library Bulletin* 50 (8): 626–27.

International Federation of Library Associations and Institutions. 2012. "Code of Ethics." Last modified December 27, 2016. https://www.ifla.org/publications/node/11092.

Jensen, Robert. 2008. "Myth of the Neutral Professional." In *Questioning Library Neutrality*, edited by Alison Lewis, 89–96. Duluth, MN: Library Juice.

Knox, Emily J. M. 2014a. "Intellectual Freedom and the Agnostic-Postmodern View of Reading Effects." *Library Trends* 63 (1): 11–26.

Knox, Emily J. M. 2014b. "Supporting Intellectual Freedom: Symbolic Capital and Practical Philosophy in Librarianship." *The Library Quarterly* 84 (1): 1–14.

Latham, Joyce M. 2009. "Wheat and Chaff: Carl Roden, Abe Korman, and the Definitions of Intellectual Freedom in the Chicago Public Library." *Libraries & the Cultural Record* 44 (3): 279–98.

Medical Library Association. 2010. "Code of Ethics for Health Sciences Librarianship." Last modified June 2010. https://www.mlanet.org/page/code-of-ethics.

National Telecommunications and Information Administration. n.d. "BroadbandUSA." http://www2.ntia.doc.gov/about.

Nelson, Sandra S., June Garcia, and Public Library Association. 2003. *Creating Policies for Results: From Chaos to Clarity*. Chicago, IL: American Library Association.

Newman, Ilana. 2018. "Hate Groups in Meeting Room B, Right Next to the Children's Books." *Medium* (blog). July 13, 2018. https://medium.com/@ilananewman/hate-groups-in-meeting-room-b-right-next-to-the-childrens-books-ccd9787003c2.

Preer, Jean. 2008. *Library Ethics*. Westport, CT: Libraries Unlimited.

Reference and User Services Association. 2017. "Professional Competencies for Reference and User Services Librarians." American Library Association. Last modified September 7, 2017. http://www.ala.org/rusa/resources/guidelines/professional.

Rubin, Richard E. 2011. "Ethical Aspects of Reference Services." In *Reference and Information Services: An Introduction*, edited by Richard E. Bopp and Linda C. Smith, 4th ed., 29–56. Santa Barbara, CA: Libraries Unlimited.

Society of American Archivists. 2011. "Core Values Statement and Code of Ethics." Last modified September 30, 2018. https://www2.archivists.org/statements/saa-core-values-statement-and-code-of-ethics.

Solove, Daniel J. 2007. "'I've Got Nothing to Hide' and Other Misunderstandings of Privacy." *San Diego Law Review* 44: 745–72.

Souter, David. 2010. "Towards Inclusive Knowledge Societies: A Review of UNESCO's Action in Implementing the WSIS Outcomes." UNESCO. http://www.unesco.org/new/en/communication-and-information/resources/publications-and-communication-materials/publications/full-list/towards-inclusive-knowledge-societies-a-review-of-unescos-action-in-implementing-the-wsis-outcomes/.

Turock, Betty J., and Gustav W. Friedrich. 2009. "Access in a Digital Age." In *Encyclopedia of Library and Information Sciences*, edited by Marcia J. Bates and Mary Niles Maack, 3rd ed., 23–33. New York: Taylor & Francis.

Twitter. http://www.twitter.com.

United Nations. 1948. "Universal Declaration of Human Rights." http://www.un.org/en/universal-declaration-human-rights/.

We Need Diverse Books. 2018. "Our Definition of Diversity." https://diversebooks.org/about-wndb/.

SUGGESTED READINGS

American Library Association. 2015. *Intellectual Freedom Manual*. 9th ed. Chicago, IL: American Library Association.

This handbook provides a comprehensive overview of the American Library Association's official positions on many issues related to intellectual freedom. The Code of Ethics, Library Bill of Rights, and the Freedom to Read Statement as well as the myriad interpretations of each are included. The ninth edition includes seventeen new or updated policy statements. Historical documents are now published in a separate supplement.

Besnoy, Amy L., ed. 2009. *Ethics and Integrity in Libraries*. New York: Routledge.

This anthology of articles from the *Journal of Library Administration* provides a wide range of views on various aspects of information ethics in libraries, including fair use law and plagiarism. It is particularly concerned with maintaining the integrity of the library as an institution that provides access to information for all.

Buchanan, Elizabeth A., Kathrine A. Henderson, and Robert Hauptman. 2009. *Case Studies in Library and Information Science Ethics*. Jefferson, NC: McFarland.

Case Studies includes both theoretical and practical insight into ethical issues in LIS. It has more than one hundred case studies and discussion questions in the areas of intellectual freedom, privacy, intellectual property, professional ethics, and intercultural information ethics.

Fallis, Don. 2007. "Information Ethics for Twenty-first Century Library Professionals." *Library Hi Tech* 25 (1): 23–36.

This article provides general background on various ethical concepts in the information professions. Fallis argues that information ethics is primarily concerned with providing access to information. He notes that codes of ethics are valuable resources for librarians and other information professionals even though their meaning is sometimes unclear and they do not always provide guidance when there are conflicts among obligations.

Hauptman, Robert. 2002. *Ethics and Librarianship*. Jefferson, NC: McFarland.

Hauptman, who conducted the famous research question experiment described earlier, offers a normative view of professional ethics in librarianship. The monograph covers many topics, including intellectual freedom, technical and access services, and reference.

International Review of Information Ethics. Stuttgart, Germany: International Center for Information Ethics, 2004. Semiannual. http://www.i-r-i-e.net/index.htm.

The *International Review of Information Ethics* is the official journal of the International Center for Information Ethics. It is primarily focused on information technology and ethics in an international context. The journal is available free of charge online, and articles may be published in English, French, German, Portuguese, and Spanish.

Isaacson, David. 2004. "Is the Correct Answer the Right One?" *Journal of Information Ethics* 13 (1): 14–18.

This article deftly explores how one might resolve dilemmas that occur when a patron is provided with the correct answer but is not happy with it.

Journal of Information Ethics. Edited by Robert Hauptman. Jefferson, NC: McFarland, 1992. Semiannual.

This journal, published in the United States, focuses on many different ethical issues, including privacy, human rights, copyright, and professional values.

Mathiesen, Kay. 2015. "Informational Justice: A Conceptual Framework for Social Justice in Library and Information Services." *Library Trends* 64 (2): 198–225.

This article provides a philosophical foundation for justice in library services, including reference.

Moore, Adam D., ed. 2005. *Information Ethics: Privacy, Property, and Power*. Seattle: University of Washington.

This book provides a short introduction to ethical theory and several short frameworks for analyzing ethical issues, including excerpts from John Stuart Mill's *Utilitarianism* and Immanuel Kant's *The Metaphysics of Morals*. It then covers specific areas of information ethics, including intellectual property, privacy, and freedom of speech.

Preer, Jean. 2008. *Library Ethics*. Westport, CT: Libraries Unlimited.

Preer's text endeavors to provide an ethical framework for decision-making that endures even when the values of librarianship are reexamined. It offers many historical cases to examine the issues of access, conflicts of interest, and confidentiality.

Reference and User Services Association. 2017. "Professional Competencies for Reference and User Services Librarians." American Library Association. Last modified September 7, 2017. http://www.ala.org/rusa/resources/guidelines/professional.

RUSA's guidelines offer standards for professional behavior in reference services. The guidelines have implications for ethics and cover areas such as access, marketing, and evaluation. Other organizations such as ASIS&T, AALL, MLA, and SAA offer guidelines for educational objectives in their respective areas. These are easily obtained online and also provide guidance for ethical behavior.

Rubin, Richard E., and Thomas J. Froehlich. 2017. "Ethical Aspects of Library and Information Science." In *Encyclopedia of Library and Information Sciences*, edited by John D. MacDonald and Michael Levine-Clark, 4th ed., 1469–83. New York: Taylor & Francis.

Rubin and Froehlich's article provides an excellent introduction to ethics in LIS. It takes the perspective that information professionals operate as both members of staff for a particular institution and members of a profession. The article covers privacy, selection, reference, copyright, administrative, access, technology-related, conflicting loyalties, and societal issues.

Solove, Daniel J. 2007. "'I've Got Nothing to Hide' and Other Misunderstandings of Privacy." *San Diego Law Review* 44: 745–72.

Solove offers a theory of privacy as a plurality of things that mitigate the power relationships between people and the modern state.

Zaïane, Jane Robertson. 2011. "Global Information Ethics in LIS." *Journal of Information Ethics* 20 (2): 25–41.

This article compares and contrasts ten national codes of ethics. The author found nine patterns, including references to human rights, copyright, and privacy, but not much mention of technology.

Chapter 3

The Reference Interview

Laura Saunders

INTRODUCTION

The reference interview is the heart of reference service. Through a structured conversation, information professionals can ensure that they understand the patron's information need and answer it as fully as possible. As discussed in Chapter 8, research shows that an effective reference interview can lead to more accurate answers (Hernon and McClure 1987) and better patron satisfaction (Durrance 1989; Radford 2006; Radford and Connaway 2009). While this chapter discusses that interview in terms of libraries, the reference interview process is applicable across many different settings and jobs. Help desk and technology specialists use the same skills when assisting a user in troubleshooting a computer problem; instructors engage in the process when helping learners to think through difficult concepts or assignments; and archivists use the reference interview to assist patrons in using archival collections. Essentially anyone who fields questions and offers guidance in finding answers can benefit from understanding the reference interview process.

While the reference interview might seem like a simple concept, it is actually complex and requires both deep knowledge of information sources and institutional collections and strong interpersonal skills to build relationships and engage in effective conversations. This chapter provides an in-depth overview of the theory and practice of the reference interview.

DEFINITION AND OVERVIEW

The reference interview can be defined as a structured conversation between an information professional and a patron in which the information professional clarifies the patron's information need and guides the patron in finding, evaluating, and using information to meet that need. According to the *Dictionary for Library and Information Science*, the reference interview is

> the interpersonal communication that occurs between a reference librarian and a library user to determine the person's specific information need(s), which may turn out to be different than the reference question as initially posed. Because patrons are often reticent, especially in face-to-face interaction, patience and tact may be required on the part of the librarian. A reference interview may occur in person, by telephone, or electronically (usually via e-mail) at the request of the user, but a well-trained reference librarian will sometimes initiate communication if a hesitant user appears to need assistance. (Reitz 2004)

The Society of American Archivists defines the reference interview within an archive setting as "a conversation between an archivist and a researcher designed to give the researcher an orientation to the use of the materials, to help the researcher identify relevant holdings, and to ensure that research needs are met" (Society of American Archivists n.d.). The Reference and User Services Association (RUSA 2013), of the American Library Association (ALA), outlines five areas of the reference interview: visibility/approachability, interest, listening/inquiring, searching, and follow-up. Building on these five areas, the reference interview can be seen as having five main steps: opening, question negotiation, search and location of information, communication of the answer, and follow-up and closure, with each step complemented by specific interpersonal behaviors.

Opening

Most reference interactions begin with a patron approaching the reference librarian with a question, whether in person or through remote services, as described in Chapter 6. To ensure easy access, reference services should be highly visible. For in-person services, this means locating the reference desk or the librarian's office in a prominent or high-traffic area, with good signage. Information for remote services should be made available in multiple points on the library website and should be clearly labeled (Schwartz 2014; van Duinkerken, Stephens, and MacDonald 2009). However, visibility does not necessarily ensure use.

There are many reasons patrons might find it intimidating to approach a reference librarian, including worry that their question might be "dumb," belief that they should be able to answer their question without help, and fear of being stereotyped (Black 2016). The subject of the question could be sensitive. For example, patrons who have recently been diagnosed with an illness, have questions about immigration and citizenship, or are questioning their sexual identity might all be worried about being judged or stereotyped if they ask questions related to these issues. Many patrons also experience library anxiety, an affective state in which a general fear of having to navigate the library or its information sources can prevent patrons from accessing the library or undermine their ability to understand and think critically about the sources they encounter (Mellon 1986). It is important for librarians to be aware of and minimize these barriers to increase the accessibility of their services.

The RUSA *Behavioral Guidelines* (2013) note that the "librarian's first step in initiating the reference transaction is to make the patron feel comfortable in a situation that can be perceived as intimidating, confusing, or overwhelming." In person, librarians might do other work at the reference desk when it is quiet. While that might be a good use of downtime, if the librarian looks busy, patrons might hesitate to interrupt. Librarians must keep an eye on their surroundings, notice patrons who might be waiting to ask a question, and, once engaged with a patron, set all other work aside and direct their full attention to that patron. To put the patron at ease, RUSA (2013) advises librarians to acknowledge patrons by making eye contact, using "open" body language such as smiling and leaning forward, and offering a greeting. Librarians can also initiate a reference transaction by asking patrons if they could use help. Librarians offering remote reference services should respond to questions in a timely manner and be sure to greet the patron before launching into the full reference interview. Wyoma van Duinkerken, Jane Stephens, and Karen MacDonald (2009) suggest using a system of triage to identify and delegate different types of questions in order to reduce wait times.

Librarians should show "a high degree of objective, nonjudgmental interest in the reference transaction" (Reference and User Services Association 2013). Most reference professionals are naturally curious and appreciate the opportunity to explore interesting questions on many different topics. But, occasionally, librarians will be faced with questions that do not pique their interest or find themselves answering the same question over and over. It is the reference librarian's job to "embrace each patron's informational need and . . . be committed to providing the most effective assistance" (Reference and User Services Association 2013). In a face-to-face interaction, librarians can convey interest through nonverbal signals such as maintaining eye contact, smiling and nodding, and facing the patron. During remote reference encounters, the librarian can maintain word contact through brief notes or responses to show that they are listening and understanding (Schwartz 2014; van Duinkerken, Stephens, and MacDonald 2009). After receiving a patron's question, the librarian might respond by saying "That's a very interesting question," before going on to clarify the question or offer an answer. Word contact can be facilitated by having some scripted prompts prepared that can be either generated by the system or quickly copied and pasted into a chat window.

Reference professionals must also be objective and nonjudgmental while answering questions. As noted earlier, patrons might share personal or sensitive information during a reference transaction, or they might ask questions the reference librarian finds unpleasant, uncomfortable, or even offensive, including questions about sex or sexuality, abortion, religion, politics, or other topics. Questions about drugs, bombs, suicide, or other topics could sound suspicious or dangerous. Regardless of the nature of the question, the librarian should strive to refrain from judging the patron or their information need and be careful not to react with surprise, alarm, or hostility. If a librarian seems surprised or put off by a patron's question, the patron might feel embarrassed, or as though they or their questions are not valued, and they might hesitate to use the service again.

That librarians have an obligation to answer a question even if it is unpleasant or objectionable is implied in the ALA Code of Ethics (2008), which instructs that "we distinguish between our personal convictions and professional duties and do not allow our personal beliefs to interfere with fair representation of the aims of our institutions or the provision of access to their information resources." In other words, while an individual librarian might be personally opposed to abortion, they should not refuse to answer a patron's question about accessing abortion or Planned Parenthood services. Dealing with uncomfortable or offensive requests is discussed in greater depth in Chapter 2, but it is worth reiterating that in most cases librarians do not know what a patron's underlying motive is for requesting such information. It is possible, for instance, that a patron requesting controversial information is a journalist doing background information for an article, a student writing a research paper, or someone who is simply curious.

Question Negotiation

Question negotiation involves a series of open- and closed-ended questions and active listening to clarify the patron's question and ensure that the librarian clearly understands the information need. At first, question negotiation might seem counterintuitive or a waste of time, but it is based on the recognition that patrons' opening questions rarely reflect their true information need. Initial questions are often "ill-formed queries" (Dewdney and Michell 1996, 520). They might be incomplete, based on faulty information or misunderstandings, or poorly phrased, and research suggests that patrons' opening questions do not reflect their actual need as much as 40 percent of the time (Dewdney and Michell 1996, 1997).

There are many reasons that patrons might not ask their "real" question immediately. If the patron is unfamiliar with the topic, they may lack the vocabulary or the background knowledge to form the question. Sometimes patrons are unsure of the purpose of reference services or the extent to which the librarian can help them, and they might begin with a question that they believe is within the scope of the service. Often, the patrons' first question will be quite broad, and it is only through question negotiation that the librarian can narrow down the topic. For instance, a patron asking for books about World War I might actually be interested in a certain battle, want to explore specific questions around weaponry, or be interested in events leading up to the war.

In some cases, the patron might have a complex question and might be breaking the question down into parts that seem manageable. A person who is starting their own business, for example, might have questions about writing a business plan, finding funding, marketing their product, exploring zoning laws for commercial properties, and so on, but they might choose just one of those areas to begin. Even questions that seem straightforward or unambiguous on the surface might mask additional or more complex questions. For example, a patron might ask if the library has cookbooks, when they are actually looking for a specific recipe. If the librarian simply sends them to the cookbook section, the patron might never find the exact recipe they want. Catherine Sheldrick Ross (2003) contends that librarians should not take any questions at face value but should always conduct a reference interview.

In most cases, question negotiation will involve a mix of open- and closed-ended questions along with active listening. Open-ended questions require more than a "yes" or "no" answer and are generally more effective in spurring dialogue. Some examples of open-ended questions include "Can you tell me a little more about your topic?" "What do you already know about this topic?" and "What more would you like to learn about this subject?" Once the focus of the question is understood, the librarian can use closed-ended questions, or questions that have a "yes" or "no" or single-choice answer, to further refine the topic. Examples of closed-ended questions include "Are you interested in books, or would you prefer Web resources?" "Have you done any previous research on this topic?" and "Do you need peer-reviewed articles?"

Throughout the reference interview, the librarian should be careful to adapt their communication style to suit the individual patron. Depending on the patron's age, language and literacy level, and depth of knowledge in the subject area, the librarian might need to adjust their own vocabulary and should always avoid using technical terminology or jargon that would be unfamiliar to most. It is not helpful to ask patrons if they checked the OPAC (online public access catalog) for an item, since most patrons will not know what the OPAC is. Instead, the librarian could ask the patron what they have already done to explore the topic.

While engaging in question clarification, the librarian should continue to use verbal and nonverbal cues to demonstrate active listening and convey interest. They should allow the patron to state their full question before asking any follow-up questions or beginning a search (Reference and User Services Association 2013) and keep their attention focused on the patron. Paraphrasing the patron's question can be useful during question negotiation. When the librarian rephrases the patron's question, they signal that they are listening and give the patron a chance to refine or refocus the question as necessary. The librarian might also state their understanding of the research goals and allow the patron to confirm or clarify their understanding (Reference and User Services Association 2013). Although the patron and librarian will continue to communicate and refine the question throughout the interview, once the librarian has a clear sense of the information need, they can begin to work with the patron to answer it. Box 3.1 provides some example patron questions with suggestions for question negotiation.

Box 3.1 Initial Questions and Question Negotiation

A patron's first question is rarely the "real" question. Following are some examples of initial questions, with a brief analysis and some suggested follow-up questions.

Do you have any books on dogs?

What sort of book does the patron want? They could be interested in nonfiction or novels featuring dogs as characters.

If the patron is looking for nonfiction, what sort of information do they need? They may want training manuals, a guide that describes the look and temperament of different breeds, or help choosing a pet. If they are looking for a pet, the librarian might ask if the patron is interested in a specific breed.

If the patron wants a novel, are they interested in a certain type of fiction? Do they want a literary novel like *The Art of Racing in the Rain* or something more inspirational, like *A Dog's Purpose*?

Where are the books on food?

What sort of information does the patron want? They could be looking for cookbooks, nutrition and diet information, or a history of food.

If the patron is interested in cookbooks, are they looking for certain styles of cooking (grilling, baking, slow-cooker), particular ethnic foods (Mediterranean, Italian, Indian, Chinese, etc.), or certain types of dishes (stews, pastas, appetizers, etc.)?

If the patron is looking for nutrition or diet information, do they have specific concerns (gluten-free, low sodium, diets for diabetics or for weight loss, etc.)?

Or, perhaps, this person is not looking for cookbooks but books about food, cooking, chefs, and so on—a memoir like *Blood, Bones, and Butter* or a history like *Cod: A Biography of the Fish That Changed the World*.

Search and Location of Information

As the RUSA *Behavioral Guidelines* (2013) state, "Search process is the portion of the transaction in which behavior and accuracy intersect." In an age of *Google* and smartphones, if patrons work with a reference professional, they expect to get added value to their search. Using specialized search skills and in-depth knowledge of information sources, the librarian can save the user time and effort by efficiently and effectively guiding them through an array of information sources and helping them evaluate the results to discover the information they need.

Successful searching often begins with identifying the type and subject of reference question. As described in Chapter 1, reference questions fall broadly into several areas, including ready reference, bibliographic verification, and research. Certain information resources are best suited to answer specific types of questions. For instance, an almanac or dictionary might be best for ready reference and an index or catalog for bibliographic verification. Further, each question will fall into one or more subject areas such as business, health, literature, or history. Specialized subject sources will often best serve these questions. Part II of this text provides overviews of resources for various types of questions and subject areas. During the search portion of the interview, librarians might begin by identifying the type and subject of the question and then determine which resources best match those categories.

During the search, communication continues to be important. The librarian should involve the patron directly in the search, explaining the steps as they go and asking for the patron's input. Chapter 4 elaborates on providing instruction as part of the reference transaction. In general, the librarian should indicate which sources they consult and share steps for using those resources, including the keywords or subject headings used to search. The librarian should ask for the patron's input on whether the results are meeting their needs and might also discuss how to evaluate the sources for authority and credibility.

While the librarian should offer instruction, the patron's level of participation will vary. In a school or academic library, students are expected to learn to find, use, and evaluate information, and the library is contributing to the educational mission of the institution by instructing students in these skills rather than just providing an answer. Corporate library patrons are more like clients, and the librarian's role is to save the firm time and money by answering questions. While corporate librarians do provide instruction, they are more likely to respond to requests with a straightforward answer. Because of the unique nature of archival collections, archival users often need to be oriented to the collection and the rules for using those materials. In a public library, the librarian should take their cues from the patron. The librarian should offer to include the patron at every step, but if the patron indicates that they just want the librarian to find the answer for them, that is generally what the librarian should do.

The patron's question might need additional refinement at this point. As they see the results of the search, the patron might gain a better understanding of the direction of their question or think of new ways to refine their ideas. The librarian should continue to engage the patron by reviewing results with them and continuing to ask questions to determine if the results are on target.

Communication of the Answer

Through search and location, the librarian and patron will arrive at either an answer to the question or another natural stopping point. When the question has a single correct answer, such as a specific statistic or the citation to a particular article, the stopping point will be obvious. However, reference professionals often spend time on more complex questions that require the compilation and synthesis of materials. For example, a patron in a corporate library might want an overview of some industry trends, a student might need to compile research for a paper, or a new parent might want to compare safety ratings on baby products. These questions take substantial time, as the librarian helps the patron compile and review relevant information. In such cases, the librarian will work with the patron to decide when a sufficient amount of information has been compiled and whether that information meets the patron's need. Often, the librarian will help the patron to get started and then check in to see if the patron needs additional help.

In other cases, patrons might need information that goes beyond the scope of the particular institution's collections or requires expert support outside of the scope of the library. A genealogist or history scholar might need to access specialized archival collections. Patrons with medical conditions, or patrons who are underhoused or homeless, might need health or other social services. In such cases, the reference professional might not be able to access the exact material that the patron needs but should be able to help the patron identify the collections or community agencies that will be able to provide that information or support. The answer to such questions might be a referral to another agency.

Interpersonal skills remain important during this part of the reference interview. Particularly important is making sure information is presented in a way that makes sense for the individual user. Some considerations in communicating the answer include the format, type, and level of information and the time frame in which the information is needed. For example, a nursing master's student, a high school student, and a new parent might all be interested in learning about vaccine safety. However, they likely will need different types and levels of information. It is the librarian's job to understand what is appropriate for the patron in terms of both their question and their background knowledge. The high school student and the nursing master's student might both have an academic interest in the topic and be interested in research, but the high school student will generally need resources written at a less-technical level than the nursing student. The nursing student might be able to understand original research articles from sources like the *Journal of the American Medical Association*, while the high school student might fare better with secondary reports on the research from publications like *Discover* magazine. While a new parent might also be interested in the research, they will likely prefer reports that synthesize the research into key takeaways that will help inform their decision-making. Guides specifically prepared for this audience by trusted sources like the Centers for Disease Control and Prevention or the American Academy of Pediatrics might be best for this group. Box 3.2 presents a selection of sample reference questions with several different audiences to consider how these different patrons might influence the resources consulted.

In guiding patrons to information resources, the reference professional should consider the patron's literacy and language level and preferred formats. A person with low vision might prefer an online resource with adjustable font size and contrast. Patrons might also have different timelines for their information needs. A scholar working on a long-term research project might be able to travel to view other collections or wait for interlibrary loans, while other patrons might be working

Box 3.2 Same Question, Different Audience

People can be interested in the same topic, but that doesn't mean that the same resources or information will satisfy each person. The following is a list of reference questions followed by different audiences who might ask about those topics. Consider what additional questions you might ask to further clarify the patron's needs. Based on the general information given here, think about what kinds of resources you might use with each patron and why.

How can I identify "fake news" and help others to recognize it?

1. Journalism undergraduate student
2. Older adult at a public library workshop
3. Middle school child

What are the leading treatments for Alzheimer's disease, and what new drugs are being tested?

1. Adult child of a recently diagnosed parent
2. Employee in research and development at a pharmaceutical company
3. Undergraduate premed student

I'm interested in conditions on the battlefield during the civil war. How did the soldiers themselves describe their experience?

1. History scholar
2. Author writing a novel set in the Civil War
3. Adult patron with a general interest

to a tight deadline. Finally, the librarian must gauge the extent of the information needed. Some patrons might need only a short answer and others a more extensive one. Regardless of the nature of the question, the librarian should provide a citation or specific resource for each answer. Even if the librarian knows the answer to a question, it is good practice for the librarian to consult a resource to share with the patron. This allows the librarian to verify the accuracy of the answer, model the search process for the patron, and provide the patron with a specific resource that they can cite or return to later.

In addition to helping the patron navigate sources, librarians should pay attention to the patron's affective state. Although not focused on imposed queries, Carol Kuhlthau's (1988) information search process model is applicable here. Kuhlthau found that as subjects moved through the research process from first being assigned a paper, to selecting a general topic, gathering information, and focusing their topic, to finally synthesizing and presenting the information, they went through a range of emotions from uncertainty, optimism, frustration, and doubt to ultimate satisfaction or disappointment. Librarians should be attuned to these emotions during the search process. If the librarian encounters patrons during a stage where they are experiencing frustration, doubt, or uncertainty, those emotions might impact their ability to articulate their needs clearly or fully engage in the search process. The librarian can acknowledge patrons' anxiety or frustration if appropriate and let them know that these feelings are common. The librarian can reassure patrons through each step of the process, pointing out when the process is going well, praising patrons for successes, and letting them know that they are making progress.

Follow-Up and Closure

Properly closing the reference interview by confirming that the patron's information need has been fully satisfied is a vital step. A patron might have initiated a reference transaction with more than one question or information need, or additional questions might arise during the search process. If the librarian closes the interview without following up, the patron might not feel comfortable asking for additional help and might leave with unanswered questions. Some research shows that patrons and librarians do not always agree on whether a question has been answered fully, and a less-than-complete answer can impact the patron's overall satisfaction with the transaction (Nolan 1992; Ross and Dewdney 1998; Saunders and Ung 2017). Asking follow-up questions like "Is there anything else I can do to assist you?" or "Do you have any additional questions?" can help to avoid these disconnects. New or additional questions can trigger a new reference interview, and the process will start again. If the patron indicates satisfaction, the librarian can close the interview. The librarian should maintain strong customer-service and interpersonal skills during the interview closure, thanking the patron for using the service and inviting them to return with any other questions. Figure 3.1 offers a model of the reference interview.

REMOTE REFERENCE INTERVIEWS

As explained in Chapter 6, reference interviews can be conducted in a variety of formats, synchronous and asynchronous, including by phone, e-mail, text or video chat, and text message. Reference interviews that take place in any format other than face-to-face are sometimes referred to as remote reference. In general, remote reference transactions will follow the same steps as the traditional face-to-face interview outlined in Figure 3.1. However, each format presents specific considerations.

Telephone Reference

The biggest challenge of telephone reference is the lack of nonverbal cues like body language and facial expression, which help gauge patron satisfaction and understanding. Without these cues, active listening becomes even more important. The librarian should be alert to cues such as tone of voice that might indicate patron understanding and satisfaction or long pauses that might suggest confusion and dissatisfaction. Because the patron cannot see the librarian, some of the typical indicators of interest and engagement such as eye contact and nodding are not relevant. However, the librarian can take other measures to convey their interest, such as paraphrasing the question and saying things like "What an interesting

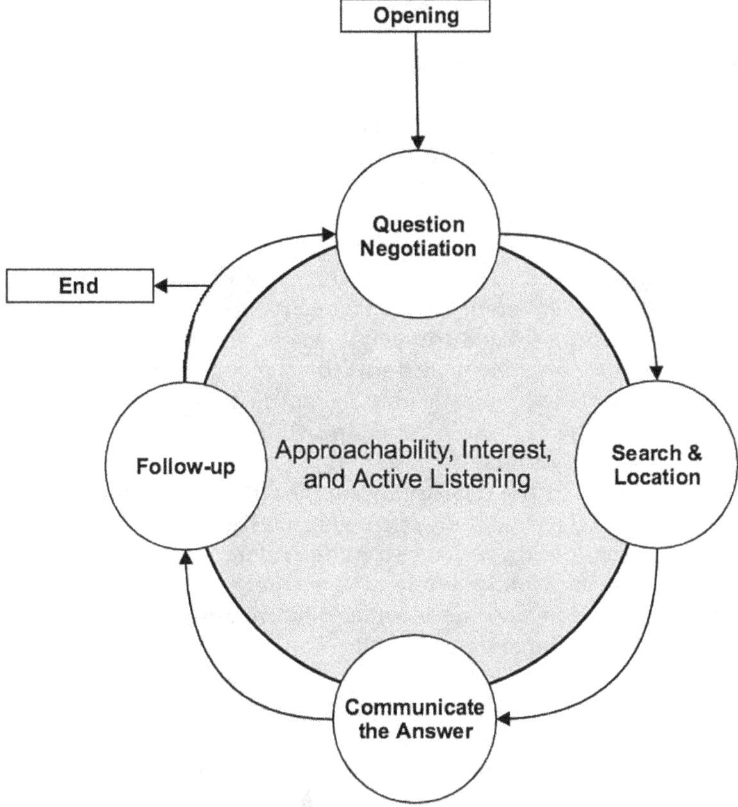

Figure 3.1 The reference interview. The interview opens with the patron's question followed by question negotiation, search and location, communication of the answer, and follow-up or closure. Approachability and interest should permeate the entire process.

question, let me see how I can help you." The librarian should be aware of their own tone of voice, as patrons can usually detect boredom, apathy, or frustration.

It can be a challenge to offer instruction with phone reference. Patrons may or may not be following along on their own computer screen and may or may not have access to the same resources as the librarian. However, the librarian can still describe the steps they are taking to locate the answer and offer to e-mail an outline of the steps and a link or citations to resources. Providing instruction by phone is time consuming and will increase the length of the interview, so the librarian should check whether the patron has the time and interest in that level of detail.

Chat Reference

Chat reference interviews have the advantage of occurring in real time but lack the verbal and visual cues of in-person and phone reference. Further, chat reference is labor intensive because, aside from the possibility of some pre-scripted notes to open and close the interview, librarians have to type their entire side of the interaction. van Duinkerken, Stephens, and MacDonald (2009) found that reference librarians in the chat environment were less likely to engage in some of the behaviors outlined by RUSA (2013), such as paraphrasing questions back to patrons, assisting patrons in broadening or narrowing the topic, or asking patrons if they had additional questions at the end of the interview. They infer these lapses are due to the time-intensive nature of the chat reference interview, which can extend to twenty minutes or more. Given the importance of these behaviors to customer satisfaction and overall success of the interview (Radford 2006; Radford and Connaway 2009), it is important for librarians to incorporate them as much as possible.

Librarians experience different levels of comfort with the chat interface. Because patrons are not watching them during chat sessions, some professionals feel less concerned if they take a moment to think through the process or if they engage in some false starts. Others find the chat format more stressful because they are concerned about leaving patrons waiting and so feel pressured to search quickly and push responses to patrons.

To increase success in the chat interview, librarians should engage in the full reference interview process, including greeting patrons and clarifying their question before beginning to search. As with phone reference, the librarian can paraphrase the question back and include brief comments like "What an interesting question" to convey interest. Tone is especially important with text. Humor and sarcasm do not always translate well online and could be mistaken for rudeness. In general, the best practice is to maintain a friendly but professional tone. The use of exclamation points or emojis can help to convey friendliness and interest, but these should be limited and used only if it seems appropriate to the audience.

As the librarian begins the search, it is helpful to tell the patron that it might take some time. Saying "I am going to search some of our databases. This might take a few moments, but I will be back with you shortly" helps to set the patron's expectations and alleviates some of the pressure to respond quickly or keep in constant word contact. Another technique is to send short chunks of information while the search is in process. For instance, after an initial search, the librarian could cut and paste some citations or send a screenshot to patrons. While the patron is reviewing the results, the librarian can continue the search. The librarian might feel a little less pressure to hurry if they know that the patron has some material to engage with while they continue to work. It also helps to remember that most patrons are not sitting at their screen waiting for the librarian to communicate with them but are probably toggling between different windows or devices and getting other work done.

As always, the librarian should include a citation for the source along with the answer. If the question is more complex, the librarian might provide brief summaries of the materials or a short explanation of their relevance, instead of just sending a list of citations. The librarian should note the sources used and, if applicable, which keywords or subject headings they used. As with any reference interview, the chat interview should end with follow-up to ensure there are no outstanding questions and a closure that welcomes the patron to return if they need further help.

E-mail Reference

Like chat, e-mail reference lacks nonverbal and tonal cues, but the challenges are compounded by its asynchronous nature. As with other forms of reference, e-mail questions usually need clarification, but without real-time conversation, the question negotiation takes longer and the delay could be frustrating. To alleviate some of that frustration, while still taking the time to ensure question clarification, the librarian can offer potential answers to the patron's initial question, while asking some clarifying questions.

If a patron e-mails saying, "I am interested in learning more about the legalization of marijuana," it is unclear if they are asking about specific legislation in their state, the general history of the legalization of marijuana, statistics related to sales, or something else entirely. Yet, if the librarian responds by only asking clarifying questions, the patron might feel as if their time is being wasted. If the librarian answers only the question being asked, the patron might not get the needed information. One approach would be for the librarian to send a response like the following:

> This is an interesting question! It would help to know a little bit more about what your interest is. Are you interested in the legalization of marijuana here in Massachusetts or across the country? I can provide you with some basic information: The public vote to legalize marijuana in Massachusetts took place on November 8, 2016. The bill putting the law into effect is H3818 and you can access the text of that bill here: https://malegislature.gov/Bills/190/H3818. Currently, 30 states and the District of Columbia have legalized use of marijuana, according to http://www.governing.com/gov-data/state-marijuana-laws-map-medical-recreational.html.
>
> Or, are you interested in a different aspect of the question? Are you interested in the federal responses, or the ongoing debate about the pros and cons of legalization? Or, are you more interested in something like the impact legalization has had on local economies, public health, etc.?
>
> I would be happy to continue to assist you in finding more information on any aspect of the topic. You can respond to this e-mail, or you can contact the reference desk at 617-555-5555.

Receiving some response will hopefully ensure the patron does not feel frustrated or put off, while the clarifying questions will help the patron understand the different types of information and support the librarian can offer. As always, it is important to invite the patron to elaborate on the needed information or return with more questions.

TONE AND PROFESSIONALISM

This chapter has emphasized the importance of interpersonal and communication skills and adherence to the RUSA *Behavioral Guidelines* (2013). This high level of customer service should be afforded to all library patrons, regardless of the format of the transaction. Indeed, the first standard of the ALA Code of Ethics (2008) states, "We provide the highest level of service to all library users through appropriate and usefully organized resources; equitable service policies; equitable access; and accurate, unbiased, and courteous responses to all requests." Unfortunately, research suggests that reference professionals sometimes fall short of these ideals and that lower levels of service might coincide with the actual or perceived racial background of the patron.

Two studies examined responses to e-mail reference questions signed with names that were distinctively associated with a particular race, gender, or ethnicity and found that librarians responded differently to patrons perceived to be of certain racial or ethnic groups. The studies found that librarians were less likely to respond to e-mails with African-American-sounding names than they were to e-mails with white-sounding names and that the responses to patrons with African-American- and Arab-associated names were less polite (Giuletti, Tonin, and Vlassopoulus 2017; Shachaf and Horowitz 2006). Patrons with white-sounding names also tended to receive longer responses, fuller answers, and a professional closure to their interaction, with the librarian providing contact information and inviting the patron to return with more questions (Shachaf and Horowitz 2006). Another study found that some reference librarians were less likely to provide complete services for questions posed by patrons who identified as or were perceived to be LGBTQ+ or questions related to LGBTQ+ materials (Curry 2005).

Both of the studies related to race examined virtual reference services. It is possible that in the remote environment, "librarians can become less self-aware and less likely to monitor their behavior and therefore more likely to react on impulses that would normally be inhibited" (Shachaf and Horowitz 2006, 503). Regardless, the results of these studies are disturbing and unacceptable. Recognizing these tendencies can be a first step in guarding against them. Librarians must be self-aware and self-reflective when providing services and ensure they are providing professional, respectful, and equitable services to all patrons in every format of the reference interaction.

SPECIAL TYPES OF REFERENCE INTERVIEWS

This chapter outlines a generic reference interview that can be applied across many different information settings and situations. However, there are some special types of reference interviews that might be called for in certain situations. For instance, Chapter 11 describes some of the unique challenges and approaches to reference with children and young adults, and Chapter 21 covers readers' advisory, a specialized reference interview in which the librarian assists the user in identifying material for leisure reading or entertainment. The following sections describe two special types of reference interviews: imposed queries and reference interview by proxy.

Imposed Queries

Discussions of the reference interview often assume that questions are self-generated or originated with the person asking it. However, some patrons ask questions they did not develop but were tasked with answering. For instance, an employee might be asked to compile a report, or a student might be assigned a research paper. These questions are sometimes referred to as imposed queries, because the patron is not asking them of their own accord but out of a sense of obligation or work commitment. The motivation for discovering the answer to such questions is more externally than internally driven, and patrons might not be as invested in the topic, although they might still be concerned with the outcome.

Melissa Gross (1999) notes that patrons with self-generated questions can provide context for the question, because it derives from their own interests and experiences. Also, if a query needs to be adapted to fit the collections or systems of the library, the patron will likely be able to provide feedback on these changes. The same is not necessarily true of imposed queries. If the patron lacks extensive background knowledge on the topic, they might find it harder to articulate the question or adapt the focus as they negotiate with the librarian.

The fact that a query is imposed does not mean the answer is unimportant to the patron. Students working on assignments will usually care about getting a good grade, and employees will be concerned with their job performance. These circumstances can make patrons even more anxious about the research process because of the high stakes. Thus, patrons with imposed queries might be less interested in the topic and yet more anxious about the outcome than patrons with internally generated questions. These factors can impact the flow of the reference interview, and Melissa Gross (1999) advises librarians to identify when reference questions are imposed as opposed to self-generated, to understand the importance of context in answering those questions, and to be empathetic to the patron during the interaction. A good, first step in responding to an imposed query, if possible, is to return to the source for additional clarification. An explanatory e-mail, work plan, or assignment prompt will often include clues to the scope of the project that the patron herself might have missed. As noted earlier, the librarian should also be cognizant of the patron's emotional state and offer support and encouragement as needed.

Reference Interview by Proxy

Another special reference interview is one that takes place by proxy, meaning the person engaging with the reference professional is not the one with the information need but is representing that person. There are a number of circumstances that can lead to a by-proxy interview, but a few common ones include a family member or caregiver who is helping a person who is ill, home bound, or otherwise unable to connect with the librarian; a person who is communicating through a language interpreter, which could include American Sign Language; or a parent who is negotiating a reference transaction for their child. The important difference between the first example and the last two is that in the first example the patron with the information need is not present, while in the last two examples, the patrons are present but are communicating through an intermediary. As with the imposed query, one of the challenges of the by-proxy interview is that the person communicating with the librarian is not the originator of the question and might not have as much personal investment or background knowledge. In addition, the original query is being filtered through the intermediary. Depending on the intermediary's understanding of the original query and topic, relationship with the patron they represent, and language or communication skills, the intermediary might inadvertently misinterpret the patron's need or skew the question. In cases where the patron and librarian do not speak the same language, libraries will rarely have professional language interpreters available. Instead, patrons might have to communicate through a staff person with limited language knowledge. Or an adult might bring a child who speaks both languages but who might not have the vocabulary or understanding necessary to navigate complex topics.

Once again, there are steps reference professionals can take to mitigate the circumstances of the by-proxy interview. If the patron is not present, librarians could offer to contact them by phone or video conference to bring the patron into the conversation. Otherwise, if the question remains unclear, the librarian should provide the proxy with whatever relevant information they can, with an invitation for either the patron or the proxy to follow up with the librarian for additional information.

When the patron is present, the librarian should include them in the interview, even if that only means making eye contact with them and speaking directly to them rather than to the interpreter. This allows the patron to feel involved and makes it obvious that the librarian is giving the patron full attention. Further, it allows the librarian to read the patron's body language, even they cannot communicate with the patron directly. As the interview progresses and more information is relayed, the librarian might be able to gauge if the patron seems confused or satisfied. In most cases, bringing the patron into the conversation will feel affirming to them and help establish the librarian as a friendly and helpful resource.

SPECIAL CONSIDERATIONS

Reference professionals spend a substantial portion of their time interacting directly with patrons, and these interpersonal interactions can give rise to some special considerations. This section outlines the topics of difficult interactions and empathetic services.

Difficult Interactions

Engaging with the public can lead to challenging interactions. At one point or another, many librarians will be faced with a patron who is rude, angry, or upset. Regardless, librarians need to remain professional and provide the highest level of service. The most important step in a difficult interaction is to remain calm and polite while trying to determine why the patron is upset. The librarian can start by asking the patron to explain the situation. When people are upset, it is important for them to feel they are being heard and taken seriously. Standard reference interview techniques such as maintaining eye contact and paraphrasing to show understanding continue to apply. Even if the patron shouts, the librarian should keep their voice calm and neutral. In fact, if the librarian makes their voice softer, that might encourage patrons to lower their voice as well.

It can be tempting to characterize angry patrons as difficult people, and the library literature and professional listservs are full of advice for dealing with "problem patrons." But making assumptions about character can be both misleading and unhelpful. Often, the librarian will not know what triggered an angry reaction in a patron. Anyone can have a bad day and take their frustration out on someone else, and, while that does not excuse bad behavior, it does suggest the patron might not be a difficult or bad person but just overreacting. While challenging, it can help to frame these scenarios as difficult situations rather than difficult people, thus making the exchange less personal and keeping the focus on the issue rather than the individual behavior.

It can help to acknowledge what has upset the patron, for instance, saying "I understand that you are upset that your fines are preventing you from checking out books." If a mistake has occurred, the librarian should acknowledge that fact and apologize. Even if the library is not at fault, it can help to frame a response with an apology and then to explain the policy or the rationale behind a decision in clear and objective terms. How the librarian phrases their response can go a long way toward escalating or defusing a situation. Whenever possible, the librarian should use positive wording and work with the patron to find a solution to the problem. Often, listening to the patron and acknowledging their feelings is enough to calm them down. With all of this said, some interactions might get more heated, and librarians should be cognizant of their own and their patron's safety. If a patron refuses to cooperate or calm down, or becomes abusive or threatening, the librarian should follow the organizational policy and safety procedures, which might include contacting security or the police.

Empathetic Services

As frontline professionals in a customer-service position, reference librarians will deal with a wide variety of people and a whole range of human emotion. As noted earlier, Carol Kuhlthau (1988) demonstrated that patrons will navigate through a range of emotions from optimism to frustration through the course of a single research project. Other studies have established the phenomenon of library anxiety, which is "a fear of the library and of using it to find research materials and may extend to librarians and other staff members" (Mellon 1986). People experiencing library anxiety may worry that they will be unable to find the information they need but might also be embarrassed to ask for help because they are ashamed to admit that they are unable to accomplish the task on their own (Campbell 2017), and they may worry that they will be judged by the librarian (Black 2016). In addition to these stressors related to the research process or the library itself, patrons might be anxious about the cause of their information need—for instance, a person recently diagnosed with an illness who is researching prognoses or a person who was recently laid off and is seeking unemployment assistance or job hunting. Occasionally, librarians will find themselves interacting with patrons who are not necessarily in search of information but are lonely and are looking for conversation. As these examples illustrate, librarians are dealing with whole people, not just discrete needs, and, as such, they need to be prepared to support their patrons' emotional as well as informational needs.

Researchers have demonstrated the relationship building is at least as important to reference service as finding the right answer. Marie Radford (1996) has established that relational aspects, including the librarian's attitude, heavily influence the patron's perceptions of the transaction's success, and these personal qualities carry over to success in the virtual environment as well (Radford 2006; Radford and Connaway 2009). In a landmark study, Joan Durrance (1989) found that patrons were willing to return to a librarian who had not been able to answer their question if that librarian had been friendly, demonstrated interest, and seemed nonjudgmental. Conversely, patrons said they would not return to a librarian they perceived as unfriendly or judgmental even if that librarian had successfully led them to the information they needed. The librarian's affect, including how approachable they appear, can determine whether a patron will approach the librarian to ask a question at all (Radford 1998).

Abigail Phillips (2017, 1) emphasizes the importance of "soft skills" to reference practice and suggests that reference professionals "may employ empathy, kindness, and sympathy to fully understand and meet the needs of patrons." In her research, she found that in addition to fulfilling information needs, librarians often find themselves providing emotional support by reassuring and encouraging patrons. She suggests that librarians are not just information or instructional providers but also a source of emotional or psychological support for some patrons and that "LIS educators and library management must make it a priority to highlight the importance of empathetic services in librarianship, encouraging pre-service and practicing librarians to embrace this critical service that libraries have been delivering patrons" (2017, 15).

While providing empathetic services, librarians need to keep a balance between empathy and professional boundaries (Phillips 2017). Information professionals are not social workers, psychologists, or counselors. While it is important for reference professionals to acknowledge, respect, and support the emotional needs of their patrons, it is equally important to recognize that some patrons will have emotional needs that extend beyond the parameters of library service. Patrons who are experiencing emotional or physical trauma or suffering from mental illness, for example, will need services beyond those that the library can provide. In such instances, the librarian must still be respectful and empathetic, but their focus should also be on providing the appropriate information to fulfill the patron's need, which in some cases could include referrals to medical, counseling, or other social services. Providing emotional support to patrons can take a toll on librarians as well. This sort of emotional labor can be exhausting and, if it is frequent, could lead to burnout. It is important for librarians to engage in self-care, including finding or creating a network of supportive colleagues, engaging in professional development activities that support growth, and taking time to recharge (Shuler and Morgan 2013). Managers also have a role to play in helping to prevent burnout in their staff. Some steps for supporting staff include avoiding overscheduling at the reference desk, setting reasonable goals and expectations, and providing opportunities for professional development and training.

CULTURAL CONTEXT IN THE REFERENCE INTERVIEW

It is important to note that the RUSA *Behavioral Guidelines* (2013) and this chapter are both written from an American perspective and therefore encourage behaviors that are culturally appropriate and considered polite for most people raised in the United States. However, information professionals will work with patrons from diverse backgrounds and must be sensitive to differences in communication. For example, the RUSA *Behavioral Guidelines* (2013) emphasize eye contact as a way of conveying interest and active listening, but in some cultures avoiding eye contact is a sign of respect, while direct eye contact could be considered rude. Similarly, neurodiverse people might find direct eye contact stressful. There are also cultural and individual differences around personal space or how close people will stand when talking with each other. In some cultures, direct communication between people of the opposite sex who are not related is considered inappropriate. Thus, while behavioral guidelines are useful as general advice, it is important for information professionals to be aware and respectful of cultural differences in communication, as discussed in further detail in Chapter 12. Whenever possible, the information professional should take their cues from the patron and adapt their verbal and nonverbal language to ensure the patron is comfortable with the interaction. Engaging in cultural convergence, or adapting speech and style to reflect the patron, is generally appreciated by the patron and can lead to a stronger rapport (Liu 2016).

CONCLUSION

Conducting a successful interview can be challenging. Reference professionals have to balance the interpersonal aspects of engaging in a conversation, asking appropriate clarifying questions, and conveying approachability and interest while employing their expert knowledge of sophisticated search techniques and a range of information sources in order to help patrons find the information they need. At the same time, the librarian is also adapting their communication style to suit the patron and providing instruction on searching and guidance on evaluating information sources. Many new professionals feel nervous or overwhelmed in the beginning, but the process gets easier with practice, and the rewards of the job can be immense. The reference interview is at the heart of the service, and a successful interview can lead to satisfied patrons. The key is to remember that the patron is the focus and that the goal is to provide the highest level of service at all times.

REFERENCES

American Academy of Pediatrics. https://www.aap.org/.

American Library Association. 2008. "Code of Ethics." Last modified January 22, 2008. http://www.ala.org/tools/ethics.

Black, Steve. 2016. "Psychosocial Reasons Why Patrons Avoid Seeking Help from Librarians: A Literature Review." *The Reference Librarian* 57 (1): 35–56. https://doi.org/10.1080/02763877.2015.1096227.

Campbell, Josephine. 2017. "Library Anxiety." *Salem Press Encyclopedia of Health.* Ipswich, MA: Salem Press.

Centers for Disease Control and Prevention. https://www.cdc.gov/

Curry, Ann. 2005. "If I Ask, Will They Answer? Evaluating Public Library Reference Service to Gay and Lesbian Youth." *Reference & User Services Quarterly* 45 (1): 65–75.

Dewdney, Patricia, and Gillian Michell. 1996. "Oranges and Peaches: Understanding Communications Accidents in the Reference Interview." *RQ* 35 (4): 520–36.

Dewdney, Patricia, and Gillian Michell. 1997. "Asking 'Why' Questions in the Reference Interview: A Theoretical Justification." *The Library Quarterly: Information, Community, Policy* 67 (1): 50–71.

Discover Magazine. 1980–. Waukesha, WI: Kalmback Media.

Durrance, Joan C. 1989. "Reference Success: Does the 55% Rule Tell the Whole Story?" *Library Journal* 114 (7): 31–36.

Giuletti, Corrado, Mirco Tonin, and Michael Vlassopoulos. 2017. "Racial Discrimination in Local Public Services: A Field Experiment in the United States." *The Journal of the European Economic Association* 17 (1): 165–204. https://doi.org/10.1093/jeea/jvx045.

Gross, Melissa. 1999. "Imposed versus Self-Generated Questions: Implications for Reference Practice." *Reference & User Services Quarterly* 39 (1): 53–61.

Hernon, Peter, and Charles R. McClure. 1987. "Library Reference Service: An Unrecognized Crisis." *The Journal of Academic Librarianship* 13 (2): 69–71.

Journal of the American Medical Association. 1883–. Chicago, IL: American Medical Association.

Kuhlthau, Carol C. 1988. "Longitudinal Case Studies of the Information Search Process of Users in Libraries." *Library and Information Science Research* 10 (3): 257–304.

Liu, Meina. 2016. "Verbal Communication Styles and Culture." *Oxford Research Encyclopedias.* New York: Oxford University Press. doi:10.1093/acrefore/9780190228613.013.162.

Mellon, Constance. 1986. "Library Anxiety: A Grounded Theory and Its Development." *College & Research Libraries* 47 (2): 160–65.

Nolan, Christopher W. 1992. "Closing the Reference Interview: Implications for Policy and Practice." *RQ* 31 (4): 513–24.

Phillips, Abigail. 2017. "Understanding Empathetic Services: The Role of Empathy in Everyday Library Work." *The Journal of Research on Libraries and Young Adults* 8 (1): 1–27.

Radford, Marie L. 1996. "Communication Theory Applied to the Reference Encounter: An Analysis of Critical Incidents." *The Library Quarterly* 66 (2): 123–37. doi:10.1086/602862.

Radford, Marie L. 1998. "Approach or Avoidance? The Role of Nonverbal Communication in the Academic Library User's Decision to Initiate a Reference Encounter." *Library Trends* 46 (4): 699–717.

Radford, Marie L. 2006. "Encountering Virtual Users: A Qualitative Investigation of Interpersonal Communication in Chat Reference." *Journal of the American Society for Information Science and Technology* 57 (8): 1046–59.

Radford, Marie L., and Lynn Silipigni Connaway. 2009. "Thriving on Theory: A New Model for Virtual Reference Encounters." Presented at the American Society for Information Science and Technology 2009 Annual Meeting, Vancouver, British Columbia, Canada. http://www.oclc.org/research/activities/synchronicity/ppt/asist09-thriving.ppt.

Reference and User Services Association. 2013. "Guidelines for Behavioral Performance of Reference and Information Service Providers." Last modified May 28, 2013. http://www.ala.org/rusa/resources/guidelines/guidelinesbehavioral.

Reitz, Joan M. 2004. *Dictionary for Library and Information Science*. Santa Barbara, CA: ABC-CLIO.

Ross, Catherine S. 2003. "The Reference Interview: Why It Needs to Be Used in Every (Well, Almost Every) Reference Transaction." *Reference & User Services Quarterly* 43 (1): 37–43.

Ross, Catherine S., and Patricia Dewdney. 1998. "Negative Closure: Strategies and Counter-Strategies in the Reference Transaction." *Reference & User Services Quarterly* 38 (2): 151–63.

Saunders, Laura, and Tien Ung. 2017. "Striving for Success in the Reference Interview: A Case Study." *The Reference Librarian* 58 (1): 46–66. doi:10.1080/02763877.2016.1157778.

Schwartz, Howard R. 2014. "The Application of RUSA Standards to the Virtual Reference Interview." *Reference & User Services Quarterly* 54 (1): 8–11.

Shachaf, Pnina, and Sarah Horowitz. 2006. "Are Virtual Reference Services Color Blind?" *Library and Information Science Research* 28 (4): 501–20.

Shuler, Sherianne, and Nathan Morgan. 2013. "Emotional Labor in the Academic Library: When Being Friendly Feels like Work." *The Reference Librarian* 54 (2): 118–33. doi:10.1080/02763877.2013.756684.

Society of American Archivists. n.d. "Reference Interview." https://www2.archivists.org/glossary/terms/r/reference-interview.

van Duinkerken, Wyoma, Jane Stephens, and Karen I. MacDonald. 2009. "The Chat Reference Interview: Seeking Evidence Based on RUSA Guidelines: A Case Study Based at Texas A&M University Libraries." *New Library World* 110 (3/4): 107–21.

SUGGESTED READINGS

Accardi, Maria T. 2017. *The Feminist Reference Desk*. Sacramento, CA: Litwin Books.

This edited collection challenges some of the traditional framings of reference service using a critical feminist lens. The various chapters examine issues such as emotional labor and ethics of the reference service, as well as the impact of intersectionality on reference work.

Harmeyer, David. 2014. *The Reference Interview Today: Negotiating and Answering Questions Face to Face, on the Phone, and Virtually*. New York: Rowman & Littlefield.

This book reviews best practices for the reference interview in a variety of formats and service models. The book presents a series of scenarios, including a full-text transcript of the interaction, followed by a series of reflections and questions to help the reader critically analyze the interaction and reflect on what might be done differently.

Knoer, Susan. 2011. *The Reference Interview Today*. Santa Barbara, CA: Libraries Unlimited.

This book provides an in-depth look at how the reference interview is enacted across all formats, including face-to-face, phone, and virtual, both synchronous and asynchronous. Knoer also discusses culturally sensitive reference service and examines some of the challenges of assisting users with disabilities.

Ross, Catherine Sheldrick. 2003. "The Reference Interview: Why It Needs to Be Used in Every (Well, Almost Every) Reference Transaction." *Reference & User Services Quarterly* 43 (1): 37–43.

Despite its publication date, the arguments and examples provided in this article continue to be relevant. Ross clearly and succinctly explains the importance of the reference interview and the reasons why it is important even for queries that seem simple and straightforward.

Ross, Catherine Sheldrick, Kirsti Nilsen, and Marie L. Radford. 2019. *Conducting the Reference Interview*. 3rd ed. Chicago, IL: Neal-Schuman.

Grounded in communication theory, this volume offers practical advice for conducting a successful reference interview across different settings and modalities. The authors cover special situations such as readers' advisory interviews and interviews with different communities, including children, seniors, and individuals with disabilities. The text also touches on ethical issues such as privacy, implicit judgment, and dealing with microaggressions; an excellent primer from established experts.

Chapter 4

Instructional Strategies for the Reference Interview

Susan Avery

INTRODUCTION

Instruction has been an essential part of reference service in libraries since at least the late 19th century. According to John Mark Tucker (1980), the modern notion of the librarian as educator emerged in 1876; Otis Richard Hall and Melvil Dewey both espoused that librarians were teachers and that libraries were not simply places to hold books. This role has evolved in conjunction with the changing mission of libraries and broader educational institutions and with new frameworks for teaching and learning. Libraries have long played an important part in promoting an educated, democratic citizenry, a role that continues to grow exponentially with the proliferation of information widely available on the Internet. In an era where multiple voices are provided platforms accessible to anyone with an Internet connection, librarians are finding their commitment to educating users growing as well. Instructional services in libraries continue to be dedicated to a common goal: understanding users' learning needs and abilities and creating effective instructional interventions to meet those needs. As such, instruction is an increasingly important reference function.

In the professional realm, associations that represent all kinds of libraries address the role of user education and instruction. The American Library Association (ALA), the American Association of School Librarians (AASL), and the Association of College and Research Libraries (ACRL), along with various international library and educational groups, have all developed standards, best practices, and outreach efforts to promote the role of libraries and librarians in the development of information literacy. In 1989, the ALA Presidential Committee on Information Literacy shared this definition of information literacy in its final report:

> To be information literate, a person must be able to recognize when information is needed and have the ability to locate, evaluate, and use effectively the needed information. Producing such a citizenry will require that schools and colleges appreciate and integrate the concept of information literacy into their learning programs and that they play a leadership role in equipping individuals and institutions to take advantage of the opportunities inherent within the information society. Ultimately, information literate people are those who have learned how to learn. They know how to learn because they know how knowledge is organized, how to find information, and how to use information in such a way that others can learn from them. They are people prepared for lifelong learning, because they can always find the information needed for any task or decision at hand.

In the intervening years, there have been numerous standards created by professional organizations and, as information formats and access have changed, variations on the definition of information literacy. While there are still debates about specific standards, practices, and approaches to instruction, the teaching role of librarians is generally acknowledged as central to promoting more productive and empowered societies. According to UNESCO (2017), "Empowerment of people through Media and Information Literacy (MIL) is an important prerequisite for fostering equitable access to information and knowledge and promoting free, independent and pluralistic media and information systems."

ROLE OF INSTRUCTION IN LIBRARIES

History of Instruction in Libraries

Library instruction has evolved over time and as information formats, access, and the educational needs of library constituencies have changed, so, too, has the focus of instruction.

The basic models have developed through the years and represent something of an evolution: library orientation, library instruction, bibliographic instruction, and information literacy. These models are neither completely linear nor mutually exclusive. Library orientations, for example, might be a vital part of an information literacy program in K–12 or higher education, but, in this context, they are one method of delivery rather than an overarching pedagogical model. A public library program might include instruction in library tools (as in the library instruction model) and critical information literacy components related to free Internet resources (consonant with information literacy instruction). Furthermore, while information literacy replaced bibliographic instruction as the dominant model in academic and school library settings in the 1990s, many librarians, in all types of libraries, refer to what they do as "library instruction." Public librarians, who often teach during individual reference transactions, might use an array of approaches that do not fit neatly into these more formal educational models. Thus, the following outline of models highlights the primary focus and purpose of instruction in group settings, even though general terms like orientation and library instruction might be used across all four models.

Library Orientation

Library orientations focus on introducing users to the library. Traditionally, orientations focused on the library as physical place and emerged as a need when libraries became larger and harder to navigate at a glance. Today, orientation activities might include an online tour of the library website, as this virtual library "space" has become increasingly complex for the end users. Print materials, such as handouts, maps, and brochures, may also serve as orienting material by providing overviews of library resources, services, and space. Library orientations can also serve as an important link to connecting a library's users with the librarians available to lend their expertise and provide further assistance.

Library Instruction

Library instruction, often referred to as user education, is focused on "know-how" and library-centered tools and resources. When libraries held only print collections, librarians trained users how to access library collections using specific tools, such as catalogs, indexes, and reference books. Library orientation and instruction often went hand in hand, although instruction in the use of library collections continued to become more diverse as collections grew in scope and complexity. By the 1970s, library instruction was a well-established (if still contested) function of most libraries. In academic libraries in particular, the 1970s witnessed a growth in practical approaches to instruction, professional infrastructure, and theoretical underpinnings. In 1971, the Library Orientation Exchange (LOEX) was established, providing a clearinghouse for instructional materials and an annual conference (LOEX 2019). Hannelore Rader (1974) created the first bibliography of research and professional publications related to library instruction.

Bibliographic Instruction

Bibliographic instruction became more prominent in the mid-1970s as collections, resources, and the information needs of users were becoming more complex. By the 1980s, "bibliographic instruction" was the term used to describe more conceptual approaches to teaching information seeking and use. New online searching technologies were changing the nature of both mediated and end-user searching. This necessitated that librarians teach transferable skills, given that learning a single strategy or library tool would not serve all library users' future needs.

Bibliographic instruction also emphasized search strategies and processes. Carol Collier Kuhlthau's (1992) work on the Information Search Process (ISP), building on George Kelly's constructivist theory of learning, was particularly influential in school and academic libraries, providing an empirically derived model of how information seekers move cognitively and affectively through a search process.

Information Literacy Instruction

Although the term was first coined in 1974, "information literacy" became the dominant user education paradigm by the 1990s. It marked a departure from bibliographic instruction in that it emphasized a wider range of information sources than traditional library resources. The goal of information literacy is to teach specific skills related to finding, evaluating, and using information. The 1990s witnessed numerous efforts to define information literacy and codify national standards of what it meant to be information literate. Since the 1990s, numerous library and professional associations across the world have developed definitions, standards, and learning outcomes for information literacy, including the ACRL; the AASL; the Society of College, National and University Libraries in Great Britain; and the former Australian and New Zealand Institute for Information Literacy. Information literacy also began to appear in academic accreditation standards (Eisenberg, Lowe, and Spitzer 2004). The Institute of Museum and Library Services (IMLS) provides a broader list of competencies in their 21st Century Skills project (IMLS n.d.), aimed at supporting museums and public libraries in their educational role. In addition to information literacy, the IMLS skills include areas of digital, financial, health, environmental, and civic literacies.

Critical information literacy is another significant trend, particularly in academic libraries (Accardi, Drabinski, and Kumbier 2010; Elmborg 2006, 2012; Kapitzke 2003). Borrowing from critical theory more broadly, proponents argue that traditional information literacy approaches tend to treat information, learning, knowledge, and even an "information literate student" as neutral and universal concepts. According to Christine Pawley (2003), this approach tends to reify these concepts or make them into things themselves. She notes how the contradiction between the stated goals of information literacy standards to promote a more broadly educated citizenry with the seemingly fixed ideas of "good versus bad" sources and "efficient" information retrieval can narrow the possibilities for individuals learning how to decide what is authoritative and valuable. James K. Elmborg (2006), building on the work of Paulo Freire, argues that critical theory can help librarians move away from the "banking concept" of education that assumes that teachers deposit knowledge into the heads of students and that learning is the product of the accumulation of this intellectual capital. Critical information literacy also proposes that librarians should address the socioeconomic underpinnings of the current information environment and issues of access, the digital divide, and information privilege, as well as broader issues of social justice (Accardi and Vukovic 2013; Gregory, Higgins, and Samek 2013; Hall 2010).

Librarians as Teachers

Are librarians teachers? Responses to this question will vary greatly. The instructional role of librarians in all library settings has grown, particularly at the start of the 21st century with the impact of the Internet as a major source of information and, in more recent years, with the advent of "fake news." Assisting users as they navigate the information landscape and evaluate information continues to offer instructional opportunities for librarians as they provide reference services. This role can be generalized to include all types of libraries.

School library media professionals have a long history of the integration of information skills into K–12 school curriculums. The *National School Library Standards* (2018b) provide an integrated framework focused on the connection between learners, school librarians, and school library standards. Commonalities among these standards are evidenced in a set of *Common Beliefs*, the first of which states that "the school library is a unique and essential part of the learning community" (American Association of School Librarians n.d.). It acknowledges the school library as a destination for learning and the role of the school librarian in ensuring access to information and "connecting learning to real-world events." The third belief states that "learners should be prepared for college, career, and life," focusing on empowering learners to persist in inquiry. During the course of the development of the standards, AASL (2018c) published several position statements focusing on specific aspects of school libraries. The "Instructional Role of the School Librarian" notes, "The school librarian plays a prominent role in instructing students, faculty, and administrators in a range of literacies, including information, digital, print, visual, and textual literacies" (American Association of School Librarians 2016). The impact of school librarians as teachers has been demonstrated by better scores on standardized tests and higher graduation rates in schools with strong library programs (Lance and Kachel 2018, 16).

Academic librarians have more consistently identified as teachers, particularly given greater instructional responsibilities. Scott Walter's (2008) exploratory study of librarians and teacher identity recognizes teaching as a "core focus" of the librarians he interviewed. Participants in his study summarized their professional identities as teachers, commenting: "The teaching function comes out in everything that you do," and "Even when I'm not in the classroom, I'm always teaching" (Walter 2008, 61). Walter himself goes on to observe the impact of curricular changes in higher education with an increasing number of instructional initiatives such as the First-Year Experience and Writing Across the Curriculum. These initiatives created additional teaching opportunities for librarians in higher education, requiring academic librarians "to focus on teaching as a core service" (Walter 2008, 65).

Librarians in public libraries can be the least likely to identify as teachers. The most common response Jessica A. Curtis received in her 2017 survey of public librarians was, "But, librarians aren't teachers." Teaching in a public library does not look the same as it does in an academic or school library; the librarian is not providing instruction for an established curriculum. However, whether or not they think of themselves as instructors, public librarians are constantly teaching their users in a variety of settings. This may occur in a one-on-one interaction or in a group setting focused on genealogy, resume writing, or technology skills. In her study Curtis found the vast majority of public librarians surveyed felt formal instruction on how to teach would be beneficial in improving their instructional skills. Sonnet Ireland (2017, 12) discussed the important role of information literacy and instruction in public libraries, noting, "School and public librarians are the first librarians that most people will interact with in their lifetimes."

Regardless of setting, instruction is a crucial role for all librarians. Box 4.1 poses a question about the role instruction is likely to play in one's work as a librarian. Thinking about this prior to beginning reference work is important in formulating instructional strategies for working with users in various library settings.

Box 4.1 Activity: What Role Is Instruction Likely to Play in Your Work as a Librarian?

Think about your potential future as a librarian. In what kind of library setting do you anticipate you will work? What do you imagine your instructional role will look like in that setting? Do you see this role as likely to change in the next five to ten years? How and why?

Instruction Standards

Regardless of library type, the role of learning and the importance of instruction in library public services have grown in recent decades. As might be expected, there is a stronger connection between reference and instruction in libraries affiliated with educational institutions. The standards and guidelines of corresponding professional associations provide supporting statements and specific language that address the expectations and potential for instruction and learning in libraries.

The "AASL Standards Framework for Learners" (2018a) emphasizes the school library as a "destination for on-site and virtual personalized learning" that focuses on "a comprehensive approach to teaching and learning by demonstrating the connections between learner, librarian, and library standards." The Public Library Association's (2018) PLA Strategic Plan 2018–2022 stresses the importance of lifelong learning as a library priority and highlights the public library as the space "where everyone is welcome to take advantage of vital services and learning." The ACRL has published numerous standards, guidelines, and frameworks that underscore the importance of instruction in the provision of library services. The "Standards for Libraries in Higher Education" (2018) includes an Educational Role principle that states, in part, "Library personnel provide appropriate and timely instruction in a variety of contexts and employ multiple learning platforms and pedagogies." The "Framework for Information Literacy for Higher Education," adopted in 2016, grew from "a belief that information literacy as an educational reform movement will realize its potential only through a richer, more complex set of core ideas." A focus on threshold concepts, those "core ideas and processes that define the ways of thinking and practicing for a discipline" (Townsend, Brunetti, and Hofer 2011, 854), is at the core of the ACRL "Framework" and serves as the foundation for the integration of information literacy into higher education.

INSTRUCTION IN REFERENCE

Opportunities for instruction abound in library settings. Instruction in libraries is not, nor should it be, limited to the library instruction classroom. Determining the role of instruction in and integrating instruction into reference services should be a priority in all libraries. However, the context of an individual library may impact the degree to which instruction is provided and how individual librarians perceive its role. In academic and school libraries there is a long-standing, strong relationship between reference and instruction based on the missions of these institutions. Instruction in public libraries and special libraries can vary greatly depending on the individual library, staffing models within that library, and the library's stated/perceived educational mission. Lorelei Rutledge and Sarah LeMire (2017, 352) encourage librarians to seek and take advantage of information literacy opportunities beyond formal information literacy instruction. They refer to such interactions as "microteaching opportunities," noting "library reference questions are a small, one-on-one version of information literacy instruction."

The Teachable Moment

Recognizing and taking advantage of the teachable moment is crucial to successfully integrating instruction into reference services. However, recognizing and understanding the role of teachable moments in the context of reference services can present challenges to the new librarian. Dictionary definitions of the teachable moment may differ, but they all emphasize their serendipitous nature. *Merriam-Webster Dictionary* (n.d.) defines a teachable moment as "a time that is favorable for teaching something, such as proper behavior." The online *Medical Dictionary* (n.d.) defines it as "an unplanned experience that gives an educator the opportunity to convey new information or ideas to his or her students." And *Wikipedia* writes the teachable moment is "the time at which learning a particular topic or idea becomes possible or easiest." In the library literature Necia Parker-Gibson (2008, 71) refers to them as "A-ha! Moments . . . when the researcher works through to some understanding." James Elmborg (2002, 461) writes, "Roughly defined, a teachable moment is one in which the student arrives at a position where he or she is open to teaching." These definitions and examples all provide a sense of the spontaneity that is at the core of the teachable moment, illustrating the need for a level of awareness on the part of the individual librarian.

Ultimately, it is important to know whether recognizing teachable moments and providing instruction in reference matter to the user. In an analysis of users in three different reference mediums (instant messaging, chat, and in person), Christina M. Desai and Stephanie J. Graves (2008, 253–54) discovered that they do. Their studies found that 46 percent, 55 percent, and 57 percent of respondents, respectively, "'definitely' wanted the librarian to teach them how to find information for themselves." Asked if they had learned anything, 96 percent, 92 percent, and 99 percent of the users surveyed indicated they had. These results caused Desai and Graves to conclude that "the ideal teachable moment can be found in reference work." Perhaps Elmborg (2002, 461) captures the essence of the teachable moment in reference work and its impact on the user best when he writes: "When a student comes to the reference desk with a genuine question, the librarian has the opportunity to participate in that moment and help the student re-construct a new, viable 'model of the world.' This is the 'teachable moment,' and every librarian should be educated to recognize and engage that moment when it comes." Teachable moments have a number of shared characteristics. They are as follows:

- Present in instruction and reference settings
- Spontaneous
- Dependent on the readiness of the recipient
- Sensitive to the needs of the user
- Serendipitous
- Likely to inform a user's future use of library resources

Recognizing and taking advantage of the teachable moment in reference requires an additional degree of awareness on the part of the librarian. While this may seem daunting to the new librarian, the following relatively simple strategies can be employed to assist in identifying and making the most of teachable moments when they occur.

- **Listen closely, without making any assumptions at the start of the reference interaction.** Conducting a complete reference interview is key at this point.
- **Be patient and flexible.** Each user is at their own point on a spectrum of understanding. Two users with seemingly the same question are likely to have very different levels of library experience and, subsequently, will need very different approaches from a librarian.

- **Look for body language cues.** The readiness of a user to take advantage of a teachable moment can often be observed in their body language. Instruction will likely be meaningless to a user who expresses no interest in learning.
- **Keep it short and to the point.** These are teachable moments! Focus on those aspects that will be most impactful at that moment.
- **Let the user do the work.** The hands on the keyboard of the computer should be those of the user, not the librarian. The librarian should stand on the side and walk the user through the process. Learning by doing provides a much more powerful experience than observing someone else as they work (adapted from Avery 2008, 112–13).

The ability to recognize teachable moments can be challenging. The questions posed in Box 4.2 provide several scenarios in which teachable moments are present.

Box 4.2 Activity: Recognizing the Teachable Moment

Examine the following scenarios for the presence of teachable moments. What might you teach the patron in each of these?

1. A patron is looking at the first set of ten results from a database search. They ask you which articles are best for their topic.
2. A patron asks for help on a search. You see they have typed in "cons of gun control" and gotten no results. They want to know why there are no articles on this topic.
3. A patron says, "I've tried every keyword I can think of in EBSCO but cannot find any good articles on the use of solar power by Native American communities."
4. A patron asks for help finding scholarly articles on steroid use in sports and asks if the *Sports Illustrated* article they found would qualify.

Thinking of teachable moments as "mini-lessons" is another way to visualize the interactions. Susan E. Beck and Nancy B. Turner (2001, 89) suggest librarians "always focus on finding the best and most efficient materials to convey the teaching point." This will avoid pushing too much information to the user and assure that an instructional opportunity or teachable moment does not lose its effectiveness. Again, conducting a complete reference interview is key to introducing meaningful and appropriate instructional elements into a reference transaction.

There are a number of strategies librarians can use to identify the instructional needs of the users they work with in reference settings. An examination of reference questions, collected informally through discussion with other librarians or more formally through the analysis of chat reference transcripts, can highlight common difficulties that library users have with a specific resource, skill, or technology. Search logs of library catalogs, websites, and other search tools can also yield similar information. Reviewing the actual questions of users themselves provides the opportunity for the most authentic assessment and understanding of the user needs exhibited in a particular library.

Numerous studies have analyzed chat reference transcripts and, while chat has been the medium for these studies, they provide a unique window into opportunities for librarians to identify user needs and implement appropriate instructional strategies. These strategies can be applied to both chat and in-person reference. Susan Avery and David Ward (2010, 42) observed some common, recurring user behaviors that provide opportunities for instruction in reference. They include "users indicating a lack of focus or clear definition of their initial research topic; users revealing a lack of knowledge of the differences between types/scholarly levels of information required for their research; users requesting knowledge of a part of the search process; users indicating uncertainty over where or how to conduct a search; and users indicating a lack of awareness of criteria for evaluating search results." In such instances, users may be stuck in a "sticky point" at which instruction from the librarian can help them move forward.

Instructional Techniques for Reference

Identifying effective instructional strategies in the provision of reference services is an important step in assuring learning occurs. Megan Oakleaf and Amy VanScoy (2010) sought to identify and link specific instructional strategies to educational theories that explain student learning in the context of digital reference. They identified three educational theories relevant to reference transactions:

- **Metacognition.** Users learn by reflecting on their own thought process, frequently defined as "thinking about thinking."
- **Constructivism and active learning.** Users construct their learning from their real-world experiences.
- **Social constructivism.** Users construct their learning from their interactions with others.

Following the identification of relevant educational theories, Oakleaf and VanScoy linked eight instructional strategies they identified with the educational theories, as described in Table 4.1. Each of the strategies was then given a "catchy" name to help facilitate recall on the part of librarians as they worked with users. Providing

TABLE 4.1 Instructional Strategy Codes: Suggested Instructional Strategies for the Reference Interview Based on Learning Theories

Codes	Description
Catch Them Being Good	• Reinforce positive information-seeking behaviors • Acknowledge and compliment; recognize user's hard work thus far
Think Aloud	• Make librarian thoughts as expert researchers transparent to users • Describe cognitive process throughout the steps of the reference transaction • Give insight into the expert information-seeking process, a window into the minds of librarians • Share failures, as well as successes, and coping strategies

Codes	Description
Show, Don't Tell	• Demonstrate the information-seeking process • Push URLs, tutorials, etc. • Direct users to open a browser window and follow along as a librarian completes steps during chat • Move beyond narration to images and interaction
Chunk It Up	• Identify additional steps the user will face after the immediate need is met • Make users aware of or offer advice about future challenges and opportunities • Step out of chat and reenter when users are ready to continue • Divide transaction into discrete, manageable chunks
Let Users Drive	• Invite users to describe or show what steps they've already taken • Encourage users to initiate actions while the librarian just observes • Allow users to make decisions and take actions
Be the Welcome Wagon	• Show enthusiasm for user requests for assistance • Explain that other information seekers wrestle with similar issues • Elicit feedback from users as newest members of information-seeking community • Recognize users' expertise
Make Introductions	• Redirect users to other reference venues if needs can be better met that way • Refer to other librarians with specialized expertise
Share Secret Knowledge	• Provide definitions for specialized community language • Confide "tricks of the library trade" to users • Explain the ethics, standards, or history of library services and policies • Describe the scope of what librarians do

Source: Oakleaf and VanScoy (2010, 384). Used with permission from the American Library Association.

librarians with an easy way to think about their actions as they relate to user behaviors can be an effective strategy for implementing instructional elements. While this study took place in a virtual reference setting, the suggested instructional strategies can readily be applied to in-person reference questions.

Gaining an awareness of and recognizing those user behaviors that are indicative of an instructional need can be a first step in the integration of instruction in reference. Avery and Ward (2010) categorized behaviors into three specific needs, each based on a user's stage in the research process. Box 4.3 provides actionable steps librarians can take to embed instruction at each of the stages. Conducting a complete reference interview and listening are critical in order to recognize a user's needs, identify what aspect of research is most troubling, and provide meaningful instruction.

Box 4.3 Reference Interview Instructional Behaviors

Stage 1: The user is exploring a topic or research question. They may need assistance in focusing their research question or topic.

The librarian can help the user

1. articulate their topic with a thesis statement or research question;
2. brainstorm key concepts and terminology associated with the topic;
3. understand types of information and what will be most appropriate in this setting (background information, research articles, statistics, etc.).

Stage 2: The user is engaged in the search process. They may need assistance creating a search strategy and understanding how to search a library database and work with results.

The librarian can

1. ask the user to share information about searches they have tried and results of those searches;
2. guide the user to an appropriate resource for accessing information and sharing why that source is appropriate;
3. help the user identify keywords and alternatives;
4. discuss the role of a search strategy and why specific words are used in the initial search;
5. guide the user through the search results and help them understand the order in which the results are returned and how to retrieve the full text of items.

Stage 3: The user is reviewing a set of search results. They may need assistance with strategies for evaluating their results.

The librarian can work with the user to

1. review the criteria for results as stated in an assignment or for an information need;
2. examine and engage with the results to determine the relevancy to the information need;
3. assist the user in revising the search based on results and unmet information needs;
4. identify additional resources that may be appropriate for further searches.

Adapted from Avery and Ward (2010, 51)

Desai and Graves (2008, 249) identified five instructional techniques in their analysis of reference transactions. These instructional practices can serve as a starting point for incorporating instruction in reference. They include the following:

- **Modeling.** Librarian finds and gives the needed information and then outlines the steps to locate it but does not make sure the patron is following along.
- **Resource suggestion.** Librarian suggests print or electronic resources such as library catalog, a database, or URL.
- **Terms suggestion.** Librarian suggests appropriate keywords, subject headings, Boolean operators, or limits.
- **Leading.** Librarian leads the patron step-by-step to the needed information.
- **Lessons.** Librarian explains library or research terminology such as the peer-review process.

In each of these situations the librarian should describe the steps he is taking and why to help the user understand why one approach is preferable to another.

For example, if a student was searching by article title, rather than journal title, in the online catalog, appropriate next steps would include (1) explaining that the catalog is a tool for locating journal titles, not article titles, and (2) showing the student the necessary steps to locate an appropriate database and demonstrating how to search for an article title. Such an approach would introduce instruction into the reference encounter and facilitate an understanding of the kinds of resources found in a catalog versus a database.

Metaphors and analogies can be very effective instructional strategies during a reference encounter. For example, teaching a user to add and save search results into an online folder while searching a library database can be compared to using a shopping cart when shopping online. Or encouraging a user to apply the skills and techniques learned while searching one database to searching another database can be likened to driving two different-model cars. The same features (windshield wipers, lights, etc.) will be present, but they are likely to be present in a different place. Brainstorming analogies with other librarians can be a good way to come up with additional ideas. However, when using metaphors and analogies it is important to keep in mind the individual user. Cultural references will likely be meaningless to those for whom English is a second language. Likewise, keep in mind that the age of a patron and their life experiences can impact whether or not a metaphor will contribute to their grasp of a concept. In all cases, the librarian should seek to impart transferable knowledge that will provide the user with the confidence to engage in the specific research task independently in the future.

Developing a system for taking notes when working with students at the reference desk, whether in person or virtually, can serve as a reminder to librarians to stress aspects of instruction and assure the reference experience is a learning experience. Librarians at the Milne Library at State University of New York, Geneseo, created a "Reference Notes" form that provides prompts for librarians as they work with students (Swoger and Hoffman 2015, 206). The prompts include the following:

- Project due date
- Research question
- Keywords/subject headings
- Databases/resources
- Other information (subject guides, strategies, types of sources, questions for professor, etc.)

Such a strategy can ensure that librarians introduce appropriate instructional elements when they work with students. A similar strategy would be to create an online form for librarians to complete during research consultations that would include information about what was covered in the consultation, suggestions for moving forward, and contact information to schedule an additional consultation. It would then be e-mailed to the student following the session. The form serves to remind students of the instructional aspects of the consultation and provide guidance as they continue work on their paper or project. In both of these examples, the opportunity for follow-up with the user stresses the availability of the librarian to continue the instruction that began in the initial reference encounter.

Understanding the User's Affective State

One resource that has stood the test of time and can serve as a valuable tool when working with users in a one-on-one setting such as the reference desk is Carol C. Kuhlthau's (1992) ISP. The ISP is introduced briefly in this chapter; a more in-depth explanation is available in Kuhlthau (2019). The ISP shows the thoughts, feelings, and actions users experience as they engage in the various phases of the research process. Developing empathy for and understanding the mind-set of a user as they engage in research and approach the reference desk can go a long way in building trust with a librarian. Library anxiety, first documented by Constance Mellon (1986), is a well-recognized condition, and developing awareness of the user's affective state can permit librarians to provide appropriate teaching strategies that match a user's needs at a given point. While the ISP was designed with secondary school students in mind, it was validated in studies of other user groups and can readily be adapted to multiple settings.

Using her ISP, Kuhlthau conceived of "zones of intervention" where students were most likely to need assistance. Expanding on this, it is possible to create a zone of intervention for each of the seven stages in the ISP. Box 4.4 illustrates what a patron is attempting to do in each of the stages, their likely emotions or feelings at this stage, and suggested interventions on the part of the librarian. Each of these stages can and should be viewed as an instructional opportunity for a librarian. By acknowledging the user's likely feelings, librarians can create empathy, which can lead to more positive interactions.

Box 4.4 Zones of Intervention

Zone 1: Initiating a research assignment
Patron feelings: Aware of a knowledge gap and lack of understanding; feelings of apprehension, uncertainty.
Librarian intervention: "Have you focused your topic yet? It can be difficult, but we can work together to find some focus."

Zone 2: Selecting a topic
Patron task: Considering potential topics and class requirements versus information available, time, etc.
Patron feelings: Brief elation, anticipation, sometimes anxiety and confusion.
Librarian intervention: "Tell me what you've done so far." "Sounds like you've got a start on focusing your topic." "Let's. . . ."

Zone 3: Exploring information
Patron task: Investigating information from initial searches, seeking to connect and make sense of what they have found.
Patron feelings: Confusion, frustration, doubt, uncertainty.
Librarian intervention: "We really do have a lot of sources available here; it can be confusing. . . ."

NOTE: This is usually the most difficult step in the process.

Zone 4: Formulating a focus
Patron task: Identifying and selecting sources that meet the needs of a focused topic.
Patron feelings: Optimism, confidence in ability to complete task.
Librarian intervention: "Sounds like you're really on track; that must feel good." "Let's. . . ."

Zone 5: Collecting information
Patron task: Gathering information to support an established focus.
Patron feelings: A sense of direction, confidence in ability to complete task, increased interest.
Librarian intervention: "You've got a great start. Tell me something about the articles you feel are especially good for your topic. . . ."

Zone 6: Preparing to present
Patron task: The culmination of the project, filling in the last-needed pieces of information.
Patron feelings: A sense of relief, sometimes satisfaction, sometimes disappointment.
Librarian intervention: "Looks like you're really wrapping things up. Is there anything you see missing in your research? We can look together. . . ."

Zone 7: Assessing the process
Patron task: Assessing the final results of the project.
Patron feelings: A sense of accomplishment or sense of disappointment.
Librarian intervention: "Tell me about your final result. . . ."

Adapted from Kuhlthau (1994)

Lisa Ellis (2004, 108) observes the impact of the user's affective state, noting, "Anxious users may not have the capacity to learn if they are preoccupied with end results of research than freely engaging in the information seeking process." She further discerns such users may need more "hand-holding" and librarians may need to rely more on a "show and tell" technique, as described by Oakleaf and VanScoy (2010). As students work through the stages of the ISP, they will move from an affective state, where they are responding to the feelings of the moment, to a cognitive state, where understanding and clarity begin to take place.

Instruction in Chat Reference

Chat reference continues to grow in popularity, particularly in academic settings. While there are many similarities to in-person reference when integrating instruction into chat reference, there are some distinct differences, and these can present challenges for librarians. First, the nonverbal cues and body language that indicate the receptivity of a user to instruction during an in-person reference encounter are absent in chat. The nonverbal cues also impact users as they, too, lack the visual cue that can help them determine who is assisting them (e.g., are they being assisted by a librarian or a student worker). Virtual reference users may also speculate whether or not they are chatting with a person. Paula Dempsey (2016, 463) documents the question "Are you a computer?" in her analysis of chat transcripts, noting the user seems pleased when the respondent indicates they are a librarian. While it is often simpler and quicker to provide the user with information rather than engaging in instruction, the value of the instructional experience must be kept in mind. For example, if a user wants to know if a library has a specific movie title, guiding them through a search of the catalog to find the movie would be appropriate instructional behavior on the part of the librarian rather than simply pushing out a link to the catalog record for the movie. Online pathfinders and how-to guides can be particularly helpful resources to share with users via chat reference.

Specific behaviors on the part of librarians are necessary to effectively take advantage of teachable moments and instruction in chat reference. Relationship building, in the sense of creating a comfortable and welcoming experience for the user, is an important first step. Instruction in reference increases the time of the transaction, and this is particularly true in chat, so letting the user know a question is complex and likely to take some time is important. Helping the user understand that the librarian is working with them not just to answer a question but to teach them how to do something independently in the future should also be conveyed, for example, "I'm going to walk you through this process, so you can do this on your own in the future."

GUIDES, PATHFINDERS, AND TUTORIALS

Research guides, handouts, and online tutorials can be a primary mode of instruction in the course of reference service. Print and online learning materials are often the most appropriate way to meet certain learning goals. For procedural knowledge, quick point-of-need instruction is more effective than demonstrating a database long before a student will actually need to use one. Creating ready-to-go instructional materials can be a successful strategy for embedding instruction in reference services. For example, if users consistently enter complete sentences as search strings into the library catalog (e.g., "articles on the economic impact of climate change regulations"), a tutorial about effective search terms might help educate users. Principles for developing good print and online materials include the following:

- **Format.** Select the most appropriate format for the learners. For definitions, text might be more appropriate, but for procedural or tool-based instruction, visuals such as screenshots or short videos will be more appropriate. Multiple formats are especially important in order to address individual learning preferences and share guides with online users.
- **Length.** Students might not have the patience to watch a long video about every possible advanced database feature or detailed search process. Chunk the information into smaller bits so that students can easily process the information and quickly go back if they need to repeat something again. Videos should be limited to one to two minutes, and address specific user questions.
- **Clarity.** Avoid jargon, distracting fonts or visuals, and clutter. Stay focused on conveying the most essential content in the most concise way possible. Have an outside reader or viewer review the content for clarity.
- **Accessibility.** For video or online content in particular, make sure that the content meets accessibility guidelines for learners with disabilities, such as video captioning.

The creation of online guides is another strategy librarians can utilize to deliver instructional materials and provide instructional support to users at their point of need. These guides are available to users twenty-four hours a day and can provide assistance with a wide variety of reference and learning needs. While *LibGuides*, a product from Springshare, has gained a significant market share and become particularly popular in this realm, individual libraries may elect to create their own guide templates. While initially a prominent tool used in academic libraries, the use of *LibGuides* is increasing in public and school libraries. Ruth L. Baker (2014) and Laurie Vaughan and Sue Smith (2013) provide tips for creating effective guides. Online guides can serve many purposes: they can support the needs of individual courses, they can focus on specific subjects or topics, or they can be how-to guides that provide the user with instruction relevant to specific library resources or aspects of the research process. Because these guides are online, they also serve as a ready resource for chat reference.

Infographics are an increasingly popular mode for information and data sharing. Bellato (2013) notes "Infographics take typically dry text-based information and

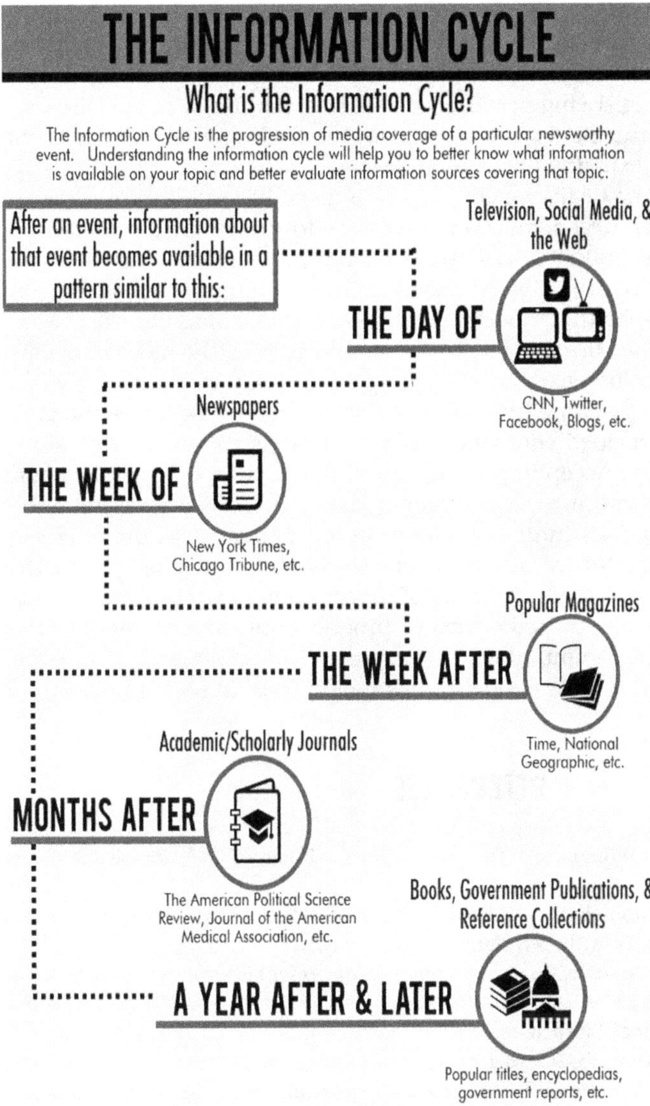
THE INFORMATION CYCLE
What is the Information Cycle?
The Information Cycle is the progression of media coverage of a particular newsworthy event. Understanding the information cycle will help you to better know what information is available on your topic and better evaluate information sources covering that topic.
After an event, information about that event becomes available in a pattern similar to this:
Television, Social Media, & the Web
THE DAY OF
CNN, Twitter, Facebook, Blogs, etc.
Newspapers
THE WEEK OF
New York Times, Chicago Tribune, etc.
Popular Magazines
THE WEEK AFTER
Time, National Geographic, etc.
Academic/Scholarly Journals
MONTHS AFTER
The American Political Science Review, Journal of the American Medical Association, etc.
Books, Government Publications, & Reference Collections
A YEAR AFTER & LATER
Popular titles, encyclopedias, government reports, etc.

Figure 4.1 The information cycle infographic. Shown is the progression of media coverage of a news story, from hours after the event unfolds through the days and weeks following up to a year or more after the event. *Source:* Used with permission from the Undergraduate Library, University of Illinois at Urbana-Champaign.

present it in a visual manner. They are concise, easily digestible, and aesthetically appealing, incorporating clever visual elements to highlight key information". Debbie Abilock and Connie Williams (2014) and Kathy Fredrick (2013) share existing tools for creating infographics and suggestions for their use in libraries. The information presented in an infographic can meet a variety of learning preferences and present information in an easy-to-understand format. Infographics can serve as an important learning tool for librarians, in that they can readily convey information and contribute to a user's learning. The infographic in Figure 4.1 visualizes the information cycle. A reference librarian can direct a user to such a tool to help them better understand why they are unlikely to find information about a particularly recent topic in a scholarly journal, for example.

FUTURE CHALLENGES

The continually changing information landscape presents numerous challenges for librarians as they seek to do their part to help create an educated citizenry that can effectively find and evaluate information sources in an era of "fake news" and conspiracy theories. The role of instruction in the reference setting is increasingly important in meeting these needs and expectations. Rapid change, new technologies, and changing user needs are themes that recur throughout the library literature. Librarians must be prepared to navigate a continually changing educational environment and information landscape, whether in a public, school, or academic library setting. Being prepared to analyze the needs of specific user populations and make strategic decisions requires much deeper knowledge of the context of education and learning needs at all levels.

While information literacy calls for librarians to move beyond library-centered education, it is even more urgent now for librarians to understand the learning needs of their patrons and stakeholders, the curriculum in formal school settings, and other contextual influences that shape their local communities. Hannelore Rader (1980, 102) argues for the importance of creating "teaching libraries," writing, "Such a library becomes directly involved in implementing the mission of educating the public through increased teaching and community outreach activities. In this type of library, the teaching function of reference service becomes the most important and highly developed component of the library's services." This statement still rings true today. Accepting our teaching role can be difficult. Elmborg (2002, 459) writes, "As librarians, we are taught that our job is answering questions. We must unlearn that definition of our job in order to teach at the reference desk." The challenge for the future is to think creatively about the most productive roles that teaching librarians from all kinds of institutions might engage in, both within and beyond our walls, to make further progress toward weaving libraries into the fabric of our local communities. It is imperative that we recognize reference services for what they can be—the library's most powerful teaching tool.

REFERENCES

Abilock, Debbie, and Connie Williams. 2014. "Recipe for an Infographic." *Knowledge Quest* 43 (2): 46–55.

Accardi, Maria T., Emily Drabinski, and Alana Kumbier. 2010. *Critical Library Instruction Theories and Methods*. Duluth, MN: Library Juice Press.

Accardi, Maria T., and Jana Vukovic. 2013. *Feminist Pedagogy for Library Instruction*. Sacramento, CA: Library Juice Press.

American Association of School Librarians. 2016. "Instructional Role of the School Librarian." Last modified June 25, 2016. http://www.ala.org/aasl/sites/ala.org.aasl/files/content/aaslissues/positionstatements/AASL_Position_Statement_Instructional_Role_SL_2016-06-25.pdf.

American Association of School Librarians. 2018a. "AASL Standards Framework for Learners." https://standards.aasl.org/framework/.

American Association of School Librarians. 2018b. *National School Library Standards for Learners, School Librarians, and School Libraries*. Chicago: ALA Editions.

American Association of School Librarians. 2018c. "Position Statements." http://www.ala.org/aasl/advocacy/resources/statements.

American Association of School Librarians. n.d. "Commons Beliefs." https://standards.aasl.org/beliefs/.

American Library Association. 1989. "Presidential Committee on Information Literacy: Final Report." Last modified January 10, 1989. http://www.ala.org/acrl/publications/whitepapers/presidential.

Association of College and Research Libraries. 2018. "Standards for Libraries in Higher Education." Last modified February, 2018. http://www.ala.org/acrl/standards/standardslibraries.

Association of College and Research Libraries. 2016. "Framework for Information Literacy for Higher Education." Last modified January 11, 2016. http://www.ala.org/acrl/standards/ilframework.

Avery, Susan. 2008. "When Opportunity Knocks: Opening the Door through Teachable Moments." *The Reference Librarian* 49 (2): 109–18.

Avery, Susan, and David Ward. 2010. "Reference Is My Classroom: Setting Instructional Goals for Academic Library Reference Services." *Internet Reference Services Quarterly* 15: 35–51.

Baker, Ruth L. 2014. "Designing LibGuides as Instructional Tools for Critical Thinking and Effective Online Learning." *Journal of Library & Information Services in Distance Education* 8 (3–4): 107–17.

Beck, Susan E., and Nancy B. Turner. 2001. "On the Fly BI: Reaching and Teaching from the Reference Desk." *The Reference Librarian* 72: 83–96.

Bellato, Nathan. 2013. "Infographics: A Visual Link to Learning." *eLearn Magazine*. https://elearnmag.acm.org/featured.cfm?aid=2556269.

Curtis, Jessica A. 2017. "The Importance of Teaching Adult Services Librarians to Teach." *Public Libraries Online* (July/August). http://publiclibrariesonline.org/2017/11/the-importance-of-teaching-adult-services-librarians-to-teach.

Dempsey, Paula R. 2016. "'Are You a Computer?': Opening Exchanges in Virtual Reference Shape the Potential for Teaching." *College & Research Libraries*, 77 (4): 455–68.

Desai, Christina M., and Stephanie J. Graves. 2008. "Cyberspace or Face-to-Face: The Teachable Moment and Changing Reference Mediums." *Reference & User Services Quarterly* 47 (3): 242–54.

Eisenberg, Michael, Carrie A. Lowe, and Kathleen L. Spitzer. 2004. *Information Literacy: Essential Skills for the Information Age*. Westport, CT: Libraries Unlimited.

Ellis, Lisa. 2004. "Approaches to Teaching through Digital Reference." *Reference Services Review* 32 (2): 103–19.

Elmborg, James K. 2002. "Teaching at the Desk: Toward a Reference Pedagogy." *portal: Libraries and the Academy* 2 (3): 455–64.

Elmborg, James K. 2006. "Critical Information Literacy: Implications for Instructional Practice." *The Journal of Academic Librarianship* 32 (2): 192–99.

Elmborg, James K. 2012. "Critical Information Literacy: Definitions and Challenges." In *Transforming Information Literacy Programs: Intersecting Frontiers of Self, Library Culture, and Campus Community*, edited by Carroll Wetzel Wilkinson and Courtney Bruch, 75–95. Chicago: Association of College and Research Libraries.

Fredrick, Kathy. 2013. "Visualize This: Using Infographics in School Libraries." *School Library Monthly* 30 (3): 24–25.

Gregory, Lua, Shana Higgins, and Toni Samek. 2013. *Information Literacy and Social Justice: Radical Professional Praxis*. Duluth, MN: Library Juice Press.

Hall, Rachel. 2010. "Public Praxis: A Vision for Critical Information Literacy in Public Libraries." *Public Library Quarterly* 29: 162–75.

Institute of Museum and Library Services. n.d. "21st Century Skills Definitions." http://www.imls.gov/about/21st_century_skills_list.aspx.

Ireland, Sonnet. 2017. "For Your Information: Using Information in Public Libraries." *Reference and User Services Quarterly* 57 (1): 12–16.

Kapitzke, Cushla. 2003. "Information Literacy: A Positivist Epistemology and a Politics of Outformation." *Educational Theory* 53 (1): 37–53.

Kuhlthau, Carol Collier. 1992. *Seeking Meaning: A Process Approach to Library and Information Services*. Norwood, NJ: Ablex.

Kuhlthau, Carol Collier. 1994. "Students and the Information Search Process: Zones of Intervention for Librarians." *Advances in Librarianship* 18: 57–72.

Kuhlthau, Carol Collier. 2019. "Information Search Process." Rutgers School of Communication and Information. http://wp.comminfo.rutgers.edu/ckuhlthau/information-search-process/.

Lance, Keith Curry, and Debra J. Kachel. 2018. "Why School Libraries Matter: What Years of Research Tell Us." *Phi Delta Kappan* 99 (7): 15–20.

LOEX. 2019. "About LOEX." http://www.loex.org/about.php.

Medical Dictionary. n.d. "Teachable Moment." https://medical-dictionary.thefreedictionary.com/teachable+moment.

Mellon, Constance. 1986. "Library Anxiety: A Grounded Theory and Its Development." *College & Research Libraries* 47 (2): 160–65.

Merriam-Webster Dictionary. n.d. "Teachable Moment." https://www.merriam-webster.com/dictionary/teachable%20moment.

Oakleaf, Megan, and Amy VanScoy. 2010. "Instructional Strategies for Digital Reference: Methods to Facilitate Student Learning." *Reference & User Services Quarterly* 49 (4): 380–90.

Parker-Gibson, Necia. 2008. "A-ha Moments, the Nearly-Now and the Implementation Dip: Finding Learning Incidents." *Behavioral & Social Sciences Librarian* 27 (2): 69–72.

Pawley, Christine. 2003. "Information Literacy: A Contradictory Coupling." *The Library Quarterly* 73 (4): 422–52.

Public Library Association. 2018. "PLA Strategic Plan 2018–2022." Last modified June, 2018. http://www.ala.org/pla/about/mission/strategicplan.

Rader, Hannelore B. 1974. "Library Orientation and Instruction—1973: An Annotated Review of the Literature." *Reference Services Review* 2 (1): 91–93.

Rader, Hannelore B. 1980. "Reference Services as a Teaching Function." *Library Trends* 29 (1): 95–103.

Rutledge, Lorelei, and Sarah LeMire. 2017. "Broadening Boundaries: Opportunities for Information Literacy Instruction Inside and Outside the Classroom." *portal: Libraries and the Academy* 17 (2): 347–62.

Society of College, National and University Libraries in Great Britain. n.d. "Information Literacy." https://www.sconul.ac.uk/tags/information-literacy.

Swoger, Bonnie J. M., and Kimberly Davis Hoffman. 2015. "Taking Notes at the Reference Desk: Assessing and Improving Student Learning." *Reference Services Review* 43 (2): 199–214.

Townsend, Lori, Korey Brunetti, and Amy R. Hofer. 2011. "Threshold Concepts and Information Literacy." *portal: Libraries and the Academy* 11 (3): 853–69.

Tucker, John Mark. 1980. "User Education in Academic Libraries: A Century in Retrospect." *Library Trends* 29 (1): 9–27.

UNESCO. 2017. "Information Literacy." http://www.unesco.org/new/en/communication-and-information/access-to-knowledge/information-literacy/.

Vaughan, Laurie, and Sue Smith. 2013. "K-12 LibGuides: A Flexible Platform for Integrating Info Lit and Promoting Your Library." *CSLA Journal* 37 (1): 21–24.

Walter, Scott. 2008. "Librarians as Teachers: A Qualitative Inquiry into Professional Identity." *College & Research Libraries* 69 (1): 51–71.

Wikipedia. 2019. "Teachable Moment." Last modified May 7, 2019. https://en.wikipedia.org/wiki/Teachable_moment.

GUIDELINES, STANDARDS, AND DEFINITIONS

American Association of School Librarians. 2018. "AASL Standards Framework for Learners." https://standards.aasl.org/framework/.

After undergoing an extensive revision, the revised AASL standards were released in November 2017. Three distinct sets of standards were created to address the learner, school librarian, and school library. They reflect "a comprehensive approach to teaching and learning by demonstrating the connection between learner, school librarian, and school library standards." The standards for learners are available free online; the standards for librarians and school libraries must be purchased through AASL.

American Library Association. 1989. "Presidential Committee on Information Literacy: Final Report." Last modified January 10, 1989. http://www.ala.org/acrl/publications/whitepapers/presidential.

A foundational document for information literacy that outlines a basic definition and need for information literacy programs and instruction across all libraries.

Association of College and Research Libraries. 2016. "Framework for Information Literacy for Higher Education." Last modified January 11, 2016. http://www.ala.org/acrl/standards/ilframework.

This document now serves as a core resource for academic instruction librarians. Rapid changes in higher education and the "information ecosystem" necessitated a document focused on "frames" of essential understandings that link closely to academic tasks. Strongly influenced by threshold concepts, the "Framework" includes concepts and dispositions intended to enable students to deepen their information literacy skills in the context of higher education.

Institute of Museum and Library Services. n.d. "21st Century Skills Definitions." http://www.imls.gov/about/21st_century_skills_list.aspx.

A list of skills applicable to patrons in libraries and museums of all types, they are intended to be adapted to an individual library's or museum's priorities and audience. Skills are focused on a wide variety of learning and creativity concepts and literacies, including visual, media, health, and environmental.

SUGGESTED READINGS

Booth, Char. 2011. *Reflective Teaching, Effective Learning: Instructional Literacy for Library Educators.* Chicago: American Library Association.

An approachable introduction to instructional design for librarians teaching in any setting, this resource provides information for all librarians involved in instruction. It includes useful frameworks and tools for designing a wide range of learning activities and materials, including face-to-face classes, print or online material, and technology-rich learning objects.

Campbell, Sandy, and Debbie Fyfe. 2002. "Teaching at the Computer: Best Practices for One-on-One Instruction in Reference." *Feliciter* 1: 26–28.

Campbell and Fyfe provide a concise and easy-to-understand list of the "Top 10 Practices for Successful One-on-One Reference Interaction." While many of these apply to an in-person interaction, many can be utilized in an online medium as well.

Clark, Ruth C., and Richard E. Mayer. 2016. *e-Learning and the Science of Instruction: Proven Guidelines for Consumers and Designers of Multimedia Learning.* 4th ed. Hoboken, NY: Wiley.

Clark and Mayer focus on the principles of multimedia instruction. They address the evidence-based research behind each principle as well as appropriate examples of the implementation of each of them.

Elmborg, James. 2002. "Teaching at the Desk: Toward a Reference Pedagogy." *portal: Libraries and the Academy* 2 (3):455–64.

From his background as a composition teacher and librarian, Elmborg shares a pedagogy for teaching at the reference desk. Focused on constructivist learning theory, he first shares why this theory is appropriate at the reference desk and goes on to move the theory into practice. This article is an essential read for every librarian who works at a reference desk.

Institute of Museum and Library Services. 2009. "Museums, Libraries, and 21st Century Skills." http://www.imls.gov/assets/1/workflow_staging/AssetManager/293.PDF.
This document provides an overview of the 21st Century Skills initiative by the IMLS. It calls for libraries and museums to take a more active and purposeful role in addressing the multifaceted needs of learners in formal and informal educational settings. It is particularly strong in advocating for public libraries and museums to be educational leaders because they are essential in extending formal schooling and meeting the needs of adult learners.

Oakleaf, Megan, and Amy VanScoy. 2010. "Instructional Strategies for Digital Reference: Methods to Facilitate Student Learning." *Reference & User Services Quarterly* 49 (4): 380–90.
While this article is focused on instruction in the context of digital reference, the strategies that Oakleaf and VanScoy share are applicable to all reference settings. Following an analysis of chat transcripts, the authors observed specific behaviors and categorized them, resulting in the instructional strategies included in the article.

Chapter 5

Consortia and Cooperation

Kelly Jo Woodside

INTRODUCTION

Many library and information science (LIS) students get all the way through graduate school with no knowledge of state libraries or regional library systems. And yet, cooperation among libraries is the force behind many of the services that reference librarians rely on to serve patrons, from interlibrary loan (ILL) to research databases to summer reading. There are several reasons why LIS students should take the time to familiarize themselves with cooperative library services and consortial arrangements. To begin with, library consortia extend services and increase capacity of individual libraries in a wide range of service areas, so knowledge of most aspects of the field is incomplete without consideration of cooperation. Indeed, most libraries belong to at least one consortium, and many participate in multiple consortia for different services, as illustrated in Box 5.1. Library employees should be prepared to engage with these organizations to maximize benefits to their own library and across the membership. Finally, library consortia offer a unique opportunity to see the big picture of the LIS field. Some facilitate benchmarking and collaboration with peer libraries, while others serve as a bridge across library type at the regional or state level.

Box 5.1 Examples of Library Participation in Consortia

Participation in consortia varies depending on the library's size and needs. The following four library examples, though not necessarily representative of their type of library, illustrate the diversity of engagement with consortial service within one state.

- **A small school library**. This library is a member of one consortium, a statewide library system. With a very tight budget, it relies on the state-funded consortium for access to key library services, including a core set of statewide databases and professional development for staff. In addition, it pays a modest fee to participate in a basic networked integrated library system (ILS) designed specifically for small libraries to help manage their collections and access ILL services.
- **A mid-sized public library**. This library is also a member of the statewide library system, relying heavily on its free courier delivery service for physical materials from other libraries, as well as its professional development and advisory services, cooperative purchasing plan, and e-books program. It is also a member of a fee-based regional network that offers a more robust ILS with direct access to resource sharing with other member libraries in the area, along with additional e-content and technical support options.
- **A community college library**. This library uses the state library system for delivery and databases, along with a regional network for its ILS and additional e-content and technical support. In addition, it is a member of another consortium for public higher education institutions, which provides shared databases, professional development, and library advocacy. It also participates in two additional cooperative purchasing consortia for additional databases and resources.
- **A research university library**. This library uses the state library system for delivery, along with some e-content and professional development. While it operates its own ILS, it maintains fee-based memberships in at least five different consortia for resource sharing and participates in two additional arrangements for joint licensing or purchase of e-content. It is also a member of a shared print initiative for academic and research libraries.

OVERVIEW OF LIBRARY COOPERATION

What is a consortium? For the purpose of this chapter, the term will include any group of libraries that pools its resources—financial, human expertise, technical, or otherwise—to achieve one or more goals beyond the capability of its individual members. As Valerie Horton and Greg Pronevitz (2015, 2) point out, such groups may be referred to by different terms, for example, "cooperatives," "networks," "collectives," "alliances," "partnerships," and "consortia."

History

Whatever one calls them, the history of library consortia reflects the overall history of librarianship. If the goal of an individual library is to organize a certain amount of information and make it accessible to a defined population, the goal of a library consortium might be understood to simply extend more information resources to a broader group of people, usually with some commonality, such as

TABLE 5.1 Development of Library Consortia: A Chronological Overview of the Major Events in the Development of Library Consortia

1876	ALA Committee on Cooperation in Indexing and Cataloguing College Libraries formed.
1898	ALA begins a shared indexing/cataloging program, which later becomes part of Wilson's International Index of Periodicals
1900	National Union Catalog first published by Library of Congress, followed by the first regional union catalog in California a year later.
1917	First ILL code adopted by ALA
1933	Formation of Triangle Research Libraries Network (TRLN), now the oldest academic library consortium in the United States. TRLN originally shared cataloging and collections among Duke University and North Carolina State University, and it continues to be at the forefront of innovative collaborative services today, adding such services as research data support and project management.
1930s	Development of many new union catalogs and establishment of early regional library cooperatives.
1940s	Growth in higher education, spurring more formalized arrangements among libraries, such as the precursor to the Center for Research Libraries in 1949.
1960s and 1970s	First period of prolific library consortia development, including OCLC, which is now a global megaconsortium. The 1970s also saw further development of regional library systems, many of which focused on expanding public library services and support, especially in rural and underserved areas, via consulting, continuing education, joint catalogs, and resource-sharing networks.
1990s through 2000s	Second period of significant consortia expansion, following development of Internet access. Group licensing and purchasing of online resources is key. Development of new specialized consortia.
2008 through 2015	Following economic recession of 2007, many library consortia closed or merged, including regional library systems, and new cooperative initiatives were limited. By the end of this period, the library consortium landscape had begun to recover, despite continued economic challenges, including limited public funding.
2020–	What will the future hold for library consortia? See the challenges and opportunities sections toward the end of this chapter for some thoughts.

Source: Timeline drawn from Alexander (1999) and Horton and Pronevitz (2015).

others in the same geographic region or at a similar institutional type. For highlights in the history of the development of library consortia, see Table 5.1.

Current Landscape

Library consortia vary widely in size, organization, and funding. Library membership ranges from the single digits—for a consortia focusing on a single metropolitan area, for example—to the tens of thousands—such as the megaconsortium

OCLC, which in 2019 claimed to represent 85,400 institutions worldwide. Most library consortia tend to be organized around one of the following factors:

- **Geography.** Libraries may collaborate with others in the same municipality, region, or state to extend services. For example, the Massachusetts Library System (MLS) provides a variety of services to approximately 1,600 libraries of all types throughout the state.
- **Library type.** Libraries may partner with similar organizations to provide services specific to that type, such as the Big Ten Academic Alliance, which focuses on the needs of major research institutions.
- **Geography and library type.** Some consortia develop membership by both geography and type, such as the Orbis Cascade Alliance, which serves academic libraries in the northwestern United States.

Consortial funding models may rely on public funds, membership fees, fee for service, grants, or some combination of these. For example, MLS services are primarily covered by funding from the state library agency, but select optional services are fee based, such as the Commonwealth eBook Collection. Membership-based consortia may impose flat fees or calculate them based on factors like community population or academic full-time equivalency.

Finally, no discussion about library collaboration would be complete without mentioning state libraries. Although state libraries are not consortia in the traditional sense, many sponsor one or more collaborative arrangements or provide consortial-type services such as resource sharing and professional development in accordance with state law. In some cases, the regional library systems mentioned earlier were created by the state to fulfill those needs at the local level, particularly in rural or underserved areas. As noted in the aforementioned timeline, however, many regional systems were merged or closed following the 2007 economic recession, leaving members to adjust to new configurations or find alternative means of support.

COOPERATIVE LIBRARY SERVICES

This section will explore common services of library consortia, including various resource-sharing arrangements, professional development, and consulting. Box 5.2 summarizes some of the services consortia offer.

Box 5.2 Activity: Examples of Consortial Activities

Library consortia engage in a wide variety of activities, including

- resource licensing
- print and electronic purchasing
- interlibrary loan/document delivery
- cooperative reference
- shared catalogs and/or discovery systems
- archival projects

- training and continuing education
- member consulting.

Questions for Reflection and Discussion:

1. Which of these activities would you find most helpful as a reference librarian? As a library director?
2. Think about the resources and services libraries might develop in the future. What role could consortia play in supporting these efforts?
3. This chapter provides examples of how a library might benefit from being part of a consortium. Can you think of an instance where a library might not benefit?
4. Library consortia have proliferated in the past twenty years. Under what circumstances might they begin to consolidate and what impact would this have on libraries?

Resource Sharing

Consortia engage in a wide variety of resource-sharing activities, including cooperative ILSs and catalogs, ILL and document delivery, and cooperative licensing and purchasing.

Integrated Library Systems and Cooperative Cataloging

As Table 5.1 shows, union catalogs were an early initiative of interlibrary cooperation, and many libraries today still rely on this service. Horton and Pronevitz (2015, 15) report that over 40 percent of library consortia provide members with a shared ILS, most of which are associated with a union catalog. Such arrangements not only offer cost-sharing benefits to participating libraries but also allow patrons to directly request materials owned by other members from within the system. For example, the academic library consortium OhioLINK operates a union catalog among its membership and also links to SearchOhio, its public library counterpart. The result is that patrons can begin in either system and easily request materials from both networks (Evans and Schwing 2016).

One consortium, Georgia's Public Information Network for Electronic Services (PINES), even went so far as to develop its own open source ILS, Evergreen. Designed specifically for the needs of small- to mid-sized mostly public library consortia, Evergreen has since been adopted by a number of other library networks, including Central/Western Massachusetts Automated Resource Sharing, Inc. (C/W MARS), and North of Boston Library Exchange (NOBLE) in Massachusetts.

Although cooperative cataloging was the impetus behind the formation of early library consortia, due to the advent of library automation and bibliographic utilities like OCLC as well as the rise of vendor-supplied cataloging records, it is not a common service of consortia today (Horton and Pronevitz 2015, 44–45). When present, cooperative cataloging efforts provide quality control of an organization's union catalog and may address the specialized needs of larger libraries. For example, the Big Ten Academic Alliance established a program to share expertise for cataloging items with specialized languages or formats across participating member libraries. Benefits include higher-quality metadata for specialized resources and smaller backlogs, both of which improve patrons' access to materials (Cronin et al. 2017).

Interlibrary Loan (ILL) and Delivery

Perhaps the classic example of library cooperation, ILL has allowed libraries to provide patrons with access to resources beyond their own collection for over one hundred years. Today that reach can extend to thousands of other libraries worldwide via OCLC's resource-sharing services, but OCLC membership costs can be prohibitive. Over one-third of library consortia provide mediated ILL services for libraries that are too small or under-resourced to work directly with OCLC, such as small- to medium-sized public libraries (Horton and Pronevitz 2105, 15). Thus patrons of these libraries have three tiers of access:

1. Items owned by the home library.
2. Items held by other member libraries in a shared ILS (as described in the previous section), which can be requested directly by the patron for pickup at the home library.
3. Items not available within the collaborative, which a consortium staff member can obtain through OCLC and forward to the home library.

A distinction in this process may be made between returnables (books and other physical items) and nonreturnables (articles, book chapters, or other items delivered to patrons as electronic copies). The latter service is sometimes referred to as document delivery. Horton and Pronevitz (2015, 15) found that about one in four library consortia provide document delivery.

If the materials to be transferred are in physical format, a shipping service is required. Many consortia provide contracted courier delivery, which offers significant cost savings to member libraries over commercial shipping services. For example, Colorado Library Consortium members save up to a collective $7.1 million per year in shipping costs by using the Colorado Library Courier System instead of relying on United States Postal Service or Federal Express (Hofschire 2012). However, despite an impressive return on investment for members, delivery service is still a significant expense for library consortia, with cost increases driven by external factors such as fuel prices and minimum wage. In response, some consortia have turned to member fees to make this service sustainable, and some have had to suspend delivery altogether.

Cooperative Licensing and Purchasing

Though a relatively recent development in cooperative library services, access to electronic content is perhaps the quintessential consortial service in these days of ever-increasing database costs, particularly for academic libraries. This can take one of two shapes:

- **Shared licensing.** Electronic resources are jointly licensed by the consortium and available to all participating members. An example is the Massachusetts Statewide Database program, a joint project of MLS and the state agency. Member input is solicited throughout the selection and procurement process, but the consortium handles the negotiation process with the vendors, as well as technical support and training once the products are in place.

- **Mediated licensing.** The consortium offers a selection of electronic resource products from which members can pick and choose (sometimes referred to as "buying clubs"). The consortium negotiates the terms of the agreement, which may be better than what libraries can obtain on their own. An example would be the Westchester Academic Library Directors Organization (WALDO), which offers consortial terms on a wide selection of online products to libraries throughout the northeastern United States.

The benefits in both models are better terms due to collective bargaining power, as well as more expertise on the part of the consortium handling the negotiation. In addition, consortia can push for further development of the products by acting as an advocate for member libraries' interests, such as improved accessibility (Horava 2018).

Consortia can also provide a stronger voice to libraries as vendors develop new pricing and delivery strategies. When e-resources were exploding in growth in the 1990s, members of the International Coalition of Library Consortia (ICOLC) organized discussions with publishing industry leaders so the two sides could share their perspectives about the changing environment (Machovec 2014). More recently, consortia have played a role in helping improve the industry standard for circulation of e-books and transition to open-access publishing models, which is discussed later in this chapter.

Finally, consortia can offer members an opportunity to explore new business models within the safety of a well-managed pilot. A patron-driven acquisition pilot for streaming video among eight libraries in western New York was ultimately discontinued at the consortial level, but it provided a "proof of concept" for the libraries to continue the service on an individual basis (Knab, Humphrey, and Ward 2016).

Beyond electronic resources, some consortia provide opportunities for cooperative purchasing of other products, such as print books, shelving, and office products. An example is MLS's agreement with the Massachusetts Higher Education Consortium, which adds library-specific vendors and extends savings to MLS member libraries of all types (Massachusetts Library System 2019).

New Directions in Resource Sharing

The changing landscape of information and higher education has produced new demands on library space, such as rooms for group work and study, media production labs, and makerspaces. Space limitations on many campuses have led libraries to explore off-site storage for less used materials and, more recently, to collaborate on shared archiving of print serials. As of summer 2019, forty-six archiving programs were listed in the Print Archives Preservation Registry (n.d.), about a dozen or so of which represent consortial arrangements. Member libraries might participate by contributing their own holdings, or as affiliate members, obtaining access to shared holdings in exchange for a fee.

A second area of recent expansion in LIS is digital repositories. Consortial efforts in this area have had mixed success. On one hand is a program like Digital Commonwealth, a nonprofit collaborative that provides support for creation, maintenance, and access to digitized cultural heritage materials from over 180 member libraries, museums, historical societies, and archives throughout Massachusetts. This project continues to grow and attract new members from a range of library sizes and types. On the other hand is the Alliance Digital Repository (ADR), a shared institutional repository operated by the Colorado Alliance of Research Libraries from 2007 through 2015. Originally comprising all eighteen Colorado Alliance members, by the time it disbanded, only seven were still participating. Key reasons for the demise of ADR were a lack of a sense of ownership of records within the system by member libraries and the challenge of establishing and maintaining a viable funding model. The alliance found few economies of scale in the model and had to make frequent adjustments to individual member contributions as others dropped out (Dean 2016). Growing interest in open educational resources (OER) offers new possibilities for digital repositories to help create, maintain, and provide access to these new materials as they are created.

Training and Professional Development

Horton and Pronevitz (2015, 15) found that training was the most commonly offered service by U.S. library consortia, with about 75 percent providing some type of professional development to members. Training may be facilitated by consortial staff, member library staff, or outside experts in a wide variety of formats, and topics range from specific application (e.g., how to use a consortial database or technology) to core library functions (e.g., reference 101, weeding, strategic planning) to broad exploration of current issues in the field (e.g., media literacy, STEAM programming, equity, and inclusion).

Since library budgets have limited funds for professional development, many consortia offer training opportunities to members at little or no cost (Horton and Pronevitz 2015, 46). In some cases, smaller libraries rely almost exclusively on consortial subsidized programs to keep their staff up to date. Unfortunately, costs to provide this training are high, and cooperative professional development is a frequent target for cuts in times of economic belt-tightening, despite the substantial cost savings member libraries can realize by seeking staff development opportunities through consortia instead of more costly options like national conferences (Machovec 2015).

Workshops and Webinars

Continuing education (CE) staff in consortia tend to be experienced professionals who are highly knowledgeable in the field. Many have specialized expertise in areas like youth services or technology, and they regularly update their skills and knowledge to share with consortia members. For example, a trainer for a geographically based consortium might attend an expensive national conference and return home to incorporate new trends and resources into free or low-cost CE for staff at member libraries.

In some cases, attendees at consortial training have an opportunity to earn professional development credits or other kinds of certification. MLS, for example, is contracted by the state of Massachusetts to provide a series of four "Basic Library Techniques" courses (reference, collection development and maintenance, cataloging, and administration), leading to alternative state certification for public library directors without a graduate library degree, an option available to municipalities with fewer than 10,000 people (Massachusetts Board of Library Commissioners n.d.). This service ensures that even the smallest town in Massachusetts has a well-prepared library leader.

Professional development may also be offered upon request to individual member libraries. Consultants from library consortia provide site-specific training on topics like customer service, copyright and open access (OA), technology, change management, and assessment.

Since travel is not always feasible, online learning is an increasingly popular option for consortial training. Consortial initiatives like the Florida Library Webinars project, administered by the Florida Department of State, Division of Library and Information Services, and managed by the Tampa Bay Library Consortium, use webinars to both extend the reach of popular trainings to members across the state, as well as make outside speakers available remotely without the expense of bringing them into town. An additional benefit is that such training can be recorded for ongoing access.

Annual Programs

Many consortia offer conferences or annual programs that provide an opportunity for members to participate in a business meeting and network with each other, as well as engage in a learning experience. One popular event at MLS is the annual Teen Summit, which features a keynote speaker on a relevant topic such as connected learning or social justice, as well as breakout sessions where attendees can learn how fellow members are engaging with that topic. As a multitype organization, MLS has also been able to offer unique opportunities for cross-type collaboration, such as the "My College Freshman Is Your High School Senior" program, which brought together librarians and faculty from colleges and high schools to discuss academic and career preparation needs of this population.

Institutes

A number of consortia also offer institutes for a more intensive professional development experience. In this model, a cohort of participants learn and develop together over a period of many months. For example, the Southeast Florida Library Information Network (SEFLIN) developed the Sun Seeker Leadership Institute to address gaps observed among their membership in succession planning and leadership development (Curry and Smithee 2009). The yearlong program includes workshops, mentor partnerships, and presentations by leaders in the field. Similarly, the Research Institute for Public Libraries (RIPL) is an immersive experience developed by the Colorado State Library and Colorado Library Consortium to train public librarians in how to collect, analyze, and use data to communicate impact.

Consulting

The broad and deep expertise of library consortia staff enable them to act as "reference librarians for librarians" and provide more in-depth consultation when necessary. Nearly half of all library consortia offer consulting as a service (Horton and Pronevitz 2015, 15). Frequent topics include technology support, program recommendations and development, space planning, and policy issues. State library or state agency staff may also consult on issues such as state law, grant-writing, trustee development, and library construction programs.

An important area of focus for consultation by many regional library systems or state libraries is planning. In Massachusetts, for instance, libraries are eligible for certain Library Services and Technology Act grant programs as long as they have a strategic plan on file with the state library agency. Consortium staff conduct workshops on the strategic planning process annually, but they also offer members a customized facilitation session with staff and/or community members to kickstart the process.

One of the best ways for consultants to better understand the challenges and issues of consortium members is to conduct site visits and talk to member library staff. For example, WiLS (formerly Wisconsin Library Services) staff visit members at least once per quarter. The insight gained from such meetings helps them plan future initiatives that respond to members' needs (Morrill and Coffin 2016).

Support for Public Services

Some library consortia are experimenting with offering direct support to their members for public services functions like instruction and reference. Examples include the British Columbia Libraries Cooperative's Library Toolshed, a repository of programming, training, and instructional materials. Likewise, the California Digital Library maintains an Instructional Materials Repository where members can share and reuse videos, handouts, slides, and other materials for library instruction. While some consortia have had success with collaborative reference, others have piloted this service and ended it due to changing technology and needs, as well as problems with quality of response to local questions (Powers et al. 2010). However, many consortia still provide opportunities for members to help each other with challenging patron questions via informal venues like e-mail discussion lists.

One notable achievement in library cooperation is the Collaborative Summer Library Program (CSLP). Established in 1987, CSLP is a grassroots collaboration that has grown to include almost all fifty states. Representatives, typically a youth services consultant from the state library or library system, gather each year to plan themes, select artwork, and develop a manual with guidance, program and promotional ideas, and additional resources to help participating libraries implement the program. Back at their own state, CSLP representatives work to disseminate information and materials about the program to libraries in their jurisdiction. For example, April Mazza, the Massachusetts representative to CSLP, then conducts workshops, webinars, and consultations on using the materials; communicates regularly with participating libraries; and collects statistics at the end of the summer (Mazza, personal communication, June 18, 2018).

For academic libraries, a growing opportunity for consortial support of teaching and learning lies in OER. Beyond the infrastructure elements noted in the resource-sharing section of this chapter, consortia are well positioned to spearhead OER initiatives by providing professional development, grants, resource guides, and other kinds of support for libraries and faculty among their membership. Affordable Learning Georgia (2018), for example, offers "Textbook Transformation Grants" and trains "campus champions" and library coordinators to advocate for open educational resources across all twenty-six campuses of the University System of Georgia.

Other Services

While resource sharing, training, and consulting account for the bulk of cooperative library services, there are many examples where consortia have branched out in different directions. Examples include a temporary staffing service for member libraries, administration of grants, accessibility testing of e-resources and library technology, video production, and support for library advocacy. Horton and Pronevitz (2015, 87–176) include a series of case studies that explore unique consortial projects. As the LIS field continues to change at a sometimes-dizzying pace, library consortial services will likely continue to develop in new directions.

CHALLENGES AND FUTURE DIRECTIONS FOR LIBRARY COOPERATION

In a recent survey, sixty consortial leaders described trends and challenges facing their organizations over the past five years and the next five years (unpublished survey, July 2018). Their responses can be broadly categorized as follows.

Funding

By far the most widespread concern in both the immediate past and future is funding. Slightly more than half of respondents reported that public funding comprises at least 25 percent of their budget, and a similar percentage described funding issues as a primary concern. Specific challenges noted were decreased or unstable state and federal public funding, along with an uncertain political environment; shrinking budgets at academic institutions; and increased costs for electronic resources, software licensing, delivery, and staffing. Two respondents mentioned the need to seek alternative sustainable funding.

Others were more optimistic, pointing to a growing state tax base, a renewed focus on pilot projects and service models, and more incentive for libraries to work together in the face of financial challenges. Nevertheless, there is an economic paradox for library consortia in times of economic difficulty: as budgets tighten, libraries are likely to consider dropping fee-based consortial memberships; however, that is exactly the time when they could most use the cost savings that consortia produce through cooperative licensing, free or low-cost professional development, and other services described in this chapter (Machovec 2015).

Demonstrating Value

Given that library consortia are competing with so many other factors for libraries' financial resources, there is tremendous pressure to demonstrate value. Historically, most library consortia have taken a quantitative approach to calculating value. For example, they emphasize the cost savings of consortial buying over purchasing e-content individually or the approximate financial value of services like consulting and professional development. MLS spends weeks each year on a complex project to calculate an individual "value of service" for each of 1,600 members. Another tactic is to calculate the return on investment for each dollar invested into the consortium. In the academic arena, the Pennsylvania Academic Library

Consortium, Inc. (2018) has recently announced CloudBased Consortial Platform for Library Usage Statistics (CC-PLUS), an initiative to develop a prototype library usage statistics tool that supports consortial functionality.

However, just as libraries have been pushed to move beyond outputs to outcomes in assessing library instruction and other services, some have suggested that library consortia need to shift from counting dollar values to demonstrating the impact their services have on members. For academic consortia, that means tying value to student learning outcomes, just as libraries themselves are doing (Chadwell 2011). But all library consortia can benefit from adding qualitative assessment measures to emphasize the value of intangible advantages provided, such as shared expertise, best practices, and market influence (Machovec 2015). A good starting point would be a process for evaluating and assessing new projects (Morrill and Coffin 2016).

Leadership Turnover

One surprising finding of the survey described previously was that five of the sixty respondents had experienced a new executive director or a change in organizational leadership in the past five years, with two of these reporting especially challenging or failed search processes. A number of additional consortia expressed concern about changes in library leadership at their member institutions. This suggests a challenge in the field in terms of management and leadership development and succession planning. The specific combination of library skills and expertise with managing people, projects, and resources in a nonprofit (and possibly political) environment may prove to be a particular challenge for consortia. More education at the graduate level, including internships, along with more outreach to promising early- to mid-career librarians, about professional opportunities in library consortia is needed.

Print to Digital

While the migration of many information resources from print to digital is far from breaking news, consortia continue to identify it as a challenge, as vendors are still trying out new pricing structures and delivery models. One survey respondent lamented that e-books are not shareable, while another noted that their member libraries are tired of "big-deal" journal subscription packages. As the information landscape continues to evolve, consortia may have an increasingly important responsibility to represent the interests of libraries and library patrons to publishers and vendors.

New Opportunities

The most commonly mentioned opportunity for new consortial initiatives was OER, with eleven of the sixty survey respondents describing increased interest in and pressure to provide OA education materials. One respondent was particularly enthusiastic about the opportunity OER might offer to develop initiatives across library type.

More broadly, library consortia can play a role in helping their members navigate the shift from traditional to OA publishing models. Support for OA ranges from assisting members in developing and sharing language for campus policies on OA to facilitating complex conversations with publishers about OA financial models. In the United States, the California Digital Library (CDL) and University of California (UC) Libraries are leading the way in cooperative approaches to OA. The Pay It Forward project (Miller 2016) brought together research libraries from California and beyond, along with publishing industry partners and scholarly communications experts to evaluate the impact of article processing charges in OA. Building on Pay It Forward, in 2018 the UC Davis Library hosted Move It Forward, a publisher workshop to explore models for transitioning journals to OA models. Also in 2018, the CDL and UC Libraries released the Pathways to Open Access toolkit to help libraries make data-driven decisions about how to move forward with OA (University of California Libraries 2018). They later hosted a working forum to help libraries beyond UC use the Pathways materials to plan OA approaches on their campuses. Since many library consortia already have long-standing relationships with scholarly publishers, they are well positioned to help facilitate challenging conversations and advise their members on OA options.

Data management is another emerging field. Certain types of consortia, especially those comprising mid- to large-sized academic libraries, may be able to provide leadership in data management via technical infrastructure, faculty training, and participation in open data initiatives.

Finally, while not new, marketing and communications is another area emphasized by survey respondents. Consortia are obliged not only to assess and market their own services but also to help libraries do the same within their communities, via training and other forms of support and advocacy. Box 5.3 offers some reflection questions based on the challenges and opportunities facing library consortia.

Box 5.3 Challenges and Opportunities Facing Library Consortia

As consortia look to the future, they face challenges as well as exciting opportunities.

Questions for Discussion and Reflection:

1. What factors do you think will impact library consortia and collaboratives in the next five to ten years? What changes will result?
2. What are the advantages and disadvantages of participating in a consortium with other institutions similar to your own library? What are the advantages and disadvantages of participating in a consortium with many different types of libraries?
3. Sustainability is a balancing act for cooperative efforts in LIS. How can consortia help make libraries more sustainable? How might member libraries help make consortia more sustainable?
4. As noted in this chapter, library consortia—like libraries—are under pressure to demonstrate value. Think about one or more of the consortial services covered in this chapter. What assessment strategies would you recommend? Why?

CONCLUSION

Library consortia and cooperative efforts are an essential part of the library and information services landscape. However, because their services are often designed to integrate seamlessly with member library operations behind the scenes, many reference librarians have a limited awareness of how consortia support their daily work. New professionals can leverage resources available to them and contribute to a sustainable environment for library consortia by seeking out opportunities to engage with these organizations, as outlined in Box 5.4.

Box 5.4 Engaging with Library Consortia

New professionals can engage with consortia in many ways.

Basic

- *Learn*. Familiarize yourself with library consortia in your area. Identify which services they provide, how to access news and updates from each organization, and whom to contact with feedback or questions.
- *Investigate*. Many libraries are members of multiple consortia. Are there consortia available that might help your library better meet its needs? Investigate options in your geographic region, as well as those that may cater to your specific type of library.
- *Advocate*. Contact your legislators to help them understand how your library community benefits from consortial services that rely on public funds, and educate your patrons to do the same.

Intermediate

- *Participate*. Ask about opportunities to serve on committees or task forces related to your professional interests. Once you have gained some experience, consider applying for a position on the executive board. However, keep in mind that when you take on such roles, you are entrusted to represent not just your individual library but the best interests of the organization as a whole (Jones 2017).
- *Collaborate*. Take advantage of networking opportunities to co-create initiatives. For example, MLS member libraries have leveraged "co-creator culture" to explore best practices, collaborate on *LibGuides*, and share instructional materials.

Advanced

- *Explore*. Consider a career in library consortia. Positions include resource-sharing technicians, software and systems managers, youth services specialists, consultants, and trainers. An internship is a productive way to explore such opportunities and develop nonprofit and organizational skills such as project management, community engagement, and communication. As one consortium leader emphasized, interns "find it interesting to see the big picture with multitype libraries at state level" (Stef Morrill, personal communication, July 2018).

- *Initiate*. Many consortia start out as informal arrangements before developing into full-fledged organizations. Indeed, the Eastern Academic Scholars' Trust (EAST) shared print initiative began as a series of discussions initiated by one local consortium and eventually grew to a self-supporting program with dedicated staff and sixty-one members in eleven states.

REFERENCES

Affordable Learning Georgia. 2018. "About Us." https://www.affordablelearninggeorgia.org/about/about_us.

Alexander, Adrian W. 1999. "Toward 'the Perfection of Work': Library Consortia in the Digital Age." *History of Academic Library Cooperative Projects* 28 (2): 1–14.

Alliance Digital Repository. Colorado Alliance of Research Libraries. https://www.coalliance.org/software/digital-repository.

California Digital Library. https://www.cdlib.org/.

Chadwell, Faye A. 2011. "Assessing the Value of Academic Library Consortia." *Journal of Library Administration* 51 (7/8): 645–61.

Collaborative Summer Library Program. https://www.cslpreads.org/.

Colorado Alliance of Research Libraries. https://coalliance.org/colorado-alliance-research-libraries.

Colorado Library Consortium. https://www.clicweb.org/.

C/W MARS. http://www.cwmars.org/.

Cronin, Christopher, Mary S. Laskowski, Ellen K. W. Mueller, and Beth E. Snyder. 2017. "Strength in Numbers: Building a Consortial Cooperative Cataloging Partnership." *Library Resources & Technical Services* 61 (2): 102–16.

Curry, Elizabeth A., and Jeannette Smithee. 2009. "Developing Leadership in a Multitype Library Consortium: Ten Years of SEFLIN Sun Seekers." *Resource Sharing & Information Networks* 20 (1): 18–34.

Dean, Robin. 2016. "Shutting Down a Consortial Digital Repository Service." *Journal of Library Administration* 56 (1): 91–99.

Digital Commonwealth. https://www.digitalcommonwealth.org/.

Evans, Gwen, and Theda Schwing. 2016. "OhioLINK—Recent Developments at a United States Academic Library Consortium." *Interlending & Document Supply* 44 (4): 172–77.

Florida Library Webinars. https://floridalibrarywebinars.org/about/.

Hofschire, Linda. 2012. "High Traffic, Low Cost: The Colorado Courier Continues to Save Libraries Millions Annually in Shipping Charges." Fast Facts—Recent Statistics from the Library Research Service. https://www.lrs.org/documents/fastfacts/302_Courier.pdf.

Horava, Tony. 2018. "The Role of Consortia in Collection Management." *Technicalities* 38 (2): 16–19.

Horton, Valerie, and Greg Pronevitz, eds. 2015. *Library Consortia: Models for Collaboration and Sustainability*. Chicago: ALA Editions.

Instructional Materials Repository. California Digital Library. https://www.cdlib.org/services/info_services/instruct/.

International Coalition of Library Consortia. https://icolc.net.

Jones, Pamela. 2017. "Why We Do That Thing We Do: What Consortia Executive Directors Want Library Directors to Know." *Journal of Library Administration* 57 (1): 114–22.

Knab, Sheryl, Tom Humphrey, and Caryl Ward. 2016. "Now Streaming: A Consortial PDA Video Pilot Project." *Collaborative Librarianship* 8 (1), Article 8. https://digitalcommons.du.edu/collaborativelibrarianship/vol8/iss1/8.

Library Toolshed. https://librarytoolshed.ca/about.

Machovec, George. 2014. "Consortia and the Future of the Big Deal Journal Packages." *Journal of Library Administration* 54 (7): 629–36.

Machovec, George. 2015. "Calculating the Return on Investment (ROI) for Library Consortia." *Journal of Library Administration* 55 (5): 414–24.

Massachusetts Board of Library Commissioners. n.d. "Librarian Certification." https://mblc.state.ma.us/jobs/certification.php.

Massachusetts Library System. https://www.masslibsystem.org/.

Massachusetts Library System. 2019. "Purchasing Cooperative." Last modified February 28, 2019. http://guides.masslibsystem.org/purchasingcoop.

Miller, Alana. 2016. "UC Davis and CDL Complete Pay It Forward Project." CDLINFO News. Last modified August 11, 2016. https://www.cdlib.org/cdlinfo/2016/08/11/uc-davis-and-cdl-complete-pay-it-forward-project/.

Morrill, Stef, and Andi Coffin. 2016. "Envisioning the Tapestry: Discovering and Planning Member-Driven Services." *Journal of Library Administration* 56 (5): 628–37.

Move It Forward. University of California Davis Library. https://www.library.ucdavis.edu/service/scholarly-communications/move-it-forward-a-publisher-workshop-to-identify-transitional-open-access-models/.

North of Boston Library Exchange. https://www.noblenet.org/libraries/.

OCLC. 2019. "OCLC Partner Programs." https://www.oclc.org/en/partnerships.html.

OhioLINK. https://www.ohiolink.edu.

Orbis Cascade Alliance. https://www.orbiscascade.org/

Pennsylvania Academic Library Consortium, Inc. 2018. "Consortia Collaborating on a Platform for Library Usage Statistics." Last updated September 2018. http://www.palci.org/cc-plus-overview/.

Powers, Amanda Clay, David Nolen, Li Zhang, Yue Xu, and Gail Peyton. 2010. "Moving from the Consortium to the Reference Desk: Keeping Chat and Improving Reference at the MSU Libraries." *Internet Reference Services Quarterly* 15 (3): 169–88.

Print Archives Preservation Registry. n.d. "Directory." http://papr.crl.edu/program/.

Public Information Network for Electronic Services. https://pines.georgialibraries.org/.

Research Institute for Public Libraries. https://ripl.lrs.org.

Southeast Florida Library Information Network. https://www.seflin.org.

University of California Libraries. 2018. "Scholarly Communication." Last modified May 10, 2019. https://libraries.universityofcalifornia.edu/about/initiatives/scholarly-communication.

Westchester Academic Library Directors Organization. http://www.waldolib.org.

SUGGESTED READINGS

Association of Specialized Government and Cooperative Library Agencies (ASGCLA). American Library Association. http://www.ala.org/asgcla/.

ASGCLA is the division of the American Library Association that serves library consortia and other library cooperatives by providing information, resources, events, and advocacy. The ASGCLA website provides numerous resources and tools for those interested in consortial work.

Chief Officers of State Library Agencies (COSLA). http://www.cosla.org/.

COSLA provides leadership to state library agencies on issues of common concern and national interest and initiates cooperative action for the improvement of library services in the United States.

Collaborative Librarianship. 2009–. Denver: Regis University. https://digitalcommons.du.edu/collaborativelibrarianship/.

This quarterly, open-access journal focuses on the scholarship of collaboration as well as the sharing of resources and expertise within and between libraries.

Esposito, Joseph. 2015. "Libraries and Consortia in the Context of a Publisher's Strategy." *The Scholarly Kitchen*. September 30. http://scholarlykitchen.sspnet.org/2015/09/30/libraries-and-consortia-in-the-context-of-a-publishers-strategy/.

A management consultant to publishers, Esposito provides an interesting point of view on the impact of consortia on small publishers and scholarly communication from the perspective of the publishers. This essay and the comments that follow provide an interesting interchange on the topic.

Horton, Valerie, and Greg Pronevitz, eds. 2015. *Library Consortia: Models for Collaboration and Sustainability*. Chicago: American Library Association.

Horton and Pronevitz cover the history, current landscape, management approaches, trends, and services that define library consortia.

International Coalition of Library Consortia (ICOLC). http://icolc.net/.

ICOLC is an international informal group that facilitates discussion on issues of common interest to participating consortia.

Machovec, George. 2013–. "Library Networking and Consortia." *Journal of Library Administration*. Philadelphia, PA: Routledge.

This regular column offers in-depth examinations of issues facing modern library consortia.

Chapter 6

Models of Reference Services

Lili Luo

INTRODUCTION

For over a hundred years, ever since Samuel Green (1876) defined the relations between librarians and library users, human-intermediated assistance provided by reference librarians has been considered a pivotal function of reference departments. An essential part of reference work is to help users find information to fulfill their information needs by every possible means.

Traditionally, reference service takes place in a reference room, or an otherwise designated area in the library, at a desk staffed by librarians and close to the reference collection. During the pre-digital age, people relied on reference librarians substantively for access to information. Since the advent of the Internet, personal computers, and other communication/networking technologies, the accessibility and availability of information have been greatly enhanced. Search engines like *Google* and *Bing*, and free Web reference resources like *Wikipedia*, have become the first stop in many people's information-seeking process. Nowadays, with the rapid development of mobile technologies, people can search for information even more easily and conveniently using various apps on their mobile devices. On the one hand, the exponential expansion of information access has reduced people's dependence on reference service; on the other hand, it offers more possibilities for reference service to be delivered beyond brick-and-mortar buildings in response to the incessantly evolving information landscape. In the past half century, reference service has migrated from a print resource-oriented service limited to a certain physical space, to a diversified service portfolio that can reach more people with more resources and less restriction of time and space.

Instead of sitting idly behind the reference desk waiting for people to visit, librarians have adopted the "going where users are" approach and offer reference service via digital venues that people commonly use for communication, such as e-mail, online real-time chat, and texting. A group of proactive reference librarians have even ventured into social Q&A sites like *Quora* and *Yahoo! Answers*, hoping to represent librarianship in a new venue, encounter users beyond the library, provide well-sourced, dependable answers to people's questions, and make people aware that librarians and libraries can be valuable sources not just for books, videos, and other materials but also for intermediated answers to questions and referral to appropriate sources and organizations (Luo 2014).

An important part of contemporary reference service is to constantly evaluate the role reference librarians can and should play in helping people fulfill their information needs. Understanding how and where people seek information in the wired world, and how their information-seeking experience can benefit from librarians' intermediation or assistance, is key to the vitality of reference service and determines how reference service is delivered. Currently, there are two main models of reference service: in person and remote/virtual. The in-person venues consist of the reference desk, research consultations, and roving reference. The remote/virtual venues include telephone, e-mail/Web form, online real-time chat, and texting.

The reference desk offers a convenient access point for users to seek assistance from librarians, but over the years the decline of reference transactions has led to challenges about its value. New staffing arrangements such as tiered reference, where paraprofessionals handle simple directional questions and refer in-depth queries to librarians, are being employed to increase efficacy. Research consultations allow library users to schedule individual meetings with a librarian. Though time consuming, such consultations are opportunities for librarians to help users deeply engage with their research projects and develop a wide range of information literacy skills. Roving reference enables librarians to be proactive, reach out to users, and provide service at their point of need, but careful planning and staff preparation is needed in order for roving to be successful.

E-mail reference service makes it possible for patrons to ask questions anytime and anywhere, as long as they have an Internet connection. It is an asynchronous service and good for nonurgent queries where an immediate response is not expected. A downside of e-mail reference is the difficulty of conducting an in-depth reference interview. To compensate, libraries offer online, real-time chat reference services where users can engage in a text-based chat session with a librarian for reference assistance. Text reference service allows users to send in queries and receive answers via texting on their mobile device.

While expanding the reach of library services, virtual reference also brings new challenges such as technological issues, concerns about privacy, and the increasing number of frivolous questions due to anonymity. In order to successfully plan and implement a suite of reference services, it is important to understand the characteristics of each in-person and remote/virtual venue as well as its advantages and disadvantages in delivering reference service.

Box 6.1 provides a summary of the two models. This chapter discusses the basics of delivering reference service under these models and concludes with a discussion of ways to keep current and stay relevant as librarians strive to meet users' needs and optimize their experience.

Box 6.1 Models of Reference Services

In person

- Reference desk
- Research consultations
- Roving reference

Virtual

- E-mail/Web form
- Online real-time chat
- Texting

IN-PERSON REFERENCE SERVICE

In-person reference services are provided through face-to-face interactions with librarians and are the most direct way for users to receive assistance in their information-seeking process. However, some library users may be reluctant to approach librarians if they are not comfortable with in-person conversations or do not speak English as their first language. If librarians at the reference desk appear to be busy or aloof, users may also feel discouraged from asking them for assistance. Thus, the first item in the Reference and User Services Association's (RUSA) (2013) "Guidelines for Behavioral Performance of Reference and Information Service Providers" is visibility and approachability, highlighting the importance of making users "feel comfortable in a situation that can be perceived as intimidating, confusing, or overwhelming."

Face-to-face interaction allows for the exchange of nonverbal information; enables librarians to transmit interpersonal, relational messages of empathy and interest found to be important to the user; and builds rapport between librarians and users (Selby 2007). The richness of communication in in-person reference services makes it the best platform for librarians to address in-depth and complex queries and to provide instruction. This section introduces three models of in-person reference service—the reference desk, research consultations, and roving reference.

Reference Desk

For easy recognition and approachability, the reference desk is usually located prominently in the library and properly labeled—popular signage includes "Reference & Information," "Ask Here," and "Research Help." To better facilitate the reference transaction, some desks have an extra monitor facing outward for users to see the librarians' searches in action so they can feel more connected and informed.

To many, the reference desk is viewed as a cornerstone of reference service and reflects values that are identified to be core to reference librarianship: convenient and equitable service to users, individually tailored personal assistance, and high professional standards (Bunge and Ferguson 1997). It represents "a critical mass of resources—human, printed, and now electronic, so configured for a convenient and predictable location so that library patrons can find the service and can find someone to help them" (Swanson 1984, 89). However, not all people believe in the value of the reference desk. Barbara Ford was one of the first to question the efficiency and effectiveness of the service provided from the reference desk and challenged the idea of the reference desk as the center of reference service (Ford 1986). Over the years, opponents of the reference desk have claimed that it is only a symbol of reference service, not the service itself (Bell 2007), and advocated the elimination of the reference desk for the following reasons:

- **Decline of reference transactions.** The shift to the online world has dramatically increased people's ability to search for information and reduced the need for reference service. For example, from 2001 to 2012, academic libraries experienced a 57 percent decline in reference transactions (Bunnett et al. 2016); from 2012 to 2017, public libraries' reference transactions decreased by 9.8 percent (Reid 2017).
- **Trivialization of queries.** Most of the queries received at the reference desk are directional (e.g., the location of the group study room) or technical (e.g., how to fix a printer jam) questions that are routine and repetitive. A 2016 study found that 85 percent of the questions posed to the reference desk were directional in nature or could be answered at the "quick lookup" level (Oud and Genzinger 2016). Such questions ignore librarians' expertise and contribute to job dissatisfaction (Aluri and St. Clair 1978; Freides 1983; Massey-Burzio 1992).
- **Expanding responsibilities of reference librarians.** With the transition to an online information world, reference librarians are faced with growing responsibilities to keep up with massive electronic resources; to deliver reference service via digital venues; to provide instruction; and to conduct outreach through liaison work, embedded services, and social media (Giordano, Menard, and Spencer 2001). Sitting behind the reference desk is no longer an efficient use of their time.
- **Emergency-style service in a nonemergency situation.** Users are inclined to view the reference desk as intended for quick replies and are under the impression that librarians function more as clerks at a service counter rather than as professionals. When the reference transaction involves an in-depth query, both user and librarian experience frustration when ringing phones and queues of users with short-answer questions compete for the librarians' attention, making the reference desk an unideal venue for consultations that could truly benefit from librarians' expertise (Freides 1983; Summerhill 1994).

These problems point to the rejection of the reference desk, not the idea of human-intermediated reference service. The opponents of the reference desk believe that it is an outmoded method of service delivery, and greater emphasis should be placed on the potential for virtual reference service to address quick-answer and repetitive queries and appointment-based, individual consultations to handle complex queries (Nolen 2010). Proponents of the reference desk, on the other hand, champion the value of "human contact," as indicated in Michael Gorman's (2001, 182) statement: "We must maintain the vital human-to-human component that typifies reference service across our history. This is an age in which human values are under strain; human contact and sympathy become more and more prized as they become rarer."

Still, even proponents recognize the problems of the reference desk. Instead of elimination, their solution is to reorganize it to enhance its efficiency. As a result, the tiered service, or the triaged service, model has been implemented to maximize use of the librarian's expertise and time, reduce stress and burnout, present an appropriate professional image, and optimize the use of human resources (LaMagna, Hartman-Caverly, and Marchetti 2016). Under this staffing model, multiple types of staff are arranged to answer user queries. The word "tiered" or "triage" refers to the varying degrees of information needs reflected in user queries. For instance, "first-tiered" questions may include directional questions, online catalog help, known-item searches, basic technology assistance, and interlibrary loan inquiries, and "second-tiered" questions may require an in-depth reference interview and comprehensive research (Poparad 2015). In some cases, paraprofessionals or trained students staff the reference desk alongside librarians, and they are responsible for answering first-tiered questions and refer second-tiered questions to reference librarians. In some other cases, they operate from a separate service point, often called the "Help Desk" or "Information Desk," to handle simple queries and make necessary referrals to librarians at the reference desk.

While the tiered or triaged service model allows differentiation of reference services and supports more effective and efficient use of librarians' time and expertise, it has its own challenges. Since this model relies on knowledge of paraprofessional staff in answering questions at their tier level and referring those that need further assistance, staff training regarding when to refer a question to a librarian is critical to effective implementation of this model. The line between simple, quick-answer queries and complex queries can be ill-defined, and inadequately trained paraprofessional staff may misjudge the nature of user queries and fail to make referrals, which ultimately will undermine the user's library experience. Meanwhile, small libraries are unlikely to have the manpower, resources, and facilities to support multiple service points. A considerable amount of time is needed for defining the mission of the separate information desk and for training the staff. Furthermore, the public is rarely aware of the difference between the service points. It could be burdensome for patrons to distinguish which questions go to which desk, and they might get frustrated if they are referred back and forth between desks, and thus the service model may not achieve its intended effect (Mosley 2007).

Some libraries combine the reference desk with other service points like the circulation desk into one location to facilitate a "one-stop shop" to conserve staffing resources and improve service access (Aho, Beschnett, and Reimer 2011; Schulte 2011). The frontline service staff are usually paraprofessionals, and they are responsible for fielding user queries and making proper referrals to on-call librarians who operate from their offices. A unified access point alleviates the concern over the "ping-pong" effect of directing patrons from one desk to another, which has been observed as a source of annoyance to many patrons (Venner and Keshmiripour 2016). Such a single service point often requires significant cross-training of library staff and effective promotion of good interpersonal and communication skills among staff members (Bunnett et al. 2016).

Despite the debate about the reference desk, a survey by Dennis Miles (2013) shows that it is still prevalent in libraries, with 66.4 percent of academic libraries still using the reference desk to offer reference services and 77.2 percent with a professional librarian at the reference desk all or some of the time. Librarians in the study indicated that the face-to-face interaction with users is the most important reason why librarians still want to offer service from the desk. They also offer other modes of reference service such as roving reference and consultations, but these services are offered in addition to the reference desk, not in place of it. While the study indicates librarians' commitment to service at the reference desk, it is worth noting the libraries surveyed in the study were mid-sized college and university libraries. Libraries of other types may have different experiences. There is no "one-size-fits-all" solution when it comes to deciding the fate of the reference desk. Careful analysis based on the library's constituents, budget, and culture is indispensable to determining the reference service model most appropriate for the library.

Research Consultations

Research consultations are individual meetings between a librarian and a user or a group of users (e.g., several students working together on a group project). Such meetings are appointment based and often take place in a private room (e.g., the librarian's office). Length of the meetings varies, often depending on the specific needs of the user. Research consultations are particularly popular among academic libraries, where students get in-depth research assistance from librarians in a quiet environment and librarians can focus exclusively on an individual student's needs (Gale and Evans 2007; Jastram and Zawistoski 2008).

Research consultations can be time consuming, especially when the demand is high. Librarians often have to prepare for the meeting by reviewing resources and consulting with colleagues. At the same time, many benefits have been identified. Research consultations are believed to be an important venue to address "student needs that were not sufficiently covered in a classroom setting" (Yi 2003, 349) and the "unique concerns of each student in a way that is not possible in larger groups" (Reinsfelder 2012, 263). If librarians consciously integrate information literacy objectives into such encounters with students, the quality of their research assistance can be greatly enhanced. Research consultations may also help promote the value of the library and nicely complement information literacy programs as some students need individual reinforcement of newly learned information skills (Faix, MacDonald, and Taxakis 2014; Gale and Evans 2007).

Trina J. Magi and Patricia E. Mardeusz (2013), in their study of students' experience with research consultations, described a number of ways that students are helped in these meetings—receiving assistance in choosing databases, identifying keywords, using search interfaces, interpreting their professors' assignments, brainstorming about how to approach their project, discussing possible topics, sharing knowledge about the subject, evaluating results for relevance and credibility, determining how disparate pieces of information could be used in a paper, and understanding how to stay organized during a semester-long research project. Students also appreciate watching the librarian work through a problem so that later they can replicate the research process. If librarians are concerned about helping students deeply engage with their research projects and develop a wide range of information literacy skills, they should consider making research consultations a component of their reference services. While research consultations are most popular in academic libraries, they are also used for in-depth or complex questions in other settings, such as supporting a history scholar navigating an archival collection or a public library patron looking for a job.

Roving Reference

Roving as a means of providing reference service started in the late 1980s and early 1990s when an increasing number of online catalog terminals and CD-ROM stations were installed in the library. More and more library users were using library computers for research, engendering a need for a more convenient way to receive help from librarians as they navigate through an overwhelming array of online information resources. A roving librarian presents a helpful, human presence in the increasingly electronic environment as they circulate in the general reference area to approach library users (especially those who look confused and might be in need of help) to offer assistance. Rather than waiting for users to come to the reference desk, roving allows librarians to be proactive, reach out to users, and provide service at their point of need. Particularly, users who are reluctant to use the reference desk for various reasons may benefit from the assistance offered by a friendly roving librarian (Courtois and Liriano 2000).

Although roving is an extension of the reference desk, it brings to play interpersonal dynamics that can be quite different from the encounters at the reference desk. Martin P. Courtois and Maira Liriano (2000) provided a series of strategies to successfully implement roving reference:

- **Prepare staff to rove.** Rovers need to project confidence and a helpful attitude, and all roving librarians need to be adequately prepared.
- **Schedule times for roving.** If the library's staffing level allows a designated rover, it is ideal to schedule roving during the busiest times as the rover can help relieve the burden of the reference desk staff, enabling them to work with users on in-depth questions.
- **Use the best people as rovers.** It is more effective to use librarians or experienced support staff as rovers in order to win trust of the user and engage them in a reference transaction.
- **Use assistants for backup or tech support.** Having assistants available to handle basic technical questions will free rovers to concentrate on helping users with more complex information needs.
- **Create an atmosphere of active learning.** The reference area can be a place for active learning where the focus is on dialogue and interaction.
- **Refer queries from the reference desk to the rover.** When queries received at the reference desk involve a follow-up on a library computer, it is more efficient to refer them to the rover.
- **Employ useful roving techniques.** Wear a nametag/badge; be mobile and do not stay too long with any one user; follow up with users to check on their progress; be discreet, and address the user before addressing their screen even when their screens are displaying ineffective search statements or error messages; think in terms of welcoming behaviors that could put users at ease; address each user instead of announcing an offer of assistance to a group of users; and be prepared for indifference when assistance is declined.
- **Document progress.** Keep statistics to monitor the content and number of roving reference transactions.

In recent years, mobile technologies have been increasingly used to support roving reference. Portable voice communication devices allow roving librarians to communicate and consult with other reference staff. The Vocera Badge is one such device, about the size of a large USB drive, usually worn around the neck like a security tag. It is often linked to telephone systems, runs on a wireless network, and works with voice commands. It is extensively used in hospitals, and now some public libraries also use it to assist with staff communication as well as for roving reference (Forsyth 2009). iPads and other tablets are also gaining in popularity among roving librarians as they allow librarians to access the library's online resources and demonstrate searches while assisting users (May 2011).

Roving reference does not necessarily have to be limited to the library. Public librarians visit community centers, farmer's markets, train stations, and parks to offer service, and academic librarians rove around campus to provide assistance. Campus-wide roving services usually take place in locations frequented by students and faculty like a campus café or a residence hall. Since librarians are outside of the library, it helps to bring some printed help guides (e.g., searching the online catalog or submitting an interlibrary loan request) for dissemination. Laptops with wireless connections and cell phones can also be helpful. The primary benefit of roving outside of the library is the informal, spontaneous engagement with patrons, especially those who do not necessarily visit the library. It helps reduce barriers to library interactions, build librarians' relationships with the user community, convey the librarians' collaborative spirit, and market library services in a high-profile way (Holmes and Woznicki 2010). Peter Bremer (2017, 108), a librarian at the University of Minnesota, opines that "at its most fundamental level a roaming librarian program can act as an ambassador." Believing that roving outside of the library allows librarians to better gauge what is happening in the community in the midst of it, instead of stuck behind four walls, Bremer shared a number of tips for successful roving outside the library.

- **Choosing the right spot is crucial.** High-traffic areas are important for visibility.
- **Timing is everything.** Picking the right hour of the day can make the difference between having tons of student contact and tabling in an empty space.
- **First impressions matter.** Besides bringing a laptop, Bremer also has signage, candy, and a short quiz, which he calls the Librarian on the Loose Quiz of Ultimate Fun. Each month features a new set of questions based on a theme. Connecting a topic with a library/campus event or a national news item is a great way to enlarge the conversation.
- **Stay awhile.** A general rule is to stay in one location at least an hour to an hour and a half. Anything less than this is generally not worth the effort of travel and setup.
- **Act like you want to be there.** Being a well-meaning wallflower staring at a computer screen will not work. When out and about, try and be proactive and engage with students and staff as they amble by. Being open and having a sense of humor pays dividends in making you more approachable. Every individual engaged with is one more person who will hopefully be more inclined to use the library and ask for help.

REMOTE/VIRTUAL REFERENCE SERVICE

When reference service is provided remotely, it enables users to receive assistance from librarians without having to be physically in the library and provides an opportunity for the library to reach out to users who shy away from in-person reference services. Before the Internet, the use of mail, telephone, and Teletype were all incorporated in remote reference service delivery (Ryan 1996). Nowadays, telephone reference is still a popular service, particularly in urban public libraries, where there are staff specially designated to handle reference calls.

As libraries adopted computing and networking technologies (especially the Internet) in the 1980s, digital media started becoming a popular choice to deliver reference services to reach a far wider audience. Digital-media-based reference services are usually referred to as either "digital reference services" or "virtual reference services." The Reference and User Services Association (2004) chose to use "virtual reference" for reference services provided digitally and defined it as the "reference service initiated electronically, often in real-time, where patrons employ computers or other Internet technology to communicate with reference staff, without being physically present. Communication channels used frequently in virtual reference include chat, videoconferencing, Voice over IP, co-browsing, e-mail, and instant messaging." Although some researchers also tend to incorporate digital/electronic resources in their definition of "virtual reference" (Tenopir and Ennis 2002), RUSA clarified this distinction by stating that "while online sources are often utilized in provision of virtual reference, use of electronic sources in seeking answers is not of itself virtual reference" (2004). Thus, resources created and distributed in digital means are not considered part of "virtual reference." Only human-intermediated reference service provided via digital media is considered "virtual reference."

Using virtual reference services, users can send their queries by e-mail or by filling out a Web form and then receive answers via e-mail, or engage in an online real-time chat reference session where they can interact with librarians synchronously and receive immediate help from the librarians. Libraries also offer text reference service (or SMS reference service), where users can text their queries to librarians and receive answers in texts as well.

Virtual reference services are often named "Ask a Librarian" or "Ask Us" on the library website. In a virtual reference transaction, the query can be seen and referred to as the answer is sought, which is convenient for librarians. Queries and answers can also be stored easily for statistical tracking or other record-keeping purposes. Frequently asked questions can help librarians decide what information should be made more accessible and available on the library website. Online information can easily be incorporated into the answers, which may help users become more aware of the vastness of the library's electronic resources. In addition, libraries can provide virtual reference services collaboratively and take turns staffing the service, making it possible to reduce cost and extend service hours.

While expanding the reach of library services, virtual reference also brings new challenges such as concerns about privacy and the increasing number of frivolous questions due to anonymity (Luo 2008). Libraries have to reconsider their service policies in response to these challenges. Librarians also have to acquire new skill sets to most successfully help users fulfill their information needs via virtual reference services. In this section, three types of virtual reference services are introduced—e-mail/Web form reference, chat reference, and text reference service, and strategies for successfully providing virtual reference services are discussed.

E-mail/Web Form Reference Service

E-mail reference services are provided either through an e-mail address to which users can send their questions directly or through a Web form that users can fill out to submit their questions. In both ways, users will receive the answer to their questions by e-mail (White 2001). While libraries were making e-mail reference services available for their users, some independent Internet-based services, usually called "AskA" services, also started offering e-mail reference services to answer questions from the general public (Lankes 1998). These services are mostly subject specialized (Pomerantz 2003). For example, Ask Dr. SOHO (SOHO 2018) answers questions about the Sun and the Solar and Heliospheric Observatory, and Ask a Linguist (The Linguist List n.d.) answers questions related to language and linguistics.

E-mail reference service has freed users from the limitations of time and location, making it possible for them to ask questions anytime and anywhere, as long as they have an Internet connection (Bushallow-Wilber, DeVinney, and Whitcomb 1996). They do not have to know whom to contact at the library, and for those whose first language is not English it might be more comfortable to compose queries in a written message than speak to a reference librarian.

Since e-mail is an asynchronous communication means, librarians are not expected to provide an immediate response. Certain pressures of time and place fall away, and user queries may be answered away from the busy reference desk, allowing librarians more time to conduct thorough searches and consult colleagues when composing the answer. The service turnaround time is usually stated on the page of the e-mail reference service; although it varies from library to library, the majority of the libraries promise to return an answer to the user's query within one to two business days.

The downside of asynchronicity is that it inevitably prevents librarians from conducting in-depth reference interviews with users (Janes and Hill 2001) and thus may lead to inadequate understanding or even misinterpretation of the user's information needs. Despite the challenges of the medium, librarians still make efforts to conduct a reference interview in e-mail reference service. However, the interview process in e-mail reference can be very lengthy. It might take weeks to conclude the reference negotiation conducted through e-mail exchanges.

Another remedy for the lack of interactivity inherent in e-mail reference service is the use of well-designed Web forms to elicit users' information needs. A structured Web form encourages users to fill in pertinent information that might have otherwise been left out but is useful for librarians answering their questions (Haines and Grodzinski 1999). Common items on a Web form include user's name and address (sometimes library card number if the service is provided only to library card holders), user status (e.g., faculty or student), and content of the user query. A more structured Web form may also ask users to provide information on the type of query (e.g., accounts or library website), subject of the query, or resources already examined. The advantage of a well-structured Web form is that it compensates for the lack of a reference interview and provides better context for users' information needs. The disadvantages include that users may not want to go through the trouble of filling out a form with many required fields and hence choose not to use the service, users may have difficulty in assigning subject categories to their questions and determining whether their questions are factual or require information sources for assistance, and the effectiveness of Web forms may be undermined by users' inappropriate understanding of the items on the form (Carter and Janes 2000). Therefore, when designing a Web form, it is important to keep a well-balanced structure that could elicit as much information from users as possible without confusing or overwhelming them. Figure 6.1 is a screenshot of the Web form at San José State University Library.

Since it is difficult to conduct a reference interview via e-mail, in their response to user queries, librarians tend to recommend patrons use other modes of reference service where they can interact with librarians in real time (e.g., desk, telephone, online real-time chat) if they have more complex queries. Such a recommendation may be included in the signature of librarians' e-mail response to user queries. It not only promotes the variety of reference services offered by the library but also

Your Question or Feedback

Question

More Detail/Explanation

Your Info

Name *

Email *

Who are you?

Select One

Type of Question *

Select One

Library card number or SJSU student ID

SJPL Branch Library (if applicable)

Select One

Phone Number

Fields marked with * are required.

Submit Your Question

Figure 6.1 San José State University Library virtual reference Web form. Shown is a screenshot of the San José University Library's virtual reference Web form. The question field is listed first to allow users to enter their question before submitting information like their name and e-mail address. Such a design is more welcoming and encouraging for users to fill out the form and submit their query.

***Source*: Reprinted with permission from San José State Library, San José State University.**

helps users better understand what types of information needs can be appropriately addressed by which modes of service and therefore use reference services more effectively and efficiently.

Online Real-Time Chat Reference Service

Libraries have experimented with real-time communication technologies to provide synchronous reference services to users since the 1990s. While several videoconferencing-based reference projects were implemented in the mid- and late 1990s, the technological shortcomings such as poor video transmission quality, limited bandwidth, and limited access to the supporting infrastructure made it difficult for "a critical mass of users" to develop for the services (Sloan 1998).

In the early 2000s, libraries adopted a simpler technology that allowed librarians and users to "chat" with each other by exchanging written messages without any visual and audio feed and started providing online real-time chat reference service. Chat reference services have since become increasingly popular and are now one of the mainstream modes of reference service. Although some libraries choose to develop in-house software for their chat reference service, most libraries provide the service via software developed by others. There are two primary categories of chat reference software: simple, and usually free, text-based chat applications like instant messengers and more full-fledged commercial software with advanced features like page-pushing or whiteboarding (Ronan 2003).

Instant messengers are applications that offer online, real-time text transmission. Providing chat reference service via instant messaging, libraries need to have a user name for patrons to add to their contact list and there initiate a chat session with librarians. The advantage of instant messengers is that they are mostly free and easy to use. Many of them also have mobile apps that users can install on their smartphones or tablets and chat. Patrons who are already using instant messaging can easily contact the library from a familiar technology. However, since instant messengers are general-purpose chat applications and not designed for reference service, librarians may find it less ideal when it comes to managing the service (e.g., logging chat transcripts and reporting usage statistics) and protecting user privacy. All of the reference transactions are recorded and archived on the servers of the instant messaging services that a library uses for virtual reference service, which poses privacy concerns because libraries have no control over how the transcripts are protected. Meanwhile, users may use different instant messengers, and therefore, the library needs to accommodate as many of them as possible and even use aggregating tools like Trillian to support chatting with users on different instant messengers from one single application. Less tech-savvy users may shy away from using the service because it requires them to download and install an instant messenger, which may be beyond their realm of technical knowledge. Another concern is that the library's information technology department may have issues with free software because of security risks. Librarians cannot exercise any control as the software changes, grows, or disappears. For example, when Meebo, a free and popular instant messenger among libraries, abruptly discontinued its service in 2012, it caused much inconvenience as librarians hurried to find a replacement in order to continue their chat reference service. Also, in recent years, major instant messengers such as AIM, Google Talk, and Yahoo! Messenger have been gradually discontinued, making it no longer a viable option for libraries to provide instant-messaging-based reference service.

An alternative to instant messengers is commercial virtual reference software. Such software is specially designed for virtual reference service and seeks to meet the needs of delivering and managing not only chat reference but also e-mail and text reference service. They are usually subscription based, and libraries use a login name to access the software service through a Web browser.

With virtual reference software, each library obtains a master account within which they can create subaccounts for all the librarians staffing chat reference service. Each librarian may use their own subaccount to log in during their shifts, and multiple librarians can be logged in simultaneously. Users access the service by typing in a widget on a Web page. Librarians can monitor the user queue on their end and are alerted when new users are online. Some virtual reference software, such as Springshare's *LibAnswers +Social*, allow librarians to monitor and respond to queries received via e-mail and social media.

Virtual reference software provides librarians more functionality than the simple exchange of texts. For example, librarians may be able to push pages to the user's screen—if they enter a URL in their message, the Web page the URL leads to will open on the user's screen. Page-pushing allows librarians to more effectively escort users in the information searching process and makes it easier for librarians to transmit electronic information to users and guide them in the navigation, given the fact that virtual reference services utilize electronic resources extensively in answering user queries (Tenopir and Ennis 2001). Another useful feature is pre-scripted messages—librarians can create frequently used scripts for their responses, such as greetings, follow-ups, and URLs of popular Web resources. This helps save typing time and thus makes the transaction more efficient. Figure 6.2 provides an example of a librarian interface for virtual reference.

When each chat session ends, a transcript of the session is saved and can be e-mailed to the user. This is convenient for users to refer back to the sources provided by the librarian. Librarians may also be able to assign a resolution code to the session to indicate whether the query is fully answered, referred to another party, or to be followed up with, which can be helpful for libraries to keep track of how the service is addressing users' information needs. In addition, virtual reference software typically enables the reporting of various service statistics such as the number of chat sessions in a specified time frame, the distribution of resolution codes, and queries from repeat users.

Since virtual reference software supports multiple simultaneous logins, librarians can communicate with each other and consult each other when answering queries. They can also transfer users to librarians from their home institution,

LibraryChat

Library: Summerville Public Library	Librarian: M. Wong
Queue Luis anon5763 RachelM anon9425	**Librarian [M. Wong]:** Welcome to LibraryChat at Summerville Public Library. How can I help you? **Patron [Luis]:** Do you have a copy of Kindred by Butler? **Librarian [M. Wong]:** I'd be happy to check! Would you prefer a print book, audio book, or another format? **Patron [Luis]:** <typing>
Scripts *click to send* Welcome Message Library Hours Catalog Link	
Librarians Online *click to transfer* L. Luo L. Saunders M. Wong	

Figure 6.2 Example of a librarian interface for virtual reference. The right-hand side displays the exchange between the librarian and the user, the upper left-hand side shows the queues of users waiting to use the service, and the lower left-hand side provides the various tools such as scripts that librarians can access to facilitate the chat session.

which often happens in a collaborative virtual reference service. In addition, virtual reference software like Springshare's *LibAnswers +Social* allows libraries to form a consortium in providing the service, reaping the benefits of reduced cost and extended service hours. In such a collaborative virtual reference service, participating libraries take turns staffing the service, and therefore, users may be connected to librarians from institutions other than their home institution. In order to best answer queries requiring local knowledge (e.g., queries pertaining to particular libraries' policies as well as the location of items within the libraries), librarians often have to transfer users to a librarian from their home institution.

Although virtual reference software offers more functionality to support chat reference service than instant messengers, there are drawbacks as well. Some libraries may find the software too costly and the learning curve too steep. There are other commercial virtual reference software options on the market; for example, LibraryH3lp is a popular option. Using LibraryH3lp, users have various options to submit their queries (e.g., through a customizable chat widget or through a mobile app), and librarians are able to answer them using a single LibraryH3lp interface. Multiple librarians can operate at the same time, sharing expertise with each other, and users can be routed to all available staff, to targeted staff subgroups, or to even individuals.

Nevertheless, no matter which software a library chooses as the platform for chat reference service, it is important to consider the following factors: usability both for users and for librarians, software stability, cost, customizability, training support, customer-service support, support for staffing flexibility, compatibility with other modes of reference service, support for mobile apps, and the need for providing chat reference service collaboratively. Clear service goals, a detailed picture of the library's wants and needs, and a thorough understanding of what each virtual reference software offers are key for a library to select a proper platform to support chat reference service. Box 6.2 provides a hypothetical scenario for discussion related to selecting a virtual reference option.

Box 6.2 Activity: Selecting a Virtual Reference Option

A library at a public university with a student population of 21,000 has been providing chat reference using a free instant messenger service. The company that provides the service has just announced that the service will be discontinued at the end of the month. The library director has asked her staff to explore new platforms for providing virtual reference, including both free and commercial services, and has asked them to consider the following factors: usability both for users and for librarians, software stability, cost, customizability, training support, customer-service support, support for staffing flexibility, compatibility with other modes of reference service, and support for mobile apps. She would also like the staff to consider whether joining a consortium would be a good option for the library.

Questions for Reflection and Discussion:

1. Which factors would you consider most important when evaluating platforms for virtual reference?
2. If you were given this task, how would you approach it?

As mentioned earlier, libraries' attempts at offering virtual reference service via videoconferencing did not succeed in the 1990s because of limitations of the technologies. In recent years such technologies have advanced tremendously and VoIP software like Skype have gained wide popularity as a tool for voice and video chat. Libraries have started exploring the use of Skype in the provision of virtual reference service. Advantages of Skype include bringing visual and nonverbal cues back to virtual reference; the ability to send links, pdfs, articles, or Jing videos via instant messages while video chatting with users; and sharing screens with users. Disadvantages include the need for installing the Skype software on one's computer, the awkwardness factor of being "on screen," and a low level of interest in the use of Skype for reference service among users (Beaton 2012). However, Skype has not yet gained ground as part of the virtual reference suite, and some early adopters such as Ohio University Libraries have discontinued the service. The lack of interest among users could be the primary cause. Skype, in the eyes of library users, may be a tool for informal communication between friends and family but not suitable for interacting with librarians. As Chad Boeninger (2010) commented when discussing Ohio University Libraries' experiment with Skype, "Our patrons may never be comfortable enough to want to call us face-to-face." Still, libraries and librarians should keep experimenting with new technologies to deliver enriched and enhanced reference service to users. The experiments may not all be successful, but they are valuable experiences nonetheless; as Boeninger (2010) summarized, "In the process, we learned about video calling software options, how to configure pages to close automatically with javascript, discovered how flaky wireless connections and computer applications can be, and much more. We also learned to be flexible, patient, and try different things to improve the service. I believe our experiences with the service have prepared us well for our next technology/reference endeavor (whatever that may be), and you can't put a price on that knowledge."

Text Reference Service

Text messaging, or texting, has become an increasingly popular communication venue. Text reference service enables library users to send in queries and receive answers via texting. Although this service, like other types of virtual reference service, makes it possible for users to use the library remotely, people often text librarians from within the library, frequently including information about exactly where they are (Pearce, Collard, and Whatley 2010). It appears that many users prefer to communicate via text even when other options for seeking assistance are available. Reasons may range from practical considerations related to what is most convenient at a given moment to a more general preference on the part of a user for a certain form of communication. For instance, patrons who are working at a library computer may find it more convenient to text a librarian than pack up their things and log out in order to visit the reference desk.

In the earlier days of text reference service, some libraries relied on a dedicated mobile device (usually a smartphone) to answer patrons' texts. The mobile-device-based delivery model is quite simple. A library needs to purchase only a cell phone with a monthly texting plan to enable text reference service. At some libraries, the cell phone is stationed at the reference desk along with other reference service points during business hours and monitored by librarians covering the reference desk; it is stashed away when it is not in use. When the reference desk is busy, an information hierarchy of importance is employed to determine query priority. Text reference questions may come after in-person, telephone, and chat reference queries (Kohl and Keating 2009). At some other libraries, the cell phone is operated independently of any other service point; it is not kept at the reference desk, and texting shifts are not connected to any other reference shifts. A different schedule is made for librarians to monitor the service, and the phone travels with the individual librarian when it is their shift. Librarians coordinate the handoffs among themselves rather than according to a formalized procedure.

One of the prominent downsides of depending on a cell phone is that it cannot be integrated into any of the existing virtual reference services and thus poses extra work for librarians. They have to master yet another technology to deliver reference service and may be reluctant to embrace this new service venue. Meanwhile, typing on a cell phone keyboard, even the most user-friendly kind, is far less comfortable than typing on a computer keyboard and may slow down the service's response time. Staffing can also be a challenge when the cell phone is not stationed at the reference desk. Without effective staffing and shift management, it will be difficult to ensure consistent and reliable service quality. These drawbacks make it unlikely for the mobile-device-based text reference service model to gain popularity among libraries.

An alternative is using computer applications to receive and respond to text reference queries, allowing librarians to work with a potentially familiar interface while offering reference service via a new venue. The learning curve is as flat as possible in terms of technology, and therefore text reference service may be greeted with a more positive attitude among librarians. Most of the commercially developed software for e-mail and chat reference service also support text reference service. For example, *LibAnswers +Social*, LibraryH3lp and Mosio for Libraries cover the whole spectrum of virtual reference service, allowing text reference service to be integrated into the library's existing e-mail or chat reference service. This integration can help minimize technology training among librarians and keep the library's virtual reference service suite streamlined with the new service addition.

Some software limits the length of librarians' responses to users' questions (Jensen 2010). Usually a reply cannot exceed two or three text messages (320 or 480 characters), and if it does, the extra part will be truncated and will not be displayed on the user's phone. However, built-in features like a character counter and a URL shortener (Weimer 2010) may also be available to help librarians to compose their responses concisely.

Most commercial software allows libraries to have a dedicated phone number that users can store in their cell phone. Generally, no special instructions are needed for texting to this number. More importantly, users' privacy is better protected as the service is run on software vendors' private servers, and access to user information is strictly limited. Some software even masks users' phone numbers and replaces it with a unique patron ID in order to further alleviate privacy concerns. Again, determining the delivery method or choosing the software for text reference is contingent upon a number of factors, and careful analysis of the library's staffing level, librarian preparedness, budget, and users' texting philosophy and behavior (not all users feel comfortable with texting librarians as they consider texting an informal way of communication among family and friends) is key to deciding on the best way to offer text reference service.

Providing Virtual Reference Services Successfully

There are two staffing models for virtual reference services. The more commonly adopted model is that reference librarians staff the service in their own offices or other locations away from the reference desk. This arrangement allows them to focus on virtual reference transactions without much distraction or interruption, which is especially advantageous when the query is complex and requires an in-depth reference interview. For libraries with an understaffed reference department, it could be challenging to have enough personnel to cover virtual reference service shifts (particularly the synchronous chat reference service where users expect an immediate response) during all library hours. Instead of limiting service hours, some libraries choose to form a consortium to provide the services collaboratively. The less popular staffing model is to staff virtual reference services from the reference desk. Under this model, priority is typically given to in-person patrons, so the information needs of online users may not be satisfactorily addressed when the reference desk is busy.

Which model to choose depends on the library's culture, user needs, budget, and staffing capacity. The most important thing is to have a well-prepared staff who are competent in providing virtual reference services. The changes in service venues have brought new challenges that require updated or new skills. For example, reference interview skills are acknowledged as one of the core skills in reference work. But conducting the reference interview is a different experience in each service venue. Although chat reference service enables the synchronous interaction between librarians and users, it cannot completely model the reference interview in the face-to-face encounter and is not an effective service venue for queries requiring in-depth question negotiation. Thus, techniques that could help librarians avoid a lengthy and cumbersome transaction become particularly important in chat reference service. Such techniques include having the ability to make appropriate referrals and recognize the need to follow up with the user. In the meantime, some of the traditional reference values like thoroughness ought to be modified in chat or text reference service. This can be challenging as reference librarians are usually expected to be thorough and detail oriented when assisting library users. Therefore, it is as important to help librarians understand the shift in expectation and make the proper mind-set adjustment as it is to equip them with requisite knowledge and skills (e.g., how to write concisely without appearing brusque and impatient).

A large part of reference librarians' expertise comes from the knowledge of general and subject-specific resources. In virtual reference, such knowledge has a particular emphasis on resources in electronic format. Librarians' familiarity with resources on the Internet and in subscription databases plays a critical role in delivering virtual reference service since users expect immediately available answers in a chat or text reference transaction; answers have to be provided electronically in order to be delivered immediately (Coffman 2003).

Commitment to user services has always been an essential competency in reference work; in virtual reference there is no exception. As a matter of fact, it is even more important in the virtual environment given that there are no nonverbal cues and users can be completely anonymous. Misunderstandings arise and inappropriate user behaviors occur, and still, librarians need to maintain a professional presence and have a customer-service mentality when dealing with users from all sorts of backgrounds and with all sorts of needs.

Every line of work has pressure. In reference service, a considerable proportion of stress comes from dealing with human beings while under time pressure, such as encountering rude users and receiving tough questions. With the advent of virtual reference, a number of new sources of pressure have aggravated the stress level. For instance, the lack of verbal and visual cues can complicate librarian–user communication and even cause anxiety and misunderstanding on both ends. Unexpected situations, like technology failure or sudden disappearance of users in the middle of a chat session, can make librarians panic. Sometimes librarians have to staff both virtual reference services and the reference desk simultaneously and juggle virtual and physical user queries, which can increase their stress level. All the pressure inherent in the virtual environment requires librarians to be able to multi-task, think quickly, manage time effectively, and be flexible and calm when dealing with difficult situations.

In virtual reference, particularly chat reference service, the ability to keep users informed by constantly notifying them of what the librarian is doing is critical to a successful transaction. In a face-to-face reference encounter, the physical presence of both the librarian and the user makes it easier to communicate the process of searching for an answer to the user's question. However, in a chat session, where no audio or visual cues exist and the entire communication is based on the exchange of written messages, librarians are faced with a more critical need to stay connected to the user. Telling the user what search activities the librarian is engaged in is an effective technique for the librarian to assure users of the "connectedness" and avoid making the user feel ignored.

The ability to use virtual reference software effectively is indispensable, especially when the service is offered through software like *LibAnswers +Social.* While software skills ensure the technical operation of a virtual reference session, online communication skills are pivotal to a successful transaction. In order to maintain a professional and yet friendly virtual presence, librarians need to be able to communicate effectively via e-mail, chat, or text, which requires a clear understanding and appreciation of online culture and etiquette and the ability to use online or texting language appropriately.

In a virtual reference consortium where members take turns staffing a collaborative service, librarians are expected to know other participating libraries' resources as well as their own so that users of other participating libraries can be well served. Usually users come to use a collaborative service with the expectation to be connected to a librarian from their own library and anticipate a conversation with a professional who knows the local library's resources well. Thus, in order for users to receive the best-possible service, librarians of a virtual reference consortium should expand their expertise to include knowledge of member libraries' resources.

An effective way to prepare librarians and help them provide virtual reference service successfully is to review transcripts of virtual reference sessions. Such transcripts will provide a concrete view of how users frame their questions in e-mail, chat, and text and what the common communication patterns are. This enables librarians to interpret user information needs more effectively and precisely and provide appropriate assistance in addressing them.

GOING WHERE USERS ARE

Reference service, since it began in the late 19th century, has evolved greatly in the way it is delivered. Nowadays it is a multimodality service where personal assistance is provided not only in person but also remotely and virtually via different venues. These venues have their own advantages and disadvantages in supporting reference transactions, and it is important that librarians have a solid understanding of them and make the best use of each venue. For example, in-person reference services at the reference desk and via research consultations are more effective in handling complex queries than virtual reference services. It would be helpful to put a statement on the library's virtual reference page, informing users that e-mail, chat, and text reference services are most effective when their queries are brief and straightforward, and if they need in-depth assistance, they are welcome to visit or call the reference desk or schedule an appointment for research consultation.

Providing users with optimal service experience is both the impetus and the goal of reference service. Users' information behavior will always change as new developments emerge in the information landscape. Librarians need to be keenly aware of this change and how this change has transformed reference services. It is imperative to constantly consider and address questions like what are users' information-seeking processes, what search strategies do they use for different information needs, where are the roadblocks, and what are their concerns when accessing digital information and services (e.g., privacy), in order to acquire a solid understanding of evolving user information behaviors, and identify the best ways to provide assistance to users via various reference venues.

Being flexible, being prepared, and being creative are three indispensable factors contributing to a successful journey of "going where users are." The rapid development of information and communication technologies requires that librarians have the flexibility to recognize and explore new service potential and adapt to new service models. Effective and efficient responses to changes in service organization and delivery cannot be achieved without being fully prepared. More often than not, librarians, faced with limited budget and staff resources, have to be creative in utilizing technologies and making staffing arrangements to conduct outreach and provide services. Going where users are, and offering services in the ways most needed, welcomed, and appreciated by them, will always remain the key for reference services to stay current and relevant.

REFERENCES

Aho, Melissa K., Anne M. Beschnett, and Emily Y. Reimer. 2011. "Who Is Sitting at the Reference Desk?: The Ever-Changing Concept of Staffing the Reference Desk at the Bio-Medical Library." *Collaborative Librarianship* 3 (1): 46–49.

Aluri, Rao, and Jeffrey W. St. Clair. 1978. "Academic Reference Librarians: An Endangered Species?" *The Journal of Academic Librarianship* 4 (2): 82–84.

Beaton, Barbara. 2012. "New Technologies for Virtual Reference: A Look at Skype and Twitter." University of Michigan. http://www.lib.umich.edu/files/departments/SkypeTwitter%20112912.pdf.

Bell, Steven J. 2007. "Who Needs a Reference Desk?" *Library Issues: Briefings for Faculty and Administrators* 27 (6): 1–9.

Bing. http://www.bing.com.

Boeninger, Chad. 2010. "So Maybe This Is Why No One Uses Our Skype Reference Service." *Library Voice* (blog). http://libraryvoice.com/technology/so-maybe-this-is-why-no-one-uses-our-skype-reference-service.

Bremer, Peter. 2017. "Librarian on the Loose: A Roving Reference Desk at a Small Liberal Arts College." *The Reference Librarian* 58 (1): 106–10.

Bunge, Charles, and Chris Ferguson. 1997. "The Shape of Services to Come: Values-Based Reference Service for the Largely Digital Library." *College & Research Libraries* 58 (May): 252–65.

Bunnett, Brian, Andrea Boehme, Steve Hardin, Shelley Arvin, Karen Evans, Paula Huey, and Carey LaBella. 2016. "Where Did the Reference Desk Go? Transforming Staff and Space to Meet User Needs." *Journal of Access Services* 13 (2): 66–79.

Bushallow-Wilber, Lara, Gemma DeVinney, and Fritz Whitcomb. 1996. "Electronic Mail Reference Service: A Study." *RQ* 35 (3): 25–36.

Carter, David, and Joseph Janes. 2000. "Unobtrusive Data Analysis of Digital Reference Questions and Service at the Internet Public Library: An Exploratory Study." *Library Trends* 49 (2): 251–65.

Coffman, Steve. 2003. *Going Live: Starting & Running a Virtual Reference Service.* Chicago: American Library Association.

Courtois, Martin P., and Maira Liriano. 2000. "Tips for Roving Reference: How to Best Serve Library Users." *College & Research Libraries News* 61 (4): 289–90, 315.

Faix, Allison, Amanda MacDonald, and Brooke Taxakis. 2014. "Research Consultation Effectiveness for Freshman and Senior Undergraduate Students." *Reference Services Review* 42 (1): 4–15.

Ford, Barbara J. 1986. "Reference beyond (and without) the Reference Desk." *College & Research Libraries* 47 (5): 492–94.

Forsyth, Ellen. 2009. "Fancy Walkie Talkies, Star Trek Communicators or Roving Reference?" *The Australian Library Journal* 58 (1): 73–84.

Freides, Thelma. 1983. "Current Trends in Academic Libraries." *Library Trends* 31 (3): 457–74.

Gale, Crystal D., and Betty S. Evans. 2007. "Face-to-Face: The Implementation and Analysis of a Research Consultation Service." *College & Undergraduate Libraries* 14 (3): 85–101.

Giordano, Peter, Christine Menard, and Rebecca Ohm Spencer. 2001. "The Disappearing Reference Desk: Finding New Ways to Support the Curriculum of a Small Liberal Arts College." *College & Research Libraries News* 62 (7): 692–94.

Google. http://www.google.com.

Gorman, Michael. 2001. "Values for Human-to-Human Reference." *Library Trends* 50 (2): 168–82.

Green, Samuel S. 1876. "Personal Relations between Librarians and Readers." *American Library Journal* 1 (November 30): 74–81.

Haines, Annette, and Allison Grodzinski. 1999. "Web Forms: Improving, Expanding and Promoting Remote Reference Service." *College & Research Libraries News* 60 (4): 271–72.

Holmes, Claire, and Lisa Woznicki. 2010. "Librarians at Your Doorstep." *College & Research Libraries News* 71 (1): 582–85.

Janes, Joseph, and Chrystie Hill. 2001. "Finger on the Pulse: Librarians Describe Evolving Reference Practice in an Increasingly Digital World." *Reference & User Services Quarterly* 42 (1): 54–65.

Jastram, Iris, and Ann Gwinn Zawistoski. 2008. "Personalizing the Library via Research Consultations." In *The Desk and Beyond: Next Generation Reference Services*, edited by Sarah K. Steiner and M. Leslie Madden, 14–24. Chicago: Association of College and Research Libraries.

Jensen, Bruce. 2010. "SMS Text Reference Comes of Age: The My Info Quest Collaborative." *The Reference Librarian* 51 (4): 264–75.

Jing. https://www.techsmith.com/jing-tool.html.

Kohl, Laura, and Maura Keating. 2009. "A Phone of One's Own: Texting at the Bryant University Reference Desk." *College & Research Libraries News* 70 (2): 104–6.

LaMagna, Michael, Sarah Hartman-Caverly, and Lori Marchetti. 2016. "Redefining Roles and Implementing a Triage Reference Model at a Single Service Point." *Journal of Access Services* 13 (2): 53–65.

Lankes, David. 1998. *Building & Maintaining Internet Information Services: K-12 Digital Reference Services.* Syracuse, NY: ERIC Clearinghouse on Information & Technology.

LibraryH3lp. https://libraryh3lp.com/.

LibAnswers +Social. Springshare. https://www.springshare.com/libanswers/.

The Linguist List. n.d. "Ask a Linguist." International Linguistics Community Online. http://www.linguistlist.org/ask-ling/.

Luo, Lili. 2008. "Chat Reference Evaluation: A Framework of Perspectives and Measures." *Reference Services Review* 36 (1): 71–85.

Luo, Lili. 2014. "Slam the Boards: Librarians' Outreach into Social Q&A Sites." *Internet Reference Services Quarterly* 19 (7): 33–47.

Magi, Trina J., and Patricia E. Mardeusz. 2013. "Why Some Students Continue to Value Individual, Face-to-Face Research Consultations in a Technology-Rich World." *College & Research Libraries* 74 (6): 605–18.

Massey-Burzio, Virginia. 1992. "Reference Encounters of a Different Kind: A Symposium." *The Journal of Academic Librarianship* 18 (5): 276–81.

May, Fiona. 2011. "Roving Reference, iPad-Style." *Idaho Librarian* 61 (2). http://theidaholibrarian.wordpress.com/2011/11/23/roving-reference-ipad-style/.

Miles, Dennis. 2013. "Shall We Get Rid of the Reference Desk?" *Reference & User Services Quarterly* 52 (4): 320–33.

Mosio. https://www.mosio.com/.

Mosley, Pixie Ann. 2007. "Assessing User Interactions at the Desk Nearest the Front Door." *Reference & User Services Quarterly* 47 (2): 159–67.

Nolen, David S. 2010. "Reforming or Rejecting the Reference Desk: Conflict and Continuity in the Concept of Reference." *Library Philosophy and Practice* (May): 1–8.

Oud, Joanne, and Peter Genzinger. 2016. "Aiming for Service Excellence: Implementing a Plan for Customer Service Quality at a Blended Service Desk." *Journal of Access Services* 13 (2): 112–30.

Pearce, Alexa, Scott Collard, and Kara Whatley. 2010. "SMS Reference: Myths, Markers, and Modalities." *Reference Services Review* 38 (2): 250–63.

Pomerantz, Jeffrey. 2003. "Question Taxonomies for Digital Reference." PhD dissertation, Syracuse University.

Poparad, Christa E. 2015. "Staffing an Information Desk for Maximum Responsiveness and Effectiveness in Meeting Research and Computing Needs in an Academic Library." *The Reference Librarian* 56 (2): 83–92.

Quora. http://www.quora.com.

Reference and User Services Association. 2004. "Guidelines for Implementing and Maintaining Virtual Reference Services." American Library Association. Last modified June 13, 2017. http://www.ala.org/rusa/resources/guidelines/virtrefguidelines.

Reference and User Services Association. 2013. "Guidelines for Behavioral Performance of Reference and Information Service Providers." Last modified May 28, 2013. American Library Association. http://www.ala.org/rusa/resources/guidelines/guidelinesbehavioral.

Reid, Ian. 2017. "The 2017 Public Library Data Service: Characteristics and Trends." *Public Libraries Online* (September/October). http://publiclibrariesonline.org/2017/12/the-2017-public-library-data-service-report-characteristics-and-trends/.

Reinsfelder, Thomas L. 2012. "Citation Analysis as a Tool to Measure the Impact of Individual Research Consultations." *College & Research Libraries* 73 (3): 263–78.

Ronan, Jana. 2003. *Chat Reference: A Guide to Live Virtual Reference Services.* Westport, CT: Libraries Unlimited.

Ryan, Sara. 1996. "Reference Service for the Internet Community: A Case Study of the Internet Public Library Reference Division." *Library & Information Science Research* 18 (3): 241–59.

Schulte, Stephanie J. 2011. "Eliminating Traditional Reference Services in an Academic Health Sciences Library: A Case Study." *Journal of the Medical Library Association* 99 (4): 273–79.

Selby, Courtney. 2007. "The Evolution of the Reference Interview." *Legal Reference Services Quarterly* 26 (1/2): 35–46.

Skype. https://www.skype.com/en/.

Sloan, Bernie. 1998. "Service Perspectives for the Digital Library: Remote Reference Services." *Library Trends* 47 (1): 117–43.

SOHO: Solar and Heliospheric Observatory. 2018. "Ask Dr. SOHO." Last modified January 26, 2018. https://soho.nascom.nasa.gov/classroom/askdrsoho.html.

Summerhill, Karen Storin. 1994. "The High Cost of Reference: The Need to Reassess Services and Service Delivery." *The Reference Librarian* 43: 71–85.

Swanson, Patricia. 1984. "Traditional Models: Myths and Realities." In *Academic Libraries: Myths and Realities: Proceedings of the Third National Conference of the Association of College and Research Libraries*, edited by Suzanne Dodson and Gary L. Menges, 84–97. Chicago: American Library Association.

Tenopir, Carol, and Lisa Ennis. 2001. "Reference Services in the New Millennium." *Online* 25 (4): 40–45.

Tenopir, Carol, and Lisa Ennis. 2002. "A Decade of Digital Reference: 1991–2001." *Reference & User Services Quarterly* 41 (3): 264–73.

Trillian. https://trillian.im/.

Venner, Mary Ann, and Seti Keshmiripour. 2016. "X Marks the Spot: Creating and Managing a Single Service Point to Improve Customer Service and Maximize Resources." *Journal of Access Services* 13 (2): 101–11.

Vocera. https://www.vocera.com.

Weimer, Keith. 2010. "Text Messaging the Reference Desk: Using Upside Wireless' SMS-to-Email to Extend Reference Service." *The Reference Librarian* 51 (2): 108–23.

White, Marilyn Domas. 2001. "Diffusion of Innovation: Digital Reference Service in Carnegie Foundation Master's (Comprehensive) Academic Institution Libraries." *The Journal of Academic Librarianship* 27 (3): 173–87.

Wikipedia. http://www.wikipedia.com.

Yi, Hua. 2003. "Individual Research Consultation Service: An Important Part of an Information Literacy Program." *Reference Services Review* 31 (4): 342–50.

Yahoo! Answers. https://answers.yahoo.com/.

SUGGESTED READINGS

Gorman, Michael. 2001. "Values for Human-to-Human Reference." *Library Trends* 50 (2): 168–82.

Gorman gives a brief history of how human-to-human reference service has evolved and provides a discussion of its future. Particularly, he elaborates on the eight values (stewardship, service, intellectual freedom, rationalism, literacy and learning, equity of access, privacy, and democracy) derived from the author's earlier work and how each relates to the practices of human-to-human reference.

Kern, M. Kathleen. 2009. *Virtual Reference Best Practices: Tailoring Services to Your Library*. Chicago: American Library Association.

Kern outlines the tools and decision-making processes that will help libraries evaluate, tailor, and launch virtual reference services that are appropriate for their specific user communities. The book departs from general guidelines and focuses on making concrete decisions about integrating virtual with traditional reference.

Luo, Lili, and Emily Weak. 2011. "Texting 4 Answers: What Questions Do People Ask?" *Reference & User Services Quarterly* 51 (2): 133–42.

This article provides a detailed view of how patrons use text reference service, especially what kinds of questions they ask and what types of information needs are fulfilled by text reference. Additional analysis of characteristics such as transaction length and interactivity provides a more in-depth picture of the nature of text reference. It strengthens the professional understanding of how to best deliver reference service via this emerging reference venue.

Magi, Trina J., and Patricia E. Mardeusz. 2013. "Why Some Students Continue to Value Individual, Face-to-Face Research Consultations in a Technology-Rich World." *College & Research Libraries* 74 (6): 605–18.

This article explores the value of research consultations from students' perspective. It examines students' views on why they schedule consultations, the kinds of assistance they receive from librarians during consultations, and what they find valuable about the consultations.

Miles, Dennis. 2013. "Shall We Get Rid of the Reference Desk?" *Reference & User Services Quarterly* 52 (4): 320–33.

This article studies the use of the reference desk in 119 academic libraries at universities offering master's level programs. It provides an empirically grounded view on the role of the reference desk at academic libraries.

Nolen, David S. 2010. "Reforming or Rejecting the Reference Desk: Conflict and Continuity in the Concept of Reference." *Library Philosophy and Practice* (May): 1–8.

Nolen provides a historical examination of the debate about the reference desk and challenges the assertion that there are two camps with diametrically opposed views of reference. He suggests that the protagonists and antagonists of the reference desk actually agree in their vision of reference, although their approaches are different.

Zemel, Alan. 2017. "Texts as Actions: Requests in Online Chats between Reference Librarians and Library Patrons." *Journal of the Association for Information Science & Technology* 68 (7): 1687–97.

Zemel examines virtual reference transcripts to demonstrate that patron requests are interactional achievements co-constituted by librarians and patrons through the exchange of text postings that are designed to be seen as requests. This article offers a new perspective on virtual reference and has practical implications for conducting the reference interview and delivering reference service in the virtual environment.

Chapter 7

Management of Reference Services

JoAnn Jacoby, M. Kathleen Kern, and Lesley K. Mackie

INTRODUCTION

Some people are born to be library directors [or reference service managers]. Not me . . . My entire goal was to be the best reference librarian I could possibly be. (Olver 2011, 6)

Aspiring reference librarians may wonder what relevance management has to them, not realizing that most professional library positions, including those at the entry level, involve a range of management and/or supervisory responsibilities. Most librarians are also involved with a variety of formal and informal leadership roles in professional associations and at their home organization. This means that almost everyone pursuing a career involving reference will have the opportunity to provide leadership for reference-related initiatives or participate directly or indirectly in the management of reference services.

David A. Tyckoson (2011, 276) asserts that a reference manager's core responsibility is deciding how much focus should be placed on each of the four foundational functions of reference services—teaching people how to use the library and its resources, answering specific informational queries, recommending sources to researchers that fit their needs, and promoting the library to the community. That determination, in turn, informs the decisions the manager must make about how services are staffed and evaluated. This is but one example of the ways managing and leading are intertwined, as further explored toward the end of the chapter.

This chapter explores the art and the science of the management of reference services, including managerial roles and expectations, hiring and managing staff, teams and communication, community relations and partnerships, planning and supporting services, policies, and developing management and leadership skills.

MANAGERIAL ROLES AND EXPECTATIONS

Librarians with responsibilities for managing reference services do so in a variety of contexts and organizational structures. Where oversight of reference services is positioned in the institution's hierarchy will shape the scope of the reference manager's responsibilities. The specific title given to positions with reference management responsibilities varies accordingly, with common examples ranging from "head" (implying oversight of a department within a hierarchical structure and direct reports) to "manager" (generally denotes direct reports within a functional unit) to "coordinator" or "team leader" (which usually means a team-based or matrix organization with staff at different levels devoting a certain amount of time to reference services). "Head of Reference" positions are less common than they once were, and with consolidation of departments the head for reference is often combined with oversight of other services such as instruction or circulation.

Responsibilities and Roles

Some roles and responsibilities are common to all managers whether the position is in a traditional hierarchical organization as a head of a reference department, in a flat organization as a reference team leader, or in an entirely different environment. One of the most frequently cited descriptions of the manager's role, Luther Gulick and Lyndall Urwick's (1937) POSDCoRB model, focuses on core functional responsibilities:

1. **Planning.** Determining goals and deciding how they will be met.
2. **Organizing.** Dividing work among units, establishing procedures to accomplish tasks.
3. **Staffing.** Making all personnel decisions, including staff hiring and evaluation.
4. **Directing.** Overseeing and assigning work to individuals.
5. **Coordinating.** Coordinating activities between units.
6. **Reporting.** Reporting on unit activities and accomplishments, keeping upper management informed about progress.
7. **Budgeting.** Determining how the unit's budget will be allocated and ensuring unit stays within budget.

These responsibilities are still salient in today's workplace but with some key differences, including a heavier managerial workload, a contact pattern more oriented toward staff working in group or team settings, and a greater emphasis on sharing information (Martin 2006; Moran, Stueart, and Morner 2013, 270). In addition, Joan Giesecke and Beth McNeil (2010, 6) emphasize the characteristics and soft skills expected of library managers by focusing on the role of the person (facilitator, creator) rather than on the task or activity (organizing, overseeing). They observe that in many libraries, the role of managers has become "more of a coach than director, more of a facilitator than a commander." Giesecke and McNeil (2010, 6–14) enumerate new roles that are more collaborative or interpersonal such as mentoring staff, facilitating conflict management, serving as a broker or negotiator for the staff or unit with upper management and other library units, and acting as an innovator who plans and manages change. These higher-level roles and competencies are the starting point for considering good management and leadership.

Competencies and Skills

Success as a reference manager requires more than executing a set of responsibilities. The Reference and User Services Association's "Professional Competencies for Reference and User Services Librarians" (2017) outlines a range of competencies that are important for frontline staff and reference managers. The skills and competencies needed to be a reference librarian—the ability to gather, organize, and analyze information; to develop a clear understanding of other's information needs; and to connect people to appropriate resources and tools—provide an excellent foundation for developing the soft skills needed to be a successful manager. Using a survey of its members, the Library Leadership and Management Association (2019) identified fourteen competencies for managers and leaders in libraries, including topics such as team building and communication skills. Each competency listed on the website is supported with further readings.

Giesecke and McNeil's (1999, 160) "Core Competencies and the Learning Organization" include a number of skill areas—such as resource management, organizational understanding, and global thinking—in which managers should work to gain deep competence. These high-level skills align with the expanded roles of managers as facilitators and creators. Soft skills such as communication, time management, and initiative serve to support the specific responsibilities discussed later in the chapter and are an important factor in providing the type of leadership often expected of reference managers.

Defining a Vision for Reference Services

Vision and the ability to translate that vision into words and actions that inspire others are the hallmarks of leadership. Where does that vision come from? Keeping up with conversations in the profession can provide inspiration or spark new ideas, but merely following trends can lead down a rabbit hole of contradictory proclamations and perspectives. Numerous articles over the past decade have reflected on the future of reference (Carlson 2007; O'Gorman and Trott 2009; Tyckoson and Dove 2015), some heralding the imminent death of reference (Campbell 1992; Kelley 2011) and others its rebirth through new technologies or its transformation from transaction-based reference services to relationship-based research support services (Gibson and Mandernach 2013; Murphy 2011; Radford 2012; Saunders, Rozaklis, and Abels 2014; Steiner and Madden 2008; Zabel 2007, 2011). The first and last chapters of this volume, on the history and future of reference services, respectively, also reflect on where we have been and how to prepare for the future. There are rich ideas here but no single path, which is not unexpected given the variety of settings and approaches taken by various librarians exploring new models of service and dealing with financial volatility.

Finding an individual path and developing vision involves at least three things on the part of the reference manager. First, it involves touching bases with the fundamentals, including the professional philosophy of service articulated in sources such as Ranganathan's *Five Laws* (1931), the ethical codes discussed in Chapter 2, and the reflections on the core functions of reference identified by Tyckoson (2011) and others in the sources cited earlier. Second, it involves developing a deep knowledge of the community, looking at both current needs and needs that are likely to emerge given changing technologies, work habits, and demographics. Finally, it involves learning to trust one's instincts and judgment, which is the key to developing an authentic vision.

HIRING AND MANAGING STAFF

In every organization of more than one person, there are different staff roles and titles. Some organizations are fluid about who can take on responsibilities, but in many library settings, positions are defined by level of education, training, and experience. Terms are traditionally used to delineate between those with an MLIS degree (professional) and those without (paraprofessional or clerical), and the reference manager must know the guidelines for the delineated staff roles at different levels. Changes in hiring are affecting these definitions as MLIS degree holders take nonlibrarian staff positions and professionals with other degrees work in libraries in specialized roles. This is particularly important in a union environment where staff classification may stipulate that only staff at a certain level of classification can work at a reference desk or as a frontline supervisor. These are important issues for the reference manager given changes to reference services configurations and staffing. Good managers know how to hire and recruit new team members who will contribute to the team, and evaluate how new and existing team members will work together to advance the reference service mission and goals.

Hiring and Recruitment

Hiring can be a daunting responsibility for a new manager, in part because of its importance. There are rules and procedures in almost every organization that facilitate the process, but the final hiring recommendation is often up to the manager or search committee. New managers should contact human resources to find out the procedures, templates, and tools that are available; this will save the manager work and ensure that the standard practices of the organization are followed. Even if specifics differ across organizations, there are some components of most hiring processes; these are developing a position description, forming a search committee, recruiting candidates, interviewing, and making a final hiring decision.

When positions become vacant or new positions are created, the need to fill them must be communicated to administration or whoever has budgetary authority over positions and salaries. This requires vision and the ability to communicate the importance of the position not just today but for the future. A good tactic is to articulate what vital work will not be done if the position is not filled as well as the benefits of filling the position to the broader organization and the community it serves. This justification of the position is also a good time to examine if the position that is needed is exactly the position that was vacated or if it is time to rethink and reconfigure the position. Sometimes, a newly structured position can not only meet the needs of the reference department better but also incorporate needs from elsewhere in the library, making the position easier to justify, particularly when budgets are tight and filling positions is a competitive process. The newly defined position should still be coherent, able to be filled by one person, and not so big in scope and responsibilities as to be unmanageable. In some cases, writing the formal position description is part of the justification process, while at other libraries it may be a later step.

The formal position description describes the responsibilities of the position as well as the required and preferred qualifications. Managers should consider carefully what is required, as candidates who do not meet those requirements may be ineligible for interviews and hiring. Anything that is not essential can be placed into a desired or preferred list. The position description should be detailed enough for potential candidates to understand the work and the requirements but not so comprehensive as to be off-putting. Including everything that might possibly be desired in a candidate could narrow the field of applicants too much, making it harder to recruit a diverse pool, and also read as a position that is not cohesive or an organization that wants more than is realistic. Human resources can advise about the inclusion of a diversity statement in the position announcement and equal opportunity guidelines. To develop a strong position description, read similar descriptions with an eye to what will attract the candidates that your organization would want. Keep in mind that the position description will often serve as an internal document post-hire to guide the work of the position as well as the foundation of the job announcement.

Depending on the organization and situation, hiring may be a solo decision of the person managing the position, may involve administrative or board approval, or may comprise a search committee which brings multiple perspectives to the hiring process. When composing a search committee, think about representation from inside and outside of the department, as there may be people external to the department who will work with the individual and who could offer a valuable perspective. A search committee is also important as it will help reduce or eliminate individual bias from the process.

After a position is approved for hiring, a job announcement needs to be posted. Where the position is posted and for how long will affect who applies. Human resources can inform on the standard recruiting process for the organization and to what extent that can be augmented to increase diversity and depth of the candidate pool. In order to better reflect their communities, libraries are actively recruiting a more diverse workforce across categories, such as race, ethnicity, and physical ability. A diverse workplace also is inclusive of people of varying religions and sexual orientations. People from a range of backgrounds and experiences will bring in a wider variety of ideas and approaches. From a reference service perspective, this can have a positive impact on outreach and connection with user populations as well as enhance the learning environment among staff.

In addition to posting the job announcement, recruiting of specific qualified candidates can be done by contacting them and inviting them to apply. This is not a promise of employment or even of an interview, but it does indicate that the person is thought to be well qualified. Some candidates who would not otherwise be looking for a job might apply if contacted directly, so this method is used more frequently, but not exclusively, for non-entry-level positions. It is important to know the rules of the organization around recruiting, but many organizations consider targeted recruitment a way to build the depth and diversity of the candidate pool.

The interview process, much like other parts of hiring, can vary dramatically depending on the organization and may take from one hour to multiple days. Two rounds of interviews, telephone or videoconference and in person, are common for some organizations and are particularly useful if there is a large number of highly qualified candidates. Regardless of format, number, and length of interviews, the most important aspect is what questions are asked of the candidate and the information that the candidate receives about the position and organization during the interview. When crafting interview questions, move beyond what is likely to be on the resume and spend time on questions likely to elicit specific examples and reveal characteristics of how the candidates think and work. For instance, questions like "What techniques do you find most effective when conducting a reference interview?" can be helpful in assessing how well the candidate's approach matches the institution's expectations. Gail Munde (2013) provides more on the hiring process, especially for academic libraries, including employment law.

After the interview process, the manager or hiring committee must select a candidate. Depending on the organization, justification of the selection choice may be required to be provided to human resources before the offer can be made to the candidate. The offer to the successful candidate and a negotiation of terms, along with other organizational requirements, such as a background check, may be completed by either human resources or the manager. Once this negotiation is complete, the other interviewed candidates are notified that they were not successful. The final step in the hiring and recruitment process is the training and orientation of the new hire to the new position, the reference team, and the organization, often with a set procedure and/or checklist. Specific training for the new position will depend on the job requirements as stated in the job description.

Performance Expectations

The position description is a starting place for setting expectations about employee responsibilities and performance, but it is certainly not the end. Position descriptions are generally overviews that do not provide measurable goals. There may be standards within the library and/or organization for employee reviews and goal-setting, or it may be up to the individual manager. Yearly or twice yearly meetings to set goals and review performance will allow alignment of work activities to organizational priorities and a formal assessment of progress. Performance expectations should include a focus on not only projects and concrete outcomes but also areas of importance to the position such as punctuality and reliability, communications, customer service, and teamwork.

Meeting with employees should not be limited to formal review cycles. Frequency of meetings between the manager and employee will depend on the needs of the employee and the manager and the type of work being supervised. Delegated projects may require closer communication in order to support the employee doing the work. New employees may need more mentoring than long-term employees.

When employees are not meeting expectations or are struggling with assigned work, documentation and regular meetings are necessary. It can be difficult and uncomfortable to tell employees that they are not meeting expectations. However, avoiding the issue only makes it worse. Consult with human resources about what processes they recommend. A common process in both union and non-union environments is a performance improvement plan, which is a tool that allows an employee the opportunity to address deficiencies and meet specific goals while their performance is monitored. Performance issues should be addressed immediately so that they are fresh in the memory of the employee and so it does not seem like the manager has stockpiled issues that then come as a surprise to the employee. Managers should strive to be clear and impartial in the communication of any issues, to seek and respect the perspective of the employee, to work with the employee to develop a plan to remediate the issues, to follow up as a manager and provide training or support for improvement, and to document the process fully. If human resources support is available, communicate with them frequently throughout the process.

TEAMS AND TEAM MANAGEMENT

> *Trusted, empowered employees provide better services (and otherwise do better) than those that are required to report to their manager before making the smallest of decisions. [Staff] appreciate managers who provide direction while they allow autonomy.* (Gordon 2005, 159)

Teams can be effective ways to organize and accomplish work. Even in the most hierarchical organizations, important functional and decision-making responsibilities, including oversight of specific areas or initiatives relating to reference services, may be assigned to teams, working groups, or committees. As Rachel Singer Gordon (2005, 138) explains, teamwork is an essential part of "a climate that encourages collaboration, cooperation, and communication [and] allows people to use individual strengths together in pursuit of library goals." Regardless of the setting, the principles of building effective teams are widely applicable when working with groups as well as when delegating specific tasks and responsibilities to individuals. Communicating to staff the information they need to do their jobs well and make appropriate decisions independently is essential to maintaining service quality, as well as productive and empowered staff at all levels.

What does it take to build an effective team? Giesecke and McNeil (2010, 24) use a definition of "team" from Jon Katzenbach and Douglas Smith (1993, 45) as "a small number of people with complementary skills who are committed to a common purpose . . . for which they hold themselves accountable." They suggest the following five factors that impact team effectiveness (Giesecke and McNeil 2010, 50–51):

- **Goals** set the direction for the group and need to be clear, specific, and shared. The team as a whole takes responsibility for achieving the goal.
- **Roles** clarify who does what, including the manager. These should be clear to all members of the team.
- **Processes** are the internal procedures that determine how the team does its work, how decisions will be made, and how the meeting should be run. Documentation of processes enables a shared understanding.
- **Relationships** in the workplace are supported by roles and processes. Teams work best when they have agreed-upon guidelines defining how different opinions and viewpoints will be addressed and how disagreements will be handled.
- **Environmental influences** are external forces that impact teamwork, including reward systems, organizational structures, resources, and policies. Managers should ensure that teams have the resources necessary to accomplish the task at hand.

Teams pose management challenges that leave them open to failure. Elaine Russo Martin (2006, 275–77) found that despite an overall positive view of the use of teams in the libraries, all participants in her study could name at least one problematic team at their institution. Some team leaders took on too much authority and did all the work, while others were uncomfortable assuming a leadership role or cited unclear lines of authority. In order to avoid assuming too much authority, a team leader should consider delegation. Effective delegation requires good communication in order to make sure the person to whom the responsibility is assigned has the information and resources they need to complete the assignment and a clear picture of the goals and parameters of the project or task. Delegation, when done right, conveys to the person receiving the assignment that they are trusted and empowered.

Participants in Martin's study emphasized the need for leaders to intervene when there was a conflict or teams were struggling, while team leaders often reported being unwilling to confront conflict with colleagues and thus risk damaging collegial relationships. If there is discord in the reference department, the manager should seek to understand the causes and mitigate appropriately. Is the source of tension a result of differences in culture or interpersonal communication style? Are the causes based on biases against a group of people? Are the causes related solely to divergent opinions about work matters? Intolerance and discrimination can be overt or subtle but must be dealt with and documented by the manager. Differences in communication style or opinions about work issues could be culturally based or personality based. An organization's human resources office may be able to suggest resources on developing cultural sensitivity. The reference manager should always remember that it is not necessary for everyone to be friends, but everyone should be respected and listened to by every other person and not just by the manager.

Ideally a team will be comprised of members with a complementary variety and depth of skills. Not only does this support completion of the work, but team members can learn cross-functionally and from more experienced colleagues. Style inventories can be a useful tool for a reference manager to assist in building complementary teams. Style inventories assess and categorize people's traits into groups that can then be used to examine common ways in which people of different styles relate, how working relationships can be improved, and how to make one's own approach to the workplace more effective. For example, learning that a supervisee prefers concrete direction can help the manager calibrate the way that they delegate and explain assignments. Some inventories aim to be holistic personality assessments such as the *Myers-Briggs Type Indicator®*, and others are specific to the workplace or other situations, like the *DiSC Profile*. Use an inventory that is well researched, even though there may be a fee, as the time that has gone into their development makes for tools that are balanced, thoughtful, and present even traditionally negative traits as challenges and opportunities. When using a style inventory with a team, an outside facilitator who knows the tool is advisable. The facilitator can frame the uses and limitations of the tool, remind people that there are no "bad" types but only differences among types, and keep team members focused on how to use the information in the workplace.

These typologies can also depersonalize character traits to make talking about them less about the individual and more on making changes that improve communication and work between people and within groups. While all team members may learn and benefit from the exercise, it is the manager who must "understand, recognize, and accommodate different work styles of the people that they supervise"

(Giesecke and McNeil 2010, 106–7) and adapt to bring out the best in the people that they supervise. Even where a manager is not a direct supervisor, learning how to adapt to others' work styles is a quality they should develop.

Teams typically work in a participatory way rather than through top-down management, although that does depend on the organization. Establishing goals, roles, and guidelines as a group can cement the team early on and also increase adherence to the guidelines. The manager or team leader is responsible for setting the tone and maintaining awareness of both the work output of the team and team dynamics (Giesecke and McNeil 2010, 55; Trotta 2006, 55–56). Communication and information flow are key, and managerial responsibilities include communications within and between teams and with other parts of the organization.

COMMUNICATION

Communicating up, down, and across the organization is an essential part of every team, including the reference team. It is vital for the reference department manager to be able to communicate with different groups and to be active in listening as well as in sharing information and ideas. The key is to take advantage of all available opportunities to tell your story, share and learn relevant evidence, and consider how reference services might evolve to serve the emerging needs of your organization and community. Henry Mintzberg's (1980) classic model of managerial work, based on long-term observations of managers on the job, identifies three informational roles that most managers play:

1. **Monitor.** Seek out information related to the broader organization and the user community as well as to professional developments in reference services and related areas, looking for relevant changes in the environment; pay attention to one's staff or team members' performance and well-being.
2. **Disseminator.** Serve as a conduit of information, sharing, interpreting, and integrating information of potential value to the reference department or team and colleagues.
3. **Spokesman.** Represent and speak for the reference department or team, transmitting information about plans, accomplishments, and policies to people outside the team.

These roles frame how communication and management responsibilities intersect.

Good communication within the reference department or team helps develop staff who are fully engaged in providing service, are empowered to share ideas, and work together to solve problems. It also helps ensure that effort is focused toward broader goals and outcomes. This is reinforced by Gordon (2005, 163) who quotes one survey respondent as stating that "managers need to share enough information with employees so that everyone understands what is happening and their place in the overall scheme of things. When employees understand the why and how of something, they are apt to do things correctly and to take ownership, responsibility for, and satisfaction from the job." Meetings and frontline communication are two methods that can assist with routine communication, whereas crisis communication can assist with responding to unexpected events.

Meetings

Regularly coming together as a group to focus on shared work and goals empowers staff and creates a positive work environment. In a connected and highly scheduled world, meetings may seem unnecessary and communicating via e-mail or some other means might appear to be a more efficient way to share information. If the purpose is one-way communication, for example, when making an announcement, e-mail or a similar technology may be appropriate, but meetings actually allow for more efficient group discussion. This is especially true for reference, where finding a time for the whole group to meet can be challenging given the demands of service schedules and other commitments. Meetings, be they in person or online, provide a venue uniquely suited to sharing information, generating ideas, problem-solving, and decision-making.

That said, calling a meeting just for the sake of meeting is not a productive approach, and running a good meeting requires some preparation and structure. One key to running meetings that all participants will find valuable is to focus on getting things done and making decisions. Being productive, however, can be successfully paired with a relaxed, collegial atmosphere, as explained by this employee describing the weekly meetings convened by one of her best managers: "One manager I had . . . had Friday morning meetings and usually someone brought bagels. . . . We'd hash out workflows, plans for the fiscal year and interdepartmental issues while enjoying a good nosh. I looked forward to these meetings, not only because of the food, but because . . . we were actually productive and felt energized and motivated to do a successful job afterward" (Gordon 2005, 164). Giesecke and McNeil (2010, 146–57) provide some excellent guidelines for running good meetings, including skills for handling problem behaviors and how to decide when a meeting is not necessary.

Small work groups or teams focused on agile work might benefit from more frequent, but less lengthy, group communication. Even groups not identified as "agile" can adapt and benefit from the shorter style of meeting. Some examples of shorter meetings are stand-up meetings, scrums (also called circle-ups or huddles), or even regular fifteen-minute coffee breaks where team members briefly check in to share progress, identify issues or next steps, and assign work priorities (Bluedorn, Turban, and Love 1999; Sutton 2012). Whatever the meeting methodology, a reference department or team that is in the habit of working through issues together will also be better prepared for times of crisis or of major change, when open communication, trust, and the habit of working together to solve problems become even more essential.

Frontline Communication

Simply walking around and observing how things are functioning at the reference desk or in people's offices can be an important way to maintain awareness and stay in communication with staff or team members. It provides an informal opportunity to work with staff to troubleshoot problems and develop a sense of how services could be improved. Doing this at least daily keeps managers in close contact with staff and the services provided.

Job aids—procedure manuals, opening and closing checklists, and computer help screens—are a form of just-in-time communication, providing crucial information and documentation when and where it is needed. Whenever possible, job aids should be integrated into existing workflows. For instance, if everyone checks the e-mail queue at the start of the reference desk shift, that would be a good place to include information about a student assignment that is generating questions. Job aids are discussed in more detail in Joe Willmore's (2006) guide.

Crisis Communications

Communication is an important tool for any reference manager; however, it is not possible to plan in advance a specific response to every situation. Library emergencies are often thought of in terms of harm to the collection (e.g., flooding, bedbug infestations), natural disasters, or threats to library visitors or personnel. Beyond this, there are a host of other situations that can occur and have the potential to grow into a crisis: protest of a public exhibit or a speaker, a personnel issue that becomes public and contentious, or harassment involving staff or patrons. Social media has accelerated the speed at which a situation can spread and become a crisis for the library. Most people who manage reference are middle managers who may not be the final decision makers or the point person for public relations, but they may be closer to the crisis event and likely supervise staff who will receive questions from the public and media.

It is key to anticipate the types of situations that might arise within your area of the organization and then determine who is responsible for decision-making and communication. In larger organizations, in particular, these might be two different people. For example, the library director might make decisions, but communications with news media might be handled through a public relations office external to the library. Even within a single library there may be multiple people involved in updating social media or the library's website, communicating with news media, and providing outreach to affected community groups.

Planning and training can also avert escalating a crisis by providing frontline staff and reference managers with guidelines for communication, including confidentiality, discretion, and clarity of roles. Staff need to know their role in crisis communication, to whom they should refer questions, and what they can provide as an appropriate response. Jan Thenell (2004, 55) advises reference managers to "reemphasize the need for the library to speak with one voice, and remind staff that there is a clear chain of command during an emergency." Thenell's book *The Library's Crisis Communications Planner: A PR Guide for Handling Every Emergency* (2004) remains a relevant guide to developing a crisis communication plan that will help reference managers make sure that nothing is overlooked or mishandled during a stressful event.

PARTNERSHIPS, COLLABORATION, AND COMMUNITY RELATIONS

Managers have a responsibility to bring information in, work with other teams and departments to align efforts toward larger organizational goals, and represent the goals and needs of their group externally (Giesecke and McNeil 2010, 57). As with many areas of their work, reference managers are well positioned to establish and nurture collaboration and partnerships across and beyond the organization.

Partnerships and Collaborations

Supportive relationships with allied departments and functions across the organization are important to the mission and success of the reference department. These relationships may include departments inside the library that are closely related to reference services, such as access services or cataloging and discovery systems, as well as community members outside the library like teachers, faculty, or community organizations that are (or can become) key partners in outreach or educational initiatives. Kay Ann Cassell and Uma Hiremath (2013, 394–97) talk about "messy partnerships" becoming increasingly common in reference services, with reference playing important, but not always clearly defined, roles in areas like electronic resource management, website management, and marketing. These often involve informal partnerships with other parts of the organization, and reference staff contributions to these areas may not be well recognized if care is not taken to make them readily apparent.

Reference departments work in a variety of ways to coordinate efforts and develop shared service programs with partners outside of the library organization. Examples include partnering with information technology departments to develop learning commons; partnering with tutoring or writing services to provide integrated support for student learning; and partnering with community organizations to provide services related to health care, small-business development, or other community needs. Opportunities to develop these services often arise as a result of ongoing relationships developed with key stakeholders throughout the organization and community, nurtured through formal and informal communication around shared goals and community needs. An important role for the reference manager is to identify potential partners and foster collaborations. If the decision is made to develop a formal partnership, then working relationships need to be developed using the team-building techniques discussed earlier, as well as more formal mechanisms like drafting written partnership agreements (Walters and Van Gordon 2007).

Community Relations

In conversations with stakeholders and community members, the reference manager should listen for trends or new directions that may influence how to best grow and develop the library's reference services. Are there new strategic directions the institution is taking that create opportunities for reference-related services, like a distance education program, a shift in curriculum, or an expanded community center? A shift in community demographics that signal changing needs or new service opportunities? A good place to start a potential partnership is to invite people to talk with you about their organization in an informal meeting without specific goals and discover through conversation where goals align.

Informal conversations can also be an opportunity to generate excitement, interest, and support for any new initiatives or projects related to reference services. Reference managers should look for opportunities to communicate the importance of reference services to key stakeholders, including higher-level managers or administrators, influential faculty or community members, and others, in order to build an awareness of the ways reference services impact outcomes they care about, such as resilient communities or student success. Fostering this awareness can help ensure that needed resources are available to sustain and support reference activities. Reference managers should start developing an "elevator speech," a simple, succinct, and memorable statement of what your reference service does and why key stakeholders should care. There are many models and guidelines available specifically for libraries on the Internet. The Association for Library Service to Children (ALSC) has developed a template for crafting an effective elevator speech, as well as a longer "coffee shop conversation," as part of their Everyday Advocacy project. An example from the ALSC website is illustrative: "I help kids and families unpack their curiosity at the library so that the kids can go out and change our world for the better" (Association for Library Service to Children n.d.). Similarly, Christine Dettlaff (2008) outlines some key arguments for the importance of reference services targeted at administrators, including some answers to the question, "Why do we still need reference services when students can find the answers so easily online?" Statements like these can be customized for higher impact by mapping them directly to the mission and strategic goals of the school, college, or university or other organization.

The same sort of two-way communication that builds strong teams within the organization is equally important to foster with the community the library serves. Some techniques mentioned earlier—walking around, observing, and making the most of day-to-day interactions—are just as effective for engaging with community members as they are with staff. From informal approaches such as attending lectures and events and scheduling lunches and coffee meetings to more formal methods such as running focus groups and surveys, the reference manager can encourage and create opportunities for staff to develop relationships with the broader community.

EVALUATION, PLANNING, AND BUDGETING

Reference managers have an important stewardship role that involves ongoing evaluation and assessment of services to inform planning and the allocation of resources. Evaluation and assessment, planning, and budgeting should be well integrated, with each component informing the other. Robert E. Dugan and Peter Hernon (2018) elegantly demonstrate this interrelationship in their guide to data-driven planning and budgeting. Their guide includes templates for planning documents, spreadsheets, and strategic plans and is a great resource for any "managerial leader."

These three interlinked activities—evaluation and assessment, planning, and budgeting—are all opportunities to share key information with higher-level administrators. This communication can and should range from the formal (e.g., annual reports, outside evaluations, or accreditation) to the informal (e.g., updates at meetings, so-called elevator speech). Service evaluation and assessment help ensure that staff time and other resources are being allocated toward services that are meaningful to the community and have the intended outcomes. Evaluation and assessment of reference services are covered in depth in Chapter 8.

Planning

Effective management involves planning for future needs and preparing for changes in the community, resource base, or services. A few approaches to planning for the future and making decisions are outlined. These supplement the techniques for looking at trends within the community as discussed earlier.

Librarians should pay attention to what is happening outside of the library's walls with an eye to new possibilities and emerging opportunities. This includes monitoring trends at other libraries, in the economy, and in technology. Excellent sources to monitor trends include the Pew Internet reports on libraries and related technology (Pew Research Center), the Public Library Data Service annual survey (Reid 2017), and the Association of College and Research Libraries' (ACRL) Top Trends in Academic Libraries (ACRL Research Planning and Review Committee 2018). The "Accidental Technologist" column in *Reference & User Services Quarterly* provides regular updates on useful reference technologies that may be helpful in keeping abreast of relevant innovations. National and state organizations and listservs, such as those discussed in Box 7.2, are good places for information on what is happening at other libraries. Trends directly observed by the manager or staff should not be overlooked: Are there a lot of tablet users in the library? How might that affect services such as the library's website and how people contact the reference librarian? Awareness of trends does not necessitate being on the leading edge of changes; different managers and organizations set their own pace.

Knowledge of reference use patterns enables the reference manager to plan changes that make the most of limited resources while offering services that are appropriate to the local user group. To be useful to decision-making, reference statistics should be more than just a tally of the number of questions received each day. Tracking reference questions by factors such as time of day, patron type, nature or subject of question, day of week or month, and mode of communication can be used to determine the best way to utilize staff. Attention to changes over time can inform the creation of a new service point, adjustments in the combination of service points, or refinement of who is staffing a service point (Todorinova et al. 2011; Ward and Phetteplace 2012). For example, if evenings are when the most challenging reference questions are received, it would make sense to staff that time of day with librarians or experienced staff. Tracking information about subjects of the questions received at the reference desk and through consultations can also inform training and collection development. Reading chat reference transcripts and e-mails is more time consuming than analyzing metadata collected about reference interactions but can also be a rich source of information for training and collection development.

Statistics about the nature of reference questions received and changes over time are a good decision-making tool, but they do not tell a complete story. Examination of trends and statistics may reveal what else needs to be known to make a well-reasoned decision. If a lot of people in the library are observed using tablets, what are they doing? Are they checking out e-books, asking reference questions, playing games, or something else? Focus groups, interviews, and listening sessions are ways to get additional, more nuanced, information from community members to further explore observed trends or survey findings.

Staff are another group whose ideas and opinions are important to decision-making. Those working the reference desk daily are best situated to alert management to emerging patterns, such as a particular shift becoming busier or an increase in questions from off-campus students. These observations can lead to an examination of existing data and/or the collection of additional information to take initial impressions to the point where they can be the basis of a change in operations.

Most reference managers also have some degree of responsibility for or influence on both staff and user spaces. For staff spaces, this involves making sure that the equipment and furniture needed to perform their work are available and may include making decisions about space and office assignments. Giesecke and McNeil (2010, 140) recommend that managers "begin by examining their employee's work area and try to see the space from the point of view of the employee." Reference managers may also have an opportunity to be involved in space planning for their service points as well as for surrounding user spaces. See Chapter 6 for ideas on how to make the most of these opportunities to ensure that service points are placed in the flow and that any redesign of service points is flexible enough to be adapted to evolving models of service delivery.

Budgeting

Reference managers may or may not have direct oversight of specific budgets other than the funds allocated for materials or collections (covered in Chapter 14), so this section covers only the basics, providing a brief overview of some key concepts related to budgeting, managing expenditures, and developing requests for specific projects or grants.

Every library has its own practices for determining which costs (salaries, supplies, equipment, collections, etc.) are assigned to the reference department and which are paid centrally and for tracking and reporting on budgets. Reference managers will most likely be responsible for monitoring monthly reconciliation reports showing balances for what funds have been expended, have been encumbered, or remain available. Knowing how to read and interpret these reports is essential, so one should not hesitate to ask other managers or the library's budget office for assistance. If the library does not provide reports, or the standard reports do not provide the detail needed, reference managers will need to develop their own internal systems to track funds. Spreadsheets can be used to track specific expenses, as well as to work with figures to calculate percentages or create graphs. Managers can delegate responsibility to someone else in the department or team familiar with the software, but as the person responsible for budgetary oversight, reference managers should review and understand any reports created by others.

Why does this matter? As Giesecke and McNeil (2010, 140) explain, "It is crucial to have accurate records and anticipate change" as this will allow the reference manager to provide advice to senior management and respond proactively in case of budget reallocations. A manager who understands the budget and knows what funds are still available will have the flexibility to take advantage of opportunities that may arise, like hiring an hourly staff member for a special project or buying equipment with funds left over near the end of the year.

Special projects and new initiatives often require funding. This may be an opportunity to request one-time money, justify a recurring allocation, or apply for a grant. Requests should include a convincing statement of need; clearly defined goals and objectives that highlight the impact the project will have on the target user community; a plan for evaluating the outcomes; an accounting of any existing resources that will be leveraged to support the project; and a budget based on sound estimates of the costs, including staff time, equipment, and any licensing or contractual fees. Granting agencies will have specific requirements and guidelines, and managers should be sure to follow them closely and consider seeking out examples of successful requests as a model. Blanche Woolls, Ann C. Weeks, and Sharon Coatney (2014) provide a step-by-step guide to developing proposals to fund new programs, and M. Kathleen Kern (2009) provides a useful overview of the process of estimating both the budget (new allocations) and costs (total costs, including existing staff time that may be reallocated) needed to support new services.

POLICIES

Many, but not all, libraries find it useful to develop a general reference service policy that provides an overarching statement of purpose, goals, and objectives and a broad strategy that will be followed to reach those goals and objectives (Katz 2002, 184–86). These policies help situate the reference services within the broader institutional mission, clarify the primary audiences served by the service, establish service priorities, let people know what they can expect from the library, and serve as a touchstone for staff. The best service policies are grounded in a shared philosophy of service and stem from a thoughtful consideration of what reference means to the institution (Kern 2009, 32).

Professional guidelines and standards provide invaluable guidance when developing policy and can support staff if a policy is challenged. The Madison Public Library's "Reference Assistance Policy," for instance, specifically cites both state statutes regarding the confidentiality of library records and the American Library Association (ALA) "Code of Ethics" (Madison Public Library Board 2001). Professional principles should inform all policies developed for reference services, and care should be taken to ensure that policies align with librarians' core values. Figure 7.1 illustrates the many factors that contribute to reference service policies, including user needs, institutional mission, legal requirements, institutional regulations, and available resources, as well as professional standards and ethics.

In addition to a general reference service policy, reference managers may be involved in creating policies regarding new modes of service delivery, such as virtual reference services, in order to clarify the scope of the service. Specific policies can help govern access to limited resources, like Internet use, in the interest of making sure that all have equal access to high-demand resources. Reference managers may also be involved in the development or revision of policies concerning general customer-service issues, like patron behavior or unattended children.

Sandra Nelson and June Garcia (2003, 8) note that one of the primary functions of policies is to provide a mechanism for library managers and staff to translate the library's service priorities into actions. Policies can indeed provide an invaluable guide to action, but as with all guides, they only provide a sense of direction and are not an inviolable set of rules. Reference managers should be prepared for likely challenges and exceptions to policies. Staff should be given explicit guidance on when rules can be modified to help people and who is empowered to make decisions about exceptions. For example, permanent staff may be able to make exceptions within certain guidelines but not student staff. Generally, policies are modified in the interest of providing more or better service. Staff should always communicate that exceptions are being made in response to the particular situation at hand. (For example, "We don't usually retrieve books for visiting scholars, but since we have staff available and your time on campus is so brief, we'll be able to have the book ready for you at the desk when you stop in tomorrow.") This will help clarify that exceptions are made in response to specific situations, not individuals or individual behavior. Even with the best written policy and a clear sense of service priorities, things can get muddy. There are times when professional judgment will be needed. Box 7.1 provides a few such examples.

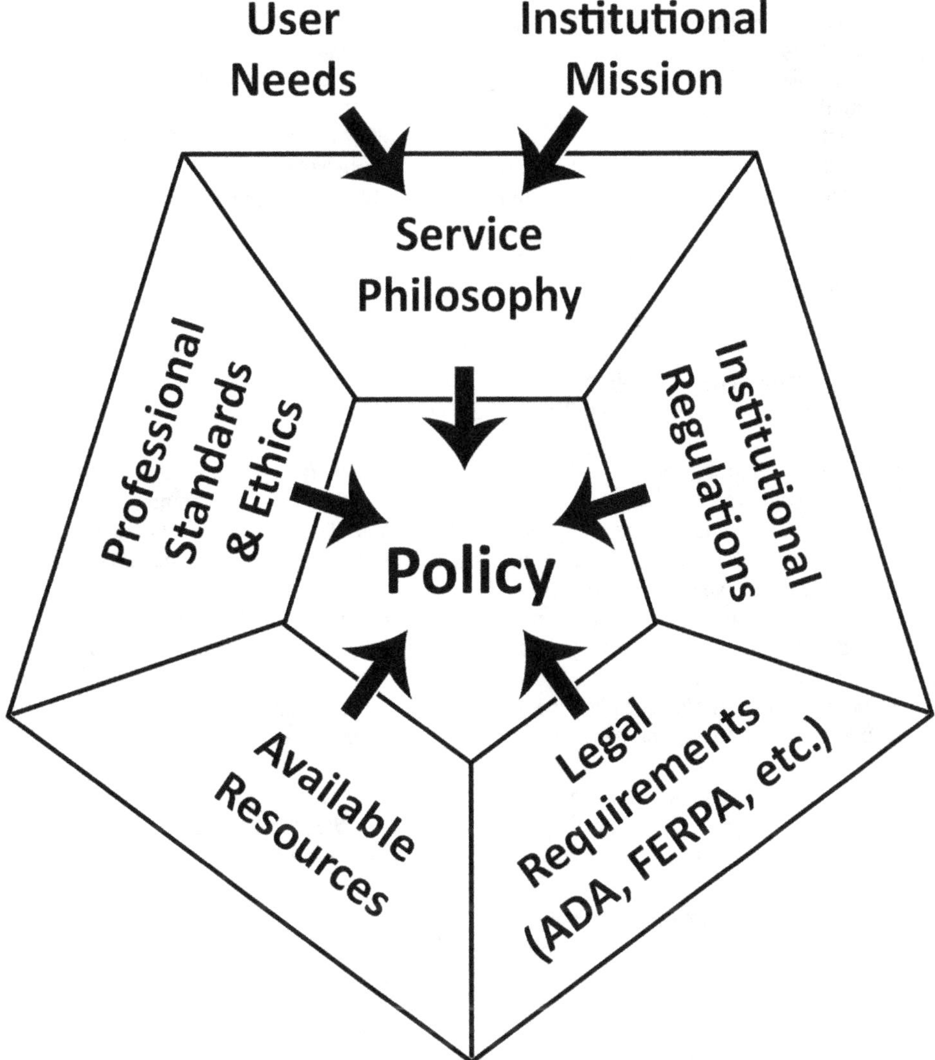

Figure 7.1 Factors that shape reference policy development. Shown are the factors that impact reference service policies: user needs, institutional mission, service philosophy, institutional regulations, legal requirements, available resources, and professional standards and ethics.

Box 7.1 Policy in Action: Balancing Principles, Politics, and the Service Imperative

Scenario 1

Community members in a public library complain about a man who is viewing pornography at a computer that they passed by on the way to the children's area.

Questions for Reflection and Discussion:

1. If no policy existed at your library, how would you tell staff to respond to this situation?
2. What factors might you consider in developing policy that balances open access to information with maintaining a welcoming and inclusive environment for people in the library, including staff? As a reference manager, what might your role be in crafting such a policy?

Scenario 2

A staff person reports that one of the regular library visitors has been making unwelcome comments on her appearance and standing so close that it makes her uncomfortable. You realize that this constitutes sexual harassment as defined by the U.S. Equal Employment Opportunity Commission (n.d.).

1. Is this sort of behavior covered by any existing policies and regulations that pertain in your community, such as Title IX guidelines prohibiting conduct that creates a hostile environment in institutions of higher education? How might you ensure that staff are aware of the implications such policies and regulations have for themselves as employees as well as service providers?
2. How might you ensure that incidents like this are reported to others in the facility to ensure safety, while respecting privacy? How would you as a manager follow up on such incident reports?
3. How might you train your staff on recognizing and responding to inappropriate behavior? When might it be appropriate for you to respond on their behalf?

Hint: A recent *American Libraries* article, "Stop Sexual Harassment in Your Library: Protecting Librarians from Inappropriate Patrons" (Ford 2017) suggests some possible responses to such inappropriate behavior, including the following:

- "That comment/behavior is inappropriate."
- "If this behavior continues, I will have someone else finish assisting you."
- "If this behavior continues, I will ask you to leave the library."

Amy Carlton (2017) focuses more specifically on how managers can empower and support staff responding to sexual harassment.

DEVELOPING MANAGEMENT AND LEADERSHIP SKILLS

Managing people is an art. . . . You can only learn it well by carefully observing, by doing, making errors, learning from those errors, mending your ways, picking the brains of successful experienced managers, and thereby incrementally improving. (Verbesy 2009, 192)

Managers learn both from the lessons they have learned from practice (often the hard way) and from the insights and experiences of others. As G. Edward Evans and Camila Alire (2013, 4–5) observe, "Course work and workshops will not ensure you will be a good manager, but these tools can improve your managerial skills." Managers who are open to learning from a variety of sources and experiences will continue to grow and develop throughout their careers.

New managers should build a network of peers, colleagues, and mentors from whom they can get advice and inspiration and with whom they can share experiences and ideas. Participating in professional associations, workshops, and leadership or management training institutes can be a way to further build this network. These sources for professional development serve a dual purpose by providing structured learning opportunities and a space for informal learning and networking. Listservs, blogs, and other social media can help build a virtual network, making them especially valuable for those for whom opportunities to travel are constrained. Other libraries, both similar and different to your own organization, as well as other service organizations and businesses, can suggest ideas and models. Many libraries will share their internal policies, procedures, annual reports, or other documentation when contacted. Most librarians are pleased to share this information, and it can be another way to build a professional network as well as helping with an immediate need for managerial information. Key resources for developing skills as a reference manager and building a professional network are provided in Box 7.2.

Box 7.2 Professional Development Resources for Library Managers

Professional associations

- *Library Leadership & Management Association (LLAMA).* LLAMA is a division of ALA focused on advancing outstanding leadership and management practices and developing excellence in current and aspiring library leaders. LLAMA brings together librarians from all types of libraries.
- *Reference and User Services Association (RUSA).* RUSA provides an excellent venue for connecting with others involved in the provision of reference services in every type of library. The Reference Services Section of RUSA includes a Management of Reference committee.
- *State and regional library associations.* These are a good way to network with those close geographically. Many offer conferences or workshops that can be attended without lengthy travel, and some offer online webinars as well.

Listservs

- Many of the organizations listed previously have listservs, and some may allow nonmembers to join the list.
- LibRef-L is a good place to monitor issues and trends and seek information and advice.

Institutes and webinars

- *WebJunction.* Sponsored by OCLC, this "learning place for libraries" hosts free webinars and courses related to library technology, management, and services. A topically organized archive of past sessions, along with links to related resources, supports self-directed learning on demand.
- *TRLN Management Academy.* This is an experiential learning program focusing on preparing mid-level academic library managers to manage complex and diverse resources with emphasis on the sound management of staff, budgets, and technology.

- *Regional or state library organizations*. Many smaller organizations offer workshops or multiday institutes for managers, sometimes focused on a specific type of library.

Journals and trade publications

- Peruse journals specific to one's particular type of library, such as *portal: Libraries and the Academy*, *Public Libraries*, and *School Library Research*.
- Browse standard reference journals like *Reference Services Review*, *Reference & User Services Quarterly (RUSQ)*, and *The Reference Librarian*.
- Management-specific journals such as *Library Leadership and Management*, *Library Management*, *Journal of Library Administration*, and *The Bottom Line* explore topics of interest to library managers.
- Professional trade publications like *American Libraries* and *Library Journal* provide an overview of developments and emerging topics across the profession.

Identifying and Developing Your Style as a Manager

Managers do things right; while leaders do the right things. (Bennis and Nanus 2007, 45)

Management and leadership are distinctive but complementary modes of action with leadership focused on developing a vision and strategy for the future and mobilizing others to help realize that vision, while management involves planning and using resources efficiently to produce the intended results (Kotter 1990). Most reference managers are expected to both manage and lead. Some people are lucky to have developed skills in both leadership and management, to apply as the situation demands, but a single individual is usually stronger in one.

Every new reference manager should undertake a frank assessment of their own strengths and weaknesses and then work to develop a strong team around them whose strengths complement their own weaknesses. Those who are more comfortable managing than leading can make a point of listening to more visionary coworkers or enlisting charismatic colleagues to help them motivate and inspire others. They can arrange opportunities for group brainstorming or other events such as charrettes or hack-a-thons to elicit innovative ideas that they can then work to implement using their managerial skills. Other strategies managers can use are gathering input from their community (e.g., through focus groups or advisory committees) and trying approaches like scenario-based planning or environmental scans that can help keep the bigger picture in focus. Conversely, strong leaders will want to build a team of people around them who are empowered to establish procedures and deadlines, organize the work of other staff or team members, and monitor and evaluate progress toward the intended result.

The management literature can be a good starting point for reflecting on and developing a personal approach and voice as a manager. Some sources promote a particular approach, while others help people determine their own leadership style. Choosing where to begin in this vast literature is an exercise in applying reference skills to find what has been well reviewed. One good place to start is to ask administrators or supervisors for suggestions as their choices can be a guide to the organizational culture or at least their aspirations for the organizational culture.

Every organization has a culture that affects how decisions are made, the management structure, and the expectations for staff at all levels. Being successful, particularly as a manager, requires understanding the organization's culture, the behaviors and norms (often unspoken), that governs how things are done and decisions are made. Carol Shepstone and Lyn Currie (2008) offer a formal process for analyzing organizational culture. Time and observation, along with talking with longer-term employees, are informal ways to learn an organization's culture.

When moving to a new organization, or when assuming a new role, it is advisable to consider how to adapt personal style to the new workplace culture. For example, top-down decisions in a collaborative culture might appear heavy handed and meet resistance, whereas a lengthy collaborative process might be seen as slow and indecisive in a culture more accustomed to leaders who are out in front with their decision-making. Successful managers will be mindful of how to work effectively within a particular organization. Box 7.3 outlines an exercise for developing an individual management philosophy based on conversations with other professionals, individual reflection, and research.

Box 7.3 Activity: Develop Your Own Management Philosophy

"Select good people, trust them, delegate authority while retaining responsibility, build true teams, and be supportive" is a good example of a management philosophy (Evans and Alire 2013, 7). New reference managers will be well served to begin developing a concise statement of their own management philosophy. To get started:

- Reflect on the good, and the not-so-good, managers you have worked for in the past. What are some of the traits you would like to emulate? That you want to avoid?
- Talk to colleagues you admire in management or leadership positions, and ask them about their management philosophies and approach. Listen for the variety of ways different leaders face similar challenges and the varied definitions of what constitutes a good result.
- Use the sources identified through the process suggested at the beginning of this section to examine some management and leadership approaches in more depth. The *Harvard Business Review* is also a great place to browse for inspiration. Which approaches resonate with you? Which fit best with your core values? With your particular strengths?

CONCLUSION

Management means making things happen, and the more people know how to make things happen, the more successful the library as a whole will be. (Applegate 2010, 4)

Reference services, in all their various forms and "messy partnerships" (Cassell and Hiremath 2013, 394), are a pivotal place where researchers and library staff engage together in the process of discovery. Reference managers help ensure that libraries continue to meet people when, where, and how services are needed. Reference managers play a central role in their organizations, with responsibility for making decisions that help shape the future of the services in an ever-evolving information landscape. Growing into this role—developing skills as a manager and an individual voice as a leader—is a process that unfolds over time and deepens with experience. Whether a reference manager by design or accident, embrace the role and you will learn and grow with every new challenge and opportunity.

REFERENCES

ACRL Research Planning and Review Committee. 2018. "2018 Top Trends in Academic Libraries." *College & Research Libraries News* 79 (6). https://crln.acrl.org/index.php/crlnews/article/view/17001/18750.

American Libraries. 1970–. Chicago: American Library Association. https://americanlibrariesmagazine.org/.

Applegate, Rachel. 2010. *Managing the Small College Library*. Santa Barbara, CA: Libraries Unlimited.

Association for Library Service to Children. n.d. "Elevator Speech." American Library Association. http://www.ala.org/everyday-advocacy/speak-out/elevator-speech.

Bennis, Warren G., and Burt Nanus. 2007. *Leaders: Strategies for Taking Charge*. New York: HarperCollins.

Bluedorn, Allen C., Daniel B. Turban, and Mary Sue Love. 1999. "The Effects of Stand-Up and Sit-Down Meeting Formats on Meeting Outcomes." *Journal of Applied Psychology* 84 (2): 277–85.

The Bottom Line. 1998–. Bingley, UK: Emerald. https://www.emeraldinsight.com/loi/bl.

Campbell, Jerry D. 1992. "Shaking the Conceptual Foundations of Reference: A Perspective." *Reference Services Review* 20 (4): 29–36.

Carlson, Scott. 2007. "Are Reference Desks Dying Out? Librarians Struggle to Redefine—and in Some Cases Eliminate—the Venerable Institution." *The Reference Librarian* 48 (2): 25–30.

Carlton, Amy. 2017. "Fighting Sexual Harassment in the Library: Knowing What to Do When Patrons Go Too Far." *American Libraries*, June 27. https://americanlibrariesmagazine.org/blogs/the-scoop/fighting-sexual-harassment-library.

Cassell, Kay Ann, and Uma Hiremath. 2013. *Reference and Information Services: An Introduction*. 3rd ed. New York: Neal-Schuman.

Dettlaff, Christine. 2008. "Managing to Keep Academic Reference Service." In *Defining Relevancy: Managing the New Academic Library*, edited by Janet McNeil Hurlbert, 161–69. Westport, CT: Libraries Unlimited.

DiSC Profile. https://www.discprofile.com/.

Dugan, Robert E., and Peter Hernon. 2018. *Financial Management in Academic Libraries: Data-Driven Planning and Budgeting*. Chicago: Association of College and Research Libraries.

Evans, G. Edward, and Camila Alire. 2013. *Management Basics for Information Professionals*. 3rd ed. New York: Neal-Schuman.

Ford, Anne. 2017. "Stop Sexual Harassment in Your Library: Protecting Librarians from Inappropriate Patrons." *American Libraries*, November 1. https://americanlibrariesmagazine.org/2017/11/01/stop-sexual-harassment-your-library/.

Gibson, Craig, and Meris Mandernach. 2013. "Reference Service at an Inflection Point: Transformations in Academic Libraries." In *Imagine, Innovate, Inspire: The Proceedings of the ACRL 2013 Conference in Indianapolis, Indiana*, April 10–13, edited by Dawn M. Mueller, 491–99. Chicago: ACRL.

Giesecke, Joan, and Beth McNeil. 1999. "Core Competencies and the Learning Organization." *Library Administration and Management* 13 (Summer): 158–66.

Giesecke, Joan, and Beth McNeil. 2010. *Fundamentals of Library Supervision*. 2nd ed. Chicago: American Library Association.

Gordon, Rachel Singer. 2005. *The Accidental Library Manager*. Medford, NJ: Information Today.

Gulick, Luther, and Lyndall Urwick. 1937. *Papers on the Science of Administration*. New York: Institute of Public Administration, Columbia University.

Harvard Business Review. 1992–. Boston, MA: Harvard Business Publishing. https://hbr.org/.

Journal of Library Administration. 1980–. Philadelphia, PA: Routledge. https://www.tandfonline.com/toc/wjla20/current.

Katz, William A. 2002. *Introduction to Reference Work*. 8th ed., 2 vols. New York: McGraw-Hill.

Katzenbach, Jon, and Douglas Smith. 1993. *The Wisdom of Teams*. Boston, MA: Harvard Business School Press.

Kelley, Michael. 2011. "Geeks Are the Future: A Program in Ann Arbor, MI, Argues for a Resource Shift toward IT." *Library Journal*, April 26. http://lj.libraryjournal.com/2011/04/technology/geeks-are-the-future-a-program-in-ann-arbor-mi-argues-for-a-resource-shift-toward-it/#.

Kern, M. Kathleen. 2009. *Virtual Reference Best Practices: Tailoring Services to Your Library*. Chicago: American Library Association.

Kotter, John P. 1990. "What Leaders Really Do." *Harvard Business Review* 68 (3): 103–11.

Library Journal. 1876–. New York: Library Journals, LLC. http://lj.libraryjournal.com/.

Library Leadership and Management. 2009–. Chicago: American Library Association. https://journals.tdl.org/llm/index.php/llm.

Library Leadership and Management Association. http://www.ala.org/llama/.

Library Leadership and Management Association. 2019. "Leadership and Management Competencies." American Library Association. http://www.ala.org/llama/leadership-and-management-competencies.

Library Management. 1979–. Bingley, UK: Emerald. https://www.emeraldinsight.com/loi/lm.

LibRef-L. https://listserv.kent.edu/cgi-bin/wa.exe?A0=LIBREF-L.

Madison Public Library Board. 2001. "Reference Assistance Policy." Last modified August 16, 2001. http://www.madisonpubliclibrary.org/policies/reference-assistance.

Martin, Elaine Russo. 2006. "Team Effectiveness in Academic Medical Libraries: A Multiple Case Study." *Journal of the Medical Library Association* 94 (3): 271–78.

Mintzberg, Henry. 1980. *The Nature of Managerial Work*. New York: Harper & Row.

Moran, Barbara B., Robert D. Stueart, and Claudia J. Morner. 2013. *Library and Information Center Management*. 8th ed. Santa Barbara, CA: Libraries Unlimited.

Munde, Gail. 2013. *Everyday HR: A Human Resources Handbook for Academic Library Staff*. Chicago: Neal-Schuman.

Murphy, Sarah Anne. 2011. *The Librarian as Information Consultant: Transforming Reference for the Information Age*. Chicago: American Library Association.

Myers-Briggs Type Indicator®. https://www.themyersbriggs.com/en-US.

Nelson, Sandra, and June Garcia. 2003. *Creating Policies for Results: From Chaos to Clarity*. Chicago: American Library Association.

O'Gorman, Jack, and Barry Trott. 2009. "What Will Become of Reference in Academic and Public Libraries?" *Journal of Library Administration* 49 (4): 327–39.

Olver, Lynne. 2011. "So You're the New Director? Twelve Points to Help You Survive the First Year." *Public Libraries* 50 (2): 6–7.

Pew Research Center. http://www.pewinternet.org/.

portal: Libraries and the Academy. 2001–. Baltimore, MD: JHU Press. https://www.press.jhu.edu/journals/portal-libraries-and-academy.

Public Libraries. 1962–. Chicago: Public Library Association. http://www.ala.org/pla/resources/publications/publiclibraries.

Radford, Marie L., ed. 2012. *Leading the Reference Renaissance: Today's Ideas for Tomorrow's Cutting-Edge Services*. New York: Neal-Schuman.

Ranganathan, S. R. 1931. *The Five Laws of Library Science.* Chennai (formerly Madras), India: The Madras Library Association.

Reference & User Services Quarterly. 1997–. Chicago: American Library Association. https://journals.ala.org/index.php/rusq.

Reference and User Services Association. http://www.ala.org/rusa/.

Reference and User Services Association. 2017. "Professional Competencies for Reference and User Services Librarians." Last modified September 7, 2017. American Library Association. http://www.ala.org/rusa/resources/guidelines/professional.

The Reference Librarian. 1981–. Philadelphia, PA: Routledge. https://www.tandfonline.com/toc/wref20/current.

Reference Services Review. 1973–. Bingley, UK: Emerald. https://www.emeraldinsight.com/loi/rsr.

Reid, Ian. 2017. "The 2017 Public Library Data Service: Characteristics and Trends." *Public Libraries Online* (September/October). http://publiclibrariesonline.org/2017/12/the-2017-public-library-data-service-report-characteristics-and-trends/.

Saunders, Laura, Lillian Rozaklis, and Eileen G. Abels. 2014. *Repositioning Reference: New Methods and New Services for a New Age.* Lanham, MD: Rowman & Littlefield.

School Library Research. 1951–. Chicago: American Library Association. http://www.ala.org/aasl/pubs/slr.

Shepstone, Carol, and Lyn Currie. 2008. "Transforming the Academic Library: Creating an Organizational Culture That Fosters Staff Success." *The Journal of Academic Librarianship* 34 (4): 358–68.

Steiner, Sarah K., and M. Leslie Madden. 2008. *The Desk and Beyond: Next Generation Reference Services.* Chicago: Association of College and Research Libraries.

Sutton, Bob. 2012. "The Virtues of Standing Up in Meetings and Elsewhere." *Work Matters.* April 3. http://bobsutton.typepad.com/my_weblog/2012/04/the-virtues-of-standing-up-in-meetings-and-elsewhere.html.

Thenell, Jan. 2004. *The Library's Crisis Communications Planner: A PR Guide for Handling Every Emergency.* Chicago: ALA Editions.

Todorinova, Lily, Andy Huse, Barbara Lewis, and Matt Torrence. 2011. "Making Decisions: Using Electronic Data Collection to Re-Envision Reference Services at the USF Tampa Libraries." *Public Services Quarterly* 7 (1–2): 34–48.

TRLN Management Academy. https://sites.google.com/site/trlnmanagementacademy/home.

Trotta, Marcia. 2006. *Supervising Staff: A How-to-Do-It Manual for Librarians.* New York: Neal-Schuman.

Tyckoson, David A. 2011. "Issues and Trends in the Management of Reference Services: A Historical Perspective." *Journal of Library Administration* 51 (3): 259–78.

Tyckoson, David A., and John G. Dove, eds. 2015. *Reimagining Reference in the 21st Century.* West Lafayette, IN: Purdue University Press.

U.S. Equal Employment Opportunity Commission. n.d. "Facts about Sexual Harassment." https://www.eeoc.gov/eeoc/publications/fs-sex.cfm.

Verbesy, J. Robert. 2009. "What I've Learned from 30 Years of Managing Libraries." *Catholic Library World* 79 (3): 192–94.

Walters, Carolyn Mary, and Elizabeth Ann Van Gordon. 2007. "Get It in Writing: MOUs and Library/IT Partnerships." *Reference Services Review* 35 (3): 388–94.

Ward, David, and Eric Phetteplace. 2012. "Staffing by Design: A Methodology for Staffing Reference." *Public Services Quarterly* 8 (3): 193–207.

WebJunction. https://www.webjunction.org/home.html.

Willmore, Joe. 2006. *Job Aids Basics: A Complete How-to Guide to Help You Understand Basic Principles and Techniques, Create and Use Job Aids Effectively, Enable Top Performance.* Alexandria, VA: ASTD Press.

Woolls, Blanche, Ann C. Weeks, and Sharon Coatney. 2014. *The School Library Manager.* 5th ed. Westport, CT: Libraries Unlimited.

Zabel, Diane. 2007. "A Reference Renaissance." *Reference & User Services Quarterly* 47 (January): 108–10.

Zabel, Diane, ed. 2011. *Reference Reborn: Breathing New Life into Public Services Librarianship.* Santa Barbara, CA: Libraries Unlimited.

SUGGESTED READINGS

Evans, G. Edward, and Camile Alire. 2013. *Management Basics for Information Professionals.* 3rd ed. New York: Neal-Schuman.

Evans and Alire provide a good balance between the practicalities of hands-on management and the broader philosophical and professional issues, further supplemented with sidebars highlighting the real-life experiences of the authors and an advisory board. The chapter on "Managing Money" is a good guide to understanding library-wide budgeting processes and cycles.

Giesecke, Joan, and Beth McNeil. 2010. *Fundamentals of Library Supervision.* 2nd ed. Chicago: American Library Association.

This book provides a practical introduction to the issues and strategies of library supervision in all areas of library work. The emphasis is on building supervisory skills and in turn creating a better working environment with motivated and productive staff. New managers, in particular, will find this work approachable and helpful with concrete suggestions.

Madden, M. Leslie, Laura Carscaddon, Denita Hampton, and Brenna Helmstutler. 2017. *Now You're a Manager: Quick and Practical Strategies for New Mid-Level Managers in Academic Libraries.* Chicago: Association of College and Research Libraries.

Written by a group of middle managers at Georgia State University, the primary audience is academic, but this is a great resource for any library manager. Plenty of practical, actionable advice is packed into a few brief chapters on topics such as "Creating a Respectful Workplace and Dealing with Problem Employees," "Mentoring and Coaching," and "Conducting Effective Meetings."

McKnight, Michelynn. 2010. *The Agile Librarian's Guide to Thriving in Any Institution.* Santa Barbara, CA: Libraries Unlimited.

Addressing librarians at all stages of their careers who want to develop skills and practices that will allow them to effectively demonstrate their worth, McKnight emphasizes evidence-based decision-making as well as strategies for communicating effectively, expanding influence, marketing, setting priorities, and managing time.

Chapter 8

Evaluation and Assessment of Reference Services

Laura Saunders

INTRODUCTION

Evaluation and assessment are processes for gathering and analyzing data to measure things like quality of resources and services, customer satisfaction, or progress toward goals. Reference professionals provide a wide range of resources and services to support users' information needs, all of which can and should be evaluated. Through a variety of techniques, reference professionals can evaluate the effectiveness and quality of their services and resources as well as the satisfaction level of users and assess progress toward goals and the impact of services.

Evaluation and assessment are both linked to accountability, the process of providing stakeholders with evidence of quality, improvement, and progress toward mission and goals. Evaluation and assessment are increasingly important in an era of greater accountability and competition. The Internet and mobile devices have made vast amounts of information instantly accessible. Patrons have many options for accessing information, some of which may be more convenient and easier to use than the library. With this competition, some libraries are seeing sharp declines in numbers of reference questions (Martell 2008). As a result, stakeholders—people with a "stake" or interest in libraries—are pressuring institutions to demonstrate their value. Some stakeholders are library users. Others might not be direct users of libraries, but they care about the services and resources libraries provide. Indirect stakeholders could include citizens whose tax dollars support the public library; parents whose children use school and academic libraries; or local, state, and federal governments that provide financial support to libraries.

In addition to demonstrating value to stakeholders, evaluation and assessment provide libraries with an opportunity to better understand their communities and services and to make informed decisions for continuous improvement (Oakleaf 2010). As frontline service providers, reference professionals interact with patrons on a daily basis and should have a sense of their patrons' opinions and perceptions of services, but that sense is not the same as hard data. Only when librarians systematically ask for feedback can they be sure that they understand the wants and needs of their community and the impact the library has on that community. The increasing importance of evaluation and assessment in libraries is reflected in projects like the Association of College and Research Libraries' (ACRL n.d.) Assessment in Action project, support for research and evaluation provided by the American Library Association's (ALA) Office for Research and Evaluation and by conferences like the Library Assessment Conference, all of which support practitioner learning related to evaluation and assessment. Through evaluation and assessment research, librarians can produce the data needed to guide their decisions, continuously improve services and programs, and provide evidence of the library's value to stakeholders.

This chapter examines the concepts of evaluation and assessment as applied specifically to reference services. It begins with definitions of terms and an overview of evaluation and assessment practices and trends, followed by specific applications to reference services. The chapter focuses on methods for evaluating the point-of-need reference transaction and related reference services. Other chapters will examine evaluation and assessment in relation to resources and managing services and people.

DEFINITIONS

While the terms are often used interchangeably, "evaluation" and "assessment" are "separate but connected concepts and processes" (Hernon, Dugan, and Nitecki 2011, 2). Evaluation involves "identifying and collecting data about specific services or activities, establishing criteria by which their success can be judged, and determining the quality of the service or activity and the extent to which the service or activity is economically efficient and accomplishes stated goals and objectives" (Hernon and Schwartz 2012, 79). Evaluation is a managerial activity and can have political implications, as managers can use evaluation data to make decisions about allocation of staff and resources. Assessment, on the other hand, refers to a process of measuring progress toward a specific outcome or goal with a focus on impact of resources and services on the community. Assessment is "any activities that seek to measure the library's impact on teaching, learning, and research, as well as initiatives that seek to identify user needs or gauge user perceptions or satisfaction. The overall goal is data-based and user-centered continuous improvement of library collections and services" (Ryan 2006, 78). Assessment centers on understanding the current state and impact of a program or service and providing feedback for improvement, while evaluation engages in measurement for the purpose of judging a program or service and determining its overall value or quality (Starr 2014). Assessment and evaluation seem like very similar concepts, and the terms are often used interchangeably, but practitioners do try to differentiate between the two.

In addition to providing proof of performance, evaluation and assessment underpin evidence-based practice. Evolving from the health sciences field, evidence-based practice entails using data to inform decision-making. In library science, evidence-based practice is described as "a means to improve the profession of librarianship by asking questions as well as finding, critically appraising and incorporating research evidence from library science (as well as other disciplines) into daily practice. It also involves encouraging librarians to conduct high quality qualitative and quantitative research" (Crumley and Koufogiannakis 2002, 62). By conducting research, librarians can gather the kind of data necessary to make good decisions regarding their programs and services. If they share their findings, they can provide colleagues at other institutions with information for evidence-based practice as well. Box 8.1 further defines evaluation, assessment, and evidence-based practice.

Box 8.1 Definitions

Evaluation is the process of determining the quality of a library's collections or services or the level of patron satisfaction with those collections or services; evaluation asks questions like "Does the library have appropriate print and online resources to answer the majority of patron inquiries?" and "Are patrons satisfied with the service they receive at the circulation desk?"

Assessment is the process of measuring the impact of a library's services and educational programs; assessment asks questions like "How has the library's new outreach program improved access to health care information?" and "After attending a workshop on resume writing, are participants using action verbs to describe their past work experience?"

Evidence-based librarianship involves incorporating research data and evidence into professional practice in order to make informed decisions; evidence-based practice asks questions like "What are best practices for providing virtual reference services?" and "How might the latest research on undergraduates' information literacy skills inform changes to the library's instruction program?"

Questions for Reflection and Discussion:

1. Find an article or example of an information-setting undertaking research to improve services. Would you characterize the study as evaluation or assessment? Why? How were the results used to improve services to patrons or the efficiency of library operations? Think about a library or information setting with which you are familiar. Are the results of this study applicable to that setting? If you were director of that library, how might you use these findings to inform your own practice?
2. Think about the type of library or information center you would like to work in. How could librarians evaluate the quality of services or programs offered there? How could the library assess the impact of those programs or services?
3. Imagine you have been hired as manager of a large reference department. Before making any major decisions, you would like to learn more about the department and its staff and services. What kinds of questions might you ask? Try formulating two evaluation and two assessment questions to gain a better understanding of the overall quality and impact of the department. How might you go about gathering evidence and data to answer these questions?

THE EVALUATION AND ASSESSMENT CYCLE

The evaluation and assessment process is often depicted as a cycle in which data is gathered and interpreted to measure progress toward goals and then to inform decision-making and establishment of new goals (Oakleaf 2009). In this

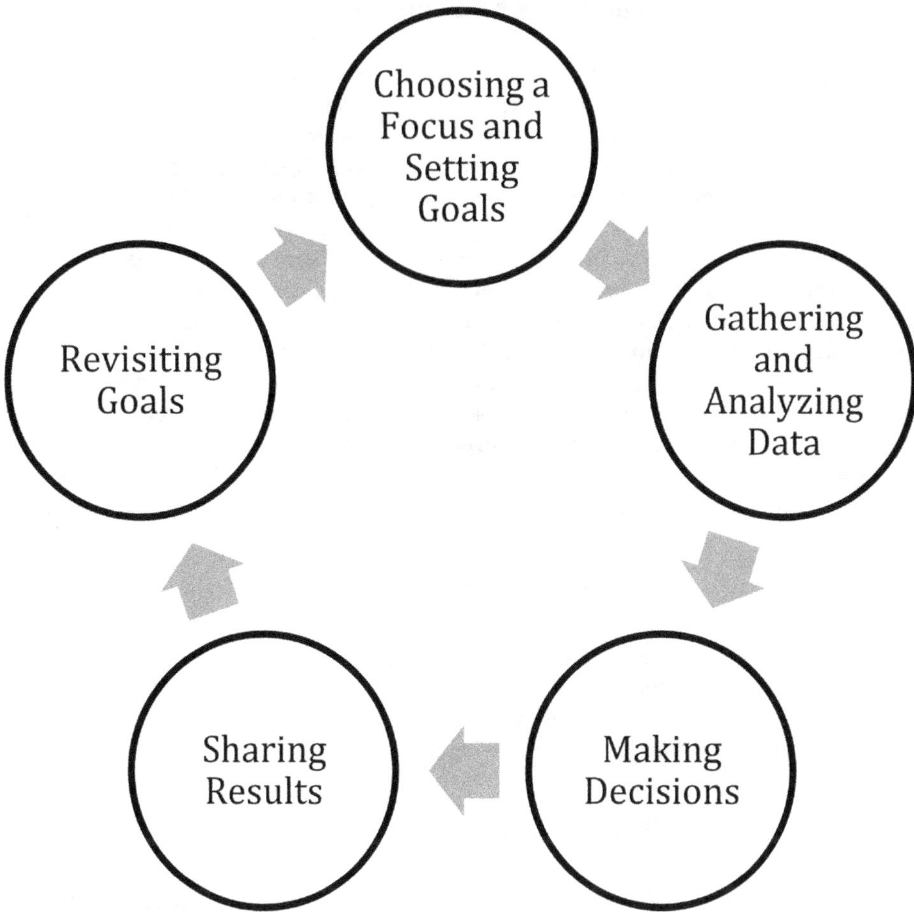

Figure 8.1 The assessment cycle: identifying goals, gathering and analyzing data, making decisions, sharing results, and revisiting goals.

sense, evaluation and assessment are iterative, meaning that as one cycle concludes, a new one begins. Figure 8.1 depicts one version of the process, involving five steps: setting goals, gathering and analyzing data, making decisions, sharing results, and revisiting goals.

Choosing a Focus and Setting Goals

The first step in any assessment project is to determine the goals and define which aspects of the service to study. For instance, librarians might study levels of customer satisfaction with virtual reference services, with a goal to achieve a 90 percent satisfaction rate. Or they could examine how accurate staff are when providing answers to questions or whether students are learning from reference transactions. The goals of the research set the standard by which results will be measured and determine what kind of data is needed and what methods are most appropriate for gathering that data.

Gathering and Analyzing Data

Once goals have been identified, data collection can begin. There are many different methods for collecting data, some of which are described in more detail here. The most important consideration when choosing a method of data collection is to consider what kinds of data are needed—for example, customer opinions and work flow processes—and then determine what method will yield that data. For instance, surveys and focus groups are often good ways of getting feedback and opinions from users.

This step does not end with the collection of data. Once the data has been gathered, it must be analyzed. The method of analysis will depend to some extent on the type of data gathered. For instance, quantitative data from surveys can be summarized using percentages and averages. If the data is qualitative, such as focus group or interview transcripts, the text will need to be read for patterns and themes in the content. Most important, however, is determining the meaning behind the data. What does it mean if 75 percent of patrons say that they are satisfied with reference services? Are there patterns or consistencies among those who are less than satisfied? How closely do these results meet the goals that staff set for themselves?

Making Decisions

The ultimate purpose of assessment research is to take action; simply gathering and analyzing data is not enough. Once data has been gathered and analyzed, it should be used to make decisions, whether about staffing, budgeting, continuing or suspending programs, or setting new goals for improvement.

Sharing Results

Communicating the results of evaluation and assessment is an important part of closing the loop and one that is too often overlooked. Stakeholder groups, from patrons to trustees to local government agencies or college provosts and presidents, will be interested to know what was learned from the research and what will be done with that information. Sharing results with people who participated in the research is one way of letting them know that their feedback is being taken seriously and that their opinions matter.

Revisiting Goals: Continuing the Cycle

Evaluation and assessment are iterative processes. Once the results have been analyzed in order to determine how well the library is meeting goals, and decisions have been made about services based on the research, the cycle begins again.

WHAT SHOULD BE EVALUATED OR ASSESSED?

Librarians have always gathered data about their resources and services, but traditionally they focused on inputs, or the resources and infrastructure of the institution, and outputs, or the products and services the library offers. Such data is valuable for tracking activities and benchmarking against peer institutions and can be useful for planning. Inputs and outputs are limited, however, because they do not measure the quality or impact of the resources or services. They tell us "how much" but not "how well." As Lynn Silipigni Connaway (2014, 1) explains:

> Input measures evaluate the library's raw materials (budget, space, collection, equipment, and staff) against standards, but are insufficient for overall assessment. Output measures quantify the work done, such as the number of items circulated, the number of reference questions answered, or the number of individuals who attended library instruction sessions, but do not relate these factors to the overall effectiveness of the library. Output measures suggest demand, performance efficiency, and customer satisfaction, but do not describe performance or identify the outcomes or benefits resulting from the use of library services and systems.

As stakeholders put greater pressure on libraries to demonstrate their value, there has been a shift in the focus from tallying inputs and outputs to evaluating quality and assessing outcomes. "Quality" refers to how good a resource or service is. Quality in reference could be measured by outside standards, such as adherence to the Reference and User Services Association's "Guidelines for Behavioral Performance of Reference and Information Service Providers" (2013), or by self-reported levels of customer satisfaction. "Outcomes" refers to the results of a library's resources or services and their impact on an individual or community. The Institute of Museum and Library Services (n.d.-b) defines outcomes as "benefits to people: specifically, achievements or changes in skill, knowledge, attitude, behavior, condition, or life status for program participants ('visitors will know what architecture contributes to their environments,' 'participant literacy will improve')," and outcome-based evaluation as "observations that can credibly demonstrate change or desirable conditions ('increased quality of work in the annual science fair,' 'interest in family history,' 'ability to use information effectively')."

Evaluation of quality and assessment of outcomes in reference services could focus on a variety of areas, including customer satisfaction with service at virtual and physical reference desks, quality and effectiveness of services, and learning outcomes of reference transactions as well as usability aspects of virtual reference services, or of physical space devoted to reference services, including design and signage. Some librarians have also engaged in cost-benefit and return-on-investment evaluation, attempting to show the economic value of the library to its community (Kelly, Hamasu, and Jones 2012). Finally, evaluation research can focus on staff performance, which could also involve assessing training programs for staff, and could encompass areas such as job satisfaction.

The choice of what to evaluate and assess is a local one. While virtually any service or resource could (and probably should) be examined, each individual library and reference department will need to determine which areas to focus on, guided by local needs, the mission of the library, and the interests of library stakeholders. An academic or school library might begin by focusing on student learning through reference interactions, while a city government might be most interested in the return on tax dollars invested in the public library or satisfaction of public library patrons. The following sections outline some traditional and emerging areas for reference evaluation: accuracy, patron satisfaction, service quality, learning, usability, and cost-benefit analysis.

Counting Reference Questions

Tracking the number and types of reference questions asked is a common activity for reference librarians in all types of settings. Librarians report these statistics to agencies such as the Institute of Museum and Library Services (IMLS) and the National Center for Education Statistics (NCES). The Integrated Postsecondary Education Data System (2015) through the NCES makes academic and school library statistics available, allowing libraries to benchmark activity against peers and making it possible to see aggregate trends in usage over time. The IMLS provides similar data for public and state agency libraries (Institute of Museum and Library Services n.d.-a).

Reference desk statistics can be tracked in a number of ways. In addition to the overall number of questions asked, librarians might track the format of the interaction (face to face, e-mail, chat, telephone, etc.). Many libraries also classify questions by type. At the simplest level, questions might be identified as reference questions, as opposed to directional or equipment questions (such as "Where is the bathroom?" or "Can you put more paper in the printer?"), which do not require specialized knowledge or the use of information resources. Reference questions can be further broken down by type, including ready-reference questions, research consultations, and readers' advisory.

Data about the number and type of reference questions fielded can inform the allocation of resources and staffing. Knowing peak days and times, and also knowing when more in-depth questions are typically asked, can assist reference managers in planning coverage for different service points (Dugan and Hernon 2002). While useful, counting reference questions is an output measure and does not offer any insight into the quality of the service or patron satisfaction. Librarians will continue to track these statistics for staffing and benchmarking purposes, but, as noted earlier, the trend is to move past input and output measures to measure quality and outcomes.

Accuracy

In a classic study, Peter Hernon and Charles McClure (1986) sent proxies (individuals recruited and trained by the researchers) to a variety of reference desks to ask questions. The researchers confirmed that each institution had a resource that could answer the question being asked. Nevertheless, nearly half of the time, the staff member at the reference failed to answer the question. Based on these results, the researchers coined the phrase the "55 percent rule" to describe the rate at which librarians provided an accurate answer to a question. Other studies of accuracy in reference transactions have varied widely, from as low as 24 percent (Profeta 2006) to as high as 80 percent (Pomerantz, Luo, and McClure 2006), with one study of virtual reference chat transcripts putting accuracy for ready-reference questions at 90 percent (Radford and Connaway 2013). Hernon and McClure's study was an important one, as it moved beyond inputs and outputs to evaluate the accuracy of the service being provided and gauged the quality of the service by examining the librarians' behaviors, including whether they engaged in a reference interview or offered a referral. However, the study has been criticized for measuring the success of the reference transaction solely by the accuracy of the librarian's answer. Issues such as the librarian's demeanor and helpfulness and the patron's satisfaction were not considered as part of the results. Later researchers have focused more on customer satisfaction and librarian behaviors as factors in the overall success of the reference interview.

Patron Satisfaction

Good customer service is crucial to any organization. People are much more likely to share bad customer-service experiences with friends and family than good experiences (Dixon, Freeman, and Toman 2010; Estep 2011), leading to a ripple effect, where one bad experience can deter others from using a service. While librarians want patrons to be satisfied with the whole range of resources and services provided, customer service is particularly important for the reference transaction, whether in a face-to-face or a virtual environment.

Joan Durrance (1989) found that a good customer-service experience was one of the most important factors in determining if a patron would return to the reference librarian with another question. Durrance found that patrons who rated the reference librarian's interpersonal skills highly were more likely to say that they would return to that reference librarian for help in the future. Patrons were much less likely to return to a librarian whom they perceived to be judgmental or uninterested in them or who made them feel uncomfortable, even if that librarian answered their question accurately. Other studies similarly found that when describing whether a reference transaction was successful, patrons were much more likely to focus on "relational aspects," such as whether the librarian was friendly and pleasant (Radford 1996), and that the librarian's friendliness strongly correlated with the patrons' overall satisfaction (Dewdney and Ross 1994). Similar criteria held true for studies of virtual reference services (Connaway and Radford 2010), demonstrating the importance of patron satisfaction to the overall success of reference services. Further, these studies indicate that the information professional's behaviors and demeanor have a strong impact on the outcome of the reference transaction. In fact, studies showed that the librarian's demeanor, and the layout of the reference desk including how approachable the space seems, can influence whether a patron will even initiate a reference transaction (Bonnet and McAlexander 2013; Cortés-Villalba, Gil-Leiva, and Artacho-Ramírez 2017).

Service Quality

Quality refers to the overall attributes or characteristics that make up a product or a service, and that would influence a person to use that service initially and to return to it in the future (Pass et al. 2006). For instance, a good-quality car should run well, last a long time, and not need repairs beyond general maintenance. While customer service relies solely on the customer's opinions—that is, the customer's subjective perception of how good a resource or service is—quality can be measured from different perspectives. In the examples given earlier, many studies found that library patrons made judgments about the quality of reference transactions based on the friendliness of the librarian. These results show that from the customer's perspective, interpersonal skills are an important aspect of quality. On the other hand, librarians often judge the success or quality of reference transactions differently. Marie Radford (1999) found that when discussing the success of a reference encounter, librarians tended to focus on the content of the question and the amount and quality of the resources available. From the librarian's perspective, providing a complete and accurate answer to the question seems to be one of the most important factors in determining quality.

When the focus of quality research is on the services provided, it is referred to as service quality. While quality can be viewed from both internal (library) and external (patron) perspectives, service quality places the emphasis on the patron. Service quality is related to satisfaction in that it relies on the patron's judgment and perceptions of their experience, and quality is generally a factor in whether a patron is satisfied. In evaluation and assessment research, however, service quality is differentiated from satisfaction. Satisfaction usually focuses on a single instance, or transaction, whereas service quality is a more general concept, encompassing the patron's overall experience (Parasuraman, Zeithaml, and Berry 1988). According to Peter Hernon and Ellen Altman (1996, 2), service quality in libraries "encompasses the interactive relationship between the library and the people whom it is supposed to serve. A library that adheres to all the professionally approved rules and procedures for acquiring, organizing, managing, and preserving material but has no customers cannot claim quality because a major element is missing: satisfying people's needs, requests, and desires for information." Basically, service quality means meeting (or exceeding) patron expectations on a consistent basis and across a variety of service points (Lewis and Booms 1983). When an organization fails to meet a patron's expectations, the failure is identified as a gap in service, and actions should be taken to improve (Bannock et al. 2003).

Librarians at the University of Mississippi measured service quality using a standardized survey that asked patrons to rate their minimum, desired, and perceived levels of quality across a range of library services. After using this survey for ten years, they conducted a longitudinal analysis and found that their customers' perceptions of staff had improved over time (Greenwood, Watson, and Dennis 2011). Another study surveyed patrons of archival reference and compared their perception of the quality of the reference transaction to their perceived importance of the service. When gaps were identified between expectations and actual quality, the staff used that feedback to improve services (Battley and Wright 2012).

Because it usually relies on patron opinions, service quality is different from what might be considered more "objective" measures of quality, such as those applied in manufacturing to determine whether to accept or reject a prototype. While some might be uncomfortable with the subjective nature of service quality, ultimately, the patron's perception is their reality. Regardless of how librarians or even another patron might rate the same service, if an individual believes they have received a lower-quality service than they anticipated, they will be dissatisfied. In other words, as noted in Box 8.2, "if customers say there is quality service, then there is. If they do not, then there is not. It does not matter what an organization believes about its level of service" (Hernon and Altman 1996, 6).

Box 8.2 Activity: Quality Service

Consider this quote: "If customers say there is quality service, then there is. If they do not, then there is not. It does not matter what an organization believes about its level of service" (Hernon and Altman 1996, 6).

Questions for Reflection and Discussion:

1. Do you agree? Why?
2. Are there any circumstances in which the organization's beliefs about its service might be more valid than those of its users?

Learning

Instruction is an important component of reference. During the reference interview, the librarian has an opportunity to guide the patron through the information search process, and it is possible that during the interaction, the patron will learn some new strategies and techniques. By assessing the extent to which learning takes place during reference encounters, librarians can demonstrate how reference services contribute to the learning mission of their institutions.

Several studies use virtual reference transcripts to assess the extent to which librarians engage in instructional activities or behaviors during the reference encounter (Passanneau and Coffey 2011; Taddeo and Hackenberg 2006). While the focus of these studies is on teaching, librarians at Wartburg College found that over 90 percent of students surveyed indicated that the librarian had taught them something during their reference encounter (Gremmels and Lehmann 2007). Similarly, librarians at Indiana University analyzed and classified reference questions as a way of assessing the information literacy levels of the patron and found these students perceived the reference interaction to be a learning experience (Cordell and Fisher 2010). Another study found that students were open to receiving instruction during chat reference, and in follow-up focus groups, those students referred back to information and strategies that they learned from librarians (Jacoby et al. 2016). Megan Oakleaf and Amy VanScoy (2010, 386) encourage librarians to "explore the direct impact of librarian instructional strategies [during virtual reference transactions] on student learning."

Usability

Usability is defined as "how effectively, efficiently and satisfactorily a user can interact with a user interface" (*Usability.gov* 2015a). Usability is part of the overall user experience, which examines ease of use and the satisfaction of a user with a system. *Usability.gov* (2015b) identifies six factors that impact usability:

1. **Intuitive design.** A nearly effortless understanding of the architecture and navigation of the site.
2. **Ease of learning.** How fast a user who has never seen the user interface before can accomplish basic tasks.
3. **Efficiency of use.** The speed with which an experienced user can accomplish tasks.
4. **Memorability.** Whether a user can remember enough to use the site effectively in future visits.
5. **Error frequency and severity.** How often users make errors while using the system, how serious the errors are, and how users recover from the errors.
6. **Subjective satisfaction.** If the user likes using the system.

As more reference services and resources move online, librarians are recognizing the need to evaluate the usability of those services and resources. Usability is important because patrons will compare library websites to the ease, speed, and convenience they are used to from services like *Google* and *Amazon*. If library sites seem too complicated or clunky, the patrons are not likely to use them. One usability study compared several formats of remote and virtual reference and found that chat seemed to be the preferred method, scoring highest for efficiency, effectiveness (in terms of task completion), and satisfaction (Chow and Croxton 2014). Librarians at the University of Saskatchewan employed usability testing as a way to plan the overall design of their virtual reference service (Duncan and Fitcher 2004). In addition to virtual reference services, usability testing can be implemented for online reference tools such as research guides (Vileno 2010).

Cost-Benefit

Stakeholders are often interested to learn the economic value of the money spent on the library. One study found that because librarians can locate information efficiently and effectively, when they were integrated into health care teams, they could save those teams $13–20 per question answered (Ganshorn 2009). Some librarians have also engaged in cost-benefit and return-on-investment evaluation, attempting to show the economic value of the library to its community (Kelly, Hamasu, and Jones 2012). One academic library estimated the cost in terms of time and money that patrons were willing to expend to get resources and services from the library and concluded that the library provided more than $4 in return on investment for every dollar spent (Kingma and McClure 2015). A systematic review of research studies found several examples of librarians in health settings saving the time of the professionals with whom they worked and contributing to the overall cost-effectiveness of the organization (Weightman and Williamson 2005).

HOW TO EVALUATE OR ASSESS

Each evaluation or assessment project has five distinct aspects that must be defined before the project is undertaken: what will be studied, who will be the focus of the study, where the study will take place, when the study will take place, and how the data will be gathered. As a whole, these five areas are sometimes referred to as the logical structure of the research project.

What

The "what" of the logical structure refers to the focus of the study: what, specifically, is being evaluated or assessed. As outlined earlier, almost any resource (e.g., website, pathfinders, collections) or service (e.g., virtual or face-to-face reference, instruction) can be evaluated. In addition to choosing an area of focus for evaluation, it is important to define what aspect of the resource or service will be evaluated (e.g., customer satisfaction, quality, learning) and which perspective will be taken (e.g., patron's, library's).

Who

The "who" is the population being studied. In some cases, the population could be very broad, such as library-card holders or genealogists, and sometimes it will be more limited, such as students of a certain age or enrolled in a certain class. The important thing is to make sure the population aligns with the focus of the study. Often, it might not be possible or practical to study an entire population. At such times, the librarians will draw a sample of the population, often trying to take a random sample or otherwise taking care to make the sample representative of the population. The suggested readings listed at the end of the chapter offer overviews of how to draw an appropriate sample for a study.

Where

The "where" of the study refers to the organization, or place, on which the study focuses, or to which it is connected. Because evaluation research is generally local in nature—that is, it is undertaken to study local services and inform decision-making within the organization—the "where" of an evaluation research project is usually the library or information setting carrying out the research.

When

"When" defines the timetable in which the research will be carried out. Selecting an appropriate time frame is important. If, for instance, a reference department wants to study customer service at the reference desk, it will need to find a time when there will be plenty of activity, with a range of patrons and questions being asked. For example, an academic library typically would not want to carry out a study during spring break, when many students will not be on campus.

How

"How" refers to the methods that will be used to collect data. There are numerous methods for studying reference services, and a comprehensive review of those methods is outside the scope of this chapter. However, a few of the more popular methods are discussed later. Suggested Readings at the end of this chapter offer more in-depth explanations of these methods, as well as overviews of additional methods not discussed here.

Definitions and Standards

Part of setting up an evaluation or assessment project involves clarifying each aspect of the study, including vocabulary and how each aspect of the study will be measured. The first step is to define the terms of the study, a process sometimes referred to as operationalization. Several of the studies described earlier employed different definitions of reference success. Some defined success at the reference desk in terms of the patron's willingness to return to the librarian, whereas others measured reference success by the accuracy or completeness of the answer supplied by the librarian. The point with operationalization is to ensure that it is clear how all aspects of the research are being defined.

Once terms have been defined, the librarians must decide how to measure each area under study. For instance, continuing with the example of reference service success, Durrance (1989) and Dewdney and Ross (1994) needed to know not just whether patrons were willing to return to the reference desk but what factors made them more likely to return. They had patrons rate the reference interactions across a number of criteria, including the different behavioral aspects of the librarian. Those criteria are the standards against which the librarian's performance was measured.

Although it is possible to define local measures, it is often preferable to find externally defined measures. Many professional associations like the ALA, the

Public Library Association, and the ACRL publish definitions, standards, and metrics that can be used for evaluation and assessment. For instance, the Reference and User Services Association (RUSA) offers the "Guidelines for Behavioral Performance of Reference and Information Service Providers" (2013), which are often used to assess librarians' performance during reference encounters. Researchers have proposed additional standards based on studies of reference services. For instance, R. David Lankes, Melissa Gross, and Charles R. McClure (2003) proposed six quality standards that could be used to evaluate virtual reference services: courtesy, accuracy, satisfaction, repeat users, awareness, and cost. External standards save librarians the time and effort of developing their own measures and allow for benchmarking and comparison across research studies that have used the same standards.

EVALUATION AND ASSESSMENT METHODS

Evaluation research can be carried out through a wide variety of methods. Most methods fall into one of two basic categories: quantitative or qualitative. Quantitative methods focus on information that can be represented numerically and might include frequency counts, percentages, and ratios. Common types of methods for gathering quantitative measures include surveys, questionnaires, or polls (with closed-ended questions); transaction log analysis (including reviews of analytics of website and e-resource use); and bibliometrics (including citation analysis). Qualitative research, on the other hand, relies on observation and description. Some common types of qualitative research include interviews, focus groups, document analysis, and unobtrusive observation.

Each methodological approach has strengths and weaknesses. Quantitative methods can often be applied to larger groups, meaning there is more likelihood of getting a representative sample whose results are generalizable to the larger population. On the other hand, qualitative methods can usually probe deeper and get at the context behind quantitative results. For instance, while a survey might tell us that patrons are satisfied with reference services, a focus group could find out why people are more or less satisfied with different aspects and probe the reasons for satisfaction and dissatisfaction. As such, it can be advantageous to use quantitative and qualitative methods together to get a fuller picture of the area under research. The following sections offer an overview of some of the more common research methods applied to reference services studies.

Surveys

Surveys are a popular method for evaluation research. When composed of closed-ended questions, or questions with a fixed set of answers from which the participant must choose, they take less time to administer than qualitative methods and generally can be analyzed more quickly, making them a good choice for large populations. Surveys can elicit a range of information, including demographics, knowledge, opinions, and awareness. In addition, surveys can include open-ended questions that allow participants to write in their own responses. These questions offer participants an opportunity to elaborate on or clarify answers to closed-ended questions and thus add qualitative aspects to the study.

Surveys are used regularly for customer-service feedback, but they have also been implemented in other ways. For instance, Gillian S. Gremmels and Karen Shostrom Lehmann (2007) used a survey to assess patrons' perceptions of learning during reference transactions. Surveys have also been used to study patrons' information-seeking behaviors in order to better understand how to support their needs through reference services (Head 2013; Mokhtari 2014) and to determine the extent to which patrons use certain technologies such as mobile devices so that services can be tailored to support access on such devices (Becker, Bonadie-Joseph, and Cain 2013; Dresselhaus and Shrode 2012). One study used a survey to determine if users understood library signage for the reference desk (O'Neill and Guilfoyle 2015). Surveying patrons on their awareness of library services and resources can be helpful in planning marketing and outreach campaigns (Del Bosque et al. 2017).

While these surveys focus on a single perspective, it is also possible for surveys to gather feedback from multiple perspectives in order to compare and contrast. For instance, the Wisconsin-Ohio Reference Evaluation Program (WOREP), developed in the 1980s by Marjorie Murfin, Gary Gugelchuk, and Charles Bunge, consisted of a two-part survey that was completed at the end of a reference transaction (Murfin and Gugelchuk 1987). One half of the survey was completed by the patron and asked about their satisfaction and about the affect and behaviors of the librarian. The other half of the survey was completed by the librarian and asked about the content of the question, how fully the question was answered, and any special considerations such as whether there were other patrons waiting for attention or whether the question was outside of the scope of the library's collection. The two portions of the survey were coded so they could be recombined and compared.

Having the two perspectives allowed the librarians to see whether their opinion of the success of the transaction matched the patron's and, if not, where the discrepancies were. For instance, librarians at Pennsylvania State University discovered that staff were overestimating patrons' satisfaction with reference transactions (Novotny and Rimland 2007). Based on their findings, the librarians implemented a training session encouraging librarians to use more resources when answering questions, to spend more time with the patron, and to offer alternatives when the desired resource was not available. A follow-up study showed that overall satisfaction improved after the training was implemented. Thus, evaluation research enabled librarians to identify a problem and to make an informed decision to improve services. Other studies based on WOREP have found that librarians and library students often underestimate the success of the reference transaction, with the patron giving the librarians a higher rating than they give themselves (Butler and Bird 2016; Saunders 2016).

Deciding whether to use an existing survey or to create a local one is an important consideration. There are established surveys like LibQUAL+® and Counting Opinions that offer valid instruments and assistance with data analysis. Many surveys are also included in research articles published in the library and information science literature or are available from the authors upon request. Still, many librarians choose to develop their own survey, perhaps for budget reasons (standardized instruments can be expensive) or in order to tailor the questions to a local audience. Generally, surveys are somewhat less time- and resource intensive to develop than other data collection instruments. However, creating a survey that will elicit reliable and valid data is not necessarily easy. Guidance on survey development can be found in the books listed in the Suggested Readings section.

Overall, surveys are an excellent way of gathering feedback on almost any topic from a wide range of community members, but they do have limits. The closed-ended nature of surveys means that they can offer a snapshot of a situation, but they cannot usually probe deeper into the explanations behind the situation. In addition, people receive surveys from many different sources, which can lead to survey burnout. If they are tired of answering surveys, patrons might not be as thorough in their answers, might not persist until the end, or might choose not to answer the survey at all. Finally, the nature and format of the survey can create barriers to response. Since surveys are written and require a certain reading level, young children, non-native speakers, and patrons with low literacy levels may be unable to participate. People without reliable Internet connections may be unable to access online surveys. On the other hand, paper surveys usually are distributed only within the physical library, thus eliminating nonusers, remote users, or anyone who simply does not visit the library during the time the survey is being distributed. Researchers must consider all of these limitations when planning surveys and decide how best to reach the largest number of patrons.

Focus Groups

Whereas surveys can be good for large samples but tend to be limited to primarily closed-ended questions, focus groups allow for greater depth by bringing together the perspectives of a group of individuals and giving them space to explore their thoughts; bounce ideas off of each other; agree, disagree, and question or challenge one another (Liamputtong 2011). Participants often learn from each other during the discussion, and researchers can see how participants' opinions influence each other. Unlike surveys, it is also possible to ask follow-up questions if a participant's answer is unclear or if they raise a particularly interesting point. In addition, focus groups can be a marketing tool in and of themselves, as participants "really appreciate the opportunity to be heard and the library is viewed as being caring enough to solicit their experiences" (Massey-Burzio 1998, 214).

Focus group methodology can be applied to any type of research problem or question, but because it emphasizes direct and open-ended feedback from participants, it can be useful for probing patrons' awareness about reference services as well as their satisfaction and opinions about those services. One study found that patrons were uncomfortable asking questions and that when they did use reference services, they found them unhelpful. Further, they complained of poor signage and indicated that they found the librarians to be generally unavailable or hard to identify (Massey-Burzio 1998). Conversely, focus group participants in another study indicated that their needs were being met by the reference desk (Fitzpatrick, Moore, and Lang 2008). Focus groups have also been used to gauge patrons' preferences for different service formats. For instance, some studies have explored patron preference for face-to-face, phone, and chat interactions (Granfield and Robertson 2008; Naylor, Stoffel, and Van der Laan 2008) or their perceptions of chat reference services (Jacoby et al. 2016), while others have examined patrons' use of mobile devices for reference support (Owen 2010).

While focus groups can be extremely useful for probing a topic deeply, with just seven to twelve participants per session focus groups reach far fewer people than surveys, meaning that the findings are limited as well. One way to maximize the strengths of each methodology while minimizing their disadvantages is to pair the two together. A survey can be used to get an overview of the community's perspectives, while follow-up focus groups can probe into the questions or concerns raised by the survey.

Observation

Observation has long been a popular method for studying reference services. As the name implies, this method involves a systematic approach to observing reference librarians in action and comparing or benchmarking their actions and behaviors against a predetermined set of criteria. Observation can be either obtrusive, meaning the subject of the study knows they are being observed though they may not know when it will happen, or unobtrusive, meaning the subject does not know they are being observed or studied. For instance, Peter Hernon and Charles McClure (1986) used unobtrusive observation when they established the 55 percent rule, as did both Durrance (1989) and Dewdney and Ross (1994) when they tested patrons' willingness to return. In each of these studies, the researchers engaged observers to ask questions at the reference desk and then report back on their experiences.

Mystery shopping is a form of unobtrusive observation employed by some libraries. Originally used in retail settings, mystery shopping involves using trained surrogates who use the services of the library in order to assess the effectiveness of the service and/or the communication, behaviors, and customer-service orientation of the employees. Mystery shoppers are not necessarily current patrons of the library but have been recruited and trained to use the library services as a regular patron would (Jankal and Jankalova 2011). For reference services, these shoppers ask a reference question and then evaluate the librarian against a set of predetermined criteria, such as RUSA's (2013) "Guidelines for Behavioral Performance of Reference and Information Service Providers." This approach has been used successfully to evaluate customer-service aspects of both academic (Kocevar-Weidinger et al. 2010) and public (Backs and Kinder 2007) libraries. The Kent Libraries in Australia offer a video describing a mystery-shopping program in which community members with disabilities act as the mystery shoppers and offer insight into how the library can better support patrons with certain needs (CILIP 2011).

Although researchers tout unobtrusive observation and mystery shopping as effective methods that can lead to actionable results, some practitioners are uncomfortable with the approach. For one thing, research involving people, known as human subjects research, typically requires the informed consent of the people involved. However, for unobtrusive observation to work, the subject has to be unaware that they are being observed. Otherwise, they are unlikely to act naturally. Librarians who decide to implement unobtrusive observation can ameliorate the problem by letting their staff know that observations are being undertaken, and discussing the purpose, without telling the librarians exactly when the observations will be done or by whom. Further, for staff to feel comfortable with the process, researchers will need to be clear that observation and mystery shopping are intended to diagnose general problems and not to target specific staff. Mihaela Banek Zorica, Tomislav Ivanjko, and Sonja Spiranec (2014) offer clear guidance on implementing a mystery-shopping program. Box 8.3 presents a short activity related to mystery shopping.

Box 8.3 Activity: Mystery Shopping

A library has decided to set up a mystery shopping study of its reference department. The director is interested in finding out how well patrons' questions are being answered (in other words, are they given full and accurate answers insofar as the librarian is able to do so) and whether they are receiving a good customer-service experience. Develop a list of questions or observation criteria for the mystery shopper to respond to after their interaction. For instance, should they note the number of sources the librarian consults? Whether the librarian makes eye contact and greets the patrons as they arrive? Create a list of five to ten things for mystery shoppers to respond to and report on.

Transcript Reviews

Reference interactions that take place by chat or e-mail usually generate a transcript that documents the transaction. These transcripts will show every aspect of the interaction, from the librarian's greeting to the reference interview questions asked, any attempts at instruction, the format of the answer provided, sources cited, and how the interview is closed. As such, virtual reference transcripts can be useful in evaluating the reference interview and the overall quality of the reference service. A number of studies have compared reference transcripts to RUSA's (2013) "Guidelines for Behavioral Performance of Reference and Information Service Providers" to see whether the librarians engaged in the recommended behaviors. Among other things, these studies have looked at whether the librarian offered a friendly greeting at the beginning of the transaction, whether they used jargon or technical terminology that might have confused the patron, and whether the librarian maintained a professional yet friendly tone (Maness, Naper, and Chaudhuri 2009; Zhou et al. 2006). In a different approach, Joanne B. Smyth and James C. MacKenzie (2006) analyzed chat reference transcripts against satisfaction surveys that users submitted upon completing a reference transaction. Comparing the two documents allowed the researchers to see what aspects of the reference transaction might influence the patron's satisfaction.

Some studies have used a review of virtual reference transcripts to improve staffing for this service (Dempsey 2017; Mungin 2017). Paula Dempsey (2017) suggests that staffing models and policies around virtual reference can impact the range of resources the librarian uses in answering questions and whether they offer instruction. Michael Mungin (2017) also noticed that at certain times librarians staffing the virtual reference service did not engage in a thorough reference interview, and this practice was associated with negative outcomes. These reviews can also examine elements such as whether the librarian is engaging in a reference interview to uncover the full information need, whether they engage in any instruction, and whether they cite sources when providing answers.

While chat reference transcripts appear to be useful assessment tools, it is important to remember that they might contain personally identifying information about patrons and/or librarians. The transcript might automatically insert the person's name as they type, or the people involved might identify themselves within the body of the conversation. In order to protect the privacy and confidentiality of anyone involved, it is good practice to anonymize transcripts before reviewing them by removing names or any other personal information first. This is important not only to protect patron privacy but also to reinforce the idea for staff that the purpose of the review is not to target individual staff members, but to look at and improve the service as a whole. Box 8.4 provides a sample chat reference transcript for analysis. Box 8.5 concludes this section on methods by providing a research scenario with reflective questions.

Box 8.4 Activity: Transcript Analysis

The following is an excerpt from a chat reference transaction. Read through and critique it, keeping the reference interview and the RUSA (2013) "Guidelines for Behavioral Performance of Reference and Information Service Providers" in mind. Does the librarian convey a welcoming tone and interest in the question? Do they ask good follow-up questions to clarify the patron's need? Are there additional questions they could have asked? How well do they seem to answer the patron's question? Do they provide a good closure to the interview?

Patron: Hi I'm looking for information for books on minerals and rocks for elementary school kids.

Librarian: Hello! Thanks for using reference chat! Let me take a minute to look through some of our resources, and I'll let you know what I find.

Patron: Thanks! That sounds great.

Librarian: I found some books that might be of interest to you. If you go to the library home page and then click on "Research & Resources," you can then browse the databases that we have. From there you can select "Children's Core Collection" from the Library and Information Science drop-down menu. Doing a keyword search for minerals and rocks will give you many results for books on the subject for elementary school kids. Unfortunately, it doesn't seem that the library owns very many of these. You can, however, request these materials through interlibrary loan. And that can be done by clicking "full-text" and then "request via interlibrary loan."

Patron: This sounds great, thank you. I'm also looking for lesson plans for students on how to identify rocks and minerals in the classroom. Are there any websites where I can find them?

Librarian: Sure. A good place to start might be the United States Geological Survey, or USGS, which has a section of resources for teachers. Here's the direct link: http://education.usgs.gov/. From there you can search educational resources for grades 3–5, with a link for geology where there's a section on Rocks and Minerals. Here's an example of one Web resource that includes a lesson plan, called Schoolyard Geology: https://www.usgs.gov/science-support/osqi/yes/resources-teachers/school-yard-geology.

Patron: This is fantastic. Thank you for your help.

Librarian: You're very welcome. Are there any other resources you're looking for?

Patron: Thank you very much, I think I got everything I needed!

Librarian: Excellent! Glad I could help.

Box 8.5 Activity: Patron Satisfaction

A library has just conducted a satisfaction survey, and the results show that patrons are not as satisfied with reference services as the staff would like them to be. When asked to rate their satisfaction with the service they receive at the reference desk, with 1 being poor and 5 being excellent, the mean response was 3.5, and the mode, or most common response, was 3. The library director has asked the head of the reference department to do some follow-up to discover more about the reasons why patrons are less than satisfied.

Questions for Reflection and Discussion:

1. What methods could be used to study reference transactions, and why? Identify three or four questions that could be used to guide your study.

CONTINUOUS EVALUATION

It is important to remember that the purpose of evaluation and assessment research is to take action. For instance, if a transcript review of chat reference services reveals that librarians seem to be missing opportunities to offer instruction during the interactions, the department head could develop a training session to help them integrate more instruction. The focus should always be on taking steps to continually improve services, not to target and take action against individuals (staff training and other efforts to improve reference services are discussed in more detail in Chapter 9). Each time a new decision, project, or service is implemented, the librarians should set new goals and then begin the assessment process again.

Another aspect of closing the assessment loop is to share the results of studies with others. Because assessment is tied to improvement, and because the data from assessment studies can be evidence of the library's value to the community, it is wise to share assessment results with stakeholders such as city managers, deans, provosts, or others who have oversight of the library. Sharing results shows that the library takes feedback seriously and could encourage more participation in future studies. Finally, librarians should consider sharing results with colleagues in other institutions so that they can learn from each other's experiences.

A CULTURE OF ASSESSMENT

Libraries continue to face greater competition from other information providers and increased scrutiny from stakeholders. Assessment and evaluation of services like reference allow librarians to generate evidence and demonstrate their value to their communities. Assessment and evaluation are also critical for checking progress toward goals, informing decisions, and continuously improving services. Given the importance of these activities, it is crucial that librarians develop a culture of assessment, making evaluation and assessment an integral part of everything they do. This means that responsibility for assessment should be a part of all job descriptions. Library directors and managers should model behavior by stressing the importance of assessment activities and by providing staff with the resources they need to engage in assessment. Reference services should be assessed regularly, and any new programs or initiatives should be developed with a plan for assessment. With such an organization-wide commitment, librarians can ensure that their services are of high quality and their patrons will continue to be satisfied.

REFERENCES

Amazon. http://www.amazon.com.

American Library Association. http://www.ala.org.

American Library Association. Office for Research and Evaluation. http://www.ala.org/aboutala/offices/ore.

Association of College & Research Libraries. http://www.ala.org/acrl/.

Association of College & Research Libraries. n.d. "Assessment in Action." http://www.ala.org/acrl/AiA.

Backs, Stephen M., and Tim Kinder. 2007. "Secret Shopping at the Monroe County Public Library." *Indiana Libraries* 26: 17–19.

Bannock, Graham, Evan Davis, Paul Trott, and Mark Uncles. 2003. "Perceived Service Quality." *The New Penguin Business Dictionary*. London, UK: Penguin.

Battley, Belinda, and Alicia Wright. 2012. "Finding and Addressing the Gaps: Two Evaluations of Archival Reference Services." *Journal of Archival Organization* 10 (2): 107.

Becker, Danielle Andre, Ingrid Bonadie-Joseph, and Jonathan Cain. 2013. "Developing and Completing a Mobile Technology Survey to Create a User-Centered Mobile Presence." *Library Hi Tech* 31: 688–99.

Bonnet, Jennifer L., and Benjamin McAlexander. 2013. "First Impressions and the Reference Encounter: The Influence of Affect and Clothing on Librarian Approachability." *The Journal of Academic Librarianship* 39: 335–46.

Butler, Kathy, and Jason Bird. 2016. "Research Consultation Assessment: Perceptions of Students and Librarians." *The Journal of Academic Librarianship* 42: 83–86.

Chow, Anthony S., and Rebecca A. Croxton. 2014. "A Usability Evaluation of Academic Virtual Reference Services." *College & Research Libraries* 75: 309–61.

CILIP: Chartered Institute of Library and Information Professionals. 2011. "Kent Libraries and Archives." YouTube video, 3:08. June 8, 2019. http://www.youtube.com/watch?v=f69sfZXEkZs.

Connaway, Lynn Silipigni. 2014. "Why Libraries? A Call for User-Centered Assessment." *BiD* 32: 1–4.

Connaway, Lynn Silipigni, and Marie L. Radford. 2010. "Virtual Reference Service Quality: Critical Components for Adults and the Net Generation." *LIBRI: International Journal of Libraries & Information Services* 60: 165–80.

Cordell, Roseanne M., and Linda F. Fisher. 2010. "Reference Questions as an Authentic Assessment of Information Literacy." *Reference Services Review* 38: 474–81.

Cortés-Villalba, Carmina, Isidoro Gil-Leiva, and Miguel Ángel Artacho-Ramírez. 2017. "Emotional Design Application to Evaluate User Impressions of Library Information Desks." *Library and Information Science Research* 39: 311–18.

Counting Opinions. http://www.countingopinions.com.

Crumley, Ellen, and Denise Koufogiannakis. 2002. "Developing Evidence-Based Librarianship: Practical Steps for Implementation." *Health Information & Libraries Journal* 19: 61–70.

Del Bosque, Darcy, Rosan Mitola, Susie Skarl, and Shelley Heaton. 2017. "Beyond Awareness: Improving Outreach and Marketing through User Surveys." *Reference Services Review* 45 (1): 4–17.

Dempsey, Paula R. 2017. "Resource Delivery and Teaching in Live Chat Reference: Comparing Two Libraries." *College & Research Libraries* 78 (7): 898–919.

Dewdney, Patricia, and Catherine Sheldrick Ross. 1994. "Flying a Light Aircraft: Reference Service Evaluation from a User's Viewpoint." *RQ* 34: 217–30.

Dixon, Matthew, Karen Freeman, and Nicholas Toman. 2010. "Stop Trying to Delight Your Customers." *Harvard Business Review* 88: 116–22.

Dresselhaus, Angela, and Flora Shrode. 2012. "Mobile Technologies and Academics: Do Students Use Mobile Technologies in their Academic Lives and Are Librarians Ready to Meet This Challenge?" *Information Technology and Libraries* 31: 82–101.

Dugan, Robert E., and Peter Hernon. 2002. "Outcomes Assessment: Not Synonymous with Inputs and Outputs." *The Journal of Academic Librarianship* 28: 376–80.

Duncan, Vicky, and Darlene M. Fitcher. 2004. "What Words and Where? Applying Usability Testing Techniques to Name a New Live Reference Service." *Journal of the Medical Library Association* 92: 218–25.

Durrance, Joan. 1989. "Reference Success: Does the 55 Percent Rule Tell the Whole Story?" *Library Journal* 114 (April 15): 31–36.

Estep, Meredith. 2011. "New Survey Shows Unhappy Customers Spread the Word." *Intelligent Help Desk* (blog), *Unitiv*. May 16, 2019. https://web.archive.org/web/20111201142235/http://www.unitiv.com/intelligent-help-desk-blog/bid/64134/New-Survey-Shows-Unhappy-Customers-Spread-the-Word.

Fitzpatrick, Elizabeth B., Anne C. Moore, and Beth W. Lang. 2008. "Reference Librarians at the Reference Desk in a Learning Commons: A Mixed Methods Evaluation." *The Journal of Academic Librarianship* 34: 231–38.

Ganshorn, Heather. 2009. "A Librarian Consultation Service Improves Decision-Making and Saves Time for Primary Care Practitioners." *Evidence Based Library & Information Practice* 4: 148–51.

Google. http://www.google.com.

Granfield, Diane, and Mark Robertson. 2008. "Preference for Reference: New Options and Choices for Academic Library Users." *Reference & User Services Quarterly* 48: 44–53.

Greenwood, Judy T., Alex P. Watson, and Melissa Dennis. 2011. "Ten Years of LibQUAL: A Study of Qualitative and Quantitative Survey Results at the University of Mississippi 2001–2010." *The Journal of Academic Librarianship* 37: 312–18.

Gremmels, Gillian S., and Karen Shostrom Lehmann. 2007. "Assessment of Student Learning from Reference Service." *College & Research Libraries* 68: 488–501.

Head, Alison J. 2013. "Learning the Ropes: How Freshman Conduct Research Once They Enter College." Project Information Literacy. Last modified December 5, 2013. https://www.projectinfolit.org/uploads/2/7/5/4/27541717/pil_2013_freshmenstudy_fullreportv2.pdf.

Hernon, Peter, and Ellen Altman. 1996. *Service Quality in Academic Libraries*. Norwood, NJ: Ablex Publishing.

Hernon, Peter, Robert E. Dugan, and Danuta Nitecki. 2011. *Engaging in Evaluation and Assessment Research*. Santa Barbara, CA: Libraries Unlimited.

Hernon, Peter, and Charles R. McClure. 1986. "Unobtrusive Reference Testing: The 55 Percent Rule." *Library Journal* 111 (April 15): 37–41.

Hernon, Peter, and Candy Schwartz. 2012. "The Assessment Craze." *Library & Information Science Research* 34: 79.

Institute of Museum and Library Services. n.d.-a "Data Catalog." Institute of Museum and Library Services. https://www.imls.gov/research-tools/data-collection.

Institute of Museum and Library Services. n.d.-b "Outcome Based Evaluation: Basics." Institute of Museum and Library Services. https://www.imls.gov/grants/outcome-based-evaluation/basics.

Integrated Postsecondary Education Data System. National Center for Education Statistics. https://nces.ed.gov/ipeds/.

Jacoby, JoAnn, David Ward, Susan Avery, and Emilia Marcyk. 2016. "The Value of Chat Reference Services: A Pilot Study." *portal: Libraries and the Academy* 16: 109–29.

Jankal, Radoslav, and Miriam Jankalova. 2011. "Mystery Shopping: The Tool of Employee Communication Skills Evaluation." *Business: Theory and Practice* 12: 45–49.

Kelly, Betsy, Claire Hamasu, and Barbara Jones. 2012. "Applying Return on Investment (ROI) in Libraries." *Journal of Library Administration* 52: 656–71.

Kingma, Bruce, and Kathleen McClure. 2015. "Lib-Value: Values, Outcomes, and Return on Investment of Academic Libraries, Phase III: ROI of the Syracuse University Library." *College & Research Libraries* 76 (1): 63–80.

Kocevar-Weidinger, Elizabeth, Candice Benjes-Small, Eric Ackermann, and Virginia R. Kinman. 2010. "Why and How to Mystery Shop Your Reference Desk." *Reference Services Review* 38: 28–43.

Lankes, R. David, Melissa Gross, and Charles R. McClure. 2003. "Cost, Statistics, Measures, and Standards for Digital Reference Services: A Preliminary View." *Library Trends* 51: 401–13.

Lewis, Robert C., and Bernard H. Booms. 1983. "The Marketing Aspects of Service Quality." In *Emerging Perspectives on Services Marketing*, edited by G. Lynn Shostack, Leonard L. Berry, and Gregory D. Upah, 99–107. Chicago: American Marketing Association.

Liamputtong, Pranee. 2011. *Focus Group Methodology: Principles and Practice*. Thousand Oaks, CA: Sage Publications.

LibQual+®. https://www.libqual.org/home.

Library Assessment Conference. https://libraryassessment.org/.

Maness, Jack M., Sarah Naper, and Jayati Chaudhuri. 2009. "The Good, the Bad, but Mostly the Ugly: Adherence to RUSA Guidelines during Encounters with Inappropriate Behavior Online." *Reference & User Services Quarterly* 49: 151–62.

Martell, Charles. 2008. "The Absent User: Physical Use of Academic Library Collections and Services Continues to Decline 1995–2006." *The Journal of Academic Librarianship* 34: 400–407.

Massey-Burzio, Virginia. 1998. "From the Other Side of the Reference Desk: A Focus Group Study." *The Journal of Academic Librarianship* 24: 208–15.

Mokhtari, Heidi. 2014. "A Quantitative Survey on the Influence of Students' Epistemic Beliefs on Their General Information Seeking Behavior." *The Journal of Academic Librarianship* 40: 259–63.

Murfin, Marjorie E., and Gary M. Gugelchuk. 1987. "Development and Testing of a Reference Transaction Assessment Instrument." *College and Research Libraries* 48 (4): 314–39.

Mungin, Michael. 2017. "Stats Don't Tell the Whole Story: Using Qualitative Data Analysis of Chat Reference Transcripts to Assess and Improve Services." *Journal of Library & Information Services in Distance Learning* 11 (1): 25–36.

Naylor, Sharon, Bruce Stoffel, and Sharon Van der Laan. 2008. "Why Isn't Our Chat Reference Used More? Findings of Focus Group Discussions with Undergraduate Students." *Reference & User Services Quarterly* 47: 342–54.

Novotny, Eric, and Emily Rimland. 2007. "Using the Wisconsin-Ohio Reference Evaluation Program (WOREP) to Improve Training and Reference Services." *The Journal of Academic Librarianship* 33: 382–92.

Oakleaf, Megan. 2009. "The Information Literacy Instruction Assessment Cycle: A Guide for Increasing Student Learning and Improving Librarian Instructional Skills." *Journal of Documentation* 65: 539–60.

Oakleaf, Megan. 2010. *The Value of Academic Libraries: A Comprehensive Research Review and Report*. Chicago: Association of College & Research Libraries.

Oakleaf, Megan, and Amy VanScoy. 2010. "Instructional Strategies for Virtual Reference: Methods to Facilitate Student Learning." *Reference & User Services Quarterly* 49: 380–90.

O'Neill, Kimberly L., and Brooke A. Guilfoyle. 2015. "Sign, Sign, Everywhere a Sign: What Does 'Reference' Mean to Academic Library Users?" *The Journal of Academic Librarianship* 41: 386–93.

Owen, Victoria. 2010. "Trialling a Service Model of the Future: Mobile Technologies in Student Support." *Multimedia Information & Technology* 26: 26–27.

Parasuraman, A., Valarie A. Zeithaml, and Leonard L. Berry. 1988. "SERVQUAL: A Multiple-Item Scale for Measuring Consumer Perceptions of Service Quality." *Journal of Retailing* 64: 12–40.

Pass, Christopher, Bryan Lowes, Andrew Pendleton, Malcolm Afferson, and Daragh O'Reilly, eds. 2006. "Quality." In *Collins Dictionary of Business*. London: Collins.

Passanneau, Sarah, and Dan Coffey. 2011. "The Role of Synchronous Virtual Reference in Teaching and Learning: A Grounded Theory Analysis of Instant Messaging Transcripts." *College & Research Libraries* 72: 276–94.

Pomerantz, Jeffrey, Lili Luo, and Charles R. McClure. 2006. "Peer Review of Chat Reference Transcripts: Approaches and Strategies." *Library and Information Science Research* 28: 24–48.

Profeta, Patricia C. 2006. "Effectiveness of Asynchronous Reference Services for Distance Learning Students within Florida's Community College System." *Community & Junior College Libraries* 14: 35–61.

Public Library Association. http://www.ala.org/pla/.

Radford, Marie L. 1996. "Communication Theory Applied to the Reference Encounter: An Analysis of Critical Incidents." *The Library Quarterly* 66: 123–37.

Radford, Marie L. 1999. *The Reference Encounter: Interpersonal Communication in the Academic Library*. Chicago: Association of College & Research Libraries.

Radford, Marie L., and Lynn Silipigni Connaway. 2013. "Not Dead Yet! A Longitudinal Study of Query Type and Ready Reference Accuracy in Live Chat and IM Reference." *Library and Information Science Research* 35: 2–13.

Reference and User Services Association. 2013. "Guidelines for Behavioral Performance of Reference and Information Service Providers." American Library Association. Last modified May 28, 2013. http://www.ala.org/rusa/resources/guidelines/guidelinesbehavioral.

Ryan, Pam. 2006. "EBL and Library Assessment: Two Solitudes?" *Evidence Based Library and Information Practice* 1 (4): 77–80. http://ejournals.library.ualberta.ca/index.php/EBLIP/article/view/136/177.

Saunders, Laura. 2016. "Teaching the Reference Interview through Practice-Based Assignments." *Reference Services Review* 44: 390–410.

Smyth, Joanne B., and James C. MacKenzie. 2006. "Comparing Virtual Reference Exit Survey Results and Transcript Analysis: A Model for Service Evaluation." *Public Services Quarterly* 2: 85–99.

Starr, Susan. 2014. "Moving from Evaluation to Assessment." *Journal of the Medical Library Association* 102: 227–29.

Taddeo, Laura, and Jill M. Hackenberg. 2006. "The Nuts, Bolts, and Teaching Opportunities of Real-Time Reference." *College & Undergraduate Libraries* 13: 63–85.

Usability.gov. 2015a. "Glossary." http://www.usability.gov/what-and-why/glossary/u/index.html.

Usability.gov. 2015b. "Usability Evaluation Basics." http://www.usability.gov/what-and-why/usability-evaluation.html.

Vileno, Luigina. 2010. "Testing the Usability of Two Online Research Guides." *Partnership: The Canadian Journal of Library and Information Practice & Research* 5: 1–21.

Weightman, Alison L., and Jane Williamson. 2005. "The Value and Impact of Information Provided through Library Services for Patient Care: A Systematic Review." *Health Information & Libraries Journal* 22 (1): 4–25.

Zhou, Fu, Mark Love, Scott Norwood, and Karla Massia. 2006. "Applying RUSA Guidelines in the Analysis of Chat Reference Transcripts." *College & Undergraduate Libraries* 13: 75–88.

Zorica, Mihaela Banek, Tomislav Ivanjko, and Sonja Spiranec. 2014. "Mystery Shopping in Libraries—Are We Ready?" *Qualitative & Quantitative Methods in Libraries* 2: 433–42.

SUGGESTED READINGS

Connaway, Lynn Silipigni, and Marie Radford. 2017. *Research Methods in Library and Information Science.* 6th ed. Santa Barbara, CA: Libraries Unlimited.

This is a thorough overview of basic research methods, clearly tailored for librarians. While it includes some sections on qualitative and historical research, the primary focus is on quantitative methods, including survey research and experiment design. It also includes a section on applied research that includes topics like Delphi studies, bibliometrics, action, and evaluation research. This book includes sections on statistical analysis, writing up results, and publishing research.

Hernon, Peter, Robert E. Dugan, and Joseph R. Matthews. 2013. *Getting Started with Evaluation.* Royersford, PA: Alpha Publication House.

Getting Started with Evaluation is a practical guide emphasizing evidence-based practice and the use of evaluation data for decision-making and planning purposes as well as continuous improvement. The volume addresses stakeholder perspectives and the development and definition of library metrics for gathering data. Separate chapters are devoted to satisfaction, service quality, and return-on-investment studies.

Matthews, Joseph R. 2017. *Library Assessment in Higher Education.* 2nd ed. Santa Barbara, CA: Libraries Unlimited.

With a focus on academic libraries, Matthews organizes his book around areas of library impact, including impact on student learning, retention, teaching, and the research environment. For each area, he provides overviews of metrics and examples of how these metrics have been measured, drawing on specific examples from across higher education. Less of a step-by-step guide, this book offers a broad overview of the assessment landscape in academic libraries, encouraging practitioners to develop their own culture of assessment.

Pickard, Alison Jane. 2013. *Research Methods in Information* Chicago: Neal-Schuman.

Pickard offers a solid and broad overview of various research methods with a focus on application in the information professions. She includes approaches to the research process, such as formulating questions and crafting research proposals, as well as attention to a range of data collection tools and instruments such as case studies, Delphi method, and ethnography, and sections on quantitative and qualitative data analysis. This handbook also includes chapters on using existing external data sets and managing research data.

Chapter 9

Training and Professional Development

Piper Martin and
Lisa Janicke Hinchliffe

INTRODUCTION

Every reference librarian has a wealth of knowledge and skills that they bring to bear in their daily work. Some of this is procedural knowledge enacted on a daily basis, such as logging in to the network, searching for a known item, or making a referral. Other knowledge is used less often but is a deep reservoir that can be drawn upon relevant to the particular reference inquiry or tool at hand. Over time, these reserves of knowledge and skills are built up and honed into advanced expertise.

Training is the organizational function that provides for the systematic and intentional development of knowledge and skills. Designing a training program requires assessing employees' existing skills and abilities, identifying gaps between what exists and what is needed to perform a job, and creating learning opportunities that address those gaps. In addition, a training and development program will include opportunities for employees to shape their career trajectories by targeting competencies in areas of leadership and management or specialized technologies that are typically not entry-level responsibilities.

This chapter provides an overview of the components of a reference training program; describes how training connects and aligns with human resources processes; and introduces basic concepts in designing, delivering, and evaluating training.

STRUCTURE OF A TRAINING PROGRAM

A training and development program is comprised of a number of different components, each of which has a distinct purpose. Typical aspects of a training program include orientation, development of job skills, and continual learning. Though different in their focus, the content of each component is likely to be interrelated and at least somewhat overlapping or repeated. For example, early training during orientation might introduce a topic, whereas later training would go more in depth into the topic. Being aware of the goals and purposes of the different components of a training program will help employees benefit from each kind of training.

Orientation and Onboarding

Libraries of all types should have an orientation process for new employees, and for those with public services responsibilities, reference will likely comprise a large part of the orientation. While models and approaches to reference have expanded recently (see Chapter 6), every library will have guidelines for how to answer patron questions. During the onboarding process, new staff will learn about the reference policies and procedures as well as about the organization's culture, practices, and goals.

"Onboarding" refers to the ongoing process of introducing a new employee to the organization (Bauer 2010, 1). There may be an event sponsored by the larger organization of which the library is a part (e.g., a college, school district, or city) called new employee orientation that offers information on benefits options, vacation and sick leave, tax withholding, and other things common to nearly any place of employment. Onboarding covers the longer process of learning how the organization operates and how the new hire's work and position fit within and contribute to their unit and the organization's mission and vision. Generally, onboarding is coordinated by a supervisor, who may use a checklist for things such as how to access departmental network drives, where to pick up keys, how to report leave, work hour expectations, and similar information (Morgan 2009, 45). The checklist may also include more in-depth, organization-specific items, such as chat reference philosophy, scope of reference services, and customer-service priorities (see Box 9.1).

The onboarding coordinator may schedule meetings with other people in the organization for the new employee. Early stages of the onboarding process might also include meetings with department members, tours of other libraries (if the library is one of several in a system or campus), introductions to staff members in other relevant departments, discussions of reference and service philosophies more generally, and scheduled reflection and processing time for the new employee to absorb all of the information. In order for the onboarding to be both effective and efficient, procedures should be led by someone with experience in the organization and should not be left for the new employee to figure out for themselves.

Box 9.1 Example Orientation Checklist

Though each library will have a unique orientation checklist reflecting the particulars of that organization, this is an example of the kind of items a new reference employee can expect to see on such a list.

On the first day:

- Keys
- Parking
- Office/desk
- Supplies
- Schedule
- Timecard
- Library tour

In the first week:

- Benefits
- Job duties and expectations
- Computer, network, and library platforms logins
- Equipment operation
- Telephone system
- Reference policies
- Organization chart

In the first month:

- Departmental logins and passwords
- Keeping statistics
- Opening and closing procedures
- Ongoing policy review
- Handling user complaints
- Performance evaluation process
- Governance and decision-making processes

Policies and Procedures

Every library will have some policies and procedures that govern the reference service. For information services or library systems that are complex, especially those providing virtual reference services from the in-person service point, there will likely be a greater number and range of policies. Typical policies and procedures may include emergency preparedness, expectations and timelines for scheduling, how to answer e-mail or chat reference questions, how to prioritize service, how to track questions, and how to use chat software. Frequently, the library will have a Web page that collocates links to all of the policies, including reference policies; alternatively, there may be a reference landing page, blog, or wiki that pulls together all of the reference-related policies and procedures. If there is a physical service point, the library will also have policies and procedures on opening and closing the space; what to do if someone calls in sick or does not show up for their shift; and how to interact with challenging patrons, unattended children, and the like. New employees should be taught how to use the telephone system and chat software and have a chance to try them out in a low-stakes training environment. Additionally, new employees should have the opportunity to shadow at the reference desk or during roving reference, sit in on one-on-one reference/research consultations, or work many of their shifts with an experienced mentor who can model appropriate behavior and explain application of general policies. Watching and learning from colleagues helps the new employee understand how the text of the policies and procedures is enacted on a day-to-day basis with a range of different patrons and situations. This observation and mentoring also reveals the culture of the library and how it puts its values into practice.

Organizational Culture and Practice

Learning the library's culture is an ongoing part of the onboarding process; in fact, the culture may take new employees more than a year to fully understand, especially if the library is a part of a larger institution such as a public library system, a university, or a state-wide consortium. In the reference context, some of the cultural values may be imbued in the text of policies, guidelines, or philosophies (e.g., is there a philosophy outlined for how to answer e-mail or chat reference questions?) and the way in which staff members interact with patrons. If there is a policy on the priority of in-person patrons over chat or e-mail, that also reflects organizational priority. Reading chat transcripts or completed e-mail questions can give potential insight into the organization's values and how they are put into practice. Supervisors and other colleagues should discuss the values and culture and allow for the new employee to ask clarifying questions as they acculturate themselves to the environment.

Job-Specific Skills

In addition to the more general orientation and reference training described earlier, each position will have job-specific skills that require development. These job skills will be articulated in job descriptions and should be updated each year as the employee, in consultation with a supervisor or advisory committee, devises new performance goals and objectives. These job-specific skills should be introduced during the orientation and reinforced during training. A combination of ongoing feedback, one-on-one meetings, and more formal performance reviews provides opportunities to ensure maintenance of the skills needed for individual positions. Reviews and one-on-one meetings should also be a time to outline aspirations for future skills acquisition to prepare the employee for greater responsibility and knowledge.

The position announcement and job description are guidance for the areas of training and development for the person in that job. In most cases, library employees whose job duties include reference will also have a range of other responsibilities (e.g., collection development or instruction), so reference training will be potentially one of a number of other training streams (Johnson 2019, 92). It is rare that a new hire will possess all of the skills and knowledge in a given job description, so some assessment of training needs may take place in order to decide training priorities. For example, while all employees who work on the reference desk should be conversant with general business resources, the business subject specialist will need to be aware of the specialty resources that are used by faculty and students in the business school. Assessments could include a brief survey, guided reflection, or conversation between the trainer and new employee to determine gaps in knowledge. Based on the results of the assessment of a new hire's existing skills, as well as a review of the job description, more personalized training procedures, goals, and objectives can be developed. The goals and objectives should be a set of clear, written performance standards so that the employee and the supervisor will know when the employee has achieved or surpassed them (Stewart, Washington-Hoagland, and Zsulya 2013, 33). As mentioned earlier, these goals will change each year as the employee masters certain skills, gains new and deeper knowledge, and begins to understand what areas of the position they would like to develop and grow.

Career Growth

Well-managed and developed training programs should not only provide opportunities for ongoing training and continual learning for employees' current jobs but also expose them to aspects of librarianship that will prepare them for the next step in their careers. This could take a number of forms, from librarians in leadership positions offering workshops on supervising or managing people to outside experts offering advanced training on cutting-edge topics in librarianship and group viewings and discussions of streaming webinar series about moving into leadership roles. Training coordinators may design sessions where newer employees can analyze their existing skills and proficiencies, reflect upon where they would like to be in the future, and brainstorm potential training and development strategies that will get them there. In this way the employees have a hand in shaping the content of the training. Box 9.2 provides an opportunity to reflect on professional development for both job-specific skills and career growth.

Box 9.2 Activity: Reflecting on Professional Development Goals

How might you, early in your career, balance acquiring skills for your current job with gaining experience for your future? As a strategy, identify two job skills you need now and two that you think would help you advance your career. How might you pursue training for each of these areas of development?

Continual On-the-Job Learning

Reference librarianship is not exempt from the fast pace of change that is observed elsewhere in today's society. New technologies, evolving expectations of users, innovations in reference models or services, and other changes necessitate continual learning that does not have a specific end. Since libraries advocate for and help patrons achieve lifelong learning, it is appropriate that library employees, as knowledge workers, also engage in ongoing learning that pushes the boundaries of existing knowledge and skills.

Efficiency and Effectiveness

Reference service is often provided at a reference desk or other frontline service point. In order to respect users' time and instill confidence that the answer is correct, staff must be ready to answer any kind of reference or research question in any format (e.g., in person, phone, chat, e-mail) in an effective and efficient manner and perform any other duties required at the service point. It may seem that working several public service shifts a week would be sufficient to practice such skills, but it is easy for certain routines to become stale and to be performed perfunctorily. Even seasoned professionals can learn from ongoing training opportunities how to better deal with different kinds of patrons, how to teach or listen more effectively, or how to more proficiently balance the competing demands of a busy reference desk.

Building the Knowledge Base

Graduate schools of library and information science offer reference courses, but even the most comprehensive course will not prepare a new employee to know exactly which source to use depending on a given question and the particular reference collection of that library. In addition, library and reference collections today are less uniform and may be constantly in flux, as online resources are subscribed to or canceled depending on budget and patron needs. Further, many public and academic libraries are digitizing or promoting unique local collections that all staff should know and be able to use. All this is to say that it is necessary for staff to learn what resources are in the reference collection at their library, be fluent in using the resources, and understand what reference or research questions those resources can best answer.

It used to be common, both in reference courses and in training of new employees, to have a list of questions that those new to working in reference would have to answer using the appropriate resource. Since the Internet has lessened the need for most people to contact the library for such ready-reference questions as current population, what year a movie debuted, and crime statistics, the questions patrons do ask have become more complex and nuanced. Continuous learning for resources should include regularly scheduled sessions on newly acquired databases, electronic encyclopedias or dictionaries, and print sources as well as online reference resources that are freely available. In order to engage employees, many libraries may solicit actual questions that staff members have received, allow staff members to lead their colleagues through the process of answering the question, and create script responses (Todaro and Smith 2006, 51). Larger academic libraries may have so many new staff or student employees each year that they schedule set training sessions on resources and tools, such as chat reference software, each semester. Large public library systems will also likely offer regularly scheduled sessions on core training topics. Chat transcript reviews can also be used to unobtrusively analyze how reference questions were answered (Ward 2003, 48) and to suggest questions that might be used for practice during training. Box 9.3 provides an opportunity to practice how real-world questions can be used for training purposes.

Box 9.3 Activity: Sample Reference Questions Practice

Librarians often use real-world questions like the following to design reference training. Imagine you are a reference department manager. How could you design a reference training program with these questions? What skills or behaviors could your trainees develop as they interact with these questions? Specifically, how would you prompt trainees to explore questions they might ask to clarify the user's information need and determine what steps to take to answer these questions?

- "I'm writing an argumentative paper (that's what my instructor told us). I need to find articles by experts about the pros and cons of pot legalization. Can you help me?"
- "Hi, I'm researching my family, and I found a branch has members who lived in your county. How can I get birth and death records for my family members?"
- "The library website says that I should be able to get the full text of this article that I need. But when I click on the link, I get an error message. What is going on?"
- "I need an image from a book in your special collections library to use in my article. What do I need to do to get a copy and reproduce that image?"

Professional Development and Engagement

Joining local, statewide, or national professional associations can be one of the most important ways to participate in ongoing training and development. For many libraries, funding travel to national conferences is increasingly out of budgetary reach, but more accessible opportunities abound. Regional or statewide chapters of the American Library Association and Special Library Association, as well as state, local, specialty, and other professional associations, offer training, conferences, networking, and educational experiences with reasonable travel and registration fees. If a library is a member of one of the associations, webinars and online classes are often offered at a discounted rate. Even serving on national committees, which once required meeting in person at conferences, has often changed to online-only meetings in an attempt to lower barriers for participation and to include a plurality of voices. New employees should expect to know what kind of professional development and engagement support and programs their library provides, and all of these opportunities should be advertised and compiled by the training program coordinator. The offerings of the Reference and User Services Association (RUSA), a division of the American Library Association, have particular relevance for reference work.

Reference positions vary widely, and different jobs have diverging professional development expectations for their employees. In addition to being aware of RUSA as a general resource, every individual should have the chance to explore and develop their own self-directed learning plan, which should reflect their job description and related responsibilities as well as their interests and aspirations. More details of how librarians may do this will be covered in later sections of this chapter, but examining the job skills and description mentioned earlier, figuring out aspects that may need more development or attention, and then calculating what needs to be learned to bridge the gap will be essential in self-directed development. Along these same lines, the development of annual goals should guide what professional development opportunities are most appropriate, and talking with colleagues who are currently engaged in various associations is enormously beneficial for librarians trying to decide where to direct their energies and engagement.

While individual learning is important, it needs also to impact the overall organizational performance in order to have a long-range benefit. As Catherine Hakala-Ausperk (2013, 121) writes, libraries should aspire to become learning organizations, that is, workplaces committed to growing the talents and skills of their employees. Although a particular individual may become an expert in a specific area, if that information and expertise are not shared with the organization, the organization will lose that valuable expertise when the individual leaves. Training coordinators should be aware of what departments or units have staff members with unique skills in order to offer those individuals an opportunity to share their skills with more people in the organization. For example, if someone in reference has a government documents focus, they should have multiple venues for sharing this knowledge so that it is not concentrated in one person alone. Ideally this knowledge would be taught in face-to-face training sessions that are recorded for employees who cannot attend or for future viewing. Best practices for design and delivery of such sessions will be covered in later sections of this chapter.

Organizations can also help employees orient themselves to the myriad professional associations referred to earlier. Those who are new to a particular library should investigate options online and talk to colleagues or mentors, but the library in which they are employed should also provide informational sessions about each association, its features, and include personal testimonies from colleagues who have served on committees or task forces.

DESIGNING AND DELIVERING TRAINING

Training programs must be carefully designed to meet the needs of a given library and its employees in order to be effective. In some cases, training can be provided by sending library employees to workshops and seminars or having them do training online. In other cases, a library may choose to develop internal training programs. As such, this chapter now turns to considerations in designing and delivering training programs.

Effective training program development includes needs assessment, identifying goals and objectives, instructional design, training delivery, and evaluation. Though an entry-level reference librarian is not likely to be tasked with responsibility for managing an overall training program, understanding how a training program is conceptualized will be useful as a new employee may be asked to lead a session sharing their expertise in a particular topic.

Needs Assessment

Determining the initial and ongoing needs that employees have for training is crucial to ensuring that the training program is appropriate to the trainees and responsive to the library's priorities and practices. In essence, a needs assessment is the process of determining what gaps exist between employees' existing knowledge and skills and the needed knowledge and skills to be effective in their jobs. Needs assessment must be ongoing to respond to changes in user groups, information structures, and resources, likely on a one- to three-year cycle depending on the complexity and size of the organization. Needs assessment will also seek to identify the aspirational knowledge and skills employees seek to develop with respect to long-term career development and succession planning. Strategies for conducting a needs assessment are numerous, including literature reviews, surveys, observations, and testing. The Suggested Readings section of this chapter includes a number of books that provide generalized outlines of library training programs.

A reference training program can also draw on various professional competency standards. The American Library Association's (2009, 3–4) "Core Competences of Librarianship" includes a section on reference and user services that provides a high-level description of the knowledge and skills central to this area of librarianship:

5. Reference and User Services

- 5A. The concepts, principles, and techniques of reference and user services that provide access to relevant and accurate recorded knowledge and information to individuals of all ages and groups.
- 5B. Techniques used to retrieve, evaluate, and synthesize information from diverse sources for use by individuals of all ages and groups.
- 5C. The methods used to interact successfully with individuals of all ages and groups to provide consultation, mediation, and guidance in their use of recorded knowledge and information.

5D. Information literacy/information competence techniques and methods, numerical literacy, and statistical literacy.
5E. The principles and methods of advocacy used to reach specific audiences to promote and explain concepts and services.
5F. The principles of assessment and response to diversity in user needs, user communities, and user preferences.
5G. The principles and methods used to assess the impact of current and emerging situations or circumstances on the design and implementation of appropriate services or resource development.

The RUSA used these competencies as the basis for articulating the specific knowledge and skills that reference practitioners should have in their "Professional Competencies for Reference and User Services Librarians" (2017). For example, please see the following:

5B. Evaluates, collects, retrieves, and synthesizes information from diverse sources

Identifies and presents highly recommended sources

1. Connects users to tools that can help them identify diverse sources of information
2. Connects users to highly recommended, carefully selected sources in many formats
3. Evaluates reference tools and sources for quality, relevance, authenticity, authority, and inclusiveness
4. Identifies any bias or point of view in an information resource
5. Creates useful research guides, web pages, bibliographies, finding aids, and other appropriate tools in areas of expertise
6. Compiles and maintains information about community resources
7. Develops programming, displays, tutorials, and other specialized instructional materials reflective of the cultural diversity of the primary community

RUSA has also promulgated the "Guidelines for Behavioral Performance of Reference and Information Service Providers" (2013), which details behavioral characteristics related to positive patron perceptions of reference service. The characteristics are grouped into five categories—visibility/approachability, interest, listening/inquiring, searching, and follow-up—and include considerations for both in-person and remote reference settings.

It is important to remember that listings of competencies typically intend to provide a comprehensive inventory of skills and abilities and so should be treated as a starting point for selecting training content and not as a checklist of everything that must be included. Surveying employees about their perceived training needs and input from supervisors about the training needs that they have observed will be very useful in developing a training program (see Box 9.4 for an activity using competencies for self-assessment). Competency statements can be the basis of such a survey. And, of course, the duties and responsibilities listed in reference job descriptions are particularly relevant for shaping the reference training program.

Box 9.4 Activity: Rate Your Competency and Improve

Select a competency from the RUSA list and rate your mastery of that competency on a scale from 1 to 5, with 1 being "unskilled in this area" and 5 being "highly skilled in this area." Consider how you could improve your competency in this area and what training might be useful for you. If you selected a competency for which you do not have much room for improvement, consider another one where you have greater room for growth and consider what training might be useful to you.

Prioritizing Needs and Sequencing Training

In addition to identifying gaps, needs assessment requires prioritizing and sequencing the order in which these discrepancies in knowledge and skills are addressed. Those things that are required to function as an employee in an organization are generally prioritized first in onboarding and orientation training. Job skills training and professional development topics are likely to be ongoing and should be prioritized based on what kinds of tasks are most commonly encountered in the position and whether others in the organization can be made responsible for a function until a new employee is trained.

In the best-case scenario, training needs are identified through an employee's annual performance review and professional development planning process. After onboarding and orientation, training to address employee performance deficits is likely to be a top priority. For example, if a library receives many reference questions related to health issues and a new employee is not familiar with *PubMed*, immediate training on the database would be warranted. Though not every performance deficit indicates a training need, many do, and providing needed employee training is the responsibility of library management (Saunders 2012, 399). Employee goals, especially those related to job responsibilities, are also a top priority for a training program. By having access to the training needs identified through the performance review process, the training coordinator can aggregate the needs across the reference unit and develop programs to meet those collective needs and recommend other resources in cases of needs that are unique and individual.

In addition to prioritization, sequencing of training is likely required. It is likely that in any given content area for training, there are skills and abilities that are prerequisites to developing other skills and abilities. For example, it will be necessary to learn the processes of logging in and navigating chat reference software before practicing answering questions using the software. The ebb and flow of reference work may also dictate sequencing and timing of content. Those new to working in an academic library will need to know about course reserves before the semester starts but can rely on referring questions of how to deposit doctoral theses in the library's institutional repository to colleagues as that is likely to be a rare question until the end of the semester as students finish their dissertations. Likewise, in a public library, annual training on federal and state tax forms and the library's policies on assisting users with these resources will likely be timed for December and January.

Finally, mandated training requirements will by their nature be high priority and their sequencing and timing likely externally dictated. Training requirements related to library records, confidentiality laws, sexual harassment prevention and reporting, and mandatory child abuse reporting are just some examples of training that may be mandatory for library employees. Though this training is not unique to the reference setting, it will impact the reference training program.

Training Program

While it can be challenging to prioritize and sequence training needs, doing so is the basis for laying out an overall training plan. In most cases, the reference training plan is likely to be an annual plan, identifying topics and their sequence (see Box 9.5). Some topics may be repeated, while others are offered just occasionally. Which training topics are repeated will reflect not only the prioritization of the content but also the number of employees who need to be trained.

Box 9.5 Example Academic Library Annual Training Calendar

August:	Reference Desk Policies and Procedures; Introduction to Basic Reference Tools; Recording Reference Transactions; READ Scale
September:	The Reference Interview in Person and in Chat
October:	Serving Diverse Populations
November:	Troubleshooting E-Resources and E-Books
December:	Supporting Stressed Students
January:	Tax Forms and Other Government Documents including Statistical Data (Census)
February:	Chat Transcript Review
March:	Newspaper Reference
April:	Annual Performance Evaluation Process
May:	Business Resources
June:	Science & Engineering Resources
July:	Multicultural and Ethnic Studies Resources

Goals and Objectives

After a needs assessment has been conducted and the overall training plan developed, librarians can turn their attention to the design and delivery of specific training sessions.

For each training session, specific objectives should be articulated. Training objectives might also be called goals or outcomes in a particular library. Regardless of what term is used, these statements indicate the intended results of the training. As such, training objectives help focus and guide training sessions, provide consistency in structuring content, facilitate selection of instructional methods, and provide a mechanism for evaluation. For the library employee, training objectives communicate training purpose, set clear expectations, and facilitate self-reflection. Objectives create a mutual understanding of content, expectations, and outcomes and therefore help make training more effective and efficient.

Most reference training sessions are orientated to practical goals and objectives because the reference work environment requires both abstract knowledge, that is, understanding concepts and principles, and applying that knowledge on the job. In other words, as a result of training, employees need to know things and to be able to do things with what they know. Employee engagement and morale can also be improved if employees understand why they are doing things. As such, while a training session should always have practical, or applied, objectives, a given session may also have objectives that reflect general knowledge and metacognition. Box 9.6 provides an example of a training session and demonstrates the inclusion of both abstract and applied objectives.

Box 9.6 Training Session Description and Objectives

Description

In this session, the facilitators will define the reference interview, identify and describe its components (both relational/interpersonal and content/answer), and discuss with participants theories that ground the reference interview (i.e., content/relational model of success and Carol Kuhlthau's zones of intervention in the search process). Participants will engage in role-playing activities to put the theories into reference interview practice. Finally, RUSA's "Guidelines for Behavioral Performance of Reference and Information Service Providers" will be reviewed.

Learning Objectives

Participants will be able to

- describe the components of the reference interview in order to conduct a well-rounded reference interview;
- summarize the theories and guidelines discussed during the session in order to evaluate how successful their reference interviews were;
- implement best practices for the reference interview at the reference desk and in chat.

When writing a training objective, the learner is always the actor in the statement. In other words, training objectives describe the results of the training or what the employee will know and be able to do. A training objective does not state what the trainer will do to facilitate the learning. What the trainer does is important, of course, but the trainer's work is documented in the plan or script for a training session as the instructional design and instructional method rather than as the training objectives. A typical phrase starting the statement of a training objective is "the employee will be able to," and that phrase is followed by a verb reflecting the kind of understanding or application that is expected.

Because training objectives are the basis for evaluating if a session is effective, ensuring that they accurately represent the intended results of the training and how it is related to on-the-job performance is very important. Employees will be frustrated if they successfully complete training but are then unsuccessful in their job performance.

Instructional Content

Instructional content is selected by reflecting on the training objectives and asking what information, experience, and reflection are required in order to achieve the objectives. Though the specific content for any particular training session cannot be detailed here, a useful way of considering the content is to distinguish among declarative, procedural, and conditional content. Declarative content is information that describes and tells *what* something is. Procedural content is information about *how* something is done. Conditional content is information about the circumstances under which particular declarative and procedural content is relevant. Conditional content tells learners "when" to use the "what" and "how" knowledge conveyed in declarative and procedural content. For example, training on what is included in local and national library online catalogs and how to search by author, title, keyword, and so forth should also include when to use the local library online catalog and when to use the national one. In this way, trainees are prepared to use their skills in the appropriate context.

Sequencing must also be considered in developing instructional content. In many cases, declarative and conditional content is the foundation for procedural content. Knowing key concepts and conditions underlies the execution of many processes. In most training sessions, the potential content that could be included is far greater than what time allows, and so decisions must also be made about what is central to the topic and what is peripheral and perhaps more of a nice-to-know rather than need-to-know. Streamlining and prioritizing content is critical to making training understandable and avoiding information overload for trainees.

Training Methods and Materials

After determining what employees need to know and be able to do and what content is necessary for the knowing and doing, decisions must be made about how to deliver the training. Selecting training methods requires considering how the training will be delivered and the skills of the trainer with respect to different instructional methods.

The primary consideration with respect to mode of delivery is whether the training be delivered online or in person. And, if it is delivered online, will it be synchronous (i.e., with a trainer present during trainee engagement with the content) or asynchronous (i.e., self-study). Online synchronous training and in-person training are similar in their structure and pacing and are commonly used in reference training programs. Online asynchronous training is less likely to be used for reference training though it is often used for mandatory training that is required for all employees such as harassment prevention training. As such, this section will focus on developing trainer-led training.

Regardless of whether the training is conducted in person or online, there are three general instructional methods that can be used: telling, showing, and coaching. For each instructional method, there is a corresponding role for the trainee: listening, watching, and doing. For each of these generalized types of methods, there are multiple specific instructional strategies and tools that can be deployed. No one instructional strategy or tool serves all situations, and their appropriateness is dependent on the training objectives, the receptivity of the trainees, and the trainer's facility with the method. Commonly, more than one method is used during a single session; for example, a training session might begin with a short lecture that incorporates multimedia, go on to trainee brainstorming in small groups, continue with the entire group discussing solutions, and end with each trainee practicing the preferred strategy individually.

Using a variety of teaching methods keeps learners involved and responsive, and every instructional strategy has certain advantages and disadvantages. It is essential that careful consideration be given to these advantages and limitations to ensure that the strategy selected for a specific instructional setting is one that will be effective. For example, a lecture is very effective at delivering a greater amount of content than other methods; however, hands-on practice with trainer coaching will be better for developing applied skills and providing feedback to the trainees. Strategy decisions must be based on careful analysis of training objectives, training content, instructional space, facilities, time, and costs. Finding the right method may also require some experimentation. The overriding consideration in the selection and sequencing of strategies, however, is the objectives of training: what the employee will be required to do.

Telling—Lecture

A lecture is a presentation in which the trainer introduces information or explains things and it is used to inform. Lectures are one-directional; that is, the trainer is telling trainees things. The goal is to transmit information, and the size of the trainee group does not impact on the delivery. Lecture is a highly efficient instructional method; however, it may be difficult to monitor its effectiveness in real time as trainees are in listening mode, and so it may not be obvious if they misunderstand or are not paying attention. Supplementing lecture with discussion can help address these challenges. Discussion involves asking questions, soliciting answers or responses, and dialogue between trainers and trainees. Discussion takes more time than lecture, and group size can impact its effectiveness; however, it is also a more engaging instructional method for trainees. Pairing lecture and discussion can be an effective strategy to attain the efficiencies of lecture and engagement of discussion. For example, a lecture on literature search strategies could be paired with a discussion of which strategies trainees have used previously and the challenges they have experienced in doing so.

Showing—Demonstration

In demonstration, the trainer performs a process, showing the learners what to do and how to do it. A demonstration is usually accompanied by explanations that point out why, where, and when the process is done. The goal is for the trainee to be able to repeat the same skills after the demonstration. Because experts are often not overtly aware of everything they are doing when they execute a process with which they are very familiar, it is critical that the trainer carefully detail the steps in the process. Many trainers find it useful to have a trainee implement the steps of the process with the trainer directing them. This is different than coaching because the trainer is still directing the specific inputs; the trainee is not working independently. Rather, this demonstration technique is used to ensure that the trainer is including every step in the process as the trainee will require direction and cannot rely on the trainer's expert tacit knowledge to know what to do next. A demonstration may also be paired with discussion.

Coaching—Planning and Monitoring Practice

In coaching, the trainee undertakes independent work. The trainer is no longer the focus of the training as they are when lecturing, facilitating discussion, or conducting a demonstration. Instead, trainees are the focus as they practice the skills and processes that they are learning. Nonetheless, while the focus is not on the trainer, for practice to be most effective, the trainer will need to have planned the practice exercises in advance and actively monitor learner performance for mistakes and confusion. During practice time, it may be necessary to have a training assistant help with monitoring depending on the size of the trainee group and how complex the practice exercises are.

Instructional Materials

Instructional materials include any and all resources that are created to support and supplement a training session. They can include guides, worksheets, videos, tutorials, and books. Perhaps the most common type of instructional material is the handout. Plain or fancy, simple or complex, handouts provide information and instructions that are needed by the learner but not easily committed to memory without practice. In some cases, the information might be needed only on rare occasions. The handout is very flexible. For training sessions that include practice time, a structured exercise will provide trainees with an opportunity to explore new resources or practice skills. In cases where practice time is not included in a training session, trainees might be required to practice on their own, guided by some sort of assignment. Many trainers will also have a set of slides or other materials that they use as visual supports for lectures, discussions, and demonstrations. Whether the materials are also provided to trainees will depend on the degree to which they contain sufficient detail to be useful as independent learning aids. Once learning objectives, content, instructional strategies, and instructional materials have been identified, it is time to pull all of the pieces together into a coherent instruction plan. New instructors will usually find it helpful to create a written outline of the session that provides an overview of the content and method of delivery and outlines any activities and assessments. Such a document does not have to be a word-for-word script but just an outline to guide the instruction. Even seasoned instructors should consider developing such documents. Not only do they help the instructor organize their thoughts before delivering the session but these outlines also enable consistency from one session to the next and provide guidance when other instructors need to step in to cover a session.

Box 9.7 contains an example of a training plan for an in-person session on conducting the reference interview.

Training Program Evaluation

Each training session should be evaluated to determine if the learners have met the objectives and if the training can be improved in any way. There are three primary considerations in evaluating a training session: learning performance, trainee reaction, and transfer of learning to job performance. A final consideration in evaluating a training session will be attending to the return on investment for training expenditures.

Box 9.7 Training Plan: Conducting the Reference Interview

This training plan is designed for a ninety-minute, in-person session for library employees who are new to working at the reference desk. In addition to lecture and discussion, trainees watch and critique videos and practice reference interview skills with a partner; thus, the training uses multiple instructional methods. The videos, created by staff at a public library and posted on *YouTube*, are relatable and often amusing, heightening trainee engagement. In addition, the relatively quick pace of watching a video, coming back together for discussion, and repeating the cycle is enjoyable for those who prefer novelty, while still following a predictable pattern for trainees who prefer routine and clear expectations. At the end of the session, a reflective component encourages trainees to self-assess their skill development and identify areas for further practice. At the same time, seeing others' reactions to the material highlights that everyone finds the reference interview challenging and is reassuring for those who are new to the topic.

- Welcome and introduction (five minutes)—The trainer welcomes everyone to the session, previews the training topic, and answers any questions.
- Lecture and discussion (twenty minutes)—The trainer reviews the steps in the reference interview, drawing on various theories from the literature and engaging learners' prior experiences as patrons or library employees.
- Reference interview critique (twenty-five minutes)—Using a series of *YouTube* videos of reference interviews, the group watches one video at a time and then discusses what the librarian did well and what could be improved. The trainer guides the conversation, but the analysis is done by trainees.
- Partner work (thirty minutes)—Trainees work in pairs to practice the reference interview using example questions and take turns role playing a librarian or patron.
- Reflective discussion and conclusion (ten minutes)—The trainer brings the group back together for a discussion of their experiences practicing the reference interview.

Outline adapted with permission from *Instructional Design for LIS Professionals* (Wong 2019)

Learning Performance and Trainee Reaction

The most immediate consideration in evaluating a training session is assessing performance in the learning setting. If trainees do not have the skills and knowledge at the end of the training session, they will not be able to implement them in the work setting. As such, learning performance assessment involves having trainees demonstrate the applications of skills as described in the training session's objectives. This also aligns with the recommendation of Lily Todorinova and Matt Torrence (2014) that training assessment be incorporated into the training itself. Such a performance will be necessarily somewhat contrived as it is in a training setting rather than on the job; however, with careful attention to design of the assessment, it is possible for the assessment to closely approximate the work setting environment. If the size of the group precludes the trainer using direct observation of the performance to evaluate the trainee's performance, the performance assessment must include a mechanism for documenting the performance for later review. This might be in the form of a worksheet, screen capture of an online process, or video recording.

Though not strictly a learning assessment, but rather a measure of reaction to the training, it is also advisable to ask employees to evaluate the training experience. If the training is effective but unpleasant, it will negatively affect motivation and engagement. Employees may resist attending training or disengage during the session. The best-case scenario is a training session that trainees enjoy and that leads to learning and improved job performance. Reaction to training is typically measured using a survey or short-answer response. For larger training programs, a focus group with a sample of participants might be used as well.

Transfer to Job Performance

Unfortunately, it cannot be assumed that an employee who demonstrates mastery in the training setting will be able to transfer that performance into the work setting (see Box 9.8). Job performance involves not only applying one's knowledge but also doing so in an environment different than the training setting. For example, an employee may be able to execute perfectly a particular process in the quiet and focused setting of a classroom but struggle to do so in the time-pressured setting of the reference desk with a line of waiting patrons. If learning does not transfer to job performance, the training was not effective and needs to be revised in light of the work setting demands for performance.

Box 9.8 Activity: From Learning to Job Performance

Reflect on a training session that you have attended either as a library employee or in another job. How could the trainer know if you were able to transfer what you learned in a workshop or training session to responsibilities in your job? What would they look for? Now consider this from your perspective as a trainee. How would you approach your supervisor if you were struggling to transfer the learning from the training to your job performance?

Return on Investment

Training programs are a financial investment. They take staff, resources, space, and time. Monitoring the overall effectiveness of the training program relative to the resources expended responds to the need to be a good fiscal steward of a library's budget. If small gains in job performance require extensive monetary investment, a particular training objective may need to be reconsidered. Perhaps it would be more effective to hire a specialist for a particular topic than to have everyone on the reference team build their skills in that area. Conversely, the training required to implement a more efficient question referral system may save a great deal of time, for both reference staff and patrons, as well as improve overall satisfaction with reference service. Understanding how investments in training affect job performance and patron experience enables the library to get the greatest benefit from the reference training program.

MANAGING TRAINING PROGRAMS

Every library and system differs in its approach to administering and delivering library services. Large public library systems may resemble large academic libraries more than either resemble their smaller counterparts, while special and school libraries diverge widely depending upon corporate practices and state and local regulations. Where library training administration may be located depends upon these various organizational structures; what should remain constant is the presence of such a unit or department, the quality of its offerings and actions, and the relevance of said opportunities to reference staff.

Some libraries are highly centralized, with departments operating for the larger system rather than the individual branch or subject-specific library. For example, in large public library systems, acquisitions and collection management may operate from one physical location in the main library, while branches may have small amounts of input or influence. Large academic libraries probably still have individual subject expert librarians making final purchase decisions for monographs or serials but may consolidate any unspent funds at the end of the fiscal year to buy one-time items for the benefit of the whole library system. Training and development is a function that is similarly situated depending on the organizational culture: it may be located in one centralized place, or it may have dedicated staff dispersed among branches or departments where the needs for training are greatest. The efficacy of the training program should be strong regardless of structure; it should be engaged with staff, responsive to feedback and local needs yet forward thinking in its offerings, and situated so that the people running the program see the big picture of the organization.

In larger library systems or corporate libraries, human resources may appear to be an appropriate home for training and development. Like training, human resources serves the entire organization and all of its staff by overseeing hiring, possibly participating in promotion and reviews, and keeping abreast of laws and regulations. It could be advantageous for the training and development coordinator and staff to be a part of a team that interacts with these issues on a regular basis so that they may, for instance, offer staff a chance to remain on top of legal changes that affect library services or policies. On the other hand, if a department or office of user/public services exists, training and development may be located there since a large portion of traditional training focuses on reference, research, and teaching/learning. This may affect other areas that also need training, so no matter the size of the library, there may be training liaisons in various departments to ensure that the correct balance of ongoing learning happens across the library system. In much smaller libraries, one person may be charged with training all staff, and so there is a possibility that they may be located in the administrative office, where there is the greatest chance for them to understand the training and development needs of the library as a whole.

The person who is coordinating the training, especially the reference training, in a library or system may have a myriad of roles. It might be a person who has a degree in organizational leadership or human resources development (instead of or in addition to a library science degree). It might be an experienced reference or public services librarian who has focused on training new employees or student workers for a considerable part of their career. A reference/research and instruction department head may have this role, or a designated training and development librarian may also have this responsibility.

CONCLUSION

Every library should have a clear commitment to professional training and development. Regardless of the type of library into which new employees enter, a thoughtful and well-paced training program needs to be in place. This may take different forms, but support for and assurance of such a program should be visible and plainly articulated. Libraries, by definition, provide the means of lifelong learning. Continuous learning, ongoing training, and challenging the skills and mind-sets of employees help reference staff help library patrons and further the growth of the profession. Individual employees cannot achieve any of these goals without the absolute commitment to ongoing learning that libraries and library systems must provide. As a frontline service very much in the public eye, those working in reference need to keep learning, be engaged on a personal and professional level, and always be attuned to the changing needs of library patrons. A robust training and development staff and program are an essential part of this crucial piece of librarianship.

REFERENCES

American Library Association. 2009. "Core Competences of Librarianship." http://www.ala.org/educationcareers/careers/corecomp/corecompetences.

Bauer, Talya N. 2010. *Onboarding New Employees: Maximizing Success.* Alexandria, VA: SHRM Publishing.

Hakala-Ausperk, Catherine. 2013. *Build a Great Team: One Year to Success.* Chicago: ALA Editions.

Johnson, Anna Marie. 2019. "Connections, Conversations, and Visibility: How the Work of Academic Reference and Liaison Librarians Is Evolving." *Reference & User Services Quarterly* 58 (2): 91–102.

Morgan, Pamela J. 2009. *Training Paraprofessionals for Reference Service.* New York: Neal-Schuman.

PubMed. National Library of Medicine. https://www.ncbi.nlm.nih.gov/pubmed/.

Reference and User Services Association. 2013. "Guidelines for Behavioral Performance of Reference and Information Service Providers." American Library Association. http://www.ala.org/rusa/resources/guidelines/guidelinesbehavioral.

Reference and User Services Association. 2017. "Professional Competencies for Reference and User Services Librarians." American Library Association. http://www.ala.org/rusa/resources/guidelines/professional.

Saunders, Laura. 2012. "Identifying Core Reference Competencies from an Employers' Perspective: Implications for Instruction." *College & Research Libraries* 73 (4): 390–404. https://doi.org/10.5860/crl-281.

Stewart, Andrea Wigbels, Carlette Washington-Hoagland, and Carole T. Zsulya, eds. 2013. *Staff Development: A Practical Guide.* Chicago: American Library Association.

Todaro, Julie, and Mark L. Smith. 2006. *Training Library Staff and Volunteers to Provide Extraordinary Customer Service*. New York: Neal-Schuman.

Todorinova, Lily, and Matt Torrence. 2014. "Implementing and Assessing Library Reference Training Programs." *The Reference Librarian* 55 (1): 37–48.

Ward, David. 2003. "Using Virtual Reference Transcripts for Staff Training." *Reference Services Review* 31 (1): 46–56. https://doi.org/10.1108/00907320310460915.

Wong, Melissa A. 2019. *Instructional Design for LIS Professionals: A Guide for Teaching Librarians and Information Science Professionals*. Santa Barbara, CA: Libraries Unlimited.

YouTube. http://www.youtube.com.

SUGGESTED READINGS

Allan, Barbara. 2013. *The No-Nonsense Guide to Training in Libraries*. London: Facet Publishing.

Allan provides a succinct discussion of developing workplace learning environments along with three main approaches: content-centered, learner-centered, and social. She explores a variety of learning and teaching methods to make training interesting, including action planning, group work, guest speakers, hands-on sessions, inquiry-based learning, problem-based learning, and the use of stories and metaphors. Additionally, she provides an overview of different ways current technologies can be incorporated into training, while acknowledging that the speed of change in this area makes it difficult to keep up to date.

Hakala-Ausperk, Catherine. 2013. *Build a Great Team: One Year to Success*. Chicago: ALA Editions.

While this book is aimed squarely at supervisors, team leaders, or managers, its content is relevant for anyone who has gone through the hiring, training, and career growth process. Organized month by month, the author's ebullient tone keeps things interesting, as do the exercises for the reader to complete. The "Month 5: Blending" chapter is of particular note for training and orientation.

Hawks, Melanie. 2013. *Designing Training*. Chicago: ACRL.

A short book in the ACRL Active Guides series that offers both theory and practice on designing effective training sessions for librarians, it is divided into four sections: designing for the adult learner, designing for takeaway value, designing for purposeful engagement, and designing for learning transfer. Reflection questions and activities for the reader are very helpful in moving one's training plan along, and sample worksheets and activities for training participants provide great templates for other applications.

Trotta, Marcia. 2011. *Staff Development on a Shoestring*. New York: Neal-Schuman.

This work is based on the assumption that the most cost-effective way to accomplish good staff training "is to design in-house training programs that turn experienced staff into proficient trainers" (ix) and so is focused on developing individualized training programs. In addition to coverage of assessing needs, developing training, using technology, and assessing training, this book discusses the manager's role in customizing job descriptions, helping staff solve problems, internal marketing, mentoring employees, evaluating performance, and recognizing effective performance. Also included are model training programs.

Chapter 10

Marketing and Promotion of Reference Services

Cassandra Graesser and Lillian Sundell-Thomas

INTRODUCTION

Having the best reference resources and services is not enough to guarantee patron use and engagement. Every library, no matter the type, needs to commit to marketing those resources and services. Most librarians do not consider themselves marketing experts. Nevertheless, they want to ensure that as many community members as possible benefit from the library's resources and services. Marketing is the key to doing this.

This chapter introduces basic marketing concepts, presents a marketing framework adapted to reference services, and provides examples of how this framework can be applied to any library. Real-world tips and suggestions are provided, including a practical discussion of commonly used marketing tools and suggested best practices.

WHAT IS MARKETING?

Many consider marketing to be selling, advertising, and promotion. While promotion is one aspect of marketing, the process, when done correctly, is much more holistic and comprehensive. Phillip Kotler, Gary Armstrong, and Lloyd C. Harris (2017, 27) describe marketing as the process used to create value for customers, build profitable relationships with them, and capture value (monetary or nonmonetary) from them. This definition is broad and may seem abstract and unclear in its application to libraries, which typically do not operate as for-profit entities. However, it can be adapted to marketing reference and library services. Library marketing is identifying whom librarians serve, determining what products and services will be most valuable to those users, promoting those products and services by demonstrating their value to users, and soliciting and listening to feedback to continually increase the value to users.

A MARKETING FRAMEWORK

Any definition of marketing, even one tailored to marketing library services, becomes more helpful when a practical framework is applied. The following list outlines a five-step marketing framework for librarians. Again, because most libraries are not profit-seeking entities and librarians do not typically consider users to be customers in the traditional sense, these steps are adapted to librarians' needs.

1. Conduct market research and assess user needs.
2. Set marketing goals and objectives.
3. Formulate a marketing plan to reach the targeted users.
4. Create value and user relationships through plan implementation.
5. Capture value from library users.

Marketing begins with understanding the needs and wants of library patrons through market research. At this stage, librarians assess the library's audience, identify user habits and characteristics, segment users into representative groups, and create user personae to better understand current and potential users. Using market research, librarians are able to set realistic goals and objectives by determining which user group(s) to target with the marketing plan and where users' needs and the library's organizational goals overlap.

Then librarians will focus their efforts into an integrated marketing plan that identifies how to create value for patrons, outlines the specific messages conveyed to users and potential users, and determines the tools to best reach them. During the implementation of the plan, value is generated, and librarians form relationships with patrons through the delivery and promotion of new services. Next, value is captured from users through increased program attendance and the increased use of services and collections. Finally, librarians must assess their marketing efforts by collecting and analyzing feedback. Each of these concepts will be expanded upon in detail in the chapter and presented along with tips to help librarians apply them in their own workplaces.

What Marketing Is Not

Not all library administrators and librarians will understand the holistic scope of marketing and may instead focus only on promotion and public relations. However, promotion and public relations that are not based on a solid understanding of the user and specific outreach goals are unlikely to be effective. For this reason, it is important that librarians understand the marketing process and are able to clearly communicate it to others in the field. Just as library jargon is confusing for those who work outside the field, marketing language can be misunderstood and used incorrectly.

The terms "promotion" and "public relations" are often used interchangeably with "marketing." There are very important differences between them, however. As illustrated in Figure 10.1, marketing begins far before promotion and continues long after one promotional campaign or press release. Promotion is simply getting the word out or telling users what the library wants them to hear. Public relations, on the other hand, has traditionally been thought of as creating content meant for journalists, reporters, and editors, and a good public relations specialist would develop strong relationships with those in traditional media (Kotler, Armstrong, and Harris 2017, 409). For promotion and public relations to be effective, they must fit within the overall marketing plan. Promotion and traditional public relations, apart from marketing, are one-way flows of information. Marketing, conversely, is a cyclical process that builds relationships with users, beginning and ending with user needs. Promotion and public relations are only parts of the process.

In today's age of marketing, the line between public relations and marketing has blurred. Librarians are now able to reach and engage with users directly, as they publish more content to their libraries' websites and social media accounts without going through traditional media. Public relations can now be defined as building a good reputation for the library by gaining positive publicity and warding off negative publicity. Despite this shift, relationships with traditional media sources can be very beneficial for libraries as part of an overall marketing plan. Even as the field of public relations grows, it still does not encompass the entire marketing process, which includes researching user needs, choosing products or services, and assessing effectiveness.

Finally, it is important to note that the term "marketing" may have a negative connotation for some. It is often associated with inauthentic methods of advertising and selling. However, when done correctly, marketing is about better serving library users by connecting them with the services they need and want. When marketing is done well, it positively benefits both librarians and library users.

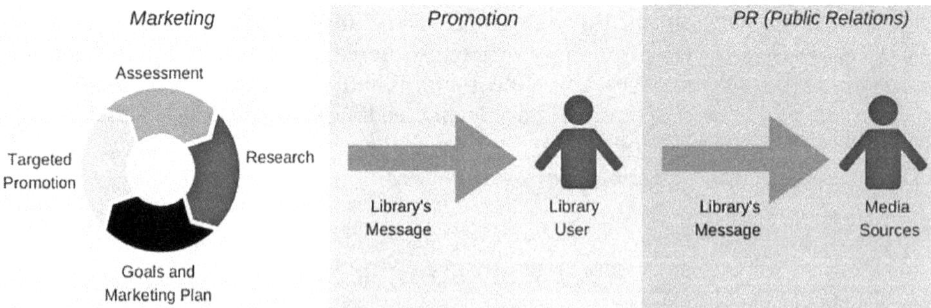

Figure 10.1 Promotion and public relations versus holistic marketing. Shown is the difference between promotion and public relations versus a holistic approach to marketing. While promotion and public relations involve direct messages to patrons and the media, holistic marketing is a cycle of targeted promotion based on research and tied to specific goals.

CONDUCTING MARKET RESEARCH AND ASSESSING USER NEEDS

The first step in any successful marketing effort is for librarians to understand the library's marketplace by conducting an environmental scan. It may be helpful to think of the marketplace as the realm in which library users or potential users would interact with library services. Market research allows librarians to gain insight into the library and its resources, understand the needs of current library users, identify potential users, and minimize risks in a marketing plan. Without asking users and potential users about their needs and desires, marketing plans will likely miss the mark. This research also provides focus and justification for the subsequently created integrated marketing plan, resulting in more successful efforts, increased usage, and improved relationships with users.

Conducting an Environmental Scan

In order to gain insight into the library's marketplace, librarians should conduct an environmental scan of the library's microenvironment, the immediate area of operation for the library, and macroenvironment, the larger societal systems within which the library operates.

For librarians, the microenvironment consists of internal resources, such as budget and staff; the communities and stakeholders the library serves; and actors close to the library that affect its ability to serve its users. Examples of actors in a library's microenvironment are a funding body (local government, for example), student groups or community organizations, the Friends of the Library, volunteers, and boards of directors. Librarians should evaluate all of the resources already available in the library and/or the reference department, previous marketing efforts, previous and potential staff involvement, and potential marketing budgets. This analysis could include strengths of the collection and other infrastructure such as technology, as well as particular skills of staff members, such as subject expertise, programming experience, or languages spoken. They should also consider their relationships with and the strengths of key stakeholders.

In order to create an effective marketing plan, librarians also must be mindful of trends and changes in society, or the larger societal forces that make up the macroenvironment. These forces can be economic, political, cultural, demographic, or environmental. For example, the demographics of the greater community, including age, education, nationality, and religion, will differ for each library. Economic changes may affect users' or the library's budget. One should remain aware of changes in tastes and trends, such as the introduction of new technology, how it is being used, and what types of user groups are most in need of these technologies. This can be done by identifying and reading relevant literature, attending conferences, and communicating with colleagues. Once gathered, this information can help librarians identify user patterns, where potential users can be found and what might convert them to *actual* users, and how value of library services can best be conveyed.

One common tool for analyzing micro- and macroenvironments is a strengths, weaknesses, opportunities, and threats (SWOT) analysis. A SWOT analysis will consider both internal (strengths and weaknesses) and external (opportunities and threats) factors. When librarians understand their institution's strengths and weaknesses, they can strategize ways to build on strengths and improve areas of weaknesses. Further, as librarians identify opportunities and threats in their external environment, they can leverage their strengths to take advantage of opportunities and avoid or minimize the impact of threats. For great examples of SWOT analyses, refer to Marie R. Kennedy and Cheryl LaGuardia's (2018) *Marketing Your Library's Electronic Resources.*

In summary, a comprehensive environmental scan typically includes

- the collection and analysis of demographics of library users and the broader community;
- the identification and assessment of market competition;
- an analysis of internal and external stakeholders;
- an examination of the library structure, focusing on resources, skills, and capabilities;
- an assessment of the internal and external use of technology and other trends in the field;
- a SWOT analysis.

Program-Specific Market Research

While environmental scans are essential and can be used to inform many activities, they may not contain information specific enough for every individual marketing campaign (e.g., how to increase program attendance by fathers aged thirty-five to forty-five with young children). When the data needed does not exist, is unreliable, or needs to be updated, librarians must conduct their own program-specific marketing research. Library marketing research can be defined as the purposeful design, collection, analysis, and reporting of data pertinent to a specific marketing situation facing a library. Before conducting additional marketing research, it is beneficial to ask other librarians in the department or organization if they are already collecting data that may be of use.

Research techniques that might be appropriate include observations, interviews, focus groups, behavioral data, surveys (mail, telephone, in library, or online), and intercept interviews. Intercept interviews, when interviewers stop others on the street or outside the library to ask them questions, can be particularly helpful when trying to reach new users. Collecting quotes, comments, and engagement rates by demographic from social media or e-mail can also prove useful. For more on types of data that are collected for assessment purposes, refer to Chapter 8.

Librarians should be mindful of the place of library marketing research within the overall process. They should determine the purpose of the research and identify the informational objectives at the outset and then continue by identifying the audience and/or potential user groups to be targeted and selecting appropriate research techniques. For example, if students often communicate through chat services, reviewing those transcripts may be beneficial. Senior citizen public library users may call the reference desk with higher frequency, and collecting quotes from phone conversations may provide more targeted data depending on marketing objectives.

After deciding upon techniques, librarians should pretest the selected techniques (e.g., surveys, collection methods). After fine-tuning, they can begin collecting and analyzing data, looking for patterns among users (which allow for user segmentation as described in the following section) and user priorities and values. Finally, market research should not end when the marketing plan is launched, but can be used to measure performance during and after the plan is implemented.

User Segmentation

Libraries cannot be all things to all users at all times. Understanding users and assessing user needs—and how they are unique—are vital to a successful marketing plan. If a library is trying to reach every potential user with a campaign, it is not likely to strike a chord with any particular user group. Without clear goals and targeted messages, the marketing will be ineffective. User segmentation and personae creation will allow librarians to assess user needs and help them define the goals and objectives of a marketing plan.

When sufficient market research has been completed, it will inform user segmentation and library user personae (see Box 10.1). Using the information gathered from the environmental scan, such as age and occupations of the population, and the data gathered from campaign-specific marketing research, librarians should look for particular recurring characteristics or patterns of use within the data, separating types of users into groups. For example, academic library users who tend to live on campus may be more likely to attend evening programs, whereas off-campus users may be more likely to use electronic resources. Segmenting users or potential users in this way allows librarians to see whose needs are being met with which services and where there is room for improvement.

Box 10.1 Activity: Thinking about Segmentation

User segmentation is a necessary piece of creating a successful marketing plan. Keeping this in mind, answer the following questions.

Questions for Reflection and Discussion:

1. Consider the users of a specific academic, public, or special library. Who is using this library, and how could this group be segmented into target audiences?
2. Using the same library as an example, brainstorm ways that user segmentation could be used to inform decision-making during the marketing process. How can defining targeted audiences improve marketing efforts?

Once the user groups have been identified, librarians should share the results with others in the library, department, and administration. If all internal stakeholders understand the targeted user groups the library aims to reach, they will undoubtedly be more supportive of marketing efforts and will make better-informed decisions.

Personae Creation

User personae are representations of a type of user that has been identified as having a specific interest in a library product or service or having a problem that a library solves. For example, the most common users of reference services at an academic library might be undergraduate students, graduate students, faculty, and staff. What needs does the library meet for undergraduate students? Undergraduate students are likely not as familiar with research and citation as faculty members and may need to know about general services provided by the library or how to evaluate source credibility. Faculty members, on the other hand, have a greater need for access to specific peer-reviewed articles and may need interlibrary loan services more frequently. When thinking about library and reference services from the perspective of user personae, the need to tailor marketing strategies to targeted user groups becomes apparent.

User personae bring focus to marketing plans, keeping users at the forefront of the process and allowing librarians to get the right message to each type of user. A persona should be created for each major group of users at the library as outlined during the user segmentation process. Each user persona is created by asking questions about the targeted audience. It should include a name; age; family members; goals; behaviors; attitudes; work experience and education levels; and potentially a story, quote, or anything else that makes the persona feel like a real library user. Personae, though generalized by necessity, are not stereotypes but are backed by the data collected through environmental scans and campaign-specific market research.

Table 10.1 shows two personae that represent user groups at hypothetical libraries. The first persona, Alexis, represents first-year undergraduate students

TABLE 10.1 Examples of Representative Personae. A Description of Two Personae That Could Represent User Groups at a Hypothetical Academic and Public Library

	Persona for Large Public University Library	Persona for Urban Public Library
Name	Alexis	Christopher
Gender	Female	Male
Age segment	Eighteen to twenty	Thirty-five to forty-five
Family	• Lives in dormitory with roommate • Mother and younger brother live at home	Wife and two children, aged two and six
Occupation/ job status	• Undergraduate student • Intern at local community media center	Work-from-home textbook editor
Education level	• High school • Zero to two years of college	Master's degree
Social interests	• Theater, social change, Quidditch team, ultimate frisbee, study groups	• Comics/zines, craft beer, homebrewing, cooking, and bicycling
Information sources	• *Buzzfeed* • *Snapchat* • *Instagram* • *YouTube* • Mobile phone alerts	• *Reddit* • *The Daily Show* • *The Atlantic* • *Vice News* • Popular nonfiction books
Adjectives	• Authentic, connected, determined	• Informed, open minded, adventurous
Needs	• Finding sources for mid-term paper • Help citing sources	• Finding books for early literacy • Interacting with other parents • Affordable activities for children

at a large public university. The second persona, Christopher, represents a user group for patrons aged thirty-five to forty-five with children at an urban public library system.

SETTING GOALS AND OBJECTIVES

Once user needs are outlined, it is easier to see what the goals and objectives of a marketing plan should be. Goals and objectives ought to be where user needs and organizational goals overlap (Solomon 2016). Librarians should consult the library's mission statement and become familiar with its strategic plan when setting goals. For example, the representative persona Christopher from Table 10.1 needs interaction with other parents and affordable activities for his children. Promoting early childhood literacy is one of his public library's missions. One resulting marketing goal, which meets his needs and the organization's goals, might be to increase parent attendance at free, early literacy programs. This goal might be reached by creating a new "Dad Storytime" that draws in parents like Christopher and their children.

Once the goals of the marketing plan have been established, it is important to make them clear to stakeholders. This will include not only library directors and managers but also all staff members. Including all staff members in the marketing process will make it much more likely to succeed. In order to produce a truly integrated marketing campaign in which all marketing efforts reinforce one another, every piece of marketing collateral (whether online or in print) and every program that is created or hosted should support and be directly tied to the goals of the marketing plan and therefore in step with serving the users' needs *and* the library's strategic plan.

FORMULATING A MARKETING PLAN

In essence, constructing an integrated marketing plan is deciding how to best meet the needs of the targeted audience, thus creating value for the targeted audience, and how to communicate the library's message to the targeted audience in a way that speaks to them. A good marketing plan will be created after considering several marketing tools and platforms and applying the most appropriate of them to the personae and/or targeted audiences. As with all stages of marketing, librarians should solicit input from a variety of staff members, as having a wide set of viewpoints is essential. Even if it is not possible to create a formal marketing committee, librarians can identify allies on staff or among library users who can contribute input during the construction of the plan.

At this step in the process, it may be helpful to consider the four Ps of the marketing mix—product, price, promotion, and place (Kotler and Lee 2007). One must first determine what "product" the library might offer to meet the needs of targeted users. For libraries, the product may be a specific reference service, a new way to offer the service, a library program, or a new database, for example. By offering the service or resource that best meets the audience's needs, librarians can actually *create value* for users. For instance, the new "Dad Storytime" mentioned earlier increases the value of Christopher's public library system by offering a program that meets his needs. Often, when considering marketing plans, librarians think of new or additional services that can meet the needs of users. Both the evaluation of potential new services and the evaluation of *existing* services are necessary. After evaluating personae needs and habits, librarians may determine that an existing service needs to be altered, marketed in a new way, or even retired if it is no longer addressing the needs or wishes of users.

At first glance, the second P, price, may not appear applicable to all libraries. Although most services are free and few libraries are interested in making a profit, many services do have a cost to users. Printing is not always free, interlibrary loan and faxing services may have fees, and some programs charge for supplies. Library patrons may also spend significant money and time traveling to the library, and learning how to access resources and services takes time. When determining which product or service meets the needs of targeted users, librarians should consider if the cost to users would be prohibitive for part of the targeted user group. Instead of focusing on profit, librarians can examine price of products and services in an effort to make them available to as many people as possible. Can the program or service be provided while still ensuring that the users who need it most are able to access it? Can costs be mitigated for those who need library products and services most?

The third P of the marketing mix is promotion. Promotion, within the framework of a well-constructed marketing plan, is telling the right things about the library to the right people. Librarians have long been involved in the promotion of their services but can still improve by ensuring that it is intentional and tailored to the goals and target audience of the marketing campaign. When considering online promotion in particular, the concept of content marketing is important. Content marketing can be defined as the creation and sharing of online material that generates interest in the library and its services. Typically this includes images, memes, videos, posts on social media networks, and blog posts. Content marketing collateral does not have to explicitly promote a library service but instead aims to tell the library's story or generate interest indirectly. A library may share a link to a video of an astronaut reading children's books in space on their *Facebook* page. This does not directly promote a library service but does promote early childhood literacy and interest users, encouraging them to engage with the library through social media. Like all promotion, great content marketing has a goal, provides value to library users, and is targeted and consistent (Solomon 2016, 16–17).

When considering place, the fourth P, librarians should be sure they are promoting to users where users are already found. One must think about both physical and online spaces and places both inside and outside of the library. For example, public library events for parents with young children could be promoted in the children's room, as well as at family-friendly local events like farmers' markets and community festivals. Library services that target new undergraduate university students might benefit from promotion in the student union, at orientation events, and through social media channels, such as *Instagram* and *Snapchat*.

Selecting Marketing Tools

While formulating the marketing plan, librarians must consider the appropriate platform(s) for promotional content. In developing personae for users, librarians should have identified how each group acquires information and the best channels for reaching targeted audiences. If *Instagram* is the best way to reach users between the ages of twenty-five and thirty, this is where librarians should be posting about services designed for this population. On the other end of the spectrum, services geared toward retirees might be better promoted in traditional print media or *Facebook*. This applies to interests as well as sheer demographics; it makes sense to hang flyers for a library comic con at a local comic book store, for example. Many marketing tools and social media platforms are discussed in depth later in the chapter.

In order for these tools to be effective, content should be tailored to the target audience as well as the communication channel. For example, librarians may partner with a local community access station to create a promotional video about fall book recommendations. The video itself could be posted to *Facebook*, but a still photograph would be an ideal *Instagram* post. Quotes recommending specific titles could be tweeted, and a book display could be created containing all the books mentioned. Librarians should not repost the same image and text across all platforms, as this can be mistaken for spam. As suggested in Table 10.2, each presentation of the content should use language specifically designed to work with the platform and engage with the target demographic.

Whether marketing and promotional material is being produced by one person or a team of ten, there should be a clear style guide and set of best practices in place to help staff create appealing and appropriate material. The style guide is essential to building a successful marketing campaign. Use of a consistent style ensures that all materials contribute to the overall organizational goals and recognizability of the library's brand. Box 10.2 provides an opportunity to evaluate and consider style consistency of library marketing materials.

Box 10.2 Activity: Evaluating Style Consistency in Marketing Collateral

Gather three to five examples of marketing collateral (e.g., welcome brochures, social media posts, flyers for events, website graphics) from the same library. If possible, collect examples of both print and digital marketing collateral.

Questions for Reflection and Discussion:

1. Is it apparent that these materials come from the same library? What do these materials convey about the library's brand, mission, or culture?
2. Do all materials use the library or event logo? Are they using the same version of the logo?
3. Do the materials use similar fonts and graphics? If so, what effect does that have? If not, why might that be important?
4. If two or more of the items promote the same event or service, is there a clear motif, graphic, or color scheme associated with it? Why might that be important?

Applying Marketing Tools to Personae

To put these ideas into practice, it is helpful to consider the two personae, Alexis and Christopher, outlined earlier in the chapter. By considering personae's needs and traits in depth as in Table 10.2, it becomes clearer how librarians might create value for these personae. The products and services that fit each persona's needs are outlined, and the costs to users, if any, are listed. Then, the places where each

TABLE 10.2 Various Marketing Research and Tools to the Library Personae Introduced in Figure 10.1.

Representative Persona	Alexis (Academic Library)	Christopher (Public Library)
User needs	• Find articles and create bibliography for mid-term paper	• Find engaging and age-appropriate books for children • Meet other parents
Meeting the user's needs (product)	• Citation help at reference desk • One-on-one instruction sessions • Pop-up citation station in high-traffic study areas	• Readers' advisory services and materials • Introduce "Dad Storytime" program
Goals (measurable outcomes)	• Increase reference questions, one-on-one appointments, use of RefWorks, and use of database searches	• Increase storytime attendance and circulation of children's materials • Grow social media following among men aged twenty-five to forty-five
Tailoring marketing content to target audience		
Why should users choose the library over other resources?	• Better grade/quality of paper • Saves time in the long run	• Expertise of staff • Engagement with other parents • Free
Where can they be reached (physical spaces, online spaces, and traditional media outlets)?	• Classes • Cafeterias • Residence halls • Campus bulletin boards • Social media: *Instagram*, *Facebook*, *Twitter*, and *Snapchat* • Campus newspaper	• Daycares and schools • Community bulletin boards • Parks • Coffeeshops • Social media: *Instagram*, *Facebook*, *Twitter*, and *Reddit* • Local newspaper (online version)
Buzzwords/language of targeted audience	• Procrastination, caffeine, late night/all-nighter	• Kid/child, childhood development, play/playgroup/playdate, community
Applying marketing tools	• Flyers in cafeteria, residence halls, bathroom stalls • Post graphics, memes, links, and guides on social media • Handouts given at instruction sessions, reference desk, and pop-up citation station	• Flyers around library and community • Post photos and videos on social media • Send information to daycares/schools • Make reading lists available in the library and on website • Recommended reads and program information in monthly newsletter

Representative Persona	Alexis (Academic Library)	Christopher (Public Library)
Identifying influencers/word-of-mouth marketing	• Orientation staff, student workers, professors • Student organization leaders	• Fathers in the community • PTA members • Circulation/frontline staff

persona can be reached, both in person and online, are considered. Finally, the tools used to best convey the value of these products to the personae are listed.

Many library marketing books and guides, including the ones listed in at the end of this chapter, provide great examples of marketing plans for specific programs. When reviewing example marketing plans, it may be advantageous to consider the four Ps of the marketing mix mentioned earlier. Box 10.3 reflects upon the relevance of the four Ps of the marketing mix during the application of marketing tools to personae.

Box 10.3 Activity: Considering the Four Ps of the Marketing Mix

The four Ps of the marketing mix are *product, price, promotion*, and *place*. Using these concepts and Table 10.2, answer the following questions.

Questions for Reflection and Discussion:

1. How are the four Ps relevant to the information found in Table 10.2? Where have the concepts of the four Ps been applied to the table?
2. Brainstorm another potential resource or service that could meet either Christopher's or Alexis's library needs. How might the four Ps determine or affect how that resource or service is offered?

Creating a Plan Timeline

To ensure success of the plan, librarians should establish a timeline detailing what needs to be done when and by whom. It is important to be realistic with the timeline and expectations for each staff member. Some staff members may be able to assist with daily tasks such as social media management, while others may be able to assist with weekly or monthly tasks. Beyond ensuring that each task is completed, a timeline also means that librarians are reaching people when they most need to be reached. Having a clear communication plan and timeline means setting limits, trusting that the most effective methods are in place, and later assessing the success of the process.

Table 10.3 shows examples of marketing campaign timelines for ongoing services designed for the example personae. Since the services being promoted are ongoing, the timeline is outlined on a continual basis. If a marketing campaign is

TABLE 10.3 Sample Marketing Campaign Timelines for the Library Personae Introduced in Figure 10.1.

	Task	Date/Frequency	Staff Member
Alexis	Social Media: *Instagram*, *Facebook*, *Twitter*, and *Snapchat*	Daily	Social media team
	In-house word-of-mouth marketing promotion	Daily	All frontline staff as appropriate/time allows
	Operate citation station pop-up	Weekly	Reference/liaison librarians
	Hang/replace flyers	Monthly	Reference/liaison librarians
	Promote services at instruction sessions	On a semester basis	Reference/liaison librarians
	Student blog posts	Once/semester	Recruit interested student staff
Chris	Restock reading lists	Daily/as needed	Children's room staff
	In-house word-of-mouth marketing promotion	Daily	All frontline staff as appropriate/time allows
	Social media: *Instagram*, *Facebook*, *Twitter*, and *Reddit*	Weekly	Social media team
	Promotion in e-newsletter	Monthly	Marketing librarian
	Hang flyers at local daycares, businesses, and community spaces	Quarterly	Marketing librarian

event specific, the timeline may be structured by date, counting down to the event. A good rule of thumb is to begin promotion at least one month to forty-five days in advance. If the event is large, promotion may need to begin earlier. Many larger library systems also promote events on a quarterly basis, and librarians should be prepared to adjust timelines to work within the library's promotional plan.

CREATING VALUE AND RELATIONSHIPS THROUGH PLAN IMPLEMENTATION

As mentioned earlier, a good marketing plan aims to create value by meeting users' needs and demonstrates that value to users and potential users. This means that value is actually created during the implementation phase of the marketing plan. Implementation generates value not only by ensuring that the most needed services are offered but also by finding new ways to engage with the community through the promotion of those services, thus forming and strengthening relationships with patrons. By letting users know that their needs have been acknowledged (or even anticipated) and met, librarians are delighting users and deepening user trust in the library. This is often the most exciting part of a marketing campaign!

As initial feedback begins to trickle in and more users become aware of new services, it may be tempting to second-guess the plan. Nevertheless, if librarians have committed to meeting users' needs and believe that their marketing plan does so in the best, most feasible way possible, they should feel confident in bringing the plan to fruition, seeing the value it creates and demonstrates to the library's community, and seeing its effects on patron relationships. Commitment to the long haul—the entire marketing plan—is important.

This does not mean that user feedback cannot be taken into account throughout the process. Adapting to users within the overall framework of a marketing plan is paramount. Having procedures in place for responding to patron feedback during campaigns, particularly on social media, is vital. Librarians should not be discouraged when particular pieces of content do not perform well but instead take note of what is and is not working and continue to deliver quality content within the scope of the marketing plan.

CAPTURING VALUE FROM LIBRARY USERS

After implementing a plan that created value for patrons by meeting their information needs, librarians must "capture," or retain, a portion of the created value. In marketing, capturing value often means to monetize created value. While this could be the case for libraries, more often librarians measure captured value as increases in the usage of programs, services, and collections. Relationships formed during the implementation of the plan can also be capitalized upon so that more patrons are using the library's services (and telling others about them!).

If librarians have followed the guidelines of this chapter, they will have set clear and defined goals for capturing value (e.g., reaching more potential users, increasing use) for the marketing plan. How is it possible to know if these goals are met and demonstrate that value is captured? No single metric will demonstrate the success of the marketing plan and its implementation, and consideration of assessment should begin before the plan is put into place and continue throughout. Before embarking upon a plan, Solomon (2016, 90) suggests considering three questions: How will marketing channels be monitored? What goals are meant to be achieved through the marketing plan? What metrics will be used to measure success?

The metrics for assessment will vary according to each library, each marketing plan, and intended goals. Typical conversion or value capture metrics for libraries include door counts/visitor counts, circulation statistics, program attendance, new library card registrations, and website visits. Today, especially in an environment that is so focused on electronic resources and content marketing, additional metrics can, and often should, be used to assess conversion and usage. Librarians can also measure online interactions, sometimes referred to as conversion rates in marketing. For example, if a librarian creates a tweet asking people to post their favorite book and 40 of the 200 people who view that tweet respond with a post, then the conversion rate for that post is 20 percent.

Metrics differ according to platform and goals but often include engagement metrics on social media platforms, including likes, shares, retweets, comments, and clicks. Many marketing channels offer built-in analytic functions. Some of these are available at no cost; others may cost money and offer more functionality. Audience size, or the number of followers, and the growth rate may also be worth tracking for specific marketing campaigns. If blog and website visits are key parts of a marketing plan, page views, unique visitors, page depth (how long visitors stay on the blog or website), and bounce rates (how many visitors visit only one page before leaving) should be measured. For e-mail campaigns and e-newsletters, it is useful to measure open rates, link clicks, unsubscribe rates, and forwards.

Not all success can be measured through statistics, and analytics. Anecdotes from comments on social media or from face-to-face conversations with library users can be used to demonstrate a campaign's success. Frontline staff can be asked to collect user stories. Though not as straightforward as statistics, these anecdotes and stories are powerful and will help show the strength of the marketing campaign. With permission, anecdotes and patron stories can be incorporated into marketing campaigns. For example, a patron who secures a job in part as a result of help from librarians may be willing to share their library story in an e-newsletter feature or even at an upcoming budget meeting.

The moment a library stops assessing its marketing plan and strategies is the moment that its marketing declines in quality. Even when a marketing plan is successful, there is room for improvement. Relationships with library users can always be strengthened; new users can always be reached. Most importantly, society, demographics, and technology change, and users will expect their libraries and library services to continue to adapt to meet their needs. Librarians should apply the information found earlier and in Chapter 8 on metrics and tools for assessment to library marketing assessment. It is important to improve upon what worked (if people liked it, try to delight them even more!), attempt to tap into the potential of good ideas that fell just short, and consider letting go of things that did not work well. Continual improvement is important so that library users and potential users can connect with resources that they need and value.

COMMON MARKETING TOOLS

Many specific marketing tools have been discussed during this chapter. While librarians will undoubtedly be familiar with some of these tools, one must consider them anew through the lens of a marketing plan. This section presents common marketing tools used by librarians in the field, as well as best practices for both print and online platforms. Digging into marketing tools is an exciting facet of the marketing process and is a great way for librarians to use their design skills and creativity.

Print

Despite the influx of online resources and interactions, libraries are physical spaces and print material is still important. Promotional materials such as flyers, table tents, and print calendars are effective ways of reaching users who already utilize the library. In public libraries, print material is particularly important for patrons who are not comfortable using computers or do not have home Internet access. While print material can be a great place for creativity and humor, it is important to keep print promotional material consistent and professional. Signage and flyers represent the library and will make an impression on users. Are patrons likely to attend a computer class if they learn about it from a handwritten note on the bulletin board? Probably not.

Most librarians are not graphic designers, and creating beautiful, professional, and eye-catching signage might be intimidating. However, there are tools to help create professional marketing materials. Many librarians use *Canva* to easily create eye-catching flyers. Photoshop and other Creative Cloud programs, as well as open-source programs like GIMP, are powerful design tools. Having material printed professionally will also make a huge impact. It may be necessary to outsource the printing of higher-profile print material to a local print shop.

Best practices for print material include the following:

- Ensure the library's name, logo, address, and contact information appear on every document.
- Create a color palate for the library and use it for all official signage.
- Limit flyers to essential information, but provide ways for users to find more information, such as links or a staff person to contact.
- Use a large font size in a color that can be seen clearly.
- Avoid putting text over patterned backgrounds or photos.

Online Marketing Tools

Library Website

Websites are often the first place potential users go to learn about the library. As such, library websites should be designed to maximize marketing potential. Home blocks with featured resources and events are an ideal place to advertise new databases or upcoming events. A news section across the top of the page is also a good place to reach audiences who are unlikely to navigate beyond the library's home page. Within the library website, there should be an up-to-date calendar with accurate descriptions of upcoming programs and a list with links to all databases and other resources and services offered by the library. Finally, it is essential that the website displays correctly on mobile devices.

When creating or updating a website, language must be considered carefully. Search engine optimization sounds like a daunting and technical task but is simply learning the most popular search terms and then using that same language on a website to ensure that user and site find each other (Potter 2012, 82). In a way, this is like using specific buzz words to attract a target audience. *Google Trends* can help differentiate between popular and antiquated language.

E-newsletter

E-newsletters are one of the best ways to send messages directly to library users. Librarians should include an e-newsletter sign-up on the website as well as on library card registration forms. Many e-mail marketing services offer templates and built-in analytics tools that not only help librarians create aesthetically pleasing newsletters but also track the open rate and click rates of the e-mail. When possible, newsletters should be tailored to reach specific audiences. For example, summer newsletters that are sent only to parents of children participating in summer reading are more likely to be opened because they are going directly to the inboxes of the target audience. Newsletters can be distributed directly to users or through listservs that reach specific audiences.

Social Media

Social media platforms are unlike other promotional channels in that they allow users to interact with and learn from each other. They are not only a place to promote services and events but also a place to receive feedback and engage directly with library users. As mentioned earlier in the chapter, these platforms can be powerful tools for public relations. Social media channels are also popular promotional tools for libraries because they are primarily free.

According to a 2018 Pew Research Center study, seven in ten Americans use social media (Smith and Anderson 2018). This demonstrates the huge opportunity for current and potential users to engage with the library and each other on these platforms. Such potential means that it is critical for librarians to think strategically about what they are posting, when they are posting it, and how they are responding to user engagement. Social media posts should relate to the library, but they must also provide value to users in order to increase followers and drive user engagement (Potter 2012, 93). Tying posts to current events and trends is a great way to add value to the library's social media presence. To illustrate, posting about a one-on-one technology help service after the holidays shows users who have been gifted devices that the library can help with a specific need.

Regardless of library type, having a strategic social media plan will improve the visibility of content posted and support engagement. Keeping the library's user personae in mind is particularly important when posting on social media. Using words and phrases that are popular for specific audiences will make content easier for that group to understand and increase engagement (Solomon 2016, 66). Clearly social media is more than a promotional channel; it is a place to create users relationships and engage users in conversation. That being said, all content should support the goals of the library. Many social media platforms have built-in analytics tools that allow users to see the most popular days/times to post content and the demographic information for users that are engaging with published content.

Facebook

Facebook remains the most widely used social media platform by a healthy margin: Pew research indicates that 68 percent of U.S. adults are *Facebook* users (Smith and Anderson 2018). The library's *Facebook* account can and should be more than just a place to promote events and collections. As discussed earlier, marketing is not a one-way street. If the library can establish itself as a known place to find entertaining, informative, and interesting content, it is more likely that patrons will choose to follow the library and continue to engage.

Facebook uses an algorithm to select the content that is displayed in a user's news feed. This means that if a user frequently likes content from a page, they are more likely to see posts from that page in their news feed in the future. If many people interact with a post, it is more likely to show up in their news feeds and also show up in their friends' news feeds. Librarians should strive to use this algorithm to their advantage by posting interesting content that many people will interact with and, in turn, other people will see. Asking questions is a good way to drive user interaction. On the other end of the spectrum, if there are long pauses between posts or posts are simply not being liked or commented on, there is a reduced chance users will see the library's content at all.

In many cases, several staff members contribute content to *Facebook*. This is another reason why a marketing plan is essential. Posting too much may overwhelm followers, but waiting days or weeks to respond to a comment reflects poorly on the library and does not promote the social nature of the platform. A plan should ensure that someone is responsible for posting and responding to user inquiries every day. *Facebook* also has built-in analytics that allow users to see popular posting times and the general demographics of page followers.

Facebook best practices include the following:

- Build brand recognition by using the library's logo as its profile picture.
- Avoid posting more than three times per day and less than two hours apart, if possible.
- Share additional content as a *Facebook* story, a newer feature of *Facebook* that is akin to the *Instagram* story.
- Use language that *Facebook* users will understand and identify with—do not use library-specific jargon, especially for a public library account.
- Encourage users to engage directly with the page by asking questions.

Twitter

As with *Facebook* and all social media platforms, *Twitter* is not simply a platform to blindly promote library events and resources but a place to interact directly with users and join larger conversations. Users can upload media, write original content up to 280 characters (also known as tweeting), retweet content, comment, or like a post. Users are able to see what others are saying by following them or by looking at popular hashtags. Hashtags are a method of categorizing content, essentially a metadata tag that allows users to view content that pertains to a particular theme. *Twitter*'s structure makes it a great place for fast-paced conversation and connection. Because of the amount of *Twitter* users and the pace at which these users react to each other, it has an ephemeral quality. *Twitter* can be an incredibly powerful word-of-mouth tool if used correctly.

Best practices for *Twitter* include the following:

- Tweet interesting content such as articles related to libraries and information literacy in general.
- Use a casual voice to make content approachable for target personae.
- Respond to users as quickly as possible, and use language that is similar to the original tweet.
- Engage in conversation.

Instagram

Instagram is a social media platform that relies heavily on images and is extremely popular among the new adult demographic. According to Pew research,

71 percent of Americans between the ages of eighteen and twenty-four use *Instagram* (Smith and Anderson 2018). The main functions are posting media such as videos and photographs, following other users, liking images, and commenting on images. There are three ways for users to post content: on their home page, which will then show up in their followers' feed; in a story, which will disappear after twenty-four hours; and as a direct message. As with *Twitter*, *Instagram* uses hashtags as a way of grouping content with a specific theme. *Instagram* has an analytics function that allows account owners to see the reach of each story and post, as well as a breakdown of the demographics of the account's audience.

Best practices for *Instagram* include the following:

- Post only high-quality and thoughtful images.
- Avoid posting more than twice a day.
- Use a relatable tone: be funny, ask questions, and so on.
- Increase engagement and post reach by using popular hashtags.
- Create a library-specific hashtag and encourage its use.

Blogs

Blogs are a casual and informative way to highlight programs, services, and collections. Because blogs allow for more text and images than other social media platforms, they are an excellent way to give users a lot of information. Therefore, blog posts are a good alternative to adding additional pages to the library's website, which could otherwise cause usability issues. As with any marketing or promotional endeavor, remember that each post is a direct reflection of the library and the quality of posts must be high.

Depending on library type, blogs can and should be used for very different purposes. Public librarians may use blogs as a way to post reading lists or photos from outreach events, while librarians at special libraries and local history collections could use blogs to promote unique collections and share ongoing research projects. Academic librarians could coordinate blog posts with events taking place on campus. A post sharing resources for citation would be successful leading up to midterms or finals, for example.

Other Platforms

There are a number of other platforms that can be used to promote library services. The following are a few examples:

- ***Snapchat***: Currently 78 percent of eighteen- to twenty-four-year-olds use this platform (Smith and Anderson 2018). Teen and Young Adult Librarians may want to explore using *Snapchat* to advertise their services.
- ***Meetup***: Essentially a community events calendar, *Meetup* is a good way to reach library users who do not use *Facebook*.
- ***Tumblr***: It is a free and easy-to-use short-form blog that supports a variety of media types, as well as text.
- ***Goodreads***: Libraries with very active book groups may want to consider using *Goodreads* as a way of organizing and promoting their groups online.

Word-of-Mouth Marketing

The library community has embraced word-of-mouth marketing (WOMM)—and for good reason. Unlike print material or social media posting, WOMM is a method of promotion that relies on human connection and shared experience. There are many definitions for WOMM, but all emphasize the basic premise that a small percentage of the population influences the rest of the population. An effective WOMM campaign taps into the power of influencer groups by engaging with them and then providing them information and tools to share their new knowledge with the rest of the community (Dowd, Evangeliste, and Silberman 2010).

An example of a library influencer could be a parent who always brings their child to storytime. This person may be involved in a school committee or other community organizations where they frequently tell others about how great storytime has been for their family. This patron is already engaging in WOMM on behalf of the library, but if a librarian takes a moment to actively engage with the patron and give them a flyer or a calendar of activities, they will be better equipped to share the information with others.

WOMM is not, as its name suggests, only a spoken activity. In fact, the library's influencers will likely use the print and digital promotional material that librarians have created to work their magic. For example, influencers might retweet a photo that the library has posted or give their friends copies of the flyer they have picked up at the library. WOMM is not a traditional promotional channel but rather a tool that amplifies all of the library's other promotional efforts.

A key concept to all marketing, but particularly WOMM, is providing services and programs that meet the needs and interests of users. This subject has been discussed in the audience assessment portion of the chapter but is important to note again. Librarians can promote an event or resources in all the right ways, but if the community does not have a need for it, there will undoubtedly be little interest. WOMM can be successful only if the library offers a service or program with which users want to engage.

Nontraditional and Guerilla Marketing

Sometimes the most unconventional approach is the one that garners the most attention. Guerilla marketing is a promotional method that relies on creativity and ingenuity rather than a large budget or sleek design. Having library staff wear capes leading up to a library-wide fandom event and yarn bombing a tree outside the library on the day of a knitting group are both low-cost ways to start conversations about library programs. Much like WOMM, guerilla marketing relies on community discussion and engagement. Users or even passersby will likely ask questions about the library's guerilla marketing tactics, and so it is essential that staff from all departments be well informed about the service or program that is being promoted.

While guerilla marketing generally catches the user off guard or is strategically designed to start conversation, nontraditional print material can also be an interesting way to promote the library. For example, a seed library launch might be promoted by printing special seed packets.

Community Partners

Building strong relationships with community partners is a free and effective way to reach larger audiences. When considering community partners, librarians should think beyond nonprofits. Local businesses or entrepreneurs are great resources for collaboration. As an example, the library's book club could meet at a local brewery or restaurant. While the location of a book club may seem like a programming decision, it doubles as marketing strategy. This kind of event will draw both library regulars and people who are enthusiastic about the brewery or restaurant. Tagging the business or adding them as a co-host in a *Facebook* event listing could greatly increase the reach of a post or event.

Traditional Media Outlets

Tapping into traditional media sources such as newspapers, local access channels, and radio stations can be a fruitful method of promoting services. Depending on the community or institution, connecting with these media sources can be a slow process. Once a relationship has been established, however, they will be key allies and even collaborators. Leaders in the traditional media world are often well connected and make great influencers and spokespeople for libraries.

Newspapers

After identifying the appropriate contact person, librarians should send local or institutional newspapers weekly program listings and, in the event of a larger initiative or new resource, more formal press releases. A weekly or monthly library column is an effective way of reaching audiences who follow the newspaper both online and in print. This is an excellent way to highlight new resources, events, and even special collections. If the editor is amenable, a librarian with an interest in writing could even write the column, thus creating little extra work for the newspaper.

Media Centers

Media centers and community access television stations often have similar goals and values as librarians, meaning these organizations will likely be willing to cross-promote services in an effort to reach a greater audience for both institutions. Once a positive relationship is established, media centers can also be powerful programming collaborators. For instance, a community access station may record a nutrition program at their city's public library and make the video available on their website and *YouTube* channel. In partnering, the community access station benefits by acquiring free quality content, while the library program is promoted to new potential users.

CONCLUSION

The marketing process can be time consuming, but it is also fun and extremely rewarding. A well-designed marketing plan will produce tangible results, such as increases in usage, attendance, and engagement. These outcomes can in turn be used to support the library's cause when justifying current or future budgets or an expansion of resources with key stakeholders. These outcomes, though obviously beneficial, are secondary by-products of the marketing process. The real benefit is creating meaningful relationships with library users, connecting people to the right library products and services for their needs, and creating lifelong library users.

REFERENCES

Canva. https://www.canva.com.

Dowd, Nancy, Mary Evangeliste, and Jonathen Silberman. 2010. *Bite-Sized Marketing: Realistic Solutions for the Overworked Librarian.* Chicago: American Library Association.

Facebook. https://www.facebook.com.

Goodreads. http://www.goodreads.com.

Google Trends. https://trends.google.com.

Instagram. https://www.instagram.com.

Kennedy, Marie R., and Cheryl LaGuardia. 2018. *Marketing Your Library's Electronic Resources: A How-to-Do-It Manual for Librarians.* 2nd ed. Chicago: ALA Neal-Schuman, an Imprint of the American Library Association.

Kotler, Philip, Gary Armstrong, and Lloyd C. Harris. 2017. *Principles of Marketing.* 7th ed. Edinburgh, UK: Pearson.

Kotler, Philip, and Nancy Lee. 2007. *Marketing in the Public Sector: A Roadmap for Improved Performance.* Upper Saddle River, NJ: Wharton School Publishing.

Meetup. https://www.meetup.com.

Potter, Ned. 2012. *The Library Marketing Toolkit.* London: Facet Publishing.

Smith, Aaron, and Monica Anderson. 2018. "Social Media Use in 2018." Pew Research Center: Internet and Technology. Last modified March 1, 2018. http://www.pewinternet.org/2018/03/01/social-media-use-in-2018/.

Snapchat. https://www.snapchat.com.

Solomon, Laura. 2016. *The Librarian's Nitty-Gritty Guide to Content Marketing.* Chicago: American Library Association.

Tumblr. https://www.tumblr.com.

Twitter. http://www.twitter.com.

YouTube. http://www.youtube.com.

SUGGESTED READINGS

Avrin, David, Jeffrey Gitomer, and Roger Sheety. 2016. *Visibility Marketing: The No-Holds-Barred Truth about What It Takes to Grab Attention, Build Your Brand, and Win New Business.* Wayne, NJ: Career Press.

Emphasizing the holistic marketing process, the authors explore the connection between market research, quality product offerings, customer service, and promotion. It is a great resource for librarians trying to demonstrate competitive advantage to users.

Barber, Peggy, and Linda K. Wallace. 2010. *Building a Buzz: Libraries & Word-of-Mouth Marketing.* Chicago: American Library Association.

Barber and Wallace give an overview of word-of-mouth marketing for librarians. They include tips, best practices, case studies, and interviews from librarians across the country.

Bizzle, Ben, and Maria Flora. 2015. *Start a Revolution: Stop Acting like a Library*. Chicago: American Library Association.

This book tells the story of the Craighead County Jonesboro Public Library in Arkansas, where Bizzle and his colleagues "revolutionized" their institution through marketing. It details a holistic approach to marketing, including traditional and nontraditional methods, with particular emphasis on community engagement and using humor to boost promotional efforts.

Media Relations Handbook for Libraries. 2012. American Library Association. http://www.ala.org/advocacy/advleg/publicawareness/campaign%40yourlibrary/prtools/handbook.

This resource provides practical media relations guidance along with examples of press releases, letters to the editor, and public service announcements.

Miller, Kivi Leroux. *The Nonprofit Marketing Guide: High-Impact, Low-Cost Ways to Build Support*. John Wiley & Sons, 2010.

This book offers tips for nonprofit marketing, emphasizing effective, low-cost methods. Miller shares useful marketing basics, as well insights for those beginning to explore content marketing.

Scott, David Meerman. 2015. *The New Rules of Marketing & PR: How to Use Social Media, Online Video, Mobile Applications, Blogs, News Releases, and Viral Marketing to Reach Buyers Directly*. Hoboken, NJ: John Wiley & Sons.

Meerman explains nuances between public relations and marketing in today's content-driven marketing world while providing marketing strategies for immediate implementation and several real-world case studies.

Chapter 11

Reference Services for Children and Young Adults

Amy S. Pattee

INTRODUCTION

While reference service to children and young people is often considered a "special case" of information work, the goal is the same as that which Dave A. Tycksoson writes in Chapter 1: to provide "direct assistance" to library patrons as they search for and evaluate information. This direct assistance includes negotiating directional queries; instructing patrons in the use of the library and its resources; providing readers' advisory; and recommending resources to satisfy a library user's informational, educational, or recreational reading needs and interests.

Professional distinction between reference services to adults and reference services to young people is a function of greater institutional, cultural, and social distinctions between young people and adults. Broadly speaking, young people are often understood in monolithic terms as "not adults," and reference and information services for young people are understood in terms of their difference from similar services libraries and information institutions provide to adults. The growing influence of childhood studies on the work of scholars and critics working in library and information science (LIS) and children's literature has led to more nuanced thinking about the young people libraries seek to serve. Additionally, contemporary recognition of the racial, ethnic, linguistic, ability, gender, sexuality, and socioeconomic diversity of the population of people once classed solely as "youth" has led to more context- and situation-attentive discussions of young people's information needs and interests. This increased and sharpened focus on the diverse information lives of young users has and will continue to shape and reshape reference and information services to young people.

YOUTH IDENTITIES AND INFORMATION NEEDS

Young people may identify or be identified in a number of institutional, social, and cultural ways. Young people most frequently identify and are identified in terms of categories associated with age; however, they also identify and are identified in terms related to ability, race and ethnicity, and gender and sexuality. As Nicole Cooke points out in Chapter 12, these identity categories are not exclusive, and most library users, including young people, claim intersecting identities. The meanings young people attach to the identities they claim—and the meanings adults associate with the same—emerge in institutional, social, and cultural contexts that construct—and, as these contexts evolve, reconstruct—the parameters of young people's information worlds.

Developmental Approaches to Identifying and Serving Young People

The American Library Association (ALA) divisions responsible for setting standards and authoring guidelines for librarians serving young people, the Association for Library Services to Children (ALSC) and the Young Adult Library Services Association (YALSA), distinguish children as people from birth through eighth grade (ALSC) and young adults as people between the ages of twelve and eighteen (YALSA). These age- and grade-based descriptions of young people position them within an explicit system of educational development and an implicit cognitive and social developmental framework on which much professional writing elaborates. As these oft-referenced schema (see Table 11.1) posit that all typically developing young people of a certain age or assigned to a specific grade in school are intellectually or developmentally similar and grow and change in a predictable, sequential, and cumulative way, age- and grade-based descriptions of young people have become markers of identity that adults and young people reference and claim to differing degrees. Consequently, theories of cognitive, social and emotional, and literacy development provide librarians with useful frameworks to guide collection

TABLE 11.1 Milestones of Social/Emotional, Cognitive, and Literacy Development of Infants, Toddlers, Preschoolers, School-aged Children, and Adolescents.

	Social and Emotional Development	Cognitive Development	Literacy Development
Infants (ages 0 – 1)	• Expresses basic emotions (e.g., happiness, sadness, anger, fear) • Recognizes basic emotions signaled by others' facial expressions and voices	• Develops an understanding of cause and effect • Develops facility with visual tracking • Begins to develop strategies to focus attention	• Demonstrates an increasing ability to communicate wants, needs, and interests using language • Engages in language "play" through song and chant • Develops the ability to recite the alphabet and recognize letters
Toddlers (ages 2 – 3)	• Distinguishes between self and others	• Understands images or pictures as symbolic representations	• Continues to increase ability to communicate wants, needs, and interests using language

	Social and Emotional Development	Cognitive Development	Literacy Development
	• Engages in selective imitation • Demonstrates pro-social and helping behavior	• Can speak in two-word sentences	• Continues to engage in language "play" through song and chant • Continues to develop the ability to recite the alphabet and recognize letters
Pre-schoolers (ages 3 – 5)	• Expresses empathy • Engages in cooperative play • Develops the ability to identify and describe own emotions • Develops an understanding of "fairness" • Recognizes and enforces social norms	• Speaks first language fluently • Recognizes counting and can conceive of simple mathematical concepts	• Continues to increase ability to communicate using language • Continues to engage in language "play" through song and chant • Continues to develop the ability to recite the alphabet and recognize letters
School Aged Children (ages 6 – 11)	• Begins to regulate own behavior • Refines understanding of the emotions of self and others • Places importance on peer group associations • Expresses sensitivity to evidence of social exclusion	• Demonstrates increasing ability to consider multiple sources of information • Thinks about own thinking and reasoning processes and strategies (metacognition)	• Hones understanding of the relationships between letters and word sounds (phonological awareness) • Applies phonological awareness to decoding and comprehension • Develops decoding fluency and increases the number of words that can be read and understood "automatically"
Adolescents (ages 12 – 18)	• Develops and refines strategies for behavior regulation • Increasingly internalizes emotional experiences • Expresses interest in or pursues romantic or sexual relationships	• Exhibits increasing facility for abstract thought • Draws conclusions using deductive reasoning	• Develops literacy across forms and genres • Fluent readers consider multiple perspectives presented in texts

Source: Allen (2017), Bjorklund and Behring (2002), Byrnes (2010), Daum (2017), Farrall (2012), Henderson, Burrows, and Usher (2017), and Svetlova and Carpenter (2017).

development, programming, and reference and information services; however, the principles of Developmentally Appropriate Practice (DAP) urge practitioners to recognize variability in individuals' development as well as the influence of cultural and linguistic contexts on the meanings individuals associate with development and the tasks typically linked to development (National Association for the Education of Young Children 2009). These principles can be usefully applied to the reference transaction with young people, as they encourage those working with the young to consider each young person as an individual with a distinct and evolving cache of abilities, capabilities, interests, and experiences that inform their information behavior.

Library collections for young people are often organized to reflect dominant developmental models and facilitate independent access to material for people who identify within this framework. For example, many libraries separate easy readers—books written and designed for young people who are just learning to decode and comprehend text—from picture books and novels to allow young people learning to read easy access to supportive material. Because Americans attending school typically learn to read in the early elementary years, an American library's easy reader collection is often associated with and recommended to young people in kindergarten, first, or second grade, making this collection one that links age and education with presumed ability. The ages of easy reader protagonists and the experiences these books describe further reflect assumptions about readership: they feature characters with knowledge, concerns, and senses of humor presumed common among members of the kindergarten through second-grade age group and introduce informational concepts to readers who, by virtue of their age, are presumed to have a limited experience of the world. A look around the typical American library reveals that many of its sub-collections are organized to reflect developmental assumptions and used in ways that affirm these assumptions: babies explore bins of board books, teen readers browse material on shelves labeled "young adult," and adults select books from the general or "adult" fiction and nonfiction shelves.

While this traditional form of organization facilitates independent access to material for patrons who identify as typical readers of easy readers, juvenile fiction, and young adult literature, young library patrons might seek resources outside of these collection boundaries or require assistance to find material that speaks to their unique abilities. For example, young readers who are fluent in fantasy might select and read material from across the library's collections of genre fiction for children, young adults, and adults; and young people completing courses for college credit might find appropriate supporting references in the adult collection. Librarians serving young people recognize both the utility and the limitations of collections organized to reflect developmental norms and, in line with DAP, should not consider this form of organization unquestioningly prescriptive. While audience-based organization provides a useful framework for patrons and librarians alike, during the reference interview, librarians should work with young people to determine where across the library they might find the most appropriate resources and material to answer an information query.

All young people may, throughout their lives or at specific points in their lives, have abilities and capabilities that fall both within and outside of standard developmental models. Because it is impossible to determine any individual's wealth of abilities and capabilities just by looking at them, the reference interview provides an opportunity for librarians to encourage agency and provide access to information to people who may be, by turns, exceptional, typical, or challenged readers;

experienced or inexperienced information seekers; and knowledgeable of or unfamiliar with a variety of topics. Applying DAP to reference services to young people means taking this variability into account by adopting an equity approach to reference services that reflects the principles of universal design.

Universal design describes the process of developing resources so that they can be used by the greatest number of people regardless of their age, size, or ability. One of the goals of universal design is "equitable use," in which a service or product is "useful and marketable to people with diverse abilities," "identical wherever possible [and] equivalent when not," and "avoid[s] segregating or stigmatizing any users" (National Disability Authority 2012). Librarians can apply the equity principle of universal design to their reference work with young people by making use of practices associated with reference services to people with disabilities in all of their reference and information transactions. Because such practices (see Box 11.1 for examples) provide developmentally appropriate opportunities for individual patrons to assert their needs and preferences, they allow for what universal designers call the "same means of use" (National Disability Authority 2012) for all patrons.

Box 11.1 Strategies for Delivering Developmentally Appropriate Reference Services to Young People

- Consider each patron an individual with their own needs, interests, and abilities, and approach each patron with an open mind.
- Avoid making assumptions about a patron's abilities or capabilities based on a perception of patron age, circumstance, or ability status.
- Provide opportunities for the patron to communicate their needs, knowledge, abilities, and capabilities during the reference interview.
- Communicate directly with the patron rather than with their caregiver or interpreter.
- Offer a demonstration while describing a process like searching the library catalog or finding a book on the library shelves.
- Offer material in a variety of formats.
- Use the patron's reading experience to determine an appropriate reading recommendation by asking what they last read and enjoyed and using that information to suggest further reading material.

(Association of Specialized Government and Cooperative Library Agencies n.d.; Middleton 2014)

DAP-informed reference service that makes service equity a goal has the potential to mitigate barriers to information and information seeking faced by both typically developing young people and young people with disabilities. For example, for a variety of reasons related to experience, size, education, and ability, young people may be challenged to use the library's online catalog, which often requires users to manipulate a mouse, type, spell, and decode and comprehend the specialized language presented in search results and library records. Finding a book on library shelves assumes the searcher understands alphabetical and numeric organization, often necessitates a tilt of the head to read titles printed on a book's spine, and may require a long reach or a deep squat to retrieve an item, all of which can be challenging for some patrons. Recognizing these potential obstacles, librarians serving young people at the reference desk should not respond to young patrons' requests for titles or information with a brusque "Did you check the catalog?" Instead, the librarian might demonstrate a catalog search after first asking if they can share their computer screen with the patron (some patrons may be bothered by the light or movement projected on a computer monitor), narrate the process, and then ask if the patron would like them to accompany them to retrieve the item. For an illustration of this process, see Box 11.2.

Box 11.2 Activity: Applying DAP to the Reference Interview

A reference interview informed by Developmentally Appropriate Practice (DAP) incorporates opportunities for patrons to establish their preferences and articulate their needs by posing questions to the library patron that allow them to describe the level of assistance, if any, they might require. As you read the following hypothetical reference interview, try to identify when and where the librarian engages with some of the specific DAP strategies listed in the Box 11.1.

Patron: Do you have *One Crazy Summer*, by Rita Williams Garcia?

Librarian: I'm not sure, but I can check and see! Can I show you how I use the library catalog to find out if a book is in the library?

Patron: Sure.

Librarian: Would it be all right if I shared my computer screen with you so that we can both see it?

Patron: Sure.

Librarian: [begins search from the catalog home screen] If you've used the library computer before, you might have seen this screen that lets you search the library's collection and tells you if the library has a book and if it's been checked out. I'm going to type the title and author of the book you just asked for here, in the box under the words "Search the Catalog" [underlines words with finger and points to search box and then narrates the search process for the patron]. . . . It looks like we have this book in a couple of different formats: you can check out a paperback or a hardback copy, an audio book, or an e-book. Do you have a preference for a certain kind of book?

Patron: I want the paperback book.

Librarian: [pulls up the record for the paperback] This screen tells me if the book is checked out or not and where I can find it in the library. Here [points], under "Call Number" I can find the book's address. I'm going to write this down on a piece of paper [writes down call number].

These letters tell me where to find the book: "J" means that it is in the "juvenile collection"—those books on the shelves by the window [points]—and WIL are the first three letters of the author's last name. The books on those shelves by the window are organized by author's last name. The books by authors whose last names begin with "A" are on the shelves near the plant [points], and the books by authors whose last names begin with "Z" are on the shelves by the computers.

Would you like to go and find the book on the shelf together?

Patron: I think I got it from here.

Librarian: Great. If you run into any trouble or can't find the book, come on back and let me know and we'll take a look together.

Culturally Competent Approaches to Serving Diverse Young People

DAP encourages adults working with young people to consider them "within the context of family, community, culture, linguistic norms, social group, past experience . . . and current circumstances" as these contexts shape young people's development and inform how they make sense of the world (National Association for the Education of Young Children 2009, 10). When applied to library services, DAP is enacted through what Patricia Montiel Overall (2009, 181) calls "culturally competent" practices that "expand . . . definitions of information [and] literacy" to reflect diverse historical, social, and cultural conceptions of these terms and ideas. Culturally competent librarians, Overall continues, reflect deeply on their own and diverse cultures; consider the influence of their cultural situation on their personal and professional beliefs and practices; seek to understand the ways in which others' cultural situations inform their own systems of beliefs and practices; and engage with members of diverse communities to create library environments, programs, and services that reflect diverse beliefs, practices, and articulated needs.

Serving Young People from Racially and Ethnically Diverse Backgrounds

The U.S. population of young people is becoming increasingly racially and ethnically diverse; by 2020, the Census Bureau predicts, over half of young people under the age of eighteen will "belong to ethnic or racial minorities" and, by 2060, 64.4 percent will belong to an ethnic or racial minority (Colby and Ortman 2015, 11). While this data suggests that the United States is moving toward greater pluralism, legacies of historical and contemporary racism continue to be felt in communities of people of color and diverse ethnicities even as they grow in size. These racist legacies contribute to barriers to information seeking experienced by young people of color who, Kafi Kumasi (2012) asserts, often feel unwelcome or like "outsiders" in the school or public library. Because a library's environment—including its collections, organization, and services—contributes to patrons' sense of the library as a place "for them" with collections and services that reflect and respect their own histories, traditions, and literatures, culturally competent service to diverse communities involves working with members of these communities to develop inclusive collections and services (Overall 2009).

The canon of children's literature has been historically monocultural and reflective of the white, Eurocentric perspectives and traditions privileged by mainstream publishers of children's literature (Horning et al. 2018; Larrick 1965). When this inequality is replicated in library collections of material for young people and when, as Kumasi (2012, 36) writes, "books with nonwhite themes and characters [are] highlighted only during cultural-heritage weeks or months," the library and its collection can be perceived as a place that "reinforce[s] whiteness as the normative and superior cultural influence." Such an emphasis on a singular history, experience, and literary and cultural tradition, Kumasi and other researchers (e.g., Mestre 2009; Overall 2009; Stivers 2017) assert, can lead to a "feeling of disconnect and exclusion" among young people of color (Hughes-Hassell and Stivers 2015, 122) that then becomes a barrier to information access.

Recent professional writing and activism in the form of the We Need Diverse Books movement have drawn attention to racial and ethnic disparities in children's literary publishing and encouraged librarians to support, purchase, and promote books by and about people of color. Informed by the work of scholar Rudine Sims Bishop (2012, 9), who argues that all people "have a right to books that reflect their own images and books that open less familiar worlds to them," librarians and other adults working with young people have adopted Bishop's "mirrors, windows, and sliding glass doors" metaphor for understanding the power of literature. Books, writes Bishop (2012, 9), can be mirrors for readers, "reflecting their own images"; can serve as "windows . . . into the realities of the multicultural world in which [readers] are living"; and can be "sliding glass doors" that allow readers to enter into a literary lived experience that is similar to or different from their own. While Bishop's argument is most often cited to promote the need for (primarily fictional) literary diversity, the "mirrors, windows, and sliding glass doors" metaphor is appropriate to information resources as well. To best capture the "realities of the multicultural world," libraries serving young people should include fiction, poetry, and informational resources that convey the perspectives and describe the knowledge traditions, histories, cultures, and achievements of people of color and of diverse ethnicities.

A belief that "it is crucial for children to 'see themselves in the book'" (Coats 2010, 111) motivates much of librarians' work to diversify their collections and promote and recommend diverse literary and informational resources. However, librarians should be wary of the limitations of this thinking when providing reference and readers' advisory services to young people. For example, if librarians conceive of the reading experience as one that can only be facilitated by way of a reader's direct identification with a character or situation, diverse literature is reduced to a singular or "niche" value, and "the experiences of other races" as lived and captured in literature are perceived as having "no relevance or meaning to any other race" (Overton 2016, 14). While readers do find pleasure and connection in material that reflects their own experiences, librarians serving young people should be wary of essentializing both the reading experience and the readers they are serving. By keeping Bishop's "mirrors, windows, and sliding glass doors" metaphor in mind, librarians can honor the range of experiences about which young people may wish to read and work to create opportunities for young people to describe the literary experiences they seek.

Librarians' perceptions of literary and informational resources—as appropriate or inappropriate mirrors, windows, or doors for young people—may be very different from young people's perceptions of the same, particularly when a librarian occupies a different institutional, social, or cultural position than the young person or people they are serving. For example, literature that privileges the stories and lived experiences of people whose voices have been historically or are contemporarily marginalized may include counter-narratives that dispute what Daniel G. Solórzano and Tara J. Yosso (2002, 32) call "majoritarian stories of racial privilege" and disrupt thinking that privileges dominant (white) narratives and experiences (Delgado 1989). Such challenges, when addressed uncritically, can lead adults working with young people who benefit from the privileges revealed and confronted in counter-narratives to relegate counter-stories to "second-tier choices" (Haddix and Price-Dennis 2013, 277). That diverse literatures, including those written by and about people of color and people who claim ethnic, cultural, and religious minority identities, are more frequently challenged or banned should encourage librarians to further advocate for this material (Adebayo 2016).

Kumasi and Sandra Hughes-Hassell (2017, 16) urge librarians to "honor the literate legacies of racialized youth" and "promote inquiry into their 'textual lineages.'" In order to honor these legacies, librarians must develop mechanisms for young people to articulate their information and reading needs and interests. One of the primary mechanisms for this articulation is the reference interview, during which librarians can use open-ended questions to encourage patrons to share what they know about a topic and what they want to know or read. Julie Stivers (2017, 15) encourages librarians to value the knowledge and contexts that inform young people's information-seeking and reading preferences and that emerge in response to the open-ended questions posed in the reference interview, and conceives of work with young people as "grounded in learning and discovering together and from each other." This advice repositions librarians as facilitators rather than gatekeepers to information and literature for young people.

Serving Young People Who Are Emergent Bilingual or Multilingual

While English is and, according to U.S. Census predictions, will remain the primary language spoken by the majority of people in the United States through 2020, throughout the country a substantial number of young people identify or are identified as English Language Learners (ELLs) and may exhibit varying degrees of proficiency reading, writing, and speaking in English. While the most recent data from the National Center for Education Statistics (2018) has demonstrated that the percentage of the population of young people receiving English language instruction in public schools has held steady at a little more than 9 percent, the proportion of young people who identify or are identified as ELLs varies significantly across the United States, with the greatest percentage of ELLs found in California (21%), Texas (16.8%), Nevada (16.8%), and New Mexico (15.7%).

Rather than being described as ELLs, young people learning English might be better understood as emergent bilingual or multilingual learners, terms researcher Mariana Souto-Manning (2016, 263) argues honor the "rich, sophisticated language and literacy practices" in which young people learning English engage in their home or community language(s). Library collections and services can honor these practices as well. Bilingual material and material written in languages other than English that reflect the knowledge, cultural, and linguistic traditions of the diversity of people in a library's service population aid in young people's bilingual and multilingual learning. As Jamie Campbell Naidoo asserts, "It is critical that children whose first language is not English have engaging learning opportunities in their first language to improve their literacy success and support development of a second language" (quoted in Payne and Ralli 2017, 27). Just as material by and about people of color reveals a library's respect for and investment in the historical and lived cultures, knowledge, and traditions of people of color, bilingual material and material in languages other than English honor the literacy traditions and experiences of emergent bilingual or multilingual young people and their families, contribute to its welcoming environment, and help to break down linguistic barriers to information access.

Emerging bilingual and multilingual learners may struggle to articulate their information needs in English and, depending on their past educational and library experiences, may feel intimidated by the reference desk and the prospect of a reference interview. Graphic signage in the languages spoken by members of the library's service community that distinguishes and draws attention to English language and bilingual material and material in languages other than English and that establishes the reference desk as a point of service can help to ease the stress that may be experienced by emerging bilingual and multilingual learners in the library. During the reference interview, librarians can apply the strategies Valentina Gonzalez (2017, 30) highlights in her description of English-language pedagogy to facilitate communication. Arguing that "the way we deliver information is key to how students receive it," Gonzalez advises teachers and librarians to use "measured speech" and "clear, explicit language" devoid of slang or figurative language to aid comprehension. Using gestures and facial expressions, drawing, or calling up images on the computer can also help to convey information and check comprehension (Carlyle 2013; Gonzalez 2017).

Serving Young People Who Identify as LGBTQIA+

Activism and legislation from the late 20th and early 21st centuries have extended previously restricted civil rights to LGBTQIA+ people and resulted in increased LGBTQIA+ visibility (for an explanation of the acronym "LGBTQIA+," see Box 11.3); however, as the ALA's Gay, Lesbian, Bisexual, and Transgender Round Table notes, "Library materials, programs, and displays related to sexual orientation and gender identity still cause controversy" (n.d., 2). This statement is particularly true in the case of library services to young people, in which the topics of gender and sexual orientation are problematically equated, in the minds of many, with sex and sexual practice deemed inappropriate or even dangerous for young people. For example, books written for young people featuring LGBTQIA+ characters or informational texts addressing sex, gender, and sexuality that include LGBTQIA+ content are disproportionally challenged and banned (Adebayo 2016). Such public concern with LGBTQIA+ material for young people can represent a significant barrier to information seeking among young people, in general, and those who identify as LGBTQIA+, specifically.

Box 11.3 What Does LGBTQIA+ Mean?

LGBTQIA+ is an acronym that stands for lesbian, gay, bisexual, transgender, queer, intersex, and asexual. The plus sign is meant to reflect inclusiveness and the diversity of identities a person who identifies as LGBTQIA+ might claim.

The LGBTQIA+ acronym describes both *sexual orientation*—a person's emotional, romantic, or sexual attraction to other people (lesbian, gay, bisexual, queer, asexual)—and *gender identity*—a person's identity, expression, and sense of themselves as a man, woman, combination of both, or none of the above (transgender, queer, intersex).

Both historically and contemporarily, people whose gender identity; gender expression; or emotional, romantic, or sexual relationships challenge *heteronormativity*, a belief system that heterosexuality is both a universal and natural norm and that gender and sexual orientation are aligned with male and female biological sex, have been criminalized, pathologized, and marginalized. The term "queer" is a legacy of LGBTQIA+ discrimination. Historically used almost exclusively as a derogatory term, "queer" has been reclaimed by many who associate the term with LGBTQIA+ pride and political activism.

(GLAAD 2016; Human Rights Campaign 2019; LGBTQIA Resource Center 2018)

While statistics collected by the Williams Institute (2016) and Gallup (Gates 2017) note that approximately 4 percent of the population identifies as LGBTQIA+, not everyone who identifies as LGBTQIA+ may be "out." Young people identifying as LGBTQIA+ may be out to different people in different degrees: they may be out to some or all members of their family but not out at school; or they might come out to their close friends but not to their classmates or teachers (Human Rights Campaign Foundation 2018). Variations in young people's disclosure of their sexuality and gender identity are directly related to their perception of physical and psychological safety in different interpersonal contexts: young people identifying as LGBTQIA+ are frequently bullied or verbally or physically threatened by those in communities in which they are out and by those who perceive their identity as LGBTQIA+ (Human Rights Campaign Foundation 2018). LGBTQIA+ people of color experience particular challenges to their senses of safety and well-being and "may encounter racism and discrimination . . . that can complicate their ability to express, explore, and/or manage their LGBTQ identities" (Human Rights Campaign Foundation 2018, 11). LGBTQIA+ young people who perceive threats to their welfare in public and institutional environments like schools may also perceive the library as a potentially unsafe space, and this perception of threat can emerge as a barrier to information seeking and access.

Reports issued by the Human Rights Campaign and GLSEN (the organization formerly known as the Gay, Lesbian, and Straight Education Network) point out and describe the benefits of inclusive curricula, teacher allies, and explicit bullying or harassment policies for LGBTQIA+ students in supportive schools (Human Rights Campaign Foundation 2018; Kosciw et al. 2016). Drawing from these examples, libraries and librarians should develop strategies to ensure that young people who identify as LGBTQIA+ feel safe and supported in the library. For example, because it can be difficult for young people who identify as LGBTQIA+ to "ascertain who is willing to be an ally . . . and who is not" (Chapman 2015, 32), librarians may need to engage in outreach to the LGBTQIA+ community of young people to establish their investment in and support for this population. Developing and promoting collections of material by, about, and in support of the experiences of LGBTQIA+ people can contribute to young patrons' perceptions of the library as a welcoming place as well (Oltmann 2016; Robinson 2016). Tracy Robinson (2016, 171, 170) recommends making LGBTQIA+ inclusive material "visible through year-round integration in book displays [and] booklists (printed and digital)" and discourages the use of distinctive spine labels that might advertise a patron's interest in LGBTQIA+ content and threaten their privacy and sense of safety, particularly if they are not out to family and friends.

Because young people interested in reading about LGBTQIA+ people may or may not identify as LGBTQIA+ themselves, librarians should avoid making assumptions with regard to the identities of patrons requesting LGBTQIA+ information or literature. Joel A. Nichols (2016, 41) encourages librarians to take a "gender-neutral" approach to library services and promotes "seeking out books with illustrations, stories, and themes that celebrate individuality and dignity in diversity, including books that do not rely on rigid gender roles" for all patrons. Furthermore, Nichols (2016, 41) advocates "using 'they' as an alternate pronoun to he or she. It is a way to neutralize the way you refer to someone whose gender you do not know or do not recognize, which might help avoid misgendering someone." Using "they" to refer to all patrons, unless and until they establish the pronouns they, themselves, use, can also help a librarian call attention to their own internalized assumptions with regard to patron identity and aid in their address and correction of these assumptions.

Library Services and Youth Identities

Young people, like adults, are people with knowledge, histories, abilities, and capabilities that emerge from their experiences as people with disabilities or typically developing people; people of color or white people; people who are mono-, bi-, or multilingual; and people who identify as straight or LGBTQIA+. Library services to young people should be attentive not only to the ways in which young peoples' information needs and information seeking might emerge from concerns or experiences related to their identities as they are lived but also to the ways in which others' biased perceptions of people who claim various identities can create barriers to information and information services. Such barriers to information arise when an institution, person, or librarian makes an assumption about the abilities or capabilities of a person based on their perception of their ability, race, ethnicity, linguistic capability, gender, or sexuality. Age represents an additional factor that contributes to both an "individual's life situation" and the information needs and interest that emerge from this context. DAP provides a model for librarians to consider the relationship between a person's "life situation" and their information needs and interests and encourages librarians to consider each young person they serve an individual, listen to and appreciate the information wants or needs they articulate in their own terms, and respond to their information requests with honor and respect.

YOUNG PEOPLE'S INFORMATION ACCESS: BARRIERS AND CHALLENGES

Librarians serving young people negotiate the same types of queries as their adult-serving counterparts; however, the contexts in which these queries emerge are often unique to young people and affect both information access and reference query negotiation. For example, although the American Library Association's (2019b) "Library Bill of Rights" asserts that "a person's right to use a library should not be denied or abridged because of origin, age, background, or views," federal law and library policies can and do construct barriers to information that effectively "abridge" young people's access to resources because of age. Assumptions about the character and nature of young people's information requests and concerns about the "appropriateness" of the material requested by or recommended to young people can lead to practices that "abridge" their access to resources as well.

Facilitating Young People's Access to Online Resources

Adults and young people turn to the Internet and digital resources to answer ready-reference questions, inform research pursuits, and provide crowd-sourced or personal readers' advisory. Federal and state mandates and laws requiring schools and public libraries to install filtering software on staff and public access computers can restrict all patrons' access to the information they seek; however, the policies libraries develop in response to these mandates can disproportionately affect young people. Lack of opportunity to "practice" online searching skills and lack of information literacy instruction that attends to the online environment can construct access barriers for young people as well. To ensure that the young people they serve are able to access the digital information and content they want and need, librarians serving young people must attend to federal and state legislation and local district, county, and library policy and develop strategies for both facilitating access to and instructing young people in the safe and effective use of digital resources.

Internet Filters, Policy, and Access

Since the 2000 implementation of the Children's Internet Protection Act (CIPA) and the subsequent or co-occurring passage of state laws requiring schools and libraries to develop policies to restrict public access to specific digital content, Internet filters have become commonplace in school and public libraries. Designed to restrict access to online images considered "obscene," "child pornography," or "harmful to minors," CIPA requires schools and libraries that receive certain types of federal funding to install filtering software on their computers to block access to potentially dangerous content and incorporate online safety instruction into their curricula (Batch 2014). While only those libraries participating in certain funding programs are required to install filters and develop online safety curricula to comply with CIPA, individual states have established laws governing how schools and libraries may provide young people with access to the Internet. Although the majority of these states do not mandate the use of filtering software and, instead, require schools and libraries to develop Internet use policies intended to prevent young people from accessing potentially harmful content, a number of states require school and/or public libraries serving young people to filter Internet access in their institutions (National Conference of State Legislatures 2016). Libraries that adhere to these regulations typically provide opportunities for adults to request that filtering software be "turned off" during an Internet use session and make allowances for "constitutionally protected content that is wrongfully filtered [to] be unblocked . . . for users of any age" (Batch 2014, 11).

Critics of filters point out that filtering software has been demonstrated to "over-block" legitimate sites and "under-block" the same content the software seeks to restrict and have documented circumstances in which constitutionally protected speech has been restricted by Internet filtering (ALA 2015; Batch 2014). More specifically, research has described and pointed out cases in which information related to health, non-dominant religions, and online resources supportive of LGBTQIA+ people and communities has been blocked by filters and noted the relevance and importance of this content to young people seeking information online (Batch 2014; Hughes-Hassell, Hanson-Baldauf, and Burke 2008; Storts-Brinks 2010). Filters may also restrict patron access to social media and interactive Web tools that allow users to upload and share content, comment on others' content, and collaborate. These restrictions, too, have been criticized in the library literature and by the ALA (2019c), which argues that prohibiting young people's access to interactive social networking tools both "den[ies] minors' rights to free expression online" and fails to address the need for education that would provide young people with "opportunities to learn and develop skills needed for responsible speech online, civil engagement, and personal-privacy protection."

Because young people are unequally affected by Internet filtering, librarians serving young people should take a proactive stance with regard to selection, policy, and management of local filters by serving on selection committees tasked with purchasing or subscribing to filtering services and contributing to local configuration and assessment. The ALA (n.d.) has published guidelines for libraries and librarians meant to advise them in their selection, management and assessment of filtering software in an effort to "minimize the negative effects of Internet content filters on intellectual freedom." For example, while many Internet filters are "pre-configured," their default settings can and should be locally manipulated to allow the greatest access possible under the law. The ALA (n.d.) encourages libraries to "avoid blocking content based on viewpoint or because the topic is controversial" and discourages blocking "entire types of content (e.g. videos or social media) or protocols (i.e. music streaming)" unless bandwidth is a significant concern. Because of the potential for patron privacy to be compromised, the ALA (n.d.) also advises libraries not to enable decryption on filters that have this capability. Librarians serving young people should not only be active participants in local configuration but also work with the library administration, board, and legal counsel to establish access policies that allow young people to request that restricted sites be unblocked either permanently or for specific and established purposes.

Digital Information Literacy

Researchers have identified a number of characteristic challenges faced by young people who are novice online information seekers, and understanding these challenges can help a librarian anticipate and respond to young people who are having difficulty finding material online. In general, young people struggle to conduct effective searches and have difficulty evaluating and selecting from among search results. For example, young people often enter natural language queries into search engines, online catalogs, and databases and frequently struggle to identify the types of appropriately specific keywords that would return useful search results (Bilal and Gwizdka 2018; Bilal and Kirby 2002; Kammerer and Bohnacker 2012). When search results are returned, young people, and inexperienced users in particular, often click indiscriminately on top results, privileging convenience and habit over in-depth evaluation and exploration (Gwizdka and Bilal 2017). In short, many young people lack what researchers Dania Bilal and Jacek Gwizdka (2018, 1038) call "search task literacy," the ability to "decipher search tasks, identify task requirements, and manipulate complex (research-oriented) versus simple (fact-finding) tasks."

Librarians can engage in what might be called "passive" reference services meant to facilitate young people's access to online information by creating webliographies of resources that feature safe and reliable content that answers young people's information needs. As LIS research has demonstrated that young people find more success browsing rather than searching information systems (Martens 2012), browse-able webliographies that are easily navigated from a launch page on the library's website represent useful resources that can aid young people's online information seeking. Because both typically developing young people and young people with disabilities may lack the fine motor skills necessary to manipulate a mouse to point to and click on small, hyperlinked targets (Hourcade 2007, cited in Martens 2012), library-developed webliographies should feature large, well-spaced, and graphic hyperlinks to ease browsing. While mouse alternatives, like trackpads, oversized trackballs, and joysticks, should always be available for library users with motor difficulties, these tools represent universal design options for young people developing motor coordination.

When conducting "active" reference using online resources or when called upon to help a young person who is actively searching the Internet, librarians should work to incorporate moments of "search task literacy" instruction within the reference transaction. For example, instead of wordlessly turning to the computer to "Google" the answer to a ready-reference question, a librarian can narrate the process, describe the search terms they used, explain how and why they chose these terms, and "think aloud" to demonstrate how they select links to pursue from the list of search results. When working with patrons who are already engaged at a public access computer, librarians can serve as teachers and research partners, helping young information seekers to brainstorm lists of potential keywords or search terms and offering suggestions for identifying the language of the information system in use or making use of features like Google's "query suggestions," which Bilal and Gwizdka (2018) state may be of particular utility to young or inexperienced searchers.

Facilitating Young People's Access to Educational Resources

Whether a young person is educated in a public or private school or at home, their educational context motivates a particular kind of information seeking that Melissa Gross (1995) has termed the "imposed query" and that describes circumstances in which a person is asked to seek, find, and report on information in response to a third party's (e.g., a teacher's) request. Most, if not all, of young people's school-related information seeking is motivated by imposed queries of greater or lesser specificity. For example, students are often tasked to find facts to complete worksheets, compile and present biographical information about a person they have been told is significant, and read and report on specific works of literature; all of these typical assignments represent imposed queries. For more information about the imposed query, see Chapter 3.

Gross (2000) suggests a number of strategies librarians can employ to negotiate imposed queries. When possible, librarians should "get ahead of the question" by paying attention to frequently asked questions, particularly when they seem to reflect particular educational demands. For example, when librarians find themselves fielding multiple queries in the space of a week about "colonial craftspeople," they might note the details of the information queries, as well as the information resources that seemed to best answer these questions for their patrons. Reference statistics like these, collected over time, can help a library identify trends in information needs as they reflect the local curriculum and its annual implementation and can help a library prepare for recurring information seeking by developing temporary reference collections of high-need material or purchasing material to meet periodic demand. Gross (2000) also encourages public librarians to work directly with teachers and school librarians to identify opportunities for collaborative service or facilitate communication about major assignments or projects in advance. This advice is reiterated in many professional handbooks for youth services librarians (e.g., Larson 2015; Peck 2014), which describe further opportunities that could emerge from such collaboration.

Negotiating an imposed query often requires a librarian to help a patron "reconstruct or discover the context" of the query, a process that might result in a reformulation of the initial question (Gross 1999). "Neutral questioning," a strategy for reference interviewing described by Brenda Dervin and Patricia Dewdney (1986), can help both the librarian and the patron discern or reconstruct the context of an information need motivated by an imposed query. Because they provide the library patron with more opportunity to voice their own understandings of their information needs, neutral questions help a librarian avoid what Dervin and Dewdney (1986, 509) call "premature diagnosis" of a user's information need (i.e., when a librarian erroneously assumes they know what a patron needs before the patron can articulate the need themselves). Librarians should be careful to treat each reference transaction—whether it is motivated by an imposed or self-generated query—individually and avoid assumptions that, Dervin and Dewdney caution, may be "wrong and hence dysfunctional or even offensive" (1986, 510). Box 11.4 provides examples of neutral questions.

Box 11.4 Examples of Neutral Questions

Brenda Dervin and Patricia Dewdney (1986) advocate for the use of neutral questioning—open-ended questions that serve to guide information seekers in their understanding and formulation of their information need and query—to determine the situation or context in which a person's information need arose, to identify what information seekers both know and seek to uncover in their information seeking, and to describe the way the information will be used with an eye toward identifying an appropriate source or sources to answer the information seeker's query.

The following questions, drawn from Dervin and Dewdney's suggestions (1986, 510), represent examples of neutral questions or prompts that could be used in a reference transaction with a young person.

- Would you tell me a little about what you know about this topic already?
- Can you tell me what you would like to know about this topic?
- What will information about this topic help you to understand or do?
- What would be the best way for you to learn about this topic?

Questions for reflection and discussion:

1. How do these questions help a librarian to discern the context of a patron's information need and encourage a patron to articulate their prior knowledge of a topic, their specific information interests, and their intentions with the information they hope to acquire?
2. Can you think of additional neutral questions to use in a reference interview?

Homeschoolers' Information Needs

While the majority of young people seeking information in response to imposed queries generated or established in an educational environment are students in public, private, or alternative schools, a growing number of young people participate in homeschooling. According to the National Center for Education Statistics (NCES), the percentage of students in the United States who are homeschooled reached 3.3 percent, approximately 1,689,726 students, during the 2015–2016 academic year (McQuiggan and Megra 2017, 18). Young people and their families may participate in homeschooling for a number of reasons: they may find traditional public and private school environments and curricula to be a poor match for their needs and interests, or they may wish to educate or be educated within a specific religious, political, or philosophical context (Baaden and Uhl 2009). Homeschooling students may be taught at home by parents or caregivers who follow or adapt lessons from curricula published by various organizations; they may participate in small group instruction within their communities; and they may complete online coursework. NCES survey data indicates that homeschooling students and their families view public libraries as a primary source of curricular material (Redford, Battle, and Bielick 2017, 13) and turn to the library for print and audio books, materials providing suggestions and instructions for learning activities, and reference resources (Marquam 2008).

Because they may or may not have access to other library collections or opportunities to receive bibliographic and information literacy instruction, the public library is an important resource for homeschooling students and their families. Recent library literature has described ways in which public libraries have developed collections and offered services to homeschooling families; however, before embarking on developing local services and collections, librarians should engage in needs assessment to determine, first, the size of the homeschooling population in their service communities and, second, to determine the kind and nature of services that might best meet this diverse population's needs (Furness 2008). Homeschooling students and their families might participate in a variety of organizations established to facilitate or support home education, and these organizations represent appropriate first points of contact for librarians interested in investigating homeschooling in their communities. Librarians interested in developing services and collections for homeschooling students and their families might look to the Johnsburg (Illinois) Public Library District's Homeschool Resource Center as an example (Slattery 2005). Open to all library patrons, the Homeschool Resource Center includes curriculum material, games and educational manipulatives, science equipment, catalogs, and books and magazines devoted to various homeschooling approaches and philosophies.

Readers' Advisory and the Question of Appropriateness

Librarians who select and recommend literature for young people are often seen as arbiters of appropriateness: public servants who, drawing from their knowledge of literature and child development and acting out of affection and concern for young people, can and should direct young people to edifying literature and protect them from material that might corrupt them or do them harm. Definitions of "appropriateness" with regard to children's literature are various and historically, socially, and culturally contingent. As Suzanne Stauffer (2014, 160) has pointed out, "appropriate" has been used to describe material that reflects, demonstrates, and encourages "socially-accepted moral values and the consequences of violating that code"; information and literature "that present[s] a safe, nurturing view of the world stripped of all adult concerns and dangers"; and works of fiction and nonfiction that employ vocabulary and language that reflect the abilities of a typically developing reader and convey information or narrative with a complexity, depth, and breadth reflecting the knowledge and literary experience of the typically developing reader. While librarians have historically applied the first two of Stauffer's definitions to their selection and recommendation of literature (Lundin 2004), contemporary professional recommendations and writing encourage librarians to adopt and apply Stauffer's third definition in their practice.

While the goal of readers' advisory with young people is the same as that associated with readers' advisory with adults—to identify and locate reading material that satisfies a patron's needs and interests—considerations related to readability and accessibility distinguish readers' advisory with young people from the same service for adults. Young people who are learning to read or are struggling with reading can have difficulty locating accessible or readable material. While a number of books published for young people are labeled with a "reading-level" designation, no single standard exists to describe the ease or difficulty of a work of literature: publishers may employ their own leveling systems or reference commercial leveling systems like Lexile, Fountas & Pinnell, or Accelerated Reader. Young people participating in literacy programs like Accelerated Reader that reward or credit students for reading books that have been assigned a specific level may request reading material by level (e.g., "I need to read a Level 5 book"), and librarians can turn to catalogs or resources published by the literacy program like the "Accelerated Reader Bookfinder" to support this specific request. However, labeling and organizing a library's collection in terms of a commercial or other reading-level designation or recommending material based on a librarian's interpretation of a person's abilities or leveled prescription for reading has the potential to restrict young people's reading in a negative way. As the American Association of School Librarians (2011) points out, "Student browsing behaviors can be profoundly altered with the addition of external reading level labels"; such labels can be considered "prejudicial," as they imply a restricted readership and narrow a reader's perception of what they can or should read.

"Viewpoint-neutral" labels that describe genre, collection, or format can aid librarians in the work of readers' advisory and guide young people in their browsing. For example, common questions posed during the readers' advisory interview (e.g., "What kind of books do you like to read?") can be fielded by both the librarian and the library's collection labels as the librarian, in response to a patron's answer (e.g., "I like graphic novels"), leads a patron to the library's shelves, recommends individual titles, and points out how to find similar works by looking at spine labels. Because readability can be a concern, the readers' advisory interview with young people may include casual assessment of individual titles to determine accessibility. Once a librarian and patron are engaged in searching or browsing, the librarian can open books of potential interest and point out features (e.g., "Look at these pictures. . . . I wonder what's happening here!" "Let's take a look at the first page of this book and see if it looks like something you might like to read.") that might aid or challenge a reader with an eye toward encouraging the reader to determine whether a title is "for them" or not.

For a variety of reasons, a young person may wish to avoid reading about certain topics or engaging with certain genres or forms, and it is the librarian's responsibility to respect a young person's reading requirements as they are articulated by the young person alone or with their family. It is not, however, the librarian's responsibility to determine the appropriateness of topics, genres, or forms on behalf of a reader who has not made their reading requirements clear. Asking a patron to point out books they have enjoyed or authors they admire can help a librarian work with the patron to identify potential read-alikes—other, similar books by the same author or within the same genre—that can satisfy their requirements and meet their reading needs. Ultimately, as Pat Scales (2010, 18) advises, librarians advising young people on their reading should "talk with [their patrons] about what they're reading, lead them to books [they] think they'll enjoy, and give them permission to reject titles they don't like."

Ensuring Young People's Access to Information

Librarians working with young people should seek to provide services that facilitate young people's access to informational and literary materials and reflect the

ALA's (2019a) "Access to Library Resources and Services for Minors" policy, which states the following:

> Librarians and library governing bodies have a public and professional obligation to ensure that all members of the community they serve have free and equitable access to a diverse range of library resources and services that is inclusive, regardless of content, approach, or format. This principle of library service applies equally to all users, minors as well as adults.

While federal and state mandates can and do inform library policies and practices that infringe upon young people's "free, equal, and equitable access" to the Internet, specifically, serving young people in libraries requires librarians to work to overcome barriers to access whenever possible (and legal). Recognizing where and how barriers to information access can arise (e.g., when a young person is struggling to interpret an imposed query or when a young person is looking for an accessible text) allows a librarian to, in the words of Gross, "get ahead" of these potential issues and affect policy, organizational practices, and services that ensure young people's information access.

ON BEHALF OF YOUNG PEOPLE: SERVING ADULTS

Librarians who work with young people are often called upon to field reference questions related to young people or young people's literature posed by adults. Parents and caregivers ask youth services librarians to recommend titles for shared reading; teachers request material to support in-class learning; schools and school systems request input when developing reading lists; and parents, caregivers, and adults working with young people seek information about young people's growth, development, and education and about local opportunities for young people in the community. While some of the material libraries offer in response to these requests is unquestionably created for young people, some of the resources librarians recommend in response to these queries might be considered "adult" or part of a more general community information collection. Depending on the organization and physical layout of the library, librarians serving young people in a "children's room" may wish to develop and make available collections of "adult" material to address the informational needs of parents, caregivers, and adults working with young people.

Many libraries organize and distinguish "parents' shelves" among collections of material for young people, and the material housed on these shelves typically includes books about child development, parenting, and education as well as brochures, pamphlets, and information about local opportunities or organizations for young people. Because placement, location, and labeling of a library's "parents' shelf" have the potential for such a sub-collection of material to function as a restricted access collection of material perceived by library patrons as "for adults," librarians should be wary of self-censorship when selecting material for the "parents' shelf." Self-censorship occurs when librarians make selection, shelving, and recommendation decisions in response to a perceived fear of community or patron reprisal. Placing fiction published for young people that features an LGBTQIA+ family among its protagonists or a plot that addresses the death of a friend or family member, or informational material published for young people about puberty and sexuality, on a library's "parents' shelf" based on a belief that material dealing with these topics is best selected by adults on behalf of young people represents a form of self-censorship. For example, while parents and caregivers may request fiction and nonfiction about death to aid in at-home bibliotherapy, placing material written for young people that addresses this topic on a parents' shelf assumes that such material has a singular function (bibliotherapy) and precludes a young person from discovering the material on their own.

LIBRARY SERVICE TO YOUNG PEOPLE: EXPANDING THE TRADITION

The first public libraries did not offer collections or services for young people and were, instead, envisioned as spaces for adult reading and education; in fact, some early libraries featured signs that warned visitors that "children and dogs [were] not admitted" to the library (Lundin 2004). Since the turn of the 20th century, when library services to young people became commonplace and the ALA established a "Section for Library Work with Children," a division of the organization that would become, in 1941, the ALSC (ALSC 2019), youth services librarians have been working to develop and refine library programs and services for young people. While a youth services librarian of today might take umbrage at an early youth services librarian's insistence on services and collections meant to mold young people into singular citizens, both would be united in their investment in a youth population that often continues to be misunderstood and underserved. Today, reference services to young people that attend to and respect the contexts in which their information needs and interests arise, allow young people to voice their needs and preferences, and provide young people with access to a diversity of material continue a service tradition established over one hundred years ago and, as librarians work directly with young people and their communities to identify information and service needs, seek to expand its benefits.

REFERENCES

Accelerated Reader. Renaissance. http://www.renaissance.com.

Accelerated Reader Bookfinder. Renaissance. http://www.arbookfind.com.

Adebayo, Olusina. 2016. "Why Diverse Books Are Commonly Banned." Association of American Publishers. Last modified September 21, 2016. http://newsroom.publishers.org/why-diverse-books-are-commonly-banned/.

Allen, Melissa L. 2017. "Cognitive Development beyond Infancy." In *Cambridge Encyclopedia of Child Development*, edited by Brian Hopkins and Ronald G. Barr, 2nd ed. Cambridge: Cambridge University Press. *Credo Reference*.

American Association of School Librarians. 2011. "Position Statement on Labeling Books with Reading Levels." American Library Association. Last modified July 18, 2011. http://www.ala.org/aasl/advocacy/resources/statements/labeling.

American Library Association. 2015. "Internet Filtering: An Interpretation of the Library Bill of Rights." Last modified June 30, 2015. http://www.ala.org/advocacy/intfreedom/librarybill/interpretations/internet-filtering.

American Library Association. 2019a. "Access to Library Resources and Services for Minors." Last modified June 25, 2019. http://www.ala.org/advocacy/intfreedom/librarybill/interpretations/minors.

American Library Association. 2019b. "Library Bill of Rights." Last modified January 29, 2019. http://www.ala.org/advocacy/intfreedom/librarybill.

American Library Association. 2019c. "Minors and Online Activity." Last modified June 24, 2019. http://www.ala.org/advocacy/intfreedom/librarybill/interpretations/minors-internet-activity.

American Library Association. n.d. "Guidelines to Minimize the Negative Effects of Internet Content Filters on Intellectual Freedom." http://www.ala.org/advocacy/intfreedom/filtering/filtering_guidelines.

Association for Library Services to Children. http://www.ala.org/alsc/.

Association for Library Services to Children. 2019. "ALSC History." American Library Association. http://www.ala.org/alsc/aboutalsc/historyofalsc.

Association of Specialized Government and Cooperative Library Agencies. n.d. "Children with Disabilities." https://www.asgcladirect.org/resources/children-with-disabilities/.

Baaden, Bea, and Jean O'Neill Uhl. 2009. "Homeschooling: Exploring the Potential of Public Library Service for Homeschooled Students." *Journal of the Library Administration and Management Section* 5 (2): 5–14.

Batch, Kristen R. 2014. *Filtering Out Knowledge: Impacts of the Children's Internet Protection Act 10 Years Later.* Chicago: American Library Association. http://www.ala.org/advocacy/sites/ala.org.advocacy/files/content/intfreedom/censorshipfirstamendmentissues/FINALCIPA_Report.pdf.

Bilal, Dania, and Jacek Gwizdka. 2018. "Children's Query Types and Reformulations in Google Search." *Information Processing and Management* 54 (6): 1022–41.

Bilal, Dania, and Joe Kirby. 2002. "Differences and Similarities in Information Seeking: Children and Adults as Web Users." *Information Processing and Management* 38 (5): 649–70.

Bishop, Rudine Sims. 2012. "Reflections on the Development of African American Children's Literature." *Journal of Children's Literature* 38 (2): 5–13.

Bjorklund, David F., and Jesse M. Bering. 2002. "Milestones of Development." In *Child Development*, edited by Neil J. Salkind. New York: Macmillan Reference USA. *Gale Virtual Reference Library.*

Byrnes, James P. 2010. "Cognitive Development." In *The Corsini Encyclopedia of Psychology and Behavioral Science*, edited by W. Edward Craighead and Charles B. Nemeroff, 4th ed. Hoboken, NJ: Wiley. *Credo Reference.*

Carlyle, Cate. 2013. "Practicalities: Serving English as a Second Language Library Users." *Feliciter* 59 (3): 18–20.

Chapman, Jan. 2015. "Become an Ally: Reach Out to Your LGBTQ Teen Community." *VOYA* 38 (4): 32–33.

Coats, Karen. 2010. "Identity." In *Keywords for Children's Literature*, edited by Philip Nel and Lissa Paul, 102–119. New York: New York University Press.

Colby, Sandra L., and Jennifer M. Ortman. 2015. "Projections of the Size and Composition of the U.S. Population: 2014 to 2060." U.S. Census Bureau. https://www.census.gov/content/dam/Census/library/publications/2015/demo/p25-1143.pdf.

Daum, Moritz M. 2017. "Cognitive Development during Infancy." In *Cambridge Encyclopedia of Child Development*, edited by Brian Hopkins and Ronald G. Barr, 2nd ed. Cambridge: Cambridge University Press. *Credo Reference.*

Delgado, Richard. 1989. "Storytelling for Oppositionists and Others: A Plea for Narrative." *Michigan Law Review* 87 (8): 2411–41.

Dervin, Brenda, and Patricia Dewdney. 1986. "Neutral Questioning: A New Approach to the Reference Interview." *RQ* 25 (4): 506–13.

Farrall, Melissa Lee. 2012. *Reading Assessment: Linking Language, Literacy, and Cognition.* Hoboken, NJ: Wiley.

Fountas & Pinnell. Heinemann. http://www.fountasandpinnell.com.

Furness, Adrienne. 2008. *Helping Homeschoolers in the Library.* Chicago: American Library Association.

Gates, Gary J. 2017. "In U.S., More Adults Identifying as LGBT." Gallup. Last modified January 11, 2017. https://news.gallup.com/poll/201731/lgbt-identification-rises.aspx.

Gay, Lesbian, Bisexual, and Transgender Round Table. n.d. "Open to All: Serving the GLBT Community in Your Library." American Library Association. http://www.ala.org/rt/sites/ala.org.rt/files/content/professionaltools/160309-glbtrt-open-to-all-toolkit-online.pdf.

GLAAD. 2016. *GLAAD Media Reference Guide.* 10th ed. Last modified October 2016. https://www.glaad.org/reference#guide.

Gonzalez, Valentina. 2017. "Secrets for ELL Success." *School Library Journal* 63 (8): 30–34.

Gross, Melissa. 1995. "The Imposed Query." *RQ* 35 (2): 236–43.

Gross, Melissa. 1999. "Imposed versus Self-Generated Questions: Implications for Reference Practice." *Reference & User Services Quarterly* 39 (1): 53–61.

Gross, Melissa. 2000. "The Imposed Query and Information Services for Children." *Journal of Youth Services in Libraries* 13 (2): 10–17.

Gwizdka, Jacek, and Dania Bilal. 2017. "Analysis of Children's Queries and Click Behavior on Ranked Results and Their Thought Processes in Google Search." Conference on Human Information Interaction and Retrieval. Oslo, Norway.

Haddix, Marcelle, and Detra Price-Dennis. 2013. "Urban Fiction and Multicultural Literature as Transformative Tools for Preparing English Teachers for Diverse Classrooms." *English Education* 45 (3): 247–83.

Henderson, Heather A., Catherine A. Burrows, and Lauren V. Usher. 2017. "Emotional Development." In *Cambridge Encyclopedia of Child Development*, edited by Brian Hopkins and Ronald G. Barr, 2nd ed. Cambridge: Cambridge University Press. *Credo Reference.*

Horning, Kathleen T., Merri V. Lindgren, Megan Schliesman, and Madeline Tyner. 2018. "A Few Observations: Literature in 2017." Cooperative Children's Book Center. http://ccbc.education.wisc.edu/books/choiceintro18.asp.

Hourcade, Juan Pablo. 2007. "Interaction Design and Children." *Foundations and Trends in Human-Computer Interaction* 1 (4): 277–392.

Hughes-Hassell, Sandra, Dana Hanson-Baldauf, and Jennifer E. Burke. 2008. "Urban Teenagers, Health Information, and Public Library Web Sites." *Young Adult Library Services* 6 (4): 35–42.

Hughes-Hassell, Sandra, and Julie Stivers. 2015. "Examining Youth Services Librarians' Perceptions of Cultural Knowledge as an Integral Part of Their Professional Practice." *School Libraries Worldwide* 21 (1): 121–36.

Human Rights Campaign. 2019. "Glossary of Terms." Human Rights Campaign Foundation. https://www.hrc.org/resources/glossary-of-terms.

Human Rights Campaign Foundation and the University of Connecticut. 2018. "2018 LGBTQ Youth Report." Human Rights Campaign Foundation. https://www.hrc.org/resources/2018-lgbtq-youth-report.

Homeschool Resource Center. Johnsburg Public Library District. http://www.johnsburglibrary.org/content/homeschool-resource-center.

Kammerer, Yvonne, and Maja Bohnacker. 2012. "Chilidren's Web Search with Google: The Effectiveness of Natural Language Queries." Proceedings of the 11th International Conference on Interaction Design and Children. Bremen, Germany.

Kosciw, Joseph G., Emily A. Greytak, Noreen M. Giga, Christian Villenas, and David J. Danischweski. 2016. "The 2015 National School Climate Survey." GLSEN. https://www.glsen.org/article/2015-national-school-climate-survey.

Kumasi, Kafi. 2012. "Roses in the Concrete: A Critical Race Perspective on Urban Youth and School Libraries." *Knowledge Quest* 40 (4): 32–37.

Kumasi, Kafi, and Sandra Hughes-Hassell. 2017. "Shifting Lenses on Youth Literacy and Identity." *Knowledge Quest* 45 (3): 12–21.

Larrick, Nancy. 1965."The All-White World of Children's Books." *The Saturday Review*, September 11, 63–65.

Larson, Jeannette. 2015. *Children's Services Today: A Practical Guide for Librarians.* Lanham, MD: Rowman and Littlefield.

Lexile. MetaMetrics. https://lexile.com.

LGBTQIA Resource Center. 2018. "LGBTQIA Resource Center Glossary." University of California, Davis. Last modified February 12, 2019. https://lgbtqia.ucdavis.edu/educated/glossary.html.

Lundin, Anne. 2004. *Constructing the Canon of Children's Literature: Beyond Library Walls and Ivory Towers.* New York: Routledge.

Marquam, Tamara. 2008. "Fable and Fact: Serving the Homeschool Population in Public Libraries." *Indiana Libraries* 27 (1): 12–18.

Martens, Marianne. 2012. "Issues of Access and Usability in Designing Digital Resources for Children." *Library and Information Science Research* 34 (3): 159–68.

McQuiggan, Meghan, and Mahi Megra. 2017. "Parent and Family Involvement in Education: Results from the National Household Education Surveys Program of 2016." National Center for Education Statistics. Last modified September 26, 2017. http://nces.ed.gov/pubsearch/pubsinfo.asp?pubid=2017102.

Mestre, Lori. 2009. "Culturally Responsive Instruction for Teacher Librarians." *Teacher Librarian* 36 (3): 8–12.

Middleton, Kathy. 2014. "Making an Attitudinal Change to Disabilities." *Public Libraries Online,* September 11. http://publiclibrariesonline.org/2014/09/making-an-attitudinal-change-to-disabilities/.

National Association for the Education of Young Children. 2009. "Developmentally Appropriate Practice in Early Childhood Programs Serving Children from Birth through Age 8." https://www.naeyc.org/resources/topics/dap/position-statement.

National Center for Education Statistics. 2018. "English Language Learners in Public Schools." Last modified May 2019. https://nces.ed.gov/programs/coe/indicator_cgf.asp.

National Conference of State Legislatures. 2016. "Children and the Internet: Laws Relating to Filtering, Blocking, and Usage Policies in Schools and Libraries." Last modified October 30, 2018. http://www.ncsl.org/research/telecommunications-and-information-technology/state-internet-filtering-laws.aspx.

National Disability Authority. 2012. "The Seven Principles." Center for Excellence in Universal Design. http://universaldesign.ie/what-is-universal-design/the-7-principles/the-7-principles.html.

Nichols, Joel A. 2016. "Serving All Families in a Queer and Genderqueer Way." *Public Libraries* 55 (1): 39–42.

Oltmann, Shannon M. 2016. " 'They Kind of Rely on the Library': School Librarians Serving LGBT Students." *Journal of Research on Libraries and Young Adults* 7 (1): 1–21.

Overall, Patricia Montiel. 2009. "Cultural Competence: A Conceptual Framework for Library and Information Science Professionals." *The Library Quarterly* 79 (2): 175–204.

Overton, Nicole. 2016. "Libraries Need Diverse Books." *Public Libraries* 55 (1): 13–14.

Payne, Rachel G., and Jessica Ralli. 2017. "Beyond Bilingual." *School Library Journal* 63 (7): 26–28.

Peck, Penny. 2014. *Crash Course in Children's Services.* 2nd ed. Santa Barbara, CA: Libraries Unlimited.

Redford, Jeremy, Danielle Battle, and Stacey Bielick. 2017. *Homeschooling in the United States: 2012.* https://nces.ed.gov/pubs2016/2016096rev.pdf.

Robinson, Tracy. 2016. "Overcoming Social Exclusion in Public Library Services to LGBTQ and Gender Variant Youth." *Public Library Quarterly* 35 (3): 161–74.

Scales, Pat. 2010. "Mature Content: To Label or Not to Label, That Is the Question." *School Library Journal* 56 (5): 18.

Slattery, Ann. 2005. "In a Class of Their Own." *School Library Journal* 51 (8): 44–46.

Solórzano, Daniel G., and Tara J. Yosso. 2002. "Critical Race Methodology: Counter Storytelling as an Analytical Framework for Education Research." *Qualitative Inquiry* 8 (1): 23–44.

Souto-Manning, Mariana. 2016. "Honoring and Building on the Rich Literacy Practices of Young Bilingual and Multilingual Learners." *Reading Teacher* 70 (3): 263–71.

Stauffer, Suzanne M. 2014. "The Dangers of Unlimited Access: Fiction, the Internet, and the Social Construction of Childhood." *Library and Information Science Research* 36 (3–4): 154–62.

Stivers, Julie. 2017. "The Critical Piece: Building Relationships with Teens of Color and Native Youth." *Young Adult Library Services* 15 (2): 12–15.

Storts-Brinks, Karyn. 2010. "Censorship Online: One School Librarian's Journey to Provide Access to LGBT Resources." *Knowledge Quest* 39 (1): 22–28.

Svetlova, Margarita, and Malinda Carpenter. 2017. "Social Development." In *Cambridge Encyclopedia of Child Development*, edited by Brian Hopkins and Ronald G. Barr. 2nd ed. Cambridge: Cambridge University Press. *Credo Reference.*

We Need Diverse Books. https://diversebooks.org/.

Williams Institute. 2016. "LGBT Data and Demographics." University of California, Los Angeles. Last modified January 2019. https://williamsinstitute.law.ucla.edu/visualization/lgbt-stats/?topic=LGBT&compare=percentage#comparison.

Young Adult Library Services Association. http://www.ala.org/yalsa/.

SUGGESTED READINGS

Naidoo, Jamie Campbell. 2014. "The Importance of Diversity in Library Programs and Material Collections for Children." Association for Library Service to Children. American Library Association. Last modified April 5, 2014. http://www.ala.org/alsc/sites/ala.org.alsc/files/content/ALSCwhitepaper_importance%20of%20diversity_with%20graphics_FINAL.pdf.

This white paper, published by the Association for Library Service to Children, outlines research describing the benefits of culturally diverse programs and material for all young people, establishes the ALSC's position in support of cultural diversity, and offers an extensive list of resources to aid librarians in materials selection and service development.

National Association for the Education of Young Children. 2019. "Developmentally Appropriate Practice." https://www.naeyc.org/resources/topics/dap.

Created by the National Association for the Education of Young Children, this section of the organization's website features a link to the DAP (Developmentally Appropriate Practice) Position Statement, which describes research and theory underpinning DAP, as well as links to short descriptions of exemplary DAP practices with young people. While this website is directed to classroom teachers, specifically, many of its DAP-related recommendations can be applied to library programming and services.

Scales, Pat, Rebecca T. Miller, and Barbara A. Genco, eds. 2015. *Scales on Censorship: Real Life Lessons from* School Library Journal. Lanham, MD: Rowman and Littlefield.

A regular columnist for *School Library Journal*, Pat Scales is an expert and advocate for intellectual freedom. This book collects Scales's responses to questions submitted to *School Library Journal* by working librarians and describes best practices for handling common challenges related to collection development, book recommendation and displays, Internet filtering, and censorship.

Chapter 12

Reference Services for Diverse Populations

Nicole A. Cooke

INTRODUCTION

An underlying philosophy of this book, articulated most explicitly in Chapter 2, is a commitment to quality reference service for *all*. Because "all" encompasses individuals with a variety of needs, successful reference service must accommodate those needs. "All," however, does not mean that all reference services are appropriate for all user groups. "One size" does not fit all when it comes to reference. No standard blueprint for reference services exists that is appropriate in all situations. Developing specialized reference services for specific, or diverse, populations within our communities is an essential corollary to developing service for the majority. Beyond the provision of basic reference services to an obvious, primary group of users, librarians need to identify special groups of users with common and equally important needs and tailor reference service to these groups.

The basis of concern for reference service to specific populations is ethical as well as legal. Librarians who provide reference services often must be advocates for members of these groups to ensure equitable access to information and materials. As noted in Chapter 2, the profession has created the "Library Bill of Rights" to emphasize its commitment to fair use of resources and openness to all users. In particular, Article I says that materials should be provided for all members of the community and "should not be excluded because of the origin, background, or views of those contributing to their creation." Article V continues by saying that people, no matter their "origin, age, background, or views," should have complete and equal access to the library (American Library Association 2019). Broadly interpreted, these articles argue that library services, which include reference services, should be made available to any and all patrons and should reflect the needs and interests of members of the community. In addition, libraries supported by public funds have a legal obligation to provide service without discrimination based on class, race, gender, sexuality, religion, or other defining social or physical characteristics.

This chapter examines models of reference service delivery to a *selection* of groups whose needs are not always recognized or well defined and not always met. This chapter does not address the reference needs of those in the business or technical sector, who would typically be served by special libraries. Instead, the focus is on groups who are defined in terms of socioeconomic, ethnic, or physical characteristics. The specific groups discussed throughout the chapter are differentiated on the basis of *cultural, social, and gender identities*, which may include *language facility* (non-English-speaking and the adult illiterate) and *sexual orientation*; *disabling conditions* (physical and developmental disabilities); and *age* (in this case, adult learners and seniors; for more on serving children and young adults, see Chapter 11). For each of these groups, defining characteristics are described, and reference techniques and policy issues associated with the group are discussed.

GENERAL PRINCIPLES FOR SERVING DIVERSE PATRONS

Within any library service community, there are nontraditional or even invisible groups to consider (such as institutionalized populations, specific ethnic or religious groups, and others), and not every group discussed here may be part of a given library's service population. And, unfortunately, this chapter cannot encompass every potential diverse population served by libraries around the world. The intent of this chapter is to give an overview of issues associated with reference service to a sampling of diverse populations. The assumption is that service to any one group is a microcosm of general reference service—that the basics of reference service are present—and the task is to adapt good reference skills and collections to serve each group. The focus should be on equitable service delivery, and services to specific populations are part of that focus and part of a systemic approach that serves all and gives library professionals the knowledge and ability to tailor and customize services when necessary. This approach requires flexibility, cultural competence, openness, and empathy toward the many diverse users who patronize libraries. It is in this spirit that this chapter is written.

Although public, academic, school, and special libraries and archives may vary in the degree to which certain reference services are provided, an equitable and responsive reference service model for diverse populations should aim to include these components:

1. Assessing the problems a member of a diverse group experiences when trying to access information and services provided by the library.
2. Conducting research that includes contact with associations and service providers about how to improve services for diverse categories of users (and how to attract nonusers).
3. Planning how to adapt the reference interview, collection development, and delivery of services.
4. Training staff to work with users with special needs or cultural differences.
5. Implementing periodic evaluation of reference services to members of diverse groups. (Based in part on Fitzgibbons 1983, 5–6)

To this end, library professionals poised to serve diverse users in these capacities should be cognizant of differences that may exist between themselves and the people they are serving. Patrons from diverse groups may have a variety of visible and invisible differences (or perhaps barriers) that could require extra attention, consultation of different resources, intercultural understanding, empathy, and so forth and could result in reluctance to use the library. This reluctance is above and beyond the library anxiety that many library users (and nonusers) experience. It becomes that much more important that the reference transaction, and other library interactions, strive to make the patron feel at ease and as though they are welcome and can be assisted.

Library professionals should strive to develop empathy and cultural competence (Box 12.1), exhibit patience, encourage patrons, ensure that patrons are aware of the helping role of the library, follow up with patrons, and admit any limitations (e.g., "no, we do not have that book, but we have something similar"). In addition, library professionals should be ready, willing, and able to work with the differing work styles, language barriers, accents, and cultural norms that patrons may possess (e.g., a man of the Muslim faith may be uncomfortable speaking with a female librarian and might be more comfortable speaking with a male colleague) (Brothen and Bennett 2013). These professional attributes benefit all patrons and particularly those from diverse user groups.

Box 12.1 Cultural Competence

A concept referenced in many disciplines, including nursing, counseling, social work, and public health, cultural competence is also important for library and information science professionals. The American Library Association (n.d.-a) defines cultural competence as "the acceptance and respect for diversity, continuing self-assessment regarding culture, and the ongoing development of knowledge, resources, and service models that work towards effectively meeting the needs of diverse populations. Cultural competence is critical to the equitable provision of library and information services."

For a more extensive discussion of cultural competence, please see Nicole A. Cooke (2016).

Reference Services in an Intersectional Society

This chapter highlights several diverse user groups, and it is worth noting the intersections of these groups (see Figure 12.1). Diverse user groups do not exist in silos; rather, most users represent multiple diversities and identities (e.g., an African-American homeless veteran is suffering from PTSD and needs assistance applying for benefits). All of these identities come with advantages and disadvantages. Recalling that a "one-size-fits-all" approach to reference is not desirable, learning how to compassionately and competently serve diverse user groups will enable library professionals to serve *all* users.

The Reference Interview

Fundamentally, how library professionals conduct the reference interview is no different with diverse users than it is with other users (Saunders and Jordan 2013).

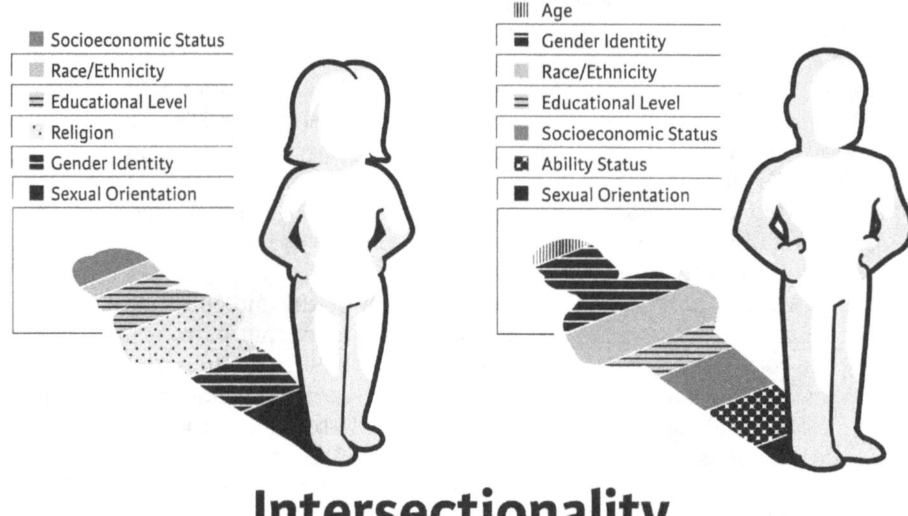

Figure 12.1 The intersectionality of diverse users (graphic by David Michael Moore). Intersectionality is shown by depicting how each individual is made up of multiple identities.

As stressed in Chapter 3, the librarian should treat all people and queries with respect and seriousness. However, with diverse users, it is especially important to anticipate some timidity and perhaps reticence toward public institutions and asking for assistance. It is crucial to be aware of and to understand both cultural and individual differences. For example, Hispanics and Latinos in the United States are from Mexico, Puerto Rico, the Dominican Republic, Cuba, the Caribbean, and countries in Central and South America. Each cultural grouping has its own traditions, value systems, and social classes, and they may speak languages *other* than Spanish. Within this array of cultural identities, it is *individuals* with unique needs and questions who come to the reference desk for help.

It is also important not to make assumptions regarding what diverse users know about libraries. Donna L. Gilton (1994) suggests that culture shock (or clash) can occur when diverse users are new to library use, not unlike the clash or discomfort that may occur when anyone visits a foreign land or engages in an unfamiliar environment. This can occur in addition to any library anxiety many users experience when using the library. "Five aspects of culture can lead to culture shock or clash: verbal communication; nonverbal communication; orientation modes, or the use of time and space; social value patterns, which include written and unwritten rules of social behavior; and intellectual modes, which include learning styles valued by the culture" (Gilton 1994, 55). All of these are applicable to library use and reference interactions.

Depending on circumstances, diverse users may not understand the concept of call numbers, be able to decipher commonly used library terms, or know how to distinguish between printed first names and surnames. In answering reference questions, slang should be avoided and the use of the library's materials explained and demonstrated, giving users the opportunity to observe and then to imitate.

Whenever possible, the librarian should escort a new library user through to the end of the process, such as locating a book or a magazine on the shelf. It is easy to mistake nods and smiles as signifying comprehension. This pitfall can be avoided by asking open-ended questions that allow patrons to communicate more precisely what they do or do not understand. It is very easy to misunderstand body language, eye contact (or lack thereof), attempts at humor, and other common communication habits (Strong 2001; Walker 2006). The librarian must abandon assumptions and concentrate on the intent of the patron's question. After a question is answered, follow-up is especially important and is vital to proper closure of the interview. The same care and consideration extended to diverse users in a physical library setting should be extended to diverse users seeking reference assistance virtually (Shachaf and Horowitz 2007). (For more on the reference interview, particularly as it pertains to diverse populations, please see Brook, Ellenwood, and Lazzaro 2015; Lam 1988.)

REFERENCE SERVICES TO PATRONS OF DIVERSE ETHNIC BACKGROUNDS

Our society is more diverse than ever, and this diversity is more than reflected in the communities served by libraries, especially public libraries. Population projections from the U.S. Census Bureau indicate that by 2030, Hispanics will make up 21.1 percent of the U.S. population, African Americans 13.8 percent, and Asians 6.9 percent. Hispanics have already replaced African Americans as the country's largest minority group. The percentage of non-Hispanic whites in the population will continue to decrease, and by 2060 non-Hispanic whites will be at 44.3 percent of the total population (U.S. Census Bureau 2018). These minority groups have quickly become the "emerging majority" (Turock 2003, 494). Religious diversity has also increased and become more prominent. In 1990, 527,000 Americans identified themselves as Muslim. By 2008, that number had risen to 1,349,000, a 156 percent increase (U.S. Census Bureau 2018, Table 75). During the same period, the number of self-identified Hindus rose from 227,000 to 582,000, also a 156 percent increase, whereas the total Christian population rose from 151,225,000 to 173,402,000 (Table 75). Although Christians are still the overwhelming majority, these latter figures represent only a 15 percent increase in that population.

Such significant data compel librarians to provide reference service that is responsive to different needs and, as stated earlier, does not have a formulaic, "one-size-fits-all" approach. Mengxiong Liu (1995, 124) notes that patrons from diverse backgrounds may not even understand how North American libraries work, as it may be a different, strange, or even unwelcome model of education and service. As individuals, their information-seeking behavior is affected by "different cultural experiences, language, level of literacy, socioeconomic status, education, level of acculturation, and value system."

Phoebe Janes and Ellen Meltzer (1990) suggest that library professionals be trained so that they will be able to address the needs of diverse users and individualize or adapt reference services as necessary. The authors suggest that invisible barriers and implicit assumptions could impact services to these users, even unintentionally. For example, reference staff could assume that their experiences, habits, and communication styles in libraries are the same for everyone and that there is little chance that they would be misunderstood. This assumption of homogeneity exists not only among individual staff but is often a larger issue of organizational culture as well. If the organization is not welcoming or understanding of patrons who are marginalized or somehow exist outside the norm of the accepted culture, these potential users will not frequent the library, no matter how wonderful the programs or extensive the collection (Elteto, Jackson, and Lim 2008). Yolanda J. Cuesta (2004) advises that staff training cover three types of techniques: techniques for engaging the community, techniques for effective communication with a diverse customer base, and techniques for analyzing the library from the community's perspective. Training could include cultural awareness and sensitivity training, information about community analysis (see Box 12.2), cultural knowledge, and linguistic competence to help staff convey information in a manner that is easily understood by diverse audiences (for more on community analysis, see Giesecke and McNeil 2001; Goodman 2011; Grover, Greer, and Agada 2010; McCleer 2013; and McDonald 1981). Cuesta (2004, 113) states, "everything and anything the library does communicates a message to the community," and staff should be aware of this and be willing to plan accordingly.

Box 12.2 Activity: Community Analysis

Community analysis is a mixture of formal and informal techniques that gives librarians a comprehensive view of their community's needs and habits; this insight can inform reference services, in addition to other services such as collection development and programming.

Using the *Community Analysis Scan Form* located on the Library Research Service website (http://www.lrs.org/public/ca_form.php), consider the community in which you live or work.

Questions for Reflection and Discussion:

1. What is the makeup of your community?
2. How well is your local public library currently addressing the represented diverse populations?
3. What improvements or enhancements would you suggest?

Ultimately, the information needs of minorities do not differ primarily because of race or ethnicity but rather because of an individual's life situation, which may include factors associated with race or ethnicity, such as cultural experiences, language, literacy, recent arrival in the United States, socioeconomic status, education, and most generally levels of acculturation (Carlson 1990) (see Box 12.3 for an example). Gillian D. Leonard (1993) extends this argument by stating that the reference requests and information needs of minority groups should pose no special challenges to a professionally trained librarian. Rather, as Patrick Andrew Hall (1991, 320) suggests, the role of *affectivity*, which is "the more intangible qualities of personal rapport and empathy," is just as important as familiarity with specific cultural experiences and sensitivity to diversity (320). Thus, although it is useful to know that people of color may regard professional distance as "a sign of rudeness or contempt" (Hall 1991, 322), it is the specific *relationship* between librarian and user that builds an effective interaction, more so than a well-intentioned, albeit blanket "politically correct" or culturally competent, approach.

Box 12.3 Activity: Avoiding the Reference Desk—Stereotype Threat

Consider this scenario posed by Patricia Katopol (2014, 1). After previous negative and frustrating experiences, Keisha again entered her school's library because she really needed some help to complete her research paper. "She looked up at the workers; some of them looked kind of young—were they real librarians? Student workers? And, as usual, they were all Caucasian, so that Keisha questioned whether she should bring her topic on Black Americans to one of them. Would they understand what she was doing and would they really be able to help her? Would they think her questions were elementary and not worthy of a graduate student? She sighed and gathered her things for the long trek to the reference desk."

Question for Reflection and Discussion:

1. If you were the librarian in line to help Keisha, how would you work with her?
2. What self-reflection and learning could you undertake to improve this scenario?

REFERENCE SERVICE TO INTERNATIONAL STUDENTS AND IMMIGRANTS

America is proverbially known as a "melting pot," and as such libraries are very familiar with international and immigrant patrons. In particular, these diverse users often come to the United State with little, or no, proficiency in the English language. Known as English as a second language (ESL), English for speakers of other languages (ESOL), English as an additional language (EAL), or English as a foreign language (EFL) learners, these populations are frequent library users and perhaps have the hardest time receiving information because they cannot communicate easily with library staff.

International Students

Academic librarians are particularly familiar with international students studying at their colleges and universities. Successful scholars in their native tongues, a lack of English mastery and different cultural norms may inhibit them while studying in the United States. "Culture can be a veil that prevents us from understanding students from other backgrounds and cultures, and it also can prevent them from understanding us. Unfamiliarity with cultural communication differences can lead to misinterpretations, misunderstanding, and even unintentional insult" (Osa, Nyana, and Ogbaa 2006, 23). Studies also suggest that international students have limited knowledge of libraries in an American context, including the idea of female librarians (Carder, Pracht, and Willingham 1997), and may not understand that the reference desk and librarians are there to assist and can be consulted for information (Dunbar 1986; Lewis 1969). As such, these patrons may be less likely to ask for assistance at an American library reference desk without outreach and training (Ganster 2011; Ishimura and Bartlett 2014; Knight, Hight, and Polfer 2010; Pyati 2003). Anxious about possible communication failures, international students are less likely to seek in person assistance, instead relying on the Internet and friends for information.

Research about the information behaviors of international students has revealed that some of these users "are accustomed to lecture, recitation, rote memory, and recall, while American students are accustomed to analyzing, synthesizing, critiquing, and expanding" (Macdonald and Sarkodie-Mensah 1988, 426). With a predilection toward print materials, international students are receptive to library instruction sessions and orientation tours, particularly those that are accompanied with print handouts, guides, slides, and visual aids. When working with international students, library professionals should ask open-ended questions and check for comprehension.

Immigrants, Refugees, and New Americans

Libraries, especially public libraries, have a long history of welcoming and serving immigrant, refugee, and New American populations (Shen 2013; Wang 2012). New residents are often financially and information poor, and consequently this diverse user group often relies on the library for access to the Internet and computers and other basic information necessary for everyday life (Bowdoin et al. 2017). Additionally, displaced and/or relocated users can require assistance with learning English (ESL classes), basic education (GED or equivalency courses), and information about citizenship. The library is also a prime source of community, health, employment, and legal information.

Using the New York Public Library as an example, particularly the Queens Public Library that serves New American populations in fifty-nine different languages (Berger 2012), libraries can serve as sites of acclimation and integration for these users. In order to be effective, which in turn facilitates the provision of reference services, librarians should survey their communities and incorporate these users into the library as much as possible (e.g., bring teenagers as pages or volunteers, invite community gatekeepers to serve on boards and committees) and establish community partnerships. Xiwen Zhang (2001) emphasizes the need to be familiar with the communities being served and developing cultural literacy; for example, there are many different and culturally distinct communities of Spanish speakers and twenty-two separate ethnic groups that make up the larger Asian community. Each group could have different language and information needs.

For users who may experience barriers due to language, it is helpful if library staff speak simply and at an easily understandable pace and avoid slang, colloquialisms, or library jargon. Language barriers can cause self-consciousness and prevent patrons from asking for assistance. Ajit Pyati (2003) suggests that libraries have extra outreach for these diverse patrons, including special resources on the library's website. Other low-stakes accommodations and actions that librarians can take include having dedicated Web pages and tutorials, specialized instruction, and orientations in other languages (Knight, Hight, and Polfer 2010); having foreign language materials in the reference and circulating collections; creating multilingual signage and handouts; and gesturing and pointing (gesturing and pointing are often perceived as rude, but can actually be helpful when there is a language barrier). Other investments, which require more time and financial commitment, involve hiring bilingual library staff and creating multilingual online catalogs.

REFERENCE SERVICES TO THE HOMELESS AND IMPOVERISHED

Libraries have often had tenuous relationships with those who are homeless, or otherwise hungry, food insecure, housing insecure, or impoverished. The homeless in particular are a diverse user group who are often viewed as problematic or troublesome, particularly if they have strong body odor, carry all of their belongings with them, stay in the library during all open hours, or use the public restrooms to bathe. In the early 1990s, the library world witnessed a public library and homeless patron engage in a series of high-stakes lawsuits. The library ejected the patron after intense encounters and complaints from other members of the community who said the homeless man smelled, used the library as a personal lounge, and created an uncomfortable environment for others. The homeless man countered, saying that by ejecting him they were denying him his basic rights to access information (Hanley 1992). This case is oft cited and characterizes the relationships many libraries have had with their homeless patrons.

The homeless are indeed sometimes mentally ill, but often they are not. The homeless, like the mentally ill, are not inherently violent or less intelligent than other patrons. The homeless are also an especially intersectional group—there are high proportions of homeless teens (Eyrich-Garg and Rice 2012; Woelfer and Hendry 2011), particularly those who are gay, lesbian, or transsexual/transgender (Winkelstein 2014). Many homeless are veterans who have been unable to find sufficient employment; many homeless are elderly, immigrants, or recently released from prison; and the homeless span every racial and ethnic group. There are many homeless people who have jobs but perhaps are underemployed and do not earn enough to secure and maintain a residence. The homeless population is more diverse than ever. In 2013 and 2014, two nationally covered news stories brought this fact to bear, one a five-part *New York Times* article that featured a homeless girl named Dasani and her family (Elliot 2013), and the second a *Chicago Sun Times* article that revealed one of the players on the world championship Little League baseball team was homeless (Sfondeles 2014). These accounts emphasize just how pervasive homelessness is and that not everyone "looks" or acts homeless. Should these children be singled out or treated any differently in the library because they are homeless?

Homeless patrons, of all ages, require quality reference services in all types of libraries (Dowd 2018; Hersberger 2003; Hersberger 2005; Muggleton and Ruthven 2012). Keith A. Anderson, Chaniqua D. Simpson, and Lynette G. Fisher (2012, 180) concur by stating: "The challenges of serving the needs of homeless library patrons are complex. Library staffs are professionally and ethically compelled to meet the informational and support needs of homeless patrons, while maintaining the decorum of the library and serving the needs of other library patrons."

Information professionals can learn how to interact with the homeless, mentally ill, or otherwise impoverished in a compassionate yet effective manner. Many feel that serving these diverse populations is the domain of social workers, and indeed, there is much overlap between librarianship and social work. Additionally, there are library systems that employ social workers and public health nurses to work *with* library staff and these diverse users (see American Library Association n.d.-b; Blank 2014; Jenkins 2014; Knight 2010; Nemec-Loise 2014; Shafer 2014). However, this can be considered a luxury that most libraries will not have. But librarians, with proper training, can be effective as providers of information and referral services. Library staff can assist homeless patrons with their financial, physical, family, work, emotional, substance abuse, and mental health issues by referring them to appropriate resources and by being empathic human beings (Anderson, Simpson, and Fisher 2012). To emphasize the point that the homeless and impoverished are no less deserving of quality and dignified services, Glen E. Holt (2006, 184) states, "The wrong library question that many public libraries might ask at this point is 'What services should my library offer to the poor?' The right question is more complex: How can my library develop and fit its services into the lives of the poor so they will benefit from what we know how to do? The differentiation is not mere words. The first question is marked by passive "supply-side" thinking about library services, i.e. 'If we offer them (i.e. services), they will come.' The second question is proactive, involving process (finding out what is needed) and outcomes."

To this end, John Gehner (2010) suggests that library professionals get out of the library and get to know this diverse user group in such a way that enables them to look beyond appearance to understand deprivation and the causes (and not the symptoms) of poverty and homelessness. This deeper understanding of circumstances can assist in the removal of barriers that socially exclude certain groups. Library staff need to "understand that charity is not dignity; dignity is inclusion" (Gehner 2010, 45). Other suggestions for providing reference services to the homeless and impoverished include delivering services at times and places that may be more convenient to these users, focusing on services relevant to homeless and poor families, and publicizing these initiatives (Holt 2006). Peter Willett and Rebecca Broadley (2011) even propose that libraries should evaluate their policies, particularly those that require proof of residency to acquire a library card; for the homeless, this may not be possible. Are there other alternatives or temporary memberships available? Julie Ann Winkelstein (2014) concurs and suggests that staff be trained specifically to work with members of this community, create partnerships with the surrounding community, and create a glossary of terms to be used in conjunction with other appropriate resources. Overall, the goal should be to create a safe and welcoming environment.

REFERENCE SERVICES TO THE INCARCERATED

Library services to the incarcerated or detained are important and often overlooked, in part because of the diverse population being served, the library locations, and a lack of resources and staff. Prison libraries are often referenced as a social justice issue and can support curriculum, hobbies and recreational reading, legal endeavors, and overall learning and improvement for those utilizing their services. Prison libraries also provide information about treatment programs (e.g., substance abuse, anger management) and can serve as a much-needed space of quiet and provide a sense of normalcy for the detained (Lehmann 2011). A marginalized population that overlaps with the mentally ill, homeless, LGBTQIA+, young adult, minority, and other diverse populations, the incarcerated particularly benefit from library services as the information gained can aid in rehabilitation, which in turn can aid in their release, reentry into society, and avoidance of recidivism (Clark and MacCreaigh 2006). Once individuals are released, libraries can also assist with the development of employment skills and computer skills. An exemplar is the

Denver Public Library, which works with the formerly detained and supports them in three areas: "job search skills and readiness, computer and Internet skills, and library awareness and understanding" (Morris 2013, 120). The library trains staff to work with this diverse population in such a way as to diffuse shame and build confidence in patrons.

Prison libraries often lack dedicated staff; some are manned with part-time staff, volunteers, or mobile librarians who enter the facility on an *ad hoc* basis (Rubin and House 1983). Other services are supported by volunteer organizations that do readers' advisory or answer basic reference questions off-site and through postal mail. Reference services can be particularly challenging in this setting. Rebecca Dixen and Stephanie Thorson (2001) state that reference service can be abbreviated and sporadic, depending on the librarian's schedule and the availability of resources. Reference interactions could last between five and ten minutes and could happen as infrequently as once a month. This makes the reference interview vitally important, and supplemental reference, via forms in the mail, is often necessary. Sheila Clark and Erica MacCreaigh (2006) speak to the range of questions that occur, from both male and female inmates, many of whom have trust (and alternately attachment) issues. The authors state that libraries are fulfilling basic information needs for these patrons, information that aids in informed decision-making about their criminal charges, their children and families, and their legal counsel. They caution library professionals providing reference assistance by stating, "while librarians cannot and should not answer any of these questions, we believe that we are duty-bound to provide our patrons with the research tools they need to answer the questions for themselves" (Clark and MacCreaigh 2006, 194). Such questions can include inquiries about legal procedures and criminal charges (please see Chapter 31).

These circumstances are even more challenging when trying to assist with legal information and research. The authors continue by discussing the need for compassion, flexibility, respect, and confidentiality while working with this population, who range greatly when it comes to backgrounds, communication skills, and educational levels. "Along with a sense of fairness, other qualities are required of all librarians who deal with the public; flexibility, high tolerance, good communication skills, awareness of cultural issues and lack of bias toward any group, emotional maturity, and a sense of humor. These skills are even more necessary for a prison librarian because of the extreme circumstances and pressured context surrounding the patrons who come to her. And often, the limited communication skills of some prisoners bring a special challenge, making the reference interview especially important" (Clark and MacCreaigh 2006, 51).

Ready-reference, readers' advisory, and legal information are especially important to this population. Glennor L. Shirley (2003, 71) cautions about material that is deemed dangerous because it could unduly incite inmates who are violent, who are sex offenders, or who have psychological issues. To that end, prison libraries experience censorship of materials, further limiting the librarian's reach and abilities. Librarians who work within prisons or detention centers, or those who work in public libraries, can aid members of this community by forging relationships "with community partners, especially with halfway houses, government agencies, correctional facilities, and other organizations that provide services to felons" (Morris 2013, 120) (see Box 12.4). Partnerships are especially important for this user group in order to maintain their progress and help them reenter society.

Box 12.4 Activity: Books to Prisoners

UC Books to Prisoners (http://www.books2prisoners.org) is a volunteer project in Urbana, Illinois, that provides books to inmates around the state. Inmates are able to write to the organization's volunteers and request reading material. Such an initiative benefits jails and prisons with library services but is particularly necessary for facilities without libraries and staff. Similar organizations exist in Seattle (http://www.bookstoprisoners.net), New York, Louisiana, Oregon, and other states around the country (http://prisonbookprogram.org/resources/other-books-to-prisoners-programs/). *LGBT Books to Prisoners*, located in Madison, Wisconsin (http://lgbtbookstoprisoners.org), extends this idea further by sending reading materials to LGBT inmates across the United States.

Questions for Reflection and Discussion:

1. What services exist to meet the information needs of the incarcerated and/or recently released in your community or region?
2. If no such services exist, how would you propose that your community's library get involved with serving the incarcerated and/or recently released?

REFERENCE SERVICE TO THE LGBTQIA+ COMMUNITY

Another growing population of diverse users is lesbian, gay, bisexual, transgender, queer/questioning, intersex, and asexual individuals (LGBTQIA+). There is debate about this label, as it is felt that it is not inclusive enough of the sexual diversity even *within* this community. Other identities include transsexual, nonheterosexual, and non-cisgender. For the purposes of this brief introduction, LGBTQIA+ will be used to discuss reference services to this community. In addition to internal diversity, the LGBTQIA+ community is particularly intersectional, and there is a growing and integral connection with services to this community particularly as it pertains to homeless, mentally ill, or incarcerated individuals. As Becky McKay (2011, 394) notes, "LGBT people have been grouped together for the purposes of research and advocacy, but LGBT communities are immensely diverse, comprising individuals of every gender, race/ethnicity, age, socioeconomic class, religion, and geographic area, just to name a few dimensions of difference. However, stigma remains one circumstance that unites these diverse constituencies." She states that the LGBTQIA+ community is especially prone to physical and mental health concerns because of fear of the medical system, and as a result, there are high rates of suicide (for more on the nuances of the LGBTQIA+ community, see Greenblatt 2011; Taylor 2002; Thompson 2012).

Ann Curry (2005), Jeanie Austin (2012, 2018), and other authors focus on LGBTQIA+ youth, but the best practices that apply to serving them in a library setting apply to the entire LGBTQIA+ community. Curry also discusses the implicit biases that may impact library professionals when serving patrons from the LGBTQIA+ community. She suggests that even if librarians at the reference desk do not outright refuse to serve these patrons or interact with them in a purposefully rude way, their demeanor and body language can indicate discomfort, hostility, or even judgment. Such nonverbal communication can deter or stifle reference interviews and interactions. Body language, and subsequently search strategies (or lack thereof) and a lack of a concluding statement or follow-up can convey a lack of objectivity and hesitancy to help LGBTQIA+ patrons. A failed reference encounter can be compounded when the library's collection and/or public catalog are not current or representative of the community, or even exclude the LGBTQIA+ community and its needs and interests. Cal Gough and Ellen Greenblatt (1992, 61) refer to this as "systemic bibliographic invisibility," when a library's collection lacks appropriate materials because they do not fit in with existing collection and classification schemes.

Curry's (2005, 72) study found that the best librarians were welcoming and "personal but not nosy," conducted a good reference interview, portrayed a level of comfort when using the words gay and lesbian, found appropriate resources, worked with the patron as opposed to telling them what to do, and referred the patron when more information was required. In general, when working with LGBTQIA+ youth or adults, librarians should appear interested in the question; appear comfortable with LGBTQIA+ topics; maintain eye contact; demonstrate a relaxed body posture; give their full attention to the patron; maintain confidentiality by being discrete; and make the patron feel at ease during the interaction (Curry 2005, 73). These best practices should of course be present in all types of libraries.

Libraries and their staff should also reflect on their behaviors and resources by conducting a SWOT (strengths, weaknesses, opportunities, and threats) analysis and adjust accordingly (Mehra and Braquet 2011). An important, and possibly overlooked, option for interacting with this community is to develop and maintain robust virtual services and resources, including chat reference, article databases, and online tutorials. Finding aids and library guides, both general and specific to LGBTQIA+ issues, can be displayed in the library and put on the library's website. These resources allow patrons to find information privately and independently; these are qualities important to the LGBTQIA+ community. "Owing to fear of stigma and rejection, LGBTQ individuals find the anonymity of online reference safer and easier for asking questions than broaching the subject face to face" (Thompson 2012, 11).

Finally, Kelly J. Thompson (2012) suggests that libraries train their staff to effectively work with this diverse user group and work toward making the library a welcoming environment overall, and Gough and Greenblatt (1992) recommend that librarians strive to handle materials and questions neutrally and equally, and stop the assumptions, stereotypes, and biases that are inherent in the larger heterosexist society.

REFERENCE SERVICES TO USERS WITH DISABILITIES

Among the specific populations for whom librarians need to develop a full range of reference services are individuals with physical and developmental differences; this includes those with visual impairments (Davies 2007), hearing impairments (Day 2000; Saar and Arthur-Okor 2013), various mobility impairments (some of which could be invisible to an observer), and those diagnosed with autism spectrum disorders (ASDs) (Anderson 2018; Anderson and Everhart 2015; Remy, Seaman, and Polacek 2014). In 1990, the Americans with Disabilities Act (ADA) was signed into law, representing "a milestone in America's commitment to full and equal opportunity for all its citizens" (U.S. Equal Employment Opportunity Commission and the U.S. Department of Justice 1992). Title II of the ADA governs public services for individuals with disabilities. Michael G. Gunde (1991, 99) concurs by stating that "library services must be provided in a manner that allows *each* eligible user with a disability to equally benefit from the local library. . . . Every decision about ADA compliance must be made on a case-by-case basis, taking into consideration the elements involved in the service or program and the needs of the library patron with a disability." A particular service for persons with disabilities can be denied only if a library can prove that it would incur an undue burden if the service was required to be offered. However, thinking in terms of "requirements" masks a simple reality. As Katy Lenn (1996, 14) observes, it "is important to remember that the purpose of legislation for the disabled is not to create special rights but equal rights."

Persons with Visual and Aural Disabilities

Developments in adaptive technology, such as speech recognition systems, screen enlargement software, and computerized Braille embossers, have transformed access to information for users with many types of disabilities. But lack of funding for high technology should not inhibit service to disabled users. Many aspects of ADA compliance are not technology intensive and serve the able-bodied population as well. A magnifying glass and an adjustable piece of furniture are two such examples. Other solutions involve forethought more than cost. If a workstation is set up on a push-button adjustable-height table with an adjustable keyboard tray, a keyboard that has large-type black-on-white keys, and two pointing devices such as a conventional mouse and a trackball, the workstation will meet the needs of wheelchair users and people who have computer-related repetitive strain injuries or carpal tunnel syndrome, as well as other dexterity disabilities (Goddard 2004). Rob Imrie (2004) advocates principles of universal design, in which products, environments, and communication systems are designed for the broadest spectrum of users. He stresses that social, attitudinal, and political shifts must first take place so that design principles and technical adaptations take place within an ethos of inclusiveness. By following this advice, libraries simultaneously meet the needs of able-bodied users as well as clientele with disabilities.

Some services and technologies that are new to mainstream audiences have engendered unexpected benefits for persons with disabilities; for example, live online chat reference service is an improvement on traditional TTY reference service. However, other unanticipated consequences have not been so welcome, such as how networked public computing workstations are often difficult to reconfigure or customize for individual users (Goddard 2004, 4). Voice recognition software requires users to build a voice file that the computer learns to "recognize," another challenge in a shared-use environment. Some technologies create noise, such as Braille embossers and voice output systems (although headphones can mitigate problems with the latter). Conversely, a workstation that is intended for users with learning disabilities should be installed in a quiet location with a minimum of distractions.

Each library needs to formulate its own service policies, using the ADA as a guideline along with publications that have been written specifically to help libraries through this process. A library, for example, may adopt the policy that when its employees are unable to provide equal, immediate delivery of service, such as photocopying the information in answer to a reference question, they will provide the material within twenty-four hours. The goal to work toward is equal treatment of all persons, the key ingredient being a positive attitude on the part of the staff. In any library, the reference department will certainly play a central role in developing and implementing services for persons with disabilities.

Both legally and ethically, librarians should evaluate the reference services they offer from the perspective of the user with a disability. This is a challenging task, given that there are numerous disabling conditions, and in any community served, the incidence of any one disabling condition may be relatively low.

Persons with Developmental Disabilities

Persons who have developmental disabilities fall into a wider variety of categories; characteristics that are often common to these disabilities are difficulties with language, communication, perception, and cognition. Some individuals may also experience problems with emotional and social development. With such a variety of characteristics, reference needs will vary, and librarians need to plan accordingly.

Despite a limited ability to manipulate information, individuals with developmental disabilities have a right to information, and reference librarians can adapt services to meet their needs. Reference interview sessions will need to be short and focused. Rephrasing or repetition may be necessary, and listening creatively will facilitate communication. The most successful materials are those that have large print, brief texts, and uncluttered pictures. Although children's materials often prove to be good reference tools, adults with developmental disabilities have a full range of adult concerns, such as vocation, social relationships, sexuality, money management, and parenting; thus, they frequently need to go beyond the resources of a children's reference collection. The adult reference collection can include titles from among the increasing number of materials related to adult literacy. Because users with developmental disabilities may be slow in processing information, it is important to have useful reference materials that circulate or to have space so that the materials may be used for extended periods of time in the library.

It is important for librarians to recognize that they may serve users with developmental disabilities through intermediaries, such as parents or attendants. Libraries should provide information about developmental disabilities, including the identification of relevant local and national organizations and agencies, so that family and caregivers can understand the conditions as well as make appropriate decisions about care. Reference librarians may offer to create bibliographies and special informational brochures about library services to be used by care providers, educators, and organizations for individuals with developmental disabilities.

Persons with Mental Illness

Another category of disability is mental illness, which is included in the ADA's definition of disability. With the deinstitutionalization of large numbers of seriously mentally ill individuals without the provision of sufficient community resources to accommodate them, many have become marginalized in society and even homeless.

The Association of Specialized Government and Cooperative Library Agencies (ASGCLA) reminds library professionals that mentally ill patrons are no more or less prone to violence than any other member of the population and should not be automatically discriminated against. ASGCLA makes suggestions for treating those with mental illness with the same respect and tolerance as with other patrons, including: do not be quick to assume that these patrons are a problem or security risk; do not assume that mental illness equates to deviant or criminal behavior; allow extra time and patience for those easily disoriented; become familiar with the wide range of behaviors associated with mental illness and encourage other patrons to do the same; be liberal with the library's signage (which allows patrons to be independent); do not over empathize in an attempt to relate to the patron; and establish community partnerships that may be able to provide additional resources (e.g., mental health clinics, group homes, homeless shelters, social workers) (Association of Specialized Government and Cooperative Library Agencies 2018).

Libraries have seen an influx of displaced people in their reference and reading rooms. Thomas E. Hecker (1996) suggests that libraries' "problem patron" response be replaced by casting the situation in terms of disability, where services and protections are provided as appropriate. But he does not intend for libraries to serve as social service agencies in the face of extreme situations: "Rather, I suggest that librarians apply the disability model to patrons with mental illness who have retained, or who have regained, a level of functioning which is still within the pale of society. Such people may exhibit symptoms which 'stretch the envelope' of our tolerance, but if tolerance will allow them to live an acceptable life within society, tolerance is the accommodation which must be accorded them" (Hecker 1996, 10).

In her book on handling problem situations in libraries, Anne M. Turner (2004, 12) proposes that it is possible to deal with the unanticipated consequences of social policy such as the presence in the library of mentally ill patrons (a broad and intersectional category of people) without compromising professional ethics and principles and also without creating draconian policies and procedures that attempt to address every conceivable situation. She suggests that libraries consider some overarching themes in their approach to library services: everyone has a right to use the library; staff should be flexible in their approach when dealing with these diverse populations; and the task of the library and its staff is to learn how to handle problem situations and *not* problem patrons.

REFERENCE SERVICES FOR OLDER ADULTS

Librarians should be cognizant of the particular needs of adult learners (Cooke 2010), and this holds true for older adults who frequent the library. Indeed, older adults may have additional special needs that require accommodating and unassuming services from the library. According to the Census, the term "elderly" refers to adults who are sixty-five years of age or older. This is one of the fastest-growing segments of our population, constituting 12.9 percent of the population in 2010 (U.S. Census Bureau 2012, Table 9); this percentage is projected to rise to 20.2 percent by 2050. Libraries should be adapting reference services to meet the needs of this growing population whose needs will be coming to the forefront in the next twenty-five years (Decker 2010).

In working with older adults, it is important to approach each person as an individual who may not share the characteristics or interests commonly associated with the elderly. One should avoid assuming that older adults experience a decline in cognitive ability because many do not. Indeed, unless disease attacks the brain, intellectual capacities can improve with age (Mates 2003, 13). Other assumptions must also be avoided; for example, reading interests may or may not change as individuals grow older, and this population may need information about sexual health and disease prevention. Older adults are not necessarily retired; they may be working full-time or part-time, or they may be underemployed and actively looking for work. Finally, many grandparents are now raising their grandchildren and consequently are very involved in technology, gaming, and other activities not readily associated with this age group. These older adults have reference needs that do not fit the mold of the stereotypical senior citizen.

Good reference service for elderly individuals includes all the basic components of good reference service for the general adult population, with particular attention to the individual needs of elderly users. In its guidelines for library service to older adults, the Reference and User Services Association (2017) exhorts libraries to provide a full slate of integrated library services to the elderly. The ALA Office for Diversity, Literacy, and Outreach Services (n.d.) provides suggestions for serving older adults that include having large print materials and magnifying equipment, having comfortable and supportive seating, having accessible shelving (so as to eliminate excessive bending or reaching for materials), having relevant information in a central location (e.g., agency brochures and flyers), and taking care that the physical building is conducive and accessible (e.g., bathrooms, elevators, and checkout stations should have support rails, computer stations should be ADA compliant, and computers might have cordless mouse devices for those with arthritis).

Reference librarians need to avoid stereotyping or patronizing older users and should develop effective communication skills so as to encourage them to ask questions and to ensure that each answer is fully understood by the user. Some older adults, for example, have had limited exposure to computers and may experience more computer anxiety than younger library users. Whereas the library was once a friendly, welcoming physical place for recreation and leisure, it now feels intimidating and impersonal. Special online catalog instruction sessions (or word-processing classes, or workshops dedicated to e-mail, Internet searching, and social media) tailored for older individuals will create a comfortable atmosphere where users can ask questions and experience self-paced practice and one-on-one coaching.

Because computer use in libraries has become so important, Barbara T. Mates (2003) devotes two full chapters of her book to the subject as it relates to seniors. She discusses hardware considerations, the problems seniors tend to have with navigation and coordination, training and marketing approaches, and website design recommendations (with special attention to color and font choices) and emphasizes the importance of teaching online safety and evaluation skills, given that many seniors may not be prepared for the preponderance of online misinformation and scam artists. Information access and training regarding health information (including information about sex and sexual health) is also increasingly pertinent (Xie and Bugg 2009). As baby boomers continue reaching retirement age, they are changing the picture of how senior citizens relate to computers.

To provide reference service to older adults, it may be necessary to offer remote delivery of materials and service. Certainly, the most common form of remote delivery of reference service to seniors is by telephone. In libraries where in-person reference service is busy and takes precedence over answering questions over the telephone, special provisions must be made to serve the homebound and the institutionalized elderly. The general rule of serving walk-in users before answering the telephone is logical but may make it difficult for the older adult to access the library. It may be necessary to set up a special telephone service for elderly (or disabled) persons who cannot easily get to the library. Also, it may be possible to take reference service to elderly individuals by including reference materials in the bookmobile collection when making stops at retirement homes, assisted living facilities, nursing homes, or senior citizen centers or by providing chat and e-mail reference service to these agencies. Training bookmobile staff in basic reference service and teaching care-facility staff to assist with online reference services would ensure that questions could be answered in a timely and predictable fashion.

It is important to communicate to older adults the reference services that are available to them and to make them feel welcome. The library can effectively market services of particular interest to older persons through library brochures, specific informational programs held in the library, and outside agencies. Reference librarians should cultivate communications with other service agencies in the community; often, specialists in services to the elderly can provide training for library staff in working with the elderly and make appropriate referrals to the library if interagency cooperation is practiced. Careful assessment of what use older citizens make of a library may reveal a need to publicize existing reference services or a way to adapt services to meet the needs and capacities of older adults. The library should not be a place where older adults encounter ageism, but rather a place that encourages and facilitates lifelong learning and healthy, independent living. In order to achieve this kind of atmosphere, Connie Van Fleet (1995) suggests that librarians serving older adults need patience, should be sensitive to unspoken needs, and need to be flexible when implementing service (e.g., in the event of diminishments in vision, hearing, or mobility).

CONCLUSION

Reference services should be offered to all persons in a library's service community regardless of their circumstances or identifying characteristics. There are several issues to be addressed by librarians responsible for ensuring that specific groups in their service community have equal access to reference service. First, librarians need to acknowledge that reference services *do* need to be adapted, or at least assessed, with respect to the needs and abilities of particular groups. Librarians need to identify groups within their community that might face obstacles to free and full access to information (see Box 12.5). It should be stressed that this assessment needs to go beyond polling or observing current users of library reference materials or services. If impediments such as physical or communication barriers exist, members of a group affected by the barriers often are nonusers of the library and thus are invisible to the librarian who observes only the behavior of the user group.

Box 12.5 Activity: Other Diverse Populations

Every community is different and dynamic; in fact, a diverse user group can be very small and unique to a particular community. This chapter covers some, but certainly not all, diverse populations that use libraries. For example, the town of Arthur, Illinois, has a large Amish community that has particular information needs (Miller and Aguilar 1984). The Oakland (California) Public Library (Oakland Public Library n.d.) has made a notable investment to serve their Asian teen population. And many communities have a significant number of children who are homeschooled and rely heavily on their local libraries (Jennings 2013).

Questions for Reflection and Discussion:

1. What diverse populations are present in your community?
2. How would you apply the aforementioned best practices and service recommendations to members of these groups?
3. If you are unfamiliar with the needs of this group, how could you learn more?

Once groups are identified, librarians need to create a plan of service for meeting the special needs of individuals in each. This plan would include determining the adaptations needed by each group, assessing the library's ability to meet identified needs, and establishing priorities for actions to be taken by the library. It is important to work with other agencies, including local ones and regional or national organizations, both to identify needs of special users and to design collections and services that meet groups' reference needs. (Box 12.6 lists some professional organizations that librarians can consult.) The library should have policies and procedures, including staff training, which enhance access to full reference services. Special adaptations to library procedures to accommodate the needs of identified groups should be incorporated in library handbooks or manuals. Librarians should work diligently with patrons of various diverse user groups without judgment or assumptions; instead, empathy and openness should guide all reference interactions, and library services in general. Finally, librarians should plan regular evaluation of services and facilities for targeted groups, so that they can keep up with, or even anticipate, changes in the population of those groups, as well as relevant changes in library technology.

Librarians need to plan reference services, assemble reference collections, and develop reference skills appropriate to the various groups in their community of users. This planning process must begin with an understanding of the diverse groups that constitute that community.

Box 12.6 Professional Organizations Related to Diversity

Not all of these organizations pertain explicitly to reference services, but they are organizations focused in some way on diversity and culture and comprise and/or serve professional librarians who engage in reference and related activities in their libraries.

American Indian Library Association (AILA)
http://ailanet.org
Asian Pacific American Librarians Association (APALA)
http://www.apalaweb.org

Association of Specialized Government and Cooperative Library Agencies
http://www.ala.org/asgcla/
ASGCLA Library Services to the Incarcerated and Detained Interest Group
http://www.ala.org/asgcla/interestgroups/iglsid
ASGCLA Library Services for Youth in Custody Interest Group
http://www.ala.org/asgcla/interestgroups/iglsyc
Association of Tribal Archives, Libraries, & Museums (ATALM)
http://www.atalm.org/
Black Caucus of the American Library Association (BCALA)
http://www.bcala.org
Chinese American Librarians Association (CALA)
http://cala-web.org
Ethnic and Multicultural Information Exchange Round Table (EMIERT)
http://www.ala.org/emiert/
The National Association to Promote Library & Information Services to Latinos and the Spanish Speaking (REFORMA)
http://www.reforma.org

REFERENCES

American Library Association. 2019. "Library Bill of Rights." Last modified January 29, 2019. http://www.ala.org/advocacy/intfreedom/librarybill.

American Library Association. n.d.-a "B.3 Diversity (Old Number 60)." http://www.ala.org/aboutala/governance/policymanual/updatedpolicymanual/section2/3diversity.

American Library Association. n.d.-b. "Extending Our Reach: Reducing Homelessness Through Library Engagement." http://www.ala.org/offices/extending-our-reach-reducing-homelessness-through-library-engagement-6.

Anderson, Amelia. 2018. "Autism and the Academic Library: A Study of Online Communication." *College & Research Libraries* 79 (5): 645–58.

Anderson, Amelia, and Nancy Everhart. 2015. "Project PALS: Ensuring Success in Libraries for Patrons with Autism." *Teacher Librarian* 43 (2): 24–25.

Anderson, Keith A., Chaniqua D. Simpson, and Lynette G. Fisher. 2012. "The Ability of Public Library Staff to Help Homeless People in the United States: Exploring Relationships, Roles and Potential." *Journal of Poverty and Social Justice* 20 (2): 177–90.

Association of Specialized Government and Cooperative Library Agencies. 2018. "Overview." Mental Health Issues. https://www.asgcladirect.org/resources/mental-health-issues/.

Austin, Jeanie. 2012. "Critical Issues in Juvenile Detention Libraries." *The Journal of Research on Libraries and Young Adults* (July 26). http://www.yalsa.ala.org/jrlya/2012/07/critical-issues-in-juvenile-detention-center-libraries/.

Austin, Jeanie. 2018. "Restorative Justice as a Tool to Address the Role of Policing and Incarceration in the Lives of Youth in the United States." *Journal of Librarianship and Information Science*: 1–15.

Berger, Joseph. 2012. "Libraries Speak the Mother Tongue." *The New York Times*, January 3, A18.

Blank, Barbara T. 2014. "Public Libraries Add Social Workers and Social Programs." *The New Social Worker* (Fall 2014). http://www.socialworker.com/feature-articles/practice/public-libraries-add-social-workers-and-social-programs/.

Bowdoin, Natalia Taylor, Chris Hagar, Joyce Monsees, Trishanjit Kaur, Trae Middlebrooks, Leatha Miles-Edmonson, Ashanti White, Touger Vang, Musa W. Olaka, Charles A. Yier,

Clara M. Chu, and Barbara J. Ford. 2017. "Academic Libraries Serving Refugees and Asylum Seekers." *College & Research Libraries News* 78 (6): 298.

Brook, Freeda, Dave Ellenwood, and Althea E. Lazzaro. 2015. "In Pursuit of Antiracist Social Justice: Denaturalizing Whiteness in the Academic Library." *Library Trends* 64 (2): 246–84.

Brothen, Erin, and Erika Bennett. 2013. "The Culturally Relevant Reference Interview." In *Library Services for Multicultural Patrons: Strategies to Encourage Library Use*, edited by Carol Smallwood and Kim Becnel, 297–302. Lanham, MD: Scarecrow Press.

Carder, Linda, Carl Pracht, and Robert Willingham. 1997. "Reaching the Whole Population: Adaptive Techniques for Reaching Students Who Fall Through the Cracks." Paper presented at the Twenty-Fourth National LOEX Library Instruction Conference, Ann Arbor, MI, May 16–18.

Carlson, David. 1990. *Adrift in a Sea of Change: California's Public Libraries Struggle to Meet the Information Needs of Multicultural Communities*. Sacramento: California State Library Foundation.

Clark, Sheila, and Erica MacCreaigh. 2006. *Library Services to the Incarcerated: Applying the Public Library Model in Correctional Facility Libraries*. Westport, CT: Libraries Unlimited.

Cooke, Nicole A. 2010. "Becoming an Andragogical Librarian: Using Library Instruction as a Tool to Combat Library Anxiety and Empower Adult Learners." *New Review of Academic Librarianship* 16 (2): 208–27.

Cooke, Nicole A. 2016. *Information Services to Diverse Populations: Developing Culturally Competent Library Professionals*. Santa Barbara, CA: Libraries Unlimited.

Cuesta, Yolanda J. 2004. "Developing Outreach Skills in Library Staff." In *From Outreach to Equity: Innovative Models of Library Policy and Practice*, edited by Robin Osborne, 112–15. Chicago: American Library Association.

Curry, Ann. 2005. "If I Ask, Will They Answer? Evaluating Public Library Reference Service to Gay and Lesbian Youth." *Reference & User Services Quarterly* 45 (1): 65–75.

Davies, J. Eric. 2007. "An Overview of International Research into the Library and Information Needs of Visually Impaired People." *Library Trends* 55 (4): 785–95.

Day, John M., ed. 2000. *Guidelines for Library Services to Deaf People*. The Hague, Netherlands: The International Federation of Library Associations and Institutions.

Decker, Emy N. 2010. "Baby Boomers and the United States Public Library System." *Library Hi Tech* 28 (4): 605–16.

Dixen, Rebecca, and Stephanie Thorson. 2001. "How Librarians Serve People in Prison." *Computers in Libraries* 21 (9): 48–53.

Dowd, Ryan. 2018. *The Librarian's Guide to Homelessness: An Empathy-driven Approach to Solving Problems, Preventing Conflict, and Serving Everyone*. Chicago: ALA Editions.

Dunbar, H. Minnie. 1986. "Bibliographic Instruction for Freshman Students at Florida International University." Paper presented at the National Conference on the Freshman Year Experience, Columbia, SC, February 18.

Elliot, Andrea. 2013. "Invisible Child." *The New York Times*, December 9. http://www.nytimes.com/projects/2013/invisible-child/index.html.

Elteto, Sharon, Rose M. Jackson, and Adriene Lim. 2008. "Is the Library a 'Welcoming Space'? An Urban Academic Library and Diverse Student Experiences." *portal: Libraries and the Academy* 8 (3): 325–37.

Eyrich-Garg, Karin M., and Eric Rice. 2012. "Cyber Behavior of Homeless Adolescents and Adults." In *Encyclopedia of Cyber Behavior*, edited by Zheng Yan, 284–91. Hershey, PA: IGI Global.

Fitzgibbons, Shirley. 1983. "Reference and Information Services for Children and Young Adults: Definition, Services, and Issues." *The Reference Librarian* 2 (7/8): 1–30.

Ganster, Ligaya. 2011. "Reaching Out to International Students: A Focus-Group Approach to Developing Web Resources and Services." *College & Undergraduate Libraries* 18 (4): 368–84.

Gehner, John. 2010. "Libraries, Low-Income People, and Social Exclusion." *Public Library Quarterly* 29 (1): 39–47.

Giesecke, Joan, and Beth McNeil. 2001. "Core Competencies for Libraries and Library Staff." In *Staff Development: A Practical Guide*, edited by Elizabeth Fuseler, Terry Dahlin, and Deborah A. Carver, 49–54. Chicago: American Library Association.

Gilton, Donna L. 1994. "A World of Difference: Preparing for Information Literacy Instruction for Diverse Groups." *Multicultural Review* 3 (3): 54–62.

Goddard, Marti. 2004. "Access through Technology." *Library Journal Net Connect* 129 (Spring): 2–6.

Goodman, Valeda D. 2011. "Applying Ethnographic Research Methods in Library and Information Settings." *Libri* 61 (1): 1–11.

Gough, Cal, and Ellen Greenblatt. 1992. "Services to Gay and Lesbian Patrons: Examining the Myths." *Library Journal* 117 (1): 59–63.

Grover, Robert, Roger C. Greer, and John Agada. 2010. *Assessing Information Needs: Managing Transformative Library Services*. Santa Barbara, CA: Libraries Unlimited.

Greenblatt, Ellen, ed. 2011. *Serving LGBTIQ Library and Archives Users: Essays on Outreach, Service, Collections and Access*. Jefferson, NC: McFarland.

Gunde, Michael G. 1991. "Working with the Americans with Disabilities Act." *Library Journal* 116 (December): 99–100.

Hall, Patrick Andrew. 1991. "The Role of Affectivity in Instructing People of Color: Some Implications for Bibliographic Instruction." *Library Trends* 39 (Winter): 316–26.

Hanley, Robert. 1992. "Library Wins in Homeless-Man Case." *The New York Times*, March 25. http://www.nytimes.com/1992/03/25/nyregion/library-wins-in-homeless-man-case.html.

Hecker, Thomas E. 1996. "Patrons with Disabilities or Problem Patrons: Which Model Should Librarians Apply to People with Mental Illness?" *The Reference Librarian* 53: 5–12.

Hersberger, Julie. 2003. "Are the Economically Poor Information Poor? Does the Digital Divide Affect the Homeless and Access to Information?" *Canadian Journal of Information and Library Science* 27 (3): 45–64.

Hersberger, Julie. 2005. "The Homeless and Information Needs and Services." *Reference & User Services Quarterly* 44 (3): 199–202.

Holt, Glen E. 2006. "Fitting Library Services into the Lives of the Poor." *The Bottom Line: Managing Library Finances* 19 (4): 179–86.

Imrie, Rob. 2004. "From Universal to Inclusive Design in the Built Environment." In *Disabling Barriers—Enabling Environments*, edited by John Swain, Sally French, Colin Barnes, and Carol Thomas, 2nd ed. 279–84. London: Sage.

Ishimura, Yusuke, and Joan C. Bartlett. 2014. "Are Librarians Equipped to Teach International Students? A Survey of Current Practices and Recommendations for Training." *The Journal of Academic Librarianship* 40 (3–4): 313–21.

Janes, Phoebe, and Ellen Meltzer. 1990. "Origins and Attitudes: Training Reference Librarians for a Pluralistic World." *The Reference Librarian* 30: 145–55.

Jenkins, Mark. 2014. "D.C. Adds a Social Worker to Library System to Work with Homeless Patrons." *The Washington Post*, August 27. https://www.washingtonpost.com/local/dc-adds-a-social-worker-to-library-system-to-work-with-homeless-patrons/2014/08/26/2d80200c-2c96-11e4-be9e-60cc44c01e7f_story.html.

Jennings, Cynthia. 2013. "Homeschoolers and Public Libraries: A Synergistic Relationship." *Maine Policy Review* 22 (1): 92–93.

Katopol, Patricia F. 2014. "Management 2.0: Stereotype Threat." *Library Leadership & Management* 28 (3): 1.

Knight, Heather. 2010. "Library Adds Social Worker to Assist Homeless." *San Francisco Chronicle*, January 11. http://www.sfgate.com/bayarea/article/Library-adds-social-worker-to-assist-homeless-3275950.php.

Knight, Lorrie, Maryann Hight, and Lisa Polfer. 2010. "Rethinking the Library for the International Student Community." *Reference Services Review* 38 (4): 581–605.

Lam, R. Errol. 1988. "The Reference Interview: Some Intercultural Considerations." *RQ* 27 (3): 390–5.

Lehmann, Vibeke. 2011. "Challenges and Accomplishments in US Prison Libraries." *Library Trends* 59 (3): 490–508.

Lenn, Katy. 1996. "Library Services to Disabled Students: Outreach and Education." *The Reference Librarian* 53: 13–25.

Leonard, Gillian D. 1993. "Multiculturalism and Library Services." *The Acquisitions Librarian* 5 (9–10): 3–19.

Lewis, Mary Genevieve. 1969. "Library Orientation for Asian College Students." *College & Research Libraries* 30: 267–72.

Liu, Mengxiong. 1995. "Ethnicity and Information Seeking." *The Reference Librarian* 23 (49–50): 123–34.

Macdonald, Gina, and Elizabeth Sarkodie-Mensah. 1988. "ESL Students and American Libraries." *College & Research Libraries* 49 (5): 425–31.

Mates, Barbara T. 2003. *5-Star Programming and Services for Your 55+ Library Customers.* Chicago: American Library Association.

McCleer, Adriana. 2013. "Knowing Communities: A Review of Community Assessment Literature." *Public Library Quarterly* 32 (3): 263–74.

McDonald, Martha J. 1981. "Structural Approaches to Community Analysis." *Indiana Libraries* 1 (2): 51–59.

McKay, Becky. 2011. "Lesbian, Gay, Bisexual, and Transgender Health Issues, Disparities, and Information Resources." *Medical Reference Services Quarterly* 30 (4): 393–401.

Mehra, Bharat, and Donna Braquet. 2011. "Progressive LGBTQ Reference: Coming Out in the 21st Century." *Reference Services Review* 39 (3): 401–22.

Miller, Jerome K., and William Aguilar. 1984. "Public Library Use by Members of the Old Order Amish Faith." *RQ* 23 (3): 322–6.

Morris, Jen. 2013. "Free to Learn: Helping Ex-Offenders with Reentry." *Public Library Quarterly* 32 (2): 119–23.

Muggleton, Thomas H., and Ian Ruthven. 2012. "Homelessness and Access to the Informational Mainstream." *Journal of Documentation* 68 (2): 218–37.

Nemec-Loise, Jenna. 2014. "A Little Extra Help—Why Public Libraries Need Social Workers." *Public Libraries Online*, September 23. http://publiclibrariesonline.org/2014/09/a-little-extra-help-why-public-libraries-need-social-workers/.

Oakland Public Library. n.d. "Asian Branch." http://www.oaklandlibrary.org/teens/your-library/teen-zones/asian-branch.

Office for Diversity, Literacy, and Outreach Services. n.d. "Services to Older Adults." American Library Association. http://www.ala.org/advocacy/diversity/librariesrespond/services-older-adults.

Osa, Justina O., Sylvia A. Nyana, and Clara A. Ogbaa. 2006. "Effective Cross-Cultural Communication to Enhance Reference Transactions: Training Guidelines and Tips." *Knowledge Quest* 35 (2): 22–24.

Pyati, Ajit. 2003. "Limited English Proficient Users and the Need for Improved Reference Services." *Reference Services Review* 31 (3): 264–71.

Reference and User Services Association. 2017. "Guidelines to Library Services for Older Adults." American Library Association. Last modified September 2017. http://www.ala.org/rusa/guidelines/guidelines-by-topic.

Remy, Charlie, Priscilla Seaman, and Kelly M. Polacek. 2014. "Evolving from Disability to Diversity." *Reference & User Services Quarterly* 54 (1): 24–28.

Rubin, Rhea Joyce, and Connie House. 1983. "Library Service in US Jails: Issues, Questions, Trends." *Library Journal* 108 (3): 173–77.

Saar, Michael, and Helena Arthur-Okor. 2013. "Reference Services for the Deaf and Hard of Hearing." *Reference Services Review* 41 (3): 434–52.

Saunders, Laura, and Mary Jordan. 2013. "Significantly Different?" *Reference & User Services Quarterly* 52 (3): 216–23.

Sfondeles, Tina. 2014. "Family of Little League Champ without a Home Base of their Own." *Chicago Sun Times*, August 28. http://archive.is/yiHQb.

Shachaf, Pnina, and Sarah Horowitz. 2007. "Are Virtual Reference Services Color Blind?" *Library & Information Science Research* 28 (4): 501–20.

Shafer, Scott. 2014. "Urban Libraries Become De Facto Homeless Shelters." *NPR News Around the Nation.* Podcast audio. April 23. http://www.npr.org/2014/04/23/306102523/san-francisco-library-hires-social-worker-to-help-homeless-patrons.

Shen, Lan. 2013. "Out of Information Poverty: Library Services for Urban Marginalized Immigrants." *Urban Library Journal* 19 (1): 1–12.

Shirley, Glennor L. 2003. "Correctional Libraries, Library Standards, and Diversity." *Journal of Correctional Education* 54 (2): 70–74.

Strong, Gary E. 2001. "Teaching Adult Literacy in a Multicultural Environment." In *Literacy & Libraries: Learning from Case Studies*, edited by GraceAnne A. DeCandido, 110–115. Chicago: American Library Association.

Taylor, Jami K. 2002. "Targeting the Information Needs of Transgender Individuals." *Current Studies in Librarianship* 26 (1/2): 85–109.

Thompson, Kelly J. 2012. "Where's the 'T'? Improving Library Service to Community Members Who Are Transgender-Identified." *B Sides*, 1–17. http://ir.uiowa.edu/bsides/22.

Turock, Betty J. 2003. "Developing Diverse Professional Leaders." *New Library World* 104 (11/12): 491–98.

Turner, Anne M. 2004. *It Comes with the Territory: Handling Problem Situations in Libraries.* Jefferson, NC: McFarland & Company.

U.S. Census Bureau. 2012. *Statistical Abstract of the United States 2012.* Washington, DC: Government Printing Office. https://www.census.gov/library/publications/time-series/statistical_abstracts.html.

U.S. Census Bureau. 2018. *Demographic Turning Points for the United States: Population Projections for 2020 to 2060.* Washington, DC: Government Publishing Office. https://www2.census.gov/library/publications/2018/demo/P25-1144.pdf.

U.S. Equal Employment Opportunity Commission, and the U.S. Department of Justice. 1992. *Americans with Disabilities Act Handbook.* Washington, DC: Government Publishing Office.

Van Fleet, Connie. 1995. "A Matter of Focus: Reference Services for Older Adults." *The Reference Librarian* 23 (49–50): 147–64.

Walker, Billie E. 2006. "Using Humor in Library Instruction." *Reference Services Review* 34 (1): 117–28.

Wang, Hong. 2012. "Immigration in America: Library Services and Information Resources." *Reference Services Review* 40 (3): 480–511.

Willett, Peter, and Rebecca Broadley. 2011. "Effective Public Library Outreach to Homeless People." *Library Review* 60 (8): 658–70.

Winkelstein, Julie A. 2014. "Public Libraries: Creating Safe Spaces for Homeless LGBTQ Youth." Paper presented at the 2014 IFLA Conference, Lyon, France, August 8.

Woelfer, Jill Palzkill, and David G. Hendry. 2011. "Homeless Young People and Living with Personal Digital Artifacts." In *Proceedings of the SIGCHI Conference on Human Factors in Computing Systems*, 1697–706. New York: ACM.

Xie, Bo, and Julie M. Bugg. 2009. "Public Library Computer Training for Older Adults to Access High-Quality Internet Health Information." *Library & Information Science Research* 31 (3): 155–62.

Zhang, Xiwen. 2001. "The Practice and Politics of Public Library Services to Asian Immigrants." *Contributions in Librarianship and Information Science* 97: 141–50.

COMPETENCIES, STANDARDS, AND GUIDELINES

Alter, Rachel, Linda Walling, Susan Beck, Kathleen Garland, Ardis Hanson, and Walter Metz. 2007. *Guidelines for Library Services for People with Mental Illnesses.* Chicago: Association of Specialized and Cooperative Library Agencies, American Library Association.

American Library Association. 2010. "Prisoners' Right to Read." http://www.ala.org/advocacy/intfreedom/librarybill/interpretations/prisonersrightoread.

Association of College and Research Libraries. 2012. "Diversity Standards: Cultural Competency for Academic Libraries." American Library Association. http://www.ala.org/acrl/standards/diversity.

Association of Specialized and Cooperative Library Agencies. 2011. *Revised Standards and Guidelines of Service for the Library of Congress Network of Libraries for the Blind and Physically Handicapped.* Chicago: Association of Specialized and Cooperative Library Agencies.

Goddard, Martha L., ed. 1996. *Guidelines for Library and Information Services for the American Deaf Community.* Chicago: Association of Specialized and Cooperative Library Agencies.

Lehmann, Vibeke, and Joanne Locke. 2005. *Guidelines for Library Services to Prisoners.* IFLA Professional Reports, No. 92. The Hague, Netherlands: International Federation of Library Associations and Institutions.

Reference and User Services Association. 2007. "Guidelines for Library Services to Spanish-Speaking Library Users." American Library Association. http://www.ala.org/rusa/resources/guidelines/guidespanish.

Reference and User Services Association. 2007. "Guidelines for the Development and Promotion of Multilingual Collections and Services." American Library Association. http://www.ala.org/rusa/resources/guidelines/guidemultilingual.

Reference and User Services Association. 2008. "Guidelines for Library and Information Services to Older Adults." American Library Association. http://www.ala.org/rusa/guidelines/guidelines-by-topic.

SUGGESTED READINGS

Drabinski, Emily, and Debbie Rabina. 2015. "Reference Services to Incarcerated People, Part I: Themes Emerging from Answering Reference Questions from Prisons and Jails." *Reference and User Services Quarterly* 55 (2): 42–48; Rabina, Debbie, and Emily Drabinski. 2015. "Reference Services to Incarcerated People, Part II: Sources and Learning Outcomes." *Reference and User Services Quarterly* 55 (2): 123–31.

Starting with a service learning assignment for LIS students, the authors analyzed reference queries from incarcerated individuals. In Part I, the authors discuss the type of queries received; in Part II, the authors discuss how the assignment met the learning outcomes for the course. The two articles reveal that information poverty can affect marginalized and vulnerable patron groups and emphasize the need to proactively expose library professionals to strategies and resources that can assist with reference provision to diverse populations.

Paris, Django. 2012. "Culturally Sustaining Pedagogy: A Needed Change in Stance, Terminology, and Practice." *Educational Researcher* 41 (3): 93–97.

An education scholar, Paris builds upon classic texts in the discipline and advocates for actively incorporating learners' cultures into the teaching and learning process. This approach is something that reference and instruction librarians should be considering and embracing in their professional practices, inside and outside library classrooms. The more library professionals understand and appreciate their patrons' backgrounds and cultural wealth, the better position they will be in to assist them with their information needs.

Pashia, Angela. 2016. "Black Lives Matter in Information Literacy." *Radical Teacher* 106: 141–3.

Pashia posits that teaching happens in library classrooms and at the reference desk during one-on-one interactions. This instruction is not neutral, just as patron questions are not neutral. As such, information professionals should be mindful of practicing critical information literacy, which encourages the incorporation of current events and media, even if they are difficult, and patrons' personal interests into reference and instruction work.

Press, Nancy Ottman, and Mary Diggs-Hobson. 2005. "Providing Health Information to Community Members Where They Are: Characteristics of the Culturally Competent Librarian." *Library Trends* 53 (3): 397–410.

Because cultural competence emerged from the applied health sciences, it is not surprising that medical library professionals were among the first to embrace the concept and that they have been discussing cultural competence in the literature for almost two decades. The authors provide concrete steps for acquiring cultural competence; the steps require effort, but they are accessible and appropriate for library professionals in any setting that provides reference and instruction services.

Sanchez, Joe. 2018. "'What Are They Doing, Like, in a Library?' Mexican-American Experiences in their High School Library." *Young Adult Library Services 16* (4): 26–30.

Sanchez explores the experiences of Mexican-American high school students and specifically investigates their social media use, study habits, and experiences with their school library. Children and young adults of color have specific historical and cultural experiences and information needs that library professionals should be aware of in order to provide the most effective and compassionate services possible to minority youth. LIS professionals need to look beyond stereotypical labels, such as "at risk," when serving non-white youth.

Part II

Information Sources and Their Use

Chapter 13

Introduction to Information Creation and Dissemination

Laura Saunders and Melissa A. Wong

INTRODUCTION

Part II of this book introduces the tools that information professionals use to locate answers and fulfill information needs. The following chapters will provide an overview of various resources grouped broadly by type or format, such as encyclopedias, bibliographies, and indexes, as well as by subject area, such as government, health, and legal information. While each chapter will introduce a variety of specific reference titles, the real focus is on the purpose, function, and utility of the resource type. In other words, while most librarians will be familiar with *Encyclopaedia Britannica*, it is more helpful to know that sources *like Britannica* are helpful for general adult audiences to get a detailed overview of a broad array of subjects and for high school and college students to engage in pre-research to gather background information on a topic. Similarly, while it is useful to be familiar with *PyscINFO* or *ABI/INFORM Global*, it is more important to know that indexes *like* these compile information—usually peer-reviewed articles but often conference proceedings, trade publications, book reviews, and other pertinent materials as well—that offers researchers in-depth access to the literature of a discipline.

In fact, as resources continue to morph online, and as libraries make difficult collection decisions with reduced budgets, it is impossible to know what specific resources any information professional will have at their disposal in any institution. Thus, rather than learning individual titles, information professionals should understand how broad types of resources work. Once a librarian understands the function, purpose, and use of resources like catalogs, bibliographies, or dictionaries, they can transfer that knowledge to evaluate and search whatever resources are available to them.

Part of understanding the purpose, function, and use of various information resources is understanding the information life cycle. Each type of information resource, and, indeed, each piece of information, passes through various phases from the initial creation of the information to its publication, which may or may not include various editorial processes, to dissemination, organization, and retrieval. Understanding the stages of the information life cycle, and the various permutations of the life cycle that apply to different information formats, can help the information professional identify the appropriate resource needed to answer a particular type of question or information need. Further, in understanding the information life cycle, librarians and other information professionals can examine the various methods for accessing different formats and types of information and can analyze where and how bias might be reflected in the sources.

This chapter provides a framework for Part II of this text. It describes the general information life cycle, as well as several variations on the life cycle specific to particular information formats. It examines trends in publishing and scholarly communication and describes how disciplinary differences impact access and use of information sources. Finally, it concludes by examining issues of bias and representation, including how these manifest in the sources upon which information professionals rely and how those professionals can recognize and minimize its impact.

THE INFORMATION LIFE CYCLE

The information life cycle describes the process through which any piece of information moves from an idea to a representation that can be saved, stored, accessed, retrieved, and shared, as illustrated in Figure 4.1 in Chapter 4.

Broadly, each piece of information—each book, article, index, and so on—goes through a five-stage cycle:

1. **Creation.** An idea or event is developed into a material representation such as a book, image, or article.
2. **Publication or dissemination.** The information representation is made available to others, either through a traditional publishing process, such as an article printed in a scholarly journal, or through a self-publishing process such as a blog post or tweet.
3. **Organization and storage.** The published information is tagged with metadata and stored in such a way that it can be discovered and accessed by others. Such "tagging" could be a formal and manual process, such as library cataloging, or could be automated, such as by a Web crawler. The information could be stored in a library, bookstore, archive, database, or the cloud.
4. **Access and retrieval.** The information is searchable and discoverable by other people. In some cases, access to the information might be limited by paywalls and subscriptions, and in other cases it may be freely available.
5. **Reuse.** The discovered information will often serve as the basis for new ideas and the cycle starts over.

While the preceding list describes a broad information life cycle through which nearly any piece of information flows, there are variations on this process that apply to specific formats and types of information.

The Information Life Cycle of News Events

When an event takes place, or news "breaks," reporting on and analysis of that news will follow a particular cycle (University of Nevada Libraries 2016). Even as the event unfolds, information will be created and shared. Depending on the severity and anticipated interest of the story, local and perhaps national broadcast news stations will follow the story and offer updates, often promoted as "breaking news" stories. At the same time, eyewitnesses and others might share news about the event through social media platforms such as *Twitter* and *Facebook*. It is worth remembering that it can be difficult to verify facts in the midst of an unfolding event. While news outlets will strive to share only verifiable facts, in the rush to post news, some outlets might share misinformation. Over the next few days, newspapers will publish stories reporting the main details of the event, while broadcast stations will continue their coverage with additional details and perhaps some early analysis. During this time, news outlets will generally correct any misinformation from initial broadcasts. Discussion of the story might continue on social media. These initial reports on a story can be considered primary source material, as it was created in the moment.

Over the next few weeks, the story might get picked up by news magazines, which will generally gather all of the details and provide an overview of the story up to that point, along with an analysis of the event's significance or effects. With time and further analysis, the story might be covered in scholarly articles and books. Often, scholarly articles will offer an in-depth examination of one aspect of the story. Books might offer a history or gather various perspectives on the story. Magazines, scholarly articles, and books are considered secondary sources, as they report on and analyze events after the fact. Eventually, the story might also be covered in tertiary sources like encyclopedias that offer summaries of significant events.

The news information life cycle can be illustrated with an event like the 2018 eruption of the volcano Kīlauea on the island of Hawai'i. The volcano began erupting in May of 2018. Major media outlets covered the eruptions almost immediately on television and online through social media and other streaming services. At the same time, residents, tourists, and members of the public shared information through outlets like *Twitter* and *Facebook*. As often happens, in the chaos immediately following the event, some inaccurate information was shared, which led to confusion about the scale of the eruption, the extent of the damage, and how much of the island was impacted. Over the next few days, news outlets continued to cover the story, verifying and correcting details and providing updated information. Since the initial eruption, scholarly articles have been written about the event, the U.S. Geological Survey (2019) has created a weekly volcano report, and *Encyclopaedia Britannica* (n.d.) has updated its entry on Kīlauea to include the 2018 eruptions.

The Information Life Cycle of Scholarly Information

Scholarly information, including scientific discoveries, has its own unique information life cycle. Scholarly information is often based on research, ranging from experimental research taking place in a lab to historical research poring over primary resources in an archive. Scholars test theories and develop ideas, which they share through journal articles or scholarly books, called monographs.

Most scholarly information goes through an extended editorial process known as peer review. During the peer-review process, book and journal editors recruit scholars to read and comment on manuscripts that have been submitted for publication. These scholars are experts in the field, and their job is to review the manuscript for overall quality and adherence to the ethical and research standards of the field. As peer reviewers read the manuscript for the quality and logic of the argument, they are also expected to assess whether researchers have employed appropriate methodologies and statistical tests, considered all of the relevant literature on a topic, and drawn reasonable inferences and conclusions based on their data. The reviewers will generally make a recommendation to the editor to publish the manuscript, reject the manuscript, or ask the author for minor or major revisions. Many publishers use a double-blind, peer-review process to reduce bias, meaning that the manuscript authors' and reviewers' identities are not revealed to each other.

While peer review is considered an important check on quality, it can slow down the publishing process, with some manuscripts taking six months to two years to move from submission to publication. It is also important to note that the peer-review process is not perfect. Although experts in their fields, peer reviewers work on a volunteer basis and are generally performing reviews as an added task on top of their own research and other scholarly and teaching responsibilities. Also, tight deadlines and lack of reviewers mean that scholars might occasionally be called on to review manuscripts that are not very well aligned with their personal areas of expertise. As a result, some mediocre, flawed, and even falsified research has occasionally passed through the review process and reached publication. In time, many of these writings have been retracted. However, the misinformation shared in these writings often persists even after retractions. Thus, when conducting literature searches, it is important for information professionals to assess each source on its own merit, regardless of whether it has been previously peer reviewed, and to teach their patrons to do the same.

While scholarly information is usually published first in academic journals and monographs, some intriguing or popular topics will eventually be picked up by mainstream news sources as well as magazines and websites. For instance, an article in the *New York Times* (O'Connor 2018) reports on a study from the *Journal of the American Medical Association*, which suggests that the quality of foods eaten may impact weight more than food quantity (Gardner, Trepanowski, and Del Gobbo 2018). Some research might eventually be covered in tertiary sources like encyclopedias. For instance, the entry on weight loss in the *Gale Encyclopedia of Fitness* cites several research studies (Avritt 2012). See Box 13.1 for an activity on the information life cycle.

Box 13.1 Activity: The Information Life Cycle

This section outlined a general information life cycle along with some variations by format. Choose a piece of information of interest to you. This could be a favorite book, an interesting newspaper or journal article, or even a tweet. See how much information you can discover about each stage of the information life cycle for that information.

Questions for Reflection and Discussion:

1. *Creation*. Who created the information? What can you learn about the author or creator?

2. *Publication or dissemination*. How was this information shared? Who might have had access to this information? Did it go through any editorial, fact-checking, or other kind of review process? How do you know?
3. *Organization and storage*. Where and how is this information stored? Has the information been organized in some way that might help you to find it (does it have a subject heading, hashtag, or other metadata attached to it)?
4. *Access and retrieval*. How might you go about finding this information? Is it listed in a library or publisher's catalog, in an index, or online? Do you need to subscribe to a third-party vendor to access it?
5. *Reuse*. Can you find any examples of the original information being reused in some way? Has it been cited somewhere? Made into a movie, television show, or even a meme? Has it been shared on social media?

Disciplinary Differences

Recognizing that scholars engage with one another by sharing their research, and that new scholarship builds on existing ideas, often attempting to replicate, extend, or challenge previous research, the Association of College and Research Libraries (ACRL) describes scholarship as a conversation (2016). In its Framework for Information Literacy for Higher Education, ACRL explains that

> research in scholarly and professional fields is a discursive practice in which ideas are formulated, debated, and weighed against one another over extended periods of time. Instead of seeking discrete answers to complex problems, experts understand that a given issue may be characterized by several competing perspectives as part of an ongoing conversation in which information users and creators come together and negotiate meaning.

ACRL (2016) goes on to note that it can be challenging for novices to enter the conversation but that "developing familiarity with the sources of evidence, methods, and modes of discourse in the field assists novice learners to enter the conversation." In other words, understanding the information landscape means not just understanding the information life cycle and the types and formats of sources as they are laid out in this textbook but also understanding that across disciplines certain kinds of information are preferred or sanctioned over others. In order to fully participate in the conversation of the field, scholars must recognize and learn to negotiate these landscapes.

For instance, while peer-reviewed journal articles are favored in most disciplines, humanities and history scholars also rely heavily on monographs. Physical scientists are often concerned with lab reports and original research reports. Many natural and social scientists are also interested in access to data sets. Historians and scholars in related disciplines like anthropology often seek access to primary and archival documents. Political scientists and journalism and communications scholars might be as interested in the newspapers of the day as they are in peer-reviewed research. The preferred format and source for each scholar depend not only on their discipline but also on the focus of their research question. A scientist involved in cutting-edge medical research will likely want only the most current data and original research reports, while a scholar studying the history of science might also be interested in the diaries, letters, and lab notes of scientific researchers.

Research suggests not only that these disciplinary differences in source preference exist but also that faculty members are interested in academic librarians expanding the range of resources they demonstrate to students during in-class instruction sessions to pay more attention to these differences (Saunders 2012). It is worth noting that different types and formats of information sources might also entail different methods of assessment. For instance, currency might be paramount for technical, medical, and scientific information but less important for historical research. When evaluating research articles in the social sciences, readers must assess the methods used, including sample sizes and statistical tests, while an assessment of a literary criticism might focus more on the logic of the argument and interpretations and the faithfulness to the source text. Just as scholars must learn the methods and sources of their discipline in order to engage in the scholarly conversation, the same holds true for the information professionals who facilitate access and guide scholars and students in their research.

ACCESS MECHANISMS

The information life cycle, along with disciplinary norms and values, influences how information is published, organized, and accessed. At the most basic level, librarians distinguish between primary, secondary, and tertiary sources. Distinct types of sources emerge at different stages in the information life cycle and are collected and accessed in specific ways. Librarians also distinguish between different types of publications, recognizing that publication type contains a clue to the information contained therein and that specific library tools were created to access different types of publications. For example, books contain more in-depth information and, because they were traditionally purchased and added to a library's collection, are identified through library catalogs, while periodical articles may be briefer, but also more up to date, and are accessed via an index.

Increasingly, the lines between these access tools are blurring. Search engines, originally created to locate websites, now draw on the content of books, periodicals, and special collections, along with websites, to provide relevant results to users. Within the library, discovery searching, discussed in Chapter 16, can provide access to all of the library's content, from books and periodical articles to reference works, special collections, and library guides. Table 13.1 summarizes the three main types of sources and their access mechanisms.

Primary Sources

Primary sources are created during the course of an event or an individual's life activities. Photographs and video footage of events; personal and business correspondence; diaries and scrapbooks; organizational records; oral histories; autobiographies; and ephemera such as pamphlets, certificates, and broadsides are all examples of primary sources. Because they provide evidence scholars can use to determine what happened at specific points in time and how those alive at the time reacted, primary sources are used extensively in history and are often associated with that discipline. However, it is important to recognize that all disciplines rely on some type of primary source material. In literature, primary sources include

TABLE 13.1 Characteristics of Primary, Secondary, and Tertiary Sources, Along with Examples and Methods of Access.

Source Type	Characteristics	Examples	Access Methods
Primary sources	Materials created during the course of an event and/or as part of a person's everyday life activities	Letters, photographs, diaries, broadsides, ephemera	Archives, personal collections, special collections
Secondary sources	Summarize or interpret events, often drawing on primary sources	Books, periodical articles, government reports	Catalogs, bibliographies, and indexes
Tertiary sources	Provide brief summaries of a topic based on secondary literature	Encyclopedias, handbooks, biographical sources	Print and online reference collections

poems, plays, short stories, and novels; in addition, scholars may seek out drafts of a literary work along with the author's diary or personal correspondence to better understand their literary intent.

Archives, special collections, and museums collect and organize primary sources in order to make them available to researchers and the general public. Traditionally, accessing these sources required a trip to the holding archive or museum to examine original documents. For famous individuals or events, one might be able to locate a collection of primary sources reproduced in book form, such as a volume containing the letters of a former president or photos from World War II. Increasingly, archives and museums are placing digital images of primary sources onto the Web, thus improving access for patrons of all ages and backgrounds. For example, the Los Angeles Public Library's *Tessa* database provides access to hundreds of thousands of digitized items from their special collections. However, such access may rely on the librarian knowing about the existence and location of a needed collection. Sites such as the *Digital Public Library of America* offer searchable access to the collections of hundreds of libraries, archives, and museums. Primary and archival sources, including methods of identifying and locating collections, are discussed in Chapter 30.

Secondary Sources

Secondary sources draw on primary sources to summarize and interpret events and topics. Secondary sources include a wide range of formats, such as books, periodical articles, and government reports, and are created for all types of audiences. Thus, secondary sources range from books that provide introductory information appropriate for an elementary school student to scholarly tomes that are hundreds of pages long, and from articles written for a current events magazine to the original research contained in a medical journal. Because secondary sources encompass such a range of resource types, topics, and intended audiences, librarians have many options for locating this type of information.

The two most common types of secondary sources are books and periodicals. Because of their length, books typically contain in-depth information on a topic. They may convey original research or draw on the existing literature to summarize what is known about a topic, present it in a new way, or make it accessible to a particular audience, such as children. Traditionally, libraries created a catalog of the books and other materials held in their collections. With the advent of the Web, libraries have created shared catalogs that allow patrons to search the holdings of multiple libraries at once. At the same time, tools such as *Books in Print* listed what was available, regardless of whether it was in a particular library's collection. Chapter 20 discusses these bibliographic tools.

Similar to books, periodicals are available for every subject and audience (see the activity in Box 13.2). Scholarly journals, which can be published weekly, monthly, or quarterly, disseminate the results of original research. Articles are accepted on the basis of peer review, where a small group of experts evaluates each article to determine if it should be published. Because articles are written by scholars and researchers for other experts, they contain evidence, disciplinary jargon, and extensive citations. Journals may also contain book reviews, editorials, and professional news.

Magazines, typically published weekly or monthly, are written for a lay audience. Magazines such as *Time* and *The Economist* focus on current events and general interest articles, while titles such as *Car and Driver* and *Sports Illustrated* are devoted to a specific topic. Articles are generally authored by journalists and undergo editorial review and fact-checking. In addition to general interest and investigative stories, magazines will include book and film reviews, interviews, and editorials. Most magazines are dependent on advertising revenue to cover production costs, and thus advertising features heavily within the pages of a typical magazine. Although library catalogs may list the journals and magazines available in a library's collections, one must use an index to locate specific articles within a publication. Chapter 22 discusses indexes in general, while other chapters in Part II recommend key indexes in areas such as business, medicine, and law.

Box 13.2 Activity: Compare Periodical Types

Skim a newspaper or general interest magazine for an article about a recent study or scientific discovery. Trace the story back to where it was originally reported in a scholarly journal (if the first article does not cite a specific source, you may be able to locate it using one of the indexes listed in Chapter 22).

Questions for Reflection and Discussion:

1. How does the language used in each article compare? Is one more technical? What sort of audience do you think each is written for?
2. How well do the facts align in each source? Do they present essentially the same findings and conclusions, or do they vary? If they vary, why might that be?
3. Can you find out anything about the authors of each article? What are their backgrounds and credentials? How might that impact their presentation of the information?
4. As a reference librarian, when might you use one of these sources over the other?

Newspapers are published daily or weekly and provide local, national, and international news along with investigative stories, editorials, and general interest articles on entertainment, fashion, sports, advice, and similar topics. Similar to magazines, articles are authored by journalists with editorial oversight. With the advent of the Internet, most traditional newspapers are available in print, online, and for libraries, through subscription databases. In addition, numerous websites provide access to current news. Chapter 23 provides an introduction to a myriad of sources for accessing current news.

Tertiary Sources

Reference sources that provide brief summaries of a topic based on the existing secondary literature are considered tertiary sources. Tertiary sources are particularly valuable when the patron needs a concise introduction to a topic, either because only a brief introduction is needed or as a precursor to further research. Encyclopedias, handbooks, and biographical resources are all examples of tertiary sources. Chapters 17–31 introduce numerous tertiary sources by both resource type and subject area.

CHANGES IN PUBLISHING

The information life cycles outlined earlier describe a traditional model of publishing in which an article, book, or other type of manuscript is developed by an author, passed through a particular editorial process which usually entails some amount of fact-checking and quality control, and then formatted and disseminated by an established publisher. Many of these publications are indexed in the sorts of resources described in later chapters of this text, enhancing their discoverability and access. For instance, newspapers like *The New York Times* are indexed in databases with a news focus, such as *Nexis Uni*, while health and medical research might be found in databases like *PubMed*. While these traditional publishers continue to be vital, changes in technology, including the advent of the Internet and World Wide Web as well as the proliferation of social media platforms, have ushered in significant changes to the worlds of scholarly and popular publishing.

Open Access and Open Educational Resources

One of the biggest changes to the traditional publishing field is the rise of open-access publishing, often referred to as OA. The Scholarly Publishing and Academic Resources Coalition (SPARC 2018) defines open access as "the free, immediate, online availability of research articles coupled with the rights to use these articles fully in the digital environment. Open Access ensures that anyone can access and use these results—to turn ideas into industries and breakthroughs into better lives."

In traditional publishing models, the end user—whether that be a reader, researcher, school, business, or library—must pay to access published material, often by buying a book or a subscription to a newspaper, journal, or magazine. However, subscription prices for journals and electronic resources have skyrocketed in recent years, placing many materials beyond the reach of even large research institutions. OA publications, on the other hand, flip the economic model by shifting the cost for publication to the author, or the grants or institutions that support them, and make the publications freely available online. Thus, OA has a democratizing effect, making previously prohibitively expensive research available to everyone for free.

OA journals function like traditional publishers to solicit, review, and publish original manuscripts. In addition, some institutions maintain OA repositories, or sites where authors can deposit a digital copy of previously published work. Some OA repositories are subject specific, such as *PubMed Central*, which focuses on biomedical literature, while institutional repositories often focus on collecting the materials created by their members. Some traditional publishers have also implemented OA options. These publishers might give authors an option to pay to publish their work as OA. Others will publish articles in a traditional paywall format first but make the article available as OA after an embargo period. Still others allow authors to deposit a pre-publication version of their work in an OA repository. Organizations that publish new material immediately in OA format are referred to as Gold OA. Organizations that provide access to pre-publication copies or move materials to OA after an embargo are referred to as Green OA.

Related to the OA movement is the open educational resources (OER) movement. UNESCO (2018) defines OER as "teaching, learning and research materials in any medium—digital or otherwise—that reside in the public domain or have been released under an open license that permits no-cost access, use, adaptation and redistribution by others with no or limited restrictions." Like OA, OER in part grew out of a concern for the rising costs of traditionally published educational materials, and the economic strain these resources put on students, schools, and libraries. OER can include textbooks, articles, training videos and tutorials, or entire courses and curricula. UNESCO points out that while OER is especially important for students and teachers in developing countries, who often do not have the resources to purchase traditional materials, OER can offer cost-saving alternatives to all. Because OER materials are either public domain or open license, they can be adapted for local use, including being translated into local languages, offering educators maximum flexibility.

It is important to note that while there are some dubious titles in the world of OA, many OA journals employ a peer-review process just like their traditional counterparts and strive to publish only high-quality, valid, and reliable research. Information professionals and concerned scholars can identify trusted OA journals and repositories through the *Directory of Open Access Journals* and the *Directory of Open Access Repositories*. The *OER Commons* and the *Open Textbook Library* are two well-established repositories of OER materials. Information professionals, educators, and students can find more resources through the *PNW OER Directory*. OA and OER are important movements aimed at increasing access to critical information sources. Information professionals have an important role to play in raising awareness about these resources, promoting their use when appropriate, and helping patrons locate, access, and evaluate these resources.

Social Media

Social media has created new avenues for sharing information and research. In some ways, social media has expanded the reach of traditional media. Individuals share links to news and magazine articles, potentially increasing readership of those articles, while authors and publishers use social media to announce new publications as part of broader advertising and outreach efforts. Social media has also created new avenues for generating and sharing information outside of established publication processes. Everyday citizens can share information, photos, and videos on microblogging platforms like *Twitter*, distributing breaking news even faster than more established news outlets or providing perspectives not covered by the mainstream media.

Social media is also a place to discuss and engage with information, whether it is the general public discussing current news or researchers analyzing a scholarly study. Although people often decry the role of social media in the spread of misinformation or the vitriolic conversations that can occur in comment boards, social media has also enabled greater interaction between scholars and the general public. For example, *Skype a Scientist* enables schoolchildren to have a guest lecture and discussion with scientists from around the world, while historians like Kevin Kruse use *Twitter* to provide fact-checking and correct historical misinformation (Pettit 2018). In academia, this democratic access can be particularly helpful for early career researchers and scholars from marginalized backgrounds who may have difficulty gaining recognition in traditional publishing channels.

ISSUES

It is a common saying that knowledge is power, and people create knowledge through their interactions and engagement with information. Thus, in its own way, information itself, and access to information, is power. Indeed, in their "Final Report" (1989), the American Library Association's Presidential Task Force on Information Literacy suggested that the ability to access, evaluate, and use information is essential to people's overall well-being and could help to balance socioeconomic inequalities. It asserted that people have a right to access information but warned that "citizenship in a modern democracy involves more than knowledge of how to access vital information. It also involves a capacity to recognize propaganda, distortion, and other misuses and abuses of information."

To fully understand and access the power of information, then, people need to be able to assess information for credibility, trustworthiness, and authority and to recognize when information is being manipulated or distorted. They have to be able to separate fact from opinion and to recognize how bias and privilege can influence the representation of information. Most people understand the need to be skeptical of information that is shared on the Internet or through social media, where anyone with access to the Internet can publish anything. However, even information from "trusted" sources can be mistaken, inaccurate, colored by bias, or limited by its perspective. The following sections outline three common issues in assessing information: misinformation and disinformation, bias, and representation.

Misinformation and Disinformation, or "Fake News"

When guiding people to resources, conducting research, or building collections, librarians should always be aware of the accuracy of the materials they consult. The term "fake news" rose in popularity when it was discovered that hackers had exploited social media platforms to launch coordinated disinformation campaigns in order to influence elections around the world. However, the phrase "fake news" is somewhat problematic, as politicians and others have often co-opted it to label news that is negative or with which they disagree, even if that news is factually accurate.

Thus, information professionals generally use the terms "misinformation" and "disinformation" when discussing issues of accuracy. Misinformation refers to inaccurate information that is accidentally shared or a mistake. As noted earlier, misinformation is often shared during breaking news stories, when it is difficult to confirm facts in the moment. Responsible writers and broadcasters will try to correct any misinformation they share as quickly as possible. Disinformation, on the other hand, is inaccurate information that is shared intentionally, with the purpose of misleading or deceiving. The fake news campaigns on social media are a type of disinformation. Chapter 23 provides an overview of and guidance on evaluating misinformation and disinformation.

Bias

The online version of the *Merriam-Webster Dictionary* (2018) defines bias as "an inclination of temperament or outlook, especially: a personal and sometimes unreasoned judgement: prejudice." People might be quick to recognize bias in certain situations. For instance, people will often assume political candidates are biased in their view on particular topics, and many people identify various media outlets as right or left leaning in their coverage of news stories. However, people will rarely think of the kinds of reference sources introduced in this textbook as potentially biased. In fact, this paragraph is a great example: when a person wishes to define a word, they will often turn to the dictionary, and whatever is written there will be accepted as definitive. Likewise, people will generally trust information they receive from encyclopedias, almanacs, or textbooks. Nevertheless, each of these resources could be biased in its representations.

According to Tanya Pai (2016), anthropologist Michael Oman-Reagan suggests that the *Oxford English Dictionary* uses sexist language in its example sentences by using negative-gendered language for words that are not inherently gendered themselves. For instance, example sentences for the word "rabid" include "a rabid feminist," and shrill includes "the rising shrill of a woman's voice." He also noted that the sentences for doctor, scientist, and smart tended to use male pronouns. Dictionary editors also make choices about which words to officially accept into their lexicon and which to leave out, and sometimes label words with terms like "offensive" or "slang." The impact of these decisions is that language favored by certain communities might not be represented in the dictionary at all or, if it is included, might be identified as somehow less acceptable or appropriate than other words.

Reference and other information sources can be biased in many other ways as well. For instance, the country of Burma was renamed Myanmar after a military uprising in 1989. Although the United Nations and many countries recognize Myanmar as the official name, the United States has not done so, and the *CIA World Factbook* still lists all relevant country information under the name "Burma." Most of the resources covered in this textbook have an English-language bias. Some resources might be biased in their scope and coverage. For instance, while the title *The Bibliography of the History of Art* sounds like it is global in its scope, it actually limits its coverage to the history of Western art. Such biases do not necessarily invalidate a resource, especially if the resource recognizes and identifies any limits to its scope and coverage within its introductory or explanatory materials. However, it is crucial for information professionals and their patrons to be aware of the potential for bias across information sources and to carefully assess each source before relying on it. Furthermore, librarians should identify and collect resources on non-Western and marginalized communities in order to ensure their collections are balanced and adequately reflect a variety of worldviews and experiences.

Representation

Related to bias are issues of representation in publishing and scholarship, or the question of whose stories are being told and whose voices are telling the stories. Issues of representation have been discussed more explicitly in the world of fiction, where movements like *We Need Diverse Books* and the *Cooperative Children's Book Center* have documented the staggering disparity between the numbers of books that include "diverse" characters and the number of books written and/or illustrated by "diverse" authors. As explained in more depth in Chapter 11, diverse books are crucial both to serve as mirrors that allow people of color, LGBTQIA+, the differently abled, and others to see themselves reflected in the books they read and to serve as windows and sliding glass doors that allow others to experience diverse perspectives. Issues of representation also surface questions of authenticity. Can a white author write authentically about characters of color or a straight author about LGBTQIA+ characters? While books by such authors might be genuinely well written, there remains a question of whether the author can authentically express the interests, concerns, and experiences of communities of which they themselves are not a part. Thus, movements like *We Need Diverse Books* seek not only to increase representation within the books but also to increase the number of authors from underrepresented communities.

While fiction and children's literature have perhaps received more attention around questions of representation, the issue extends to nonfiction, reference, and scholarly works as well. April Hathcock (2016) notes that "there is a wealth of experiences, knowledge, and perspectives that is largely unseen and unheard in mainstream scholarship. Indeed, scholarly communication and academic discourse largely reflect the systemic biases we find in broader society." Charlotte Roh (2016) provided a breakdown of some of the issues of representation and diversity in scholarly publishing, noting, for instance, that according to a *Publisher's Weekly* survey, 89 percent of publishers are white and that 70 percent of peer-reviewed scientific articles are authored by men, while only 27.2 percent of scholarly articles are written by women. Importantly, Roh (2016) notes that this lack of diversity can impact content as well, essentially creating a "feedback loop in scholarship that privileges and publishes the majority voice, which is often white and male." Needless to say, the problem extends to other forms of publication as well. For instance, lack of diversity in journalism can impact both what stories are covered by news outlets and how stories of marginalized communities are covered. The Internet and social media platforms have helped to balance the issue somewhat, by giving voice to underrepresented communities and space to share their own stories. However, this impact is limited, especially since social media and other self-published materials like blogs are often not sanctioned as part of "legitimate" scholarly conversation.

The problem of representation extends to the library field as well. The field itself severely lacks in diversity, with 87.1 percent of American Library Association (ALA) members identifying as white (Roh 2016). Just as with publishing, this lack of diversity impacts library systems and service models. For instance, classification systems such as Dewey and the Library of Congress often reflect the bias of the white, Christian, heteronormative men who created them. Even the traditional reference model, which requires patrons to initiate contact by approaching a librarian, often at a physically imposing reference desk, privileges users who understand the system and expect the librarian to be ready to assist them. Yet, as described in Chapter 3, there can be many physical, emotional, and cognitive barriers to people asking for such assistance. The lack of diversity can also impact librarians of color, many of whom report experiencing microaggressions on the job (Swanson, Tanaka, and Gonzalez-Smith 2018).

Information professionals have an obligation to recognize and work against the limits of lack of representation. Indeed, the ALA Library Bill of Rights (2019) exhorts librarians to collect widely and seek out diverse materials by stating that "materials should not be excluded because of the origin, background, or views of those contributing to their creation" and that librarians "should provide materials and information presenting all points of view on current and historical issues. Materials should not be proscribed or removed because of partisan or doctrinal disapproval." Beyond simply seeking out more diverse materials, information professionals must also reflect on their own practice and the systems within which they work in order to identify and work against systemic and implicit bias.

CONCLUSION

In providing a framework for Part II of this textbook, this chapter illustrates that the work of a reference professional entails much more than being familiar with source types like dictionaries or even specific titles like the *Oxford English Dictionary*. Rather, the work involves a deep understanding of the purpose, function, and use of a wide range of source titles and types, beginning with an understanding of how information is created, disseminated, stored, and accessed, as well as a familiarity with a variety of publishing models and their purposes and limitations. The work also involves an ability to analyze and evaluate information across subjects, disciplines, and source types and to critically reflect on information sources and systems in order to recognize and limit the impact of bias, misinformation and disinformation, and lack of representation. The majority of Americans say they believe the library helps them to find trustworthy and reliable information and to help them find the information they need to make decisions (Geiger 2017). Information professionals must recognize the responsibility that goes with that trust and be vigilant in their own assessment of information as they select resources for their collections, assist users in accessing information, and teach users the skills to assess information on their own.

REFERENCES

American Library Association. 1989. "Presidential Committee on Information Literacy: Final Report." http://www.ala.org/acrl/publications/whitepapers/presidential.

American Library Association. 2019. "Library Bill of Rights." Last modified January 29, 2019. http://www.ala.org/advocacy/intfreedom/librarybill.

Association of College and Research Libraries. 2016. "Framework for Information Literacy for Higher Education." American Library Association. http://www.ala.org/acrl/standards/ilframework.

Avritt, Julie Jordan. 2012. "Weight Loss." In *The Gale Encyclopedia of Fitness*, edited by Jacqueline L. Longe. Farmington Hills, MI: Gale. *Credo Reference*.

Encyclopedia Britannica n.d. Kilauea. https://www.britannica.com/place/Kilauea.

Gardner, Christopher D., John F. Trepanowski, and Liana C. Del Gobbo. 2018. "The Effect of Low-Fat vs. Low-Carbohydrate Diet on 12-Month Weight Loss on Overweight Adults and the Association of Genotype Pattern or Insulin Secretion." *JAMA* 319 (7): 667–79.

Geiger, Abigail. 2017. "Most Americans—Especially Millennials—Say Libraries Can Help Them Find Reliable, Trustworthy Information." Pew Research Center. August 30. http://www.pewresearch.org/fact-tank/2017/08/30/most-americans-especially-millennials-say-libraries-can-help-them-find-reliable-trustworthy-information/.

Hathcock, April. 2016. "Making the Local Global: The Colonialism of Scholarly Communication." *At the Intersection: Blog about the Intersection of Libraries, Law, Feminism, and Diversity*. September 27. https://aprilhathcock.wordpress.com/2016/09/27/making-the-local-global-the-colonialism-of-scholarly-communication/.

Merriam-Webster Dictionary. 2018. "Bias." https://www.merriam-webster.com/dictionary/bias?utm_campaign=sd&utm_medium=serp&utm_source=jsonl.

O'Connor, Anahad. 2018. "The Key to Weight Loss Is Diet Quality, Not Quantity, a New Study Finds." *The New York Times*, February 20. https://www.nytimes.com/2018/02/20/well/eat/counting-calories-weight-loss-diet-dieting-low-carb-low-fat.html.

Pai, Tanya. 2016. "Why People Are Calling the Oxford Dictionaries Sexist." *Vox*. January 30. https://www.vox.com/2016/1/30/10871598/dictionary-sexism.

Pettit, E. 2018. "How Kevin Kruse Became History's Attack Dog." *The Chronicle of Higher Education*, December 21. https://www.chronicle.com/article/How-Kevin-Kruse-Became/245321.

Roh, Charlotte. 2016. "Library Publishing and Diversity Values: Changing Scholarly Publishing through Policy and Scholarly Communication Education." *College & Research Libraries News* 77 (2). https://crln.acrl.org/index.php/crlnews/article/view/9446/10680.

Saunders, Laura. 2012. "Faculty Perspectives on Information Literacy as a Student Learning Outcome." *The Journal of Academic Librarianship* 38 (4): 226–36.

Scholarly Publishing and Academic Resources Coalition. 2018. "Open Access." https://sparcopen.org/open-access/.

Swanson, Juleah, Azusa Tanaka, and Isabel Gonzalez-Smith. 2018. "Lived Experience of Academic Librarians of Color." *College & Research Libraries* 79 (7). https://crl.acrl.org/index.php/crl/article/view/16850/19187.

UNESCO. 2018. "Open Educational Resources OER." https://en.unesco.org/themes/building-knowledge-societies/oer.

University of Nevada Libraries. 2016. "The Information Life Cycle." https://vimeo.com/175421451.

U.S. Geological Survey. 2019. "Hawaiian Volcano Observatory Weekly Update." Last modified July 19, 2019. https://volcanoes.usgs.gov/volcanoes/kilauea/status.html.

LIST OF SOURCES

ABI/INFORM Global. Ann Arbor, MI: ProQuest. https://www.proquest.com/products-services/abi_inform_global.html. Subscription required.

Bibliography of the History of Art. http://www.getty.edu/research/tools/bha/.
Books In Print. Ann Arbor, MI: ProQuest. http://www.booksinprint.com. Subscription required.
Car and Driver. 1955–. Ann Arbor, MI: Hearst. Monthly.
CIA World Factbook. https://www.cia.gov/library/publications/the-world-factbook/.
Cooperative Children's Book Center. https://ccbc.education.wisc.edu/books/pcstats.asp.
Digital Public Library of America. https://dp.la/.
Directory of Open Access Journals. http://www.doaj.org.
Directory of Open Access Repositories. http://www.opendoar.org.
The Economist. 1843–. London, UK: The Economist Group. Weekly.
Encyclopaedia Britannica. http://www.britannica.com/.
Facebook. http://www.facebook.com.
New York Times. https://www.nytimes.com/.
Nexis Uni. New York: LexisNexis. https://www.lexisnexis.com/. Subscription required.
OER Commons. https://www.oercommons.org/.
Open Textbook Library. https://open.umn.edu/opentextbooks/.
Oxford English Dictionary. http://www.oed.com.
PNW OER Directory. https://sites.google.com/site/pnwoer/.
PsycINFO. Washington, DC: American Psychological Association. http://www.apa.org/pubs/databases/psycinfo/index.aspx. Subscription required.
PubMed. https://www.ncbi.nlm.nih.gov/pubmed/.
PubMed Central. https://www.ncbi.nlm.nih.gov/pmc/.
Skype a Scientist. https://www.skypeascientist.com/.
Sports Illustrated. 1954–. New York: WarnerMedia. Monthly.
Tessa. Los Angeles Public Library. https://tessa.lapl.org/.
Time. 1923–. New York: Time, Inc. Weekly.
Twitter. http://www.twitter.com.
We Need Diverse Books. https://diversebooks.org/.

SUGGESTED READINGS

Cope, Jonathon. 2010. "Information Literacy and Social Power." In *Critical Library Instruction: Theories and Methods*, edited by Maria T. Accardi, Emily Drabinski, and Alana Kumbier, 13–27. Sacramento, CA: Library Juice Press.

This chapter offers a solid introduction to critical approaches to thinking about information as it is situated within political and economic systems.

Ettarh, Fobazi. 2018. "Vocational Awe and Librarianship: The Lies We Tell Ourselves." *In the Library with the Lead Pipe.* January 10. http://www.inthelibrarywiththeleadpipe.org/2018/vocational-awe/.

Fobazi Ettarh describes vocational awe as the notion that many librarians hold that libraries are inherently good institutions. Fobazi argues that this awe tends to imply that libraries are beyond critique and thus interferes with attempts to challenge the inherently oppressive structures that permeate much of library practice and service, and contributes to burnout and low salaries. This article invites reflection by deconstructing the mythos of the sacred library and identifying and naming oppressive structures so that they can be challenged and changed.

Hathcock, April M., and Stephanie Sendaula. 2017. "Mapping Whiteness at the Reference Desk." In *Topographies of Whiteness: Mapping Whiteness in Library and Information Science*, edited by Gina Schlesselman-Tarango, 247–56. Sacramento, CA: Library Juice Press.

This chapter, part of a larger work on whiteness in library and information science, specifically examines whiteness at the reference desk. The authors discuss the microaggressions that librarians of color face in a field so heavily dominated by white women and in particular how the work, settings, and expectations of reference can function to reinforce systems of whiteness and oppression. The chapter ends with straightforward advice for combatting microaggressions and dismantling the system of whiteness within reference service and practice.

Schlesselman-Tarango, Gina. 2017. *Topographies of Whiteness: Mapping Whiteness in Library and Information Science*. Sacramento, CA: Library Juice Press.

This book confronts issues of whiteness, representation, and bias in the field of library and information science broadly. With chapters authored by researchers and practitioners, the book examines the history of whiteness in the profession and how that history has shaped service and practice. The book also explores contemporary lived experiences of librarians of color and proposes ideas for challenging oppressive systems within the field.

University of Nevada Libraries. 2016. "The Information Life Cycle." https://vimeo.com/175421451.

This brief and entertaining video illustrates the life cycle of information using a fictional example of an alien landing. The video demonstrates the coverage, treatment, and dissemination of information from moments after an event occurs through the days, weeks, and years that follow.

Chapter 14

Selection and Evaluation of Reference Sources

Carol A. Singer

REFERENCE SOURCES

The varied types of services that make up the work of reference librarians were the focus of Part I of this text. However, a reference librarian can provide excellent reference service only if an equally excellent reference collection is available to be consulted. As Rosanne Cordell (2014, 53) writes, "The selection and management of these sources continues to be a time-consuming part of reference work, but these are essential for timely and accurate reference assistance. One cannot depend exclusively on open Web searching on-the-fly to provide the highest quality of assistance." This chapter reviews common types of reference sources used in reference work and discusses how to develop and manage a reference collection. This chapter lists and discusses the criteria used to evaluate reference sources and introduces resources that assist in the development of a reference collection. This chapter explores the similarities and differences in the inclusion of print materials, licensed electronic sources, and freely available Internet resources.

What Is a Reference Source?

A wide variety of sources might be included in a reference collection. Even when reference collections were expected to include only print resources, they were still composed of many kinds of resources. Given the current incredible variety of electronic resources that could be considered to be part of the reference collection, deciding which resources to include in a reference collection is even more challenging.

In 1893, E. C. Richardson defined a reference book as "a book which is to be consulted for definite points of information (rather than read through), and is arranged with explicit reference to ease in finding specific facts" (1893, 254). Current definitions reflect the inclusion of nonprint resources in reference collections. The *ALA Glossary of Library and Information Science* defines "reference source" as "Any *source* used to obtain authoritative *information* in a *reference transaction*. Reference sources can include, but are not limited to, printed *materials*, *databases*, *media*, the *Internet*, other *libraries* and institutions, and persons both inside and outside the library. Synonymous with *reference work*" (Levine-Clark and Carter 2013, emphasis in original). Most reference collections continue to include print sources, although many print collections have grown smaller in recent years, as libraries transition to a reference collection that is composed primarily of online resources. Many titles that were originally published as print books are now online, while new reference sources are frequently only available as licensed online resources. The number of freely available reference sources on the Internet continues to increase, making it even more difficult to define the boundaries of the reference collection. Margaret Landsman (2005, 19) writes, "The ability to search full text, though, turns every collection of online texts into a reference collection and provides an automatic concordance for every title. Titles can no longer be tidily separated into 'reference works' and 'general collection.'"

Types of Sources

Reference sources may be categorized by format, such as books, microforms, tangible electronic formats (e.g., CD-ROM), or online formats (e.g., Internet). Another method of defining reference sources is to group them loosely into those that contain information and those that refer the user to the source of the information. However, compilations that contain information frequently refer the user to other sources of information, while compilations that primarily refer the user to other sources sometimes contain sufficient information that the user does not need to use the source being referenced. Many of these types of sources are treated in later chapters of this book. Government publications, although not a single type of source, are treated in Chapter 26, as these publications are frequently housed in a separate collection.

Trends in Reference Publishing

In many libraries, the print reference collection is diminishing in size as the online reference collection is expanding. Today, most librarians and library users begin by consulting online resources when searching for information. Some online reference sources simply duplicate a print reference source, while others go beyond the capabilities of a print reference source by utilizing technological abilities that expand the type of information available in the print publication. Online reference sources are acquired as a single title or as part of an aggregated database. Aggregated databases provide the publications of one or many publishers. One example of a database that provides access to reference sources of many publishers is *Credo Reference*. As of early 2020, the database included more than 3,400 reference books from more than 100 publishers.

Adam Hodgkin (2002), who developed *xrefer*, which became *Credo Reference*, defines what he sees as the advantages of this type of aggregated database:

1. By combining reference works together at one URL, the reference service becomes much better known to potential users and easier to find.
2. By tackling a number of reference works, there are economies of scale in production and development.
3. The user's search session is likely to be much more powerful and fruitful, since a collection of reference resources "behind" a common interface can be meta-searched. By firing a search term at the "collection of books," the user finds hits across the whole library, and this is a procedure impossibly time-consuming with any modest collection of print books.

Although some full-text databases include only the text of reference books, it is common for them to mix reference materials with other resources such as periodicals, newspapers, pamphlets, manuscripts, letters, audio and video files, or dissertations. *SBRnet*, the *Sports Business Research Network*, features market research, directories, data, facility reports, and full-text periodical articles. EBSCO's *Consumer Health Complete* includes reference works such as the *American Medical Association Complete Medical Encyclopedia*, plus periodical articles and medical images.

Some databases aggregate primary source materials with other resources, such as the *Rock and Roll, Counterculture, Peace and Protest: Popular Culture in Britain and America, 1950–1975* database, which provides access to manuscripts, government files, underground magazines, fanzines, letters, photographs, pamphlets, video files, posters, and memorabilia. *Accessible Archives* is composed of a series of databases, including historical newspapers and magazines, county histories, and books.

This rapidly expanding variety of databases is invaluable to the reference librarian. It allows librarians and patrons to access resources that would have previously been unavailable. Aggregators of reference materials can make it possible to provide access to more resources than would be available if each were purchased individually. However, utilizing aggregators may also end the practice of carefully choosing each book in a reference collection. If an already acquired aggregator includes an encyclopedia on a particular subject, the library might not be able to also afford a similar title that is deemed to be superior. Because aggregators are expensive and include only the publications of a select group of publishers, one unintended result of acquiring aggregated databases could be a reference collection with less diversity of content and viewpoint.

REFERENCE COLLECTION DEVELOPMENT AND MAINTENANCE

It is the responsibility of reference librarians to select a collection of appropriate reference sources and to arrange and maintain these sources, so they support the reference services of the library. Planning is extremely important to ensure that the collection matches the needs of the community served by the library and of the reference staff.

Components of the Collection

Although an increasing number of libraries make the majority of purchases in electronic formats, some librarians still find reasons to continue purchasing new print reference books. Some sources may only be available in print, may be less expensive in print, or may be easier to use in print. For instance, an atlas with oversized pages might give a better sense of scale than an online source. A print citation manual allows the writer to easily flip back and forth between pages and refer back to their document without toggling screens. Finally, when a school owns a full set of encyclopedias, students can use different volumes at the same time. A library may also have a substantial number of users who do not want to use a computer or there may be inadequate or nonexistent Internet service.

Even when the content of the print and online formats is identical, the online format may offer superior functionality. The superior searching capability often found in online formats is one reason many reference collections are transitioning to these formats, resulting in the cancellation or nonpurchase of print sources. In addition to comparing content, librarians must also consider the comparative cost, the desirability of a purchase or a subscription, ease of use, search capabilities, unique features of each format, and the potential reaction of library users to the format. Because circumstances change, each acquisition requires a fresh decision.

Reference Collection Development

Because reference materials are expensive, budgets are tight, and the available resources are more abundant than ever before, it is imperative that the reference collection is carefully planned and not assembled in a haphazard manner. This text describes many of the most common types of resources found in a reference collection, but there is no such thing as a "one-size-fits-all" reference collection as every library's user community is different. The reference collection manager should consider the needs not only of the mainstream culture but also of marginalized groups who may have information needs which may not be supplied by the mainstream press. In addition, it is valuable for library users in all parts of the community to experience a multiplicity of viewpoints.

Box 14.1 identifies the many collection development decisions that reference collection managers must make.

Box 14.1 Collection Development Decisions

Reference collection managers must decide whether or not to:

- purchase or subscribe to newly published titles
- acquire a resource in a tangible or virtual format
- buy a new edition of a title already in the collection
- buy a supplement to a title already in the collection
- cancel a title that is freely available on the Internet
- cancel a title that is now contained in an aggregated database
- continue to receive serials or standing orders
- acquire online resources as an Internet resource or load the material locally
- coordinate collection development decisions with other libraries
- purchase resources as part of a consortium in order to save money
- repair a book or purchase a replacement
- remove materials from the collection in response to a complaint
- weed or review the collection

(Singer 2012, 19–20)

A collection development policy can provide guidance and help ensure that decisions are made in a fair and equitable manner. Such a policy serves several purposes, in addition to being the basis for decision-making about the collection. It defines the purpose of the collection and describes what should or should not be included. It encourages continuity during personnel changes. It can help a librarian provide justification for a requested budget. It can explain why materials were included or excluded. It can enable a librarian to justify a resource whose presence in the collection has been challenged.

The process of writing a reference collection development policy can also be a valuable exercise. Daniel Liestman (2001, 86) writes, "The actual process of creating a policy is beneficial as it forces the library staff to consider unspoken/unrecorded assumptions about the reference collection. In order to successfully manage a reference collection, a library's staff must possess a shared understanding of their reference philosophies as well as the users' current and anticipated information needs. . . . Developing such a document provides the opportunity for those involved to come to a consensus about major goals for the collection and reference service." Box 14.2 identifies potential parts of a reference collection development policy, and Box 14.3 contains a practice activity on examining a collection policy.

Maintenance of any reference collection is a continuous process. Some types of materials can become swiftly outdated, such as directories, road maps, or rulebooks. Some print resources are updated on a regular schedule, while others are updated irregularly by supplements, pocket parts, or transmittal sheets. The librarian must be alert for online resources that are more current than the available tangible resources.

Box 14.2 Collection Development Policies

Reference collection development policies may include the following:

- Purpose of the collection development policy
- Person(s) charged with responsibility for collection development
- Purpose of the reference collection
- Target audience(s)
- Budgeting and funding
- Selection criteria
- Resources to aid in selection of materials
- Preferred format(s)
- When, or if, to purchase duplicates
- Preferred language(s)
- Circulation of tangible reference materials
- Treatment of specific resource groups
- Resource sharing with other libraries
- Collection maintenance
- Weeding and reviewing the collection
- Timeline for policy revision

Box 14.3 Activity: Evaluating a Collection Development Policy

Many library collection development policies are found on the Web. Reviewing some of these policies can provide valuable experience before you begin writing a collection development policy for your library. Begin this exercise by locating and reading a reference collection development policy.

Questions for Reflection and Discussion:

1. Who is responsible for collection development? Are there other individuals or groups who should provide significant input? How would this best be accomplished?
2. Who is the target audience for this collection? Are there other potential audiences who have not been listed? If so, who are they and how could their needs be included?
3. Choose a section of the policy you would like to change. Why did you choose this section? How would you change it?

Arrangement of the Collection

Reference collections may be arranged in a variety of ways. Tangible collections may be arranged in call number order regardless of type of resources. Some libraries divide the collection by type of book, such as encyclopedias, dictionaries, atlases, biographical sources, indexes and abstracts, legal materials, or job hunting materials. The majority of the collection may be arranged in call number order, with a few categories of specific materials in separate spaces, such as atlas cases or dictionary stands. Most reference collections designate a section of shelving near the reference desk as a ready-reference collection, which contains resources that are frequently used.

Inclusion of special formats, such as CD-ROMs, microforms, or maps, should be carefully considered to ensure maximum ease of access and use for both reference librarians and library users. This is particularly true of formats that require the use of specialized equipment. Appropriate signage and directions for use are essential to ensure that these resources and any necessary equipment will be easy to identify and use.

As libraries decrease the size of their tangible reference collection, they frequently increase the size of their virtual reference collection. As a result, reference librarians are frequently involved in the redesign of the library's user interface or the part of the library's Internet presence that provides access to electronic resources in order to assist library users in identifying the most appropriate online sources for their needs. Box 14.4 provides an activity related to website design for reference sources.

Weeding the Collection

Weeding or deselecting materials is an extremely important part of maintaining a usable, current collection. Maria Isabel Fernandes (2008, 205) defines weeding

Box 14.4 Activity: Organizing Databases

Electronic resources must be organized in order to be discoverable and accessible. Not all libraries choose to organize these resources in the same fashion. Look at the following Web pages to see how some libraries have organized their databases:

Boston University: http://library.bu.edu/az.php
Toledo-Lucas County Public Library: http://www.toledolibrary.org/research
Oakland Public Library: http://oaklandlibrary.org/online-resources/articles-and-databases
University of New Mexico: https://elibrary.unm.edu
University of Tennessee Knoxville: https://libguides.utk.edu/databases

Questions for Reflection and Discussion:

1. What are the advantages and disadvantages of each organizational scheme?
2. Which organizational scheme is better for a public library? Would that scheme also be the best for a college or university library?
3. Which organizational scheme would you choose for your own library? Why?

as "the process of removing materials from the collection. It is the process by which librarians control the overall health of a collection." Some librarians find weeding difficult or distasteful, which can result in a print collection that is dusty, cramped, and out of date. An online collection can become crowded with incorrect URLs, out-of-date editions, and resources that no longer serve any useful purpose or have lost significant functionality.

When weeding either the print or online collection, taking the time to plan before acting is critical. A number of questions should be answered before beginning to weed. Will the entire collection be weeded or only a portion? Who will do the weeding? Who will assign the areas to be weeded? Will people outside the reference department be involved? What criteria will be used to determine what to keep and what to remove? Who will make the final decision if there are disagreements? What will happen to the books that are removed from the reference collection? Who will decide which books to replace with newer editions? What will be done about missing books?

If the weeding project will cause a significant disruption to the work of other departments, this must be taken into consideration when planning the timeline. Communication is one of the most important aspects of planning and managing a weeding project. All those who are involved or affected by the project must be kept informed.

If the weeding will be a continuous project, with only a small section being weeded at one time, planning may not need to be as elaborate. In a continuous weeding project, one person might make the initial decisions about what to weed. These books can be held for review by other reference librarians, subject specialists within the library, or constituencies outside the library. After review, the books can be transferred to the circulating collection, sent to off-site storage, or withdrawn. Depending on the policies of the library, withdrawn items might be sold, donated, recycled, or discarded.

In a major weeding project, the collection to be weeded might be divided into sections and each person involved given the responsibility of making initial weeding decisions in one or more sections. At this point, the basic steps listed above will be followed. In a major weeding project, managing the process is crucial. One or more persons must be designated to track progress; ensure that reviewers have adequate opportunity to make decisions and resolve disagreements; ensure that books reach their final destination; decide what to do about missing books; and order replacement copies or more current books.

The criteria for removing books from the collection will vary, depending on the goals of the project and the mission of the library. See Box 14.5 for some common reasons for weeding books, and Box 14.6 for a practice activity.

Box 14.5 Reasons for Weeding Reference Books

Reasons for weeding reference books can include the following:

- Lack of use
- Availability of online or other formats
- Not being listed in selection aids
- Not being sufficiently comprehensive
- Duplicating information in other sources
- Not citing sources for further exploration
- Out-of-date information
- Availability of a newer edition
- Duplicate copies in the collection
- Poor condition
- More appropriate for the circulating collection
- Written in a language that few library users can read (Singer 2012, 96–97)

Box 14.6 Activity: Evaluating Reference Books

A university library reference department has in its collection a multivolume encyclopedia published in the 1950s in the European duchy of Transmogrania. Of course, it is written in Transmogranian, a language that none of the reference staff can read. This encyclopedia remains in the lists of reference works because it is a standard, authoritative work on all aspects of Transmogranian life and culture. A survey of the reshelving of reference works in the department shows that none of the volumes were reshelved during the six months in which the survey was conducted. As always, the reference librarians are finding that shelf space is inadequate, and one reference librarian suggests removing the encyclopedia from the reference collection.

Questions for Reflection and Discussion:

1. Would you (a) keep the encyclopedia in reference, because it is a standard reference work; (b) transfer the encyclopedia to the general stacks, where it will become a circulating title; or (c) get rid of the encyclopedia by donating it to the only faculty member on campus who can read Transmogranian?
2. Are there alternative solutions?

Now suppose that one of your expert Web-surfing librarians has discovered that the government of Transmogrania has established a website that contains very thorough, current information about the duchy of Transmogrania in both Transmogranian and imperfect English.

Question for Reflection and Discussion:

1. Does the availability of this resource affect your decision about the encyclopedia?

Weeding the online reference collection may be more difficult than weeding the print collection, because e-books are frequently not loaded on local servers. If e-books were purchased as part of an aggregated database, the library may not be able to remove individual titles from the database.

The first step in weeding the e-book collection is to determine which books can be removed from the collection or from the access points to the collection. It is a waste of time to identify e-books that ought to be removed if there is no mechanism for the librarian to remove them. Once those that can be removed or whose presence in the collection can be suppressed have been identified, the process for weeding will be similar, allowing for the difference between working with tangible and virtual books. One or more lists of the books to be reviewed must be prepared. Once weeding decisions have been made, the method used to remove the e-book from the collection will vary depending on how the library acquired the e-book, the way(s) in which library users access the e-book, and the license agreement. If the e-book is on a library server, the e-books can probably be removed from the server. However, most e-books will be on servers controlled by a database vendor. The library may not have the choice of removing the e-book itself and may only be able to remove evidence of the e-book from the library catalog and from any other media the library uses to provide access to the e-book.

Some of the criteria used are similar to those used to weed the print collection, such as lack of use, not being listed in the selection aids used by the library, not being sufficiently comprehensive, duplicating information in other sources, not citing sources for further exploration, containing outdated information, availability of a newer edition, or being written in a language that few library users can read. However, other criteria are important when reviewing online resources, such as the ability of library users to identify and access the e-book or the usefulness of the user interface.

Reference databases should also be reviewed regularly. This might be performed by a single person, there may be a meeting of reference librarians to review databases, or there may be a meeting of all stakeholders within the library to review databases. Librarians may also need to consult with stakeholders outside the library. With the proliferation of databases and the amount of work required to prepare for a database review, it is very tempting to put off this important task. If possible, review all databases as a group to ensure that duplication is kept to a minimum. Participants should examine changes in content or functionality that may alter the need for the database. This is also a good time to consider new databases that might be added to the suite of available databases or might replace a currently available database. Before the meeting, a list of databases should be prepared that includes at least the title, the database producer, cost, and usage data. Participants should also know before the meeting if the budget must be reduced or if the reference department will have additional funds to spend. Even if the budget remains the same, databases normally increase in price, so one or more databases may need to be cancelled. Box 14.7 is an activity in evaluating databases.

Box 14.7 Activity: Which Databases to Cancel?

Cancelling a database or subscription is rarely an easy decision. Many factors may be considered, but one common one is the usage of the resource. Usage figures may be evaluated as straightforward numbers or may be used in conjunction with the cost of the resource to compute the cost per use.

For this exercise, assume your library subscribes to the databases on the list provided by the Wyoming State Library at https://gowyld.libguides.com/libraryinfo/home. It is time to decide which of these databases will be renewed; however, the budget is not going to be sufficient to pay for all of them. Review the usage statistics on that website and choose two to three databases to cancel.

Questions for Reflection and Discussion:

1. Why did you choose these particular databases?
2. Would you make the same cancelation decision for each of those libraries or would you keep the database for one or more of the libraries? Why?
3. What did you learn from the usage data?
4. What other information would have improved your ability to make an informed decision?

Numerous articles discuss how reluctant some librarians are to weed the collection. One way to overcome this reluctance is to use onion weeding, that is, to weed, or peel off, one layer at a time. Librarians can choose any category that they perceive as being easier to review. A librarian might begin by reviewing old travel guides, books that have not been reshelved for at least ten years, older directories, duplicate volumes, books that are also available online, or any other category that seems to promise easier decisions. Remember, the decision was made to review the category, not to weed everything within that category without examining it. Some of the books within that category may be kept because they are still useful. Once the first category of books has been reviewed, the librarian can choose another category to review. For many librarians, weeding becomes easier with practice.

EVALUATION OF SOURCES

As part of developing a reference collection, each source must be evaluated to see if the material is appropriate for the collection and of sufficiently high quality. Because most libraries are spending a significant portion of the budget on online resources and these resources tend to be more expensive, there are sometimes fewer selection decisions than when the collection was composed mostly of books. Instead of making a decision about each reference book, the reference librarian might make a decision about an aggregated database in which there are hundreds of titles. This chapter covers general evaluation criteria that apply to many types of reference resources. Chapters 17 through 31 include sections on the evaluation of particular types of sources. Using these criteria will assist the reference librarian in developing a superior reference collection that meets the needs of the library. Box 14.8 identifies the evaluation criteria for print and/or electronic resources.

Box 14.8 Evaluation Criteria

Evaluation criteria that may be used for all formats:

Content
Authority
Format

Evaluation criteria that may be used for electronic resources:

User interface
Branding and customization
Provision of full text
Accessibility
Cost and licensing

Evaluation criteria that may be used for print resources:

Physical attributes
Indexing
Cost

Content

The first thing most librarians consider when choosing reference materials is the relevancy of the content to their service community. Because most budgets are insufficient to purchase all desired titles, the reference collection manager must consider the collection holistically, looking for gaps. The librarian should try to anticipate necessary changes in the content of the collection caused by the addition of new courses or degrees, demographic changes, or changes in the business climate.

Particular attention should be paid to the composition of a library's constituency. The librarian must consider, not just library users, but potential users, including marginalized groups. The reference collection should include resources that reflect the information needs and viewpoints of all groups within the library's constituency.

The librarian should consider the scope and intent of a resource and its accuracy, completeness, and currency. Since most reference books are not available for examination before ordering, the librarian must frequently rely on book reviews or other selection aids to assist in making acquisition decisions. The desired completeness of the content will vary, depending on the purpose the book will play in the reference collection and on the intended audience.

The expected level of currency of a reference source will vary depending on the type of source. An online index of newspaper articles might be updated daily, but other online indexes of magazines or journals might only be updated weekly or monthly. A print reference book might not include an event until one or more years after the event takes place. If a print reference book is updated by pocket parts, transmittal sheets, supplements, or yearbooks, the librarian should consider acquiring these additions. Some libraries prefer to order online versions of reference sources that require regular updates.

Illustrations should support the content of the resource, should enhance the usefulness of the content, and should be of excellent quality. Black-and-white illustrations might be acceptable for some sources, but some topics and audiences will demand color.

The content of the book or online resource should match the age and/or reading level of the intended audience. Publishers who produce books intended for a school audience frequently indicate the age or grade level of intended users, although librarians should still use professional judgment in selecting titles. If the library serves a diversity of ages or reading levels, the reference collection should reflect that diversity.

Authority

Ideally, the author, publisher, and/or database producer should have an excellent reputation for producing reference materials. If desired, academic credentials or publishing history can be checked. The catalog or website of the publisher can be explored to see what types of resources are issued by this company and if any of these have received awards. If the library already owns titles by the author or publisher, these can be examined.

If the book or e-book includes multiple entries, each entry should be signed. The librarian can check author credentials of selected entries. Some resources include a list of authors, with academic credentials.

It is generally easier to identify and purchase resources that have authority within the mainstream culture. The librarian should consider if there are authors, publishers, and/or database producers that would be authoritative representatives of underrepresented groups. A task force at the MIT Libraries (2017, 13) asserts that mainstream publishing does not adequately represent the viewpoints of marginalized groups in American society and concludes, "In order to disrupt this stream and incorporate non-majority voices, we must deliberately acquire materials through non-traditional publication channels."

Format

In addition to print or electronic formats, reference sources can be produced as microforms, maps, CD-ROMs, globes, or field identification cards. The format should contribute to the usability of the content and enhance the user's ability to find pertinent information in the source.

Elisabeth Leonard (2014, 12) describes the results of a survey in which librarians were asked if they preferred print or online reference sources. Sixty percent of librarians from public libraries had no preference, while 35 percent preferred online reference sources. Only 22 percent of academic librarians showed no preference, while 68 percent preferred online sources. Thirty-one percent of special librarians reported that they had no preference, while 50 percent preferred online sources. Katherine Hanz and Dawn McKinnon (2018, 6) conducted a survey of Canadian academic librarians and found that 80 percent preferred e-books for general reference, 77 percent preferred e-books for specialized reference, and 62 percent preferred e-books for citation manuals.

Respondents to a 2010 Association of Research Libraries (Bleiler and Livingston 2010, 58–59) survey listed the most important selection criteria for electronic resources as cost (39 percent) and compatibility with library systems (12 percent). The criteria they rated as very important were relevance to current curricula (49 percent), relevance to current faculty research (47 percent), uniqueness of content (46 percent), inflation history (43 percent), and cost per use (42 percent).

College and university students listed the most important features in an e-book as presence of page numbers (75 percent); adjustable text size (67 percent); readability on phones and tablets (64 percent); and bookmarking, highlighting, and note writing (60 percent) (*Academic Student Ebook Experience Survey 2018* 2018, 5).

Online Resources: User Interface

User interfaces can vary enormously, but most people prefer a graphically clean, well-organized, and easy-to-read interface. The user interface should be appropriate for the content of the online resource and the intended audience. Over time, users' expectations change, so the user interface should reflect contemporary graphical and functional preferences. If the user interface remains the same, over time it looks increasingly outdated. Functionality should be updated and enhanced as new and improved technologies become available.

Many databases offer a basic search page that may be as simple as a single search box. They may also offer an advanced search page that includes multiple search boxes, limiters, and other search options. Some offer alternative types of search pages, such as a visual search or a Boolean search page. Databases that index any type of text usually offer at least the ability to search by author, title, and keyword. However, there may be many other types of search fields, such as subject terms, person's names, geographic locations, company names, or the institutional affiliations of the author(s). These specialized search fields should be appropriate to the content and also to the intended user group. See Chapter 16 for detailed information on search strategies.

Some online resources offer the ability to search a controlled vocabulary. The quality of the thesaurus, including the existence of subject term definitions, cross-references, and pertinent subheadings, should be examined. If an online resource includes items written or produced by marginalized groups, preference should be given to resources that use updated/politically correct terminology as indicated by the marginalized community, instead of using only the terms and language of the dominant culture.

The help screens should be easy to locate and negotiate. They should be context sensitive so that clicking on the Help link on a page of search results will display a selection of Help topics related to search results.

Lists of search results should be consistently organized, and the fields in the entries should be easily identifiable. It should be obvious how the result list was sorted, whether by relevance or some other method, and the sorting method should be simple to change. Search limiters on results pages should enhance the user's ability to identify and retrieve the most useful results.

The ability to work with search results in varied ways may be crucial to users. Frequently, the user can save, print, or e-mail individual entries or groups of entries that have been placed in a virtual folder. Users want the ability to print a range of pages with a single command. Some users may wish to export citations to bibliographic management software.

Online Resources: Branding and Customization

When people come to the library to use reference sources, they are reminded they need and want resources provided by the library. When they access reference sources from their home or business, it is not as obvious that the resources are acquired and managed by the library. This is particularly true for users who connect directly to the online resources they use most often, bypassing the library website. Many librarians want to remind library users and the people who fund the library that these resources were provided by the library. One way to do this is to brand their online resources. Many online resources allow for the addition of a library logo or text that indicates access is provided by the library.

Many databases also offer opportunities for libraries to further customize the user interface of an online resource. It is common for the library to have the opportunity to add a logo and/or text or a pop-up box that provides access to the library's chat reference service. Libraries may be able to customize some aspects of functionality, such as which search form is displayed on the landing page of the database. Libraries may be able to alter the text on some buttons, choose which limiters appear on the search page, choose the order in which limiters appear, or make other types of customizations.

Online Resources: Provision of Full Text

If the database indexes full-text articles or other documents, the convenient availability of full text may be one of the most important factors in selection. Library users typically want to be able to easily access the full text of articles, dissertations, company reports, or other textual sources once that source has been identified. The most convenient option is for the database to also supply the full text. If the full text is not in the database, the ability to link to the full text in another of the library's databases is the next most desirable option. At the very least, the database should have the ability to indicate if the library owns the full text of the item being indexed. The ability to identify and access full text may be a deal-breaker when choosing online resources because so many library users are accustomed to the convenience of instant full-text online.

Even when the entry for an item indicates that it is available as full text, some of the content may be missing, such as illustrations, a page on which an article is continued, appendices, or other materials that were present in the print version.

Databases that supply full text usually provide an HTML file and/or a pdf. HTML files are smaller and load more quickly but might not include illustrations or indicate page breaks. The pdf is generally a much larger file but should be an image of the print page, so users will be able to cite the exact page on which a particular piece of text is found. Some databases offer the option of listening to audio files of full text. Sue Polanka (2010, 116) writes, "Visualizing information, hearing the pronunciation of a word, or listening to the content in its entirety can be a tremendous help, particularly to those with learning or physical disabilities and ESL learners."

The currency of any resource that indexes library materials can be crucial. Currency is more important if the source is issued daily, such as a newspaper or the *Federal Register*. Reference e-books sometimes also have currency problems. If a new edition of an e-book is published, the database provider sometimes deletes the older edition from the database when the new edition is added. If the library does not purchase the new edition, library users would have access to neither edition. However, if there are multiple editions of an e-book in the database, library users may unknowingly access the out-of-date edition instead of the newest edition.

Online Resources: Accessibility

A number of accessibility issues should be considered when selecting online reference sources. The ability to access online resources remotely is frequently a deal-breaker. The provisions made for accessibility for those with visual or auditory disabilities may be an important factor in selecting resources. An increasing number of library users want to use library resources on a mobile device. The library may have subscribed to a web-scale discovery service and want all online resources to be available through that service. The library may subscribe to a service that indexes the entries in e-books and want all reference e-books to be accessible through that service.

For many libraries, if a database cannot be accessed remotely, it is not a desirable purchase. College and university students and faculty need to be able to use materials off campus, especially as the number of online courses increases. Public libraries acquire resources to be accessed by users in a city, county, or regional area. Companies and other organizations have employees who work at home or another location.

Database companies have made various provisions so users with visual or other disabilities are able to use the resource successfully (Tatomir and Tatomir 2012). This might involve text-only web pages, audio files for full-text articles, provision for the site to interface with particular software, closed captioning for video files, or other types of accommodation.

The demand for mobile access is so widespread that most databases from major database producers offer a mobile-optimized web page and/or a mobile app. The *2014 Pearson Student Mobile Device Survey* reveals that 62 percent of students in grades 4–12 use a smartphone regularly and 53 percent use a tablet regularly. Smartphones are regularly used by 44 percent of students in elementary school, 58 percent of those in middle school, and 75 percent of those in high school. Tablets are used by 66 percent of students in elementary school, 58 percent of those in middle school, and 42 percent of those in high school (Pearson 2014b, 24). The same survey reveals that 83 percent of college students use a smartphone regularly and 45 percent use a tablet regularly (Pearson 2014a, 20).

If the library has subscribed to a web-scale discovery service, all library reference sources will ideally be accessible from that service. Accessibility by the library's web-scale discovery service may be a deal-breaker, or the use of online resources not accessible through the discovery service may decline to the point that they are cancelled.

Reference Universe provides another way to discover the contents of some of the library's reference books because it indexes the contents of many of those books. If the library subscribes to this service, librarians may choose to purchase only reference books that are included in this database.

Online Resources: Cost and Licensing

Cost models vary widely for online resources. The acquisition of an online resource might be a purchase, a subscription, or some more creative arrangement. An online resource that has been purchased, or for which the perpetual access has been purchased, might require an annual maintenance fee. Some online resources that appear to library users to be a single database might actually be a group of separate databases or titles with the content available in units, each of which can be acquired individually. The library might have purchased perpetual access for some portions of the overall online resource but have a subscription for other portions of the resource.

Pricing of online resources can be influenced by variables such as the number of FTE students, the number of library branches, the number of majors in an academic department, the number of residents in a library district, the number of simultaneous users, the number of computers that have access to the resource, or the ability to provide remote access. The price may also be negotiable, particularly in a poor economy when fewer libraries can afford to acquire new online resources. Membership in a library consortium, discussed in detail in Chapter 5, might help a library manage costs for online resources.

In most cases, libraries subscribing to an online resource will need to sign a license with the database provider. A license will usually define who is allowed to use the online resource; restrictions to using such features as printing, saving, or e-mailing; the ability to use individual items for electronic reserve or interlibrary loan; the availability of technical support; the library's liability; and provision of usage data. If the library has already acquired at least one online product from the database vendor, it may be possible to add the new resource to the existing license rather than negotiate a new license. If the online resource was acquired through a consortium, the consortium might negotiate and administer the license, relieving the librarian of that responsibility. Because the license is a legal instrument, librarians will sometimes consult an attorney, particularly if some of the elements of the license are problematic. Whether or not an attorney is required, in many libraries there will be only one person who is authorized to negotiate licenses. Chapter 15 provides additional information on price models and licensing for online resources.

Box 14.9 provides a practice activity to select a database for a reference collection.

Box 14.9 Activity: Choose a Database

In this scenario, you will be responsible for choosing databases for a particular library. You can choose to work for one of the following (imaginary) libraries:

- James R. Weir Public Library in Whittier, California
- Margaret Whitlinger Memorial Library at Freeport State University, Kentucky
- Franz Holscher High School Library in Augusta, Georgia

You are trying to decide if your library should subscribe to one of the imaginary databases listed here. Although the databases are not in the same subject area, you have sufficient funds for only one of them. Which would you choose and why?

Note that you can devise additional information about your library and/or the sources, if that will support your decision.

- *Hot Topics Pro & Con*. Full-text sources on multiple sides of important current issues.
- *Movie Abstracts*. A searchable database of scholarly articles on film.

- *Diversity eBooks*. e-books written by authors from marginalized communities.
- *Languages to Go*. Video lessons for more than thirty languages.
- *Green Issues*. Books and articles on a wide variety of environmental topics.
- *Marketing Full Text*. A collection of marketing research reports.
- *All the News*. Clips of television news stories from major networks that aired during the past year.

Print Resources: Physical Attributes

Reference books that are expected to last for many years should have sturdy binding that will withstand use by numerous people. The quality of the binding is less likely to be important for a book that is expected to be useful for a limited period, such as a weather almanac or a travel guide. Paper binding may be acceptable for sources such as a monthly issue that will be replaced by an annual bound volume. Photocopying of either paper or cloth-bound books sometimes causes the binding to crack, making rebinding necessary. If a book is expected to be so heavily used that it will need to be rebound, the inner margins of the book should be sufficiently generous for the book to be rebound without losing part of the text.

The quality of the paper is more likely to be important for a book that is expected to have a long shelf life because deteriorating paper may not be able to be rebound, if rebinding is necessary. Poor-quality paper may also become brittle and fall out of the book, or the page may be creased and split at the point of the crease so that part of the page falls out.

Print Resources: Indexing

Indexes and other finding aids in a reference book or set should be easy to locate and appropriate to the content and the target audience. The language used should enhance the ability of users to identify and access the desired information. If the indexes cover a multivolume set, index entries should include both volume and page numbers, so library users are not forced to hunt through multiple volumes in order to find the correct page. If a multivolume set was issued one volume at a time, the index may not arrive until the entire set has been published. If the library owns the previous edition, it may be necessary to retain the older edition, with its indexing, until the entire new edition has been received.

Print Resources: Cost

Print reference books are usually purchased one at a time. The library may obtain a discounted price by buying books on sale, purchasing from a company that offers a reduced price as the library's regular purchasing agent, or receiving a discount as a member of a consortium. If a multivolume set is received one volume at a time, the individual volumes may be cheaper if the library places a standing order for the series. Some reference books are accompanied by free access to the e-book edition, although this access may only be for a limited time.

Materials such as annuals and yearbooks are frequently purchased as a subscription or standing order. Subscriptions are usually an annual fee that pays for everything received during the year, appropriate for monthly, quarterly, or annual publications. Libraries use standing orders for items that are received irregularly, such as pocket parts or transmittal sheets, because the library is billed as materials are received. Utilizing a standing order to acquire the volumes of a multivolume set received one volume at a time ensures that the library does not miss a volume and saves processing time over creating a separate order for each volume. Budgeting for standing orders can be a challenge because the librarian may not be able to predict the number of volumes received throughout the year.

COLLECTION DEVELOPMENT OF FREE INTERNET SOURCES

The number of reliable freely available Internet sites that can be used for reference work continues to expand. In some cases, these sources are so heavily used that they compete with or replace long-established reference works. Some librarians use online booksellers, such as *Amazon.com*, to obtain purchasing information about books, instead of using *Books in Print*. Instead of purchasing movie review guides, a library might use *IMDb*, the *Internet Movie Database*.

Using freely available Internet sources is sometimes problematic. They can vary enormously in quality. They may disappear without notice or remain on the Internet, but cease to be updated. Some questions to ask when evaluating a freely available Internet source are:

- Who is the author? What are the author's credentials? What is the author's point of view?
- Is the site sponsored by or associated with an organization? What is its purpose?
- Who is the intended audience?
- What is the purpose of the information? To entertain? To inform? To sell a product or service? To influence?
- Is the content presented clearly? Is the site easy to navigate?
- Is the content accurate?
- Is the content provided in sufficient depth?
- If currency matters, is the content current?

Including freely available Internet sites and databases in the list of library-provided resources is useful when providing reference service to those who are outside the boundaries of the public library district or those who are not faculty, staff, or students of a college or university library because some licensed resources may not be available for use by these groups.

SELECTION AIDS

A number of tools provide assistance in selecting reference resources. Review sources, issued periodically, provide critical and descriptive reviews of newly issued print and/or electronic titles. Guides to reference sources identify important reference titles and can also be useful when reviewing the reference collection to identify gaps. Both are invaluable in identifying high-quality reference materials. However, the reference librarian must still have a thorough knowledge of both the reference collection and the needs of the library's community in order to build a collection that will fully support reference service for the library's diverse clientele.

Sources of Reviews

In an ideal world, the reference librarian would be able to personally examine each reference source before ordering it. That is rarely possible, but there are a number of sources of reviews that can assist the librarian. The best review sources will vary by type of library, as each of the sources in this section is intended for a particular audience.

American Reference Books Annual is a comprehensive compilation of reviews for English-language print and online reference sources, primarily published in the United States and Canada. As of early 2020, the accompanying online database, *ARBAonline*, included more than 19,000 reviews published from 1997 to the present.

Booklist, a semimonthly publication, includes signed reviews of English-language reference books and electronic reference sources. The reviews of reference works, along with reviews of nonreference resources, are then made available in a searchable database at the *Booklist Online* website.

The *Charleston Advisor: Critical Reviews of Web Products for Information Professionals*, a quarterly journal, publishes extensive reviews of both licensed and free online resources.

Choice: Current Reviews for Academic Libraries publishes signed reviews of reference books and online resources of interest to college and university libraries. The reviews are made available online at the *Choice Reviews* website.

Choice and the *Charleston Advisor* have combined to produce *ccAdvisor*, a subscription-based Internet database of reviews of databases, Internet sites, and tools.

Library Journal publishes a section of signed reviews of print and online reference sources. These reviews are also available on the *Library Journal* website. *Library Journal* publishes an annual supplement on new and forthcoming reference resources.

School Library Journal publishes a section of signed reviews of print and online reference sources suitable for school libraries. The reviews are also available on the *School Library Journal* website.

Reference & User Services Quarterly (*RUSQ*) publishes a section of signed reviews of print and online reference sources. *RUSQ* publishes several annual lists of reference materials chosen by committees of the American Library Association's Reference and User Services Association. The Emerging Technologies Section's (ETS) Best Free Web Sites Committee chooses an annual list of selected freely available websites. These reviews are also posted on the ETS website, which includes a combined index to all of the reviews from this list published beginning in 1999. Committees of the Business Reference and Services Section choose an annual list of the best business information sources and a list of the best business websites, both published in *RUSQ*.

This is only a sample of the available reviews in serials. Many subject-specific serials include reviews of reference books about the subject covered by the journal.

If the library orders books from an online vendor database, then that database might include book reviews. Databases already available in the library may also include full-text sources that publish reviews of reference books. A free source of book reviews might be a consortium's catalog or the catalog of a large library as many library catalogs now include book reviews.

The most useful reviews are those which describe the source, critically examine it, and compare it to similar sources. In addition to reading any available reviews, the librarian may wish to arrange for a trial of any online resource. This can be particularly valuable if the trial is available to the user groups most likely to use this particular source.

Guides to Reference Sources

The American Library Association (ALA) publishes *Reference Sources for Small and Medium-Sized Libraries*, most recently in 2014. The target audience for this guide is school and public libraries. Subject-oriented guides to reference books can also be very helpful. A few examples of this type of publication are the *ALA Guide to Sociology and Psychology Reference*, *Introduction to Reference Sources in the Health Sciences*, and *Information Resources in the Humanities and the Arts*.

Older guides may be useful for reviewing the existing reference collection. ALA has published a number of editions of the *Guide to Reference*. Although the *Guide to Reference* has ceased publication, it may be useful for evaluating older reference works. *The New Walford* is a three-volume set: *Volume 1: Science, Technology, and Medicine* (2005), *Volume 2: Social Sciences* (2008), and *Volume 3: Arts, Humanities, and General Reference* (2008). This British publication includes entries for print and electronic reference sources.

Guides to reference sources are useful for both collection development and reference work. As a collection development tool, they can be used as a resource for evaluating the content of the reference collection and as a guide to selection of new resources. They can also guide the reference librarian to the most appropriate source to answer a question in a subject area with which the librarian is not familiar.

REFERENCE COLLECTIONS IN TRANSITION

Reference collections have been in transition ever since the first electronic reference sources became available in the early 1970s. They will continue to transition as libraries downsize their print collections and acquire an ever-increasing variety of online resources. Some librarians refer to their print collection as a legacy collection, implying that the print collection has become something of an antique. Nevertheless, publishers continue to issue print reference books and libraries continue to buy them. Until librarians no longer see the need to provide a print reference collection, both print and electronic reference collections must be developed and maintained to effectively support all the types of reference services that are available to assist library users.

REFERENCES

Academic Student Ebook Experience Survey 2018. 2018. Library Journal. https://s3.amazonaws.com/WebVault/research/2018_AcademicStudentEbookExperience.pdf.

Bleiler, Richard, and Jill Livingston. 2010. *Evaluating E-resources*, SPEC Kit 316. Washington, DC: Association of Research Libraries.

Cordell, Rosanne. 2014. "Optimizing Library Services—Managing the 21st-Century Reference Collection." *Against the Grain* 26 (4): 53–54.

Fernandes, Maria I. 2008. "Ready Reference Collections: Thoughts on Trends." *Community & Junior College Libraries* 14 (3): 201–10.

Hanz, Katherine and Dawn McKinnon. 2018. "When Librarians Hit the Books: Uses of and Attitudes Toward E-Books." *Journal of Academic Librarianship* 44 (1): 1–14.

Hodgkin, Adam. 2002. "Integrated and Aggregated Reference Services: The Automation of Drudgery." *D-Lib Magazine* 8 (4). http://www.dlib.org/dlib/april02/hodgkin/04hodgkin.html

Landsman, Margaret. 2005. "Getting It Right—the Evolution of Reference Collections." *The Reference Librarian* 91/92: 5–22.

Leonard, Elisabeth. 2014. *The State of Reference Collections.* SAGE. https://studysites.sagepub.com/repository/binaries/pdfs/StateofReference.pdf

Levine-Clark, Michael, and Toni M. Carter, eds. 2013. *ALA Glossary of Library and Information Science.* Chicago: American Library Association, s.v. "reference source".

Liestman, Daniel. 2001. "Reference Collection Management Policies: Lessons from Kansas." *College & Undergraduate Libraries* 8 (1): 79–112.

MIT Libraries, Collections Directorate Diversity, Inclusion, and Social Justice Task Force. 2017. *Creating a Social Justice Mindset: Diversity, Inclusion, and Social Justice in the Collections Directorate of the MIT Libraries.* https://dspace.mit.edu/handle/1721.1/108771

Pearson. 2014a. *Pearson Student Mobile Device Survey 2014. National Report: College Students.* Last modified May 16, 2015. http://www.pearsoned.com/wp-content/uploads/Pearson-HE-Student-Mobile-Device-Survey-PUBLIC-Report-051614.pdf

Pearson. 2014b. *Pearson Student Mobile Device Survey 2014. National Report: Students in Grades 4–12.* Last modified May 4, 2014. http://www.pearsoned.com/wp-content/uploads/Pearson-K12-Student-Mobile-Device-Survey-050914-PUBLIC-Report.pdf

Polanka, Sue. 2010. "Interactive Online Reference." *Booklist* 106 (9/10): 116.

Richardson, E.C. 1893. "Reference-Books." *Library Journal* 18 (7): 254–57.

Singer, Carol A. 2012. *Fundamentals of Managing Reference Collections*, ALA Fundamentals Series. Chicago: American Library Association.

Tatomir, Jennifer Nasasia, and Joanna Catarina Tatomir. 2012. "Collection Accessibility: A Best Practices Guide for Libraries and Librarians." *Library Technology Reports* 48 (7): 36–42.

LIST OF SOURCES

Accessible Archives. Malvern, PA: Accessible Archives. http://www.accessible-archives.com/. Subscription required.

ALA Guide to Sociology and Psychology Reference. 2011. Chicago: American Library Association.

Amazon.com. http://www.amazon.com/.

American Medical Association Complete Medical Encyclopedia. 2003. New York: Penguin Random House. Available in *Consumer Health Complete.*

American Reference Books Annual. 1970–. Edited by Shannon Graff Hysell. Santa Barbara, CA: Libraries Unlimited.

ARBAonline. Santa Barbara, CA: Libraries Unlimited. http://www.arbaonline.com/. Subscription required.

Best Free Reference Web Sites Combined Index. 1999–. RUSA ETS Emerging Technologies Section. http://www.ala.org/rusa/awards/etsbestindex.

Booklist. 1905–. Chicago: American Library Association. 22 issues per year.

Booklist Online. Chicago: American Library Association. http://www.booklistonline.com/. Subscription required for full access.

Books in Print. New York: R.R. Bowker. http://www.booksinprint.com/. Subscription required.

ccAdvisor. Middleton, CT: American Library Association and the Charleston Company. http://www.ccadvisor.org/. Subscription required.

Charleston Advisor: Critical Reviews of Web Products for Information Professionals. 1999–. Denver: The Charleston Advisor. Quarterly. http://www.charlestonco.com/index.php. Subscription required for full access.

Choice: Current Reviews for Academic Libraries. 1964–. Middletown, CT: Association of College and Research Libraries. 11 issues per year.

Choice Reviews. Middletown, CT: Association of College and Research Libraries. http://www.choice360.org/products/reviews. Subscription required.

Consumer Health Complete. Ipswich, MA: EBSCO. https://www.ebsco.com/products/research-databases/consumer-health-complete. Subscription required.

Credo Reference. Credo Reference. http://search.credoreference.com/. Subscription required.

Federal Register. 1936–. Washington, DC: Office of the Federal Register. Daily. https://www.federalregister.gov/.

Guide to Reference. (1996). Edited by Robert H. Kieft. Chicago: American Library Association.

IMDb: Internet Movie Database. http://www.imdb.com/.

Information Resources in the Humanities and the Arts. 6th ed. 2013. Edited by Anna H. Perrault and Elizabeth S. Aversa. Santa Barbara, CA: Libraries Unlimited.

Introduction to Reference Sources in the Health Sciences. 6th ed. 2014. Edited by Jeffrey T. Huber and Susan Swogger. Chicago: Neal-Schuman.

Library Journal. 1876–. New York: Library Journals, LLC. 20 issues per year. http://lj.libraryjournal.com/.

The New Walford Guide to Reference Resources. 3 vols. 2005–2008. London: Facet.

Reference & User Services Quarterly (RUSQ). 1997–. Chicago: American Library Association. Quarterly. https://journals.ala.org/index.php/rusq/index.

Reference Sources for Small and Medium-Sized Libraries. 8th ed. 2014. Edited by Jack O'Gorman. Chicago: American Library Association.

Reference Universe. Sterling, VA: Paratext. http://reference.paratext.com/. Subscription required.

Rock and Roll, Counterculture, Peace and Protest: Popular Culture in Britain and America, 1950–1975. Marlborough, UK: Adam Matthew Digital. http://www.rockandroll.amdigital.co.uk/. Subscription required.

SBRnet: Sports Business Research Network. Princeton, NJ: Sports Business Research Network. https://www.sbrnetportal.com/. Subscription required.

School Library Journal. 1954–. New York: Media Source. Monthly. http://www.slj.com/.

SUGGESTED READINGS

Brumley, Rebecca. 2009. *Electronic Collection Management Forms, Policies, Procedures, and Guidelines Manual With CD-ROM.* New York: Neal-Schuman Publishers.

This compilation of policies, procedures, guidelines, and forms from academic and public libraries provides a treasure trove of information to assist the reference collection manager. It includes resources for administration, collection development, equipment, accessibility, copyright, and position descriptions.

Detmering, Robert, and Claudene Sproles. 2012. "Reference in Transition: A Case Study in Reference Collection Development." *Collection Building* 31 (1): 19–22.

Detmering and Sproles describe the changes made to the University of Louisville reference collection development policies and print collection as a result of changing reference practices, budget limitations, and the implementation of a learning commons. The librarians used a revised policy to evaluate serials and standing orders, weed the reference collection, and plan the future development of the collection.

Kessler, Jane. 2013. "Use It or Lose It! Results of a Use Study of the Print Sources in an Academic Library Reference Collection." *The Reference Librarian* 54 (1): 61–72.
The University at Albany, State University of New York implemented a study to determine the use of their reference collection. Kessler discusses procedures used for the study, which found only 7.1 percent of the volumes in the reference collection were used at least once during the fall semester.

Larson, Jeannette. 2012. *CREW: A Weeding Manual for Modern Libraries*. Austin, TX: Texas State Library and Archives Commission. https://www.tsl.texas.gov/ld/pubs/crew/index.html.
The CREW guide to weeding was written primarily for small- and medium-sized public libraries, but it is also useful for other libraries. It explains the process of weeding, from planning to disposal of unwanted materials. One chapter focuses on weeding reference collections.

Miller, Eve-Marie. 2016. "Making Room for a Learning Commons Space: Lessons in Weeding a Reference Collection through Collaboration and Planning." *Serials Librarian* 71 (3–4): 197–201.
Due to the potential of instituting a learning commons, the reference librarians at Santa Rosa Junior College planned and executed a program to weed their reference collection. This article details the planning and procedures and evaluates the importance of communication within the department and with the other departments involved.

Singer, Carol A. 2012. *Fundamentals of Managing Reference Collections*. Chicago: American Library Association.
This volume summarizes the basics of managing a print and online reference collection. Topics covered include collection development policies, staffing, selection, acquisitions, budgeting, licensing, collection maintenance, weeding, consortia, discovery and access. The book also includes a *Reference Collection Development Policy Template*.

Verminski, Alana and Kelly Marie Blanchat. 2017. *Fundamentals of Electronic Resources Management*. Chicago: American Library Association.
Verminski and Blanchat cover the basics of managing electronic resources in libraries, including purchase models, evaluation of resources, open access resources, licensing, maintenance, statistics, and marketing. The volume includes an open access resource rubric and a checklist to assist in reviewing a license.

Chapter 15

Licensing and Managing Electronic Resources

Michael Rodriguez

INTRODUCTION

Library collections are shifting from physical to electronic formats. Academic libraries in the United States on average spend 60–70 percent of their collections budgets on electronic books and reference materials, journals, and databases (American Library Association 2015). Similarly, public and school libraries spend rising portions of their buying power on e-books, e-audiobooks, and streaming media. Electronic formats offer major benefits to patrons and libraries alike—they expand access, bolster usage, and enable spaces to be repurposed to meet evolving patron needs.

Notwithstanding these benefits, acquiring and managing e-resources is challenging and complex. Physical materials are simpler—they are ordered, delivered, cataloged, circulated, and weeded if they no longer meet patron needs. Only the copyright laws of the library's jurisdiction limit use of physical materials. On the other hand, e-resources encompass all manner of content types (journals, books, videos, and primary sources), delivery platforms (ever-changing publisher websites), and technologies (knowledge bases, analytics tools, file formats, and much more). Navigating this maze, librarians must set up and maintain online access and discovery for the life cycle of each e-resource—painstaking work that requires a high level of comfort with ambiguity.

Most important, librarians must negotiate prices and licenses for each e-resource they acquire. Pricing is fluid, with list prices calculated and discounted based on countless variables, including individual librarians' skill at negotiating with vendors. Negotiators strive to minimize legal risk and maximize value on investment for their libraries and patrons. This means getting the lowest prices and broadest terms of use, obligating vendors to deliver consistent and reliable service, and making contract compliance easy for everyone involved. Some libraries employ an acquisitions librarian to handle negotiations, but most libraries are not big or specialized enough to dedicate a salary line to this role. Reference librarians may end up selecting e-resources for acquisition, negotiating with vendors, reading contracts, and troubleshooting access.

Even librarians not involved in licensing or e-resources management directly still need to understand and participate in licensing. Public services staff work directly with patrons and have the clearest sense of patron needs and experiences. Does this database provide the most useful content? Is this e-book platform more user friendly than others? Academic librarians, meanwhile, may serve as subject specialists. They liaise with faculty and build subject collections. Reference librarians and subject specialists should communicate their insights and content expertise back to library negotiators, ensuring that license terms meet patron needs. Reference librarians may find themselves troubleshooting access or explaining to patrons the permissible uses of an e-resource. Consequently, all types of library workers in all types of libraries benefit from understanding the fundamentals of licensing electronic resources. These fundamentals include the e-resources life cycle, pricing models, terms of use, negotiation strategies, and market awareness.

MANAGING THE ELECTRONIC RESOURCES LIFE CYCLE

Licensing is just one vital part of a much larger electronic resources life cycle. Jill Emery and Graham Stone (2013) developed a framework called Techniques for Electronic Resource Management (TERMS). Electronic resources management cycles through the following stages: (1) investigating new content, (2) acquiring new content, (3) implementing or setting up access and discovery to content, (4) maintaining and evaluating e-resources on an ongoing basis, (5) conducting annual reviews, and (6) canceling and replacing e-resources. TERMS 2.0 will add preservation to the mix, highlighting the importance of permanent sustainable access to born-digital resources, which theoretically could vanish if a publisher goes out of business. These stages are fluid. Not every e-resource cycles through all these stages every year.

Investigation

First, librarians investigate an e-resource to see if it is worth acquiring. Content criteria should include the following: Does the e-resource meet identified patron needs and align with the library's mission and goals? Is content unique? Next, investigators should check user interfaces against criteria such as mobile responsive design, advanced searchability, compatibility with major Web browsers, accessibility for people with disabilities, and intuitive navigation. Next to consider are technical specifications. Would access work through the library's preferred methods of patron authentication? Is usage data available and do those statistics meet industry standards for precision and transparency? Does the e-resource integrate into the library's online catalog or discovery service? Are machine-readable cataloging (MARC) records provided and do they meet quality standards? Vendors usually offer free temporary access to e-resources under investigation so librarians can invite patrons to test out an e-resource to determine if it meets their needs and is intuitive to use. Reference and information services librarians interact with patrons regularly and know their communities' needs, so their input at this stage is valuable. Librarians should also get price quotes at this early stage to establish if acquiring the e-resource is financially feasible.

Acquisition

Should the e-resource meet the purchase criteria and funding is available, the acquisition process can begin. Acquisition hinges on negotiation of pricing and license terms. Vendors sell e-resources under annual subscription or one-time purchase models. The most common model is to pay annual fees for ongoing access. Academic libraries frequently negotiate perpetual rights to access and use e-journal issues published during the subscription period. For other e-resources, access to content is generally terminated if the library stops paying the subscription fees or if a predetermined usage threshold is reached. The alternative is for the library to pay a one-time fee to keep e-resources "in perpetuity." Even so, some vendors charge annual fees for e-resources purchased in perpetuity, seeking to recoup their costs for hosting the e-resources online.

Once the purchase model and price are negotiated, the license comes next. Sometimes, an existing license will cover the new purchase, or the library and vendor will agree that no license is needed. Vendors—particularly smaller companies without legal departments—go this route to reduce labor costs, recognizing that most libraries are low-risk business partners. However, the best practice is for libraries and vendors to reify rights and responsibilities in a license. In particular, libraries acquiring perpetual rights to content should always negotiate licenses to safeguard those rights under law. Licenses are arguably less important for subscriptions under which libraries are not acquiring long-term rights to content or for inexpensive, low-profile products such as single streaming videos. In such cases, simply including the basic terms of use—interlibrary loan rights, length of term, and so on—on the invoice or purchase order can substitute for a formal license.

If formal documentation of terms of use is needed, the first step is to check if the library can piggyback onto a group or consortial license, or if the parties are willing to accept the Shared Electronic Resource Understanding, or SERU (standardized terms of use based on U.S. national standards), in lieu of a full-blown license (National Information Standards Organization 2019). Using group licenses, or SERU, saves librarians time and effort, but, more important, libraries working together can draw on their collective buying power to negotiate better deals. Licensing, negotiation, and the role of consortia will be examined in depth later in this chapter.

Implementation

After acquisition comes implementation, although both stages may happen concurrently. Librarians set up access to the e-resource, pushing out a stable uniform resource locator (URL) to the various interfaces where patrons go to search, including the library's website, discovery tool, A-Z database list, and research guides. Librarians may need to ask information technology staff outside the library to help configure and test patron authentication. Typical authentication methods are Internet protocol addresses and proxy servers, though increasingly libraries are using authentication systems like Shibboleth and OpenAthens. When available, MARC records should be added to the catalog. Librarians must test access thoroughly to enable a smooth launch. The library's name, logo, or other branding should display on each e-resource's web platform, and marketing should inform patrons of the e-resource's availability and utility. Documentation and vendor-provided training, whether onsite or online, help librarians and patrons get the most from newly implemented e-resources. Single e-journals or other minor e-resources require much less time and effort to implement than, say, a newspaper database or a big e-journal package.

Maintenance

After implementation, librarians should monitor and maintain e-resources to ensure that they keep functioning as needed. Periodic checks on URLs ensures that access is turned on and stays on to all components of acquired e-resources. Monitoring is needed because access is often unreliable. Libraries may unexpectedly lose access to individual e-book or e-journal titles but still have access to the rest of a collection—this is usually due to poor inventory management by the vendor. Large-scale downtime may mean that vendors shut off access assuming the library had opted not to renew their subscription that year. In that case, librarians simply check their payment records and contact the vendor to restore access. On other occasions, e-resource downtime may result from Web server glitches or changes to e-resource URLs that vendors did not communicate properly to customers. Sometimes, loss of access arises from library mistakes, for example, if the wrong metadata records were loaded into the catalog, remote patron authentication was misconfigured, or access points were never actually added to the catalog in the first place (yes, this happens!).

No matter the cause, librarians should have communication protocols in place to address loss of access. These communication protocols should address how and when to contact vendors to restore access and explain why access was lost, to notify other library staff in case of questions from patrons, and sometimes to post messages on the library's e-resource portal to alert patrons to loss of access. Libraries should also distribute widely an e-mail address or simple online form so that patrons can report access problems quickly and easily to the library's e-resources management staff.

Evaluation

In addition to ensuring vendors hold up their end of the bargain, libraries should conduct a systematic review of e-resources each year, ensuring ongoing value. Accurate usage reporting is essential. Usage reports should follow international standards defined in the latest release of the COUNTER Code of Practice. Usage reports commonly take the form of spreadsheets listing downloads, views, and unique logins per month. If the annual review turns up low usage or other problems, then librarians should review the e-resource for cancellation or replacement. Note that usage data is sometimes inconsistent and difficult to interpret, as not all vendors follow the same global COUNTER standard. Librarians must clean up and normalize data, for instance averaging out abnormal dips and spikes in the numbers across various months. In some cases, libraries can automate the import of standardized usage reports into local systems through the Standardized Usage Statistics Harvesting (SUSHI) protocol (National Information Standards Organization n.d.). Context and qualitative data are important, too; therefore, e-resources managers should gather feedback from subject-matter experts and patrons and should remember that little-used e-resources may still be essential. A Spanish-language e-journal or a medieval studies bibliography might see relatively low usage but might be vital to providing equitable library services or sustaining a small but mighty academic department. To build and sustain healthy collections, librarians must cultivate market awareness, watching for new or improved e-resources as well as familiarizing themselves with industry standards.

Cancellations are sometimes complicated. If a library cancels an e-resource, stakeholders should be consulted and notified early and often. Effective communication prevents disruption to patrons' work and forestalls complaints. Licenses may contain multiyear commitments or require that vendors be notified of cancellation decisions long in advance of the subscription's end date, so librarians should review licenses carefully for such restrictions as well as for any perpetual or post-cancellation rights to access content. If the cancelled e-resource is slated for replacement, the electronic resources life cycle starts afresh with the investigation and acquisition phases.

Preservation

A core but often overlooked e-resources management principle is to ensure that content licensed in perpetuity survives in perpetuity. Publishers go out of business. Electronic files decay and become unreadable. Servers crash. In addition to knowledge's inherent social and scholarly value, preservation of licensed content sustains library investments. As most libraries lack staff or infrastructure to host e-resources themselves, librarians must negotiate licenses that obligate vendors to document and deliver sustainable preservation strategies. These strategies vary. One popular digital preservation service is Portico from ITHAKA, a not-for-profit organization that puts e-resources in a dark archive; should the publisher go out of business or for any reason stop providing access (a *trigger event*), Portico turns on access for the publisher's customers. Portico preserves electronic journals, books, primary sources, and other material types and serves more than 600 content providers and 1,000 libraries. Other content providers and libraries crowdsource preservation through LOCKSS (Lots of Copies Keeps Stuff Safe) or CLOCKSS (Controlled LOCKSS), in which libraries collectively back up materials on their own servers (Mering 2015). However, if preservation is to be achieved, librarians must ensure publishers are contractually bound to deliver sustainable preservation solutions. Preservation is an issue only if libraries purchase content in perpetuity. Many public and small academic libraries subscribe to mostly aggregator databases that provide subscription access only but not perpetual rights.

IMPACT OF LICENSES

Licenses are critical at each stage of the e-resources life cycle. Licenses define the rights and responsibilities of everyone involved. Licenses may prohibit remote access, limit number of simultaneous logins, restrict downloading or sharing, or impose other restrictions that reduce the content's usefulness. The gravest risk is a license whose terms of use are so watered down that libraries and their communities pay top dollar for what amounts to temporary, read-only access to content. Restrictive licenses encourage vendors to monetize common usages by charging extra fees to allow text and data mining or authorize library-affiliated researchers to reproduce figures and excerpts from licensed materials in their own publications. Monetization increases financial burden on researchers and establishes troubling precedents for scholarly communication.

Licenses also impact internal library workflows and systems. Overly restrictive licenses may force labor-intensive changes to patron authentication and remote access technology, while unusual lending restrictions force interlibrary loan staff to reverse the trend toward automation and handle lending requests manually in order to comply with the license agreement. Meanwhile, licenses that lack rigorous vendor performance obligations may lead to libraries struggling with frequent access outages or troublesome workflows to get metadata needed to make e-resources discoverable by patrons. Vendors who are rivals may refuse to share metadata with each other's proprietary knowledge bases and discovery tools. Without licenses to protect library and patron interests, value on investment declines. As reference and information services librarians often select or recommend e-resources for acquisition, they should understand how license agreements impact value and how purchasing decisions reward actors, good and bad, in this ecosystem.

Last but not least, academic library licenses hold the potential to transform scholarship. Many academic libraries are stuck with "big deals," subscription bundles containing dozens or even thousands of e-journals, whose cost increases at an average fixed rate of 5–6 percent every year (EBSCO 2018). In addition to eroding libraries' budgetary flexibility and ability to respond to shifting patron needs, these big deals undermine scholarship and public knowledge. They restrict access to philanthropically or publicly funded science to institutions and individuals who can afford expensive subscriptions. A single e-journal subscription can cost an institution up to $10,000 per year. A single e-book can cost $500. Equally problematic, authors generally sign away their intellectual property rights to publishers, but those publishers rarely or inadequately compensate the authors, editors, and peer reviewers who make scholarship possible. Elsevier and other commercial publishers boast soaring profit margins in the range of 30–40 percent—higher than big technology or pharmaceutical companies like Apple and Pfizer (Lewis 2016, 50). While vendors reap the profits, library budgets are generally falling or frozen. Increasingly, libraries are challenging these inequitable and unsustainable business practices. But achieving sustainability requires negotiating to redefine how access is granted and how pricing is determined.

PRICING MODELS

Vendor pricing models vary according to what the market will bear, number of patrons served, and which types of libraries and intended usage are involved. Sometimes, vendors take a one-price-fits-all approach, but most have defined pricing tiers. Vendors want to sustain revenue growth year over year. This impetus leads them to raise prices (typically 3–7 percent a year) and sometimes revamp the basis of pricing. For instance, academic publishers might switch from a pricing model based on the library's historical print journal subscriptions to a model based on the college's current head count. Standard increases of 5 percent per year mean that e-resources double in cost every twenty years, outpacing the average U.S. inflation rate (around 2 percent a year). Librarians must understand how pricing works and be ready to renegotiate every year.

"List price" refers to the price posted on fliers, Web pages, and quotes distributed by the vendor. List prices bear only slight relation to production costs or value to consumers—vendors charge whatever they think the market will bear. Vendors inflate list prices so that they can mark down prices during negotiations, profiting but letting customers feel good about the deal. Prices are negotiable and variable. The most common forms of list pricing are based on a combination of population served and organization type, but these are just two of many approaches. Following is a summary of pricing models, followed by Tables 15.1–15.7, which illustrate what pricing models might look like by library type. Box 15.1 provides an activity on calculating subscription costs.

TABLE 15.1 Academic Libraries: Pricing Model Based on Enrollment Tiers

Full-Time Equivalent	Cost ($)
1–1,000	9,995
1,001–2,000	13,945
2,001–5,000	16,775
5,001–10,000	27,495
10,001–20,000	37,340

TABLE 15.2 Public Libraries: Pricing Model Based on Population Tiers

Population Served	Cost ($)
<7,500	775
7,501–15,000	953
15,001–30,000	1,737
30,001–50,000	2,443
50,001–75,000	3,707
75,001–150,000	4,886

TABLE 15.3 Academic Library: Pricing Model Based on Enrollment and Institution Type

Full-Time Equivalent	Four-Year Institutions ($)	Art Schools ($)	Law Schools ($)	Medical Schools ($)	Miscellaneous Schools ($)
1–999	845	510	637	510	510
1,000–2,999	1,657	510	637	510	510
3,000–4,999	2,533	510	637	510	510
5,000–11,999	4,122	510	637	510	510
12,000–24,999	5,270	510	637	510	510
25,000–39,999	6,791	510	637	510	510
40,000–999,999	8,075	510	637	510	510

TABLE 15.4 Academic Library: Pricing Model Based on Enrollment and Multiple Subscriptions

Full-Time Equivalent	With Academic E-Book ($)	Without Academic E-Book ($)
1–2,499	1,500	2,250
2,500–5,999	3,000	4,500
5,000–7,499	4,845	7,268
7,500–9,999	6,565	9,848

TABLE 15.5 Academic Library: Pricing Model Based on Enrollment and Product Quantity

Full-Time Equivalent	Price per Journal				
	1 journal:	2–10 journals:	11–20 journals:	21+ journals:	All journals:
1–999,999	$452	$428	$404	$380	$309

TABLE 15.6 Academic Library: Pricing Model Based on Enrollment and Budget

Full-Time Equivalent	Budget ($)				
	1–499,999	500,000–749,999	750,000–999,999	1,000,000–2,499,999	2,500,000–9,999,999
1–1,999	709	1,241	1,772	2,304	2,832
2,000–3,999	756	1,323	1,890	2,457	3,020
4,000–999,999	945	1,654	2,363	3,072	3,776

TABLE 15.7 Public Library: Pricing Model Based on Population and Branches

Population Served	Library Price Per Person ($)	Library Minimum Per Branch ($)	Consortium Price Per Person ($)	Consortium Minimum Per Branch ($)
<15,000	0.063	810.00	0.06	780
15,001–50,000	0.055	1,818.25	0.05	1,725
50,001–200,000	0.032	3,872.25	0.03	3,685
200,001–500,000	0.024	7,675.50	0.023	7,290
500,001–1,000,000	0.017	14,847.25	0.016	14,125
>1,000,000	0.014	21,280.00	0.013	20,260

- **Flat pricing.** Prices are the same for every institution, regardless of size or type. Under this model, impecunious community colleges and public libraries would pay the same price as research-intensive universities do. Flat pricing is common for single e-books, single e-journals, and other e-resources that are singular and/or relatively inexpensive.
- **Organization types.** Most vendors offer different pricing tiers for corporate, academic, public, community college, school, and special libraries. A community college with 30,000 students is going to have less available money to buy e-resources than a research university with similar enrollment. Most vendors recognize and build that distinction into pricing. SkillSoft and O'Reilly, which sell mostly to corporations, charge libraries a fraction of what they charge Fortune 500 companies for the same e-books bundle.
- **Population served.** Prices hinge on the full-time equivalent (FTE) student enrollment or other total population served by the library. For hospital libraries, the population served may refer to the number of beds or doctors; for public libraries, it may be the number of residents or taxpayers in the county or municipality. For example, if a resource costs $1 per patron, then a library serving 3,000 patrons pays $3,000. Population-based models are often calculated in combination with institutional rankings or other criteria.
- **Relevant population served.** For niche products, pricing may hinge on the portion of the subscriber's population likeliest to use the e-resource in question. In academic libraries, this is "relevant" FTE. For instance, vendors may price financial information based on how many students are majoring in business. Even if a vendor does not offer this model for subject-specific e-resources, librarians can lobby for lower pricing on this basis.
- **Academic classification.** For academic libraries, the Carnegie Classification is very important. Overseen by a nonprofit organization, the Carnegie Classification categorizes institutions of higher education on the basis of research intensiveness (Center for Postsecondary Research n.d.). For pricing purposes, vendors assume that doctoral-granting institutions will get more usage and value from e-resources than lower-tier institutions such as regional universities or community colleges.
- **Number of patrons/seats.** Some e-resources are licensed for a limited number of unique logins accessing the e-resource simultaneously, for example, five users at a time. For e-books and specialized or low-in-demand databases, this model is a way for libraries to control costs. However, this seat-based model is losing popularity. It is a legacy of the 1990s and early 2000s, when data storage was expensive and e-resources lived on compact discs. Patrons get frustrated if turned away from a website, so unlimited access is usually the way to go.
- **Number of sites.** Sometimes, vendors price e-resources on the basis of how many library branches, campuses, or other physical locations ("sites") are part of the institution. This is an archaic model based on the print era, when each campus or branch library had its own print subscriptions. As libraries switched from print to electronic formats, these duplicate subscriptions were consolidated. However, vendors tried to keep the revenue by charging based on number of sites. Site-based pricing warrants pushback from libraries.
- **Remote access.** Especially for public libraries, vendors may try to charge on the basis of whether patrons must be physically present at a library in order to access the e-resource or whether they are permitted to access remotely from work or home using their library card number. Academic library licenses allow remote access by default in most cases; public librarians will still need to fight for remote access for their patrons at a fair price.

Box 15.1 Activity: Calculate E-Resource Pricing

The vendor JSTOR offers a simple online calculator for institutions to calculate the cost of their e-journal subscriptions. Go to https://purchase.jstor.org/quotecart and follow the prompts. You will be taken to a page where collections and titles are displayed alongside their list prices for institutional type and size you selected. Few vendors offer this degree of transparency, but JSTOR's calculator suggests how other vendors may calculate asking prices for products.

Discounts

In many cases, vendors offer custom quotes that go beyond the parameters of a pricing model. While lacking transparency, this practice enables librarians to negotiate potentially major discounts, ranging from 10 percent to 80 percent, and deals that may not deliver cost savings but confer other advantages to the library, such as more flexible license terms or free extra content. Following are some common situations in which vendors are incentivized to offer major discounts.

- **Bulk purchasing.** Vendors usually give significant discounts when libraries buy multiple costly products within a certain timeframe (typically in the same fiscal year) or when multiple libraries combine forces to form a consortium and negotiate as a group (see Chapter 5 for more discussion of consortia).
- **Financial hardship.** If a library is experiencing a budget crisis, vendors may be willing to freeze or even reduce renewal pricing and offer extra discounts on new acquisitions.
- **Multiyear deals.** In this model, costs decrease if the library agrees to a longer-term commitment (e.g., a three-year commitment rather than a year at a time).
- **Relationships.** Vendors may offer special discounts to strategic partners and brand-loyal or high-volume customers or if the negotiators share a good relationship.
- **Timing.** Vendors often offer bigger discounts if their fiscal year is winding down and they are trying to hit sales targets in order to earn bonuses or meet financial projections.

LICENSE TERMS AND CONDITIONS

The first skill that library negotiators must learn is how to interpret and rewrite vendor licenses. Often, these licenses run between five and twenty pages long, crowded with text and packed with legalese indecipherable to anyone but lawyers or others trained in contract law. But as explained previously, good license terms and conditions are vital to maximizing the library's value on investment and minimizing legal risk. This means gaining expansive terms of use, obligating vendors to deliver consistent and reliable service, and making compliance easy. Vendors have similar goals for themselves but may wish to make money on types of usage that libraries want at no extra cost (e.g., data mining rights for academic libraries or patron access from home for public libraries). License negotiation is important and time-consuming work for both sides.

Fortunately, library negotiators are not alone. Academic library consortial groups such as California Digital Library (CDL) and the NorthEast Research Libraries Consortium (NERL) in the United States, Canadian Research Knowledge Network and Ontario Council of University Libraries in Canada, and Jisc in the United Kingdom have developed model licenses to serve as templates for negotiation. In the United States, the best-known model is the LIBLICENSE Model License from the Center for Research Libraries, last modified in October 2018 (Center for Research Libraries 2018). The CDL hosts a licensing toolkit that, while designed for use by the University of California, lets other libraries benchmark and learn from the CDL's methods (California Digital Library 2018). Another approach to licensing is the National Information Standards Organization's Shared Electronic Resource Understanding (SERU), which sets forth standardized, simple terms of use and performance expectations for both vendor and library. Given SERU's ambiguous legal standing, however, the bulk of publishers and libraries have not embraced this standard. No model licenses have seen widespread adoption among public or K–12 libraries.

In addition to model license language, most libraries are required to comply with state and federal laws and institutional regulations. States such as Connecticut require all vendors to sign ethics affidavits and accept contract provisions mandated by the legislature. States such as California have unusually robust state laws requiring that digital educational resources be fully accessible for patrons with disabilities. Meanwhile, states such as Texas may require only that their own state laws govern contracts. Some libraries are allowed to handle licensing in house; others are required to submit licenses to external review by central procurement or legal offices. While regulated less than state or public institutions are, private colleges and schools may have administrative requirements that librarians must follow as a condition of employment.

Licensing follows a consistent overall workflow. Once an e-resource has been identified for acquisition, the librarian should contact the vendor, gather information including price quotes, and obtain an editable copy of the vendor's license (optimally in Microsoft Word or LibreOffice format). After informing the vendor of the need to negotiate changes to the license, librarians should draw on LIBLICENSE and other model licenses to mark up the vendor's license, tracking changes within the document. Often librarians can simply copy and paste provisions from the model license into the vendor license, removing language from the vendor license that conflicts with the desired terms and conditions. Sometimes, the vendor will accept the library's changes without question; at other times, a dialogue takes place between library and vendor that can last for days, weeks, or even months. Eventually, agreement is reached and both parties sign. Either party may walk away from a deal if the pricing or terms are unacceptable and neither party is ready to compromise to the extent demanded by the other. Librarians should have a backup plan and stakeholder communication process in place should negotiations fall through. Box 15.2 describes commons licensing terms.

Box 15.2 Licensing Terms

1. *Governing law*. Licenses should specify the governing law and jurisdiction of the courts as that of the state where the institution is located or else not say ("remain silent").
2. *Indemnification*. Vendors must indemnify and hold harmless the library in the event any materials sold to the library infringe the intellectual property rights of third parties. But libraries should never agree to indemnify or hold harmless the vendor for any reason.
3. *Confidentiality*. Librarians should reject any confidentiality or nondisclosure provisions in vendor licenses, keeping the door open to sharing license terms or prices with other libraries and enforcing a degree of transparency on a normally opaque marketplace.
4. *Filtering*. Some school and public libraries must block or restrict age-inappropriate or explicit materials in order to comply with the Children's Internet Protection Act (CIPA) or community standards. Licenses should allow for the use of technology protection measures, or the vendor should provide child-friendly editions of e-resources.
5. *Cancellation*. The license should state what happens if a library cancels a subscription, in particular whether it is granted post-cancellation perpetual use rights and, if so, to what content. Multiyear licenses should include an opt-out clause in the event of budget cuts.
6. *Perpetual rights*. If acquiring perpetual use rights to content, libraries should ensure that licenses guarantee these rights and describe mechanisms for providing access in the event the vendor goes out of business or ceases to provide online access.
7. *Breach*. Licenses should not impose performance obligations on the library other than a general statement of using reasonable efforts to prevent unauthorized use.

Authorized Patrons and Uses

8. *Authorized users*. Licenses should permit e-resource access to anyone with valid library credentials plus "walk-ins" who are physically present at the library, whenever possible. For academic libraries, authorized users should include students, faculty, staff, and walk-ins. For public libraries, authorized patrons should include library cardholders as well as walk-ins. For special libraries, more restrictions may apply. For example, hospital library licenses may limit access only to physicians and perhaps nurses and other clinical staff.
9. *Authorized sites*. Licenses should define the institution as a single site and as broadly as possible, with one license covering all campuses, branches, or other physical locations.
10. *Remote access*. Academic library licenses generally allow offsite access by default, but public libraries may need to pay extra for offsite access for genealogy, business, and other e-resources that are also sold on the corporate or direct-to-consumer markets.
11. *Copying*. Licenses should permit patrons to print, download, and display reasonable amounts of licensed materials and include materials in course packs and reserves.

12. *Fair use*. Copyright law and fair use guidelines should supersede any license restrictions.
13. *Interlibrary loan*. The license should stipulate whether interlibrary loan is allowed and should exclude, to the extent possible, any restrictions on method or frequency of loans.
14. *Scholarly sharing*. Within reason, patrons should be allowed to share reasonable amounts of licensed materials with other individuals not affiliated with the library.
15. *Text/data mining*. Licenses should authorize patrons to conduct text and data mining on licensed materials, disseminate the results, and make results available for use by others.

Vendor Performance Obligations

16. *Level of service*. Vendors should guarantee prompt and effective customer service and technical support and should agree to e-resource uptime of 99 percent per year.
17. *Discovery*. Vendors should provide complete MARC records for all licensed materials and work with other vendors to integrate e-resources into discovery services.
18. *Patron privacy*. Vendors should guarantee the integrity of their systems against external attack, use industry-standard data encryption and other cybersecurity practices, and not disclose any personally identifiable patron information to third parties.
19. *Accessibility*. Vendors should commit to complying with the Americans with Disabilities Act (ADA) to ensure equitable access for patrons with disabilities. Librarians can ask for a Voluntary Product Accessibility Template to indicate the vendor's extent of compliance with U.S. federal Section 508 standards on Web accessibility.
20. *Means of access*. Licenses should specify authentication support for Internet protocol addresses, proxy servers, or library card numbers. Licenses should note if the vendor supports single sign-on authentication services such as Shibboleth or OpenAthens.
21. *Usage data*. Licenses should commit the vendor to providing usage data and should indicate whether usage reports comply with the most recent COUNTER standards.

NEGOTIATION

Negotiation is an important skill for every librarian who licenses or manages e-resources. Negotiation takes place when two or more parties (each with different needs and goals) seek out common ground to resolve a conflict or matter of mutual concern. Negotiation is fundamentally a dialogue that produces compromise. In the context of e-resource licensing, negotiators seek to reach equilibrium between (1) what the vendor charges and what the library is prepared to pay and (2) the ideal terms for the library versus the ideal terms for the vendor. To maximize value for the library and its patrons, librarians should negotiate the best possible license and business terms with vendors. Even better, individual libraries should combine forces, leveraging collective expertise and buying power to get better deals than any one library could negotiate on its own.

Collective Action

Collective action is the future of licensing. Instead of negotiating licenses independently, increasingly libraries are leveraging their collective buying power to not only get better deals but also transform the means by which e-resources are created and disseminated. In Europe, national consortia such as the UK's Jisc, Germany's Max Planck Society, and the Netherlands' UKB negotiated with major publishers to switch their licensing models from traditional subscriptions to "read-and-publish" models. Read-and-publish enables authors at participating institutions to make their works freely available online ("open access") at no cost to the authors. The CDL is pursuing similar efforts in the United States. Other major U.S. consortia include NERL, which negotiates on behalf of thirty core member libraries and over one hundred affiliates. State library systems such as the Florida Academic Library Services Cooperative negotiate and often subsidize e-resources for all in-state public and academic libraries. To achieve economies of scale, libraries should work in consortia whenever feasible.

Win-Win Negotiation

Librarians should try not to approach negotiation as a zero-sum game where libraries win and vendors lose or vice versa. This attitude is detrimental. Instead of framing the relationship as adversarial, library negotiators should strive for win-win scenarios in which everyone benefits and positive working relationships are sustained over time. The adversarial approach may prove effective in one-off situations, but it tends to burn bridges. In most cases, librarians and vendor representatives are in a long-term business relationship, so it behooves both parties to negotiate respectfully, candidly, and in good faith. The most successful negotiators improvise. They think outside the box, show humor, empathize, and persist. Above all, they find the leverage.

Leveraging Context

Prior to beginning negotiations in earnest, librarians should understand the vendor's priorities, strategies, and personalities. Vendors are not monolithic. They include profit-driven companies owned by private equity firms or publicly traded, family-owned businesses, and not-for-profit enterprises. Many focus on content, some focus on software and services, and others manage a diversified portfolio. Some compete directly with other vendors; others are the sole sources for certain e-resources. Each of these types has different interests and concerns. Each company also has its own distinctive corporate personality, commonly reflected in the methods and goals of its salesforce. By understanding vendors, librarians can deduce the most effective negotiation tactics for them to use. Think contextually! Is the vendor scrambling to meet a target and ready to cut deals to earn bonuses or boost its earnings report? Can the library entertain competing bids from rival vendors for similar e-resources? If the pricing model is population served, can the librarian convince the vendor to count only the group (e.g., French speakers or business students) likeliest to use the e-resource? Librarians can almost always negotiate a better deal than the first offer, but success requires spotting and using contextual cues. Box 15.3 offers some tips on negotiation.

Box 15.3 Negotiation as Process

1. Prepare.
    a. Determine your objectives and rank them in order of priority.
    b. Develop a timetable and stakeholder communication plan.
    c. If part of a team, figure out how to work together.
2. Research.
    a. Research the vendor, product, pricing models, and standard license terms in advance.
    b. Ask for a vendor organizational chart so you can ensure decision-makers are present.
    c. Ask for the vendor's desired timeline.
3. Meet.
    a. Frame the negotiation by spelling out what you expect to achieve.
    b. Listen more than you speak. Ask vendors to explain and justify their positions.
    c. Leverage data such as usage reports to support your arguments.
    d. Aim high. Do not be afraid to ask for your ideal solution.
4. Persist.
    a. Do not accept the first offer and do not be discouraged or frustrated by rejection.
    b. Compromise but get something you want in exchange for each concession you make.
    c. Be firm but polite (for as long as possible) and do not take things personally.
5. Achieve.
    a. Desired outcome? Get the agreement in writing. Verbal agreements are meaningless.
    b. Have a fallback plan if the desired outcome proves impossible to attain.

Relationship Management

Building and managing vendor relationships facilitates successful win-win negotiations. While some negotiators are uncomfortable with personalizing professional relationships—and it is fine to keep interactions strictly professional—some of the most successful negotiators build interpersonal rapport by identifying shared likes and experiences as an initial step toward finding common ground, as well as using humor appropriately to ease tensions. A confident demeanor, sensitivity to nuance, active listening, probing with open-ended questions, and trying to see situations from the other party's perspective are ingredients for successful negotiation.

Relationships also create opportunities for strategic partnerships and market influence, which translates into leverage. In a dynamic e-resources market, librarians can achieve greater success at the negotiation table by studying that market and knowing options and vendors well. Effective relationship management may lead to invitations to serve on focus groups and advisory boards to influence product development and strategies. Professional conferences, especially the Charleston Library Conference and the Electronic Resources and Libraries Conference, offer opportunities to meet vendor leadership and identify trends and new products. Librarians can use conferences and e-mail lists to network and benchmark with peers, learning how other libraries' negotiations are going and what license and business terms they have been able to negotiate.

Ethics

Notwithstanding the need for vendor relationships, librarians should beware of allowing personal rapport to influence business decisions. Librarians should not build relationships in ways that may violate professional ethics or government regulations, such as allowing vendors to furnish expensive dinners and drinks. Librarians should avoid the appearance of conflict of interest, even if they feel confident in their own independence. Appearances matter.

CONCLUSION

Electronic publishing and libraries are a multi-billion-dollar global industry. In 2012, the latest year for which figures were available, public libraries in the United States spent $200 million on e-resources. Meanwhile, U.S. academic libraries invested $2.8 billion in collections, mostly on e-resources. Most primary and secondary school libraries have much smaller budgets for collections (American Library Association 2015). Librarians tend to be uncomfortable with wheeling and dealing, but as implied by the American Library Association's (2008) core values libraries have a collective social responsibility to make information access as universal and as equitable as possible, for the public good. In societies where scholarship has been commodified, achieving this better world requires understanding market forces and working with vendors, to whom libraries funnel billions of dollars a year. Librarians should recognize their role in the information marketplace and embrace using that power for the benefit of the communities they serve. Serving their communities effectively enables libraries and librarianship to thrive.

REFERENCES

American Library Association. 2008. "Professional Ethics." Last modified January 22, 2008. http://www.ala.org/tools/ethics.

American Library Association. 2015. "Library Operating Expenditures: A Selected Annotated Bibliography." Last modified April 2015. http://www.ala.org/tools/libfactsheets/alalibraryfactsheet04.

California Digital Library. 2018. "Licensing Toolkit." Last modified May 15, 2018. https://www.cdlib.org/services/collections/toolkit/.

Canadian Research Knowledge Network. https://www.crkn-rcdr.ca/en/home.

Center for Postsecondary Research. n.d. *The Carnegie Classification of Institutions of Higher Education*. Indiana University. http://carnegieclassifications.iu.edu/.

Center for Research Libraries. 2018. "Model Licenses." Last modified October 24, 2018. http://liblicense.crl.edu/licensing-information/model-license/.

Charleston Library Conference. http://www.charlestonlibraryconference.com/.

CLOCKSS. https://clockss.org/.

COUNTER. https://www.projectcounter.org.

EBSCO. 2018. "2019 EBSCO Serials Price Projection Report." https://www.ebsco.com/blog/article/2019-ebsco-serials-price-projection-report.

Electronic Resources and Libraries. http://www.electroniclibrarian.com/.

Emery, Jill, and Graham Stone. 2013. "Techniques for Electronic Resource Management." *Library Technology Reports* 49 (2).

Florida Academic Library Services Cooperative. https://libraries.flvc.org/.

Jisc. https://www.jisc.ac.uk/.

Lewis, David W. 2016. *Reimagining the Academic Library*. Lanham, MD: Rowman & Littlefield.

LOCKSS. https://www.lockss.org/.

Max Planck Society. https://www.mpg.de/en.

Mering, Margaret. 2015. "Preserving Electronic Scholarship for the Future: An Overview of LOCKSS, CLOCKSS, Portico, CHORUS, and the Keepers Registry." *Serials Review* 41 (4): 260–65. https://doi.org/10.1080/00987913.2015.1099397.

National Information Standards Organization. 2019. "Shared Electronic Resource Understanding (SERU)." https://groups.niso.org/workrooms/seru/.

National Information Standards Organization. n.d. "Standardized Usage Statistics Harvesting Initiative (SUSHI)." https://www.niso.org/standards-committees/sushi/.

NorthEast Research Libraries Consortium. http://www.nerl.org/.

Ontario Council of University Libraries. https://ocul.on.ca/.

OpenAthens. https://openathens.org/.

Portico. https://www.portico.org/.

Shibboleth. Internet2. https://www.internet2.edu/products-services/trust-identity/shibboleth/.

TERMS: Techniques for Electronic Resource Management. https://library.hud.ac.uk/blogs/terms/.

UKB. https://www.ukb.nl/english.

SUGGESTED READINGS

Ashmore, Beth, Jill E. Grogg, and Jeff Weddle. 2012. *The Librarian's Guide to Negotiation: Winning Strategies for the Digital Age*. Medford, NJ: Information Today.

Three experienced library negotiators argue that (1) negotiation is a fundamental skill for information professionals, and (2) negotiation is hard, particularly for librarians without any formal training in the skill. In addition to theories and techniques of effective negotiating, the authors examine the influence of gender on negotiation.

Fisher, Roger, William Ury, and Bruce Patton. 2011. *Getting to Yes: Negotiating Agreement without Giving In*. 3rd ed. New York: Penguin.

Classic 1981 bestseller offering theory and techniques for principled win-win negotiation. The authors encourage negotiators to "separate the people from the problem," "focus on interests not positions," "invent options for mutual gain," "insist on using objective criteria," and "know your BATNA (Best Alternative to a Negotiated Agreement)."

Halaychik, Corey, and Blake Reagan. 2019. *Library Licensing: A Manual for Busy Librarians*. Santa Barbara, CA: Libraries Unlimited.

Coauthored by a librarian and a university procurement officer, this is an invigorating plunge into the storm-tossed waters of licensing. Halaychik and Reagan address licensing fundamentals, best practices, structuring a license, and negotiation, highlighting the importance of research and relationship building for achieving success.

Harris, Lesley Ellen. 2018. *Licensing Digital Content: A Practical Guide for Librarians*. 3rd ed. Chicago: ALA Editions.

From an attorney and copyright law expert, this guide demystifies licensing for librarians. Harris talks through the lingo and answers frequently asked questions. Although basic, this handbook is probably the single best introductory text to licensing e-resources.

Lipinski, Tomas A. 2013. *The Librarian's Legal Companion for Licensing Information Resources and Services*. Chicago: ALA Neal-Schuman.

A lawyer and library school administrator, Lipinski guides intermediate-to-advanced readers through the ins and outs of licensing. He deconstructs typical license agreements and answers 126 frequently asked questions. Lipinski also examines other license types, such as end-user license agreements and media and open-source licenses.

Ross, Sheri V. T., and Sarah W. Sutton. 2016. *Guide to Electronic Resource Management*. Santa Barbara, CA: Libraries Unlimited.

Ideal for newcomers. Ross and Sutton examine selection and assessment of e-resources, access and discovery, vendors and the marketplace, national information standards, and the implications of licensing for scholarly communication and open access writ large.

Chapter 16

Search Strategies for Online Sources

Melissa A. Wong

INTRODUCTION

Early online databases utilized complex search and retrieval systems, and individual researchers, for the most part, did not have the time or inclination to learn the necessary codes and formulas for successful searching. Now, these databases have migrated to the Web and, in place of highly structured search command languages, most of these services provide a point-and-click interface with a "fill in the box" search window designed for easy searching. Results are displayed on the screen for review and with a few more clicks, very often, the user will be connected to the full text of the source online, ready to be read, downloaded, imported into the user's own database, or printed.

One consequence of the change in the primary audience for electronic resources is a change in the way reference librarians use their expertise and understanding of databases. In the past, their role was to serve as an intermediary between the complex database search system and the person needing the information. Now it is to guide the user to the appropriate information resource and serve as coach and tutor for the end user conducting the search. In this role, an understanding of the concepts and mechanics of information retrieval is essential for reference librarians. It can be argued that it is more important to fully understand a search system when one is a coach because of the consequences of an error. If, as an experienced searcher, one misremembers a feature, the resulting search failure is readily apparent and can be corrected immediately. If one makes a similar error as a coach, the inexperienced user may not recognize the error and its implications, never understanding why the search failed.

This chapter examines the deep structure of databases and explains the concepts and mechanics of information retrieval. In addition, because librarians increasingly use free Internet sources for reference work, the chapter presents strategies for effectively searching the Web.

TYPES OF DATABASES

Many types of databases exist in libraries, including catalogs, indexes and abstracts, e-journal collections, and reference tools. Although similar search strategies can be used in all types of online resources, librarians should understand the different content found in these resources.

Catalogs

A *catalog*, sometimes referred to as an *online public access catalog*, *OPAC*, or *online catalog*, lists items available in a library's collection, including their location, call number, and circulation status (whether they are checked out or available). In addition to books, the catalog will list videos, music, audio books, and other materials. The catalog will list the periodicals a library subscribes to, although it will not list specific articles within a publication. In addition to maintaining a local catalog, libraries may participate in a regional, statewide, and/or national catalog, all of which exist to identify the materials available within specific libraries. Catalogs are discussed in more detail in Chapter 20.

Indexes and Abstracts

An *index* lists the contents of periodicals and sometimes other types of publications, such as conference proceedings and book chapters, in order to provide access to articles by author, title, and subject. If the database also contains short summaries of the articles, called abstracts, it is technically called an *abstract*, however in reality the term "index" is often used to refer to any database that is primarily intended to provide subject access to the contents of periodicals.

Because of the space limitations of the print format, indexes traditionally contained only the bibliographic record for an item. As they migrated to the Web, many began to offer not only citations and abstracts but also the full text of articles. These are often referred to as *full-text databases*, although they may not contain the full text of all the indexed articles due to copyright restrictions.

Indexes are created by commercial companies and sold to libraries; thus they reflect materials available somewhere in the bibliographic universe, not the holdings of a specific library. This can confuse patrons, since an index available on the library's Web page may list material not available at the library where the patron is searching.

Indexes typically cover a specific subject area. For example, *America: History and Life* indexes journals on the history of the United States and Canada, while *PsycINFO* covers literature in psychology and the behavioral and social sciences. In addition, indexes can be aimed at a particular audience. For example, both *PubMed* and *Consumer Health Complete* cover health and medicine, but *PubMed* is intended for physicians and biomedical researchers and indexes scholarly journals, while *Consumer Health Complete* is aimed at patients and caregivers and contains encyclopedia and magazine articles, book chapters, and videos. Indexes are discussed in more detail in Chapter 22.

E-Journal Collections

The term "e-journal" may be used to describe a journal that is published only online but usually refers to any online access to articles from any type of periodical, including journals, magazines, or trade publications. Therefore, although somewhat a misnomer to librarians who understand the differences between types of periodicals, the term "e-journal" is often used for electronic access to any kind of periodical.

Libraries have access to e-journals in many ways. In some cases, they subscribe to individual titles or bundles of titles directly from the publisher and access content through the publisher's website. In other cases, they subscribe to a collection like *JSTOR* that pulls together content from multiple publishers. Open access efforts have also provided online access to journal literature through single title websites, collections of open access titles like *PLOS*, and repositories for individual articles like *PubMed Central*.

Reference Tools

Libraries provide access to a wide range of reference tools in online formats, including encyclopedias, dictionaries, and collections like *Credo Reference* and *Oxford Reference*. These resources, many of which are discussed in detail in Chapters 17–31, can be free or subscription based and vary widely in their content.

STRUCTURE OF ONLINE DATABASES

Regardless of content, a *database* is a set of information items, called *entries*, formatted into defined structures with additional elements designed to assist retrieval. Entries can be a basic bibliographic citation with the authors' names and the source; it can be an enhanced citation including subject headings and abstracts; or it can be the full text of an article or a report. In addition to text, entries can be media items such as photos, musical selections, or video clips.

Each element of an entry, such as the author's name or the title of the work, is assigned to a *field*. Fields are defined, organized, and labeled according to the rules of the database. Typically, each field has a particular format for the elements within it. For example, an author's name is likely to be structured with the surname first, followed by a comma and some elements of the forenames. This structure for names is ubiquitous, appearing in the telephone directory, personal address books, endnotes, and the like. The more formal term for the kinds of structures and elements used to organize and index information is "metadata."

Metadata is "data about data" or "data associated with data." People encounter, use, manipulate, and create metadata many times every day. One example is the daily newspaper. Each part of the newspaper is assigned to a section and, in the world of print, a page. Online, articles are grouped into browsable categories such as "Local News," and each article has a particular URL. The section is a metadata element, as is the page number or URL. Each article is composed of many elements, and each element has a role to play in the display, arrangement, and retrieval of the article. For example, pieces of metadata attached to a headline drive the display so that the headline appears in a larger, bolder font than the body of the article; other pieces of metadata allow the newspaper's users to search for words in the headline and retrieve the needed article.

In the robust online databases found in libraries, the kinds and roles of metadata grow in complexity. This database design with metadata elements is the result of very deliberate decisions by database producers and has consequences for searching. Box 16.1 provides a made-up example of how a typical entry from a telephone directory could be structured in a database:

Box 16.1 Sample Database Entry

Record Number:	qs122333
Record Type:	residential
Surname:	Hunkle
Forename:	Walter
Middle Initial:	A
Title:	DDS
Street:	123 Maple Avenue
City:	Hometown
State:	NE
Telephone:	555-123-4567

From this simple example, one can see the kind of decision-making that is required to build a database with enough structure for it to be functional. The developers have to anticipate all the forms of the information and take into account all the possible variations.

Field labels allow for three essential tasks: sorting, formatting, and searching. The sorting can be imagined as a series of sets of slots. Each record will be sent through the appropriate slot at each level for further sorting. At each level, the sorting becomes finer. For example, in print directories, the initial sort would be at the record type, which determines the segment of the directory; the second level would be alphabetical by surname; the third level would be alphabetical by forename; and so on. Decisions about how to deal with compound surnames or hyphenated forenames would be built into the sorting software. In a print source, the arrangement of entries is static; in an online database, entries can be sorted dynamically, depending on the needs of the user. In this example, results could be displayed by name or by address.

Once the records are sorted, the field labels would be used to determine formatting. In a print directory, the name of a person or an organization might be in bold and left justified. Additional information, such as an address and phone number, might be set in lighter typeface and indented under the name. In an online database, the title of an article might appear at the top of the record in bold, with the author, source, and date of publication appearing underneath in a smaller typeface.

Finally, correctly populated fields of metadata enable accurate searching. When searching for a name in a print directory, users will first turn to the correct section

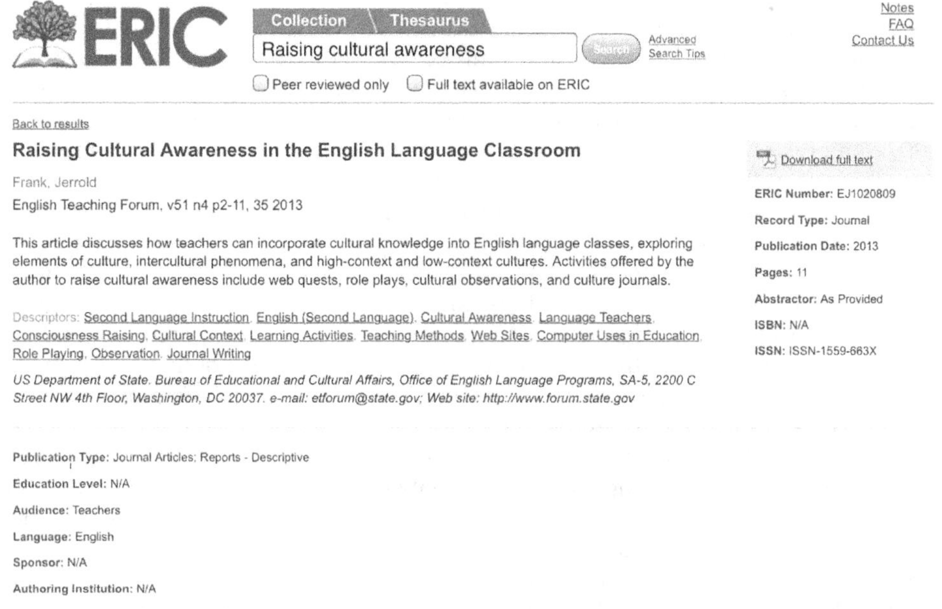

ERIC

Collection | Thesaurus

Raising cultural awareness

Search | Advanced Search Tips

Peer reviewed only | Full text available on ERIC

Notes
FAQ
Contact Us

Back to results

Raising Cultural Awareness in the English Language Classroom

Frank, Jerrold

English Teaching Forum, v51 n4 p2-11, 35 2013

This article discusses how teachers can incorporate cultural knowledge into English language classes, exploring elements of culture, intercultural phenomena, and high-context and low-context cultures. Activities offered by the author to raise cultural awareness include web quests, role plays, cultural observations, and culture journals.

Descriptors: Second Language Instruction, English (Second Language), Cultural Awareness, Language Teachers, Consciousness Raising, Cultural Context, Learning Activities, Teaching Methods, Web Sites, Computer Uses in Education, Role Playing, Observation, Journal Writing

US Department of State. Bureau of Educational and Cultural Affairs, Office of English Language Programs, SA-5, 2200 C Street NW 4th Floor, Washington, DC 20037. e-mail: etforum@state.gov; Web site: http://www.forum.state.gov

Download full text

ERIC Number: EJ1020809
Record Type: Journal
Publication Date: 2013
Pages: 11
Abstractor: As Provided
ISBN: N/A
ISSN: ISSN-1559-663X

Publication Type: Journal Articles; Reports - Descriptive
Education Level: N/A
Audience: Teachers
Language: English
Sponsor: N/A
Authoring Institution: N/A

Figure 16.1 Sample entry from ERIC. In this example of a database entry, some metadata fields, such as those for the descriptors, record type, and language, are labeled, while others, such as the article's title and author, are not.

of the directory and then search alphabetically, trusting that the entries are displayed in the correct order. In an online database, metadata allows one to search within specific fields, so one can search for books authored *by* Malala Yousafzai rather than books *about* her (or vice versa).

When applied to a database of bibliographic citations, this database-building process becomes very complex. Even a very basic metadata structure within an index has to deal with a huge variety of names, journal titles, languages, abbreviations, volume and issue numbering, and pagination. All of the relevant data elements must have a field that supports their form. For example, ISSN numbers need to be eight characters long, ISBN numbers ten (or thirteen, depending on the date of the item). To be of more use, the database structure must be explicitly built and labeled to support subject headings, descriptors, identifiers, and other elements that can be added to the record. Figure 16.1 shows a sample database entry.

THE ROLE OF THE SEARCH ENGINE AND INTERFACE

A database is a collection of information in the form of metadata. To be searchable, it needs a *search engine* that determines how search queries will be handled. Although the term "search engine" is usually used to describe tools that search the free Web, such as *Google* and *Bing*, any electronic database with a search feature could be said to have a search engine.

The *default search* determines how the database interprets queries and searches metadata to produce a list of results. For example, if a user enters a two-word query like "dog training," the default search determines if the two words are searched separately or as a phrase and whether a word variation like "dogs" would be retrieved. In an author search, the default might be to search the author field as well as related fields like those for editors and contributors in order to create a comprehensive list of a writer's works available in the database.

Since database vendors aim to create a product that can be searched by a non-expert, databases are given a search screen, or *interface*, through which users can access the database and determine the search capabilities of the system. The interface dictates how search boxes, limiters, and other features display on the screen. Many interfaces offer both a basic search screen with a single search box and an advanced search screen that provides numerous additional options. Interfaces may also offer features designed to make searching easier, such as autocomplete, where the database anticipates the word a user is typing and offers complete search terms, and a "did you mean?" spell-check. The interface will also dictate how results are displayed, such as listing entries in alphabetical, date, or relevance order, and placing facets, recommended search terms, or similar entries near the results list.

In some cases, a vendor creates a unique interface designed to maximize access to content in a specific database. However, interface design is a complex undertaking, and many vendors create a general interface that is used for most of the databases they offer; thus, online resources can look virtually the same but have very different content. This can be confusing for patrons, who may tell the librarian, "I've already searched there" when in fact they have unknowingly searched a different database than the one the librarian is recommending.

SEARCH STRATEGIES FOR DATABASES

The structure of a database and the search engine interact to create information retrieval possibilities. Most of the decisions a searcher makes are done to achieve an appropriate balance between precision and recall. "Precision" refers to getting *only* relevant material. "Recall" refers to getting *all* the relevant material. In a world where language is unambiguous and indexing is perfect, precision and recall would be the same, but in reality they are largely incompatible goals. For example, the word "program" represents multiple concepts, including a television show, an event held in the library, a playbill given at the theater, and a set of instructions for a computer. A search on the term "program" for one of these concepts will retrieve unrelated material that refers to other meanings of the term, reducing precision. On the other hand, because of synonyms and changes in terminology over time, there may be a multitude of terms to describe a single concept and searching for every possible term to achieve perfect recall is a demanding task. Whether aiming to improve precision or recall, some of the more important tools librarians can use for effective searching are field searching, controlled vocabulary, Boolean logic, proximity operators, and truncation and wildcards.

Field Searching

Because the parts of a record are organized in fields, it is possible to limit a search to a particular field. Common field searches include author, title, date, language, and type of publication or media. Some databases offer search options specific to a particular type of content. For example, *American National Biography* offers the option to search for people by place of birth or occupation, while *ProQuest Dissertations & Theses Global* has an option to search by advisor.

In most interfaces, the basic search screen offers few to no field search options, while the advanced search screen offers numerous field search options. In addition, when displaying a list of search results, many interfaces now offer the ability to refine one's results by *facets* such as type of publication and date. These facets are really field searches with a new look and name, designed to improve the search experience for novice users. Box 16.2 offers a practice activity using search fields.

Box 16.2 Activity: Using Search Fields

WorldCat is a free database of the holdings of libraries worldwide. Go to *WorldCat* at http://www.worldcat.org and review both the initial search screen and the advanced search screen. Next, try to locate the following:

1. A film version of the ballet *Coppelia*.
2. Spanish-language children's books about soccer.
3. Books about Amish life and culture published within the last five years.

Questions for Reflection and Discussion:

1. What search options are available on the initial search screen?
2. What additional search options are available on the advanced search screen?
3. What search options were most useful in the practice searches?
4. When looking at a list of results, what facets did *WorldCat* offer to further refine your search?

Controlled Vocabulary

Catalogs and indexes are meant to provide enhanced access to information resources by allowing users to identify resources on a particular topic. Therefore, records include *subject headings* that describe the content of the item. In theory, the person creating the catalog or index can label the item with any terms they want; however, this would get messy very quickly, as different people choose different terms to describe the same idea: for example, should the database use "Native Americans," the term commonly used in the United States; "First Nations," a term used primarily in Canada; or the more widely descriptive "indigenous"? Therefore, catalogs and indexes use a set of *controlled vocabulary* to create consistent subject headings.

A well-known set of controlled vocabulary used by most libraries in the United States to catalog books is the *Library of Congress Subject Headings*. However, there are other sets of controlled vocabulary. For example, *PubMed* uses *Medical Subject Headings* (*MeSH*). Just as *MeSH* provides a controlled vocabulary more appropriate for medical literature, most indexes use a controlled vocabulary that provides more nuanced access to the literature of a particular field.

A master list of the controlled vocabulary that shows the definitions of terms and the relationships between them is called the *thesaurus*. Thesauri are arranged in a hierarchy of broader and narrower terms that allow the user to identify the most precise term for their topic; *see* and *use* references direct users to preferred entries. Box 16.3 shows a hierarchy of terms that could be created for controlled vocabulary related to fruit.

Box 16.3 Example of a Thesaurus Entry for Fruit

Fruit

- Chinese Gooseberry—*use* Kiwifruit
- Citrus
  - Grapefruit
  - Lemons
  - Limes
  - Oranges
- Eggfruit—*use* Lucuma
- Kiwifruit—*use for* Chinese Gooseberry
- Kumquats
- Lucuma—*use for* Eggfruit
- Pome
  - Apples
  - Pears

In this case, "fruit" is the broader term that encompasses "citrus" and other types of fruit; narrower subject headings exist for specific types of citrus and pome fruit, while *see* references direct the user from the popular term "Chinese gooseberry" to the preferred term "kiwifruit."

In an online database, a link to the thesaurus can usually be found from both the basic and advanced search screens. Box 16.4 provides a practice activity using thesauri to identify controlled vocabulary.

Box 16.4 Activity: Using a Database Thesaurus

The *Educational Resources Information Clearinghouse* (*ERIC*) is an index to books, articles, conference proceedings, and other literature in the field of education. Go to *ERIC* at http://www.eric.ed.gov and click on "Thesaurus." Use the thesaurus to answer the following questions:

1. When searching *ERIC*, what is the difference between "home schooling" and "home instruction"?
2. How does the *ERIC* thesaurus define "learning disabilities"?

Your library may also offer access to *ERIC* through a subscription-based service from EBSCO, ProQuest, or another vendor. Although the thesaurus will be the same as in the free version, the vendor may offer a richer thesaurus browsing experience. Try the same searches again. How does your experience differ?

PubMed is an index to literature in the field of medicine. Go to *PubMed* at http://www.pubmed.gov and click on "MeSH Database" to access the thesaurus. Use the thesaurus to answer the following questions:

1. What is the official subject heading for a sore throat?
2. Look up "myocardial infarction." What is the broader term? What are the narrower terms?
3. In *MeSH*, what is the preferred subject heading for "learning disabilities"? How does the definition compare to the one in *ERIC*?

Boolean Logic

Boolean logic is a form of symbolic logic named after George Boole, the 19th-century English mathematician who developed it. Boolean logic uses common words as logical operators to create and manipulate sets. Some of these operators are *and*, *or*, and *not*.

The Boolean operator *or* creates a set by making an item eligible for inclusion if it meets at least *one* of the stated criteria: an item would be included in a set if it meets the condition A *or* the condition B *or* the condition C, and so on. In creating a set of citrus fruit, one might use the following Boolean string: oranges *or* grapefruit *or* lemons *or* limes. This set is more inclusive than a set that has a single criterion for acceptance, for example, oranges. The Venn diagram for *or* is shown in Figure 16.2.

The Boolean operator *and* creates a more restrictive set by requiring that an item meet *both* the conditions stated: an item would be included only if it meets condition A *and* condition B. One could use the Boolean *and* to create a set containing only those books written by Isaac Asimov that contained the word "robot."

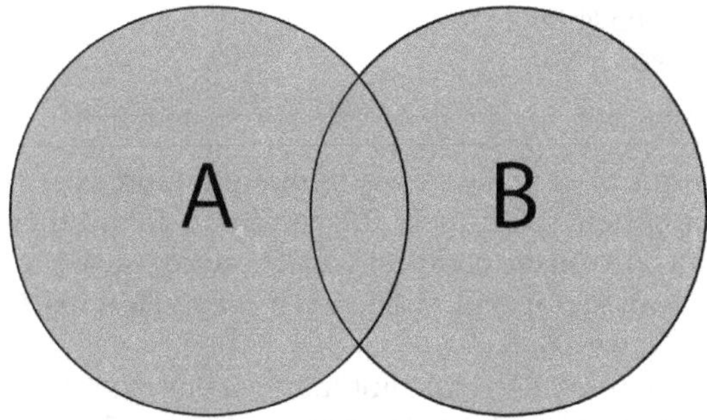

Figure 16.2 A Venn diagram for the Boolean operator *or*. Each circle represents database entries containing a search term; both circles are shaded to show that all the items from either search term would be retrieved by the search "A or B."

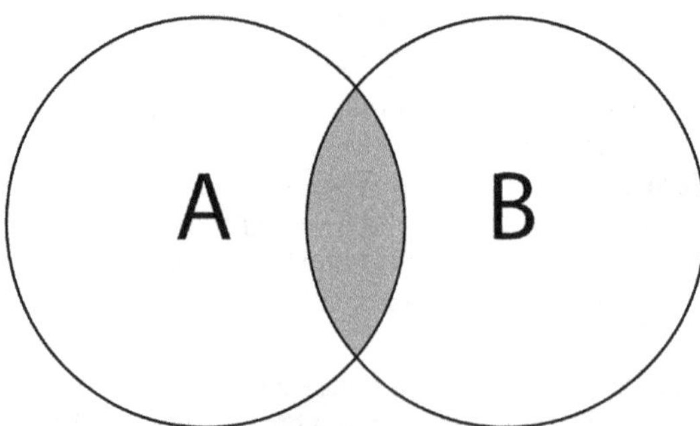

Figure 16.3 A Venn diagram for the Boolean operator *and*. Each circle represents database entries containing a search term; the shaded area where the two circles overlap represents the items that would be retrieved by the search "A and B."

The Boolean string would be "Isaac Asimov *and* robot." The Venn diagram for *and* is shown in Figure 16.3.

The Boolean *or* and *and* are concepts that the beginning searcher may have trouble keeping straight, because the use of the terms is at odds with ordinary usage. In ordinary usage, "or" implies a choice where to select one item is to exclude the others, whereas the Boolean *or* expands and includes all of the items. For example, in a restaurant a breakfast order may include the option of toast or a muffin or a bagel. Here, the English "or" means the customer may select one item from the list. In a database, the same search string would be a request to retrieve any articles that used at least one of these terms (or, all the bread in the restaurant!).

In ordinary usage, "and" adds all the items joined by the "and," while the Boolean *and* selects only items that include all the named elements. In a restaurant that allows one to choose one item from column A *and* one from column B *and* one from column C, the result will be a plate that contains three items. The result of a Boolean search for A *and* B *and* C is one item that contains all three elements, an unlikely dish in any restaurant. Box 16.5 also illustrates the use of the Boolean *and* compared to ordinary usage.

Box 16.5 When Librarians Shop for Groceries

If you send a reference librarian to the store to buy sugar and flour and eggs, they will return with a cake.

The Boolean operator *not* is also used to make a more restrictive set of results. It first creates a set of items that meet the condition A and then *removes* from the set those items that also meet condition B. To create a set of trees that are not deciduous, the Boolean string would be "trees *not* deciduous." The Venn diagram for *not* is shown in Figure 16.4.

Boolean operators can be used in combination. For example, a librarian seeking articles about reference services to children might use the search "reference *and* children *or* youth." However, this search could be interpreted by the database in one of two ways, leading to two very different sets of results:

- If the database reads the search string from left to right, it will create a set of articles about "reference *and* children" and then, based on the *or* statement, add

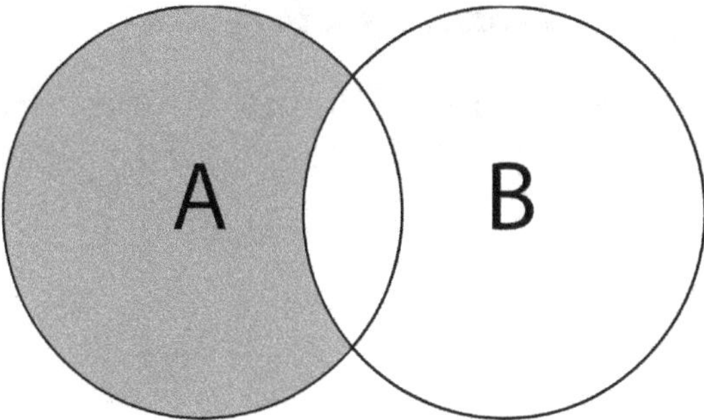

Figure 16.4 A Venn diagram for the Boolean operator *not*. Each circle represents database entries containing a search term; the shaded area in circle A shows the items that would be retrieved by the search "A not B."

all the articles about "youth." This will produce results in which a large number of articles are about youth but not necessarily about reference services for youth.

- If the database prioritizes *or* searches first, it will create a set of articles about "children *or* youth" and then limit that set to only the articles that mention "reference" based on the *and* statement. This will produce a small set of results that is on topic for the librarian's needs.

Extending this example, the search string "children *or* youth *and* reference" would produce different results because the order of operations has been changed. Librarians can use the help menu in a database to determine how a database will interpret a search query with multiple Boolean operators. However, a more efficient method is to tell the database which action should be done first by placing it in parentheses, a process called *nesting*. In this example, the correct search query would be "reference *and* (children *or* youth)" or "(children *or* youth) *and* reference." Box 16.6 provides practice using Boolean logic.

Box 16.6 Activity: Predicting the Results of Boolean Operators

Consider these statements:

- (mice *or* rats) *and* pets
- (mice *or* rats) *not* pets
- mice *or* rats *and* pets
- (mice *and* rats) *and* extermination
- (mice *or* rats) *and* extermination
- (mice *or* rats) *and* food
- (mice *or* rats) *and* food *not* extermination

Questions for Reflection and Discussion:

1. What kind of documents would be retrieved with each set of statements?
2. Imagine that a patron is interested in having a small rodent, such as a mouse or hamster, as a pet but had not yet selected what type of animal to get. What search string(s) would you recommend?

Proximity Operators

Proximity operators enable the user to state how close search terms should appear to one another. The most common use of proximity operators is to create a phrase, such as "gun control" or "eating disorders." In almost all databases, phrase searches are created by enclosing the search terms in quotation marks.

Proximity operators can also be used to indicate that search terms should be found "with" or "near" one another, if not actually adjacent. Although not all databases allow for this kind of search, in those that do, typically *with* (or *w*) indicates that words should be found in the order indicated, while *near* (or *n*) indicates that words can be found in any order. A combination of the operator and a number are used to indicate how close the words should be. Examples follow:

- "electronic health records"—locates articles that use the exact phrase "electronic health records"
- electronic *and* "health records"—locates articles that use the exact phrase "health records" and the term "electronic" but not necessarily together
- electronic *w5* "health records"—locates articles with the term "electronic" followed by the exact phrase "health records" within five words (e.g., in a title like "As Hospitals Move into the Electronic Era, Health Records Go Digital")
- electronic *n5* "health records"—locates articles with the term "electronic" and the exact phrase "health records" within five words of one another (e.g., in a title like "Hospitals Move Health Records Online in Electronic Patient Care Systems")

Using quotation marks to create phrases is one of the simplest and most powerful tools in a librarian's search arsenal. The *with* and *near* operators are less common in everyday searching but can be useful tools when searching the full text of books or other data-rich resources.

Truncation and Wildcards

Truncation refers to shortening a word or eliminating some characters from a longer term to pick up variants. For example, when a user searches for the truncated term "librar*," the database will retrieve items that contain the term "library" or "libraries" or "librarians" or "librarian" or "librarianship." The truncation symbol varies from system to system, although the asterisk (*) is the most commonly used.

Truncation can take place to the left, to the right, or in the middle of the core characters. Truncation can also involve the replacement of several characters or a single character. In the previous example, because the truncation occurred to the right of the core characters, it is called right-hand truncation. If the truncation occurs to the left of the core characters, it is left-hand truncation. For example, left-hand truncation with the core characters "ship" would retrieve records containing the terms "librarianship," "guardianship," "statesmanship," "leadership," "starship," and more.

When truncation occurs in the middle of the core characters, it is called a *wildcard*. An example would be "Labo#r" where the "#" is the wildcard symbol. If this were a single-character substitution system, in which the symbol can stand for either nothing or a single character, this term would pick up items that contained the terms "labor" or "labour." If it were a multiple-character system, in which the symbol can stand for more than one alternate character, the set could include "labor," "labour," "laborer," and "labourer."

Frequently, systems allow one to select a single-character or multiple-character truncation or wildcard method in order to tailor the search to one's needs. Truncation and wildcard searching allow the user to acknowledge and compensate for some amount of uncertainty in the source information, as well as for other, more predictable variations in the database. At the same time, the searcher must take care to avoid unwanted hits, such as "readjustment" from a search for a truncated term such as "read*".

While the Boolean operators *and*, *or*, and *not* are used consistently in most databases, the symbols used for proximity, truncation, and wildcards vary widely. Librarians can use the help menu of a database to determine the correct symbols to use. Boxes 16.7 and 16.8 provide practice activities related to searching.

Box 16.7 Activity: Using Boolean Operators

GreenFILE is an index to scholarly journals and government documents in the environmental sciences. Go to *GreenFILE* at https://www.ebscohost.com/academic/greenfile and search for information about one or more of the following:

1. environmentally friendly building materials
2. toxins from mines
3. simple living

Questions for Reflection and Discussion:

1. What Boolean search strings were most helpful for finding information about each topic?
2. Did you try other search strategies and if so what strategies were most helpful?

Box 16.8 Activity: Learning about a New Database

An important skill for librarians is the ability to analyze a new database and learn to search it effectively. You can do this by reading promotional literature from the publisher, reading the help screens, and conducting practice searches. For this activity, go to your library's list of databases and select an unfamiliar database.

1. Use the help menu to locate a description of the database. What kind of information can be found in this database? Who is the intended audience? What kinds of patrons would benefit from using this database?
2. Review the basic and advanced search screens. What kinds of searches can be conducted? Are there any search options that are unique or particularly appropriate for the topics covered by this database? What operators and search limits are available?
3. Try some practice searches. Are the results what you expected? If not, can you determine why?
4. Do you like this interface? Why or why not?

SEARCHING THE WEB

While the online databases offered by libraries are highly structured compilations of carefully vetted information, the Web is not. Anyone can publish on the Internet, either through the creation of a formal Web page or blog or by posting to one of the innumerable websites dedicated to discussion or user-generated content. No process exists to vet this information as accurate, reliable, or up to date; thus, high-quality information exists side by side urban legends, rumors, half-truths, and deliberately misleading information. And, while individual websites may be well curated and organized, the Web as a whole does not have an overarching organizational system designed to facilitate information retrieval.

Despite these drawbacks, the Web can be an excellent source of information for almost any need. Educational organizations, government agencies, companies, organizations, and even individual authors provide free, reliable information on almost any topic imaginable, sometimes in more detail than one can find in commercially published sources. Librarians should be familiar with websites that are relevant to their patrons' needs, since such sites can ease the search for reliable information online. Chapters 17 to 31 recommend many such sites on a variety of topical areas.

Search Engines

Search engines crawl the Web on a regular basis, following links and indexing Web pages as well as resources like pdf documents, images, and videos. The goal of most search engines is to index as much of the Web as possible, although some search engines will focus on selected types of information and no search engine has indexed the entire Web. (The phrase "deep Web" or "hidden Web" is often used to refer to pages a search engine cannot access, such as those behind corporate firewalls or within proprietary databases.)

When a user queries a search engine, the search engine uses its vast index of the Web to present the user with a list of results. Because the Web is so extensive and searches can easily return thousands and even millions of results, search engines attempt to rank results so that the first few are the ones most likely to meet a user's need. The exact algorithms used to rank a set of results are a closely guarded secret for any search engine, but are generally based on a combination of the presence and placement of keywords and popularity, with popularity measured by how often other high-quality sites link to the particular site.

In many cases, these algorithms do deliver highly relevant results. At the same time, they can deliver results that are biased or exclusionary. Bess Sadler and Chris Bourg (2015) point out that using popularity as measured by how often other sites link to a given site "creates a majority-rules definition of relevance that masquerades as neutrality." In addition, savvy Web designers who understand how search engines identify and rank sites can use metadata and cross-linking to influence search engine rankings. Organizations and businesses routinely use this process, called *search engine optimization*, to push their results to the top of a search. Researcher Safiya Noble (2012, 2018) has identified how search algorithms are not neutral but reflect and replicate the biases inherent in society, prioritizing search results that reinforce stereotypical depictions of women, people of color, and other marginalized communities.

Search engines are free to users, and the companies that provide them are often supported by advertising revenue. In addition to websites retrieved from the search engine's index, a results page will display paid advertisements, often designed to look very similar to actual search results. Although these ads may be labeled as such, research shows that 50 percent or more of users have difficulty distinguishing between ads and organic search results (Charlton 2016; Vincent 2015). Even "organic" results may prioritize the search engine's other products and partners, such as video, review, and shopping sites that are themselves supported by advertising (Noble 2018).

Google indexes billions of Web pages and features a simple search interface with a single box for inputting text. The search results include links and images, ads, search suggestions, and the option to limit by facets such as images, videos, news, and shopping. Increasingly, *Google* will go beyond offering links to websites to provide direct access to the information it thinks the user needs. For example, a search for "Pantages Theatre" results in an address, map, and schedule of upcoming shows along with links to the official homepage and other sites with information about the theater. *Google*'s SafeSearch option allows the user to block potentially objectionable content from search results.

Bing also features a simple search box but has a more elaborate homepage that features an image of the day, complete with embedded, relevant searches to inspire browsing and links to current news stories. Search results include links and images, ads, search suggestions, and in some cases a sidebar of related information. *Bing* has a SafeSearch option as well as a Search History feature.

DuckDuckGo bills itself as a search engine that does not track users. A simple search box provides recommendations as users search. Search results include a brief definition of the topic with an image, links, clearly labeled ads, and the option to limit to videos or images. A particularly useful feature of *DuckDuckGo* is that in searches for specific places, such as the Pantages Theatre, it labels the official site in the list of results.

Specialized search engines provide access to niche material on the Web. The *Wayback Machine* provides access to archived copies of Web pages and can be useful for locating material that no longer exists in its original location, such as a Web page that was taken down or past versions of pages. *Wolfram Alpha* is a computational search engine that provides statistics, facts, and other numerical data rather than links to external pages. A Source link at the bottom of the results provides citations for and links to source material. Some search engines provide information of interest to specific communities. For example, Noble (2018, 151) highlights *Blackbird* as a search engine that attempts to surface material relevant to the Black community. Librarians interested in identifying additional specialized search engines can find numerous such lists on the Web (e.g., Hines n.d.).

SEARCH STRATEGIES FOR THE WEB

Most search engines offer a simple search box, and it may not be obvious whether one can use Boolean operators and other advanced search strategies. The lack of an advanced search page or help menu may further stymie librarians accustomed to the more complex search possibilities offered by databases. However, most search engines do offer some advanced search options; one can often find more detailed information by searching for the name of the search engine and a phrase like "search help" or "advanced search" (e.g., Bing search help, Google advanced search).

Boolean Operators and Truncation

Search engines typically permit the use of Boolean operators. The most common strategy is to use quotation marks to create a phrase (e.g., "gun control"). In addition, usually the *or* operator can be used, while a dash is used to eliminate results, similar to the *not* operator (e.g., bats -baseball). Truncation is often applied without any express action on the part of the searcher. Each search term is matched to a set of words with the same stem and all the variants are queried in the search engine's index.

Limiting by Site and URL

Each address on the Web must be registered to assure its uniqueness, and naming conventions govern the appearance of the domain name or URL. In the United States, the top-level domain names have one of several main. endings: .edu, .org, .com, .gov, .net, and so on. Each ending lets the user anticipate the kind of organization or service that is available through that website. Although the categories are not absolute, in general, ".edu" is used for educational organizations, ".org" for nonprofit organizations, ".com" for commercial sites, ".gov" for units of government, and ".net" for organizations that support Internet access and Web services.

In other parts of the world, there are similar patterns governing domain name conventions. In countries outside of the United States, domain names generally include an abbreviation for the country of origin as well as an element designating the kind of service provider. For example, the URL for a commercial site in Australia might look like http://mycompany.com.au.

Many search engines allow one to limit a search to a domain name or URL. For example, in *Google*, the search "admissions site:.edu" would limit the search to Web pages from educational institutions, while the search "flu prevention site:cdc.gov" would limit the search to Web pages from the Centers for Disease Control and Prevention.

Other Types of Search Limits

In addition, search engines offer specialized search options for specific types of information. For example, *Bing*'s image search returns only image files and includes the option to limit by attributes such as color, size, and usage rights.

Google's shopping option returns only items available for purchase and includes the option to filter results by price, color, brand, and other features.

PUTTING IT ALL TOGETHER: LOCATING INFORMATION ONLINE

Searching for information online is a complex process that involves the following steps:

1. Conducting the reference interview
2. Deciding where to search
3. Developing a search query
4. Searching, revising, and searching again
5. Saving and managing search results

Conducting the Reference Interview

The first step in any successful reference transaction is a reference interview to ensure the librarian accurately understands the patron's information need. Strategies for a successful reference interview are given in Chapter 3. In addition, some chapters in Part II of this book provide tips for particular types of reference interviews, such as those for readers' advisory (Chapter 21), business (Chapter 28), and legal (Chapter 31) questions.

Deciding Where to Search

Based on information gained in the reference interview, the librarian selects an appropriate resource to search for information. If the patron needs a basic explanation of a scientific term, the most appropriate place might be an online encyclopedia. If the patron needs scholarly journal articles, the most appropriate place would be an index or open-source article repository. If the patron is seeking a list of all the television adaptations of the show *The Office*, a fan site or *Wikipedia* might provide the most comprehensive, up-to-date answer. In selecting an appropriate resource, librarians should consider not only the depth and amount of information needed but also the age and educational level of the patron, the subject of the query, the need for a specific format such as a book or DVD, and whether the patron needs an immediately available item or can wait for an interlibrary loan.

Developing a Search Query

Once the librarian has selected a resource, they will need to create a search query. This can be done by brainstorming keywords or using the thesaurus to identify appropriate controlled vocabulary and linking terms into a query using Boolean operators, truncation, and so forth. In addition, the librarian should consider whether the database offers any limiters or search features that would be useful for the given query.

For example, if the patron is searching for information about whether elephants show grief when a member of the group dies, a brainstormed list of search terms might include "elephants," "grief," "mourning," "emotion," "death," "die," and "dying." These could be combined into a simple search string such as *elephants and death and grief* or a more complicated search string such as *elephants and (death or die or dying) and (grief or mourn* or emotion)*.

A few quick searches in the selected database can be helpful in developing a search query. One can put in a few keywords to confirm that the database is likely to be productive and get a rough estimate of the quantity of available materials. Scanning a few records can point the way to improving the search; one record may have a subject heading that encapsulates the search topic more effectively than the keywords with which one began.

Searching, Revising, and Searching Again

Once searching begins in earnest, one should keep in mind that the first search is rarely the best search. Rather, it represents a starting point from which the librarian can critically evaluate search results for clues about improving the search. A search that brings back only a few results may indicate that the librarian has not yet identified the best search terms; the librarian can continue to brainstorm alternate vocabulary or consult the thesaurus for subject headings. The librarian should also consider whether a broader search term or even another database would yield better results. On the other hand, a search that brings back an overwhelming number of results may indicate that the librarian needs to narrow the search through the use of additional terms or database limiters.

Librarians can also use a strategy of *citation pearl growing* to build a set of relevant results. Once an on-topic record has been located, it can serve as a jumping-off point for further searches. Most obviously, librarians can use the subject headings from one record to identify additional relevant records. Many databases will suggest "articles like this one" to assist patrons in identifying promising material. Librarians can also run additional searches for selected authors or within likely journals or other publications.

Librarians can also remind patrons to mine footnotes and bibliographies to identify additional materials on their topic. A few databases will assist patrons in doing this, most notably *Web of Science*, which allows one to trace articles through footnotes going both forward and backward in time. *Google Scholar* is also working to link articles through citations, as are some databases from EBSCO and ProQuest.

In the case of complex searches, it may be helpful to keep notes about the search process. Inevitably, as the search for an elusive piece of information progresses, one forgets where one has searched and which search terms have been tried. Jotting down the databases and search queries that have been used can prevent frustration and the potential for unwittingly repeating unsuccessful searches. Some databases offer a *search history* feature that allows the user to not only see a list of all searches that have been attempted but also repeat searches, combine search queries, and compile sets of results from multiple searches.

Saving and Managing Search Results

For simple queries, such as the definition of a word, it may be sufficient for the librarian to point to an entry on the screen or help the patron print a brief record. In the case of more complex searches, the librarian may want to assist the patron in saving records for later use. Most databases allow the user to collect records in a "folder" to print, e-mail, or download at the conclusion of a search session or to create an account where they can save searches and collect records over time. Librarians can also assist patrons in using reference management tools like *EndNote* and *Zotero* to collect and manage citations.

HELPING PATRONS LOCATE INFORMATION ONLINE

Although librarians can use their extensive knowledge of the library's resources to select an appropriate database or reference tool for a given topic, patrons may not have the necessary experience to do the same. Therefore, one of the responsibilities of reference librarians is to present the library's resources in such a way that patrons can identify where to search for information.

Many libraries provide an alphabetical or subject-based list of databases. These pages can direct patrons to useful resources, although they rely on the patron to browse pages and lists to identify the most appropriate places to search. Lists that combine catalogs, indexes, reference tools, and reliable websites provide more comprehensive access to the library's resources, but as lists grow they become more cumbersome to use. In addition, such pages may require that library users understand the difference between a catalog, index, and reference tool and what kind of information can be found in each.

Another option for helping users is librarian-authored guides. These guides, often devoted to a particular topic, list recommended reference tools and indexes and provide search strategies and general advice germane to the topic. In addition to research topics, guides can cover readers' advisory, citation styles, and even information on local services. A popular product for authoring Web-based guides is *LibGuides*, a service that hosts a library's guides and provides templates to ease the process of organizing and formatting entries, linking to databases and websites, and updating content as needed. In addition, *LibGuides* allows librarians to reuse content across multiple guides, share content with colleagues, and integrate multimedia and social media.

Recognizing that lists and guides may not be enough to enable patrons to make full use of the library's resources, librarians are turning to federated search and discovery tools to provide patrons with a single search box through which to search multiple resources, including the library's catalog, subscription databases, local repositories and digital collections, and even selected websites. As Michael Levine-Clark, John McDonald, and Jason S. Price (2014, 249) note, "Searching across multiple resources at once makes it much easier to find information, especially for students who might not understand the difference between an article index and a library catalog, and even for more experienced researchers who may not know the best subject-specific resource for locating articles. With the growth of interdisciplinary research, discovery services make it easier to gather information from a variety of disciplinary viewpoints at once."

The technology underlying federated searching and discovery systems differs, resulting in different search experiences for patrons. In federated searching, the patron's query is relayed to selected databases; each database is searched and a list of results is displayed to the user. (In some cases, a list of the databases searched is displayed with the number of results found, an attempt to simplify the presentation of results, although this requires the patron to enter each database to see the list of actual results.) Early federated search efforts suffered from slowness and an inability to de-duplicate or rank records, resulting in a potentially overwhelming list of disorganized results (Wang and Mi 2012, 232–33). More recent federated searching products have increased search speed and provided improvements in de-duplication as well as more advanced search features and faceted results (Wang and Mi 2012, 234). Currently available products include *360 Search*.

Discovery services, on the other hand, create an index of content and associated metadata from selected sources, allowing for a richer, faster search experience as well as better de-duplication and results ranking. As a result, most libraries have moved from federated search to discovery systems. Current products include *EBSCO Discovery*, *Primo*, *Summon*, and *WorldCat Discovery*.

CONCLUSION

Today's modern databases offer robust search options for patrons and librarians alike. For patrons, interface designers offer simple search boxes combined with features like auto-complete, spell-check, and faceted searching that enable even novice searchers to refine their search results. For librarians, these same interfaces permit the use of sophisticated strategies like Boolean operators, truncation, and wildcard searching that can improve the precision and recall of searches.

REFERENCES

Charlton, Graham. 2016. "Do 50% of Adults Really Not Recognize Ads in Search Results?" *Search Engine Watch*. Last modified April 26, 2016. https://searchenginewatch.com/2016/04/27/do-50-of-adults-really-not-recognise-ads-in-search-results/?_ijcid=1530034791870|19.663421614.1530034759384.6b0959b8.

Hines, Kristi. n.d. "40 Advanced and Alternative Search Engines." *Kissmetrics*. https://blog.kissmetrics.com/alternative-search-engines/.

Levine-Clark, Michael, John McDonald, and Jason S. Price. 2014. "The Effect of Discovery Systems on Online Journal Usage: A Longitudinal Study." *Insights* 27 (3): 249–56.

Noble, Safiya Umoja. 2012. "Missed Connections: What Search Engines Say About Women." *Bitch* 54 (Spring). https://safiyaunoble.files.wordpress.com/2012/03/54_search_engines.pdf.

Noble, Safiya Umoja. 2018. *Algorithms of Oppression: How Search Engines Reinforce Racism*. NY: New York University.

Sadler, Bess, and Chris Bourg. 2015. "Feminism and the Future of Library Discovery." *code{4}lib Journal* 28 (April 15). http://journal.code4lib.org/articles/10425

Wang, Yongming, and Jia Mi. 2012. "Searchability and Discoverability of Library Resources: Federated Search and Beyond." *College & Undergraduate Libraries* 19 (2–4): 229–45.

Vincent, James. 2015. "Teens Can't Tell the Difference Between Google Ads and Search Results." *The Verge*. Last modified November 20, 2015. https://www.theverge.com/2015/11/20/9768350/google-ads-search-results-ofcom

LIST OF SOURCES

360 Search. Ann Arbor, MI: ProQuest. http://www.proquest.com/products-services/360-Search.html. Subscription required.

America: History and Life. Ipswich, MA: EBSCO. https://www.ebscohost.com/academic/america-history-and-life. Subscription required.
American National Biography 1999. New York: Oxford University Press. Supplements, 2000–. http://www.anb.org. Subscription required.
Bing. http://www.bing.com/.
Blackbird. http://www.blackbirdhome.com/.
Consumer Health Complete. Ipswich, MA: EBSCO. https://www.ebscohost.com/public/consumer-health-complete. Subscription required.
Credo Reference. Credo Reference. http://search.credoreference.com. Subscription required.
DuckDuckGo. https://duckduckgo.com/.
EBSCO Discovery Service. Ipswich, MA: EBSCO. https://www.ebscohost.com/discovery .Subscription required.
EndNote. Philadephia: Thomson Reuters. http://endnote.com/.
ERIC. Washington, DC: Institute of Education Sciences. http://eric.ed.gov. Available online from EBSCO, ProQuest, and other vendors.
Google. http://www.google.com.
Google Scholar. https://scholar.google.com/.
GreenFILE. Ipswich, MA: EBSCO. https://www.ebscohost.com/academic/greenfile.
JSTOR. Ann Arbor, MI: JSTOR. http://www.jstor.org/. Subscription required.
LibGuides. Miami, FL: Springshare. https://springshare.com/libguides/. Subscription required.
Library of Congress Subject Headings. Library of Congress. http://authorities.loc.gov/.
Medical Subject Headings. National Library of Medicine. https://www.nlm.nih.gov/mesh/.
Oxford Reference. New York: Oxford. http://www.oxfordreference.com/. Subscription required.
PLOS. https://www.plos.org/.
Primo. Des Plaines, IL: Ex Libris. https://www.exlibrisgroup.com/products/primo-library-discovery/. Subscription required.
ProQuest Dissertations & Theses Global. Ann Arbor, MI: ProQuest. http://www.proquest.com/products-services/pqdtglobal.html. Subscription required.
PsycINFO. Washington, DC: American Psychological Association. http://www.apa.org/pubs/databases/psycinfo/. Subscription required.
PubMed. http://www.ncbi.nlm.nih.gov/pubmed.
PubMed Central. http://www.ncbi.nlm.nih.gov/pmc/.
Summon. Des Plaines, IL: Ex Libris. https://www.exlibrisgroup.com/products/summon-library-discovery/. Subscription required.
Wayback Machine. Internet Archive. https://archive.org/index.php.
Web of Science. Philadelphia: Thomson Reuters. http://wokinfo.com/. Subscription required.
Wikipedia. https://www.wikipedia.org/.
Wolfram Alpha. http://www.wolframalpha.com/.
WorldCat. http://www.worldcat.org.
WorldCat Discovery. Dublin, OH: OCLC. https://www.oclc.org/en/worldcat-discovery.html. Subscription required.
Zotero. Corporation for Digital Scholarship. https://www.zotero.org/.

SUGGESTED READINGS

Beall, Jeffrey. 2011. "Academic Library Databases and the Problem of Word-Sense Ambiguity." *The Journal of Academic Librarianship* 37 (1): 64–69.

Beall looks at how word-sense ambiguity, or the fact that one word can have multiple meanings, affects precision in searching as well as efforts like machine translation and text mining. This is a thoughtful exploration of a contemporary problem in information management.

Brown, Christopher C., and Suzanne S. Bell. 2018. *Librarian's Guide to Online Searching: Cultivating Database Skills for Research and Instruction.* 5th ed. Santa Barbara, CA: Libraries Unlimited.

Brown and Bell provide an excellent guide to online databases and search strategies. Following early chapters on search strategies, the authors cover core titles and discipline-specific search strategies for the sciences, social sciences, humanities, statistics, and more.

Noble, Safiya Umoja. 2018. *Algorithms of Oppression: How Search Engines Reinforce Racism.* New York: New York University.

Noble demonstrates how search engine rankings are influenced by bias within search algorithms as well as advertising. An important read for all information professionals.

Pope, Julia T., and Robert P. Holley. 2011. "Google Book Search and Metadata." *Cataloging & Classification Quarterly* 49 (1): 1–13.

The authors discuss the importance of good metadata in helping users discover resources and explore the problem of high rates of error in the metadata used in *Google Books.*

Robbins, Jennifer Niederst. 2012. *Learning Web Design: A Beginner's Guide to HTML, CSS, JavaScript, and Web Graphics.* 4th ed. Sebastopol, CA: O'Reilly.

For those who want more detailed information on the structure of the Internet and web pages, chapter 2, "How the Web Works," provides a brief, accessible introduction.

Uyar, Ahmet, and Farouk M. Aliyu. 2015. "Evaluating Search Features of Google Knowledge Graph and Bing Satori: Entity Types, List Searches, and Query Interfaces." *Online Information Review* 39 (2): 197–213.

The authors examine efforts by major search engines, particularly *Google* and *Bing,* to deliver not just webpages in response to a user's query but actual content that answers the implied question.

Chapter 17

Ready-Reference Sources

Opetoritse A. Adefolalu

INTRODUCTION

What Is Ready Reference?

As explained in Chapter 1, the term "ready reference" describes the provision of straightforward, factual answers for patrons posing very specific questions. Box 17.1 provides a few real-life examples. Ready-reference queries usually have

Box 17.1 Ready-Reference Recollections: Example Queries

Following are some of the ready-reference questions the author has received while working at public, school, and academic libraries. In some cases, it may be easy to guess in which type of library the question was received."What's a hickey?"

- "What is the opus number of Beethoven's *Moonlight Sonata*?"
- "Is City Hall open today?"
- "What sports were practiced at the Olympic games in ancient Greece?"
- "Why are chili peppers spicy?"
- "Who was the first Black chess grandmaster?"
- "What are the walking directions from here [Inglewood, CA] to Torrance?"

only one right answer, and, as the name implies, a reference librarian will ideally be equipped to provide the requested answer readily. The books, databases, websites, and other materials at the reference librarian's disposal principally suited to answer these types of questions are known as ready-reference resources.

Why Do People Ask Ready-Reference Questions?

It may seem strange that, in the age of the Internet, someone would ask a ready-reference question when they could simply run a search on their closest broadband, Wi-Fi, or 4G connected device. Despite all the offerings of modern technology, many people continue to come to the library for even their basic information needs. Generally, these seem to be people who

- trust libraries and librarians as reliable sources of information;
- do not have access to or are not comfortable using other means of answering their questions;
- simply enjoy the interaction of asking ready-reference questions (see Box 17.2 for an example).

Box 17.2 Ready-Reference Recollections: "Where Is the President?"

While working in one public library, the author and his colleagues received almost daily phone calls from a patron who always asked the same question: "Where is the president today?" We would gladly find the answer for her (usually using the "President's Public Calendar" generated by Factba.se), after which she would ask two more questions before thanking us and hanging up.

The second and third questions were usually various trivia items, but without fail the first of the three would be about the president's whereabouts. While we of course couldn't know her ultimate motive, it seemed to be something of a pastime for her, and she would occasionally make small talk with us between her inquiries.

When Should Ready-Reference Services Be Provided?

At times, the line between ready-reference and research consulting can become blurred, and it is important to conduct a standard reference interview whenever a patron poses a query. Patrons will likely initiate a ready-reference interview by asking questions with fixed answers, but some patrons may use these narrow inquiries as an indirect approach to a more complicated information need. Librarians can use open and neutral questions about the scope, depth, and origin of the patron's underlying information need to determine the best service approach. Usually it will become clear early on in the interview whether the patron is in need of a quick, factual answer or a more involved consultation. Chapter 3 provides more in-depth guidance on conducting the reference interview.

READY-REFERENCE COLLECTION DEVELOPMENT

Ready-reference services are only as effective as the materials used to provide them. This section provides an overview of some general strategies for developing and maintaining a strong ready-reference collection. For a full examination of reference collection development, see Chapter 14.

Setting the Scope

The first step in any collection development project should be to determine the desired breadth and depth of the collection based on the library's goals and the patrons' information needs. Thus, the ready-reference collection of a small town public library will look very different from that of a major university's main library. If the library has an established collection development policy, librarians should refer to it for guidance. If not, the librarians should consider whether or not they would benefit from creating one.

It is important to know who the library's patrons are, what information they need, and what kinds of resources they prefer to use when deciding what will and will not be included in the collection. For example, initially it may seem like the most efficient approach would be to rely primarily on free and subscription-based online resources such as *Credo* and *Oxford Reference* rather than regularly purchasing expensive physical books that will become outdated. Large universities, where faculty and students rely on remote access, would likely benefit from such an approach, especially those that offer off-campus degree programs. However, for a mid-sized public library serving a population with low digital literacy rates this approach would likely cause accessibility and usability issues. Chapter 8 provides more information on how to assess the needs of the library's community.

Selection and Evaluation

Librarians should consider accuracy, authority, breadth and depth, accessibility and usability, and pricing when evaluating potential sources for the ready-reference collection. Of course, it would be impossible to personally examine all of the resources that might be of use to the library. For this reason, selection aids are published to help librarians develop their reference collections. Tools such as *American Reference Books Annual*, *Reference and User Services Quarterly*, and *Library Journal* contain guides, lists, and critical reviews to assist in the selection and evaluation process.

Accuracy

Perhaps the most important criterion, accuracy is measured by the currency, objectivity, and factuality of the information provided. The editorial staff cannot catch all errors, and even renowned and well-established reference works can contain erroneous or outdated information. The most basic defense against inaccuracy is to keep materials on the ready-reference shelf up to date. Placing standing orders for annually released reference works, such as yearbooks and almanacs, can help ensure that the collection stays current. When considering or using online sources, librarians should determine how regularly the content is updated.

It is equally important to investigate what biases may be present in a source, especially with regards to controversial topics such as race, war, and sexuality. While purportedly factual sources like specialized handbooks, government websites, and newspapers would ideally provide objective information, in reality they tend to reflect the interests and beliefs of certain constituents over others. An infamous example that remained unaddressed until 1987 was the inclusion of homosexuality as a mental illness in the *Diagnostic and Statistical Manual of Mental Disorders*, the principal reference text for psychiatric diagnoses in the United States. While it may not be possible to develop a collection free of bias, librarians should equip themselves to provide balanced, multifaceted answers by purchasing reference resources representing divergent perspectives.

Authority

A work gains authority from the staff and institutions responsible for its content and publication. The publisher is often a quick indicator of authority, with eminent university presses such as Oxford and Harvard, distinguished organizations such as the Public Broadcasting Services (PBS) and the British Broadcasting Corporation (BBC), and departments of government ranking among the most respected distributors of content. Editors and contributing authors considered to be leading experts in their field are also a sign that a work is highly authoritative.

General reference sources like databases, almanacs, yearbooks, and encyclopedias often compile data from multiple other works, making it a bit more complicated to assess their authority as a whole. Skimming through the references, titles, and contributing authors is a good way to get an idea of authority in these cases. In individual entries, references should have enough detail to lead to the original source where additional information would be found. The endless multitude of sources available through the Web has also complicated the process of appraising authority. This is arguably most true when answering questions about current events, making it essential that today's ready-reference collection include several reliable local and national news sources to avoid reliance on unverified information.

Breadth and Depth

Breadth refers to the range of information a source covers, while depth refers to the level of detail provided. A general ready-reference collection will focus on achieving a wide breadth with just enough depth to guide the patron toward deeper research. Basic sources such as almanacs and encyclopedias may provide only a few paragraphs for most articles, therefore sacrificing depth for breadth. Even more detailed sources like yearbooks, which may have multiple sections on certain topics, may value breadth over depth in their coverage.

The ready-reference collections of libraries specializing in certain subjects will include sources that are narrow in breadth but boast exceptional depth, such as subject manuals and periodicals. A university with a prominent jazz program, for example, is almost certain to carry magazines like *Downbeat*, which cover the latest developments and album releases within the genre. Public, school, and university library ready-reference collections should include local community sources, which are similarly limited in scope and vary in depth depending on their purpose. Articles in a school yearbook may be relatively light reading but provide valuable local information not found elsewhere, whereas local government websites may include comprehensive data, statistics, and other minute details about a city or county.

Accessibility and Usability

Accessibility describes the extent to which patrons are able to access and use a source and is often discussed with regard to serving patrons with disabilities. Both public and private libraries are legally required to make information as accessible as possible for patrons with visual, hearing, reading, and other disabilities that could affect their use of services. The means of meeting accessibility standards have been greatly advanced by the capabilities of digital technology, especially on the Internet. For example, many reference databases and websites include text-to-speech features that will read content aloud for the user, and Web browsers like Google Chrome have such features built in for use on any website. Other expected accessibility features in online reference sources include closed captioning for video material, alternative text coded to describe images for those who cannot see them, and navigability of the website without a mouse and/or fine motor skills. In addition, the ability to utilize resources from outside the library improves access for patrons who have difficulty traveling to the library.

The usability of a source refers to how conveniently and comfortably it can be used. For print and other non-digital sources, usability relates to the layout of indices and tables of contents, font sizes, use of white space, inclusion of pictures and illustrations, complexity of the language, and other factors affecting how easily and pleasurably a source can be read. Many of these same presentation concerns carry over to online sources but with the additional task of assessing the user interface. Librarians should evaluate potential sources to ensure that searching and browsing tools, navigation menus, help pages, and other website features are adequately effective and intuitive.

A major factor in determining the importance of accessibility and usability in a ready-reference collection is whether or not patrons will use the resources on their own. Traditionally, ready reference is a service provided by the reference librarian; however, advances in information technology and literacy have made it increasingly possible for patrons to perform their own ready reference. Many sources for ready reference can double as tools for general research, such as subject handbooks and research databases. The library will need to make an accurate assessment of the needs and capabilities of its community in deciding whether to invest in resources intended for independent use or those that might require the expertise of trained librarians.

Pricing

In a perfect world this category would be unnecessary, but unfortunately cost is almost always a limiting factor in a library's acquisitions process. Some print resources such as single-volume encyclopedias, almanacs, yearbooks, and handbooks offer good value at relatively low cost, but in most cases new editions will need to be purchased regularly to maintain accuracy. Subscriptions to large databases offer continuous access to a multitude of up-to-date resources but can be expensive. Since subscription prices often vary based on the number of titles included and the number of users that will have access, it may be more cost effective to limit database use to the reference desk and a few designated public research computers. Subscription prices for online periodicals such as local newspapers also vary based on the range of issues made available and degree of access granted. Discounts are often offered for online resource subscriptions when purchasing as part of a consortium of institutions and when subscribing to multiple products from the same vendor.

SPEEDY STARTER SOURCES

Speedy starter sources are the first line of defense at the reference desk. Often, they can be used to answer simple factual questions within a matter of seconds. Even when they do not provide a definitive answer, they may help the reference librarian and the patron discover background knowledge that will be useful when moving on to more extensive sources.

Google

Google has become a ubiquitous information source, so much so that the word "google" is now colloquially used as a verb. Some have suggested that *Google's* services, and those of the Internet in general, are eliminating the traditional role of libraries as information providers, a notion that casts the two entities in an unnecessary conflict (Barker 2016). A more optimistic and constructive viewpoint is to see *Google* and similar online resources as additional tools expanding the librarian's arsenal, as is evidenced by publications such as *Harnessing the Power of Google: What Every Researcher Should Know* (Brown 2017) and *The Complete Guide to Using Google in Libraries: Research, User Applications, and Networking* (Smallwood 2015).

It is worth noting that *Google is not a source in and of itself* but an engine that pulls information from billions of sources all over the World Wide Web, from government websites to travel blogs to panoramic images of street corners (see Box 17.3). The search engine uses complex algorithms to sort results by relevance to the user's query, but due to the sheer breadth of data users are sometimes led to undesired information. The reliability of search results can also be questionable, especially in cases of self-published and crowdsourced domains such as blogs, forums, and wikis.

These shortcomings exemplify the complementary relationship between *Google* and libraries; *Google* has made it possible to access virtually infinite resources, and librarians are equipped with the information literacy skills necessary to navigate this ocean of knowledge. *Google* is often the fastest option when dealing with simple facts, definitions, and popular culture (as is explored in Box 17.4), but its convenience can invite complacency. When using *Google* at the reference desk, librarians should be sure to identify the root source and evaluate it on criteria such as currency, authority, and objectivity. If, for example, a search leads to a news website that does not include author names or publication dates with its articles, it would be remiss to use the source as the final answer to a patron's question.

Box 17.3 Ready-Reference Recollections: Google Maps

Google offers an online location and navigation service called *Google Maps* that can be very useful when helping patrons with directional questions. The service includes a street view feature allowing users to virtually survey an area. The author once had a patron at the reference desk who wanted information about a corporate building near his apartment but couldn't remember the name displayed on the façade. The patron named the intersection where he lived and using *Google Maps*' street view, the author was able to find an image of the storefront that included the name.

Google Search's simplistic interface belies its many innovative features, which can prove particularly useful for ready reference. The engine is compatible with natural language, making it possible to search the exact question a patron asks. The search bar also uses word prediction software to complete queries based on popular searches; problematically, however, some suggestions stem from frequently searched stereotypes and other harmful biases (Noble 2018). The predictive software will also generate lists, display images, and even provide short answers alongside search results. A "Tools" tab on the results page offers useful filters such as the date and time of an article's publication or the size and color of an image. More advanced features such as natural language Boolean options and the ability to search pages within a specific website are available in *Google*'s advanced search.

Box 17.4 Activity: Knowing When to Google—Part I

The author once received a call at the reference desk from a patron with three questions:

1. Who was the previous owner of the Los Angeles Clippers?
2. What work is Rupert Murdoch doing these days?
3. Does Sir Elton John live in England or the United States?

Try to answer all three questions using *Google*. Then, answer them using a subscription-based reference database.

Questions for Reflection and Discussion:

1. Which approach did you find most effective?
2. What do these questions have in common that makes one approach better suited than the other?
3. How reliable did the sources found through *Google* seem based on the criteria discussed previously?

Almanacs

Almanacs collect a multitude of facts, statistics, and lists into one conveniently organized volume, usually published annually. Almanacs are most useful as sources of statistical, historical, biographical, and directory information.

To make their breadth and depth reasonably navigable, many print almanacs utilize special tabs, page markings, and multiple indices in addition to a table of contents, while online almanacs employ various searching and browsing features.

Almanacs are divided into two broad categories. The first is the traditional almanac containing calendars accompanied by astronomical and meteorological data. A venerable example is *The Old Farmer's Almanac* first published in 1792 as a continuation of Benjamin Franklin's famous *Poor Richard's Almanack*. In addition to detailed weather forecasts, it includes a historical database of weather conditions for 2,000 locations in North America dating back as far as 1946. The pages on gardening are bolstered by planting tables and source lists for seeds and flowers, while the astronomy pages chart various celestial events such as the moon phases, comet and meteor appearances, and sunrise and sunset times.

The second category is the modern almanac containing general information and statistics. Modern almanacs are typically more extensive and include information on prominent people and organizations, current and historical events, popular culture, geography, practical advice such as first aid treatment, statistics such as sports records, and much more. The perennially bestselling *World Almanac and Book of Facts*, for example, begins with a list of "Number Ones" such as the world's wealthiest people, its most populous countries, and the year's most important events. The remainder of the almanac contains a wealth of information on health, sports, politics, countries, the arts, entertainment, and science. Another well-known almanac is *Guinness World Records*, an annual listing of world records for both human feats such as the largest pizza ever made and naturally occurring phenomena such as the most dangerous ant.

Another reputable modern almanac is *Infoplease*, the online successor to the *Information Please Almanac* first published in 1947. Its contents are integrated with the *Random House Unabridged Dictionary* and *The Columbia Dictionary*, supplementing an already comprehensive reference source. Keyword searching, topical indices, and a browsable directory offer users a number of navigation options. Commonly used resources such as a conversion calculator and the periodic table of elements are also available through easy access links.

Some almanacs target younger users, such as *The World Almanac for Kids* and the online *Factmonster.com*. These almanacs emphasize browsability, featuring colorful, graphically oriented designs and topic pages based on common school subjects. The articles are written with simplified language and scope appropriate for elementary and middle school students. They make suitable stepping stones for supporting early information literacy in libraries serving children.

Most modern almanacs are broad in their geographic scope, but others cover a specific area, such as the *Canadian Almanac and Directory* and the *Texas Almanac*. Almanacs focusing on specific subjects can also be found, such as Christopher Antonio Brooks's *The African American Almanac* and Karl Zinmeister's *The Almanac of American Philanthropy*. Librarians should consider the needs and interests of their patron population when selecting specialized almanacs.

AGGREGATOR REFERENCE DATABASES

Aggregator reference databases are similar to search engines, but instead of drawing information from the Internet they utilize a curated collection of sources.

While still covering a broad range of knowledge, databases place greater focus on depth than the resources discussed in the previous section. For many libraries, online databases that access multiple publications make up the core resources in this category.

Although databases are often associated with in-depth research, they can prove handy for ready reference, as well. This is especially true in academic libraries, where students are more likely to pose questions about obscure topics. Through the integration of versatile sharing tools such as citation generators, pdf e-mailing, and cloud sharing to services such as *Google Drive*, *Facebook*, and *Twitter*, databases have embodied the practices of modern scholarship.

Publishers offer a wealth of databases suitable for ready reference. The differences between these products range from target audience to user interface design to exclusive publication access rights. This section examines three major databases used by public, school, and academic libraries alike: *Credo Reference*, *Gale Virtual Reference Library*, and *Oxford Reference*. All three are full-text databases that provide access to the entire contents of the titles they contain.

Credo Reference

Credo Reference offers access to hundreds of specialized subject encyclopedias, general encyclopedias, dictionaries, handbooks, and more that provide background information on almost any topic. These resources are organized into "core collections" designed to target the needs of different types of libraries. The core collection for school libraries offers 350 titles best suited for grades 7–12, the academic core collection offers 600 titles spanning all disciplines, and the public library core collection offers 700 titles for users of all ages and interests. Libraries can also subscribe to subject collections in areas such as special education, Islam, and artificial intelligence. General sources such as the *Britannica Concise Encyclopedia*, *The Columbia Encyclopedia*, and *Merriam-Webster's Collegiate Dictionary* are also included.

Credo Reference is primarily designed for narrow and deliberate searching and offers users a number of ways to locate needed information. Basic, image, and title searching are available from each page, and an advanced search option allows the use of Boolean operators presented in natural language (e.g. "with all of the words," "without the words"). Search results can be limited by collection, subject, media type, date of publication, and article length. The search interface can also be customized to include links that will search the same query in other databases within the library system, including the library catalog. Figure 17.1 shows the *Credo Reference* home page with the basic search screen.

Credo's search options are supplemented by the option to browse by subject, collection, title, and topic. Hundreds of topic pages act as springboards for finding related articles, images, and videos. An additional brainstorming tool called "Mind Map" expands topical browsing by presenting a dynamic visual diagram of topics related to a given query. Each time the user clicks on a topic within the diagram, a new branching map is generated (see Figure 17.2 and Box 17.5). Another dynamic feature included in *Credo* is a set of in-page tutorials that can be launched by clicking the question mark icon at the top of every page.

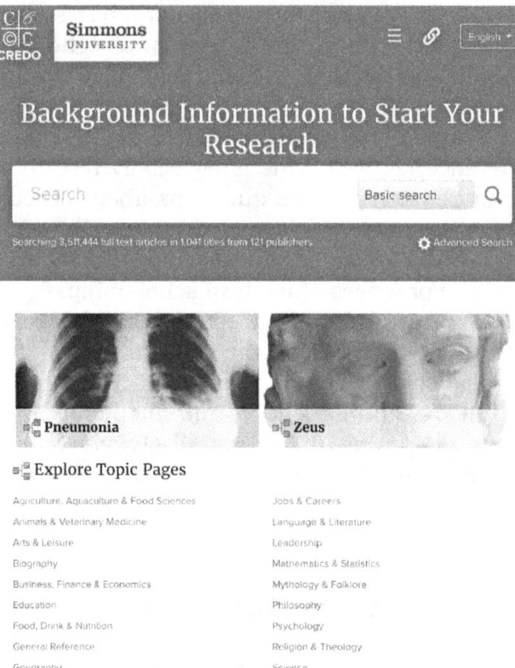

Figure 17.1 *Credo Reference*. This screenshot of the home page shows the search bar for a basic search and options to browse by topic.

Used with permission from *Credo Reference*.

> ### Box 17.5 Activity: Mind Map Practice
>
> Run a search for "library" using *Credo Reference*'s Mind Map feature and spend some time clicking through the related topics. How well does the diagram contextualize the initial search term? How might this feature be useful when helping patrons?

Gale Virtual Reference Library

Gale Virtual Reference Library offers full-text access to hundreds of premier reference books. Unlike other reference databases, however, there are no preset collections tailored for specific libraries or subjects. Instead, librarians will need to choose what titles they want to include and, if desired, categorize into custom collections. While many works such as the *New Encyclopedia of Africa* are Gale's own publications, prominent titles from external publishers, such as *Baker's Biographical Dictionary of Musicians*, are also available.

Gale's searching options are particularly robust. Keyword, subject, publication, and full-text searches can be run from the simple search bar at the top of every page (see Figure 17.3). The advanced search utilizes standard Boolean operators and an expanded set of search filters including document title, image caption, volume

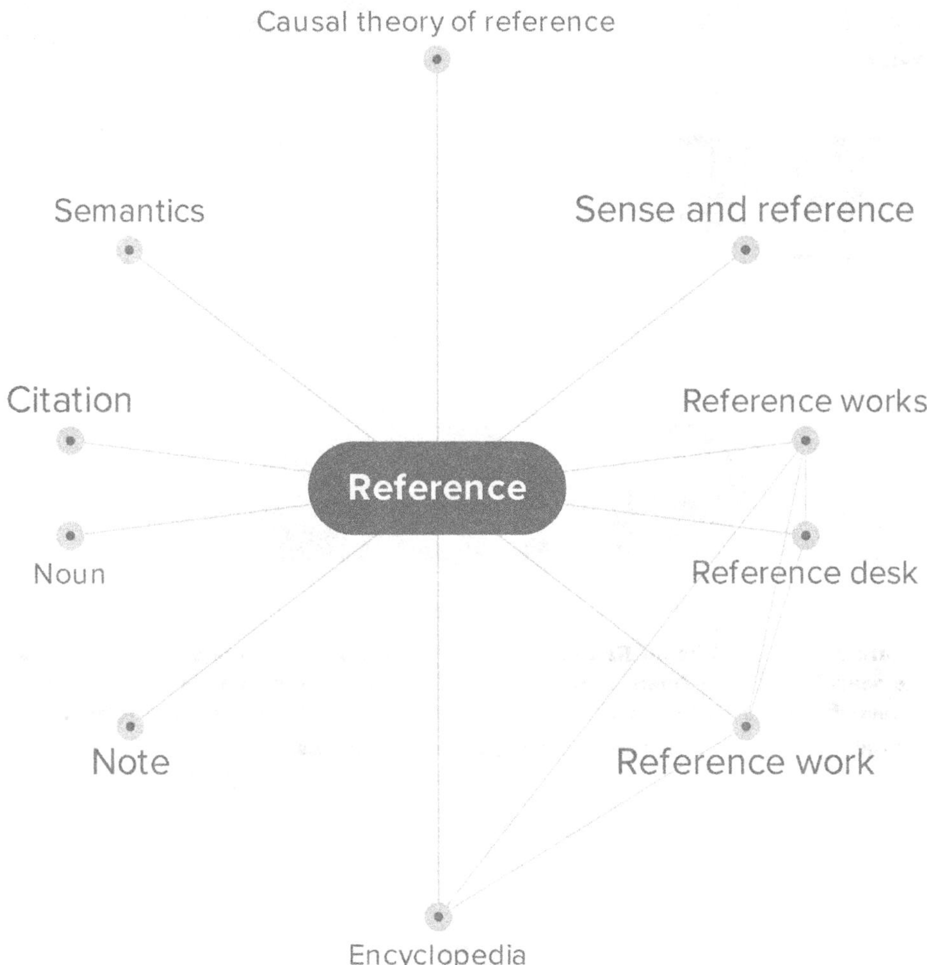

Figure 17.2 *Credo Reference* Mind Map. This screenshot shows an interactive mind map for the search term "reference". When users click a related term, the map reorients to make that the major search term. When users close the Mind Map box, *Credo* presents a list of articles related to the major searh term.
Used with permission from Credo Reference.

number, and ISBN. Additional options allow filtering by media type, intended audience, content complexity level, and more (see Figure 17.4). Similar options to limit results are available on the search results page. This flexibility allows for multiple approaches to finding a specific resource, even when working off of incomplete information (see Box 17.6). Promising entries can be saved using the "My Folder" feature, and the search history for the current session can be reviewed at any time under the "More" button. Text selections within individual articles can be highlighted and even annotated for future reference.

Gale's browsing features include the "Subject Guide Search," a thesaurus-like listing of the different subject terms linked to a given query, and the "Topic Finder"

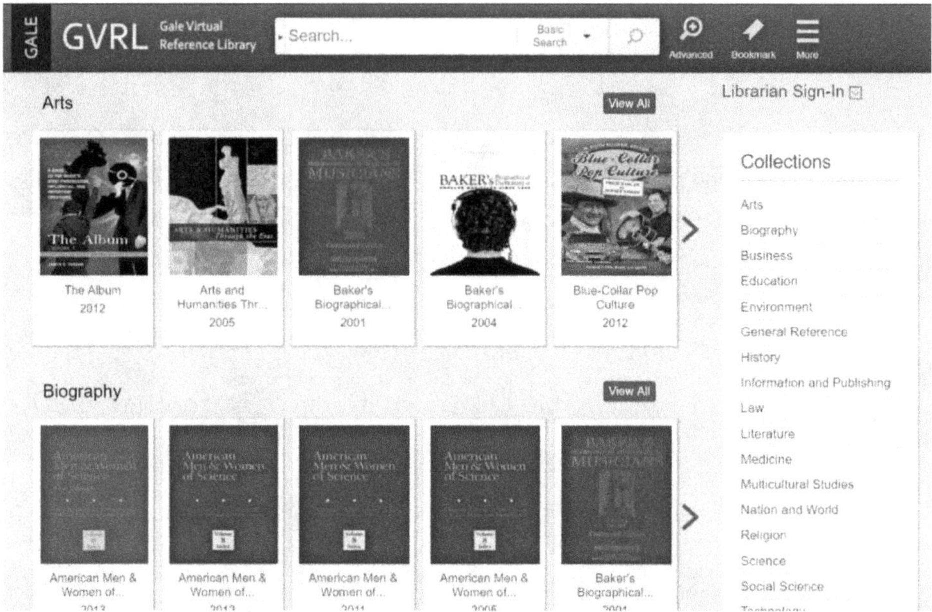

Figure 17.3 ***Gale Virtual Reference Library's*** **home page. This screenshot shows the search bar for a basic search and options to browse by title and collection. Screenshot from** ***Gale Virtual Reference Library.*** **© Gale, a part of Cengage, Inc. Reproduced by permission. www.cengage.com/permissions.**

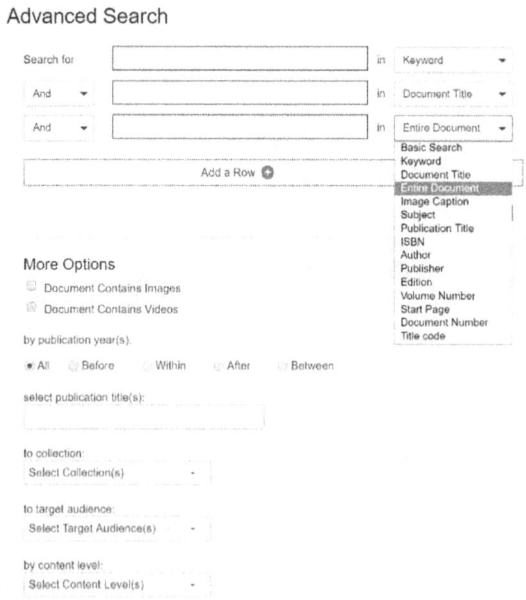

Figure 17.4 ***Gale*** **Advanced Search. This screenshot shows advanced search options, including the option to combine terms and add search limits. Screenshot from** ***Gale Virtual Reference Library.*** **© Gale, a part of Cengage, Inc. Reproduced by permission. www.cengage.com/permissions.**

brainstorming tool, which returns a graphical representation of the top search results for a query. There is also a quick-access dictionary feature under the "More" icon that searches a default dictionary chosen during the database setup.

Box 17.6 Activity: Knowing When to Google—Part II

Imagine you are a reference librarian working at a university with a large film studies program. A student comes to the reference desk looking for an article on horror movies. Through the subsequent reference interview, you learn that the student is attempting to rediscover a specific article that another librarian helped him find in one of the library's online databases sometime last semester. The article made several references to the work of a particular psychoanalyst whom the student would like to research further, but he cannot remember the name. He does not remember which publication it was, either, but knows that the title included the word "death" and that the database had a black and gray banner across the top. He is certain he will recognize the psychoanalyst's name when he hears it and is hoping you can help him find out what it is.

Try to find the name of the psychoanalyst, first using *Gale Virtual Reference Library* and then using *Google*. As the student's description hints, *Gale* was the database in which he first encountered the article; however, it is possible to locate the name using *Google*, as well. See Box 17.9 toward the end of this chapter for the answer.

While the scenario presented in Box 17.6 may seem contrived, such cases are far from unheard of in academic and school libraries. The hypothetical search illustrates three main advantages research databases have over *Google* in these contexts. First, the reference librarian and the student are afforded a shared frame of reference that sets a relatively narrow scope for the initial search. The student's recollection of a black and gray banner is the digital age equivalent of a patron recalling that their desired book had an orange cover, yet, while the latter scenario is frequently a sign of a comically hopeless search, the former is almost as good as a URL to a seasoned reference librarian. Second, the searching capabilities of research databases are far more precise than those of *Google*. Even *Google's* advanced search options are too broad to track down a specific publication using only the subject and one word from the title. Third, guiding students in database use familiarizes them with the structure of academic discourse. Interactions like these highlight the blurred line between ready-reference and research consulting, preparing students to confidently navigate disciplinary scholarship.

Oxford Reference Library

Oxford Reference Library provides full-text access to Oxford University Press reference publications as well as a selection of works from partner publishers. It contains about two million entries from dictionaries, companions, quotation books, and encyclopedias, some of which are only available online. Titles are automatically added and updated as new publications are released, and libraries can choose content by subject and title. The articles are divided into twenty-five core subject areas, ranging from essentials like literature and history to less commonly featured areas such as media studies and name studies. Two other levels of subscription for *Oxford Reference* are also available: *Oxford Quick Reference*, a short-entry collection drawing from academic subject, language, and quotation dictionaries, and *Oxford Reference Premium*, a combination of *Oxford Quick Reference* and *Oxford Reference Library*, which includes an additional selection of specialized titles.

Unlike most databases, the interface of *Oxford Reference* emphasizes browsing options over those for searching. The design seems to take as much inspiration from the format of online library guides such as *LibGuides* as it does from that of traditional online databases, balancing the essential elements of precise searching with ample opportunities for guided discovery. Images on the home page link to overview pages for each core subject and provide contextualizing background information, author features including interviews, and links to sample entries, timelines, blogs, maps, and more. The "Subject" tab at the top of each page contains links that run a search for all entries and titles in each core subject. The "Historic Timelines" feature also lends itself to both browsing and searching. Split into 270 entries, the timelines survey major historical events from 1,000 BCE to the present, with special entries dedicated to selected countries and regions. Timeline pages include cross-references to one another, as well as links to relevant subject areas and articles.

While *Oxford Reference*'s browsability is front and center, its searching functionality is robust as well. While an advanced search option is interestingly absent, Boolean operators work within the basic and subject search available at the top of every page. More refined searching can be accomplished using the facets available on the search results page. Multiple subject limiters can be applied simultaneously, as well as descriptive metadata filters such as entry title, book title, contributor, and caption. Results can also be limited by the type of reference resource, media type, and availability within the subscription.

YEARBOOKS

Yearbooks, also referred to as "annuals," are publications released annually with detailed information on major events, statistics, and other notable items from a particular year. They also provide information about influential organizations, people, places, and other broadly impactful entities. The form of the content ranges from timelines, statistical surveys, and directories to brief biographies and essays. It should be noted that the date given on the spine reflects the publication year; the information in the yearbook comes from the preceding year. While similar in scope to a modern general almanac, yearbooks provide more in-depth coverage. For example, while an almanac might include the final scores of matches from the latest World Cup, a yearbook is more likely to have a game-by-game description of the tournament. This makes yearbooks valuable tools for both contemporary and historical research, as they may provide greater detail about past events compared to other reference sources. The library's collection should include older yearbooks covering landmark events in addition to the latest publications, especially in scholastic and academic settings where students can utilize past editions for history assignments. *The Statesman's Yearbook*, edited by Barry Turner, the *Britannica Book of the Year* (discontinued after 2018), and *The Europa World Year Book* are a few well-known examples of yearbooks.

For information on yearbooks published by schools as directories of the student body, see the "Local School Resources" section of "Local Sources" later in this chapter.

ENCYCLOPEDIAS

Encyclopedias, discussed in more detail in Chapter 19, are excellent tools for ready reference. They have long been the quintessential reference tool, seeming to cover every topic imaginable. Although traditional print encyclopedias are giving way to online alternatives, the popularity of Web-based encyclopedias such as *Wikipedia* evinces the durability of the format.

SPECIALIZED SUBJECT SOURCES

While many of the sources discussed earlier in this chapter provide a concise introduction to a multitude of subjects, the sources addressed in this section contain thorough information about a specific topic. This makes them well suited for in-depth research; however, they also lend themselves well to ready reference for subject specialists, often carrying succinct answers to obscure questions.

Handbooks and Manuals

The labels of "handbook" and "manual" are used more or less interchangeably to refer to reference works that provide in-depth information on a particular subject or topic. Generally, these works are very limited in scope, addressing narrow subjects such as chemistry, psychology, medicine, and film. Handbooks and manuals are meant to be used by students or professionals in the field being covered, and as a result the language used and concepts discussed may be too advanced for general readers. Some notable handbooks and manuals include the *CRC Handbook of Chemistry and Physics*, *The Diagnostic and Statistical Manual of Mental Disorders*, and the *Oxford Companion* series.

Many handbooks organize the foundational information and data of a discipline into charts, tables, formulas, and other diagrams well suited for quick reference. Step-by-step instructions on performing certain tasks such as diagnosing an illness or properly citing sources is supplemented by statistical information, historical background, scholarly critiques, bibliographies, and references to relevant organizations. Writing style guides such as *The Chicago Manual of Style*, *The Publication Manual of the American Psychological Association*, and the *MLA Handbook* are perhaps the most well-known resources of this type and are essentials for any public, academic, or high school library. Handbooks and manuals are most likely to be used in special libraries such as law, music, medical, and academic libraries. Because handbooks and manuals tend to require some prior knowledge of the subject matter and/or organizational structures, librarians should familiarize themselves with the most frequently used titles in their collection.

Popular Media Databases

Many patrons come to the reference desk looking for information on popular literature, music, and film that may not be covered by traditional resources. Questions about the reading order of a comic book series, the accolades of a hit album, and the filmography of an up-and-coming actress can often be answered using free online websites dedicated to those topics. Three example sites are *Goodreads*, *AllMusic*, and *IMDb*.

Goodreads is a social media platform where users can share and discuss books they have read or want to read. The website has individual pages for over two billion books added by its seventy-five million users ("About Goodreads" n.d.). By design, almost all of the content is user generated and fairly subjective. Thus, as with other popular open-source reference tools, the reliability of the information can be questionable. That being said, the site can be very useful for answering fact-based reader advisory questions such as "What is the ninteenth book in the *Jack Reacher* series?" and "What books make up 'The Toni Morrison Trilogy'?" Books can be searched for by title, author, or genre.

One of several sister websites owned and maintained by the company All Media Network, *AllMusic* is an extensive music database with detailed information on over three million albums and over thirty million songs, as well as articles on specific bands, musicians, record labels, and more. The website's features include biographies, reviews, discographies, recording dates, album credits, award information, music samples, and links to streaming services. Music can be browsed by genre, mood, or theme, and the search feature includes advanced filtering options such as release date, recording type, and *AllMusic*'s quality rating.

IMDb, the Internet Movie Database, is an online database of information on film and television and is a subsidiary of Amazon. The database has entries for nearly five million movies and television shows and over 400,000 actors, directors, producers, and other cast and crew members. The site's advanced search tool boasts incredible precision, offering dozens of filtering options such as awards, nominations, plot description, production company, sound mixing system, and country of origin.

LOCAL SOURCES

From helping a lifelong resident track down information on an event from her childhood to giving a new parent statistical comparisons of elementary schools, reference librarians frequently handle questions related to local knowledge. In some cases, the library may play the role of an archive, housing the only freely accessible copies of certain items. Collecting and preserving reference materials tailored to the unique needs and interests of the town, city, university, school, or organization the library services is essential to maintaining relevance.

Local Government Websites

State, county, and city websites often provide information that can be used to answer patrons' questions about government holidays, employment opportunities, local representatives' contact information, voting instructions, annual budgets, city council meeting schedules, Section 8 apartment listings, and other practical concerns. For public libraries, especially, city and county websites can be critical resources for serving the community's everyday needs. In some cases, the library website itself may be a subsection of the city's website. Public librarians will likely find it beneficial to become as familiar with certain sections of local government websites as they are with the library's own website and even to provide links from the latter to the former. It may be useful to keep printouts of some government documents permanently available at the reference desk for patrons who prefer physical formats.

Local Periodicals

Local periodicals serve as the most direct source of information on your library's community, containing information on the latest events, developments, and concerns. Whether it's the city's gazette, the undergraduate paper, or the university magazine, periodicals are the finger on your community's pulse. They can be of great use when answering questions like "Who won last night's Little League game," "What was the protest on the quad about last week," and "Who gave the keynote address at the last American Library Association conference?" In many small cities and towns, daily and weekly newspapers remain the most up-to-date sources of fundamental information such as apartment listings, job openings, and obituaries. Many local papers publish their content online as well as in print; however, the library may be required to purchase a subscription for online access.

Local School Resources

While the relevance of school resources is obvious in the case of school and academic libraries, public libraries may also find patrons frequently asking about local school matters at their reference desks. Much of this information should be available through the school district's or the university's website, and librarians will want to maintain familiarity with the sites of the most prominent schools. Building partnerships with teachers, principals, and other librarians in the area is also key to staying informed. Ideally, school librarians and public librarians serving the same community will have a working relationship, and each should be aware of what resources the other offers.

Academic calendars are probably the most heavily used sources in this category, listing important dates, holidays, and administrative events throughout the academic year (see Figure 17.5 for a sample academic calendar). Most school websites also have event calendars listing dates for special programs, dances, standardized testing, field trips, and other important activities. Information on after-school activities, clubs, sports teams, and other extracurricular activities may be available online, but for accurate details you will most likely need to refer patrons to officials from the school or university.

Many schools have annual yearbooks created by staff and/or students to document the most memorable events of a particular year. These yearbooks also include a directory of all students who attended the school during that year complete with individual, class, and team/club photographs. Yearbooks can be invaluable heirlooms for visiting alumni and community members at times such as class reunions or a classmate's passing, as well as when a former student becomes particularly successful or famous (see Box 17.7). Playbills, concert programs, performance recordings, and other records of school events are similarly meaningful pieces of the student body's history. School and academic librarians should contact the organization(s) in charge of producing school papers, yearbooks, and other records to ensure that the library always receives at least one copy. Public libraries should also consider acquiring the yearbooks of local schools as part of their community reference archive.

Dr. Janice K. Jackson
Chief Executive Officer

2018-2019 CPS CALENDAR
ELEMENTARY AND HIGH SCHOOLS

AUGUST				
		1	2	3
6	7	8	9	10
13	14	15	16	17
20	21	22▲	23	24
27•	28+	29+	30+	31+

NOVEMBER				
			1Q	2#
5	6	7	8	9
12*	13	14ESPT	15HSPT	16
19	20	(21)	22*	23*
26	27	28	29	30

FEBRUARY				
				1#
4	5	6	7	8
11	12	13	14	15
18*	19	20	21	22
25	26	27	28	

MAY				
		1	2	3
6	7	8	9	10
13	14	15	16	17
20	21	22	23	24
27*	28	29	30	31

SEPTEMBER				
3*	4	5	6	7
10	11	12	13	14
17	18	19	20	21
24	25	26	27	28

DECEMBER				
3	4	5	6	7
10	11	12	13	14
17	18	19	20	21
/24/	/25/	/26/	/27/	/28/
(31)				

MARCH				
				1
4	5	6	7	8
11	12	13	14	15
18	19	20	21	22
25	26	27	28	29

JUNE				
3	4	5	6	7
10	11	12	13	14
17	18Q	19#	20•	21e
24e	25e	26e	27e	28

OCTOBER				
1	2	3	4	5
8*	9	10	11	12
15	16	17	18	19
22	23	24	25	26
29	30	31		

JANUARY				
	(1)	(2)	(3)	(4)
7	8	9	10	11
14	15	16	17	18
21*	22	23	24	25
28	29	30	31Q	

APRIL				
1	2	3	4Q	5#
8	9	10ESPT	11HSPT	12
/15/	/16/	/17/	/18/	/19/
22	23	24	25	26
29	30			

JULY				
1	2	3	4	5
8	9	10	11	12
15	16	17	18	19
22	23	24	25	26
29	30	31		

LEGEND

Q End of Quarter
\+ Teacher Institute Days
\# School improvement Days
* Holiday
Day of non-attendance for students
Anticipated Window for Summer Programs
( ) Schools closed-- no salary paid

// Schools closed—salary paid except as provided by budgetary action
HSPT High School Parent-Teacher Conference Day (Report card pickup)
ESPT Elementary Parent-Teacher Conference Day (Report card pickup)
e Emergency day-school in session if student days fall below state requirement
◆ Each school is provided 2 professional development days
▲ School clerks begin working on Wednesday, August 22, 2018

***HOLIDAYS**

September 3	Labor Day	January 21	M. L. King Day
October 8	Columbus Day	February 18	President's Day
November 12	Veteran's Day	May 27	Memorial Day
November 22, 23	Thanksgiving Holiday		

Please note: December 25 and January 1 are holidays for the district offices.

Figure 17.5 Sample academic calendar. This academic calendar from the Chicago Public Schools shows the days school will be in session as well as holidays for students and employees.

Used with permission from the Chicago Public Schools.

Box 17.7 Reference Desk Recollections: Showcasing Alumni

The author previously worked in the library of the Chicago Vocational Career Academy (formerly Chicago Vocational High School), which is the alma mater of distinguished comedians Kel Mitchell and the late Bernie Mac. The yearbooks containing their pictures were extremely popular items, so much so that they unfortunately went missing. It is advisable to keep such rare materials in a secure location and only make them available upon request.

CONCLUSION

As the numerous and varying resources described in this chapter suggest, there is more than one correct way to approach ready-reference service. The word "ready" gives a connotation of speed but is better understood as a confirmation of the reference librarian's preparation. Providing the short, well-defined answers that are archetypal of ready reference is not always a short, well-defined process. By building familiarity with these myriad resources, the librarian develops the versatility necessary to meet any query with confidence. This familiarity grows not only from study but from frequent practice. Box 17.8 provides an opportunity for such practice with sample ready-reference questions. Box 17.9 provides the answer to the activity discussed in Box 17.6.

Box 17.8 Activity: Ready-Reference Practice

Read the following ready-reference scenarios and decide what resource(s) you would use to answer each patron's question. If possible, try going to a library and using the materials in the reference collection to answer the questions as best you can. Then ask the librarians and see what resources they use.

1. A young girl around the age of five comes to the children's department desk and asks, "Why is the sun yellow?"
2. An elderly man comes to the adult reference desk and explains that he has a cell phone provided by the government program Lifeline. The phone was given to him without a manual, and he would like you to help him find one online that he can print. The phone model is ZTE Tempo X.
3. Three college students enter the university music library and timidly approach the reference desk. They tell you that they are not sure if this is the right place to ask, but they have a question about an instrument. They recently attended a performance on campus featuring instruments from around the world, and one was a horn called the "abu." The performers said it was from Africa but they did not say which country, and the students are hoping you can help them find out.
4. A young couple with an infant comes to the reference desk upset about how few streetlights are present in their neighborhood, expressing how they feel the lack of lighting contributes to high crime rates in the area. They would like to know who is responsible for the distribution of streetlights and to have any contact information available for that entity.

Box 17.9 Knowing When to Google: Answer to Part II

The name that the hypothetical student is looking for is Carl Jung. With access to a *Gale Virtual Reference Desk* subscription that includes the *Macmillan Encyclopedia of Death and Dying*, the exact article the student read could be found by running an advanced search for entries with "horror" in the subject field and "death" in the publication title. The title of the article is "Horror Movies," written by James F. Iaccino, and Carl Jung's psychoanalytic theory is mentioned in the fourth paragraph. While less precise, a basic search for "horror movies death" will still retrieve the same article within the top five results.

REFERENCES

"About Goodreads." n.d. *Goodreads*. https://www.goodreads.com/about/us.

Barker, Steve. 2016. "In Age of Google, Librarians Get Shelved." *Wall Street Journal*, January 10, 2016. https://www.wsj.com/articles/in-age-of-google-librarians-get-shelved-1452461659.

Brown, Christopher C. 2017. *Harnessing the Power of Google: What Every Researcher Should Know*. Santa Barbara, CA: Libraries Unlimited.

Noble, Safiya Umoja. 2018. *Algorithms of Oppression: How Search Engines Reinforce Racism*. New York: New York University Press.

Smallwood, Carol. 2015. *The Complete Guide to Using Google in Libraries: Research, User Applications, and Networking*. Lanham, MD: Rowman & Littlefield.

LIST OF SOURCES

The African American Almanac. 2011. Edited by Christopher Antonio Brooks. Detroit, MI: Gale Cengage Learning.

AllMusic. https://www.allmusic.com.

American Reference Books Annual. 1970–. Edited by Shannon Graff Hysell. Santa Barbara, CA: Libraries Unlimited.

Baker's Biographical Dictionary of Musicians. 2001. Edited by Laura Diane Kuhn and Nicolas Slonimsky. New York: Schirmer Books. Available online as part of *Gale Virtual Reference Library*.

Britannica Book of the Year. 1938–2018. Chicago: Encyclopaedia Britannica. Annual.

Britannica Concise Encyclopedia. Chicago: Encyclopaedia Britannica. Available online as part of *Credo Reference*.

Canadian Almanac & Directory. 1847–. Toronto: Grey House Publishing Canada. Annual.

The Chicago Manual of Style, 17th ed. 2017. Chicago: The University of Chicago Press.

The Columbia Encyclopedia. 1936–. New York: Columbia University Press. Available online as part of *Credo Reference*.

CRC Handbook of Chemistry and Physics. 1913–. Boca Raton, FL: CRC Press. Annual. Available online as part of the Taylor & Francis Group.

Credo Reference. Credo Reference. http://search.credoreference.com/. Subscription required.

Diagnostic and Statistical Manual of Mental Disorders, Fifth Edition (DSM-5). 2013. Washington, DC: American Psychiatric Association. http://psychiatryonline.org/. Subscription required.

DownBeat. 1934–. Elmhurst: Maher Publications. Available online at http://downbeat.com/. Subscription required.

The Europa World Yearbook. 1989–. London: Europa Publications.

Facebook. http://www.facebook.com.

Factba.se. https://factba.se.

Factmonster.com. Boston, MA: Information Please. http://www.factmonster.com.

Gale Virtual Reference Library. Farmington Hills, MI: Gale Cengage Learning. http://www.cengage.com. Subscription required.

Goodreads.com. https://www.goodreads.com.

Google. https://www.google.com.

Guinness World Records. 1956—. New York: Guinness World Records. Annual. http://www.guinnessworldrecords.com.

IMDb. https://www.imdb.com.

Infoplease. http://www.infoplease.com.

LibGuides. Springshare. https://springshare.com/libguides/.

Library Journal. 1876–. New York: Library Journals, LLC. https://www.libraryjournal.com/.

Merriam-Webster's Collegiate Dictionary. 1898–. Springfield, MA: Merriam-Webster. Available as part of *Credo Reference*.

MLA Handbook. 2016. 8th ed. New York: The Modern Language Association of America.

The New Encyclopedia of Africa. 2008. Edited by John Middleton and Joseph Calder Miller. Detroit: Thomson/Gale. Available online as part of *Gale Virtual Reference Library*.

The Old Farmer's Almanac. 1792–. Dublin, NH: Yankee Publishing. Annual. http://www.almanac.com.

Oxford Companions. 1932–. New York: Oxford University Press.

Oxford Quick Reference. New York: Oxford University Press. http://www.oxfordreference.com/. Subscription required.

Oxford Reference Library. New York: Oxford University Press. http://www.oxfordreference.com/. Subscription required.

Oxford Reference Premium. New York: Oxford University Press. http://www.oxfordreference.com/. Subscription required.

Publication Manual of the American Psychological Association, 7th ed. 2020. Washington, DC: American Psychological Association.

Reference & User Services Quarterly (RUSQ). 1997–. Chicago: American Library Association. https://journals.ala.org/rusq.

The Statesman's Yearbook. 1864–. Edited by Barry Turner. Basingstroke, Hampshire: Palgrave Macmillan. Annual. https://www.palgrave.com/gp/book/9781349953202. Subscription required.

Taylor & Francis Group. London: Informa UK Limited. https://taylorandfrancis.com/. Subscription required.

Texas Almanac. Texas State Historical Association. http://texasalmanac.com/.

Twitter. http://www.twitter.com.

Wikipedia. http://www.wikipedia.org.

The World Almanac and Book of Facts. 1868–1876, 1886–. Mahwah, NJ: World Almanac Books. Annual. http://www.infobasepublishing.com/. Subscription required.

The World Almanac for Kids. 1996–. Mahwah, NJ: World Almanac Books. Annual.

Zinsmeister, Karl. 2017. *The Almanac of American Philanthropy*. Washington, DC: The Philanthropy Roundtable.

SUGGESTED READINGS

Katz, Bill. 1998. *Cuneiform to Computer: A History of Reference Sources*. Lanham, MD: Scarecrow Press.

For those interested in the origins and evolution of almanacs, encyclopedias, and other reference sources, this book provides an in-depth introduction.

Rettig, James. 1992. *Distinguished Classics of Reference Publishing*. Phoenix, AZ: Oryx Press. https://archive.org/details/DistinguishedClassicsOfReferencePublishing.

This wonderful history of famous reference books includes many of the works discussed in this chapter, including *The Chicago Manual of Style*, *Encyclopaedia Britannica*, *The Encyclopedia of Associations*, *Emily Post's Etiquette*, *Guinness Book of Records*, *Robert's Rules of Order*, *The Statesman's Yearbook*, the *World Book Encyclopedia*, and *The World Almanac*.

Chapter 18

Dictionaries

Stephanie Davis-Kahl

USES AND CHARACTERISTICS

Purpose: Past and Present

Dictionaries have long been the tool by which people from all walks of life find definitions, pronunciations, usage, and etymology of words. They are fascinating glimpses into how words and their meanings are shaped by aspects of our culture and society such as commerce, technology, entertainment, trends, politics, and globalization:

> Dictionaries . . . are often all too human products, able to reflect the social and cultural assumptions of the time in which they are written, and telling, as a result, their own stories of society, culture, innovation and ideals. Who writes a dictionary—and when and where—are factors which, in significant ways, will change and influence the kind of dictionary that is produced. (Mugglestone 2011, xii)

This point is underscored when considering heritage and endangered languages. According to the United Nations Educational, Scientific, and Cultural Organization (UNESCO) (n.d.), "A language is endangered when its speakers cease to use it, use it in fewer and fewer domains, use fewer of its registers and speaking styles, and/or stop passing it on to the next generation." For communities with dwindling numbers, or communities with fewer native speakers of a language, "Dictionaries of endangered languages represent especially important products of language documentation, in part because they are usually the most familiar and useful genre of linguistic representation to endangered community members" (Kroskrity 2015, 140).

In the last century, dictionaries have expanded their reach from providing textual definitions to integrating images and visual information, audio, and multimedia, all excellent developments for a wide range of users, including children, teachers, librarians, and English language learners. Creative authors have compiled dictionaries on novel topics, exemplified by two MIT Press titles: François Caradec's (2018) *Dictionary of Gestures* and John Bevis's (2010) *Aaaaw to Zzzzzd: The Words of Birds*. Publishers of dictionaries are active on social media, providing useful and valuable commentary on national events, linking essays about word usage and history and sharing "word of the day" posts. By far the most exciting development in the dictionary's long history is the now-ubiquitous availability of dictionaries on the Web and as apps, extending the value, accessibility, and versatility of the dictionary as a format in and of itself. However, with progress comes tension, as the commercial viability of print dictionaries has come under scrutiny, even for the *Oxford English Dictionary*, a highly regarded and well-known dictionary (Flanagan 2014). Funding for another well-respected and award-winning publication, the *Dictionary of American Regional English* (*DARE*), continues thanks to federal agencies, private foundation funding, and individual contributions.

History

Although a short word list from the 7th century BCE was found in central Mesopotamia, today's dictionary has its roots in Greece and later in Italy, from the 1st century CE into the Middle Ages. In the early Middle Ages, manuscripts often included *glosses*, marginal or interlinear notes, to define or translate words. Oftentimes, glosses from different works were collected and printed as a standalone publication. Clerics, spelling reformers, and teachers heavily influenced the development and creation of dictionaries. These could be divided into two schools of thought: the first stressed standardizing the language (i.e., dictionary as authority, a *prescriptive* approach), whereas the second emphasized recording language as it was used by the people (i.e., dictionary as reflection of reality, a *descriptive* approach). An excellent example of the divergence between the two perspectives is illustrated by the reaction to one of the first dictionaries compiled in America, Caleb Alexander's *The Columbian Dictionary of the English Language*, published in 1800. According to the *Encyclopaedia Britannica*, "it received abuse from critics who were not yet ready for the inclusion of American words" (Read 2005, 280).

Although Britain's contribution to the evolution of the dictionary is exemplified best in the massive and incomparable *Oxford English Dictionary* (*OED*), it is worth noting that dictionaries created up until the 18th century were authored by amateur lexicographers. John Kersey the Younger published *The New English Dictionary* in 1702, the first work to be compiled by a professional lexicographer. Another major name in the history of dictionaries is Samuel Johnson, a poet and critic, whose *Dictionary of the English Language* (1755) included quotations showing the usage of the word as well as a definition. Johnson's *Dictionary* went through multiple editions and was even imported to America for schoolchildren.

Kinds of Information Found in Dictionaries

The goal of a dictionary usually dictates layout, breadth, depth of coverage, and the information included in each entry. A standard, general dictionary will contain pronunciation (including syllabication and emphasis), definitions, function, variant spellings, and an example of usage. Entries may also include more in-depth information, such as etymological history, dates of use, and—depending on the objective, scope, and size of the publication—an illustration or photograph. A specialized subject or discipline-focused dictionary will go into more detail in its definition, examples, and usage but may omit elements found in a general dictionary such as pronunciation. Dictionaries are generally organized alphabetically, but visual dictionaries, in which the focus is on associating terms with their corresponding objects, are often organized by subject. Dictionaries in electronic form can include enhancements such as links for cross-references, audio samples of correct pronunciation, or visual representations of synonyms.

Types of Dictionaries

General dictionaries are one of two types: abridged and unabridged. An *abridged* dictionary is usually based on a larger work, such as the two-volume *Shorter Oxford English Dictionary on Historical Principles*, which has fewer than 3,900 pages, whereas the full twenty-volume *OED* has 22,000 pages. The goals of an abridged dictionary are convenience, conciseness, and selectivity. An *unabridged* dictionary strives to be comprehensive in its goal to record and reflect the usage and definition of words in use at the time of the dictionary's creation. Also, an unabridged dictionary provides more information about its contents than an abridged dictionary. Whereas an abridged dictionary may include only a word's definition, part of speech, pronunciation, and usage, an unabridged dictionary may include variant spellings; word etymology and dates of use; lengthy notes about usage including examples, synonyms, or word history; and color pictures. Specialized types of dictionaries focus in depth on particular aspects of words, such as etymology or synonyms (see Box 18.1). Examples of these specialized types are discussed later in this chapter.

Box 18.1 Specialized Dictionaries

- **Etymological dictionary**. An etymological dictionary gives the history of individual words with linguistic derivation and examples from writings of the past.
- **Slang dictionary**. A slang dictionary defines terms used in ordinary, informal speech. These terms may include jargon, obscenities, or ephemeral words that go in and out of use quickly.
- **Thesaurus**. A thesaurus contains synonyms and antonyms, usually without definitions. Its purpose is to provide writers with alternate or more specific words.
- **Dual-language dictionary**. A dual-language dictionary has two sections, the first being a dictionary of terms in one language with definitions in a second language. The second section is the reverse, with terms in the second language and definitions in the first language.
- **Dialect dictionary**. A dialect dictionary gives regional variants and usage for words within a language. It may include some slang.
- **Usage dictionary**. A usage dictionary prescribes how a word should be used, based on the way it has been used in the past.

EVALUATION

When evaluating dictionaries, an assessment of their authority and accuracy is essential. Scope considerations include both the number and the content of entries, and also paramount is the clarity of definitions and examples. Because a growing number of titles are available in electronic form, a comparison of the features of print and electronic formats becomes important in relation to the user community's needs.

Authority

Authority can be difficult to ascertain in the case of large, unabridged, comprehensive dictionaries because they are usually the product of editorial staffs of publishers. As a consequence, investigating the authority of the publisher is usually a more productive endeavor. In the United States and Canada, several publishers are well known for the quality of their previously published work: Houghton Mifflin, Merriam-Webster, NTC/Contemporary, Random House, Macmillan USA, and World Book. Internationally, Dorling Kindersley (DK) is noted for its visual dictionaries, and Cambridge University Press and Oxford University Press are noted for their overall reputation and quality of content. In addition, attention should be paid to university presses, which often publish dictionaries of regional interest, with a focus on slang or regionalisms. In general, judging the authority of a dictionary can be informed by professional or user reviews; reviews in the library literature; posting queries to mailing lists or blogs; and browsing catalogs or bookstores.

Accuracy and Currency

The three key factors in judging a dictionary's accuracy and currency are spelling, definition, and usage. Spelling should be up to date, keeping pace with how a word's spelling might have changed in common use. The inclusion of variant spellings is also important for loanwords that have been subsumed into a language from other languages or dialects, such as the word *airplane*, which is an alteration of the French word *aéroplane*. Typically, dictionaries also demonstrate where hyphens should go if necessary. This is a helpful feature especially with terms that sometimes appear as a single word, for example, e-mail or spell-check. Definitions of words should be succinct and clear, without using the word itself. It is important to note here that some dictionaries organize definitions chronologically, whereas others order definitions by the most to the least commonly used. In addition, a comprehensive unabridged dictionary will include several, if not many, definitions, but a general desk dictionary will usually limit itself to commonly used definitions. The same holds true for usage, which is fundamental to understanding how the word is used in context, not only grammatically but also in modern connotations. For example, the word "cookie" has three definitions listed in *The American Heritage Dictionary of the English Language* (2011, 403):

1. A small, usually flat and crisp cake made from sweetened dough.
2. *Slang* A person, usually of a specified kind: *a lawyer who was a tough cookie.*

3. *Computer Science* A collection of information, usually including a username and the current date and time, stored on the local computer of a person using the World Wide Web, used chiefly by websites to identify users who have previously registered or visited the site.

Some dictionaries create their own usage examples, and others use phrases or sentences from literature, poetry, science, or news to demonstrate usage.

Format

The Web catalyzed a wave of evolution in dictionaries. In contrast to dictionaries that were once static representations of language and word use, publishers and communities are now taking advantage of the fluid and mobile nature of technology and putting it to excellent use. Pre-Internet, Merriam-Webster would receive about 1,000 letters every year from dictionary users with new definitions, corrections, and questions. By 2003, they were receiving 1,000 e-mails per month (McQuade 2003, 1688).

A plethora of free and subscription-based dictionary websites are active on the Internet. Some are from standard publishers and include additional online content. An example is *Merriam-Webster Online*, which includes extras such as word games, word of the day, free downloads such as dictionary toolbars, and links to free and fee-based apps. Some subscriptions offer extra features such as more terms and definitions and ad-free searching. In evaluating and selecting which online dictionaries to link from a library website, criteria to consider are similar to criteria used to evaluate print dictionaries with the additional factors of ease of navigation, ease of printing, and quick response time. Crowdsourced dictionaries such as *Urban Dictionary* and meta-dictionaries that bring together several different sources such as *Wordnik* are other examples of new uses and formats for dictionaries as a source not only of definitions but also of correct and colloquial usage of words and phrases. While these sources may contain language considered offensive or obscene, they also function as democratizing, since they provide definitions for slang and jargon typically not found in traditional dictionaries.

Major dictionary publishers have developed apps for mobile phones and tablets. App-based dictionaries create a new set of usability issues for developers and users. Readability on a small screen, ease of navigation, cost, links between words, integration of audio and graphics, and internal/external linking to related terms in addition to the criteria listed here are all factors for librarians to consider. An important consideration to some is choosing an offline app versus an online app. An offline app requires the user to download the dictionary's database, which may cause storage space constraints, as opposed to searching an app's online database. The comprehensiveness of a dictionary's database may also be sacrificed in an offline app. The functionality of a dictionary app, regardless of whether offline or online, is analogous to print. Readability of text is vital, as is the ability to enlarge text or change the layout of a screen. Complexity of entries might be constrained on an app due to small screens, so users may not be able to access features such as images, usage examples, or word origins. However, one advantage of a dictionary app is the option to say a word to search it and to hear the pronunciation spoken. Some apps have translations or thesauri built in, while others only provide a basic definition.

In print, online, and mobile app dictionaries, aesthetics make a difference. Because dictionaries are traditionally text with some pictures (if any), layout is a key factor in assessing usability. Good use of white space, color choices, use of boldface or italics for emphasis, use of different fonts, and size of typeface all have an impact on the ease of locating a definition and readability. In some cases, how a page looks may seem frivolous; however, for users who are visually impaired or who just prefer not to squint over a screen or page of small words, user-friendly aesthetics will improve the user experience and comprehension of the text, page, or screen. Accessibility is also key for readers with visual disabilities. Effective layouts help screen readers "read" pages aloud, and the option to enlarge or change the background color is also beneficial.

Scope

No matter the format, a dictionary's scope is often communicated in its introduction or an "about" section, usually written by the primary author or lead editor. In addition to explaining the purpose and content of the dictionary, the introduction often contains information such as abbreviations and acronyms, pronunciation guides, names of contributors, and how the dictionary came to be compiled and published. This information will help gauge whether the dictionary will supplement or replace other items in the current reference collection, and its content will help decide if the dictionary is age appropriate (i.e., children, college students) and contains a useful amount of information. For instance, language derivation is less important for children than visual representations and a clear pronunciation guide. Last, some dictionaries may include charts, tables, and time lines that make up a sort of miniature ready-reference collection. Such information is definitely helpful but, for many libraries, not a requirement for selection, given that libraries will have other materials such as almanacs and encyclopedias that include such information.

Comparing Similar Dictionaries

In evaluating dictionaries that cover similar topics, regions, or time periods, an excellent rule of thumb is to choose a few words, look them up in each dictionary, and compare the elements of the dictionary entry discussed earlier in this chapter. The words selected should represent commonly used terms, slang, technical jargon, and rarely used words. Other considerations include the presence of a chart or legend explaining the abbreviations used to represent word derivation, part of speech, stress marks, and regionalisms.

SELECTION

With the many varieties of dictionaries available, assessing the value of a particular dictionary is vitally important. Ideally, this process should begin with an exploration of user needs. No matter the type of library, there are often several choices for purchasing dictionaries. Therefore, in the public library setting, the librarian must consider the needs of children, adolescents, adults, and senior citizens. Also important is the demographics of the community; as the ethnic makeup of the community changes, so do the reading and reference needs of library users. In a school library, dictionaries (as all reference works in general) should be useful for a range of ages, reading levels, curricula, and topics. In addition, teachers' and administrators' needs should be addressed, so a more comprehensive dictionary or a dictionary specific to education may be a good purchase depending on other factors such as cost. In academic libraries, considerations include type of institution. For example, a research university's students, faculty, and staff will differ from those of a school of art and design. In any academic library, the balance between curriculum and research needs is key to creating a responsive reference collection. There is no one-size-fits-all solution to selecting dictionaries, especially when considering more specialized, subject-focused dictionaries. Fortunately, publishers provide a wide range of options for dictionaries, so libraries have many choices. For sources for review and evaluation, please see Chapter 14.

Electronic Options

Electronic options for dictionaries include both freely available and subscription-based titles and mobile apps. Features of some specific titles are discussed in the following section. Electronic dictionaries may be single titles or aggregations of titles that can be searched simultaneously. The best-known title available by subscription is the *OED Online*, the electronic version of the *OED*. An example of a single, freely available title is Joan M. Reitz's *Online Dictionary for Library and Information Science* (*ODLIS*), based on the print *Dictionary for Library and Information Science*. The online version supports browsing by initial letter in a word or phrase and searching either headwords or headwords and definitions. Like many subject-specific titles, entries include only definitions. Extensive hyperlinks connect terms within a definition to entries elsewhere in the dictionary. In addition, several entries include links to other websites for additional explanations of terms. Increasingly, multiple dictionaries are available as part of collections in electronic form. For more information on aggregator reference databases in ready-reference collections, please see Chapter 17.

Tools are also available to facilitate simultaneous searching of freely available dictionaries on the Web. In addition to *Wordnik* (described previously), *OneLook Dictionary Search* indexes words in more than 1,000 online dictionaries and provides a range of search options in addition to exact match, such as "*bird" to find words and phrases that end with "bird." When a word is searched, the resulting list of matches identifies the titles of sources that provide a definition, allowing the user to select the one(s) likely to be most authoritative.

Selection tools for finding mobile dictionary apps are as easy as visiting a device's online app store. User reviews can be helpful as an initial filter for quality, ease of searching, ease of navigation, and comprehensiveness. There are also occasionally reviews of dictionary apps from technology and education blogs, which give a more nuanced and in-depth view of selected apps. In general, dictionary apps are free or low-cost, so testing different apps on different devices is not cost prohibitive. One notable exception is *The American Heritage Dictionary* app, which costs $14.99. For hardcore dictionary users, the cost is most likely worth it given the stellar reputation of the text and the number of words included in the fifth edition (over 300,000). Updates to the dictionary are included in the initial price, and a thesaurus is available as an in-app purchase.

IMPORTANT GENERAL SOURCES

This section focuses on several kinds of dictionaries and related tools that are found in typical school, public, or academic library reference collections. Under each category, a few representative titles are described. For information on titles not discussed here, the reader may consult the sources for reviews listed earlier and relevant articles in the Suggested Readings section.

Unabridged Dictionaries

Though unabridged dictionaries are expensive to develop and maintain, the quality ones continue to keep high standards in comprehensiveness, description, and usage. First, a note on the prodigious use of the name "Webster" in the dictionary world is required. Though Merriam-Webster purchased the copyright from Noah Webster in 1843, the name "Webster" is still used by multiple publishers. The name "Webster" has become a sort of colloquialism for the word "dictionary," and this is reflected in the publishing world.

Noah Webster's first unabridged dictionary, *An American Dictionary of the English Language*, appeared in 1828, and the first Webster's dictionary published by Merriam was released in 1847. The latest in the modern series of the Webster's unabridged dictionary, *Webster's Third* (first published in 1961), is infamous for the decision of its editors to be descriptive in its style and content rather than prescriptive. Traditionalists were unsupportive of the inclusion of colloquial and slang words, but others welcomed the change as a true reflection of how new words and phrases contribute to the English language (for more on the controversy, see sources in the Suggested Readings).

Its most current edition, titled *Webster's Third New International Dictionary, Unabridged*, was published in 2002 (a new edition is underway). The print edition includes a complimentary one-year subscription to *Merriam-Webster Unabridged* online, which provides access to additional definitions. Each edition contains nearly a half-million entries with pronunciation, part of speech, definition, example of usage, etymology, labels (obsolete, slang, dialect, regional), cross-references, and more. In the matter of pronunciation as well, description over prescription holds true; entries reflect "general cultivated conversational usage, both formal and informal, throughout the English-speaking world" (Merriam-Webster 2002, 4a). The 2002 edition of *Webster's* also included a new label especially for scientific and technical terms: International Scientific Vocabulary (ISV). ISV labels denote current, in-use words with uncertain language of origin, such as "endoscope" and "cholesterolemia" (Merriam-Webster 2002, 16a). The dictionary is also available online and as an app, either free of cost or for a fee. Both the online and app versions are updated with new entries regularly.

Another authoritative publisher of unabridged dictionaries is Random House. A revised, single-volume edition of the *Random House Webster's Unabridged Dictionary* was published in 2005 with an updated word list, definitions, and etymologies. In addition, the dictionary includes illustrations, maps, and supplements in the form of lists, tables, time lines, style guides, and more. Like other dictionary publishers, Random House also boasts an ever-growing database of new words, new uses for words, and updated definitions. It is also worth mentioning that

Random House published the *Random House Webster's American Sign Language Dictionary: Unabridged* in 2008.

Etymological Dictionaries

The *OED* is by far the most comprehensive etymological dictionary available. The story of the *OED* is a fascinating history of an incredible human achievement that began in 1857 and continues to the present day (see Suggested Readings at the end of this chapter). The publication has had countless contributors throughout its development and reflects the technology of its time; it was made available in microfilm in 1971, on CD-ROM in 1992, and on the Web in 2000. The most recent edition in print was published in 1989, combining the text of the first edition, published between 1884 and 1928, with four supplements published between 1972 and 1986. Three volumes of supplements, the *Oxford English Dictionary: Additions Series*, were subsequently published in 1993 (two volumes) and 1997 (one volume). The second edition contains nearly 300,000 main entries, a 15 percent increase over the first edition, but, more important, the second edition also contains 34 percent more text, with expanded citations, usage examples, and notes. The *Additions Series* not only contained new words such as "Bechdel test" and "precariat" but also added new meanings to older words; for example, to the entry for the word "read," editors added the following definition: "To interpret or translate (genetic information); *spec.* to extract genetic information from (a particular sequence of nucleic acids), or to extract from a given sequence the genetic information necessary to synthesize (a particular substance)" (Simpson and Weiner 1993, 1:220). The *OED Online* is now home to the second edition and the *Additions Series*, and on its website the Help section lists the new words added to the database on a quarterly basis. The quarterly updates to the *OED Online*, which began in 2000, are considered to be its third edition. The *OED Online* can be considered as a database with extensive searching options, from simple word and proximity searching to Boolean searching across one or more fields (such as headword, definition, and etymology) in the dictionary entries. The quotations illustrating word usage are also searchable.

Though the full twenty-volume second edition is usually out of the price range of most public and school libraries, Oxford University Press has several smaller options for these libraries. The *Shorter Oxford English Dictionary* is a two-volume set that is currently in its sixth edition, published in 2007. It is also available as a fee-based app. The *Oxford Dictionary of Word Origins* was published in 2010 and provides narrative descriptions of words, tracing their development through other languages and time periods to present-day English, including regionalisms and older spellings. The *Shorter OED* and the *Oxford Dictionary of Word Origins* are excellent options for those libraries that choose not to purchase the full *OED*. Another choice is Eric Partridge's *Origins: An Etymological Dictionary of Modern English*. Though not as comprehensive as the *OED*, it is equally informative and useful as a single-volume etymological dictionary. The most attractive aspect of *Origins* is its focus on current and modern language, with more than 20,000 words, as well as lists of prefixes and suffixes.

For readers interested in Canadian English, the second edition of the *A Dictionary of Canadianisms on Historical Principles* was published digitally in 2017. Building on the legacy of the first print edition, the digital project was funded by the Canadian government, universities, and the Dictionary Society of North

America. The Canadian English Lab at the University of British Columbia leads this effort to document historical changes in Canadian English.

Desk Dictionaries

Desk dictionaries are usually single-volume and more concise than an unabridged dictionary. Content is more focused on current usage and more up to date, with rare, technical, and obsolete words and definitions omitted. Etymologies are usually abbreviated or do not appear in a desk dictionary, and appendices usually contain supplemental lists of things such as weights and measures, abbreviations, names, and dates. The biggest difference between the desk dictionaries discussed in this section is layout; any of the works listed would be excellent choices for home, school, or office.

The American Heritage Dictionary of the English Language is well known for its readable and aesthetically pleasing layout. Words are in boldface, printed with a dark blue ink, and appear in syllabicated form, distinguishing them from accompanying pronunciation, part of speech, definitions, brief etymological note (when included), usage examples, and variant forms (also when included). Illustrations are in both black and white and color, and nearly every page has a mini-guide to pronunciation. The revised fifth edition, published in 2016, includes over 10,000 new words, including "cryptocurrency" and "rando," and over 4,000 new images. The dictionary is also available for a fee as an app.

The *Merriam-Webster's Collegiate Dictionary* is part of the Merriam-Webster family of publications. The strength of the *Collegiate Dictionary* lies in its content, taken from the Merriam-Webster word database. The eleventh edition, published in 2014, contains about 10,000 new words, more examples of usage, idioms, and updated definitions. Illustrations are black-and-white drawings, and entries include the usual pronunciation, brief etymology, and usage examples. With Merriam-Webster's stellar reputation, libraries may want to consider a subscription to Merriam-Webster's online products in addition to or instead of purchasing print, depending on factors such as user needs and budgets. The app version includes Voice Search, an integrated thesaurus, and user-generated Favorites.

School Dictionaries

Dictionaries for children and young adults are published by nearly every reputable dictionary publisher, including Oxford University Press, Houghton Mifflin, Macmillan, Merriam-Webster, and World Book, leaving readers to decide between a visual or a textual focus. Visual dictionaries can be exciting ways to introduce new words to children, with bright colors, images, and simple definitions. Textual dictionaries may be more appropriate for older children, depending on reading ability and grade level. In each case, important criteria for selection include clear layout, easy-to-understand definitions, and enough words to interest and educate a child using the dictionary. Large print and the highlighting of main words are both helpful at this level, as are simple examples of usage. Dictionaries are available for specific age groups, organized alphabetically and by subject, both with their advantages and drawbacks. For settings serving children and young adults, having a few of both types of dictionaries is a wise choice. Because use of the word "children's" or "student" in the title does not always correspond to a specific age range or grade level, evaluation of such a dictionary should include determining the target audience. For example, Merriam-Webster has a series of four titles: *Merriam-Webster's First Dictionary* (grades K–2; published in 2012), *Merriam-Webster's Elementary Dictionary* (grades 3–5; published in 2019), *Merriam-Webster's Intermediate Dictionary* (grades 6–8; last published in 2016), and *Merriam-Webster's School Dictionary* (grades 9–11; last published in 2015). Dorling-Kindersley (DK) continues to set the standard for visual dictionaries, especially for children, with the 2017 publication of the *Ultimate Visual Dictionary*. For older readers, *The American Heritage Student Dictionary* is focused on providing more detailed information such as etymology and usage notes. The *World Book Dictionary* is a two-volume set with more than 225,000 entries and 3,000 illustrations. Words likely to be used by students are clearly defined, and usage examples are included.

Dual-Language Dictionaries

In the case of dual-language dictionaries, the options available include everything from mini-abridged dictionaries for travelers to comprehensive dictionaries for scholars and academics to dictionary apps and translation apps. Specialized dictionaries for those traveling on business, dictionaries for students studying abroad, and dictionaries devoted to single subjects such as food are also abundant. In the case of foreign languages, the authority of the publisher is key. Cassell's, HarperCollins, Cambridge University Press, and Larousse have an excellent reputation in the world of dual-language dictionaries, and Oxford University Press also publishes dual-language dictionaries suitable for a range of readers. In addition to print titles available from Oxford, *Oxford Language Dictionaries Online* includes bilingual dictionaries in Arabic, Chinese, French, German, Hindi, Italian, Russian, and Spanish with up-to-date translations of words and phrases, illustrative examples, and native speaker audio pronunciation of words.

Visual dictionaries are a well-established format for dual-language dictionaries and useful to both language learners and travelers. As previously noted, DK is a well-known publisher in this area, with titles such as *Mandarin-English Visual Dictionary* and *English for Everyone: English Grammar Guide*. DK's *5 Language Visual Dictionary* includes English, French, German, Spanish, and Italian. The book is organized by broad categories, including people, appearance, health, home, services, shopping, food, leisure, and more. Each image is accompanied by the word printed in a different font according to its language. Images are all in color and are pleasing to the eye. The book also includes helpful short phrases, such as "Do you have any vegetarian dishes?" and "Where can I park?" An index of all the words in the dictionary, arranged alphabetically by language, is also included. This type of book would be an excellent addition to any type of library with either foreign-language or English-language learners. The *Merriam-Webster's Compact 5-Language Visual Dictionary* is equally as robust, with over 1,100 pages with illustrations and words (with masculine, feminine, and neutral version notes) organized clearly into broad categories such as "House and Do-it-Yourself," "Transportation," and "Animal Kingdom."

A large number of dual-language dictionaries in many languages can be accessed on the Web, including online counterparts of the print versions from major publishers listed here. A number of free websites can serve as aids to translating from one language into another as well, such as *WordReference.com* and *Reverso.com*. Translation apps are now commonplace, including *Google Translate* and the *iTranslate* suite of apps. One unique element of *Google Translate* is Word Lens, which allows the user to take pictures of words for a translation using the built-in camera.

Dialect and Regionalisms Dictionaries

One of the most fascinating types of dictionaries is that which chronicles the evolution and use of language from a specific geographic area. Three such works are the *Dictionary of American Regional English* (*DARE*), the *Dictionary of the American West*, and the *Dictionary of Smoky Mountain English*. The first is legendary in its scope: 10 years, 1,000 communities, nearly 3,000 informants, and 80 fieldworkers, ultimately totaling more than two million responses to the survey created by the American Dialect Society (ADS). The ADS had planned *DARE* since the beginning of the society in the late 1800s and held on to this goal through the Depression and two World Wars, finally appointing an editor in the 1960s. Thanks to federal funding, the editors and staff developed a survey (included in an appendix) to record the use of English throughout the country. Responses from informants, a listing of whom is included, complemented other primary and secondary sources of usage, such as oral histories, diaries, letters, regional fiction, and newspapers, to name a few. *DARE* contains entries for single words, phrases, and compounds, with each entry including parts of speech, etymology, geographical and usage labels, definitions, and cross-references for variant spellings. *DARE* lives up to its goal of "testify[ing] to the wondrous variety and creativeness of human language, and specifically of the English language as it is used regionally in the United States" (Cassidy, Hall, and Von Schneidemesser 2013, xxii). *DARE* continues its work with plans to begin a new round of fieldwork and to continue developing the *Digital DARE*.

Michael Montgomery and Joseph Hall's *Dictionary of Smoky Mountain English*, published in 2004, achieves a similar level of comprehensiveness for the "traditional and contemporary folk language of Appalachia" (Montgomery and Hall 2004, vii). Based on the life work of Joseph Hall, a trained phonetician who studied Appalachian English over his entire career, the book chronicles and identifies two centuries' worth of words, phrases, and definitions from three generations of members of the Appalachian community. In fact, Hall's work was consulted by the editors of *DARE*. Like *DARE*, other primary and secondary sources, such as documents, recordings, and transcripts from archives, historical societies, and libraries were also used to create the word and definition list. Entries include definitions, usage examples and their supporting citations, variant spellings, labels, and cross-references. The book also includes fascinating historical material, such as informative chapters about the grammar and syntax of the Great Smoky Mountain areas.

Win Blevins's *Dictionary of the American West* began as a pamphlet for book editors unfamiliar with the vernacular of the American West. As the author researched and wrote, his goal expanded to "restore some of the full richness of the history of the West" (Blevins 2001, vii). The book is fascinating given that the American West was home to a wide diversity of people: Native Americans, Mormons, Hispanics, French Canadians, Mexicans, enslaved peoples, and immigrants from Europe, to name a few. The book's entries include definitions, some black-and-white illustrations and photos, a history of how the word came to be used, and, occasionally, examples of use. The book's introduction is a captivating overview of the history of the area and also lists books on the topic of the American West.

English Language Learner Dictionaries

For English language learners, the major dictionary publishers have excellent options for all ages. *Merriam-Webster's Essential Learner's English Dictionary* and *Merriam-Webster's Advanced Learner's English Dictionary* both are suitable for classrooms, public and school libraries, and academic libraries with education departments. For learner dictionaries, clarity of definitions and usage is key; visuals are also important. Oxford University Press has a series of titles for kindergartners through adults; their website also features a Teacher's Club with classroom activities. The *Oxford Picture Dictionary*, currently in its third print edition, includes a dedicated site for teachers, while the *Oxford Picture Dictionary for Learners of English* includes an audio component. The *Oxford Advanced American Dictionary for Learners of English*, published in 2011, contains not only definitions but also words in context and an Academic Word List for students.

Slang and Euphemism Dictionaries

The most entertaining types of dictionaries are those that keep a record of the various words in our language that do not appear, as a rule, in general dictionaries. The word "slang" has several synonyms, including "vernacular," "colloquialism," "mumbo jumbo," "vulgarity," "lingo," and "jargon." In general, slang is either language used by a specific group, such as teenagers, or language that is informal and conversational, often used for added effect. Euphemisms are closely related to slang at first glance, given that both are colloquialisms, but the difference is that euphemisms seek to restate or deflect a harsh, perhaps-too-realistic term or phrase. For example, the term "person of interest," when used by police, usually equates with the word "suspect" or "witness." Both slang and euphemisms can be geographic- and occupation-based as well.

Words, at least the ones used in conversation, are a fascination for people. Publications recording the rise and fall of slang and euphemisms exist for libraries as well as for consumers' personal libraries. Aaron Peckham, the creator of *Urban Dictionary*, also released a print edition of the online dictionary in addition to calendars and flashcards, titled *Urban Dictionary: Freshest Street Slang Defined*. Two titles offer a look into how colorful language evolved over time: Rob Chirico's *Damn!: A Cultural History of Swearing in Modern America* traces the use of expletives through the latter part of the 20th century, using pop culture, politics, and the media as primary sources. Rosemarie Ostler's *Dewdroppers, Waldos, and Slackers: A Decade-by-Decade Guide to the Vanishing Vocabulary of the Twentieth Century* is broader in scope and provides more of a historical look at slang generally. *Dictionary.com* has sites dedicated to slang and emoji, and the *Internet Slang Dictionary & Translator* searches both words and acronyms used frequently in texting. Several apps for both Android and iOS assist with defining slang terms and acronyms, such as *Chat Slang* (which includes a list of text slang for parents), and specialized jargon for specific occupations, foreign languages, or topics.

More traditional reference sources for current colloquialisms are available as well. Jonathon Green published his comprehensive and celebrated *Green's Dictionary of Slang* in 2010, with over 100,000 definitions and over 400,000 citations. The first two volumes of the *Random House Historical Dictionary of American Slang* were published in 1994 and 1997. For librarians who seek to show the development of the English language in America from colonial times to the present day, this would be an excellent source. *The Routledge Dictionary of Modern American Slang and Unconventional English* provides an authoritative source for contemporary American slang with 25,000 entries accompanied by citations and examples of usage. The second edition of *The New Partridge Dictionary of Slang and Unconventional English*, a two-volume set, contains over 60,000 entries and is unique in its international focus, bringing in entries from several English-speaking countries around the world. Entries include not only definitions but dates and citations to common usage as well. *New Partridge* begins with 1945, but readers who want a historical perspective on slang can consult the older edition of *Partridge*, which remains the best record of British slang antedating 1945.

A source that provides a different, geographic perspective is R.W. Holder's *How Not to Say What You Mean: A Dictionary of Euphemisms*. Published by Oxford University Press, the fourth edition of this resource covers American and British euphemisms, both contemporary and traditional. The most interesting aspect of this dictionary is the number of words shared by both countries. Each entry contains the main word, definitions, usage examples or citations, and notes, such as "obsolete" or "American." C.J. Moore's *How to Speak Brit: The Quintessential Guide to the King's English, Cockney Slang and Other Flummoxing British Phrases* and *British English A to Zed: A Definitive Guide to the Queen's English*, edited by Norman W. Schur, Eugene Ehrlich, and Richard Ehrlich, while less scholarly, are more portable guides to usage of British colloquialisms.

McGraw-Hill's Conversational American English: The Illustrated Guide to the Everyday Expressions of American English edited by Richard Spears stands out from the rest with its focus on English language learners. The book contains more than 3,000 expressions organized by broad theme, such as "Making Friends," "Polite Encounters," and "Small Talk." The goal of the dictionary is to help new English speakers not only understand the idiomatic phrases being used in conversation but also use English correctly in conversation. For librarians looking for an abridged slang dictionary, either *The American Heritage Dictionary of Idioms*, which contains 10,000 expressions, or the *Dictionary of Contemporary Slang*, by Tony Thorne, which contains more than 7,000 words in its updated fourth edition published in 2014, would be worthwhile investments.

Thesauri and Usage Guides

A thesaurus is an invaluable tool to anyone who writes for work or pleasure and for English language learners. Essentially a dictionary of synonyms and antonyms, a thesaurus helps novice and expert writers alike add variety and clarity to their work.

First published in England in 1852 by physician Peter Mark Roget, *Roget's International Thesaurus* is the standard thesaurus of choice. Currently in its seventh edition, *Roget's* is organized not alphabetically but instead by category. Fifteen classes of words contain more than 1,000 categories, and 325,000 synonyms, antonyms, and phrases serve to guide readers, writers, and speakers to the best word or phrase for their purpose. Classes are broad, such as "Place," "Natural Phenomena," "Measure and Shape," "Behavior," and "Language." Categories are more detailed; for example, under the class "Mind and Ideas," categories include "Comparison," "Discrimination," "Judgment," and "Theory and Philosophy." Cross-references and quotations help to add meaning and context to each category and entry, and an alphabetical index helps users locate specific words when necessary. Lists of words without synonyms appear in sidebars throughout the book with their related class; for instance, names of muscles and bones appear in the "Body" class. The layout of the book is clear and helpful to the reader, with main words in bold and numbered for easy location. *Roget's 21st Century Thesaurus* and *The Concise Roget's International Thesaurus* are both desk versions of the original.

In addition to *Roget's*, Oxford University Press has entered the thesaurus market with its usual quality and authority. The *Oxford American Writer's Thesaurus* is suitable for middle school and high school students, as is the *American Heritage Student Thesaurus*. For college students, the *Merriam-Webster's Collegiate Thesaurus* and *Roget's* are suitable, and online both *Merriam-Webster Online* and *Dictionary.com* include a thesaurus search option in addition to the dictionary. For new speakers of English, the *Oxford Learner's Thesaurus* is an excellent complement to any of the dictionaries referenced in this chapter.

Academic libraries invest heavily in general thesauri but should also be aware of discipline-specific works that will aid students and scholars in their research. The *Thesaurus of Psychological Index Terms*, published by the American Psychological Association (APA), was last published in print in 2007, but the APA posts updates of new terms to their website and integrates new terms into the PsycINFO database. Likewise, the eighth edition of the *Thesaurus of Aging Terminology*, published by the AARP in 2005, is also available online. *The Art and Architecture Thesaurus*, published by the Getty Research Institute of the J. Paul Getty Trust, is now searchable online.

Usage guides are another important resource for writers. These go one step further than a general desk dictionary by providing quotations and citations illustrating grammar and word use. Two examples published in the last decade are given here. The third edition of *Garner's Modern American Usage*, published by Oxford University Press in 2009, not only includes nouns, verbs, adjectives, idioms, and exclamations but also explains distinct jargon such as "commercialese" and "computerese" and figures of speech such as the "zeugma." In addition to examples of word and phrase use, *Garner's* includes a lengthy bibliographic time line of usage guides and a bibliography of sources used to gather examples. The third edition of *Common Errors in English Usage*, based on the popular website of the same name, is a good choice for new or native English learners for its readable and authoritative approach to improving speaking and writing.

Abbreviation and Acronym Dictionaries

Dictionaries of abbreviations and acronyms are key sources for any type of library, especially those that serve writers, researchers, journalists, or students. The sheer number of abbreviations and acronyms in the United States alone is mind-boggling, so a quality dictionary is an essential reference tool. The two largest and perhaps most comprehensive publications are Gale's *Acronyms, Initialisms & Abbreviations Dictionary* and its counterpart, *Reverse Acronyms, Initialisms & Abbreviations Dictionary*. Each is a multivolume set covering abbreviations and acronyms from specific subjects and disciplines, associations, organizations, companies, and periodical titles. The latter is organized alphabetically by abbreviation, and the former is organized alphabetically by organization name. Published annually, the two sets easily stand alone as core sources. There are also numerous publications for special subjects, such as medicine, politics, business, and law, among others. Because abbreviations dictionaries are usually compiled and published by publishing houses within specific disciplines or industries, the information is usually authoritative and credible. There are several online acronym dictionaries, including *AcronymFinder.com* and *Dictionary.com*'s acronym finder.

Quotation Dictionaries

Another core source for any reference collection is a dictionary of quotations. Questions from users may focus on the source of a particular quotation or on how a quotation appeared originally; reasons for researching quotations can vary from a planned toast at a wedding to a speech for a class or event or even to the settling of a bet. However, if a quotation book has a decent index, quotations can be easy to locate and verify. In addition to the two sources noted in this section, librarians may like to supplement their collections with more focused quotation books, such as dictionaries of song lyrics, movie quotations, political speeches, Shakespeare, or quotations specific to weddings, graduations, birthdays, retirements, and other special occasions.

The core quotations source is *Bartlett's Familiar Quotations*, now in its eighteenth edition, published since 1855. With 25,000 quotations from more than 2,000 authors, *Bartlett's* covers a wide variety of subjects, time periods, and people, from the Bible and Shakespeare to contemporary figures such as former president Barack Obama and songwriter Patti Smith. It is arranged chronologically and includes an author index and a keyword index to provide and enhance access. Its moderate price puts it within the reach of many libraries' budgets, and for the content and history contained in *Bartlett's* it should be part of every library's collection. In 2013, *Barlett's Familiar Black Quotations*, edited by Retha Powers with an introduction by Henry Louis Gates, Jr. was published.

Other publishers have emulated *Bartlett's* and developed their own quotation books. Oxford University Press has an impressive array of choices, from the general and comprehensive to the specialized. The *Oxford Dictionary of Quotations*, now in its eighth edition, is another core source for libraries of any type. Like *Bartlett's*, sources of quotations come from traditional works and from elements of modern culture. An excellent keyword index helps the reader locate authors and verify quotations, and informative sidebars contribute to the comprehensive nature of the work. Citations provide context for quotations, and cross-references help readers find quotations on related topics. Oxford also publishes many other quotation dictionaries focusing on literature, science, politics, law, business, humor, and other specific topics, industries, or occupations.

SEARCH STRATEGIES

Questions about definitions of words or phrases can be among the most important interactions between librarian and user. Sometimes just giving an example of how to correctly use a word or illustrating a word's definition with a sentence can help a reader understand a topic in a whole new way. Librarians need to be cognizant of both the tools and the many ways users can approach them. The key to understanding how to use a specific dictionary is to make a list of words and look them up in different dictionaries to compare and contrast the clarity, completeness, and credibility of the sources and to experience first-hand how the same words are treated in different dictionaries. The introduction and any how-to-use-this-book section is a valuable tool to review so that the information in the book can be used to its fullest extent. For some of the more subject-specific dictionaries and word books, such sections are crucial to understanding the organization of and access methods to retrieve the information within the book.

Just as one must work to become familiar with the scope and organization of print titles, the features and search capabilities of electronic sources, both available free of cost and subscription based, need to be explored so that an informed choice can be made as to when turning to the Web is likely to be more efficient and effective than consulting print sources. Depending on the source, electronic format dictionaries may allow users to differentiate between exact and "near" spellings and to search other elements of an entry (definition, quotations, word usage, word history) in addition to the entry word. The capability to simultaneously search multiple sources increases the chances of locating the information sought. Enhancements such as audio pronunciation go beyond the capabilities of print resources, as do visual representations of words and their synonyms and antonyms.

Readers of all ages, from children to adults to senior citizens, have a need for dictionaries, which can explain the wide variety of print and online dictionaries available today. Reference librarians have the enviable task of getting to know the character and strengths of the dictionaries, quotation books, and thesauri in their collections for the benefit of the users in their community. As the example in Box 18.2 illustrates, it is important to develop an appreciation for the range of answers that different sources can provide for even a seemingly simple definition question. Understanding why the information is sought and how it will be used can be helpful in developing a search strategy to guide the user to the sources most likely to be helpful in responding to a particular word-related question.

Box 18.2 Search Strategy: Defining "Suffragette"

In seeking a definition, it would be natural to begin with a desk dictionary such as *Merriam-Webster's Collegiate Dictionary*, where one finds the following definition for suffragette:

> *n* (1906): a woman who advocates suffrage for women. (2006, 1248)

This is not particularly informative. *The American Heritage Dictionary of the English Language* adds a bit more detail but still requires the user to look further if unfamiliar with the meaning of "suffrage":

> An advocate of women's suffrage, especially in the United Kingdom. (2011, 1742)

The *OED Online* provides a more detailed definition, accompanied by numerous examples of the word's use in context, beginning with a quotation from the 1906 *Daily Mail*:

> A female supporter of the cause of women's political enfranchisement, *esp*. one of a violent or "militant" type.

Thus far, only general dictionaries have been consulted. A search of subject-specific dictionaries yields definitions reflecting the particular perspective of each. Some examples include the following:

In *Dictionary of American Government and Politics*, the term does not appear; however, there is a nearly two-page entry on women's suffrage that begins as follows, "The term 'women's suffrage' refers to the economic and political reform movement aimed at extending the suffrage, or right to vote, to women. Its origins are often traced back to the United States in the 1820s" (Watts 2010, 329).

According to *The SAGE Dictionary of Sociology* (2006, 294), "This 19th-century term denotes the right to vote in elections. The feminine 'ette' ending was added to denote those women who in the early part of the 20th century campaigned to have voting rights extended to women."

Finally, one can turn to a usage guide, *The American Heritage Guide to Contemporary Usage and Style* (2005), to differentiate between "suffragist" and "suffragette":

> The word *suffragist*, meaning an advocate of the extension of political voting rights, especially to women, is used of both men and women. The word *suffragette*, which refers only to female suffragists, became popular in the early 20th century and was favored by many female British suffragists as well as some groups and individuals who mocked women's attempts to gain suffrage. In the United States, however, the word *suffragist* was preferred by advocates of women's suffrage, who regarded *suffragette* as a sexist diminutive.

REFERENCES

The American Heritage Dictionary of the English Language, 5th ed. 2011. Boston: Houghton Mifflin Harcourt.

Blevins, Win. 2001. *Dictionary of the American West: Over 5,000 Terms and Expressions from Aarigaa! to Zopilote*, 2nd ed. Seattle: Sasquatch Books.

Cassidy, Frederic G., Joan Houston Hall, and Luanne Von Schneidemesser, eds. 2013. *Dictionary of American Regional English.* Cambridge, MA: Belknap Press of Harvard University Press.

Flanagan, Padraic. 2014. "RIP for OED as World's Finest Dictionary Goes Out of Print." *The Telegraph*, April 20. http://www.telegraph.co.uk/culture/culturenews/10777079/RIP-for-OED-as-worlds-finest-dictionary-goes-out-of-print.html.

Kroskrity, Paul V. 2015. "Designing a Dictionary for an Endangered Language Community: Lexicographical Deliberations, Language Ideological Clarifications." *Language Documentation & Conservation* 9: 140–57.

McQuade, Molly. 2003. "Defining a Dictionary." *Booklist* 99: 1688.

Merriam-Webster. 2002. *Webster's Third New International Dictionary of the English Language, Unabridged.* Springfield, MA: Merriam-Webster.

Montgomery, Michael B., and Joseph S. Hall, eds. 2004. *Dictionary of Smoky Mountain English.* Knoxville: University of Tennessee Press.

Mugglestone, Lynda. 2011. *Dictionaries: A Very Short Introduction.* New York: Oxford University Press.

Read, Allen Walker. 2005. "Encyclopaedias and Dictionaries." *Encyclopaedia Britannica*, 15th ed., Vol. 18, 257–86. Chicago: Encyclopaedia Britannica.

Simpson, John, and Edmund Weiner, eds. 1993. *Oxford English Dictionary: Additions Series.* New York: Oxford University Press.

United Nations Educational, Scientific, and Cultural Organization. n.d. *Frequent Asked Questions on Endangered Languages.* http://www.unesco.org/new/en/culture/themes/endangered-languages/faq-on-endangered-languages/.

LIST OF SOURCES

5 Language Visual Dictionary. 2016. Revised and updated. New York: DK Publishing.

AcronymFinder.com. https://www.acronymfinder.com/.

Acronyms, Initialisms & Abbreviations Dictionary: A Guide to Acronyms, Abbreviations, Contractions, Alphabetic Symbols, and Similar Condensed Appellations, 51st ed. 2017. Farmington Hills, MI: Gale Cengage Learning.

Alexander, Caleb, and American Imprint Collection (Library of Congress). 1800. *The Columbian Dictionary of the English Language: In which Many New Words, Peculiar to the United States, and Many Words of General Use, Not found in Any Other English Dictionary, Are Inserted. . . : To which Is Prefixed, a Prosodial Grammar, Containing, a Short Dissertation on Vowels and Consonants : To the Whole is Added Heathen Mythology, Or, A Classical Pronouncing Dictionary.* Printed at Boston: By Isaiah Thomas and Ebenezer T. Andrews.

The American Heritage Dictionary of the English Language, 5th ed. 2016. Revised and updated. Boston: Houghton Mifflin Harcourt.

The American Heritage Dictionary of the English Language. 2018. [Mobile app]. Boston: Houghton Mifflin Harcourt.

The American Heritage Dictionary of Idioms, 2nd ed. 2013. Boston: Houghton Mifflin Harcourt.

The American Heritage Guide to Contemporary Usage and Style. 2005. Boston: Houghton Mifflin.

The American Heritage Student Dictionary, 4th ed. 2019. Boston: Houghton Mifflin Harcourt.

The American Heritage Student Thesaurus, Updated edition. 2015. Boston: Houghton Mifflin.

The Art and Architecture Thesaurus. 2017. The Getty Research Institute. Last modified March 7, 2017. http://www.getty.edu/research/tools/vocabularies/aat.

Bartlett's Familiar Quotations: A Collection of Passages, Phrases, and Proverbs Traced to Their Sources in Ancient and Modern Literature, 18th ed. 2012. Boston: Little, Brown.

Barlett's Familiar Black Quotations: 5,000 years of Literature, Lyrics, Poems, Passages, Phrases and Proverbs from Voices Around the World. 2013. Boston: Little, Brown.

Bevis, John. *Aaaaw to Zzzzzd: The Words of Birds: North America, Britain, and Northern Europe.* 2010. Cambridge, MA: MIT Press.

Blevins, Winifred. 2008. *Dictionary of the American West: Over 5,000 Terms and Expressions from Aarigaa! to Zopilote*, 2nd ed., expanded and revised. Fort Worth, TX: TCU Press.

Caradec, François. 2018. *Dictionary of Gestures: Expressive Comportments and Movements in Use around the World.* Translated by Chris Clark. Cambridge, MA: MIT Press.

Chat Slang. 2018. [Mobile app]. Minneapolis, MN: Sharpened Productions.

Chirico, Rob. 2014. *Damn!: A Cultural History of Swearing in Modern America.* Durham, NC: Pitchstone Publishing.

Common Errors in English Usage, 3rd ed. 2013. Sherwood, OR: William, James & Co.

The Concise Roget's International Thesaurus, 7th ed. 2011. New York: Harper.

Dictionary of American Regional English. 5 vols. 1985–2013. Cambridge, MA: Belknap Press of Harvard University Press, http://www.daredictionary.com. Subscription required for full access.

Dictionary.com. http://dictionary.reference.com/.

Dollinger, Stefan, and Margery Fee, eds. 2017. *DCHP-2: A Dictionary of Canadianisms on Historical Principles*, 2nd ed. With the assistance of Baillie Ford, Alexandra Gaylie and Gabrielle Lim. Vancouver, BC: University of British Columbia. http://www.dchp.ca/dchp2/.

English for Everyone: English Grammar Guide. 2016. London: Dorling Kindersley Limited.

Garner, Bryan A. 2009. *Garner's Modern American Usage*, 3rd ed. New York: Oxford University Press.

Google Translate. 2018. [Mobile app]. Mountain View, CA: Google, Inc.

Green, Jonathon. 2010. *Green's Dictionary of Slang*. London: Chambers.

Holder, R. W. 2007. *How Not to Say What You Mean: A Dictionary of Euphemisms*, 4th ed. New York: Oxford University Press.

Internet Slang Dictionary & Translator. NoSlang.com. http://www.noslang.com/.

iTranslate. 2018. [mobile app]. Pischeldorf, Austria: Sonico GmbH.

Johnson, Samuel. 1755. *A Dictionary of the English Language: In which the Words Are Deduced from Their Originals, and Illustrated in Their Different Significations by Examples from the Best Writers : To which Are Prefixed, a History of the Language, and an English Grammar*. London: Printed by W. Strahan, for J. and P. Knapton.

Kersey, John. 1702. *The New English Dictionary*. London: Printed for H. Bonwicke & R. Knaplock.

Mandarin-English Visual Dictionary. 2015. New York: DK Publishing.

Merriam-Webster Dictionary. 2018. [Mobile app]. Springfield, MA: Merriam-Webster.

Merriam-Webster Online. Springfield, MA: Merriam-Webster. http://www.merriam-webster.com/.

Merriam-Webster Unabridged. Springfield, MA: Merriam-Webster. http://unabridged.merriam-webster.com/. Subscription required for full access.

Merriam-Webster's Advanced Learner's English Dictionary. 2017. Springfield, MA: Merriam-Webster.

Merriam-Webster's Collegiate Dictionary, 11th ed. 2014. Springfield, MA: Merriam-Webster.

Merriam-Webster's Collegiate Thesaurus, 2nd ed. 2010. Springfield, MA: Merriam-Webster.

Merriam-Webster's Compact 5-Language Visual Dictionary. 2010. Springfield, MA: Merriam-Webster.

Merriam-Webster's Elementary Dictionary. 2019. Updated and expanded edition. Springfield, MA: Merriam-Webster.

Merriam-Webster's Essential Learner's English Dictionary. 2010. Springfield, MA: Merriam-Webster.

Merriam-Webster's First Dictionary. 2012. Springfield, MA: Merriam-Webster.

Merriam-Webster's Intermediate Dictionary. 2016. Revised and updated edition. Springfield, MA: Merriam-Webster.

Merriam-Webster's School Dictionary. 2015. Springfield, MA: Merriam-Webster.

Montgomery, Michael, and Joseph Hall. 2004. *Dictionary of Smoky Mountain English.* Knoxville: University of Tennessee Press. http://artsandsciences.sc.edu/engl/dictionary/dictionary.html.

Moore, C. J. 2014. *How to Speak Brit: The Quintessential Guide to the King's English, Cockney Slang, and Other Flummoxing British Phrases*. New York: Gotham Books.

The New Partridge Dictionary of Slang and Unconventional English, 2nd ed. 2013. New York: Routledge.

OED Online. Oxford: Oxford University Press. http://www.oed.com. Subscription required for full access.

OneLook Dictionary Search. http://www.onelook.com.

Ostler, Rosemarie. 2005. *Dewdroppers, Waldos, and Slackers: A Decade-by-Decade Guide to the Vanishing Vocabulary of the Twentieth Century*. New York: Oxford University Press.

Oxford Advanced American Dictionary for Learners of English. 2011. New York: Oxford University Press.

Oxford American Writer's Thesaurus, 3rd ed. 2012. New York: Oxford University Press.

Oxford Dictionary of Quotations, 8th ed. 2014. Oxford: Oxford University Press.

Oxford Dictionary of Word Origins. 2010. New York: Oxford University Press.

Oxford English Dictionary, 2nd ed. 1989. 20 vols. New York: Oxford University Press.

Oxford English Dictionary: Additions Series. 1993–1997. 2 vols. New York: Oxford University Press.

Oxford Language Dictionaries Online. Oxford: Oxford University Press. https://languages.oup.com/. Subscription required for full access.

Oxford Learner's Thesaurus: A Dictionary of Synonyms, 4th ed. 2012. Oxford: Oxford University Press.

Oxford Picture Dictionary, 2nd ed. 2008. New York, NY: Oxford University Press.

Oxford Picture Dictionary for Learners of English. 2016. Oxford: Oxford University Press.

Partridge, Eric. 1937. *A Dictionary of Slang and Unconventional English.* New York: Macmillan.

Partridge, Eric. 2008. *Origins: An Etymological Dictionary of Modern English.* New York: Routledge.

Peckham, Aaron. 2015. *Urban Dictionary: Freshest Street Slang Defined.* New ed. Kansas City, MO: Andrews McMeel.

Random House Historical Dictionary of American Slang, 1st ed. 1994–2007. 2 vols. New York: Random House.

Random House Webster's American Sign Language Dictionary: Unabridged. 2008. New York: Random House.

Random House Webster's Unabridged Dictionary, 2nd ed. 2005. Revised and updated edition. New York: Random House.

Reitz, Joan M. *Dictionary for Library and Information Science.* 2004. Westport, CT: Libraries Unlimited.

Reitz, Joan M. n.d. *Online Dictionary for Library and Information Science (ODLIS).* Santa Barbara, CA: ABC-CLIO. http://www.abc-clio.com/ODLIS/odlis_A.aspx.

Reverse Acronyms, Initialisms & Abbreviations Dictionary: A Companion Volume to Acronyms, Initialisms & Abbreviations Dictionary, with Terms Arranged Alphabetically by Meaning of Acronym, Initialism Or Abbreviation, 51st ed. 2017. Farmington Hills, MI: Gale Cengage Learning.

Reverso.com. http://www.reverso.com.

Roget's International Thesaurus, 7th ed. 2011. New York: HarperCollins.

Roget's 21st Century Thesaurus in Dictionary Form: The Essential Reference for Home, School, or Office, 3rd ed. 2008. Bridgewater, NJ: Baker & Taylor.

Routledge Dictionary of Modern American Slang and Unconventional English. 2013. New York: Routledge.

The SAGE Dictionary of Sociology. 2006. Thousand Oaks, California: SAGE.

Schur, Norman W., Eugene Ehrlich, and Richard Ehrlich. 2013. *British English A to Zed: A Definitive Guide to the Queen's English*, 3rd ed. New York: Skyhorse.

Shorter Oxford English Dictionary. 2018. [Mobile app]. San Diego, CA: MobiSystems.

Shorter Oxford English Dictionary on Historical Principles, 6th ed. 2007. 2 vols. New York: Oxford University Press.

Spears, Richard. 2011. *McGraw-Hill's Conversational American English: The Illustrated Guide to the Everyday Expressions of American English.* New York: McGraw-Hill.

Thesaurus of Aging Terminology, 8th ed. 2005. Washington, DC: AARP. http://assets.aarp.org/rgcenter/general/thesaurus.pdf.

Thesaurus of Psychological Index Terms. 2012. Washington, DC: American Psychological Association.

Thorne, Tony. *Dictionary of Contemporary Slang*, 4th ed. 2014. London: Bloomsbury.

Ultimate Visual Dictionary. 2017. Revised and updated edition. New York, New York: DK Publishing.

Urban Dictionary. http://www.urbandictionary.com.

Watts, Duncan. 2010. *Dictionary of American Government and Politics.* Edinburgh, Scotland: Edinburgh University Press.

Webster, Noah. (1828) 1970. *An American Dictionary of the English Language.* New York: Johnson Reprint Corp.

Webster's Third New International Dictionary of the English Language, Unabridged. 2002. Springfield, MA: Merriam-Webster.

Wordnik. San Francisco, CA: Planetwork NGO. http://www.wordnik.com.
WordReference.com. http://www.wordreference.com.
The World Book Dictionary. 2011. 2 vols. Chicago: World Book.

SUGGESTED READINGS

Brewer, Charlotte. 2007. *Treasure-House of the Language: The Living OED*. New Haven, CT: Yale University Press.

This book brings the history of the *Oxford English Dictionary* forward from the completion of the first edition in 1928 to its current electronic form in the 21st century.

Jones, Mari, and Sarah Ogilve. 2013. *Keeping Languages Alive: Documentation, Pedagogy and Revitalization*. London: Cambridge University Press.

Jones and Ogilve bring together an international list of authors, both academic and community members, to discuss the work being done to document endangered languages for the future.

Kendall, Joshua C. 2008. *The Man Who Made Lists: Love, Death, Madness, and the Creation of Roget's Thesaurus*. New York: Berkley Books.

This biography of Peter Mark Roget (1779–1869) traces Roget's life and the thesaurus project that occupied his retirement years, with the first edition published in 1852.

Landau, Sidney I. 2001. *Dictionaries: The Art and Craft of Lexicography*, 2nd ed. London: Cambridge University Press.

Landau offers a description of how dictionaries are researched and written, with particular attention given to how computers have changed modern lexicography. The final chapter addresses legal and ethical issues.

Mugglestone, Lynda. 2011. *Dictionaries: A Very Short Introduction*. New York: Oxford University Press.

The *Very Short Introductions* series from Oxford University Press is a gem of a collection, and this slim, 134-page volume on dictionaries is no exception. In six chapters, Mugglestone covers not only the basic facts about dictionaries but also their cultural, social, and historical significance.

Skinner, David. 2012. *The Story of Ain't: America, Its Language, and the Most Controversial Dictionary Ever Published*. New York: HarperCollins.

David Skinner has written an entertaining and vivid history of the controversial *Webster's Third*. The editor of *Webster's Third*, Philip Gove, courted furor and dismay from readers when he and the editorial board of the dictionary decided to completely overhaul and revolutionize the content of the venerated source, including the addition of the word "*ain't*."

Stamper, Kory. 2017. *Word by Word: The Secret Life of Dictionaries*. New York: Pantheon.

Stamper's book is both entertaining and educational. Her perspective on dictionaries and the English language, informed by her expertise as a professional lexicographer and former associate editor at Merriam-Webster, is lively, frank, and fascinating.

Steinmetz, Sol. 2010. *There's a Word for It: The Explosion of the American Language Since 1900*. New York: Harmony Books.

Steinmetz, a lexicographer with several books to his name, investigates and illuminates all the various ways the English language has changed and grown over the past 114 years. Organized by decade, each chapter begins with a succinct history lesson for the reader, and then lists out by year the new words in use.

Winchester, Simon. 2003. *The Meaning of Everything: The Story of the Oxford English Dictionary*. New York: Oxford University Press.

Winchester provides an interesting history of the first edition of the *Oxford English Dictionary*, including prior efforts to document the English language beginning in the 17th century. He describes the people and processes involved in the project over a seventy-year period concluding with completion of the first edition in 1928.

Chapter 19

Encyclopedias

Melissa A. Wong

INTRODUCTION

The encyclopedia has long been the quintessential reference tool—a source that seems to cover any topic imaginable and one many people remember learning to use at an early age. More than any other book, the encyclopedia has long been associated with an educated mind. In the 20th century, traveling salesmen sold encyclopedias door to door, and many families bought an encyclopedia for their school-aged children. The home encyclopedia set provided ready access to information for school reports and symbolized the family's commitment to education and knowledge. Thus, it seems only fitting that A. J. Jacobs's (2004) memoir about reading the entire *Encyclopaedia Britannica* is titled *The Know-It-All: One Man's Humble Quest to Become the Smartest Person in the World.*

In the past decade, print encyclopedias have given way to robust online products that combine multiple titles in two or more languages, enhanced multimedia content, and supplementary resources such as newspaper and magazine articles, primary documents, and curricular tools. At the same time, free, volunteer-authored encyclopedias such as *Wikipedia* and the *Stanford Encyclopedia of Philosophy* have emerged on the Internet. Whether the encyclopedia is a multivolume work such as the *World Book*, a single volume on one specific subject, or an online multimedia resource, the goal remains implicit: to provide a summarized compendium of multidisciplinary knowledge in a verifiable, organized, and readily accessible manner.

USES AND CHARACTERISTICS

Because of the broad nature of information available in encyclopedias, they can be used to answer many types of questions, including ready-reference and biographical questions. However, librarians and patrons most often turn to encyclopedias for general background information, such as an explanation of photosynthesis or construction techniques used to build the Golden Gate Bridge. Although librarians working with adult patrons may gravitate toward titles written for adults, children's encyclopedias are particularly helpful in this regard, since they provide simplified explanations accompanied by illustrations.

Encyclopedias are also useful as "pre-research" tools since they provide succinct overviews, cross-references to related topics that help novice researchers make connections and see information in a broader context, and often links or citations to more in-depth information found in outside sources. They may identify important controversies and unanswered questions that can serve as fruitful research avenues, particularly for students.

Subject encyclopedias can provide a comprehensive review of a specialized subject or insight on a topic from a particular vantage point. For example, *Brill's Encyclopedia of Hinduism* can be used to look up not only information about Hindu religious practices but also topics like gift giving and travel and their significance in Hindu culture.

EVALUATION AND SELECTION

Even libraries with minimal budgets should have a few standard general and subject-specific encyclopedias in their ready-reference collection. In addition, librarians can bookmark freely available, authoritative titles such as the free *Encyclopaedia Britannica* in order to provide quick and easy access to reliable information for both librarians and patrons (see Box 19.1 for an example of evaluating a free online encyclopedia).

Box 19.1 Activity: *Stanford Encyclopedia of Philosophy*

Access the community-edited *Stanford Encyclopedia of Philosophy* at https://plato.stanford.edu and skim at least three entries.

Questions for Reflection and Discussion:

1. How thorough were the entries you reviewed?
2. What can you learn about the author of each entry?
3. What can you learn about the sources of information?
4. How would you rate this encyclopedia using the evaluative criteria discussed in the chapter?
5. Would you use this source for reference and, if so, for what types of questions?

Audience

All encyclopedias, even general ones, are written for a particular audience. Clearly, the *Dictionary of Mechanical Engineering* sees its audience as adults who have a professional interest in engineering. *Worldmark Encyclopedia of the Nations* is appropriate for readers at the ninth grade level and above, while *Our Country's Presidents: A Complete Encyclopedia of the U.S. Presidency*, with its short entries, numerous illustrations, and larger print, is aimed at young readers. Some titles aim to serve a wide audience and can be used by children, young adults, and adults. Although targeted at primary and secondary school students, *World Book Encyclopedia* prides itself as being suitable as a "family reference tool," and librarians may find it useful for adult users seeking a simple explanation of a topic.

Subject matter, writing style, and presentation all determine an encyclopedia's audience. In an encyclopedia for adults, a plethora of photographs and illustrations and a dearth of textual content might indicate a lack of substance; however, in the case of encyclopedias for children, this scenario would be welcome, particularly if the photographs and illustrations are current and targeted to a child's viewpoint. In print titles, page layout also figures prominently. Minimal or excessive "white space," poor placement of illustrations, and incorrect choice of fonts for headers and text will detract from content, no matter how scholarly or substantive the title. In online encyclopedias, the appearance and functionality of the interface as well as the content should be appropriate for the intended user. Products for children should be visually appealing; offer simple, intuitive search and browse options; and provide content written at the appropriate level along with engaging multimedia, while products for adults should offer advanced search options that enhance access along with more sophisticated content.

Coverage and Objectivity

In general encyclopedias, coverage should be even across all subjects, although some subjects, by their very nature, will be given greater emphasis. For example, general encyclopedias published in the United States contain far more information about the United States than other countries. In order to assess whether an encyclopedia is balanced with respect to subject coverage, one can examine the length and depth of articles written on a variety of subjects. Librarians should pay particular attention to how well a title integrates non-Western topics and perspectives that have historically been underrepresented, such as the accomplishments of women and people of color. In addition, librarians should pay careful attention to coverage within articles. With respect to controversial issues such as the death penalty or abortion, does the article present both sides? Is inflammatory language used or is the article entirely objective in its treatment? A librarian must also consider photographs, illustrations, sounds, and digital images. Do images portray women solely in traditional settings? Does the title devote equal media space to all ethnic groups?

Authority

As with any reference source, authority, or the staff responsible for the content, has immense value when making a selection decision. Editors guide decisions about topical coverage and ensure that articles conform to style and length guidelines. Ideally, articles will be authored by specialists in the field. Author credit may appear at the beginning or end of individual articles and as a list elsewhere within the publication or site. Some articles may not provide an author credit; therefore, one might conclude that the editorial staff, in concert with a subject expert, wrote those pieces.

Currency

It is a Herculean task to revise a multivolume encyclopedia. Consequently, publishers may update only a portion of a print encyclopedia with each new edition, particularly in the case of annual publications. Online resources have no limitations on the level and frequency of updates, and most publishers update their online versions regularly. For example, within days of American Pharaoh winning the Belmont Stakes, *Encyclopaedia Britannica* had updated not only the entry on the Triple Crown but also entries for trainer Bob Baffert and jockey Victor Espinoza. However, not all articles will be targeted for regular updates, and librarians should take care to confirm time-sensitive information in more than one source.

Arrangement

In larger print works, the arrangement of volumes impacts usability. Children's encyclopedias are often arranged so that one volume encompasses an entire letter of the alphabet, ensuring, for example, that entries beginning with M are not split between two volumes, which can be confusing for younger users. Although the alphabetical arrangement is the most common, it is not the only possible arrangement. The *Encyclopedia of American History* is arranged chronologically, with individual volumes devoted to a specific time period and the entries within organized alphabetically. Some encyclopedias aimed at young children, such as *The New Children's Encyclopedia*, organize each volume around a broad topic, such as continents or technology.

Interface

In selecting an online resource, the librarian should give careful consideration to the interface used for searching and reading. The design needs to be age appropriate, user friendly, and intuitive in order to readily and effortlessly guide users to desired information. The main page should be well designed with multiple search and browsing options. Resources targeted at a wide range of age ranges may even offer a choice of interfaces. For example, *Britannica School* offers different search screens for elementary, middle, and high school users.

The option to use Boolean operators such as *and*, *or*, and *not* and phrase searching can make a search more precise and productive. However, because not all users have experience using Boolean logic, many titles allow for natural language searching, where the user types in a question such as "What was England's role in the American Civil War?" and the search engine returns articles containing any of the question's keywords ("England," "American," "Civil," and "War"). Although this latter method lacks precision and yields a number of false hits, the user will presumably retrieve some relevant articles that could lead to other related information. Most products automatically spell-check searches and offer alternate spellings of words, which can greatly ease a user's search for information, and rank retrieved articles for relevance, thus allowing the user to quickly locate relevant information.

Choosing between Print and Online Formats

Many standard titles are available in both print and online formats. Online titles offer the option to search and browse, providing enhanced access to content, and are often enriched with additional illustrations, multimedia such as video and audio clips, primary source materials, and even magazine and journal articles. Features such as "Today in History," prominent links to timely topics, and trivia or puzzle-type games add visual appeal and encourage users, particularly children, to explore the resource. This additional content can make the online version a very attractive purchase, although it is important to verify that such features enhance the educational value of the encyclopedia and are not merely shallow or distracting.

Ultimately, librarians need to examine a variety of issues in choosing between print sources and their online counterparts. In addition to cost and access issues, librarians need to consider shelf space, preservation goals, and user needs. A large academic or public library may subscribe to online encyclopedias in order to provide their users access to information from homes and offices. A small school library with limited computer workstations, however, might find that a print encyclopedia provides the best access since multiple volumes can be used simultaneously.

IMPORTANT GENERAL SOURCES

The best known of the traditional encyclopedias, *Encyclopaedia Britannica* is also the most detailed and scholarly. Now solely online, *Britannica* is available in versions for school, public, and academic libraries. Textual content is supplemented with full-color images, maps, videos, and audio clips; content is updated monthly. All *Britannica* interfaces offer prominent search and browse options, media, biographies, and a world atlas. Special features include access to the *Merriam-Webster's Collegiate Dictionary* and eye-catching links like "Demystified" and "On this Day." Interfaces are mobile friendly for use on smartphones and tablets. Table 19.1 summarizes available Britannica products.

Britannica Library, designed for public libraries, offers separate interfaces for children, young adults, and adults, each of which links to content drawn from three separate encyclopedias written for different reading levels. The product also provides access to thousands of magazine and journal articles and primary source materials, a useful addition for small libraries with limited resources.

Britannica Academic offers the most advanced content with signed articles authored by experts in each field. It also offers enhanced content beyond the encyclopedia, including magazine and journal articles, primary source materials, a daily newsfeed with articles from the BBC and *New York Times*, and the World Data Analyst with up-to-date statistical profiles of countries worldwide.

TABLE 19.1 Encyclopedia Databases Available from Britannica, Showing Title, Access Model, Audience, and Language.

Title	Access	Audience	Language
Britannica Kids	Free Limited content	Students (grades K–12)	English
Encyclopaedia Britannica	Free Limited content	Students (grades 6–12) Adults	English
Britannica School	Subscription	School Libraries (grades K–12)	English
Britannica Library	Subscription	Public Libraries	English
Britannica Academic	Subscription	Academic Libraries	English
Britannica Escolar	Subscription	Students (grades K–8)	Spanish
Britannica Moderna	Subscription	Students (grades 9–12) Adults	Spanish
Universalis Junior	Subscription	Students (grades K–5)	French
Encyclopaedia Universalis	Subscription	Students (grades 6–12) Adults	French

Britannica offers a free version of its encyclopedia under the name *Encyclopaedia Britannica.* Although more limited in content than the subscription-based products, the free version contains substantial articles on thousands of topics along with images and multimedia. This free version is an excellent resource for librarians to verify facts and locate brief background information.

For Canadian audiences, *The Canadian Encyclopedia* does an admirable job of providing information on a wide variety of Canadian personalities, places, events, and achievements. Previously published in print and as a CD-ROM, the encyclopedia is now produced as a free website available in both English and French. The site also offers the *Encyclopedia of Music in Canada* and selected content from *Maclean's* magazine. Features such as interactive maps, timelines, and exhibits invite the user to explore the site.

In the realm of free resources, *Wikipedia*, the online encyclopedia that anyone can author and edit, is undoubtedly the most well known. Authors are asked to maintain an objective point of view, include only verifiable information, and provide references. Unlike more traditional encyclopedias, there is no editorial system that certifies articles or their authors prior to "publication." Instead, *Wikipedia* assumes other users will check for and correct erroneous information. Each article includes a discussion page where individuals can explain a change they have made or otherwise discuss the article's content.

Because of the open authorship, reviews of *Wikipedia* have been mixed. An early study published in *Nature* found that science articles in *Wikipedia* were nearly as accurate as those in *Britannica*, with three errors per article on average for *Britannica* and four for *Wikipedia* (Giles 2005). Studies also have found that errors and vandalism in *Wikipedia* are quickly fixed. At the same time, studies have noted that *Wikipedia*'s articles can provide uneven treatment of topics; thus, while the information given in an article is generally accurate thanks to eager fact-checkers and editors, the same article can be missing important aspects of a topic that a more conventional source would include (Read 2006). Studies have also found that controversial topics are particularly prone to repeated editing, making their accuracy and objectivity at any given time suspect (Wilson and Likens 2015). In addition, as the encyclopedia has become more ubiquitous, concerns have arisen about a Western bias to content (Giles 2013, Luyt 2018), gender bias in content and authorship (DeDeo 2018, Luyt 2018, Paling 2015), and efforts to pay public relations firms and experienced editors to edit *Wikipedia* entries to promote products or remove unflattering information (Pinsker 2015).

One of the advantages of *Wikipedia* is its sheer size; in late 2018, the site had over 5.8 million articles in its English-language version. *Wikipedia* covers topics from the scholarly (phenomenology) to the mundane (San Pedro, California) and the trivial (a comparison chart of characters from eleven different versions of the television show *The Office*). Thus, the encyclopedia can be a source of information on even the most unusual of topics. In addition, *Wikipedia*'s open editing structure means articles can be updated almost simultaneously with world events.

Although librarians should be wary of consulting *Wikipedia* for ready-reference factual information, the encyclopedia can be a valuable resource for general background information and pre-research information. Bibliographies and cited references, when present, can direct researchers to additional sources of information, and careful reading of the discussion page associated with a topic can reveal diverse points of view worthy of further study. Box 19.2 examines *Wikipedia* in more detail.

Box 19.2 Activity: Comparing Encyclopedias

Compare coverage in *Wikipedia* and a general encyclopedia using three topics:

- A controversial topic such as vaccinations or climate change.
- An event or a person that was recently in the news.
- A topic about which you have some in-depth knowledge.

Questions for Reflection and Discussion:

1. Which source is more up to date?
2. Which source is more balanced and objective?
3. In each source, how would you rate the quality and style of writing?
4. Which source offers more helpful guidance for further study?

SOURCES FOR CHILDREN AND YOUNG ADULTS

Because young readers represent a variety of abilities and audiences, one finds a variety of titles to choose from in both print and online formats. Typically, the format of these titles mirrors those targeted to adults although pages may be more colorful and lavishly illustrated. For young students in particular, font sizes may be larger and there may be less text on a page so as to not overwhelm the reader. However, the principal difference between titles for children and those for adults lies in content. Children's encyclopedias focus on topics popular with children as well as those covered in the school curriculum. Explanations are simplified and the writing style and vocabulary are adjusted for the intended audience, whether young readers or more advanced students.

General Encyclopedias

In the realm of encyclopedias for children, some print titles continue to exist, even as online products grow richer and more popular. Of the general, multivolume sets for children, the most prominent is the *World Book Encyclopedia*. The 2019 revision has twenty-two volumes. Articles vary in length and treatment depending on the subject matter and intended audience. The "mouse" article targets young readers and includes age-specific vocabulary, whereas the "cell" article targets advanced readers. Many of the lengthier articles, like the one on leaves, use a graduated approach; that is, authors use simple concepts and vocabulary at the beginning of the article and build toward incorporating more advanced ideas and vocabulary at its conclusion. Technical terms are italicized, and their meanings are given within the context of the sentence or within parentheses. Articles are arranged alphabetically using the word-by-word method and cross-references play a significant role.

World Book is heavily illustrated. The 2019 revision has over 25,000 illustrations, the vast majority in color, including photos, illustrations, and maps. *World Book* conveys much of its information in tables and charts that are set apart from the text on a given page. This method makes the layout more visually appealing and acts as a vehicle for helping readers digest what they have read thus far. For example, the "tree" article has twenty-three illustrations covering, among other things, the parts, growth cycle, and uses of trees; instructions on correctly planting and growing a tree; and a guide to over seventy-five tree species that includes an illustration of each tree with and without leaves and detailed views of the leaf, seed, and bark.

World Book also offers the *Discovery Encyclopedia*, a thirteen-volume set aimed at new readers, reluctant readers, and English-language learners. The encyclopedia focuses on high interest topics and informational text. Most articles are brief, but special feature articles contain more detailed treatments. Pages are colorful and articles are heavily illustrated.

World Book is available electronically through a suite of products known as *World Book Online*. The online version contains the complete contents of the print set plus thousands of more articles, as well as additional illustrations and multimedia. *World Book Kids* is aimed at younger students and features a simple search feature and the option to browse articles, along with games and fun activities. *World Book Student* is intended for elementary and middle school students. Optimized for tablets, it also features a dictionary and atlas, a citation builder, current news articles, and the option to create an account and save content. For teachers, content is correlated to educational standards and many articles are labeled by Lexile level, a measure of reading difficulty. *World Book Advanced*, for high school students and adults, includes all of the content and features of *World Book Student* along with access to thousands of e-books, periodical articles, and primary sources. *World Book Discover*, a version for English-language learners, struggling readers, and adult learners, features specially written articles, a visual dictionary in multiple languages, a text-to-speech option, and a section titled "Life Skills" with information on topics like health care and applying for jobs. Table 19.2 summarizes available *World Book* titles.

TABLE 19.2 Encyclopedia Products Available from World Book, Showing Title, Format, Audience, and Language.

Title	Format	Audience	Language
World Book Encyclopedia	Print (22 volumes)	Students (grades K–12)	English
Discovery Encyclopedia	Print (13 volumes)	Students (grades K–3) English-language Learners	English
World Book Online	Subscription	Students (grades K–12) Adults	English
World Book Kids	Subscription	Students (grades K–3)	English
World Book Student	Subscription	Students (grades K–8)	English
World Book Advanced	Subscription	Students (grades 9–12) Adults	English
World Book Discover	Subscription	Students (grades K–3) English-language Learners	English
Enciclopedia Estudiantil Hallazgos	Subscription	Students (grades K–8) Adults	Spanish
L'Encyclopédie Découverte	Subscription	Students (grades K–8)	French

As discussed earlier in this chapter, *Britannica*'s online products offer rich textual material supplemented by extensive illustrations and multimedia. For children, *Britannica School* offers interfaces for elementary, middle, and high school audiences. Each interface draws on content from one of three age-appropriate encyclopedias, although once an article has been located, students can adjust the reading level and complexity of the content while remaining in their chosen interface. Options to change the font size and have text read aloud further improve accessibility for students with special needs. On-screen tools make it easy for students to bookmark, save, and print content. In addition to articles and multimedia content, *Britannica School* offers access to primary source documents for classroom and research use. At the high school level, there are resources to assist students with the research and writing process, book reviews, and presentations. Teachers can take advantage of a Lesson Plan Builder to integrate content into the classroom.

Another major online title for children and young adults is *Scholastic Go!* Content is based on two venerable encyclopedias that have now ceased publication, the *New Book of Knowledge* and the *Encyclopedia Americana*, with supplemental content from additional science and social science encyclopedias. The site offers over 115,000 articles, each labeled with Lexile level and correlated to educational standards, along with interactive maps, videos, articles from over 1,100 newspapers in 73 languages, and links to vetted Web resources.

Single-Volume Encyclopedias

Many excellent single-volume encyclopedias are available for children, often focusing on a specific subject area. These can be kept in a non-circulating reference collection to provide breadth of coverage for students working on school assignments or seeking an answer to a specific question; alternatively, they can be integrated with the circulating collection to provide reading material for students interested in a particular topic.

The New Children's Encyclopedia has over 4,000 entries organized into broad topics like "Space" and "The Human Body." Entries feature simple explanations and flashcard style facts, often integrated into engaging timelines, charts, and illustrations. Excellent cross-section diagrams accompany articles on topics like the planet Earth and fossil fuels. *Our Country's Presidents: A Complete Encyclopedia of the U.S. Presidency* provides profiles of all the U.S. presidents arranged in chronological order. Profiles are heavily illustrated and include biographical information, descriptions of contemporary events, and assessments of the president's policies and initiatives. *The Kingfisher Animal Encyclopedia* covers 2,000 animals and is organized by classification. Each section includes information about a group of animals and profiles of specific species. Entries on specific species include common and scientific names, environment and distribution, size, and behavior. Kingfisher makes many encyclopedias for children, including *The Kingfisher History Encyclopedia* and *The Kingfisher Science Encyclopedia.*

SUBJECT ENCYCLOPEDIAS

Varying in price and size, subject encyclopedias give more in-depth coverage to a specific field of knowledge. Inexpensive single-volume titles such as *Encyclopedia of Native Tribes of North America, The Concise Encyclopedia of Poultry Breeds,* and *The St. James Encyclopedia of Hip-Hop Culture,* although highly specialized, can function as cost-effective alternatives that facilitate ready-reference access to subjects underrepresented in the overall library collection. Some mid-sized sets, such as the *Worldmark Encyclopedia of the Nations* or *Women in World History,* can also add immediate depth to a library's collection for a reasonable cost.

As with their more general counterparts, subject encyclopedias have largely moved online, although some single-volume and mid-sized sets are still available in print. Larger comprehensive titles are usually offered as stand-alone subscription databases, while smaller sets are available as individual e-books through products like *Gale Virtual Reference Library.* Multi-title databases such as *Credo Reference* and *Oxford Reference,* both discussed in more detail in Chapter 17, are an economical way to expand the library's collection of subject encyclopedias as well as other types of resources.

One of the most important subject encyclopedias is *AccessScience,* an online product unsurpassed in scope and coverage. From the initial screen, users can search, browse alphabetically or by topic, or jump straight to multimedia resources. An advanced search screen allows Boolean searching and offers a variety of search limits. Articles are authored by experts, including a number of Nobel Prize winners, and written to accommodate a wide variety of readers, from the layperson to the specialist. Each entry begins with a definition and a general overview of the topic. The entry then progresses from the general to the specific in an effort to provide comprehensive coverage of the topic. In addition to over 8,500 articles and 19,000 images and animations, *AccessScience* includes more than 3,000 biographies, which can be browsed by name or by scientific discipline. Articles are enhanced with hyperlinks, definitions, bibliographies, and links to primary literature. A Nobel Prize section provides a list of all prize winners, including those for literature, peace, and economics, with links to relevant articles. Images, animations, and videos can be viewed online or downloaded for use in the classroom. A section for educators provides curriculum maps to facilitate classroom use. *AccessScience* also offers a widget that can be embedded in course management systems and a mobile version for tablets and smartphones.

A second important science encyclopedia is *Grzimek's Animal Life Encyclopedia*, available as an e-book through *Gale Virtual Reference Library*. The seventeen-volume set contains over 700 articles and 12,000 color illustrations. Each article provides an overview of a family (e.g., slit-faced bats), including biology, habitat, behavior, and conservation status, followed by more detailed information on individual species. Information is presented in both narrative and tabular form, and each article is accompanied by at least one distribution map. Articles end with a list of resources for further study. Users can view articles as either a continuous article or a pdf of the original print entry.

Access Science and *Grzimek's* are both suitable for high school students and adults. For younger children, a potential purchase is the *Discovery Science Encyclopedia*. Aimed at new readers, reluctant readers, and English language learners, this nine-volume encyclopedia covers all areas of science as well as some social science topics. Articles are heavily illustrated with photos, diagrams, and maps.

Oxford Research Encyclopedias provides encyclopedia-style overview articles for disciplines in the humanities, social sciences, and sciences. All articles are written by experts, dated, and peer-reviewed. Articles include a table of contents, hyperlinks to endnotes and outside resources, a citation tool, and the option to save annotations to a personal profile. Users can browse individual titles, search within a specific title, or search all titles simultaneously. In late 2018, *Oxford Research Encyclopedias* included titles in fifteen disciplines with ten more in development.

The *Encyclopedia of Religion*, most recently revised in 2005, contains approximately 3,300 articles on religion and spiritual practice. The *Encyclopedia of Religion* takes a valuable cross-cultural approach, highlighting practices and beliefs in different faiths and countries. Because of this cross-cultural approach and because one of the goals of the encyclopedia is to place religion in the context of daily life, the content is relevant to users interested in art, history, sociology, and other fields. Articles are arranged alphabetically, and longer articles include a table of contents. Cross-references and bibliographies, many with annotations, are located at the end of articles. Composite articles start with an overview of a topic (e.g., "Afterlife") followed by articles that explore the topic in the context of a particular faith or place (e.g., "Afterlife: Oceanic Concepts," "Afterlife: Jewish Concepts"). Interestingly, this edition retained approximately fifty prominent articles in their original form, providing updates in a second article subtitled "Further Considerations." All articles are signed and dated.

The five-volume *Worldmark Encyclopedia of the Nations* is another essential title for most libraries. Country information is contained in four volumes that are organized by continent, with country entries organized alphabetically within each volume. Each entry starts with basic country facts, followed by detailed information organized under fifty subheadings. These subheadings are numbered and are consistent across all entries to aid users in finding the desired information. Information is presented primarily in narrative form, although some tabular data is given. Illustrations are black and white and consist of the coat of arms and flag, as well as a map of each country. A full-color regional map is printed at the front of each volume. Volume One provides detailed information about the United Nations, as well as information on polar regions, tables of statistical data, and an index. (Unfortunately, the index's location in the first volume is counterintuitive to most users and it is easily overlooked.) Although librarians would want to verify some information in a more up-to-date source, the *Worldmark Encyclopedia of the Nations* continues to be an excellent source for succinct background information about a nation's history, politics, economy, and culture.

A companion work is the *Worldmark Encyclopedia of Cultures and Daily Life*, a five-volume title that focuses on ethnic and cultural groups. Arranged alphabetically by culture or nationality, the encyclopedia uses frequent cross-references to direct the user to related articles and, in the case of groups with more than one popular name, to the main entry. Each entry contains basic facts such as the group's population, location, and religion as well as detailed descriptions of characteristics like language, clothing, folklore, rites of passage, educational traditions, family life, and work. Both *Worldmark Encyclopedia of the Nations* and *Worldmark Encyclopedia of Cultures and Daily Life* are available through *Gale Virtual Reference Library*.

In the arts, two prominent titles are *Oxford Art Online* and *Oxford Music Online*. *Oxford Art Online* is based on the thirty-four-volume *Dictionary of Art*, a venerable encyclopedia covering art and artists from all time periods and regions of the world. It includes 200,000 peer-reviewed articles with bibliographies and cross-references, over 19,000 images, a dictionary of art terms, research tools such as timelines and subject guides, and access to additional Oxford resources on art. *Oxford Music Online* brings together content from five encyclopedias and two music dictionaries with additional material written solely for the online platform. Its 52,000 articles, authored by experts, and 30,000 biographies include bibliographies, music samples, and cross-references. The product also provides research tools for students.

NON-ENGLISH-LANGUAGE ENCYCLOPEDIAS

Increasingly, encyclopedia publishers are offering content in Spanish, French, and other languages. Non-English-language encyclopedias may be based on a publisher's other encyclopedia titles and typically include general content with additional articles appropriate to the language of publication, translation dictionaries, news articles, and a wealth of multimedia images and videos. These encyclopedias can be valuable additions to libraries supporting bilingual and multilingual communities, English-language learners, and students studying other languages.

Britannica offers two French-language products, *Encyclopaedia Universalis* for young adults and adults and *Universalis Junior* for elementary school children, and two Spanish-language products, *Britannica Moderna* for young adults and adults and *Britannica Escolar* for elementary and middle school students. World Book publishes the Spanish-language *Enciclopedia Estudiantil Hallazgos* and the French-language *L'Encyclopédie Découverte*. Both Britannica and World Book products can be purchased as stand-alone resources or in combination with other online holdings for seamless access in multiple languages.

SEARCH STRATEGIES

The first step in developing a search strategy is to determine the nature of the question. Encyclopedias can be used to verify factual information but are most useful when a patron needs a concise overview of a topic or is seeking background information. If current information is required, frequently updated databases or websites are preferable. Titles with a national or regional slant usually have more information about these geographic areas, while subject encyclopedias can provide more in-depth information or a unique perspective on a topic. For difficult or hard-to-find information, the search capabilities of online resources and the breadth of multi-title databases like *Credo Reference* and *Oxford Reference* are better choices.

For the patron who asks "I am writing a report about Martin Luther King. My teacher said that he wrote a speech about a dream. Where can I find it?" an online encyclopedia enhanced with multimedia would be a good choice. Not only does *Britannica Library* provide an article about Dr. King as well as links to the text of his "I Have a Dream" speech, it also includes a video clip of Dr. King delivering that speech. The student would benefit from reading and listening to this speech and might gain a better understanding of the impact Dr. King had on U.S. history.

For the patron who asks "Where can I read about the structure of DNA?" a subject encyclopedia might be the first place to look. In particular, *AccessScience* lends itself to this question because it is the standard for in-depth information on science and technology. However, for younger users, *World Book* or the *Discovery Science Encyclopedia* would provide comparable information written at a level they would better understand.

Oftentimes, librarians will use more than one encyclopedia to completely answer a patron's question. As Box 19.3 illustrates, librarians can use a general source for introductory information and then specialized sources to find more in-depth or focused information.

Box 19.3 Search Strategy: What Would You Like to Know about Giraffes?

A library patron approaches the desk and asks for information on giraffes. The free *Encyclopaedia Britannica* provides a short article accompanied by photos and a video. After reviewing the article, the patron indicates that more information is needed. Which source would be best?

If the patron is a child working on a school project, *World Book* would be a good choice. In the print version, the article is almost two pages long and is accompanied by multiple illustrations. The article addresses physical appearance and reproduction, as well as the family life of giraffes, how they move, and their interaction with people. In addition to two photos, one of which shows how giraffes bend to the ground to lick salt or drink, there is an illustration of the giraffe's skeleton, an illustration of its footprints, and a world map showing distribution. The online *World Book Student* provides a similar article; while there are fewer illustrations, it includes videos of giraffe behavior.

For the older student, *Britannica Library* provides a moderate-length article with two photos and a video. This article has more detail than its print counterpart and lists the nine subspecies of giraffes. *Grzimek's Animal Life Encyclopedia* has twelve pages on the family Giraffidae, which includes giraffes and okapis. The article includes in-depth information and numerous photos. One section provides scientific names and descriptions for the nine subspecies, as well as photos illustrating their markings and a short discussion of current scientific debates about whether all nine are truly distinct subspecies.

In addition to a brief article on giraffes, *AccessScience* has a lengthy article on the order artiodactyla with a detailed discussion of unique features of the ankle joint, skulls and teeth, and cranial appendages. There is also an analysis of how the order has evolved and the relationship of giraffes to other animals. *Oxford Reference* provides access to the *Encyclopedia of Mammals*, which contains a detail-rich article about giraffe physiology and behavior. Further exploration reveals links to poetry and literary references to giraffes, an entry for the constellation Camelopardalis, which represents a giraffe, and a discussion of "camelopard" as an archaic name for a giraffe, opening up further avenues of exploration for the patron.

Wikipedia provides an extensive article with a table of contents, an illustration with the complete scientific classification and conservation status, numerous photos (including one of the tongue and one of giraffes bending down to drink), a map of the distribution of all nine subspecies, and an illustration of the skeleton. The article provides information on evolution, anatomy and morphology, behavior, and conservation, as well as giraffes in art and culture. The entry ends with a list of references and links to further information on other sites. By consulting an additional free encyclopedia, *Wildscreen Arkive*, the librarian may locate numerous additional images and videos as well as links to further information.

CONCLUSION

In print or online, encyclopedias are valuable resources for topical overviews, pre-research information, and fact-checking. Many traditional titles have migrated online to provide enhanced access to textual content along with supplemental multimedia and research resources, while databases like *Gale Virtual Reference Library* and *Credo Reference* provide ready access to multiple subject-specialized titles.

REFERENCES

DeDeo, Simon (@simondedeo). 2018. "Donna Strickland, One of This Year's Nobel Laureates. . . . " *Twitter*. October 6. https://twitter.com/SimonDeDeo/status/1048611161049063424.

Giles, Jim. 2005. "Internet Encyclopaedias Go Head to Head." *Nature* 438 (December 15): 900–901.

Giles, Jim. 2013. "Wiki-opoly." *New Scientist* 218 (April 13): 38–41.

Jacobs, A. J. 2004. *The Know-It-All: One Man's Quest to Become the Smartest Person in the World*. New York: Simon & Schuster.

Luyt, Brendan. 2018. "Wikipedia's Gaps in Coverage: Are Wikiprojects a Solution? A Study of the Cambodian Wikiproject." *Online Information Review* 42 (2): 238–49.

Paling, Emma. 2015. "Wikipedia's Hostility to Women." *The Atlantic*. October 21. https://www.theatlantic.com/technology/archive/2015/10/how-wikipedia-is-hostile-to-women/411619/#arbcom.

Pinsker, Joe. 2015. "The Covert World of People Trying to Edit Wikipedia—For Pay." *The Atlantic.* August 11. http://www.theatlantic.com/business/archive/2015/08/wikipedia-editors-for-pay/393926/.

Read, Brock. 2006. "Can Wikipedia Ever Make the Grade?" *Chronicle of Higher Education* 53 (10), October 27.

Wilson, Adam M., and Gene E. Likens. 2015. "Content Volatility of Scientific Topics in Wikipedia: A Cautionary Tale." *PLoS One* 10 (8): 1–5.

LIST OF SOURCES

AccessScience. New York: McGraw-Hill. http://www.accessscience.com/. Subscription required.

Atkins, Tony, and Marcel Escudier. 2013. *Dictionary of Mechanical Engineering.* London: Oxford University Press. Available online as part of *Oxford Reference.*

Bausum, Ann. 2017. *Our Country's Presidents: A Complete Encyclopedia of the U.S. Presidency.* Washington, DC: National Geographic Books.

Britannica Academic. Chicago: Encyclopaedia Britannica. https://britannicalearn.com/products/. Subscription required.

Britannica Escolar. Chicago: Encyclopaedia Britannica. https://britannicalearn.com/products/. Subscription required.

Britannica Kids. https://kids.britannica.com.

Britannica Library. Chicago: Encyclopaedia Britannica. https://britannicalearn.com/products/. Subscription required.

Britannica Moderna. Chicago: Encyclopaedia Britannica. https://britannicalearn.com/products/. Subscription required.

Britannica School. Chicago: Encyclopaedia Britannica. https://britannicalearn.com/products/. Subscription required.

Burnie, David. 2011. *The Kingfisher Animal Encyclopedia.* New York: Kingfisher Encyclopedias.

The Canadian Encyclopedia. Historica Foundation. https://www.thecanadianencyclopedia.ca/en.

Commire, Anne, and Deborah Klezmer, eds. 1999–2002. *Women in World History: A Biographical Encyclopedia.* 17 vols. Farmington Hills, MI: Gale Cengage Learning. Available online as part of *Gale Virtual Reference Library.*

Credo Reference. Credo Reference. http://search.credoreference.com/. Subscription required.

Discovery Encyclopedia. 2017. 13 vols. Chicago: World Book.

Discovery Science Encyclopedia. 2015. 9 vols. Chicago: World Book.

Enciclopedia Estudiantil Hallazgos. Chicago: World Book. https://www.worldbook.com/digital.aspx. Subscription required.

Encyclopaedia Britannica. http://www.britannica.com/.

Encyclopaedia Universalis. Chicago: Encyclopaedia Britannica. https://britannicalearn.com/products/. Subscription required.

Gale Virtual Reference Library. Farmington Hills, MI: Gale Cengage Learning. http://www.cengage.com. Subscription required.

Grzimek's Animal Life Encyclopedia. 2nd ed. 2003–2004. 17 vols. Farmington Hills, MI: Gale Cengage Learning. Available online as part of *Gale Virtual Reference Library.*

Hams, Fred. 2015. *The Concise Encyclopedia of Poultry Breeds.* London: Southwater.

Jacobsen, Knut A., ed. 2014. *Brill's Encyclopedia of Hinduism.* Boston, MA: Brill. Available online at http://referenceworks.brillonline.com/browse/brill-s-encyclopedia-of-hinduism. Subscription required.

Johnson, Michael, and Richard Hook. 2014. *Encyclopedia of Native Tribes of North America.* 2nd ed. Austin, TX: Firefly Books.

Jones, Lindsay, ed. 2005. *Encyclopedia of Religion.* 2nd ed. 15 vols. Detroit: Macmillan Reference. Available online as part of *Gale Virtual Reference Library.*

The Kingfisher History Encyclopedia. 2012. New York: Kingfisher Encyclopedias.

L'Encyclopédie Découverte. Chicago: World Book. https://www.worldbook.com/digital.aspx. Subscription required.

Macdonald, David W. 2007. *The Encyclopedia of Mammals.* 3rd ed. New York: Oxford University Press. Available online as part of *Oxford Reference.*

Nash, Gary B., ed. 2009. *Encyclopedia of American History.* 11 vols. New York: Facts on File.

The New Children's Encyclopedia. 2013. New York: Dorling Kindersley Publishing.

Oxford Art Online. New York: Oxford University Press. http://www.oxfordartonline.com/public/. Subscription required.

Oxford Music Online. New York: Oxford University Press. http://www.oxfordmusiconline.com/public/. Subscription required.

Oxford Reference. New York: Oxford. http://www.oxfordreference.com/. Subscription required.

Oxford Research Encyclopedias. New York: Oxford. http://oxfordre.com/. Subscription required.

Scholastic Go! http://www.scholastic.com/digital/go.htm. Subscription required.

The St. James Encyclopedia of Hip-Hop Culture. Farmington Hills, MI: Gale Cengage Learning. Available online as part of *Gale Virtual Reference Library.*

Stanford Encyclopedia of Philosophy. Stanford University. http://plato.stanford.edu.

Taylor, Charles. 2017. *The Kingfisher Science Encyclopedia.* New York: Kingfisher Encyclopedias.

Universalis Junior. Chicago: Encyclopaedia Britannica. https://britannicalearn.com/products/. Subscription required.

Wikipedia. http://www.wikipedia.org.

Wildscreen Arkive. Wildscreen. http://www.arkive.org/.

World Book Advanced. Chicago: World Book. https://www.worldbook.com/digital.aspx. Subscription required.

World Book Discover. Chicago: World Book. https://www.worldbook.com/digital.aspx. Subscription required.

World Book Encyclopedia. 2019. 22 vols. Chicago: World Book.

World Book Kids. Chicago: World Book. https://www.worldbook.com/digital.aspx. Subscription required.

World Book Online. Chicago: World Book. http://www.worldbook.com/. Subscription required.

World Book Student. Chicago: World Book. https://www.worldbook.com/digital.aspx. Subscription required.

Worldmark Encyclopedia of Cultures and Daily Life. 3rd ed. 2017. 5 vols. Farmington Hills, MI: Gale Cengage Learning. Available online as part of *Gale Virtual Reference Library.*

Worldmark Encyclopedia of the Nations. 14th ed. 2017. 5 vols. Farmington Hills, MI: Gale Cengage Learning. Available online as part of *Gale Virtual Reference Library.*

SUGGESTED READINGS

Jacobs, A. J. 2004. *The Know-It-All: One Man's Humble Quest to Become the Smartest Person in the World.* New York: Simon & Schuster.

Entertaining and informative, this book describes the author's attempt to read the entire *Encyclopaedia Britannica* and what he learned in the process.

Rettig, James. 1992. *Distinguished Classics of Reference Publishing.* Phoenix, AZ: Oryx Press. https://archive.org/details/DistinguishedClassicsOfReferencePublishing.
This wonderful history of famous reference books includes many of the works discussed in this text, including *The Chicago Manual of Style, Encyclopaedia Britannica, The Encyclopedia of Associations, Emily Post's Etiquette, Guinness Book of Records, Robert's Rules of Order, The Statesman's Yearbook,* the *World Book Encyclopedia,* and *The World Almanac.*

Chapter 20

Bibliographic Sources

Linda C. Smith

INTRODUCTION

Knowledge of bibliographic tools is essential for assisting users in identifying resources on various topics or verifying the existence of and locating a particular publication. This chapter covers those bibliographic tools that provide the most comprehensive coverage of books or serials or both. These tools have been made far more accessible and versatile through their availability as Web-based resources, enabling librarians in all types of libraries to answer a wide range of bibliographic questions.

USES AND CHARACTERISTICS

Many of the most challenging questions that a reference librarian faces are bibliographic puzzles involving the verification of incomplete or inaccurate information when a user wants to find a particular book or other resource in the library. The librarian must then determine the following:

1. Do the library's catalog records show that the library owns the item?
2. If not, is the user looking for an item that really exists? That is, has it actually been published? Or is the user looking for a type of item not indexed in the catalog?
3. Is the user's information correct or only partially correct? For example, could the author's name be misspelled?
4. If the information is not completely correct, did the user get the information about the item from a reliable source, or has it perhaps been garbled in an oral communication?

The librarian must decide what path to take to recreate the information in correct form or to verify that the information is correct. A seemingly simple question may turn into a puzzle requiring the use of multiple sources, including catalogs and bibliographies.

The process of bibliographic control generally means providing two different kinds of access to information: bibliographic access, letting the user know of the existence of the work; and physical access, letting the user know where the work can be found. To achieve the aims of bibliographic control, three major types of reference sources have evolved: bibliographies, library catalogs, and shared cataloging networks. In general, bibliographies list works or parts of works regardless of their physical location. Library catalogs aim to list the works located in or accessible online from one or more libraries. Shared cataloging networks serve both functions, providing complete machine-readable cataloging copy and a list of libraries that own the item reflected in the catalog record.

Patrick Wilson in *Two Kinds of Power* (1968, 13) defines universal bibliographic control as the creation of an "exhaustive inventory" of all the works that have ever been published. Although extremely noble, such an aspiration toward universal bibliographic control is unattainable and has become even more elusive given the proliferation of self-published works (Wesner-Early 2017). However, progress has been made through the cooperative efforts of national libraries, national standards organizations, and the efforts of the shared cataloging networks in various countries. Especially in the digital realm, there is increasing interest in extending the access provided by bibliographic control to encompass archival and museum collections as well as library collections (Marcum 2014).

Types of Bibliographies and Catalogs

In the print environment, a bibliography is a list of works compiled on some common organizing principle, such as authorship, subject, place of publication, or chronology. The primary arrangement of the list is usually alphabetical, although a subject classification scheme, such as the Dewey Decimal Classification System, may be used. Secondary arrangement schemes may also be employed, such as by date when the primary arrangement is by author. As explained in Chapter 16, electronic resources provide a superior bibliographic product because most fields or elements of the bibliographic record are searchable and extremely precise queries can be formulated.

National bibliographies list the materials published in a particular country. In addition, the scope may be enlarged to include works written about the country or in the language of the country, regardless of the place of publication. Material written by the citizens of the country, wherever published, may also be included. Trade bibliographies are produced by commercial publishers and serve to provide the information necessary to select and acquire recently published materials. The predominant form of trade bibliography is the in-print list. Subject bibliographies are lists of materials that relate to a particular topic.

The terms "current" and "retrospective," as applied to bibliographies, refer to the time period covered by the items selected for inclusion in the bibliography. A current bibliography lists books or other items published close to the time at which the bibliography is compiled. A retrospective bibliography covers materials published during an earlier time period. Compilations of current bibliographic sources turn into retrospective sources when the time period covered recedes into the past.

Library catalogs exist to serve the users of a particular library by listing the holdings and location of materials accessible to users in that library. Union catalogs (or union lists) identify the material held in the collections of more than one library. Library consortia (see Chapter 5) may create union catalogs for their member libraries. In the case of union lists of serials, it is quite common to find not only the list of libraries holding a particular title but also a record of which volumes each library holds.

Kinds of Information Contained in Bibliographies and Catalogs

The data elements in a bibliography entry depend largely on the intent of the publication. Current national bibliographies exist in part to facilitate the international exchange of cataloging data in a standardized format. Therefore, the entries reflect the information available in machine-readable cataloging records. In addition to author, title, and publication data, each entry usually includes subject headings, content notes, and suggested classification numbers. Name entries, both personal and corporate, are standardized. Ordering information such as price is often included.

Because trade bibliographies are produced for the use of book dealers, they contain information that is essential for book purchases. Examples include price, availability, publishers' addresses, and International Standard Book Number (ISBN). The International Standard Serial Number (ISSN) serves a similar role, uniquely identifying each serial title.

Use of bibliographies depends on the type of information needed. If one needs simply to verify the existence of an item, a source giving short entries may be sufficient. If one needs both to identify and to locate copies, a union list is necessary. If the intent is to purchase materials, information such as price, ISBN, and availability is definitely required.

The content of catalog records reflects the cataloging code in use by the organization creating the records. Increasingly, catalog records are being enriched with additional content such as tables of contents, images of book jackets, narrative summaries of the book's contents, and even excerpts from book reviews.

EVALUATION

Evaluation of bibliographies and library catalogs is primarily concerned with the following criteria: authority, accuracy, scope, access points, and currency of the included material. In response to criticism regarding limitations in existing approaches to subject access, additions and changes are being made to standard subject headings as explained in the discussion of enhancements to subject access.

Authority

Authority concerns the qualifications of the compiler or sponsor. Compiling a national or trade bibliography is a massive undertaking, usually involving the resources of a major publisher, national library, or governmental agency. Therefore, the issue of authority usually concerns the compilers of smaller subject bibliographies or resources found on the Web. Do the compilers have the educational background or academic stature to justify their roles in compiling these bibliographies? Does the organization sponsoring the bibliography have a particular political agenda or viewpoint?

Accuracy

To accomplish bibliographic control, the accuracy of the bibliographic data describing each item is essential. In catalogs this also entails standardization of forms of entry for authors and subjects. A basic tenet of cataloging is the principle of collocation, which means that similar materials are gathered together at a single location. An essential requirement for achieving collocation is maintenance of authority control, whether of authors' names, subjects, or titles. For example, author-name authority control ensures that all existing permutations of an author's name are linked so that all works written by that individual are gathered together at a particular location in the catalog. Subject authority control has as its objective the gathering together in one place of items on a particular topic. The sheer size of the bibliographic universe has made authority control one of the biggest challenges in cataloging today (Gorman 2004).

Scope

The scope of any reference tool is of primary importance when evaluating its usefulness. Parameters determining scope can include place of publication, language, time period, type of materials, format, or subject. For retrospective sources, *Guide to Reference Books* (see Cargill 1996) gives clear and concise descriptions of the scope. For currently published works, the introductory material in a print source or the "about" section of a website should be studied.

Access Points

A print bibliography or catalog will have a primary form of arrangement, such as by author, possibly supplemented by one or more indexes. For online sources, options for searching and limiting are generally much more numerous. For example, the typical card catalog generally had entries for authors, titles, and subjects interfiled alphabetically. Online catalogs likewise enable searching by author, title, and subject as well as by keyword and other elements of the record such as ISBN/ISSN. It may also be possible to limit the search by such elements as date, format, or language.

Currency

Currency refers to the delay, or lack thereof, between the date of publication and the time at which the publication is entered in the bibliography. Publications designed for the book trade should offer the most recent information to fulfill the intent of their publications: providing information on currently available materials. Book trade publications may also list publications announced for publication but not yet published.

Enhancements to Subject Access

Michael Buckland (2017, 105) articulates the dilemma facing compilers of bibliographies and catalogs: "Most bibliographies and catalogs have a single topical index, but include material of interest to more than one community. Since each community has slightly different linguistic practices, no one index will be ideal for everyone and, perhaps, not for anyone." *Library of Congress Subject Headings* (*LCSH*) is the controlled vocabulary of choice not only for library catalogs but for many other bibliographic tools as well. Over the years *LCSH* has been criticized for its choice of terms, especially on the ways that various groups of people—often marginalized groups of people—have been identified. Sanford Berman (1971) was the first of many authors to identify problematic subject headings, including obsolete and racist or sexist terms, and recommend alternatives. This led, for example, to changes such as *Romanies* replacing *Gipsies*, *Mexican Americans* replacing *Mexicans in the U.S.*, *Developing countries* replacing *Underdeveloped areas*, and the deletion of *Sexual perversion* as a cross-reference from *Homosexuality* (Knowlton 2005).

The process of updating *LCSH* is gradual and deliberate (Ferris 2018). Knowlton (2005) demonstrates that many of Berman's suggestions have been implemented, while other headings remain unchanged. Dissatisfaction with the pace of change in *LCSH* and the mismatch between *LCSH* and terminology more likely to be used by those searching the catalog has led to proposals to augment the controlled vocabulary of subject headings through social tagging (Rafferty 2018). Tagging allows users to generate keywords to describe, categorize, or comment on books and other information objects. Potential benefits of this approach include the possibility of multiple interpretations expressed in users' vocabularies (Spiteri 2016). User tags can provide opportunities to include terminology that reflects the needs of local communities, including terms in languages other than English. In addition, users assigning tags are more likely to have read or listened to items than the librarians who have the task of assigning subject headings to library materials.

Studies demonstrate that both the controlled vocabulary of *LCSH* and tags have value for retrieval. Toine Bogers and Vivien Petras (2017) found that controlled vocabulary terms and tags seem to provide complementary contributions; some information needs are best addressed using controlled vocabulary terms, while others are best addressed using tags. Removing either is likely to decrease retrieval performance. For example, they found that unique tags work much better than controlled vocabulary for fiction book requests, while controlled vocabulary showed a tendency to work better for non-fiction book requests. Similarly, a study by Tina Gross, Arlene G. Taylor, and Daniel N. Joudrey (2015) demonstrated that some records retrieved by keyword searches would be lost without subject headings. They concluded that *LCSH* offers benefits of consistency, accuracy, and control often lacking in a free-text approach drawing on tagging done by users. See Box 20.1 for an example of subject headings versus tags. The tags demonstrate lack of control in singular/plural forms, level of specificity, and choice among synonyms. They also illustrate that tags introduce topics and concepts beyond those expressed by the chosen *LCSH*.

Box 20.1 Comparing Subject Headings and Tags for the Same Book

Wilkerson, Isabel. 2010. *The Warmth of Other Suns: The Epic Story of America's Great Migration*. New York: Random House.

LCSH:

African Americans—Migrations—History—20th Century; Migration, Internal—United States—History—20th Century; Rural-urban migration—United States—History—20th Century

Tags:

African American; African American history; African Americans; American history; Black history; Chicago; civil rights; great migration; history; Jim Crow; migration; migrations; race; race relations; racism; segregation

SELECTION

Many of the sources discussed in this chapter would be found in most libraries. Most often, the choice is fairly clear-cut; only one source will fill a particular need. Occasionally, there may be a choice between format, print or electronic, with the latter likely more expensive. In that case, the librarian needs to assess whether the cost is justified by added value for reference work, perhaps due to greater currency or more access points to the content. As more tools become freely available on the Web, the librarian may also need to determine whether a purchased or licensed resource provides information or search capabilities not yet matched through freely available sources. For example, the Online Computer Library Center (OCLC) provides *WorldCat.org* on the open Web and *WorldCat* as a licensed resource.

IMPORTANT GENERAL SOURCES

The following discussion covers those bibliographic tools that provide the most comprehensive coverage of books or serials or both. The focus is tools that continue to be updated. For guidance to retrospective titles, such as the *National Union Catalog, Pre-1956 Imprints*, the *Guide to Reference Books* provides an effective means for identifying and learning about the vast array of bibliographic sources that have been published. The *National Union Catalog, Pre-1956 Imprints*, a set of 754 volumes, included works published before 1956 and held by major American and Canadian libraries. It was an important resource for verifying bibliographic information and locating copies of books before the availability of *WorldCat*. This section of the chapter covers *WorldCat* and digital initiatives, followed by sections on library catalogs, current bibliography, sources of purchasing information, serials sources, and recommended lists.

WorldCat

The most important bibliographic source in today's library is produced by the shared cataloging network OCLC. Founded in 1967 as the Ohio College Library Center, OCLC is a "global library cooperative that provides shared technology services, original research and community programs for its membership and the library community at large" (OCLC n.d.). The cooperative encompasses almost 17,000 library members in 113 countries. As of January 2019, OCLC's *WorldCat*, the world's largest and most comprehensive catalog of library resources, includes more than 444 million bibliographic records (albeit with some duplication) with more than one new record added every two seconds. These records represent more than 2.7 billion items held by participating libraries. Coverage encompasses books, serials, audiovisual materials, musical scores, maps, archives/manuscripts, and electronic resources in 491 languages. These records are accessible in two ways: through the licensed database *WorldCat* and freely available to the world in the form of the simpler *WorldCat.org*. Given its scope, *WorldCat* can be used to identify materials available in a subject area, in a particular format or by a particular author; to verify citations; and to locate libraries holding a title.

In 2005, OCLC announced the Open WorldCat Initiative, with the goal of making library holdings more visible on the Web (McCullough 2015). *WorldCat.org* opens up *WorldCat* so that any Web user can search the database and link to online catalog records. *WorldCat.org* offers a single search box (with options to search everything or only books, DVDs, CDs, or articles), faceted browsing (refining an initial search by year, audience, content, format, language, author, or topic), and a general streamlining of the interface. There are also social features, including the possibility for users to add tags or reviews. Libraries holding an item are also displayed as part of the search results. In addition, OCLC works with partners such as *Wikipedia* to include links from title-level book displays back to *WorldCat.org* and from there to local libraries.

The licensed version of *WorldCat* has a sophisticated advanced search, allowing selection from more than twenty options when entering search terms, including author, title, or subject as words or phrases as well as elements such as publisher and series. Limiting options include year, audience (any, juvenile, not juvenile), content (e.g., fiction, biography), format, language, and location. Retrieval results provide detailed bibliographic information, bring together different editions and formats of the title searched, and identify holding libraries.

Digital Initiatives

As projects to digitize large numbers of books proceed, one can supplement searches of the document surrogates found in catalog records with a search of the full-text of a growing number of books. Launched in 2004, *Google Books* is currently the most ambitious digitization project, allowing a simple Web search of book contents or an advanced search of combinations of fields such as keyword or phrase, language, title, author, publisher, subject, and publication date. While acknowledging the concerns that have been raised about the lack of quality in the metadata and lack of quality control in the mass-digitization process (Weiss 2016), Dorothy A. Mays argues that *Google Books* can enrich what a library can offer its patrons. She notes that in addition to books, "there is a wealth of non-monograph ephemera, including government documents, retail catalogs, maps, city reports, directories, and illustrations that can be mined for genealogical and historical research" (Mays 2015, 23). Google scans two types of materials: works that are in the public domain (pre-1924 as of January 1, 2019) and books published in 1924 or after that are likely still under copyright protection. The pre-1924 books are fully searchable and almost always can be read in their entirety online. In the case of books published in 1924 or after, what can be viewed depends on the copyright status of the book. Full view is possible if the book is out of copyright or if the publisher or author has asked that the book be made fully viewable. Limited preview of selected pages is possible if the author or publisher has given permission. Otherwise, a "snippet view" is provided: information about the book plus a few sentences to display the search term or terms in context. If no text is available online, then basic bibliographic information about the book is provided. Entries for each book include a "find in a library" link to *WorldCat.org* (Chen 2012). A court decision in October 2015 clarified the legality of *Google Books* (Meyer 2015).

Other noteworthy projects providing access to digitized content include the *HathiTrust Digital Library* and the *Digital Public Library of America* (*DPLA*). Started in 2008, *HathiTrust* is a partnership of academic and research institutions offering a collection of millions of titles digitized from libraries primarily in North America (Anderson 2017). It is characterized by a robust search engine that provides the option of searching the full text or the catalog with well-organized metadata. Eamon P. Duffy (2013) documents the ways in which this library metadata benefits search strategies. In *HathiTrust*, documents in the public domain are available for view and download. Documents currently protected by copyright are available for full-text searching; search results indicate the number and location of occurrences of search terms across titles in the *HathiTrust* database, with more than half the titles in languages other than English. The *DPLA* launched in the spring of 2013. It collocates the metadata of over thirty-three million publicly accessible digital assets (including text, images, videos, and sound recordings), unifying access to previously siloed collections of digitized content from libraries, archives, museums, and historical societies (Ismail 2017).

Naomi Eichenlaub (2013) highlights the common challenges faced by such efforts to broaden access to content through digitization: copyright, orphan works (a copyrighted work for which the copyright owner cannot be contacted), and the quality of metadata and the content resulting from the digitization process. Despite these barriers, such projects dramatically extend access not only to records of materials but also to the contents of many more of the items themselves.

LIBRARY CATALOGS

For many years, the library catalog was the primary means of locating and accessing items in a library's collection; indeed, the function of the catalog was to display the holdings of a particular library. Over the last several decades, however, the catalog's function has evolved so that it not only reflects the library's collection but also acts as an access mechanism to resources beyond the library, whether housed in other libraries in a consortium or available in electronic form. Although the records that make up a library's catalog may be drawn from a shared cataloging network such as OCLC, such records may be tailored to the specific library's collection, such as through the addition of a local call number or volume holdings statement. Consulting a database like *WorldCat* answers the question "Does an item exist?" Consulting the local catalog answers the questions "Does the library own or provide access to the item?" and "Where can the item be found?"

A library's catalog is cumulative, including materials held in a collection, regardless of date of publication or date of acquisition. In a library consortium, the contents of the catalog may be a combination of several libraries. In these instances, the catalog is known as a union catalog. When the catalog is not fully representative of a library's collection, this fact should be made clear to users and librarians. For example, if an academic library maintains an institutional repository including the research output of scholars affiliated with the institution such as electronic theses and dissertations, the contents are not necessarily included in the library's catalog. The library catalog may also not fully represent the library's holdings of e-books and e-journals, so the user should be made aware of other finding tools for such content. As noted in Chapter 16, implementation of Web-scale discovery systems seeks to combine catalog access with access to other resources such as online databases.

Historically, the catalog provided three major types of access points for a given item: author, title, and subject. Authority control ensures that author names and subject headings are represented consistently. The *Library of Congress Authorities* includes authority headings for subject, name, title, and name/title combinations. Given the ease of access to catalogs across the world, as demonstrated by *LibWeb*: *Library Servers via WWW*, it is important to be aware that libraries in other countries do not necessarily conform to the authority control practices followed by the Library of Congress. The *Virtual International Authority File* is a collaborative effort that identifies the authoritative form of a given name in different countries.

For bibliographic verification tasks, most often it is preferable to search *WorldCat* rather than individual library catalogs. Either successful or negative search results cost the librarian very little time. However, the presence of locally produced cataloging copy that might not be present in *WorldCat* occasionally merits searching catalogs individually. Subject bibliographers may wish to search a local collection to determine its holdings in a particular area of strength. In addition to the online catalog, conditions of use, hours of operation, and other worthwhile information may be found on a library's website.

Online catalog design has become more user centered. Such catalogs are characterized as "next generation" (Burke and Tumbleson 2016, 19), with features that may include a single search box, a state-of-the art Web interface, enriched content (book cover images, user tags, reviews), faceted navigation (refining results based on dates, languages, formats, locations, etc.), relevancy ranking of search results, spelling suggestions, recommendations of related materials, and opportunities for user contributions. Such catalogs take lessons from online booksellers like *Amazon*, which include more information about each title than a typical catalog provides and seek to involve users in activities like providing reviews of titles. In the case of catalogs, enriched book content can be licensed from ProQuest. *Syndetics Unbound* allows libraries to customize catalog record displays by including such elements as cover images, summaries, authors' biographies, tables of contents, excerpts, series, recommendations of similar titles, professional reviews, reading level, and awards. In addition, reader reviews, ratings, and tags drawn from *LibraryThing*, a social cataloging website, can be included. This inclusion of user-generated metadata responds to the concern noted previously regarding the limitations and biases of *LCSH*.

United States

Currently, the products and services of the Library of Congress and the shared cataloging network OCLC are the dominant elements in the provision of bibliographic control in the United States. The *Library of Congress Online Catalog* is a database of more than seventeen million catalog records for books, serials, manuscripts, maps, music, recordings, images, and electronic resources in the Library of Congress collections. Search options include Browse (titles, authors/creators, subjects, call numbers), Keyword Search anywhere in the catalog record, or Advanced Search combining terms and applying limits.

Libraries Outside the United States

LibWeb: Library Servers via WWW provides access to library catalogs from around the world, grouped by broad geographic area: United States; Europe; Canada; Australia, New Zealand & the Pacific; Asia; Africa and the Middle East; Mexico and the Caribbean; Central America and South America. As one example, *Aurora* is Library and Archives Canada's online catalog of published material. Its companion service, *Voilà*, Canada's National Union Catalogue, is a single point of access to the collections of libraries across Canada. It contains records for books, magazines, maps, music, and more, including items in formats for the print- or hearing-impaired. Both *Aurora* and *Voilà* are hosted by OCLC.

CURRENT BIBLIOGRAPHY

Current bibliographic sources are heavily used by librarians because they provide a timely list of books and other media at the time of publication and often in advance of publication. Librarians use these listings to perform the core functions of libraries: selection, reference, and cataloging. Subject access to newly published books allows both librarians and users to determine those books that have been published on the topic of interest. In addition, reference librarians use them to answer reference questions, including the verification of bibliographic citations. National bibliographic agencies have a broader societal ambition when producing current bibliographic sources: to capture the record of the national publishing output for posterity.

U.S. Bibliography

In the United States, the only title being published that meets the definition of a current bibliography is the *American Book Publishing Record* (*ABPR*), a monthly publication from Grey House Publishing. *ABPR* provides full cataloging information for over 10,000 new titles as they are published. It is arranged by the Dewey Decimal Classification System, with author and title indexes complementing the primary arrangement. Separate sections for adult fiction and juvenile fiction are arranged alphabetically by main entry author or title. In addition, the subject guide, arranged alphabetically, directs the user from the subject headings to the corresponding Dewey Decimal Classification System numbers. The annual *ABPR*, published in March, is compiled from the twelve monthly issues.

National Bibliographies from Other Countries

The International Federation of Library Associations and Institutions (IFLA) Section on Bibliography maintains a *National Bibliographic Register*, with information about and links to more than forty national bibliographies from countries in Europe, Asia, Africa, the Caribbean, and South America. The Section's Working Group on Guidelines for National Bibliographies maintains a website *Best Practice for National Bibliographic Agencies in a Digital Age.*

SOURCES OF PURCHASING INFORMATION

In-print lists identify titles that are currently available from publishers. Because books may remain in print for a number of years, the current list can also be useful in identifying material published much earlier. In reference work, in-print lists are often used to determine whether an announced book has been published, whether a later edition of a work has been published, or what volumes of a series are still in print. The primary advantage of the in-print list is that it consolidates book purchasing information from thousands of publishers into one integrated list.

Other resources now rival the in-print list in usefulness. Almost all publishers worldwide now produce catalogs available through the Web. Frequently, these electronic catalogs provide more accurate up-to-date information than that available from in-print lists. *Amazon* and *Barnes & Noble* provide easily searchable basic bibliographic and pricing information for millions of books in multiple formats, videos, and CDs. However, as Melissa De Fino (2013) cautions, *Amazon*'s data is not organized or indexed in a way that is conducive to research but rather designed to improve sales. The quality, search capability, and organization of bibliographic information important to researchers are lacking. Accurate and objective metadata is what sets library catalogs apart from commercial databases like *Amazon*.

Currently, a business unit of ProQuest, Bowker dominates the in-print list field. The Web-based *Books In Print* offers information on over twenty million books, audiobooks, e-books, and multimedia global titles, including in-print, forthcoming, and out-of-print items. It is available at two subscription levels: United States Edition for U.S. publications and Global Edition for U.S., UK, Canadian, European, and Australian publications. It offers multiple search options. The basic search includes subject, title, author, publisher, series title, and character options. Advanced search allows for even more precise searching through combinations of various fields and a variety of limits such as language, country of publication, audience, date range, and Dewey range. In addition to detailed bibliographic and order information, records for titles may include reviews and suggestions of similar titles.

Grey House Publishing issues a number of titles, based on the Bowker data, in print form. *Books In Print* (*BIP*) is an annual listing of books available from U.S. publishers, with a midyear supplement. *Forthcoming Books*, published four times a year, lists books projected to be published within the next several months. *Subject Guide to Books In Print* arranges the content of *BIP* by subject, based primarily on the *Library of Congress Subject Headings* assigned to the books. *Children's Books In Print* and the *Subject Guide to Children's Books In Print* list material selected by age level. Other titles cover specific formats: *Books Out Loud: Bowker's Guide to Audiobooks* and *Complete Video Directory* are examples.

SOURCES FOR SERIALS

The most comprehensive source of bibliographic information about serials is *Ulrichsweb*, a database with entries for 300,000 serials of all types, including academic and scholarly journals, e-journals, peer-reviewed titles, open access titles, popular magazines, newspapers, newsletters, and more (Meeks 2018). Proprietary subject headings encompass 977 subject areas and titles are in 200 languages. Entries in *Ulrichsweb* provide data such as ISSN, publisher, frequency, language, subject, indexing and abstracting coverage, full-text database coverage, and reviews written by librarians. The status of each title, whether active or ceased, is clearly indicated. The basic search prompts for title, ISSN, or search term; advanced search allows one to enter additional terms and limit by status (e.g., active, ceased), serial type, content type, and language. Icons indicate peer-reviewed, online, and open access titles. Box 20.2 illustrates the use of advanced search features.

In recent years, there has been growth in open access journals, publications that make the full text of their articles freely available on the web (see Chapter 22 for more discussion of open access). The *Directory of Open Access Journals* has been developed to simplify identification of and access to these scientific and scholarly journals. As of March 2019, the directory included 12,852 journals from 129 countries, with 9,914 searchable at the article level.

Box 20.2 Search Strategy: Astronomy Magazines

Following the total solar eclipse that occurred on August 21, 2017, a public librarian noticed increased interest in astronomy among library users, both youth and adults. The library subscribed to general science magazines like *Discover* and *Scientific American* but none specific to astronomy. Seeking to identify titles for possible inclusion in the collection, the librarian consulted *Ulrichsweb*. Choosing Advanced Search, she entered "Astronomy" as a subject term and limited to Status=Active; Serial Type=Magazine; Content Type=Consumer; and Language of Text=English. Several titles matched this strategy, including *Astronomy*, *Griffith Observer*, *Sky & Telescope*, and *StarDate*. Each of these four included reviews from *Magazines for Libraries* and ordering and price information, helpful guidance in deciding which titles to add to the library's collection.

RECOMMENDED LISTS

Recommended lists are highly selective evaluative bibliographies, used by librarians in three integral ways: building a collection to meet the needs of users, measuring (evaluating) the library collection against these standard lists, and advising readers. In carrying out these activities, one must keep in mind that recommended lists are created for an average collection, whereas the librarian is collecting for a particular library with a unique user population. A few examples of some well-known recommended lists are discussed in this chapter. Chapter 14 may be consulted for titles that provide lists of recommended reference books, and Chapter 21 provides thorough coverage of tools for readers' advisory use.

The *Core Collections* database is available online from EBSCO. Subsets including the most highly ranked titles are distributed in print by Grey House Publishing: *Children's Core Collection, Middle & Junior High Core Collection, Senior High Core Collection, Young Adult Fiction Core Collection, Graphic Novels Core Collection, Fiction Core Collection*, and *Public Library Core Collection: Nonfiction*, with the latter two recommending titles for a general adult audience. Titles included are selected by the *Core Collections* team employed by EBSCO and the *Core Collections* Advisory Group, comprising public, academic, and school librarians who are experts in their fields. Entries include complete bibliographic information, an annotation and subject headings, grade level and Dewey classification, recommendation level, and links to reviews, similar books, and other books by the author. Print volumes have author, title, and subject indexes. Fiction entries are arranged by author and nonfiction by Dewey.

Resources for College Libraries (*RCL*) covers nearly 85,000 titles targeted at an undergraduate audience in a broad range of subjects, including the traditional liberal arts and sciences curriculum, business, computer science, education, engineering, and health sciences. *RCL* resources are selected by subject specialists, including both academic librarians and faculty members. Primarily a collection development tool, the database provides titles of print and electronic books, websites, and databases. The database is searchable by keyword, subject, title, author, and publisher. Advanced search allows combinations of terms and limits by such criteria as audience, Dewey or Library of Congress classification range, and format.

Magazines for Libraries is an annotated list by subject of more than 5,100 periodicals, both print and electronic journals. Subject specialists limit selection to those titles they consider to be most useful for the average elementary or secondary school, public, academic, or special library. *Magazines for Libraries* also serves as a readers' advisory tool for the user who wants to select a magazine in a subject area of particular interest. Annotations from *Magazines for Libraries* are included in *Ulrichsweb*. The *Magazines for Libraries Update* blog includes annotations for selected open access and niche titles of interest.

Oxford Bibliographies consists of subject modules covering the literature on specific topics, primarily in the humanities and social sciences. Each collection has its own editor in chief and editorial board. Each bibliography identifies the essential literature of its topic, providing introductory overviews, identifying standard works if they exist, and providing evaluative and comparative annotations of relevant books, articles, primary sources, online resources, and other formats of material deemed essential to an overview of the subject. Broad subject areas range from anthropology to medieval studies to music. Examples of specific bibliographies within these subject areas are "material culture," "feudalism," and "folk music."

SEARCH STRATEGIES

Verification is necessary when trying to identify, and eventually locate, a given item. Often, the bibliographic information presented by a library user to the reference librarian is so incomplete that a good deal of ingenuity must be used to locate a copy. The sources of incomplete citations can vary from partial information gathered from a chance reference on a television or radio talk show to a poorly constructed bibliography in a scholarly book. Practice and experience make the process easier, but there are a number of factors to keep in mind when deciding where to start.

For most bibliographic quests, a search begins with *WorldCat*. The speed, ease of searching, and depth and breadth of coverage make this the first choice in almost all cases. However, a study by Jeffrey Beall and Karen Kafadar (2005) and a follow-up study by Christine DeZelar-Tiedman (2008) demonstrate that there are still a significant number of bibliographic records, especially for old and rare materials, found in the *National Union Catalog, Pre-1956 Imprints* that are not found in a search of *WorldCat*. To fully answer a patron's question, the librarian may need to look at several tools and may well find pieces of the bibliographic puzzle in each of them. Knowledge of these sources will assist the librarian in deciding which tools to examine and, in some cases, may narrow the search to only one tool that will give a particular type of information.

Box 20.3 Search Strategy: A Book on Homeschooling

An out-of-town researcher appeared at a university library's reference desk. A colleague at her home institution had recommended a book by Eva Boyd. The book was about a single mother who homeschooled her son, who then completed college by age seventeen. She remembered neither the date of publication nor the title of the book. The first step was searching the university library's own catalog. Because the university had a strong collection in the field of education, it was assumed that the book would turn up immediately as the result of an author search. No author with the name of Eva Boyd appeared in the list of authors. A widening of the catalog search to include the holdings of the consortium of which the library was a part resulted in one book by Eva Jolene Boyd on the subject of stagecoach travel in the American West, *That Old Overland Stagecoaching*. A search of *WorldCat.org* and *Books In Print* on the Web turned up more books by the same author, Eva Jolene Boyd. Finally, the librarian revised her strategy on *WorldCat.org*. A subject search on "Home Schooling" and keyword author search "Eva" produced several matches, including *About Face: A Redirection in Education* by Eva Seibert. The alternative title is "How Both Sons of a Single Mother Were Homeschooled and Admitted to College by the Time They Were Twelve." The record indicated that the book was self-published, and only two holding libraries were listed, neither close by. The librarian turned to *Amazon* to determine whether a copy was available inexpensively. Several sources for purchase were identified, with one copy priced as low as $8.00.

The search in Box 20.3 illustrates several points. First, one should note that current English usage indicates that the word "homeschooling" should be spelled as one word, yet *LCSH* uses two words. When one goes back and checks the electronic *Books in Print* entry for the book, the entry shows only one subject heading: Education—Aims and Objectives. At no place in the *Books In Print* entry does the concept "home schooling" appear. Had the librarian relied on only one source, this query would never have been answered. This case shows how resourceful and creative reference librarians must be when tackling complex bibliographic questions. Name and title variations, or uncertainties regarding specific editions of works or which libraries might own these editions, are just a few of the difficulties that may arise from a seemingly simple request for a book. Often, the librarian must carefully question the user and consider all available resources to successfully answer bibliographic reference questions.

CONCLUSION

The future of bibliographic tools and the capabilities they offer reference librarians will be shaped by new developments in bibliographic control. In November 2006, the Library of Congress convened the Working Group on the Future of Bibliographic Control. Its final report, titled *On the Record*, concluded that "the future of bibliographic control will be collaborative, decentralized, international in scope, and Web-based. Its realization will occur in cooperation with the private sector, and with the active collaboration of library users. Data will be gathered from multiple sources; change will happen quickly; and bibliographic control will be dynamic, not static" (2008, 4). As the discussion of major bibliographic tools in this chapter has shown, librarians now benefit from the ready availability of web-based resources that are international in scope and support advanced search capabilities. Gaining a thorough familiarity with these resources and any future enhancements in their content and search options increases the likelihood that librarians can successfully solve bibliographic puzzles when users seek assistance.

REFERENCES

Anderson, Rick. 2017. "HathiTrust." In *Encyclopedia of Library and Information Sciences*. 4th ed., 1757–62. Boca Raton, FL: CRC Press.

Beall, Jeffrey, and Karen Kafadar. 2005. "The Proportion of NUC Pre-56 Titles Represented in OCLC WorldCat." *College & Research Libraries* 66 (5): 431–35.

Berman, Sanford. 1971. *Prejudices and Antipathies: A Tract on the LC Subject Heads Concerning People*. Metuchen, NJ: Scarecrow Press.

Bogers, Toine, and Vivien Petras. 2017. "An In-Depth Analysis of Tags and Controlled Metadata for Book Search." In *iConference 2017 Proceedings*, Vol. 2, 15–30. https://www.ideals.illinois.edu/handle/2142/98869.

Buckland, Michael. 2017. *Information and Society*. Cambridge, MA: MIT Press.

Burke, John J., and Beth E. Tumbleson. 2016. "Search Systems and Finding Tools." *Library Technology Reports* 52 (2): 17–22.

Cargill, Mary. 1996. "Bibliography." In *Guide to Reference Books*. 11th ed., edited by Robert Balay, 1–105. Chicago: American Library Association.

Chen, Xiaotian. 2012. "Google Books and WorldCat: A Comparison of Their Content." *Online Information Review* 36 (4): 507–16.

De Fino, Melissa. 2013. "Amazon for Technical Services Librarians: Making Order of the Jungle." *Technical Services Quarterly* 29 (4): 280–91.

DeZelar-Tiedman, Christine. 2008. "The Proportion of NUC Pre-56 Titles Represented in the RLIN and OCLC Databases Compared: A Follow-Up to the Beall/Kafadar Study." *College & Research Libraries* 69 (5): 401–6.

Duffy, Eamon P. 2013. "Searching HathiTrust: Old Concepts in a New Context." *Partnership: The Canadian Journal of Library and Information Practice and Research* 8 (1). https://doi.org/10.21083/partnership.v8i1.2503.

Eichenlaub, Naomi. 2013. "Checking in with Google Books, HathiTrust, and the DPLA." *Computers in Libraries* 33 (9): 4–9.

Ferris, Anna M. 2018. "Birth of a Subject Heading." *Library Resources & Technical Services* 62 (1): 16–27.

Gorman, Michael. 2004. "Authority Control in the Context of Bibliographic Control in the Electronic Environment." *Cataloging & Classification Quarterly* 38 (3–4): 11–22.

Gross, Tina, Arlene G. Taylor, and Daniel N. Joudrey. 2015. "Still a Lot to Lose: The Role of Controlled Vocabulary in Keyword Searching." *Cataloging & Classification Quarterly* 53 (1): 1–39.

Ismail, Lizah. 2017. "Digital Public Library of America." *The Charleston Advisor* 19 (2): 25–30.

Knowlton, Steven A. 2005. "Three Decades Since *Prejudices and Antipathies:* A Study of Changes in the Library of Congress Subject Headings." *Cataloging & Classification Quarterly* 40 (2): 123–45.

Marcum, Deanna. 2014. "Archives, Libraries, Museums: Coming Back Together?" *Information & Culture* 49 (1): 74–89.

Mays, Dorothy A. 2015. "Google Books: Far More Than Just Books." *Public Libraries* 54 (5): 23–26.

McCullough, John. 2015. "OCLC and Discovery." In *Reimagining Reference in the 21st Century*, edited by David A. Tyckoson and John G. Dove, 327–33. West Lafayette, IN: Purdue University Press.

Meeks, Kim. 2018. "*Ulrichsweb* Review." *Journal of Electronic Resources in Medical Libraries* 15 (1): 26–35.

Meyer, Robinson. 2015. "After 10 Years, Google Books Is Legal." *The Atlantic*, October 20. http://www.theatlantic.com/technology/archive/2015/10/fair-use-transformative-leval-google-books/411058/.

OCLC. n.d. "About OCLC." https://www.oclc.org/en/about.html.

Rafferty, Pauline. 2018. "Tagging." *Knowledge Organization* 45 (6): 500–16.

Spiteri, Louise E. 2016. "Managing User-Generated Metadata in Discovery Systems." In *Managing Metadata in Web-Scale Discovery Systems*, edited by Louise E. Spiteri, 165–94. London: Facet Publishing.

Weiss, Andrew. 2016. "Examining Massive Digital Libraries (MDLs) and Their Impact on Reference Services." *The Reference Librarian* 57 (4): 286–306.

Wesner-Early, Caryn. 2017. "Self-Publishing Online." In *Encyclopedia of Library and Information Sciences*. 4th ed., 4054–61. Boca Raton, FL: CRC Press.

Wilson, Patrick. 1968. *Two Kinds of Power: An Essay on Bibliographical Control.* Berkeley, CA: University of California Press.

Working Group on the Future of Bibliographic Control. 2008. *On the Record.* Washington, DC: Library of Congress. https://www.loc.gov/bibliographic-future/news/lcwg-ontherecord-jan08-final.pdf.

LIST OF SOURCES

Amazon. https://www.amazon.com.

American Book Publishing Record. Amenia, NY: Grey House Publishing. Monthly with annual cumulation.

Aurora. Ottawa: Library and Archives Canada. https://bac-lac.on.worldcat.org/discovery.

Barnes & Noble. https://www.barnesandnoble.com.

Best Practice for National Bibliographic Agencies in a Digital Age. IFLA Working Group on Guidelines for National Bibliographies. https://www.ifla.org/node/7858.

Books In Print. Amenia, NY: Grey House Publishing. Annual with semiannual supplements.

Books In Print. Ann Arbor, MI: ProQuest. http://www.booksinprint.com. Subscription required.

Books Out Loud: Bowker's Guide to Audiobooks. Amenia, NY: Grey House Publishing. Annual.

Children's Books In Print. Amenia, NY: Grey House Publishing. Annual.

Children's Core Collection. 23rd ed. 2017. Amenia, NY: Grey House Publishing. Also available online from EBSCO as part of *Core Collections.*

Complete Video Directory. Amenia, NY: Grey House Publishing. Annual.

Core Collections. Ipswich, MA: EBSCO. https://www.ebsco.com/products/research-databases/core-collections. Subscription required.

Digital Public Library of America. https://dp.la/.

Directory of Open Access Journals. https://doaj.org/.

Fiction Core Collection. 19th ed. 2018. Amenia, NY: Grey House Publishing. Also available online from EBSCO as part of *Core Collections*.

Forthcoming Books. Amenia, NY: Grey House Publishing. Quarterly.

Google Books. https://books.google.com.

Graphic Novels Core Collection. 2nd ed. 2019. Amenia, NY: Grey House Publishing. Also available online from EBSCO as part of *Core Collections*.

Guide to Reference Books. 1th ed. 1996. Edited by Robert Balay. Chicago: American Library Association.

HathiTrust Digital Library. https://www.hathitrust.org/.

Library of Congress Authorities. Library of Congress. https://authorities.loc.gov.

Library of Congress Online Catalog. Library of Congress. https://catalog.loc.gov/.

Library of Congress Subject Headings. Library of Congress. http://authorities.loc.gov/.

LibraryThing. https://www.librarything.com/.

LibWeb: Library Servers via WWW. http://www.lib-web.org/.

Magazines for Libraries. 27th ed. 2018. Edited by Cheryl LaGuardia. New Providence, NJ: ProQuest. Also available online as part of *Ulrichsweb*.

Magazines for Libraries Update. Ann Arbor, MI: ProQuest. http://www.proquest.com/blog/mfl/.

Middle & Junior High Core Collection. 13th ed. 2017. Amenia, NY: Grey House Publishing. Also available online from EBSCO as part of *Core Collections*.

National Bibliographic Register. IFLA Section on Bibliography. https://www.ifla.org/node/2216.

National Union Catalog, Pre-1956 Imprints. A Cumulative Author List Representing Library of Congress Printed Cards and Titles Reported by Other American Libraries. 1968–1981. 754 vols. London: Mansell.

Oxford Bibliographies. Oxford: Oxford University Press. http://www.oxfordbibliographies.com. Subscription required.

Public Library Core Collection: Nonfiction. 17th ed. 2019. Amenia, NY: Grey House Publishing. Also available online from EBSCO as part of *Core Collections*.

Resources for College Libraries (RCL). Ann Arbor, MI: ProQuest. http://www.rclweb.net. Subscription required.

Senior High Core Collection. 21st ed. 2018. Amenia, NY: Grey House Publishing. Also available online from EBSCO as part of *Core Collections*.

Subject Guide to Books in Print. Amenia, NY: Grey House Publishing. Annual.

Subject Guide to Children's Books In Print. Amenia, NY: Grey House Publishing. Annual.

Syndetics Unbound. Ann Arbor, MI: ProQuest. https://proquest.syndetics.com/. Subscription required.

Ulrichsweb. Ann Arbor, MI: ProQuest. http://ulrichsweb.serialssolutions.com/. Subscription required.

Virtual International Authority File. https://viaf.org/.

Voilà. Ottawa: Library and Archives Canada. https://www.bac-lac.gc.ca/eng/services/national-union-catalogue/Pages/national-union-catalogue.aspx.

Wikipedia. https://www.wikipedia.org/.

WorldCat. Dublin, OH: OCLC. https://www.oclc.org/en/worldcat.html. Subscription required.

WorldCat.org. Dublin, OH: OCLC. https://www.worldcat.org/.

Young Adult Fiction Core Collection. 2nd ed. 2017. Amenia, NY: Grey House Publishing. Also available online from EBSCO as part of *Core Collections*.

SUGGESTED READINGS

Brown, Christopher C., and Suzanne S. Bell. 2018. *Librarian's Guide to Online Searching: Cultivating Database Skills for Research and Instruction.* 5th ed. Santa Barbara, CA: Libraries Unlimited.

This text has a helpful chapter on searching bibliographic databases and full-text e-books, with a focus on *WorldCat, WorldCat.org*, the library's own catalog, *Google Books*, and *HathiTrust.*

Chambers, Sally, ed. 2013. *Catalogue 2.0: The Future of the Library Catalogue.* Chicago: ALA Neal-Schuman.

This collection of papers provides a state-of-the-art examination of the library catalog and an exploration of where it may be headed.

Hall, Danielle. 2004. "Mansell Revisited." *American Libraries* 35 (4): 78–80.

Hall highlights the decrease in usage of the *National Union Catalog* by U.S. libraries, coinciding with the growth of *WorldCat.* She provides a brief history of this ambitious publication project, commenting that "even as the project progressed, the profession recognized that this 'greatest single instrument' would be the last great bibliographic effort in a paper format."

Joudrey, Daniel N., Arlene G. Taylor, and Katherine M. Wisser. 2018. *The Organization of Information.* 4th ed. Santa Barbara, CA: Libraries Unlimited.

This introductory text gives an excellent overview of the principles of organizing recorded information of various types. Within a broad context, the authors enable the reader to see how organization facilitates use.

Kornegay, Rebecca, Heidi E. Buchanan, and Hildegard B. Morgan. 2009. *Magic Search: Getting the Best Results from Your Catalog and Beyond.* Chicago: American Library Association.

The authors explain the *Library of Congress Subject Headings* system, particularly the subdivisions and how they can be used to improve keyword search results.

Library of Congress. 2017. *The Card Catalog: Books, Cards, and Literary Treasures.* San Francisco: Chronicle Books.

The text traces the history of bibliographic practices from 5,000 years ago in ancient Mesopotamia to modern-day catalogs and features many images of original catalog cards and early edition book covers.

Mann, Thomas. 2015. *The Oxford Guide to Library Research.* 4th ed. New York: Oxford University Press.

Three chapters in this guide provide guidance on search strategy specific to bibliographic sources: "Subject Headings and the Library Catalog," "Published Subject Bibliographies," and "Locating Materials in Other Libraries."

Roberto, K. R., ed. 2008. *Radical Cataloging: Essays at the Front.* Jefferson, NC: McFarland.

This collection of critical and scholarly essays includes criticisms of traditional Library of Congress cataloging and identifies methods of making cataloging more inclusive and helpful to library users.

Chapter 21

Readers' Advisory Services and Sources

Neal Wyatt

INTRODUCTION

Discovery tools shape how the seemingly ineffable is defined and found. Companies such as Netflix, Match.com, and Spotify have invested millions in such processes, telling subscribers that they know what makes a movie enjoyable, a partner desirable, and one song evocative of another. Book discovery is part of this same movement, with mathematical formulas guiding reading choices. It is also driven by circles of influence with celebrities of all kinds, through an ever-expanding range of outlets, venturing to tell readers what is worth exploring. Magazines, newspapers, social media, and next-door neighbors do as well. Where do librarians fit into a conversation fueled by big data and high-impact influence?

Librarians practicing readers' advisory (RA) service occupy the space between discovery and suggestion. Their work is interwoven into the primary reason most users visit the library: to access and discover books (see De Rosa et al. 2011; Horrigan 2016; OCLC and American Library Association 2018; Zickuhr, Rainie, and Purcell 2013). Advisors help readers learn the addictive joys of J. K. Rowling's *Harry Potter and the Sorcerer's Stone* when they are young and the sustaining pleasures and gratifications of Colson Whitehead's *The Underground Railroad* when they grow older. RA librarians help readers discover underappreciated gems, as well as books lighting up social media and dominating the bestseller lists. They suggest titles to readers based upon conversations about what readers like and dislike and what they desire in their reading experiences. Author by author, title by title, RA librarians assist readers in negotiating the most complex process of discovery—understanding what one likes to read (listen to, watch, even play) and why.[1]

EDUCATION, PLACEMENT, AND DUTIES OF READERS' ADVISORY LIBRARIANS

Most RA librarians are self-taught (see Anderson 2016; Schwartz and Thornton-Verma 2014; Van Fleet 2008). They learn to practice RA through trial and error and in-house training, reading RA books and articles, attending conference sessions, and modeling peers. In addition to book and reading-related skills, advisors must also be accomplished in many of the same areas as reference, collection development, and cataloging librarians, as each contributes to the ways readers borrow, access, and discover books. Like reference librarians, advisors study to be expert searchers, practiced in the art of developing nuanced and intricate search strategies. Like collection development librarians, advisors acquire a thorough knowledge of the publishing industry and understand the cycles of the publishing calendar. Like catalogers, RA librarians learn to characterize the essence of a wide variety of books succinctly and master the operations of a controlled vocabulary.

While there is an ongoing movement to bring RA services to those who use academic libraries, and while school librarians are in the vanguard of the service in K–12 institutions (for discussion of academic RA and how RA is practiced in K–12 institutions see Behler 2011; Brookbank, Davis, and Harlan 2018; Nesi 2012), readers' advisory service is most widely practiced in public libraries, where it is part of a broad range of responsibilities that public service/reference librarians undertake.[2] In a smaller number of libraries there are staff who devote most of their attention to RA while different aspects of public service are delivered from a separate location. In addition to public services librarians, advisors can also be based within the collection development or technical services departments, working as selectors and catalogers as well as frontline librarians. Regardless of where they are housed, advisors must collaborate with colleagues in order to offer the best service to readers. Multiple aspects of library operations—from circulation policies to the selection of the integrated library system (ILS) to what the service desks are termed—shape the form and extent of RA duties.

What are those duties? RA librarians talk with patrons about books and reading. They do so at the service desk, over the phone, in the stacks, and via online forms and social media. Advisors suggest books to readers, based upon a system of appeal terms (descriptors that capture specific points of reader engagement). They identify read-alikes, read-arounds, and sure bets; create displays; and develop reading guides of all types.[3] Advisors also create programs to further the aims of RA, such as book discussion groups, author visits, and summer reading, as well as supporting community reading efforts and hosting book events beyond the library's walls. Advisors read widely, venturing far beyond their own personal preferences (see Box 21.1 for guidance). They monitor publishing trends and keep abreast of popular authors and titles. They track changes in fiction genres and nonfiction types and note emerging authors just starting to gain attention. RA librarians advocate for the importance of reading in the lives of those they serve and strive to create an environment in which reading and book discovery is a familiar and accessible service of the library.

Box 21.1 Activity: Creating a Reading Plan

Advisors need to be readers and strategic ones at that. Developing an intentional reading plan to ensure wide exposure to key authors, genres, and subgenres is an important part of fulfilling the role of advisor. This professional reading is different from personal reading and develops knowledge and depth across all genres and material types. There are many ways to create a reading plan and following are descriptions of four approaches. For each book read, advisors should think about why the book is popular, consider its central appeals, speculate as to what kinds of readers will enjoy it, and identify possible read-alikes. It is also helpful to discuss discoveries with colleagues and library patrons.

Five Book Challenge

First devised by Ann Bouricius (2000, 67–68), this reading plan asks advisors to read five books in a given genre over the course of a year. The goal is to become familiar with the specific appeals of a genre and its range of subgenres. Wyatt and Saricks (2019, 261–262) offer a genre-spanning list of suggestions for those needing help getting started.

Reading Pathways

This reading plan, building from a *Book Riot* feature, provides a way to become familiar with an author's style, interests, and genre affiliations. Pick an author and research the titles for which that author is most admired (fan favorites, award winners, and best reviewed). Read these books, noting how they relate and differ from one another and how the author develops their style and concerns over time.

Classic Sure Bet and New Sure Bet Genre Titles

Sure bets are books that hold broad appeal for a wide range of readers. They are good books to have in the proverbial RA back pocket as reading them instills confidence and advances RA knowledge in a strategic manner. Pick one classic sure bet, a title fans of the genre often reference. Then pick a new sure bet, one published in the last year that is in the same genre. Read both back to back, starting with the classic. Consider how the genre both keeps key appeals and has changed over time.

Read Awards

Pick a book award and a category (best novel, best short story collection, best debut) and read both the winner and the short list. Reading this way connects advisors to the works held in high esteem by authors, fans, and critics. Such a reading plan can also provide insight into trends and inform key author and sure bet selections.

Question for Reflection and Discussion:

1. What are the major appeals of the genre/author/titles? How can they be best expressed and shared with readers?
2. How many books does an advisor need to read in order to feel comfortable with a genre?
3. How can advisors ensure they are reading broadly and strategically?
4. What might be other ideas for reading plans that ensure both depth of knowledge and awareness of contemporary trends?

READERS' ADVISORY THEORY: APPEAL

Appeal is the foundational theory of readers' advisory work. It is a set of terms that describes the multiple attractions readers have to books and with the reading experience. More broadly, it is a framework advisors use to translate what a reader enjoys about one book into a set of descriptors that can be applied to others. Advisors use appeal to help readers better understand their reading interests as well as to make suggestions, identify read-alikes and sure bets, and understand genres. Prior to the development and widespread adoption of appeal, many advisors struggled to routinely develop satisfying suggestions and identify a range of authors that pleased readers. Instead they made suggestions based upon genre classification, subject headings, popularity, their own reading preferences, or a vague intuition that one book felt similar to another.

Systems of appeal are most frequently expressed as a list of elements with accompanying descriptions and definitions. There are three systems commonly used by advisors.

Joyce Saricks and Nancy Brown

Joyce Saricks and Nancy Brown (1989, 40–73) developed the most widely used system of appeal. It consists of four elements—pacing, characterization, story line, and setting—and was first formally published in their landmark book *Readers' Advisory Service in the Public Library*.

Pacing captures how quickly a novel progresses through the story arc and readers' perception of that speed. Characterization refers to the types of characters in a novel and the manner in which they are brought to life. Are they developed over time through their dialogue, actions, and inner thoughts or are they fully formed and described from the outset and easily understood and known? Story line encompasses several elements including the point of view from which the story is told and the amount of dialogue in a novel. This latter concern was Saricks and Brown's effort to distinguish novels of action from those that revolve around relationships. They believed that books with a great amount of dialogue were "talking" books, those in which characters and their relationships were the center focus. Story line is most centrally concerned, however, with the authors' treatment of, and intentions toward, the story itself. Treatment refers to the kind of story being told. One author might approach an espionage novel from the standpoint of the mission, tracing the elements of spy craft and emphasizing the danger and escape. Another author could pen an espionage novel with a stress on the moral ambiguity of the situation and the cost of the mission on the agent's psyche. Intention refers to the author's approach, be it a serious examination of an issue, a romp, or a soap opera. Setting, as Saricks and Brown wish the term to be understood, does not just mean place or time but also background detail: the description that sets a book into a particular world. Settings readers notice tend to be rich and expansive, such as the treacherous landscape and mythic details of Sarah Perry's *The Essex Serpent*, rather than those that are thin and imprecise, such as the quickly sketched and little noted settings Saricks and Brown refer to as "wallpaper."

Saricks has continued to study appeal and has written subsequent editions of *Readers' Advisory Service in the Public Library* (see Saricks 2005b; Saricks and Brown 1997) along with her "At Leisure with Joyce Saricks" columns in *Booklist* magazine. Through these outlets, she has revised some of the terminology she and

Brown first developed, changing the term "setting" to "frame' and adding the concepts of tone and mood as well as language and style to her list of appeal elements. Saricks's term "frame" has been widely adopted, and many advisors use it in place of the word "setting" as frame more clearly marks a distinction between setting as "time and place" and setting as "background detail."

Building off of the work of Catherine Sheldrick Ross (discussed later), Saricks uses the term "mood" to define the emotional state of the reader. She defines "tone" as the feeling an author creates in a book. Like Ross, Saricks believes that readers' moods are critical and can almost entirely account for a reader not enjoying a suggestion. She also holds that tone can be as important as pacing in the determination of what a reader will enjoy (Saricks 2010, 21).

Saricks uses the terms "language" and "style" to account for the fundamentals of writing quality and "stylistic flourishes" and also for a wider range of language and style concerns, such as language that is "clever, natural, ornate, polished, lyrical, smart, witty, breezy, or pun-filled" and styles that are "anecdotal, journalistic, scholarly, complex, unusual, or experimental" (2013, 19).

Nancy Pearl

Nancy Pearl (1999, xii-xiii) defines four elements of appeal: setting, story, character, and language. Pearl has used these divisions to create a metaphor that describes the way a reader engages with a book. The "doorway" system of appeal posits that all books have a front door, the main entrance through which readers connect to a given work (Pearl 2012, 18). While all books have all four doorways, the size of the doors frequently operates on a sliding scale. A large story doorway, for example, often decreases the aperture of the language doorway. Sometimes, appeal elements work hand in hand, however. A sizeable setting doorway might require an equally large language doorway, creating a French door effect. Pearl discusses books in terms of their doorways, linking works with large setting doorways to each other in ways that are similar to how Saricks links books with quick pacing and twisty plots to one another.

What might strike advisors first about Pearl's framework is its seeming correspondence to Saricks and Brown's. Both include a stress on setting, story, and characters. However, Pearl defines these terms differently. In her framework, setting refers to both the geographical and the temporal locations of a novel and the degree to which a particular place or time is fully evoked (rather than Saricks and Brown's use of the word to also mean frame). Pearl uses "story" to indicate the "what happens" and the "what happens next" aspects of the novel. It is this use of the term that has become the most widely adopted definition within RA service. Few advisors, even if they use the term "story line," understand that term to mean anything more than a story summary. Pearl's use of the term "character" does overlap with Saricks and Brown's, but her interest is in whether or not the most important part of a novel is its characters, rather than the events in which they feature. Language indicates style and word craft. In Pearl's use of the term, it means writing of a particularly high quality.

Catherine Sheldrick Ross

In 1982, professor Catherine Sheldrick Ross began interviewing avid readers. Over the course of two decades, she and her graduate students interviewed over 300 readers, developing a rich collection of data addressing why people read, how they select titles, and the elements that contribute to enjoyment. Based upon this data, Ross (2001a, 2001b) has created an appeal framework that includes eleven elements: mood, cost, physical size, subject, treatment, impact, character, pacing, action, setting, and ending.[4]

Mood, which Ross frequently expresses as the "reading experience wanted" (Ross, 2001a, 17), is the central revelation found through her interviews. Ross posits that readers choose titles based upon their emotional state at the time of selection. If readers are under stress when making selection choices, they tend to gravitate toward books that offer reassurance and validation. If they are in a state of equanimity, then readers are more likely to seek new experiences (such as unfamiliar authors or genres) and are able to enjoy books that challenge their beliefs or offer less predictable stories.

Cost addresses the effort it takes to read a book. If a novel requires a great deal of background knowledge or uses obscure vocabulary, for example, it can be more difficult, or costly, in terms of degree of work required of the reader. If a book is very long, it also has a higher cost in terms of commitment. If a novel is deeply depressing or harrowing, it exacts an emotional cost.

Subject, treatment, impact, character, pacing, action, setting, and ending are more traditional appeal elements, several of which Saricks and Brown as well as Pearl have also identified. As was the case with Pearl, however, some of Ross's terms convey different meaning. Ross understands "subject" to encompass what she terms the "what's-this-book-about-question" (Catherine Sheldrick Ross, personal communication), which includes its story as well as its genre or nonfiction type. Ross's term "treatment" aligns with part of Saricks and Brown's aspect of story line in that both address the approach an author takes to the story. Ross also includes the emotional content of the book under a consideration of treatment (an aspect Saricks calls tone). Impact is related to both treatment and mood and addresses the emotional effect a book has on a reader and readers' preferences in that regard. Some readers do not enjoy ironic books or those with black humor. Others do not enjoy works they consider saccharine. Character includes not just a concern for dimensionality versus stereotypes but also the actual kind of characters in the novel, such as strong female heroines, alpha males, or zany private detectives.

Ross uses the concept of pacing to address the level of engagement a reader has with the unfolding story. She also gathers here a concern about dialogue versus descriptions of events, people, and places. Action addresses how the story is developed, through its unfolding events or the thoughts and development of its characters. These concerns of pacing and action are echoed by Saricks and Brown as well as Pearl, as each, using different terms, makes a distinction between books in which story, character, or language is the principal attraction.

In discussing setting, Ross addresses what she terms "the nature of the world represented" (2001b, 92). Like Pearl, this concept covers the level of detail and description of the geographic and temporal setting, but moving beyond both Pearl and Saricks and Brown, Ross means the term to define the similarity between the fictional world and a reader's reality in terms of the essential truths of the novel. Ending addresses the way a novel concludes, such as happily, predictably, or unresolvedly.

See Box 21.2 for a list of terms used in these various appeal systems, but note that the differences between appeal schematics are less important than the concept of appeal itself. Learning an appeal framework, applying it to one's own reading preferences, and developing a customized approach to appeal based upon interactions with patrons are key steps in learning to be an advisor.

Box 21.2 Appeal Term Summary

The following table shows the most widely used appeal terms in contemporary RA. Be aware that a common term, such as "setting," may hold different meanings between frameworks.

Joyce Saricks/ Nancy Brown	Nancy Pearl	Catherine Sheldrick Ross
Pacing	Setting	Mood
Characterization	Story	Cost
Story Line	Character	Physical Size
Setting [Frame]	Language	Subject
Tone/Mood		Treatment
Language/Style		Impact
		Character
		Pacing
		Action
		Setting
		Ending

It is critical that advisors understand the appeal framework and how it describes and classifies the reading experience. One relied-upon method to practice and appreciate appeal is to create a reader profile (see Box 21.3). Joyce Saricks gives credit for this idea to Debra Wordinger (Joyce Saricks, personal communication). It is an exercise Saricks has since expanded upon in a *Booklist* column (2005a), offering advisors a chance to consider their own reading preferences and practice applying appeal terms to those preferences. The exercise illustrates the powerful ways appeal serves to classify the reading experience and the difficulty readers may have expressing their likes and dislikes.

Box 21.3 Activity: Understanding Your Own Appeal Preferences—Creating a Reader Profile

Getting Started

- List three to five books you have enjoyed and three to five books you have not.
- For each title, list as many reasons as possible for your like and dislike. Be specific. For example, rather than writing "I liked the story," push further and list "I enjoyed the Cinderella, ill-treated and then made good, aspects of the story."

- Continue examining each title and listing reasons for your response. Consider all aspects of why you did or did not enjoy the work.
- Once you have exhausted your own list of reasons, review the appeal terms defined previously and make sure each has been addressed. Expand your profile as needed.
- Review your notes, looking for similar comments and appeal terms in your analysis of each book you enjoyed and each you did not.
- List the areas of positive overlap and apply appeal terms to each. Are there repeated instances of several appeal terms?
- List the areas of negative overlap and apply appeal terms to each. Again, are there repeated instances of appeal concepts? Are they in opposition to the aspects you enjoyed? Do they deepen your understanding of what you enjoy or change how you understand your preferences?
- Have you identified any appeal terms that do not affect your reading enjoyment?

Creating the Profile

- List three to five titles you count as outstanding examples of books you enjoy. For each, summarize the reasons why they are favorites, using appeal terminology.
- List your most important appeal elements as indicated by the frequency each was a reason you enjoyed a given title.
- List the aspects of books you do not enjoy, again using appeal terminology.

Putting the Profile to Use

Exchange profiles with classmates or colleagues. Read each other's work and ask questions to clarify meaning and point out areas that are not as precise as others. Revise accordingly and then exchange profiles again, using them as the basis to suggest new titles to one another. Discuss why each title was offered and why it might be enjoyed.

READERS' ADVISORY PRACTICE: THE CONVERSATION

Readers' advisory service involves the sharing of books between readers, one of whom happens to be the advisor. Traditionally, the process of talking with readers and making book suggestions has been termed an "interview," aligning the process with the reference interview. In many ways, the RA conversation is similar to the reference interview described in Chapter 3. Both the reference interview and the RA conversation blend art and craft. To do either well requires a certain degree of deftness, but for each the processes can be learned and skill and adroitness can be acquired through practice. Both the reference interview and the RA conversation require a willingness to be open to possibilities and to think creatively. Each also demands skill, knowledge, confidence, and, most of all, a positive, welcoming, and professional approach. Ultimately, however, the RA conversation is different from a reference interview, with different starting points, processes, expectations, and outcomes.

Foremost is a difference in goals. Unlike a reference interview, in which a patron seeks assistance in finding an answer to an information query, the RA conversation is not focused upon informational outcomes but on the experience itself. At its best and most felicitously practiced, the RA conversation achieves several objectives. The offering of book suggestions is the most obvious result. However, RA conversations should also provide readers the opportunity to share books and reading experiences and to have their interests in reading supported and reflected back. Conversations should help readers articulate their reading likes and dislikes and teach readers how to browse the collection and evaluate and select titles. Conversations should also teach readers and then continually reinforce the concept: that the library is a place where reading—of any kind and of any type—is appreciated and encouraged. Finally, conversations should invite readers back to the library and—it is to be hoped—back to further conversations, so that they feel sustained in a lifetime of reading. These goals of suggestion, support, and education shape the RA conversation.

While many interactions with patrons ultimately conclude with book suggestions, a conversation that does not close with suggestions can be equally successful. RA conversations can conclude with an advisor teaching a patron to use a database or a website; with a guided tour of the collection, pointing out the new bookshelf, sure bet cart, display areas, and sections of the collection broken down by genre; with an invitation to join the library's book discussion group; or with the advisor promising to send a title list to the reader later on that week. Ultimately, the patron and advisor might just enjoy a rich and affirming conversation about books and their importance in their lives.

Even given the divergence of goals and outcomes between reference and RA encounters, the broad outline of the RA conversation shares much with the steps governing the reference interview. As such, advisors are well served following many of the best practices developed for the provision of reference services. The Reference and User Services Association's (RUSA) "Guidelines for Behavioral Performance of Reference and Information Service Providers" (2013) offers expansive recommendations for how advisors should generally proceed through the conversation and establish rapport. Basing the RA conversation upon its general structure, it is possible to identify four parts of the RA counterpart: initiation of the conversation, appeal identification, title suggestion, and an invitation to continue the conversation.

Initiate the Conversation

Most patrons are not aware that RA is a part of the library's core mission. RA services of all kinds are less obvious, and often less obviously promoted, than traditional information-seeking services, computer access, and circulation services. Few libraries have dedicated RA desks and few have staff devoted solely to RA services (see Schwartz and Thornton-Verma 2014). For these reasons, and many more, it is common to encounter readers who do not know that asking for help finding a book to read for pleasure—beyond the basics of location or availability—is a service they can expect from the library. Accordingly, one of the greatest challenges advisors face is starting the conversation itself. Few readers will approach a service desk labeled "Information" or "Reference" and ask what to read now that they have finished all the N. K. Jemisin books. It is incumbent upon advisors to be proactive and help readers engage in these conversations.

Start by meeting readers where they are. Walk around the library and approach readers at the new bookshelf, display locations, computer sign-up, the gathering spaces during story time, and in the stacks. Offer assistance by asking, "Are you finding everything you're looking for?" Readers are likely to be more open to RA services when they encounter a librarian more casually or while in the process of looking for a book. Even if patrons initially refuse the offer of assistance, they have learned that librarians are happy to offer reading suggestions.

Many libraries offer form-based and social media RA to initiate the conversation.[5] The advantages of these types of readers' advisory services are many. They allow readers to request assistance at a direct point of invitation (the form or platform itself), learning that such requests are part of the library's services. They allow readers to think more carefully about what they desire, lessening concerns over articulating likes and dislikes. Additionally, form-based RA in particular affords advisors time to find suggestions without the pressures of patrons waiting for them to do so or while other patrons wait in line.

Determine Needs: Appeal Identification

Once a reader has entered into a discussion with an advisor, the next step is to determine needs. Some readers might simply want to talk about books and authors they enjoy while others may wish to continue the conversation from a book discussion the previous night. Many, however, will be seeking something to read and desire help with that process. The rest of this discussion assumes an advisor is helping a patron with this type of inquiry. The first step is to prompt for appeal descriptions. Ask open-ended questions that guide readers toward sharing features of works they have enjoyed. Prompts such as "What are some [books/authors] you have enjoyed in the past?" and "Tell me about a book you have recently enjoyed" often work because they allow readers to share what they can articulate, directing their attention toward the aspects of a work they most enjoyed. The opposite question, "Tell me about a book you have recently disliked," works just as well and allows readers the freedom to admit that they found a book wanting.

If readers cannot describe a particular book or author, ask them to describe a movie or television show. As all forms of storytelling share a basis of appeal, movies and television shows can provide an equally useful place to start a conversation. For example, advisors can learn just as much by discovering that a reader enjoys the TV shows *Miss Fisher's Murder Mysteries* or *Babylon Berlin* as knowing that the reader enjoys the Flavia de Luce mysteries by Alan Bradley or the Darktown series by Thomas Mullen.

Advisors can also offer options to help readers describe their desired experience. Pose contrasting pairs of features such as "Are you in the mood for a book that is fast and thrilling with a great story or would you enjoy one filled with interesting characters and fewer adventures?"

Once readers begin to talk about the kind of reading experience they are seeking, listen carefully for appeal clues. Readers will not necessarily use appeal terminology but they will say things that relate to appeal, such as

- "I could not put the book down. I stayed up all night reading."
- "I was fascinated by ideas in the book; it really got me thinking about cloning."
- "I fell in love with the book; it was so wonderful, comforting, and special."
- "I liked the characters. They were interesting and complicated."
- "It was scary. That was great."
- "It was a super story, very twisty and surprising."
- "I was really captured by how evocative and poetic it was. I think I paid attention to each sentence. It took a while to read but I loved it."
- "It was a quick read. It kept me entertained on the plane."

Advisors should next translate those descriptions into the appeal framework and determine what the reader is emphasizing. A reader who says something similar to "It was a quick read. It kept me entertained on the plane and was twisty and surprising" is stressing pacing and story over other concerns. A reader who says "I was really captured by how evocative and poetic it was" is stressing style. Based on elements the reader shares, advisors next create an appeal summary to match what the reader is seeking. This process is critical to do well and with care. Advisors should take time to confirm that they have understood the reader by restating the appeal elements. Advisors might say, "It sounds like you enjoy books that keep you turning the pages and have gripping and clever plots. Is that right or are you in the mood for something else?" Giving readers an out by including something similar to "or are you in the mood for something else" allows them to correct the appeal summary without having to challenge the authority of the librarian—an action many might be reluctant to do.

After the opening segment of the conversation, once readers have shared what they desire, advisors need to determine if there are certain formats, types, or genres in which readers are particularly interested. Knowing the genre a reader enjoys can help narrow choices, but do not assume that a single genre is the limit of the suggestion range. Genre blends are common and regularly introduce readers of one genre to the pleasures of another. Also, do not draw on the fiction collection alone. There are many narrative nonfiction titles that will please readers, and films, audiobooks, and graphic novels may also be included.

Advisors should determine if readers wish to avoid any topics, treatments, or certain levels of sex, violence, or profanity. However, the question itself is a tricky proposition as it can unintentionally suggest that the advisor thinks there are books that should be avoided and knows the level of sex, violence, and profanity in every title offered. This thorny problem is best approached by simply asking readers if there is anything they do not want to read (rather than listing possible affronts) and then suggesting that once a few titles are identified that readers check reviews to find more specific information.

Suggest Titles

It is at the point of making suggestions that many advisors feel trepidation. It can be a daunting undertaking. With practice and experience, the process does become easier but there will always be titles and authors that stump even the most experienced advisor, titles advisors cannot find anything about, or those so unique that they are hard to match with other works. With the right approach, however, making suggestions can be deeply enjoyable as advisors and readers share the pleasures of discussing books and discover new titles to explore.

Equipped with an appeal profile, an idea of the authors and titles enjoyed in the past, and any specifics to avoid, advisors can proceed to think of, search for, and find suggestions. The variety of methods for doing so are too lengthy to detail here and vary by advisor based upon their own depth and breadth of reading, the in-house tools at their disposal (such as key author templates and genre sure bet lists), the RA resources their library owns or they can access, as well as the actual holdings of their collection. There is, however, a body of time-tested advice advisors typically share with each other:

- Relax. Readers do not expect advisors to have encyclopedic information on every book ever written. Making suggestions is part of a conversation, not a speed-round on a game quiz show.

- Just as in reference service, there are many tools that contain answers to RA questions. Readers do not expect advisors to rattle off a list of suggestions for every book ever written and advisors should not expect that of themselves.
- Keep the search focused on the specific appeal elements the reader mentioned.
- Focus on the reader. Advisors should keep their own reading tastes out of the equation unless they directly overlap with the reader's. Even then, avoid comments such as "I love Chitra Banerjee Divakaruni and know you will too" as this leaves the reader little room to disagree.
- Suggest proven, reader-tested title and author matches. Even if readers have already read them, it helps confirm appeal and lets readers know the advisor is on the right track. Suggesting such titles also helps further narrow the search once readers comment upon their particular favorites.
- Start with fan favorites, sure bets, and award winners within a few connected genres that are known for sharing the appeals the reader enjoys.
- Collaboration is encouraged. It is always appropriate to ask for assistance from coworkers. It is also perfectly fine to e-mail a colleague in another library or post a query to a discussion list or social media.
- It is absolutely appropriate to offer to send readers a list of suggestions at a later date to allow for more time for research.

Invite Readers to Continue the Conversation

Every RA conversation should conclude with an invitation to continue the dialogue. Invite readers to share what they think of the suggestions with a closing sentence such as "I hope you come back and let me know what you think. If you really enjoy any of these we can find more and if you do not like some of them that will help me pinpoint better suggestions—we have plenty to choose from." Advisors can also mention they will keep an eye out for further titles and will be happy to share more the next time they see the patron. Doing so sets the stage for further conversations and establishes the library as a part of the patron's reading life. Advisors also might wish to point out any additional RA services the library offers as part of wrapping up a session. For example, if the library offers a form-based RA service, let the reader know that suggestions can be received via e-mail as well. Advisors can also share guides to authors and genres or free book-based newsletters. Box 21.4 offers practice integrating each aspect of the RA conversation.

Box 21.4 Activity: Identifying Read-Alikes

An advisor meets a reader in front of the new book display and asks if he can help the patron find a specific title. The reader responds that she is looking for the newest book by Alyssa Cole but it seems all the copies are checked out. The librarian offers to help find books in the same style and manner as Cole and the reader is happy to hear a few suggestions.

Questions for Reflection and Discussion:

1. Given that the librarian is in front of the new bookshelf, how might that shape the start of the RA conversation?
2. What are some of the questions the librarian needs to ask the reader?

3. How will the librarian know which appeal elements are most important to the reader?
4. What will the librarian need to know about Cole's books in order to make suggestions?
5. What resources might identify read-alikes?
6. What are some ways the librarian can successfully end the conversation?

Activity: Places to Start Reading

A readers' advisory librarian comes upon a patron sitting in the stacks, with every book by Stephen King pulled out and scattered on the floor. The advisor asks if the reader needs any help and gets the reply, "How do you tell which one is the best? A friend told me I would love Stephen King but how am I supposed to know where to start?"

Questions for Reflection and Discussion:

1. What might be some ways the advisor can immediately ease the reader's frustration?
2. How do appeal elements factor into this question?
3. What aspects about the reader's preferences and King's body of work would help determine the best starting title?
4. Who might have created the most useful guides to aid in answering this question?
5. What elements in a review or an RA resource would provide help in determining an answer to the reader's question?
6. How many choices of starting titles might the librarian offer? What might be a good way to introduce each different title?
7. How should the advisor conclude the conversation?

Dealing with Special Concerns in the Reader's Advisory Conversation

Book Judgment

As Catherine Sheldrick Ross, Lynne (E. F.) McKechnie, and Paulette Rothbauer (2018, 147–9) have shown through their studies of readers, browsing for books is often a disheartening process. It is difficult for many readers to identify what they enjoy about a reading experience and thus the search for such elusive titles can be fruitless and frustrating. Beyond the difficulties of selection, reading itself is culturally weighted. Many people have opinions on what is a "good" book and few readers are lucky enough to reach adulthood without someone telling them what they are reading is "trashy," be that a parent, teacher, friend, or complete stranger.

Advisors have to work against this baggage. They need to help patrons become comfortable in their reading choices and confident in the selection process. As such, their work is guided by the core philosophy that all types of reading are to be supported in the library and that all types of books—from the most denigrated "pulp" paperback novel to the most lauded award-winning biography—are valuable to the readers who enjoy them. Betty Rosenberg (1982, 5) created the standard philosophical tenet that supports this idea in readers' advisory service: "never apologize for your reading tastes." The professional correlation to Rosenberg's law is that advisors should never make others feel as if they need to apologize for their reading tastes either. "Advisors act as appreciators rather than critics" is the way Joyce Saricks frames it (2007, 33).

When working at a service desk or talking with readers in the stacks, advisors should take care to respond to readers in a positive way regardless of the books they are seeking. This means that an advisor's reaction to learning that a reader enjoys fantasy novels, armchair travel, or erotica must be the same as upon learning that they enjoy mysteries, memoirs, or street lit. An individual advisor might think that chick lit is silly or that Westerns are pulp but those opinions have no place in a professional transaction. All kinds of reading provide opportunities for enjoyment, learning, and reflection. One never knows what book will trigger the creation of a lifetime reader or what work will open a new world of discovery. It is the advisors' job to actively support all reading explorations and interests.

To that end, advisors should school their facial expressions as much as possible, always reacting with interest to a reader's preferences. Advisors should curb any negative verbal reactions as well. While it is to be hoped that no advisor would respond to a reader with an astonished "Really?" it is easy to unthinkingly express comparable thoughts during an off-the-cuff conversation. For example, saying something similar to "I don't know that author, we don't have many fans of that kind of romance here" has the same effect and tells readers that what they read is not valued in the library (for more on this see Orr and Herald 2013). To counter unintentional responses, advisors should practice positive replies (see Box 21.5) and develop a toolkit of phrases that they feel comfortable using.

Box 21.5 Positive Replies

Develop phrases that are honest and apply to all types of reading. Such responses let readers know they are in good company and affirm their reading choices. Generic responses might include the following:

- "That is a very popular [genre/author]."
- "I have heard lots of buzz about that [book/author]."
- "I am so happy to hear you enjoyed [title/author]."
- "The hold list for that title is very long; you are in great company!"

If advisors happen to be fans of the author/genre/type a reader mentions, then even more enthusiastic responses are appropriate:

- "I just [finished/started] that. Tell me what you thought about it."
- "I really enjoy [genre/type] as well. Tell me about some of your favorites."
- "I just read a great review about [title]. What did you most enjoy?"

The point is to develop responses that feel authentic and natural so that immediate positive reactions become instinctual.

Author Diversity

Advisors often work on the fly, pulling books from displays, the new bookshelf, sure bet carts, and the stacks. They rely upon tested, proven matches to quickly help readers. That can mean suggestions dwindle to a few key, well-known names and that less publicized authors, debut authors, and those published by smaller presses are less frequently included in the suggestion process, put on display, or included in booklists. This lack of diversity in the range of authors suggested is compounded by a lack of diversity in the race, gender, and ethnicity of the authors themselves. It is a problem reflected in our collections, which are often less varied than they should be, and in the tools we use to build those collections, which can offer scant help to easily identify diverse authors across all genres. It is a problem in the broader publishing world, too, where fewer diverse authors get published, reviewed, receive mainstream publicity, make the bestseller lists, and get included in year-end "best of" lists.

This is regrettable and frustrating, but it is also a situation librarians can directly confront by reaching beyond the easy, familiar suggestion to include authors of color, non-U.S. authors, LGBTQIA+ authors, and others who are often left out of the conversation. Advisors can start by ensuring that a broad spectrum of authors are included in displays, put on the new bookshelf, and included in RA materials. Advisors can also widen the range of authors and titles they use as default suggestions, creating a richer and more diverse set of initial answers. Moreover, advisors can be leading sources of information for readers wanting to see themselves reflected in their reading and for those who wish to broaden their perspective. Advisors can do so by curating sources that publicize diverse authors, sharing them with readers who may have a hard time finding titles on their own. A few to note include *African American Literature Book Club*; *Asian Review of Books*; *GLBT Reviews*; Lambda Literary Awards; *Latino Book Review*; *QBR the Black Book Review*; the many lists focused on diverse authors posted on *Book Riot* and *Goodreads*; and library resources such as *EarlyWord*'s "Diversity Titles, Upcoming, LibraryReads Consideration" list, the "Diversify Your Readers' Advisory Resource List" created by librarians Anna Mickelsen and Alene Moroni (2018), features in *Booklist*, *Library Journal*, and *NoveList* (it is possible to search by "Author's Cultural Identity" and/or "Author's Nationality" and then to limit the search by year, genre, starred review, or award winner). In addition, advisors can point out awards for literature in translation, automatically widening the scope of authors they draw upon in their work and which readers might explore (see the Awards section later).

Wrong Answers

Given the multiple variables in RA conversations, it should not be surprising that there are no right answers, only possibilities. The fact that there are no right answers, however, does not mean that there are no wrong answers. Mismatched read-alikes and hasty suggestions that strike a reader as tone deaf can arise from not listening carefully to the reader, not applying appeal, and not understanding the genre or type of book under discussion. While there is a great deal of room to think of suggestions, and while readers most often appreciate a wide range and large scope when considering titles offered, it is critical to listen and respond appropriately. Suggesting books to readers and supporting their reading interests is not work to be undertaken lightly with the thought that connections between titles can be casually made. Any book will not do. It must be a book within a range of correct possibilities. It does a disservice to the reader to approach RA with the mind-set that all mysteries set in an English village are the same or any book with time travel will suit a reader who likes time travel. The RA conversation may be less formal in its tone than a traditional reference interview but its standards for excellence are not less exacting.

READERS' ADVISORY SOURCES

Uses and Characteristics

RA resources aid in the identification of read-alikes, sure bets, key authors, and genre conventions. Resources also assist advisors in the ongoing work of keeping abreast of publishing trends and forthcoming titles. RA resources answer questions such as the following:

- What is the best book by Haruki Murakami?
- Can I start this series with its most recent title or do I have to go back to the beginning?
- Who writes works similar to Sarah Waters's?
- What was the name of that book [celebrity of the moment] talked about yesterday?
- What is slipstream fiction?

For a field that covers every aspect of the library's collection, RA resources are a concentrated body of literature. ALA Editions and Libraries Unlimited (LU) publish the majority of the print resources used by advisors. The major library information vendors, such as EBSCO and Gale, produce the few RA databases. Trade review sources are also concentrated to four primary publications: *Booklist*, *Kirkus Reviews*, *Library Journal*, and *Publishers Weekly*. Consumer review sources remain fairly centralized as well. For variety and range, librarians can look toward the multitude of book-related Internet sites.

Evaluation

Format

RA resources have four primary formats: books, subscription databases (and related catalog enhancement services), print journals (and their online counterparts), and a wide variety of free sources on the Web. Each offers different benefits. RA books include annotations written by readers' advisors who know how to craft descriptions that go beyond story summary to detail appeal and offer read-alikes. Subscription databases have a variety of access points and indexing that supports complicated searches accounting for a range of factors important to readers. Print journals and their Web editions offer advance notice of forthcoming titles with content specifically directed toward librarians. Because of their diversity in approach, topic, and content, free Web resources offer advisors information that is rarely covered in a more formal printed text or database, helping advisors to tap into the thinking of experts in a genre and offering advance notice of what fans are reading and thinking. RA librarians are well served by including all four formats in their work, as it is in their combination that advisors can most successfully keep abreast of title information, increase their knowledge of genres and key authors, and offer suggestions readers will enjoy.

Authority

The qualifications of those creating and/or contributing to an RA print resource are of critical importance. As many advisors are self-taught, the books they use to help readers are among those they also use for continuing education. As such, these sources have significance beyond the ways they are used in any individual RA encounter: they shape how RA services are understood and practiced. RA librarians should evaluate resources based upon the authority and expertise of the authors, the approach they take, and the guidance they provide in addition to other standard elements of assessment.

The authority of a database rests largely on the reputation of its publisher; the accuracy, timeliness, and thoroughness of its bibliographic entries; the depth of its indexing; and the reliability of its read-alike suggestions. Sustained use is the best indicator of reliability and accuracy although having practicing RA librarians involved in its production as either contributors or on an advisory board is also a factor to note.

The four primary trade journals mentioned previously offering book reviews for public libraries are uniformly highly regarded and should be considered standard and authoritative resources.

Authority as applied to websites can be hit or miss. Many are produced by librarians and other experts in the publishing world with deservedly strong reputations, but a number of review sources are little more than personal musings, which, while interesting, are not sufficiently authoritative to base a suggestion upon alone. As is true with all Web sources, advisors should practice rigorous evaluation before relying upon a single source for RA information.

Scope

Scope varies by format but each type of RA resource should be evaluated based upon its date range, material types included, content of entries, and the thoroughness of indexing. Advisors work with both front and backlist titles and thus the required date range will vary by inquiry. Books and databases offer the deepest coverage, including older titles that are still relevant to readers. Journals and websites typically focus only on new and forthcoming titles. Patrons routinely seek information on fiction and nonfiction, audiobooks, comics, film, and TV series, and resources that cover each of these areas are increasingly vital.

Central to evaluation as well is depth of content. What is possible to include varies based on the format of the resource, with databases having the most complete entries, followed by books. Journals typically offer the most complete bibliographic data. A story summary/review including appeal should be considered a standard for all RA resources regardless of format. Summaries or reviews that do not include appeal might be useful for purposes other than RA, but without an indication of such elements as pacing, characterization, tone, style, and setting, their RA use is limited. To the extent a resource is designed to aid advisors in making suggestions, reliable read-alikes, with an explanation as to why a title is suggested as a read-alike, should also be considered standard. RA usefulness is further enhanced when entries suggest the best starting point for a series or author and list all the awards a title has won. Full series information is expected in database entries. Databases should additionally be evaluated based upon the more expansive content possible for entries. Full reviews, ideally from multiple trade journals, are of key consideration, as are jacket covers (of sufficient size to see enough detail to visually recognize the book).

Indexing is only an evaluative element of databases and books although the ease of searching a website should be considered as well. At a minimum, books should be indexed by author, title, and subject. A higher standard of indexing includes an index of appeal, award winners, subject/theme, and other specialized entry points. Databases offer the richest indexing. In addition to the standards governing books, databases can be evaluated based upon the expansiveness of their genre and subject tracings and the extent to which they support searching by starred reviews, geographic and temporal setting, keyword, and author demographics such as nationality, ethnicity, and gender.

Currency

All book resources are in some ways out of date the moment they are published due to the volume and speed of the publishing cycle. However, because librarians rely upon their backlist holdings to form the spine of the collection, many book resources do not age as quickly as might be feared. Titles by authors who have ceased writing can serve equally well for suggestions and read-alikes as the buzziest title by a debut author. That being said, currency remains an important consideration. Older resources will not include titles that become sure bets and genre classics after the resource is published, nor will they include new titles that serve as excellent read-alikes for older titles. Readers tend to focus on what is new and if advisors rely upon dated resources to suggest titles, they risk seeming out of touch. Currency is also a concern when benchmark author examples are dated. This is particularly troublesome for advisors who are not sufficiently familiar with a genre to recognize authors whose work has been superseded by changes in reader taste and/or cultural and genre trends. The best practice is to update as new editions become available and retain older editions for more exhaustive research.

Review journals and websites are the most current resources advisors can use. Journals routinely publish reviews months prior to street date release, as do many websites. Databases should mirror library review sources in their currency.

Selection

RA resources are seldom reviewed in the library media. Many of the print resources are written by librarians connected to the journals themselves, making reviews inappropriate. RA databases are not routinely reviewed either, often gaining focused attention only when major updates have been made or new databases are introduced. Few free websites are formally reviewed, if even mentioned, by the library media. This dearth of review attention requires selectors to seek other ways of identification and selection.

Reviewing examination copies is a time-tested method. It can often be the only way to ascertain the nature of the resource, the depth of genre coverage, and the extent of whole collection coverage.[6] Publisher exhibits at conferences offer selectors an opportunity to inspect print books. If conference attendance is not possible, consider interlibrary loan or visiting a neighboring library with significant RA holdings.

Conferences also provide the occasion to compare each of the major RA databases and examine catalog enhancement services. Database providers can arrange in-library trials as well. Each database should be compared for cost, usefulness, accuracy, appeal indexing, search capabilities, ease of use, and catalog integration. Enhancement services can be viewed by searching subscribing libraries' catalogs. Advisors should perform typical searches to see the range of material supplied and carefully consider which aspects will support their work and enrich patrons' experiences.

Asking advisors about the resources they find most useful is another excellent method of selection. The RA community is an active and friendly one, always ready to offer opinions about the best resources and tools. If selectors cannot examine sources, posting a query to an RA discussion list such as Fiction_L or CODES-L is likely to elicit a number of opinions. This method is useful for books and databases but is likely most useful for the identification and selection of free Internet resources. The scope of such resources is so vast and ever-changing that the insight of other advisors who have found useful sites is critical.

IMPORTANT GENERAL SOURCES

These resources address the collection needs of public libraries intending to offer robust RA services for adults. Readers' advisory for children and teens are specialized fields with specific service goals and resources. Those interested in learning more about the provision and resources of either can do so by consulting works such as *The Readers' Advisory Guide to Teen Literature* by Angela Carstensen (2018), *The Whole Library Handbook: Teen Services* by Heather Booth (2014), *Serving Teens Through Readers' Advisory* also by Booth (2007), and *Readers' Advisory for Children and 'Tweens* by Penny Peck (2010).

Genre Bibliographies and Read-Alike Guides

Genre bibliographies introduce the history and subdivisions of a genre as well as list its key authors, essential titles, and important series. They are essential tools, as they provide a depth of knowledge beyond what advisors can often gain from solely their own reading. The basic format of a genre bibliography is a title listing followed by a brief annotation. Organizational schemes are typically by genre or subgenre, depending on the breadth of the resource, but can include divisions by appeal. Appeal classifications, when used, are not specific enough to determine read-alikes. Further reading is sometimes included in an entry but appeal-specific suggestions are rare.

The standard genre bibliography is *Genreflecting*, edited by Diana Tixier Herald and Samuel Stavole-Carter (2019). Long considered a core text in the field, the eighth edition includes an introduction to RA services followed by chapters on popular genres and formats.

Read-alike guides differ from genre bibliographies in that their main purpose is to suggest specific appeal-based read-alikes for key titles and authors. They are indispensable tools of RA as they provide actionable suggestions to advisors and readers based upon key authors, essential titles, and important series. Similar to genre bibliographies, read-alike guides additionally offer a depth of knowledge about a given genre and include subgenre information. Annotations tend to be longer than those found in genre bibliographies and include appeal elements in their descriptions. Because of their approach and the requirement of developing read-alikes for featured titles, these guides include less extensive title listings than genre bibliographies although many are supplemented with suggested reading lists.

The standard read-alike guide is *The Readers' Advisory Guide To* series published by ALA Editions. Each title in the series is devoted to a particular genre and includes chapters that address the genre's appeal, history, development, and subgenres. The core of each book is a set of chapters devoted to key titles and authors with read-alikes, extensive annotations, and appeal descriptions of both the main book and read-alikes.

Journals

Professional review journals help advisors stay ahead of the publishing curve by reading about forthcoming titles before they appear in consumer sources, thus preparing advisors for the moment readers learn about a title themselves. Journals also provide advisors with appeal-rich reviews. Their comments about pacing, setting, depth of characterization, and other appeal aspects allow advisors to learn the appeal profile of a book prior to publication. Some review sources, most notably *Booklist* and *Library Journal*, often suggest read-alikes within the body of the review itself. Advisors strive to keep up with what their patrons read, and that means following popular consumer media as well, such as the book coverage in *Entertainment Weekly*, National Public Radio (NPR), *People*, *The New York Times*, and *USA Today*. It also means being alert to the local sources within a given community, such as the free weekly paper, local radio, and websites.

Databases and Catalog Enhancement Services

RA databases have become foundational tools for advisors. Currently EBSCO's *NoveList* and Gale's *Books & Authors* are the most widely used. While they differ in approach and additional content, both allow advisors to quickly look up a title and find subject, genre, and setting information as well as a basic story summary. *NoveList* is particularly notable for its innovative appeal indexing, multi-point searching, depth of subject headings, and range of coverage (including audiobooks). *Books & Authors* offers an inviting "Who, What, Where, When" search process that allows for inputs based on character, subject, location, and time period and graphically displays the overlapping results. Libraries can extend the valuable information found in RA databases by placing it directly within the catalog's bibliographic record via cataloging enhancement services. Such services encourage readers to share their own read-alike suggestions and reviews, widening and extending the RA conversation.

Internet Resources

Readers' Advisory and Book-Centric News

Keeping on top of the endless outpouring of new books and publishing news is necessary work for advisors. Several sites provide assistance. *Library Journal*'s "Book Pulse" offers a daily update for RA and collection development librarians, while their "Prepub Alert" supplies advance notice of upcoming books and the splash they are likely to make. *EarlyWord* provides an invaluable spreadsheet of current and forthcoming book adaptations as well as monthly insider reports from librarians about advance reader copies. *Literary Hub* concentrates on literary fiction and nonfiction and offers a short set of daily links to news stories and articles.

Shelf Awareness is geared to booksellers but is of great use to librarians in covering book news. In their "News" section, *Publishers Weekly* provides breaking news about the publishing world.

Collaborative Readers' Advisory Aids

The RA world is a highly collaborative one, full of advisors, trade journal editors, and others willing to help find a suggestion or unravel a question. (See Box 21.6 for an example search relying upon this collaborative approach.) Three resources are particularly worth tracking: Fiction_L, The Adult Reading Round

Box 21.6 Search Strategy: A Read-Alike for Jesmyn Ward's *Sing, Unburied, Sing*

An advisor encounters a reader in the stacks, aimlessly pulling books off the shelf and putting them back. The advisor offers assistance saying, "Can I help you find anything to read or are you content to browse on your own?" The patron accepts the offer responding, "I could use some help. I cannot find anything I think I would like." The following dialogue takes place:

Advisor: "That happens to me all the time too. Can you tell me about a book you have enjoyed? We can work from there."

Reader: "I liked *Sing, Unburied, Sing* a lot."

Advisor: "What did you like about it?"

Reader: "That it was so moving and visceral and made me think all the time I was reading it."

Advisor: "That is a great description. Are you searching for another book like that?"

Reader: "Yes, that would be good. Something that feels important to read and which I want to keep reading too."

Advisor: "All right, let's see what we can find. Since *Sing, Unburied, Sing* was very popular with many of our readers and it was a *New York Times*/PBS book club pick, we made a list of suggestions for further reading. We can start there and then look for more titles too." The advisor shows the list to the reader. Since the guide is annotated, there is sufficient appeal-based description for the reader to identify a book she wants to check out. The librarian consults the catalog, sees the book is on the shelf, and walks with the reader into the stacks to pull it. Along the way the advisor says, "Would you like more books or are you happy just checking out this one?"

Reader: "I would like something else too. I like to have more than one book going at a time."

Advisor: "Certainly, let's do a quick search of read-alikes online and see what we find." The advisor searches the Web for "read-alikes *Sing, Unburied, Sing*" and finds a resource authored by staff at *Booklist*. One of the suggestions is Stephanie Powell Watts's *No One Is Coming to Save Us*, which the reader thinks she will like based on the description. It is on the shelf, too. As they go to pull the book the reader thanks the advisor, who responds, "We are always happy to help. If you don't like these, come back and we will find you something else. We have plenty of options. And if you do like them, let us know and that will help us find you even more great titles to enjoy."

Table (ARRT), and CODES Conversations. Begun in 1995, Fiction_L is an electronic mailing list to which queries about read-alikes, title identification, book groups, genre studies, and more are shared with a large community of librarians who help by offering suggestions and best practices. ARRT posts exhaustive reports from their lengthy genre studies that advance the confidence and knowledge of all who follow along. CODES Conversations, run by the Collection Development and Evaluation Section (CODES) of RUSA, gather hundreds of librarians together for electronic e-mail conversations related to specific topics such as "RA as a Technical Service" and "Working with Titles You Have Not Read." In addition to these dedicated RA tools, many advisors post read-alike lists on their library websites. Searching for a particular book or specific author along with terms such as "read-alike[s]" or "if you like" will often return a number of librarian-crafted read-alike suggestions.

Book Sites

There are too many sites devoted to books to even scratch the surface here. However, a few are of such use they are worth pointing out. *The Millions* is an online magazine devoted to literary and general fiction. It includes an eclectic and far-ranging collection of essays, reviews, commentaries, links, and lists. Advisors should not miss the "Most Anticipated" posts, in which *The Millions* surveys the literary landscape of the year, offering a reading list of key authors far in advance of publication date (the site then breaks up that list, and adds to it, for a monthly accounting as well). *Fantastic Fiction* provides a cornucopia of book-related information based on author bibliographies, new titles, and forthcoming releases. The true gem of the site is the list of 260 top authors. For each author, details of their newest book, a full backlist broken by series where applicable, and a list of titles the author recommends is supplied. *Book Riot* is the quirky kind of book resource readers can get lost in for hours only to emerge with a list of titles they want to borrow. Of particular note are the "Reading Pathways," a three-book sequence designed to introduce a reader to an author. As noted previously, it is an idea advisors might want to model as well as a good place to start one's own reading explorations. *IndieBound* is the website of independent bookstores. Its aim is to promote its members, but advisors refer to it monthly to see what has made the "Indie Next List," a group of titles suggested by booksellers who hand-sell books much as advisors do. *LibraryReads* is a group that models much of what *IndieBound* has done, from a library perspective. *Book Marks* (a part of *Literary Hub*) offers a survey of new books getting critical attention. They provide an overview of the review consensus with excerpts from and links to each review. The site also includes a survey of the best-reviewed books each week.

Beyond these general and omnibus sites, there is a range of specific genre sites such as *Reading the Past*; *RA for All: Horror* (both written by librarians); *Stop, You're Killing Me*; and *Smart Bitches Trashy Books*. Such sites help advisors identify sure bets and new titles. Some offer read-alike suggestions as well, and all help RA librarians stay current with genre developments.

Awards

Pressed to find titles with staying power in the ever-growing universe of possible book suggestions, advisors can identify key authors, sure bets, and trends by following book awards. New awards highlight genres and subgenres of interest. Discarded categories in established awards alert advisors to what is losing favor.

Award short lists, and longlists, offer advisors an easy way to review the best of a given year as judged by authors, readers, and critics. Multiple winners, within a year and across years, highlight sure bets and key authors. Although awards are often criticized as lacking diversity and rewarding power players, they can also be cultural markers of change and help spotlight new voices too. Following them with an inquiring and creative eye is an important skill for advisors to develop.

The major librarian-selected awards include the Black Caucus of the American Library Association Literary Awards and the CODES Listen List, Notable Book List, Reading List, and Sophie Brody Medal. A panel that includes librarians selects the Andrew Carnegie Medals for Excellence in Fiction and Nonfiction.

Important national and international literary and nonfiction awards include the following:

- Costa Book Awards
- Governor General's Literary Awards
- *Kirkus* Prize
- *Los Angeles Times* Book Prize
- Man Booker Prize
- NAACP Image Awards, Literature
- National Book Awards
- National Book Critics Circle Awards
- Nobel Prize
- PEN Literary Awards
- Pulitzer Prize
- Women's Prize for Fiction

Genre awards to note include the following:

- Arthur C. Clarke Award (Science Fiction)
- Bram Stoker Award (Horror/Dark Fantasy)
- Edgar Awards (Mystery)
- Hugo Awards (Science Fiction and Fantasy)
- International Thriller Writers Thriller Awards (Thriller/Suspense)
- Nebula Awards (Science Fiction and Fantasy)
- RITA Awards (Romance)
- Spur Awards (Westerns)
- Walter Scott Prize (Historical Fiction)
- World Fantasy Award (Fantasy)

There are important awards beyond these as well, including The Eisner Awards for comics; Lambda Literary Awards for LGBTQIA+ titles; and the Best Translated Book Award, The Man Booker International Prize, The National Books Awards Translated Literature, and the PEN Translation Prize for works in translation. Year-end "best of" round-ups are also important. Key lists include those issued by the library trade journals; several public libraries, including the Chicago Public Library and The New York Public Library; Amazon; *Entertainment Weekly*; NPR; *The New York Times*; and *The Washington Post*.

The Internet of Books

Much RA takes place online. Advisors offer read-alikes, explore and comment upon RA issues, and share resources and ideas. Beyond librarian-created outlets (library-owned or personal), there are social reading and cataloging sites such as

Goodreads and *LibraryThing* that support a thriving online conversation about books and book selection. Both allow users to catalog their own books, post personal reviews, and conduct conversations with fellow members. Such sites, as well as *Instagram*, *Twitter*, *Facebook*, and any number of blogs, create a vital community of readers and an ongoing—and fascinating—conversation about books.

Advisors can profit from engaging with these resources and contributing to them. Following readers' conversations on these platforms provides intimate access to how fans talk about books with each other and serves as one measure of the popularity of authors (thus aiding in identifying new key authors and sure bets). Advisors can also use such sites to share books with patrons, create an online presence within a community of dedicated readers, and create groups that support book discussion. Further, these free community-made and generated resources mine a deep well of interests and span a wide range of suggestors, providing access to titles that advisors do not know themselves, that were not reviewed, and that represent a broader range of genres and publishers. RA can often winnow itself down to best-of lists, award winners, and buzzy titles getting heavy attention. The bounty of social media sites helps balance the usual suspects with a rich tapestry of additional choices.

These sites, and countless others, help readers find books to enjoy. Learning to browse the bookish Web, and find a book one enjoys, is a key skill that advisors can help readers master. See Box 21.7 for several methods.

Box 21.7 Helping Readers Learn to Browse Online

After a successful RA conversation, a reader tells a librarian, "I wish I could do this myself, for when the library is not open or I am too busy to come by." The following exchange occurs:

Advisor: "You are always welcome to call us or use our chat service if you do not want to drive over here, but I am also happy to help you maximize your book search efforts at home. I think the key is to think of it as a treasure hunt for possibilities. A good place to start is with ready-made lists that provide a book summary, or even better, reasons why you might be interested in a title. The library website links to several." The advisor shows the reader *LibraryReads*, *Indie Next*, and *The Millions* monthly lists, pointing out how to find each and giving a quick overview of the lists and their qualities. The advisor then says, "You can also just wander from a general jumping off search that captures what you hope to find, such as 'books I could not put down' or 'books that will sweep you away.' One site will lead to another and provide links to even more to explore. You can follow authors you like on *Twitter* or *Instagram* and they will suggest books. You might stumble across a list of books someone would take to a desert island, all from a genre you love. Keep a running list of things that catch your interest. And remember, you don't have to have a result in mind. You are simply building possibilities."

Reader: "If I find a book that sounds interesting, how do I research it further?"

Advisor: "That is a good question. You can look in a number of places; it is just a matter of finding some sources you like. *Goodreads* might work, or *NoveList*, or *Amazon*, or you can look it up in our catalog. That will show you if we have it and often provide links to more information about the book as well. Also, bring your list in the next time you come by, or call or chat with us about it, and we can use it to find even more books you might like and share what we know about what you have found."

Reader: "I will do that. Any other ideas? I want to find books more specific to my tastes, and also not always new."

Advisor: "Try searching by genres you like. From our work together I know you enjoy historical fantasy. Try searching for that and add a search term such as 'under the radar.' You will get more lists, but they will be things like 'gems not to miss' or 'underrated' or the '10 best books no one reads.' You can also search awards and look at past winners or even do a search on the best historical fantasy novels but put in 'of 2015' rather than this year; that way you find books you might have missed and books that will be on the shelf rather than with a long holds list. Another trick is to search for things that are close to what you enjoy and see what branching out nets you. For you, maybe search for historical fiction with magic rather than historical fantasy, or historical fiction with witches or magicians."

Reader: "Oh. Could you help me find some of those now?"

Advisor: "Absolutely."

CONCLUSION

Practicing RA well, with skill, care, and attention is an undertaking central to the library's mission. Many of the terms staff, directors, and board members wish to associate with libraries, words such as "service," "engagement," "enjoyment," "community," "education," and "enlightenment," are fulfilled when advisors help patrons discover books they relish.

The process of successfully pairing reader and book depends upon a protocol that includes listening to and engaging with the reader, understanding the dynamics of appeal, and practicing the steps of the RA conversation. It involves the deft use of the right resource at the right time and a deep knowledge of popular authors, titles, and genres. It further depends upon understanding that the provision of RA service is a cycle that has no real end and is instead a continuous process of reading, sharing, and learning—such that one conversation can enhance another and that one book can connect outward to many others in a chain of read-alikes. Critically, it requires a thoughtful, professional approach that situates RA services within the same high standards librarians have traditionally demanded of themselves in the provision of reference services. There might not be a more daunting question than "can you help me find something good to read?" (see May et al. 2000) but there are not many questions as potentially joyful and important within a library either.

NOTES

1. For ease of reading, and because novels were the initial subject of RA, this chapter uses the terms "reader," "reading," and "novel" to represent the individuals, activities, and objects of readers' advisory work. However, these terms are intended to be understood in their broadest context, with listening, watching, looking, and playing understood as activities "readers" undertake and audiobooks, nonfiction, graphic novels, films, music, and games as the additional subjects of RA work.

2. Although this chapter addresses public services and RA librarians, the provision of RA is also the responsibility of circulation staff, both at the checkout desk and when shelving books in the stacks. Often, it is in these locations that readers are most receptive to conversations about reading and book selection.

3. Read-alikes are titles that share similar appeal. Read-arounds are titles that amplify or extend the subjects and themes of a book. They are not based upon appeal. Sure bets are titles that please a wide range of readers, typically titles that have intriguing story lines and well-developed characters.

4. Ross (2001a, 2001b) uses slightly different explanations and terms in her discussions of appeal over the course of her research, as she refines concepts and gathers new data. These two sources contain the most complete explanations of her theories and findings, although each presents those findings in different forms. I have elected to use her most common terms when summarizing her work. However, advisors should be aware that it is entirely possible to list Ross's concepts in different ways and thus the number of appeal terms attributed to her (and the terms themselves) can vary.

5. Neil Hollands (2006) lays out much of the groundwork for asynchronous RA. For examples of RA forms and social media use, see *Williamsburg Regional Library*, "Looking for a Good Book"; *The Seattle Public Library*, "Your Next 5 Books"; *New York Public Library*, "The Librarian Is In Podcast"; and *EarlyWord*'s "GalleyChat" conversations on Twitter.

6. Whole collection RA includes the entire scope of the collection (fiction, nonfiction, comics, poetry, music, audiobooks, films, and digital collections), as well as those resources available freely online.

REFERENCES

Anderson, Stephanie H. 2016. "Trends and Directions in RA Education." *Reference & User Services Quarterly* 55 (3): 203–9.

Behler, Anne. 2011. "Leisure Reading Collections in College and University Libraries: Have Academic Librarians Rediscovered Readers' Advisory?" In *Reference Reborn: Breathing New Life into Public Services Librarianship*, edited by Diane Zabel, 133–42. Santa Barbara, CA: Libraries Unlimited.

Bouricius, Ann. 2000. *Romance Reader's Advisory: The Librarian's Guide to Love in the Stacks*. Chicago: American Library Association.

Brookbank, Elizabeth, Anne-Marie Davis, and Lydia Harlan. 2018. "Don't Call It a Comeback: Popular Reading Collections in Academic Libraries." *Reference & User Services Quarterly* 58 (1): 28–39.

De Rosa, Cathy, Joanne Cantrell, Matthew Carlson, Peggy Gallagher, Janet Hawk, and Charlotte Sturtz. 2011. *Perceptions of Libraries, 2010: Context and Community: A Report to the OCLC Membership*. Dublin, OH: OCLC. http://www.oclc.org/content/dam/oclc/reports/2010perceptions/2010perceptions_all.pdf.

EarlyWord. "GalleyChat." *Twitter*. https://twitter.com/hashtag/ewgc?src=hash.

Hollands, Neil. 2006. "Improving the Model for Interactive Readers' Advisory Service." *Reference & User Services Quarterly* 45 (3): 205–11.

Horrigan, John B. 2016. "Libraries 2016." *Pew Research Center*. Last modified September 9, 2016. http://www.pewinternet.org/2016/09/09/2016/Libraries-2016/.

May, Anne K., Elizabeth Olesh, Anne Weinlich Miltenberg, and Catherine Patricia Lackne. 2000. "A Look at Reader's Advisory Services." *Library Journal* 125 (September 15): 40–43.

Nesi, Olga M. 2012. *Getting Beyond "Interesting": Teaching Students the Vocabulary of Appeal to Discuss Their Reading*. Santa Barbara, CA: Libraries Unlimited.

New York Public Library. "The Librarian Is In Podcast." *Podcast audio*. https://www.nypl.org/voices/blogs/blog-channels/librarian-is-in.

OCLC and American Library Association. 2018. *From Awareness to Funding: Voter Perceptions and Support of Public Libraries in 2018*. Dublin, OH: OCLC. https://doi.org/10.25333/C3M92X.

Orr, Cynthia, and Diana Tixier Herald. 2013. *Genreflecting: A Guide to Popular Reading Interests*. Santa Barbara, CA: Libraries Unlimited.

Pearl, Nancy. 1999. *Now Read This: A Guide to Mainstream Fiction, 1978–1998*. Englewood, CO: Libraries Unlimited.

Pearl, Nancy. 2012. "Check It Out with Nancy Pearl: Finding That Next Good Book." *Publishers Weekly* 259 (March 19): 18–19.

Reference and User Services Association. 2013. "Guidelines for Behavioral Performance of Reference and Information Service Providers." http://www.ala.org/rusa/resources/guidelines/guidelinesbehavioral.

Rosenberg, Betty. 1982. *Genreflecting: A Guide to Reading Interests in Genre Fiction*. Littleton, CO: Libraries Unlimited.

Ross, Catherine Sheldrick. 2001a. "Making Choices: What Readers Say about Choosing Books to Read for Pleasure." *Acquisitions Librarian* 25: 5–21.

Ross, Catherine Sheldrick. 2001b. "What We Know from Readers about the Experience of Reading." In *Readers' Advisor's Companion*, edited by Kenneth D. Shearer and Robert Burgin, 77–95. Englewood, CO: Libraries Unlimited.

Ross, Catherine Sheldrick, Lynne (E. F.) McKechnie, and Paulette Rothbauer. 2018. *Reading Still Matters: What the Research Reveals about Reading, Libraries, and Community*. Westport, CT: Libraries Unlimited.

Saricks, Joyce G. 2005a. "At Leisure with Joyce Saricks: Writing a Reader Profile; or, What I Like and Why." *Booklist* 102 (October 1): 35.

Saricks, Joyce G. 2005b. *Readers' Advisory Service in the Public Library*. 3rd ed. Chicago: American Library Association.

Saricks, Joyce G. 2007. "At Leisure with Joyce Saricks: RA Today." *Booklist* 103 (February 15): 33.

Saricks, Joyce G. 2010. "At Leisure with Joyce Saricks: Tone and Mood." *Booklist* 106 (April 1): 21.

Saricks, Joyce G. 2013. "At Leisure with Joyce Saricks: Updating Appeal—Language and Style." *Booklist* 109 (March 1): 19.

Saricks, Joyce G., and Nancy Brown. 1989. *Readers' Advisory Service in the Public Library*. Chicago: American Library Association.

Saricks, Joyce G., and Nancy Brown. 1997. *Readers' Advisory Service in the Public Library*. 2nd ed. Chicago: American Library Association.

Schwartz, Meredith, and Henrietta Thornton-Verma. 2014. "The State of Readers' Advisory: Time, Lack of Training, and Shifting Staff Expertise Present Challenges, but Both High- and Low-Tech Tools Can Help to Deliver Better RA." *Library Journal* 139 (February 1): 30.

Seattle Public Library. "Your Next 5 Books." https://www.spl.org/programs-and-services/authors-and-books/your-next-5-books.

Van Fleet, Connie. 2008. "Education for Readers' Advisory Service in Library and Information Science Programs: Challenges and Opportunities." *Reference & User Services Quarterly* 47 (3): 224–9.

Williamsburg Regional Library. "Looking for a Good Book." http://www.wrl.org/books-and-reading/adults/looking-good-book.

Wyatt, Neal, and Joyce G. Saricks. 2019. *The Readers' Advisory Guide to Genre Fiction*. Chicago: American Library Association.

Zickuhr, Kathryn, Lee Rainie, and Kristen Purcell. 2013. "Library Services in the Digital Age." *Pew Research Center*. Last modified August 10, 2013. http://www.pewinternet.org/2013/08/10/library-services-in-the-digital-age/.

LIST OF SOURCES

Adult Reading Round Table. http://www.arrtreads.org/.

African American Literature Book Club. https://aalbc.com/.

Amazon. http://www.amazon.com.

Andrew Carnegie Medals for Excellence in Fiction and Nonfiction. http://www.ala.org/awardsgrants/carnegieadult/.

Arthur C. Clarke Award. http://www.clarkeaward.com/.

Asian Review of Books. https://asianreviewofbooks.com/content/.

The Best Translated Book Award. http://www.rochester.edu/College/translation/threepercent/index.php?s=btb.

Black Caucus of the American Library Association. Literary Awards. https://www.bcala.org/bcala-awards/literary-book-award.

Book Marks. https://bookmarks.reviews/.

"Book Pulse." *Library Journal*. https://www.libraryjournal.com/?global_search=BOOK+ PULSE.

Book Riot. http://bookriot.com/.

Booklist. 1905–. Chicago: American Library Association. 22 issues per year.

Books & Authors. Farmington Hills, MI: Gale Cengage Learning. https://www.gale.com/c/books-and-authors. Subscription required.

Booth, Heather. 2007. *Serving Teens Through Readers' Advisory*. Chicago: American Library Association.

Booth, Heather. 2014. *The Whole Library Handbook: Teen Services*. Chicago: American Library Association.

Bram Stoker Award. http://horror.org/bram-stoker-awards/.

Carstensen, Angela. 2018. *The Readers' Advisory Guide to Teen Literature*. Chicago: American Library Association.

CODES Conversations. http://www.ala.org/rusa/sections/codes/convos.

CODES-L. http://lists.ala.org/sympa/lists/divisions/rusa.

Costa Book Awards. http://www.costa.co.uk/costa-book-awards/welcome/.

EarlyWord. "Diversity Titles, Upcoming, LibraryReads Consideration." https://docs.google.com/spreadsheets/d/1nyuBdpdWxKZaIEuGHxmeiW85-YzGGlsVytp_MQUezBY/edit#gid=0.

EarlyWord: The Publisher | Librarian Connection. http://www.earlyword.com/.

Edgar Awards. http://www.theedgars.com/.

The Eisner Awards. https://www.comic-con.org/awards/eisner-awards-current-info.

Entertainment Weekly: Books. http://www.ew.com/ew/books/.

Facebook. https://www.facebook.com/.

Fantastic Fiction. http://www.fantasticfiction.co.uk/.

Fiction_L. https://listserver.cuyahogalibrary.net/scripts/wa.exe?A0=FICTION_L.

GLBT Reviews. https://www.glbtrt.ala.org/reviews/.

Goodreads. https://www.goodreads.com/.

Governor General's Literary Awards. http://ggbooks.ca/.

Herald, Diana Tixier, and Samuel Stavole-Carter, eds. 2019. *Genreflecting: A Guide to Popular Reading Interests*. Santa Barbara, CA: Libraries Unlimited.

Hugo Awards. http://www.thehugoawards.org/.

Indie Next List. http://www.indiebound.org/indie-next-list.

IndieBound. http://www.indiebound.org/.

Instagram. https://www.instagram.com/?hl=en.

International Thriller Writers Thriller Awards. http://thrillerwriters.org/programs/*thriller-awards*/.

Kirkus Prize. https://www.kirkusreviews.com/prize/.

Kirkus Reviews. 1933–. New York: Kirkus Media. Biweekly.

Lambda Literary Awards. http://www.lambdaliterary.org/overview-of-llf-awards/.

Latino Book Review. https://www.latinobookreview.com/.

Library Journal. 1876–. New York: Media Source. 22 issues per year.

LibraryReads. http://libraryreads.org/.

LibraryThing. https://www.librarything.com/.

The Listen List. http://www.ala.org/rusa/awards/listenlist.

Literary Hub. https://lithub.com/.

The Los Angeles Times Book Prize. http://events.latimes.com/festivalofbooks/book-prizes/.

Man Booker Prize. http://www.themanbookerprize.com/.

Man Booker International Prize. https://themanbookerprize.com/international.

Match.com. https://www.match.com/.

Mickelsen, Anna, and Alene Moroni. 2018. "Diversify Your Readers' Advisory Resource List." In *Massachusetts Library Association Conference*, Framingham, MA, May 21–23, 2018.

The Millions. http://www.themillions.com/.

NAACP Image Awards, Literature. https://naacpimageawards.net/.

National Book Awards. http://www.nationalbook.org/.

The National Books Awards, Translated Literature. https://www.nationalbook.org/awards-prizes/national-book-awards-2018/?cat=translated-literature.

National Book Critics Circle Awards. http://bookcritics.org/awards/.

National Public Radio: Books. http://www.npr.org/books/.

Nebula Awards. https://nebulas.sfwa.org/.

Netflix. https://www.netflix.com/.

The New York Times: Books. http://www.nytimes.com/pages/books/index.html.

The Nobel Prize. http://www.nobelprize.org/.

The Notable Book List. http://www.ala.org/rusa/awards/notablebooks.

NoveList. Ipswich, MA: EBSCO. http://www.ebscohost.com/novelist. Subscription required.

Peck, Penny. 2010. *Readers' Advisory for Children and 'Tweens*. Santa Barbara, CA: Libraries Unlimited.

PEN Literary Awards. http://www.pen.org/literary-awards.

PEN Translation Prize. https://pen.org/pen-translation-prize/.

People. https://people.com/.

"Prepub Alert." *Library Journal*. https://www.libraryjournal.com/?global_search=PREPUB+ALERT.

Publishers Weekly. 1872–. New York: PWxyz, LLC. Weekly.

Publishers Weekly. "News." https://www.publishersweekly.com/pw/by-topic/industry-news/publisher-news/index.html.

Pulitzer Prize. http://www.pulitzer.org/bycat.

QBR the Black Book Review. https://www.qbrbookreview.com/.

RA for All: Horror. http://raforallhorror.blogspot.com/.

The Readers' Advisory Guide To. Joyce Saricks and Neal Wyatt, series eds. Chicago: ALA Editions.

The Reading List. http://www.ala.org/rusa/awards/readinglist.

"Reading Pathways." *Book Riot*. http://bookriot.com/category/reading-pathways/.

Reading the Past. http://readingthepast.blogspot.com/.

RITA Awards. https://www.rwa.org/Online/Online/Awards/RITA_Awards/RITA_Award.aspx.

Saricks, Joyce G. 2004–2016. "At Leisure with Joyce Saricks." *Booklist*. Chicago: American Library Association. Monthly.

Shelf Awareness. http://www.shelf-awareness.com/booktrade.html.

Smart Bitches Trashy Books. http://smartbitchestrashybooks.com/.

The Sophie Brody Medal. https://www.rusaupdate.org/awards/sophie-brody-medal/.

Spotify. https://www.spotify.com.

Spur Awards. http://westernwriters.org/spur-awards/.

Stop, You're Killing Me! http://www.stopyourekillingme.com/.

Twitter. https://twitter.com/?lang=en.

USA Today: Books. http://www.usatoday.com/life/books/.

Walter Scott Prize. http://www.walterscottprize.co.uk/.

Washington Post. https://www.washingtonpost.com.

Women's Prize for Fiction. http://www.womensprizeforfiction.co.uk/.

World Fantasy Award. http://www.worldfantasy.org/.

Wyatt, Neal, and Joyce G. Saricks. 2019. *The Readers' Advisory Guide to Genre Fiction.* Chicago: American Library Association.

SUGGESTED READINGS

Dali, Keren. 2014. "From Book Appeal to Reading Appeal: Redefining the Concept of Appeal in Readers' Advisory." *The Library Quarterly* 84 (1): 22–48.

Dali extends the considerations of appeal by exploring the distinction between book-oriented and reader-oriented appeal elements and by situating appeal within a wider consideration of reading practices.

Lee, Jin Ha, Rachel Ivy Clarke, Hyerim Cho, and Travis Windleharth. 2017. "Understanding Appeals of Video Games for Readers' Advisory and Recommendation." *Reference & User Services Quarterly* 57 (2): 127–39.

Based on a large-scale study, this article uses the concepts of appeal and whole collection RA to explore how RA works with gamers and games rather than readers and books. It urges advisors to think broadly about the materials they suggest and provides a useful and contemporary investigation into the ways RA service is advancing.

Orr, Cindy. 2015. *Crash Course in Readers' Advisory.* Santa Barbara, CA: Libraries Unlimited.

Orr offers a fresh and accessible introduction to the field by reviewing the research on reading and readers, outlining the tools and techniques of RA, and discussing how to create a reader-centered library. She further reviews best practices, supplies an exhaustive reading list, and examines the current and future state of RA.

Ross, Catherine Sheldrick. 2014. *The Pleasures of Reading: A Booklover's Alphabet.* Santa Barbara, CA: Libraries Unlimited.

Using the alphabet as an organizing skeleton, Ross explores 30 areas related to reading and readers' advisory service. The chapters are uniformly accessible, inviting, and illuminating. They serve not only as an introduction to a number of RA elements but also as a model way of thinking deeply and broadly about the field.

Ross, Catherine Sheldrick, Lynne (E. F.) McKechnie, and Paulette Rothbauer. 2018. *Reading Still Matters: What the Research Reveals about Reading, Libraries, and Community.* Westport, CT: Libraries Unlimited.

This essential text explores the history of reading, how readers develop, the reading experience, and the importance of reading. It provides critical background on why RA service is important and the factors that should influence its provision. The chapters include case study examples, lists of suggestions for how librarians can improve the reading environment, and a bibliography for further reading in each topic area.

Saricks, Joyce G. 2005. *Readers' Advisory Service in the Public Library.* Chicago: American Library Association.

This is the foundational text in the field; the book that helped shape the future and direction of contemporary RA service. It first defined appeal in a standardized form, detailed the duties of RA librarians, and outlined the range of RA services. Not only does Saricks's book, now in its 3rd edition, still provide the most complete explanation of appeal, but it also reviews the tools of RA, discusses how to conduct the RA conversation, offers guidance on the necessary background for advisors, and considers ways to market RA services.

Trott, Barry, and Neil Hollands. 2011. "Contemporary and Future Roles for Readers' Advisory in Public Libraries." In *Reference Reborn: Breathing New Life into Public Services Librarianship*, edited by Diane Zabel, 117–31. Santa Barbara, CA: Libraries Unlimited.

In their overview of RA practices and services, Trott and Hollands detail traditional and new methods of RA service, discuss the benefits of RA in libraries as a countermeasure to declining reference queries, and explore eight elements shaping the future of RA. Among these are whole collection, changes in genres and technology, the future of appeal, and methods of marketing.

Wyatt, Neal. 2014. "We Owe Our Work to Theirs: Celebrating the Twenty-Fifth Anniversary of *Readers' Advisory Service in the Public Library*." *Reference & User Services Quarterly* 54 (2): 24–30.

This article presents an examination of *Readers' Advisory Service in the Public Library* on the occasion of its twenty-fifth anniversary. It provides a detailed account of the formulation of appeal and explores how the times in which Saricks and Brown worked shaped both appeal and the provision of RA service. Excerpts from an audio interview with Saricks and Brown are included.

Chapter 22

Indexes and Abstracts

Linda C. Smith

INTRODUCTION

A library's catalog generally does not provide access to the entire contents of a library's collection. The catalog may confirm the holdings of a periodical title but not its contents, a poetry collection but not individual poems, and the title of an author's collected works but not an individual essay. Indexes and abstracts can more fully reveal resources not covered in the general catalog, as well as the existence of additional resources not held in a given library's collection. Increasingly, indexes and abstracts are Web-based and integrate access to the full text of publications. They thus facilitate both discovery of and access to a wide range of materials needed by library users.

USES AND CHARACTERISTICS

Indexes such as periodical indexes usually list the authors, titles, or subjects of publications without comment. Abstracts, on the other hand, present a brief summary of content. Many abstracting services rely on author abstracts (or translations thereof) rather than having staff read each article and abstract it (a very costly practice). Abstracts serve as an aid in assessing the content of a document and its potential relevance, and they continue to be valued (Koltay 2010).

Although indexes and abstracts existed before 1900, there was a dramatic growth in their number during the 20th century, as the scholarly community demanded improved access to a growing number of publications. The advent of the Web made it possible for librarians to subscribe to indexing and abstracting databases that the user could search and view over the Web, dramatically expanding their availability and usefulness.

In the first two decades of the 21st century, increasingly questions have been raised about the future of indexes and abstracts, especially those covering specialized subject areas (Chen 2010; Tucci 2010). A growing number of publications are available in full text online, with the entire text searchable for occurrences of the keywords sought, potentially reducing the need for document surrogates such as indexes and abstracts. Nevertheless, Dennis Auld (1999) argues that the skills of classifying, indexing, aggregating, and structuring content still are needed in the Web environment. Traditional databases remain superior in their ability to describe, organize, and connect information in a consistent, structured way. Indexes and abstracts are often thought of as value-added services because a human indexer has analyzed the document content and developed a document surrogate, including indexing terms drawn from a thesaurus or other controlled vocabulary. It is assumed that this effort benefits the user by improving retrieval performance, enabling the identification of the best set of items for the user's purposes: "Abstracts are one antidote to information overload. Indexing is another. . . . The value added by well-written abstracts and appropriate thesauri are more important than ever" (Ojala 2012, 5).

Publishers of indexes and abstracts are introducing a number of enhancements to better meet user needs: inclusion of abstracts in what were formerly only indexing services; inclusion of full-text articles in what were formerly only abstracting services; marketing of different subsets of a service to meet the needs of different sizes and types of libraries; creation of rich networks of links between indexes and multiple full-text resources; enhanced retrospective coverage; and improved searching capabilities (see Chapter 16). Library users increasingly demand rapid access to full texts, and indexes and abstracts are evolving to support that. This has led to what can seem to be a bewildering array of choices for librarians seeking to make selections among competing indexes and abstracts, increasing the need for careful evaluation.

Scholarly Communication

Because many indexes and abstracts focus on coverage of the scholarly literature, they need to respond to changes in scholarly communication practices: the processes for disseminating research results and other scholarship. In this context, peer review is an important activity as a means of quality control. Before articles are published in a scholarly journal, one or more of an author's peers are invited to review the work and provide critical input. A peer-reviewed journal will not publish articles that fail to meet the research standards established for a given discipline. Recognizing the importance of peer review, indexes and abstracts may restrict their coverage to peer-reviewed journals or enable limiting a search to peer-reviewed journals when their scope also encompasses other types of publications.

As long as the means of publishing scholarly journals was limited to print, access to the scholarly literature depended on the payment of subscription fees to build collections of print journals. With the growth in electronic publishing, the prevailing scholarly communication system of *toll access*—requiring payment in the form of journal subscriptions—is being challenged by those advocating *open access*, who want access to scholarly content made freely available to all (Anderson 2018, 197). There are multiple strategies for enabling open access, depending on a journal's policy: gold (open access journal, all articles accessible), green (author deposits a copy of the article in an institutional or disciplinary repository that makes it accessible), or hybrid (the author pays an article-processing charge to provide open access to an individual article in a subscription-based journal). To these categories, Bo-Christer Björk (2017) adds the emergence of a fourth, which he terms "black": illegal article copies retrievable from academic social networks or pirate sites. In general, indexes and abstracts provide access to gold or hybrid open access articles where they exist, but they cannot alert the user to the existence of a green open access version available in an open access repository. This is beginning to change as index publishers find ways to enable discovery of green open access materials (Clarivate Analytics n.d.). As open access repositories increase in number and scope, the need for such discovery tools increases (Herther 2017). Given the rapid changes in open access, the *Open Access Directory*, a compendium of lists about open access to science and scholarship, is a useful guide to learning more. The *Directory of Open Access Journals* indexes and provides access to high-quality, open access, peer-reviewed journals. *OpenDOAR*, a directory of open access repositories, includes information on the content types (e.g., journal articles, theses and dissertations, conferences papers, reports) within scope for each.

Scholarly communication is also concerned with understanding the impact of research that has been disseminated through publication. Traditionally, citations in scholarly literature were used as an indicator, with higher citation counts generally interpreted to represent higher impact. (For more discussion see the section on citation indexes later in this chapter.) Altmetrics provide a new way to measure the impact of research (Cave 2017, 44): "The use of altmetrics aims to capture a broader view of scholarly research by tracking the activity of this research as it is viewed, shared, critiqued, cited, and built upon." Some database vendors such as EBSCO are now integrating access to altmetrics data as part of the record for retrieved articles by partnering with Plum Analytics. PlumX Metrics encompass five categories: usage, captures, mentions, social media, and citations (Plum Analytics n.d.). As Rick Anderson (2018, 189) cautions, "The question of whether and how scholarly impact can (and whether it ought to) be measured continues to be a controversial one, so this area is likely to remain volatile for the foreseeable future."

EVALUATION

As reference librarians use indexes and abstracts in reference work, they evaluate and choose titles that will best reveal the contents of their own collections or that will refer users to needed information beyond library walls. Important characteristics to consider are format, scope, authority, accuracy, access points, and any special features that enhance effectiveness or ease of use.

Many of the indexes and abstracts discussed in this chapter are devoted to a particular type of publication, such as periodicals or dissertations. More specialized services devoted to indexing and abstracting the literature of a discipline often try to encompass many different types of publications to provide more comprehensive coverage in one source. Other differences arise if there are restrictions on place and language of publication of the source materials. Some indexes and abstracts cover only English-language material; others try to identify material relevant to a particular subject area in any language and from any part of the world. To determine the scope, it is necessary to rely on database descriptions found in documentation provided by the database producer or vendor. Many publishers of periodical indexes are now posting lists of indexed journals on their websites, making comparison among competing services easier (Chen 2006).

Format

While some indexes and abstracts still have a print counterpart, most current indexes exist only in electronic form with much more powerful search capabilities, including more access points and the possibility of refining searches by using Boolean logic to combine terms (see Chapter 16 for a discussion of search strategy). However, because many databases do not cover the literature before the mid-1960s, searches of indexes and abstracts for older literature must rely on the print versions, where they exist, for the period of interest.

Scope

Several characteristics define the scope of indexes and abstracts, including the publication dates covered and the types of materials indexed. The time covered does not necessarily coincide with the period of publication because the publisher may go back and index some older material valuable to the users of the index. For example, *Science Citation Index Expanded* has now extended its coverage back to 1900, although it originally began publication in the 1960s. An advantage of searching indexes and abstracts online is that the contents are automatically cumulated, with updates as often as daily.

Types of materials covered are another aspect of scope. Indexes and abstracts differ in the number of publications covered and the depth or specificity of the indexing. General periodical indexes tend to index all substantive articles from the periodicals selected for indexing, whereas subject-specific indexes and abstracts are more likely to index selectively from a much larger list of periodicals, with indexers identifying those articles of most relevance to the subject scope of the service. Some indexes and abstracts are more inclusive in the types of articles indexed, indexing such things as letters to the editor and editorials, whereas other services restrict their coverage to research articles. As the number of electronic-only and, more recently, open access journals has grown, publishers of indexes and abstracts have had to develop criteria for covering such titles.

Authority

The reputation of the publisher or sponsoring organization and the qualifications of the editorial staff determine the authority of indexes and abstracts. Publishers of indexes include commercial firms, professional associations, and government agencies. EBSCO, Gale, and ProQuest are the major commercial publishers of indexes and abstracts. The Modern Language Association, publisher of *MLA International Bibliography*, is an example of a professional association, and the National Agricultural Library, publisher of *AGRICOLA*, is an example of a government agency.

Accuracy

The quality of indexing and accuracy of bibliographic citations affect the usefulness of indexes. Questions to consider include the following: Are all authors associated with an indexed item included in the author index? Are all major facets of the content of the article represented by entries in the subject index? Accuracy can also apply to both author and subject indexing. Author names should be spelled in the index as they are spelled in the work. Unfortunately, indexing guidelines for some indexes and abstracts dictate that only initials of given names be retained, even when a fuller form of the name appears on the original publication. This can make it difficult, when searching authors, to distinguish between different authors who share a common surname and initials. Accuracy of subject indexing depends on the indexer's ability to represent the content of a publication using terminology drawn from the controlled vocabulary (thesaurus or list of subject headings) to be used in indexing. Cross-references should be included where needed to lead from a form not used to the proper form or to link related terms. Some indexes include augmented titles, where the indexer supplements the original article title with additional terms to characterize the article's content more completely. Abstracts should provide an accurate summary of the original article's content.

Access Points

Indexes and abstracts in electronic form generally offer many options for searching in addition to author name and subject. These may include such elements as keywords from title and abstract, journal title, and author affiliation. Documentation provided by the publisher can be studied to learn more about the structure of a database record and which elements can be searched or used to limit the results, as explained more fully in Chapter 16.

Special Features

When indexes and abstracts are evaluated, any special features that enhance their usefulness should be noted. Examples include a list of periodicals or other sources indexed and a published list of subject headings. The list of sources indexed is helpful in providing a clear indication of the materials covered as well as complete bibliographic information for those materials not available locally. This can be helpful in acquiring documents, whether ordering copies for inclusion in the library's collection or making requests through interlibrary loan or a document delivery service. A published list of subject headings can help in formulating effective search strategies because the user can see a comprehensive list of terms available to the indexer and thus have a better chance of locating the appropriate terms to search. This is especially the case for those lists of subject headings that include scope notes or instructions for indexers, explaining how particular terms are to be used in indexing (and hence in searching). A growing number of indexing and abstracting services are developing approaches to ease the task of locating the full text of documents covered by their services, such as including the full text of documents as page images or searchable full text. Because databases may include indexing of articles in languages other than English, both the extent of coverage of non-English content and how easy it is to access should be assessed (Albarillo 2016).

When a library subscribes to multiple indexing and abstracting databases and full-text resources, it can be a challenge to determine whether the full text of an article cited in one database is available in another resource. Link-resolving software makes this task easier by creating a bridge between databases, enabling users to easily go from a journal citation in one database to the full text of the journal article in another database (Breeding 2012).

SELECTION

Indexes and abstracts are often expensive reference tools. Selection of titles for a particular collection must take into account the characteristics of that collection as well as the needs of users for access beyond what is already provided by the library's catalog. *Ulrichsweb*, described in Chapter 20, can be searched for serial type "abstract/index." In addition, for each periodical listed, *Ulrichsweb* provides an indication of the indexes and abstracts that include the periodical in their coverage.

Needs of Users

Indexes and abstracts selected for a particular library collection should reflect the types of information and publications that library users wish to access. Given the increasing availability of full text online as part of indexing and abstracting databases, selection of such a database also gives users access to these full-text documents in electronic form. General periodical indexes could be useful in libraries of all types. Selection of indexes devoted to particular subject areas will reflect the subject interests of the library's users. Citation indexes, with their emphasis on scholarly literature, will be of most use in academic and special libraries. Indexes to special types of materials such as dissertations or patents are also likely to be found most often in academic and special libraries. Selection of indexes to reviews should reflect user demand for this information. Indexes to literary forms can prove useful wherever collected works and anthologies make up part of the collection. Usage of indexes and abstracts in electronic form can be measured, providing a tool to guide the choice of which resources to retain and which to cancel when licenses come up for renewal (International Coalition of Library Consortia 1999; Pesch 2017).

Cost

The discussion of licensing in Chapter 15 identifies a number of factors affecting the cost of indexes and abstracts. As explained in Chapter 5, increasingly libraries are gaining access to electronic databases through participation in consortial licensing arrangements, which may reduce the price paid by each participating library.

Most of the major index publishers have several products, usually for different types of libraries and often in different size packages, so librarians can choose which package they need and can afford. For example, EBSCO has four general titles for public libraries (*MasterFILE Complete*, *MasterFILE Elite*, *MasterFILE: Main Edition*, and *MasterFILE Premier*) and four general titles for academic libraries (*Academic Search Complete*, *Academic Search Elite*, *Academic Search Premier*, and *Academic Search Ultimate*) as well as products for elementary, middle, and high school library use. They differ in the number of periodical titles indexed, the number of titles in full text, the types of titles (scholarly vs. popular; intended age level), and supplementary materials included together with the indexed titles. (For example, the *MasterFILE* databases include the full text of selected reference books, primary sources, videos, photos, maps, and flags in addition to periodicals.)

Uniqueness

Although overlap in sources indexed is one indicator of the degree of uniqueness of indexes, the access points and search capabilities provided by the indexes must also be considered. Two indexes could cover many of the same periodicals, but the subject indexing may give the user different ways of approaching the content in each. Thus, examination of overlap in materials covered must be supplemented by an assessment of the approaches provided to those materials by the different indexes.

Although many indexes and abstracts are available on only a single system, others may be available on more than one, such as *PsycINFO*, which is distributed by both EBSCO and ProQuest. In such a case, librarians need to consider the selection factors for electronic sources discussed in Chapter 14, including the user interface, branding and customization, and accessibility.

Full-Text Coverage

Given the growing demand for the full text of periodicals and other publications in electronic form, criteria for selecting these resources deserve special consideration. Unfortunately, "full text" does not have a standard definition when applied to electronic publications with print counterparts. At the article level, "full text" may include the main text but not any sidebars or illustrations (Chen 2005). At the issue level, "full text" may include major articles but omit such things as letters to the editor, short columns, book reviews, and advertisements. At the journal level, one expects "full text" to cover all the issues of the publication, including any supplements. As Walt Crawford (2000) notes, these differences may result in a loss of important context for the content.

Factors to consider in comparing full-text databases include which titles are covered in various subject areas (and whether any are unique, not covered elsewhere), coverage dates, currency, policy on inclusion of article types and illustrations, whether text is searchable or only displayable, indexing, output formats, and pricing. Delivery of full text in a Web environment also opens up the possibility of creating links among articles, reflecting the relationships among them.

As journal publishers experiment with the electronic medium, the situation becomes even more complex. Because of possible differences between the electronic and print versions of the same title, indexing and abstracting services may have difficulty deciding which version to index. Reference librarians also need to be aware of the different models of supplying full text that have emerged in the Web environment: publisher-supplied full text; third-party or aggregator-supplied full text; and distributed, "linked" full text, in which an indexing or abstracting service links to publisher-supplied full text (Tenopir 1998).

IMPORTANT GENERAL SOURCES

This chapter describes some of the most widely held general periodical indexes, subject-oriented periodical indexes, citation indexes, indexes for special types of materials, indexes of reviews, and indexes for different literary forms. Only a few of the available indexing and abstracting databases devoted to coverage of the literature of a specific subject area can be mentioned in this chapter as examples.

General Periodical Indexes

General periodical indexes are held by all types of libraries. They index periodicals covering current events, hobbies, popular culture, and school curriculum—related areas. The *Readers' Guide to Periodical Literature* has filled this need since 1901 (Biggs 1992). It continues to be published in print quarterly with an annual cumulation, providing subject and author access to articles in 300 of the most popular general-interest periodicals published in the United States and Canada. EBSCO provides online access to *Readers' Guide* with coverage beginning in 1983 as well as to *Readers' Guide Retrospective: 1890–1982.* The *Alternative Press Index*, which began publication in 1969, seeks to provide subject indexing for more than 300 periodicals and newspapers covering alternative or radical points of view. It is updated semiannually in print and quarterly online through EBSCO, with coverage from 1991. EBSCO also provides retrospective coverage from 1969 through 1990 in *Alternative Press Index Archive.*

EBSCO, Gale, and ProQuest all produce multiple databases that index periodicals and provide increasing quantities of full text, with products ranging from those for school libraries to those intended for large academic and public libraries. These competing products continue to change their coverage, both of titles indexed and of titles available in full text, and search capabilities. Therefore, librarians need to follow these developments to determine which approaches to providing access to periodicals best meet the needs of the library's users and which are affordable. Publisher websites are very helpful for current listings of product offerings. Increasingly, these databases encompass material in addition to periodicals, such as selected reference books. Box 22.1 compares the coverage of the most comprehensive multidisciplinary database offered by the three major vendors as of early 2019.

Box 22.1 Comparison of Major Multidisciplinary Databases

EBSCO, *Academic Search Ultimate*:

More than 10,000 journals and magazines in full text in many different subject areas and including both English-language and native-language titles from countries in Asia, Oceania, Europe, and Latin America; additional content includes reports, books, and more than 74,000 videos from the Associated Press.

Gale, *Academic OneFile*:

More than 19,000 journals, books, news sources, and reports are indexed, with more than 9,000 journals in full text; some non-English language titles, including French, German, Portuguese, Spanish, and Turkish; additional content includes podcasts and transcripts from NPR and CNN and videos from BBC World Learning.

ProQuest, *ProQuest Central*:

This resource provides access to forty of ProQuest's complete databases, with a variety of content types across over 175 subjects, making this the broadest single research resource in the world. In addition to journals, coverage includes news, market information, dissertations, conference proceedings, working papers, and videos.

Comparison among these offerings should consider not only how many of their titles are full text but also how far their backfiles extend, how many of their titles are unique, and how many of their titles are peer reviewed. In addition, librarians need to be aware that the most recent issues of a journal may be embargoed: to protect subscriptions, journal publishers may not immediately release the full text of their most recent issues for inclusion in these aggregated collections.

Google released *Google Scholar* in a beta version in 2004 to enable free searching of the scholarly literature. Because it is simple to use, free, and available to anyone with access to the Web, *Google Scholar* has rapidly gained in popularity. Nevertheless, a number of questions have been raised. As William Badke (2009, 49) notes, *Google Scholar* "is not like the carefully structured, library-based databases we treasure." Concerns include its selection criteria for "scholarly" materials being unknown, its scope and currency being unknown, and its formatting of citations for items retrieved being very nontraditional (Badke 2013). Nevertheless, it provides a way to search across many disciplines and sources simultaneously. Christopher Brown (2017, 31) observes that *Google Scholar* complements indexing and abstracting databases "in providing depth of discovery, citations to subsequent articles, and exposure to related articles that many find useful." An advanced search interface is available with the option to search words or phrases in the title only or across the entire article, search by author or source publication, and limit by date. Retrieved items are ranked by relevance but this can be changed to sort by date. Because there is no controlled indexing vocabulary, subject search terms must match the vocabulary in the articles. Recognizing that many of their users are turning to *Google Scholar* despite its potential shortcomings, librarians are partnering with Google to include links to their resources as part of *Google Scholar* search results (Google n.d.). In addition to being interactive with a library's link resolver to provide full-text access, *Google Scholar* expands the full-text collection of the library beyond what is accessible through paid subscriptions and database content via its ability to ferret out free full text for open access titles, including items in open access repositories (Chen 2013).

Major retrospective indexing projects are becoming available in electronic form, overcoming a long-standing weakness of most online indexes. For example, *Periodicals Index Online* from ProQuest provides access to citations for more than 18,000,000 periodical articles from more than 6,000 journals from as early as 1665 in the arts, humanities, and social sciences, including titles in several non-English, Western European languages. Libraries can gain access to the digitized full text of more than 750 of these journals through *Periodicals Archive Online* from ProQuest.

Although indexes like *Readers' Guide* include some magazines of interest to children, other products are targeted specifically at children. Examples include EBSCO's *Primary Search*, a full-text database covering 100 popular elementary school magazines; EBSCO's *Middle Search Plus*, with the full text of more than 170 popular middle school magazines; Gale's *Onefile: High School Edition* for middle and high school students, indexing more than 2,000 titles; and ProQuest's *ProQuest Central Student*, with the full text of over 10,000 titles for high school student use. In addition to the journal content, these resources include supplementary reference material useful to students such as encyclopedias, dictionaries, biographical sources, primary source documents, videos, and images of photos, maps, and flags.

Two indexes provide good coverage of Canadian periodicals. *CPI.Q*, available from Gale, indexes more than 1,300 Canadian periodicals (both English and French) from 1980 to the present, with full text from more than 700 periodicals. This resource also covers newspapers, including *The Globe and Mail*, as well as reference material related to Canada, such as travel handbooks. ProQuest's *Canadian Business & Current Affairs (CBCA) Database* combines full-text and indexed content from three *CBCA* database subsets (Business, Education, and Reference & Current Events). Coverage includes indexing for over 1,800 publications, with full text for more than 700. Materials include journals, newspapers, and transcripts from several well-known CBC programs.

As library users become more diverse, libraries need to consider databases in languages other than English. *Informe Académico* from Gale provides a wide range of full-text Spanish- and Portuguese-language scholarly journals and magazines both from and about Latin America. The interface is configured for Spanish-speaking users, allowing them to analyze topics and conduct research in Spanish.

Subject-Oriented Indexes

Multidisciplinary databases such as *Academic Search Ultimate*, *Academic OneFile*, and *ProQuest Central* can provide some coverage of many different subject areas, but indexes focused on a specific subject area often enable more complete and effective searching of the literature in that subject area. One index commonly found in public and academic libraries is ProQuest's *PAIS Index*. It contains citations to journal articles, books, government documents, statistical directories, research reports, conference papers, Web content, and more. *PAIS Index* includes publications from more than 120 countries throughout the world, with coverage back to 1915. In addition to English, some of the indexed materials are published in French, German, Italian, Portuguese, Spanish, and other languages. It does not index journals cover to cover, instead selecting articles relevant to public policy. In introducing a library user to this index, it is helpful to point out the types of publications indexed, given that different strategies may be needed to locate periodicals, books, and documents in the library's collection.

EBSCO, Gale, and ProQuest all have a range of databases indexing the literature of broad subject areas as well as some more specialized in focus. In many cases, they have acquired databases originally developed by another publisher, such as EBSCO's purchase of H.W. Wilson. The company websites can be consulted for a listing and descriptions of available subject-oriented databases. While some subjects are covered by a unique database available from a single vendor, such as the *ATLA Religion Database* from EBSCO, other subjects are covered by competing products. For example, ProQuest's *ABI/INFORM Global* and EBSCO's *Business Source Complete* are rich sources of business journal literature.

The relative value of general periodical indexes, periodical indexes with a more specific subject focus, and Web resources will vary by discipline. Specialized subject databases often include coverage of a range of publication types, such as conference proceedings and books, as well as journals, where these are important to the discipline. In addition, the subject indexing may draw on a specialized thesaurus reflecting concepts and terminology specific to that discipline. See Table 22.1

TABLE 22.1 Major Subject-Oriented Indexes

Humanities and Arts	
Art	*Art & Architecture Source*
Film	*Film & Television Literature Index*
Literature	*MLA International Bibliography* *Literature Resource Center*
Music	*Music Index*
Religion	*ATLA Religion Database*
Social Sciences	
Education	*ERIC*
History	*America: History and Life*
	Historical Abstracts
Library and Information Science	*Library & Information Science Source*
	LISA: Library and Information Science Abstracts
Political Science	*PAIS Index*
Psychology	*PsycINFO*
Sociology	*Sociological Abstracts*
Women's and Gender Studies	*GenderWatch* *LGBT Life*
Sciences	
Agriculture	*AGRICOLA*
Biology	*Biological Abstracts*
Chemistry	*SciFinder*
Engineering	*Ei Compendex*
Geology	*GeoRef*
Physics	*Inspec*

for examples of some widely used subject-oriented indexes. See Chapters 28, 29, and 31 for more discussion of indexes for business, medical, and legal materials.

Citation Indexes

The periodical indexes described thus far allow the user to find articles written by the same author or indexed under the same subject heading. Citation indexes allow the user to locate items based on a different type of relationship: the links created when authors cite earlier works by other authors (or even some of their own previously published works). The primary use of a citation index is to find, for a particular publication known to the searcher, later items that have cited it. Clarivate Analytics publishes three indexes that allow the user to carry out such searches in broad subject areas: *Science Citation Index Expanded*, *Social Sciences Citation Index*, and *Arts & Humanities Citation Index*, searchable singly or in combination online as part of *Web of Science Core Collection*. All three are international in scope, covering many journals published outside the United States as well as the major U.S. titles in each subject area. Coverage of other types of publications by *Web of Science Core Collection* has been expanded with the addition of *Conference Proceedings Citation Index*, *Book Citation Index*, and *Emerging Sources Citation Index*, listing peer-reviewed journals of regional importance. Citation networks are an inherently hypertext approach to navigating the literature. *Web of Science Core Collection* has three types of internal links among records in the database: "cited references" lead to the items cited by a publication (going backward in time), "times cited" links lead to the items citing a publication (going forward in time), and "related records" identify other publications that have overlapping items cited with the publication of interest. *Web of Science Core Collection* also provides external links to the full text of journal articles indexed in the database. If the library subscribes to a given journal, then the user can link from the record in *Web of Science Core Collection* to the full text of the journal article. Box 22.2 provides an example of a search using *Web of Science Core Collection*.

The dominance of *Web of Science Core Collection* in the citation searching arena has now been challenged by both fee-based and freely available resources (Duffy 2018). Elsevier's *Scopus* has particular strengths in coverage of the scientific and medical literature but covers journals in the social sciences and arts and humanities as well. Its coverage includes over 23,700 peer-reviewed journals, including more than 4,000 gold open access as well as books and conference papers. Some discipline-specific indexes as well as full-text journal databases have introduced citation-searching capabilities (Herther 2015). Finally, *Google Scholar* includes a "cited by" link as part of the bibliographic information for items retrieved through a search. Péter Jacsó (2010) cautions that citation counts displayed in *Google Scholar* are often in error because they are generated automatically and not through the careful editorial process exercised in compiling *Web of Science Core Collection* and *Scopus*. Yet *Google Scholar* has merit in retrieving citations made by documents not readily found elsewhere, such as online theses, technical reports, and course syllabi. An exhaustive search for cited references requires searching more than one resource. Librarians are becoming more involved in assisting in gathering citation as well as altmetric data as indicators of impact, so familiarity with citation indexes is becoming increasingly important (Roemer and Borchardt 2015).

Box 22.2 Search Strategy: Bias in Algorithms

A computer science student enrolled in a course on ethical and professional issues in computer science had listened to the NPR TED Radio Hour episode "Can We Trust the Numbers?" and found the interview with Cathy O'Neil titled "Do Algorithms Perpetuate Human Bias?" to be of particular interest. Searching the online catalog, she had found the library's e-book copy of O'Neil's 2016 book *Weapons of Math Destruction: How Big Data Increases Inequality and Threatens Democracy*. Now the student needed to locate recent scholarly research on the topic and sought advice through her college library's e-mail reference service. The librarian who handled the question recognized *Web of Science Core Collection* as a likely tool for such a search, since it would enable the student to locate more recent scholarly publications citing and discussing O'Neil's concerns about bias in algorithms. Completing a cited reference search in *Web of Science Core Collection* using "O'Neil*" as the cited author (allowing variant forms of the cited author's name), "Weapons*" as the cited work, and "2016" as the cited year, he found multiple citations to the book as the cited work. Recent citing article titles included "Potential Biases in Machine Learning Algorithms Using Electronic Health Record Data," "Preventing Discrimination in the Automated Targeting of Job Advertisements," and "Detecting Racial Bias in Algorithms and Machine Learning." He e-mailed the student instructions on how to repeat the cited reference search and navigate the links in *Web of Science Core Collection* and encouraged her to contact the reference desk again if she had further questions.

Indexes for Special Types of Materials

The indexes discussed thus far in this chapter provide good coverage of periodicals but are not helpful for gaining access to some other special types of materials that may be important in certain library collections. Academic library users frequently want access to dissertations. Indexes devoted to these and other special types of materials, such as conference proceedings and research reports, can be useful for both collection development and reference work. This section describes the indexes for dissertations. Other indexes to special materials are described in more specialized guides to reference sources, such as books on patent searching (Hitchcock 2017).

Research for the doctorate is reported in dissertations, many of which are deposited with *ProQuest* to enable their use outside the institution in which the research was originally completed. The *ProQuest Dissertations & Theses Global* database provides historical and ongoing coverage for North American works and growing international coverage, with many dissertations available in full text. Increasingly, universities are encouraging students completing a dissertation to deposit it in electronic form, and the *Networked Digital Library of Theses and Dissertations* website supports a global search for electronic theses and dissertations. The *EBSCO Open Dissertations* project is aggregating metadata for electronic theses and dissertations from participating research universities and libraries around the world and enabling access through a Web portal.

Indexes of Reviews

Reference librarians may be asked to assist the user in locating reviews of books. Although periodical indexes can sometimes help with such requests, it may be more efficient and effective to use indexes specifically designed for this purpose. Four tools available to libraries include EBSCO's *Book Review Digest Plus* and *Book Review Digest Retrospective*, Gale's *Book Review Index Plus*, and EBSCO's *Book Index with Reviews*. *Book Review Digest*, with coverage from 1903, provides excerpts of and citations to reviews of current juvenile and adult fiction and nonfiction in the English language. It continues to be published in print but is more easily consulted online, where it exists in two parts: *Book Review Digest Retrospective*, covering 300,000 books, and *Book Review Digest Plus*, with coverage from 1981 forward. For the current database, contents include at least a citation to every book review from more than 5,000 indexed journals. Excerpts from reviews or full reviews are included for many books. *Book Review Index Plus* contains entries for more than five million reviews from 1965 to the present, with links to many full-text reviews. Citations are drawn from thousands of periodicals and newspapers. *Book Index with Reviews* includes citations for reviews of thousands of books, music, e-books, audiobooks, and movies, with more than 700,000 reviews in full text. Of course, there are several freely available sources of book reviews on the Web, including online bookseller sites such as *Amazon* and *Barnes & Noble*. These sites include both published reviews (termed "editorial reviews") and "customer reviews" submitted by users of the site. Chapter 21 identifies many sites useful for readers' advisory. The book review index databases identified in this section remain valuable for the wide range of sources of book reviews that they index and for their retrospective coverage of books both in and out of print.

Indexes for Different Literary Forms

Library collections in school, public, and academic libraries generally include many collected works: poetry anthologies, collections of plays or short stories, and collections of essays. Unless the contents of these volumes are analyzed during the cataloging process and the analytical entries made searchable directly in the library's catalog, the user of the catalog cannot easily determine whether the library holds an anthology that includes a particular play, short story, poem, or essay. EBSCO publishes three indexes that provide access to the contents of collections by author and subject: *Essay & General Literature Index*, *Play Index*, and *Short Story Index*.

Essay & General Literature Index is an author and subject index to essays published in collections, with particular emphasis on materials in the humanities and social sciences. It encompasses works published in the United States, the UK, and Canada, and it is now available online in two parts: a retrospective index covering the period 1900–1984 and a regularly updated index for the period from 1985 forward.

Play Index contains entries for more than 34,000 plays, published individually or in collections, dating from 1949 to present, and is updated on a weekly basis to incorporate new content. The scope includes one-act plays, plays in verse, musicals, radio and television plays, classic drama, and monologues. Various limits can be placed on the search, including age level, number of female and male cast members, and genre.

Short Story Index is now available online in two parts: a retrospective index covering the period 1915–1983 and a regularly updated index for the period from 1984 forward, including stories written in or translated into English and published in collections. *Short Story Index* is searchable by author, title, subject, keyword, date, and source, or by any combination of terms. Additionally, limits can narrow searches even further by document type (e.g., detective and mystery story, science fiction). A print volume is published annually by Grey House Publishing.

Indexes to poetry anthologies provide author, title, and subject indexing to poems printed in collections. In addition, titles such as *The Columbia Granger's*

Index to Poetry in Anthologies provides access by first line and last line because that may be the information the user remembers rather than the poem's title. The most recent print edition of *The Columbia Granger's* covers anthologies published through May 31, 2006, including 85,000 poems by 12,000 poets. Several of the anthologies are collections of poetry translated from other languages, as well as poems published in Spanish, Vietnamese, and French. Because the most recent edition does not cover all anthologies indexed in the previous editions, the latter should be retained to allow access to poems found only in older anthologies.

The Columbia Granger's World of Poetry Online includes 250,000 poems in full text in English and other languages and 450,000 citations. Search options include title, first line, last line, full text, subject, and author. Other reference material includes biographies and bibliographies on poets and commentaries on poems. Gale's *LitFinder* provides a repository of full-text literature including more than 130,000 full-text poems and nearly 700,000 poetry citations and excerpts as well as several thousand short stories, essays, speeches, and plays in full text. Basic and advanced search modes allow users to search by keyword, author, subject, work title, work date, nationality, gender, and more.

SEARCH STRATEGIES

The reference interview is an important part of assisting library users in accessing indexes and abstracts. Many users may be familiar only with *Google* or other Web search engines. As a starting point for database selection, it is important to determine the subject of interest and direct the user to the most appropriate indexes for the subject and type of material desired. Because online databases are often limited in the time period covered, library users must be aware that using only these tools for literature searching may lead to inadequate coverage of the published literature.

If a library user is in search of an article that is known to have appeared in a certain periodical but for which no other information is available, the librarian can consult an index or abstract that covers the periodical in order to identify the complete bibliographic information and possibly a link to the full text. The entry for the periodical in *Ulrichsweb* provides notations to indicate coverage by indexes and abstracts. Because many indexes and abstracts cover periodical titles only selectively, it may be necessary to look in more than one index to find the particular article sought. Indexes may also differ in time lag for indexing the same article. For topical searches, it is likewise necessary to identify the index or indexes most likely to provide the best coverage of the topic. As noted in Chapter 14, electronic resources must be organized in order to be discoverable and accessible. Reference librarians are frequently involved in the redesign of the library's user interface or the part of the library's Web presence that provides access to electronic resources in order to assist library users in identifying the most appropriate databases or other online sources for their needs.

For the first-time user of an index, some instruction may be necessary. This is also an opportunity to advise on search strategy. It may also be necessary to explain how to interpret the various components of a bibliographic citation as well as how to locate materials in the library's collection. Knowing the scope of the various indexes and abstracts is essential in selecting the most appropriate sources when verifying a citation or searching for information on a subject. Awareness of the conventions used by a particular database for author indexing is essential to doing a thorough search for works by an author. Familiarity with the approaches to subject indexing used in each index or abstract is necessary to select the sources most likely to have the terminology required in searching a particular subject. If the librarian is unfamiliar with the topic sought, it may be necessary first to check reference books such as encyclopedias and dictionaries to develop a list of related terms under which to search. Indexing vocabularies are not standardized, so it may be necessary to reformulate a subject search when checking multiple indexes and abstracts. Access to online sources allows the use of terms appearing in titles, abstracts, and possibly full text in addition to terms selected from controlled vocabularies.

In order to simplify access to multiple indexing and abstracting databases, as discussed in Chapter 16, many libraries are implementing some type of federated searching or Web-scale discovery. As Mark Dehmlow (2015, 2) cautions, "Because of the nature of merging billions of scholarly records into a single system, discovery systems will never be able to provide the same experience as a native A&I system." Discovery systems and indexing and abstracting databases are serving two separate needs: discovery systems provide quick access to full text, while indexing and abstracting databases provide "precision discipline-specific searching for expert researchers" (Hawkins 2013). Sarah P. C. Dahlen and Kathlene Hanson (2017) argue that subject-specific indexing and abstracting databases still play an important role for libraries that have adopted discovery layers, because subject-specific databases provide a less overwhelming set of search results as well as better options for advanced searching within a discipline. At present, records from all indexing and abstracting databases licensed by the library may not be integrated into a library's discovery system. Ideally, in the future, discovery systems can be enhanced to guide users back to indexing and abstracting databases based on terms in their search queries when they need to go beyond what can be found easily through the discovery system.

Because discovery systems cannot take advantage of unique features in particular databases, most expert searchers prefer to exploit the specific access points and search features provided by individual databases in order to produce thorough searches. As Miriam Drake (2008, 22) observes, "effective information finding . . . requires users to know the type and quality of required information, to have extensive knowledge of sources, to understand how to build effective search strategies, and to have the experience to evaluate results." Knowing that user needs vary, the librarian should seek to understand the kind and quality of information desired by the user before starting an index search. If the user just wants general, non-scholarly articles on a subject, then multidisciplinary periodical indexes are places to begin. Should the user's interest be more specialized, however, the librarian can assist the user in finding appropriate subject-oriented indexes and developing strategies to exploit their capabilities. Box 22.3 illustrates such a collaboration between a user and a librarian.

Box 22.3 Search Strategy: Citizen Science

A college student in an environmental policy course came to the reference desk looking for assistance in locating resources for a paper related to the role of the general public in gathering data that could be used to inform environmental policy. She had been watching the PBS series *The Crowd & the Cloud* that explores citizen science and learned about the Christmas Bird Count project and how data gathered on an annual basis can be used in guiding conservation efforts. She was seeking a wider range of examples.

To become more familiar with the topic, the librarian started with a catalog search using "citizen science" as title words. The top-ranked book was *Citizen Science: Public Participation in Environmental Research* (2012), available as an e-book with several chapters of interest, including the first titled "Overview of Citizen Science." No other book in the catalog had the assigned subject heading "Environmental Sciences—Research—Citizen Participation," so the librarian and student decided to explore available indexing and abstracting databases next. The librarian showed the student the A–Z Databases page on the library's website and how to limit by subject to "Environmental Science" and by database type to "citation and abstracts." Three databases were labeled as "best bets": *CAB Abstracts*, *GreenFILE*, and *Scopus*. Scanning the descriptions of the twenty-seven other databases in this category, the student noted *Wildlife & Ecology Studies Worldwide* as another promising title for her topic. The librarian suggested doing a subject search for "citizen science" and "environment*" in each database and then looking at indexing terms for relevant articles to refine the search using vocabulary specific to that database to further expand the search. For example, using this approach, the student found articles using the subject terms "citizen science" and "environmental databases" in *Wildlife & Ecology Studies Worldwide*, with titles such as "Citizen Science of Marine Protected Areas: Case Studies and Recommendations for Integration into Monitoring Programs" and "Citizen Science for Policy Development: The Case of Koala Management in South Australia." The librarian explained how to link to the full text of articles available in the e-journals in the library's collection. In reviewing the record for the first article, the student noted a PlumX Metrics logo and asked the librarian what that meant. Together, they clicked the link and found information about eighteen captures, nine tweets, and one citation of this article within a few months following its publication. The second article, published three years earlier, had much more extensive usage, capture, and social media metrics, as well as six citations by subsequently published articles that also looked promising, such as "Citizen Science in Water Quality Monitoring: Mobile Crowd Sensing for Water Management in the Netherlands." Encouraged by these initial results, the student continued the search of the "best bets" databases on her own to find additional examples for inclusion in her paper.

CONCLUSION

In performing searches of indexes and abstracts and in guiding library users in search strategy development, today's reference librarian must be able to locate the appropriate databases and take full advantage of the search capabilities. This requires a sophisticated understanding of specifics regarding content, organization, and interface. Almost anyone can find something from an electronic index without any knowledge of searching. It requires skilled searching to find precisely what is needed rather than everything with the same general keyword. As more libraries adopt Web-scale discovery services (Breeding 2018), librarians must continue to assess the role of indexes and abstracts in enabling discovery of and access to materials needed by library users.

REFERENCES

Albarillo, Frans. 2016. "Evaluating Language Functionality in Library Databases." *International Information & Library Review* 48 (1): 1–10.

Anderson, Rick. 2018. *Scholarly Communication: What Everyone Needs to Know*. New York: Oxford University Press.

Auld, Dennis. 1999. "The Future of Secondary Publishing." *Online & CD-ROM Review* 23 (3): 173–78.

Badke, William. 2009. "Google Scholar and the Researcher." *Online* 33 (3): 47–49.

Badke, William. 2013. "Coming Back to Google Scholar." *Online Searcher* 37 (5): 65–67.

Biggs, Mary. 1992. "'Mom in the Library': *The Readers' Guide to Periodical Literature*." In *Distinguished Classics of Reference Publishing*, edited by James Rettig, 198–210. Phoenix, AZ: Oryx Press.

Björk, Bo-Christer. 2017. "Gold, Green, and Black Open Access." *Learned Publishing* 30 (2): 173–75.

Breeding, Marshall. 2012. "E-resource Knowledge Bases and Link Resolvers: An Assessment of the Current Products and Emerging Trends." *Insights* 25 (2): 173–82.

Breeding, Marshall. 2018. "Index-Based Discovery Services: Current Market Positions and Trends." *Library Technology Reports* 54 (8): 5–33.

Brown, Christopher C. 2017. "Google Scholar." *The Charleston Advisor* 19 (2): 31–34.

Cave, Richard. 2017. "Altmetrics." In *Encyclopedia of Library and Information Sciences*. 4th ed., 44–47. Boca Raton, FL: CRC Press.

Chen, Xiaotian. 2005. "Figures and Tables Omitted from Online Periodical Articles: A Comparison of Vendors and Information Missing from Full-Text Databases." *Internet Reference Services Quarterly* 10 (2): 75–88.

Chen, Xiaotian. 2006. "Overlap between Traditional Periodical Indexes and Newer Mega Indexes." *Serials Review* 32 (4): 233–37.

Chen, Xiaotian. 2010. "The Declining Value of Subscription-Based Abstracting and Indexing Services in the New Knowledge Dissemination Era." *Serials Review* 36 (2): 79–85.

Chen, Xiaotian. 2013. "Journal Article Retrieval in an Age of Open Access: How Journal Indexes Indicate Open Access Articles." *Journal of Web Librarianship* 7 (3): 243–54.

Clarivate Analytics. n.d. "Open Access." https://clarivate.com/webofsciencegroup/solutions/open-access/.

Crawford, Walt. 2000. "Here's the Content—Where's the Context?" *American Libraries* 31 (3): 50–52.

Dahlen, Sarah P. C., and Kathlene Hanson. 2017. "Preference vs. Authority: A Comparison of Student Searching in a Subject-Specific Indexing and Abstracting Database and a Customized Discovery Layer." *College & Research Libraries* 78 (7): 878–97.

Dehmlow, Mark. 2015. "A & I Databases: The Next Frontier to Discover." *Information Technology & Libraries* 34 (1): 1–3.

Drake, Miriam A. 2008. "Federated Search: One Simple Query or Simply Wishful Thinking?" *Searcher* 16 (7): 22–25, 61–62.

Duffy, Jane C. 2018. "Web of Science." *The Charleston Advisor* 20 (1): 52–54.

Google. n.d. "Library Support." http://scholar.google.com/scholar/libraries.html.

Hawkins, Donald T. 2013. "Information Discovery and the Future of Abstracting and Indexing Services: An NFAIS Workshop." *Against the Grain.* Last modified August 6, 2013. http://www.against-the-grain.com/2013/08/information-discovery-and-the-future-of-abstracting-and-indexing-services-an-nfais-workshop/.

Herther, Nancy K. 2015. "Advanced Citation Searching: Moving from Single Sourced Research to a Potential Future of Unlimited Connections." *Online Searcher* 39 (3): 44–48.

Herther, Nancy K. 2017. "Open Access Repositories: Revealing the Mother Lode of Research to the World." *Online Searcher* 41 (6): 34–39.

Hitchcock, David. 2017. *Patent Searching Made Easy: How to Do Patent Searches on the Internet and in the Library.* 7th ed. Berkeley, CA: Nolo.

International Coalition of Library Consortia. 1999. "Guidelines for Statistical Measures of Usage of Web-Based Indexed, Abstracted, and Full-Text Resources." *Information Technology & Libraries* 18 (3): 161–63.

Jacsó, Péter. 2010. "Metadata Mega Mess in Google Scholar." *Online Information Review* 34 (1): 175–91.

Koltay, Tibor. 2010. *Abstracts and Abstracting: A Genre and Set of Skills for the Twenty-First Century.* Oxford: Chandos Publishing.

Ojala, Marydee. 2012. "An Abstract Concept." *Online* 36 (2): 5.

O'Neil, Cathy. 2016. *Weapons of Math Destruction: How Big Data Increases Inequality and Threatens Democracy.* New York: Crown Publishers.

Pesch, Oliver. 2017. "COUNTER Release 5: What's New and What It Means to Libraries." *Serials Librarian* 73 (3/4): 195–207.

Plum Analytics. n.d. "PlumX Metrics." https://plumanalytics.com/learn/about-metrics/.

Roemer, Robin Chin, and Rachel Borchardt. 2015. "Altmetrics, Bibliometrics: Librarians and the Measurement of Scholarship." *American Libraries* 46 (9/10): 29.

Tenopir, Carol. 1998. "Linking to Full Texts." *Library Journal* 123 (6): 34, 36.

Tucci, Valerie. 2010. "Are A&I Services in a Death Spiral?" *Issues in Science and Technology Librarianship* 61 (Spring). http://www.istl.org/10-spring/viewpoint.html.

LIST OF SOURCES

ABI/INFORM Global. Ann Arbor, MI: ProQuest. https://www.proquest.com/products-services/abi_inform_global.html. Subscription required.

Academic OneFile. Farmington Hills, MI: Gale. https://www.gale.com/c/academic-onefile. Subscription required.

Academic Search Complete. Ipswich, MA: EBSCO. https://www.ebsco.com/products/research-databases/academic-search-complete. Subscription required.

Academic Search Elite. Ipswich, MA: EBSCO. https://www.ebsco.com/products/research-databases/academic-search-elite. Subscription required.

Academic Search Premier. Ipswich, MA: EBSCO. https://www.ebsco.com/products/research-databases/academic-search-premier. Subscription required.

Academic Search Ultimate. Ipswich, MA: EBSCO. https://www.ebsco.com/products/research-databases/academic-search-ultimate. Subscription required.

AGRICOLA. Washington, DC: U.S. Department of Agriculture. https://agricola.nal.usda.gov/.

Alternative Press Index. 1969–. Baltimore, MD: Alternative Press Center. http://www.altpress.org/mod/pages/display/8/index.php?menu=pubs. Available online from EBSCO. https://www.ebsco.com/products/research-databases/alternative-press-index. Subscription required.

Alternative Press Index Archive. Ipswich, MA: EBSCO. https://www.ebsco.com/products/research-databases/alternative-press-index-archive. Subscription required.

Amazon. https://www.amazon.com.

America: History and Life. Ipswich, MA: EBSCO. https://www.ebsco.com/products/research-databases/america-history-and-life. Subscription required.

Art & Architecture Source. Ipswich, MA: EBSCO. https://www.ebsco.com/products/research-databases/art-architecture-source. Subscription required.

Arts & Humanities Citation Index. Philadelphia: Clarivate Analytics. https://clarivate.com/products/web-of-science/databases/. Available online as part of *Web of Science Core Collection*. Subscription required.

ATLA Religion Database. Chicago: American Theological Library Association. https://www.atla.com/products/prodinfo/Pages/ATLA-RDB.aspx. Available online from EBSCO. https://www.ebsco.com/products/research-databases/atla-religion-database. Subscription required.

Barnes & Noble. https://www.barnesandnoble.com/.

Biological Abstracts. Philadelphia: Clarivate Analytics. https://clarivate.com/products/web-of-science/databases/. Subscription required.

Book Citation Index. Philadelphia: Clarivate Analytics. https://clarivate.com/products/web-of-science/databases/. Available online as part of *Web of Science Core Collection*. Subscription required.

Book Index with Reviews. Ipswich, MA: EBSCO. https://www.ebsco.com/products/research-databases/book-index-reviews. Subscription required.

Book Review Digest. 1903–. Amenia, NY: Grey House Publishing.

Book Review Digest Plus. Ipswich, MA: EBSCO. https://www.ebsco.com/products/research-databases/book-review-digest-plus. Subscription required.

Book Review Digest Retrospective. Ipswich, MA: EBSCO. https://www.ebsco.com/products/digital-archives/retrospective-indexes/book-review-digest-retrospective. Subscription required.

Book Review Index Plus. Farmington Hills, MI: Gale. https://www.gale.com/c/book-review-index-plus. Subscription required.

Business Source Complete. Ipswich, MA: EBSCO. https://www.ebsco.com/products/research-databases/business-source-complete. Subscription required.

CAB Abstracts. Wallingford, UK: CABI. https://www.cabi.org/publishing-products/online-information-resources/cab-abstracts/. Subscription required.

Canadian Business & Current Affairs (CBCA) Database. Ann Arbor, MI: ProQuest. https://www.proquest.com/libraries/academic/databases/cbca.html. Subscription required.

The Columbia Granger's Index to Poetry in Anthologies. 13th ed. 2007. Edited by Tessa Kale. New York: Columbia University Press.

The Columbia Granger's World of Poetry Online. New York: Columbia University Press. http://www.columbiagrangers.org/. Subscription required.

Conference Proceedings Citation Index. Philadelphia: Clarivate Analytics. https://clarivate.com/products/web-of-science/databases/. Available online as part of *Web of Science Core Collection*. Subscription required.

CPI.Q. Farmington Hills, MI: Gale. https://www.gale.com/c/cpiq. Subscription required.

Directory of Open Access Journals. https://doaj.org/.

EBSCO. https://www.ebsco.com/.

EBSCO Open Dissertations. https://biblioboard.com/opendissertations/.

Ei Compendex. Amsterdam, The Netherlands: Elsevier. https://www.elsevier.com/solutions/engineering-village/content/compendex. Subscription required.

Emerging Sources Citation Index. Philadelphia: Clarivate Analytics. https://clarivate.com/products/web-of-science/databases/. Available online as part of *Web of Science Core Collection*. Subscription required.

ERIC. Washington, DC: Institute of Education Sciences. https://eric.ed.gov/

Essay & General Literature Index. Ipswich, MA: EBSCO. https://www.ebsco.com/products/research-databases/essay-general-literature-index. Subscription required.

Essay & General Literature Index Retrospective: 1900–1984. Ipswich, MA: EBSCO. https://www.ebsco.com/products/digital-archives/retrospective-indexes/essay-general-literature-index-retrospective. Subscription required.

Film & Television Literature Index. Ipswich, MA: EBSCO. https://www.ebsco.com/products/research-databases/film-television-literature-index. Subscription required.

Gale. https://www.gale.com/.

GenderWatch. Ann Arbor, MI: ProQuest. https://www.proquest.com/products-services/genderwatch.html. Subscription required.

GeoRef. Alexandria, VA: American Geosciences Institute. https://www.americangeosciences.org/georef/georef-scholarly-information. Subscription required.

Google. https://www.google.com/.

Google Scholar. https://scholar.google.com/

GreenFILE. Ipswich, MA: EBSCO. https://www.ebsco.com/products/research-databases/greenfile. Subscription required.

Historical Abstracts. Ipswich, MA: EBSCO. https://www.ebsco.com/products/research-databases/historical-abstracts. Subscription required.

Informe Académico. Farmington Hills, MI: Gale. https://www.gale.com/c/informe-academico. Subscription required.

Inspec. London: The Institution of Engineering and Technology. https://www.theiet.org/resources/inspec/. Subscription required.

LGBT Life. Ipswich, MA: EBSCO. https://www.ebsco.com/products/research-databases/lgbt-life. Subscription required.

Library & Information Science Source. Ipswich, MA: EBSCO. https://www.ebsco.com/products/research-databases/library-information-science-source. Subscription required.

LISA: Library and Information Science Abstracts. Ann Arbor, MI: ProQuest. https://www.proquest.com/products-services/lisa-set-c.html. Subscription required.

Literature Resource Center. Farmington Hills, MI: Gale. https://www.gale.com/c/literature-resource-center. Subscription required.

LitFinder. Farmington Hills, MI: Gale. https://www.gale.com/c/litfinder. Subscription required.

MasterFILE Complete. Ipswich, MA: EBSCO. https://www.ebsco.com/products/research-databases/masterfile-complete. Subscription required.

MasterFILE Elite. Ipswich, MA: EBSCO. https://www.ebsco.com/products/research-databases/masterfile-elite. Subscription required.

MasterFILE: Main Edition. Ipswich, MA: EBSCO. https://www.ebsco.com/products/research-databases/masterfile-main-edition. Subscription required.

MasterFILE Premier. Ipswich, MA: EBSCO. https://www.ebsco.com/products/research-databases/masterfile-premier. Subscription required.

Middle Search Plus. Ipswich, MA: EBSCO. https://www.ebsco.com/products/research-databases/middle-search-plus. Subscription required.

MLA International Bibliography. New York, NY: Modern Language Association. https://www.mla.org/Publications/MLA-International-Bibliography. Available online from EBSCO. https://www.ebsco.com/products/research-databases/mla-international-bibliography. Subscription required.

Music Index. Ipswich, MA: EBSCO. https://www.ebsco.com/products/research-databases/music-index. Subscription required.

Networked Digital Library of Theses and Dissertations. http://search.ndltd.org/.

Onefile: High School Edition. Farmington Hills, MI: Gale. https://www.gale.com/c/onefile-high-school-edition. Subscription required.

Open Access Directory. http://oad.simmons.edu/oadwiki/Main_Page.

OpenDOAR. http://v2.sherpa.ac.uk/opendoar/.

PAIS Index. Ann Arbor, MI: ProQuest. https://www.proquest.com/products-services/pais-set-c.html. Subscription required.

Periodicals Archive Online. Ann Arbor, MI: ProQuest. https://www.proquest.com/products-services/periodicals_archive.html. Subscription required.

Periodicals Index Online. Ann Arbor, MI: ProQuest. https://www.proquest.com/products-services/periodicals_index.html. Subscription required.

Play Index. Ipswich, MA: EBSCO. https://www.ebsco.com/products/research-databases/play-index. Subscription required.

Primary Search. Ipswich, MA: EBSCO. https://www.ebsco.com/products/research-databases/primary-search. Subscription required.

ProQuest. https://www.proquest.com/.

ProQuest Central. Ann Arbor, MI: ProQuest. https://www.proquest.com/products-services/ProQuest_Central.html. Subscription required.

ProQuest Central Student. Ann Arbor, MI: ProQuest. https://www.proquest.com/products-services/databases/ProQuest-Central-K12.html. Subscription required.

ProQuest Dissertations & Theses Global. Ann Arbor, MI: ProQuest. https://www.proquest.com/products-services/pqdtglobal.html. Subscription required.

PsycINFO. Washington, DC: American Psychological Association. https://www.apa.org/pubs/databases/psycinfo/index.aspx. Subscription required.

Readers' Guide Retrospective: 1890–1982. Ipswich, MA: EBSCO. https://www.ebsco.com/products/research-databases/readers-guide-retrospective-1890-1982. Subscription required.

Readers' Guide to Periodical Literature. Amenia, NY: Grey House Publishing. Available online from EBSCO. https://www.ebsco.com/products/research-databases/readers-guide-periodical-literature. Subscription required. Quarterly with annual cumulation.

Science Citation Index Expanded. Philadelphia: Clarivate Analytics. https://clarivate.com/products/web-of-science/databases/. Available online as part of *Web of Science Core Collection.* Subscription required.

SciFinder. Columbus, OH: CAS. https://www.cas.org/products/scifinder. Subscription required.

Scopus. Amsterdam, The Netherlands: Elsevier. https://www.scopus.com. Subscription required.

Short Story Index. Amenia, NY: Grey House Publishing. Annual. Available online from EBSCO. https://www.ebsco.com/products/research-databases/short-story-index. Subscription required.

Short Story Index Retrospective: 1915–1983. Ipswich, MA: EBSCO. https://www.ebsco.com/products/digital-archives/retrospective-indexes/short-story-index-retrospective. Subscription required.

Social Sciences Citation Index. Philadelphia: Clarivate Analytics. https://clarivate.com/products/web-of-science/databases/. Available online as part of *Web of Science Core Collection.* Subscription required.

Sociological Abstracts. Ann Arbor, MI: ProQuest. https://www.proquest.com/products-services/socioabs-set-c.html. Subscription required.

Ulrichsweb. Ann Arbor, MI: ProQuest. http://ulrichsweb.serialssolutions.com/. Subscription required.

Web of Science Core Collection. Philadelphia: Clarivate Analytics. https://clarivate.com/products/web-of-science/web-science-form/web-science-core-collection/. Subscription required.

Wildlife & Ecology Studies Worldwide. Ipswich, MA: EBSCO. https://www.ebsco.com/products/research-databases/wildlife-ecology-studies-worldwide. Subscription required.

SUGGESTED READINGS

Anderson, Rick. 2018. *Scholarly Communication: What Everyone Needs to Know.* New York: Oxford University Press.

Anderson provides an overview of the scholarly communication system and a range of significant issues associated with it, such as open access and metrics and altmetrics.

Brown, Christopher C., and Suzanne S. Bell. 2018. *Librarian's Guide to Online Searching: Cultivating Database Skills for Research and Instruction.* 5th ed. Santa Barbara, CA: Libraries Unlimited.

Following early chapters on search strategies, this text provides thorough coverage of core database titles for the humanities, social sciences, sciences, statistics, and more.

Cleveland, Donald B., and Ana D. Cleveland. 2013. *Introduction to Indexing and Abstracting.* 4th ed. Santa Barbara, CA: Libraries Unlimited.

This book provides practical examples of the procedures for indexing and abstracting and includes numerous resource lists helpful for practitioners as well as students.

Holmberg, Kim. 2016. *Altmetrics for Information Professionals: Past, Present and Future.* Waltham, MA: Chandos Publishing.

Encompassing bibliometrics, scientometrics, informetrics, webometrics, and altmetrics, the book gives special attention to the potential and problems in using altmetrics.

Keyser, Pierre de. 2012. *Indexing: From Thesauri to the Semantic Web.* Oxford: Chandos Publishing.

Keyser describes various traditional and novel indexing techniques, giving a broad and comprehensible introduction to indexing.

Mann, Thomas. 2015. *The Oxford Guide to Library Research.* 4th ed. New York: Oxford University Press.

Several chapters in this guide provide helpful discussions on search strategy for effective use of indexes and abstracts. See in particular the chapters on "Subject Headings and Descriptors in Databases for Journal Articles," "Keyword Searches," "Citation Searches," and "Special Subjects and Formats."

Chapter 23

News Sources

Barbara A. Alvarez

INTRODUCTION

News sources are crucial for the dissemination of current events, political issues, and public affairs. According to the American Press Institute (n.d.), news "keeps us informed of the changing events, issues, and characters in the world." News sources are powerful tools and essential to a functioning democracy because they inform citizens of what is happening on a local, national, and international level. They also give citizens the ability to form their own opinions and take action through consumer choices, voting, volunteering, and other means.

Library patrons use news sources for a variety of reasons. Sometimes, they simply want to stay informed, while other times they want to find more information on a particular topic. Whatever the reason, patrons and reference librarians are able to select from a plethora of sources, including print and online publications, live broadcasts, podcasts, and social media, many of which have not previously been readily and widely available. Whether patrons are looking for recent news coverage on a particular topic, conducting research for a school paper, or seeking information of general interest, they are presented with more news source options now than ever before.

However, not all news sources are created equal. News sources may go beyond providing facts to present information in such a way as to persuade the reader into a certain belief, idea, or action. And sometimes the news is not accurate, either because it is outdated information or because factually untrue articles are accidently or purposefully published. Even for information professionals, it may be overwhelming to ascertain which sources are reliable in the sea of news sources. However, it is essential that librarians understand the different types of news sources and how to properly evaluate them in order to provide credible information to patrons.

This chapter discusses a variety of news source formats and types and examines how to evaluate news sources to successfully direct patrons to reliable information that will meet their needs.

PAST TO PRESENT

News dissemination is hardly new. Before the written word was prevalent, stories were passed by word of mouth and sometimes inscribed on stone, clay, and papyrus. However, since the elite were primarily the ones who knew how to read and write, information and news were largely created, controlled, and contained by those in political or religious authority (Burkhardt 2017, 5). For example, during the Medieval Ages, monks in monasteries painstakingly hand-copied biblical texts to spread Christianity (Corwin 2016). It was the invention of the modern printing press by Johannes Gutenberg in the 15th century that made it possible for information to be spread to the masses.

As printing techniques improved, production became more affordable, and literacy spread, different formats for sharing information were created. For example, government officials could pay for an expensive subscription service to receive weekly newsletters about politics, government, and war. Additionally, pamphlets that detailed wars in surrounding countries were printed in response to public interest. However, it was not until the 19th century that newspapers became a staple of information dissemination (Pettegree 2014, 12).

In the United States, in 1791, the First Amendment, which guarantees freedom of speech and press, became part of the Bill of Rights. However, production costs still limited newspaper circulation to the elite. In 1833, Benjamin Day turned newspaper production on its head. Taking advantage of technological advances from the Industrial Revolution, Day created *The Sun* newspaper, which could print 18,000 copies in one hour. Additionally, Day sold newspaper space to businesses who wanted to advertise. This allowed him to sell the newspaper for one penny and reach a wider audience. *The Sun* focused on daily happenings, police reports, and local coverage to attract and engage readers. This new form of coverage led to newspapers cropping up all over the country.

Technological advances continued to impact news coverage and access. When Samuel Morse invented the telegraph, newspapers could receive current news briefs from around the world (*Understanding Media and Culture* 2016, 12). The mid-20th century brought radio and television to the public. For the first time, the general public was able to listen to and watch news unfold. They were also bombarded with advertisements in new ways. Because listeners and viewers did not have to pay any subscription fees as they would for a newspaper, networks sold airtime to advertisers in exchange for radio or television programs with commercials and brand promotions (Ponce de Leon 2016, 2).

During World War II, news programs became a regular part of the broadcasting schedule. Sig Mickelson (1998, 8), head of the news division of CBS, writes that news "helped create an image that was useful in attracting audiences and stimulating commercial sales, not to mention maintaining favorable government relations. . . . News met the test of 'public service.'" Initially, CBS had two 15-minute news programs, on Thursdays and Fridays at 8:00 p.m., with NBC hosting a short news broadcast on Sunday evenings. Beginning in 1948, as televisions became more prominent in

American homes, networks launched nightly news broadcasts (Ponce de Leon 2016, 7, 8).

In 1963, CBS and NBC expanded the news from fifteen minutes to thirty minutes; in 1967, ABC followed suit. The prevalence of news broadcasts allowed Americans to rely on them for information about presidential elections, the assassination of John F. Kennedy, the Vietnam War, and other important events. That same year, President Lyndon B. Johnson signed the Public Broadcasting Act, which established the Corporation for Public Broadcasting, with the goal of providing educational, noncommercial media to the public (Chrypinski 2017).

Cable television ushered in another new era. Originally intended to provide broadcasting to Americans in remote locations through wires and antennas, operators discovered that high-quality images could be sent via satellite. This ushered in a host of entrepreneurs who could provide their own channels and programs outside of the confines of traditional broadcasting (Ponce de Leon 2016, 166). In 1979, C-SPAN was founded, broadcasting sessions from the House of Representatives, as well as hearings and press conferences (Ponce de Leon 2016, 169). In 1980, CNN, the first live, all-news channel was launched with round-the-clock coverage (Ponce de Leon 2016, 127). Simply put, cable television gave viewers more options for watching television and news.

In order to compete with cable news, networks started to feature documentary-style news programs like *20/20*, which provided more detailed coverage of a specific topic. Additionally, news shows started to air in the early morning and late at night (Lurie 2012).

The development of the Internet further improved people's access to news. The World Wide Web was launched in 1989, making it possible for organizations, businesses, and individuals to create their own websites to share information. By 1994, major news outlets like CNN and *The Chicago Tribune* had developed websites (Sanburn 2011). As more people gravitated toward accessing news on the Internet, different types of news platforms emerged. For example, sites like *Yahoo!* and *America Online* gathered articles from varied news sources into one space. Additionally, many print publications created supplementary or born-digital news sites, presenting content that was produced digitally from the start rather than adapted to digital formats (Sanburn 2011).

By the turn of the century, the Internet evolved into a content creation mechanism as well as an information repository. People could now write and distribute information through websites, blogs, videos, podcasts, and social media. Additionally, readers could interact with news publications, providing instant feedback about their reporting.

Now, digital news sources, live broadcasts, podcasts, apps, and social media, have revolutionized how news is created and consumed. No longer do people need to wait for the nightly news or their morning newspaper to find out what is going on in the world; a simple scroll through their social media timeline or a notification from an app at 3:00 a.m. can do the same.

TYPES OF NEWS SOURCES

People now have a myriad of ways to access news. According to a Pew Research Center study, 47 percent of Americans prefer watching the news as opposed to reading or listening to it. Additionally, 44 percent of Americans prefer television, while 34 percent choose the Internet as their viewing platform. Furthermore, those who prefer to read the news are more likely to do so online (63%) instead of in print (17%). In fact, Americans younger than 50 years old largely choose the Web to get their news for reading, watching, and listening (Atske 2018). In addition, the lines between different formats are becoming increasingly blurred, as traditional print papers generally offer online access, often enhanced by additional audio and visual content. With digital resources, an entirely new category of new sources has not only been created but has expanded the versatility of existing print, visual, and audio news formats, as described in the following passages.

Subscription-Based Publications

Subscription-based news sources include newspapers and periodicals that are printed daily, weekly, or monthly. These are typically obtained through paid subscriptions and delivered to one's home or an institution, organization, or business. Many of these print publications also have websites that readers can access with their paid subscription. These websites often include bonus news features such as recorded interviews, live updates, and interactive media. Some websites will provide a limited amount of free access to non-subscribers.

In addition, many major news publishers have developed apps for mobile phones and tablets. These apps provide a combination of news articles, video and audio content, and images. Some apps are created in tandem with an existing newspaper such as *The New York Times*. While the app itself is usually free, access to the content requires a newspaper subscription. Other news apps are free and based on Internet sites like *HuffPost*. Although libraries do not typically offer apps as part of their collection, librarians should be familiar with these apps and their utility for patrons who wish to acquire them on their personal devices.

Free Websites

Some websites, typically supported by advertising, offer free access to news information. Articles may be authored by professional journalists or freelancers, or the website may accept contributions from anyone who creates an account and submits an article, such as the online publishing platform *Medium*. Some sites serve as news aggregators, pulling content from multiple sources across the Internet.

Multimedia

Multimedia news sources include news broadcasts, political and cultural commentary, radio shows, and podcasts and can be watched on television or accessed via the Internet. News broadcasts are aired live on both network and cable television and recordings of entire broadcasts and/or selected portions can often be accessed online. Programs featuring political and cultural commentary, such as *PBS NewsHour* and *Hardball with Chris Matthews*, may be presented as a live broadcast and/or a prerecorded program.

Radio shows are often aired live, but have given way to the popularity of prerecorded podcasts. Both news radio shows and podcasts can be produced daily, weekly, or monthly. While some shows provide general, current news information, some shows go into greater detail on a particular topic such as politics, business, or the financial markets.

Databases

News databases offer access to multiple news publications in one source; these databases are designed for libraries and are subscription based. Librarians and patrons can search by keyword or construct advanced searches by publication, date, geographic location, and other criteria to find current and historical news.

FAKE NEWS

In recent years, librarians and the general public have become increasingly concerned about "fake news," an umbrella term that can be used for any inaccurate news story, although it is often used to imply that the information was deliberately misleading and may be slung at any news piece with which one disagrees. While some news is unintentionally inaccurate, the creation of fake news can be motivated by political interests to disrupt elections and public policy issues. It can also be used to generate money; some creators of fake news sites make thousands of dollars per month through advertisements (Ohlheiser 2016).

In some cases, fake news is the result of misinformation, or incorrect information. It is not intended to be deceitful and is often spread mistakenly before a correction can be made. Misinformation can also arise from outdated information. While old articles may have been accurate at the time of publication, they can be superseded by new facts, so it is important for librarians to ensure that any news information they recommend to patrons is current.

In other cases, fake news is based on disinformation, false information that is specifically distributed to influence a group of people, or propaganda, where facts are manipulated in order to persuade people or excite their emotions. Oftentimes, disinformation and propaganda are distributed through "click-bait," articles with eye-catching and outlandish headlines that are meant to pique readers' interest in order to get them to click on the link to read a story. The goal of click-bait may be to spread disinformation or simply to generate clicks that convert to advertising dollars for the website hosting the article. Boxes 23.1 and 23.2 provide activities to explore misinformation, disinformation, and propaganda more closely.

Box 23.1 Activity: The Many Faces of a Story

Search the Web for a recent event and skim a variety of news sites, blogs, and social media platforms.

Questions for Reflection and Discussion:

1. Can you find examples of accurate reporting, misinformation, disinformation, and propaganda about the same event?
2. Do the sources have different narratives or information? If so, how might these differences impact the reader's perception of the event?
3. Are any of these sources examples of click-bait?

Box 23.2 Activity: Creating Fake News

Find an article from a legitimate news source. Read the article and take note of any quotes, statistics, or people that stand out. Using only the details from the article, write a new narrative, with a sensational headline, that skews the original information. For added measure, find an image to pair with the news article. Share your news piece with a classmate.

Questions for Reflection and Discussion:

- How did you transform the original piece into fake news?
- How does the image you selected support the new narrative of the story or impact the reader's response to the story?
- How did your classmate react?
- What surprised you about creating your own fake news?

Deliberately fake news can be hard to spot, even to the most trained eye. Wynne Davis (2016) provides useful tips for evaluating news sites, including the following:

- **Look at the website address:** Often fake news websites will use domains that look very similar to popular URLs. They may even use the same logos and branding on the fake website. For example, http://abcnews.com.co mimicked http://abc.go.com to spread false information.
- **Check the date of the article.** Is this a new story or out of date? In this social media–driven world, old news is recycled easily.
- **Read the "About Us" page.** This can give you an indication of when the website was created, what the organization stands for, and where they get their information.
- **Look at multiple sources.** Compare what you have read on different websites or resources to see if you find confirming or contrasting information.
- **Fact-check.** Look at third-party fact-checking resources, like *Snopes*, to verify the statements made in the news story.
- **Use a reverse image search machine.** Does the photo match the story? Upload the image or copy and paste the website URL to *Google Images* to see if the photo comes from a different event.

In addition to the pointers mentioned here, the International Federation of Library Associations and Institutions (2017) created an infographic with eight steps to use when determining if a news source is reliable, reprinted here (see Figure 23.1).

EVALUATION OF SOURCES

Due to the abundance of news sources, reference librarians must determine which formats and sources will be the most useful for the patron's needs. In

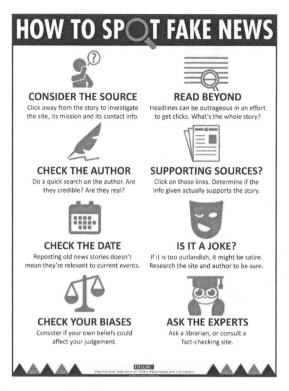

Figure 23.1 How to spot fake news. This infographic from IFLA suggests eight steps to determine if a news source is reliable: consider the source; read beyond the headline; check the author, date, and supporting sources; determine whether the piece is satire; check your own bias; and consult experts.

***Source*: International Federation of Library Associations and Institutions (CC BY 4.0)**

speaking with the patron, it is important to conduct a comprehensive reference interview in order to fully determine the type and depth of the information that the patron wants to access. Then, as the librarian searches, each news source must be evaluated to determine if it is a credible resource that adequately answers the reference question.

Format

In the realm of news, print publications abound. Many libraries subscribe to print newspapers and magazines for patrons who wish to browse and read current news. These print publications can also be consulted for past stories, although most librarians and patrons find it more efficient to search and access older articles through a publication's website or a news database. Some news sources have no print equivalent, either because they were born digital or because they are audio-visual in nature. In these cases, librarians will need to search the Web or an appropriate database to locate copies of the needed resource.

For breaking news, freely available Internet news sources, like press services such as the *Associated Press* and *Reuters*, can be helpful for immediate information.

Often, these stories are still developing, so they should be approached with a level of caution. Consulting articles from different news outlets on the same subject may provide more complete, or confirming, information.

Authority

Librarians should take into consideration the origins of a news source, such as the publisher or site sponsor and the author, and how that may impact the type of news coverage that is provided. Some sites allow users to post news and articles with little to no oversight, while others put articles through an editorial process, including revisions, proofreading, and fact-checking. If the publisher has a reputation for delivering news with a particular slant, bias, or viewpoint, the librarian should warn the patron of this potential bias.

News blogs and free content sites that provide articles on current events and breaking news often rely on freelance writers and/or reader contributions. Some sites only accept articles from writers who have previously been published or have a level of expertise on the subject, while others allow anyone to be a contributor. Librarians should examine the author's expertise, qualifications, or credentials to write about a particular topic.

Purpose

All news pieces, whether print or online, have their own objectives. In print newspapers, the section in which an article is published may indicate whether its purpose is to inform or persuade; online, these clues are often less obvious, and librarians should carefully consider the purpose of the source as well as individual articles and broadcasts.

- **News story.** A news story reports the facts of a situation based on the journalist's investigation of the issue, interviews with relevant sources, and related reports or records. The purpose of a news story is to provide information to the reader/viewer without inputting superfluous details, insights, or commentary.
- **Feature.** A feature article is typically the main "story" of a periodical. It provides information like a news story but will be longer and often provides analysis, a conclusion, and/or the writer's personal observations and judgments.
- **Opinion piece.** An opinion piece gives an individual or group's perspective, typically on a controversial issue or topic. Frequently referred to as an OpEd, or an opinion letter to the editor, an opinion piece is meant to persuade readers into understanding the writer's perspective, and perhaps, changing their opinion.
- **Editorial.** An editorial is a piece written on behalf of a publishing house or agency that reflects the organization's opinion on a relevant political, social, or cultural topic.
- **Advertisement.** Some advertising is clearly structured to look like an ad, while in other cases it can be more difficult to discern. Called "native advertising," these ads are interspersed in newspapers and periodicals in a format that looks like the rest of the publication. They provide information on a topic, at times included with research or interviews from others, while offering a solution. The solution, however, is typically a product, service, or program that the company wants to sell.

Accuracy and Objectivity

The intention of a reputable news publication is to provide accurate and objective coverage of an incident or event. Professional journalists seek reliable sources of information and adhere to ethical standards, including "seek truth and report it," "minimize harm," "act independently," and "be accountable and transparent" (Society of Professional Journalists 2014).

Journalists have different means of obtaining information about events, and some means are considered more trustworthy than others. Primary sources are physical or verbal sources of information that provide a first-hand account of an occurrence. Primary sources may be written reports, letters, e-mails, speeches, interviews, audio or video footage, official records, meeting minutes, government documents, leaked documents, sales receipts, reports, statistics, and artifacts. Secondary sources are created after the fact and typically provide an analysis or perspective on an occurrence. These include commentary, criticisms, textbooks, journal articles, and histories, as well as reviews of books, movies, and articles. The code of ethics makes it clear that journalists are responsible for the accuracy of their reporting, part of which includes ensuring that their sources of information, whether primary or secondary, are reliable and trustworthy.

Journalists can help establish their accuracy and trustworthiness by being transparent about their sources whenever possible. Reliable news sources indicate the people, places, and documents from which they received their information, a process called attribution. When something is quoted as "on the record," the material may be published and attributed to the source, allowing the reporter to quote names and include specifics. Non-attributable (or on-background) material may be published but not attributed. This occurs when a reporter interviews someone who would like to remain anonymous. Journalists prefer on-the-record sources for accuracy and transparency, but occasionally it will not be possible to have an "on the record" interview (Ingram and Henshall 1991, chapter 9).

In addition to looking for these markers of reputable journalism, librarians should take into consideration whether an article or a resource is slanted to promote a particular view of a person, event, or issue. For example, the images used to illustrate a story may be intended to evoke an emotional response from the reader, such as unflattering photos of an individual that literally and figuratively cast that person in a bad light.

Librarians should also be aware of confirmation bias: the tendency to seek out or trust sources and articles that confirm what an individual already believes to be true. In addition, Internet search algorithms adapt to user reading habits and preferences, so news sources that are displayed through search engines may be limited to sources and perspectives that the user routinely consults or with which the user already agrees. Librarians can raise awareness of these biases and help patrons craft searches and consult resources that will point them to more accurate and objective information.

Currency

The currency of the news piece should also be considered. The ease and immediacy with which information can be shared online and through social media means that breaking news stories are often shared before all of the details have been verified. It is imperative to check the publication date and determine whether there are updated versions of a story.

SELECTION

In making news source selections, the librarian should consider the mission of the library and the demographics of the community that it serves. For example, an academic library will undoubtedly have different reference requests than a rural public library. Additionally, librarians should assess the digital landscape of their community, such as the accessibility of Wi-Fi and prevalence of mobile phones and tablets, before deciding whether to select physical or electronic news sources.

Although the Internet has made it possible to access an abundance of free news sources, it is still important for libraries to have a variety of print and online news sources available to meet different reading preferences. Librarians should also consider the circulation policies of the library. For example, oftentimes, newspapers and magazines are only available for circulation after the month in which they were published; in the meantime, the item is only available for in-library use. Therefore, it may be advantageous for the library to have digital access to the newspaper or magazine to serve the widest audience of readers.

IMPORTANT GENERAL SOURCES

Current News

Current news can be accessed in a variety of ways. For the most recent news, patrons and librarians can browse print newspapers and magazines or consult websites for major news publications. If the patron wants access to a wider array of publications, they may consult news aggregator sites, such as *Google News*, which display current headlines from a wide array of news sites and allow patrons the option to search by keyword and browse specific sources and topics. *Google News* allows users to search by topic, location, and source. Additionally, one can create a Google account and "favorite" articles and save search criteria. Furthermore, *Google News* can curate stories and sources based on search histories and reading habits. While this is a very easy way to access the news, it should be noted that the article links that appear in the search results redirect the reader to the news source, which may require a subscription to access the full-text story.

The websites for subscription-based newspapers like *The New York Times* and *The Wall Street Journal* typically provide access to current and older articles. Users can search by author, topic, date, or subject. Local and regional newspapers often have electronic access as well, although these websites may have limited access to older articles and the search functions may be less sophisticated. As mentioned earlier, the websites for traditional print publications often include a combination of free and subscriber-based content; if the needed information is not freely available, librarians can consult a subscription-based newspaper database.

America's News from Newsbank provides access to 3,000 full-text sources on recent and current news, including newswire articles and broadcast transcripts. Additionally, it provides access to the largest collection of obituaries and death notices, both of which can be difficult to find on the Internet. NewsBank's *Access World News* contains more than 528 million current and archived articles from 172 countries, as well as add-on databases for local news, such as the Boston Metro Collection and the Los Angeles Metro Collection. Users can search by topic, special report, region, date, and type of news source and create a personal account to save articles.

EBSCO's *Newspaper Source Plus* has twenty-eight million full-text articles from over 1,500 newspapers. Users can perform a basic or advanced search, and full-text articles are available in HTML format and as pdfs. Notably, *Newspaper Source Plus* has an image collection, so one can search for historical and current photos of people, places, maps, and flags in black and white or color. EBSCO also offers *Regional Business News*, which provides full-text coverage for more than seventy U.S. and Canadian business publications, including *The Washington Post* and *PR Newswire US*. Resources in *Regional Business News* include news transcripts, trade publications, magazines, and newswires.

ProQuest's *Recent Newspapers* provides digital editions of news from the late 2000s to the present, minus a three-month embargo, and includes over fifty digitized editions of the most-requested newspapers. *Recent Newspapers* is both browsable and fully searchable at page level. Newspaper titles can be purchased regionally or individually. ProQuest also offers *Global Newsstream*, which provides global, contemporary news coverage from more than 2,500 sources, including newspapers, wire feeds, blogs, podcasts, and websites. *Global Newsstream* provides access to same-day publication on over 250 titles, article translations for 13 languages, and a multi-lingual interface supporting 18 different languages.

Historical Newspapers

While some resources provide access to contemporary news, other resources provide access to historical news articles, including older editions of existing publications as well as publications that have been discontinued. ProQuest's *Historical Newspapers* offers the complete text of newspapers like *The Chicago Tribune* and *The New York Times* going back to their inception. Users can search or browse by keyword, publication, date, and location. Users can also limit by document type, like birth notices, advertisements, and classifieds. Libraries can subscribe to the entire database, regional collections, or specific titles. ProQuest also offers access to historical newspaper databases *Black Newspapers*, *American Jewish Newspapers*, and *Chinese Newspapers Collection*.

Newspapers.com Library Edition, also distributed by ProQuest, offers access to partial and complete content from over 4,000 U.S. and global newspapers with coverage from the 1700s to the 2000s. Users can browse publications and perform basic or advanced searches, although search functions are somewhat limited and require the user to understand and perform their own Boolean searching. The most valuable aspect of this database is the option to "clip" and save articles.

NewsBank offers *America's Historical Newspapers*, which provides more than 1,100 fully searchable newspapers from all fifty states dated from 1690 through 1922. In addition to searching by article type and keywords, users can narrow down results by U.S. presidency and/or historic era. Articles can be printed or saved digitally.

Google Newspaper Archive provides a freely available selection of digitized, historical newspapers. From 2008 to 2011, Google scanned almost one million pages from 2,000 global newspapers. Although the company shut down the project, the database is still available to access. *Google Newspaper Archive* offers very limited search options: one can search by newspaper title or topic. Additionally, some of the scans are shoddy, or were scanned without the use of optical character recognition software, making it impossible to search the text. Nevertheless, this free service is worthwhile because it provides access to many small newspapers from around the globe and offers shareable links (Keller 2011).

The Library of Congress's freely available *Chronicling America: Historic American Newspapers* has a digitized selection of newspapers from 1789 to 1963. The plethora of newspapers may feel overwhelming, but one can search for ethnic newspapers or narrow the search by language, making this one of the more inclusive newspaper databases. Articles can be downloaded as text, pdf, or JPEG.

Newspaper Indexes

When searching for older and/or specific articles, newspaper indexes are valuable tools, especially since not all newspapers have been digitized in their entirety. Although the index will not give access to the full-text newspaper article, it will direct one to the original news article by publication title and date. Some newspaper indexes provide an alphabetical list of news articles organized by general subject headings or noteworthy names, while others are searchable by keyword.

Elephind is a freely accessible index that has links to digitized articles from over three million newspapers around the world. The goal of *Elephind* is to centralize all historical newspapers into one database, eliminating the need to visit each site. While *Elephind* itself does not have the digitized newspaper, it directs users to the newspaper site that does. Similarly, the *International Coalition on Newspapers* (*ICON*) provides links to past, present, and prospective digitization projects of historical newspapers. As stated on its site, the purpose of *ICON* is to focus on "digital conversion efforts, not full-text collections of current news sources." Additionally, genealogy websites, like *Ancestry.com*, often have newspaper indexes.

Perhaps the best place to find a list of indexes is the Library of Congress's *Chronicling America*, noted previously. Their website provides a table with links to the newspaper index archive, with dates available, and stating whether there is access to a full-text article. Additionally, its *U.S. Newspaper Directory* (1690–present) can help a researcher identify a title and see where the newspaper or index is located.

Broadcasts and Transcripts

For patrons who prefer to watch or listen to news, free video and radio options abound. In addition to tuning in on their home televisions and radios, patrons can access current and archived video and audio news via program websites and through sites specializing in videos and podcasts. In some cases, these sites also provide transcripts of programs that can be used by patrons with hearing disabilities or for keyword searching.

Perhaps the most popular site to search for news videos is *YouTube*. While not necessarily created to be a news platform, many news outlets have *YouTube* channels where they upload live content and/or broadcasts that were recently aired. The Internet Archive offers access to U.S. news shows through its *TV News Archive*. A basic search yields results that can be refined by news program, TV producer, year, language, and topic. Furthermore, *TV News Archive* has special collections that consolidate videos on a specific topic into one location. The Internet Archive also has a collection of news and public affairs radio programs. Many of these video and radio clips are public domain and can be downloaded. Some news outlets have posted historical news content. The Associated Press's *AP Archive* has 1.7 million global video news stories dating from 1895.

American Archive of Public Media, a collaboration between the Library of Congress and WGBH Media Library & Archives, hosts a collection of public radio and television content. In addition to virtual exhibits and special collections, users can easily search by one of their suggested categories; "news," "global affairs," "government," and "public affairs" are just some of the topics for finding video and radio news clips. Additionally, the website has a map of the United States that locates which organizations contribute to the site. *American Archive of Public Media* does provide access to transcripts, but these are largely limited to the media that is already hosted on their website.

Vanderbilt Television News Archive has over one million records of regularly scheduled newscasts from *ABC*, *CBS*, *NBC*, *CNN*, and *Fox News* from 1968 to present. Transcripts are available for some newscasts. Media can be lent out to anyone for a service fee, although it is not a nominal cost. However, colleges and universities can become subscribers to give students access. Researchers can visit and access the entire archives in Nashville, Tennessee, at Vanderbilt University.

C-SPAN, founded in 1979, provides unedited coverage of congressional proceedings, and the *C-SPAN Video Library* is an invaluable resource. The *Library* hosts every program aired on *C-SPAN* since 1987; nearly 250,000 hours of content can be easily searched by date, organization, people, topic, or legislative bill. The site has program transcripts as well as extensive indexes to make searching user friendly. All of the content is free for research and educational purposes.

Transcripts for many television and radio news programs can be found in subscription databases, where they can be searched by keyword, program, and date. *Nexis Uni* has television and radio transcripts from *ABC*, *CBS*, *CNN*, *NBC*, *NPR*, and more, while *Factiva* indexes transcripts for *ABC*, *BBC*, *CBS*, *CNBC*, *CNN*, *Fox News*, and *NPR*. *NewsBank* has transcripts from over 500 sources.

Images

They say that a picture is worth a thousand words, and in this digital world there is no shortage of images. Nearly all news websites have a section of photojournalism. Websites like *Reuters*, *BBC News*, and *The New York Times* allow readers to see curated albums from news stories or stand-alone photo stories. Librarians should caution patrons that these images are not necessarily free for use. When looking at the photos, it is important to review copyright restrictions and terms of use listed on the website before sharing.

Other news images are available for purchase through websites, like *Getty Images* and *AP Images*. Images can be searched by title or topic, browsed by collection, or located by a tagged subject heading. Images can be purchased individually or in bulk, although they are not inexpensive and copyright restrictions still apply. Nevertheless, these websites are valuable as the images typically accompany descriptive captions that can be useful for context and research purposes.

Fact-Check Websites

With all of the different sources online and in print, it can be difficult to discern what is true and what is skewed, even after using the evaluation guidelines outlined in this chapter. In moments like this, it is helpful to use a third-party source such as a fact-check website. A credible fact-check resource should be nonpartisan and not beholden to any financial institutions or advertising companies. Additionally, it should use skilled journalists or researchers who can access credible sources.

There are a number of websites that check on the validity of political news and statements made by elected officials. *Politifact.com* won the 2009 Pulitzer Prize for National Reporting of the 2008 U.S. election. Their website rates the validity of statements made by elected officials. Additionally, the site has specific sections by topic, region, and people. Most notable is the "Truth-O-Meter," which rates statements on a truth scale, with "pants on fire!" being the most factually incorrect. *FactCheck.org* is a nonpartisan, nonprofit "consumer advocate" that focuses on the factual accuracy of U.S. politics by reviewing debates, speeches, television ads, interviews, and news releases. The site also has a section called "Viral Spiral," which debunks stories and rumors that spread on the Internet.

For those who want to bulk up on fact-checking skills and journalism knowhow, *Poynter*, from Poynter Institute for Media Studies, a non-profit school for journalism, is a great resource. The website provides information and updates about technology and tools used in digital journalism, ethics and trust in the media, and reports from different investigative journalism projects. The website also offers a free course, *Hands-On Fact-Checking: A Short Course*, that provides ninety minutes of content about identifying reliable sources and handling misinformation. It can be taken as a self-directed course or used as a classroom resource for teachers.

Climate Feedback is hosted by a network of scientists throughout the world who respond to claims about climate change. Scientists review articles that are published in major media outlets, discussing the accuracy of the claims and the interpretations of data. There is also a "claim reviews" section that scores statements by public officials as "incorrect," "inaccurate," "misleading," "unsupported," and "mostly correct."

Although a general fact-check website, *Snopes* checks everything from political statements to famous quotes and urban legends. There is a "Fact Check" section that debunks the latest rumors, as well as another section called "Hot 50" that lists the topics that are currently most popular on the website. Users can also do a search by keyword or website URL. Each claim on *Snopes* is given a rating, a debrief of where the claim originated, and a list of sources that were used to debunk the rumor. The ratings include tags like "legend," "scam," "outdated," and "miscaptioned."

AllSides consists of a multi-partisan team that delivers "balanced news and civil discourse." Topics are linked to different news sources to give perspectives from across the political spectrum. In addition to news articles, the website has a "bias rating" for different news sources. There is even a Google Chrome extension called "Bias Finder," which rates news sites on the *AllSides* bias scale.

News Sources for Children

News sources are not only for adults; children are also interested in current events and need to know how to navigate the news. The News Literacy Project is a national education nonprofit that helps students learn to evaluate news sources. The organization, in partnership with the Facebook Journalism Project, offers free access to *Checkology*, a virtual course for educators to help students learn to detect misinformation, evaluate biases, and critique headlines and news stories.

A variety of websites provide news for younger audiences. *TweenTribune* from the Smithsonian makes news articles readable by grade and/or Lexile level. Users can browse by topic, and articles can also be read in Spanish. However, the website is a curated selection of news articles for each education level and users are limited in their search options.

DOGO News organizes news by category, current events, student grade level, and popularity. Users can create an account and comment on articles, making it an interactive platform for children to engage with others and share their perspectives. Additionally, there are reviews and ratings for the latest books and movies.

TIME for Kids allows young users to read articles on current events and trends by grade and Lexile level. The website is a customizable experience that lets readers select articles to be displayed in Spanish or read aloud. Additionally, select words are highlighted in articles; when clicked, a pop-up box appears with the word's definition, an audio of the pronunciation, and a related image.

CONCLUSION

There have been many dramatic changes in how news is created, accessed, and shared, and these sources will undoubtedly continue to evolve. From newspapers, radio, and TV to podcasts, live broadcasts, apps, databases, and aggregators, the options feel limitless. As news sources have become more prevalent and varied, the challenge of discerning fact from fiction has also increased. As reference librarians, it is important not only to stay current with new platforms but also to be vigilant on journalistic practices and changes. In addition, librarians have a responsibility to teach patrons how to find credible sources and evaluate information. Although this work may seem daunting, it is actually an incredible opportunity to show that no matter how many news source adaptations and revisions occur, there is always a reliable resource: the reference librarian.

REFERENCES

American Press Institute. n.d. "What Is the Purpose of Journalism?" https://www.americanpressinstitute.org/journalism-essentials/what-is-journalism/purpose-journalism/.

Atske, Sara. 2018. "Americans Still Prefer Watching to Reading the News—And Mostly Still Through Television." *Pew Research Center's Journalism Project*. Last modified December 3, 2018. http://www.journalism.org/2018/12/03/americans-still-prefer-watching-to-reading-the-news-and-mostly-still-through-television/.

Burkhardt, Joanna M. 2017. "Chapter 1: History of Fake News." *Library Technology Reports* 53 (November): 5–9.

Chrypinski, Steve. 2017. "The 50th Anniversary of the Public Broadcasting Act." *Michigan Radio*. November 7, 2017. https://www.michiganradio.org/post/50th-anniversary-public-broadcasting-act.

Corwin, Victoria. 2016. "Medieval Book Production and Monastic Life." *Dartmouth Ancient Books Lab*. Last modified May 24, 2016. https://sites.dartmouth.edu/ancientbooks/2016/05/24/medieval-book-production-and-monastic-life.

Davis, Wynne. 2016. "Fake or Real? How to Self-Check the News and Get the Facts." *All Tech Considered: Tech, Culture, and Connection.* National Public Radio. December 5, 2016. https://www.npr.org/sections/alltechconsidered/2016/12/05/503581220/fake-or-real-how-to-self-check-the-news-and-get-the-facts.

Ingram, David, and Peter Henshall. 1991. *The News Manual: A Professional Resource for Journalists and the Media.* Poroman Press. https://www.thenewsmanual.net/index.htm.

International Federation of Library Associations and Institutions. 2017. *How to Spot Fake News* (digital image). *Wikimedia Commons.* https://commons.wikimedia.org/wiki/File:How_to_Spot_Fake_News.pdf.

Keller, Jared. 2011. "Google Shuts Down Newspaper Archive Project." *The Atlantic Monthly,* May 22. https://www.theatlantic.com/technology/archive/2011/05/google-shuts-down-newspaper-archive-project/239239/.

Lurie, Hannah J. 2012. "An Abridged History of Network Television News." *Humphrey Fellows at Cronkite School of Journalism and Mass Communication—ASU.* Last modified October 29, 2012. http://cronkitehhh.jmc.asu.edu/blog/2012/10/an-abridged-version-of-the-history-of-network-television-news.

Mickelson, Sig. 1998. *The Decade that Shaped Television News: CBS in the 1950s.* Westport, CT: Praeger.

Ohlheiser, Abby. 2016. "This Is How Facebook's Fake-news Writers Make Money." *The Washington Post.* November 18. https://www.washingtonpost.com/news/the-intersect/wp/2016/11/18/this-is-how-the-internets-fake-news-writers-make-money/?utm_term=.b8b4c040bff1.

Pettegree, Andrew. 2014. "Print, Politics & Prosperity." *History Today* 64 (February): 11–17.

Ponce De Leon, Charles L. 2016. *That's the Way It Is: A History of Television News in America.* Chicago: University of Chicago Press.

Sanburn, Josh. 2011. "A Brief History of Digital News." *TIME.* February 1. http://content.time.com/time/business/article/0,8599,2045682,00.html.

Society of Professional Journalists. 2014. "SPJ Code of Ethics." Last modified September 6, 2014. https://www.spj.org/ethicscode.asp.

Understanding Media and Culture: An Introduction to Mass Communication. 2016. Minneapolis, MN: Open Textbook Library.

LIST OF SOURCES

20/20. https://abcnews.go.com/2020/.

ABC. https://abc.go.com/.

Access World News. Naples, FL: NewsBank. https://www.newsbank.com/libraries/public/solutions/us-national/americas-news. Subscription required.

AllSides. https://www.allsides.com/.

America Online (AOL). New York, NY: Verizon Media. https://www.aol.com/.

America's Historical Newspapers. Naples, FL: NewsBank. https://www.readex.com/content/americas-historical-newspapers. Subscription required.

America's News. Naples, FL: NewsBank. https://www.newsbank.com/libraries/public/solutions/us-national/americas-news. Subscription required.

American Archive of Public Media. Library of Congress and WGBH. http://americanarchive.org/.

American Jewish Newspapers. Ann Arbor, MI: ProQuest. https://www.proquest.com/products-services/hnp_ajn_shtml.html. Subscription required.

Ancestry.com. Lehi, UT: Ancestry LLC. https://www.ancestry.com/. Subscription required.

AP Archive. http://www.aparchive.com/.

AP Images. http://www.apimages.com/.

Associated Press. https://apnews.com/

BBC News. http://www.bbc.com/news.

Bias Finder. https://chrome.google.com/webstore/detail/bias-finder/jojjlkfeofgcjeanbpghcapjcccbakop?hl=en-US.

Black Newspapers. Ann Arbor, MI: ProQuest. https://www.proquest.com/products-services/histnews-bn.html. Subscription required.

CBS. https://www.cbs.com/.

C-SPAN. https://www.c-span.org/.

C-SPAN Video Library. http://www.c-spanvideo.org/about.

Checkology. The News Literacy Project. https://checkology.org/.

The Chicago Tribune. https://www.chicagotribune.com/.

Chinese Newspapers Collection. Ann Arbor, MI: ProQuest. https://www.proquest.com/products-services/hnp_cnc.html. Subscription required.

Chronicling America: Historic American Newspapers. Library of Congress. https://chroniclingamerica.loc.gov/.

Climate Feedback. https://climatefeedback.org/.

CNN. https://www.cnn.com/.

DOGO News. https://www.dogonews.com/.

Elephind. https://www.elephind.com/.

Facebook Journalism Project. https://www.facebook.com/facebookmedia/solutions/facebook-journalism-project.

FactCheck.org. Annenberg Public Policy Center. https://www.factcheck.org/.

Factiva. New York: Dow Jones & Company. https://www.dowjones.com/products/factiva/. Subscription required.

Fox News. https://www.foxnews.com/

Getty Images. https://www.gettyimages.com/.

Global Newsstream. Ann Arbor, MI: ProQuest. https://www.proquest.com/products-services/globalnewsstream.html. Subscription required.

Google Images. https://images.google.com/

Google News. https://news.google.com/.

Google Newspaper Archive. Mountain View, CA: Google. https://news.google.com/newspapers.

Hands-On Fact-Checking: A Short Course. International Fact-Checking Network at the Poynter Institute and the American Press Institute. https://www.poynter.org/shop/fact-checking/handson-factchecking/.

Hardball with Chris Matthews. https://www.msnbc.com/hardball/.

Historical Newspapers. Ann Arbor, MI: ProQuest. https://www.proquest.com/products-services/pq-hist-news.html. Subscription required.

HuffPost. New York, NY: The Huffington Post. https://www.huffingtonpost.com/.

International Coalition on Newspapers (ICON). Center for Research Libraries. http://icon.crl.edu/.

Internet Archive. https://archive.org/.

Medium. https://medium.com/.

MSNBC. https://www.msnbc.com/.

NBC. https://www.nbc.com/.

New York Times. https://www.nytimes.com/.

The News Literacy Project. https://newslit.org/.

NewsBank. Naples, FL: NewsBank Inc. https://www.newsbank.com/. Subscription required.

Newspapers.com Library Edition. Ann Arbor, MI: ProQuest. https://www.proquest.com/products-services/Newspaperscom-Library-Edition.html. Subscription required.

Newspaper Source Plus. Ipswich, MA: EBSCO. https://www.ebsco.com/products/research-databases/newspaper-source-plus. Subscription required.

Nexis Uni. New York, NY: Lexis Nexis Group. https://www.lexisnexis.com/en-us/support/nexis-uni/default.page. Subscription required.

NPR. https://www.npr.org/

PBS NewsHour. https://www.pbs.org/newshour/.
PolitiFact. Poynter Institute for Media Studies. https://www.politifact.com/.
Poynter. Poynter Institute for Media Studies. https://www.poynter.org/.
Recent Newspapers. Ann Arbor, MI: ProQuest. https://www.proquest.com/libraries/public/databases/ProQuest-Recent-Newspapers.html. Subscription required.
Regional Business News. Ipswich, MA: EBSCO. https://www.ebsco.com/products/research-databases/regional-business-news. Subscription required.
Reuters. https://www.reuters.com/.
Snopes. https://www.snopes.com/.
TIME for Kids. New York: Marc & Lynne Benioff. https://www.timeforkids.com/.
TV News Archive. The Internet Archive. https://archive.org/details/tv.
TweenTribune. Smithsonian Institute. https://www.tweentribune.com/.
U.S. Newspaper Directory. Library of Congress. https://chroniclingamerica.loc.gov/search/titles/.
Vanderbilt Television News Archive. Vanderbilt University. https://tvnews.vanderbilt.edu/. Subscription required.
Wall Street Journal. https://www.wsj.com/.
Yahoo!. http://www.yahoo.com.
YouTube. https://www.youtube.com/.

SUGGESTED READINGS

Bartlett, Bruce R. 2017. *The Truth Matters: A Citizen's Guide to Separating Facts from Lies and Stopping Fake News in Its Tracks*. California: Ten Speed Press.
At only 135 pages, this book packs in a lot of information about the changing landscape of media and journalism. Topics include learning the difference between primary and secondary sources, how to assess polls and statistics, and how to properly use Wikipedia.

Cooke, Nicole A. 2018. *Fake News and Alternative Facts: Information Literacy in a Post-truth Era*. Chicago: ALA Editions.
Cooke explains behaviors and attitudes that have contributed to the rise of fake news. Additionally, she discusses how users can identify fake news on the Internet, and how to help patrons think critically about information.

De Abreu Belinha S. 2019. *Teaching Media Literacy*. 2nd ed. Chicago: ALA Neal-Schuman.
Intended for K-12 learners, this book focuses on fake news/alternative facts and critical thinking while accessing information on a national and global level. Lesson plans and activities are included to help students understand fake news and digital literacy.

Hands-On Fact-Checking: A Short Course. International Fact-Checking Network at the Poynter Institute and the American Press Institute. https://www.poynter.org/shop/fact-checking/handson-factchecking/.
This 90-minute, self-guided course teaches learners to identify reliable sources and spot misinformation. It can be used individually or as a class lesson plan.

Hargreaves, Ian. 2014. *Journalism: A Very Short Introduction*. Oxford: Oxford University Press.
Hargreaves explores contemporary journalism, its changing landscape with digital media, how it has impacted the field, and how readers connect with the news. He also explores the civic responsibilities of journalists and the current need for Freedom of the Press.

Housand, Brian C. 2018. *Fighting Fake News!: Teaching Critical Thinking and Media Literacy in a Digital Age*. Waco, TX: Prufrock Press.
Specifically for elementary and middle school classrooms, this resource includes activities and lessons that prepare students to approach digital and media literacy with a critical eye. It goes over how to properly locate, evaluate, and share information.

Madison, Ed, and Ben DeJarnette. 2018. *Reimagining Journalism in a Post-truth World: How Late-night Comedians, Internet Trolls, and Savvy Reporters Are Transforming News.* Santa Barbara, CA: Praeger.

The authors discuss the new landscape of journalism from late-night political commentary to newspapers adapting to the digital age. They also explore ideas on contemporary journalism and the challenges that it faces.

Niblock, Sarah. 2010. *Journalism: A Beginners Guide.* Oxford: Oneworld.

Niblock talks about the fundamentals of journalism, including ethics and what challenges contemporary journalists face with digital media. She also discusses "infotainment"—the intersection of entertainment and news.

"State of the News Media." Pew Research Center. http://www.pewresearch.org/topics/state-of-the-news-media/.

This annual report provides data about how media is created, published, distributed, and utilized across different demographics in the United States. The report helps make sense of the different information sources and their impact on society.

Chapter 24

Geographical Sources

Matthew D. MacKellar

INTRODUCTION

"From the moment settlements became more permanent, and thus their natural environment made more familiar, people have named these environments and any surrounding places that were changed by their presence" (Smits 2014, 329). Geography is a practice of naming, classifying, and measuring the natural environment, and thus "geographical sources" are those that engage in this practice in different ways and for varied purposes. Geography is a diverse field that analyzes both the physical features of the earth and human activity upon the earth—but especially the interaction of these two aspects. Although humans think of themselves as analytically distinct from the earth, they are of course part of the physicality of earth, both affecting and being affected by it. Even seemingly purely abstract geographic phenomena, such as political borders, affect the usage and thus physical features of the land. Place is an essential context for all human life, events, and societies, and geographical sources seek to elucidate various aspects of this context.

With the continued process of globalization, it has become a truism to say that the world has gotten smaller. However, this does not mean that this smaller world is better known—in fact it simply increases the number of geographical questions people may have as they travel, study, interact, and do business with other people from around the world. The need to supply these interactions with accurate, timely, and helpful information has never been greater. Further, many academic specialties are becoming increasingly interdisciplinary and utilizing more geospatial analysis in their research, and thus librarians—whether generalists at an academic library or public librarians—must expand their knowledge of and skill with geographical sources in order to meet these information needs (Todd 2008, 14, 18).

USES AND CHARACTERISTICS

The subfields of geography are manifold—including physical geography, human geography, historical geography, economic geography, political geography, as well as cartography, aerial photography/remote sensing, mapping software, and geographic information systems (GIS). As such, the information needs of those seeking reference services vary widely, ranging from seeking a simple map of local environs to information regarding soil types in a distant place, to a diachronic representation of shifting political boundaries, to a representation of the distribution of wealth in the neighborhoods of an urban center. Further, users may be seeking not only to passively receive information but rather to craft their own visualizations of geospatial data using interactive mapmaking software with overlays, geographic information systems, and more.

Performing reference services with regard to geographical sources involves not only awareness of the breadth of resources available but also facility in using them in all their variety, with their particular features, strengths, and limitations. Depending on the level of knowledge of the user and their information needs, which must be ascertained through the reference interview (discussed in Chapter 3), different resources will be appropriate. For a grade school student seeking to know where Akron, Ohio, is and what other cities may be near it, use of ready-reference tools such as a gazetteer or an atlas will be sufficient. For a college student studying the hydrological patterns of the Yaak Valley in Montana, more specialized charts, maps, and GIS may be necessary. A sense of confidence in their knowledge of these various sources and their use will allow librarians to calibrate their reference services accordingly. This chapter seeks to aid in building such knowledge and confidence with regard to geographical sources and thus to enable more agile and accurate geographical reference services.

EVALUATION

As with most areas of information science in this era of digitization and the Internet, the task of geographical reference is both aided and complicated by the plethora of sources available. On the one hand, for example, because of the wide accessibility of digitized geospatial representations via the Internet, a LIDAR (light detection and ranging) project is readily available from the State of Kansas GIS Data Access & Support Center (2017); on the other hand, nearly anyone can publish findable geographical information on the Internet without the usual vetting or quality control of publishers or professional associations.

This calls for use of the classic criteria of evaluation, as discussed in Chapter 14. The *currency* of the source must be considered. Often, the date of a map or geospatial representation is present on the map itself, though usually in small print and/or at the margins of the representation. With *Google Street View* in *Google Maps*, for instance, the date of the image is in the border at the lower right edge of the image. Sometimes, adjacent images or map sets can have divergent dates, so it is important to be wary. The currency of a source is of course more important for some inquiries than others: the average property values of a neighborhood may change significantly from year to year, but the location of the mountain range outside of town will not. For historical geographical sources, currency is not the issue, but the accuracy and relevance of the date of the source for the research question is significant. As with all inquiries, a healthy degree of skepticism may be warranted: charts and maps may be misidentified in terms of their year of provenance, so this information should be evaluated in corroboration with other criteria discussed here.

The *authority* behind a source must also be considered, and here the librarian has the fortunate circumstance that many geographical sources come from long-standing respected institutions such as the National Geographic Society, U.S. Geological Survey, and Rand McNally. Information from unknown sources can still be quite helpful and accurate, but it should of course be cross-checked with other sources, especially if the question at hand is weighty or future research hinges upon it.

As with the other criteria, knowing the user and their information needs is crucial when evaluating the *scope* and *comprehensiveness* of a source. A simple atlas might be comprehensive enough if the location of a city is all that is needed; however, if the inquiry is about the number of cities and towns in a given county, then a more thorough and detailed map would be needed. Likewise, the scope of the resource should be suitable for a task. A gazetteer can supply the proper contemporary spelling of a place name, but a geographical encyclopedia might be necessary to ascertain some of the history and relevance of that place, as an encyclopedia is intended to offer a broader range of information than a gazetteer.

SELECTION

The cardinal rule when it comes to selection of reference materials for a collection is the needs of the user group. This will help with selecting what sources and how many should be purchased in print for ready reference, whether free online sources will be adequate or subscription-based electronic sources need to be purchased, and so on. A consideration of the ever-finite resources of money for purchasing, storage space (both physical and electronic), and staff time for cataloging the materials must be made. If the library or information center serves an historical purpose or has many users interested in historical geography, then keeping antiquarian maps and atlases may be warranted; if users are more interested in contemporary geospatial research, investment in subscription-based GIS resources is probably the better choice. If physical space is limited, the selector might have to be quite judicious in selection, since many geographical sources tend to be oversized and/or bulky, such as paper maps and atlases. It is also important to consider what resources are readily available via other local institutions and consortia, though many geographical sources may not be eligible for interlibrary loans, due to their size and handling requirements.

Another selection consideration is which format might be most helpful for the user group. Electronic versions of maps, charts, and atlases may allow for customization by the user, adding or subtracting relevant layers of information, and saving pdfs or JPEGs of specific maps. This ease of access and customization is certainly a strength of electronic versions, but often print maps and atlases are easier to read, given the size and level of detail of these sources. Scrolling around a detailed, large map on a computer screen can sometimes be akin to exploring a field by looking at one's feet, whereas a high-quality print of a map on a large sheet can give the whole picture of the geographical situation and help the patron make connections between parts of that map and judge relative distances. With regard to gazetteers, dictionaries, and encyclopedias, electronic versions offer greater searchability, while print versions are easier to browse and make serendipitous discoveries.

Research suggests that local and regional materials are much more frequently sought than geographical materials that cover states, regions, or countries that are farther away (Scarletto 2011, 134). Information needs about more distant locales might be adequately met via free online resources. Thus, a wise collection development strategy would be to maintain more sources on local regions, even at the expense of the breadth of the collection. It makes sense to have a good print topographical map of the immediate region ready for the frequent questions that can be answered with this at-hand tool, rather than trying to have a comprehensive set of maps for every area on the globe or trying to guess which distant geographical areas might happen to be in demand.

The flip side of selection is deselection, or weeding. Studying the usage patterns of one's community can help with these decisions as well. Resources frequently consulted should be kept readily at hand, of course; those with low usage yet historic or intellectual value could be sent to long-term storage; high usage, vulnerable resources might be good candidates for digitization efforts. (Here, one thinks especially of maps that need to be unfolded to be used, as every unfolding and refolding weakens the paper and increases the risk of tearing.) It is also important to consider which items in the collection are relatively unique and might serve a legacy function. Such items might be worth preserving even if they are little used, or it might be advisable to digitize them so as to increase the accessibility of such rare sources. Since digitizing geographical sources often involves large format scanners and increased data storage space, judicious decisions must be made in this area (Scarletto 2011, 125, 135).

IMPORTANT GENERAL SOURCES

The variety and number of geographical sources are immense, but there are certain general sources which are an essential part of any ready-reference collection and can handily answer a good portion of the standard geographical reference questions. These include gazetteers, thesauri, dictionaries, and encyclopedias. While the distinctions between these three types of sources can grow a little fuzzy, they each serve a purpose and knowing these terms can aid in the discoverability of such resources.

Gazetteers

Gazetteers are alphabetical lists or directories of geographic places and features, often used in conjunction with an atlas or a map. In those instances, they provide further details about these items, such as alternate spellings, distances between points, population size, and presence of recreational features. Other gazetteers are not tied to specific maps or atlases and thus serve as a kind of geographical dictionary, providing brief information about geographical entities. While print gazetteers can be easily browsed, electronic gazetteers usually offer a robust set of search options, enabling the discovery of specific information such as proper spelling, variant names, coordinates, and elevation.

The *GEOnet Names Server* (*GNS*) is an official, searchable repository of geographic names outside of the United States, as sanctioned by the U.S. Board on

Geographic Names (US BGN) and hosted by the National Geospatial Intelligence Agency. It was started in 1994 for the use of the federal government and public information and contains over twelve million names, including variants and non-Roman script spellings, for over seven million geographic features. The "GNS Search—Text Based Page" supports extensive advanced search options, such as searching within a given country, historical records, levels of population, type of locality (drainage basin, battlefield, etc.), type of vegetation, hydrographic features, and undersea features. Search results display the name; whether the name is officially approved, unverified, provisional, or variant; the administrative division of the locality; latitude and longitude; Military Grid Reference System (MGRS) coordinates; feature code; and an option to display the locality in *Google Maps* or *MapQuest*. Note that the "Open Geospatial Consortium (OGC) Viewer Page," which is supposed to provide graphical map search options, has persistent functionality and time out failures as of the time of this writing.

The *Geographic Names Information System* (*GNIS*) serves a very similar function as the *GNS*, except that it covers the United States, Antarctica, and undersea features and is hosted by the U.S. Geological Survey. As a directory and repository of official names for geographical features in the United States, it also includes variant spellings and a "Feature ID," a unique identifier for each geographical feature. The search form allows inquiry by a number of access points including name, state, county, Feature ID, feature class, elevation, and BGN decision date. Search results provide feature name, Feature ID, class, county, state, latitude and longitude, elevation, map, and entry date. Specific entries also provide history, description, variant names, and citation information. It is worth noting that, due to budgetary constraints, some cultural or manmade feature names are no longer updated in the *GNIS* as of October 1, 2014.

A flagship gazetteer tending more toward encyclopedic thoroughness is *The Columbia Gazetteer of the World*, an electronic, fee-based resource containing over 170,000 entries on physical geography, industry, trade, demography, agriculture, history, transportation, and variant names and spellings—all written, edited, and updated by geographical scholars. Though it prides itself on extensive coverage of all the countries of the world, even small ones such as Djibouti and Andorra, it focuses extensively on large countries, with 38,745 entries for the United States, including all incorporated places and many unincorporated locales. It contains a glossary of geographical terms, an alphabetical browsing option, and a quick search option to search either the place names of entries or in the full text of the entries. It should be noted that the place name search uses the search terms in the exact order they are given, whereas the full-text search will find the search terms in any order that they appear. The advanced search offers easy-to-use select/deselect options to limit the search by type of place (ancient city, bayou, state park, etc.), continent, country, latitudinal and longitudinal coordinates, and various statistical criteria (area, elevation, population, etc.). Search results are returned listing the name, type of place, country, and region, which helps eliminate any ambiguity in results. Specific entries list the type of place, location, coordinates, pronunciation, description and history, citation suggestions, and options to print, e-mail, or save the result.

Thesauri

Geographical names can be confusing for a number of reasons, including names that are homonyms, exonyms (names used by outsiders), endonyms (names used by locals); transliteration issues; transcription problems; and obsolescence (Smits 2014, 330). Names may change because of historical and political changes. Especially in the period of decolonization in the second half of the 20th century, many names changed in formerly colonized locales such as Africa, South America, and Asia. For instance, the geographical entity formerly known as Southern Rhodesia became modern-day Zimbabwe after gaining independence from its British colonizers. Geographical thesauri exist to connect differing names for related geographical entities and to disambiguate entities with the same or similar names, showing the semantic relationships between terms.

The Getty Thesaurus of Geographic Names began in 1987 as an effort by the J. Paul Getty Trust to compile and synthesize geographical terminology into a controlled vocabulary to aid in cataloging, retrieval, and research. This global thesaurus contains over four million administrative names and physical features, modern and historical terms, and seeks to show equivalence between synonyms and hierarchical relationships between geographical wholes and parts. Like the *GNIS*, the *Getty Thesaurus* uses unique numeric identifiers in order to integrate linked data. It references published sources so that its authority is transparent and it is committed to being a fee-free resource. Entry results list the name, place type, numeric identifiers, latitude and longitude, variant names, hierarchical position (its relation to larger geographical entities of which it is a part), and its source(s) of information.

Dictionaries and Encyclopedias

Numerous quality geographical dictionaries and encyclopedias exist. However, there is little consensus as to the top geographical books. In fact, one study found that 86.9 percent of geography books were listed only once in the geography *LibGuides* consulted (Dougherty 2013, 265–67). Still, these are some recommended titles to start with:

Merriam-Webster's Geographical Dictionary has been around since 1949 and is currently in its third edition. It contains over 48,000 entries and gives spelling, variants, pronunciation, location, and other essential information. It focuses on the United States and Canada but aims to provide entries on locations and features of the most interest to general readers. It contains a quick reference glossary, helpful for rapidly ascertaining what an "atoll" is, for instance, and a useful list of geographical terms in other languages, such as "dong" being Vietnamese for "plain," which can add levels of meaning to place names.

The *GIS Dictionary* is a free, online listing of brief definitions of terms related to GIS, cartography, geographic data, and software. It is hosted by Esri (Environmental Systems Research Institute) and can be browsed alphabetically or searched with a simple search box that also returns other possible matches, allowing some degree of fuzzy searching. It is a streamlined, quick, free source for definitions related to GIS.

For more in-depth entries about broader topics in geography, rather than a directory of place names, *A Dictionary of Geography* by Susan Mayhew (2015) is a well-respected source. While it only contains about 3,100 entries, it covers both physical and human geography, delving into broader concepts such as meteorology, ecology, and population, along with cartography and place names. It is a helpful ready-reference source for finding out about "biometeorology" or "territorial seas."

If this source takes a small step along the continuum between dictionaries and encyclopedias, the *Encyclopedia of Human Geography* takes a full step. It contains

300 entries written by scholars in the important area of human geography, an interdisciplinary field exploring the interactions between humans and physical space and places, involving economic, urban, political, and cultural geographies, as well as geographic theory, cartography, and GIS. While entries are arranged alphabetically, a readers' guide presents these entries by subdiscipline, giving topical coherence. This is a useful resource if questions about topics like "suburbanization" or "diffusion" are sought. All entries provide a list of related subjects and suggested reading for further research.

The *Encyclopedia of Geography* provides 1,224 essays in six volumes that aim to reasonably capture the current state, significant ideas, and different methodologies in the modern-day study of geography. As with the previous source, in addition to the alphabetical listing of entries, a readers' guide groups the entries according to physical geography, human geography, nature and society, GIS, history of geography, and people, organizations, and movements. Entries include numerous pictures, illustrations, and charts, as well as lists of related subjects and further readings. Encyclopedias such as these can bridge the gap between simple listings, such as those found in dictionaries and gazetteers, and complex monographs or journal articles. As such, they can provide reliable, in-depth articles for those who are neither beginners nor geographical scholars.

MAPS

Maps are probably the resource people first think of when they consider geographical sources. As has been seen already, they are certainly not the only sources of geographical information, but they remain central to the pursuit of geographical knowledge, both for their ability to concatenate a lot of information in a contained visual space and because so much of what they aim to depict is visual and spatial. This means that geographical data can translate more readily to maps than other kinds of visualizations that depict nonspatial data. However, this does not mean that maps are somehow a one-to-one representation of the physical world. All maps are crafted artifacts that choose which data to include and which to omit, the methods of symbolizing geographical information, and the perspective of their portrayal, including boundaries, scale, and map projection. Further, maps do not just exist in a vacuum; they are created by specific people and organizations for specific purposes, ranging from educational to recreational and commercial. As with any other text, one must be aware of the rhetoric and purposes behind a map: What is it trying to accomplish? What is it trying to persuade the viewer to believe? What are its possible biases or oversights? For examples, see Figure 24.1 and Box 24.1.

An important principle of map usage and interpretation is to recognize the different types of maps—many of which will be discussed here—and to use them only for their intended purpose. Thus, the map in the visitors' guide for a national park should be used to locate the visitors' center, major roadways, or attractions within the park but not for backcountry trail navigation. On the other hand, a *Trails Illustrated* topographic map would be ideal for navigating a backcountry trail, but it should not be used to locate the visitors' center, as the symbol for this feature is likely to be out of scale and possibly located with a degree of imprecision so as not to cover over any of the symbols more central to the map's purpose, such as contour lines or trail indicators.

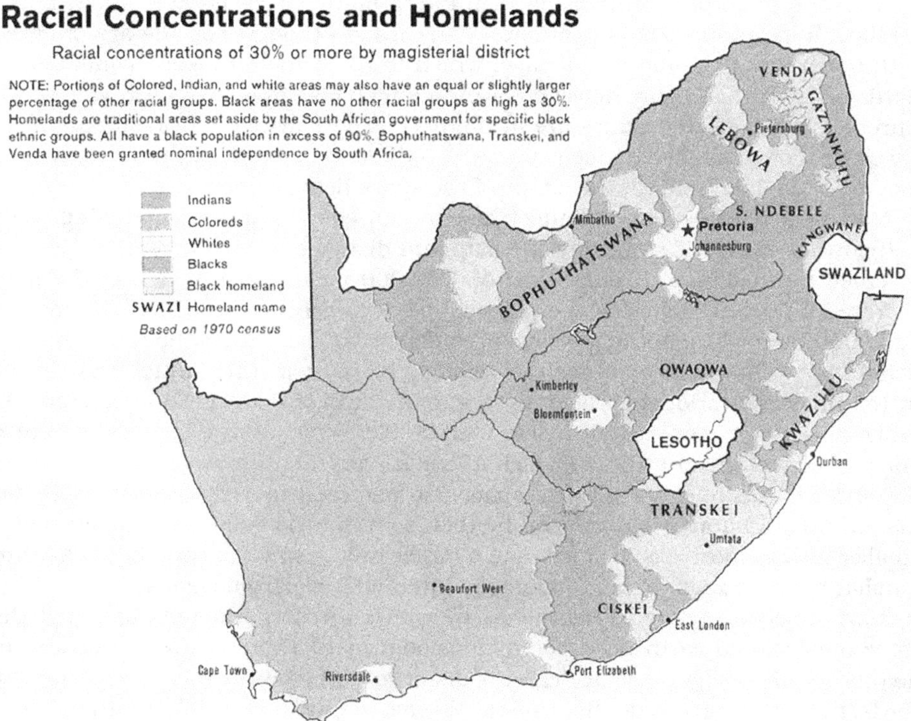

Figure 24.1 "Racial Concentrations and Homelands 1979," from the U.S. Central Intelligence Agency, from Map No. 503971. In this map of South Africa, note the outmoded language ("Coloreds") and ideology of racial control, in which only some areas are designated as "homelands" for the indigenous Black population. Courtesy of the University of Texas Libraries, The University of Texas at Austin.

Box 24.1 Activity: Map Bias

Consider the map found at the following URL, which is titled "African Religions and Missions 1913" from the *Literary and Historical Atlas of Africa and Australasia* by J.G. Bartholomew (Courtesy of the University of Texas Libraries, The University of Texas at Austin.): http://legacy.lib.utexas.edu/maps/historical/africa_religion_1913.jpg

Discuss the following questions:

1. All maps select certain information to highlight at the expense of other information. What information and perspective does this map emphasize?
2. What useful historical geographical information does this map provide, and how does that reflect the era of its creation?
3. What biases might you notice in the terminology chosen?
4. Do you think it is possible to produce a map that is without bias in its visual and terminological presentation? Why or why not?

A second important principle of map interpretation and usage is knowing the symbols and perspective of the map. Many maps—though not all—are oriented with north being the top of the page, which leads to the erroneous conflation of north being "up" and may reflect a Euro-American bias in mapmaking, since both Europe and the United States are in the northern hemisphere. It is important to check the compass rose to determine which direction is north on the map, which may be altered to better fit the shape of the space being depicted.

Map scale can also greatly affect how a map conveys information. Map scale is the ratio between distance on the map and distance in the physical world represented by that map. A map scale of 1:50,000 means that 1 inch of the map represents 50,000 inches in the physical world, or, conversely, that the map is 1/50,000ths the size of the physical area depicted. The greater the ratio, the less detail will be shown, as every inch on the map has to depict that much more space in the physical world, thus leading to streamlining of details. Thus, a 1:24,000 scale map will be more detailed than a 1:100,000 scale map. Maps will often also show scale with a bar scale, in which a length shown on the bar scale represents the specified distance in physical space—so one inch may represent a mile, for instance. Patrons may be confused by this, so it may be helpful to explain that a smaller ratio is more "zoomed in" than a larger ratio, as most users these days are familiar with the zoom in/out options on interactive electronic maps.

Map projection refers to the means by which the map attempts to depict the three-dimensional earth on a two-dimensional map. There is no perfect way to do this, so all maps have some degree of distortion, which is further exacerbated by the fact that the earth is neither completely smooth nor spherical but rather exhibits topography and bulges around the equator due to the rotation of the earth. Maps attempt to show equivalence (equal area), conformality (shape), distance, and direction. Depending on the purpose of the map, particular map projections may be chosen that maximize one property of the map at the expense of others. For instance, a Mercator projection is conformal, preserving true direction and thus being useful for navigational maps. However, the areas closer to poles are distorted in size, thus making Greenland and Antarctica appear disproportionately large. On the other hand, the Albers equal area projection is conical, keeping the meridians (markers of longitude) straight but curving the parallels (markers of latitude). This projection provides accurate size relationships and directions over regions but is rather distorting when picturing the entire world. In other words, every map projection is a trade-off between vying factors, so it is helpful to be aware of these compromises and possible distortions, especially when there is a possible mismatch between the purpose of a map and the projection used. It is standard cartographic practice to denote the map projection used somewhere on the map, usually by the legend or bar scale. For a detailed description of the physics of map projection, the various standard projections, and their strengths and weaknesses, helpfully illustrated throughout, please consult the entry "Map Projections" in the *Encyclopedia of Geography* described previously (Hill 2010, 1843–49).

Lastly, most maps also have a symbol legend, tailored to the needs of that map, to serve as a concise way to mark information on the map. While there tends to be some standardization of symbols across maps, this cannot be assumed, and frequent reference to the legend is advisable. In addition, many maps also include latitude and longitude coordinates and/or Universal Transverse Mercator (UTM) notations. UTM is a two-dimensional coordinate system developed in the 20th century that divides the earth into 60 zones of 6 degrees longitude each. Given the transverse Mercator projection used, which is conformal, there is very little distortion within these regions that are narrow from east to west but large from north to south. Usually, the map details will specify which coordinate system is in use, with the numbers along the edges of the map often being color coordinated.

Maps cannot portray everything about a physical space and the geospatial data relevant to it, and if a given map tried to do so it would be rendered essentially useless by the density and clutter of vying information and accompanying symbols. Therefore, maps are developed for specific purposes, thus limiting the scope of a given map to a reasonable set of data to portray. Some of the major types of maps one is likely to encounter and need in the course of performing geographical reference services are detailed in the following sections.

Topographic Maps

Topographic maps are those that seek to reflect the reality that the earth's surface is not perfectly flat by depicting vertical variations through various symbols on the map, including relief shading and contour intervals. Of course, this is particularly relevant for areas in which there are dramatic vertical variations—such as mountainous regions—or for purposes which require a close knowledge of topography, such as maps for hiking or hydrological maps for tracing water flow and drainage basins. Topographic maps are most notable for the presence of contour lines, which connect places of equal elevation and thus cumulatively build a three-dimensional picture of land. Usually, every fifth contour line is labeled with its particular elevation, and the map specifies the standard elevation difference between lines, known as the contour interval. Depending on the steepness of the terrain, the contour interval of a map can vary widely from 5 feet per line to 100 feet per line, so it is vital for interpreting a topographic map to be aware of the contour interval. It takes some practice to quickly and accurately read a topographic map and be able to identify features such as ridges, valleys, and peaks: narrowly spaced contour lines depict very steep terrain, whereas widely spaced contour lines depict more gradual elevation changes. Many topographic maps also use relief shading to enhance the three-dimensional appearance of the map, which can make them easier to read (see Figure 24.2).

Topographic maps are often used for trail maps, for obvious reasons. The National Geographic Society produces and sells the *Trails Illustrated* map series, which consists of over 250 different topographic maps in mainly recreational areas of the United States, though some maps "spill over" into Canada and Mexico. These maps are vetted for accuracy by local land managers and are printed on waterproof, tear-resistant paper, making them ideal for backcountry use—or repeated reference use. One helpful tip when trying to determine distances along trails—which rarely move in straight lines—is to measure the trail length on the map with a flexible material like string that can follow the curves of the trail and then hold that length of string up against the bar scale for measurement.

Prior to 2009, the United States Geological Survey (USGS) produced handcrafted topographic maps based on field work and aerial photography, but now the *US Topo* project produces topographic quadrangles—some 57,000 of them in total—from the digital GIS databases of the *National Map* and is thus is able to update its topographic maps of the United States on a three-year cycle and make them available free of charge from the *National Map* website. Over time, additional data layers are added to the maps, such as road data, National Forest boundaries, state and county boundaries, timber coverage, railroad tracks, and shaded relief

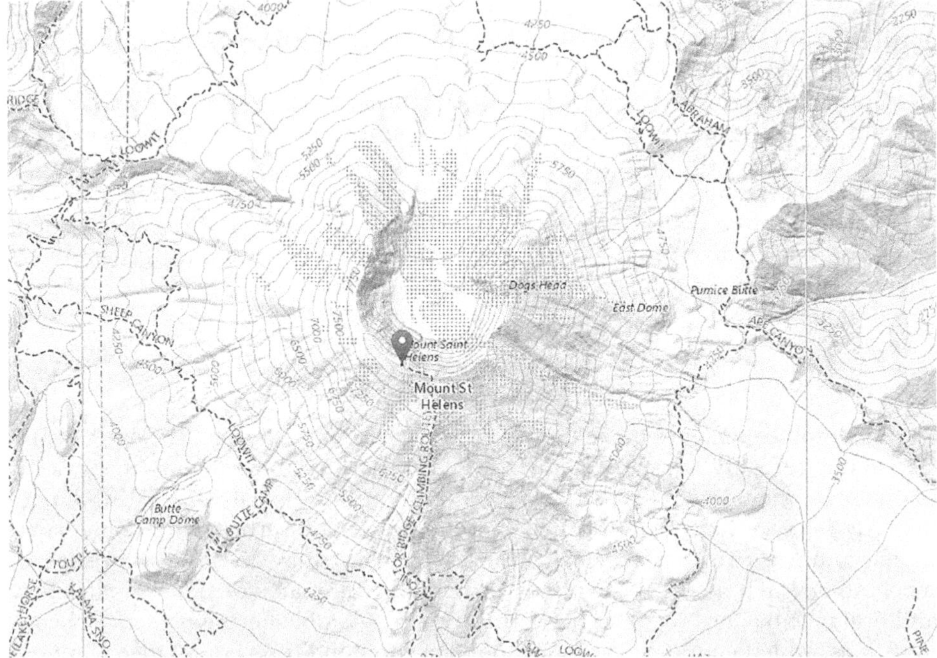

Figure 24.2 USGS topographical map of Mount St. Helens. Note the contour lines and shading used to indicate elevation changes.

data. While the older, hand-drawn maps are renowned for their graceful appearance and smart text placement and design, the new *US Topo* maps include orthophotos (aerial photos adjusted to be to scale and accurate overlays to maps) and updated coordinate data (including UTM coordinates), along with the accessibility of being free digital products. However, digital images of the older, hand-drawn maps are still available for download (see following passages).

Though there are several portals for *US Topo* products, the most reliable and user friendly is the USGS Store. It can be searched by location from a simple search box, or the user can browse around a map, zooming in and out, and dragging to scroll as needed. The latitude and longitude of the position the cursor is hovering over is displayed as well. Once the desired location is identified, the map layers button on the side of the screen can be activated, displaying options for USGS Topo, USGS Imagery Topo, EsriUSA Topo, and Esri World Topo maps. Double-clicking brings up the available products for that location, helpfully including historic maps of that area as well as the most current version. Results can be refined by map year and map scale, and products can be viewed either as a free pdf download or as a printed map shipped from the USGS warehouse for a reasonable price and shipping fee. The resulting pdf is a high-quality image with plenty of detail and helpful information at the bottom, including the date of provenance of various aspects of its data, map scale, symbol legend, contour interval, UTM grid information, and identification of neighboring quadrangles in all directions.

While access is clearly greatly improved by having these maps available instantaneously and free of charge as digital downloads, for those still needing paper copies of the maps, they are available through the USGS store. Given what was said previously about the disproportionately high demand for local maps and the fact that topographic maps are the most popular map type (Scarletto 2011, 133), it would likely make sense for a library to purchase the quadrangles for the surrounding area to have on hand for ready reference. If a library already owns historic USGS quadrangles, they are prime candidates for preservation for their legacy value.

Sanborn Fire Insurance Maps

Keeping with the theme of demand for local maps, many users seek maps of their property, town, or village over the years. The Sanborn Map Company published detailed maps of approximately 12,000 cities and towns in the United States during the 19th and 20th centuries. Originally, these maps were used by fire insurance companies to evaluate risk and underwrite fire insurance policies, but now these maps are essential for showing the built environment of urban areas in the United States over time. These maps were published up until 1977, typically at a 1:600 scale on 21 × 25-inch sheets of paper bound into volumes. As with all maps, they were made for a specific purpose—they bear a specific color-coding that indicates the building materials used in each mapped structure, for instance. For proper interpretation of the maps, it is vital to pay heed to the symbol keys included with the maps and to be aware that use of these symbols changed with time. Introductory material to the volumes typically described the fire protection measures and capacity of that community, detailing of schools, churches, and businesses, as well as a list of all incorporated and unincorporated locations in that volume. These materials and the maps themselves are invaluable for the historical geography of urban areas (see Figure 24.3).

The *Sanborn Maps* digital collection at the Library of Congress website contains over 25,000 sheets from more than 3,000 city sets throughout the United States and includes some maps from Canada and Mexico. The collection is searchable by a simple search box at the top of the page and browsable through a series of limiters on the left side of the page, allowing for refinement of the results by date, location, and subject. Search results list the title, publishing date, notes, digital ID, description, and allow download of the image(s) in either GIF or JPEG formats. High-quality scans of the images are also available for viewing on the website, including options for zooming, rotating, or clipping the images.

The University of California, Berkeley, hosts the *Union List of Sanborn & Other Fire Insurance Maps* on their website. This list is organized by state and details the holdings of Sanborn maps by various libraries around the country. Selecting a particular state will produce a listing by town or city, showing how many sheets are held from which years for that community and the location of those holdings. Where pertinent, links to online repositories for relevant images are given. There is also a bibliography and a web page that summarizes all the institutions in each state that own Sanborn maps.

Other Maps

There are as many different kinds of maps as there are interests in physical and human geography. Here are a few and some suggestions of where to find them:

- The Departments of Transportation in most states maintain highway maps, intended for the navigational aid of motorists, and often also have county maps,

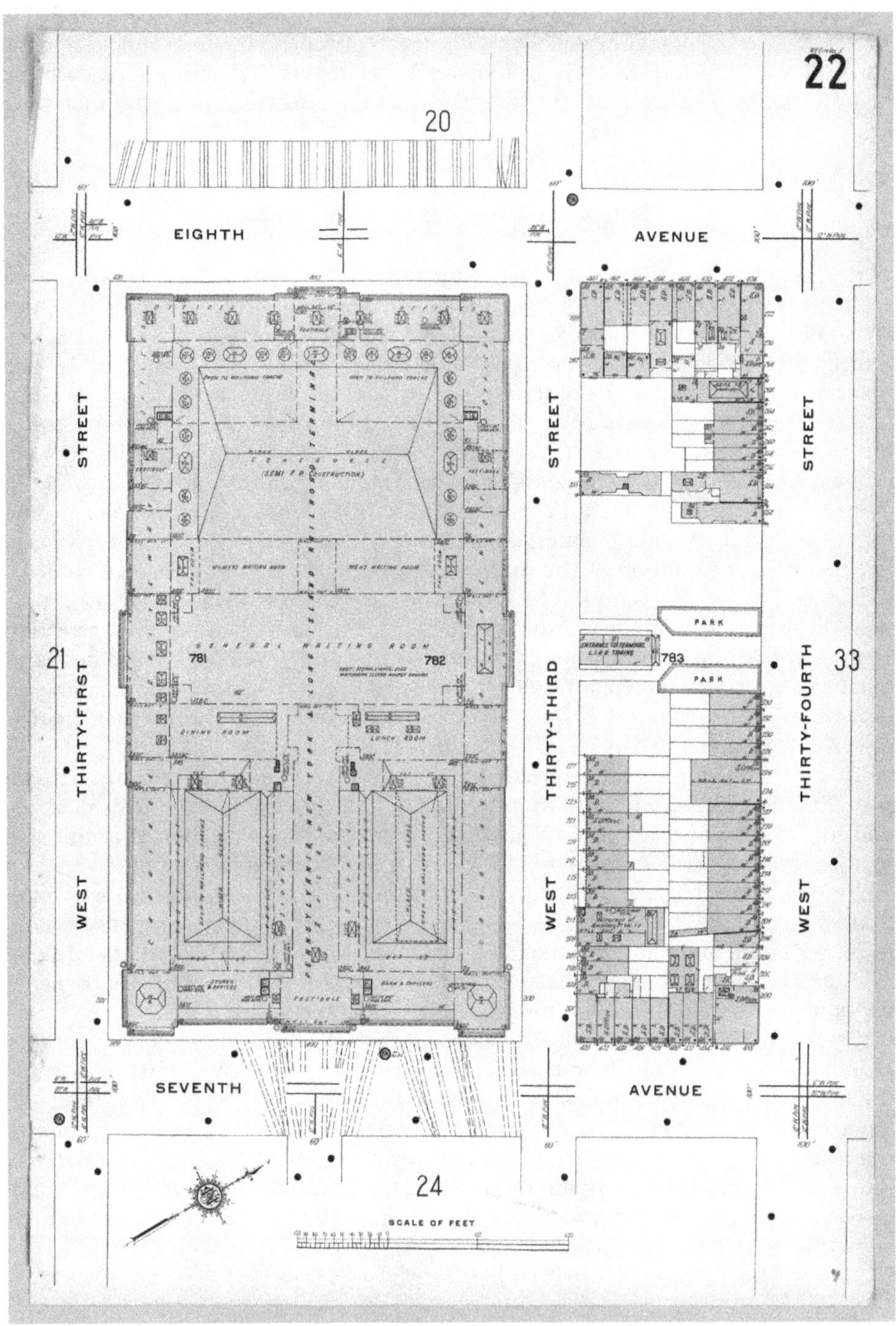

Figure 24.3 1911 Sanborn map of Manhattan. Note the internal architectural details of the railroad terminal depicted at left, including separate "Writing Rooms" for men and women. In the full color version, different tones are used to depict various building material types in the buildings at right.

Courtesy of the Library of Congress, Geography & Map Division.

bicycle maps, and scenic byways maps. These are typically available for free download at each state's Department of Transportation website.

- Nautical charts often show maritime areas and coastal regions, including water depths, land topography, coastline details, navigational hazards, and tide information. Such charts are produced by the National Oceanic and Atmospheric Administration (NOAA) in the United States and by the International Hydrographic Organization (IHO) internationally.
- Hydrologic unit maps depict various hierarchical levels of watersheds in a geographical area, which can be helpful in tracing the drainage areas of rivers and lakes. In the United States, the USGS maintains the *Hydrologic Unit Maps*.
- Cadastral maps depict the boundaries and legal ownership of plots of public land in a given area. The *Cadastral Survey* of the Bureau of Land Management produces and maintains such maps in the United States.
- Aeronautical charts help with the navigation of aircraft by depicting landmarks for navigation, obstructions, airspace boundaries, airports, populated areas, route guidance, radio frequencies, and more. The Federal Aviation Administration (FAA) maintains and sells printed aeronautical charts, and interactive digital aeronautical charts are freely available from the SkyVector website.

Map Collections

In this digital age, librarians are fortunate to have tens of thousands of out-of-print, rare, hard-to-access maps immediately available and searchable free of cost via the Internet. Following are a few of the more notable digital map collections:

- The *Perry-Castañeda Library Map Collection*, hosted by the University of Texas at Austin, has digitized 70,000 of the more than 250,000 maps in its collection. These are mostly historical, public domain maps that are made available to the public free of charge in JPEG format and sometimes pdf. The maps are searchable as well as browsable by a number of categories, including geographical regions, historical, thematic, and topographic. Helpfully, the collection regularly updates a list of maps relating to current national and world events right on its landing page.
- The *David Rumsey Map Collection* is physically housed at the Stanford University Library but has an online catalog of over 86,000 maps available, including rare maps from the 16th through 21st centuries. There are unique collections of celestial, maritime, and pictorial maps, as well as antique atlases and globes. The LUNA viewer technology on the website allows the user to rotate, zoom, or place several of the high-resolution images side by side. A significant amount of metadata is available for each image, which also allows images to be discovered through the advanced search. There is also a visually appealing browsing portal that allows refinement by time, place, person, and type of map. The website allows exporting of images into zipped JPEG files of various sizes.

ATLASES

At first glance, atlases might appear to just be collections of maps, which they are, of course, but they are also much more. Atlases collect maps for a number of reasons and include interpretive apparatuses with them. Some atlases have developed maps that were intended to be presented together, such as road atlases.

Other atlases bring together disparate maps under some kind of thematic coherence, such as an atlas of historical maps of North America. Some atlases are meant for desktop reference, others for handy "pocket" reference, and others for travel. This affects the size, binding, selection of maps, and information and symbols presented within the atlas. In other words, one should not assume that all atlases are the same. The following are some notable atlases of various types of which to be aware.

Rand McNally has been making maps since 1872 and made its first road map in 1904. It was even the first to use a numbered highway system, which was later accepted by federal and state highway authorities. Its *Rand McNally Road Atlas* has long been a standard in the field. It is published annually and includes road maps for every state in the United States, organized alphabetically, along with an overview map of the United States and maps of Canada and Mexico. Inset maps on the pages detail cities, national parks, and other significant locations. The atlas also—as is typical—includes a gazetteer, listing the distance between cities, providing a directory of cities and landmarks in various states and provinces, and notable information about each state such as population, land area, nickname, and largest city. The atlas features a large page size (10.875″ × 15.375″) and a folded binding that lays flat, not obscuring any of the map area in the page gutter. Rand McNally also produces the *Motor Carriers' Road Atlas*, intended for commercial truckers, which is laminated for durability and spiral-bound for ease of reference. It includes safe truck routes, warning about low clearances, weigh station locations, and other information useful to commercial truckers.

Several other standard atlases serve similar purposes but on a global scale. The *National Geographic Atlas of the World* is in its tenth edition and features hundreds of maps from around the world, including detailed regional maps of Australia, the Mediterranean Sea, and others, as well as maps of the oceans and space. Its gazetteer includes over 150,000 place names and informational graphics about population, climate, human migration, and flags and facts about the world's nation states. It has a large page size (12.1″ × 19″) designed for detailed tabletop viewing. The *Oxford Atlas of the World* is the only annually updated world atlas, which means it reflects the latest political and geological changes. It includes hundreds of full-color maps from around the world, satellite imagery of the earth, a comprehensive "Gazetteer of Nations," and a thorough textual introduction to the aims and concerns of world geography. The page size is 14.6″ × 11.4″, which is a little smaller and more square than the National Geographic atlas.

There are also a number of handy pocket atlases that combine high-quality maps with a portable size. Oxford University Press publishes its *Pocket World Atlas*, which is only 7.1″ by 4.6″ and 240 pages. It contains maps from every region of the world, often dividing large countries into multiple maps. Elevation and terrain are shown by coloration of the maps, and each page has a color code, bar scale, and inset map to locate the larger map on the world map. There are 15,000 entries in its gazetteer, as well as maps of worldwide time zones, flight paths, distances, world climate, and twenty-four city plan maps.

Dorling Kindersley (DK) has a reputation for publishing outstanding, visually attractive nonfiction titles and their pocket atlas, *Essential World Atlas*, is no exception. Despite their small size, the maps are more readable than other pocket atlases, and the book contains a gazetteer, a photo directory of world flags, and discussions about geology, population, languages, politics, overseas territories and dependencies, and a glossary. This atlas is 6.1″ × 8.5″, which is a little larger than the Oxford pocket atlas; however, it should still be noted that, given the small page size, the maps of both these atlases tend to disappear somewhat into the gutter at the center of the book, obscuring some features. Clearly, the maps of a pocket atlas do not have the detail or readability of a large size atlas, but they are much more portable, which could be handy for the student or world traveler. In this era of online digital maps, travelers could easily find more detailed and searchable maps on their mobile devices, but pocket atlases bring together a lot of information in a small space and do not depend upon charged batteries and Internet connectivity.

Finally, there are numerous thematic atlases that serve more specific purposes than national or world atlases. James Trefil's *Space Atlas* (2012), for instance, provides full-color maps and labeled photographs of celestial bodies such as the moon, planets, constellations, and galaxies. Like most atlases, it includes a gazetteer of facts about planets, moons, deep sky objects, an index of names, and a glossary of terms. The *Color Landform Atlas of the United States* is a free online atlas maintained by Ray Sterner and the Johns Hopkins University Applied Physics Laboratory that assembles and maintains maps of each state of the United States. The maps for most states include shaded relief maps, county maps, satellite imagery maps, and historic Rand McNally 1895 maps. *New Worlds: Maps from the Age of Discovery* by Ashley Baynton-Williams and Miles Baynton-Williams (2008) contains over 120 reprints of historical maps starting from 1475 CE tracing European exploration of the world. The early maps especially are notable for the presence of mermaids, dragons, and other mythical beasts representing geographic unknowns and fears. This atlas is useful for tracing the evolution of Euro-American understandings of the world as well as cartographic conventions, misconceptions, and developments. Some atlases get even more specific, such as *The Historical Atlas of New York City*, which uses a series of maps, photographs, charts, and text to follow the development of New York City from its earliest days until present times. Sources like these that convey historical geography of particular places can be helpful, specialized sources for a given library, depending on that library's user population needs and interests. With all atlases, the source, comprehensiveness, purpose, and accuracy of the resource must be considered and the resource used for its intended purpose.

INTERACTIVE ONLINE MAPS

Maps and geographical sources used to be viewable, indexable, and searchable—but essentially static sources. A massive impact of Internet, digital, and mobile technologies has been the development of fully interactive geographical sources, especially *Google Maps* and *Google Earth*. Not only can these sources be panned, zoomed, and scrolled—like other digital maps—but they can also be customized, explored, crowdsourced with photos and reviews, and utilized to give real-time navigation to users via global positioning systems, popularly referred to as GPS. In addition to the obvious personal and commercial uses of such technology, increasingly libraries are using these interactive geographical sources as finding aids for their collections (by geoindexing their collections of maps, photos, letters, etc.), for organization and delivery of location-oriented collections, and for instruction in geography and geographical sources (Dodsworth and Nicholson 2012, 104–106). Such interactive maps are quick, easy to use, and easily updated, unlike paper atlases, where one must look a place name up in the gazetteer of a paper atlas, locate the correct map page, and then find the place.

Google Maps

Google Maps began in 2005 as a web application providing street maps, satellite imagery, and the 360° *StreetView*, which are georeferenced, integrated digital photographs taken from the street level that allow the user to "walk" a particular street or location. The street map level is searchable by address, business/organization name, or even type of location (one can search for "hotels" or "coffee," for instance). Such searches or browsing by the buttons for "restaurants," "hotels," "bars," and so forth creates a data overlay that shows locations, names, and even sometimes prices of the places in question. If integrated with a user's mobile device, the street map is customized and ever-evolving, showing the user's home, workplace, and other locations she has visited in the past. These maps can be zoomed, dragged and dropped to move, and centered on the user's current location, all using the buttons in the lower-right side of the screen.

Google Maps also offers a satellite imagery view that has overhead images of locations, with an option for turning on or off the location labels (again using the three-horizontal-line menu in the upper left of the screen). This option can be useful for assessing urban density, natural features, the size and location of parking lots and alleys (which just appear as blank spots on the street map view). The date of the imagery can be found in the lower-right side of the screen and can be interesting to see changes with time, though Google updates this imagery regularly. This view can be rotated by holding the Ctrl key and the mouse button to drag the view and then reset with north to the top of the screen by clicking on the compass rose. The view can also be tilted to give a sense of depth to the image by toggling the "3D/2D" button in the lower-right side of the screen. This can be helpful for giving users a better sense of the actual appearance of locations, as it allows for greater depth perception while still maintaining the helpful overview of a map.

In both street map and satellite imagery modes, the user can right-click on a location and select "What's here?" to get the address, latitude and longitude, and a preview image of that location. Clicking "add a destination" after right-clicking a location will add that location to the list of waypoints in the navigation bar to the left of the screen, allowing the user to produce a complex set of directions that will guide him through a series of waypoints rather than to a singular destination. Selecting "measure distance" after right-clicking on a location will enable the user to drop two waypoints, and *Google Maps* will display the distance between those two points in both feet and meters, with a scaled distance line in between. Lastly, right-clicking and selecting "print" allows the user to print the current map and enter a title or any relevant notes to the top of the map. All of these options are potentially useful for library users seeking specific, customized maps, information, and directions.

Lastly, *Google Street View* is enabled by clicking on the little yellow icon of a human in the lower-right corner of the screen. Streets that are *Street View* enabled are marked in blue and places with 360° photo spheres appear as blue circles. These spheres and other geotagged photos are marked with the date of the photo and the photographer, making this a crowdsourced, interactive map. With its "walkable" street-level photography, *Street View* can be invaluable in helping users recognize a place and assess features such as what the parking is like or whether there are stairs or other accessibility impediments to a building. All of these contribute to the public's access and ease of use of public and private spaces. While some have raised privacy concerns regarding these extensive photographs of public places, Google does attempt to blur out specific faces if people are in the picture.

The activity in Box 24.2 compares *Google Maps* with another popular online mapping platform.

Box 24.2 Activity: Comparing Map Interfaces

Search for "1600 Pennsylvania Ave NW, Washington, DC 20500" in both *Google Maps* and *MapQuest*. Then use the route-finding features to get directions to this address from your current location. Consider the following questions:

1. What different kinds of information does each resource present? Which interface is easier to use and why?
2. Under what circumstances might each resource and its information be particularly helpful?
3. Do you see any contradictions in information presented? How might you account for that?
4. Now search this same address in *Google Earth*. How is this interface different, and when might this resource be more pertinent to certain user needs?

Google Earth

Google Earth is a free, downloadable computer application that goes a step further than *Google Maps* by using satellite imagery to render a 3-D model of the earth, including urban, rural, and wilderness areas. The application loads with an impressive scene of gliding up to the earth from space. From there, the user can move, zoom, or rotate the earth as they wish, either simply to explore or to find a specific place. Alternately, individual addresses and places can be typed into the search box, after which the application will visually "fly" the viewer to the place in question. The search function also tolerates fuzzy searches; for instance, a search for "highest point in Scotland" will zoom to Ben Nevis. The capabilities of *Google Earth* are especially apparent in wilderness places with elevation, as the user can turn the view to not just look down at the feature in question but move around it laterally, like a bird or airplane.

Google Earth features various data layers that can be toggled, including borders, roads, 3-D buildings, weather, and topical geolocated insets called "Global Awareness." Users can place virtual pins in places to save them as their favorites, as well as add images, record a tour, and save and print customized images. The specific satellite, aerial photography, or GIS data that was used to produce the imagery currently in sight is displayed at the bottom of the screen, as is the date of the imagery. Slider controls allow the user to see the sunlight across the location during the course of a day or to see historical imagery of that location, allowing changes over time to be observed.

Google Earth Pro is now the standard free version of the application, and, amazingly, it also includes interactive maps of the sky (constellations and galaxies) and 3-D globes of both the moon and Mars. These have fewer features than the renderings of the earth, but they include geotagged information like the locations of the Apollo missions on the moon and the routes of the Mars landers.

Other Resources

While there are no other free 3-D rendering applications quite like *Google Earth*, there are a number of other free web mapping services like *Google Maps*. *Bing Maps* offers much of the same functionality as *Google Maps*, including road, aerial, and street-side views, as well as navigational aids. However, the Bird's Eye view (the equivalent of the 3-D mode in *Google Maps*) has been mostly disabled, though it is still available to view from certain locations. In some ways, the interface is cleaner than Google's, such as the simple "Traffic" button at the top of the screen that shows current traffic conditions, whereas Google's button is in a side menu. *MapQuest* also has much of the same functionality as the other web mapping applications but with an attractive topographic map as its landing map. There are a number of easily accessed layers that can be activated for travelers and consumers, such as finding nearby hotels, food, gas, grocery stores, and airports. However, the interface is cluttered by a number of ads that encroach upon the map space.

GEOGRAPHIC INFORMATION SYSTEMS

GIS has been defined as "a computerized system for managing data about spatially referenced objects. GISs differ from other types of information systems in that they manage huge quantities of data, require complex concepts to describe the geometry of objects, and specify complex topological relationships between them" (Khosrow-Pour 2013, 392). Particularly with the turn toward interdisciplinarity in geographical studies, GISs are increasingly used to collect, integrate, and express vast amounts of georeferenced information, such as county maps depicting poverty rates and city maps depicting literacy rates over a period of time by ethnicity. These systems combine different kinds of data into visualizations such as maps and 3-D representation so as to detect patterns and trends. These visualizations typically involve layers of data that are organized geographically and can produce real-time information and/or be queried.

Esri (Environmental Systems Research Institute) has become perhaps the most widely known commercial GIS company. It started in 1969 as a computer mapping system to help land resource managers and has evolved into a software company offering several tiers of products that can perform spatial analytics and show remote sensing, real-time GIS, and 3-D visualizations of data. ArcReader is a free data viewer for Esri-created GIS data; Esri also produces the ArcGIS, ArcGIS Pro, ArcGIS Enterprise, and ArcGIS Online software products. In addition, Esri offers a number of free tutorials about various aspects of GIS, though the user is required to make an account. As mentioned in the section on geographical dictionaries, Esri also maintains a free online dictionary of terms related to GIS. Other notable commercial GISs include Autodesk, ERDAS IMAGINE, and MapInfo Pro.

There have been various open source GIS software platforms since 1978. Some of the more common include *GRASS* (*Geographic Resources Analysis Support System*) *GIS*, which was started by the U.S. Army Corps of Engineers and now contains more than 350 modules to render maps and geospatial displays on a variety of operating systems. *MapWindow GIS* is another open source GIS platform built on Microsoft.NET technology and available under Mozilla Public License distribution. It is currently used by the U.S. Environmental Protection Agency for some of its projects and modifiable through various plug-ins.

There are a number of online platforms that present free data visualizations resulting from GISs, often in Esri shapefiles that can be read and further manipulated with GIS software. The *National Map* offers geospatial representations of national hydrography, including data sets that integrate information about stream levels, fish populations, water quality, and invasive species; and the 3D Elevation Program, which uses light detection and ranging (lidar) to update flood maps and provide more accurate elevation data for aviation maps. *The Atlas of Historical County Boundaries*, hosted by the Newberry Library in Chicago, collects and presents maps and data about the formation, boundaries, and changes to all county boundaries in the United States through time and makes this data available as shapefiles with accompanying metadata. The United Nations Environment Programme (UNEP) maintains the *UNEP GEO Data Portal*, which is a GIS of environmental and economic development data, offering datasets about climate, pollution, forests, and population. It offers online maps, graphs, tables, metadata, and the option to download the data as an HTML file, a Microsoft Excel spreadsheet, or an Esri shapefile. In addition, many states maintain collaborative repositories of GIS data, which can be easily found online, such as the *State of Kansas GIS* or the *GIS Data Depot* of St. Johns County, Florida.

REFERENCE SOURCES ON COUNTRIES AND CULTURES

While many geographical sources are primarily visual in nature, such as maps and atlases, many users will want to find factual information about various aspects of different countries and cultures. The information sought might be political, economic, environmental, historical, social, cultural, or agricultural in nature. In today's increasingly globalized world, it is all the more important to have easy access to this sort of information. There are a number of convenient sources in both print and online to answer these sorts of questions. In addition, encyclopedias often offer information of this nature; two notable titles are the *Worldmark Encyclopedia of the Nations* and the *Worldmark Encyclopedia of Cultures and Daily Life* (see Chapter 19).

The World Factbook was produced by the CIA for government officials starting in 1962 but has been made available for the public in print since 1975 and online since 1997. It gathers information from numerous government agencies and published sources, combining them in a useful resource that features regional and world maps, flags of the world, and specific sections on each country that include information on geographic area, elevation, land use, environmental agreements, population, ethnic groups, languages, religions, median age, birth rates, life expectancy, government type, administrative divisions, national holidays, political parties, national anthem, gross domestic product, labor force, unemployment rates, poverty rates, exports and imports, monetary exchange rates, energy, communications, transportation, military and security, terrorism, and international disputes pertaining to that country. In addition to this wealth of detailed information, a particularly useful feature of the online *Factbook* is the "country comparisons" feature, which produces a ranked list of countries by eighty statistical subfields, such as land area, population, and literacy rates, providing helpful context for various statistics. Since it is a public domain resource, it is freely available online.

Europa World Plus is a well-respected, subscription-based online world year book that includes extensive, regularly updated geographical information, details of world events, and statistics. It offers advanced search options and is browsable by countries/territories, regions, and organizations. Entries for particular countries feature a quick reference of area, population, finances, government, and images of the country's flag and map. There are links to detailed textual information about that country's geography, history, economy, as well as directories with contact information for various governmental agencies. It also features a customizable country comparison feature in which user-selected countries are compared side by side according to selected statistics. One downside of the resource is that it is structured as a "nest of links," requiring numerous mouse clicks to access specific information, decreasing its usability.

The Statesman's Yearbook has been printed annually since 1864 and includes facts about and analysis of all the world's countries, including biographies of world leaders. It also includes articles about the United Nations, European Union, International Olympic Committee, African Union, and many other international organizations. Entries for particular countries include a map; population; key historical events; major provinces and their population; social statistics; climate; constitution and government; current governmental office holders; military; energy; industry; trade; and social, religious, and cultural information, along with suggestions for further reading. This pricey print resource is more readable and concise than other sources but without the country comparison and advanced search features of the online resources, though it is also available as an e-book with limited search functions.

CultureGrams is a ProQuest subscription-based online information resource about countries and cultures that is delivered in a World Edition, which covers the countries of the world; a States Edition about the states of the United States; a Provinces Edition, covering the provinces and territories of Canada; and a Kids Edition, providing a view of life in various countries from the vantage point of a child. All editions are multi-sensory and written at a more introductory level than some of the other resources described in this section, featuring appealing infographics, audio clips of national anthems, videos, pictures, interviews, recipes, and concise country, state, or province data. Helpfully, this resource focuses upon the cultural aspects of different societies, discussing greetings, gestures, eating customs, family traditions, recreation habits, and so on. *CultureGrams* also allows the user to customize their own tables and graphs and then download them as CSV files. The Kids Edition provides an even more streamlined discussion of each geographical entity and includes a "Life as a Kid" section.

Lastly, the United Nations maintains several free online repositories of statistics and information about the world's countries. *UNdata* is maintained by the United Nations Statistics Division and features glossaries, tables, and advanced search capabilities to access information such as country profiles, regional profiles, and specialized databases about crime, education, energy, agriculture, gender, and human development. The country profiles provide concise information about population, capital city, economic factors, social indicators, and environmental aspects, including data points from a variety of different years for quick comparison. *UNCTADstat* is maintained by the United Nations Conference on Trade and Development and includes much more detailed economic and development data, including fact sheets, country profiles, and infographics. It also has a data center with comprehensive tables of statistics on all varieties of global economic data.

CONCLUSION

Reliable geographic information is all the more important in today's globalized world, and technology has made geographic information even more accessible and detailed. Specialized map collections, once only available in-person, are now accessible to anyone with an Internet connection. Comprehensive encyclopedias, databases, and GIS provide unprecedented levels of information with a few clicks of a mouse. Even print atlases and maps benefit from the level of detail and up-to-date information provided by modern satellite and computer technologies. But as it ever has been, the task of the librarian is to help guide the patron to reliable information and tools calibrated to their needs and inquiry. It is hoped that this relevant, accurate information will not only dependably reflect the physical features of the earth but also meaningfully guide human activity in interaction with the earth into the future.

REFERENCES

Dodsworth, Eva, and Andrew Nicholson. 2012. "Academic Uses of Google Earth and Google Maps in a Library Setting." *Information Technology & Libraries* 3 (2): 102–17.

Dougherty, Kate. 2013. "The Direction of Geography LibGuides." *Journal of Map and Geography Libraries* 9 (3): 259–75.

Hill, Miriam Helen. 2010. "Map Projections." In *Encyclopedia of Geography*, edited by Barney Warf. Thousand Oaks, CA: SAGE Publications.

Khosrow-Pour, Mehdi. 2013. "Geographic Information System (GIS)." In *Dictionary of Information Science and Technology*. Hershey, PA: IGI Global.

Scarletto, Edith. 2011. "Collection Development Guidance through Reference Inquiry Analysis: A Study of Map Library Patrons and Their Needs." *Journal of Map and Geography Libraries* 7 (2): 124–37.

Smits, Jan. 2014. "Geographical Thesauri: Choices to Be Made in an Ever-Growing International Context." *Journal of Map and Geography Libraries* 10 (3): 329–46.

Todd, Julia L. 2008. "GIS and Libraries: A Cross-Disciplinary Approach." *Online* 32 (5): 14–18.

LIST OF SOURCES

ArcGIS. Esri. https://www.esri.com/en-us/home.

ArcGIS Enterprise. Esri. https://www.esri.com/en-us/home.

ArcGIS Online. Esri. https://www.esri.com/en-us/home.

ArcGIS Pro. Esri. https://www.esri.com/en-us/home.

ArcReader. Esri. https://www.esri.com/en-us/home.

The Atlas of Historical County Boundaries. The Newberry Library. https://publications.newberry.org/ahcbp/index.html.

Autodesk. https://www.autodesk.com.

Baynton-Williams, Ashley, and Miles Baynton-Williams. 2008. *New Worlds: Maps from the Age of Discovery*. London: Quercus Editions Ltd.

Bing Maps. https://www.bing.com/maps/.

Cadastral Survey. Bureau of Land Management. https://www.blm.gov/programs/lands-and-realty/cadastral-survey.

The Columbia Gazetteer of the World. New York, NY: Columbia University Press. http://www.columbiagazetteer.org. Subscription required.

CultureGrams Online Edition. Ann Arbor: ProQuest. https://online.culturegrams.com/. Subscription required.

David Rumsey Map Collection. Cartography Associates. https://www.davidrumsey.com/home.

ERDAS IMAGINE. Hexagon Geospatial. https://www.hexagongeospatial.com/products/power-portfolio/erdas-imagine.

Essential World Atlas. 9th ed. 2016. New York, NY: Dorling Kindersley Publishing.

Europa World Plus. London: Routledge. http://www.europaworld.com/pub/. Subscription required.

Gale Virtual Reference Library. Farmington Hills, MI: Gale Cengage Learning. http://www.cengage.com. Subscription required.

Geographic Names Information System (GNIS). United States Board on Geographic Names. https://geonames.usgs.gov/domestic/.

GEOnet Names Server (GNS). United States Board on Geographic Names. http://geonames.nga.mil/gns/html/.

The Getty Thesaurus of Geographic Names. The J. Paul Getty Trust. http://www.getty.edu/research/tools/vocabularies/tgn/.

GIS Data Depot. St. Johns County Government. www.sjcfl.us/GIS/DataDepot.aspx.

GIS Dictionary. Esri. https://support.esri.com/en/other-resources/gis-dictionary.

Google Earth. https://google.com/earth/.

Google Maps. https://www.google.com/maps/.

GRASS GIS. Open Source Geospatial Foundation. https://grass.osgeo.org.

Homberger, Eric. 2015. *The Historical Atlas of New York City: A Visual Celebration of 400 Years of New York City's History.* 3rd ed. New York, NY: St. Martin's Griffin.

Hydrologic Unit Maps. United States Geological Survey. https://water.usgs.gov/GIS/huc.html.

International Hydrographic Organization. http://www.iho.int/.

MapInfo Pro. Pitney Bowes. https://www.pitneybowes.com/us/location-intelligence/geographic-information-systems/mapinfo-pro.html.

MapQuest. https://www.mapquest.com.

MapWindow GIS. https://www.mapwindow.org/#home.

Mayhew, Susan. 2015. *A Dictionary of Geography,* 5th ed. Oxford: Oxford University Press.

Merriam-Webster's Geographical Dictionary. 3rd ed. 2007. Springfield, MA: Merriam-Webster.

National Geographic Atlas of the World. 10th ed. 2014. Washington, DC: National Geographic.

National Map. United States Geological Survey. https://nationalmap.gov.

National Oceanic and Atmospheric Administration. http://www.noaa.gov.

Oxford Atlas of the World. 24th ed. 2017. New York, NY: Oxford University Press.

Perry-Castañeda Library Map Collection. The University of Texas at Austin. https://legacy.lib.utexas.edu/maps/.

Pocket World Atlas. 5th ed. 2005. New York, NY: Oxford University Press.

Rand McNally. https://www.randmcnally.com.

Rand McNally 2019 Motor Carrier's Road Atlas. 2018. Chicago, IL: Rand McNally.

Rand McNally 2019 Road Atlas. 95th ed. 2018. Chicago, IL: Rand McNally.

Sanborn Maps. Library of Congress. https://www.loc.gov/collections/sanborn-maps/.

SkyVector Aeronautical Charts. https://skyvector.com.

State of Kansas GIS: Data Access & Support Center. 2017. *LiDAR 2017.* http://kansasgis.org/catalog/index.cfm?data_id=2643&show_cat=5.

State of Kansas GIS. http://www.kansasgis.org.

The Statesman's Yearbook 2018: The Politics, Cultures and Economies of the World. 2017. London, UK: Palgrave Macmillan.

Sterner, Ray. *Color Landform Atlas of the United States.* Johns Hopkins University Applied Physics Laboratory. http://fermi.jhuapl.edu/states/states.html.

Trails Illustrated Maps. National Geographic Society. https://www.natgeomaps.com/trail-maps/trails-illustrated-maps.

Trefil, James. 2012. *Space Atlas: Mapping the Universe and Beyond.* Washington, D.C.: National Geographic.

UNCTADstat. United Nations Conference on Trade and Development. http://unctadstat.unctad.org/EN/Index.html.

UNdata. United Nations Statistics Division. http://data.un.org/Default.aspx.

UNEP GEO Data Portal. United Nations Environmental Programme. https://geodata.grid.unep.ch/.

Union List of Sanborn & Other Fire Insurance Maps. University of California, Berkeley. http://www.lib.berkeley.edu/EART/sanborn_union_list.

US Topo. United States Geological Survey. https://store.usgs.gov/map-locator.

Warf, Barney, ed. 2010. *Encyclopedia of Geography.* Thousand Oaks, CA: SAGE Publications.

Warf, Barney, ed. 2006. *Encyclopedia of Human Geography.* Thousand Oaks, CA: SAGE Publications.

The World Factbook 2018–2019. 2018. New York, NY: Skyhorse Publishing.

The World Factbook. Central Intelligence Agency. https://www.cia.gov/library/publications/the-world-factbook/index.html.

Worldmark Encyclopedia of Cultures and Daily Life. 3rd ed. 2017. 5 vols. Farmington Hills, MI: Gale Cengage Learning. Available online as part of *Gale Virtual Reference Library.*

Worldmark Encyclopedia of the Nations. 14th ed. 2017. 5 vols. Farmington Hills, MI: Gale Cengage Learning. Available online as part of *Gale Virtual Reference Library.*

SUGGESTED READINGS

Dodsworth, Eva H. and Andrew Nicholson. 2015. *Using Google Earth in Libraries: A Practical Guide for Librarians.* Lanham, MD: Rowman & Littlefield Publishers.

This text provides a more in-depth discussion of the capacities of *Google Earth* and the ways it might be embedded in library services and instruction for users of different ages. It also discusses how to integrate *Google Earth* into a library's discovery tools and includes tutorials and sample classroom activities.

Johnson, Jenny Marie. 2003. *Geographic Information: How to Find It, How to Use It.* Westport, CT: Greenwood.

This text is written by a map and geography librarian at the University of Illinois at Urbana-Champaign and includes detailed discussions of the nature and uses of various geographical sources, including GIS, remotely sensed images, and aerial photographs.

Chapter 25

Biographical and Genealogical Sources

Jeanne Holba Puacz

USES AND CHARACTERISTICS

From investigating potential corporate board members to learning about presidents for school reports, from exploring personal genealogical relationships to researching figures for dissertations, biographical questions abound at the reference desk. At all types of libraries and for all sorts of reasons, patrons ask questions about the lives of others. While the questions may focus on the lives of local personages or family members, they will more commonly focus on the lives of the famous and the infamous.

In order to determine what sources are most appropriate and helpful, it is necessary to evaluate both the sources available and the needs of the patrons. Source evaluation and selection should encompass such considerations as scope, accuracy, currency, format, and cost, among others. The types of questions commonly received, the depth of response generally required, and the age and educational level of the average patron are often included in an evaluation of user needs.

In addition to classic biographical sources such as *Current Biography*, the *Who's Who* titles, and *Encyclopedia of World Biography*, a number of excellent aggregate sources have evolved that greatly reduce the time required for many biographical searches. Sources such as *Biography in Context*, *Biography Reference Bank*, and *Biography Reference Center* allow simultaneous searching of numerous biographical sources, and many of the results are available in full text. These sources allow cumulative access to and searching of multiple editions, titles, and series.

When pursuing biographical information, search strategy will be affected by a number of factors. How much information is needed, how quickly it is needed, and by whom it is needed must be considered. The number and type of sources consulted for an elementary student will, obviously, be more limited than the sources consulted for a graduate student. The subject of the biographical search, and what is already known about the subject, will also impact the search process. Information concerning a well-known historical figure is often readily available, even if the patron is unsure about the spelling of the name, the time period, or the subject area in which the biographee was most influential. Unfortunately, searches for information pertaining to lesser-known individuals can be significantly hampered by a lack of such knowledge.

Although it is true that, as William Katz (2002, 2) said, "answering reference questions may involve the resources of the whole library, and, for that matter, libraries and collections elsewhere," there are a number of standard sources with which any student of reference should become familiar. In addition to the classic biographical sources, standard encyclopedia and indexing sources can also be extremely useful when pursuing information about people. Many specialized biographical sources exist, so many that it is impossible to know all of them. Therefore, guides to biographical sources have been produced to assist librarians in locating specialized sources to meet the needs of their patrons. Primary sources, such as vital records, city directories, census data, and the like may be necessary for some types of questions. However, because this research may go beyond the scope of the local resources, it is important for the reference librarian to know where to direct patrons so that they can obtain the documents they need.

Although a number of biographical sources may be considered universal, in that they include persons regardless of their nationality, their subject of interest, or whether they are living or dead, many titles are subdivided into a variety of categories. These subdivisions can be classified by the type of information the source provides, the type of persons included in the source, or the format of the source itself. The strengths and limitations of each category of source, as well as the goal of the patron's research, must be considered when choosing the sources to be consulted.

Direct versus Indirect

Biographical sources are typically designated as either direct or indirect. This designation refers to the type of information that the sources provide. Direct sources provide information within the source itself, whereas indirect sources indicate which sources should be consulted to obtain information. Indexes, such as *Biography and Genealogy Master Index* and *Biography Index Past and Present*, are illustrations of indirect biographical sources. These titles provide just enough information about the person of interest for identification purposes and then point the patron to where they can find supplementary data. Sources that provide any type of bibliography, list of works consulted, or recommended sources for further reading easily qualify for both categories. *Encyclopedia of World Biography* and *Contemporary Authors* provide both direct and indirect access to information. *Biography in Context*, *Biography Reference Center*, and *Biography Reference Bank* also provide both types of information.

Current versus Retrospective

Biographical sources are frequently categorized by the type of persons included in the work and are commonly designated as being either current or retrospective. Persons included in the current sources are generally assumed to be living at the time of publication, and the *Who's Who* variety of source serves as a representative example. Retrospective sources are understood to provide information about persons from the past and to include only those who are deceased. *Oxford Dictionary of National Biography* and *American National Biography* are two such retrospective sources. A number of sources provide information on both current and retrospective figures. *Current Biography* only profiles current individuals but provides access to obituaries for deceased individuals who were previously included. *Biography in Context*, *Biography Reference Center*, and *Biography Reference Bank* regularly include both living and deceased individuals.

International versus National

Biographical sources are often classified as either international or national in scope. *Who's Who in the World* and *Encyclopedia of World Biography* are international in coverage and include persons regardless of ethnicity or country of origin. National sources restrict their coverage to individuals born in the nation in question or to those persons of prominence in that nation. *Who's Who in America* and *American National Biography* are two examples of sources that are limited nationally in their scope. Sources may be further restricted to cover only a particular region of a country, as with *Who's Who in the Midwest*, or to cover only a particular field of interest, such as *American Men and Women of Science*.

Alternative Sources

While persons included in major biographical works have, obviously, obtained some level of fame, the area in which they have achieved their status may dictate the sources where they can be found. Those of longstanding fame or outstanding achievement, such as classical Greek poets or past presidents of the United States, are likely to be included in the standard biographical tools. Individuals of sport or entertainment fame may be restricted to sources with good coverage of individuals of broad popular interest, such as *Current Biography* and *Biography.com*.

Newspapers and magazines can serve as excellent sources of biographical information, particularly for those persons who are newly famous, fleetingly famous, or famous for notorious or criminal reasons. The notorious may be excluded from the standard biographical sources; this does nothing, however, to lessen interest in these individuals, and periodicals may be able to fill the gap (see Chapters 22 and 23). Periodical indexes act as an excellent supplement to the traditional biographical sources by providing access to very current information before the standard sources have been updated. *Biography in Context*, which integrates periodical coverage, primary sources, and websites into their biographical entries, has recognized the value of these sources and has attempted to facilitate access. It should be noted that while some periodical indexes offer full-text access to referenced articles, they may be limited in full text for retrospective coverage.

Encyclopedias can also act as supplementary biographical sources (see Chapter 19). Encyclopedia articles can provide concise and helpful overviews concerning the person sought and are quite useful for historical figures. Encyclopedias, particularly those created for young people, can be excellent sources for pictures. Valuable information may also be included in topical encyclopedia articles for subjects related to the field of interest of the individual in question; therefore, it is important that the access points or indices of the encyclopedia be consulted.

The web can serve as another outstanding alternative for very current information or difficult-to-locate persons. In addition to some of the well-known biographical websites, such as *Biography.com* and *Infoplease Biography*, a wealth of biographical information may be gleaned from the web. Personal websites of the famous (and infamous), company websites that provide profiles of corporate officials, and access to the content of smaller, local newspapers via their websites are a few examples of potential web resources that may be tapped. Social networking sites, such as *Facebook* and *LinkedIn*, where users are encouraged to post and share autobiographical information, have the potential to provide more complete access to lesser-known individuals. Collaborative web sources, such as *Wikipedia*, may also serve as supporting sources in biographical searches. Personal, corporate, and general websites, as well as collaborative sources, often lack any editorial control; thus, it is extremely important to review each site critically and evaluate each entry carefully for bias, accuracy, completeness, reliability, and currency.

EVALUATION

It is imperative for librarians to carefully evaluate the numerous sources available and to work diligently to direct patrons to those sources deemed to be of the highest quality. Through careful collection development, librarians should strive to ensure that patrons are consulting sources that are current, accurate, comprehensive, and easy to use.

Currency

When evaluating currency, it is important to consider how quickly, how often, and how thoroughly the work is updated. The entries in retrospective sources generally do not need regular updating and will be updated only if significant new information about a figure is uncovered. However, because lives and fortunes can change very quickly, it is extremely important for current sources to be regularly and thoroughly updated. Outdated entries may provide incorrect and inaccurate information to the researcher. Many sources, particularly electronic tools, have regularly scheduled updates; however, others are updated less frequently, offering updates and revisions only when new editions are released. Some sources that are available electronically and also published serially, such as *Contemporary Authors* and *Current Biography*, periodically revise entries to keep the information provided more accurate. During the evaluation process, careful attention should be paid to the editorial policy regarding updates.

Accuracy and Authority

Issues of accuracy and authority can be considered on several levels. When evaluating any reference work, it is important to investigate what kinds of reviews the source received and whether the work has been included in any guides to reference works. The reputation of the publisher can also serve as a good indicator of the overall quality. Gale, Oxford, ProQuest, and EBSCO are some of the known and trusted names in biographical reference publishing.

A consideration that is somewhat unique to biographical works is the source of the biographical data. Often, the biographees themselves are asked to provide information. Theoretically, self-compiled information will be superior as it will be most accurate. However, the accuracy of the reported information is dependent upon the honesty and thoroughness of the individual entrant. While the entrant may not provide factually incorrect information, the information may be edited to provide a more flattering, if not more complete, picture. If the information located in a source seems at all questionable or incomplete, it is advisable to consult additional sources.

Scope and Comprehensiveness

The scope statement of the source will indicate which individuals are eligible for inclusion. A clearly worded and well-defined statement of scope will help to lend legitimacy to the source and its entries. Common ways to limit scope include whether the entrants are living or deceased, residents of a particular country or region, or employed in a particular field. Inclusion of as many individuals as possible that meet the stated scope results in a more comprehensive source. If prominent individuals who meet the stated scope are overlooked, the overall legitimacy of the source will suffer. Likewise, if individuals who do not meet the qualifications set down by the scope statement are included, the quality of the source should be questioned.

Format

The usefulness of a source, even a source that contains information of the highest quality, may be greatly diminished if the source is difficult to use. The source and its information can be rendered useless if it is inaccessible due to poor organization or lack of access points. The number and type of available indexes in a print source will greatly impact the overall effectiveness of the work. Electronic sources have great potential in terms of searching and accessibility. Many sources allow for searching essentially all of the fields of the record, searching a number of factors in combination, or even searching the entire contents of the database by keyword (see Figure 25.1). The feature of electronic sources that allows for cumulative searching of multiple editions of a title, as with *Biography and Genealogy Master Index*, is an advantage for any searcher. Likewise, the option to search many biographical sources concurrently, as allowed for by aggregate sources such as *Biography in Context*, *Biography Reference Center*, and *Biography Reference Bank*, can make biographical searching much faster and easier.

Careful attention should be paid to the spelling of names when using electronic sources. Electronic sources may not return a result if the name is spelled incorrectly, which may lead patrons to believe that the individual is not included in the source. Increasingly, sources will offer close matches, suggest alternative spellings, or offer an alphabetical browse feature in order to assist the searcher in locating the correct individual.

People Search				
Search for:		in	Name ▼	
And:		in	Place of Birth ▼	
And:		in	Place of Death ▼	
More Options:				
Occupation:	▼			
Nationality:	▼			
Ethnicity:	▼			
Gender:	Male		Female	
Birth Year:	is ▼			
Death Year:	is ▼			

Figure 25.1 Advanced search in biographical databases. Shown is an example search screen that enables searching by a combination of multiple fields, such as occupation, nationality, and gender.

Cautions

Many early biographical works, particularly those from 19th- and early 20th-century America, were essentially vanity publications. Prominent citizens were offered inclusion in the source for a fee and the publishers would profit. While these works are now useful to scholars as historical snapshots of the era and locale, they are not without bias. Many vanity publications continue to exist in the biographical realm, and some publishers may use "who's who" phrasing in their titles in an effort to lend credibility. Any publication that requires an individual to purchase a copy of the title before they are included, or that offers to include an individual for a fee, should be viewed as suspect. Librarians should use tact when discussing these titles with patrons who have received invitations for inclusion.

Quality and completeness of information included in biographical entries has varied greatly over time. Whether done deliberately or subconsciously, biographers can be selective in their coverage. The Victorian era was notorious for including only acceptable and complimentary information in biographies. Obituaries, which can be useful biographical sources, are also often considered to be more complimentary than complete. Therefore, knowing what sources have been consulted during the creation of a biographical work and knowing where to look to locate additional information can be quite helpful to researchers. As it is often necessary to consult multiple sources in order to obtain a clear picture of an individual, references and recommendations for further research can be important components of biographical works.

SELECTION

Needs of Users

Although some sources are useful at multiple levels, the needs of the users of specific types of libraries will impact each library's selection of biographical tools. Biographical works with essay length entries, written at age-appropriate levels for the students being served and that provide illustrations, are likely to be more useful than sources with directory information in a school library. Such sources will be far more useful to students as they work to complete reports and projects on prominent individuals. Likewise, it is expected that they will also be more useful to the student users of academic libraries. However, sources with directory entries may be extremely useful to the staff and faculty users of the library. Identifying researchers specializing in particular fields, locating colleagues at different educational institutions, and obtaining contact information for potential donors are just a few of the possible uses of such sources at academic libraries. Sources that provide very current contact information and brief biographical data are often the most useful biographical sources for users of special libraries. The narrative entries provided by dictionary sources are likely to provide substantial retrospective information and, thus, be less useful in these settings. As it is difficult to anticipate the broad range of questions that may be faced in a public library, it is important to provide a cross-section of sources. Both dictionary and directory sources, in a progression of difficulty and detail, should be made available for use.

Cost

Unfortunately, budgetary restrictions prevent libraries from collecting all the sources that might be helpful to their patrons. Therefore, in addition to evaluating sources for quality and usefulness, price must also be considered. The uniqueness of works considered for a collection should be taken into account and titles with similar scope statements should be studied closely; it is unlikely that smaller libraries truly need or can afford titles that duplicate coverage.

Increasingly, electronic versions of sources are becoming available. Discounts may be offered for libraries wishing to subscribe to both the electronic and the print version of a source, which can provide additional access without significant extra cost. Electronic aggregate sources that provide full-text access to numerous classic biographical sources may enable libraries to provide access to more sources than they would otherwise be able to afford. Consortial pricing, which may result in discounts, should be investigated for those sources that may be useful to multiple libraries in an area. A number of biographical sources are freely available on the Web; *Biography.com* and *Infoplease Biography* are examples of free resources that can supplement any collection.

IMPORTANT GENERAL SOURCES

A number of regularly used sources of widely accepted worth are discussed in this chapter. Several of the entries in the Suggested Readings section at the end of this chapter can be used to identify more specialized biographical sources suitable for particular collections.

Directories

Who's Who directories, in one variation or another, are traditionally used biographical sources. They provide succinct, non-critical access to biographical facts for currently prominent individuals, including name, age, education, family, and contact information. Inclusion is restricted to those deemed to be of "reference interest" and is dictated by an individual's achievements. Achievement may be measured by positions of leadership or responsibility held, significant creative or educational works, public speaking, publishing, or noteworthy contributions to the community. Those selected for inclusion are sent a questionnaire and are asked to provide information about their life, family, career, and achievements, which is compiled in a standardized format. It should be noted that although the *Who's Who* sources have generally been found to be reliable, the answers provided by the biographees may not undergo any editorial review and the depth of content and currency for entries can vary significantly.

Marquis Biographies Online provides aggregate, searchable access to twenty-four Marquis *Who's Who* titles. *Who's Who in the World* and *Who's Who in America* are included, as are regional and topical *Who's Who* titles. *Who Was Who in America*, a title intended to provide retrospective coverage, is also available. In total, more than 1.5 million individuals are included in this database, which may be searched by fifteen fields including name, occupation, gender, degrees, colleges or universities, year of graduation, hobbies, and religion. These fields may be searched individually or in combination to create specific search statements. Many countries of the world produce some type of *Who's Who* directory, providing information about their prominent citizens, such as *Canadian Who's Who*, *Who's Who in the World*, and *The International Who's Who*.

A specialized directory useful for finding biographical information on contemporary scholars is *American Men and Women of Science* (*AMWS*). *AMWS* includes biographical entries on nearly 151,000 living scientists from the United States and Canada. Entries include birth date and place, field of specialty, education, career history, awards, memberships, research/publication information, and contact information. *AMWS* is available online independently, as part of *Biography in Context* and through the *Gale Virtual Reference Library*. It should also be noted that significant information about current scholars, such as contact information, research interests, publications, awards, and fellowships, is often readily available by visiting the website of the scholar's academic institution.

Indexes

Biography and Genealogy Master Index includes citations from more than 2,000 publications that provide biographical information. Currently, the index provides access to more than seventeen million citations relating to over five million individuals. The number of citations is continually rising, as an estimated 600,000 new entries are added every year and existing citations are retained, not removed. Although the source provides little biographical data within its entries—just name, birth, and death dates—it effectively points the researcher, via source citations,

Results for Basic Search: (Riley, James Whitcomb)

Mark	Riley, James Whitcomb (1849-1916) 102 Citations
Mark	Riley, James Whitcomb (1849-) 1 Citation
Mark	Riley, James Whitcomb (d1916) 1 Citation
Mark	Riley, James Whitcomb 1 Citation
Mark	Riley, James Whitcomb (1852?-1916) 1 Citation
Mark	Riley, James Whitcomb (1853-) 1 Citation
Mark	Riley, James Whitcomb (1853-1916) 4 Citations
Mark	Riley, James Whitcomb (1854?-1916) 1 Citation

Figure 25.2 Authority control in biographical batabases. An example of search results that lack authority control and consist of multiple forms of entry for the same individual.

to published biographical information. The database is updated twice a year and allows for cumulative searching of the entire print series. A note of caution regarding *Biography and Genealogy Master Index* lies in the method of including names. Names and dates are included as they appear in the title that has been indexed; no attempt is made at authority control. Therefore, a single individual may have multiple entries under various forms of the same name (see Figure 25.2).

Biography Index Past and Present provides access to more than 1.2 million book and article citations. These citations are not limited to biographies and autobiographies but include interviews, obituaries, letters, diaries, memoirs, juvenile literature, reviews, and bibliographies. Coverage includes persons from the past and the present, of all nationalities and from all fields of interest. Unlike *Biography and Genealogy Master Index*, authority control is employed to ensure easy access to individuals regardless of possible name variations. The source is available online individually or via *Biography Reference Bank*. The online source may be searched cumulatively, is updated daily, and provides retrospective coverage going back to 1946.

Biographical Dictionaries

Current

Current Biography, which began publication in 1940, is a useful biographical source, enduringly popular with users and librarians. Complete with photographs, family life, and physical descriptions of the biographees, *Current Biography* provides accurate and readable essay-length biographies of international personalities. Subjects tend to have had some impact on American life and are often important figures in popular culture. The print source is published monthly, with sixteen to eighteen profiles in each issue as well as brief obituaries for past entrants who are recently deceased. The monthly issues are gathered into an annual yearbook that also contains additional current and cumulative indexing. The title is also available electronically as *Current Biography Illustrated*, and the database contains the entire contents of all print issues, more than 30,000 articles and obituaries and 35,000 images. This source is also included in *Biography Reference Bank*.

Containing profiles of almost any published American writer, including novelists, poets, columnists, cartoonists, screen and television writers, and more, *Contemporary Authors* is an extremely comprehensive choice for biographical information about authors. Produced by Gale since 1962, it references more than 120,000 authors. Described as a bio-bibliographical guide, the work contains biographical details, references to recent news about the author, biographical and critical references, and more. Modern writers and significant writers from the early 20th century from around the world are included and, when possible, biographical information is provided directly from the entrant. The source is available online individually, as a part of *Biography in Context* or as part of Gale's *Literature Resource Center.*

Newsmakers is designed to provide profiles of prominent contemporary individuals from various backgrounds and professions. Like *Current Biography, Newsmakers* covers all fields, from government and business to entertainment and sports. Issues appear quarterly and are gathered annually into a cumulative volume. Also published by Gale, *Contemporary Black Biography* focuses on important persons of African heritage. Each volume contains at least fifty-five biographies. Name, occupation, nationality, and subject indexes are included in each volume. Both *Newsmakers* and *Contemporary Black Biography* are available through the *Gale Virtual Reference Library* or as part of *Biography in Context.*

Current and Retrospective

Encyclopedia of World Biography, including its supplements and updates, contains almost 8,000 biographical sketches of current and historical figures. In addition to the more expected historical entrants, movie, television, and music stars are included. The text is eminently readable and, thus, accessible to students as well as the general public. Illustrations and bibliographical references are provided for many of the entries and extensive indexing is available. The source is well organized and easily usable in print, but it is also available as part of *Biography in Context.*

African American National Biography contains over 4,000 entries written and signed by distinguished scholars under the direction of editors in chief Henry Louis Gates, Jr., and Evelyn Brooks Higginbotham (2013). The coverage spans almost 500 years, from 1528 to the present day. The scope includes slaves, abolitionists, writers, politicians, business people, athletes, lawyers, and civil rights leaders. Each entry is followed by a section of suggestions for further reading. Indexes allow access by category or area of renown and by birthplace. There are also lists of African American prizewinners, medalists, members of Congress, and judges. The regularly updated entries are available online as part of the *Oxford African American Studies Center. Contemporary Hispanic Biography* presents biographical information pertaining to prominent individuals of Latino heritage. The source includes Hispanic people of various nationalities and in numerous fields, from art, music, and literature to science, politics, and business. The source is available in print, as an e-book, or online as a database.

Retrospective

Dictionary of American Biography, or *DAB*, is a massive work containing narrative biographical accounts for more than 19,000 prominent deceased Americans. All entries are evaluative, written by scholars, and focused on the public life of the featured individual. Some personal information is also included, as are bibliographical references for further reading. The first volumes of this source were published in the late 1920s, with the index following in the late 1930s; updates and supplements provide coverage through 1980, and a comprehensive index was published in 1990. Although long accepted as an excellent reference source, like many sources from the early 20th century, it lacks of diversity; entries for women and minorities are quite limited. As it is now dated, researchers should consult additional sources, when possible, to guarantee accuracy and thoroughness. Continuing biographical coverage of deceased Americans in the tradition of the *DAB*, *The Scribner Encyclopedia of American Lives* provides access to thousands of entries and is available in print, online, and via the *Gale Virtual Reference Library*.

Compared to *DAB*, *American National Biography* (*ANB*) is an equally massive, but far more recent, biographical work focusing on significant deceased Americans and individuals of consequence in America. Although some figures featured in *American National Biography* are also in *DAB*, *ANB* has worked diligently to expand coverage and include persons overlooked by *DAB*, especially women, minorities, and precolonial figures. Entries are signed, are lengthy, include bibliographical references, and often include illustrations. The source is available in print and electronically with the online version regularly revised, updated, and expanded. Online access points include gender, birth and death dates, and occupations. Serious scholars who are researching figures included in both *ANB* and *DAB* should consult both entries.

Dictionary of National Biography was originally published in the late 1800s to profile deceased persons of distinction from Great Britain and Ireland. A new edition, titled *Oxford Dictionary of National Biography*, is available electronically and in print. This edition features more than 60,000 deceased persons of significance in Britain. The popular and the scholarly, the ancient and the modern, are all included in this award-winning revision. In the regularly updated online version, search options include searches by person, full text, bibliographic references, contributors, or images.

The major source for historically important Canadians is the *Dictionary of Canadian Biography* (*DCB*). The print version of the *DCB* is arranged chronologically rather than alphabetically, and each volume contains essays about individuals who contributed to a specific period of Canadian history. Free online access to the set is available, including content from forthcoming volumes. The online *DCB* supports searching by name or keyword and limiting by date range, gender, or occupation.

Developed by the Australian National University, the *Australian Dictionary of Biography*, which is available in print or online, contains over 12,000 entries on persons who were representative in Australian history. Coverage currently extends to 1990, with plans to extend coverage to subsequent decades. Browsing may be done by name or by occupation, and the advanced search feature enables access by dates and place of birth/death, religious influence, cultural heritage, occupation, and gender.

World Biographical Information System Online (*WBIS Online*) offers biographical access to over six million individuals. Information from the 4th century BCE to the present is included, as is the content of twenty-nine of K. G. Saur's biographical archives series. International in scope, entrants represent all countries, professions, and areas of renown. *WBIS Online* includes index listings as well as digitized copies of many original biographical articles.

Retrospective sources may also focus on particular ethnic or gender groups or professions. Examples include *Dictionary of Scientific Biography* (*DSB*) and its supplement *New Dictionary of Scientific Biography*. Articles describe work and career and conclude with a bibliography of works by and about each scientist. The two publications exist in an online version called the *Complete Dictionary of Scientific Biography* and are available as part of the *Gale Virtual Reference Library*. *Notable American Women*, published in three parts, provides scholarly essays on historically significant American women from 1607 through the 20th century. Each entry contains a life history covering personal and career events and concludes with a list of primary and secondary sources for further research. Electronic access is available via *Credo Reference*.

Aggregate Sources

Although general aggregators of online reference sources, such as *Credo Reference*, include a growing number of biographical titles, several aggregate sources devoted to biographical information provide even richer coverage. *Biography in Context*, an easy-to-use online source, provides biographical access to more than 650,000 individuals and integrates contextual articles and media to clarify the overall impact of the featured individuals. Entries are regularly expanded and continual updates are made to reflect current events. It is universal in scope, including current and historical figures from around the world and from all areas of interest. Biographical information from more than 170 titles from Gale and its partners, including, but not limited to, *Newsmakers*, *Contemporary Authors*, and *Contemporary Black Biography* are indexed and made available full-text. Full-text articles from hundreds of magazines and newspapers are included in this comprehensive database, as are websites, illustrations, and audio/video clips. This media-rich content does much to ensure that the researcher will find something at the desired level on the individual in question. Quick name searching, advanced searching, and biographical facts searching (by birth/death years and places, nationality, ethnicity, occupation, gender) make this a useful tool for novices and experts alike. The convenience and time savings of searching so many standard and accepted reference works at one time are significant.

Biography Reference Bank is an aggregate tool available online from EBSCO. This source provides biographical information for more than 750,000 individuals, with over 3.5 million total records. *Biography Index*, *Current Biography*, *World Authors*, *Junior Authors & Illustrators Series*, and more are combined with biographical material from other reference publishers (such as Greenwood Publishing and Oxford University Press) to provide the substance for this resource. In addition to narrative biographies, more than 35,000 images and links to more than 650,000 full-text periodical articles are provided, as are interviews, reviews, speeches, and obituaries. This extensive database allows searching by name, profession, place of origin, gender, ethnicity, birth and/or death date, titles of works, and keywords. As with *Biography in Context*, the overall convenience and time that may be saved by accessing these numerous titles via one interface and one search is substantial.

Similar in function to *Biography in Context* and *Biography Reference Bank*, *Biography Reference Center* provides access to both brief and extensive biographies as well as related supporting articles. The database boasts over 430,000 full-text biographies, including access to the content of *Biography Today*, as well as selected content from a number of respected reference titles such as *American National Biography*, *Encyclopedia Britannica*, and the Congressional Biography entries from *America Reference Library: Biography*. The database supports keyword searching and users can also opt to locate biographies by browsing a variety of categories, including occupation, nationality, and publication.

Free Web Resources

Biography.com began as an outgrowth of the Arts & Entertainment channel's popular *Biography* television program. Providing access to more than 7,000 biographical entries, the database is not limited to those who have been featured on the program; however, the coverage for those who have been featured is more extensive. Although emphasizing coverage of figures in popular culture, historical figures and scholars are also included. This user-friendly and familiar site is a worthwhile free source of legitimate biographical information. *Infoplease Biography*, an affiliate of the *Infoplease* almanac, provides access to more than 30,000 brief biographical entries. These listings can be searched by name, browsed by occupational category, or browsed by race and ethnicity. *The Biographical Dictionary* is a crowdsourced database that provides entries for numerous individuals of current interest. This source invites users to edit existing biographical entries or even create entries for themselves. Thanks to this wiki model, the scope of the entries is quite broad and the database can be a useful starting point for research. As with any community-created website, findings should be evaluated for accuracy and authority.

Book-Length Biographies

Biographical queries are perennially popular at the reference desk and some users do not wish to stop their investigation with mere articles. Recommendations for book-length biographical works may also be requested. Both factual and fictionalized book-length biographies exist, and the librarian should take care to ascertain which type of coverage is desired. Standard readers' advisory sources, such as those discussed in Chapter 21, may be useful, and readers' advisory tools with a biographical or historical focus should also be consulted. Daniel Burt's (2001) *The Biography Book* provides recommendations for factual biographies, biographical novels, fictional portraits, and even juvenile biographies, while Burt's (2003) *What Historical Novel Do I Read Next?* and Donald K. Hartman and Gregg Sapp's (1994) *Historical Figures in Fiction* each focus on fictionalized accounts. Recommendations for hundreds of memoirs, biographies, and autobiographies are available through *Read on Biography* and *Read on Life Stories*. Theatrical and cinematic adaptations of biographies may also be of interest to users. *The Biography Book* provides references to both, and free Web sources, such as the *Internet Movie Database*, may also be helpful.

SEARCH STRATEGIES

When developing a search strategy to locate biographical information, a number of factors should be considered, such as what the patron knows about the individual being sought, what the patron is hoping to learn about the individual, and at what level the information is needed. Whether the person is well known or obscure, whether the coverage should be scholarly or popular, whether the user is sure of the spelling or unsure of even the name, there are sources and strategies that can be employed to attempt to locate the required information.

When the subject of the search is well known, it is possible, even likely, that the problem will not lie in being able to find something about the individual; rather, it will lie in finding too much. When there is an abundance of information available, the librarian may find it wise to assist the patron in evaluating the search results to determine which sources are most appropriate. When the individual sought is not well known, finding anything may become an issue, and it may be necessary to employ sources with a regional or local focus. If the patron knows very little about the individual being sought, it can be very difficult to narrow the search or even to be sure that the located results are for the correct person. It is extremely important for the librarian to obtain any and all information possible from the patron. Information that the patron may feel is insignificant or information that the patron is hesitant to share because they are unsure of its accuracy may well be the information that the librarian will need in order to conduct a successful search. It may also happen that a patron claiming to need biographical information about an individual in fact needs information related to that person's work instead. Thus, a thorough reference interview, investigating everything from where the patron heard of the individual to any variations on the name or spelling of the name, to what the patron is actually hoping to find, is essential and no detail at this stage should be discounted.

Biographical information exists in a range of depth and completeness, from thorough, scholarly articles to popular, gossipy coverage. In order to perform a successful reference transaction, it is necessary for the librarian to ascertain the level of coverage desired by the patron. It is unlikely that an elementary school student would find an article from the *Dictionary of American Biography* useful and readable or that a graduate student would find a single profile from *Current Biography* sufficient for research; however, it is equally unlikely that a librarian can assume what level of coverage is most appropriate for a patron. Therefore, in order to avoid misunderstandings and assumptions, the librarian should try to investigate the level and depth of coverage desired during the interview process. If the patron is hesitant to clarify the level needed, the librarian may wish to consider offering a number of sources at varying levels of complexity. The patron can then choose the desired source, thus indicating to the librarian the type of coverage preferred if additional information is necessary.

Factual Data

If the patron is looking for brief, factual data, such as birth or death dates, full name, education, or contact information, biographical directories are excellent sources. If the individual is famous, basic information such as nationality and whether the individual is still alive may be known to the patron and the librarian. If so, it may be possible to go without hesitation to the appropriate directory. *Marquis Biographies Online* is a noteworthy possibility for living figures. As this source includes regional and topical *Who's Who* titles, multiple sources can be consulted quickly and easily. In addition to biographical directories, encyclopedia articles may well prove an effective resource for general, factual data about well-known individuals.

Single-volume universal biographies, which do not restrict by time, place, or subject and include both the living and the dead, have long served as starting points for biographical research. Titles of this type include *Merriam-Webster's Biographical Dictionary* and *Chambers Biographical Dictionary*. Both sources are available electronically, *Merriam-Webster's* via *Biography in Context* and *Chambers* via *Credo Reference*; however, neither source has been recently updated. Therefore, *Biography in Context, Biography Reference Bank,* and *Biography Reference Center*, which are regularly updated electronic aggregate sources, may now be the best approach for initial research.

When the subject in question is not known to the librarian and the patron can provide little detail, the librarian may find it efficient to consult an indirect source, such as *Biography and Genealogy Master Index*, in order to determine in which titles the individual will be found. If available, an electronic source such as *Biography in Context* can act as both an indirect and a direct source for this type of question. A single search in such a source can provide a variety of information as well as references to additional content in the event there is need to pursue the subject further.

Narrative Biographies

If the patron is looking for essay-length coverage, and the individual is well known, it may be possible to progress directly to an appropriate source. Important historical figures of British descent may be available in the *Oxford Dictionary of National Biography*; historical figures of American heritage may be found in either the *Dictionary of American Biography* or *American National Biography*. If the person sought is fairly well known but the nationality of the person is in question, a source such as *Encyclopedia of World Biography*, which is international in scope, may provide an entry. If the figure sought is well known but currently famous or popular, sources such as *Current Biography* or even *Biography.com* may be most appropriate. As noted here, if very little is known about the individual being sought, an indirect source such as *Biography and Genealogy Master Index* or an aggregate source such as *Biography in Context* or *Biography Reference Bank* should be consulted early in the search in order to locate information with a minimum of lost time and fruitless searching.

If the user is hoping to locate detailed or exhaustive coverage of an individual, a number of steps will be required. Indirect biographical sources should be consulted to obtain references to articles that are available in the standard biographical reference tools. Then the articles located should be consulted for any bibliographic references or recommendations that may be included. Information about the individual of interest may also be available in non-biographical periodical articles. Sources such as *Biography in Context, Biography Reference Bank, Biography Reference Center*, or even a general periodical index can provide access to such articles. If the user is hoping to obtain as much information about the person in question as possible, the existence of a full-length biography or autobiography of the individual should be investigated. The library catalog, available union catalogs such as *WorldCat*, as well as biographical bibliographies (such as *The Biography Book* and related titles listed in this chapter's Suggested Readings), may be consulted to determine if such a work is available.

Subject Inquiries

A number of sources are designed to help searchers locate information on individuals prominent in a particular subject area or vocation. Sources such as *Contemporary Authors, Something about the Author, American Men and Women of Science, Oxford Art Online*, and *Oxford Music Online* are just a few of the numerous subject-specific sources available. These specialized sources, due to their more limited scope, often include a larger number of entrants from the field and information at a greater level of detail. If the profession or field of the individual sought is known to the patron, these subject-specific sources may be a good starting point. If it is not known whether a subject-specific source is available, a guide to biographical sources (see Suggested Readings) should be consulted for further information. A number of excellent subject-specific free websites also may be consulted for biographical information. *Union List of Artist Names* (*ULAN*), *Internet Movie Database* (*IMDb*), *AllMusic, POTUS: Presidents of the United States*, and *The First Ladies* are just a few of the subject-specific free websites that can provide reliable biographical information. Professional directories, although limited in the biographical information they provide, may also serve a purpose in biographical searching. These directories often provide an opportunity to verify the name, licenses, and educational credentials of individuals who are not included in more standard biographical sources.

Authors and writers are particularly well covered in many general biographical sources. Additionally, there are a number of excellent sources that focus on this vocation. Authors and illustrators of works for children are well covered in Gale's *Something about the Author*. If the subject of the search might be considered a writer by any definition, *Contemporary Authors* should be checked for coverage. *Dictionary of Literary Biography*, a related work to the *Contemporary Authors Series*, is also an excellent source of biographical information for literary figures. These sources, which provide thorough cross-referencing, can be quite valuable when dealing with questions of pseudonyms. *Contemporary Authors, Contemporary Authors New Revision Series, Dictionary of Literary Biography*, and more are available electronically via Gale's *Literature Resource Center*. As this aggregate source also includes works focusing on literary criticism, it is a particularly effective resource for those searching not only for biographical information about an author but also for critical information about the author's works. *Contemporary Authors* and *Contemporary Authors New Revision* are also included in *Biography in Context*, which may be more widely available than *Literature Resource Center*, especially in smaller libraries.

It is not uncommon for a librarian to be asked to help a patron identify an individual who fits a particular set of biographical criteria. Often related to school assignments, librarians may be faced with the challenge of finding an individual of a certain nationality, race, or ethnicity who is prominent in a particular field or profession. Searches of this type have been, historically, difficult and labor intensive. However, with the powerful search capabilities and excellent access points of the electronic biographical sources, such searches have become much simpler, as illustrated in Box 25.1. *American National Biography, Oxford Dictionary of National Biography, Biography in Context, Biography Reference Center*, and *Biography Reference Bank*, among others, allow searching by a variety of criteria such as gender, vocation, ethnicity, place of birth, date of birth, and date of death.

Box 25.1 Activity: Combining Criteria in Biographical Searching

An elementary student was assigned to write a report on a male photojournalist of African American descent. Such a task seemed hopeless to the student and his grandmother when they approached the reference desk; however, with the assistance of *Biography in Context*'s Person Search, an appropriate individual was identified in a matter of minutes. The librarian used the various options in the search interface to specify Occupation=photojournalist, Ethnicity=African American, and Gender=male. The search resulted in ten matches, including John H. White, a photojournalist for the *Chicago Sun-Times*. The search yielded links to three articles on White in *Contemporary Black Biography*, *Contemporary Authors Online*, and *Who's Who Among African Americans*.

Use *Biography in Context* or another online biographical database to locate the following:

- Photojournalists of an ethnicity of your choice
- African American woman in the medical or health care fields in the 19th century
- Someone born on your birthdate

Questions for Reflection and Discussion:

1. What search limits were available? Which were most helpful for these searches?
2. Can you think of other reference scenarios where these search limits would be useful?

Images

If a picture of the subject is required, there are a number of sources that may be useful. While some may feel that images are only sought by schoolchildren writing reports, a vast amount of information that may not be readily available elsewhere can be gleaned from the image of an individual. Details of a person's appearance are not regularly included in many of the traditional sources; however, the searcher may observe that information firsthand if an image is available. Standard biographical sources, such as *Encyclopedia of World Biography* (online via *Biography in Context*) and *Current Biography* (online via *Biography Reference Bank*) generally provide images of their entrants. In many electronic sources, it is possible to limit the search to entries with illustrations. Encyclopedias, especially those designed for young people, can serve as an excellent source for images. Web search tools, such as *Google Images*, may provide quick electronic access to hard-to-find pictures. Images relating to the work of the individual in question, such as campaign posters and political cartoons, may provide additional insight and perspective. When dealing with requests for images, the librarian may be faced with the dilemma of having to explain to patrons why no photographs exist for certain figures of historical significance. It is important for the librarian to remain patient and tactful when explaining the time limitations of photographic technology and to offer artists' renderings as a possible alternative.

Recently Deceased

Individuals who are recently deceased may, for a brief period, still be listed in the current sources; however, after they are removed from the current sources, it may take some time before they are included in the retrospective sources. During this gap, it may be necessary to consult alternative sources. Electronic resources that are regularly updated, particularly sources that include newspaper, magazine, or journal articles, may fill this need. Biographical sources that index periodicals, such as *Biography Reference Center*, *Biography in Context*, and *Biography Reference Bank*, as well as general periodical indexes, may be extremely useful.

Obituaries

Obituaries can provide a wealth of biographical information on the famous as well as on the lesser known. Obituaries for famous individuals may be accessed in a number of ways. The *New York Times Obituaries Index* is a standard source to use when searching for obituaries of the well known. The index is available in print or obituaries can be searched online from the *New York Times* archive. The online *New York Times* archive may be searched for citations free of charge; however, full-text coverage must be purchased. *Current Biography* provides short obituary notices with references to the *New York Times* obituaries for past biographees. The content of *Current Biography* and, thus, the obituaries, is available electronically. *Biography and Genealogy Master Index* may also be used to find some obituary references. Often, obituaries will be published even for lesser-known figures, particularly in the local newspaper of the person's hometown. Historically, the obituaries published in these small-town newspapers became inaccessible over time. While the newspaper itself may have been preserved in microform, access to the contents of the said paper was often quite limited due to a lack of indexing. Currently, a number of retrospective indexing and digitization projects are helping to save these valuable records from obscurity. Librarians should be sure to investigate this possible avenue of access for obituaries published in local papers. Because newspaper websites may make their obituary sections freely available, searches using a web search engine such as *Google* may also yield a needed obituary.

Local and Lesser-Known Personalities

If the patron is attempting to locate information on local or lesser-known personalities, it will be necessary to alter the search strategy and sources employed. As patrons can pose queries about anyone and comparatively few persons are ever included in biographical reference sources, biographical requests for the local and lesser-known can be daunting. However, it is important to remember that virtually all persons are listed somewhere, even if only in local sources. Locally compiled and created resources, particularly local newspapers, are excellent potential sources. Vital records, city directories, or yearbooks from local institutions may also provide biographical insights. Until recently, using such sources necessitated research visits and interlibrary loan requests. Now, as many libraries and institutions have begun creating databases of local history information and records, much information is available via the web. Visiting the websites of the libraries in the area where the individual lived or achieved prominence should give some indication as to what information is available electronically, or, if not yet available online, what is available in print. If sources are available to be consulted remotely, the librarian should explain their accessibility and worth to the patron to ensure the patron's ability to exploit them. If the sources are not available for use remotely, the librarian should explain what sources are held, what they may contain, and what options exist for consulting those sources, including interlibrary loan, document delivery, or site visits. *Facebook*, *LinkedIn*, and other social networking sites that invite users to share autobiographical information may serve as useful sources of biographical information for the lesser known. Even if the persons in question have not been included in the standard biographical sources, they may have chosen to share details on these sites. Similarly, collaboratively created web sources, such as *Wikipedia*, may provide significant amounts of information about minor celebrities. As with any information that is obtained from sources that are not under consistent editorial control, the information located on social networking and collaborative sites should be evaluated fully for accuracy.

GENEALOGICAL INFORMATION

Genealogical queries are a subset of biographical questions and are quite popular, especially in public libraries and in libraries that house a special collection focusing on family or local history. Because of their popularity, it is necessary for all reference librarians to be familiar with some of the basic genealogical sources. A number of excellent electronic options exist when searching for genealogical information, including both freely available and subscription tools.

Subscription databases, such as *Ancestry Library Edition*, *HeritageQuest Online*, and *Findmypast*, provide extensive coverage and access to works of genealogical research. *Ancestry Library Edition* includes access to Census data, draft registrations, passenger and immigration lists, the Social Security Death Master File, also known as the Social Security Death Index (SSDI), and more. *HeritageQuest* is also helpful for United States Census information and is notable for indexing thousands of genealogical texts and journals. *Findmypast* provides searchable access to over four billion census, historical, and directory records with a British, Irish, and Australian focus. *FamilySearch*, a free resource from the Church of Jesus Christ of the Latter-day Saints, shares introductory information about conducting genealogical research and also provides access to various databases of nondenominational genealogical information. Accessible content includes the catalog of the Church's Family History Library, indexes of birth and marriage registers that have been transcribed from microfilm, and the *International Genealogical Index*. *Cyndi's List of Genealogy Sites on the Internet* provides a categorized index to genealogical resources on the Web, serving as a free starting point for online research.

Numerous genealogical sites and tools have been created and posted by volunteers. Projects such as the *RootsWeb* and the *USGenWeb* are examples of tools created by dedicated genealogical volunteers. *RootsWeb* hosts a multitude of surname discussion groups and also provides access to significant primary source material, such as obituaries, tax lists, and local histories. *The USGenWeb Project* is facilitated by volunteers and is organized by state and county. The project provides access to geographically arranged genealogical discussions and content. *Find a Grave*, a moderated site containing much crowdsourced information about graves and cemetery records, is another example of a volunteer-driven resource. As with all crowdsourced content, information should be evaluated for accuracy and authority.

As when searching for information on local personalities, genealogical requests may necessitate consultation of primary source materials, whereby the reference request may quickly move into the realm of research. Primary source materials such as birth, death, and marriage certificates; census records; and tombstones provide a wealth of genealogical and biographical information but can be very time consuming and labor intensive to locate. The responsibility of the librarian usually does not lie in conducting the research for the patron; rather, it lies in conveying to the patron the types of sources that may be available, the information that they may contain, and direction on how to locate and obtain the records. Libraries, genealogical groups, and historical societies often hold a wealth of archival sources that may be available to researchers. Additionally, many of these organizations are working to make digitized content available electronically from their websites. As noted, *Ancestry Library Edition*, *HeritageQuest*, and *FamilySearch* all provide access to some primary source documents. The National Archives and Records Administration hosts a *Resources for Genealogists* site that provides access to and information about immigration records, land records, census information, military service records, and more.

The National Archives and Records Administration also provides a more detailed guide to immigration information on its *Immigration Records* page. For immigrants to the United States, naturalization records may be available from the U.S. Citizenship and Immigration Service (USCIS). The USCIS hosts a website, *Genealogy*, which details the available records and how they can be requested. Immigration records may also be available from the immigrant's port of entry to the United States. Large and historically significant ports of entry, such as Ellis Island and Castle Clinton Monument, host websites providing online access to records and information. Immigration records for Angel Island, the major West Coast immigration station, are housed in the National Archives.

Land and property ownership records can provide valuable information. *Land Records*, from the National Archives and Records Administration, provides information about locating and obtaining records of land transfers from the U.S. government to private ownership. *General Land Office Records*, from the Bureau of Land Management, provides some access to federal land conveyance records. *Sanborn Maps*, which were originally used to assess fire insurance risk, provides detailed histories of many U.S. localities. While archives often hold paper copies of their local *Sanborn Maps*, the collection is available electronically as *Digital Sanborn Maps* from ProQuest.

FICTIONAL PERSONALITIES

Reference questions may arise that are presumed to be biographical in nature but, in fact, focus on a fictional personality instead of an actual person. While the librarian may determine that the name in question is that of a fictional personality, it may require some tact when conveying this information to a patron who believes the person to be real. Literary characters, gods, or epic heroes may be the focus of such inquiries. General and subject encyclopedias, such as those focusing on literature, folklore, mythology, and religion, may be helpful when searching for references to fictional figures. Individuals who were alive at some point but who have since attained legendary status, such as saints, folk heroes, and outlaws, may also pose unique challenges. Biographical studies of saints are often quite glorified, frequently to the point that it is considered hagiography. Legends surrounding folk heroes and outlaws (and especially outlaws who have evolved into folk heroes) are often exaggerated as well, and careful checking will be required to verify occurrences as fact.

CONCLUSION

A plethora of quality sources exist that provide biographical information. Evaluating, selecting, and recommending biographical sources is an important aspect of reference work at most libraries. Questions about the lives of people are popular with patrons of all ages, and librarians must be prepared to assist these patrons in their research. Enhanced knowledge of biographical tools, strategies, and tips will empower librarians to better meet the reference needs of their patrons.

REFERENCE

Katz, William. 2002. *Introduction to Reference Work.* 8th ed. Boston: McGraw-Hill.

LIST OF SOURCES

All Music. http://www.allmusic.com.

American Men and Women of Science. 2012. Detroit: Gale Research. Available online as part of *Gale Virtual Reference Library* and *Biography in Context.*

American National Biography. 1999. New York: Oxford University Press. Supplements, 2000–. Available online: http://www.anb.org. Subscription required.

America Reference Library: Biography. Orem: Western Standard Publishing Company.

Ancestry Library Edition. Ann Arbor, MI: ProQuest. http://ancestrylibrary.proquest.com. Subscription required.

Australian Dictionary of Biography. http://adb.anu.edu.au.

Biographical Dictionary. http://www.s9.com/.

Biography and Genealogy Master Index. Detroit: Gale Group. https://www.gale.com/c/biography-and-genealogy-master-index. Subscription required.

Biography in Context. Detroit: Gale Cengage Learning. https://www.gale.com/c/in-context-biography. Subscription required.

Biography Index Past and Present. Ipswich, MA: EBSCO. https://www.ebscohost.com/academic/biography-index-past-and-present. Subscription required.

Biography Reference Bank. Ipswich, MA: EBSCO. https://www.ebsco.com/products/research-databases/biography-reference-bank. Subscription required.

Biography Reference Center. Ipswich, MA: EBSCO. https://www.ebsco.com/products/research-databases/biography-reference-center. Subscription required.

Biography Today. Detroit: Omnigraphics. Available online as part of *Biography Reference Center.*

Biography.com. http://www.biography.com.

Burt, Daniel S. 2001. *The Biography Book: A Reader's Guide to Nonfiction, Fictional, and Film Biographies of More Than 500 of the Most Fascinating Individuals of All Time.* Westport, CT: Oryx Press. Available online: http://ebooks.abc-clio.com/?isbn=9780313017261.

Burt, Daniel S. 2003. *What Historical Novel Do I Read Next?* Detroit: Gale.

Canadian Who's Who. Toronto: University of Toronto Press. http://canadianwhoswho.ca. Subscription required.

Castle Clinton Monument. The Battery Conservancy. https://www.nps.gov/cacl/index.htm.

Chambers Biographical Dictionary. 2011. London: Chambers Harrap. Available online as part of *Credo Reference.*

Complete Dictionary of Scientific Biography. 2008. Detroit: Scribner. Available online as part of *Gale Virtual Reference Library.*

Contemporary Authors. 1962–. Detroit: Gale Cengage Learning. Available online as part of *Gale Biography in Context* and *Literature Resource Center.*

Contemporary Authors New Revision Series. 1982-. Detroit: Gale Cengage Learning. Available online as part of *Gale Biography in Context* and *Literature Resource Center*

Contemporary Black Biography. 1992–. Detroit: Gale Cengage Learning. Available online and as part of *Gale Biography in Context.*

Contemporary Hispanic Biography. 2002–. Detroit: Gale Cengage Learning. Available online as part of *Gale Virtual Reference Library.*

Credo Reference. Credo Reference. http://credoreference.com. Subscription required.

Current Biography. 1940–. Ipswich, MA: EBSCO. Available online as part of *Current Biography Illustrated* and *Biography Reference Bank.*

Current Biography Illustrated. Ipswich, MA: EBSCO. https://www.ebsco.com/products/research-databases/current-biography-illustrated. Subscription required.

Cyndi's List of Genealogy Sites on the Internet. http://www.CyndisList.com.

Dictionary of American Biography. 1928–1937. New York: Scribner. Supplements, 1944–1980. Available online as part of *Biography in Context* and *Hathi Trust Digital Library.*

Dictionary of Canadian Biography. 1966-. Toronto: University of Toronto Press. http://www.biographi.ca/en/index.php.

Dictionary of Literary Biography Complete Online. Detroit: Gale Research. Available online as part of *Literature Resource Center.*

Dictionary of Scientific Biography. 1970–1980, 1990. New York: Scribner. Available online as part of *Gale Virtual Reference Library* and *Hathi Trust Digital Library.*

Digital Sanborn Maps. Ann Arbor, MI: Proquest. http://sanborn.umi.com/. Subscription required.

Encyclopaedia Britannica. http://www.britannica.com/.

Encyclopedia of World Biography. 1998. Detroit: Gale Research, Inc. Supplements, 1999–. Available online and as part of *Biography in Context.*

Facebook. https://www.facebook.com.

FamilySearch. Salt Lake City, Utah: Church of Jesus Christ of Latter-Day Saints. http://familysearch.org/.

Find a Grave. http://www.findagrave.com/.

Findmypast. http://www.findmypast.co.uk/.

The First Ladies. https://www.whitehouse.gov/about-the-white-house/first-ladies/.

Gale Virtual Reference Library. Farmington Hills, MI: Gale Cengage Learning. http://www.cengage.com. Subscription required.

Gates, Henry Louis, Jr., and Evelyn Brooks Higginbotham. 2013. *African American National Biography.* New York: Oxford University Press. Available online as part of *Oxford African American Studies Center.*

Genealogy. U.S. Citizenship and Immigration Services. http://www.uscis.gov/genealogy.

General Land Office Records. Bureau of Land Management. https://www.glorecords.blm.gov/default.aspx.

Google. http://www.google.com.

Google Images. http://images.google.com.

Hartman, Donald K., and Gregg Sapp. 1994. *Historical Figures in Fiction.* Phoenix, AZ: Oryx.

HeritageQuest Online. Ann Arbor, MI: ProQuest. http://www.proquest.com/products-services/HeritageQuest-Online.html. Subscription required.

Immigration Records. National Archives and Records Administration. http://www.archives.gov/research/immigration/.

Infoplease Biography. http://www.infoplease.com/people.html.

International Genealogical Index United States. Salt Lake City, UT: Church of Jesus Christ of Latter-Day Saints, Genealogical Dept. Available online as part of *FamilySearch.*

International Who's Who. 1935–. Abingdon-on-Thames, UK: Routledge.

Internet Movie Database (IMDb). http://www.imdb.com/.

Junior Authors & Illustrators. 2000. New York: H.W. Wilson Co. Available online as part of *Biography Reference Bank*.

Land Records. National Archives and Records Administration. http://www.archives.gov/research/land/.

LinkedIn. https://www.linkedin.com.

Literature Resource Center. Detroit: Gale Cengage Learning. https://www.gale.com/c/literature-resource-center. Subscription required.

Marquis Biographies Online. New Providence, NJ: Marquis Who's Who. http://www.marquiswhoswho.com/. Subscription required.

Merriam-Webster's Biographical Dictionary. 1996. Springfield, MA: Merriam-Webster. Available online as part of *Biography in Context*.

New Dictionary of Scientific Biography. 2007. Farmington Hills, MI: Charles Scribner's Sons. Available online as part of *Gale Virtual Reference Library*.

New York Times. New York: New York Times. https://www.nytimes.com/.

New York Times Obituaries Index. 1858–. New York: New York Times. http://www.nytimes.com/pages/obituaries/index.html.

Newsmakers. Detroit: Gale Cengage Learning. Available online as part of *Biography in Context* and *Gale Virtual Reference Library*.

Notable American Women: 1607–1950. 1971. Cambridge, MA: Belknap Press of Harvard University Press. Available online as part of *Credo Reference* and *Alexander Street Press*.

Notable American Women: A Biographical Dictionary Completing the Twentieth Century. 2004. Cambridge, MA: Belknap Press of Harvard University Press. Available online as part of *Credo Reference* and *Alexander Street Press*.

Notable American Women: The Modern Period. 1971. Cambridge, MA: Belknap Press of Harvard University Press. Available online as part of *Credo Reference* and *Alexander Street Press*.

Oxford African American Studies Center: The Online Authority on the African American Experience. New York: Oxford University Press. http://www.oxfordaasc.com/. Subscription required.

Oxford Art Online. Oxford: Oxford University Press.

Oxford Dictionary of National Biography. 2004. Oxford: Oxford University Press. Supplements 2009–. http://www.oxforddnb.com. Subscription required.

Oxford Music Online. Oxford: Oxford University Press.

POTUS: Presidents of the United States. http://potus.com/.

Reisner, Rosalind. 2009. *Read On Life Stories: Reading Lists for Every Taste*. Santa Barbara, CA: Libraries Unlimited.

Resources for Genealogists. National Archives and Records Administration. http://www.archives.gov/research/genealogy/other-websites/database-links.html.

Roche, Rick. 2012. *Read On Biography: Reading Lists for Every Taste*. Santa Barbara, CA: Libraries Unlimited.

RootsWeb. http://www.rootsweb.ancestry.com/. Subscription required.

The Scribner Encyclopedia of American Lives. 1998–. Detroit: Charles Scribner's Sons. Available online as part of *Biography in Context* and *Gale Virtual Reference Library*.

Social Security Administration. *Social Security Administration Death Master File*. Washington, D.C.: Government Publishing Office. https://dmf.ntis.gov/. Available online as *Social Security Death Index (SSDI)* online as part of *Ancestry Library Edition*.

Something About the Author. Detroit: Gale Cengage Learning. https://www.gale.com/c/literature-something-about-the-author/. Subscription required.

Union List of Artist Names (*ULAN*). Getty Research Institute. http://www.getty.edu/research/tools/vocabularies/ulan/.

USGenWeb Project. http://usgenweb.org/.

Who Was Who in America, 1897–2007. 1942–. New Providence, NJ: Marquis Who's Who. Available online as part of *Marquis Biographies Online*.

Who's Who. 1849–. London: A & C Black. Available online: http://www.ukwhoswho.com. Subscription required.

Who's Who in America. 1900–. New Providence, NJ: Marquis Who's Who. Available online as part of *Marquis Biographies Online.*

Who's Who in the Midwest. 1949–. New Providence, NJ: Marquis Who's Who. Available online as part of *Marquis Biographies Online.*

Who's Who in the World. 1972–. New Providence, NJ: Marquis Who's Who. Available online as part of *Marquis Biographies Online.*

Wikipedia. https://www.wikipedia.org/.

World Authors. 1990–. New York, NY: Wilson. Available online as part of *Biography Reference Bank.*

World Biographical Information System Online. Berlin: De Gruyter. http://db.saur.de/WBIS. Subscription required.

WorldCat. Dublin, OH: OCLC. http://www.worldcat.org.

SUGGESTED READINGS

Mann, Rupert. 2006. "Searching the *Oxford Dictionary of National Biography.*" *The Indexer* 25 (1): 16–18.

Mann explains how the option to "Search for biography of person" can exploit the metadata associated with each name to enable retrieval on alternative forms, such as maiden and married surnames.

Reference and User Services Association. 2007. *Guidelines for a Unit or Course of Instruction in Genealogical Research at Schools of Library and Information Science.* American Library Association. http://www.ala.org/rusa/resources/guidelines/guidelinesunit.

These guidelines provide an outline of the expertise needed to support library users undertaking genealogical research, including basic genealogical research methodology and major genealogy research resources. Notes accompanying the guidelines identify several sources useful in developing this expertise.

Reference and User Services Association. 2007. *Guidelines for Developing a Core Genealogy Collection.* American Library Association. http://www.ala.org/rusa/resources/guidelines/guidelinesdeveloping.

These guidelines describe the services, resources, and staff necessary to create and maintain a collection suitable for genealogical research. They are designed to help libraries build core genealogy collections and plan for basic genealogical reference assistance.

Searing, Susan E. 2007. "Biographical Reference Works for and about Women, from the Advent of the Women's Liberation Movement to the Present: An Exploratory Analysis." *Library Trends* 56 (2): 469–93.

Searing compiled a database of more than 400 English-language biographical dictionaries and collective biographies devoted to women and published in the period 1966–2006. The data was analyzed to identify trends in subject content over this period. She also highlights problems with some sources, including duplicative content, subjectivity, and factual errors and omissions. A bibliography of sources used in this study, grouped by decade, is available at https://www.ideals.illinois.edu/bitstream/handle/2142/3534/SearingWomensBiogRef-final.pdf?sequence=2.

Skarl, Susie. 2014. "This Is Your Life." *College & Research Libraries News* 75 (7): 394–406.

Skarl provides a guide to authoritative online biographical sources for notable individuals, both living and deceased, in an effort to aid students in their research. Noted sites include those from non-profit organizations, government entities, universities, and media outlets. The guide does not intend to be comprehensive, but, rather, to serve as a gateway to information about noteworthy individuals.

Wleklinski, Joann, M. 2010. "Get a Life" *Online* 34 (1): 40–44.

Wleklinski evaluates a number of online biography resources, such as *Biography Resource Center* (now *Biography in Context*) and *Biography Reference Bank.* Biographical results from the general web search tool, *Google*, are also analyzed.

Chapter 26

Government Information

Sarah Erekson

INTRODUCTION

Government information offers an exciting, unique area of reference service. Government information exists to accomplish a particular civic mission, that is, to openly record a government's activities and inform the public. Governments produce resources and publications that educate, enlighten, and entertain, although the original purpose is not for profit. The result is that government information covers nearly every imaginable topic.

Government documents are used by officials, the general public, statisticians, social workers, scientists, students, retirees, teachers, parents—in short, by almost anyone who has an information need. In addition to formal government depositories, most libraries, regardless of type, size, or location, provide government information to users. Many library practitioners use government information every day. It is not just for specialists anymore, and, of course, it never was.

This chapter focuses on strategies for discovering, locating, and using government information. It discusses the most indispensable government documents and information sources. U.S. federal government information sources are stressed, with related sources and tools from nongovernmental or commercial sources discussed as appropriate. Canadian government information is covered in its own section. Selected state, local, and intergovernmental sources, such as the United Nations (UN), are also discussed. Strategies for reference and research services using government information are integrated throughout.

GOVERNMENT INFORMATION: A BRIEF HISTORY

Government information has existed since governments were first formed, but systems for distributing it have evolved. Official channels for disseminating U.S. federal government information began with the *U.S. Constitution*, Article 1, Section 5, requiring Congress to keep and publish a journal of its proceedings. After half a century of contracting with private printers with poor results, Congress founded the Government Printing Office, now known as the Government Publishing Office (GPO), in 1861.

In 1895, the General Printing Act streamlined and expanded government information distribution into a system of depositories of public documents called the Federal Depository Library Program (FDLP). This act also mandated the creation of a catalog of all such documents, the first effort at systematic, ongoing bibliographic control of government documents.

During the 20th century, the federal government itself expanded quickly and with it the production of government information. In 1962, Congress passed a law specifically requiring depository libraries to allow all members of the public to have access to the documents. This law created a networked system of depository libraries including hubs or regional libraries that coordinated with spokes or selective libraries. This provided for flexibility for some libraries to select only what was useful to their users and also helped ensure easy access to all documents through the regional libraries that are required to receive and keep a copy of everything distributed. The end of the 20th century saw the proliferation of nonprint formats, such as microfiche, diskettes, CD-ROMS, and remotely accessible electronic information, that is, websites. Despite having minimal or no cataloging before the advent of the Online Computer Library Center (OCLC) database, bibliographic records for modern government documents are readily available and metadata for historic documents are slowly being added.

Open Government Information

Bringing government documents to the people to help make government accountable and transparent is a key principle of a formal government information distribution system. However, access to information has been formally and informally bolstered with two other movements: access to information laws (in the United States, known as freedom of information acts or FOIA) and open government initiatives.

Using access to information laws, individuals can directly request information or records that are not otherwise made publicly available. Journalists and activists have used this type of request to bring attention to government activities that are newsworthy or scandalous ("Closing the Books" 2018). For questions about accessing U.S. federal records, the following titles should be helpful. *Your Right to Federal Records: Questions and Answers on the Freedom of Information Act and the Privacy Act* and *A Citizen's Guide on Using the Freedom of Information Act and the Privacy Act of 1974 to Request Government Records* H.R. Rpt. 109–226 (2005) both outline the procedures that individuals can use to obtain access to federal records and agency files. Other levels of government, such as state and local, will have processes associated with their own access to information laws.

Pivotal to the open government movement is legislation like the *Government in the Sunshine Act* (1975). The bill's sponsor, Senator Lawton Chiles of Florida, noted that "democratic self-government and an informed citizenry just naturally go hand in hand, making essential the conduct of public business in the open, 'in the sunshine.' Only with such openness can the public judge and express, through its vote or voice, whether governmental decisions are just and fair" (118 Cong. Rec. 26902 [1972]).

Sunshine laws sought to ensure that government business meetings were open for the public to attend. When government operations were done in brick and mortar offices or face-to-face meetings, public attendance created a sense of openness and transparency. Now, most government activities utilize information and communication technologies (ICTs), so bringing the activities into the open becomes more complex.

Thus, the concept of open government becomes "increasing public access to government information through modern digital technologies" (Leveille 2015). In this new context, increasing access has the same intention as sunshine laws: to enhance citizen participation and create government accountability and responsiveness. As a subset of open government information, open government data is machine-readable data produced by government bodies or at government expense that can be "freely used, reused, and redistributed by anyone, only subject to (at the most) the requirement that users attribute the data and that they make their work available to be shared as well" (Ubaldi 2013). Open government data also includes the intent that the user can do something with the data.

Open governments may host data and digital information in portals wherein the public can access and transform these data. Taking advantage of digital technologies can be a boon to governments, encouraging citizen activism and soliciting expertise. On the other hand, relying solely on these portals creates barriers to access in populations with limited skills in data manipulation. For example, while crime data for a large city may be readily available through an open data portal, many stakeholders are not able to pull out needed statistics. Annual reports may be cumbersome to produce, but they provide snapshots and analysis that are lacking in a data portal.

Government data portals create open access to processes and details, providing the public the ability to hold agencies accountable and the opportunity to see patterns. This allows people to be a check on government power. In addition, people interact with governments using modern digital technologies or ICTs for a number of other reasons: accessing government programs and services, answering specific legal questions, obtaining permits and licenses, or requesting assistance from a government agency (Fisher, Becker, and Crandall 2010). Library roles in assisting patrons in these interactions may include facilities (i.e., public access computers or space for government agency liaisons to assist users filling out online-only forms), programming (i.e., one-on-one technology coaching or computer classes), or expertise (i.e., reference staff familiarity with local e-government websites).

In 2007, Darrell M. West did a survey of state and federal e-government in the United States. Some of the issues he identified were reliability, security and privacy, accessibility for people with disabilities, adaptability to various devices, and readability. Ten years later, these are still major hurdles. Analysis done in 2017 by the Information Technology and Innovation Foundation on U.S. government websites found that most federal websites continue to fall short on these critical standards (Castro, Nurko, and McQuinn 2017).

USES AND CHARACTERISTICS

U.S. government documents are officially defined as "informational matter which is published as an individual document at Government expense, or as required by law" (44 United States Code 1901). Basic government information sources include the laws and official records of government entities, information of an administrative nature, demographic and economic data, technical or scholarly reports, and informational matter for general use by the public. The percentage of current U.S. federal government information available online is extremely high, and trending ever closer toward 100 percent. GPO's emphasis is on discovery and stewardship of government information, regardless of format, and it continues to work hard in the areas of identification of materials, cataloging and metadata, preservation, and ensuring perpetual access to government information in all formats.

On a significantly smaller scale, state governments produce a similar range of state government information. State governments may rely upon electronic formats to satisfy legal requirements and provide no-fee information access to depositories and the public, although some still maintain formal depository systems. Local governments, foreign-country governments, and intergovernmental organizations (IGOs), such as the North Atlantic Treaty Organization and the United Nations, create government information, although the output and volume of these entities vary greatly. Nonetheless, e-publishing, websites, databases, and e-government services have increased the availability of all levels of government information and resulted in better access for many patrons.

Organization of Documents

U.S. federal government documents use a unique classification system called the Superintendent of Documents system, referred to as SuDoc. Unlike Dewey or Library of Congress, the SuDoc system is based on the issuing agency, that is, provenance rather than subject. Class numbers are based on agency, subagency, and publication series, type, or form. For example, the SuDoc number for *Nail Gun Safety: A Guide for Construction Contractors*, L 35.8:N 14, is constructed as follows.

SuDoc numbers are devised and assigned by GPO to materials in all formats as outlined in the *Superintendent of Documents Classification Guidelines*. Although

TABLE 26.1 Example of a SuDoc Number

L				Department of Labor
	35			Occupational Health and Safety Administration (OSHA)
		.8		Handbooks, manuals, and guides
			:N 14	Cutter for title word "Nail"
				Nail Gun Safety: A Guide for Construction Contractors

some libraries have classified and integrated documents into their regular collections using the Library of Congress or Dewey classification schemes, the SuDoc system is universal and used in many standard bibliographies, such as the *Catalog of U.S. Government Publications*. The SuDoc classification scheme allows the user to find a particular item and/or browse an agency or subagency's publications on the shelves. Understanding the SuDoc system remains essential for reference, classification, and access purposes. It comprehensively illustrates every U.S. government unit, relationships within these units, changes over time, and the publishing output of the units, historically and currently. Other levels of government information may be classified by similar schema based on provenance. Some classifications systems may be well documented and useful as a finding aid, such as the UN Document Symbols; other systems may be homegrown.

Web domain names also represent an authoritative type of information organization. Most U.S. government information is at the .gov domain, although the U.S. Department of Defense uses. mil for most of its websites. Quasi-governmental entities, such as the Smithsonian Institution, may use another; Smithsonian's is .edu. The UN uses the .org domain. Most state governments use either a variation on their postal abbreviation and .us or the state name with .gov. Other national-level governments generally use their assigned country extension.

Uses of Government Information

As mentioned before, users of government information can be nearly anyone, but how and why someone needs government information can impact the librarian's reference strategy. Perhaps the patron needs an answer to factual questions about the government, its personnel, or its activities. Or perhaps the patron does not ask for government information specifically, but the wealth of historical information about the country, its geographic and political units, and its people contained in government information fulfills the information need. In the following section, the major types of reference activity utilizing government documents are highlighted.

A major category of reference use of documents is bibliographic verification, or supplying bibliographic information about a particular document. The question may take the form of "What is the *Serial Set* volume number of House Document 91–102?" or "This citation says the call number is ED 202716, what does that mean?" Upon identification of the item or source, the question becomes how to find the desired document within the library's tangible collection or online. Similarly, government reports and statistical tables are cited daily in newspapers and other media, and a librarian may be asked to find the original source (Kline 2013). Increasingly, search engines can identify current known-item requests. Familiarity with major government surveys, series, abbreviations, and acronyms is fundamental to the search process.

Answering questions about legislation and public laws is standard practice in government information reference service. A patron may be looking for a specific fact, such as the date the president signed a bill into law, or may be interested in the status of proposed legislation and need either a succinct overview or in-depth coverage. Locating official versions of these publications, whether in print or in electronic format, can be straightforward, as long as an accurate citation is available or can be easily ascertained.

Usually, current information is needed, but historical queries are common. Local collections and online repositories of digital collections are heavily utilized, and referrals to other libraries and archives occur frequently. Another major type of assistance revolves around statistical information and data sets (covered in Chapter 27).

EVALUATION

Government information sources often are the only authoritative source on a subject. There may be no similar sources with which to compare their currency and accuracy. Evaluation of reference tools from the government therefore depends mainly on comparing features, format, indexing, ease of use, local need, and price, as well as the inclusion of complete and accurate citations to the original sources.

Commercially published reference sources provide background, present additional factual information, and offer analyses on politics, socioeconomic matters, and public officials, even critiques, and help to supplement the vast array of government-produced information tools. For instance, a patron interested in legislation might prefer the *CQ Weekly*, a weekly magazine that surveys current public policy, significant legislation, and other activities of Congress and includes major votes and other activities, to the often-more-difficult task of examining the primary source materials found in *Congress.gov*, a legislative research system discussed later in the chapter.

Government information should be evaluated as to its nature, purpose, and audience. For instance, much agency government information is by nature designed to be strictly factual and may be considered accurate. Proceedings, records, and most statistical undertakings are relatively straightforward, and the research involved is done by career staff, scientists, and statisticians. Other government information is potentially subject to disagreement, depending on politics and interpretations of specific issues. Finally, the intended audience may vary by website. *Ben's Guide to the U.S. Government* has components that are written for elementary readers; these sections may gloss over some of the intricacies of the Constitution and the branches of government. Similarly, agency posts on social media may be intended to quickly spread the word on a current issue. Returning to the agency source may be needed to get the full picture.

It is important to remember that nongovernmental sites, perhaps a university or even a private company, may host digital versions of government documents. These may not be official versions, but depending upon the user and the purpose, such digital versions may be more than sufficient.

SELECTION

The dramatic reduction of government information in print format has clearly altered the selection and acquisition of government information. The traditional method of acquiring government documents was for a library to be part of the FDLP, through which some 1,000 depository libraries would select "classes" (a designation for a particular title, series, or type of publication from a particular government entity) of depository items and receive these from GPO at no cost. The law required libraries to house and retain the materials and make them available to the general public.

Because of the preponderance of online government information, selection of government information by depositories is becoming a two-part process: first, identify those titles necessary to receive in tangible formats, and, second, identify what online government information requires localized discovery tools. However, plenty of government information is not distributed through depository programs. Identifying government information, especially local, state, and international publications, is an important skill in the digital publishing environment. In most cases, these digital documents do not have persistent URLs or assurances of permanent access. This may mean that long-term access to these publications is in jeopardy if the only way libraries provide access to these publications is by pointing to websites.[1]

To a degree, government information selection is not significantly different from any other selection process: one must be aware of the needs of users. Although most federal depositories will want to select the essential titles, decisions of what else to acquire are informed by local needs. Librarians in rural libraries located among public lands might make sure they are receiving pertinent publications from the U.S. Forest Service or the Bureau of Land Management. Similarly, librarians in the Delaware suburbs of Philadelphia might want to make sure they receive *Census of Population and Housing* volumes not only about Delaware but about Pennsylvania and Maryland as well. Although the basic government information sources are easily identified—discussed later in this chapter—the less common sources needed by patrons of a particular library have to be identified through librarians' alertness and sensitivity to their users' needs and reliance upon standard government information collection tools.

GENERAL SOURCES ON THE U.S. FEDERAL GOVERNMENT

Government-produced reference sources fall into many categories. This section identifies sources that can be used to locate information on and publications from a wide variety of federal government entities.

The Federal Depository Library Program and the GPO

As mentioned earlier, the standard system of acquiring and providing access to U.S. federal government information is the FDLP, which distributes tangible and electronic materials and provides bibliographic records. The essential finding tool for federal documents is the *Catalog of U.S. Government Publications*. The free online *Catalog* contains bibliographic records and is updated on a daily basis.

Govinfo is another GPO tool. *Govinfo* provides full-text access to documents and other publications from all three branches of the federal government. As a Trusted Digital Repository, *Govinfo* has undergone an extensive audit for organization, process, and permanence. The community is assured that publications found in *Govinfo* are authentic and complete electronic versions that will be preserved in perpetuity.

General and Agency Websites

The U.S. General Services Administration's *USA.gov* tool functions as the official, primary portal to access federal government information online. Similar to a search engine, *USA.gov* points to webpages within government domains. In English and Spanish versions, *USA.gov* offers access to government information based on topics and services. If the query is about government "services," *USA.gov* should be the starting point. Unlike websites and databases in the private sector, the *USA.gov* website was built according to accessibility standards and is easily navigable using software like Zoom Text or Jaws.

Depending upon the type of query, federal government agency websites may be just as useful, more up to date, and more convenient. In other cases, using a search engine or *USA.gov* may return recent government monographs or digitized historical documents. However, several categories of government information remain outside the reach of search engine indexing (for instance, technical reports), or their nature does not lend itself to discovery via a general search engine (bills and bill status, laws and codes, and specific statistical information). These types of government information require knowledge of, and skills with, the specialized sources to be discussed in this chapter.

Directories

One standard way to obtain information about the federal government is to consult its official handbook, the *United States Government Manual*, which has been published annually since 1935 and is now online. The *Manual* describes the federal government (see Figure 26.1) and provides mission statements, descriptive information, organizational charts, and directory information for legislative, judicial, and executive agencies and offices as well as for independent boards, commissions, committees, and quasi-official agencies. Entries cover dates of establishment, key personnel, major subagencies, and programs and services. It is a convenient source for locating contacts, including those for public information inquiries and regional offices.

The websites of the House of Representatives and the Senate are a rich source of directory information. The traditional government handbook that covers Congress is the comprehensive, biennial *Congressional Directory*. This tool provides brief biographies and committee appointments of senators and representatives and directory information for them, their office staff, and congressional committee staff. It includes descriptions and maps of congressional districts and zip codes. Although the *United States Government Manual* presents useful descriptions of agencies and their programs, the *Congressional Directory* usually provides personnel information.

Various other directories are published commercially, so unlike nearly all sources discussed in this chapter, they are not free online or available via the FDLP. In some instances, these provide directory information deeper than is provided free online. Some are descriptive, such as the *Washington Information Directory*, which includes brief information about the programs or purpose of an agency or congressional committee, as well as the address, telephone number, and names of directors or committee members and staff. The *Washington Information Directory* also covers nongovernmental groups interested in federal activities; these include associations, lobbying organizations, and foundations.

Individual federal agencies sometimes publish their own directories, phonebooks, guides, or handbooks that give the user more detailed information about the programs, services, and organization of an agency and that also may provide factual material for reference purposes. One example is the *Social Security Handbook*, which tells what the Social Security Administration programs encompass and how to apply for benefits.

Historical Indexes and Guides

Through most of the 18th and 19th centuries, most U.S. executive agencies submitted annual reports to Congress about their activities. These appeared as part of the *United States Congressional Serial Set*. Historically, the *Serial Set* was a shifting composition of congressional publications, communications from the president and other executive agencies, or anything else chartered or commissioned by Congress and was the primary vehicle for publishing and distributing all federal government information. Many items issued in the *Serial Set* were also issued and classed as executive agency or departmental documents. The *Checklist of United States Public Documents 1789–1909*, consisting of lists of the *Serial Set* volumes and the departmentally classed documents, is a useful tool to find and manage historical publications.

While it is a major publication, known item and subject searches with the *Serial Set* can be difficult. Luckily, this collection has been the subject of digitization efforts since the early part of the 21st century. Commercial databases are thorough and user friendly, but most of the publications are freely available in the digital repository *HathiTrust*.

THE GOVERNMENT OF THE UNITED STATES

THE CONSTITUTION

LEGISLATIVE BRANCH

THE CONGRESS

SENATE HOUSE

ARCHITECT OF THE CAPITOL
CONGRESSIONAL BUDGET OFFICE
GOVERNMENT ACCOUNTABILITY OFFICE
GOVERNMENT PUBLISHING OFFICE
LIBRARY OF CONGRESS
UNITED STATES BOTANIC GARDEN

EXECUTIVE BRANCH

THE PRESIDENT
THE VICE PRESIDENT

EXECUTIVE OFFICE OF THE PRESIDENT

COUNCIL OF ECONOMIC ADVISERS
COUNCIL ON ENVIRONMENTAL QUALITY
NATIONAL SECURITY COUNCIL
OFFICE OF ADMINISTRATION
OFFICE OF MANAGEMENT AND BUDGET
OFFICE OF NATIONAL DRUG CONTROL POLICY
OFFICE OF SCIENCE AND TECHNOLOGY POLICY
OFFICE OF THE UNITED STATES TRADE REPRESENTATIVE
OFFICE OF THE VICE PRESIDENT
WHITE HOUSE OFFICE

JUDICIAL BRANCH

THE SUPREME COURT OF THE UNITED STATES

ADMINISTRATIVE OFFICE OF THE UNITED STATES COURTS
FEDERAL JUDICIAL CENTER
TERRITORIAL COURTS
UNITED STATES COURTS OF APPEALS
UNITED STATES COURT OF APPEALS FOR THE ARMED FORCES
UNITED STATES COURT OF APPEALS FOR VETERANS CLAIMS
UNITED STATES DISTRICT COURTS
UNITED STATES COURT OF FEDERAL CLAIMS
UNITED STATES COURT OF INTERNATIONAL TRADE
UNITED STATES SENTENCING COMMISSION
UNITED STATES TAX COURT

DEPARTMENT OF AGRICULTURE
DEPARTMENT OF COMMERCE
DEPARTMENT OF DEFENSE
DEPARTMENT OF EDUCATION
DEPARTMENT OF ENERGY
DEPARTMENT OF HEALTH AND HUMAN SERVICES
DEPARTMENT OF HOMELAND SECURITY
DEPARTMENT OF HOUSING AND URBAN DEVELOPMENT
DEPARTMENT OF THE INTERIOR
DEPARTMENT OF JUSTICE
DEPARTMENT OF LABOR
DEPARTMENT OF STATE
DEPARTMENT OF TRANSPORTATION
DEPARTMENT OF THE TREASURY
DEPARTMENT OF VETERANS AFFAIRS

INDEPENDENT ESTABLISHMENTS AND GOVERNMENT CORPORATIONS

ADMINISTRATIVE CONFERENCE OF THE UNITED STATES
AFRICAN DEVELOPMENT FOUNDATION
BROADCASTING BOARD OF GOVERNORS
CENTRAL INTELLIGENCE AGENCY
COMMODITY FUTURES TRADING COMMISSION
CONSUMER FINANCIAL PROTECTION BOARD
CONSUMER PRODUCT SAFETY COMMISSION
CORPORATION FOR NATIONAL AND COMMUNITY SERVICE
DEFENSE NUCLEAR FACILITIES SAFETY BOARD
ENVIRONMENTAL PROTECTION AGENCY
EQUAL EMPLOYMENT OPPORTUNITY COMMISSION
EXPORT-IMPORT BANK OF THE UNITED STATES
FARM CREDIT ADMINISTRATION
FEDERAL COMMUNICATIONS COMMISSION
FEDERAL DEPOSIT INSURANCE CORPORATION
FEDERAL ELECTION COMMISSION
FEDERAL HOUSING FINANCE AGENCY
FEDERAL LABOR RELATIONS AUTHORITY
FEDERAL MARITIME COMMISSION
FEDERAL MEDIATION AND CONCILIATION SERVICE
FEDERAL MINE SAFETY AND HEALTH REVIEW COMMISSION
FEDERAL RESERVE SYSTEM
FEDERAL RETIREMENT THRIFT INVESTMENT BOARD
FEDERAL TRADE COMMISSION
GENERAL SERVICES ADMINISTRATION
INTER-AMERICAN FOUNDATION
MERIT SYSTEMS PROTECTION BOARD
NATIONAL AERONAUTICS AND SPACE ADMINISTRATION
NATIONAL ARCHIVES AND RECORDS ADMINISTRATION
NATIONAL CAPITAL PLANNING COMMISSION
NATIONAL CREDIT UNION ADMINISTRATION
NATIONAL FOUNDATION ON THE ARTS AND THE HUMANITIES
NATIONAL LABOR RELATIONS BOARD
NATIONAL MEDIATION BOARD
NATIONAL RAILROAD PASSENGER CORPORATION (AMTRAK)
NATIONAL SCIENCE FOUNDATION
NATIONAL TRANSPORTATION SAFETY BOARD
NUCLEAR REGULATORY COMMISSION
OCCUPATIONAL SAFETY AND HEALTH REVIEW COMMISSION
OFFICE OF THE DIRECTOR OF NATIONAL INTELLIGENCE
OFFICE OF GOVERNMENT ETHICS
OFFICE OF PERSONNEL MANAGEMENT
OFFICE OF SPECIAL COUNSEL
OVERSEAS PRIVATE INVESTMENT CORPORATION
PEACE CORPS
PENSION BENEFIT GUARANTY CORPORATION
POSTAL REGULATORY COMMISSION
RAILROAD RETIREMENT BOARD
SECURITIES AND EXCHANGE COMMISSION
SELECTIVE SERVICE SYSTEM
SMALL BUSINESS ADMINISTRATION
SOCIAL SECURITY ADMINISTRATION
TENNESSEE VALLEY AUTHORITY
TRADE AND DEVELOPMENT AGENCY
UNITED STATES AGENCY FOR INTERNATIONAL DEVELOPMENT
UNITED STATES COMMISSION ON CIVIL RIGHTS
UNITED STATES INTERNATIONAL TRADE COMMISSION
UNITED STATES POSTAL SERVICE

Figure 26.1 Organizational chart of the U.S. government. Shown is the organization and reporting structure of the legislative, executive, and judicial branches of government as well as departments, independent establishments, and government corporations. Reprinted from the *United States Government Manual.*

One of the trickiest aspects of working with government information is discovering historical publications, especially items that were never descriptively cataloged, have not been scanned and placed online, *and* predate the *Catalog of U.S. Government Publications*' creation in 1895. For these items, specialized historical indexes are necessary. A number of private and government-sponsored ventures attempt to index government publications before 1895. An example is Benjamin Poore's *A Descriptive Catalogue of the Government Publications of the United States, September 5, 1774–March 4, 1881*. An excellent annotated list of such titles is available on the National Archives' site, *Library Resources for Administrative History: Indexes to Legislative and Executive Publications*.

Another useful source for tracking historical government publications is the *Guide to U.S. Government Publications*, popularly known as "Andriot" after its founding author. It is arranged by SuDoc number and therefore by agency and includes defunct and discontinued agencies and classes alongside the current ones. It is a valuable tool for understanding publication patterns of historical and current agencies.

Specialized Catalogs and Indexes

The preceding sources are mostly broad and relatively comprehensive access points to government information. For in-depth or comprehensive research, government information users may need to go beyond search engines, general catalogs, or indexes. This section focuses on important examples of other types of government information that require specialized tools, including archival material, technical reports, and patents and trademarks.

The National Archives and Records Administration's (NARA) website is the major point of entry to archived government information. It includes the *National Archives Catalog* and the *Guide to Federal Records in the National Archives of the United States*. NARA's digital collections are extensive: users can access 126,500 digitized historical documents, photographs, and images in the *National Archives Catalog* as well as founding documents. For educators, there is *DocsTeach*, with digitized primary sources, lesson plans, and tools to create educational activities. *Archives.gov* also offers specific guides for researching family history or veteran service records.

Scientific and technical reports represent another type of government publication for which specialized indexes may be the better finding aid or for which e-repositories may be available, either subscription based or free. The premier example, the National Technical Information Service (NTIS), is the source for scientific, technical, engineering, and business reports on government-funded projects. The first year of publication was 1899, and at present there are over 3 million reports covering over 350 subject areas. The best option for access is NTIS's *National Technical Reports Library*, which is open to all users, both domestic and international. Other useful repositories include *Technical Report Archive and Image Library TRAIL* and *HathiTrust*. It is also worthwhile to do a Web search for a known technical report as reports indexed by NTIS can sometimes be found elsewhere on the Web.

Patents and trademarks specifically deal with intellectual property of inventors and businesses. The United States Patent and Trademark Office (USPTO) provides a system for public access to an invention, while protecting the economic and intellectual rights of the inventor. The basics are covered in the companion publications *General Information Concerning Patents* and *Protecting Your Trademark: Enhancing Your Rights through Federal Registration*. Patent and Trademark Resource Centers are libraries that provide specialists and tools to conduct patent and trademark research. However, one can now accomplish fairly extensive patent and trademark research on the Web. The USPTO website now has searchable databases of all patents and trademarks ever issued. In addition, *Google* has uploaded the majority of patents from USPTO into its own patent search database.

LEGISLATIVE INFORMATION

Law and its creation delineate a major area of government information reference service. Primary legal sources are published by government, available to depositories, and in the purview of the government information professional. This section focuses on the most important information needs that occur related to statutory and administrative, and in brief judicial law. Legal materials are discussed in greater detail in Chapter 31.

The Legislative Process

It is essential that the government information provider acquire and maintain an in-depth understanding of the legislative process. Comprehension of this process and an awareness of the resultant publications ensure librarians are able to locate the most authoritative information. The legislative process will vary based on jurisdiction; that is, how the U.S. federal legislature works may have similarities to state legislatures or local governments, but the latter will likely not produce the same quantity or quality of documentation throughout their legislative processes.

Statutes begin as legislative proposals, usually in the form of "bills" or "resolutions." Upon introduction, each House or Senate bill or resolution is printed and numbered sequentially within a specific Congress, and here lies the first publication that a user may need: the text of a bill as introduced.

The numbering is important, given that the bill will often be referenced by number. For instance, the first bill introduced in the Senate during a session of Congress will be given the number "S.1," and the second bill will be "S.2," and so on. Note that each session of Congress lasts for two years; so "S.1" for the 116th Congress will either become law or die by the end of the two-year duration of the 116th Congress. If it does not become law, a new version (which could be identical) would need to be introduced again in the next Congress, at which time it would receive a new number and begin the process anew. Further, each two-year session of Congress consists of a "first" and "second" session, usually one for each calendar year. Box 26.1 offers some tips on how to search for laws, especially when patrons only know the popular name of the law.

Once a bill has been introduced, it is usually referred to a congressional committee. The committee may hold hearings on the bill, and then transcripts of these may be published. Committee hearings contain the oral and/or written testimony of both legislators and experts on the subject at hand. Contentious issues usually have several experts testifying on both sides of an issue, making the hearings of particular use to students, the public, and casual and serious researchers alike.

If the committee decides to move the measure to the next stage, consideration by the full chamber, the bill is "reported" out of committee and accompanied by a

Box 26.1 Activity: Search Tips for Locating Laws by Popular Name

It is common for high-profile legislation to have a popular, though unofficial, name. A recent example is "Obamacare." The actual title of that bill was the *Patient Protection and Affordable Care Act* (2010). If a patron requests the text of a bill using the popular name, the first task for the librarian will be to figure out exactly which bill is being requested. In this instance, the enacted bill was from the 111th Congress, H.R. 3590, which became Public Law 111–148. For legislation that is less well known, using *Shepard's Acts and Cases by Popular Names* should provide the citation to find the text in the *Statutes at Large*.

Another example is when a user is looking for the text of famous historical legislation like the *Voting Rights Act*. If the user doesn't know exactly when it was passed, a simple Web search may produce information such as the full title (*An Act to Enforce the Fifteenth Amendment to the Constitution of the United States and for Other Purposes*) or the citation in the *Statutes at Large* (79 Stat. 437). The text of the *Voting Rights Act* as it was passed in 1965 is available on *Govinfo*.

The PATRIOT Act is the popular name of a law often discussed in library and information sciences. Can you find the full title of this law and a copy of its text? The answer is provided at the end of the chapter, in Box 26.4.

written Senate or House report. The report contains the latest version of the proposed legislation and may provide insight, such as an overview of the proposal, a cost estimate, and supplemental views. In some cases, committee prints are necessary, providing in-depth analyses about a policy, subject, or issue of the legislation.

Once a bill has come out of a committee, it may be debated on the floor of the chamber and then voted on. These debates appear in the *Congressional Record*, and the vote activity is recorded there as well. If passed, it is sent to the other chamber to follow a similar path. Upon passage by both chambers, it is sent to the president for consideration. Note that occasionally identical pieces of legislation, or extremely similar pieces legislation, could make their way through both chambers concurrently. If this is the case and both bills pass their respective chambers, a "conference" of senators and representatives is appointed to iron out the differences between the two bills. The result and details of the conference are published in "conference reports."

Finally, once signed by the president, the legislation is known as a "public law" and is assigned a sequential number based on the session of Congress in which it was passed (e.g., Public Law 114–86). Then the law is compiled into the bound series the *United States Statutes at Large*. The *Statutes at Large* provide a chronological arrangement of the laws in the exact order that they were enacted, with the text of the law as passed (see Figure 26.2).

The current law of the land is contained in the *United States Code* (*USC*). The *USC* is the codification by subject matter of the general and permanent laws of the United States divided into fifty-three titles. See Box 26.2 for tips for searching the U.S. Code.

PUBLIC LAW 114–86—NOV. 5, 2015 129 STAT. 675

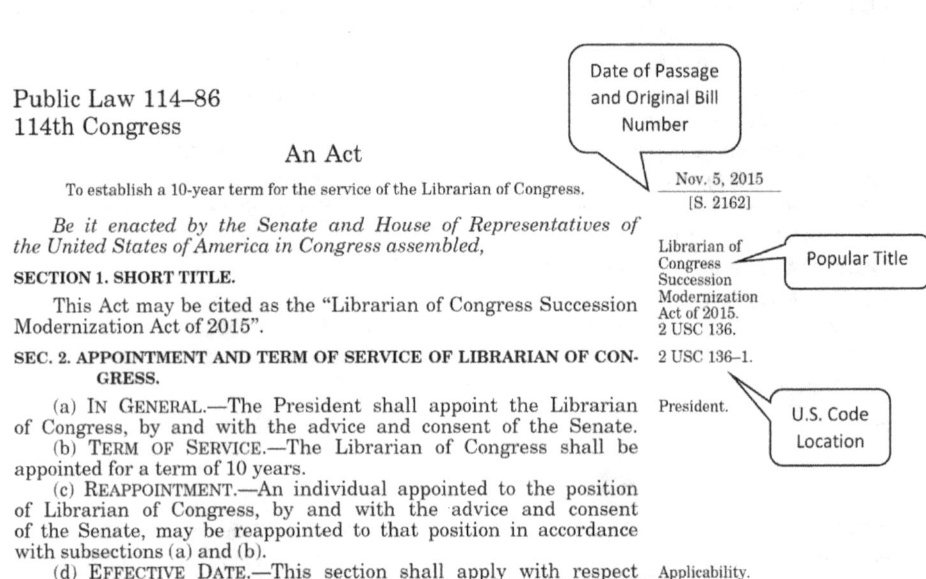

Public Law 114–86
114th Congress

An Act

To establish a 10-year term for the service of the Librarian of Congress.

Nov. 5, 2015
[S. 2162]

Be it enacted by the Senate and House of Representatives of the United States of America in Congress assembled,

SECTION 1. SHORT TITLE.

This Act may be cited as the "Librarian of Congress Succession Modernization Act of 2015". Librarian of Congress Succession Modernization Act of 2015. 2 USC 136.

SEC. 2. APPOINTMENT AND TERM OF SERVICE OF LIBRARIAN OF CONGRESS. 2 USC 136–1.

(a) IN GENERAL.—The President shall appoint the Librarian of Congress, by and with the advice and consent of the Senate. President.

(b) TERM OF SERVICE.—The Librarian of Congress shall be appointed for a term of 10 years.

(c) REAPPOINTMENT.—An individual appointed to the position of Librarian of Congress, by and with the advice and consent of the Senate, may be reappointed to that position in accordance with subsections (a) and (b).

(d) EFFECTIVE DATE.—This section shall apply with respect Applicability.

Figure 26.2 Example of a Public Law from the *United States Statutes at Large*. This example shows an excerpt of the text of a public law, with annotations identifying the public law number, U.S. Statutes at Large citation, date of passage and original bill number, popular title, and U.S. Code location.

Bills and resolutions, hearings, reports and committee prints, floor debates, votes, presidential actions, laws, and other congressional publications are the tangible representations and textual records of the legislative process. Upon completion, the entire process is often referred to as a law's *legislative history*.

Box 26.2 Search Tip: U.S. Code

One public law may amend several titles of the *United States Code*, for example, Public Law 107–273, *21st Century Department of Justice Appropriations Authorization Act* includes changes to the *United States Code* on subjects like juvenile justice and criminal procedure (Title 18 Crimes and Criminal Procedure, Title 28 Judiciary and Judicial Procedure, and Title 42 The Public Health and Welfare) as well as the interstate shipment of wine directly from a winery (Title 27 Intoxicating Liquors). Marginalia in the *Statutes at Large* indicate the *USC* titles affected, and legislative histories often list specifically the titles and sections affected by the public law.

Legislative Research: Guides and Indexes

The Library of Congress's *Congress.gov* and the congressional section of *Govinfo* are the permanent, no-fee gateways to bills and resolutions, legislative actions, congressional publications, and related information.

Congress.gov has the full text of most congressional publications, except hearings. *Congress.gov* offers an abundance of information: title, text, and sponsors/cosponsors; related bills; bill status; cost estimates related to the legislation provided by the Congressional Budget Office; useful summaries of the legislation from the Congressional Research Service; detailed legislative histories with links to publications; and even subject terms.

Alternatively, GPO's *Govinfo* also covers legislation, with browsable and searchable collections of congressional bills, documents, hearings, reports, and the *Congressional Record*, as well as the *Statutes at Large* and the *United States Code*. In addition to the electronic versions of congressional publications, tangible versions are maintained by all regional and many selective federal depository libraries.

ProQuest Congressional is a subscription service offering access to congressional activity. Furthermore, it provides more detailed coverage and indexing of historical legislation and congressional documents. Value-added features like legislative history, regulatory history, and relevant newspaper articles round out the database.

CQ products are likely to appeal to those who desire readable background information on political activities but not necessarily primary documents from Congress. These users can consult *CQ Weekly*, *CQ Almanac*, and *CQ Researcher*. *CQ Weekly* and *CQ Almanac* provide the user with a well-organized, succinct account of national politics and congressional, presidential, and judicial consideration of major issues affecting the American public. *CQ Researcher* offers in-depth, unbiased coverage of political and social issues, including regular coverage of topics as diverse as health, international affairs, education, the environment, technology, and the economy.

Of course, new media are covering Congress as well. Various blogs and *Twitter* feeds from reporters, scientists, and even representatives feature congressional news as well, from every conceivable political angle.

EXECUTIVE BRANCH PUBLICATIONS

The Executive branch includes the Office of the President and numerous agencies and departments. The president may make law, although such overt law-making is generally limited to executive orders, which detail some function of how the government will operate and do not often have large policy implications, and proclamations, which tend to be more ceremonial. Executive branch agencies and departments are responsible for enforcing the laws enacted by Congress.

Presidential Documents

All presidential actions, such as executive orders and proclamations, along with the text of speeches, press conferences, bill-signing ceremonies, and other activities, are recorded in the *Compilation of Presidential Documents*, available in *Govinfo*, which is eventually compiled into the bound *Public Papers of the President*.

The White House's website is also a source for information about presidential activity and publications, although it is not as comprehensive as the *Public Papers*.

Regulatory Documents

Executive agencies and departments enforce laws via rules and regulations or detailed requirements pertaining to the actual implementation of statutory law. Central to the regulatory process is the publishing of *proposed* rules and regulations, followed by a public comment period, and completed with publication of *final* rules. The comment period is normally thirty, sixty, or ninety days. Most agencies accept comments electronically or in writing. The publishing and distribution of the proposed regulations give citizens, officials, and experts the opportunity to comment on and critique them in advance of the final ruling. These administrative rulings, notices, and comments, as well as presidential executive orders and proclamations, appear in the daily *Federal Register*.

Federalregister.gov, the online version, allows for advanced searching and provides other tools for tracking specific areas of regulation. The website presents the same information as the print publication but has various value-added features such as linking to pertinent Public Laws and *United States Code* sections and the option to subscribe to notifications on topics.

Final rules and regulations, and presidential executive orders and proclamations, are incorporated into the *Code of Federal Regulations* (*CFR*), the codification of the general and permanent rules from executive departments and agencies of the federal government. The *CFR* compiles and codifies all current, in-force regulations into a subject arrangement, just as the *United States Code* does for statutory law. *Govinfo* has direct links to the daily *Federal Register* and the current and historical volumes of *CFR*. An online version, which is an unofficial compilation, is published as the *e-CFR*.

JUDICIAL BRANCH PUBLICATIONS

Courts may issue decisions on some aspect of law that is unclear or disputed. Such decisions, when considered significant by the courts, are published and make up what is called *case law*. The Supreme Court's *United States Reports* have been the only judicial decisions that were (and still are) printed by the U.S. government as government documents. Other court decisions, when they were published at all, have traditionally been published by private publishers, and access required subscriptions to large, expensive sets or databases. Government information specialists and others now have the option of using the fee-based *Public Access to Court Electronic Records* (*PACER*). Case and docket information from federal appellate, district, and bankruptcy courts and the *PACER* Case Locator form this centralized system. Case law and other legal materials are discussed in Chapter 31.

CANADIAN GOVERNMENT INFORMATION

Like their U.S. counterparts, the Canadian government disseminates information products that are up to date, authoritative, accessible online, and indispensable as reference tools. The Canadian government's official website, *Canada.ca*, is in English and French. The site's organization is user friendly, even for novices such as tourists, providing ready access through this initial page to the most significant and in-demand types of information. It is a great starting point for most topics, including jobs, immigration, travel, business, health, and taxes, and has convenient links to "how the government works" and "open government" in the footer.

Unlike their U.S. counterparts, Canadian government documents and information sources are no longer disseminated in tangible formats. The Depository Service Program used to administer a program somewhat analogous to the GPO's Federal Depository Library Program. However, due to several conditions, like website consolidation and streamlining, budget cuts, and the political climate, the program ceased distribution of tangible materials to the depository libraries in 2013 (Wakaruk 2014).[2]

The Canadian Depository Services Program's move to electronic-only publishing may seem to limit access. However, the Government of Canada (2017) shows commitment to the open government movement, hoping to foster "open, honest, and sincere engagement and constructive two-way dialogue between the Government of Canada and the interested stakeholders and citizens which results in better policies, programs, and services for Canadians" through open government information. Documented biennially in *National Action Plan on Open Government* (see, e.g., *Canada's 2018–2020 National Action Plan)*, Canada's advancements include creating the *Open.canada.ca* website and data portal; creating the position of minister of digital government; and establishing new digital standards and policy.

Canadian Government Information Online

The *Government of Canada Publications* catalogue contains more than 430,000 publications, including over 310,000 that are digital publications that can be downloaded. Libraries can access cataloging metadata and permanent URLs to items in the catalogue. Since 2015, *Weekly Acquisitions Lists* are the source for identifying electronic publications from federal departments and the Parliament.

Canadiana is a one-stop shop for digitized primary source materials of Canadian history, including government information, a boon to genealogists, students, and scholars. The site is a Trusted Digital Repository, meaning that it has gone through a certification process to assure the library and archival communities that these scanned materials will be preserved and accessible. *Canadiana* is made up of several digital collections including *Héritage* (scanned archival collections) and *Early Canadiana Online* (scanned manuscripts and early printed materials). Most importantly, *Canadiana Online* includes a government publications collection of historical colonial, provincial, and federal government documents. *Canadiana.org* recently merged with the Canadian Research Knowledge Network (CRKN), an important outcome being the removal of the subscription paywall for accessing the collections.

Canadian Legislative Documents

The *Canadian Parliamentary Guide/Guide Parlementaire Canadien* is an annual publication that details the current membership of the legislative and judicial branches of the government. It includes biographical information on the members of the Senate and House of Commons, the Supreme Court and Federal Court of Canada, and the provincial legislatures, as well as historical information such as results of general elections dating back to 1867.

The *Parliament of Canada* website includes extensive and current information about Parliament and its processes. "The Learn about Parliament" section provides overviews of the government structure and the legislative process as well as teacher resources, games, and classroom activities. Primary sources from Parliament, including bills and debates, are now published online and are widely accessible using the *Parliament of Canada* website. *LEGISinfo*, a research tool on Canadian legislation from the Senate, House of Commons, and Library of Parliament, has information about current legislation before Parliament. *Canadian Parliamentary Historical Resources*, a digital collection from the Library of Parliament, has the Debates and Journals of both houses from the first to the thirty-fifth Parliaments (1867–1996).

The *Canada Gazette*, the official newspaper of the Government of Canada, is now published online. *Part I* contains notices and proposed regulations; *Part II* gives the text of official regulations; and *Part III* publishes Acts of Parliament.

For general information about the parliamentary system of government in Canada, refer to recent texts such as *The Canadian Regime: An Introduction to Parliamentary Government in Canada* (Malcolmson and Myers 2016). For more comprehensive information on Canadian federal legislation, library research guides such as *Finding Historical Federal Legislation* (Koscielski 2018) from Simon Frasier University may prove useful.

Other Sources about Canadian Governance

The *Canadian Almanac & Directory*, from Grey House Publishing Canada, is an expansive compendium of directory information for governmental and non-governmental organizations, and it includes coverage for municipalities. *Governments Canada*, also published by Grey House, is a directory of government officers from the federal, provincial, and municipal governments in Canada. Other features include analysis of election spending and a glossary of acronyms. *Government Information in Canada* (Wakaruk and Li 2019) provides an overview of current systems for disseminating government information at the Canadian federal and provincial levels.

STATE, LOCAL, AND INTERNATIONAL GOVERNMENT PUBLICATIONS

Just as accessing U.S. and Canadian government information has nuances and requires expertise, access to international, foreign national, state, and local government information also requires specialized knowledge of the systems that produce and disseminate government information at those levels of governance.

State Government Information

Whereas much of U.S. federal government information is managed by the GPO and its FDLP, the coordination of state information may or may not be controlled or systematized. Some states offer depository programs wherein libraries can receive state government publications. Other states may have systems similar to the current Canadian Depository Services Program with all-electronic production and dissemination.

Most state governments publish directories to their agencies and officials. Like their federal counterparts, state agency websites contain directory and other factual information, which is in some cases extensive. *Book of the States*, published biennially, also offers a wealth of factual information about individual states in one place that may be unmatched online. *Book of the States* is the standard ready-reference source to check for recent information on state officials, state legislatures, and the state judiciary, as well as on state elections and finances. Whether seeking information on the qualifications of secretaries of state, the methods for the removal of judges and filling of vacancies, or allowable state investments, this source is the place to start. State mottoes, flowers, songs, birds, and so forth are also given, although a quick review of a state website may also provide this type of information.

The amount and variety of state information in electronic format has increased rapidly. Legislative information, business and economic data, and agency reports are representative of the types of information that are currently available to the public on the Web. Using these electronic sources to answer questions about state issues has become the norm. Librarians should be aware of how their own state catalogs and distributes its documents and what the best sources are for identifying those documents.

While legal resources are covered in greater detail in Chapter 31, states usually mimic the federal government in the publication of their state statutory law and state administrative (or regulatory) law. The titles, however, may not correspond directly to the titles of federal publications. "Statutes" can mean different things at different levels. For instance, the Illinois equivalent to the *United States Statutes at Large* is called *Laws of the State of Illinois*, and its equivalent to the *United States Code* is called the *Illinois Compiled Statutes*. In recent years, making the primary legal materials of states available online has been advocated by professional organizations and users. Electronic versions of state legal materials may be available, but they may not be free, official, or preserved. States that have passed the *Uniform Electronic Legal Materials Act*, legislative text developed by the Uniform Law Commission (2011) with legal and legislative advisors, have assured citizens that digital versions of state statutes, administrative rules, and other legislative documents are accessible, authenticated, and preserved.

Local Government Information

In the large arena of government information librarianship, the documents that are closest to home may be the hardest to obtain or to access. Local governments, like state governments, may not have obligations or mandates to "deposit" their works with libraries. Local government structures may be different from the three-branch system of checks and balances at the federal level. For example, legislative and executive functions may not be as strictly separated as they are at state or federal levels. Also, there may be a number of layers of governance at a local level; local taxing bodies or districts may overlap (Stanton 2013). Finally, producers of local information may be unaware of the potential for partnership with libraries for information dissemination. At these local and regional levels, government officials may not be aware of the long-term access, subject expertise, and scholarship that working with librarians can bring (Poon 2019). If the attitude is "it's available on our website" and "we don't need to waste server space with these capital plans that are ten years old," then there is a real need for government information specialists to step in and help preserve access to local government information within their communities.

That said, some cities and municipalities have repositories for local publications. Sometimes, these fall into the category of archives; at other times, these materials are kept at the public library.

Foreign Governments and Intergovernmental Organizations

Available in print and online, the *Europa World Year Book* is an excellent guide to foreign governments and international or intergovernmental organizations. This resource provides names, addresses, and telephone numbers for foreign governments and their major agencies, as well as major intergovernmental organizations (IGOs). Going straight to the websites of IGOs or foreign governments may help users get statistics, publications, and other information free of cost, but they are often in the vernacular and may be difficult to navigate. And while all countries surveyed by the Inter-Parliamentary Union had government websites, services, content, usability, and accessibility varied widely and correlated with economic status and stability of the country (World e-Parliament Report 2018). Library subject guides for IGOs and other national-level governments, such as the *List of IGOs: Getting Started* and *List of Foreign Governments: Getting Started*, from Northwestern University Library are also useful sources.

Both foreign and IGO documents may have been cataloged and be discoverable via a library catalog. The UN, the largest IGO, has several access tools and databases. Unlike most other instances in the chapter, the UN does not use the terms "publications" and "documents" interchangeably. A UN document is material or text created by a principal organ or subsidiary agency of the UN during the course of its business. An example of a UN document would be the "Universal Declaration of Human Rights," which was adopted as a resolution by the United Nations General Assembly in 1948. A UN publication is issued by the UN to the general public and is available for sale. An example of a UN publication would be *Civil Society, Conflicts and the Politicization of Human Rights* (Marchetti and Tocci 2011). Guides to researching UN information, both documents and publications, are available through the United Nations' Dag Hammarskjold Library. *UN Resources and Documents* is a good access point for the various databases of the United Nations.

SEARCH STRATEGIES

Current government information is nearly all online and mostly free. Locating a known, recent government publication can usually be accomplished through a general Web search or a library's discovery tools, including the online catalog. When characteristics of a publication are known but the title is not, a civics-informed strategy often may be successful, namely, navigating to the website of the appropriate government agency or branch and browsing for the desired information.

When specific legislation or information about a bill is sought, search *Congress.gov*, which provides easy access to bills, their text, their status in the legislative process, and documents related to the bill. To locate the documents of the regulatory process, search the *Federal Register* or the compiled-by-subject *Code of Federal Regulations*, both available on *Govinfo*. As Box 26.3 illustrates, when searching government websites it is important to keep in mind that government agencies might use their own vocabularies, which could differ greatly from popular or natural language terms in use for the same topic.

Box 26.3 Search Tip: Appropriate Terminology

A library patron may be interested in locating the most recent regulations related to personal ownership and operation of a drone. Unfortunately, a search in *Govinfo* using the word "drone" does not return any regulations from the Federal Aviation Administration (FAA), the relevant regulatory agency. The FAA uses the term "unmanned aircraft system," although the related term "unmanned aerial vehicle" also produces some relevant results. Armed with the appropriate terminology, searches produce better results.

The *Catalog of U.S. Government Publications* continues to be a key bibliographic tool for verifying and locating government publications. If a Web search is unsuccessful or inappropriate, or if the needed item is older, search the *Catalog*. The *Catalog* benefits from the usual bibliographic advantages, such as subject headings and author information featuring the issuing agency. As indicated previously, a number of specialized tools exist to aid the search for historical government information as well.

For Canadian government information, pursue a strategy similar to that for the United States. Start with the official Canadian government website, and also search the *Weekly Checklist* for Canadian government documents. Canadian legislative information may be accessed via Parliament's website.

State laws, legislation, and regulations are usually found via state-specific sources somewhat akin to federal sources. The reference librarian should learn the appropriate tools for the state or states of interest to the library's clientele. The *Federal Depository Library Directory* may be a useful tool in situations when a query received from a distance may be better answered by a specialist at the requestor's local depository.

Moreover, a cardinal rule in government information reference situations is that "if you can't answer the question or find the source, ask a colleague." The importance of networking and utilizing local resources cannot be overemphasized on the road to success as a government information specialist. For example, Queen's University Library has a well-organized, research guide *Government Information: Canada* that highlights the major tools, publications, and types of information resources about the Canadian federal and provincial government. Using colleagues' guides can be a great place to start research, especially for unfamiliar subjects.

CONCLUSION

Government information may be seen as a different and difficult area of reference service. Essentially, government information librarians not only have to understand how government works and where to find documentary evidence of its operations, through their reference interaction they have the chance to empower citizens interacting within government systems. Regarding recent redesigns of standardized tests from the College Board to include robust coverage of the U.S. Constitution, Stefanie Stanford, chief of global policy for the College Board, was quoted as saying, "Understanding how government works is the essence of power. To be a strong citizen, you need to know how the structures of our government work and how to operate within them" (Friedman 2019). By developing knowledge of sources of government information and associated search strategies, reference librarians can ensure public access to government information. Given the range of material published by the government, librarians in any setting can enhance service to their users by more fully integrating government information sources and assistance into reference services.

Box 26.4 presents the answer to the activity discussed in Box 26.2.

Box 26.4 Activity: Find the Full Title and Text of the Law Popularly Known as the PATRIOT Act or the USA PATRIOT Act

The full title is Uniting and Strengthening America by Providing Appropriate Tools Required to Intercept and Obstruct Terrorism Act of 2001 (note that the title creates the acronym "USA PATRIOT"). The bill was passed by the 107th Congress on October 26, 2001, and became Public Law 107–56 (Pub. L. 107-56, Oct. 26, 2001, 115 Stat. 272). A pdf copy of the text can be accessed through the United States Code website: https://uscode.house.gov/statutes/pl/107/56.pdf.

NOTES

1. Jacobs (2014) outlines risks to online government information. Digital preservation standards and practices continue to evolve. One organization assessing, certifying, and assuring libraries of the trustworthiness and permanence of digital repositories is the Center for Research Libraries. For an overview of other national and international digital preservation standards and initiatives, see Oehlerts and Liu (2013).

2. Historical background and a complete discussion of the early history, evolution, problems, and status of the Canadian Depository Services Program through the late 1980s can be found in Dolan (1989). The author describes the official origins of the program, the role of various agencies, and the pressures that combined to form the depository system that was in place until recently. As well, archived issues of the *Weekly Checklist* 13–49, 13–50, and 13–51 focused on the history of the Depository Services Program. For more background on the changes to the Depository Services Program in Canada, see Smugler (2013) and Wakaruk (2014).

REFERENCES

21st Century Department of Justice Appropriations Authorization Act. 2002. Pub. L. No.107–273, 116 Stat. 1758.

Canada's 2018–2020 National Action Plan on Open Government. 2018. Ottawa: Treasury Board of Canada. https://open.canada.ca/en/content/canadas-2018-2020-national-action-plan-open-government.

Castro, Daniel, Galia Nurko, and Alan McQuinn. 2017. *Benchmarking U.S. Government Websites.* Information Technology and Innovation Foundation. Last modified November 27, 2017. https://itif.org/publications/2017/11/27/benchmarking-us-government-websites.

"Closing the Books—Smart Management: A Growing Number of Governments Seem Bent on Limiting Access to Public Records." 2018. *Governing Magazine (USA)*, June 1, 60.

Dolan, Elizabeth. 1989. *The Depository Dilemma: A Study of the Free Distribution of Canadian Federal Government Publications to Depository Libraries in Canada.* Ottawa: Canadian Library Association.

Fisher, Karen E., Samantha Becker, and Michael Crandall. 2010. "eGovernment Services Use and Impact through Public Libraries: Preliminary Findings from a National Study of Public Access Computing in Public Libraries." Paper presented at 43rd Hawaii International Conference on System Sciences, Koloa, HI, January 5–8, 2010. https://ieeexplore.ieee.org/document/5428291.

Friedman, Thomas. 2019. "The Two Codes Your Kids Need to Know." *The New York Times*, February 12. https://www.nytimes.com/2019/02/12/opinion/college-board-sat-ap.html.

Government in the Sunshine Act. 1975. Pub. L. No. 94–409, 90 Stat. 1241.

Government of Canada. 2017. "What Is Open Dialogue?" Last modified December 20, 2017. https://open.canada.ca/en/frequently-asked-questions.

Jacobs, James A. 2014. "Government Records and Information: Real Risks and Potential Losses." Paper presented at Leviathan: Libraries and Government Information in the Age of Big Data, Chicago, IL, April 24–25, 2014. https://www.crl.edu/sites/default/files/d6/attachments/events/Jacobs%20Slides%204-18.pdf.

Kline, Sims D. 2013. "Documents in the News: A Review of Articles in the *New York Times.*" *DttP: Documents to the People* 41 (Summer): 22–26.

Koscielski, Yolanda. 2018. *Finding Historical Federal Legislation: Research Guide.* Simon Fraser University Library. Last modified October 10, 2018. https://www.lib.sfu.ca/help/research-assistance/subject/criminology/legal-information/historical-federal-legislation.

Leveille, Valerie. 2015. "Through a Record Management Lens: Creating a Framework for Trust in Open Government and Open Government Information." *Canadian Journal of Information and Library Science* 39 (2): 154.

Malcolmson, Patrick, and Richard Myers. 2016. *The Canadian Regime: An Introduction to Parliamentary Government in Canada.* 6th ed. Toronto, ON: University of Toronto Press.

Marchetti, Raffaele, and Nathalie Tocci. 2011. *Civil Society, Conflicts and the Politicization of Human Rights.* Shibuya-ku, Japan: United Nations University Press.

Oehlerts, Beth, and Shu Liu. 2013. "Digital Preservation Strategies at Colorado State University Libraries." *Library Management* 34 (1–2): 83–95.

Patient Protection and Affordable Care Act. 2010. Pub. L. No. 111–248, 124 Stat. 119.

Poon, Linda. 2019. "Should Libraries Be the Keepers of Their Cities' Public Data?" *CityLab*, February 11. https://www.citylab.com/life/2019/02/libraries-public-information-city-data-digital-archive/581905/.

Smugler, Sherrie. 2013. "Facing Change: A Perspective on Government Publications Services in Canadian Academic Libraries in the Internet Age." GODORT Occasional Paper 9. American Library Association. http://www.ala.org/rt/sites/ala.org.rt/files/content/godortcommittees/godortpublications/OP9-smugler.pdf.

Stanton, Dan. 2013. "State and Local Documents Spotlight: A Whole Lotta Local Going On." *DttP: Documents to the People* 41 (Fall): 14–16.

Ubaldi, Barbara. 2013. "Open Government Data: Towards Empirical Analysis of Open Government Data Initiatives." *OECD Working Papers on Public Governance*, No. 22. Paris: OECD Publishing. https://doi.org/10.1787/5k46bj4f03s7-en.

Uniform Law Commission. 2011. "Uniform Electronic Legal Material Act." https://www.uniformlaws.org/committees/community-home/librarydocuments?communitykey=02061119-7070-4806-8841-d36afc18ff21&tab=librarydocuments.

United Nations. 1948. "Universal Declaration of Human Rights." http://www.un.org/en/universal-declaration-human-rights/.

Wakaruk, Amanda. 2014. "What the Heck Is Happening Up North? Canadian Government Information, Circa 2014." *DttP: Documents to the People* 42 (Spring): 15–20.

West, Darrell M. 2007. "State and Federal Electronic Government in the United States." https://www.brookings.edu/wp-content/uploads/2012/04/0826_egovernment_west.pdf.

World e-Parliament Report. 2018. Inter-Parliamentary Union. https://www.ipu.org/resources/publications/reports/2018-11/world-e-parliament-report-2018.

LIST OF SOURCES

Ben's Guide to the U.S. Government. Government Publishing Office. https://bensguide.gpo.gov.

Book of the States. 1965–. Lexington, KY: Council of State Governments. Annual.

Canada.ca. Government of Canada/Gouvernement du Canada. https://www.canada.ca/index.html.

Canada Gazette: Parts I, II, and III. Government of Canada/Gouvernement du Canada. http://www.gazette.gc.ca/.

Canadian Almanac & Directory. 1947–. Toronto, ON: Grey House Publishing Canada. Annual.

Canadian Parliamentary Guide/Guide Parlementaire Canadien. 1909—. Toronto, Ontario: Grey House Publishing Canada. Annual.

Canadian Parliamentary Historical Resources. Library of Parliament. http://parl.canadiana.ca/.

Canadiana. Canadiana.org. http://www.canadiana.ca/.

Catalog of U. S. Government Publications. Government Publishing Office. http://catalog.gpo.gov/.

Census of Population and Housing. United States Census Bureau. http://www.census.gov/prod/www/decennial.html.

Checklist of United States Public Documents 1789–1909, Congressional: to the close of Sixtieth Congress, Departmental: to the end of the calendar year 1909. 1911. Government Printing Office. https://digital.library.unt.edu/ark:/67531/metadc1029.

Code of Federal Regulations. Government Printing Office. http://www.ecfr.gov.

Compilation of Presidential Documents. Government Publishing Office. https://www.govinfo.gov/app/collection/CPD.

Congressional Directory. 1888–. Government Publishing Office. Biennial. https://www.govinfo.gov/app/collection/CDIR.

Congress.gov. http://congress.gov.

Congressional Record. 1873–. Washington, DC: Congress, Daily when Congress is in session. https://www.govinfo.gov/app/collection/CREC. Also available via *Congress.gov.*

CQ Almanac. 1945–. Washington, DC: Congressional Quarterly. Annual. https://library.cqpress.com/cqalmanac/. Subscription required.

CQ Researcher. 1991–. Washington, DC: Congressional Quarterly. Weekly. https://library.cqpress.com/cqresearcher/. Subscription required.

CQ Weekly. 1946–. Washington, DC: Congressional Quarterly. Weekly. https://library.cqpress.com/cqweekly/. Subscription required.

DocsTeach. National Archives and Records Administration, Education Division. https://www.docsteach.org.

e-CFR: Electronic Code of Federal Regulations. Government Publishing Office. http://www.ecfr.gov/cgi-bin/ECFR?page=browse.

Europa World Year Book. Europa Publications. http://www.europaworld.com. Subscription required.

Federal Depository Library Directory. Government Publishing Office. https://www.fdlp.gov/about-the-fdlp/federal-depository-libraries.

Federal Register. 1936–. Washington, DC: National Archives and Records Administration. Daily. https://www.federalregister.gov/.

General Information Concerning Patents. 2015. United States Patent and Trademark Office. https://www.uspto.gov/patents-getting-started/general-information-concerning-patents.

Google Patents. http://patents.google.com.

Government Information: Canada. Queen's University Library. http://library.queensu.ca/gov.

Government of Canada Publications. http://publications.gc.ca/site/eng/home.html.

Governments Canada. Toronto, ON: Grey House Publishing Canada. Annual.

Govinfo. Government Publishing Office. https://www.govinfo.gov.

Guide to Federal Records in the National Archives of the United States. 2nd ed. 1998. 3 vols. Washington, DC: GPO. http://www.archives.gov/research/guide-fed-records/.

Guide to U.S. Government Publications. 1953–. Farmington Hills, MI: Gale. (Commonly called "Andriot.")

HathiTrust. https://www.hathitrust.org.

Illinois Compiled Statutes. Illinois General Assembly. http://www.ilga.gov/legislation/ilcs/ilcs.asp.

Laws of the State of Illinois. https://www.illinois.gov/Government/Pages/LawsAndConstitution.aspx.

LEGISinfo. Ottawa, Ontario: Library of Parliament. http://www.parl.gc.ca/LEGISinfo/.

Library Resources for Administrative History: Indexes to Legislative and Executive Publications. National Archives. http://www.archives.gov/research/alic/reference/admin-history/publication-indexes.html.

The National Archives Catalog. National Archives and Records Administration. http://www.archives.gov/research/arc/.

National Technical Reports Library. National Technical Information Service. https://ntrl.ntis.gov/NTRL.

Northwestern University Library. 2019. *List of Foreign Governments: Getting Started*. http://libguides.northwestern.edu/ForeignGovernmentList.

Northwestern University Library. 2019. *List of IGOs: Getting Started*. http://libguides.northwestern.edu/IGO.

Open.canada.ca. https://open.canada.ca/en.

PACER, Public Access to Court Electronic Records. http://www.pacer.gov.

Parliament of Canada. http://www.parl.gc.ca/default.aspx?Language=E.

Poore, Benjamin Perley. 1885. *A Descriptive Catalogue of the Government Publications of the United States, September 5, 1774—March 4, 1881*. Washington, DC: Government Printing Office.

ProQuest Congressional. Bethesda, MD: Congressional Information Service/ProQuest. http://congressional.proquest.com/congressional/search/basic/basicsearch. Subscription required.

Protecting Your Trademark: Enhancing Your Rights Through Federal Registration. 2018. United States Patent and Trademark Office. https://www.uspto.gov/sites/default/files/documents/BasicFacts.pdf.

Public Papers of the President. 1929–1933, 1945–. Washington, DC: Government Publishing Office. https://www.govinfo.gov/app/collection/PPP.

Shepard's Acts and Cases by Popular Names: Federal and State. 1999. 3 vols. Colorado Springs, CO: Shepard's Cumulative supplements.

Social Security Handbook. 1960–. Social Security Administration. https://www.ssa.gov/OP_Home/handbook/handbook.html.

Superintendent of Documents Classification Guidelines. United States Government Publishing Office. https://www.fdlp.gov/classification-guidelines/introduction-to-the-classification-guidelines.

Technical Report Archive and Image Library (TRAIL). http://www.technicalreports.org/trail/search/.

Twitter. http://www.twitter.com.

United States Code. 1994–. Government Publishing Office. https://www.govinfo.gov/app/collection/USCODE.

United States Congress House Committee on Government Reform. 2005. *A Citizen's Guide on Using the Freedom of Information Act and Privacy Act of 1974 to Request Government Records: Second Report*. H.R. Rpt. 109–226. Washington: Government Printing Office. https://fas.org/sgp/foia/citizen.html.

United States Congressional Serial Set. 1817–. Washington, DC: Congress.

United States Government Manual. 1935–. Washington, DC: Office of the Federal Register. Annual. https://www.govinfo.gov/app/collection/GOVMAN.

United States Reports. Supreme Court of the United States. https://www.supremecourt.gov/opinions/boundvolumes.aspx.

United States Statutes at Large. 1789–. Washington, DC: Government Publishing Office. Annual. https://www.govinfo.gov/app/collection/STATUTE.

UN Resources and Documents. Dag Hammarskjold Library, United Nations. https://library.un.org/content/un-resources-documents.

USA.gov. General Services Administration. http://www.usa.gov.

U.S. Constitution. National Archives. http://www.archives.gov/exhibits/charters/constitution_transcript.html.

Voting Rights Act of 1965. 79 Stat. 437. PL 89–110.

Wakaruk, Amanda, and Sam-chin Li. 2019. *Government Information in Canada: Access and Stewardship*. Edmonton, Alberta, Canada: University of Alberta Press.

Washington Information Directory. 1975/76–. Washington, DC: Congressional Quarterly. Annual.

Weekly Acquisitions List. Government of Canada Publications. http://publications.gc.ca/site/eng/weeklyAcquisitionList/lists.html.

Weekly Checklist of Canadian Government Publications. Ottawa, ON: Government of Canada. http://publications.gc.ca/site/eng/weeklyChecklist/archivedIssues.html?sy=2001.

White House. https://www.whitehouse.gov/.

Your Right to Federal Records: Questions and Answers on the Freedom of Information Act and the Privacy Act. General Services Administration. https://www.gsa.gov/cdnstatic/Your_Right_to_Federal_Records.pdf.

SUGGESTED READINGS

Caro, Susanne. 2018. *Government Information Essentials*. Chicago: ALA Editions, an imprint of the American Library Association.

This recent edited collection covers practical advice for new government information professionals. It acknowledges the current landscape of librarianship which includes teaching and training, advocacy, and the interconnectedness of this specialty within the larger institution.

Drake, Miriam, and Donald T. Hawkins, eds. 2016. *Public Knowledge Access and Benefits*. Medford, NJ: Information Today.

Chapters in this book discuss the challenges in collecting, preserving, updating, and disseminating the large quantities of information generated daily by public sources. Of particular interest is the chapter by James A. Jacobs and James R. Jacobs on "Beyond LMGTFY*: Access to Government Information in a Networked World."

DttP: Documents to the People. Chicago: American Library Association, Government Documents Round Table. https://journals.ala.org/index.php/dttp/index.

An important source for articles, news items, and other information on government publications, technical reports, and maps; related governmental activities; documents librarianship; and Round Table matters.

FDLP Academy. https://www.fdlp.gov/about-the-fdlp/fdlp-academy.

This training resource is a collection of webinars on topics essential to the government information librarian. Trainings are presented by GPO staff, other federal agencies, and government information specialists from the community.

Free Government Information (FGI). http://freegovinfo.info/.

Every government information specialist and depository librarian's favorite blog, *FGI* focuses on open government information through collaboration, education, advocacy, and research among librarians, government agencies, nonprofits, researchers, journalists, and others.

Hartnett, Cassandra J., Andrea L. Sevetson, and Eric J. Forte. 2016. *Fundamentals of Government Information: Mining, Finding, Evaluating, and Using Government Resources*. 2nd ed. Chicago: ALA Neal-Schuman.

This publication is the go-to-source for new and seasoned depository librarians and other practitioners who provide government information references services, whether basic or advanced. A quick look or a longer consult can help any stymied reference librarian confronted with a request for government information.

Latham, Bethany. 2018. *Finding and Using U.S. Government Information: A Practical Guide for Librarians*. Rowman & Littlefield.

This publication is exactly what the subtitle describes: a practical guide. It covers current issues that the new professional will encounter with depth and breadth. Handy especially for those who may accidentally find themselves in charge of government information.

Sevetson, Andrea, ed. 2013. *The Serial Set: Its Make-up and Content*. Bethesda, MD: ProQuest.

This recent compilation discusses various subjects, formats, and time periods covered in the *United States Serial Set*.

Sunlight Foundation. http://www.sunlightfoundation.com/.

This organization is dedicated to protecting and expanding access to government information.

Welch, Susan, John Gruhl, Sue Thomas, and MaryAnne Borrelli. 2014. *Understanding American Government*. 14th ed. Boston, MA: Wadsworth/Cengage Learning.

This title is an engaging textbook on American government and politics. An introductory chapter on the role of government in America is followed by chapters covering such topics as units of government (e.g., Congress, the Presidency, the Judiciary) and important issues such as civil liberties and civil rights.

Chapter 27

Data and Statistical Sources

Celina Nichols McDonald

INTRODUCTION

Although humans have been collecting data since the Babylonians gathered economic data and recorded it on clay tablets in 4,500 BCE (Grajalez et al. 2013), the technological advances at the end of the 20th and start of the 21st centuries propelled production of and demand for data and statistics to unprecedented highs. Before the 1970s, data and statistics were only available in physical formats like paper and microform. Starting in the mid-1970s, libraries began providing access to machine-readable data files via diskettes and remote services like Dialog. Since then, patrons' needs for statistics and data have increased in frequency and complexity.

Today, data and statistical literacy are required and taught by the institutions and communities libraries serve:

- K–12 institutions have introduced data literacy into their curricula;
- Undergraduates learn how to create, analyze, and cite data using sophisticated software;
- Graduate students and faculty across all disciplines use specialized data sets for their research; and
- Public and private sector businesses use data and statistics for many of their decisions.

Due to the vast amounts of data available through a variety of sources and mediums, data and statistics reference questions can be a daunting prospect for many librarians. The purpose of this chapter is to help readers navigate reference questions by introducing them to data and statistics concepts, key resources, and search strategies.

WHAT ARE DATA AND STATISTICS?

While many people use the terms "data" and "statistics" interchangeably, a more nuanced understanding of the two terms and their differences can help librarians provide better assistance to their patrons. This chapter will use definitions from the *Oxford English Dictionary*, which defines "data" as "related items of (chiefly numerical) information considered collectively, typically obtained by scientific work and used for reference, analysis, or calculation" (*OED Online* 2015a). "Statistics" is defined as "a numerical characteristic of a sample (as opposed to a characteristic of the population from which it is drawn)" (*OED Online* 2015b).

In addition to the definitions established here, librarians should understand how the terms are defined in different disciplines to ensure that there is no miscommunication when a patron asks for assistance. For example, sociologists may use the *Blackwell Dictionary of Sociology*, which defines "data" as "facts that social scientists gather, analyze, and interpret" (Johnson 2000, 76). In the health sciences, *The Dictionary of Nursing Theory and Research* defines "data" as "pieces of information (numerical and/or verbal) collected during a research study comprising the empirical evidence" (Powers and Knapp 2011, 40). The common thread throughout the disciplines is that data is the initially unprocessed information collected in the course of a study that is then aggregated or synthesized to support an interpretation.

Like "data," the word "statistics" has a variety of meanings to different groups. The *Dictionary of Nursing Theory and Research* defines a statistic as "a summary measure of the data for a sample, such as a sample mean, a sample standard deviation, or a sample correlation coefficient" (Powers and Knapp 2011, 173–74). In contrast, the *Blackwell Dictionary of Sociology* defines statistics as "a set of mathematical techniques used to organize, analyze, and interpret information that takes the form of numbers" (Johnson 2000, 308).

In addition to understanding the definitions of data and statistics as they apply to different subjects, librarians should learn common terms and phrases that are used when people talk about numeric information (See Table 27.1 for a list of terms and their definitions.). Understanding these terms will greatly facilitate a librarian's communication with patrons as well as clarify the characteristics of patrons' requests that will be used to develop a search strategy for the data they need.

TYPES OF DATA AND STATISTICS

Official and Unofficial

Several different schemes can be used to categorize data and statistics. The source of the data is one such scheme. Although data and statistics are produced by a wide variety of sources, the most meaningful distinction is between official and unofficial sources.

Official data and statistics are those collected by intergovernmental, federal, state, and local government agencies. A patron looking for demographic, business, agricultural, or environmental statistics will find a treasure trove of official information to meet their information needs. For example, users can find a wide range of general data on Canada, the United States, and Mexico collected by

TABLE 27.1 Definitions of Data and Statistical Terms.

Term	Definition
Big Data	A large collection of data; the term is frequently used to refer to a collection of data that requires specialized software to analyze.
Codebook	A book or file that contains information about how a study or survey's data was collected, processed, and analyzed.
CSV	A type of file format that can be used by most mathematical software. CSV stands for "comma separated value," wherein a comma is used to demarcate different fields.
Data Cleaning	To prepare data for analysis by reviewing the content to ensure the data is accurate and in a format that can be analyzed.
Data Mining	Searching large data collections to find new information, such as previously undiscovered relationships between data sets.
Data Set	Collection of related data such as data from a survey.
Meta-Analysis	A systematic review of data or statistics that has been analyzed previously.
Raw Data	Unprocessed numeric information that has not been cleansed or analyzed.
Text Mining	Similar to data mining, text mining occurs when someone searches large collections of textual data to find new relationships between content.

Statistics Canada, the U.S. Census Bureau, and Instituto Nacional De Estadística y Geografía, respectively. More targeted data is often available from specialized government entities, such as weather data gathered by the National Oceanic and Atmospheric Administration (NOAA) or the *Uniform Crime Reporting Program* from the Federal Bureau of Investigation. Most official publications are available free of charge in electronic formats. In the United States, many tangible government publications are also distributed free of charge to federal depository libraries (see Chapter 26).

Whereas official data and statistics originate with government entities, unofficial data and statistics encompass all other publishers, including researchers, non-profit and for-profit companies, and so forth. It is important to note that the use of the term "unofficial" does not signify that the data and statistics are unreliable; it merely indicates that they do not emerge from the operating needs of a government entity. For example, many businesses subscribe to databases from companies such as Nielsen (United States), Abacus Data (Canada), and Kantar Marketplace (United Kingdom) to conduct market research. An example of an authoritative and significant unofficial data source is the Roper Center. Created in 1957, the Roper Center has become one of the most important sources for data on the American public's opinion of political candidates (Hart 2015). In years when there are presidential elections, librarians are likely to receive questions from patrons seeking information about public opinion polls cited by a news source. Along with Gallup, Roper is a valuable tool for politicians and the public to measure the success of a campaign.

Public, Restricted Access, and Inaccessible Data

Another important factor to consider when helping patrons find and use data and statistics is the accessibility of the numeric information, which can be categorized as public, restricted, or inaccessible. At the lowest end of the spectrum, there is public data, which has no impediments to its use. For example, official data and statistics disseminated online or in a tangible format to libraries are public data that anyone can use. At the next level, there is restricted access content, which is only available to users who meet the content provider's access requirements. Common reasons for restricted access are as follows:

- Subscription-/membership-only materials
- Privacy/security concerns
- Researcher/producer's discretion

Content can be restricted based on content, subscription, or membership requirements. Databases such as *ProQuest Statistical Insight* or the Minnesota Population Center's *Integrated Public Use Microdata Series* are restricted to subscribers or membership. Raw data generated through the United States Decennial Census or human subject research is restricted based on its content. With all restricted data, the ease of access will depend on the content, content provider, and library user. While subscription and membership products may offer user-friendly interfaces that make the data relatively easy to access, their license agreements often place complicated restrictions on the reuse of that data. Sometimes, people can access data after personally identifiable information has been stripped out of it. In other instances, people who pass a rigorous application process and visit approved research locations can access raw data.

The third level of accessibility is temporarily or permanently inaccessible data due to the sensitivity of the contents, such as confidential, proprietary, or classified government information. As mentioned previously, the U.S. Decennial Census raw data is stripped of personally identifiable information prior to its original publication. For seventy-two years after initial collection, the raw data is inaccessible to the greater public to protect the subjects' privacy for the duration of their lives. On other occasions, data is inaccessible to users without a formal government security clearance due to national security concerns.

Micro, Aggregated, and Secondary Data: The Data Life Cycle

Data is often conceptualized as going through a life cycle with distinct phases corresponding to various steps in the research process. Over the course of this life cycle, the data itself undergoes changes as it passes through the microdata, aggregated data, and secondary data phases. When the data is initially collected, each individually collected unit (an individual's survey question response, the result of an experimental trial on a single subject, etc.) is called microdata. At this stage, no changes have been made to the data, and personally identifiable information is often still included; for this reason, microdata is the type of data most likely to be subject to access restrictions.

Aggregated data is numeric information derived from microdata after it has been cleaned and analyzed by the content creator. Examples of aggregated data are facts (the observed mass of the Higgs boson), statistics (mortality rates broken down by demographic categories), or analytical conclusions (evidence supporting the effectiveness of a public health campaign). Publicly accessible data is almost always aggregated data.

After researchers have concluded the analysis of their data and published the results of the study, the data life cycle continues. Subsequent research is often performed on the published data, either by the original researchers or by others, transforming the aggregated data into secondary data. Secondary data is aggregated data that has been published and reused to verify the researchers' conclusions or for a new study. The statistically analyzed data can also be reused as secondary statistics, often by combining it with the results of other similar studies to generate more statistically significant conclusions. A common technique in the health sciences is the systematic review with meta-analysis, which combines the results of several published clinical trials using statistical analysis techniques to determine the strength of evidence for a medical intervention.

For most reference librarians, the most frequently encountered user need is to find data and statistics that the user can then put to secondary use in a research project. The user's specific need will help determine the type of data most appropriate for their purposes. Understanding the data life cycle will make it easier for a librarian to determine if micro, aggregate, or secondary data will be most useful for the user.

Cross-Sectional, Time-Series, and Longitudinal Data

Cross-sectional, time-series, and longitudinal data sets relate to the time period over which the data was collected. A cross-sectional data set is collected at a single point in time. Survey responses, measurements taken on a single experiment, and information collected from travelers' customs declaration forms at the end of a flight from Amsterdam to Moscow are all examples of cross-sectional data.

Time-series data is collected in regular intervals over a period of time. An example of time-series data is the data gathered by the STAR*D trial funded by the National Institute of Mental Health, which studied the efficacy of different depression treatments. Data was gathered from participants in twelve-week intervals until their depression went into remission. Researchers followed up with the patients again, one year after they went into remission.

Longitudinal data is collected over an extended period of time, often spanning multiple decades. Longitudinal data is often the most difficult to find because of the expense and level of commitment required to ensure the success of a study that may span decades. As a result, longitudinal data sets are some of the most frequently reused, with the data collected from a single longitudinal study often leading to dozens of publications, even years after the original study was published. Census data is a prominent example of an ongoing longitudinal data set. Just like any other source of information, data sets should be cited, but citing different types of data sources can be tricky. Box 27.1 discusses issues related to citing data sources.

Box 27.1 Activity: Citing Data in Bibliographies

While citing statistics and figures from a single resource is straightforward, citing reused data can be a complicated and even problematic endeavor. For example, a patron analyzing demographic statistics published between 1950 and 2000 only needs to worry about properly citing the creator of the data. On the other end of the spectrum, citing metadata harvested from a search on a vendor database can be a violation of a publisher's terms of use. To address these kinds of issues, a librarian will need to review any applicable licensing agreements. Many libraries have published data citation guides on their pages to help their users properly attribute their resources in their bibliographies.

DataCite is a nonprofit organization that assists researchers in finding data and also provides guidance on citing the data sets. Visit the *DataCite* website (https://datacite.org/) and try searching for data sets on a topic of interest.

1. What kinds of sources do you find? Are they official or unofficial?
2. Are the sources mostly original data sets or secondary analysis?
3. What guidance is provided in how to cite the data sets that you find?

EVALUATION OF SOURCES

It is important to have a collection development policy with set criteria for evaluating any potential acquisitions and withdrawals, and data and statistics sources are no exception. Thematically, the criteria by which data and statistical publications are evaluated mirrors other parts of reference collections; however, there are some aspects that are unique to statistical and data resources. It is not enough to just look at the group that gathered the data, who funded the study that led to its collection, and the institution that published it; a truly thorough review will also examine the data's content and the methods by which it was collected. Understanding data collection methods and best practices is especially important for librarians because a library's reputation is based in large part on the credibility of the resources it provides. Librarians should take the steps needed to provide quality resources to minimize the chances of their users' research being invalidated due to a reliance on faulty data.

Authority

Previous chapters have discussed the importance of the author and publisher establishing the authority of a source. In addition to these considerations, librarians should also look at the funding source when evaluating data and statistics. In many professions, people judge the value of research based on who funded it. For example, a 2012 study published by the *New England Journal of Medicine* found that doctors trusted NIH-funded studies more than those that received funding from pharmaceutical companies (Kesselheim et al. 2012). Studies funded by pharmaceutical companies were generally distrusted due to the potential conflict of interest between the researcher's objectivity and the funding agent's business objectives.

Citations of a data set can also be a useful tool in establishing its authority, as it provides a general measure of how a data set is regarded within its discipline. *Data Citation Index*, a database published by Thomson Reuters, is a useful tool for determining how often a data set has been cited and by whom. Exploring the citing articles to understand the context of the citation can also inform the librarian of the quality of the data.

Accuracy

It is important to assess data collection methods as carefully as possible when evaluating data and statistical materials. When presenting data to patrons, it may be helpful for the librarian to be able to explain factors that might complicate its accuracy. For example, longitudinal studies may suffer from data collection methods that vary from year to year, resulting in improper comparisons across time. If possible, librarians should determine if a study or data set has been contradicted or revised by later research, as in the high-profile case of a study published in *Lancet* (Wakefield et al. 1998) linking vaccinations to autism that was later debunked. Some data sets include "data quality flags" that identify any variables that have been edited for analysis due to incomplete or illegible responses. One way to ascertain this is to look up the article produced by the study and see if it has been retracted. One widely followed blog, *Retraction Watch*, provides up-to-date and comprehensive information on retracted articles.

Currency

Collected data is almost invariably linked to the time that it was collected. Thus, it is extremely important to understand the user's needs and whether current or historical data will answer their questions. Both the date of the data's collection and that of its publication are valuable pieces of information. If the 1990 census data set was published in 1991, the librarian may need to see if a more recent edition or corrected copy supersedes the original edition. If the data is the product of research, it can be important to determine if it has been debunked by later studies.

Scope and Comprehensiveness

The scope and comprehensiveness of the collection should be determined by the level of service the library intends to provide to support users of data and statistics (see Box 27.2). A collection development policy should be established that deals with levels of service and criteria for including and excluding materials from the collection. The policy should include formats collected, the subject scope to be covered, criteria and schedule for weeding, and a preservation plan to ensure data does not become corrupted or otherwise unusable.

Box 27.2 Activity: Levels of Service

The early 1990s saw a dramatic increase in demand for data services as a result of the 1990 Decennial Census being distributed to Federal Depository Libraries. Since the 1991 publication of Jim Jacobs's seminal article "Providing Data Services for Machine-Readable Information in an Academic Library," librarians have been trying to define the right level of service to support their users' data and statistical needs. Because authors differ on the number of levels and what services are provided for each stage, this section introduces a simplified version of the levels of service (Jacobs 1991).

Level One: Basic Services

The library acquires and catalogs some materials and helps users search for materials held by other institutions. Users have access to computers with an office software suite, such as Microsoft Office or LibreOffice, both of which include programs that help people work with numeric information. Reference librarians at these institutions should be knowledgeable of general resources and where a patron can go to get more advanced assistance. A school media library may purchase materials from *Facts on File* through Infobase, which is recommended for K–12 users. For complex questions, librarians refer patrons to other departments or organizations that provide specialized support. This level of service would be appropriate at small public, school media, special, and academic libraries, where there is little demand for data and statistics.

Level Two: Intermediate Services

At this level, the library subscribes to general data and statistical databases as well as popular subject-specific databases. The library also purchases data sets on request and makes specialized software packages available on the public-use computers. The library does not provide technical support or guidance regarding the software's use; however, librarians do offer consultations to library patrons who need help finding data and statistics. Librarians have access to and can help patrons search databases for content. Reference librarians at these institutions should be knowledgeable of general resources as well as more popular sources. This level of service can typically be found at large public research, academic, and special libraries.

Level Three: Advanced Services

The library subscribes to a large number of databases providing subject-specific data and statistical information. At least one dedicated data services librarian works with researchers to curate original research for the library's collection and an employee provides statistical analysis support to researchers. This may include helping the researcher design the study, clean data, and process it using specialized software. This level of service is generally found at large research, academic, and special libraries.

When making decisions regarding the level of service to be provided by the library, librarians should carefully examine their users' needs and the library's financial resources before developing a formal policy and plan for providing the services, no matter how simple, because they will inform all staff and guide acquisitions decisions.

Visit the website of an information organization of your choice, and answer the following questions:

1. Can you find a data policy or plan for this institution?
2. If so, what level of service does this institution offer to its users?
3. If you cannot find a data policy or plan, can you infer the level of service from other clues on the website? For instance, is there a LibGuide with information on finding and using data? Does the institution subscribe to any of the data sources highlighted in this chapter?

Format

The question of format is a complicated issue when evaluating data and statistical information because content is delivered through a variety of mechanisms and machine-readable file formats. In terms of delivery mechanisms, content is stored in analog and digital formats. Analog materials are tangible materials that can be used without the aid of a computer, such as paper and microfiche. Digital materials contain information stored in a machine-readable format that can only be accessed with the aid of a computer or an Internet-connected device. These materials may be stored on local physical carriers such as CD-ROMs or accessed online. While analog materials are less likely to be rendered unusable due to changes in technology, they are vulnerable to environmental factors such as temperature and humidity. Depending on factors such as the storage medium, file format, and backup strategy, digital materials may also be susceptible to both environmental and technological changes. For example, in the early 1990s, the Government Publishing Office distributed the 1990 Census on CD-ROM. At the time, CD-ROMs were considered a stable long-term storage solution. Since then, studies, have shown the usable life of a CD-ROM to be anywhere from fifteen months (Zurkirch and Reichart 2000) to five years (Lawrence, Connaway, and Brigham 2001).

SELECTION

Needs of Users

Libraries of different types may rely on a variety of tools or measurements to evaluate their patrons' needs and determine appropriate collection policies. For example, a school librarian, in addition to getting demographic information about the students, should also obtain course syllabi to understand what kind of projects the students will be bringing to the library and anticipate their needs. Public libraries, with a more diverse set of users, will need to base their selection decisions on a more complicated set of criteria, examining both their community as a whole and their library users in particular. Many libraries avoid tracking patron-specific data due to privacy concerns, so they must pursue alternate means of gathering data on user needs. For example, tracking reference questions and materials' circulation and in-house use can help the librarian gain insight into the topics of interest, format preferences, and level of technical expertise of their users. Any analysis of the library's user demographics and their needs should be included in the collection development policy.

Cost

Different types of data and statistical sources are associated with different cost considerations. As is often the case, the primary distinction is between print and electronic formats. On a basic level, print content has a single, up-front cost, while electronic content, even if purchased, generally comes with an annual access fee. Another cost that should be considered for both formats is the cost of maintaining the collection. Acquiring and cataloging the data, storing it, and ensuring long-term access, particularly for digital formats that will likely need to be migrated periodically to remain usable, all have associated costs. While electronic data in many formats can be used with basic text editors or common spreadsheet programs, others may require the purchase or licensing of specialized software needed to access or manipulate the data. There may be additional costs depending on the library's level of service and the user's needs.

Storage and Organization

After acquiring a data or statistical resource, the library must make provisions for storing, organizing, and providing access to it. Data and statistical resources are commonly classified by the subject of the information rather than collocating all such resources in a single area. Library staff members may prefer to create a central data and statistics collection, particularly in the electronic domain. However, the staff then needs to be careful that selectors communicate with each other to minimize overlap and gaps in the collection.

Traditionally, print and microform data and statistical publications have been housed according to their format, usually at or near information services desks. In institutions where the library has taken on a more active role in acquiring or curating digital data resources, librarians must also be cognizant of other considerations such as the hardware, database architecture, and user interface design needed to store, organize, and make the data accessible. In particular, libraries embarking upon or already serving as institutional repositories for data and statistics should pay attention to the organization and access to materials stored on library servers. This is an extensive topic, and librarians with the responsibility of supporting an institutional repository should refer to a more in-depth work on data curation such as *Research Data Management: Practical Strategies for Information Professionals* (Ray 2014).

Supplemental Tools

When acquiring electronic data sets and statistics, librarians also need to consider what technology and supplemental tools may be needed, particularly if they plan to offer data services beyond the most basic level. For example, most data sets come with a codebook that explains the fields in the data, the questions that were used in data collection, how the data was acquired and processed, and so on. Users need this information to make sense of the data, and it should be in a format that can be loaded into SPSS or other specialized data analysis tools.

Providing access to specialized software is also important. Some are cost prohibitive for most patrons, and many require expertise in order to use effectively.

One area of data analysis that has seen significant growth in recent years is text mining. Although people in different fields, especially biomedicine, have been text mining since the 1990s, in recent years the practice has expanded to the humanities and social sciences disciplines (Hearst 1999). Some free tools are available, such as the Google Books Ngram Viewer, which allows users to numerically analyze the frequency of words and phrases used in a corpus of millions of books going back to 1800. Other text-mining projects may require access to content from specific subscription databases and use of special statistical software. In these cases, the library staff must negotiate with the vendor for the researcher to make use of the database's content beyond the access allowed by general license agreements. In some cases, researchers who are unaware of this condition may attempt to download whole collections from a vendor database in violation of the library's license agreement, which can result in a disruption in service (Van Noorden 2012).

Because of the increase in text mining, libraries and publishers are being compelled to learn how to allow complete access to collections without losing control of the copyrighted materials. Typically, the library must subscribe to the database and purchase additional access to allow the researcher to download the corpus to be analyzed. This access must be negotiated carefully on a case-by-case basis, typically initiated by a user's request, but due to the cost of enhanced access the library will usually want to purchase the content outright for it to be cost effective. Text mining is a new frontier for librarians, where even text can be transformed into numerical information. *The Text Mining Handbook: Advanced Approaches in Analyzing Unstructured Data* by Ronen Feldman and James Sanger (2007) is a seminal introductory title that can help reference librarians deepen their understanding of text mining.

IMPORTANT GENERAL SOURCES

The goal of this chapter is to highlight some key guides and sources that reference librarians will frequently use to answer patron questions. Due to the vast range of available sources and frequency with which useful sources are introduced, it is not possible to list all information sources or even list all of the best ones. Data and statistical guides and sources change frequently as researchers find new ways to share numeric information online. If a reader is unable to access a source, the Internet Archive's *Wayback Machine* website can often be used to gain access to archived websites, including older versions of existing websites as well as sites that have been deleted.

Whereas data and statistics are increasingly available for use, there has been a marked decrease in the number of general guides to resources. One particular area that has not kept pace with the information boom is print guides. The rapid expansion, rapid rate of change, and instability of online content has caused authors to be reluctant to attempt to track these resources in a print publication. Therefore, many print publications tend to be older and out of date; however, there are a significant number of excellent online guides. One standout guide is *Data & Statistics Research Guides* from Michigan State University, which includes information for finding data and statistics in overlooked areas such as the arts, religion, and linguistics. Canadian librarians may find the University of Ottawa's *Data and Statistics* useful for finding and using official Canadian statistics. For users searching for international data and statistics, *International Statistics and Data* from the University of Illinois at Urbana-Champaign is an online guide with an extensive collection of links to data in other countries and from a variety of sources.

Books dedicated to finding data and statistics are rare because they quickly become outdated. As a result, there are few books that can guide librarians to different resources. One such publication is Julia Bauder's (2014) *Reference Guide to Data*, which is an essential title for the reference shelf. It is organized by subject and serves as a guide to finding data from a variety of sources from the United States and other nations, both general and specialized.

Statistics Sources: A Subject Guide to Data on Industrial Business, Social, Educational, Financial and Other Topics for the United States and Internationally, an annual bibliographic guide to official and unofficial statistics, can be a good publication for libraries of all types and sizes to have in their collections. A two-volume set, *Statistics Sources* is a comprehensive guide that can help a librarian quickly identify the best source for statistical information.

Another guide that can be an asset to all types of libraries, especially public and school media libraries, is *Datapedia of the United States: American History in Numbers* (Kurian and Chernow 2007). An accessible source on data and statistics about the United States from 1789 to 2003, the book is highly recommended because it has many tables, is easy to read, and is full of citations to its source materials.

Finding guides to unofficial resources tends to be more difficult than finding guides for official sources. Unofficial resources tend to be more unstable than official sources. If a reference librarian needs help finding unofficial sources, the *World Directory of Non-Official Statistical Sources* is a useful guide to keep in the reference collection.

OFFICIAL RESOURCES

The resources included in this section are official data and statistics resources from the originating agency or another government body. Official numeric information that is accessed through an aggregator such as *Data-Planet* are explored as unofficial resources. Official resources can help reference librarians assist patrons of all ages and reading levels find data and statistics about

- population and demographics;
- economics, industry, finance, and business;
- health and vital statistics;
- energy (fossil fuels, renewable, natural);
- environment, forestry, water, fish and wildlife;
- agriculture, livestock, and crops.

Almost all official data and statistics resources are available online free of cost to the general public, making them essential and affordable sources for content. Official information is especially strong for subjects in the social sciences such as anthropology, business, political science, economics, education, the environment, history, geography, and psychology. Because official data covers a multitude of subject areas and dates, there is a tremendous amount of information, which can make it difficult to find official data on a particular topic. This section of the chapter will focus on data and statistical products from the United States, Canada, and the United Nations. Because of the affordability, scope, and relevance to a wide range of users of different reading levels and abilities, there will be a greater focus on official resources than on unofficial sources. Readers are encouraged to consult the *Reference Guide to Data Sources* by Julia Bauder (2014) to get a more complete list of data and statistical sources.

U.S. Resources

Over one hundred U.S. federal departments and agencies publish data and statistics, thirteen of which are considered the primary producers. These agencies are

TABLE 27.2 Data and Statistics Available from U.S. Federal Agencies.

Agency	Description
Bureau of Economic Analysis	Regional, national, and international trade data.
Bureau of Justice Statistics	Arrest, crime incidence, law enforcement, and penal data and statistics.
Bureau of Labor Statistics	Labor, compensation, employment and unemployment statistics; workforce, career, and industry data and statistics; *Consumer Price Index*.
Bureau of Transportation Statistics	State and national transportation statistics including rail, air, and motorway statistics.
Census Bureau	Censuses of population and housing, economic, and governments; *American Community Survey*.
Economic Research Service	U.S. Department of Agriculture crop, food supply, consumption, and market data and statistics.
Energy Information Administration	Energy use, trade, and market data and statistics.
National Agricultural Statistics Service	Crop and livestock data and statistics; *Census of Agriculture*.
National Center for Education Statistics	K–12, secondary, and postsecondary data and statistics; student achievement and assessment data and statistics; school, library, and school district data and statistics.
National Center for Health Statistics	Birth, mortality, and health data and statistics; this agency includes data for specific ailments and conditions as well as current issues such as obesity.
National Center for Science and Engineering Statistics	Science and engineering statistics including demographic profiles of the work force.
Social Security Administration Office of Research, Evaluation, and Statistics	Social security recipient and program data and statistics.
Statistics of Income IRS	Individual, nonprofit, and for-profit taxation information.

listed in Table 27.2, with information on their major data-gathering programs and publications. Common topics of reference questions requiring U.S. governmental data or statistics include population, business, workforce, education, health, agriculture, and criminal justice. Because of the depth and breadth of the data and statistical information available from the U.S. government, a few agencies are highlighted in more detail.

For general informational needs, *Data.gov* can often help a librarian find the data and statistics they need. *Data.gov* serves as a single access point to more than 188,000 data sets on a variety of subjects, such as agriculture, business, environment, education, health, and criminal justice. Librarians at academic institutions may find *Data.gov* of greater assistance than those at public and school libraries.

The U.S. Census Bureau is one of the most important sources for statistics about the U.S. population, government, and business. Their content is published in tangible and electronic formats. In addition to the familiar *Census of Population and Housing*, they also collect and publish valuable data in the *Economic Census*, *Census of Governments*, and *American Community Survey*. The Census Bureau also conducts surveys for or with other federal agencies and departments such as the *American Housing Survey* for the Department of Housing and Urban Development and the *Current Population Survey* with the Bureau of Labor Statistics. A complete listing of surveys is available from the Census Bureau's website.

While the United States Census Bureau collects and disseminates some of the most important data for modern libraries, their tools can be very frustrating for librarians and the public due to their complexity and rapidly changing landscape. As of July 2019, *data.census.gov* is the primary source of Census Bureau data, while previously popular online tools such as *American Factfinder* and *DataFerrett* now have limited usefulness due to technological restrictions such as server space and dated software. In fact, ingestion of new data into *American Factfinder* was stopped in June 2019. One of the benefits of *data.census.gov* is that users will have a single source for different census products such as the *Economic Census*. Because census tools are regularly being updated to accommodate the growing body of data, users are advised to regularly visit the Census Bureau's website to sign up for webinars or watch training videos to stay abreast of the latest developments and learn about new functionalities.

The Bureau of Labor Statistics (BLS) provides numeric information about employment, compensation, and consumer trends. Major publications include the *Consumer Price Index*, *Employment and Earnings*, *Employment Cost Index*, and *Monthly Labor Review*, all of which were published in print until 2007 and 2008, when they became electronic-only publications. One of their most frequently cited sources is *Employment and Earnings*, which contains city, state, and national employment, unemployment, and compensation statistics. For reference librarians who are helping people learn about the cost of different products and services, the *Consumer Price Index* is a valuable publication. In addition to providing data and statistics about the workforce, the BLS produces *Employment Cost Index*, which contains information about total expenditures by employers per employee.

The National Center for Health Statistics is a valuable official source for health statistics and data. They publish a multitude of reports such as the *National Vital Statistics Reports* and the *National Health Statistics Reports*, which contain birth, death, and other health statistics for the United States. They also publish annual reports that focus on current trends and issues through *Health, United States*, which is an annual publication available in print and on the agency's website. People who would like to build custom tables that contain the information they need will find *Health Data Interactive* a useful online tool for health statistics. Users can build custom tables by report, subject, geographic location, race, age, and urban/rural.

The National Center for Education Statistics is an excellent source for data and statistics on education topics. One of the best sources to consult is the *Digest of Education Statistics*, an annual publication that is currently published only in electronic format. The publication contains statistics derived from many different surveys and programs conducted throughout the year and compiles statistics about all levels of education, from pre-kindergarten to secondary education, public and private schools, staffing, libraries, crime in schools, achievement, and employment. The *Condition of Education* is another good source for data and statistics about current issues such as crime in schools.

In addition to its regular publications, the National Center for Education Statistics has developed online tools for its different survey programs. Someone who is searching for data about a school district can use *Search for Public School Districts*. Someone else who wants to find statistics related to students' academic achievement in different subjects can consult the "Data Explorer" on the *National Assessment of Educational Progress* website.

For librarians who are asked questions about U.S. food production, costs, nutrition, or people's eating habits, two excellent sources of data and statistics are the U.S. Department of Agriculture's (USDA's) Economic Research Service and the National Agricultural Statistics Services. The National Agricultural Statistics Services collects and disseminates agricultural industry data and statistics, including the quinquennial *Census of Agriculture*. As with many publications, the most recent census is currently available electronically. The Economic Research Service publishes reports about farm productivity, market data for specific crops, and data about people's access to and consumption of food. The easiest way to find and use current data and statistics from the Economic Research Service is to visit their website's "Data Products" page, which has a full listing of files, applications, and charts. School media librarians may find the *Atlas of Rural and Small-Town America*, *Food Access Research Atlas*, and *Food Environment Atlas* particularly useful. The user-friendly, brightly colored atlases are well designed for middle and high school students. They can create subject- and location-specific maps, which can then be exported as images or pdfs. For research-oriented questions, librarians can consult the U.S. Department of Agriculture's *Economics, Statistics, and Market Information System*, a database that provides access to reports and data sets from five USDA agencies and Cornell University. Users can access and download historical and current publications about crop, livestock, and market data and statistics.

Users looking for crime and justice statistics can find data from the Federal Bureau of Investigation (FBI) or the Bureau of Justice Statistics (BJS). The FBI's *Uniform Crime Reporting Program* is a vital resource for crime-related statistics. Publications such as *Crime in the United States*, *Law Enforcement Officers Killed and Assaulted*, *Hate Crime Statistics*, and the *National Incident-Based Reporting System* will meet most users' needs. The BJS provides access to crime and justice data and statistics. Many users, particularly young readers, may find both bureaus' websites challenging because of the frequent use of technical terms. Another challenge can be knowing which agency produces content on a specific topic. For example, users who are looking for statistics about the number of civilians killed by police officers should consult the BJS for statistics from their *Arrest-Related Deaths* (which gathered data from 2003 to 2012) and *Mortality in Correctional Institutions* (formerly *Deaths in Custody*) programs. In the future, this may change. In January 2019, the FBI began gathering data for their upcoming *National Use-of-Force Data Collection*.

Canadian Sources

In contrast to their southern neighbor, Canada has a centralized system for collecting and disseminating data. Most official Canadian data and statistics are collected and disseminated by Statistics Canada, which provides access to content on a broad variety of topics, including agriculture, business, crime and justice, economics, education, energy, health, income, labor, population, science, transportation, and the environment. In addition to Statistics Canada, eleven other agencies also generate data and statistics (see Table 27.3). For many librarians from all types of libraries, Statistics Canada's data and statistics can meet most, if not all, users' needs.

One resource that many librarians will find essential is the reference section of the *Statistics Canada* website. On the reference page, users can find guides, codebooks, dictionaries, and reference publications such as *Canada Year Book*. The *Canada Year Book* is a comprehensive collection of tables and statistics from all the censuses, surveys, and statistics collections published by Statistics Canada. Coverage includes publications and surveys on topics such as agriculture, education, economics, crime and justice, labor, and transportation. Although users can access archival copies of the *Canada Year Book* online, no new editions have been published since 2012.

Canada at a Glance is a small, quick-reference publication for current statistics in the most common areas, such as population, agriculture, health, education, commerce, justice, and travel. *Canada at a Glance* is one of the few publications that is still published in print, in addition to the electronic version.

For historical data and statistics, *Historical Statistics of Canada* is a useful publication for reference collections. Available in print and online, *Historical Statistics of Canada* provides easy access to official statistics dating from the Canadian Confederation in 1867 to the mid-1970s. The online version allows data access in a variety of file formats, including comma separated value, which can be manipulated by almost all statistical software programs, including Microsoft Excel.

TABLE 27.3 Data and Statistics Available from Canadian Government Agencies.

Agency/Department	Description
Bank of Canada	Banking and financial statistics.
Canada Revenue Agency	Individual and business income statistics.
Canadian Grain Commission	Grain data and statistics including exports and tax.
Immigration and Refugee Board of Canada	Refugee data and statistics.
Military Grievances External Review Committee	Military grievance data and statistics.
National Defence and Canadian Forces Ombudsman	National defense data and statistics.
National Energy Board	Energy market and use data and statistics.
Natural Resources Canada	Forest and natural resources data and statistics.
Office of the Commissioner of Official Languages	Language use data and statistics.
Parole Board of Canada	Parole statistics.
Statistics Canada	Population, education health, economic, criminal justice, and agricultural data and statistics from the national statistics office for Canada.

In addition to the data and statistics available from Statistics Canada, the Government of Canada provides *Open Data* which, like *Data.gov*, serves as a single portal to official data from all branches of the government. Statistical information can also be found from federal agencies and divisions such as the Canada Revenue Agency.

United Nations

The United Nations (UN) is one of the best resources for international data and statistics. Although the UN has their own statistics division, UN-affiliated organizations like the World Health Organization, International Monetary Fund, World Bank, and United Nations Educational, Scientific and Cultural Organization (UNESCO) also publish statistics.

The goal of the United Nations Statistics Division (n.d.) is to be the "apex entity of the global statistical system." In that capacity, the division collects and disseminates data and statistics about and for the international community. Several databases and publications can help a librarian answer data and statistics questions.

For a librarian or library user who prefers accessing content online, *UNdata* is an inter-organizational database that makes it possible to search UN and partner organizations' statistical publications. Users searching *UNdata* can also find statistics from organizations such as the UNESCO Institute for Statistics, International Monetary Fund, United Nations Population Division, and World Health Organization. In addition to the search function, a glossary, list of included data sets, and country information are available via *UNdata*.

Another excellent online resource is *UN COMTRADE Database*, a database with more than 1.5 billion records that serves as a comprehensive source for international trade data. Highly technical, *COMTRADE* is recommended for advanced users. For most data and statistics questions reference librarians receive, *UNData* will meet the patron's needs.

In addition to their databases, the UN and its affiliates continue to publish materials in print and electronic formats. One such publication is the *Statistical Yearbook*, an annual report that strives to be a comprehensive collection of statistics assembled from UN divisions and affiliated organizations. The *Statistical Yearbook* is divided into four parts:

- World and region
- Population and social statistics
- Economic activity
- International economic relations

In addition to being available in print, every edition of the *Statistical Yearbook* published since 2006 is also available electronically, making it convenient for users to download and analyze its data.

Two other vital UN Statistics Division publications are the *World Statistics Pocketbook* and *Monthly Bulletin of Statistics*. Both publications are good multidisciplinary statistical sources, potentially useful to library users with a wide range of needs. The former is a compilation of statistics for 224 counties and locations around the world. Agriculture, finance, health, tourism, labor, and population are among the subjects covered in the *World Statistics Pocketbook*. The *Monthly Bulletin of Statistics* contains 50 tables of economic, population, labor, energy, and transportation statistics for more than 200 countries. Published for more than eighty years, the *Monthly Bulletin* is now available in print and electronic formats. Online users also have the option of downloading tables.

In addition to the general sources already mentioned, the UN and their affiliates publish subject-specific statistics. For example, the *Energy Statistics Yearbook*, *Demographic Yearbook*, and *International Trade Statistics Yearbook* are annual compendiums that have a smaller target audience than the general sources. Many UN publications are available in different tangible and digital formats. The most recent editions of the publications are available for purchase. It is also possible to purchase historical materials. For example, librarians can purchase the *Demographic Yearbook* for 1948–1997 in CD-ROM format.

UN affiliates publish a significant number of official sources of useful international statistics and data. UNESCO Institute for Statistics publishes titles like the *Global Education Digest*, an annual publication with statistics that assess children's access to education, identify achievement gaps, and analyze environmental factors affecting student learning. Another affiliate that publishes valuable information is the World Health Organization. Their *World Health Report*, a biennial publication with health statistics from 194 participating countries, may be of particular use to librarians in all types of libraries. Librarians who work with students from middle school to graduate school can find the content useful to answer questions such as the following:

- What is the life expectancy for males and females in Afghanistan?
- What country has the lowest rate of infant mortality?
- What country has the highest number of people infected with the HIV virus?

The statistics from the World Health Organization can also be accessed using the *Global Health Observatory Data Repository*. In this database, users can download and customize the tables included in the *World Health Report* as well as content from other sources.

Dozens of other UN divisions and affiliates provide access to data and statistics. Librarians are encouraged to visit the *UN Statistics Division* website. There are links to a number of resources from different UN divisions, affiliates, and nations from around the world.

Sources for Children and Young Adults

For school librarians, helping their patrons find and use suitable data and statistics sources can be problematic. Most official sources focus on adult users when they design websites and publish materials. Subscription-based content may be economically infeasible or require purchasing decisions at the district level or higher. Following are some free official online sources for data and statistics that are accessible to young readers:

- ***USDA for Kids.*** The USDA's page for food, crop, livestock, and agricultural information including links to games, information about research, and guides for educators.
- ***Statistics in Schools.*** The U.S. Census Bureau's website is a resource for educators who wish to teach their students about data and statistics. It includes information about activities, games, apps, and resources that can be used to educate students on statistics.

- ***Data in the Classroom.*** Links to educational resources from the U.S. federal government that can help educate students on how to find and use data, including lesson plans, activities, and links to official and unofficial data sources.
- ***Secretary-General's Envoy on Youth.*** United Nations portal to help educate and engage young people in the UN, it includes information about the United Nations as well as links to statistics about children.

In addition to these sources, there are a number of other resources available. School librarians should stay abreast of current trends in their profession by reading professional publications and signing up for listservs, where they can communicate with and receive advice from their peers.

UNOFFICIAL RESOURCES

A tremendous number of subscription and free databases make data and statistics available. Even databases that are primarily text focused, such as *ProQuest Legislative Insight*, can provide data in the form of text. This section focuses on databases that provide access to data and statistics, feature interdisciplinary content, and support library users at all types of libraries. The goal is to highlight databases that many libraries should include in their essential or high-priority lists.

Subscription-Based Databases

Data-Planet is a helpful broad-based data and statistical resource, available as either *Data-Planet Statistical Datasets* or *Data-Planet Statistical Ready Reference*. The two versions provide access to the same content; the primary difference between the two interfaces is the ability to customize tables. First-time users for both databases will probably be able to find and extract relevant information but performing analysis via the user interfaces may require manipulation of the data. For example, if someone who is using *Data-Planet Statistical Datasets* wants to create a time series chart that correlates arrest rates, unemployment, and government policies, they can select the following facets from the list:

1. Arrests by race from 1980 to present;
2. Presidencies during that time by political party;
3. Unemployment statistics.

Since these data sets cover different time spans and are aggregated in different units (monthly, yearly, etc.), the user will need to remove surplus data by downloading and modifying it using Microsoft Excel or another statistical software package to produce a usable chart. Because of its complexity, *Data-Planet Statistical Datasets* is recommended for academic and research institutions, where students, professors, and researchers frequently work with large data sets.

Another excellent database is *ProQuest Statistical Insight*, which provides electronic access to official and unofficial data and statistics from a multitude of sources, including the United States, Canada, and the United Nations. For example, *Statistical Insight* includes content from the *American Statistics Index*,

Statistics Reference Index, and the *Index to International Statistics*, all of which have also been published in microfiche. Furthermore, *Statistical Insight* serves as a single access point for data from federal and international agencies.

Two other products many librarians find useful are *ProQuest Statistical Abstracts of the World* and *ProQuest Statistical Abstract of the United States*, both of which can replace discontinued products like the Census Bureau's *Statistical Abstract of the United States*. Both databases are excellent resources to find quick population, housing, and economic statistics. These resources are recommended for all libraries, especially public and academic libraries because they can meet the needs of many users.

In many public and academic libraries, the institution subscribes to several business databases that may be useful in answering statistical questions. One such database is Standard & Poor's *NetAdvantage*, which provides access to data on individual companies, industries, and the *Daily Stock Price Record*, which provides information on stocks, bonds, and futures prices. Many other business databases provide valuable data for researchers (see Chapter 28). Business librarians consider these databases essential, and in fact for some academic libraries they are mandatory because the departments they serve may lose accreditation if the library does not subscribe to the databases. More specialized business databases are the Roper Center's *iPOLL Search* and *Gallup*, which supply public opinion data and statistics.

In addition to databases that provide access to newer and/or specialized content, there are several sources for historical statistics. Librarians from the United States may find *Historical Statistics of the United States* (Carter et al. 2015) from Cambridge University Press to be a helpful database. This database provides access to statistical content that can be difficult to find in other sources. For example, users can find crime and arrest information back to 1910. Law enforcement agencies did not begin regularly recording official crime data and statistics until 1930, when the FBI was given the responsibility to do so.

The last database to be highlighted in this section is the Inter-University Consortium for Political and Social Research (ICPSR), which is not truly a subscription database; however, the institution must pay a membership fee and belong to the consortium to be able to have full access to its data repository. ICPSR is a repository for social science research data. Although many universities and colleges participate, federal agencies also use and deposit content. Librarians who receive advanced questions that seem to have no easy-to-find solution are advised to search ICPSR to ascertain if any of its data sets contain the content the patron needs. For example, undergraduate students who need data about how sentencing affects inmates' actions can find that information at ICPSR. Much of the data is curated from research projects conducted by academics, government entities, and researchers. To be included in the ICPSR database, data must meet several requirements, including the types of files and information that must be submitted with the data. This is a valuable resource for large academic libraries and a must-have for many researchers. Members include academic, government, and special libraries from around the world. Although ICPSR has existed since 1962, in recent years increasing numbers of faculty and graduate and undergraduate students have sought access to data available through ICPSR.

Free Sources

Since the early 2000s, there has been a marked increase in the number of open access online data repositories, with a dramatic impact on the data and statistics landscape. Whereas governments and intergovernmental organizations previously had a monopoly on free data and statistics, universities, consortia, academics, and publishers are entering the market in growing numbers. Because many of the resources included in this section are specialized and have narrow scopes, reference librarians will find these resources helpful when trying to find data and statistics that cannot be found in any of the usual places. For many resources, patrons will need to use specialized software like SPSS to process the data.

An example of a highly specialized database is the *Global Terrorism Database*. Although open access, it deals with a specialized subject and target audience. The *Global Terrorism Database* was created by the National Consortium for the Study of Terrorism and Responses to Terrorism, which was created by the University of Maryland and Department of Homeland Security.

No section on open access unofficial data and statistics sources is complete without mention of the Minnesota Population Center at the University of Minnesota, which provides access to United States and international demographic data resources through the Integrated Public Use Microdata Series (IPUMS). All of the content is available free of charge, but users must register for access if they want to download any of the information. Through IPUMS, registered users can access *IPUMS-USA*, *IPUMS-International*, *Current Population Survey*, *Integrated Health Interview Series*, and the *North Atlantic Population Project*. This database can be very useful when one is unable to find data and statistics elsewhere. For example, a student asking for maternal and infant mortality statistics for Sierra Leone may have difficulty finding that information on the UN's website, but the information is readily available from IPUMS. Users can create their own tables and then download the data set.

Since the wide array of openly available data sets is impossible to capture in a brief overview, librarians in search of data are advised to consult one or more of the continuously updated directories of such sources. Simmons University's School of Library and Information Science hosts the *Open Access Directory* (*OAD*), which helps users find open access content online from official and unofficial sources. *OAD* is most useful when trying to find data that seems outside of the scope of most databases. For example, if an archaeologist needs help finding data and statistics, the *OAD* can provide a link to the *Archaeology Data Service*. It can also help connect users to unique types of repositories such as *Databrary*, an online video database from New York University.

A site that is similar to the *OAD* is the *Registry of Research Data Repositories* (*Re3Data*). *Re3Data* is an international registry of data collections from around the world. Additionally, the registry lists repositories for audio-visual, images, word documents, and other types of data files. Users can search using its search function or they can browse by subject, country, or type of content.

SEARCH STRATEGIES

Librarians have many ways to approach finding data if they know the source of the data needed. Starting with the source is frequently the most direct way to find the data. For example, if a librarian gets a question about the number of barrels of crude oil imported by the United States in the previous month, starting directly at the Department of Energy website is likely to yield quick results.

The reference interview for patrons seeking data and statistical information should draw out some specific pieces of information not commonly needed in other cases. The appropriate units of analysis for the user's question should be understood by the librarian, although it is not necessary to use those terms with the user. The time period to be analyzed is also of great importance and should be established as soon as possible.

If the librarian is not sure of the best source for the data, depending on users' needs they can do several things. One of the most common ways is to use *Google*. Librarians can conduct keyword searches and then depending on the type of source that is needed restrict results to a specific site or type of site by typing "site:" followed by the preferred ending (e.g., site:un.org or site:.gov).

Another way to search is to conduct a general search for a secondary source. For example, if the patron needs farm industry information and they are unsure if it is available through NASS (National Agricultural Statistics Service), the Economic Research Service, the Bureau of Labor Statistics, or the Census Bureau, they may wish to consult a secondary source or statistical aggregator database such as *Data-Planet* or *ProQuest Statistical Insight*. For Canadian libraries, the *Statistics Canada* website makes it possible for users to search multiple agencies at once to ascertain which agency has published the most useful information.

CONCLUSION

As library users gain experience and facility with data and statistics, their queries become more advanced. Therefore, there is an increasing need for librarians who have a deeper understanding of data and statistics and can provide the appropriate level of support. While not all librarians need to be data experts, they still need to understand the types and usage of data; know how it can be evaluated, accessed, and manipulated; and be able to recommend general sources of data. Providing and facilitating access to data and statistics presents a valuable opportunity for librarians to develop stronger relationships with their patrons and demonstrate the value of their library to its community.

REFERENCES

Feldman, Ronen, and James Sanger. 2007. *The Text Mining Handbook: Advanced Approaches in Analyzing Unstructured Data*. Cambridge: Cambridge University Press.

Grajalez, Carlos Gómez, Eileen Magnello, Robert Woods, and Julian Champkin. 2013. "Great Moments in Statistics." *Significance* 10 (6): 21–28.

Hart, Darlene. 2015. "The Roper Center." Roper Center. https://ropercenter.cornell.edu/.

Hearst, Marti A. 1999. "Untangling Text Data Mining." In *Proceedings of the 37th Annual Meeting of the Association for Computational Linguistics on Computational Linguistics*, 3–10. Association for Computational Linguistics. http://dl.acm.org/citation.cfm?id=1034679.

Jacobs, Jim. 1991. "Providing Data Services for Machine-Readable Information in an Academic Library: Some Levels of Service." *Public Access-Computer Systems Review* 2 (1). https://journals.tdl.org/pacsr/index.php/pacsr/article/view/6033/5665.

Johnson, Allan G. 2000. *The Blackwell Dictionary of Sociology*. Malden, MA: Blackwell Publishers.

Kesselheim, Aaron S., Christopher T. Robertson, Jessica A. Myers, Susannah L. Rose, Victoria Gillet, Kathryn M. Ross, Robert J. Glynn, Steven Joffe, and Jerry Avorn. 2012. "A Randomized Study of How Physicians Interpret Research Funding Disclosures." *New England Journal of Medicine* 367 (12): 1119–27.

Lawrence, Stephen R., Lynn Silipigni Connaway, and Keith H. Brigham. 2001. "Life Cycle Costs of Library Collections: Creation of Effective Performance and Cost Metrics for Library Resources." *College & Research Libraries* 62 (6): 541–53.

OED Online. 2015a. "Data, N." Oxford University Press. http://www.oed.com/view/Entry/296948. Subscription required.

OED Online. 2015b. "Statistics, N." Oxford University Press. http://www.oed.com/view/Entry/189322. Subscription required.

Powers, Bethel A., and Thomas R. Knapp. 2011. *Dictionary of Nursing Theory and Research*. New York: Springer Publishing Company.

Ray, Joyce M., ed. 2014. *Research Data Management: Practical Strategies for Information Professionals*. Charleston Insights in Library, Archival, and Information Sciences. West Lafayette, IN: Purdue University Press.

United Nations Statistics Division. n.d. "About." Welcome to the UNSD. https://unstats.un.org/home/.

Van Noorden, Richard. 2012. "Trouble at the Text Mine." *Nature* 483 (7388): 134–35.

Wakefield, Andrew J., Simon H. Murch, Andrew Anthony, John Linnell, D.M. Casson, Mohsin Malik, Mark Berelowitz, et al. 1998. "Ileal-Lymphoid-Nodular Hyperplasia, Non-Specific Colitis, and Pervasive Developmental Disorder in Children." *The Lancet* 351 (9103): 637–41.

Zurkirch, Manfred, and Inge Reichart. 2000. "Environmental Impacts of Telecommunication Services." *Greener Management International* 32: 70.

LIST OF SOURCES

Abacus Data. http://abacusdata.ca/.

American Community Survey. Census Bureau. https://www.census.gov/programs-surveys/acs/.

American FactFinder. Census Bureau. https://factfinder.census.gov/faces/nav/jsf/pages/index.xhtml.

American Housing Survey. Census Bureau. https://www.census.gov/programs-surveys/ahs.html.

Archaeology Data Service. http://archaeologydataservice.ac.uk/.

Arrest-related Deaths. Bureau of Justice Statistics. https://www.bjs.gov/index.cfm?ty=dcdetail&iid=428.

Atlas of Rural and Small-Town America. Department of Agriculture. https://www.ers.usda.gov/data-products/atlas-of-rural-and-small-town-america.aspx.

Bauder, Julia. 2014. *Reference Guide to Data Sources*. Chicago, IL: American Library Association.

Bureau of Justice Statistics. https://www.bjs.gov/.

Bureau of Labor Statistics. https://www.bls.gov/.

Canada at a Glance. 1995–. Ottawa, ON: Statistics Canada. Annual. https://www150.statcan.gc.ca/n1/en/catalogue/12-581-X.

Canada Revenue Agency. https://www.canada.ca/en/revenue-agency.html.

Canada Year Book. Statistics Canada. https://www65.statcan.gc.ca/acyb_r000-eng.htm.

Carter, Susan B., Scott Sigmund Gartner, Michael R. Haines, Alan L. Olmstead, Richard Sutch, and Gavin Wright. 2015. *Historical Statistics of the United States: Millennial Edition*. Cambridge: Cambridge University Press.

Census Bureau. https://www.census.gov/.

Census of Agriculture. Department of Agriculture. https://www.agcensus.usda.gov/.

Census of Governments. Census Bureau. https://www.census.gov/econ/overview/go0100.html.

Census of Population and Housing. Census Bureau. https://www.census.gov/prod/www/decennial.html.

Condition of Education. Department of Education. https://nces.ed.gov/programs/coe/.

Consumer Price Index. Bureau of Labor Statistics. https://www.bls.gov/cpi/.

Crime in the United States. Department of Justice. https://ucr.fbi.gov/ucr-publications.

Current Population Survey. Census Bureau. https://www.census.gov/programs-surveys/cps.html.

Data Citation Index. Eagan, MN: Thomson Reuters. http://wokinfo.com/products_tools/multidisciplinary/dci/. Subscription required.

"Data Explorer." https://nces.ed.gov/nationsreportcard/data/.

Data in the Classroom. https://www.data.gov/education/classroom/.

"Data Products." Department of Agriculture. https://www.ers.usda.gov/data-products.aspx.

data.census.gov. https://data.census.gov/cedsci/

Data.gov. https://www.data.gov/.

Data-Planet: The Universe of Data. Bethesda, MD: Conquest Systems. https://homepage.data-planet.com/. Subscription required.

Databrary. New York University. https://nyu.databrary.org/.

DataCite. https://datacite.org/

DataFerrett. Census Bureau. https://dataferrett.census.gov/.

Demographic Yearbook. United Nations Statistics Division. https://unstats.un.org/unsd/demographic/products/dyb/default.htm.

Department of Agriculture. https://www.usda.gov.

Department of Energy. https://www.energy.gov/.

Digest of Education Statistics. Department of Education. https://nces.ed.gov/programs/digest/.

Economic Census. Census Bureau. https://www.census.gov/programs-surveys/economic-census.html.

Economics, Statistics, and Market Information System. Department of Agriculture and Cornell University. https://usda.library.cornell.edu/.

Employment and Earnings Online. Bureau of Labor Statistics. https://www.bls.gov/opub/ee/.

Employment Cost Index. Bureau of Labor Statistics. https://www.bls.gov/news.release/eci.toc.htm.

Energy Statistics Yearbook. United Nations Statistics Division. https://unstats.un.org/unsD/energy/yearbook/default.htm.

Facts on File. Infobase. https://www.infobase.com/product/schools/issues-controversies-online-2/. Subscription required.

Food Access Research Atlas. Department of Agriculture. http://www.ers.usda.gov/data-products/food-access-research-atlas.aspx.

Food Environment Atlas. Department of Agriculture. https://www.ers.usda.gov/data-products/food-environment-atlas.aspx.

Gale Virtual Reference Library. Farmington Hills, MI: Gale Cengage Learning. http://www.cengage.com. Subscription required.

Gallup. https://www.gallup.com/home.aspx.

Global Education Digest. UNESCO Institute for Statistics. https://en.unesco.org/gem-report/statistics.

Global Health Observatory Data Repository. World Health Organization. https://apps.who.int/gho/data/view.main.

Global Terrorism Database. University of Maryland. https://www.start.umd.edu/gtd/.

Google. http://www.google.com

Hate Crime Statistics. Department of Justice. https://www.fbi.gov/services/cjis/ucr/hate-crime.

Health Data Interactive. Centers for Disease Control and Prevention. https://www.cdc.gov/nchs/hdi.htm.

Health, United States. Centers for Disease Control and Prevention. https://www.cdc.gov/nchs/hus.htm.

Historical Statistics of Canada. Statistics Canada. https://www5.statcan.gc.ca/olc-cel/olc.action?objId=11-516-X&objType=2&lang=en&limit=0.

Instituto Nacional De Estadística y Geografía. https://www.inegi.org.mx/.

Integrated Public Use Microdata Series. University of Minnesota and Minnesota Population Center. https://usa.ipums.org/usa/.

Inter-University Consortium for Political and Social Research. https://www.icpsr.umich.edu/icpsrweb/landing.jsp.

International Trade Statistics Yearbook. United Nations Statistics Division. https://unstats.un.org/unsd/tradekb/Knowledgebase/International-Trade-Statistics-Yearbook-ITSY.

iPOLL. Ithaca, NY: Roper Center for Public Opinion Research. https://ropercenter.cornell.edu/ipoll/. Subscription required.

Kantar Marketplace. https://www.kantarmarketplace.com/ix/DataMarketPlace/PublicKantarMarketPlace/index/.

Kurian, George Thomas, and Barbara Ann Chernow. 2007. *Datapedia of the United States: American History in Numbers.* 4th ed. Lanham, MD: Bernan Press. Available online as part of *Gale Virtual Reference Library.*

Law Enforcement Officers Killed and Assaulted. Department of Justice. https://www.fbi.gov/services/cjis/ucr/leoka.

Monthly Bulletin of Statistics Online. United Nations Statistics Division. https://unstats.un.org/unsd/mbs/app/DataSearchTable.aspx.

Monthly Labor Review. Bureau of Labor Statistics. http://www.bls.gov/mlr/.

Mortality in Correctional Institutions. Bureau of Justice Statistics. https://www.bjs.gov/index.cfm?ty=dcdetail&iid=243.

MSU Libraries. n.d. *Data & Statistics Research Guides.* Michigan State University. http://libguides.lib.msu.edu/datastatguides.

National Assessment of Educational Progress. Department of Education. https://nces.ed.gov/nationsreportcard.

National Center for Education Statistics. Department of Education. https://nces.ed.gov.

National Center for Health Statistics. Centers for Disease Control and Prevention. https://www.cdc.gov/nchs/.

National Health Statistics Reports. Centers for Disease Control and Prevention. https://www.cdc.gov/nchs/products/nhsr.htm.

National Incident-Based Reporting System. Department of Justice. https://www.fbi.gov/services/cjis/ucr/nibrs.

National Oceanic and Atmospheric Administration. https://www.noaa.gov/.

National Use-of-Force Data Collection. Federal Bureau of Investigation. https://www.fbi.gov/services/cjis/ucr/use-of-force.

National Vital Statistics Reports. Centers for Disease Control and Prevention. https://www.cdc.gov/nchs/products/nvsr.htm.

NetAdvantage. New York: Standard and Poor's Capital IQ. https://www.capitaliq.com/ciqdotnet. Subscription required.

Ngram Viewer. Google Books. https://books.google.com/ngrams.

Nielsen. https://www.nielsen.com/us/en.html.

Open Access Directory. Simmons University. http://oad.simmons.edu/oadwiki/Main_Page.

Open Data. Government of Canada/Gouvernement du Canada. https://open.canada.ca/en/open-data.

ProQuest Legislative Insight. Ann Arbor, MI: ProQuest. https://www.proquest.com/products-services/legislativeinsight.html. Subscription required.

ProQuest Statistical Abstract of the United States. Ann Arbor, MI: ProQuest. https://www.proquest.com/products-services/statabstract.html. Subscription required.

ProQuest Statistical Abstracts of the World. Ann Arbor, MI: ProQuest. https://www.proquest.com/products-services/proquest-statistical-abstracts-world.html. Subscription required.

ProQuest Statistical Insight. Ann Arbor, MI: ProQuest. https://www.proquest.com/products-services/Statistical-Insight.html. Subscription required.

Registry of Research Data Repositories (Re3data.org). https://www.re3data.org.

Retraction Watch. https://retractionwatch.wordpress.com/.

Roper Center. https://ropercenter.cornell.edu/

Search for Public School Districts. National Center for Education Statistics. https://nces.ed.gov/ccd/districtsearch/.

Secretary-General's Envoy on Youth. United Nations. https://www.un.org/youthenvoy/.

*STAR*D.* National Institute of Mental Health. https://www.nimh.nih.gov/funding/clinical-research/practical/stard/index.shtml.

Statistical Abstract of the United States. 1878–2012. Census Bureau. https://www.census.gov/library/publications/time-series/statistical_abstracts.html.

Statistical Yearbook. United Nations Statistics Division. https://unstats.un.org/unsd/syb/.

Statistics Canada. http://www.statcan.gc.ca/start-debut-eng.html.

Statistics in Schools. Census Bureau. https://www.census.gov/schools/.

Statistics Sources: A Subject Guide to Data on Industrial Business, Social, Educational, Financial and Other Topics for the United States and Internationally. 1992–. 2 vols. Farmington Hills, MI: Gale Cengage Learning. Available online as part of *Gale Virtual Reference Library.*

UN COMTRADE Database. United Nations. https://comtrade.un.org/.

UNdata. United Nations Statistics Division. https://data.un.org/.

Uniform Crime Reporting Program. Federal Bureau of Investigation. https://www.fbi.gov/services/cjis/ucr.

United Nations Statistics Division. https://unstats.un.org/home/.

University Library. *International Statistics and Data.* University of Illinois at Urbana-Champaign. https://www.library.illinois.edu/govinfo/u-of-i-unit-library-homepage/researchtools/statistics/interstats/.

University of Ottawa Library. n.d. *Data and Statistics.* University of Ottawa. https://uottawa.libguides.com/friendly.php?s=DataandStatistics-en.

USDA for Kids. Department of Agriculture. https://www.fsis.usda.gov/wps/portal/fsis/topics/food-safety-education/teach-others/download-materials/for-kids-and-teens.

Wayback Machine. Internet Archive. https://archive.org/web/.

World Directory of Non-Official Statistical Sources. 2000. London, UK: Euromonitor PLC.

World Health Report. World Health Organization. https://www.who.int/whr/.

World Statistics Pocketbook. United Nations Statistics Division. https://unstats.un.org/unsd/publications/pocketbook/.

SUGGESTED READINGS

Bauder, Julia. 2014. *The Reference Guide to Data Sources.* Chicago, IL: American Library Association.

This is a good introductory book that explains key concepts in data and provides an in-depth listing of a wide range of data sources. The book is organized by subject and is indexed, with a helpful appendix on citing data. The first chapter is especially helpful, exploring the different types of data, publishers, and the process of searching for data. The rest of the book is useful to refer to for specific reference needs. The listing of sources includes a substantial description of each agency and the data it provides.

Geraci, Diane, Chuck Humphrey, and Jim Jacobs. 2012. *Data Basics: An Introductory Text.* Ann Arbor, MI: Inter-university Consortium for Political and Social Research. http://3stages.org/class/2012/pdf/data_basics_2012.pdf.

Data Basics is an important monograph by pioneers in the area of data and statistics services for libraries. It provides a good introduction to data services and provides valuable insight for librarians intending to offer such a service. It lays a solid foundation for understanding data and statistics and their position in libraries, examining the entire life cycle of data, and providing one of the best overviews of preservation issues with data currently available.

Kellam, Lynda M., and Katharin Peter. 2011. *Numeric Data Services and Sources for the General Reference Librarian.* Chandos Information Professional Series. Oxford: Chandos Publishing.

This handbook provides a more advanced look at data and its use and examines the data life cycle in detail. This book can be very helpful for a library that wishes to provide advanced data services. The book's intended audience is academic librarians.

Rice, Robin C., and John Southall. 2016. *The Data Librarian's Handbook.* Chicago: American Library Association.

This handbook provides a thorough guide to nearly all aspects of data librarianship, beginning with an overview of the changing role of and attitudes toward data. In addition to building a data collection and supporting the development of data literacy skills, the book delves into issues of developing data policies and management plans, data sharing, and maintaining a data repository.

Chapter 28

Business Sources

Celia Ross

INTRODUCTION

The increasing ubiquity of business-related questions combined with the complexity and challenges involved in answering them makes knowledge of business information sources and research strategies a valuable component of any general reference librarian's repertoire. This chapter introduces strategies for handling business questions and emphasizes a variety of business reference resources that all reference librarians should be familiar with.

STRATEGIES FOR BUSINESS REFERENCE

Types of Business Reference Questions

The process of business reference begins with the question itself. Business reference questions can come in many shapes, sizes, and degrees of complexity but typically can be broken into a few broad categories:

- Company information
- Industry information
- Consumer information
- Financial or investing information

Of course, there are additional categories, including international questions, small business questions, and legal questions. However, starting with these broad areas can provide a foundation upon which to build a search strategy for a particular question and ultimately enhance one's understanding of business reference resources. Box 28.1 provides some examples, and Box 28.2 provides a practice activity.

Box 28.1 Search Strategies: Categorizing Business Reference Questions

The following questions have been simplified using the categories listed earlier:

- Who are the top executives at Apple, Inc.? *Company*
- How can I find information on the smoothie industry? *Industry*
- What is the target market for the Fitbit and other wearable fitness products? Who else makes products like Fitbit? *Consumer/Industry/Company*
- What was the stock price of Kmart on Black Friday in 2000? *Investing*

Some of these questions, especially the last one, will turn out to be quite challenging, but by categorizing them you have given yourself and your patron something to work with and reduced some of their initial complexity. As you become more familiar with business reference, you will know which resources to start with based upon how you have categorized the question. See Box 28.4 later in the chapter for more discussion on the last question.

Box 28.2 Activity: Putting Categories to Use

Work with your classmates to come up with additional examples of business questions and then work collaboratively to apply categories to them. Keep the questions available and review them again once you have explored some of the resources covered later in this chapter.

The Business Reference Interview

Because business questions are often an amalgam of multiple questions covering a variety of topics, an important first step is to parse out a complex business question into its more specific component parts. A thorough reference interview will help identify the general categories and subcategories at the root of the question (see Chapter 3).

Beyond the standard reference interview queries, questions that can help direct the business reference search include the following:

- What are some keywords you would use to describe this company or industry?
- Do you have an example of a company that operates in this industry?

- Do you have an example of some relevant data that we could track back to its source?
- If we could find exactly what you are looking for right now, what would it look like?

Business research is often more of a hunt for clues than for answers. Once the core facets of the question have been identified (using some of the categories noted earlier), then the appropriate resource(s) can be determined, and the search for clues and answers can begin. Keep in mind that the more specific or granular a question, the more difficult it may be to find an answer. Many business reference questions are multilayered, and trying to answer everything at once can impede the process. Chip away at each piece of the puzzle rather than setting out to find everything at once.

Asking "Who Cares?"

Asking "Who cares?" is a framework that works well with many types of business questions. Asking "Who cares?" is industry agnostic and can help to uncover relevant companies and industry terminology to refine and finesse the search. Ask "Who cares?" to answer questions such as the following:

- Are there industry or consumer groups that focus on this topic?
- Are there databases that include coverage of this industry or these types of companies?
- Are there scholarly papers on this topic?
- Are there government agencies or local municipal groups that collect data in this area?
- Has a research guide been created that addresses this subject?
- Is there a known expert or other go-to resource in this field?

Once the question of "Who cares?" has been posed, then comes the challenge of looking for the answer(s). Beginning with a combination of article databases and open Internet searching can turn up relevant clues that will be useful throughout the course of the search. When using this kind of "Who cares?" brainstorming to identify likely sources of information, the key to success will be a combination of creativity, search prowess, perseverance, and timing.

The "Who cares?" framework can also be used to identify library guides and other research tools that may provide useful suggestions. The Business Reference and Services Section (BRASS) of the American Library Association (ALA) has a *Business Reference Essentials* guide that serves as a great starting point and includes links to research guides, blogs, periodicals, and associations on the topic of general business research. Another way to identify potentially useful guides is to search relevant keywords (e.g., "bonds" or "finance") and add in the phrase "library guide" or just "library." Limiting a search on *Google* to "site:.edu" will bring up only academic library guides and is another helpful strategy. Even if the resources highlighted on another institution's guide are not available to the patron, a good guide will still inform an understanding of the topic and provide indications as to whether the search is moving along the correct trajectory.

See Box 28.3 for an example of how to incorporate "Who cares?" into a reference interaction.

Box 28.3 Search Strategy: Asking "Who Cares?" and Looking for Information about Nike's Target Market

A student is looking for information on running clothes and, specifically, Nike's running clothes for women. After determining that the student is working on a class assignment, the librarian suggests that the student say more about the project. The following dialogue takes place:

Student: "I have information about Nike as a company, but I can't find anything specifically about their female customers or about their running clothes."

Librarian: "We will look for Nike and women and apparel, but let's break this question into a few parts. We'll look for information on Nike and their consumers in general using some article databases which we'll search together. We can also look for women and fitness trends. We'll also look for information about running clothes in general or maybe the overall sportswear or fitness apparel market."

Student: "Yes, I'm interested in fitness apparel and things like workout clothes or athletic clothes like the kind Nike and Under Armour make."

Librarian: "Great. You're already helping with some of the terminology and names of competitors. I can also point you to some databases that 'care' about athletic apparel or female consumers. We can also Google: sports apparel association, to find some industry associations that might have some data."

Student: "This sounds like it will take a lot of time. I thought you could just point me to one place where I could find the answer."

Librarian: "Well, business research takes some time and you usually have to search and then re-search some of the databases looking for clues. Often you won't find an exact answer and you'll have to extrapolate and make some logical guesses based on what you *can* find. Companies like Nike and Under Armour don't want their competitors to be able to find out all about their strategies and business practices, so they don't publicize this kind of information or make it easy to find. The good news is, this kind of research is like any skill and the more you do it, the better you'll get at it. The next time you have an assignment like this, you'll be that much farther up the learning curve."

Student: "OK. We better get started then. The paper is due tomorrow."

IMPORTANT GENERAL SOURCES

Some key resources will form the foundation of a solid business reference collection and serve as useful starting points for many business reference questions. The next section highlights a number of these by their primary business topic and/or functionality. Many of these resources cross categories but are listed under the area in which they have the strongest content.

Periodical Resources

Article searching is a key part of thorough business research. Whether a business reference question involves a company that is public, private, or subsidiary, an article search is always recommended as articles are often the only sources of information for private and subsidiary companies and/or smaller, more niche types of industries.

The key to a successful article search on business topics is to brainstorm on keywords that relate to the topic and then add terms like "statistics," "data," "trends," or "attitudes" and similar vocabulary to the search. If possible, start with some of the specialized business article databases highlighted later in this chapter to begin this search. These same strategies can also be applied to an Internet search in order to turn up relevant trade associations and other potential sources of data.

As mentioned earlier, remember to parse out the main themes rather than search for everything all at once. As the search progresses, be on the lookout for synonyms to the main keywords that have been identified (e.g., clothing or apparel; utilities or energy; bonds or corporate finance). Incorporate these keywords into the search in order to expand or narrow the scope as necessary and always be on the lookout for other potential clues, such as references to a particular study, a relevant competitor or process, or an expert or association.

Google Scholar falls somewhere between an article database and the free Internet and can provide potential business research leads and information. Use *Google Scholar* to search for keywords to see what kinds of papers have been published and what data sources they utilize. Even without full access to some of the sources listed, it will be helpful to know what resources are relevant. Mine the bibliographies of papers and use the "Cited by" feature to locate similar research. *Google Scholar* can provide a welcome respite, too, from searching the open Internet, where some industry keyword searches will return only commercial sites.

Some databases specifically target business publications such as trade journals, scholarly business journals, and business case studies, including ProQuest's *ABI/Inform*, EBSCO's *Business Source Complete*, *SAGE Business Cases*, and *SAGE Business Researcher*. Many general article and news databases such as *Factiva*, *LexisNexis*, Gale Cengage Learning's *General* and *Academic OneFile*, and *NewsBank* can contain relevant information, as can subject-specific article databases such as *PsycINFO* and *EconLit*.

Librarians can also identify local newspapers and business publications and search those. Two publishers, Crain Communications and American City Business Journals (ACBJ), each produce a number of publications focusing on a specific city. Crain's covers fewer areas and focuses on Midwestern cities such as Chicago, Detroit, and Cleveland. Crain's also publishes *Crain's New York Business*. ACBJ covers more than sixty market areas including larger cities such as Atlanta, Boston, Phoenix, and San Francisco and smaller cities such as Buffalo, Dayton, Santa Barbara, and Wichita. These types of regional publications can be a useful resource, especially for harder-to-find private company and industry information.

Multi-Content Databases

Some business resources have a little bit of everything in them, including company information as well as industry profiles and articles. Usually, these types of databases act as an aggregator, pulling in content from a number of different sources and giving users a one-stop portal to lots of different types business research information.

- ***D&B Hoovers* (formerly *OneSource/Avention*).** Primarily a directory of public and private companies, including subsidiaries. Content also includes analyst reports, news articles, company filings and financial data.

- ***Business Insights: Global.*** Includes a number of business reference titles, including *Business Rankings Annual, Market Share Reporter*, the *International Directory of Company Histories*, and *Ward's Business Directory*. It also contains full-text articles from trade journals and some company, country, and industry comparison and screening tools. Additional content includes financial and investment reports.
- ***Mergent Online.*** Covers mainly publicly traded U.S. and international companies, although a *Mergent Intellect* module is available as an add on containing Dun & Bradstreet's private company data. Company profiles include history, financial statement data going back over fifteen years, and management profiles.
- ***Statista.*** Covers a wide variety of industries and consumer demographics, aggregating data from a number of free and fee-based sources into one intuitive interface. Data sources are thoroughly cited and entries point to related results for further exploration. Some data on larger companies and defined industries are compiled into what are referred to as *Statista* dossiers.
- ***MarketLine.*** Contains company and industry profiles. Most company profiles include a strengths, weaknesses, opportunities, threats (SWOT) analysis section, and many of the industry reports include a Porter's five forces analysis (buyer power, supplier power, new entrants, threat of substitutes, and degree of rivalry).

SOURCES FOR COMPANY INFORMATION

Business reference questions often involve a search for company information. A patron may want to identify companies in a particular industry, prepare for a job interview, identify a company's competitors or suppliers, or learn more about a company's products and services. More often than not, basic information about a company such as the headquarters location or an executive's name can be found with a simple Internet search. The company information questions that are brought to the reference desk will be more challenging and may lean toward competitive intelligence queries such as a company's supply chain strategies or marketing practices or advertising spending. Because of this complexity, understanding company information resources and what can and cannot be found in them plays a key role in becoming adept at business reference.

Determining whether a company is publicly traded, private, or a subsidiary of a larger parent company is an important first step in company research. The free *Hoovers.com* website (different than the *D&B Hoovers* database) is one place to check for basic company information, including whether one company is a subsidiary of another. Another quick way to check whether a company is public or not is to perform an Internet search for the company's name and add in the word "ticker." If the company is public, generally its ticker symbol will come up as well as links to additional information about its performance in the stock market.

Be aware that while some databases cover both public and private companies, some cover only public companies and a search for a private entity or a subsidiary company will turn up nothing. In general, it will be much more difficult to find a great deal of information on private companies.

There are many strategies for finding company information and numerous resources that are part of the company information landscape. While there is no single best practice for this kind of searching, the University of Florida Business Library's *Company Research* is a useful step-by-step guide that can direct the process.

Company Directories

If a patron needs to generate a list of companies and/or filter by certain criteria (e.g., number of employees, industry, sales, or geography), company directory databases offer the filtering and export capabilities that will help them make the most of the data. Some business directories are available in print format, although many publishers are moving to online-only formats. However, most online directories include only the most recent listings, so for historical business research purposes a print directory may be the only resource that can provide snapshots of specific past time periods.

Examples of key company directories include the previously mentioned *D&B Hoovers* and the following:

- ***ReferenceUSA.*** This directory has powerful screening and crisscross capabilities (using a number to look up an address or vice versa) for more than twelve million public and private U.S. businesses.
- ***Orbis.*** This includes coverage of millions of companies across the globe, many of them private. Companies can be screened by a number of different criteria, including keywords from the business description. Unique among many company directory tools, *Orbis* retains coverage of inactive companies, making historical research going back to about the mid-1990s possible.
- ***Leadership Directories.*** These focus on providing contact information at various companies, government organizations, nonprofits, and law offices. The print versions of the *Leadership Directories* are colloquially known as the "Yellow Books," although various *Leadership Directories* are also available online.
- ***Million Dollar Database.*** This directory covers millions of private (and public) companies in more than 200 countries. Information includes founding dates and in some instances sales estimates, officer names, state of incorporation and titles, and functions of company officers.
- ***Ward's Business Directory of U.S. Private and Public Companies.*** This focuses on approximately 100,000 domestic companies, of which about 90 percent are private. Entries include company description and contact information as well as some ranking information and other screening capabilities.
- ***Thomas Register of American Manufacturers.*** This register is a freely available resource for identifying who makes, distributes, or supplies a product.
- ***Corporate Affiliations.*** Sometimes referred to as "Who Owns Whom?" this listing profiles public and private companies and provides a visual representation of their affiliates, subsidiaries, and divisions. Coverage is strongest for U.S. companies and includes information such as founding dates and top competitors.

Websites, Annual Reports, and SEC Filings

When searching for company information, reviewing the company's website is recommended. Retail and other consumer product sites often focus on the e-commerce side of their mission and serve primarily as a sales portal, but a careful search for an "About Us" section (or a link to "For Investors" or "Investor Relations" for public companies) can lead to information about the corporate side of the business.

Most public companies will make their annual report available somewhere on their website as well as link to their filings with the Securities & Exchange Commission (SEC). Both the annual report and its SEC-filing counterpart, the 10-K, contain valuable information about the company. An annual report serves as an informational tool for the company's shareholders. It generally will contain pictures and graphics and can give its reader a sense of the company's style and culture. A useful resource for making the most of the information found in an annual report is IBM's *How to Read Annual Reports*. The 10-K is a less colorful document than the annual report but will contain useful information in the form of a business description section and other data about the company. Sometimes, additional clues can be found on the website in the form of links to subsidiaries or information about executives or specific initiatives the company is pursuing.

Intelligize from LexisNexis is a database that offers the ability to search across all SEC filings and also offers other corporate and legal documents. Some websites offer searchable annual reports and SEC filings. *Historical Annual Reports* from ProQuest includes reports of Fortune 500 and other large companies dating back to the mid 1800s. *AnnualReports.com* can be searched by company, stock exchange, and industry or sector. *Rank and Filed* bills itself as "SEC Filings for Humans" and provides a visual look at companies and when they file, what they file, their stock ownership, executives and boards of directors, and more.

FINANCIAL AND INVESTING INFORMATION

For a librarian without a background in corporate finance or accounting, finding information related to a company's financial or investment performance can be a challenge. Two useful resources that can serve as primers in this area are William G. Droms and Jay O. Wright's (2015) *Finance and Accounting for Nonfinancial Managers: All the Basics You Need to Know* and the *Guide to Financial Statements* from IBM.

Two popular databases for investment research are *Value Line* and *Morningstar*. The *Value Line Investment Survey* divides companies into categories based on their market capitalization size. Companies are further divided by industry sector. Industries and companies are ranked according to a proprietary *Value Line* analysis. Online subscriptions also offer mutual fund coverage and "special situations" surveys that focus on a more aggressive and risk-oriented investment strategy, among other content. *Morningstar* is another source of stock price and other market information as well as personal finance guides and tools. It is well known for its coverage of mutual funds and also includes information on other types of funds as well as bonds.

Some websites offer company investment and financial data. *Big Charts* contains current and historical stock quotes and allows for screening and comparison of companies, as do sites like *Yahoo! Finance*. *Investopedia.com* is a useful go-to source for all types of investment topics. Descriptions are clear, and terminology is linked to definitions. In addition to providing overviews of topics, from stock market basics to wealth management, it offers tutorials and exam preparation information for users who wish to take their financial skills to the next level.

Often, business researchers need raw data points; these can be daily stock prices, bond ratings, currency exchange rates, revenue data, and so on. These kinds of data requests can quickly turn unwieldy, either because a consistent run of data going back a number of years is needed or because it involves complicated financial or economic data points or some combination of these challenges. Some of the key financial and market databases that are used to answer these types of questions and which can be found in many larger academic settings, especially those with PhD programs, include the following:

- Global Financial Data's *GFDatabase*
- S&P Global Market Intelligence *Capital IQ* database
- *Bloomberg*
- *Eikon* (formerly *ThomsonONE*)
- *FactSet*
- *Compustat Research Insight*
- The *Center for Research in Security Prices (CRSP) U.S. Stock Databases* database
- *Datastream*
- *Wharton Research Data Services* (*WRDS*). *WRDS* is not a specific database, per se, but a platform that can be used by researchers to manipulate and view large data sets, such as those produced by *Compustat* and *CRSP*, both of which are available as subscriptions via *WRDS*.

A lot of investing occurs outside of the stock market. Private equity (PE) firms are funding established companies to help them grow, and venture capital (VC) firms are looking for start-up companies to take a chance on as an investment. Between companies themselves, mergers and acquisitions (M&A) are happening, sometimes resulting in a whole new entity or sometimes just a larger parent company. This type of information can provide clues as to whether a private company has acquired another company, been bought themselves, or been invested in, making it useful in private company research.

Some resources to be aware of that cover PE and VC activity include the following:

- *CrunchBase*
- Bureau van Dijk's *Zephyr*
- *PrivCo*
- *Intelligize*
- *CB Insights*
- *Pitchbook*
- *Prequin*

In general, only institutions with large finance or entrepreneurial programs will subscribe to these professional products. In most cases, academic subscriptions will be limited to small population segments (e.g., only MBA students or only students in a certain course) and downloading and other functionality will be limited.

Historical Market Information

Many of the investment sites noted earlier, like *Yahoo! Finance* and *Morningstar*, offer daily, weekly, and monthly stock prices going back a number of years. Finding historical stock prices can be a challenge, however, if the company in question has undergone changes over time such as merging with another company or ceasing to exist due to bankruptcy or other circumstances. See Box 28.4 for a helpful example of this kind of scenario.

Traditionally, microform versions of newspapers such as the *New York Times* and *Wall Street Journal* were the go-to resources for basic historical stock price research because the business section of each would contain a record of that day's stock and other market prices. Unfortunately, beginning around 2006, many newspapers, including the *New York Times* and *Wall Street Journal*, stopped printing daily stock prices, and thus their microform versions will not help if a post-2006 price is being sought.

The *Daily Stock Price Record* from Standard & Poor's has been a trusted resource for historical stock prices since the early 1960s. Three editions cover stocks traded on the New York Stock Exchange, the American Stock Exchange, and the Nasdaq market. Listings in the print version are alphabetized by company. Online access to stock prices for defunct and inactive companies is available through *NetAdvantage* and *Capital IQ*, mentioned earlier. Similarly, *Mergent Online* offers an inactive company module that contains stock price information for those entities.

For clues about a company's past and changes it might have undergone, a search of news sources should provide helpful clues. Additionally, publications like the *Capital Changes Reporter* and the *Directory of Obsolete Securities* can help.

Box 28.4 Search Strategy: Finding a Historical Stock Price

A good example of a seemingly straightforward historical stock price question was presented in Box 28.1: what was the stock price of Kmart on Black Friday in 2000?

After confirming that the patron is indeed referring to the Friday after the U.S. Thanksgiving holiday and searching the Web to find the actual date it occurred in 2000 (November 24), the next logical step would be to use one of the many stock price tools available and simply look up Kmart. However, most stock price databases will not contain stock information for Kmart on this date.

A little digging will turn up news of the merger of Kmart and Sears in 2006. Out of this merger, the company now called Sears Holdings (ticker symbol: SHLD) was formed, and Sears and Kmart each became obsolete. Immediately, their respective ticker symbols, S and KM, no longer were tied to them. Further complicating things, Kmart filed for bankruptcy in early 2001, not long after Black Friday, so Kmart's status as "inactive" may have happened even sooner than the merger date.

Mergers and bankruptcies and similar kinds of changes in a company's status are clues to the researcher that standard stock price tools, even some of the fee-based database tools, are unlikely to have the information they are seeking. Instead, they will have to turn to a specialized tool such as the *Daily Stock Price Record* or dig through old newspaper microfiche.

Kmart's stock closed at $6.06 (sometimes reported as 6–1/6) on Friday, November 24, 2000, according the *Daily Stock Price Record* as accessed via *NetAdvantage*.

Company Rankings and Market Share

Often, a patron will want to know where a company ranks among their peers/competitors or how much of the industry's market share is owned by the company. This information is challenging to find for a number of reasons, including the fact that industries can be difficult to define and that companies can do more than one thing but will not necessarily break out their performance in all areas and make the data available for general consumption. Many times, a ready-made ranked list of companies and their market shares will not be found but instead will have to be constructed by the patron using a variety of sources.

Business Rankings Annual from Gale Cengage Learning is one of the few resources available that focuses on company and product ranking data. This publication is available in a searchable online form through *Business Insights: Global* database as well as through their *Gale Directory Library* product. Also available through *Business Insights: Global* and the *Gale Directory Library* is the *Market Share Reporter*. Both resources aggregate articles, reporting market share and ranking information from across various business publications and trade journals. If a relevant entry is found in either database, it can be used as a pointer toward additional resources, such as an updated ranking, or to provide additional keywords and terminology for later searching.

Both Crain Communications and ACBJ publish an annual *Book of Lists* for the cities they focus on. These can be useful resources for finding lists of companies that have been compiled throughout the year in the rest of the publication. Very specialized lists, including area executives who are paid the most money, the state's largest manufacturers, the leading small business lenders in the region, and the top health care institutions, are compiled in these titles. Each individual publication's website will sometimes make some of the list content available, as well, but in general librarians should add the relevant *Book of Lists* to the collection, especially if the library is located near one of the major metropolitan areas covered.

Additional information on rankings or market share can sometimes be found by doing an article or Internet search. Searching with a search string like "(top or best or ranking) and (market size or market share or share of industry)" and relevant keywords can lead to—if not an actual ranked list or market share data to start—useful clues that can help to guide the rest of the search.

Using Social Media for Company Research

Social media sources such as *LinkedIn*, *YouTube*, and *Twitter* should also be considered as potential sources of information on companies and executives. Many companies have a social media presence that can provide insights into their marketing and other strategies. Searching *Twitter* for mentions of a company name or a product can turn up useful clues, as can looking on *LinkedIn* for executives' profiles. A search in *YouTube* can sometimes provide a glimpse onto a factory floor or demonstrate a new manufacturing technology.

SOURCES FOR INDUSTRY INFORMATION

Although they may start as seemingly straightforward, industry questions can be a challenge especially if an industry is niche, new, or dominated primarily by private companies. Often, the industry in question comprises all three of those characteristics. Many questions that do not start off with a focus on industry will shift gears during the course of the search because it will be necessary to search for industry information in order to fully understand a company and/or consumers.

Industry Resources

Databases vary in the scope of their coverage, and many of the databases mentioned in the Multi-Content Databases section, such as *MarketLine* and *Statista*, also include industry information. Gale Cengage Learning's *Business Insights:*

Global, mentioned earlier, contains content from the *Encyclopedia of American Industries*, the *Encyclopedia of Global Industries*, and the *Encyclopedia of Emerging Industries*, which are also available as print products. Each of these titles provides insights into their respective topics, including local and suburban transit in the United States, global aquaculture, boutique wineries, and green construction. Librarians should check the publication date of entries and supplement with additional sources when necessary.

Other resources that cover multiple industries include *IBISWorld*, which is especially good for very niche industries, *Standard & Poor's Global Industry Surveys*, the *Freedonia Focus Report Collection*, and *Plunkett Research Online*.

For additional tips on resources and search strategies, the University of Florida Business Library has a useful *Industry Research Tutorial*, and Harvard's Baker Library has a number of helpful industry research guides.

Many database products target specific industries, such as technology, sports, energy, health care and medicine, and automotive. A few examples of these types of databases include the *Automotive News Data Center* and *GlobalData Power*, which focuses on the alternative and other energy industries. Specialized databases focusing on technology topics include *Gartner* and *Forrester*. The *Sports Market Analytics* (formerly *Sports Business Research Network* or *SBRNet*) database covers college and professional sports as well as fantasy sports and e-sports.

Patrons doing an open Internet search will often stumble across expensive market research reports that seem to have all the information they need and then be disappointed when they discover that their library does not have it. While most libraries will not subscribe to these kinds of reports—nor would they be able to afford to purchase them individually—they can still serve as useful sources for looking at the industry in question. There is often a free registration feature that will provide access to the table of contents for the report and possibly some snippets of data or mentions of the companies covered in the report. Some databases such as *MarketResearch.com Academic* and *EMIS University* aggregate reports from across a number of report publishers.

Industry Classification Codes

In the United States, the North American Industry Classification Codes (NAICS) and the Standard Industrial Classification (SIC) System codes broadly classify the industry areas in which a company operates. These codes and others can be useful tools when doing research on an industry or looking into a company's competitors. The quickest way to look up NAICS classifications (and to find their corresponding SIC codes) is to use the U.S. Census's *North American Industry Classification System* site.

A company can have more than one SIC or NAICS code: a primary code to identify its main area of business and additional codes to indicate other areas of activity. Note that using SIC and NAICS codes will not necessarily produce an exhaustive, comprehensive list of an industry's players; these codes are just one of many industry research tools, and not every industry has a related code.

NAICS and SIC are the closest to universal schemes compared with others likely to be found in the typical business reference setting. While not all industry resources utilize NAICS or SIC codes in their indexing, being aware of these classification systems enables the best use of those that do.

SOURCES FOR CONSUMER INFORMATION

As with industry research, often a successful consumer and market information search will involve searching in article databases and on the open Internet; however, many databases do cover consumers and their markets, as well as some print resources.

Passport from Euromonitor contains profiles of consumer-focused markets such as food, beverages, apparel, beauty and personal, retail, and travel. *Passport* covers more than one hundred countries and provides historical and forecast market data for consumer products as well as demographic, economic, and marketing statistics for each country. Market share and brand share data for numerous products are included, and quick top-level economic data can be pulled to compare trends across countries and time. But the real wealth of information comes from the consumer data side of the product; for example, users can find out how much people spent on pet food or on diapers in France as compared with the whole world.

Mintel is another resource focused on industries from a consumer perspective. In addition to covering the consumer side of industry sectors such as automotive, financial services, household care, and technology, *Mintel* categorizes its reports by themes such as Healthy Lifestyles, Austerity and Value, and Premium and Luxury. There are also demographic categories such as Millennials, Mothers, Singles, and Teens. *Mintel* reports focus primarily on the U.S. and UK markets, although there is some international coverage. Reports are robust and include brand analysis, purchase and price information, packaging data, market size, forecast information, and more.

From social media habits to wine consumption and more, *Statista* is worth a search when looking for anything related to consumers. *Statista* also offers a Global Survey tool that presents additional information around consumer behavior and brand preferences. Similarly, *eMarketer* provides a lot of consumer data regarding online habits. A robust demographics section includes Internet users by age and race as well as frequency of use. Consumer attitudes about various online industries and mobile technologies and social media are also included. A digital atlas shows the total population, total number and percentage of Internet users, households with broadband, and mobile phone users on a country-by-country basis. Data are forecast out for five years.

RKMA Market Research Reports are a set of twelve handbooks covering marketing topics and consumer markets such as sports, retail, health care, and entertainment. Available in print or online, these serve as useful primers.

The U.S. Census Bureau's *American Factfinder* database is a freely available source for population, housing, economic, and geographic information. Much of the data is available down to ZIP code and census tract levels and includes coverage of not only the decennial census but also other census surveys, including the economic census, annual economic surveys, and the annual American Community Survey.

MRI+ provides information on demographics, lifestyles, product, brand usage, and advertising media preferences reported by a sample of more than 25,000 U.S. consumers. And *Simmons OneView* provides survey data on the demographic, psychographic, and media use characteristics of users of products, brands, and services. Like *MRI+*, academic access to the surveys is generally embargoed by at least two years.

Many consumer information databases offer mapping capabilities. These products provide geographically based demographic and consumer data, like households with income over a certain amount in specified ZIP codes, which state buys the most frozen pizza, or other information that may help the user paint a more robust picture of the target market or consumer product being researched. They can also be used in business location analysis and research. Users would require some amount of training and exploring on each of these resources to fully make use of all its functionality and content. Some such resources include:

- *Business Decision*
- *Business Decision Academic*
- *DemographicsNow*
- *Business Analyst*
- *ReferenceUSA's Consumers/Lifestyles* and *New Movers/Homeowners* modules
- *SimplyAnalytics*
- *Social Explorer*

ADDITIONAL SOURCES

International Information

Understanding a country is often key to understanding a particular company, its products, customers, suppliers, and other stakeholders. Many industries function across international borders, as well, so tracking down information on the global market is important. The following resources are strong in their coverage of country economic indicators and/or business and industry topics globally.

- *Passport*
- *World Bank Data*
- *Doing Business*
- *GlobalEDGE*
- *Business Monitor Online*
- *EIU.com*
- *EMIS University*
- *OECD iLibrary*

For more information on these and other resources, the *International Business* guide from the American Library Association's BRASS is an excellent guide to finding more information on this topic and includes coverage of the resources mentioned here and many more.

Small Business and Entrepreneurship

Small business and entrepreneurship are increasingly popular and vital areas of research in libraries. Often, these topics go beyond the scope of the types of company and industry research that a general academic or public library reference desk can support, such as patent searching, business financing or legal questions, or deep dives into trends in innovation. However, like any challenging business research topic, there are always ways to creatively approach these types of questions and provide the patron with some useful material. In fact, many of the resources and strategies that have been covered in this chapter will be useful in assisting small business and entrepreneurial patrons. A useful book on the topic is

Luise Weiss, Sophia Serlis-McPhillips, and Elizabeth Malafi's (2011) *Small Business and the Public Library: Strategies for a Successful Partnership.*

Additionally, the following resources focus specifically on small business.

- *Small Business Reference Center*
- *Entrepreneurial Studies Source*
- *GALE Business: Entrepreneurship* (includes access to the *Business Plans Handbook* and the *Encyclopedia of Small Business*)
- *ProQuest Entrepreneurship*

EVALUATION AND SELECTION

Like business reference questions, business reference resources also come in many shapes, sizes, and degrees of complexity. Some business reference resources are better than others, depending on the task at hand. In addition to categories like company information, industry information, financial or investing information, or consumer information that a resource may cover, business reference resources can be differentiated by other criteria including functionality such as data exporting capabilities. Subject coverage and other content can overlap among resources, but each will have particular areas of strength, whether it is their interface, their depth of coverage of a certain discipline or topic, their ability to export data in a particular way, or their unique material or expansive scope. Often, it will be necessary to search in multiple resources, all the while keeping an eye out for clues or pointers toward other potential sources of information. In the end, the best business resource is a skilled information professional who can think creatively about how to approach any question and adeptly navigate the myriad of potential resources.

Cost

Regardless of their expense, the selection of business resources must take into account the overall needs of users as well as the existing collection to determine overlapping content from other resources. Librarians should consider how each resource complements the other and how they collectively serve to support their respective audiences. Budgets, as well as users' needs, will vary depending upon whether the setting is academic, public, or corporate. Cost-benefit analysis should also include a consideration of the learning curve involved in thoroughly utilizing the resource in question and the number of users it would serve and whether it is a physical print publication, an online database, or a tool that needs a dedicated terminal or some other specialized software or expertise to run.

Beyond an investment of money in business information sources, librarians should factor in an investment of time for training and other professional development related to business. Training should focus on specific database interfaces and content as well as on business reference in general. Business information sources are valuable only if they are utilized by librarians and patrons, so something that sits overlooked on a shelf or unused because no one is trained in its content or how to navigate it will only be a wasted expense.

Uniqueness

Commercially published business information tools often offer at least some level of unique content—how unique it is may be a factor in pricing. Some business databases produce their own content, while others aggregate information from multiple sources. As mentioned earlier, content among business reference databases can overlap, so it is important to compare and contrast to avoid duplication and double-spending.

A good business librarian will, over time, become something of a "database whisperer" and be able to creatively exploit the databases and other available resources. Becoming familiar with some of the many business database products starts with understanding not only the database's subject coverage but also some of the underlying content and how the business information is organized in each. Chapter 16, in Box 16.8, provides a practice activity that models learning about an unfamiliar database.

In terms of building a business reference collection, remember that no single resource will exhaustively cover all business reference topics. Librarians should consider their user base and strive to include a mix of resources. A robust business reference database collection might include, for example, one or two business article databases, one or two databases with company or industry information, one or two databases with international content, one or two directory databases, one or two finance and investment databases, and one or two small business databases.

It can be helpful to identify a peer institution and compare business collections and seek inspiration from innovative subject guides. Reaching out to other librarians, either directly or via some of the channels mentioned in Box 28.6, to request feedback and insights on business collection development is also recommended. For more on business database holdings at various academic institutions, see Kyunghye Kim and Trip Wyckoff (2016).

Reviewing Tools

A number of reviewing tools focus on business resources or occasionally cover business-related topics. The BRASS's *Selected Core Resources for Business Reference* is a curated guide to resources in topics ranging from banking and electronic commerce to health care management, taxation, and more. BRASS also selects and publishes an annual list of the year's *Outstanding Business Reference Sources* in the Winter volume of the *Reference & User Services Quarterly* journal. A number of journals include coverage of business reference resources including the *Journal of Business & Finance Librarianship* and *Business Information Review*.

The University of Florida Business Library's *Business Books: Core Collections* has been a useful tool highlighting selections of the best business and economics books published since 2000. These lists can be used to compare against local holdings and provide a robust resource on the readings on the major aspects of business, including consumer behavior, accounting, and management.

Best of the Business Web is published by Robert Berkman, coeditor of the *Information Advisor's Guide to Internet Research*. Monthly newsletters covering business research sites get sent out to subscribers.

Former Wharton librarian Terese Terry maintains the *BizRefDesk* site. With a tagline "land of the free & the good," it is a bare-bones but frequently updated blog highlighting useful, reputable sources for industry and economic data.

CONCLUSION

Business research, like any skill, is mastered through practice over time. To become adept at business reference, it is less important to exhaustively know the content and functionality of every single business database than to approach each question with creativity and flexibility. Business information is everywhere, as are business questions. Any librarian should expect to face at least a few business reference questions at some point in their career. Hopefully, the resources and strategies covered in this chapter will help when the time comes. See Box 28.5 for some tips on how to put it all together and Box 28.6 for resources for further learning.

Box 28.5 Search Strategy: Putting It All Together

Review the questions you and your classmates were prompted to gather in Box 28.2. Select one or two and brainstorm ways you might approach them and the resources you would use. Then work individually on the questions and regroup later to discuss your findings.

Questions for Reflection and Discussion:

1. Do these questions seem as daunting as they did before reading this chapter?
2. What search strategies did you use? Did you break out the questions into their broad facets? Did you ask yourself "Who cares?" and identify relevant trade groups or other information sources?
3. What databases and other sources did you end up using? Did you hit roadblocks and if so what alternate strategies did you try?

Box 28.6 Other Professional Resources

Identifying library guides was suggested earlier in this chapter as a strategy for finding information on challenging business reference topics. Behind these guides are the people who created them. Individually and collectively, these intrepid business librarians are an amazing source of information and support and should not be overlooked.

The BRASS division of ALA's RUSA has been referred to already in this chapter. One of the core missions of BRASS is to assist business librarians in the work that they do. Additionally, getting involved with BRASS is a great way to expand your professional development and leadership horizons. For ALA members with an interest in business reference, BRASS is a welcoming and supportive ALA home base. The Special Libraries Association has a similar group of helpful and productive business librarians in the form of their Business and Finance Division (B&F). Both BRASS and SLA's B&F are key organizations for anyone looking for business reference assistance or for guidance with the profession of business librarianship in general. Don't forget to look for regional and local business librarian groups in your area, too.

Another key resource for business librarians is the *BUSLIB-L* e-mail group. A Listserv log-in ID is required, but members of the list have access to a wealth of business information in the form of the *BUSLIB-L* searchable archives as well as to the more than 1,500 members who make up the group and who are ready and willing to share their vast knowledge of complicated business research topics.

There are a number of publications that are useful in keeping up on business reference. The *Journal of Business & Finance Librarianship*, mentioned earlier as a source of product reviews, also publishes peer-reviewed articles and studies related to business libraries and business librarians. *Business Information Review*, also mentioned earlier, is another peer-reviewed source of articles with a knowledge management focus. And Information Today is a publisher of a number of periodicals of interest to business librarians, including *ONLINE*, *Information Today*, and *Online Searcher*.

Finally, some individual business librarians publish blogs that not only are helpful for keeping up on business resources but also can serve as inspiration for how to teach business research. Two examples are highlighted here, but there are many others to discover. Chad Boeninger is the librarian behind Ohio University's (OU) *Business Blog*, which he uses to highlight the best databases and other resources for business researchers. OU students are the main target audience, but helpful instructional videos that guide users through the ins and outs of market research using specific databases serve as great examples and templates for librarians to replicate for their own patrons. Steve Cramer's *This Liaison Life* blog has a tag line of "adventures of an embedded business librarian." It features posts related to teaching business research, professional reading, and guest posts from other business librarians.

REFERENCE

Kim, Kyunghye, and Trip Wyckoff. 2016. "What's In Your List?: A Survey of Business Database Holdings and Funding Sources at Top Academic Institutions." *Journal of Business & Finance Librarianship* 21 (2): 135–51.

LIST OF SOURCES

ABI/Inform. Ann Arbor, MI: ProQuest. http://www.proquest.com/products-services/abi_inform_complete.html. Subscription required.

Academic OneFile. Farmington Hills, MI: Gale Cengage Learning. http://assets.cengage.com/pdf/bro_academic-onefile.pdf. Subscription required.

American City Business Journals. American City Business Journals. http://acbj.com/brands/bizjournals. Subscription required for full access.

American City Business Journals. Book of Lists. American City Business Journals. https://promo.bizjournals.com/bookoflists/. Subscription required for full access.

American Factfinder. Census Bureau. http://factfinder.census.gov/faces/nav/jsf/pages/index.xhtml.

AnnualReports.com. http://www.annualreports.com/.

Association for Research on Nonprofit Organizations and Voluntary Action (ARNOVA). Indianapolis: ARNOVA. http://www.arnova.org/.

Automotive News Data Center. Crain Communications. http://www.autonews.com/section/datacenter?cciid=internal-anhome-dcnav. Subscription required.

Baker Library. Harvard University. http://www.library.hbs.edu/guides/.

Best of the Business Web. Rochester, NY: Best of the Business Web. http://www.bestbizweb.com/.

Big Charts. MarketWatch. http://bigcharts.marketwatch.com/.

BizRefDesk. http://www.bizrefdesk.com/.

Bloomberg. http://www.bloomberg.com/professional/education/. Subscription required.

Boeninger, Chad. *Business Blog.* Ohio University Libraries. https://libguides.library.ohio.edu/business/businessblog/.

Business Analyst. Redlands, CA: Esri. http://www.esri.com/software/businessanalyst. Subscription required.

Business Decision. CIVICTechnologies. http://civictechnologies.com/businessdecision/. Subscription required.

Business Decision Academic. CIVICTechnologies. http://civictechnologies.com/businessdecision/. Subscription required.

Business and Finance Division. Washington, DC: Special Libraries Association. http://bf.sla.org/.

Business Information Review. 1984–. Thousand Oaks, CA: Sage. Quarterly. http://bir.sagepub.com/.

Business Insights: Global. Farmington Hills, MI: Gale Cengage Learning. https://www.gale.com/c/business-insights-global. Subscription required.

Business Monitor Online. New York: Business Monitor International. https://bmo.bmiresearch.com/authentication/login/. Subscription required.

Business Plans Handbook. Farmington Hills, MI: Gale Cengage Learning. Available online as part of *Business Insights: Global* and *GALE Business: Entrepreneurship.* Subscription required.

Business Rankings Annual. Farmington Hills, MI: Gale Cengage Learning. Available online as part of *Gale Directory Library* and *Business Insights: Global.* Subscription required.

Business Reference and Services Section. American Library Association. http://www.ala.org/rusa/sections/brass.

Business Reference and Services Section. 2019. *Business Reference Essentials.* American Library Association. Last modified January 2, 2019. http://brass.libguides.com/BusinessReference.

Business Reference and Services Section. 2018. *International Business.* American Library Association. Last modified December 4, 2018. http://brass.libguides.com/internationalbusinesscore.

Business Reference and Services Section. *Selected Core Resources for Business Reference.* American Library Association. http://www.ala.org/rusa/sections/brass/brassprotools/corecompetencies/corecompetenciessmall /.

Business Source Complete. Ipswich, MA: EBSCO. https://www.ebscohost.com/academic/business-source-complete. Subscription required.

BUSLIB-L. https://sites.google.com/site/buslibl/.

Capital Changes Reporter. Riverwoods, IL: Wolters Kluwer. https://www.cchgroup.com/capitalchanges. Subscription required.

Capital IQ. New York: S&P Global Market Intelligence. https://www.spglobal.com/marketintelligence/en/index. Subscription required.

CB Insights. New York: CB Insights. https://www.cbinsights.com. Subscription required.

Center for Research in Security Prices US Stock Databases. Chicago: University of Chicago. http://www.crsp.com/products/research-products/crsp-us-stock-databases. Subscription required.

Compustat Research Insight. New York: S&P Global Market Intelligence. https://www.spglobal.com/marketintelligence/en/?product=compustat-research-insight. Subscription required.

Corporate Affiliations. Dayton, OH: LexisNexis. http://www.corporateaffiliations.com/. Subscription required.

Crain's Book of Lists. City varies. Detroit: Crain Communications. https://www.crainsdetroit.com/data-lists/38566/2018-book-lists. Subscription required for full access.

Crain's New York Business. Detroit: Crain Communications. https://www.crainsnewyork.com/. Subscription required for full access.

Crain's Regional Business Publications. Detroit: Crain Communications. https://www.crain.com/capabilities/brands/. Subscription required for full access.

Cramer, Steve. *This Liaison Life: Adventures of an Embedded Business Librarian* (blog). http://liaisonlife.wordpress.com.

CrunchBase. San Francisco: AOL. https://www.crunchbase.com/. Subscription required.

D&B Hoovers. Short Hills, NJ: Dun & Bradstreet. http://www.hoovers.com/. Subscription required.

Daily Stock Price Record: American Stock Exchange. 1962–. New York: Standard and Poor's. Annual. Available online as part of *NetAdvantage* and *Capital IQ*.

Daily Stock Price Record: NASDAQ. 1993–. New York: Standard and Poor's. Annual. Available online as part of *NetAdvantage* and *Capital IQ*.

Daily Stock Price Record: New York Stock Exchange. 1962–. New York: Standard and Poor's. Annual. Available online as part of *NetAdvantage* and *Capital IQ*.

Datastream. New York: Thomson Reuters. https://financial.thomsonreuters.com/en/products/tools-applications/trading-investment-tools/datastream-macroeconomic-analysis.html. Subscription required.

DemographicsNow. Farmington Hills, MI: Gale Cengage Learning. https://www.gale.com/c/business-demographicsnow /. Subscription required.

Directory of Obsolete Securities. South Plainfield, NJ: Financial Information Incorporated. http://www.fiinet.com/products/libraries-universities. Subscription required.

Doing Business. World Bank Group. http://www.doingbusiness.org/.

Droms, William G., and Jay O. Wright. 2015. *Finance and Accounting for Nonfinancial Managers: All the Basics You Need to Know*. 7th ed. New York: Basic Books.

EconLit. Nashville: American Economic Association. https://www.aeaweb.org/econlit/. Subscription required.

Eikon. New York: Thomson Reuters. http://thomsonreuters.com/en/products-services/financial/trading-platforms/thomson-reuters-eikon.html. Subscription required.

EIU.com. St. Louis: The Economist Group. http://www.eiu.com/. Subscription required.

eMarketer. New York: eMarketer. http://www.emarketer.com/. Subscription required.

EMIS University. London: Euromoney Institutional Investor. https://www.emis.com/university. Subscription required.

Encyclopedia of American Industries. Farmington Hills, MI: Gale Cengage Learning. Available online as part of *Business Insights: Global*.

Encyclopedia of Emerging Industries. Farmington Hills, MI: Gale Cengage Learning. Available online as part of *Business Insights: Global*.

Encyclopedia of Global Industries. Farmington Hills, MI: Gale Cengage Learning. Available online as part of *Business Insights: Global*.

Encyclopedia of Small Business. Farmington Hills, MI: Gale Cengage Learning. Available online as part of *Business Insights: Global* and *GALE Business: Entrepreneurship*. Subscription required.

Entrepreneurial Studies Source. Ipswich, MA: EBSCO. https://www.ebscohost.com/academic/entrepreneurial-studies-source. Subscription required.

Factiva. New York: Dow Jones and Company. http://new.dowjones.com/products/factiva/. Subscription required.

FactSet. Norwalk, CT: FactSet Research Systems Inc. http://www.factset.com/. Subscription required.

Forrester. Cambridge, MA: Forrester Research, Inc. https://www.forrester.com.

Freedonia Focus Report Collection. Cleveland: Freedonia Group. http://www.freedoniagroup.com/FocusReports.aspx. Subscription required.

GALE Business: Entrepreneurship. Farmington Hills, MI: Gale Cengage Learning. https://www.gale.com/c/business-entrepreneurship. Subscription required.

Gale Directory Library. Farmington Hills, MI: Gale Cengage Learning. https://www.gale.com/databases/gale-directory-library. Subscription required.

Gartner. Stamford, CT: Gartner, Inc. https://www.gartner.com.

General OneFile. Farmington Hills, MI: Gale Cengage Learning. https://www.gale.com/c/general-onefile. Subscription required.

GFDatabase. San Juan Capistrano, CA: Global Financial Data. https://www.globalfinancialdata.com. Subscription required.

GlobalData Power eTrack. London: GlobalData. http://power.globaldata.com/. Subscription required.

GlobalEDGE. Lansing: Michigan State University. http://globaledge.msu.edu/.

Google. http://www.google.com.

Google Scholar. http://scholar.google.com.

Guide to Financial Statements. Armonk: IBM. http://www.ibm.com/investor/help/guide/.

Historical Annual Reports. Ann Arbor, MI: ProQuest. https://www.proquest.com/products-services/pq_hist_annual_repts.html. Subscription required.

Hoovers.com Short Hills, NJ: Dun & Bradstreet. http://www.hoovers.com/. Subscription required for full access.

How to Read Annual Reports. Armonk, NY: IBM. http://www.ibm.com/investor/help/reports/.

IBISWorld. Los Angeles: IBISWorld. http://www.ibisworld.com. Subscription required.

Information Advisor's Guide to Internet Research. Medford, NJ: Information Today. http://www.informationadvisor.com/.

Information Today. Medford, NJ: Information Today. http://www.infotoday.com/IT/default.asp.

Intelligize. Reston, VA: LexisNexis. https://www.intelligize.com. Subscription required.

International Directory of Company Histories. 1998—. Farmington Hills, MI: Gale Cengage Learning. Annual. Available online as part of *Business Insights: Global*.

Investopedia.com. http://www.investopedia.com/.

Journal of Business & Finance Librarianship. 1990–. Florence, KY: Taylor & Francis Group. Quarterly. http://www.tandfonline.com/toc/wbfl20/current.

Leadership Directories. New York: Leadership Directories. https://www.leadershipdirectories.com/Hub/Business.aspx. Subscription required.

LexisNexis. Dayton, OH: LexisNexis. http://www.lexisnexis.com/en-us/products/lexisnexis-academic.page. Subscription required.

LinkedIn. https://www.linkedin.com/.

Market Share Reporter. Farmington Hills, MI: Gale Cengage Learning. Available online as part of *Gale Directory Library* and *Business Insights: Global*. Subscription required.

MarketLine. London: Progressive Digital Media. http://www.marketline.com/. Subscription required.

MarketResearch.com Academic. Rockville, MD: MarketResearch.com. https://www.marketresearch.com/academic/. Subscription required. /

Mergent Intellect. New York: Mergent by FTSE Russell. https://www.mergentintellect.com/. Subscription required.

Mergent Online. New York: Mergent by FTSE Russell. https://www.mergentonline.com/login.php. Subscription required.

Million Dollar Database. New York: Mergent by FTSE Russell. https://www.mergentmddi.com/. Subscription required.

Mintel. Chicago: Mintel Group. http://www.mintel.com/.

Morningstar. Chicago: Morningstar. http://www.morningstar.com/. Subscription required for full access.

MRI+. New York: GfK MRI. http://www.mri.gfk.com/en/gfk-mri.html. Subscription required.

NetAdvantage. New York: S&P Global Market Intelligence. https://www.capitaliq.com/help/sp-capital-iq-help/netadvantage-on-sp-capital-iq.aspx /. Subscription required.

New York Times. http://www.nytimes.com/.

Newsbank. Naples, FL: NewsBank. http://www.newsbank.com/. Subscription required.

North American Industry Classification System. Census Bureau. http://www.census.gov/eos/www/naics/concordances/concordances.html.

OECD iLibrary. Washington, DC: Organisation for Economic Co-operation and Development. http://www.oecd-ilibrary.org/. Subscription required.

ONLINE. Medford, NJ: Information Today. http://www.infotoday.com/online/default.shtml.

Online Searcher. Medford, NJ: Information Today. http://www.infotoday.com/online searcher/default.shtml.

Orbis. London: Bureau Van Dijk. http://www.bvdinfo.com/en-gb/our-products/company-information/international-products/orbis. Subscription required.

Passport. London: Euromonitor International. http://www.euromonitor.com/passport. Subscription required.

Pitchbook. Seattle: Pitchbook. https://pitchbook.com/. Subscription required.

Plunkett Research Online. Houston: Plunkett Research. http://www.plunkettresearchonline.com/. Subscription required.

Prequin. New York: Prequin. https://www.preqin.com/. Subscription required.

PrivCo. New York: PrivCo. http://www.privco.com/. Subscription required.

ProQuest Entrepreneurship. Ann Arbor, MI: ProQuest. http://www.proquest.com/products-services/pq_entrep.html. Subscription required.

PsycINFO. Washington, DC: American Psychological Association. http://www.apa.org/pubs/databases/psycinfo/index.aspx. Subscription required.

Rank and Filed. http://rankandfiled.com/.

Reference & User Services Quarterly (RUSQ). 1997–. Chicago: American Library Association. Quarterly. https://journals.ala.org/rusq/index.

ReferenceUSA. Multiple modules. Papillion, NE: Infogroup. http://www.referenceusa.com/Home/Home. Subscription required.

RKMA Market Research Reports. Miramar, FL: Richard K. Miller & Associates. http://www.rkma.com/. Subscription required.

SAGE Business Cases. Thousand Oaks, CA. https://us.sagepub.com/en-us/nam/sage-business-cases. Subscription required.

SAGE Business Researcher. Thousand Oaks, CA. https://us.sagepub.com/en-us/nam/author/sage-business-researcher. Subscription required.

Simmons OneView. Costa Mesa, CA: Experian. http://www.experian.com/marketing-services/simmons-oneview.html. Subscription required.

SimplyAnalytics. New York: Simply Analytics. http://simplyanalytics.com. Subscription required.

Small Business Reference Center. Ipswich, MA: EBSCO. https://www.ebscohost.com/public/small-business-reference-center. Subscription required.

Social Explorer. New York: Oxford University Press. http://www.socialexplorer.com/. Subscription required.

Sports Market Analytics. Princeton, NJ. SBRnet. http://www.sportsmarketanalytics.com/home.aspx.

Standard & Poor's Global Industry Surveys. http://www.spcapitaliq.com/our-capabilities/our-capabilities.html?product=industry-surveys. Available online as part of *Capital IQ* and *NetAdvantage*. Subscription required.

Statista. New York: Statista. http://www.statista.com/. Subscription required for full access.

Thomas Register of American Manufacturers. New York: Thomas Publishing Company. http://www.thomasnet.com/.

Twitter. https://twitter.com/.

University of Florida Business Library. 2018. *Business Books: Core Collections*. Last modified December 4, 2018. http://businesslibrary.uflib.ufl.edu/businessbooks.

University of Florida Business Library. 2015. *Company Research*. Last modified December 8, 2015. http://businesslibrary.uflib.ufl.edu/companyresearch.

University of Florida Business Library. 2019. *Industry Research Tutorial*. Last modified January 1, 2019. http://businesslibrary.uflib.ufl.edu/c.php?g=114645&p=746469.

Value Line Investment Survey. http://www.valueline.com/.

Wall Street Journal. https://www.wsj.com/

Ward's Business Directory of U.S. Private and Public Companies. Farmington Hills, MI: Gale Cengage Learning. Available online as part of *Gale Directory Library* and *Business Insights: Global*. Subscription required.

Weiss, Luise, Sophia Serlis-McPhillips, and Elizabeth Malafi. 2011. *Small Business and the Public Library: Strategies for a Successful Partnership*. Chicago: ALA Editions.

Wharton Research Data Services. Philadelphia: Wharton University of Pennsylvania. https://wrds-web.wharton.upenn.edu/wrds/. Subscription required.

World Bank Data. World Bank Group. http://data.worldbank.org/.

Yahoo! Finance. http://finance.yahoo.com/.

YouTube. https://www.youtube.com/.

Zephyr. London: Bureau van Dijk. https://zephyr.bvdinfo.com/. Subscription required.

SUGGESTED READINGS

Heckman, Lucy. 2011. *How to Find Business Information: A Guide for Businesspeople, Investors and Researchers*. New York: Praeger.

A helpful introduction, this title includes good coverage of business guides, including some older seminal publications in the field. Other chapters cover finding industry and company information, the stock market, insurance, accounting and taxation, marketing and advertising, management, small business, and entrepreneurship. Appendices cover acronyms and abbreviations, major business libraries, business-related government agencies, and major stock and securities exchanges.

Moss, Rita W. 2012. *Strauss's Handbook of Business Information: A Guide for Librarians, Students, and Researchers*. 3rd ed. Santa Barbara, CA: Libraries Unlimited.

A business reference standard, *Strauss's Handbook* provides an overview of basic resources and then covers specific topics such as company information, industry information, credit and banking, and real estate. Appendices decode acronyms and abbreviations, point to sources for business case studies, and identify key economic indicators, among other helpful topics. An updated edition is anticipated in 2020.

Ross, Celia. 2019. *Making Sense of Business Reference: A Guide for Librarians and Other Research Professionals*, 2nd ed. Chicago: ALA Editions.

This book attempts to demystify the process of business reference and is described by the author as "part business reference source guide, part business reference therapy." General business reference strategies and sources are covered as well as those useful in company research, industry research, investment research, consumer and market research, business statistics, international business, and small business. An appendix includes a collection of "stumpers" that feature business reference questions and sample strategies for answering them.

Wasserman, Paul, Verne Thompson, and Virgil Burton III, eds. 2015. *Encyclopedia of Business Information Sources*. 32nd ed. Farmington Hills, MI: Gale Cengage Learning. This annual publication presents a wide variety of terms and topics such as adhesives, affluent market, and baking industry, all arranged alphabetically. Each entry points to relevant abstract and indexing sources, directories, ratio sources, handbooks, databases, periodicals, research centers, trade associations, and more. Note that this title is available through Gale Cengage Learning's *GALE Business: Entrepreneurship*.

Chapter 29

Health and Medicine Sources

Maura Sostack and Rebecca Davis[1]

INTRODUCTION

It would be difficult to find someone who has not, at some point during their lifetime, sought out medical or wellness information. Health talk is everywhere. Consider the fact that media outlets employ health news journalists (Association of Health Care Journalists n.d.), a number of whom are physician reporters (Linden 2010). On July 1, 2019, a simple *Google* phrase search for "consumer health information" produced 837,000 hits. The "Social Life of Health Information" research findings reveal that individuals not only seek health information online but also post their medical conditions via *Twitter*, *Facebook*, and blogs (Fox 2014). Health professionals also seek out medical information on a regular basis. Physicians, nurses, pharmacists, and other health care providers all need access to up-to-date medical information to care for their patients, while biomedical researchers rely heavily on bibliographic databases such as *PubMed* to inform their work.

This chapter provides an introduction to reference work for questions related to health and medicine. It begins with a brief introduction to types of health information and medical terminology and then describes key sources and search strategies for both consumer and professional health information.

USES OF HEALTH AND MEDICAL INFORMATION

Health and medical information can be categorized into five discrete "use cases," each with unique, yet sometimes overlapping, sources. When librarians encounter a health-related question at the reference desk, considering which "use case" the query best matches can help the librarian determine which sources and search strategies to use in the search for information.

1. **Consumer health information.** Users of health and wellness information include patients, someone who receives health care services; caregivers, a term reserved for a family member or close friend who cares for individuals who are physically or mentally ill (caregivers usually have no formal clinical training and often are not paid for their services); and the general public.
2. **Patient education materials and discharge instructions at the point of care.** The term "point of care" (or POC) means the location at which patient services and care, either inpatient or outpatient, are delivered. Educating patients at the point of care is an essential component of the clinician-patient encounter. Users of these materials include allied health professionals, dentists, nurses, pharmacists, and physicians as well as dental, medical, nursing, and pharmacy students and residents. Patients and their families, along with caregivers, are the recipients. The vast majority of these materials are distributed in print format.
3. **Medical information at the point of care.** From physicians keeping a print copy of a differential diagnosis handbook stashed in their white coats, to residents using symptom checker software on their tablets, the availability of referential clinical information at the point of care has always been a mainstay of clinical practice. Users include allied health professionals, dentists, nurses, pharmacists, and physicians as well as dental, medical, nursing, and pharmacy students and residents.
4. **Biomedical research information**. Biomedical researchers are individuals who experiment, observe, test, and analyze diseases. They may work at large universities, in private industry, and with state and federal agencies. Researchers most often have postgraduate degrees and many have dual PhD and MD degrees. Biomedical scientists are individuals employed by hospitals and independent laboratories. Virology, medical microbiology, clinical chemistry, cytology, and histopathology are broad areas of biomedical laboratory work. Both professions require biomedical research information to inform their experimental and clinical work.
5. **Health care business, economic, and technology information**. Hospital and health system executives, health economists, and health informaticists require information about health care management and technology on a regular basis.

MEDICAL TERMINOLOGY

Librarians providing reference services in a public library or a hospital-based, patient resource center may encounter questions like the following:

- "I find it difficult to make a fist and my hands are very stiff lately. My doctor told me I have osteoarthritis. Can you help me find information about osteoarthritis?"
- "My doctor prescribed a drug to help with my arthritis pain. On the prescription note, he wrote 'take this medicine b.i.d.'" What does "b.i.d." mean?
- "My sister has smoked four packs of cigarettes a day for the last forty years and was recently told she has developed COPD." What is COPD?

Medicine, like all professions, has its own language. For the uninitiated, medical terminology can be confusing, even intimidating. Medical vocabulary includes terms often built from Greek and Latin word parts:

- **Root:** Core or fundamental meaning of a word.
- **Prefix:** Attached to the beginning of the word root and provides additional information.
- **Suffix:** Attached to the end of the word and provides additional information.
- **Combining vowel:** Usually the letter "O" and placed between two word roots or the root and suffix.

Thus, the word "osteoarthritis" can be deconstructed as follows:

- **Oste.** Of Greek derivation and means "bone."
- **Arth.** A word root meaning "joint."
- **O.** The combining vowel.
- **itis.** A suffix meaning "inflammation."

Therefore, "osteoarthritis" means "inflammation of the bone and joint."

Not all medical vocabulary is built from Greek or Latin word parts. Medical eponyms are the names of individuals, places, or things. "Lou Gehrig's disease" is the eponym for the medical term "amyotrophic lateral sclerosis." Medical acronyms are formed from the first letter of several words. "COPD" is the acronym for the medical term "chronic obstructive pulmonary disease." In some cases, medical abbreviations are shortened forms of a word or phrase. "b.i.d." means twice a day, from the Latin *bis in die*.

Understanding these common origins of medical terminology can help librarians negotiate the reference interview and search for health information. Both Barbara Cohen's *Medical Terminology: An Illustrated Guide* (2016) and Danielle LaFleur and Myrna LaFleur-Brooks's *Basic Medical Language* (2013) offer an informative overview. Librarians who provide a high volume of health and medical reference services, particularly those in medical libraries, may find it helpful to enroll in a medical terminology course. A number of free, Web-based medical terminology resources include medical acronyms, eponyms, abbreviations, and, to assist with pronunciation, talking dictionaries.

MEDICAL, NURSING, AND ALLIED HEALTH PROFESSIONALS

When answering questions about health and medicine, it can be helpful to understand the type of medical professionals that work within the health care system.

- **Allied health professionals.** A diverse group of health care providers that includes occupational, physical, and respiratory therapists; speech and language pathologists; dietitians, radiology technicians, and laboratory personnel.
- **Clinician.** A health professional who works directly with patients. Clinicians are distinguished from other types of health workers, such as those involved in biomedical laboratory work.
- **Dentist.** An individual educated, trained, and licensed to practice dentistry and/or oral surgery. Dentists treat diseases and conditions of the teeth and gums. In

the United States, a dentist's postnominal credential is "Doctor of Medicine in Dentistry" (DMD).

- **Nurse.** An individual educated, trained, and licensed to practice nursing. In the United States, a nurse's postnominal credential is either "Registered Nurse" (RN) or "Licensed Practical Nurse" (LPN).
- **Pharmacist.** An individual educated, trained, and licensed to dispense prescription medications. In the United States, a pharmacist's postnominal credential is "Doctor of Pharmacy" (PharmD).
- **Physician.** An individual educated, trained, and licensed to practice medicine. In the United States, a physician's postnominal credentials are either "Medical Doctor" (MD) or "Doctor of Osteopathy" (DO). Many refer to physicians as doctors, that is, "My doctor prescribed an antibiotic for my strep throat." MDs practice allopathic medicine, which emphasizes the treatment of diseases and illness through the use of drugs and medications. Allopathic medicine tends to focus on a specific body part and is concerned with the process of disease. MDs may become certified in a medical specialty and subspecialty through standards established by twenty-four American Board of Medical Specialties (ABMS) certifying boards. DOs practice osteopathic medicine, which emphasizes preventive care, the integration of the body's systems, and allowing the body to heal without overusing medications. DOs may earn board certification in an osteopathic specialty or subspecialty through the American Osteopathic Association Board Certification program.
- **Podiatrist.** An individual educated, trained, and licensed to practice podiatric medicine. Podiatrists diagnose, treat, and prevent foot disorders. In the United States, a podiatrist's postnominal credential is "Doctor of Podiatric Medicine" (D.P.M).
- **Resident.** A physician in training. The individual has graduated from medical school with a DO or an MD degree and is employed, usually at a community or an academic health system, in postmedical school training. The residency period lasts three to seven years depending on the type of medical specialty training.

Patrons may wish to verify the credentials of their physician. The ABMS's *Certification Matters* website provides free access to check physician certification. *Board Certified Docs* is a subscription-based service designated by the ABMS as its official display agent and primary source verification of its data.

CONSUMER HEALTH INFORMATION

Research suggests that health information is among the most commonly sought topics both online and in libraries. Pew Research Center findings reveal that 59 percent of Internet users have looked online for health information within the past year and 77 percent of these health information seekers began their last session using a general search engine such as *Google* (Fox and Duggan 2013). Unfortunately, once these information seekers find something that piques their interest, they may not check the source or date of the health information they find. Pew Research also shows that the vast majority of these health information seekers feel overwhelmed and confused by the amount of information they find and frustrated by their inability to find what they were looking for (Fox and Fallows 2003).

As they struggle to make sense of the vast amount of health information available online, the "public library is one of the first places where many consumers turn to search for health information" (Zionts et al. 2010, 350). One survey found that "84 percent of librarians were asked more than 10 health-related questions per week," indicating that consumers are coming to libraries for assistance with finding health information (Linnan et al. 2004, 182). These statistics indicate that public librarians must be familiar with and able to evaluate an array of consumer health resources.

Consumer health resources provide timely, reliable, and accurate health care information written at a level appropriate for patients and caregivers. These resources are intended to help nonmedical professionals learn about medical topics, such as diseases and treatments, communicate with medical professionals, and make appropriate health care decisions. Consumer health resources include free websites provided by federal agencies and professional medical organizations and subscription-based databases of periodical articles and patient education materials.

The Health Information Reference Interview

When assisting a patron in the search for health information, a thorough reference interview is key to providing timely and accurate information. Barriers and challenges include the following:

- Health issues evoke strong, complicated emotional responses. Patrons may be upset, confused, and somewhat angry.
- Patrons may have hidden literacy problems.
- Patrons may be caregivers asking questions for a friend or relative. The librarian is now dealing with second-hand information.
- The librarian may be hesitant to ask probing, personal questions.

Chapter 3 provides guidance for the reference interview, including in situations where the patron may be asking for a friend or family member. Additional tips for the health reference interview include the following:

- If possible, move the conversation to a private space within the library.
- Practice active listening skills.
- Be mindful of clues to possible low literacy problems and offer information in varied formats and at varied reading levels.
- Never interpret medical information or make any direct or indirect inferences regarding diagnosis. Make sure the patron understands you are not a health care provider, but a provider of health care information.
- Use both verbal and printed disclaimer statements, for example, "Materials in ABC Library represent the opinions of the authors and are intended to complement, not substitute for the advice of your healthcare professional."

The Reference and User Services Association's (2015) "Health and Medical Reference Guidelines" also provide advice for the reference interview.

Ethical Considerations in the Health Reference Interview

As discussed with legal sources in Chapter 31, librarians must make a distinction between helping consumers find information and giving what could be perceived as health or medical advice. While some patrons might ask consumer health questions out of curiosity or general interest, often questions are motivated by personal health issues. For example, a patron might have questions about a new diagnosis, whether to try a gluten-free diet, or alternative treatment options for an existing condition. In each of these cases, the patron is likely planning to use the information to inform a critical decision. While assisting the patron in finding and evaluating information, librarians should avoid any suggestion that they are providing advice or endorsing a course of action. Such advice could have a critical effect on the health of the patron or others. Additionally, librarians are not aware of other existing health issues that patrons may have or medications they are taking. Even in situations that seem relatively harmless or where the evidence seems clear, librarians should make a clear distinction that they can assist patrons with finding health information, but cannot give advice, and suggest the patron consult with a doctor or healthcare professional.

Privacy and confidentiality are an important part of any reference transaction, but perhaps especially so with health information given its sensitivity. Both the ALA Code of Ethics (American Library Association 2008) and the Medical Library Association (MLA) Code of Ethics (Medical Library Association 2010) emphasize confidentiality. Librarians should strive to protect patron privacy during the reference transaction and refrain from discussing the transaction with others unless consulting with a colleague for assistance.

Health Literacy

The Institute of Medicine defines health literacy as "the degree to which individuals have the capacity to obtain, process, and understand basic health information and services needed to make appropriate health decisions" (2004, 2). However, 36 percent of Americans, or nearly ninety million people, are considered functionally illiterate (Somers and Mahadevan 2010). Linda Murphy-Knoll (2007, 205) writes, "low health literacy is so common in America that it puts at risk countless numbers of patients who cannot comprehend the information required to seek or receive quality healthcare." Population-based survey findings for both adult and health literacy research have shown that individuals aged sixty-five years and older, those who have not completed high school, and minority populations are more likely to have health literacy challenges. Even highly educated individuals have difficulty understanding admission forms, discharge instructions, and medication regimens. The majority of health information is written at eighth- through eleventh-grade reading levels. When emotions run high, as they do when a patient or caregiver is dealing with illness, these materials can be difficult to decipher. Box 29.1 provides additional information about health literacy.

Box 29.1 Activity: Understanding Health Literacy

To better understand the scope of the problem of limited health literacy, watch "Health Literacy and Patient Safety: Help Patients Understand," a twenty-three -minute video produced by the American Medical Association Foundation (https://www.youtube.com/watch?v=cGtTZ_vxjyA).

Questions for Reflection and Discussion:

1. For patients that lack health literacy skills, what problems do they encounter?
2. When helping patrons who are seeking health information, what can librarians do to ensure the patron can read and understand the information?

Some information providers specialize in easy-to-understand medical information. MedlinePlus has an Easy-to-Read section that provides access to consumer health resources on a wide variety of topics written at second-, fifth-, and eighth-grade readings levels. The Plain Language Action and Information Network (PLAIN) is a group of U.S. federal employees from various agencies who support the use of clear communication in government writing. Their *Plain Language in Healthcare* Web page provides information and links to health literacy resources. The Taubman Health Sciences Library at the University of Michigan created an interactive *Plain Language Medical Dictionary*. Users can search or browse for a term, and its plain language equivalent appears.

The National Patient Safety Foundation's *Ask Me 3* educational program was designed to help improve communication between patients and their health care providers. *Ask Me 3* refers to three questions every patient should ask their health care provider: What is my main problem? What do I need to do? Why is it important for me to do this? The Agency for Healthcare Research & Quality, part of the U.S. Department of Health & Human Services, has developed "Questions to Ask Your Doctor," a list of questions patients should ask prior to, during, and after seeing their health care provider. In addition, a free, interactive "Question Builder" tool is available to help patients to prepare for health care appointments.

Evaluation and Selection of Consumer Health Resources

Other sections of this chapter address collection development considerations of professional health and medical sources. Librarians dealing with consumer health information have some additional criteria to consider. Unreliable and out-of-date medical information abounds on the Internet, and it is important to carefully evaluate any information one finds. Numerous groups and associations have developed criteria for evaluating consumer health resources. These criteria can guide librarians as they select materials for the collection, including websites that might be linked on a library's Web page. In addition, these criteria can be shared with patrons during the reference interview and in instructional sessions. The list of "20 Questions for Evaluating Consumer Health Information" in Box 29.2 provides a framework to determine the accuracy, authority, objectivity, currency, and coverage of a consumer health website. Box 29.3 provides an opportunity to practice using this framework.

Box 29.2 Twenty Questions for Evaluating Consumer Health Information

1. What is the URL?
2. Who runs the site?
3. Why was the site created?
4. What do the site creators want from the reader?
5. Who is paying for the site?
6. Are there advertisements on the website?
7. If so, are the advertisements in line with the site's purpose?
8. Does the information on the website favor the site's owner?
9. Is a celebrity used to promote the information on the website (if there is a celebrity endorsement, librarians should check whether the celebrity has medical credentials)?
10. Is the health and wellness information posted on the website reviewed by medical experts?
11. Where did the information come from?
12. Are there bibliographic references provided?
13. Does the information on the site make unbelievable claims?
14. Is the site up to date?
15. Is there a way to contact the site's owner through its website?
16. Is there a privacy statement?
17. Do users need to register to access information?
18. Do users need to pay to access information?
19. If so, does the site require users to register and store debit or credit card information?
20. What happens to personal information if the user registers?

Janet Papadakos et al. (2014) found that consumer health librarians tend to follow certain criteria in their collection development, though these are not always spelled out in their policies. While these criteria may be unwritten, the librarians largely base their policies on the National Library of Medicine Collection Development Guidelines, the Medical Library Association guidelines, the HONcode for Health On the Net Foundation, and the Consumer and Patient Health Information Section of the Medical Library Association. The collection development criteria that ranked the highest among the consumer health librarians were relevance, credibility, currency, and accessibility (Papadakos et al., 2014). All four of these criteria are mentioned throughout this chapter when discussing the criticality of finding health information and the need for consumers to have access to relevant, reliable, and credible information. In addition to these criteria, consumer health librarians emphasize "practicality which refers to including practical information or tips for consumers and their family members" and a "disclaimer statement that cautions consumers that they should not substitute information provided for professional medical advice" as practice-based criteria used for collection development policies for consumer health resources (Papadakos et al., 2014, 81). Ideally, the collection development policy in a library should address consumer health resources in addition to the rest of the collection. See Box 29.3 for an activity on evaluating consumer health websites.

Box 29.3 Activity: Evaluate a Consumer Health Website

Using the twenty questions in Box 29.2, evaluate one or more of the following consumer health websites:

- GenF20Plus (http://www.genf20-usa.com/index.html)
- Harvard Health (http://www.health.harvard.edu/)
- Healthy People 2020 (http://www.healthypeople.gov/)
- Healthyroads (https://www.healthyroads.com/)
- Kripalu Center for Yoga & Health (http://kripalu.org/)
- Suzanne Somers (http://www.suzannesomers.com/)
- U.S. Anti-Doping Agency (http://www.usada.org/)

Questions for Reflection and Discussion:

1. During your evaluation process, did you find the website to provide enough information to enable you to answer all twenty questions?
2. If you could not answer all 20 questions, were the missing pieces of information problematic enough that you could not recommend the site?

CONSUMER HEALTH WEBSITES

Librarians should be familiar with reliable consumer health websites that can be used for general health information as well as sites for specific conditions and diseases such as cancer, diabetes, heart disease, HIV/AIDS, and stroke. Patrons often want to find information quickly, and knowing which resources to use can save time.

General Consumer Health Information

MedlinePlus, maintained by the National Library of Medicine, is the premier consumer health website. Patrons can browse health topics or search by keyword; entries include well-organized overviews of diseases and conditions, health topics, and treatments, and links to reliable websites for additional information. *MedlinePlus* also offers a medical dictionary, illustrations, and educational videos and tools which allow consumers to learn about anatomy, diseases, and conditions, along with medical topics. The "Understanding Medical Words Tutorial" can equip users with knowledge of medical terms before and after visiting a healthcare professional. Information on core topics is provided in multiple languages, and, as mentioned earlier, there is a plain language section.

The Centers for Disease Control and Prevention (CDC) is a federal agency that works to protect the United States from health or safety threats by providing consumers with public health information. The CDC site provides a wealth of information, data, and statistics on topics such as alcohol use, autism spectrum disorder, birth defects, cancer, healthy aging, immunizations, obesity, and smoking and tobacco. Data and statistics are updated regularly as the information becomes available. In addition to diseases and conditions, the site offers information on healthy living, travelers' health, emergency preparedness, and topics such as environmental, work, and global health.

Familydoctor.org, sponsored by the American Academy of Family Physicians, also covers a variety of topics such as family health, mental health, kids and teens, disease and conditions, prevention and wellness, and additional health resources. The site provides health tools like a dictionary, symptom checker, and BMI checker. A health management section provides information on insurance and bills, self-care, and working with one's doctor.

The "Patient Care & Health Info" section of the Mayo Clinic website is one of the most well-known general health resources because of the reputation of the Mayo Clinic. In addition to extensive health and wellness information, the site offers a symptom checker that allows users to input symptoms and receive links to potentially relevant diseases and conditions. Mayo Clinic also offers products and services including health books, a healthy living program, and clinical services.

The National Institute on Aging has excellent health information specifically for seniors. The site highlights health issues of particular relevance to older adults, such as cognitive health, exercise and diet, and advance care planning, and is designed with large type and high-contrast colors. The site can be searched or browsed.

Specific Diseases and Conditions

The American Cancer Society is one of the leading consumer resources on cancer. Their website provides information on all types of cancer, treatments, and research news with statistics and data about cancer. In addition, the site provides information on how to stay healthy along with support resources. The website also has testimonials from people who have cancer and those who are currently in remission. There is a live chat option so patients and caregivers can ask questions and quickly receive an answer. For those interested in volunteering or political activism, a "Get Involved" section provides information.

CancerCare offers information and support services such as counseling, support groups, educational workshops, financial assistance, and community programs. Much like the American Cancer Society, patrons can search by diagnosis or topic; find information for patients, survivors, and caregivers; or learn how to get involved through fundraising or creating a Team CancerCare page to raise awareness. There is also a page dedicated to pets with cancer with information for pet owners.

The National Cancer Institute is another credible resource for consumers. This website has information on different types of cancer, but the focus is on medical research and the goal is to keep consumers up to date with studies being conducted, funding opportunities, and national events. There is also a live chat option along with a toll free number to call for more information.

The American Diabetes Association has a plethora of information from assessing one's risk for diabetes, living with diabetes, and food and fitness, to research news and advocacy information. A Diabetes Basics tab provides definitions of common terms, symptoms of diabetes, and information about Type I and Type II diabetes, along with a section debunking diabetes myths. Resources for those living with diabetes include what it means to be recently diagnosed, complications, health insurance, treatment and care, information for parents and children, and patient rights and where to go for help. The Food and Fitness tab has information about diet, meal planning, and recipes. The site also provides clinical guidelines, patient education material, professional books, research resources for professionals and patients, and student and practice resources.

The website for the National Institute of Diabetes and Digestive and Kidney Diseases addresses diabetes as well as related diseases. The site is primarily devoted to research and funding news; however, it does provide consumer information related to diabetes, digestive diseases, kidney disease, weight management, diet and nutrition, endocrine disease, blood disease, and more under the Health Information tab.

For information on heart disease and stroke, the American Heart Association is an excellent resource. The website features a prominent user-friendly search box on the home page; patrons can also browse for information. One of the first tabs at the top of the home page is for Heart Attack and Stroke Symptoms, which gives consumers an opportunity to easily explore those symptoms. The site addresses a variety of topics about healthy eating, lifestyle, fitness, and CPR and other emergency training.

The American Stroke Association is a division of the American Heart Association, and the two sites follow a similar design. On the American Stroke Association's site, a Stroke Symptoms tab at the top of the page provides information about the "What to Do" if someone is exhibiting stroke symptoms. This site has information about risk factors, types of stroke, effects, treatment, life after stroke, help and support, and healthy living, along with content for medical professionals, and getting involved. The National Stroke Association emphasizes support resources and communities for stroke survivors and caregivers.

For patrons seeking information about HIV and AIDS, AIDS*info* has guidelines, information about understanding HIV/AIDS, drug information, clinical trials, research, and an updated glossary. The content under Understanding HIV/AIDS includes fact sheets, infographics, a glossary, and awareness day pages. This tab along with the Drug and Clinical Trials tabs will be most useful to consumers.

Another useful site is *The Body: The HIV/AIDS Resource*, which provides information on the history of HIV/AIDS, HIV risks and symptoms, HIV testing, starting HIV treatment, life with HIV, HIV drugs in development, and more. As with the majority of the consumer sources, there are tabs on Advocacy and Policy and News where patrons can find the latest developments on HIV/AIDS along with information on support resources.

Medications and Supplements

Patrons may also have questions about over-the-counter and prescription medications and/or supplements. The Drugs and Supplements section of *MedlinePlus* has information about over-the-counter medicines, prescription drugs, and herbs and supplements. Patrons can browse by the brand or generic name; entries include cross-references between brand and generic names as well as combination products, indicated uses, dosage, side effects, and special precautions. *Drugs.com* and *RxList* also provide consumer health information on over-the-counter and prescription medications, along with more advanced information for physicians and pharmacists.

Pills often have a similar shape or color, or one forgets what that "little pink pill" is actually for. An important aspect of reference work is to point patrons to the right resource to help them visually identify medications. A number of websites, including *Drugs.com*, *RxList*, *Pill Identifier* from the AARP, and the NLM's *Pillbox*, provide free access to interactive pill identifier "wizards."

Family Resources

Many consumer health questions arise within a family context, as parents and caregivers tend to the health of their children, elderly relatives, and other family members. The CDC's *Parent Information* website provides answers to many health questions that parents may have and offers links to additional information on each topic. The site includes sections on pregnancy, infants and toddlers, children, and teens, as well as a section on parenting information for health care professionals and researchers. Each section covers a broad range of topics including diseases and conditions and age-appropriate safety information. Additionally, a "Popular Parent Topics" page features an extensive list of common health topics that parents may want to explore. A search box and A–Z index allow for additional access to topics. The parenting videos section offers videos and interactive activities with advice on how to handle "real-life parenting challenges."

HealthyChildren.org was created by the American Academy of Pediatrics and has information for parents from the prenatal stage through young adulthood and provides parents with advice on physical, behavioral, and emotional issues that affect children and teens. Another resource librarians can recommend to parents is *Parent Toolkit*, which provides information and videos on a wide range of health and development topics along with links to an array of reputable sites for further information. The site can be browsed by age or topic, and a search box allows users to search in English or Spanish.

A variety of sites provide nutrition tips and advice for parents to help build healthy eating and exercise habits. *ChooseMyPlate.gov* from the U.S. Department of Agriculture, the "For Kids" section of *eatright*, and *SuperKids Nutrition* all focus on nutrition and eating habits. *Salud America!* is specifically dedicated to fighting obesity among Latino children. This website also features bilingual videos and infographics in addition to tips to help reduce obesity.

The American Dental Association's *Mouth Healthy* provides oral care and dental advice for children at every age level. For parents seeking information related to sleep, the National Sleep Foundation has a section on children and teens.

Children and Teens

Several resources are geared specifically for children and teens to use on their own, although as with any patron, librarians should remind children and teens to consult with a medical professional for health questions. While *Healthychildren.org* is a good family resource, the sections for grade school children, teens, and young adults are written at a level appropriate for younger readers. There are subsections for grade school children (five to twelve years) on fitness, nutrition, puberty, and school with articles on babysitting, friendship, gender identity, shyness, and more. The subsections for teens (twelve to eighteen years) provide information on dating and sex, fitness, driving safety, school, substance abuse, and nutrition along with articles about body piercings, managing money, summer jobs, acne and skin problems, and much more. Although there are no subsections for them, young adults (eighteen to twenty-one years) can find articles focused on graduating from high school, drinking in college, college applications and financial planning, campus safety, common health problems at college, and more. It is notable that while the site provides articles on gender identity and transgender topics for grade school children and parents, there are no articles on those topics for teens or young adults.

Librarians may also refer children and teens to *Healthfinder.gov*, which is managed by the U.S. Department of Health and Human Services. Similar to the *Parent Toolkit*, *Healthfinder.gov* links to reliable websites on different health-related topics, many of which have games, puzzles, videos, and other interactive activities to help children learn more about their health. Sites like *Best Bones Forever! Girlshealth.gov*, and *GoGirlGo!* are targeted specifically to girls, while

PACER's *Kids Against Bullying* and *Teens Against Bullying* offer bullying support and prevention tips for a range of ages. Similar to the *Parent Toolkit*, the sources on *Healthfinder.gov* are categorized by topics instead of an alphabetical listing that would make this resource more user friendly. Instead of referring children or teens to the *Healthfinder.gov* main page, it might be helpful to point them to specific websites depending on their questions as some users might find the site overwhelming.

KidsHealth provides information on children and young adults' health, growth, and development with sections written for parents, children, and teens. Content is in English and can be translated to Spanish, while a search box provides additional access. *KidsHealth* covers a variety of topics of interest to children and teens, including safety, puberty, feelings and emotions, and sexual health, and is updated regularly. Like *Healthfinder.gov*, *KidsHealth* has interactive activities including a section to submit questions for expert answers, with content written at an age-appropriate level.

LGBTQIA+ Health Issues

People in the LGBTQIA+ community face health disparities linked to societal stigma, discrimination, and denial of their civil and human rights (*Healthypeople.gov* n.d.), which can lead to health concerns and questions different from the general population. *Healthypeople.gov*, which is managed by the U.S. Department of Health and Human Services, is dedicated to collecting health data on the LGBTQIA+ community and offers resources and evidence-based information specifically for this community. The "Overview" page describes the goals of the site and includes access to statistics, reports, and references for further research. Because "sexual orientation and gender identity questions are not asked on most national or state surveys" (*Healthypeople.gov* n.d.), this website fills a gap by providing some statistical data about the LGBTQIA+ community.

The National LGBT Health Education Center, a program of the Fenway Institute, has "educational programs, resources, and consultation to health care organizations with the goal of optimizing quality, cost-effective health care for lesbian, gay, bisexual, and transgender (LGBT) people" (National LGBT Health Education Center n.d.). This website has sections on data and statistics, LGBTQIA+ health and transgender health specifically, and includes webinars, learning modules, resources and readings, and stories from people in the LGBTQIA+ community. "Publications" and "News and Events" sections allow users to browse and learn more about each health-related topic.

Social Media and Health Information

Patrons may have questions about using blogs and social media sites such as *Facebook* and *Twitter* for health information, from sites convened by individuals or groups to those run by official associations and organizations. Yuehua Zhao and Jin Zhang (2017, 278) note that individuals tend to "engage in online support groups for health information because they provide social support and empathy." Users can read about and communicate with others who have experience with the same health issues that they are or a family member is currently battling. "With the access to information on the social media platforms, people find useful information more effectively and personally than traditional information retrieval through search engines" (Zhao and Zhang 2017, 270).

While patrons may naturally gravitate toward these support groups, librarians should exercise caution in recommending such groups, warn patrons to check that the information they receive is credible and current, and advise them to consult a health care professional before acting on advice received through such a site. Social media sites supported by an official government agency or a professional association, which often have a .gov or .org domain, may be more credible. If a site lacks such official support, if the organizers lack professional credentials, or if the site does not indicate the individual or organization associated with it, then the resource is likely not credible. Librarians can assist patrons in finding out as much as they can about the people hosting the forum, including their educational background, sources of information, sources of funding, whether they publish any materials, and whether they appear to have a particular bias. Librarians and patrons should also check the currency of any posted content as health information changes over time.

CONSUMER HEALTH DATABASES

Librarians and patrons can access a wealth of consumer health information through subscription databases. These databases combine reference works, book chapters, magazine and journal articles, patient education resources and, oftentimes, multimedia into browsable and searchable collections of detailed, reliable information suitable for patient, caregivers, and students conducting research.

Gale's *Health & Wellness Resource Center* is suitable for public, school, and academic libraries. It provides access to reference works, periodical articles, and multimedia. The home page allows for keyword searching or browsing in four major categories: diseases and conditions; drugs; diagnostics and tests; and therapies, treatments, and surgeries. Results can be sorted using a number of limiters, including resource type and language. Gale also offers *Health and Medicine*, which covers additional periodicals, including medical journals.

EBSCO offers *Health Source: Consumer Edition* for public and school libraries. The database provides access to articles from magazines and reference works, patient education brochures, and clinical reports in English and Spanish. EBSCO also offers *Consumer Health Complete* for public, high school, and academic libraries, which provides more extensive coverage of periodicals, including medical journals; evidence-based health reports; illustrations and videos; and material written specifically for teens and seniors. The company's *Alt HealthWatch* indexes periodicals, including peer-reviewed journals, that focus on complementary, holistic, and integrated approaches to health and wellness.

PROFESSIONAL MEDICAL INFORMATION

Health care providers need reliable, accurate, and up-to-date clinical information at the point of care. Characteristic information-seeking behavior by a hospital-based clinician may look like this:

- A pulmonologist (a physician who specializes in lung diseases) sends a text message to the hospital-based librarian and asks, "I am teaching third year medical

TABLE 29.1 Comparison of Health Databases and Point-of-Care Resources.

	Databases	Point of Care Resources
Content	Citations, abstracts, and full text for journal articles and conference proceedings.	Summaries or structured evidence reviews on a clinical topic.
Purpose	Conduct topic-specific, in-depth research.	Assist clinicians in making patient care decisions.
Role in Health Care	In-depth research results sourced to write systematic reviews and meta-analyses that, in turn, inform clinical practice guideline development.	Systematic reviews and clinical practice guidelines are the building blocks used to produce digested summaries available through online point-of-care resources.
Search Options	Boolean and proximity operators, truncation, controlled vocabulary, field searching, and hedge limits.	Simple search box employing natural language search techniques.

students about various drug therapies for asthma. Can you do a *MEDLINE* search for review articles going back five years?"

- During daily patient care rounds in the hospital's intensive care unit, an Intensivist (a physician who specializes in critical care medicine) asks the clinical librarian to find evidence-based practice guidelines discussing the use of beta-lactam antibiotics for treatment of severe sepsis.

Biomedical researchers also have sophisticated medical information needs. For example, a researcher with a PhD in epidemiology may request a comprehensive literature search on published studies discussing the use of chest X-rays to affirm an asthma diagnosis in adults. This is a comprehensive, highly sensitive literature search for quality studies to answer the narrowly focused question, "What is the added value of chest radiography to affirm an asthma diagnosis in adults?" Biomedical researchers use information gleaned from literature searches to inform their own research and to create clinical practice guidelines for clinicians to use at the point of care.

Medical librarians have at their disposal a number of resources to answer clinical and research questions. Some of these are electronic, point-of-care resources, while others are biomedical bibliographic databases (see Table 29.1).

Evaluation and Selection of Medical Resources

For almost four decades, the Brandon-Hill lists were the most widely used collection development instruments utilized by hospital-based medical and nursing school librarians. Librarians Alfred Brandon and Dorothy Hill developed three lists:

1. *Brandon/Hill Selected List of Print Books and Journals for the Small Medical Library*, published from 1965 through 2004 (Hill and Stickell 2001)

2. *Brandon/Hill Selected List of Print Nursing Books and Journals*, published from 1979 through 2004 (Hill and Stickell 2002)
3. *Brandon/Hill Selected List of Print Books and Journals in Allied Health*, published from 1984 through 2004 (Hill and Stickell 2003)

One drawback of the Brandon-Hill lists as libraries have transitioned to a mixed print and electronic resources model is that they list only print resources. However, although publication of the lists ceased over a decade ago, many hospital-based librarians still use the lists as a guide in their collection development process.

When the Brandon-Hill lists ceased publication, the void was filled by *Doody's Core Titles in the Health Sciences* (DCT) from Doody Enterprises (Fischer 2005). Basic and premium versions of DCT are available on an annual, subscription basis. The basic edition includes a title list organized by subject area for 121 health care specialties and the ability to search and filter results. Entries include title scores and "Essential Purchase" recommendations made by librarian selectors. The premium edition includes all the features of the basic edition, plus the full reviews and star ratings of all titles in Doody's Review Service. Library selectors score each title on five collection development criteria:

1. Authoritativeness of author and publisher
2. Scope and coverage of subject matter
3. Quality of content including timeliness
4. Usefulness and purpose
5. Value for the money

Founded in 1946, Rittenhouse Book Distributors provides print and electronic books in medicine, nursing, and allied health. Librarians can access the "Browse Categories" section of the Rittenhouse website and filter results by "Display Doody Star Rated Titles Only." If budgets are tight, this free service can be used as part of a librarian's collection development process.

Essential Nursing Resources (*ENR*) is a product of the Interagency Council on Information Resources in Nursing. Hospital and academic medical center librarians find the *ENR* a useful nursing collection development resource. In addition, the Nursing and Allied Health Resources Section (NAHRS) of the Medical Library Association published the "NAHRS 2012 Selected List of Nursing Journals," which can be used to guide selection.

Databases

MEDLINE is internationally recognized as *the* database for biomedical research. A product of the National Library of Medicine (NLM), *MEDLINE* contains over twenty-one million article citations from more than 5,600 journals in the life sciences with a focus on biomedicine. *MEDLINE* records are indexed using NLM's Medical Subject Headings (MeSH). Many *MEDLINE* citations link to free full-text articles archived in *PubMed Central* and other open access repositories like *Biomed Central*, making *MEDLINE* a useful resource for even small libraries with limited journal holdings. If articles are not available freely, users can link from a *MEDLINE* citation to the publisher or other full-text provider.

NLM licenses *MEDLINE* to a number of database providers and publishers including Elsevier, EBSCO, OVID, and Clarivate Analytics, all of which provide subscription-based access via their own search interfaces. In addition, *MEDLINE* is freely available as *PubMed*. Medical and large academic libraries may prefer to offer *MEDLINE* through one of the above-mentioned commercial interfaces that can integrate *MEDLINE* with other databases and the library's e-journal holdings; however, the free *PubMed* version offers a robust search interface and is an excellent option for libraries with limited budgets.

With almost 4 million citations and 4,000 journals indexed dating back to the late 1930s, the *Cumulative Index to Nursing and Allied Health Literature* (*CINAHL*) is widely regarded as the definitive nursing and allied health database. It includes citations to journal articles, books and book chapters, conference proceedings, and practice guidelines. In addition, for those seeking nursing literature, *MEDLINE* indexes more than 700 nursing journals and searches can be limited to the nursing journals subset.

Point-of-Care Resources

For clinicians at the point of care, biomedical researchers, and senior executives, the phrase "find me the evidence" works its way into almost every health and medical-related reference interview and request. The need to access the best available evidence quickly at the point of care, along with the rapid adoption of mobile technology by clinicians, spawned a new type of health care electronic resource information tool: the clinical decision support e-resource, also known as a point-of-care e-resource. These clinical support e-resources offer digested summaries, many of which are evidence-based, on clinically relevant health care topics. Instead of a clinician doing their own primary research, information services companies, publishers, and nonprofits are doing it for them and writing a research summary. This summary informs how a clinician makes clinically sound decisions at the point of care.

Numerous well-regarded clinical decision support e-resources are available. Although these require a subscription and are most likely to be found in a medical library or large academic library supporting a medical school, some provide patient-appropriate information or limited free content that may be of interest to patrons in all types of libraries.

An EBSCO product, *DynaMed* is a clinical decision support tool that provides access to more than 3,200 topics and practice guidelines at the point of care. Owned by Wiley-Blackwell, *Essential Evidence Plus* is an evidence-based, point-of-care clinical decision support tool providing access to over 13,000 topics, guidelines, and diagnostic calculators. *JAMAevidence*, an American Medical Association product licensed through McGraw-Hill, is a portal to evidence summaries and clinical decision-making tools and calculators. *TRIP Database* (TRIP originally stood for Turning Research Into Practice) is a clinical search engine that simultaneously searches evidence-based sources of systematic reviews, practice guidelines, and critically appraised topics and articles. And finally, *UptoDate* is an evidence-based clinical decision support resource. Research is synthesized with evidence-based recommendations for use at the point of care.

For nurses, there are two well-regarded point-of-care tools. Elsevier's *ClinicalKey for Nursing* is a portal to evidence-based nursing resources and drug monographs, while EBSCO's *Nursing Reference Center* is an evidence-based resource that includes care sheets and point-of-care drug information.

Evidence-Based Medicine

What is evidence-based medicine (EBM)? In a 1996 editorial published in the journal *BMJ*, David Sackett, one of the "godfathers" of the evidence-based medicine movement, described EBM as "the conscientious, explicit, and judicious use of current best evidence in making decisions about the care of individual patients. The practice of evidence-based medicine means integrating individual clinical expertise with the best available external clinical evidence from systematic research" (71). Sackett's definition continues: "increased expertise is reflected in many ways, but especially in more effective and efficient diagnosis and in the more thoughtful identification and compassionate use of individual patients' predicaments, rights, and preferences." The EBM triad is shown in Figure 29.1.

Sackett makes reference to individual patients and individual "clinical expertise." Two decades later, this definition of EBM has changed, and the scope broadened to include the use of evidence in guidelines and policies that apply to entire populations. The phrase "is there any evidence to show . . ." or "what does the evidence say . . ." permeates every decision-making level of any health care system.

So where do librarians go to find the evidence? EBM research begins with a well-built clinical question that contains four distinct components, referred to as PICO:

- **P**=Patient(s) or Population
- **I**=Intervention
- **C**=Comparator
- **O**=Outcome

Librarians and biomedical researchers collaborate to write PICO questions, harvest search terms, select databases to search, and choose date parameters. Librarians search bibliographic, biomedical databases, and cull information from research organizations, government agencies, and clinical trial data repositories. Citation results are imported into bibliographic software programs like EndNote or Mendeley for evaluation by researchers. Figure 29.2 provides an example of a PICO

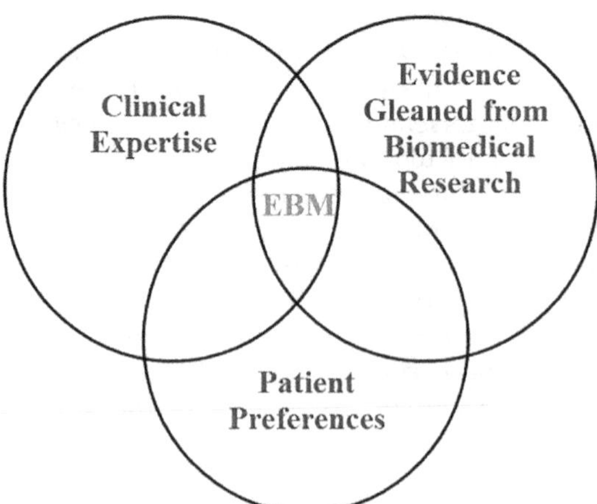

Figure 29.1 The EBM triad. Evidence-based medicine is a combination of a physician's clinical expertise, evidence gleaned from the biomedical literature, and patient preferences.

question using the example of a biomedical researcher seeking information about the use of a chest X-ray to affirm a diagnosis of asthma.

A number of organizations work to promote EBM and provide evidence-based reviews. As noted earlier, the Agency for Healthcare Research and Quality (AHRQ) is part of the U.S. Department of Health and Human Services. Its mission is to "produce evidence to make health care safer, higher quality, more accessible, equitable, and affordable, and . . . to make sure that the evidence is understood and used" (Agency for Healthcare Research and Quality 2017). Since 1997, AHRQ has awarded five-year contracts to health care research institutions in the United States and Canada to function as evidence-based practice centers (EPCs). As of May 2019, there are twelve AHRQ-designated EPCs (Agency for Healthcare Research and Quality 2019). Researchers at EPCs search biomedical literature on a variety of clinical and health care services topics and publish their research results in evidence reports. These evidence reports, among other things, inform clinical practice guidelines. They can be accessed via the *Evidence Reports* section of the AHRQ website.

Founded as a not-for-profit in 1993, Cochrane (n.d.-a) is international in scope with a mission to "promote evidence-informed health decision-making by producing high-quality, relevant, accessible systematic reviews and other synthesized research evidence." Members of Cochrane Review Groups research and publish

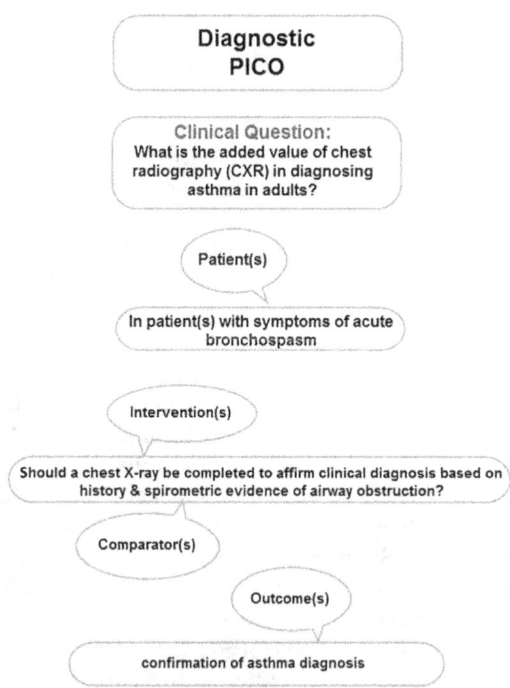

Figure 29.2 An example PICO search. The figure shows how the searcher takes a clinical question regarding the value of chest radiography in diagnosing asthma in adults, defines the population (patients with symptoms of acute bronchospasm), identifies the potential intervention and comparators (chest X-ray to confirm clinical diagnosis based on history and spirometric evidence of airway obstruction), and identifies the outcome (confirmation of asthma diagnosis).

systematic reviews on specific clinical topics, which are used by clinicians worldwide, at the point of care, to make evidence-based treatment decisions. Of particular interest to librarians is the Cochrane Information Retrieval Methods Group (IRMG). The IRMG recognizes that "a broad and sensitive literature search to retrieve the maximum number of relevant published and unpublished studies is a crucial component of an unbiased systematic review" (Cochrane, "More About Us" n.d.-b). Cochrane reviews can be accessed through the *Cochrane Database of Systematic Reviews.*

Joanna Briggs Institute (JBI) is an international not-for-profit division of the School of Translational Science at the University of Adelaide, South Australia. The Institute conducts research on health-related topics, with a focus on nursing practice, and publishes their results in the journal *JBI Systematic Reviews and Implementation Reports*, available as part of JBI Resources.

Located in Hamilton, Ontario, Canada, the Health Information Research Unit (HIRU) is a component of the Clinical Epidemiology and Biostatistics Department at McMaster University. HIRU's mission is to "improve the effectiveness and efficiency of health care by providing innovative evidence-based information products and systems to health professionals, patients, policy makers, and the public" (*Health Information Research Unit* 2016). Their database, *McMaster Plus*, is created by the McMaster Health Knowledge Refinery. Studies published in journal articles are selected and indexed using a critical appraisal process. Studies are then rated by clinicians who work at the point of care using McMaster's Online Rating of Evidence system.

Clinical Practice Guidelines

Evidence-based research findings inform the writing and publication of clinical practice guidelines. Many health care organizations author their own clinical practice guidelines, but the retrieval process, via medical society and association websites, is very often time-consuming. What was needed was a one-stop shopping experience. AHRQ established, in partnership with the American Medical Association, the National Guideline Clearinghouse. The goal of the clearinghouse is to make it easier for clinicians and patients to access, free-of-charge, evidence-based clinical practice guidelines.

With offices in London and Manchester, England, the National Institute for Health and Care Excellence (NICE) guidelines are evidence-based, point-of-care recommendations for health care provided in England. Most NICE guidelines are available free of charge. *DynaMed*, EBSCO's subscription-based point-of-care clinical decision support resource, does an excellent job gathering and organizing clinical practice guidelines by topic. Created in 1984, and supported by the AHRQ, the U.S. Preventive Services Task Force (USPSTF) comprises experts in preventive and evidence-based medicine. The Task Force makes evidence-based recommendations about preventive services such as screenings, counseling services, and preventive medications. The *USPSTF Information for Consumers* provides evidence-based recommendations for patients and caregivers with information on ways to prevent illness and stay healthy.

Clinical Trial Repositories

A clinical trial is a research study designed to evaluate new drugs or treatments, prevention measures, diagnostic tests, and prognostic tools. Retrieval of results reported in trial repositories and republished in journal articles, conference abstracts, or posters is an integral part of an EBM literature search. *ClinicalTrials.gov* is a global repository of clinical trial studies, limited to human participants. The U.S. National Institutes of Health maintains this trial repository.

Database Hedges

Regardless of preferred searching platform, *MEDLINE* is the bibliographic database of choice to begin an EBM literature search. High recall is the end goal, and to achieve this, librarians need to use validated search hedges. A hedge is a combination of controlled vocabulary and natural language words and phrases used to search for American and British spellings of concepts and terms. The purpose of using a hedge, rather than preset filters found in bibliographic databases, is to improve search recall of clinically important studies.

Librarians and researchers collaborate to create and validate hedges. Many are publicly available. The most well known is the McMaster Hedge Project. Using hedges developed at McMaster University, *PubMed Clinical Queries* provides a quick way to find evidence in *MEDLINE* via the *PubMed* search platform. The *Clinical Queries* page is designed to filter one search by three clinical research areas: Clinical Study Categories, Systematic Reviews, and Medical Genetics. While quick and convenient, a search in *Clinical Queries* cannot take the place of information retrieved from comprehensive, mediated literature searches.

HEALTH CARE BUSINESS INFORMATION

It is essential for librarians to be well versed in resources on the business aspects of health care. Health care executives will contact librarians to request information about health care reform, health information technology, institutional accreditation, and continuing education and certification programs.

Health Care Business

Doody's Core Titles evaluates and rates titles in health economics and the delivery of health care. Two essential health care business journals are *Health Affairs* and the *Milbank Quarterly*. *Health Affairs* publishes feature articles, editorials, and blog postings on health policy, quality, reform, and spending issues. Since 1986, The Milbank Memorial Fund, a health care research policy organization, has published the *Milbank Quarterly*. This peer-reviewed journal publishes original health care policy research and editorials.

Health Insurance

During the Great Depression of the 1930s through the early 1940s, hospital admissions dropped, as did hospital and physician profits. Hospitals began to offer health insurance plans. In December 1929, Baylor University Hospital enrolled public school teachers, at 50 cents a month, for guaranteed 21 days of hospital care. This model grew into the Blue Cross Hospital Insurance Plan.

U.S. presidents Theodore Roosevelt, Franklin D. Roosevelt, and Harry S. Truman proposed national health care programs. None were successful until 1965, when President Lyndon B. Johnson signed the Social Security Amendments of 1965 (P.L. 89–97: Title XVIII and XIX of the Social Security Act) creating Medicare and Medicaid. This was the first time in U.S. history Americans sixty-five years of age and older and low-income individuals and families were guaranteed health insurance coverage.

Administered by the Centers for Medicare and Medicaid (CMS), an agency within the U.S. Department of Health and Human Services, Medicare is a complicated alphabet soup of insurance coverage options. The best place to begin a Medicare and Medicaid information search is the U.S. federal government's Medicare and Medicaid websites.

Signed into law in 1997, and reauthorized in 2009, the Children's Health Insurance Program (CHIP) provides health insurance coverage for children and their families who cannot afford private health insurance or qualify for Medicaid. The best place to learn about CHIP is *InsureKidsNow*, the website operated and maintained by CMS.

Enacted into law on March 23, 2010, the Patient Protection and Affordable Care Act is referred to as the Affordable Care Act, the ACA, or colloquially as "Obamacare." Key provisions eliminate lifetime limits on insurance benefits, prohibit rescission of health policies, and require insurance companies to cover preventive health services and immunizations. Information on the ACA for individuals, families, providers, and insurers is available at *HealthCare.gov*. In addition, the Henry J. Kaiser Family Foundation website has a wealth of nonpartisan health care reform research and information, including updates on legal challenges to the ACA. The activity in Box 29.4 explores resources on the ACA in more depth.

Box 29.4 Activity: ACA Updates

Select one of the following scenarios:

- You are the newly minted medical reference librarian at a four-hospital health system. The Chief Nursing Officer walks into your library and asks you to recommend a few websites that she can easily access to keep her updated on ACA changes.
- You are the newly minted consumer health librarian for a medium-size public library system. Your patron, a public health policy student, is researching challenges to the ACA.

Questions for Reflection and Discussion:

1. Using the twenty-point consumer website evaluative criteria, would you recommend the Kaiser Family Foundation site to both the Chief Nursing Officer and the student? Why or why not?
2. Would you recommend *Healthcare.gov* instead of *Health Reform*? Why or why not?

ADDITIONAL RESOURCES

Health Care Foundations and Private Research Organizations

Health care foundations and research organizations sometimes produce publicly available reports that can be useful to patrons. Established in 1991, the Henry J. Kaiser Family Foundation is a private, independent, non-profit organization that develops its own health policy analysis research and manages its journalism and communications programs. All Kaiser products are available free of charge. The Institute of Medicine (IOM), established in 1970, is the health division of the National Academies. It is an independent, non-profit organization. Much of the health care research performed by the IOM originates with requests from the U.S. Congress, federal agencies, or public and private organizations. Established by the founder of Johnson & Johnson, the Robert Wood Johnson Foundation provides grants with the goal to improve the health and health care of all Americans. Grant awards go to projects to combat childhood obesity, expand health insurance coverage, and improve the cost and quality of health care. Reports and research produced by the RWJ Foundation are available free of charge.

The National Network of Libraries of Medicine

Whether one is a consumer health librarian working in a public library setting, a clinical librarian providing information to clinicians at the point of care, or part of a biomedical research team, one of the most important resources available is the National Network of Libraries of Medicine (NN/LM). The NN/LM is composed of a nationwide network of hospital and health science libraries and information centers. NN/LM members are supported through eight regional offices called Regional Medical Libraries (RMLs). RMLs offer e-learning and in-person classes to support the effective use of NLM information products and services, such as *MedlinePlus*. Most of these learning opportunities are free. Many NN/LM hospital and health science libraries have consumer health collections and provide interlibrary loan services to public libraries. A number of these libraries employ consumer health librarians who provide reference services to the general public and assist public librarians in answering difficult health questions.

CONCLUSION

Information needs for health and medical information come from inside and outside the health care system because health happens everywhere. And the need for timely and accurate health care information happens everywhere. Patients, caregivers, and the general public tend to access consumer health information via the Internet, and librarians can play a role in directing them to reliable, up-to-date sources. Inside the health care system, clinicians at the point of care need access to digested, evidence-based summaries on topics of clinical relevance. To inform their work, biomedical researchers need access to bibliographic databases and clinical trials repositories. It is incumbent on librarians to choose the right resource for the clientele they serve.

NOTE

1. The editors would like to acknowledge the work of Maura Sostack in writing the inaugural version of this chapter for the fifth edition of the textbook, and for her substantial work revising portions of the chapter for this edition. We would like to thank Rebecca Davis for her contribution of additional consumer health resources in this edition.

REFERENCES

Agency for Healthcare Research and Quality. 2017. "About AHRQ." Department of Health & Human Services. Last modified November 2017. http://www.ahrq.gov/cpi/about/index.html.

Agency for Healthcare Research and Quality. 2019. "Evidence-Based Practice Centers (EPCs)." Last modified May 2019. https://www.ahrq.gov/research/findings/evidence-based-reports/centers/index.html.

American Library Association. 2008. "Code of Ethics." Last modified January 22, 2008. http://www.ala.org/tools/ethics.

Association of Health Care Journalists. n.d. "History of AHCJ." http://healthjournalism.org/about-history.php.

Cochrane. n.d.-a "About Cochrane." http://www.cochrane.org/about-us.

Cochrane. n.d.-b "More About Us." http://irmg.cochrane.org.

Fischer, Karen S. 2005. "Doody's Core Titles in the Health Sciences (DCT)." *Journal of the Medical Library Association* 93 (3): 409.

Fox, Susannah. 2014. "The Social Life of Health Information." Pew Research Center. January 15. http://www.pewresearch.org/fact-tank/2014/01/15/the-social-life-of-health-information/.

Fox, Susannah, and Deborah Fallows. 2003. "Internet Health Resources." Pew Research Center. July 16. https://www.pewinternet.org/wp-content/uploads/sites/9/media/Files/Reports/2003/PIP_Health_Report_July_2003.pdf.pdf.

Fox, Susannah, and Maeve Duggan. 2013. "Health Online 2013." Pew Research Center. January 15. https://www.pewresearch.org/internet/2013/01/15/health-online-2013/.

Health Information Research Unit. 2016. McMaster University. Last modified February 9, 2016. http://hiru.mcmaster.ca/hiru/.

Healthypeople.gov. n.d. "Lesbian, Gay, Bisexual, and Transgender Health." Last updated January 1, 2020. https://www.healthypeople.gov.

Institute of Medicine. 2004. *Health Literacy: A Prescription to End Confusion.* Washington, DC: National Academies Press.

Linden, Tom. 2010. "Reporting by TV Docs in Haiti Raises Ethical Issues." *Electronic News* 4 (2): 60–64.

Linnan, Laura. A., Barbara M. Wildemuth, Claudia Gollop, Peggy Hull, Christie Silbajoris, and Ruth Moning. 2004. "Public Librarians as a Resource for Promoting Health: Results from the Health for Everyone in Libraries Project (HELP) Librarian Survey." *Health Promotion Practice* 5 (2): 182–90.

Medical Library Association. 2010. "Code of Ethics for Health Sciences Librarianship." Last updated June 2010. https://www.mlanet.org/page/code-of-ethics.

Murphy-Knoll, Linda. 2007. "Low Health Literacy Puts Patients at Risk: The Joint Commission Proposes Solutions to National Problem." *Journal of Nursing Care Quality* 22 (3): 205–9.

National LGBT Health Education Center. n.d. Last updated December 4, 2019. https://www.lgbthealtheducation.org/.

Papadakos, Janet, Aileen Trang, David Wiljer, Chiara Cipolet Mis, Alaina Cyr, Audrey Jusko Friedman, Mauro Mazzocut, Michelle Snow, Valeria Raivich, and Pamela Catton. 2014. "What Criteria Do Consumer Health Librarians Use to Develop Library Collections? A Phenomenological Study." *Journal of the Medical Library Association* 102 (2): 78–84.

Patient Protection and Affordable Care Act, 42 U.S.C. § 18001 et seq. (2010).

Reference and User Services Association. 2015. "Health and Medical Reference Guidelines." American Library Association. http://www.ala.org/rusa/resources/guidelines/guidelinesmedical.

Sackett, David L. 1996. "Evidence Based Medicine: What It Is and What It Isn't." *BMJ* 312 (7023): 71–72.

Somers, Stephan A., and Roopa Mahadevan. 2010. "Health Literacy Implications of the Affordable Care Act." Center for Health Care Strategies. https://www.chcs.org/media/Health_Literacy_Implications_of_the_Affordable_Care_Act.pdf.

Zhao, Yuehua, and Jin Zhang. 2017. "Consumer Health Information Seeking in Social Media: A Literature Review." Health Information and Libraries Journal 34 (4): 268–83.

Zionts, Nancy D., Jan Apter, Julianna Kuchta, and Pamela K. Greenhouse. 2010. "Promoting Consumer Health Literacy: Creation of a Health Information Librarian Fellowship." *Reference & User Services Quarterly* 49 (4): 350–9.

LIST OF SOURCES

AIDS*info*. https://aidsinfo.nih.gov/.

Alt HealthWatch. Ipswich, MA: EBSCO. https://health.ebsco.com/products/alt-healthwatch. Subscription required.

American Board of Medical Specialties. http://www.abms.org/.

American Cancer Society. https://www.cancer.org/.

American Diabetes Association. http://www.diabetes.org/.

American Heart Association. https://www.heart.org.

American Osteopathic Association. "AOA Board Certification." https://certification.osteopathic.org/

American Stroke Association. https://www.strokeassociation.org.

AskMe3. The National Patient Safety Foundation. http://www.ihi.org/resources/Pages/Tools/Ask-Me-3-Good-Questions-for-Your-Good-Health.aspx.

Best Bones Forever! https://www.bestbonesforever.org/.

Biomed Central. http://www.biomedcentral.com/.

Board Certified Docs. Atlanta, GA: Elsevier. http://www.boardcertifieddocs.com/abms/static/home.htm. Subscription required.

The Body: The HIV/AIDS Resource. https://www.thebody.com/.

CancerCare. https://www.cancercare.org/.

Centers for Disease Control and Prevention. https://www.cdc.gov/.

Centers for Disease Control and Prevention: Parent Information. https://www.cdc.gov/parents/.

Certification Matters. American Board of Medical Specialties. http://certificationmatters.org/.

ChooseMyPlate.gov. http://www.choosemyplate.gov.

ClinicalKey for Nursing. Atlanta, GA: Elsevier. https://www.elsevier.com/solutions/clinicalkey-for-nursing. Subscription required.

ClinicalTrials.gov. https://clinicaltrials.gov/.

Cochrane Database of Systematic Reviews. London: Cochrane. https://www.cochranelibrary.com/cdsr/reviews. Available as part of Cochrane Library.

Cochrane Library. Hoboken, NJ: Wiley. https://www.cochranelibrary.com/advanced-search?q=&t=1. Subscription required

Cohen, Barbara Janson. 2016. *Medical Terminology: An Illustrated Guide.* 8th ed. Philadelphia, PA: Lippincott Williams & Wilkins.

Consumer and Patient Health Information Section. Medical Library Association. https://www.mlanet.org/caphis.

Consumer Health Complete. Ipswich, MA: EBSCO. https://www.ebsco.com/products/research-databases/consumer-health-complete. Subscription required.

Cumulative Index to Nursing and Allied Health Literature (CINAHL). Ipswich, MA: EBSCO. https://health.ebsco.com/products/the-cinahl-database. Subscription required.

Doody's Core Titles in the Health Sciences. Oak Park, IL: Doody's Enterprises. http://www.doody.com/dct/default.asp. Subscription required.

Drugs.com. http://www.drugs.com/.

DynaMed. Ipswich, MA: EBSCO. https://dynamed.ebscohost.com/. Subscription required.

Easy-to-Read. *MedlinePlus.* http://www.nlm.nih.gov/medlineplus/all_easytoread.html.

eatright. http://eatright.org.

EndNote. http://endnote.com/.

Essential Evidence Plus. Hoboken, NJ: Wiley. http://www.essentialevidenceplus.com/. Subscription required.

Essential Nursing Resources. 26th ed. 2012. Silver Spring, MD: Interagency Council on Information Resources in Nursing.

Evidence Reports. Agency for Healthcare Research and Quality. http://www.ahrq.gov/research/findings/evidence-based-reports/search.html.

Facebook. http://www.facebook.com.

Familydoctor.org. http://www.familydoctor.org.

Girlshealth.gov. https://www.girlshealth.gov/.

GoGirlGo! https://www.womenssportsfoundation.org/programs/gogirlgo/.

Google. http://www.google.com.

Health & Wellness Resource Center. Farmington Hills, MI: Gale Cengage Learning. https://www.gale.com/c/health-and-wellness-resource-center. Subscription required.

Health Affairs. 1981–. Bethesda, MD: Project HOPE. Monthly. http://www.healthaffairs.org/.

Health and Medicine. Farmington Hills, MI: Gale Cengage Learning. https://www.gale.com/c/health-reference-center-academic. Subscription required.

Health Source: Consumer Edition. Ipswich, MA: EBSCO. https://www.ebsco.com/products/research-databases/health-source-consumer-edition. Subscription required.

Healthcare.gov. https://www.healthcare.gov/.

Healthychildren.org. https://www.healthychildren.org.

Healthfinder.gov. https://www.healthfinder.gov.

Healthypeople.gov. https://www.healthypeople.gov.

The Henry J. Kaiser Family Foundation. http://kff.org.

Hill, Dorothy R., and Henry N. Stickell. 2001. "Brandon/Hill Selected List of Print Books and Journals for the Small Medical Library." *Bulletin of the Medical Library Association* 89 (2): 131–53.

Hill, Dorothy R., and Henry N. Stickell. 2002. "Brandon/Hill Selected List of Print Nursing Books and Journals." *Nursing Outlook* 50 (3): 100–13.

Hill, Dorothy R., and Henry N. Stickell. 2003. "Brandon/Hill Selected List of Print Books and Journals in Allied Health." *Journal of the Medical Library Association* 91 (1): 18–33.

Institute of Medicine. http://iom.nationalacademies.org/.

InsureKidsNow.gov. http://www.insurekidsnow.gov/.

JAMAevidence. New York, NY: McGraw-Hill. http://jamaevidence.com/. Subscription required.

JBI Database of Systematic Reviews and Implementation Reports. 2003–. Adelaide: Joanna Briggs Institute. Monthly. https://journals.lww.com/jbisrir.

Kids Against Bullying. https://pacerkidsagainstbullying.org/.

KidsHealth. https://kidshealth.org/.

LaFleur, Danielle S., and Myrna LaFleur-Brooks. 2013. *Basic Medical Language*. 4th ed. St. Louis: Elsevier.
Mayo Clinic. https://www.mayoclinic.org/.
McMaster Hedge Project. http://hiru.mcmaster.ca/hiru/HIRU_Hedges_home.aspx.
McMaster Plus. http://hiru.mcmaster.ca/hiru/HIRU_McMaster_PLUS_projects.aspx.
Medicaid.gov. http://www.medicaid.gov/.
Medicare.gov. https://www.medicare.gov/.
MEDLINE. https://www.nlm.nih.gov/bsd/pmresources.html.
MedlinePlus. http://www.nlm.nih.gov/medlineplus/.
Mendeley. https://www.mendeley.com/.
Milbank Quarterly. 1923–. New York, NY: Milbank Memorial Fund. Quarterly. http://www.milbank.org/the-milbank-quarterly.
Mouth Healthy. http://www.mouthhealthy.org.
National Cancer Institute. http://www.cancer.gov.
National Guideline Clearinghouse. https://www.ahrq.gov/gam/index.html.
National Institute for Health and Care Excellence. https://www.nice.org.uk/guidance.
National Institute of Diabetes and Digestive and Kidney Diseases. https://www.niddk.nih.gov/.
National Institute on Aging. https://www.nia.nih.gov/.
National LGBT Health Education Center. https://www.lgbthealtheducation.org/.
National Network of Libraries of Medicine. http://nnlm.gov/.
National Sleep Foundation. https://www.sleepfoundation.org/.
Nursing and Allied Health Resources Section. 2012. "NAHRS 2012 Selected List of Nursing Journals," Medical Library Association. https://sites.google.com/site/nahrsnursingresources/selected-journals-list.
Nursing Reference Center. Ipswich, MA: EBSCO. http://www.ebscohost.com/nursing/products/nursing-reference-center. Subscription required.
Parent Toolkit. https://www.parenttoolkit.com.
Pill Identifier. AARP. https://healthtools.aarp.org/pill-identifier.
Pillbox. National Library of Medicine. https://pillbox.nlm.nih.gov/.
Plain Language in Healthcare. https://www.plainlanguage.gov/resources/content-types/healthcare/.
Plain Language Medical Dictionary. Taubman Health Sciences Library. University of Michigan. http://www.lib.umich.edu/plain-language-dictionary.
PubMed. http://www.ncbi.nlm.nih.gov/pubmed.
PubMed Central. http://www.ncbi.nlm.nih.gov/pmc/.
PubMed Clinical Queries. http://www.ncbi.nlm.nih.gov/pubmed/clinical.
"Question Builder." Agency for Heathcare Research and Quality. https://www.ahrq.gov/patients-consumers/question-builder.html.
"Questions to Ask Your Doctor." 2012. Agency for Healthcare Research and Quality. http://ahrq.gov/patients-consumers/patient-involvement/ask-your-doctor/index.html.
Rittenhouse Book Distributors. https://www.rittenhouse.com/Rbd/Web/Default.aspx.
Robert Wood Johnson Foundation. http://www.rwjf.org/.
RxList. http://www.rxlist.com.
Salud America! https://salud-america.org/.
SuperKids Nutrition. https://www.superkidsnutrition.com/.
Teens Against Bullying, https://pacerteensagainstbullying.org/.
TRIP Database. http://www.tripdatabase.com/.
Twitter. http://www.twitter.com.
UptoDate. Boston: Wolters Kluwer. http://www.uptodate.com/home. Subscription required.
USPSTF Information for Consumers. http://www.uspreventiveservicestaskforce.org/Tools/ConsumerInfo/Index/information-for-consumers.

SUGGESTED READINGS

Groopman, Jerome E. 2007. *How Doctors Think*. Boston: Houghton Mifflin.

This book enables the reader to understand how physicians process information gleaned from their patients and how they understand illness. According to Groopman, for the most part, doctors get it (diagnosis) right, but when they get it wrong, the fallout can be monumental. Most diagnostic errors are due to doctors' perceptions and sometimes stereotypical beliefs about their patients. Much of what is written about the doctor–patient dialogue is from the patient's perspective meaning, how do patients more effectively communicate with, and become partners with, their healthcare team? Groopman's tome offers much needed insight into how doctors process information. And this insight, in turn, can help patients.

Huber, Jeffrey T., and Susan Swogger. 2014. *Introduction to Reference Sources in the Health Sciences*. 6th ed. Chicago, IL: ALA Neal-Schuman.

This guide to reference sources is essential for anyone considering a career providing medical or health sciences reference services. The authors present their information in four parts: Health Reference in Context, the Reference Collection, Bibliographic Sources, and Information Sources. Published in 2014, this edition includes new chapters on health information–seeking behaviors, point of care, and global health sources. There is also an increased emphasis and focus on highlighting electronic resources since these resources are ubiquitous in medical reference work.

Kohn, Linda T., Janet M. Corrigan, and Molla S. Donaldson, eds. 1999. *To Err Is Human: Building a Safer Health System*. Committee on Quality of Health Care in America; Institute of Medicine. Washington, DC: National Academy Press.

On November 29, 1999, the Institute of Medicine (IOM) released its groundbreaking "To Err is Human" report in which the IOM made a staggering pronouncement: medical errors account for upwards of 98,000 hospital deaths in the United States each year, and most of these errors are preventable. The findings of this report ushered in what is known as the patient safety era whereby patients and their families must be part of the care process. This report was one of the first to put the spotlight on health literacy issues.

Nordenström, Jörgen. 2007. *Evidence-Based Medicine in Sherlock Holmes' Footsteps*. Malden, MA: Blackwell Publishers.

Understanding the EBM process can be overwhelming. This very useful, easy-to-read book provides an introduction to the basic concepts of evidence-based medicine. This fun (yes fun!) text takes the reader through the literature searching process to a step-by-step approach to critically appraising results.

Osborne, Helen. 2013. *Health Literacy from A to Z: Practical Ways to Communicate Your Health Message*. 2nd ed. Burlington, MA: Jones & Bartlett Learning.

Osborne's text was included in the 2015 edition of the essential collection of *Doody's Core Titles*. Chapters are organized around "Starting Points" with an introduction to key concepts, followed by "Strategies, Ideas and Suggestions" that contain how-to tips. "Stories from Practice" discusses real-life health literacy experience, and "Sources to Learn More" includes a bibliography of books, journal articles, podcasts, and other resources. This book is extremely practical and easy to read, and librarians providing consumer health reference will find Osborne's strategies and ideas invaluable.

Spatz, Michele. 2014. *The Medical Library Association Guide to Providing Consumer and Patient Health Information*. Lanham, MD: Rowman & Littlefield.

Spatz covers all aspects of consumer health information services: from ethical issues to needs assessments; from budgeting and funding to strategic partnerships, to meeting the needs of diverse groups such as children, teens, LGBTQ+ individuals, and patients with low literacy. This book provides a foundation from which to build effective and efficient consumer health reference services.

Sultz, Harry A., and Kristina M. Young. 2014. *Health Care USA: Understanding Its Organization and Delivery*. 8th ed. Sudbury, MA: Jones & Bartlett Learning.

The 8th edition of this classic text provides a wide-ranging overview of the United States healthcare system. New to this edition are analyses of the progress and impact of the Affordable Care Act, and new information on efforts to reduce medical errors such as the Institute for Health Care Improvement's 100,000 Lives Campaign. Readers are provided with historical overviews of Medicare and Medicaid programs and the role that managed care plays as the primary method of insuring most Americans.

Wood, M. Sandra. 2014. *Health Sciences Librarianship*. Lanham, MD: Rowman & Littlefield.

This text is useful to those tasked with managing the day-to-day operations of a medical or health sciences library. Chapters are organized in four main parts: The Profession, The Collection, User Services, and Administrative Services. The chapter authors emphasize how technological advances have changed the role of the health science librarian, specifically the expectation of virtual reference services and 24/7 access to resources. Additionally, the authors discuss the "library without walls" concept and the idea of embedded librarianship.

Chapter 30

Primary and Archival Sources

Shelley Sweeney

"The palest ink is better than the best memory."—Chinese proverb

INTRODUCTION

Although primary sources and archival records were opened up for research in the 1800s, they were more or less inaccessible to all but the most privileged and dedicated scholars. Today, most such records are open to everyone. They are attractive to students interested in experiential learning and creating mash-ups, scholars who are including more original resources in their research, and members of the public who have more time on their hands and have such hobbies as genealogy and local history. But what has led to the democratization of primary sources and archival records is the advent of the Internet and the digitization of resources. Suddenly, instead of users having to physically get to archives in obscure locations during short opening hours, they can go online and get access to millions of photographs, documents, audio recordings, and myriad other formats, whenever it is convenient to them. However, because of the newness and unfamiliarity of these resources, many users in all types of libraries require reference assistance, and this is where the reference librarian comes in.

Primary Sources and Archival Records

Primary sources or archival records can be used to respond to a wide variety of reference requests. But what exactly are they? Unfortunately, not all historians and teachers agree on the definition. The Society of American Archivists' (SAA) *Glossary* defines a primary source as "material that contains firsthand accounts of events and that was created contemporaneous to those events or later recalled by an eyewitness" (Pearce-Moses 2005). Such materials can include the following:

- Diaries
- Memoirs
- Oral history interviews
- Newspaper articles about contemporaneous events
- Records of court cases
- Official government documents
- Ephemera

Primary sources are often contrasted with secondary sources, which are sources that are produced after the event by someone who did not experience the event. Secondary sources can contain summaries, interpretations, authorial opinions, and commentary, and are often compilations of information from various sources. Scholarly publications, textbooks, and encyclopedias would be typical formats of secondary sources. Sometimes, secondary sources can contain primary sources within them, such as histories that contain eyewitness accounts.

Archival records are defined as "materials created or received by a person, family, or organization, public or private, in the conduct of their affairs that are preserved because of the enduring value contained in the information they contain or as evidence of the functions and responsibilities of their creator" (Pearce-Moses 2005). The key consideration is that these materials were produced in the normal course of daily activity and record or support that activity in some way. Typical formats of such materials include:

- Textual records, such as correspondence
- Photographs
- Maps
- Architectural plans
- Drawings and sketches
- Sound recordings
- Audiovisual records

Figure 30.1 provides an example of an archival photograph; such "old" photographs can be the main focus of historical study or just useful for adding color to student essays and illustrating texts on historic topics. Records can be analog or digital; increasingly, archives are "born digital." Artifacts, microforms, and published materials can sometimes be considered part of archival records, although typically artifacts are collected by museums, and microforms and published materials by libraries. It usually depends on the relationship between the materials. If, for instance, an archival collection included design drawings and correspondence for the creation of a medal, an archives might keep the medal as part of the collection. Likewise with literary archives, it is not unusual for an archives to keep the final published version of a work with drafts of the same.

Although a single item might be considered an archive, typically archives consist of a group of materials that have organic relationships between the component parts based on the activities of the creator or creators. The fact that archival

Figure 30.1 Aboriginal man with braids and earring, 1880, Connie Macmillan Collection, from the University of Manitoba Archives & Special Collections, the Libraries, Accession Number: UM_pc284_A11-086_001_0001_003_0001.

records are typically a grouping of materials affects everything from how they are described, to how they are retrieved, and how they are used.

Primary sources can be published summaries of selected archival documents, often referred to as "calendars." In the British tradition, these so-called calendars provide the substance of the selected documents in chronological order, which can save a great deal of time when researchers need to pin down the exact documents they need (Sweetman 2008). In addition, if the documents are in a foreign or an ancient language, the calendar will provide a translation. These calendars provide very rigorous and specific descriptions that can obviate the need to consult the originals and can be used as primary sources. In the North American tradition, however, the calendars are more likely to be simple lists pointing the researcher to the appropriate materials.

Primary sources can also be published compilations of selected archival documents; this can include facsimiles, which attempt to reproduce the original records as closely as possible. These publications reproduce important series of documents relating to a particular event, for instance, such as the Anglo-Chinese opium wars (Waley 1958), or the correspondence of someone important, such as American president Theodore Roosevelt (Roosevelt 1951–1954). Although such publications were more popular in the 20th century, it is still fairly common for organizations and authors to publish important documents, although increasingly these compilations of archival texts are being produced online. For example, InteLex's *Past Masters* includes the complete letters of Jane Austen.

Other Words for Primary Sources and Archival Records

Primary sources are almost always called "primary sources." In rare circumstances, they can also be referred to as original sources or evidence. Archival records can be referred to in a number of different ways by both users and creators: archival materials or collections, archives, the archive, records, original records, documentation, documents, papers, and manuscripts, among others. They are often referred to as being rare, unique, and original. Furthermore, although users are unlikely to use this term, Canadian and international archivists and archival websites often refer to a creator's "fonds." This term refers to all the archival records created or collected by a person, a family, or an organization. American archivists are more likely to refer to record groups or collections.

Although all archives are considered primary sources, not all primary sources would necessarily be considered archives. A verbatim interview in a standalone publication could be considered a primary source, but neither the interview nor the publication would be considered archival. They lack all the defining characteristics of an archives: they were neither created in the conduct of daily activity nor selected to be permanently retained, for example.

In general, users do not care whether they are accessing primary sources or archival records. They just want the answer to their questions. It is usually only professors and teachers who will specify that their students need to use primary sources. For the purposes of this chapter, references to primary sources will be considered separately from original archival records.

USES

The types of reference requests that primary sources and archival records can best help answer will likely fall into five categories. When referring a patron to primary sources or archival records, the reference librarian should mentally categorize the reference request, because determining the best resources will depend upon the category. The categories are as follows:

1. **Class assignments.** Users have been given an assignment that requires they use primary sources: "My teacher wants us to go through old newspapers and find stuff about soldiers from our town during the Second World War" or "My professor wants me to use primary sources to do an assignment on the Civil Rights movement and the paper's due tomorrow."
2. **Searching for facts.** Users want to know a specific fact or facts that cannot be found in more traditional reference sources: "I want to find out whether X ever held a position in Y company" or "Can you tell me when X graduated from university?"
3. **Seeking answers to specific questions.** Users have specific questions in mind but are unsure what records might meet their needs: "I am going to write the history of the Garden Club of Allegheny County and would like to find as much information about it as I can" or "I am researching my family tree and I want to know more about the X family of New York City."
4. **Looking for known records.** Users are looking for specific known records or specific types of records: "Where would I find papers relating to Harriet Tubman?"

5. **Looking for records to enforce rights.** Users are looking for records that will help enforce their rights: "I need to prove I attended Residential School to receive compensation" or "I have to provide evidence of my birthdate to get my pension."

A good reference interview will elicit the scope of the user's question and the level or amount of information required, and particularly the deadline by which to have the information. It also helps a great deal to know what outcomes the users are hoping for. Are they going to write a five-page paper or are they writing a *magnum opus* and require as much information as possible no matter how long it takes them to acquire it? All of the information solicited will help the reference librarian decide whether primary or archival sources are best used to answer the information need.

Class Assignments

Primary sources are fairly easy and straightforward to use when a class assignment requires a student to use them, or for quick and ready reference. Archival records, because of their volume, the hierarchies, the complex relationships between the various parts of the collections, the indirect nature between descriptions and contents, and the lack of granularity in the descriptions, can be tricky and often time consuming and laborious to use. In addition, there is no guarantee that the records will have what the student is looking for or enough information to fulfill a class assignment. When there is a time limit, primary sources are best, but digitized archival records might also be appropriate for class assignments, depending on the request.

Searching for Facts

If the information need is to determine a specific fact, either primary sources or archival sources could be employed. If the required fact is about a person, a family, or an organization and popular reference sources cannot answer the question, then potentially the private papers of those entities might have the answer. Correspondence written by the person, family, or representative of an organization to another entity would also be good to consult.

If the user needs an answer about a specific event, then primary sources would be a good place to start. If these did not provide the answer, then the user would need to tie the event to a particular person, family, or organization, and employ archival records.

Seeking Answers to Specific Questions

The same decision would need to be made if the user has a specific question in mind but is unsure what materials to use. Where requests are broad, the reference librarian needs to assist researchers in narrowing down their requests. For instance, "I want to find the causes of the American Civil War" is too broad for archival records unless the user wants to spend a significant amount of time, even years, on the request. In that case, contemporary newspapers might be appropriate, but such a request would still be time consuming. A more specific request, such as "I want to know how Union soldiers viewed the American Civil War," could be answered by reading letters from soldiers.

A request such as "I want to know how many women worked in Chinese laundries in San Francisco in the 1920s" is so narrow and so specific that it quite likely will not result in any answers because of the lack of records. Depending on their needs, the researcher could consider looking at the 1930s instead, when the Chinese Consolidated Benevolent Association and the Chinese Hand Laundry Alliance were formed, in case these institutions might have produced records on their members. There may also have been government inquiries into the laundry business that produced records. It is important to keep in mind that the absence of information about women might just mean that women were not considered important enough to include in the records.

Thus, unless users are planning on spending significant amounts of time, they will not be able to quickly answer general historical questions through examining primary sources or archival records. For detailed histories, fresh analyses of historical issues, specific questions, and to enforce rights, however, normally archival records are the *only* materials that can satisfy such requests.

Looking for Known Records

When a researcher comes to a reference librarian asking for specific records or record types, it is always good to probe deeper through a reference interview to ensure the patron understands what they are asking for. Once assured that they know the records will answer their needs, the librarian can assist them to find the institution that would most likely hold the records.

Looking for Records to Enforce Rights

This is a special category. If patrons are seeking records relating to the enforcement of rights and the cases have a historic dimension, reference librarians should send them to the most appropriate archival institutions because often such records are only in hardcopy form and not online. An example of such a case might be records relating to a toxic waste cleanup. Those seeking redress would need to do extensive research into records relating possibly to the government department that investigated and regulated the cleanup, the company involved in producing the toxic waste, the departments of health that followed up on the cleanup, and so on.

IDENTIFYING RECORDS

Linking Topics to Records

For all searches, if the researcher does not yet have a good understanding of their topic, the librarian should advise the user to read secondary sources, if any exist, and extract all names of people, families, and organizations that appear in the literature. The researcher should also confirm all the changes in names of these entities. For example, in the past women virtually always changed their names when they got married, and many still do. It is important to know both their single and married names. Organizations often change their names over time, reflecting changes in purpose. The researcher should also look for language or naming that is unique to the topic. For instance, in the early part of the 20th century, people from Czechoslovakia were referred to as Bohemians. Then they were referred to as Czechoslovaks. Over time and particularly once the country split into two separate countries in 1993, people were referred to as Czechs and Slovaks. It is critical to know all names associated with the topic because archival records are organized by the name of the creator, or in some instances, by the name of the donor. This is referred to as the provenance of the archives.

This seemingly arcane practice of identifying all archival records by their creators is not simply to recognize the importance of who created the records, although that is critical to determining the value of the records, but because the creator's name is the only certain way to consistently identify archival materials. There is no title on archival records, the dates may not be precisely known, and the number of subjects is often too many to narrow down to only a few. But if one knows who created the materials, what their life story is, and particularly what functions they performed during their lifetime, then the contents of the archive might be inferred. Box 30.1 provides two examples of creators, one private and one corporate, and how one might use details of their histories to determine what questions their records might answer.

Box 30.1 Search Strategy: Determining Likely Topics Covered by Archival Records

Knowing the life history of Amelia Earhart, an American pilot, aviation pioneer, and author, who mysteriously disappeared during a round-the-world flight in 1937, would give one a good indication of what one might expect to find in her private papers. One might look for information on female pilots, early aviation history, the role of and public reaction to female pilots, the mechanics of early flight, and the commercial aspects of aviation in the 1920s and 1930s, for instance. Users interested in unusual careers for women in the early 20th century might have a difficult time in coming up with the name "Amelia Earhart," but reading biographies of outstanding American women would probably lead them to her name and hence her papers.

The Hudson's Bay Company is a retail store based in Canada that started off life as a fur trading company after receiving an English royal charter in 1670. The company at one time was one of the largest landowners in the world, owning huge swaths of territory in Western Canada. Knowing its history even superficially, one would expect to find information about British attitudes toward North America, the fur trade, international shipping and selling, as well as modern retailing and corporate ownership. Plunging further into the company's history, however, reveals that employees of the company were expected to keep detailed records of their daily business and general observations and that these records can and do provide information on the local indigenous populations, weather, the lives of fur trappers, and a whole lot more. Researchers wanting to investigate the effects of global warming in Canada over a sustained period of time would ask themselves who or what organization was creating records in the 1700s that might have included observations of the weather? This would lead them to the Hudson's Bay Company archives.

In addition to determining the names of all of the people connected to the topic, the user should note all the locations associated with those people, keeping in mind that place names may have changed over time as well. This will help the librarian identify the institutions most likely to hold relevant records. The context of creation is everything.

Finally, by consulting secondary scholarly works, the researcher will be able to compile a list of the archival records that other scholars have cited; these citations will provide helpful shortcuts to archival records to give some impetus to the search.

The Value of Records

Archival records and to a lesser extent primary sources are valued for their impartiality. Because the records were created in the normal course of daily activity, they were written neither for an audience nor with the intent to present a particular point of view; in other words, they are unmediated. They will still reflect the biases of their creators however, and acknowledging the context of creation is very important in determining those biases. This must be taken into account when researchers use the materials. Additionally, the records will reflect the biases and opinions of the archivists who chose which records would be acquired, and how they would be described and made available.

Archivists talk about the *evidential* and *informational* value of archives. The evidential value of a record is, according to the SAA *Glossary*, "the quality of records that provides information about the origins, functions, and activities of their creator" (Pearce-Moses 2005). The informational value is "the usefulness or significance of materials based on their content, independent of any intrinsic or evidential value" (Pearce-Moses 2005). Census records are evidence of a government's enumeration of its citizens, but genealogists use those same census records in order to find information about their relations.

Archivists also refer to the *authenticity* and *reliability* of archival records. The authenticity of records refers to the fact that they are what they purport to be based on internal and external evidence, such as their formats and physical characteristics, the way they are structured, and the information they hold. Archivists also refer to the unbroken line of custody for archives; that is to say, they can trace who held the records from the original creator to the time when the archives received them. That custody provides some measure of assurance that the records were indeed created by the person, persons, or organization identified as the creator(s). The reliability of records indicates that they are worthy of trust. Primary sources are less likely to provide evidence of functions performed by a creator and thus may be less authentic and reliable because they have been stripped of their context or they never had any context beyond publication to begin with. They do, however, have information that can be utilized.

Selecting the Most Appropriate Types of Records

Once the librarian has a good grasp of what the researcher needs, and the user knows all the names and geographical locations connected to their topic, the next step is to determine the best resource the researcher can use. There are two types of resources that a librarian can point patrons to: reproductions of records, or descriptions of those records, held by a variety of commercial and noncommercial organizations, and original records in various formats that were collected by institutions. In both cases, records can be analog or digital.

Reproductions

The easiest option for users is to use records that have been published or are online. A professional has already selected the documents for their relevance or for their importance to a particular topic. With published individual documents, the records are usually transcribed, so there is no need for the researcher to have to deal with cursive handwriting or strange fonts. Increasingly, cursive is becoming more and more difficult to read for younger members of society who have not been taught cursive in school. In addition, quite often the historical context and significance of the documents will be outlined in an introduction. There can be commentary on each document included as well, with a helpful index at the end. All of these tools make these publications a gentle way to introduce neophytes to the use of primary sources and archival records.

Reproductions of records can be found in analog format most often in libraries and rare book rooms and in electronic format on the websites of archives and through commercial online databases licensed by libraries. Organizations also mount reproductions of their records; for example, the United Nations has mounted treaties on its website.

Published physical texts of documents can be found in library catalogs; when they are grouped around a person, family, or organization or under a particular topic, they will have subject headings to assist in discovering them. Christine Bone, Associate Librarian at the University of Manitoba Libraries, notes that the subdivision "Archives" should be attached in the subject heading field to the name of a particular person, family, or organization that created the records (personal communication). The heading "Archives" can also be attached more broadly to classes of persons, ethnic groups, types of organizations, and so on. The subdivision "Sources" is generally added to historical subject headings when the item contains predominantly primary sources, that is to say, published primary sources or archival records *about* a subject. Alternatively, if the documents are of a specific format, that term may be used instead, for example "Diaries" or "Correspondence." "Personal narratives" can be used with wars and other events. With organizations and types of industries, "Records and correspondence" will be added to distinguish these types of records (although a search using "Correspondence" would capture this too). The term "Letters" can also be used for very general correspondence not associated with any particular person, organization, or event, so it would be less useful in finding archival materials but might be helpful as a last resort.

So, the subject terms that will capture most published primary sources and archival records are as follows:

- Archives
- Sources
- Diaries
- Correspondence
- Records and correspondence
- Personal narratives
- Letters

Using words such as "papers," "letters," and "documents" in a keyword search along with the subject of interest is also a possible way to track them down, particularly if there has been an inconsistent use of subject terms.

Digital reproductions of records can be in commercial databases or freely available. Commercial databases typically group materials by theme or subject. They may be licensed by libraries for patron use, or, in some cases, individual researchers can pay for access by subscription. Free resources would be those offered by archives, libraries, research centers, and consortia on their websites. Many university libraries and research centers provide links to these reproductions. For example, a regional group calling itself the Triangle Legal History Seminar, connected to a number of universities, provides a page on *Legal History on the Web*, which provides an exhaustive list of links to dozens of free sources of primary materials on legal history.

Original Records

When reproductions are not available, researchers, and the librarians helping them, look for original records. How can the librarian determine which repository would be appropriate to send users to, either physically or virtually? This is when the researcher's background work focusing the topic; collecting the names of all the people, families, and organizations connected to the topic; and finding the geographic locations where these entities carried out their activities becomes essential.

Do the records actually exist? If they exist, have they been kept? If they have been kept, have they been donated or sold to a public institution? If they have been deposited in, or sold to, a repository, can one find that institution? If one can find the place where have they been placed, have they been processed and cataloged? All of these questions have to be answered in the affirmative to determine if records are available for research. There is absolutely no way to tell whether records might have been created or not, but one can make an educated guess. Governments are required to create records, prominent individuals often create records in their daily activities, and certain types of private organizations, such as religious organizations, typically create records. One can only hope that the organizations or people kept the records they created. Whether they decided to donate the records, keep the materials in their family or organization, or destroy them is completely unknowable. There is an economic incentive to place records in public institutions. Most archives can provide tax receipts for the value of records of private individuals and organizations, and some wealthier institutions purchase records.

Finding the institution where records have been placed can sometimes be challenging. Private individuals and organizations do not always make sensible decisions about where to deposit their records. And there exist enormous backlogs of unprocessed, late-20th-century records that were acquired by archives in great volumes in a very short period of time. Thus, even if logic tells one that an institution should have appropriate records for a reference request, it does not mean that those records either exist or are available. One must accept that archival research is more challenging than research into primary sources or published material, but the thrill of the chase is often, for researchers, a huge part of the allure.

Primary sources often end up being acquired by special collections within libraries or special libraries and are often discoverable through library catalogs. Archival records can be found in a variety of institutions, including special collections departments within libraries, and in a significant number of cases, the collections can only be found through a search of the institutions' own websites or by contacting the institution.

However, to begin a search for collections of really prominent individuals, the librarian can conduct a *Google* search, such as "where are archives relating to X?" This will likely bring up a number of sites that have archival material relating to that person. "Where are archives relating to Harriet Tubman?" for instance, brings up links to records relating to Tubman, the African American abolitionist and humanitarian, from the National Archives and Records Administration and the Library of Congress, among others. For organizations, it is best to check the website of that organization first. Even if the organization does not maintain its own archives, they may have information about where their records are kept.

For collections related to people who are not prominent and for defunct organizations, generally one can say that the place where the entities carried out their activities will determine where the users should start their search. For example, one would expect to find the archives of the Hawaiian government in Hawai'i, and one would expect to look for the papers of prominent Hawaiians in Hawaiian repositories, at least in the first instance. As to how to determine the type of organization that might hold the records, there is an overlying structure that provides pointers as to what institutions might hold the actual records the users need. Carrying the previous example forward, one would expect to find the archives of the Hawaiian government at the Hawai'i State Archives. The personal papers of prominent Hawaiians, particularly those who likely would have deposited after institutions were created in Hawai'i, might be found in a variety of institutions, such as the University of Hawai'i at Mānoa Library.

Important institutions at the national level in the United States are the Library of Congress and the National Archives and Records Administration (NARA). The Library of Congress was established in 1800, originally to collect books, but by 1897 the new Manuscript Division acquired 25,000 manuscripts, which became the basis for collecting the records of private individuals. NARA was established considerably later in 1934 and is responsible for collecting federal government records or private records with a strong federal connection. NARA is also responsible for the confusingly named Presidential Libraries, which are not libraries per se, but primarily house the archives of each president. Below the national level, almost every state has a state archives, or often a state archives and library combined, for government records, and a state historical society for private records. In a number of states, the state archives and the historical society are combined. State archives particularly in the south also have significant holdings of private records. Many of the larger cities have their own archives or departments responsible for records management that will also look after archives. Sometimes private records at the city level will be held by history centers located within municipal public libraries. The majority of universities will have archives, most housed in the library. Some will only have university archives that collect university records, and some will have only a special collections department that collects private records, but a significant number will have both. Religious organizations usually have archives at all administrative levels except individual churches.

A number of major businesses have archives, such as the Ford Motor Company at The Henry Ford and the Coca-Cola Company, but many business archives exist only to serve their parent organizations, and much of their work has to do with patent and trademark rights, so it is sometimes difficult for external researchers to get access to these archives. In addition to business archives, there are a number of archives that serve parent organizations, such as the NSDAR archives of the Daughters of the American Revolution and the archives of the Boy Scouts of America, held by the National Scouting Museum.

In Canada, the National Library and the National Archives merged to form Library and Archives Canada in 2004. The National Library collected literary manuscripts, music archives, and maps, in particular. In Canada, all governmental archives made a special point of collecting private records of interest; this is something Canadian archivists refer to as "total archives." That collection effort did not stop nongovernmental libraries and archives from collecting private records, a role that has become increasingly important as today many governmental institutions have sharply cut back on their collecting of private records. University archives, religious archives, and municipal archives are the major collectors outside of federal and provincial archives. There are very few independent business archives. Many companies have placed their records with public institutions, such as the Hudson's Bay Company archives at Archives of Manitoba, and the Eaton's Company archives at the Archives of Ontario, both provincial archives.

Internationally, similar structures can be found in most countries, although they will have individual differences among them. In Britain, for instance, many of the major estates have significant family archival holdings.

Thus, one can see that archives are closely associated with organizations. With the exception of universities, which tend to have broad collecting mandates, most records are kept by their creating institutions: religious records by religious organizations, government records by governments, business records by businesses, and so on. A general Web search is a good place to start as many archives have a strong presence on the Internet. There are also various websites and guides that can help users look for appropriate institutions in each country as outlined in the Sources by Country or Region section.

Descriptions of Records

Once the librarian and the patron have pinpointed the institution that holds the records of interest, then either the librarian can assist the patron in navigating the descriptions of records or the patron will do the searching on their own and will be responsible for selecting the records that best suit their needs. Some institutions will have the descriptions of their records online, some will have in-house databases of descriptions, and some will still have manual systems. For online and database descriptions, users will likely be able to search the descriptions. With manual systems, there will likely be indexes to the contents. In virtually every case, users will be searching for the names of the individuals they have identified connected to their topic, although archives have begun to add subject headings to the descriptions of their holdings, and many have created thematic Web pages.

At the top level, each named collection will be described through such information as biographical sketches of the creators, dates of the records, extent and type of records, and the scope and contents of the collection. In the United States, this is referred to as the "collection description." In Canada, archivists will refer to these global descriptions as "RAD descriptions," that refers to fonds or collection-level descriptions according to the Canadian standard, the *Rules for Archival Description* (Bureau of Canadian Archivists 2008). Figure 30.2 provides an example of a global level description.

Below these high-level descriptions will be finding aids, inventories, or file lists. These aids assist the user in determining the specific contents of each collection. See Figure 30.3 for an example of a file-level inventory.

Hamilton Family fonds

Call Number:	Mss 14, Pc 12, Tc 70 (A.79-21, A.79-41, A.79-52, A.79-56, A.79-65, A.80-08, A.80-25, A.81-09, A.86-56)
Title:	Hamilton Family fonds.
Dates:	1919–1986.
Extent:	2.5 m of textual records and other material
Biographical sketch:	Dr. T.G. (Thomas Glendenning) Hamilton was born in Agincourt, Ontario in 1873. In 1883, his family moved west to Saskatchewan and was among the first pioneer families to settle in Saskatoon. After his father died in 1891, his mother moved the family to Winnipeg where young T.G. Hamilton attended Manitoba College. He graduated from medical school in 1903, completed his internship at the Winnipeg General Hospital in 1904, and commenced practice in the district of Elmwood within Winnipeg. In 1915, he was President of the Manitoba Medical Association. Hamilton also served on the Public School Board for nine years, one year as chairman. He was also elected a member of the provincial legislature in 1914-1915. In 1918, soon after his young son's death, he began to experiment with psychic phenomena. His aim was the investigation of paranormal phenomena such as rappings, psychokinesis, ectoplasms, and materializations under scientific conditions that would minimize any possibility of error. His work became known in the United Kingdom, Europe, and the United States. In 1923, T.G. Hamilton was appointed to the Executive of the Canadian Medical Association as a representative for Manitoba; he held thie position until 1931. Between 1926 and 1935, he presented eighty-six lectures and wrote numerous articles that were published in Canada and abroad. Dr. Hamilton's wife, Lillian, carried on his paranormal experimentations following his death in 1935.
Custodial history:	The fonds was donated to University of Manitoba Archives & Special Collections by T.G. and Lillian's daughter, Margaret Hamilton Bach, and her daughters in several instalments between 1979 and 1986.
Scope and content:	The fonds is primarily related to Dr. T.G. and Lillian Hamilton's investigations of psychic phenomena spanning the years 1918 to 1945. The subject matter of the records includes rappings, clairvoyance, trance states and trance charts, telekinesis, wax molds, bell-ringing, transcripts and visions, as well as teleplasmic manifestations. The records are in the following various formats: scrapbooks, seance attendance records and registers, affidavits, automatic writings, correspondence, speeches and lectures, newsclippings, journal articles, books, photographs, glass plate negatives and positives, prints, slides, tapes, manuscripts, and promotional materials related to major publications. All positive prints taken from the photographic negatives have been retained with the written records of the experiments which they illustrate. Almost all the glass plate negatives were photographed for archival purposes, and the black and white glossy print collection is also available. A library of related books and journals which accompanied the collection has been separately catalogued and is available.
Restrictions:	There are no restrictions on this material.
Finding aid:	Printed finding aids are available in the Archives reading room

Figure 30.2 Global level description of the Hamilton Family collection at the University of Manitoba Archives & Special Collections.

Box	Folder	**Seance Attendance Registers:**
8	1	March 29, 1925–December 9, 1926—includes MSS & typed formats.
	2	January 20, 1927–December 29, 1929. Typed format, 1927 only.
	3	January 5, 1930–February 19, 1933.
	4	February 22, 1933–May 22, 1935.
	5	May 8, 1935–June 8, 1936. Original notes by Gladys and Dr Bruce Chown.
		Seance Directories:
Box	Folder	
8	6	Index April 1923–September, 1927.
	7	R.L.S. seance output index, April 1923–July 1925.
	8	"Book I—R.L.S. directory 1923–1927," MSS & typed format.
Box	Folder	
9	1	"Book II—R.L.S. Alone 1923–1925."
	2	"Book III—Directory 1925–1927."
	3	"Book IV—Directory 1927."
		Affidavits for Seance Sittings:
Box	Folder	
9	4	May 13, 1928—Bell Ringing
	5	September 23, 1928—Bellchords & Teleplasm.
	6	November 4, 1928—Spurgeon Face.
	7	November 25, 1928—5 Faces.

Figure 30.3 File-level inventory for the Hamilton Family collection at the University of Manitoba Archives & Special Collections.

Finding aids and inventories describe the contents of the collection using hierarchical levels of description such as the following:

- Group/fonds
- Subgroup/sousfonds
- Series
- Subseries
- File
- Item

A series is an intellectual grouping of like materials. "Correspondence," for example, might be a typical series title. File lists are simple lists of files in a collection without any attempt to distinguish groupings. A number of Canadian and other international archives employ something called the series system, which focuses descriptions on the series level and then links each series to all the creators and to all the files that belong to the series. This is particularly useful for describing government archives where names, functional responsibilities, and composition of departments frequently change. In these systems, users will begin by searching series descriptions.

It is important to remember two things: item-level finding aids are very rare and usually confined to special formats, such as photographs and maps, and not every archives has had the funds to retrospectively re-catalog their collections when they have changed access systems. Thus, an archives can have some holdings described one way and some holdings described another way, such as by a published guide, a card catalog, paper finding aids, and/or online finding aids.

Using Archives at the Institution

> I get slightly obsessive about working in archives because you don't know what you're going to find. In fact, you don't know what you're looking for until you find it.
>
> —Antony Beevor (quoted in Orr 2009)

If the librarian directs the researcher to approach a suitable institution, the researcher should first locate the institution's website, if such exists. Many institutions have restricted hours and special conditions for individual holdings based on donor restrictions and privacy concerns. In addition, a number of larger archives now store their collections in off-site storage once they run out of space in their main facilities. This can result in a day or longer wait time after materials have been requested. Making contact with the archives in advance will overcome these issues and will also help pinpoint the best materials to use for the request in advance of the visit. Staff might be able to predict the likelihood of finding the required information in the selected materials and might possibly assist in forwarding the researcher to a more appropriate location, saving the researcher a wasted trip.

If the researcher has a factual question that can be answered in a relatively brief period of time, most institutions will provide the answer directly to the researcher without the researcher having to come to the archives. If, however, the reference question requires a significant amount of time, or decisions need to be made along the research path (is this information important enough to continue the search here?), then the repositories will request that the researcher physically come to the archives or library and do the research themselves or will suggest that a research assistant be hired to do the research on the user's behalf. Once the researcher has actually gone to the archives, the archivists or librarians at the repository will guide the researcher through the access process. They will also explain more fully the nature and meaning of any restrictions that might apply to any of the records the user is interested in and help the researcher begin his search. Once records have been found, staff will assist the researcher in understanding the records and the context of their creation and provide support for getting any needed copies of records.

SOURCES BY COUNTRY OR REGION

The following discussion presents important websites and databases of primary and archival sources according to American, Canadian, UK, European, and International categories, followed by thematic categories. Newspaper sources are discussed in Chapter 23; sources related specifically to genealogical research are discussed in Chapter 25. Databases and websites are growing exponentially as archives, libraries, research centers, and commercial entities rush to provide access to these previously inaccessible resources. As universities in particular see these resources as one of the few ways to distinguish their institutions, they are making significant efforts to digitize their collections. This list provides a useful starting point of major collections of materials.

As has been noted, there is a strong geographic component to archival resource discovery. The following list separates institutions by country. The general rule is that one can expect to find the records of a country or its citizens in that country. Unfortunately, however, that is not always entirely true. North American universities often see their collecting mandates as very broad and hence acquire records from international sources.

United States

The National Archives and Records Administration (NARA) has holdings dating back to 1775, numbering literally billions of records of all types. Naturally, for a collection so large, there are a number of online tools and helpful instructional pages. In addition to an online catalog, there are a microfilm catalog and a number of archival databases that provide access to special formats. There is also a specialized guide to federal records. In addition to these finding aids, there is a specialized tool for researching veterans' service records. Actual copies of some of NARA's records have been digitized in conjunction with a number of organizations, such as *Google* and the University of Texas at Austin. A number of iconic documents, including the Constitution, the Louisiana Purchase, and Thomas Edison's patent application for the light bulb are available on NARA's *America's Historical Documents* page.

The *Library of Congress* website provides a wealth of information on the holdings of the Library of Congress. The main thrust of the collection is American history and culture through historic newspapers, sound recordings, prints, photographs, and U.S. legislative information and through the veterans' history project and website archiving. Finding aids to personal papers, such as the Alexander Graham Bell family papers and the Jackie Robinson papers, indicate what users might find if they come to the Library of Congress. However, the overwhelming majority of papers described were created by men, giving a decidedly lopsided view of American history. The Library of Congress's *American Memory* website presents selected collections that have been digitized. There is a cautionary note: the library has migrated some of its collections to a new system. Their intention is to eventually migrate all of the collections. Collections that have been migrated no longer appear in internal *American Memory* search results and browse lists. To search all Library collections (including *American Memory*) one must use the general search and browse options on the Library's main page.

The Smithsonian, a complex of nineteen museums and nine research centers and affiliates, provides both descriptions of holdings and online collections through its website, *Smithsonian*. Included are the Archives of American Art, the Smithsonian Archives, and the Smithsonian Libraries. In addition, many of the museums also have their own archives, such as the National Museum of the American Indian (NMAI), that go beyond the archives of the actual individual institution. *The Archive Center* of the NMAI actively collects the records of contemporary Native American artists, writers, activists, and organizations. Photographs from the archives can be accessed from the general *Collections Search* website.

ArchiveGrid was begun by the Research Libraries Group and contains over four million records for archival material held by over 1,000 different archives, libraries, museums, and historical societies. Coverage includes collections from around the world, but is primarily from institutionsin the United States. One can easily see which organizations are included. What is less obvious is that the material that is included is archival material that was cataloged for library catalogs and so therefore often more nearly resembles published primary sources or single archival records. From the Folger Shakespeare Library, for example, one can see a description of a handwritten book of recipes from 1675 from Thomas Sheppey. This would be useful for anyone researching food, customs, and so on. But is this the only item the Folger holds from this individual? Does the recipe book make up a part of a larger collection? Where did it come from and how did the Folger get it? Answers to these questions would make the item more useful to any serious scholars. Thus, *ArchiveGrid* is a useful starting point for identifying institutions with relevant material, but librarians might need to point the researcher to the institutions to learn more relevant information. The *Digital Public Library of America* is a portal that provides integrated access to more than ten million digitized items from libraries, archives, and museums throughout the United States. The website supports searching by topic, place, and date.

Web-based directories can assist in locating particular types of collections of primary and archival sources. *State Archives and Libraries* provides links to various state archives. Although many of the links are broken, the site provides the names of the state repositories that researchers can use in Internet searches. The *Lavender Legacies Guide* produced by the SAA's Lesbian and Gay Archives Roundtable is good for finding records relating to the lesbian and gay communities in North America. The *Directory of Corporate Archives in the United States and Canada* includes companies that maintain their historical records themselves, as well as other sources of company records.

Canada

Library and Archives Canada is the main repository for federal government records and many private records of national importance. An improvement in the user interface with the *Library and Archives Canada* website has made searching finding aids easier, as has the new version of *Collection Search*. There are also specialty portals for the most popular types of uses: genealogy and family history, censuses, military records, and portraits. The site is available in Canada's official languages, French and English.

Most of the provinces and territories in Canada have provincial archival organizations that maintain databases that include collection-level descriptions. Although the coverage varies from database to database, these portals are generally important sources to find records held by small- and medium-sized archival institutions, particularly those that are unable to support their own descriptive databases. When seeking information from larger organizations, such as university archives, it is generally better to go straight to the websites of those institutions as the holdings will be fuller and more up to date than what is included in these portals. The Canadian Council of Archives provides access to an online *Directory of Archives*.

A major source of radio broadcasts and television footage is the archives of the Canadian Broadcasting Corporation (CBC), the national public radio and television broadcaster. The *CBC Digital Archives* provides excellent online access to its most popular broadcasts. It also has a music archive of original CBC commissions, a library of CBC publications, and a photo collection made up primarily of publicity shots taken by the CBC's own photographers in the 1950s, 1960s, and 1970s.

United Kingdom

The National Archives provides a strong search tool that allows users to search the records from the Archives as well as over 2,500 archives across the United Kingdom. Users can also narrow the search down to just those held by the National Archives. As might be expected from the National Archives, the results are excellent.

A Directory of Rare Book and Special Collections in the UK and Republic of Ireland, edited by B. C. Bloomfield (1997), lists information on approximately 1,200 libraries, archives, museums, and private holdings providing details on the contents of these institutions as well as their locations and contact information. Although the majority of this information is about published books, manuscripts held by these institutions are also included.

Europe

Archives Portal Europe provides for a federated search across sixty million descriptive units of archives contained in 865 institutions as well as important details such as their location, access conditions, and hours of service. *Europeana* allows users to explore millions of items from a range of Europe's leading galleries, libraries, archives, and museums. Items include books and manuscripts, photos and paintings, television and film, sculpture and crafts, diaries and maps, sheet music, and recordings. The Czech Republic has produced *Manuscriptorium*, a subaggregator for *Europeana*, which provides access to "historic book resources," including manuscripts, maps, charters, and university theses. Materials display in their original language although the interface is in eleven different languages. *Manuscriptorium* is both a catalog of descriptions of online holdings and a collection of a smaller number of digitized images.

European History Primary Sources is a joint initiative of the Library and the Department of History and Civilization of the European University Institute in Florence, Italy. It provides a one-stop location for visiting archives and libraries of primary and archival sources throughout Europe.

Other Countries

There are many sites all over the world that feature the archives of that country, particularly offered by national institutions. The drawback of course is that users must understand the language of the country. However, one website that is close to home and provides access in English is at the Library of Congress. The Library of Congress, with support from UNESCO, has created the *World Digital Library*. In addition to books, there are archival materials from a wide variety of institutions, such as the Bibliothèque nationale de France and the Tetouan Asmir Association of Morocco. The strength of the website is that it provides all navigation tools, bibliographic information, and content descriptions in seven languages: Arabic, Chinese, English, French, Portuguese, Russian, and Spanish. Additionally, the metadata and descriptions can be listened to using text-to-voice conversion in all of these languages.

RESOURCES BY SUBJECT

There are many websites and subscription-only online databases that focus on specialized subjects, providing an easier way for users interested in subjects or topics, rather than individuals, to do their research. Many of these databases include materials from both the United States and Canada and occasionally other countries. Most sites are a hybrid of archival, primary, and published sources. Even the archival material on these sites would be considered more primary sources, however, for though the publishers cite the origins of the material, they present each document on its own as if it were a publication. It would take a great deal of digging to get back to the repository where the original is described to see what other records might enhance the user's understanding of the context. The great strength of these databases is the ability to search across materials because of the detailed metadata attached to each image. These websites are mostly digitized documents, although occasionally there may be descriptions and actual finding aids as well.

Gale Primary Sources allows users to search across a number of primary source collections including: *Archives of Sexuality and Gender*; *Indigenous Peoples: North America*; *Nineteenth Century Collections Online*; *Slavery and Anti-Slavery: A Transnational Archive*; and *Women's Studies Archive: Women's Issues and Identities*, among others. Some of the scanned documentation is very poor, with text cut off and very low-resolution facsimile images that are difficult to decipher.

ProQuest has its own subscription database of archival documents on American history from the 18th to the 20th centuries called *ProQuest History Vault*. Although the main emphasis is on Southern, African American, and women's history, there is also material relating to political science, military and diplomatic history, immigration, and so on.

American Foreign Policy

For general historic U.S. government documents, there are a number of websites to explore (see Chapter 26). In addition, however, there has been a growing interest in foreign policy and security. There are official publications from the American government, for instance, the book series *Foreign Relations of the United States*, which is published by the Office of the Historian in the U.S. Department of State. This series presents the official record of major U.S. foreign policy decisions and significant diplomatic activity and includes declassified records from foreign affairs agencies. The series began publication in 1861. *HeinOnline* provides access to these volumes from 1861 to 1980, or users can go to the *Historical Documents* website of the U.S. Department of State Office of the Historian and search the volumes covering the presidencies from the Truman administration to the Carter administration from 1945 to 1980.

ProQuest provides subscription access to the *Digital National Security Archive*, which consists of declassified documents dealing with U.S. foreign policy and intelligence and security issues from post–World War II to the 21st century. From this site, there is access to the intriguingly named "CIA Family Jewels Indexed." ProQuest has indexed this file, which dates from 1973 and documents the illegal activities that the CIA was engaged in, such as assassinations, interrogations, surveillance, and so on. You can freely access *The CIA's Family Jewels* without ProQuest's helpful index from *The National Security Archive* at George Washington University. They also provide access to other unpublished and published declassified documents on issues including U.S. national security, foreign policy, diplomatic and military history, and intelligence policy.

African Americans

Although *Black Thought and Culture: African Americans from Colonial Times to the Present* by Alexander Street Press presents primarily published material by leaders within the Black community, it also contains pamphlets, letters, and other primary sources. The collection is intended for research in Black studies, political science, American history, music, literature, and art. Adam Matthew's *Slavery, Abolition and Social Justice* is designed as an important portal for slavery and abolition studies, bringing together documents and collections dating from 1490 to 2007. Another good site is Vanderbilt University's *Slave Societies Digital Archive*, which preserves and makes available endangered documents relating to Africans and their descendants in the Atlantic world.

American History

A number of commercial online resources provide information on American history. Alexander Street Press offers a number of databases relating to various themes. *Early Encounters in North America: Peoples, Cultures and the Environment* documents the relationships among peoples and their environment in North America from 1534 to 1850. *North American Immigrant Letters, Diaries, and Oral Histories* provides access to private records about immigration to America and Canada, including letters, diaries, pamphlets, autobiographies, and oral histories, and dates from around 1840 to the present, although the predominant dates are from 1920 to 1980. Both *North American Immigrant Letters* and *Early Encounters* provide only transcriptions, which strip the text of context but make it easier to use for people who do not read cursive handwriting.

Sage Knowledge has produced *Historic Documents*, which is an online version of the Historic Documents print editions. Published annually since 1972, the Historic Documents volumes present transcriptions of approximately 100 documents covering the most significant events of the year. Because these are single documents, it makes it very difficult to get a sense of the context.

Human Rights

Many websites have sprung up, particularly in the last decade, featuring human rights archives and primary sources. Often these sites have been created by university libraries to assist in the preservation and dissemination of human rights materials for academics and students. These types of records are fragile not only because of the circumstances of their creation, often in countries struggling with poverty and extreme environmental conditions, but also because the records themselves are often the targets of destruction. These archives are not necessarily always physical. In some cases, the organizations have been digitizing the documents and returning them to their country of origin. In others, institutions or agencies have retained original documents. For instance, the U.S. Secretary of Defense's *Conflict Records Research Center*, active until 2015, held onto the physical records of the Saddam Hussein regime, a move not entirely without controversy. The access conditions for each of these archives vary widely, depending upon the sensitivity of the information, their dates, and so on.

The Columbia University Libraries' *Center for Human Rights Documentation & Research* holds a variety of archival collections including records of Amnesty International USA and Human Rights Watch. The center also holds the *Human Rights Web Archive*, a searchable collection of archived copies of human rights websites created by nongovernmental organizations, national human rights institutions, tribunals, and individuals. The Duke University Libraries' *Human Rights Archive* has been acquiring records and papers of human rights advocates. Their collections are as diverse as Radio Haiti records and the Southern Poverty Law Center collection of extremist literature. The University of Texas Libraries of the University of Texas at Austin maintains the *Human Rights Documentation Initiative*, which helps to preserve vulnerable records of human rights activities around the world. Significant holdings include the Free Burma Rangers, the Genocide Archive for Rwanda, and the Guatemalan National Police Historical Archive.

The University of Southern California's *Shoah Foundation* has an archive of nearly 52,000 testimonies of survivors and witnesses to the Holocaust. The foundation is also incorporating collections of testimonies on the Cambodian, Rwandan, and Armenian genocides. The *Human Rights Collection* at Archives & Special Collections at the Thomas J. Dodd Research Center of the University of Connecticut includes such archives as the U. Roberto (Robin) Romano digital photographs of child labor and the African National Congress Oral History Transcripts Collection.

The *National Centre for Truth and Reconciliation* at the University of Manitoba in Winnipeg is the site for the records of the Truth and Reconciliation Commission of Canada. This includes recorded testimonies of survivors of the Canadian Indian Residential School system and digital copies of records relating to the schools from the federal government and churches, as well as records relating to the Settlement process, which established the commission.

Indigenous Peoples

There are a number of key websites in North America and internationally dedicated to preserving records relating to indigenous peoples. In the United States, *The Plateau Peoples' Web Portal* provides access to archival records held in Washington State University's Manuscripts, Archives and Special Collections, the Northwest Museum of Arts and Culture, and private donors, among others. In Canada, the *Reciprocal Research Network* at the University of British Columbia holds museum items focused on Northwest Coast museum collections as well as nearly 300,000 photographs, including historic photos, from twenty-four partner institutions. The Métis National Council's *Historical Online Database* is a Web-interfaced database that contains genealogical information on individuals of the historic Métis Nation. The website also contains scans of many of the original documents represented in the database; many of the documents were created by other organizations and institutions.

Internationally, the *Australian Institute of Aboriginal and Torres Strait Islander Studies* provides access to descriptions about original photographs, rare serials, photographs, moving images, and sound recordings on Australia's indigenous population through the Mura catalog. Two hundred people who were in care or were child migrants were interviewed by the National Library of Australia for the *Forgotten Australians and Former Child Migrants Oral History Project*. In New Zealand, there are Māori archives held by a number of institutions including *Archives New Zealand* and the *National Library of New Zealand*.

There are a number of online subscription databases relating to indigenous people. *American Indian Histories and Cultures* from Adam Matthew includes manuscripts, artwork, photographs, and newspapers dating from contact to the mid-20th century. Gale's *Indigenous Peoples: North America* covers collections from across Canadian and American institutions that provide insight into the cultural, political, and social history of Native Peoples from the 17th into the 20th centuries. Alexander Street Press provides access to biographies, autobiographies, oral histories, reference works, manuscripts, and photographs in the database *North American Indian Thought and Culture*. Again, the coverage is North American.

Women

An excellent general site for finding resources on women is the *Women's History Research in Archives* guide at UW-Madison Libraries. It provides links to sites on professional women, women of color, Jewish women, lesbian archives, and websites devoted to women's archives in different parts of the United States and around the world. Alexander Street Press has two online resources relating to women. *North American Women's Letters and Diaries: Colonial to 1950* includes transcriptions of both published letters and diaries and unpublished materials from individuals writing from Colonial times to 1950. *Women and Social Movements in the United States 1600–2000* brings together images, documents, scholarly essays, and commentaries on women's reform activities.

SOURCES FOR SPECIFIC MEDIA

Sometimes users are looking for particular media or formats, such as oral histories or sound and moving image archives. This is a popular way for organizations to group primary and archival sources, particularly with photographs. The following section provides information about sources for these various types of materials. General sources discussed above will also include these types of media.

Digital Archives

The Internet Archive's *Wayback Machine* is hosted in the United States. It is a service that allows people to visit archived versions of sites on the World Wide Web. Visitors to the *Wayback Machine* can type in a URL, select a date range, and then begin surfing on an archived version of the Web. This is an extremely useful resource, but the harvesting has not been consistent, so not all changes to a website will necessarily be represented and often links to external and even sometimes internal Web pages are broken.

Oral Histories

Oral History Online from Alexander Street Press is a database of English language oral histories, including Ellis Island oral history narratives and exclusive Black Panther Party interviews. The interface is not always easy to use as some links to resources take the user to the collecting institution where it is necessary to conduct another search. *American Rhetoric* is a massive multimedia site that contains over 5,000 full-text, audio, and video versions of public speeches, legal proceedings, lectures, debates, interviews, and other recorded media events, and 200 short audio clips from well-known speeches, sermons, popular songs, and media events by politicians, actors, preachers, and other noteworthy personalities.

Photographs

There are a number of free and commercial sites dedicated to providing access to historic photographs. Many of the sites provide access to both still and moving images. The *AP Images* photo archive features state, regional, and national photos from North America as well as international photos. The historical section in particular features iconic photographs of people, places, objects, and events in various themed categories such as sports and entertainment. *Artstor* provides access to nearly two million digital images that cover the arts, architecture, humanities, and the sciences from museums, photo archives, scholars, and artists. Although *Artstor* bills itself as an image library, there are a number of primary source collections, including Magnum Photos, the Thomas K. Seligman Archive, and a selection from the Condé Nast Archive of Photography, among others.

Flickr is a free photo sharing service. A number of archives and libraries have established photostreams. One of the most important is the Library of Congress, which has uploaded nearly 23,000 images from its collections. Unfortunately, the results from searching *Flickr* for primary or archival images are hit and miss. Few libraries and archives have really taken to the site to disseminate their holdings. But searching on the *Flickr Commons*, launched in 2008, provides an easier way to discover primary and archival images. The quality of the images and the metadata is sometimes lacking, but *Flickr Commons* can be a good place to start for a beginner.

George Eastman House has its own historic *Photography* collection, which contains a selection from their large photo collection. Daguerreotypes, 19th-century British and French photography on paper, and 19th-century American holdings have been uploaded onto *Flickr Commons* and are freely available.

Millions of images, both photos and drawings, from *Life* magazine dating back to as early as the 1860s have been uploaded into *Google Images* and can be searched by adding "source:life" to any *Google Images* search or searched from the *Life* photo archive page. Most of these images were never published. These images can be used for personal, noncommercial use without having to pay for the use.

Sound and Moving Images

There are a number of websites for accessing moving images that could be considered primary sources. On *YouTube*, if the phrase "old commercials" is entered into the search bar, advertisements from 1940 to 1970 will be retrieved, including television advertisements. *ResearchChannel* on *YouTube* provides one-stop shopping for videos from research and academic institutions on such topics as the hurricane-climate connection and the origin of cancer. The videos are a mixture of documentaries and oral interviews.

The *Internet Archive* includes films, video, community video, television shows, and advertisements on its site. Many film titles created by U.S. corporations, non-profit organizations, trade associations, community and interest groups, and educational institutions included in the Prelinger Archives are accessible through the *Internet Archive.*

The *Open Video Project,* sponsored by the Interaction Design Laboratory at the School of Information and Library Science, University of North Carolina Chapel Hill, is a growing repository of both clips and full digital video and digitized video in the historical, documentary, educational, public service, and ephemeral arenas.

CONCLUSION

Major publishers and a number of archives and libraries have tried to bridge the gap between users who are accustomed to searching by subject and the standard arrangement of archival resources listed by creator by developing websites focused on a particular subject. If users are trying to complete assignments, or they do not need a specific answer, these websites are usually sufficient. These websites can also be good places to start a more in-depth search. But for specific answers and for any intensive research that relies on facts related to specific people and events, archives are usually the only way to find the answers. By using a method of matching topics to persons, and then matching the persons to a geographic place, the reference librarian can often determine where likely collections will reside and point the patrons there online first, and then to the physical location as a follow up.

REFERENCES

Bureau of Canadian Archivists. 2008. *Rules for Archival Description.* Ottawa: Bureau of Canadian Archivists.

Orr, Deborah. 2009. "Antony Beevor: 'History Has Not Emphasised Enough the Suffering of French Civilians During the War.'" *The Independent,* June 6, 2009. http://www.independent.co.uk/news/world/europe/antony-beevor-history-has-not-emphasised-enough-the-suffering-of-french-civilians-during-the-war-1696148.html.

Pearce-Moses, Richard. 2005. *A Glossary of Archival and Records Terminology.* Chicago: Society of American Archivists. https://www2.archivists.org/glossary.

Sweetman, H. S. 2008. *Calendar of Documents Relating to Ireland Preserved in Her Majesty's Public Record Office.* Burlington, ON: TannerRichie.

LIST OF SOURCES

America's Historical Documents. National Archives and Records Administration. http://www.archives.gov/historical-docs/.

American Indian Histories and Cultures. Chicago: Adam Matthew. http://www.amdigital.co.uk/m-collections/collection/american-indian-histories-and-cultures/. Subscription required.

American Memory. Library of Congress. http://memory.loc.gov/ammem/index.html.
American Rhetoric. http://www.americanrhetoric.com/.
AP Images. New York: Associated Press. http://www.apimages.com/historical-photo-archive. Subscription required for full access.
Archive Center. National Museum of the American Indian. http://nmai.si.edu/explore/collections/archive/.
ArchiveGrid. Dublin, OH: OCLC. http://beta.worldcat.org/archivegrid/.
Archives New Zealand. http://archives.govt.nz/.
Archives of Manitoba. http://www.gov.mb.ca/chc/archives/.
Archives of Ontario. http://www.archives.gov.on.ca/en/index.aspx.
Archives Portal Europe. The Hague, Netherlands: APEx project. http://www.archivesportaleurope.net/.
Archives of Sexuality and Gender. Farmington Hills, MI: Gale Cengage Learning. https://www.gale.com/primary-sources/archives-of-sexuality-and-gender. Subscription required.
Artstor. New York: Artstor. http://www.artstor.org/index.shtml. Subscription required.
Australian Institute of Aboriginal and Torres Strait Islander Studies. http://www.aiatsis.gov.au/main.html.
Bibliothèque nationale de France. http://www.bnf.fr/en/tools/a.welcome_to_the_bnf.html.
Black Thought and Culture: African Americans from Colonial Times to the Present. Alexandria, VA: Alexander Street. http://alexanderstreet.com/products/black-thought-and-culture. Subscription required.
Bloomfield, B.C., ed. 1997. *A Directory of Rare Book and Special Collections in the UK and Republic of Ireland*. London: Library Association.
CBC Digital Archives. CBC/Radio Canada. http://www.cbc.ca/archives/.
Center for Human Rights Documentation & Research. Columbia University Libraries. http://library.columbia.edu/locations/chrdr.html.
CIA Family Jewels Indexed. Ann Arbor, MI: ProQuest. https://proquest.libguides.com/dnsa/familyjewels. Subscription required.
The CIA's Family Jewels. The National Security Archive. https://nsarchive2.gwu.edu/NSAEBB/NSAEBB222/.
The Coca-Cola Company. http://www.coca-colacompany.com/history/.
Digital National Security Archive. Ann Arbor, MI: ProQuest. https://www.proquest.com/products-services/databases/dnsa.html. Subscription required.
Digital Public Library of America. http://dp.la.
Directory of Archives. Canadian Council of Archives. http://www.cdncouncilarchives.ca/directory.html.
Directory of Corporate Archives in the United States and Canada. Society of American Archivists. http://www2.archivists.org/groups/business-archives-section/directory-of-corporate-archives-in-the-united-states-and-canada-introduction.
Early Encounters in North America: Peoples, Cultures and the Environment. Alexandria, VA: Alexander Street. http://alexanderstreet.com/products/early-encounters-north-america-peoples-cultures-and-environment. Subscription required.
European History Primary Sources. European University Institute. http://primary-sources.eui.eu.
Europeana. http://www.europeana.eu/.
Flickr. https://www.flickr.com/.
Flickr Commons. http://www.flickr.com/commons.
Folger Shakespeare Library. https://www.folger.edu/.
Foreign Relations of the United States. Getzville, NY: HeinOnline. https://home.heinonline.org/titles/Foreign-Relations-of-the-United-States-FRUS/. Subscription required.
Forgotten Australians and Former Child Migrants Oral History Project. National Library of Australia. http://www.nla.gov.au/oral-history/forgotten-australians-and-former-child-migrants-oral-history-project.

Gale Primary Sources. Farmington Hills, MI: Gale Cengage Learning. https://www.gale.com/primary-sources. Subscription required.

Google Images. https://images.google.com/.

The Henry Ford. http://www.thehenryford.org/.

Historic Documents. 1972–. Thousand Oaks, CA: Sage.

Historical Documents. Office of the Historian. U.S. Department of State. https://history.state.gov/historicaldocuments.

Historical Online Database. Métis National Council. http://www.barbau.ca/content/metis-national-council-historical-online-database.

Human Rights Archive. Duke University Libraries. http://library.duke.edu/rubenstein/human-rights/.

Human Rights Collection. Archives & Special Collections at the University of Connecticut Libraries. https://humanrights.uconn.edu/human-rights-research-at-uconn/.

Human Rights Documentation Initiative. University of Texas Libraries. University of Texas at Austin. https://repositories.lib.utexas.edu/handle/2152/4022.

Human Rights Web Archive. Columbia University Libraries. https://hrwa.cul.columbia.edu/.

Indigenous Peoples: North America. Farmington Hills, MI: Gale Cengage Learning. https://www.gale.com/c/indigenous-peoples-north-america. Subscription required.

Internet Archive. https://archive.org/

Lavender Legacies Guide. Society of American Archivists. http://www2.archivists.org/groups/lesbian-and-gay-archives-roundtable-lagar/lavender-legacies-guide.

Legal History on the Web. Triangle Legal History Seminar. http://law.duke.edu/legal_history/portal/primary-sources.html.

Library and Archives Canada. https://www.bac-lac.gc.ca/eng/Pages/home.aspx.

Library of Congress. http://www.loc.gov/.

Life Photo Archive Hosted by Google. http://images.google.com/hosted/life.

Manuscriptorium. National Library of the Czech Republic. http://www.manuscriptorium.com.

Māori. Archives New Zealand. https://archives.govt.nz/search-the-archive/researching/research-guides/maori.

The National Archives. http://discovery.nationalarchives.gov.uk/.

National Archives and Records Administration. http://www.archives.gov/.

National Centre for Truth and Reconciliation. University of Manitoba. http://nctr.ca/map.php/2015.html.

National Library of New Zealand. https://natlib.govt.nz/.

National Scouting Museum. Boy Scouts of America. http://www.philmontscoutranch.org/Museums.aspx.

The National Security Archive. The George Washington University. https://nsarchive.gwu.edu/.

Nineteenth Century Collections Online. Farmington Hills, MI: Gale Cengage Learning. https://www.gale.com/primary-sources/nineteenth-century-collections-online. Subscription required.

North American Immigrant Letters, Diaries, and Oral Histories. Alexandria, VA: Alexander Street. http://alexanderstreet.com/products/north-american-immigrant-letters-diaries-and-oral-histories. Subscription required.

North American Indian Thought and Culture. Alexandria, VA: Alexander Street. http://alexanderstreet.com/products/north-american-indian-thought-and-culture. Subscription required.

North American Women's Letters and Diaries: Colonial to 1950. Alexandria, VA: Alexander Street. http://alexanderstreet.com/products/north-american-womens-letters-and-diaries. Subscription required.

Northwest Museum of Arts and Culture. https://www.northwestmuseum.org/

NSDAR Archives. National Society Daughters of the American Revolution. https://www.dar.org/archives.

The Open Video Project. School of Information and Library Science. University of North Carolina at Chapel Hill. http://www.open-video.org/.

Oral History Online. Alexandria, VA: Alexander Street. http://orhi.alexanderstreet.com. Subscription required.

Past Masters: Full Text Humanities. Charlottesville, VA: InteLex Corporation. http://www.nlx.com/home. Subscription required.

Photography. George Eastman Museum. https://www.eastman.org/photography.

Plateau Peoples' Web Portal. http://plateauportal.wsulibs.wsu.edu/html/ppp/index.php.

Prelinger Archives. https://archive.org/details/prelinger&tab=about.

ProQuest History Vault. Ann Arbor, MI: ProQuest. http://www.proquest.com/libraries/academic/primary-sources/historyvault.html. Subscription required.

Reciprocal Research Network. http://www.rrncommunity.org/.

ResearchChannel. YouTube. https://www.youtube.com/user/ResearchChannel.

Roosevelt, Theodore. 1951–54. 8 vols. *Letters*. Edited by Elting E. Morison. Cambridge. MA: Harvard University Press.

Shoah Foundation. University of Southern California. https://sfi.usc.edu/.

Slave Societies Digital Archive. Vanderbilt University. https://www.slavesocieties.org/.

Slavery, Abolition and Social Justice. Chicago: Adam Matthew. http://www.amdigital.co.uk/m-collections/collection/slavery-abolition-and-social-justice/. Subscription required.

Slavery and Anti-Slavery: A Transnational Archive. Farmington Hills, MI: Gale Cengage Learning. https://www.gale.com/primary-sources/slavery-and-anti-slavery. Subscription required.

Smithsonian. http://www.si.edu/.

State Archives and Libraries. Clear Digital Media. http://statearchives.us/index.htm.

Tetouan Asmir Association of Morocco. https://www.tetouanasmir.org/.

Waley, Arthur. 1958. *The Opium War Through Chinese Eyes*. Stanford, CA: Stanford University Press.

WayBack Machine. Internet Archive. https://archive.org/web/.

Women's History Research in Archives. University of Wisconsin-Madison Libraries. http://researchguides.library.wisc.edu/c.php?g=177948&p=1168872.

Women and Social Movements in the United States 1600–2000. Alexandria, VA: Alexander Street. http://womhist.alexanderstreet.com/. Subscription required.

Women's Studies Archive: Women's Issues and Identities. Farmington Hills, MI: Gale Cengage Learning. https://www.gale.com/c/womens-studies-archive-womens-issues-and-identities. Subscription required.

World Digital Library. Library of Congress. http://www.wdl.org/en/.

YouTube. https://www.youtube.com/.

SUGGESTED READINGS

Cook, Terry. 1997. "What Is Past Is Prologue: A History of Archival Ideas since 1898, and the Future Paradigm Shift." *Archivaria* 43 (Spring): 17–63.

This article by the giant of archival science, Terry Cook, is written for the archival practitioner, but is a seminal work that explores the evolution of thinking about archives that will give non-archivists good insight into the archival profession.

Duranti, Luciana, and Patricia C. Franks, eds. 2015. *Encyclopedia of Archival Science*. Lanham, MD: Rowman & Littlefield.

This work provides definitions for all major aspects of archival science written by experts in the field. This does not present theories and concepts in plain language, but for those interested in learning more without having to wade through lengthy articles, this will be the place to start.

Harris, Verne. 2007. *Archives and Justice: A South African Perspective.* Chicago: Society of American Archivists.

Verne Harris, who was Director of the South African History Archive and archivist for South Africa's Truth and Reconciliation Commission, has been the Head of the Memory Programme at the Nelson Mandela Foundation's Centre of Memory and Dialogue since 2004. This is a volume of his best writing about archives during the period of post-apartheid democracy.

Jimerson, Randall C. 2009. *Archives Power: Memory, Accountability, and Social Justice.* Chicago: Society of American Archivists.

This text revolves around the role of the archivist, but the context of that role will be important for librarians who are wondering about the importance of archives. Rand Jimerson considers the intersection of archives, memory, identity, accountability, and social justice. He feels there is a renewed emphasis on remembrance, evidence, and documentation in order to make governments accountable and transparent.

Millar, Laura, and Association of British Columbia Archivists Small Archives Committee. 1994. *A Manual for Small Archives.* 2nd ed. Vancouver: Association of British Columbia Archivists.

This textbook, although dated, provides a very good overview of archival practice for people who may be responsible for an archives but do not have any training. As such, this work is useful for reference librarians who might want to get an overview of archives practice.

O'Toole, James M., and Richard J Cox. 2006. *Understanding Archives and Manuscripts.* Chicago: Society of American Archivists.

This is an American text for students and beginning practitioners. It gives a good overview of the history of the archival profession, the organization of archival records, and the theory and practice of archives in an increasingly electronic world.

Chapter 31

Legal Sources

Paul D. Healey

INTRODUCTION

Law and legal issues permeate American life. For this reason, legal questions are very common at the reference desk of almost any library. In the past, it was generally not possible for librarians to provide much in the way of legal reference service, except at specialized law libraries, because legal reference materials were expensive, were highly technical in nature, and required lots of shelf space.

The Web has changed much of this. Although specialized legal research tools used by attorneys are still very expensive and difficult to use, most basic legal materials are freely available in authoritative forms on the Web, and librarians in all kinds of libraries now have access to the tools and information required to provide basic reference service for legal questions.

Unfortunately, legal reference questions raise at least two major issues. First, there exists the possibility of personal legal liability for a reference librarian who does not handle a legal reference question in the right way. Second, the highly technical and complex nature of many legal questions remains a formidable barrier to providing appropriate legal information.

This chapter begins by looking at the professional and legal issues that arise when handling legal information requests and discusses how to handle them appropriately. This is followed by a discussion of the technical nature of legal information in order to provide the reader with some background on these issues. Finally, the chapter provides an overview of the array of print, online, and web-based resources that are currently available for providing legal reference service.

PROFESSIONAL ISSUES IN PROVIDING LEGAL REFERENCE

As with any area of reference, good legal reference service requires some familiarity with available resources and an understanding of how those resources might serve a user's needs. With legal reference, however, additional issues arise. How a user intends to use legal information and how the reference librarian interacts with that user are very important.

Liability

Legal reference is relatively unique in that it is one area of reference service where the librarian's actions could conceivably lead to legal liability. This is because it is theoretically possible that providing legal reference service could be construed as giving legal advice and thus constitute the unauthorized practice of law.[1] As of the date of this writing, no reference librarian has ever been charged with unauthorized practice of law for providing legal reference services but the risk, if theoretical, is still real.[2]

Before exploring the nature of this potential liability, and how to avoid it, it may be helpful to explore why library users are searching for legal information, and how this affects the liability issue. Put simply, people who seek legal information can be divided into two groups: those who are searching for legal information for some general purpose and those who are looking for legal information in order to pursue their own legal interests.

People who are seeking legal information for some general purpose, such as writing a paper on a legal topic or simply to inform themselves, but are not pursuing their own legal interests are generally not a matter of concern. The key distinction is that the information request is not related to the individual's own legal interests. Such users can be treated like any other reference service user. The issue of liability arises only when the librarian's reference activities involve acting like a lawyer by providing legal information that could be seen as legal advice.

The second group consists of library users who are seeking legal information in order to pursue their own legal interests. These people may be engaged in a variety of activities, from litigation to divorce or drafting their own will, as the possibilities for involvement in legal issues are many and varied. The key issue here is that the library user is seeking legal information in order to protect or pursue their personal legal interests.

It is this fact that raises the liability issue for librarians. Although one might imagine that it would be clear-cut what activities constitute the practice of law, in fact the practice of law has never been clearly defined.[3] The giving of legal advice is one of the activities that appears in all definitions of the practice of law. Giving legal advice is only broadly defined, but in some instances, it could include providing legal information, which raises the issue of liability for librarians. Unfortunately, although many researchers have pursued the topic over the years, no one has been able to draw a clear line between what constitutes appropriate legal reference service and what constitutes legal advice (for further reading on this issue, see Healey 2002).

Avoiding Liability

In order to avoid liability, librarians should present themselves as an expert on finding information, but not as experts on the information they find. This is a dictum with plenty of gray areas, but the distinction is crucial.

Although the concept of giving legal advice remains frustratingly undefined, at its heart is the idea of one person advising another person what to do to protect their legal interests. If a reference librarian were to suggest to library users what area of law to research, or what legal form might meet their needs, that could constitute advising them on how to pursue their own legal interests, and thus constitute legal advice. As a librarian responding to a legal reference question, the key point is to avoid exercising any kind of legal judgment in providing legal information.

It is clearly acceptable for a librarian to answer questions that might be referred to as ready reference. A specific request for a statute or a form, when the item requested is clearly identified, does not involve a legal judgment. Similarly, answering a request for information on a legal topic is not a problem when the answer is to refer the user to a resource that they can explore to answer their own question. However, getting involved in the question itself, including offering opinions on appropriate legal solutions to the problem, should be strictly avoided.

One of the potential dangers is the urge to relate personal experiences when responding to questions. A librarian who has been through a divorce or written a will might be tempted to offer his perspective based on that experience. The message here is to strictly avoid such an urge. Librarians simply must restrict themselves to providing the information the user is seeking.

Other Professional Issues

In addition to liability, other professional issues arise when providing legal reference service to people who are pursuing their own legal interests. While none of these rises to the level of a liability issue for the librarian, the ethical problems they create are quite real. These issues are also not unique to legal questions but are definitely important in this context.

The first issue is confidentiality. Librarians have a strong ethic of confidentiality at the reference desk (for more on confidentiality in the reference transaction, see Chapter 2). In the case of legal questions, the library user may be dealing with an issue that is extremely personal, and potentially embarrassing. Under the circumstances, protecting confidentiality becomes crucial. Talking about a user's question with others could not only prove embarrassing or difficult for the user, but could in some cases lead to harm. Imagine a person trying to find a legal way out of an abusive domestic relationship. Loose talk about that person's situation could actually put that patron in danger. Confidentiality with legal reference questions is a must.

The second issue is conflict of interest. While this issue is rare at the reference desk, in a legal dispute it is not unreasonable to assume that people on different sides of the dispute might seek information at the same reference desk. In such a situation, it is important to treat both library users fairly and equally and to refrain from becoming personally involved in the issue. This problem also reinforces the need for confidentiality.

A third issue is reliance and harm. In law, reliance takes place when a person believes that they can trust advice they have been given. If they rely on erroneous advice, they could be harmed in some way. Many library users see reference librarians as educated professionals and readily accept and trust the information they get at the reference desk. For most purposes, this is desirable, and it is desirable in legal reference, so long as the patron understands that they are being given information and not legal advice.

If library users seeking legal information get the impression that the librarian is an expert on law, and the librarian offers an opinion or advice, they may rely on the librarian to their detriment. This is particularly a problem in specialized law libraries, where many of the librarians are, in fact, legally trained. However, even in a nonlaw library, it would be possible for a librarian to act in such a way that library users get the impression that they are getting expert information. Even if it did not lead to allegations of giving legal advice, it would be unfortunate if this led to reliance and subsequent harm. It is far better to simply supply information as requested and let users make their own assessment of the information they receive and decide how to use it.

A Restrained Approach to Legal Reference

Librarians are dedicated to providing access to information for all library users, generally striving to answer reference questions fully and completely. To hold back information or skimp on a response feels wrong as a professional. However, the legal and professional issues discussed previously demonstrate that it is theoretically possible for a librarian answering legal reference questions to cause problems for users, or even be accused of unauthorized practice of law. The result is a requirement that librarians take a more restrained approach to answering legal reference questions. This approach protects both the librarian and the user.

When presented with a legal question, librarians should provide complete, fair, and balanced information to the extent possible. Librarians should avoid becoming involved in the question or the research, avoid appearing to be an expert on the topic, and avoid giving any kind of advice (see Box 31.1).

Box 31.1 Responding to Requests for Legal Advice

Library users with legal questions often do not understand that librarians cannot give them a direct answer and sometimes become frustrated. When a user asks a question that would require a legal answer (e.g., "How do I file for divorce?" or "What is the law on. . .") the best response is to remind the user that you cannot answer the question itself, but you can help them find information on it.

Examples of good responses include the following:

- "I can't answer that question for you, but I can show you some materials that might let you find the answer."
- "That's a legal question, and I'm not a lawyer. However, we do have some legal resources that might help. Let me show them to you."
- "Legal questions are quite complicated. We have some materials that I can show you that might help."

The important point is to make sure that users don't feel that you have answered a legal question for them. Keep in mind the following ideas when dealing with legal questions:

- Do not get personally involved. Even if you have experienced a similar legal situation, stay in role as a librarian and restrict yourself to helping the user find information.
- Another library may have better resources. If there is a reasonably close law library open to the public, you may want to refer the user to that library.
- Do not be shy about suggesting that a user seek legal counsel. Often, a user has already considered this option and rejected it, but once the user encounters the difficulty of doing legal research or representing themselves, they may reconsider.

BASIC CONCEPTS IN LEGAL INFORMATION

Law is a very complicated and technical subject. While it is best that librarians take a restrained approach to answering legal reference questions, some knowledge of the structure of law and the structure of legal materials will be useful in locating information in response to a legal question.

The Structure of Law in the United States

The American system of government is a federal system. This means that rather than being one country with subdivisions, the United States consists of fifty separate states, each with the sovereign power to make law, united under a federal government, which can also make laws. The federal government and fifty sovereign state governments are all structured in roughly the same way and generally make law in the same form. The federal and state governments are each set up by, and operate under, a constitution, and in each case the constitution calls for three branches of government, with a legislature, a court system, and an executive branch.

The federal government is intended to have limited lawmaking powers. Speaking broadly, the U.S. Constitution empowers the federal government to handle matters that affect the entire country, for example, manage the military and relations with other countries; manage the relations between the separate states; and regulate affairs in certain specific areas listed in the Constitution, such as copyright and bankruptcy. All other lawmaking is reserved to the states.

Each state government has a broad mandate for lawmaking, and most matters affecting day-to-day life are regulated by state law. The only limit on this power is that the states cannot make laws that violate the federal or their state constitution, and they cannot intrude on areas that are reserved to the federal government. Apart from these exceptions, the states can make law on any matter that they choose.

In this system, all three branches of federal and state governments make law. The legislature makes law in the form of statutes, the judiciary makes law in the form of case law, and the executive branch makes law in the form of regulations. The states are further divided into smaller governmental units, including counties, cities, and towns. These smaller units of each state can often also make law, referred to as ordinances or local laws.

Jurisdiction

The federal structure of American government creates a complicated landscape for law. For any given legal issue, the first question to answer is usually that of jurisdiction. Jurisdiction is defined as the official power to make laws or legal decisions and is delineated by sovereign body, geography, and other factors. Any given form of law, whether a statute, a case, or a regulation, is only controlling in its own jurisdiction.

One of the primary divisions in jurisdiction is between federal and state law. For example, if someone wants to find information on filing for bankruptcy, the relevant jurisdiction is federal, because the U.S. Constitution reserves bankruptcy as a federal matter. On the other hand, if someone wants information about divorce the answer will lie in state law, because divorce is a state matter. Of course, each state is its own jurisdiction, so someone who lives in Illinois will want information on Illinois divorce law, rather than from some other state.

These examples are just for purposes of illustration. An extended discussion of jurisdiction is beyond the scope of this chapter (for further reading on this topic, see Healey 2014). However, being sensitive to jurisdiction as an issue is important in rendering legal reference services.

Form of Law

A very common question asked at the reference desk is some variation of "I would like the law about X." Finding that law has two parts. The first is determining the relevant jurisdiction as described previously. The second question has to do with the form of law involved. This could be a constitution, a statute, a case, a regulation, or a local ordinance of some kind. This section describes each of these in turn.

Constitutions

The most fundamental form of primary legal material is a constitution. Constitutions have several functions. First, they set up the form of government. The federal and state constitutions each lay out the three branches of government and decree how people will be elected or appointed to posts in those branches. The constitution also decrees what the powers of the government will be and in what areas it will be allowed to make and enforce laws. Finally, the constitution sets out liberties for the people. These liberties cannot be taken away by any law or action of the government. A constitution is a fundamental form of law and governs many disputes about the propriety of other laws.

Statutes

Statutes are what most people commonly think of as the law. Statutes are created by the legislature and are published in organized, topical form in codes.

Case Law

Case law is law made by the courts in the form of legal decisions by appellate courts. The American legal system has a large and active body of case law. Case law, and its importance, results from two aspects of the American judiciary. The first is the ability of the courts to interpret legislation and review statutes for their constitutionality. The second is because courts can actually make law, called common law, in areas where there is no legislation.

Both federal and state courts have the power to review any statute to be sure it does not violate provisions of the relevant constitution. This is a basic protection built into the American system of government and is a major part of the checks and balances between the branches of government. If a court finds that a law violates some provision of the constitution, it can invalidate all or part of the statute.

Courts in the United States also have the power to interpret legislation from their jurisdiction when the meaning of a statute is not clear. This means the court can determine what a statute actually means, and the court's decision must be followed in working with the statute in the future.

In the United States, there are areas of law that are generally not governed by legislative statutes or rules. These areas of law, most commonly torts, contracts, and property, are instead governed by law made by the courts.

The body of common law in America is extensive and very difficult to work with. Cases are not organized by topic in the way statutes are, and any one case can be affected by subsequent cases that overrule, limit, or interpret it. Private publishers have developed professional tools to help with case research, but these are very expensive and can be difficult to understand and use. For this reason, a user who wants to do extensive case research is probably best referred to a law library for assistance.

Regulations

Regulations are a very important form of law and are widespread in the United States. Regulations are made by the executive branch of government, and their function is to provide details for the enforcement of a statute. Regulations have traditionally been somewhat difficult to locate. The Web is changing this, but access to regulations can take some effort.

Ordinances and Local Laws

In addition to federal and state law, local governments also make laws, often referred to as ordinances. Local governments can include county and municipal bodies. The nature of these local units and the lawmaking powers they have vary widely from state to state. Perhaps not surprisingly local law has been the most difficult to find for research purposes, although again the Web is improving this situation.

Several private publishers provide the service of codifying local ordinances at the request of a local government. This is important because it provides a published code of local ordinances that can be distributed and consulted. In addition, most of these private publishers also place their codes on the Web, which provides free access to all. Many libraries will want to obtain a copy of their relevant local ordinances, and will also want to be aware of what local ordinances they can find online, particularly for local governments that they would not normally pay to acquire.

Legal Issue

When a library user asks a law-related question at the reference desk, the question might involve finding a simple fact or discrete item, what might be called ready reference, or it might require more involved research. Sometimes, a patron will ask for a discrete item for which there is a citation or reference. In this case, it is a matter of locating the item. Often, however, the reference question is not about a particular item, but about a legal issue. It would be impossible to provide a comprehensive guide to researching all legal issues. However, Table 31.1 provides a brief overview of the jurisdiction and type of law for some common legal issues.

TABLE 31.1 Jurisdiction and Type of Law for Common Legal Issues

Note for Any Issue:
If the question involves litigation on any topic in state or federal courts, the patron will also need information on court rules of procedure and evidence and potentially also jury instructions and local court rules. Litigation rules are an entire set of procedures that must be followed, in addition to the subject matter of the suit.

Issue:	Bankruptcy
State or Federal:	Federal
Type of Law:	Statute (Title 11 of the *U.S. Code*), with case law interpretation
Notes:	Personal exemptions are sometimes covered by state statute.
Issue:	Contracts
State or Federal:	State
Type of Law:	Case law
Notes:	Commercial disputes may be covered by the *Uniform Commercial Code*, which is part of the state's statutes.
Issue:	Criminal
State or Federal:	State (most commonly) or federal
Type of Law:	Statute, with case law interpretation
Notes:	People facing criminal charges should be strongly encouraged to seek legal counsel.
Issue:	Debt (credit, collections, foreclosure)
State or Federal:	State or federal, possibly a combination
Type of Law:	Statutes and regulations
Notes:	Many issues will involve the Fair Debt Collection Practices Act (FDCPA), 15 U.S.C. § 1692, or the Consumer Finance Protection Bureau.

(*Continued*)

TABLE 31.1 (Continued)

Issue:	Divorce and custody
State or Federal:	State
Type of Law:	Statute, with case law interpretation
Notes:	Very common legal question; generally lots of self-help materials available.
Issue:	Employment discrimination
State or Federal:	State or federal (most commonly)
Type of law:	Statute, with case law interpretation
Issue:	Employment (other than discrimination)
State or Federal:	State
Type of Law:	Statute, with case law interpretation
Issue:	Housing discrimination
State or Federal:	State or federal (most commonly)
Type of Law:	Regulations (mostly) and statute
Notes:	"Section 8," now called the Housing Choice Voucher Program, refers to Section 8 of the Housing Act of 1937 (42 U.S.C. § 1437f).
Issue:	Intellectual property (copyright and patent)
State or Federal:	Federal
Type of Law:	Statute, with case law interpretation
Issue:	Landlord-tenant
State or Federal:	State
Type of Law:	Statutes
Notes:	Most states have a specific landlord-tenant statute. However, case law might be relevant.
Issue:	Professional malpractice (a form of tort)
State or Federal:	State
Type of Law:	Case law
Notes:	Usually medical or legal, but other professions as well, particularly licensed professions.
Issue:	Torts (accidents, injuries, etc.)
State or Federal:	State
Type of Law:	Case law
Issue:	Wills, estate planning, probate
State or Federal:	State
Type of Law:	Statute
Notes:	Many states have a separate probate code. Also, if going to court, there may be special probate court procedural rules.

TYPES OF LEGAL MATERIALS

A distinction should be made between two fundamentally different forms of legal materials: primary and secondary. In one sense, the difference between primary and secondary legal materials is quite simple. Primary legal materials are the law, while secondary legal materials are everything else. Although this distinction can be expressed simply, it would benefit from some further explanation.

Primary Legal Materials

Primary legal materials are those that constitute the law itself; they are items that can be used as controlling law or precedent in their jurisdiction. The three forms of primary legal materials that are referred to most commonly are statutes, case law, and regulations. In addition, a full description of primary legal materials would include constitutions and local laws and ordinances.

Secondary Legal Materials

Secondary legal materials are those that have the law as their subject, but are not themselves law. A vast and varied array of secondary legal materials is available, but the majority of these secondary legal materials are both extremely expensive and highly technical in nature. For this reason, they are generally not available except in specialized law libraries.

Some secondary legal materials that all librarians should know about include some basic tools. Some examples are legal encyclopedias and legal dictionaries, which would be reasonable to find in a nonlaw library, and a vast number of websites that offer legal information free of cost or at a low cost.

Attorney-Oriented Materials

A number of secondary legal publications are used by legal professionals that would normally only be found in a specialized law library, or in a subscription database. These resources are useful to legal professionals and scholars, and so they are often referred to in other sources. Based on such a reference, a library user might ask for these secondary sources at the reference desk. If that resource itself is needed, it will be necessary to refer the user to a law library. However, sometimes the information the secondary source provides can be found in other ways. As a result, it might be useful to describe a few of the most common secondary sources and what they do.

Treatises

Legal treatises are written by experts to provide an in-depth explanation of a particular area of law. Large law libraries will contain most of the prominent legal treatises in print form, and if the treatise is in print form, it might be possible to obtain it through interlibrary loan.

Restatements

Restatements are created for each area of common law and look at the common law across all fifty states to summarize the law in the form of a set of rules. Restatements are useful to scholars and the courts as a way of assessing what the most common form of the common law is for a given topic.

Looseleaf Practice Sets

Legal publishers have produced a wide variety of publications intended to assist lawyers as they practice in a particular area of law. These sets have traditionally been referred to as *looseleafs* because they were published in a physical format that allowed for the insertion of new pages within each volume. Many legal practitioners use the term "looseleaf" to mean any practice aid set.

Looseleafs will commonly provide editorial and expert information on the topic, along with references and summaries of the relevant law, and often forms, practice checklists, reference materials, and other helpful material. Many looseleafs come with a current awareness service on that topic. Looseleafs require a subscription to be kept up to date. Most looseleafs have migrated online and are available through subscription databases provided by their publisher.

Subscription Legal Databases

As mentioned earlier, the major private legal publishers make their materials available through online subscription databases. These databases are tools aimed at legal professionals and tend to be very expensive. Although it is unlikely that a nonlaw library will have access to any of these, it might be helpful to know something about them because of their prominence in the legal publishing field. As of this writing, there are three major legal database providers.

LexisNexis was the original online legal database, launched in 1973. It contains primary law from the federal government and all fifty states, along with a vast array of other legal materials, including material published by its parent company, Reed Elsevier.

West Publishing, now a subsidiary of Thomson Reuters, has been the premier publisher of American law since the 19th century. West created *Westlaw*, its online legal database, in the 1970s in competition with *LexisNexis*. *Westlaw* contains all of the primary law from all U.S. jurisdictions, as well as a vast array of secondary sources published by West and Thomson Reuters. *Westlaw* also benefits from having the proprietary Key Number System, the only comprehensive topical index to American case law.

Bloomberg Law, a relative newcomer to the legal database field, describes itself as an integrated legal research and business intelligence solution. In addition to providing primary legal materials and some professional finding aids, the database includes materials from the Bureau of National Affairs.

One subscription legal database that might be available in an academic or a large public library is *Nexis Uni*. This product by LexisNexis is aimed at universities, colleges, and large public libraries. It provides access to LexisNexis news and legal databases and contains case law, statutes, regulations, and some law review articles, as well as access to the Shepard's Case Citator. If an institution subscribes to *Nexis Uni*, it should be the librarian's primary tool for answering legal reference questions.

EVALUATION AND SELECTION OF LEGAL MATERIALS

Most librarians will want to have access to some legal materials. The blossoming of free Web-based materials makes this even more compelling. This section will discuss how to evaluate legal materials being considered for the collection, and then some considerations for selection.

Evaluating Legal Materials

A number of factors should be considered when evaluating legal materials, including authority, currency, completeness, and bias or slant.

Authority

It is very important that legal information come from authoritative sources, particularly with primary legal materials. Authoritative sources include the government itself, state bar associations,[4] accredited law schools, intergovernmental and quasi-governmental organizations,[5] and established legal publishers with a solid reputation. Before purchasing or relying on a legal source, it would be best to check the authority of its publisher or provider.

Currency

Laws are constantly being changed, and many legal concepts and issues exist in a state of flux. Because of this, it is essential that any legal material be current. With law, out-of-date materials not only are less useful but also can actually be harmful. For this reason, out-of-date legal materials should generally be removed from a library's collection, unless they are being retained for archival or historical purposes.

Completeness

In order for legal materials to be fully useful, they must provide complete access to the relevant law. For example, many statutes have been interpreted by courts in a way that affects how they are understood and used. As such, having a current set of statutes is only part of the required information, because access to the relevant case law is also needed to fully understand the statute. Completeness is an important issue, and one that most libraries cannot solve fully without access to specialized legal materials. However, when evaluating a Web-based resource, completeness should be considered.

Bias or Slant

Because law is such a fundamental topic, and because aspects of law are often controversial, bias or slant in legal materials is always possible. This comes up most commonly with websites and publications produced by advocacy and special interest organizations. Certainly many, if not most, such organizations provide a fair and balanced view of the law in their area of concern, but some do not. Librarians must be on the lookout for bias when evaluating such materials.

Selection of Legal Materials

Primary legal materials, particularly statutes, cases, and regulations, have traditionally been available free of cost or at a low cost directly from the government. These materials are now almost entirely available online. Primary legal materials are also available from private publishers, who include a variety of research aids and added information. For most libraries, privately published legal materials will be too expensive to collect and keep updated. In addition to their expense, privately published legal materials tend to be complex tools designed for use by trained legal professionals. As such, they can have limited utility for regular library users.

Thus, most librarians will rely on free websites for access to the statutes, cases, and regulations of their state and of the federal government. Some librarians may want to collect selected secondary materials as well, such as legal dictionaries and encyclopedias, and perhaps some legal self-help books on particular topics.

Print Sources

Print resources for legal reference are mostly a dying breed. Probably, the most common primary legal item found in print is the U.S. Constitution. Because it is a relatively short document, it can be found both published on its own in various forms and included in many other publications. For instance, all statute sets, both federal and state, contain the text of the U.S. Constitution. However, the Constitution is also widely available online free of cost, both from the government and other sources.

State constitutions are included in statute sets for their state. As with the U.S. Constitution, state constitutions are readily available online, usually on the state legislature Web page as well as other sources.

GENERAL AND SECONDARY LEGAL RESOURCES

This section discusses general resources for legal reference. Most of these resources are Web-based, but some are in print. This section will cover affordable secondary materials in print, online legal dictionaries and encyclopedias, free websites, general research guides, federal law research guides, legal forms, and referral resources. Box 31.2 provides advice on helping a patron with legal questions utilizing primarily free legal resources, and Box 31.3 provides a practice exercise.

Box 31.2 Where to Start?

Helping a library user get started on a legal question can be daunting. A good place to start is to determine if a user is seeking information about some aspect of law or is seeking a particular item, such as a specific case or a form. If a user is looking for a particular item, you can use the resources in the following sections of this chapter to help them. If a user does not have a particular item that they are looking for, it is best to start with general information, even if their question sounds fairly specific.

Box 31.3 Activity: Filing for a Divorce without an Attorney

Work with your classmates to discover what resources you can find for someone who wants to file for a divorce in your area without using an attorney.

Task 1. Start general. If your library has a legal encyclopedia, you might start there. If not, consult online encyclopedias such as the Legal Information Institute's *Wex*. See what general background information on divorce you can find.
Task 2. Look for state or local self-help resources. Can you find an online legal self-help site in your state that has information on filing for divorce?
Task 3. Look for attorney referral and low-cost or free legal aid resources in your area.

Questions for Reflection and Discussion:

1. How useful was the general legal information on divorce that you found? Do you think it would be useful to a library user trying to understand the divorce process?
2. Did you find self-help divorce resources specific to your state? Did they appear to be geared toward a layperson audience? Were they available in any language other than English?
3. Did you find any local attorney referral resources? Describe what you found. Were you able to determine if the low-cost or free legal services agencies in your area handle divorces? If so, what are the income guidelines for those services? Do they take any divorce client within the income guidelines, or do they also require additional factors, such as the presence of domestic abuse?
4. Are there any other resources you feel you would need in order to assist a library user looking for information on divorce?

Referral Resources

Many times a user will approach the reference desk with a legal question that is beyond the scope of help provided by a library. It is always a good idea to suggest that a user with a significant legal issue consult a legal professional. Referral resources can help with finding a lawyer or a public law library. If a library handles lots of legal questions from the public, it would be a good idea to contact local referral sources, or nearby law libraries, to discuss when and how librarians can make referrals.

If there is a law school in the vicinity, it would be good to check with them about their policy for public access. Not all law school libraries are open to the public. A good alternative is a state, court, or county law library. Most of these are open to the public. Again, it is a good idea to check with the library first to get to know their access policies.

It is almost always a good idea to refer users to a lawyer if it becomes clear that they are trying to handle a legal problem without help. Users who meet income guidelines might even qualify for low-cost or free legal representation. Most state bar associations have a referral service that is often a good first stop. Otherwise, "Find an Attorney" at *AttorneyPages* and "Find a Lawyer" at *FindLaw* are good alternatives. For referrals to legal aid, librarians can use *LSC Programs*.

Secondary Legal Materials in Print

Most secondary legal materials in print will be too expensive, and in many cases too hard to use, to be of interest to a public or academic library. However, there are some basic, relatively low-cost items that any library might want to obtain in print form. These include a legal dictionary or an encyclopedia, and legal self-help books.

Legal Dictionaries and Encyclopedias

Legal dictionaries define legal terms and can be very useful for pursuing any legal topic. The most popular legal dictionary is *Black's Law Dictionary*, published by Thomson Reuters and available in hardcover for less than $100. Online legal dictionaries are also available, often free of cost, but a print version is a handy resource for any reference desk.

Many librarians will also find it useful to have access to a general legal encyclopedia. The *Gale Encyclopedia of American Law*, third edition, is a good choice for most libraries and is available in print or as an e-book. There are also legal encyclopedias aimed at legal professionals, such as *American Jurisprudence 2nd* or *Corpus Juris Secundum*, both published by Thomson Reuters, but these are both very expensive and aimed at a technically trained audience.

Some online legal dictionaries and encyclopedias are available free of cost. While these sources can be quite good, they are generally not as comprehensive as purchased products. *Wex*, from Cornell University Law School, is both a dictionary and an encyclopedia. In addition, *Nolo* provides some very good information on its website free of cost. Among other things, they provide a *Free Dictionary of Law Terms and Legal Definitions* as well as a fairly extensive legal encyclopedia with information on a broad variety of topics under the name *Free Legal Articles & FAQs*. These resources are excellent for quick reference and basic legal information.

Legal Self-Help Sources

Legal self-help books are intended to explain the law to laypersons and often guide nonlawyers through a legal process. Although such books are not without controversy and even resistance from the bar, there is no risk to a library for providing them as part of their collection.

The most prominent publisher of self-help legal books is Nolo, which provides books on a wide variety of legal topics, including many that are state specific. Nolo's publications are generally considered authoritative and are available through the *Nolo* website.

Other self-help resources may be available from a local legal services office or county or state bar association. Often, these groups have pamphlets and short books they distribute free of cost or at a low cost that they might be willing to provide to the library.

Free Websites

Several free online resources provide a broad spectrum of reliable, authoritative legal information. These sites are worth noting here in general, although they will each appear later in the chapter in relation to specific kinds of material. These are great go-to sites to have on hand when providing legal reference services.

The *Legal Information Institute* (*LII*) is produced and maintained by the law library at Cornell University Law School. It was one of the first general resources made available on the Web and continues to be one of the most useful and robust. It is basically a portal, in that most of the material it supplies is via links to other sources. This is an excellent first stop when looking for legal information.

Govinfo is a site maintained by the U.S. Government Publishing Office (GPO). It provides access to legal materials from all three branches of the federal government, and much more besides.

General Research Guides

Other sites provide guidance in finding basic legal information. Most of these sites not only cover federal law topics but also provide good information at the state level. Most of these guides offer links to resources by specific jurisdiction.

The American Association of Law Libraries, through their Legal Information Services to the Public Special Interest Section, offers the free *Public Library Toolkit*. These are toolkits aimed at average public libraries for answering legal reference questions. The toolkits would work well in most academic libraries too, particularly if they are open to the public. There are specific toolkits for each state. Another good basic source of state law information is the *LII*'s "Law by Source: State" page.

Federal Law Research Guides

These guides are designed to provide access to a broad variety of federal legal resources on the Web. Both of the guides here are produced by major law schools and are generally kept up to date.

The *LII* has a page called the "Federal Law Collection." This provides a comprehensive set of links to federal resources. New York University School of Law, through their Hauser Global Law School Program, has produced *A Guide to the U.S. Federal Legal System Web-based Public Accessible Sources*. It nicely mixes links with explanatory material and is also quite comprehensive.

Legal Forms

Forms are used widely in legal issues, both in court actions and in transactional situations such as contracts and wills. Keep in mind that there is not always a form for every legal situation, and not all forms are available on the Web. For local court forms, it is usually best to check the website of the local clerk of court. Also, remember that librarians should never select a particular form for a user or help a user fill it out. Those activities could constitute the unauthorized practice of law.

The *FindLaw* website has a very comprehensive page of links to forms, called "State Specific Legal Forms for All States." *LLRX.com* is a site oriented toward legal professionals, but it has good resources for everyone. Their page of forms is very rich and has forms from almost all jurisdictions, some down to county level.

PRIMARY LEGAL RESOURCES

This section provides information about finding the law itself, specifically constitutions, statutes, case law, regulations, and local ordinances. Information about the type of law is provided, as well as suggested sources for finding a particular type of law.

Constitutions

Because constitutions serve such a fundamental purpose, it is fairly common to get requests for them. Fortunately, there are plenty of sources for constitutions on the Web.

The U.S. Constitution is widely available on the Web. For an official version, a good site is the *U.S. Constitution* page at the National Archives. The U.S. Constitution has been heavily interpreted and analyzed over the course of its existence. Although the material is very complex, the United States Congress provides a very good annotated version of the Constitution at *U.S. Constitution Annotated.*

Each state's official government website should have that state's constitution in full text. Most commonly this will be on the state legislature's site.

Statutes and Legislative Materials

Legislation is created by the legislative process. The documentation of the legislative process, referred to as legislative history, is often used to determine the intent of the legislature in creating a particular law (for more on researching legislative history, see Chapter 26). The legislative process produces individual laws, which are published as session law and made publicly available. Relevant individual session laws are then compiled by topic into a code.

Session Law and Codes

In each legislative session, bills are introduced by legislators and considered by the legislative body. Those bills that successfully pass through that process emerge as individual laws. These individual laws are called session laws and are collected for publication in a session law set. The session law set is an official publication of the legislature and contains each law passed in chronological order. This set is published after each legislative session. Session laws are also available on the legislature website.

Once session law has been published in the session law set, it is codified. In codification, the individual laws from all legislative sessions are arranged by topic. Any amendments to prior laws are placed in context, and repealed laws are edited out. The result is a publication of all legislation currently in force, arranged by topic and referred to as a code. The code allows a user to see the statutory law on a particular topic as it exists right now, regardless of when the underlying pieces of session law were passed, and without any former language that has been repealed or amended.

It is important to note that not all session law ends up in the code. While most legislation will be included, at least while it is still in force, some session laws are not suitable for codification and are not included. One category of legislation that does not get codified is session laws that by their nature change yearly. The most prominent examples of this would be appropriation session laws and the annual budget. Another category of laws that are not codified are those of minor import, sometimes referred to as private laws. Private laws are session laws that only affect a small number of persons or entities, and therefore do not have general effect. Some examples would be laws that name a public building or that grant citizenship to a foreign national as a reward for rendering service to this country (for more information, see Mantel 2008).

The code is therefore the primary tool for consulting statutes. Because new laws are passed regularly, a code must be updated regularly. An out-of-date code is not only less useful but can actually be dangerous, because code sections important to the researcher may have been changed subsequent to its publication. Virtually, all state legislature websites now contain the current state code, although usability varies. In addition, most states still publish their code in print for a reasonable price.

Annotated Codes

Because the courts in America have the power to interpret legislation, finding the language of a statute may be only part of the answer to a user's question. In order to fully understand a code section, the researcher will need to be aware of any court decisions that have interpreted or otherwise directly affected that statute. Private publishers have solved this problem by publishing something called an annotated code. An annotated code contains all of the language of the official code, but each code section is interspersed with notes about court decisions that have interpreted that section, along with references to other related materials. Annotated codes are available for the federal *United States Code* and for each of the fifty states.

An annotated code is obviously a very useful tool for statutory research. Unfortunately, annotated codes are very expensive in print or online form and require a substantial annual subscription fee to be kept up to date. For library users doing substantial research in statutes, it might be worthwhile to refer them to a law library that has access to the relevant annotated code.

Federal Statutes

Congress.gov is generally the best place to start federal legislative research. It can be searched by bill number or title as well as keyword. Entries provide a summary and the full text of legislation in addition to a list of sponsors, and actions and votes taken. *Congress.gov* also provides browsable lists of public laws passed in each two-year session of Congress and access to the *United States Code.*

While *Congress.gov* is the official source of the *United States Code*, it is also widely available on the Web, as are other federal legislative materials. A good source, although it is not official, is the *LII.* Box 31.4 provides further advice on locating statutes.

State Statutes

Each state's legislature website will have the most recent version of the state code and usually will also have additional information, such as bills, past versions of the code, and other legislative materials. Two resources that provide access to all or most state codes are *State Home Page and Legislature Links* from MultiState Associates and *State Law and Code Links* from FreeAdvice.

Box 31.4 Activity: Finding a Statute

Asking for the text of a particular statute is a common reference question. Unfortunately, the way legislation and statutes work can make finding the statute itself complicated.

Issue 1. Session law vs. code. As discussed earlier, statutes begin life as session, a single law that is published in a session law set. From there, it is codified, meaning it is placed in topical context in the code. Unfortunately, it is very common for people to request a session law, when what they really want is the code.

For example, a user might want to read some part of the Americans with Disabilities Act. However, this title refers to the session law. Almost always users want to see provisions of it in the code. It is important to be clear as to which form of the law the user wants.

Issue 2. Popular names. Many session laws are given a popular name, especially at the federal level. Popular names always refer to the session law. As with the previous example, popular names do not indicate where a session law is codified. Fortunately, most code publishers provide a popular names table that will cross-reference the session law with its location in the code. If no popular names table is available, a Web search engine can often find the information.

Issue 3. Searching codes. Searching online for a code section can be very frustrating. Many state legislature sites have limited search capabilities. Even in well-developed databases, searching for code sections is frustrating because codes inevitably do lots of cross-referencing, which leads to many false hits in a search.

The best approach to searching a code is to use a finding aid such as the index, if available, or the table of contents.

Work with your classmates to discover the text of "Megan's Law."

1. Start by looking at Megan's Law on *Wikipedia*. How helpful is the information? Does it provide a link or citation to the text of the federal Megan's Law? Is the citation to the session law or the *U.S. Code*?
2. Find the federal Megan's Law in the *U.S. Code*. What finding aid did you use to find the law? Was it easy or difficult to find?
3. See if your state also has a Megan's law. Go to a site that provides your state code, such as your state legislature website. What finding aids does the site provide? Is there a popular names table? Is there a searchable index? Can you determine if your state has a Megan's Law?

Case Law

Case law has always been the most difficult form of primary legal material to work with. This is because, as mentioned earlier, case law is not published in a way that organizes it by topic, and because when a case is affected by later cases, such as by being overruled or limited in scope, those changes are not reflected in the original case.

Case law is published in books called reporters. Reporters publish cases in the order they are issued by the courts. Traditionally, case law was published by the court itself in an official reporter. In addition, private legal publishers, most notably West Publishing, publish case law from state and federal courts. Case law is also published in private legal databases, as discussed later.

Most courts now publish their cases online, on the court's website. However, the problems of organization and updating remain, and online publication of cases tends to go back only a few years, meaning cases from past years are not available on a court's website.

The good news is that case law is now more available than ever, and mostly free of cost. The bad news is that the tools required to find cases by topic and update the treatment of those cases are still mostly the purview of private publishers whose products are very expensive.

Case Citation

Cases are identified and located by their citation. A case citation includes the names of the primary parties involved, information about the reporter in which the case is published, the court issuing the case, and the year. Although all of this information is present in a case citation, the highly technical nature of the citation system can make this very confusing.

For purposes of illustration, a standard case citation looks like this:

Garratt v. Dailey, 279 P.2d 1091 (Wash. 1955)

The citation provides the names of the parties (*Garratt v. Dailey*), the location of the case in the reporter set (279 P.2d 1091), and in the parentheses, the jurisdiction (the Supreme Court of Washington) and the year the decision was rendered (1955).

The reporter information in a case citation is key to locating the case in order to read it. In the earlier example, the reporter information—279 P.2d 1091—is parsed as follows: The central abbreviation P.2d indicates that the reporter being referenced is from the second series of the *Pacific Reporter*, a publication of state case law published by the West Publishing company. The first number, 279, indicates that the case is in volume 279 of the second series of the *Pacific Reporter*. The final number, 1091, is the beginning page number of the case in volume 279.

West Publishing established a national set of reporters in the 19th century for all state and federal case law, and references to their reporters are the most commonly found citations.[6] However, many cases, including the example here, are published in two reporters: the relevant West reporter and the official reporter of the issuing court, which in this case is the Washington Supreme Court. The citation to this case in the official reporter looks like this:

Garratt v. Dailey, 46 Wash. 2d 197, (1955)

In this case, the reporter information indicates that the case appears in volume 46 of the Washington Reports, second series, starting on page 197. The text of the case in this reporter will be identical to that in the West *Pacific Reporter*. Finally, many case citations will contain the citation information for both the official reporter and the West reporter. Such a cite looks like this, with the official reporter information listed first:

Garratt v. Dailey, 46 Wash. 2d 197, 279 P.2d 1091 (Wash. 1955)

With few exceptions, this system of designating cases by reporter volume and starting page number continues to dominate, in spite of the fact that cases are now published almost exclusively online. As of this writing, several jurisdictions have designed online citation systems, but no one system has emerged as dominant, and in most jurisdictions, the reporter system is still the only citation system in use.

One final note on finding a case by its citation: when presented with a case citation, do not hesitate to try a Web search engine. Many cases are published on the Web in various forms, and searching the citation will often find them. In particular, check *Google Scholar* which, as described in the case law resources later in this chapter, provides access to case law from most jurisdictions. Box 31.5 provides additional advice on locating court decisions.

Box 31.5 Where's That New Case?

Legal cases often make the news, and library users often want to read the decision itself. The Web has made legal decisions much more available than they were previously, but there are still challenges.

Challenge 1. Case name and citation. News reports very rarely include full citation information for a legal decision. In that event, the most important information to look for is the last name of one or more of the parties, along with the identity of the issuing court. These two pieces of information will often allow you to search the court's website for the opinion.

Challenge 2. Trial court decisions. Published case law is made up of appellate court decisions. Trial court decisions are not considered legal precedent, and therefore are not published. In addition, many trials are decided without any kind of a written opinion. For instance, a jury verdict is simply a finding of guilty or not guilty in criminal cases, or liable or not liable in civil cases. No other opinion exists. Even when a judge issues the trial court decision, it is often a similar finding, without a written decision.

Trial court judges sometimes do issue written opinions, but there is no system of publication or distribution for such decisions. While trial court decisions are usually a public record, traditionally the only way to access them has been to go to the courthouse and view the case file. However, this situation is in flux. Most courts are adopting online docket systems, and these often contain all documents filed in a case. If such documents are viewable by the general public, it would then be possible to find trial court decisions online.

Court Rules and Dockets

Many people doing research on a legal topic may be involved in litigation. In addition to access to other forms of law, they will need access to court rules and dockets. Court rules are the rules that the courts follow during litigation and appeals. There are generally separate sets of rules for civil litigation, called the rules of civil procedure; criminal litigation, called the rules of criminal procedure; the production of evidence, called the rules of evidence; and appeals of court decisions, called the rules of appellate procedure. These bodies of rules are generally the same throughout the jurisdiction. In other words, there is one set of rules of civil procedure for all of the federal courts and one set for the courts in each state. However, in addition to these jurisdiction-wide rules, there are often local court rules that govern the administration and conduct of local courts.

In addition to rules, each court will have a docket system. The docket is primarily a scheduling and deadline system, but modern online systems will also include the actual documents filed at each stage of the litigation. Dockets can be used to check on the progress of particular litigation and to find and download documents that have been filed in a case, such as motions, briefs, and orders. Dockets are public records, but many are not free of cost. For example, the federal court docket system, PACER, charges a small per-page fee for downloading documents.

Court rules, and often docket access, can usually be found on the website of the particular court involved. If in doubt as to which site to consult, start with the state's Supreme Court or state court's website. At the federal level, the *Court Website Links* provides an interactive map of federal courts. Rules and dockets for many courts, both state and federal, are also available on *LLRX Court Rules, Forms and Dockets.*

Case Law

Google Scholar provides access to case law from most jurisdictions. Select case law under the *Google Scholar* search bar. U.S. Supreme Court opinions are among the most commonly sought legal cases. Most prominent or famous U.S. Supreme Court cases are available on the Web and can be found using *Google Scholar.* In addition, the U.S. Supreme Court website has a directory of where to find opinions, both online and in print, at *Where to Obtain Supreme Court Opinions.*

For a U.S. Circuit Court of Appeals decision, *Google Scholar* is once again a good choice. Other sources tend to be limited to decisions from the last ten to twenty years. Each circuit court of appeals has its own website, and most have at least some decisions available. The previously mentioned *Court Website Links* can be used to locate the website of the desired circuit court. Another partial database of decisions is the *Public Library of Law*, which has cases from 1950 to the present.

It is not possible to provide specific access to each state's court resources in this chapter. For recent court opinions for a particular case, it is best to check that state's court website. The National Center for State Courts has a helpful page of links to all state court websites, including individual courts in most states. It is a good starting point for finding state court opinions online. *Google Scholar* has an extensive collection of state court decisions and allows searchers to pick a particular jurisdiction for searching.

Regulations

Regulations are promulgated by executive agencies when the legislature passes a statute that requires regulations in order to be properly enforced. Laws that direct an agency to promulgate regulations are referred to as enabling legislation; an agency can only make regulations when an enabling statute directs them to.

In many ways, regulations at both the federal and state levels are published in the same way as legislation. There is an initial publication of the regulation, much like session law, and then current regulations are gathered by topic into a code, referred to as an administrative code. In the case of regulations, however, there is actually a two-step process for the initial publication of regulations. Regulations are first published as proposed regulations; there is generally then a comment period, during which anyone can send comments on the proposed regulation to the agency. After the comment period, the regulations are issued in final form and it is these final regulations that are codified.

Proposed and final regulations are published in a publication of the executive branch, usually referred to as a register. At the federal level, regulations are published in the *Federal Register*, which is published each day that the executive branch operates. All proposed and final regulations, requests for comments, and other materials of the executive branch of the federal government appear in the *Federal Register*. Most states have a similar publication, although state registers are often published weekly rather than daily.

Each jurisdiction also has an administrative code, which contains all of the regulations currently in force arranged by topic. As with statute codes, administrative codes are regularly updated and will normally be the preferred source for regulations. At the federal level, the regulatory code is called the *Code of Federal Regulations*.

Executive agencies not only draft rules but also enforce their rules. This means that agencies have their own court systems, called administrative courts, which render decisions. Sometimes, these decisions are published on the Web, but often they are not. Administrative action is a fairly advanced topic for research, and again someone with such a question is probably best referred to a law library.

When library users are searching for a particular rule, it might be worth inquiring if they need the text of the rule itself or are looking for what the rule requires. The reason for this is that regulations can be very dense and hard to parse, making the effect of a regulation hard to discern. Because of this, the agencies that promulgate and enforce the rules often provide practical, accessible information on a rule's effect on their websites.

Federal regulations are the most commonly requested regulations at the reference desk. Fortunately, all current federal regulations are available free of cost from websites maintained by the Federal government. *Regulations.gov* is a site the federal government has set up to encourage public participation in the regulation drafting process. It provides a good first stop for regulations research. The *Federal Register* is available from the GPO from 1994 onward through the *FederalRegister.gov* website. The current *Code of Federal Regulations* is available on *Govinfo* on a page referred to as the *eCFR*. This version of the *CFR* is updated daily, and although it is not an official version of the *CFR*, it is produced by the office that produces the official *CFR* and can be trusted. Finding the relevant federal agency can be a challenge. Fortunately, *USA.gov* has a fairly comprehensive "A-Z Index of U.S. Government Departments and Agencies."

State governments also issue regulations, working in a manner very similar to the federal government. Of course, each state is different, so librarians would be advised to do a little research to discover the rules resources available for their state. A good starting point for finding state rules is the website of the Administrative Codes and Registers Section of the National Association of Secretaries of State, *Administrative Rules*.

Ordinances and Local Law

Ordinances and local laws have historically been the hardest laws to find. The Web has helped immensely as many local communities now put their ordinances and laws on their websites. Prior to the Web, and continuing today, several private publishers have served as publishers of local ordinances for municipalities. While these were previously published only in book form, they are now commonly also published on the Web. Because publishers have only the ordinances and codes that they publish, librarians may wish to determine which sites have the ordinances relevant for their library.

Municipal Code Corporation is the largest publisher of local law and has the most comprehensive site with *Code Library*. A number of other municipal law publishers provide partial or regional coverage. *Municipal Codes* from Code Publishing has partial coverage, as do *Codes Online* and *eCode360*. Historically, *Code Library* from Coded Systems also offered partial coverage, mostly for western states; as of early 2020, *Code Library* was merging its system with *eCode360*.

CONCLUSION

Reference questions about legal issues are very common in most libraries. Helping users with legal questions can be daunting, both because of the complex nature of legal issues and legal materials, and because of fears of liability. However, with proper preparation, such questions can be handled effectively and fruitfully.

While the possibility of liability arising from answering legal reference questions is real, such a possibility is highly unlikely. The best way to minimize this risk is to refrain from presenting as a legal expert or presenting an opinion about the actual legal issue being researched. Instead, the librarian should concentrate on being an expert at finding the information sought.

The amazing array of legal resources available on the Web has made effective legal reference a possibility in any library. The most important starting point for the librarian is to understand the basic structure of legal materials. With that in hand, most legal questions can be handled effectively using Web resources. For very complex or difficult issues, the user can be referred to an expert, either a specialized law librarian or a legal professional.

Like any other area of expertise, facility with legal materials comes with practice and experience. Mastering legal materials can be very rewarding and extremely useful to the user who needs the librarian's research expertise.

NOTES

1. This issue also potentially applies to providing reference service on medical issues and indeed in any area of knowledge that relates to a licensed profession, if the act of providing information could reasonably be seen as providing the professional expertise of the licensed profession. For more information on this, see Paul D. Healey (2008).

2. This assertion is based on searches of the literature and of news and legal databases by the author first performed in 1994 (Healey 1995, 519–21) and regularly updated since then through December of 2018.

3. The actual definition of the practice of law varies from state to state, although most states base their definition, at least in part, on the American Bar Association's *Model Definition of the Practice of Law* (2003).

4. State bar associations often act on behalf of the state Supreme Court in disciplining lawyers and setting rules for legal practice. As a result, materials published by state bar associations are generally considered authoritative.

5. Examples include the Uniform Law Commission, which drafts suggested laws for all fifty states; The National Center for State Courts and the National Conference of State Legislatures, which provide guidance and resources for state court systems and state legislatures, respectively; and the American Law Institute, which gathers legal experts and government officials to provide guidance on legal issues.

6. *Wikipedia* has a brief but good explanation of the West National Reporter System that includes abbreviations, maps, and dates of coverage ("National Reporter System" 2019).

REFERENCES

American Bar Association. 2003. *Model Definition of the Practice of Law*. Last modified August 11, 2003. http://www.americanbar.org/groups/professional_responsibility/task_force_model_definition_practice_law.html.

Healey, Paul D. 1995. "Chicken Little at the Reference Desk: The Myth of Librarian Liability." *Law Library Journal* 87 (Summer): 515–33.

Healey, Paul D. 2002. "Pro Se Users, Reference Liability, and the Unauthorized Practice of Law: Twenty-Five Selected Readings." *Law Library Journal* 94 (Spring): 133–38.

Healey, Paul D. 2008. *Liability Issues for Librarians and Information Professionals*. New York: Neal-Schuman.

Healey, Paul D. 2014. *Answering Legal Reference Questions: How and Where to Find the Answers*. Chicago: ALA Editions.

Mantel, Matthew. 2008. "Private Bills and Private Laws." *Law Library Journal* 99 (Winter): 87–100.

"National Reporter System." 2019. *Wikipedia*. http://en.wikipedia.org/wiki/National_Reporter_System.

Pacific Reporter. 1883–. Eagan, MN: West Publishing.

LIST OF SOURCES

"A-Z Index of U.S. Government Departments and Agencies." *USA.gov*. https://www.usa.gov/federal-agencies/a.

Administrative Rules. National Association of Secretaries of State. http://www.administrativerules.org/administrative-rules/.

American Jurisprudence. 2nd ed. 2004–2015. Eagan, MN: Thomson Reuters. Available online as part of *Westlaw*.

American Law Institute. http://www.ali.org/.

Black's Law Dictionary. 10th ed. 2014. Eagan, MN: Thomson Reuters.

Bloomberg Law. http://www.bna.com/bloomberglaw. Subscription required.

Code of Federal Regulations. Government Publishing Office. http://www.ecfr.gov.

Code Library. Coded Systems. http://www.codedsystems.com/codelibrary.html.

Code Library. Municipal Code Corporation. http://www.municode.com/library/.

Codes Online. Sterling Codifiers. http://www.sterlingcodifiers.com/#codes.

Congress.gov. http://www.congress.gov/.

Corpus Juris Secundum. 2003–2016. Eagan, MN: Thomson Reuters.

Court Website Links. United States Courts. http://www.uscourts.gov/about-federal-courts/federal-courts-public/court-website-links.

eCode360. General Code. https://www.generalcode.com/resources/ecode360-library/.

"Federal Law Collection." Legal Information Institute. Cornell University Law School. http://www.law.cornell.edu/federal.

Federal Register. Government Publishing Office. https://www.federalregister.gov/.

"Find a Lawyer." *FindLaw*. http://lawyers.findlaw.com/.
"Find an Attorney." *AttorneyPages*. http://attorneypages.com/.
FindLaw. http://www.findlaw.com/.
Free Dictionary of Law Terms and Legal Definitions. Nolo. http://www.nolo.com/dictionary/.
Free Legal Articles & FAQs. Nolo. http://www.nolo.com/legal-encyclopedia.
Gale Encyclopedia of American Law. 3rd ed. 2011. Farmington Hills, MI: Gale Cengage Learning. Available online as part of *Gale Virtual Reference Library*.
Gale Virtual Reference Library. Farmington Hills, MI: Gale Cengage Learning. http://www.cengage.com/. Subscription required.
Google Scholar. https://scholar.google.com/.
Govinfo. Government Publishing Office. http://www.govinfo.gov/.
A Guide to the U. S. Federal Legal System Web-based Public Accessible Sources. Hauser Global Law School Program. New York University. http://www.nyulawglobal.org/globalex/United_States1.htm.
"Law by Source: State." *Legal Information Institute*. Cornell University Law School. http://www.law.cornell.edu/states/.
Legal Information Institute. Cornell University Law School. http://www.law.cornell.edu/.
LexisNexis. San Francisco, CA: LexisNexis. http://www.lexisnexis.com/. Subscription required.
LLRX Court Rules, Forms and Dockets. LLRX. http://www.llrx.com/courtrules.
LSC Programs. Legal Services Corporation. http://www.lsc.gov/find-legal-aid.
Municipal Codes. Code Publishing. https://www.codebook.com/listing.
The National Center for State Courts. http://www.ncsc.org/.
National Conference of State Legislatures. http://www.ncsl.org/.
Nexis Uni [LexisNexis]. San Francisco, CA: LexisNexis. http://www.lexisnexis.com/en-us/products/lexisnexis-academic.page. Subscription required.
Nolo. http://www.nolo.com.
PACER. Administrative Office of the U.S. Courts. https://www.pacer.gov/.
Public Library of Law. http://www.plol.org/Pages/Search.aspx.
Public Library Toolkit. Legal Information Services to the Public Special Interest Section. American Association of Law Libraries. https://www.aallnet.org/lispsis/resources-publications/public-library-toolkit/.
Regulations.gov. http://www.regulations.gov/.
State Home Page and Legislature Links. MultiState Associates. https://www.multistate.us/state-govt-websites.
State Law and Code Links. FreeAdvice. http://law.freeadvice.com/resources/statecodes.htm.
"State Specific Legal Forms for All States." *FindLaw*. http://www.uslegalforms.com/findlaw/.
Uniform Law Commission. http://www.uniformlaws.org/home.
United States Code. Congress. http://uscode.house.gov/.
U.S. Constitution. National Archives. https://www.archives.gov/founding-docs.
U.S. Constitution Annotated. Congress. http://www.congress.gov/constitution-annotated.
Westlaw. Eagan, MN: Thomson Reuters. http://www.westlaw.com. Subscription required.
Wex. Legal Information Institute. Cornell University Law School. http://www.law.cornell.edu/wex/.
Where to Obtain Supreme Court Opinions. Supreme Court of the United States. http://www.supremecourt.gov/opinions/obtainopinions.aspx.

SUGGESTED READINGS

Healey, Paul D. 2002. "Pro Se Users, Reference Liability, and the Unauthorized Practice of Law: Twenty-Five Selected Readings." *Law Library Journal* 94 (Spring): 133–38.
This article surveys the literature that addresses the issue of providing legal reference services to members of the public. As the article shows, there is a broad diversity of

opinion as to whether legal reference service constitutes legal advice, and where the line between reference service and legal advice might be.

Healey, Paul D. 2008. *Liability Issues for Librarians and Information Professionals.* New York: Neal-Schumann.

This book addresses the concept of liability for librarians. Legal issues arising from providing legal reference services are covered in Chapter 7.

Healey, Paul D. 2014. *Answering Legal Reference Questions: How and Where to Find the Answers.* Chicago: ALA Editions.

This book covers much of the information covered in this chapter, only in much greater detail. It also includes an appendix that lists Web-based legal resources for all fifty states and the federal government.

How to Research a Legal Problem: A Guide for Non-Lawyers. 2014. American Association of Law Libraries. https://www.aallnet.org/wp-content/uploads/2018/01/HowToResearchLegalProblemFinal_2014.pdf.

In this guide, law librarians explain the research process for non-lawyers. The guide is a free service of AALL.

Locating the Law. 6th ed. 2018. Public Access to Legal Information Committee. Southern California Association of Law Libraries. https://scallnet.org/publications/.

Although aimed at California librarians and California law, this free publication contains some excellent information on providing reference services on legal topics.

Public Library Toolkit. Legal Information Services to the Public Special Interest Section. American Association of Law Libraries. https://www.aallnet.org/lispsis/resources-publications/public-library-toolkit/.

This Web resource provides information on collecting and using legal materials for public and academic libraries. In addition to general information, the guide provides a specific toolkit for each state.

Part III

The Future of Reference Service

Chapter 32

Creating the Future of Reference Service

Amy VanScoy

INTRODUCTION

The chapters of this book have covered all manner of knowledge and skills concerning reference service. You have learned about the reference interview, strategies for searching, and a wide variety of reference sources. However, there is more to reference service than knowledge and skills. It is also a way of thinking. Excellent reference service includes attitudes and beliefs that make professional practice more than simply a set of behaviors.

Some shared attitudes and values have been covered in this book, such as putting the patron at the center of the interaction and the importance of equal access for all patrons. However, the profession's shared values are not the only ones that will guide your practice; you will develop a personal philosophy of reference. Your attitudes and beliefs will be influenced by your reflection, your vision for reference service, and the kinds of experiences you have as a practitioner.

Throughout this book, you have been absorbing the wisdom of reference experts. They have shared both broad and deep knowledge. But now that you are at the end of the book, it is time to take what you know and go make a difference in your professional work. As you develop your own expertise, you need to develop your personal reference philosophy that will shape and guide your practice. This philosophy will articulate what you believe about information seeking and reference service. It will guide your daily practice and help you communicate to others the values, attitudes, and beliefs that inform and motivate what you do. You can think of your career as a journey to create the future of reference service based, not just on policies and procedures, but on values, attitudes, and beliefs about reference service. This chapter will guide you in reflecting on reference practice and creating a vision for reference service with the goal of developing a reference philosophy to help create the future you envision.

BE YOUR OWN FUTURIST

Much has been said and written about the future of reference service. Listening to and reading the predictions of futurists in the profession can provide food for thought and lively conversation with colleagues. However, these speculations about the future may be only marginally helpful to a practicing librarian because they can fall short of the core principles of reference service. Speculations about whether or not reference desks will exist or what new technologies will be used to provide service do not contribute to high-level thinking about reference practice. They reduce reference practice to the level of furniture and technological fads. These concepts are not the basis for a real vision for practice and how it can be continuously improved. In addition, it is critical not to sit back and listen to what the futurists tell you will or should happen. In today's world, change tends to come from below, from people on the front lines who see opportunities for improvement.

THEMES TO CONSIDER IN ENVISIONING THE FUTURE

Creating a vision is the first step in any strategic planning exercise. As you plan your career, envisioning the impact you want to have is key for charting a course toward your desired future. As part of this process, it might be useful to reflect on some key themes—the patron-professional interaction, technology, entrepreneurship and creativity, social justice and allyship, the confines of space, and the search process in context.

Patron-Professional Interaction

The interaction between the patron and the information professional has always been the core of reference service. This is such a given that it is easy to lose sight of the interaction and focus energy on the opportunities and challenges of technologies, physical spaces, and other issues that are more concrete. However, the patron-professional interaction needs attention for continuous improvement.

A key component of the patron-professional interaction is interpersonal relations. Marie L. Radford's (2006) and Radford and Lynn Silipigni Connaway's (2009) research has demonstrated the importance of relationship building in reference service. Using extensive virtual reference data, Radford and Connaway developed a model for success in virtual reference that includes both a content dimension (whether the interaction addressed the patron's information need) and a relational dimension (whether the interaction addressed the patron's interpersonal need). They found that both the relational and the content dimensions were important for success in reference service, with the relational dimension actually being more important to the patron. In the last few years, we have seen a resurgence of interest in relationship-building initiatives, such as embedded librarians and community reference, both of which are intended to build and strengthen relationships between the professional and their local clientele.

Another key aspect of interacting with patrons is listening. Listening gets its own step in the reference interview guidelines, but sometimes librarians do not recognize it as a professional skill, claiming, "I didn't really do anything. All I did was listen." However, good listening is a significant professional skill. While the librarian who is listening may appear passive, listening is an active state and much work is happening during this activity. Listening supports the concept of the reference dialogue (Doherty 2006) by allowing the patron to take some control and shape the direction of the interaction. In talking through their research issue with the listening librarian, a course of action or new insight may occur to the patron.

An essential skill related to good listening is empathy. Although empathy is often associated with emotions and sympathy, cognitive empathy is about trying to understand another person. This understanding allows the librarian to grasp the other's reasoning and provide them with service that really meets their needs, rather than the needs you assume they have. Empathy is increasingly viewed as a skill that can be learned, not a personal characteristic. Young (2015, 38) breaks down the practice of empathy into two parts. The first part is "develop empathy," which you do through listening and thinking about what you heard. The second part is "apply empathy," which you do through trying to use the other person's reasoning process when creating something or collaborating with them (rather than relying on your own ideas of what makes sense) and through supporting them via your products or services. Developing and applying empathy allows you to understand the patron's mind-set and to provide them with better service.

Relationship building, good listening, and empathy are only a few of the many aspects of interacting effectively with patrons. The most important point is that the interpersonal aspect is of critical importance in reference service and should be actively considered when envisioning the future.

Technology

Discussions of the future of reference service nearly always involve discussions of technology. Technology has always been an important tool in providing reference service, even when that technology was not digital, and envisioning the future of reference service definitely requires exploration and creative thinking about technology. However, the applications or devices themselves are not where the improvement in reference service lies. The improvement lies in how you exploit these applications and devices and, in addition, how you use these applications or devices to think differently about your practice. You should approach new technologies not as specific tools that you could implement but as new ways to think about what you do. Think about the latest gadget that your patrons are using as a window into what they like, how they want to interact, and how they see their world.

For example, years ago, when people started flocking to *Second Life*, a collaborative virtual world, librarians went there, too (Luo 2008). They explored the virtual world, set up in-world professional communities, and created libraries and reference desks. When *Second Life* succumbed to the next online fad, there was some scoffing about how silly these reference desks in *Second Life* had been. If you view this experimentation as being solely about staffing a reference desk in a virtual world, then the experiment does appear to be a bit of a failure. However, if you view it as a group of professionals investigating what their patron are doing, meeting users where they are, and exploring, experimenting, and pushing the boundaries of the traditional environment where reference service occurs, then the *Second Life* experiment may well have been a total success.

- What did librarians learn about virtual worlds?
- What did they learn about their patrons?
- How did their beliefs about reference service and interactions with patrons change as a result of this experimentation?

The answers to these questions are much more important than how many reference interactions actually occurred at the reference desks in *Second Life.*

Keep in mind that technology does not necessarily improve reference service. Recall Dave A. Tyckoson's words from Chapter 1 that technology is "a tool that enhances library service," but he continues, "it does not fundamentally change the nature of that service." Like the card catalog or an iPad, cool new technology is simply a tool that you can exploit to provide better service. Be suspicious of a conference presentation that claims that a particular technology will revolutionize your service. Instead, seek out presenters who propose discussing how a new technology might help you think outside the box about your work or presenters who discuss how the technology can give you insights into how your patrons use technology.

Thinking about new technology not just as a tool to be evaluated but also as a way to better understand your patrons is a mind-set that requires practice. Box 32.1 provides an example of this way of thinking.

Box 32.1 Case Study: *reddit*

reddit is an online forum used by millions of people. The largest group of users is young adult males, but the fact that this group represents only 15 percent of the total users shows that the *reddit* community is diverse (Duggan and Smith 2013). Users post and comment on information, images, and questions, and there is a sense of community with shared acronyms and behavior patterns. What can librarians learn from *reddit*? Misguided librarians might investigate the site and then reject it as a means of communication not suitable for reference service. Others might try to figure out how they can answer user questions within the *reddit* format. But the real questions to ask are as follows:

- Why is *reddit* so popular?
- What about this particular format draws millions of people every day to share and ask for information?
- What does *reddit* tell us about our current users?
- What does it tell us about their issues and concerns?
- What does it tell us about how they like to communicate?

The answers to these questions might provide new ideas for creating new services or modifying existing services to appeal to the information-sharing and -seeking behaviors of some users.

Developing an attitude of experimentation with technology may be the best way to keep your practice on the cutting edge and fend off the routine and disappointment that leads to burnout. For some librarians, experimentation with technology comes naturally. For those who do not feel a thrill at the discovery of a new smartphone app, remember that it is not really about the technology: it is about the users. So, find some users who are thrilled by new technology and tap into their excitement. Seek out a coworker using a device you do not recognize. Identify a blog or *Twitter* account that discusses or reviews new technologies. Find out what young people in your area are using by chatting with a few who visit your library regularly, asking to have some time with the teen advisory board, or talking to the YA librarian about what they are observing. Look outside the library literature to people and publications in computer science or education, such as the website *TechCrunch* or the magazine *Wired*. And always think, "How could I use this to provide better service?"

Entrepreneurship and Creativity

Creating a future for reference service requires an entrepreneurial spirit. Creating the change you want to see in reference service requires creative thinking and initiative. Of course, any new initiatives require critical analysis and careful planning before implementation, but those creative ideas have to come from somewhere.

There is a common misperception that creativity is a trait of only certain people or that it spontaneously occurs, as if by magic. In reality, creativity occurs as a result of concerted effort over time. *Creative people* are the ones who consistently apply themselves to the task—gathering and processing new information, interacting with and reflecting about this new information, and setting aside and revisiting their ideas.

Box 32.2 Generating Creativity through an Idea File

There are many strategies for developing creative ideas. An incredibly simple but effective strategy is the *idea file* suggested by Robert Boice (1994).

- Create an idea file—a simple file folder for something you want to think creatively about: reference services, programming or events, instruction, or a conference presentation, for example.
- Every time you think of or run across a related idea, jot down the idea and put it in your idea file. Ideas may come from professional articles, articles from other fields, blogs, tweets, and even science fiction films!
- Every week, go through your folder, reading and reorganizing the ideas in your file. Move them around, grouping ideas together to see them in different ways. Feel free to jot additional thoughts on any idea in the file.

Eventually, the act of rereading and reorganizing the ideas will create connections between the ideas and will help you see them in new ways. These connections and insights will be the seeds of innovative services, inspiring lesson plans, intelligent programs, and useful presentations.

Steven Johnson (2006), who has written several books on innovation, explains that great ideas do not come in "eureka" moments, but rather they evolve over time as one assembles small ideas garnered from different sources. In his engaging TED Talk, he says, "We take ideas from other people, from people we've learned from, from people we run into in the coffee shop, and we stitch them together into new forms and we create something new. That's really where innovation happens" (Johnson 2006). Librarians can facilitate the development of great ideas by creating a space where different kinds of people come together to share ideas.

Like creativity, entrepreneurship is not a gift but a skill. What can we learn from entrepreneurs that we can apply to reference service? One concept is that of "failing fast." The worst thing you can do with a start-up company is to fail slowly. This draws out the agony and prevents you from moving on to something new that might be more successful. This is not a familiar concept for librarians. Librarians tend to carefully examine an issue, do the necessary research, bring everyone to consensus, and wait until they are absolutely sure of success before launching a new service. Often, services are launched as pilot projects with limited hours and a limited duration. This cautious approach may occasionally save a library from a failed initiative, but it consumes significant time and resources that could have been spent on simply giving the service a try. Failing fast in reference service might look like seizing on some new technology, blasting out advertising via every possible channel, and jumping into the new service 100 percent with every staff member on board. If patrons love it, great! Then time can be spent on figuring what they really love about it and how it can be maintained. If patrons hate it, no problem! At least you will know quickly that it was a bad idea and you can turn your time and resources to something else. Of course, failing fast requires a culture that supports innovation and risk taking. Librarians need to feel supported in being creative and entrepreneurial.

Another key concept for innovative thinking is that it is okay to be wrong. As conscientious stewards of community resources, librarians are sometimes reluctant to experiment with new services or programs. As wrongness expert Kathryn Schulz (2010, 5) says, "Wrongness is a vital part of how we learn and change. Thanks to error, we can revise our understanding of ourselves and amend our ideas about the world." Experimentation, even with its associated risk of being wrong, is an excellent way to learn what works for our users. So, future information professionals: do not be afraid to be occasionally wrong! An attitude of perseverance and acceptance of mistakes can lead to continuous improvement and innovation in reference service.

Social Justice and Allyship

An important aspect of librarianship in general and particularly for reference service is social justice. While this has been a common thread through the history of reference service, recently it has received more explicit attention. Numerous conferences have chosen social justice as their theme, and a quick search will reveal several new books related to social justice in librarianship. In Chapter 2, "Ethics," you read about the professional value of equal access to information. The "digital divide" limits some users' access to information. Simply by helping a user to log into a computer and navigate to a website, you may have helped to narrow this divide. Offering financial literacy programming and being patient with users who are not tech-savvy are ways that librarians facilitate equal access.

Beyond treating all users as equal in your practice, you can be a force for social good. Beyond just valuing diversity and inclusion, your practice can make positive change in small and large ways. Not all users share your understanding that libraries are places where they belong. Making a young person, a family, or a new member of the community feel welcome in your library conveys that libraries are for everyone. As the "face" of the library, professionals providing reference service are in a unique position to notice opportunities and create a *safe space* atmosphere for all users. If you have collection development or programming responsibilities, you can select materials and plan programs that reflect diverse cultures and viewpoints. Perhaps most importantly, you can reach out to the community to work together toward a common goal. In developing their Library Community Convergence Framework, Bharat Mehra and Ramesh Srinivasan (2007) advocate "proactive action" to create an "image of the library as a social catalyst" rather than a mere bystander.

Librarians are in a powerful position to serve as allies—members of a dominant social group that actively work to dismantle systems of oppression. A key element of successful allyship is working with members of the community to help them help themselves. Because librarians value listening and dialogue and have excellent skills in this area, they are particularly suited to being good allies. In a useful resource called *Community Tool Box*, the Work Group for Community Health and Development (n.d.) provides a concrete and substantial discussion of allyship and how you can work toward being an effective ally. According to the *Community Tool Box*, "we need to get to know people, find out what they're up against, and support them in their struggles. That's a lot of what allies do—get involved and support people, instead of staying on the sidelines."

Nicole Cooke (2017) advocates being an "active bystander" as a way of implementing social justice in your practice. What does it mean to be an "active bystander"? Cooke argues that social justice requires that you look for opportunities in your environment to take action. She explains how to be an active bystander with these four behaviors:

- Be aware of your surroundings.
- Interpret and assess the situation.
- Feel a responsibility to act.
- Intervene safely.

As with practicing allyship, being an active bystander puts your values into your reference practice.

For libraries to be effective institutions for social justice, professionals must develop the cultural competence necessary to effectively serve the wide variety of users they will encounter. Patricia Montiel Overall's (2009, 192–98) cultural competence model for LIS professionals provides a framework for self-evaluation and concrete examples of steps professionals can take to develop in this area. Overall identifies three domains of cultural competence and provides strategies for improving one's competence in each area, such as examining one's own cultural identity (cognitive), engaging in conversation with people from other cultures (interpersonal), and translating library signage (environmental). What cultural competence skills do you need to develop to build the kind of inclusive reference service you want to see in the future?

The Confines of Space

Librarians sometimes see reference service as happening solely at a "reference desk." While this is changing somewhat with the idea of mobile services, it has not completely changed. Librarians sometimes neglect to view an interaction with a patron as reference service when it does not occur at the reference desk but perhaps in the context of instruction or in a building outside the library. It is important to realize that reference service can happen outside the confines of your regular shift at the reference desk.

Most librarians have experienced the *feeding frenzy* sensation. When they leave the traditional reference desk to help a patron at a computer or in the stacks, suddenly all the patrons around them are asking questions. This phenomenon demonstrates how important it is to get out in the areas where users are looking for and using information. This may be as simple as leaving the reference desk to help a user in the stacks, or it may be as far afield as providing service in a community center, a faculty office, or a laboratory, for example.

When people agonize that "reference is dead," they really mean that reference desks, as monolithic pieces of furniture, are dead. Reference service thrives beyond the reference desk, in the library building, in the community, and in the world. Successful reference desks often do not look like those of the past—they may be combined with other services, be replaced by other types of furniture, or be more like an Apple Store genius bar with librarians moving about the space. So move out of your comfort zone and expand your notion of the "reference area" to include the entire library, the entire school, or the entire community.

The Search Process in Context

It is becoming clear that the future of reference service involves more than searching for and locating information. Information seeking is one component of a broader activity for users—a broader activity that information professionals have the skills and knowledge to improve. If you think about the context for the patron's information seeking, you can begin to see opportunities to fill.

When searching was extremely difficult, users needed the help of a professional to locate bits of information in esoteric reference books or to locate scholarly papers in unintuitive databases. Today, searching for and locating information still has its challenges, but users with reasonable information literacy skills can often manage this task. Some have perceived this change as a crisis for reference service, but it is really an opportunity.

A useful model for thinking about how to expand reference service beyond its traditional context is Carol Kuhlthau's Information Search Process model (2004). Kuhlthau's model describes the stages of the search process through which users progress—initiation, selection, exploration, formulation, collection, and presentation—including the thinking and feeling of the user and the actions that they take. Although librarians have always helped patrons at all stages of the information search process, by necessity most of their attention has been focused on the collection stage, when patrons were searching for and locating information. As access to information has become easier, professionals now have the opportunity to focus more on pre-searching activities, such as topic selection and focus reformulation, or post-searching activities, like managing information and presenting results. These activities may be even more intellectual and less mechanical than search and retrieval. As these stages of the search process are associated with more challenging affective states for patrons, such as uncertainty, frustration, and disappointment, supportive reference assistance might be most welcome.

Experienced librarians usually have a proud story about the time they asked a patron to tell them about a topic and, through the ensuing conversation, helped the patron to clarify and develop their thinking about the topic. The reference interview is not simply a diagnostic tool to inform searching but also an opportunity for synergy in thinking about the patron's information need. Simple encouragements like handing patrons some markers to sketch out their topic on a whiteboard or handing them some sticky notes to jot down their ideas can encourage patrons to take advantage of professionals' skills and knowledge about the pre-searching phase. Pre-searching activities like topic selection can be enhanced as well by providing and instructing patrons in concept-mapping software and other applications that enhance creativity and clarify thinking.

Post-searching activities can include providing and instructing patrons in the use of citation management or note-taking software such as NoodleTools or instructing patrons in evaluation criteria and ensuring that they are applying these criteria. Lots of productivity apps can help users to organize and present their ideas. For example, providing access to and support for apps, such as Gingko, an online notecard system, could be a way of supporting information use and communicating to patrons the vital and extensive role of reference professionals. Thinking beyond the collection stage to the other stages of the information search process can create opportunities and help you provide useful service.

THINKING LIKE A REFERENCE LIBRARIAN

In other professions, the focus of professional work has shifted from knowledge and skills to professional thinking. While knowledge and skills are certainly important, focusing on how professionals who provide reference service think about their work is also important and may provide the greatest opportunity for professional development after the novice phase. In my research, I have tried to get inside the mind of the reference librarian to understand the thoughts and feelings that shape good reference work (VanScoy 2013, 2016; VanScoy and Bright 2017). Despite the diverse ways that librarians think about their work, we can see some patterns: a focus on the patron, feelings of pride and failure, dealing with complexity and uncertainty, and appreciation of learning new things. You can do your own exploring by asking librarians to share their experiences or to think aloud while you shadow them at work.

Thus, in moving through one's career, it is important to continue to develop new skills and knowledge by reading the professional literature; attending webinars, conferences, and training; and maintaining professional dialogue with both local and distant colleagues. However, it is also important to continue to develop one's professional thinking. Professional thinking is the values, attitudes, and beliefs of the librarian. The key to examining and developing your professional thinking is reflective practice.

Reflective Practice

Reflective practice may sound like a buzzword, but it prevents you from simply going through the motions of your work and helps you to practice reference deliberately and mindfully. In general, it means thinking about and questioning your practice. As a professional, it can be easy to submit to the pressure to constantly produce. If there are no questions or projects that demand your attention, you will likely have projects you have been meaning to get around to. In this fast-paced line of work, it can be hard to take time to reflect and ask yourself the kinds of probing questions that lead to creative ideas and improvement in service.

Reflective practice might manifest itself as thinking about a reference interaction after it is finished and asking yourself if it went well or went poorly, deciding what you did effectively and what you could have done better, and then considering what you might do in the future to improve your practice. You can go further than this, as well, by examining how your values, attitudes, and beliefs affected your practice. But how do you know how they affected it if you do not know what they are?

Developing Your Reference Philosophy

It is important to examine your values, attitudes, and beliefs about reference service. These things affect your practice whether you are aware of them or not. Throughout this book, you have been presented with scenarios that challenge you to think about what you would do in a given situation. These scenarios are designed to prompt you to think about your values, attitudes, and beliefs in terms of ethics and social justice, for example. As you remember from Chapter 1, Wyer (1930) presents various orientations toward reference service: "conservative," moderate," and "liberal" levels of service.

Information professionals have diverse beliefs about the purpose of reference service. Table 32.1 (VanScoy 2012) lists some different roles a librarian may play based on their reference philosophy. Some of the purposes in the table may resonate with you.

What will be your style? A useful exercise might be to write a "reference philosophy" with the same deliberate reflection as a teacher writes a "teaching philosophy."

TABLE 32.1 Roles a Librarian May Play Based on Their Personal Philosophy of Reference.

Roles for Reference Librarians	Professional Beliefs Motivating These Roles
The Information Provider	The goal of reference is to provide answers to questions.
The Instructor	The goal of reference is to teach skills in library and information use.
The Communicator	The goal of reference is a flow of accurate information and a human connection between the user and the resources.
The Relationship Builder	The goal of reference is a productive, long-term relationship between librarian and user.
The Guide or Advisor	The goal of reference is to guide and advise users.
The Counselor	The goal of reference is to develop lifelong information users through mentoring or coaching.
The Partner	The goal of reference is a balance of power and expertise between librarian and user.

A teaching philosophy usually begins with a discussion of what the instructor believes about learning. How does it happen? What makes learning happen? How does teaching facilitate learning? This section of the philosophy may refer to specific theories. The next section discusses how the instructor's beliefs about learning influence their teaching. This section usually includes some specific examples of what the instructor does in the classroom because of their beliefs. The teaching philosophy can also talk about how the instructor assesses their teaching and how the instructor has improved and developed. A teaching philosophy statement has multiple uses. Most important, producing the statement is an opportunity for the instructor to deliberately reflect on their teaching. It also allows the instructor to articulate their philosophy, so that it can be shared with others. In practical terms, it can be shared with a prospective employer, so that the employer can see what the instructor believes and how this belief is manifested in practice.

A reference philosophy is useful for the same reasons. Taking the time to reflect on one's practice and articulate one's beliefs may be enlightening. One's attitudes, values, and beliefs about reference service change over time, so doing this exercise as a student in an LIS program, as an early career librarian, and later as an expert librarian could provide satisfying evidence of your professional development and journey from novice to expert. While an employer is unlikely to request a reference philosophy statement, a job candidate who clearly articulates their values, attitudes, and beliefs about reference service and describes in detail how these manifested themselves in their past experience is likely to seem a more competent candidate than an applicant who has not reflected on these things. Box 32.3 provides questions to guide your reflection as you develop a reference philosophy.

Box 32.3 Activity: What Is Your Reference Philosophy?

First, consider your beliefs about users and their experience of information seeking and use.

- What are your beliefs about information seeking and use?
- What are your beliefs about the user experience?
- Are there concepts about the user experience from this book or other courses that really speak to you (e.g., the Information Search Process model, library anxiety, the imposed query)?

Second, consider your beliefs about reference service.

- How can reference service address the needs, problems, and challenges of information seeking and use that you described previously?
- Which techniques introduced by this book support your beliefs about reference service (e.g., searching, listening, communicating, instruction, relationship building)? Are some techniques more important than others? If so, which ones and why?
- What do you think about the balance between instructing users and providing them with information?
- What do you think about developing relationships with users?

Next, consider how these beliefs influence your practice or how you would like them to influence your practice.

- How do these thoughts manifest themselves in your practical experience?
- If you do not have work, volunteer, or field experience in libraries, what practical experience do you have that might be related, such as tutoring or customer service?

Finally, consider how you assess the quality of your reference service.

- By what standards do you judge your practice?
- What areas for improvement have you identified and how did you go about improving your practice as a result?

The process of articulating a reference philosophy goes back to thinking like a librarian and acting upon your values, attitudes, and beliefs. If you believe that instruction is of critical importance but you notice that in all of your virtual reference transcripts you provide URLs with little instruction, how can you reconcile belief and practice? If instruction truly is important, how can you increase the instructional aspects of your virtual reference work?

In addition, you may have practices that were dictated to you by training or library policies. As a staff member or student worker, you may have been instructed to practice in a certain way. But as a librarian, you need to develop a sense of professional judgment, decide what the profession should be, and work to make it that way. This begins with reflecting about what you have been told to do and reconciling it with your professional beliefs. Consider again an example from virtual reference: if you have been told that a virtual reference transaction should take fifteen minutes or less and to transfer any patron to another medium after fifteen minutes, consider the values, attitudes, and beliefs behind this policy. Does this policy reflect your values, attitudes, and beliefs? If not, you should work to communicate this and make changes that will improve service to your patrons.

Developing a Portfolio

Another mechanism for reflecting on your practice is developing a portfolio of your work. This is an effective practice from teaching and other professions, where professionals consider their values, attitudes, and beliefs and gather evidence to support them. The exercise of compiling a portfolio of your professional work should not simply be to show others what a fantastic job you are doing but also to reflect on your values, attitudes, and beliefs and demonstrate how they manifest themselves in practice (see Box 32.4).

Box 32.4 Activity: Create a Reference Service Portfolio

Your reference service portfolio not only provides evidence of your experience providing reference service but also demonstrates that you have thought carefully about what it means to provide good service and that you engage in reflective practice and assessment.

What might go into a reference service portfolio?

- Anonymized transcripts of your virtual and/or e-mail reference interactions. Do not just choose the best ones or the ones where you found the answer. Choose ones that demonstrate specific values. For instance, if you feel that relationship building is a key component of reference service, find an example of a transcript in which you made an extra effort to develop a relationship with the user. Add to the transcript a brief reflection about how your behaviors reflected your beliefs and how this improved the experience in some way for the user.
- Summaries of consultations with users in which you describe in detail the user, their need, what you did with the user, and the end result, including the impact of your service.
- Examples of Web pages or online tutorials you have developed. Explain how these pages or tutorials anticipate user needs and demonstrate your reference philosophy.
- Reports from supervisors or even fellow students who have observed you providing reference service.

Developing Your Professional Brand

Patrons still sometimes associate information professionals with reference books and do not understand the broad range of expertise they have. Even some library administrators retain this conservative view, insisting that reference desks are no longer being used, so reference service is no longer necessary. While this is frustrating, it is not a reason to give up on the vital work that you do. Try to see these frustrating encounters as opportunities, even teachable moments. Develop an *elevator speech* that succinctly and pleasantly reveals the mission of the contemporary reference professional.

Creating a personal brand for your reference service may be an effective way to do this. Using your professional Web page, your presentations and service activities, your *Twitter* feed, and other tools, you can create an image for yourself as the kind of information professional you want to be. This brand can be helpful in communicating your value in cover letters and job interviews. It is an ongoing, always developing process, but it will keep you fresh and help keep you focused on your professional mission.

Your professional brand will involve much more than reference service. All professionals need a broad range of knowledge and skills in order to be flexible and to succeed in today's multifaceted positions; however, your reference philosophy should play some role in this suite of expertise. If you do not see yourself providing reference service as a major part of your work, consider how your reference philosophy contributes to the kind of work you plan to do—how does an understanding of the user experience or expert searching skills contribute to your future work? How do you want to portray yourself to potential employers? How do you want to be viewed by your future colleagues? How do you want to be perceived when you give workshops, present at conferences, or blog about your work? Here are some images that might resonate with you: tech savvy, ally and advocate, nexus for scholars on campus, dynamic and innovative, inspiring instructor, creative problem solver (see Box 32.5).

Box 32.5 Activity: Creating Your Professional Brand

What Is Your Existing Brand?

What you are communicating about yourself now? Search for yourself online and analyze what you find about yourself.

- Do pages about you show up at the top of the results list? If not, you may want to work on optimizing pages so that potential employers see your work first.
- What kinds of pages exist that communicate your work? Have you created a professional website, a professional blog, a *LinkedIn* profile, a *Twitter* feed, or a student profile page?
- What message do these pages convey about you as an information professional? Do they reflect your reference philosophy or your professional attitudes and values?

How Can You Improve Your Brand?

After searching for yourself, you may have already come up with some ideas, such as creating a professional website or setting up a *LinkedIn* profile. As you are creating and editing pages about yourself, however, think about your reference philosophy and other professional attitudes and beliefs. How can you communicate these attitudes and beliefs through your online presence?

- Make a statement on your website that communicates your philosophy.
- Include excerpts of your work or testimonials from patrons or supervisors that illustrate these beliefs in practice.
- Add photographs to your site if you feel that some aspects of your philosophy might be better communicated with images.
- Ask colleagues to endorse you on *LinkedIn*.
- Create a professional *Twitter* feed where you tweet about things that support your reference philosophy and your brand.
- Include ideas from your brand in your cover letters to reinforce the impression that potential employers have seen online.
- Make sure that your brand is consistent across all of your professional sites and profiles.

CONCLUSION

Reference service is and will continue to be a vibrant and essential service in libraries and information agencies. Systems will continue to improve and become more intuitive, and information will become easier to find. However, the interaction between the patron and the information professional will remain a key offering of libraries and information centers. Beyond this certainty, the future of reference service is up to you to envision and create. As M. Kathleen Kern (2014, 284), experienced reference librarian and former president of the American

Library Association's Reference and User Services Association, has written, "Take the action of trying the new, but don't lose sight of the purpose. Know that your actions shape the future." Use the knowledge and skills discussed in this book, along with your thinking and reflection about them, to create your vision of the future of reference service.

REFERENCES

Boice, Robert. 1994. *How Writers Journey to Comfort and Fluency: A Psychological Adventure.* Westport, CT: Praeger.

Cooke, Nicole A. 2017. "Librarians as Active Bystanders: Centering Social Justice in LIS Practice." In *The Portable MLIS: Insights from the Experts*, edited by Ken Haycock and Mary-Jo Romanick, 2nd ed., 39–47. Westport, CT: ABC-CLIO.

Doherty, John J. 2006. "Reference Interview or Reference Dialogue?" *Internet Reference Services Quarterly* 11 (3): 97–109.

Duggan, Maeve, and Aaron Smith. 2013. "6% of Online Adults Are reddit Users." *Pew Research Internet Project.* Pew Research Center. Last modified July 3, 2013. http://www.pewinternet.org/2013/07/03/6-of-online-adults-are-reddit-users/.

Gingko. https://gingkoapp.com/.

Johnson, Steven. 2006. "Where Good Ideas Come From." *TED.* https://www.ted.com/talks/steven_johnson_where_good_ideas_come_from?language=en.

Kern, M. Kathleen. 2014. "Continuity and Change, or, Will I Ever Be Prepared for What Comes Next?" *Reference & User Services Quarterly* 53 (4): 282–85.

Kuhlthau, Carol C. 2004. *Seeking Meaning: A Process Approach to Library and Information Services.* 2nd ed. Westport, CT: Libraries Unlimited.

LinkedIn. http://www.linkedin.com.

Luo, Lili. 2008. "Reference Service in Second Life: An Overview." *Reference Services Review* 36 (3): 289–300.

Mehra, Bharat, and Ramesh Srinivasan. 2007. "The Library-Community Convergence Framework for Community Action: Libraries as Catalysts of Social Change." *Libri* 57 (3): 123–39.

NoodleTools. https://www.noodletools.com/.

Overall, Patricia Montiel. 2009. "Cultural Competence: A Conceptual Framework for Library and Information Science Professionals." *The Library Quarterly* 79 (2): 175–204.

Radford, Marie L. 2006. "Encountering Virtual Users: A Qualitative Investigation of Interpersonal Communication in Chat Reference." *Journal of the American Society for Information Science and Technology* 57 (8): 1046–59.

Radford, Marie L., and Lynn Silipigni Connaway. 2009. "Thriving on Theory: A New Model for Virtual Reference Encounters." Presented at the American Society for Information Science and Technology 2009 Annual Meeting, Vancouver, British Columbia, Canada. http://www.oclc.org/research/activities/synchronicity/ppt/asist09-thriving.ppt.

Reddit. http://www.reddit.com.

Schulz, Kathryn. 2010. *Being Wrong: Adventures in the Margin of Error.* New York: Harper Collins.

TechCrunch. https://techcrunch.com/.

Twitter. http://www.twitter.com.

VanScoy, Amy. 2012. "Inventing the Future by Examining Traditional and Emerging Roles for Reference Librarians." In *Leading the Reference Renaissance: Today's Ideas for Tomorrow's Cutting-Edge Services*, edited by Marie L. Radford, 79–94. New York: Neal-Schuman.

VanScoy, Amy. 2013. "Fully Engaged Practice and Emotional Connection: Aspects of the Practitioner Experience of Reference and Information Service." *Library & Information Science Research* 35 (4): 272–78.

VanScoy, Amy. 2016. "Making Sense of Professional Work: Metaphors for Reference and Information Service." *Library & Information Science Research* 38 (3): 243–9.

VanScoy, Amy, and Kawanna Bright. 2017. "Including the Voices of Librarians of Color in Reference and Information Services Research." *Reference & User Services Quarterly* 57 (2): 104–14.

Wired. 1993–. San Francisco, CA: Advance Magazine Publishers. Twelve issues per year.

Work Group for Community Health and Development. n.d. "Section 5. Learning to Be an Ally for People from Diverse Groups and Backgrounds." *Community Tool Box*. http://ctb.ku.edu/en/table-of-contents/culture/cultural-competence/be-an-ally/main.

Wyer, James I. 1930. *Reference Work: A Textbook for Students of Library Work and Librarians*. Chicago: American Library Association.

Young, Indi. 2015. *Practical Empathy: For Collaboration and Creativity in Your Work*. New York: Rosenfeld Media.

SUGGESTED READINGS

Kern, M. Kathleen. 2014. "Continuity and Change, or, Will I Ever Be Prepared for What Comes Next?" *Reference & User Services Quarterly* 53 (4): 282–85.

Written while Kern was president of the Reference and Users Services Section of ALA, this essay responds to the doubts and concerns that we encounter as we embark on a career in librarianship. Her honest and rational message fills me with hope and determination every time I read it.

Radford, Marie L. 2008. "A Personal Choice: Reference Service Excellence." *Reference & User Services Quarterly*, 48 (2): 108–115.

In this essay, prolific scholar and former reference librarian, Marie Radford, offers inspiring examples and sage advice. With enthusiasm and infectious energy, Radford challenges us to embrace change and go beyond the status quo in our reference service.

Index

Page numbers followed by *t* indicate tables and *f* indicate figures.

About the Contributors

OPETORITSE A. ADEFOLALU, Librarian, Formerly Inglewood Public Library

BARBARA A. ALVAREZ, Doctoral Student, University of Wisconsin-Madison

SUSAN AVERY, Instructional Services Librarian and Associate Professor, University of Illinois at Urbana-Champaign

NICOLE A. COOKE, Augusta Baker Chair in Childhood Literacy and Associate Professor, School of Library and Information Science, University of South Carolina

REBECCA DAVIS, Assistant Professor, School of Library and Information Science, Simmons University

STEPHANIE DAVIS-KAHL, Collections & Scholarly Communications Librarian, Illinois Wesleyan University

SARAH EREKSON, Regional Government Documents Librarian, University of Florida

CASSANDRA GRAESSER, Digitisation Librarian and Social Media Manager, University of Queensland

PAUL D. HEALEY, Senior Instructional Services Librarian and Associate Professor of Library Science, University of Illinois College of Law

LISA JANICKE HINCHLIFFE, Coordinator of Information Literacy and Instruction and Professor, University of Illinois at Urbana-Champaign

JOANN JACOBY, Director, Tutt Library, Colorado College

M. KATHLEEN KERN, Director, Miller Learning Center Library Commons, University of Georgia

EMILY J. M. KNOX, Associate Professor, School of Information Sciences, University of Illinois at Urbana-Champaign

LILI LUO, Professor, School of Information, San José State University

MATTHEW D. MACKELLAR, Community Engagement Librarian, Skokie Public Library

LESLEY K. MACKIE, Head of Research Services, Tutt Library, Colorado College

PIPER MARTIN, Reference Services and Instruction Librarian and Assistant Professor, University of Illinois at Urbana-Champaign

CELINA NICHOLS McDONALD, Government Documents, Law, & Criminology Librarian, University Libraries, University of Maryland

AMY S. PATTEE, Associate Professor, School of Library and Information Science, Simmons University

JEANNE HOLBA PUACZ, Adjunct Lecturer, School of Information Sciences, University of Illinois at Urbana-Champaign

MICHAEL RODRIGUEZ, Collections Strategist, University of Connecticut

CELIA ROSS, Senior Associate Librarian, Kresge Library, Ross School of Business, University of Michigan

CAROL A. SINGER, Professor, Library Teaching & Learning Department, Bowling Green State University

LINDA C. SMITH, Professor Emerita, School of Information Sciences, University of Illinois at Urbana-Champaign

MAURA SOSTACK, Independent Search Specialist

LILLIAN SUNDELL-THOMAS, Deputy Director of Libraries, Somerville Public Library

SHELLEY SWEENEY, University Archivist & Head of Archives & Special Collections, University of Manitoba Libraries

DAVE A. TYCKOSON, Research Services Librarian, California State University, Fresno

AMY VANSCOY, Associate Professor, Department of Library & Information Studies, Graduate School of Education, University at Buffalo

KELLY JO WOODSIDE, Consultant, Massachusetts Library System

NEAL WYATT, Contributing Editor and Readers' Advisory Columnist, *Library Journal*

About the Editors

MELISSA A. WONG holds degrees from Augustana College, Rock Island, Illinois (BA, English) and the University of Illinois at Urbana-Champaign (MS, library science). During her career, she has served as a librarian at the University of Southern California and as the library director at Marymount College (now Marymount California University) in Rancho Palos Verdes, California. She has been an adjunct instructor at the University of Illinois at Urbana-Champaign School of Information Sciences since 2001 and currently teaches courses in reference, instruction, academic librarianship, and library management.

LAURA SAUNDERS holds degrees from Boston University (BA, English) and Simmons University (MS and PhD, Library and Information Science). She is an Associate Professor at Simmons University School of Library and Information Science, where she has been a faculty member since 2011. She teaches courses in reference, information literacy and instruction, academic librarianship, and intellectual freedom and censorship. During her career, she has served as a librarian at Simmons University and as a library assistant at the Medford Public Library, Massachusetts.

More Praise for *Reference and Information Services: An Introduction, 6th Edition*:

"Reference is alive and well, which is demonstrated by this collection of essays! The editors have included an impressive list of authors who are experts in reference service practice and research. The chapters range from an overview of sources and their uses to the history, ethics, management, evaluation, and delivery of reference services to diverse populations. The final chapter on creating the future of reference service is provocative and inspiring."

—Lynn Silipigni Connaway, Ph.D., Director of Library Trends and User Research, OCLC Research

"What a pleasure to see the 6th edition of Reference and Information Services: An Introduction. Embracing recent developments in technology and an increasing social consciousness, this edition makes a wise and comprehensive contribution to today's reference service. As someone engaged in reference and information literacy for over 30 years, I strongly recommend it to LIS students and practicing librarians."

—William Badke, Associate Librarian, Trinity Western University, British Columbia, Canada